Helsinki
Leningrad
ESTONIA
Riga
LATVIA
LITHUANIA
Kaunas
EAST PRUSSIA
Moscow
Tula
Smolensk
Vitebsk
Minsk
Gomel
Kursk
U. S. S. R.
VOLGA R.
Voronezh
MAXIMUM GERMAN ADVANCE 1941-42
Stalingrad
VISTULA R.
Warsaw
Kharkov
POLAND
Kiev
DNIEPER R.
DON R.
Cracow
Dnepropetrovsk
Rostov
ZECHOSLOVAKIA
Krasnodar
Budapest
RUMANIA
UNGARY
Yalta
Ploesti
BLACK SEA
Belgrade
Bucharest
UGOSLAVIA
BULGARIA
ALBANIA
Ankara
Brindisi
GREECE
TURKEY
Athens
SYRIA
N
Damascus
MEDITERRANEAN SEA
Amman
Derna
TRANSJORDAN
Tobruk
Alexandria
Benghazi
Cairo
El Alamein
EGYPT
palacios
P9-DWJ-451

Mainstream of America Series ★

EDITED BY LEWIS GANNETT

EXPERIENCE OF WAR

The United States in World War II

Books by Kenneth S. Davis

EXPERIENCE OF WAR

THE HERO

A PROPHET IN HIS OWN COUNTRY

MORNING IN KANSAS

RIVER ON THE RAMPAGE

THE YEARS OF THE PILGRIMAGE

SOLDIER OF DEMOCRACY

IN THE FORESTS OF THE NIGHT

EXPERIENCE OF WAR

The United States in World War II

KENNETH S. DAVIS

MAPS BY RAFAEL PALACIOS

1965 DOUBLEDAY & COMPANY, INC., Garden City, New York

LIBRARY OF CONGRESS CATALOG CARD NUMBER 65–12374

PRINTED IN THE UNITED STATES OF AMERICA

To Four Friends Who Helped:

Tilton M. Barron
Edward C. Camp
Mrs. Norma Passage
Thurston Taylor

Contents

MAPS

Prefatory Note

This is a book about the American experience of World War II. It is not designed to be a formal academic history, though every effort has been made to assure its factual accuracy. Rather, its essential purpose is literary in that it attempts to rescue from the erosions and abstractions of Time something of what Webster's Dictionary, in the definition of "experience," calls the "actual living through an event or events; actual enjoyment or suffering."

My sustaining hope through a long and arduous labor has been that the final work would have the effect of immediacy while indicating the general shape of the war and the flow of time through it and from it to now. The reader will know, better than I can possibly know as I write this, whether or not, or to what extent, the hope has been realized.

K.S.D.

Princeton, Massachusetts
August 31, 1964

"Only connect . . ."

E. M. FORSTER, *Howard's End*

"Connectedness is of the essence of all things. . . . No fact is merely itself."

ALFRED NORTH WHITEHEAD, *Modes of Thought*

"Our whole Universe is but an infinite Complex of Forces; thousandfold, from Gravitation up to Thought and Will; man's Freedom environed with Necessity of Nature: in all which nothing at any moment slumbers, but all is forever awake and busy. The thing that lies isolated and inactive thou shalt nowhere discover. . . ."

THOMAS CARLYLE, *The French Revolution*

Book One

THE ROAD TO WAR

1

To the Edge of the Abyss

i. *A Walk in Evening Fog*

On the evening of Friday, February 24, 1939, a short, disheveled man with grizzled hair upon his head and a worried frown upon his face took a walk along the East River in New York, accompanied by his wife, Florence, and a small brown dachshund named Einstein.[1] It was a walk which neither the man nor his wife would ever forget.

The night sky was clear above central Manhattan, but a fog rose up from the river and spread across Sutton Place, along which they walked slowly northward. Foghorns moaned across invisible waters. Near lights were blurred, far ones blotted out. The great Queensboro Bridge was but a shadow looming ahead, mysterious, vaguely menacing, as they who walked through dissolving walls of mist yet remained walled in, their privacy bounded by a chill white secret silence. The woman felt that they were alone, and in grave danger. The man's voice, talking about what he had seen and heard that afternoon, was hushed.

For William L. Laurence, science reporter for the New York *Times*, had just come from a meeting of the American Physical Society held in Lecture Hall 401 of Columbia University's Pupin Hall. There, sitting beside Columbia physics professor John R. Dunning among two hundred other scientists, he had listened to the second installment of a story that had begun for him a month before at a meeting of physicists in Washington's Georgetown University. To that earlier meeting, Copenhagen's Niels Bohr and Rome's Enrico Fermi (the latter now a refugee from Mussolini's Italy) had brought the exciting, the astounding news that an experiment conducted in Germany had resulted in the splitting apart, or fission, of uranium atoms. To today's meeting, Fermi, Bohr, and others had brought news of the experimental confirmation, in Denmark and America, of the German results. Fermi had also mentioned the probability that each nucleus as it split would shoot out two or three subatomic particles known as neutrons which, knocking around among uranium atoms, might induce further fissions. There was, in other words, the possibility of an explosive chain reaction in a mass of uranium of an as-yet-undetermined "critical size." The terrifying human significance of this was more quickly and completely realized by Laurence than it had been by most of the American scientists in the room. His profession as journalist required him to translate science into human terms, and the process was stimulated by the fact that he had been born a Lithuanian Jew and that his invalid mother and half-blind brother yet lived in his native village.

Within minutes after this day's meeting had ended, Laurence had asked Fermi and Bohr directly if uranium-235 might not be used to make a bomb. The two scientists had looked at one another through a pause long enough to make Laurence feel distinctly uncomfortable.

"It was as though I had committed a *faux pas*," he said to his wife that night.

Then—slowly, carefully—Fermi had replied that it was much too early to tell about such things. One must avoid "hasty conclusions." "It has not yet been proved that a chain reaction would actually occur." At least twenty-five, possibly fifty years of work would be necessary before Laurence's question could be firmly answered.

"I think he overestimated the time," said Laurence to his wife. "I think he *deliberately* overestimated it."

For as they walked at night beside the river, Laurence could actually *feel* a chill fog of secrecy gathering here and there in the realm of his professional interest. Later it might seem to him that even this early, as the foghorns moaned and the river mists swirled around him, he discerned the shapes of things soon to come into his professional field. Just a few days from then, physicists in Columbia University and in Paris would prove experimentally that neutrons were indeed emitted when uranium fissioned, as theory had predicted, which meant that a chain reaction was indeed possible. At once, led by Leo Szilard, a group of foreign-born physicists who had fled to America from a Europe menaced by Nazi-Fascism would begin to press toward twin objectives: the restriction of publications in nuclear physics which might help the dictatorships toward atomic bombs, and the gaining of governmental support of such developments in America. They were to be frustrated in the first instance by the refusal of F. Joliot-Curie in Paris to agree to it, and in the second by the apathy and ignorance of military officialdom.

Fermi, for instance, would make a direct approach to the Navy in Washington on the morning of March 17, it being generally acknowledged that the Navy was more receptive to new ideas than the Army. This would be on the day after Hitler, in cynical violation of the Munich Pact, had taken over the whole of Czechoslovakia—and Fermi knew well that Czechoslovakia had the only considerable uranium deposits in Europe. He would see two youthful lieutenant commanders who would listen politely as the Italian, handicapped by imperfect English, struggled to impress upon them the significance of the new discoveries. When he had finished, they would ask him, politely, to keep them informed of future developments. For agonizing months thereafter, scientists in America would note, helplessly, one sign after another that physicists and chemists of Nazi Germany were being concentrated in the Kaiser Wilhelm Institute where they worked with uranium . . .

All this portended in Laurence's mind, that late February night of 1939. He and his wife came to an iron fence at the dead end of Fifty-seventh Street. They stood there beside the fence watching the wraiths of mist, breathing the dank river smell—and she listened in increasing agitation as he told her in his hushed voice about his fears.

ii. *A Night in the White House*

Viewed from the lonely eminence of the White House's upper study, it had been in nearly every respect a miserable spring and summer. The President and his Secretary of State, sitting in their shirt-sleeves, awaiting the arrival of invited Congressional leaders, felt the night's hot darkness as an oppressive weight upon their spirits. Cordell Hull, especially, was glum—so much so he could not make adequate response to the President's half-hearted attempts to cheer things up. Almost nothing had gone right, almost nothing now went right. And neither man had any real belief that the impending conference would make a difference . . .

True, the tide of isolationist sentiment had ebbed considerably since that October day in 1937 when the President, speaking in the very shadow of Colonel McCormick's Gothic tower in Chicago, had suggested that peace-loving nations join in a "quarantine" of the "aggressors" whose lawlessness he likened to a contagious physical disease. If war engulfed Europe, "let no one imagine that America will escape," he had said with all the grim earnestness he could project.[2] He was not likely to forget the popular response. It had been dismaying. Far from mobilizing public opinion behind a foreign policy that might halt the dictators short of war, far from strengthening his hand as he dealt with them, the speech had produced precisely the effects most encouraging to democracy's enemies and most likely to render him impotent in world power politics. Disapproval was vehement and seemingly almost universal. Roosevelt had been forced to admit tacitly that he had made a political miscalculation, that in the crucial matter now in hand too much haste did indeed make waste. Tragic waste. Yet haste there must be . . .

Since then, public opinion polls had recorded a widespread change of mind.[3] The ruthless bombing of helpless Chinese all through the spring of 1938, the almost incredible barbarities of Japanese infantrymen, the increasing severity of Nazi persecutions of Jews in Germany, the repeated ruthless aggressions of Hitler and Mussolini—all these had forced millions of formerly isolationist Americans to conclude that something (opinions varied as to what) must be done by the United States to thwart the insatiable ambitions of the Japanese militarists, the Nazi-Fascist dictators. Many who had theretofore accepted the simple view that wars are caused by commercial rivalries and interests, and by these alone, now began to doubt and even reject it. More and more Americans began to recognize other causative factors—factors having little or nothing to do with economics. A paranoid megalomania, a perverted sexuality expressed through ruthless power lusts, the profound moral outrage joined to an "instinct" of self-preservation which such evil inevitably provoked—these, too, were causative. Thousands of Americans who had been most vehemently pacifist in the early 1930s now realized that their pacifism stemmed from a yet deeper commitment, a commitment to human freedom and humane values. The same moral energies that had fed it now fed their antifascism.

Roosevelt, trying hard to gauge the shift of sentiment in order to stay just a little ahead of it in public speech and action, had measured it too small in the late autumn of 1938, in the opinion of several of his advisers. These also felt that he failed to exercise desperately needed leadership as the practical failure and moral contemptibility of Chamberlain's "appeasement" policies became daily more apparent. Ickes urged him to take the people fully into his confidence in a full-length presentation of the gravity of the situation, preparing the way for needed drastic revisions of foreign policy. Roosevelt refused. What was the use? he had asked, with a touch of bitterness. The people would not believe him . . .

For he knew (none better) that his power of leadership was less at that moment than it had been at any other since his first inaugural—less inwardly as well as outwardly. Early in the preceding summer, disregarding the advice of Jim Farley and other party leaders, he had entered actively into the primary campaigns in an effort to "purge" certain Democratic Senators and Representatives who had opposed his major policies, especially his scheme to enlarge the Supreme Court. He had met with a humiliating rebuff; only one of his intraparty foes had been defeated; and the event, so largely and clearly the consequence of his own mistake, could hardly fail to diminish (for the moment) his faith in his own good judgment. There had followed the first Tuesday in November, adding injury to insult: the Republicans had almost doubled their strength in the House, from 88 to 169, while increasing it by eight in the Senate, and nearly all these new opponents were strongly isolationist. In concert with anti-New Deal Democrats they had enough votes to thwart the Executive's legislative program, and they could be counted upon to oppose with special vehemence every effort to ally the United States with other nations in an effort to halt fascist aggression.

So as 1938 ended and 1939 began, Roosevelt had felt that he could not risk another major rebuff. His Annual Message to Congress, January 4, was therefore as ambiguous as the American mind seemed in general to be in the face of totalitarianism—bold in its expression of the ideals we would defend, timid in its concrete proposals for defending them. The

Message had even failed to issue a clear and forthright call for repeal of the compulsory embargo provisions of the Neutrality Act, though these were as a straitjacket on foreign policy. There had followed a winter and spring crowded with disasters. The final crushing of Czechoslovakia, Hungary's carving of Ruthenia from the dying body of Czechoslovakia, the seizure of Memel from tiny Lithuania, the renewed and more threatful demands that Danzig be returned to Germany and that free access to it across the Polish "corridor" be granted Germany—all these events, fathered in Berlin, came to explosive birth during the last half of March. It became evident that Poland was to be the next major target of Hitler's aggression. In Spain, the last stubborn Loyalist resistance to Franco had collapsed by the end of the month. Japan, meanwhile, laid claim to islands scattered over a large area southwest of Manila, posing a clear threat to the Philippines. In early April, Mussolini seized Albania. Everywhere the aggressors were on the march. Nowhere were they effectively opposed.

In the whole dark picture, the only faintly luminous spots were the sparks struck from British and French public opinion by the sword that murdered Prague. Frenchmen and Englishmen who had cheered the Munich Pact in hysterical relief were now outraged in such numbers that Chamberlain and Daladier were forced to abandon "appeasement" as an openly avowed policy. This might well presage the end, ultimately, of Hitler's dreams of world conquest, but it did nothing to lessen the urgency of Roosevelt's central problem, for it meant that early war in Europe was more likely.

Of course, the whole of the ill-conceived Neutrality Act ought to be repealed, and promptly, but the President wasted no energy in the wish that this was possible. It just wasn't—not in the present state of public opinion. But surely repeal of the Act's compulsory embargo provisions would now recommend itself as an absolute necessity to so many members of Congress that its swift passage was insured.

There had been enough dawdling, in all conscience!

When the embargo repeal bill was introduced, Roosevelt was persuaded by his recent sad experiences, and by Administration leaders in Congress, that its chances of passage would be improved if he followed a strictly "hands off" policy. Senator Key Pittman of Nevada, chairman of the Senate Foreign Relations Committee, was of this opinion. He also expressed the conviction that the bill would pass handily—this despite the fact his committee's members included William E. Borah of Idaho, Arthur H. Vandenberg of Michigan, Hiram W. Johnson of California, and Robert M. LaFollette, Jr., of Wisconsin, each a man of great personal force whose isolationism, being a matter of principle, seemed actually to harden to the precise extent that popular support of it softened, thus offsetting the political effectiveness of the latter development. Pittman continued optimistic from January into April. "Two weeks more . . ." was his standard cheerful reply to inquiries made approximately every two weeks by Hull or Roosevelt, ". . . two weeks more and we'll be getting somewhere."[4]

By the second week of April, however, when Hull at last pressed him sharply, he confessed he had been mistaken; in point of fact, as things stood now, the chances of repeal were very slight.

On the other hand, the chances of general European war beginning soon, perhaps within days, were now very great, according to secret messages moving through State Department channels.

At this point, Roosevelt had engaged in a piece of spectacular personal diplomacy. He had sent identical messages to Hitler and Mussolini asking them to give assurance that their armed forces would not "attack or invade the territory" of thirty-one nations, which he specifically named. They included Poland, Denmark, the Baltic States, The Netherlands, and France. Cheered in democratic countries and the Soviet Union, the message had not been answered directly by either Hitler or Mussolini. The latter dismissed it publicly in a single scornful sentence of a speech. Hitler seized upon it as a unique propaganda opportunity, delaying his answer until April 28, when he dealt with it point by point, and at length, in a speech to the Reichstag. He had "taken the trouble" to ask each of the States mentioned two questions: *First*, did it feel itself threatened in any way by Germany? *Second*, had it authorized the President to make his proposal? "The reply was in all cases negative. . . ." He then addressed himself to Roosevelt by name: "Mr. Roosevelt! I fully understand that the vastness of your nation and the immense wealth of your country allow you to feel responsible for the history of the whole world and for the history of all nations. I, sir, am placed in a much more modest and smaller sphere. . . ." Whereupon, with heavy but effective irony, he proceeded to ring every change in the repertoire of American isolationism so perfectly that some believed the speech to have been composed in Germany's Washington Embassy.[5]

Certainly the isolationist leaders reacted to it as the Nazis wished. They rejoiced in what they deemed to be Roosevelt's smarting discomfiture. "He asked for it," said North Dakota's Senator Gerald P. Nye . . .[6]

Nor did the President fare better in his now-active intervention in the Congressional battle over neutrality legislation. The House finally passed a new neutrality bill in late June, but it bore little resemblance to the bill that had been introduced—it retained essentially the old compulsory embargo provisions. As for the Senate, it refused to pass a new bill at all: on July 11 the Foreign Relations Committee voted 12–11 not to report out the Administration measure. It was as if Congress were determined to validate every slur cast by the dictators upon democracy's inability to rise to heroic challenges, upon its inefficiency, its indecisiveness, its inevitable quality of the lowest common denominator . . .

It was on the morrow of his Senate rebuff that the President had decided, as a last forlorn hope, upon the conference he now awaited in the White House's upstairs study. And thus it was that his cheeriness was forced; Cordell Hull's glumness was the prevailing mood. Insects buzzed against the screens. Dry leaves rustled in a dry wind across the White House lawn. The black night of Tuesday, July 18, 1939 rolled out of Europe over the Atlantic and the Republic's drought-blighted eastern seaboard, rolled across the Appalachians and the Old Northwest, covered the prairies of Illinois and the cornfields of Iowa, and met evening light at last upon the High Plains of Kansas (dust clouds swirled up there against a red sunset behind gangplows that turned mile on mile of golden wheat stubble under the earth), while on a big chintz-covered couch beside an empty fireplace in a room whose walls were lined with books and hung with colored prints, whose desk bore a ship model and framed photographs and a clutter of other Rooseveltiana, the President of the United States leaned back at his seeming ease and blew smoke toward the ceiling from a cigarette in a long holder cocked at its usual jaunty angle—

And waited . . .

By nine o'clock they were all assembled, and the mood of the room was changed. Hull and Steve Early, the White House press secretary, greeted the arrivals at the door and gestured toward a table in one corner which bore a tray of whiskies, gin, vermouths, and assorted wines. Roosevelt was glad to see that most of the men had shed their coats and held drinks in their hands as they took their seats. He had wanted this meeting to take place in an atmosphere of relaxed, casual camaraderie and had gone so far in his own effort to create it as to joke with the Vice-President, whom he cordially disliked, over the proper way to make an old-fashioned.[7]

Watching and waiting for the proper psychological moment to open the discussion, he let his gray-eyed gaze dance over the assemblage. He might have seen it as fairly representative of the regional differences and social class structure of America, and of her range of character types. There were Key Pittman, who had been in the Alaska gold rush in '98 and now represented a silver constituency, Nevada; the Vice-President, John Nance Garner from Texas, whose cherubic countenance (intense blue eyes, bushy white brows, a cherry-red complexion) masked the ruthless acquisitiveness and political conservatism characteristic of his old Texas constituency; Minority Leader Charles L. McNary of Oregon, whose shrewd manipulatory intelligence joined to a basically cynical tolerance (Old Guard Republicans were often angered by his lack of intransigent partisan feeling) might well be useful to the President this night; McNary's second-in-command, Warren R. Austin of Vermont, an earnest and studious man whose New England conscience shaped a basic attitude that contrasted sharply with the Minority Leader's and who, convinced that America's failure to join the League of Nations was a major cause of present international anarchy, had long been appalled by his party's prevailing isolationism; Senate Majority Leader Alben W. Barkley of Kentucky, an amiable and affable man whom no one could seriously dislike but whose general intelligence was questioned by many; and the Secretary of State, formerly Senator Cordell Hull of Tennessee, the only leading figure in contemporary politics to have been born (sixty-seven years before) in a log cabin—a man of gentle courtly manners and cautiously conservative outlook who, nevertheless, had the fiery temper (rigorously controlled for the most part), the stubborn tenacity, and the personal honor code of a first-class fighting man. Others were also present . . .

But the man on whom Roosevelt most narrowly focused—the dominant personality among his opposition in that room—was the old but far from feeble lion of Idaho, Senator William E. Borah. A man of large physique, large courage, and large generosity, Borah was also possessed of a monumental moral egotism. Long ago, in a far safer world than 1939's, he had accepted Washington's Farewell Address, or what he conceived to be its central message, as the eternal Rock on which the Church of foreign policy was founded. As an Absolute Moral Principle, his isolationism had ever since been impervious to whatever factual evidence and logical argument might be brought against it, for it was that by which he measured their truth and goodness. Even the moral authority of Jesus Christ, clearly expressed, would have been helpless against it. Borah himself had said so. "If the Saviour of mankind would revisit the earth and declare for a League [of Nations] . . ." he had cried during the League battle, "I would be opposed to it."[8]

Obviously, if Jesus Christ could not be persuasive of Borah on what Borah clearly regarded as a moral question, Roosevelt could never hope to be. The most he could hope for was to counteract Borah's influence over that night's meeting. And it may have been a felt need to match his chief opponent's moral fervor with his own on the other side, thus neutralizing such "morality" altogether and leaving practical minds free to deal with crucial practical matters—it may well have been this which determined the manner in which Roosevelt finally opened the discussion. Certainly his first words came as something of a shock amidst the conviviality, though this too could have been a calculated effect.

"Perhaps it would be the proper thing," he said solemnly, "to open this meeting with prayer. For our decision may affect the destiny of not only our *own* people but of all the peoples of the world."

He did not, however, offer prayer. Instead he plunged grimly into the business at hand. For more than an hour he reviewed the events—the repeated fascist aggressions, the repeated yieldings of the democracies—which had brought the world to the very edge of the abyss. That it *was* truly the edge he strove to impress upon his listeners by every means at his command while Borah, as Roosevelt warily noted, grew increasingly restive. War *could* break out at any moment. The "possibility" of its doing so before the next regular session of Congress was "very strong" as things now stood but would be much weakened if the embargo were repealed.

He told why this was so, in his conviction—and obviously so. He referred to his own repeated efforts to save the peace.

"But now I've fired my last shot," he concluded. "I think I ought to have another round in my belt."[9]

Then it was Hull's turn, and he was more emphatic in his prediction of dire events, and far more emotional in his assessment of them, than the President had been. If general war came, America's vital interests, perhaps her very survival, would be at stake. Moreover (he said this flatly), the war *would* come by the end of summer—unless Congress repealed the embargo. Repeal would reduce what was not a certainty to a fifty-fifty proposition. . . . He looked toward the Presidential couch.

Roosevelt, leaning forward, nodded and spoke, saying that the nation was indeed endangered by the extreme isolation of Senator Nye . . .

"There are others, Mr. President!"

The lion of Idaho had been unable any longer to restrain himself, and Roosevelt, somewhat taken aback, turned to him.

"What did you say, Senator Borah?"[10]

"I said there are others, Mr. President. Senator Nye is not alone . . ." And he went on boldly to challenge the Executive's premises. "There is not going to be any war in Europe. At least not soon. Germany is not ready for it. All this hysteria is manufactured and artificial."

He spoke dogmatically, assertively, and Roosevelt could see that Hull bristled at the implied insult. Quickly, the President turned to his Secretary of State.

"Cordell," he said, "what do you say to that?"

"All I can say . . ." And Hull was controlling himself with difficulty. ". . . is that I wish Senator Borah would come to my office and look over the cables coming in. I feel satisfied he would modify his views."

Borah, shaking his lionesque head, addressed himself to the President. "I've listened to what the Secretary of State has to say about the information he has . . ." The tone was smug, almost contemptuous. ". . . but I have my own sources of information in Europe that I regard as more reliable than those of the State Department, and I can say to you that there is not going to be any war."

There followed a moment of stunned, embarrassed silence. A red-faced Cordell Hull struggled to hold back tears of helpless anger. The President leaned back in his couch, his eyes closed. The Senator from Idaho, his mouth clamped tightly shut, tilted his formidable jaw forward and upward. Garner at last broke the silence with a mild joke, attempting with some success to restore ease to the company.

Later, when the opinions of others in the room were being canvassed, someone asked for Hull's view on a point someone else had raised. The Secretary replied bitterly that he had nothing more to contribute "in the light of the complacent way Senator Borah has brushed aside the whole mass of facts we have in the State Department." Whereupon Senator Austin spoke up in support of the Administration position, insisting that "the time has come to repeal this impossible act." McNary, though he later told Barkley he thought the President was right, was noncommittal.

The hour of midnight now approached. As the discussion lagged, Garner asked Barkley point-blank if he had enough votes to override the committee action and bring the repeal issue up for vote on the Senate floor. Barkley admitted he did not. Each of the others, individually asked by Garner, made the same estimate of the voting situation. If their answers dismayed the Vice-President he hid the fact well as he shrugged, his bright blue eyes twinkling toward the President from beneath their white-thatched brows.

"Well, Captain," he said, "we may as well face the facts. You haven't got the votes and that's all there is to it."[11]

Roosevelt acknowledged this good-humoredly. He had done the best he could, he said. He did feel, however (glancing toward Steve Early), that the public had a right to know where the responsibility lay in this matter—

"There'll be no difficulty about that," interrupted Borah, assertively.

Well, then, said the President, summoning Early to his side. Swiftly, as the White House clocks struck twelve and the morning of July 19 began, two brief communiqués were drafted, to be handed to the reporters waiting downstairs. One stated the consensus of the Senators present, Republican and Democratic alike, that no action on neutrality legislation could be obtained at this session of Congress. The other said: "The President and the Secretary of State maintained the definite position that failure by the Senate to take action now would weaken the leadership of the United States in exercising its potent influence in the cause of preserving peace among other nations in the event of a new crisis in Europe between now and next January."[12]

iii. *Sultry, Sullen August: The Abyss*

> "In the real dark night of the soul it is always three o'clock in the morning."
>
> F. SCOTT FITZGERALD

In early August, the President went up to Hyde Park to become for a few hot days Squire Roosevelt, the country gentleman, driving around his estate in his Ford (especially built for him, with hand controls) and taking his ease with friends on a porch that looked down sloping green acres over the Hudson. But he was still President. Every day he talked on the phone with Under Secretary of State Sumner Welles, in Washington, and every day the concentrated essence of the news Welles gave him from abroad was more bitter to his taste—or would have been had not his palate become, by this time, numbed.

The belated efforts of Chamberlain and Daladier to entice Soviet Russia into a military alliance with their countries, guaranteeing Poland's territorial integrity, were obviously failing. The event had been predictable and to some extent discounted in Washington ever since the iron-hard anti-Western Vyacheslav Molotov had replaced the genial Maxim Maximovich Litvinov (his collective security policy in ruins about him) as Soviet Commissar for Foreign Affairs in early May. Why, after all, should Stalin seriously consider such a pact? Its probable effect would be precisely that Hitlerian drive to the east which had for so long been the wish behind British and French policy. During the Czech crisis of September 1938, Russia had announced her readiness to fulfill her treaty obligations, which required her to go to the aid of an attacked Czechoslovakia *provided* that the French did so—and the French, of course, were most solemnly pledged to do so. Instead of accepting this opportunity to face Hitler (and doubtless face him down) with an overwhelming combination of powers, the men of Munich, ignoring Russia, had preferred to render impotent a well-trained and -armed Czech army of a million and a half men, plus a formidable Czech air force; to abandon a fortified frontier running across excellent defensive terrain; and (ultimately) to add to Nazi armaments the production of the vast Skoda works. Immediately following the final crushing of Czechoslovakia in mid-March, the Soviet Union had made yet another attempt toward collective action, proposing a six-power conference to discuss ways and means of stopping Hitler. Chamberlain had dismissed the suggestion as "premature." If this was utter madness it had, from Stalin's point of view, a discernible method: a Nazified Czechoslovakia, flanking Poland on the south, was as a spear aimed at the Ukraine. And since the men of Munich remained in control of their governments, what reason did Stalin have to believe that Britain and France would actually aid him with an effective western front if Hitler should drive on through Poland toward Moscow? Obviously, he had none. One major snag in the present negotiations, as a matter of fact, had been Poland's stubborn refusal, sustained by Paris and London, to permit Soviet troops to enter her territory from the east if the Nazis moved in from the west—a refusal that meant that Soviet troops could engage the Germans only after the latter stood on Russian soil. . . . On June 29, Andrei Zhdanov, one of the men closest to Stalin, published in *Pravda* an article expressing his opinion that "the British and French Governments are not out for a real agreement acceptable to the U.S.S.R. but only for talks about an agreement in order to demonstrate before the public opinion of their own countries the alleged unyielding attitude of the U.S.S.R. and thus facilitate the conclusion of an agreement with the aggressors."[13]

But if the failure to form a Western alliance with Russia had been expected, if the accumulating evidence of it therefore held no new alarms and terrors for the American Executive, there was another development which, if not wholly unexpected, was almost incredible and altogether ominous. If anything had seemed certain amidst the shifting sands and fogs of European politics it had been the implacable enmity between

Hitler's Germany and Stalin's Russia. The assumption of it, justified by an abundance of historical evidence, remained basic to Anglo-French policy. What after all *was* Fascism as a historic movement save a violent reaction against Communism? Opposition to the latter was its very *raison d'être*, and both Hitler and Stalin had said so—ceaselessly, vociferously—in their domestic as in their foreign propaganda. If such propaganda were at all effective, and there was much evidence that it was highly so, it must by now have generated an energy of mutual popular hatred so powerful as to render impossible any accommodation whatever between the two nations even if the dictators themselves should wish it. Of this, British and French policymakers were convinced when they finally and reluctantly opened negotiations with the Russians. They refused to take seriously the proposal to Molotov by the German Ambassador in Moscow, in early May, that a Russo-German trade agreement be negotiated; they took even less seriously Molotov's counterproposal that the economic agreement be part of a more general political settlement.

American diplomacy, however, less ideological in its assumptions than that of the European democracies, registered definite if necessarily secret alarm. Two former U. S. Ambassadors to the Soviet Union—William C. Bullitt, now Ambassador to France, and Joseph E. Davies, now Ambassador to Belgium—issued early warnings that a Nazi-Soviet pact, far from being impossible, became increasingly probable with every British and French rebuff of Soviet overtures; and in June and early July there came repeated warnings from the present U. S. Ambassador in Moscow, Laurence A. Steinhardt, that the probable grew rapidly toward the certain. In response to this, Roosevelt in early July had sent a personal message to Stalin via the Soviet Ambassador, who returned to Moscow on leave, warning the Russian dictator that Hitler would certainly attack Russia as soon as France was disposed of if Stalin now encouraged the latter development by entering into an agreement with the Nazis.[14] There was small likelihood that such a message, in such circumstances, would have any influence on Stalin's final decision. Certainly there was no indication that it had had. On the contrary, every sign now pointed to the swift conclusion of the dreaded pact. Roosevelt had hardly the time to don casual country clothes, after his arrival in Hyde Park, when Welles informed him over the private wire from the State Department that Molotov and the German Ambassador to Russia, Count Frederic Werner von der Schulenburg, seemed close to agreement and that the terms reportedly included a new partition of Poland between their respective States.

He was now very tired. In Washington's sultry heat, his anxious burdens had worn his nerves to a frazzle—and neither his burdens nor the heat were lessened to any important degree in the Hudson River Valley. What he badly needed was a complete change, a sea change, and he had scheduled one to begin on August 12: on that day he embarked on the Navy cruiser *Tuscaloosa* for a coasting voyage along northern New England. It was on the *Tuscaloosa*, then, that Roosevelt learned of Hitler's increasing pressure on Poland through the third week of August. The Nazi dictator would no longer be satisfied by the return of Danzig to the Reich; he now demanded the Corridor itself . . .

On August 24, in the Kremlin in Moscow, representatives of Germany and Russia signed a ten-year non-aggression pact. The news of it exploded as a bombshell upon the unsuspecting publics of Britain and France and the United States, shattering for the moment the very foundations of their thought about world power relationships. Roosevelt learned of it as the *Tuscaloosa* sailed south and west in the sunset light. Next morning, a black Friday, he debarked at New Jersey's Sandy Hook and hurried to Washington where his train was met at the Union Station by Sumner Welles. The Under Secretary briefed his superior on the latest developments as the two men rode in the limousine up Pennsylvania Avenue toward the White House.

* * *

Midnight came and passed. America hurtled through night toward the blood-red dawn of September 1, 1939. The telephone rang beside his bed. Instantly wide awake, he picked up the receiver.

"Who is it?"

"This is Bill Bullitt, Mr. President."

"Yes, Bill."

"Tony Biddle has just got through from Warsaw, Mr. President. Several German divisions are deep in Polish territory, and fighting is heavy. Tony said there were reports of bombers over the city. Then he was cut off. He tried to get you for half an hour before he called me."

Roosevelt glanced at his watch. It was ten minutes till three.

"Well, Bill," he said, "it's come at last. God help us all."[15]

II

In the Valley of Indecision

i. *Dr. Sachs Calls Upon the President*

As his visitor entered, Franklin Roosevelt's gaze was bent upon the desk whose litter of letters and memoranda, books and photographs and nautical mementoes, was expressive not only of his unchanneled administrative techniques, so irritating to the neat and tidy, but also of the man's personality, his mind, his interests. Many had found him diverse and unpredictable, as impossible to classify as America herself. His methods were multiform and erratic, but he had a bone-deep commitment to the rights, the dignity, the sacred value of the human person. In his own person he might be deemed an uncompleted or yet-building bridge between an era that had put a *versus* between freedom and organization and an era wherein freedom would be realized (or might be, for the issue remained in doubt) *through* organization.

His visitor of the moment saw him so . . .

Dr. Alexander Sachs, seating himself across the desk from the President, was a man of forty-six who looked like Ed Wynn. He wore his curly hair overlong and his bespectacled eyes had a humorous glint. The prose he talked (and wrote) was as elaborate as Wilkins Micawber's. He was fond of "adumbrating his thesis," as, mentally nourished by a "pluralism of sources," he viewed present developments from the "vantage point of cultural-technological history."[1] But if he required translation to be understood, such translation was well worth making. Far from being the Perfect Fool whose characterization had made Wynn famous, Sachs was one of the keenest of those keen minds who had fed ideas into the New Deal.

He was himself a "pluralistic mind." Born in Russia, he had been formally educated in science, philosophy, jurisprudence, and sociology, and had later become an economic counseler whose expensive advice was sought by some of the nation's wealthiest investors. Thus he was able to focus and fuse mental energies normally widely separated, and with only a few weak connections between them, in overly specialized America. It was in this capacity that he now placed himself before the President of the United States.

The date—October 11, 1939, a Wednesday—might prove worth marking by future historians. On it, and through Sachs, science in America made its first definite if groping and tentative effort to form a working alliance with the Executive power of government . . .

As generally happens when a major scientific breakthrough is scored, the January 1939 announcement of nuclear fission had been followed by a veritable explosion of fruitful research in the newly opened area. Such progress, if gratifying, continued to be dismaying to humane men—and especially to the foreign-born physicists—who knew how science was brought into the service of totalitarian States. There was a blood-tie between physics and high officialdom in Germany: C. F. von Weiszäcker of the Kaiser Wilhelm Institute was the son of the German Under-secretary of State: and through that tie the Nazi government might be immediately responsive to new physical knowledge. There was no tie at all between physics and government in America, and in the view of agitated foreigners the native American physicists had an insufficient urge to shape one. Certainly they had no idea how to do it.

Yet it must be done! And at once!

Leo Szilard from Hungary was convinced of it. So were Fermi, Eugene Wigner from Hungary, Edward Teller from Hungary, and Victor Weisskopf from Austria. Albert Einstein, too, became deeply concerned when, in Princeton, he read a report by Szilard and Fermi in the *Physical Review* indicating that the hitherto remote possibility of a chain reaction (Einstein himself had regarded it as a virtual impossibility)[2] was now distinctly and even immediately possible. Szilard, the active center, the leader, of what became known as the "Fermi Five," was glad to learn of Einstein's concern, for by that time he had become convinced of two things: First, that to obtain the kind of governmental action now needed the President himself must be moved to act and, Second, that the only scientist in America who could obtain private audience with the President, and whose advice would be carefully listened to, was Einstein. Accordingly, in July, the "Five" had approached Einstein with the request that he call upon the President.

The moment must have been one of excruciating moral choice for the author of Relativity who was also, with Gandhi, one of the two most famous exponents of non-violence in this most violent of centuries. But what, in 1939, were the actual alternatives? Was the choice between violence and non-violence? Or was it between more or less violence? If the latter, surely the less violent, the less destructive end would be served if whatever explosive power might come from fission were in American rather than in Nazi hands. . . . At any rate, Einstein, though he refused to attempt a personal visit with Roosevelt, agreed to sign a personal letter addressed to the President. Wigner and Szilard immediately set about drafting it. Einstein signed it on August 2, 1939.

There remained the problem of making sure the letter came to the President's personal attention. It must be given into Roosevelt's hand by someone to whom the President would listen, and who would be qualified to answer questions. The "Five" were unable to find such a man. Weeks passed. Poland was invaded: World War II began. It was then that the "Five" turned, almost desperately, to Alexander Sachs. He was a friend of Szilard's and had discussed with him, Wigner, and Einstein the possibility of a fission bomb and the probability (though they thought it a certainty) that the Germans aimed at making one; moreover, he dared to demand, and he knew how to command, Roosevelt's full attention. . . . In retrospect, it appears that no better choice could have been made.

Certainly there were reasons why the President might have found it difficult to concentrate on the matter Sachs had in hand that day.

The world yet reeled from the shock of Nazi blitzkrieg in Poland. Within a few hours after the telephone call which awakened Roosevelt September 1, the German Luftwaffe had virtually destroyed the Polish air force. Within a few days, Nazi ground forces had pinched off and encircled major portions of the Polish army. Within four weeks Warsaw had fallen, all effective Polish resistance had been crushed, and the bleeding, conquered land was divided between Germany and the Soviet Union. The Polish conquest with its demonstration of seemingly invincible Nazi military power had been accompanied and followed by what Senator Borah soon dubbed a "phoney war" in the West where, in fact, there had been no fighting at all; and on October 10, in a brief speech inaugurating the Winter Relief for 1939, Hitler asserted that Germany "has no cause for war against the Western Powers" and that he personally had a "readiness for peace." Meanwhile, there were disturbing developments in northeastern Europe. The Soviet Union had begun to press demands upon Finland for cession of territory needed, the Russians claimed, for the proper defense of Leningrad.

All these developments had, of course, repercussions in Washington. Each added to the pressures on Roosevelt personally—and as the Chief Executive of a divided America he must bear them, respond to them with a mind that was far from whole and a will torn between contradictory drives. Ambiguity was of the essence of his official words and deeds that autumn, its nature revealed in the very first of his public reactions to the New World War. This was a radio Fireside Chat delivered on September 3, just a few hours after a weary Neville Chamberlain had broadcast from London that a state of war existed between his country and Germany. "You must master at the outset a simple but unalterable fact in modern foreign relations between nations," Roosevelt had said.

"When peace has been broken anywhere, the peace of all countries everywhere is in danger. . . ." But he also said, "Let no man or woman thoughtlessly and falsely talk of America sending its armies to European fields. . . ." In the very sentence in which he said emphatically that the United States was and would remain a neutral nation, he admitted that he could not ask "that every American remain neutral in thought as well." And he had compounded all this ambiguity with closing sentences that were a ringing appeal to the country's pacifist sentiments: "I have said not once but many times that I have seen war and that I hate war. . . . As long as it remains within my power to prevent it, there will be no blackout of peace in the United States."[3] Two days later the Executive issued a formal declaration of American neutrality and placed an embargo on arms and munitions to all belligerents, as he was required to do by the Neutrality Act.

But he also renewed, with more urgency than ever, his request for a revision of the Neutrality Act. He summoned a special session of Congress and, when it convened on September 21, called for repeal of the embargo provisions and the substitution for them of a requirement "that all purchases . . . be made in cash, and all cargoes . . . carried in the purchasers' own ships, at the purchasers' own risk . . ." This, he said, would make the United States more truly "neutral," since the present arrangement denied to a "seapower . . . its ancient right to buy anything anywhere" and gave a "definite advantage" to a "land power" whose survival did not depend on imports.

Clearly, the "neutrality" which the Administration espoused was not unqualified—it was weighted on the side of the Allies (and, incidentally, Japan). The opposition to it, perforce, was a "neutrality" weighted on the side of Hitler's Germany. And it was significant of the deep confusions of the time that truly dedicated Christian pacifists, having only these two equivocal "neutralities" to choose between, tended to choose the one which aided the fomenter of war, Adolf Hitler. They stood, if uneasily, on the side of Colonel Charles A. Lindbergh who, on September 15, suddenly shed his taciturn habits, his abhorrence of personal publicity, in order to make a radio address heard by an audience as large as the President's—an address whose call for "neutrality" was based on grounds perilously near the racism of Nazi doctrine and actually identical with the Nazi propaganda line on the "cause" of World War II. (Said Lindbergh: "These wars in Europe are not wars in which our civilization is defending itself against some Asiatic intruder. There is no Genghis Khan or Xerxes marching against our Western nations. This is not a question of banding together to defend the white race against foreign invasion. This is simply one more of those age-old struggles within our own family of nations—a quarrel arising from the errors of the last war. . . ." And who had made the errors? The "victors of that war!"[4]) Roosevelt had listened grimly.

The battle lines between the two kinds of "neutrality" were clearly drawn by this second week of October. Roosevelt could draw comfort from this and from the fact that his opponents weakened themselves by the very vehemence of their attack. They were usually intemperate; they were often absurd. Ex-President Herbert Hoover argued that Britain and France did not need American aid! Senator Nye saw "nothing ahead of America but hell" if the Administration policy were followed. Democratic Senator Bennett Champ Clark of Missouri went so far as to assert (in perfect agreement with Goebbels) that the British and French proved they were the real "aggressors" in this war when they refused to accept the peace which Hilter now offered them! Such nonsense may have aided the Administration when, just the day before Dr. Sachs' call at the White House, it scored an unexpected victory in the Senate, defeating by a vote of 65–26 a Republican attempt to amend the Neutrality Act, separating embargo repeal from the cash-and-carry provision.

Nevertheless the issue remained in doubt; many Americans remained susceptible to the kind of argument Lindbergh had made in his national radio broadcast a month before and would doubtless make again three days later. For on the evening of Friday the thirteenth, on prime radio time, the hero was to make a second broadcast, this one to "clarify his stand" in opposition to Neutrality Act revision. (The war had been "brought about by the desire for strength on the part of Germany and the fear of strength on the part of England and France," Lindbergh would say. Also: "Our bond with Europe is a bond of race and not of political ideology. . . . It is the European race we must preserve. . . . Racial strength is vital—politics a luxury. If the white race is ever seriously threatened, it may then be time for us to take our part for its protection. . . ." Etc.[5])

Sachs was of course aware of the swirling, far-reaching pressures upon the harried man who nevertheless, this golden October day, looked up from the cluttered desk with a smile. He was aware, too, that nothing in Roosevelt's education prepared him for the kind of decision-making which Sachs' communication was to require. The curriculum followed by a Hudson River patrician through Groton and Harvard at the turn of the century included no adequate introduction to physical science, and a lifetime devoted to the law and politics had not remedied the deficiency. To catch and hold the President's attention in these circumstances required a knowledgeable skill. One must know of the President's shield of loquacity, habitually raised against those who pressed requests he felt unable, or was unwilling, to grant. (Sachs, who was himself the opposite of taciturn, knew Roosevelt to be a master at "taking over" a conversation so completely that his baffled petitioner was unable to "get a word in edgewise.") One must know that the President was notably ear-minded, gathering from choice as well as necessity far more of his information from listening than from reading. And, finally, one must be bold . . .

"Mr. President," began Dr. Sachs, with a puckish grin, "I want you to know I paid for my trip to Washington. I can't deduct it from my income tax. So won't you please pay attention?"

Roosevelt laughed.

And Sachs went quickly on to say that the documents he now had in his hand were of such importance that he wished to make certain, before he left, that their contents had actually been communicated to the Executive mind. He would, therefore, with the President's permission, read them aloud.

Roosevelt smilingly nodded, seemingly unperturbed by the implication.

The first document, said Sachs, and the key one, was a letter to F. D. Roosevelt from Albert Einstein. He read it slowly, carefully, emphasizing the major points:

". . . in the course of the last four months it has been made probable through the work of Joliot in France as well as Fermi and Szilard in America—that it may become possible to set up a nuclear chain reaction in a large mass of uranium, by which vast amounts of power and large quantities of new radiumlike elements would be generated. Now it appears almost certain that this could be achieved in the immediate future. . . . This new phenomenon would also lead to the construction of bombs, and it is conceivable . . . that extremely powerful bombs of a new type may thus be constructed. A single bomb of this type, carried by boat and exploded in a port, might very well destroy the whole port together with some of the surrounding territory. . . . In view of this situation you may think it desirable to have some permanent contact maintained between the Administration and the group of physicists working on chain reactions in America. One possible way of achieving this might be for you to entrust with this task a person who has your confidence and who could perhaps serve in an unofficial capacity."

The Einstein letter also pointed out that there was "some good" uranium ore in the "former Czechoslovakia," whence all sales had been halted by the Nazis, but that "the most important source of uranium is the Belgian Congo." Sachs then read aloud a memorandum from Szilard urging that large amounts of pitchblende (containing uranium) be brought to the United States from the Congo. Finally, there was a letter to Roosevelt from Sachs himself, stressing the probability that work on a uranium bomb was being rapidly advanced in Germany and that its unique possession by Hitler, assuming the bomb proved feasible, might well mean a Nazified world. This, too, Sachs read aloud. He then handed all three documents to the President, who at once examined the Einstein letter carefully.

Roosevelt looked up at his visitor, obviously impressed.

"What you are after," he said, no longer smiling, "is to see that the Nazis don't blow us up."

"Precisely," said Sachs.

The President pressed a button. There entered his military aide, Brigadier General Edwin M. Watson, whose benignly paternal appearance and manner caused everyone to call him "Pa."

"Pa," said Roosevelt, handing over the two letters and the Szilard memorandum, "this requires action . . ."[6]

In point of fact, no effective action was to be forthcoming from Sachs' visit. Indeed, the appointment of an Advisory Committee on Uranium, which was its only actual consequence, may have retarded rather than stimulated fission work in America, by lulling with a sense of false security the American scientists through many months of intense and growing danger.[7] But of course the good doctor could not know this as he took leave of the President and went into "Pa" Watson's office to consult on the nature and membership of the Committee. When he walked out beneath the White House portico into autumn sunlight he was, as he deserved to be, a little proud of the manner in which he had handled his assignment, and happily convinced that there would emerge from it, very soon, important developments.

ii. *Fire Smolders in Europe, Then Bursts into Flame*

Through the winter of 1939–40, no fire was apparent on the Western Front in Europe, and scarcely any smoke. The opposing armies lived at peace in their steel-and-concrete fortifications, which they extended and improved in full view of each other. Only in northeastern Europe was there a licking tongue of flame . . .

On November 30, in apparent expectation of easy victory if not actually a welcome from disaffected Finns, Stalin launched a five-pronged attack upon Finland. The aggressors were met by a murderous fire from highly skilled and heroically determined defenders. The political effect upon the Western Allies was electric. Within two weeks after the attack had begun, Soviet Russia had become the only State ever to be expelled from the League of Nations for aggressive acts. Within two months, France, so strangely passive in her declared war upon the Nazis, was preparing to send an expeditionary force of fifty thousand to fight Russia in Finland, and the British were following suit, though with smaller forces. Both were blocked only by the refusal of neutral Norway and Sweden to permit the passage of foreign troops across their territories. Then, in February 1940, after weeks of quiescence amidst the snows and glooms of northern forests, a Russia disabused of false notions massed artillery on the scale of Verdun and the Somme. By mid-March it was all over: the Kremlin dictated peace terms considerably harsher than those originally offered the government in Helsinki. Flame died out in the northeast.

In March, too, a watching world shuddered at the spectacle of a new and daringly imaginative version of blitzkrieg, an amphibious operation which mocked Britain's vaunted command of the seas.

Denmark, whose defense was impossible, fell within hours and with no more than token resistance. This was to be expected—all that was required for such a conquest was ruthlessness, and of ruthlessness the Nazi stock was unlimited. But Norway seemed a different matter. Yet within ten hours after the assault was launched at dawn on Tuesday, April 9, 1940, Oslo and every major Norwegian port, from Narvik in the far north to Kristiansand at the southern tip of the peninsula, was in German hands. How had this dark miracle been achieved? A watching world, dazed by what it saw, found it easy to believe that Norway had been betrayed from within. And indeed she had been. There was in Oslo a certain Major Vidkun Quisling, whose actions at this time were to make his name synonymous with "traitor."

But far more important than treason in achieving the over-all result were surprise and daring and careful planning—an audacity and skill that exploited to the utmost the weaknesses (the slowness of movement, the inadequacies of materiel) which plagued the British, while employing a theretofore unprecedented combination of land, sea, and air tactics.

By early May there were many high governmental officials and soldiers in France and the Lowlands who were more certain than their German counterparts that the German legions were invincible in battle; that the Fuehrer was a mystic genius, a hero drawing inspiration from supernatural sources; and that resistance to the Nazi will and arms was therefore futile if not suicidal. They had premonitions of doom which were in the nature of self-justifying prophecy: by expecting disaster they helped to insure it when, shortly before the dawn of May 10, 1940, the Germans attacked without warning across the frontiers of Holland, Belgium, and tiny Luxemburg, whose governments—despite the urgings of London and Paris, despite the object-lessons of Poland and Scandinavia and 1914—had persisted in a rigid neutrality. "The hour has come for the decisive battle for the future of the German nation," Hitler cried as his armor roared along Low Country roads and his planes swept the skies above them. ". . . the struggle which begins today will decide the fate of the German people for a thousand years. . . ."

Numerically, the opposing armies were evenly matched on that historic Friday. Between the North Sea and Switzerland, 136 German divisions faced 135 French, British, Belgian, and Dutch. The latter possessed what had proved to be an immense advantage in the First World War—a defensive posture in carefully prepared fortifications from which they should be able to inflict (if war in 1940 were as war had been in 1914–18) three casualties upon the attackers for every one they suffered themselves. This "advantage," however, was an illusion which should not have survived Poland and did not survive the opening days of the present battle.

Five days sufficed for the complete subjugation of Holland. A dark night of tyranny closed down upon the dazed and bleeding land shortly after sunset on May 14, when the commander of the Dutch forces ordered his troops to lay down their arms. And on that same earth-shaking day, the fates of Belgium and France were sealed.

The initial response by the French and British was based on the assumption that the mountains and forests of the Ardennes in southeastern Belgium were impassable by a large modern army and that the main weight of the attack must therefore come on the enemy's right wing.[8] The events of May 14 proved this assumption wholly wrong. The Allies concentrated on the fortress line between Namur and Antwerp, actually outnumbering the Germans nearly two to one in that area.[9] But suddenly, without warning, their enemies burst into and through the Ardennes with such a mass of swift-moving heavy armor, preceded by such sky-darkening hordes of tactical bombers as the world had never seen before. Sedan, scene of the French catastrophe of 1870, became now the scene of even greater catastrophe. The center of the Allied line was pierced, and behind the line was nothing—nothing with which to oppose the columns of German tanks that swept behind and around masses of troops, capturing prisoners by the thousand and towns by the dozen at little or no cost to themselves.

The heaviest weight of the German attack now thrust toward the sea, cutting by May 25 the southern and eastern communications of the Allied left wing which, squeezed into a tightening pocket reaching inland from the Strait of Dover, included the French First Army, the French XVI Corps, the British Expeditionary Force, and, to the north, the Belgian Army. The situation of these troops was desperate. Three days later it appeared hopeless. For in the early morning of May 28—without prior consultation with his allies, against the unanimous advice of his cabinet ministers (whom he was as monarch constitutionally obligated to obey), and with a single hour's notice to Lord Gort, the British commander—Leopold III, King of the Belgians, in his capacity as commander-in-chief of the Belgian Army, surrendered unconditionally to the enemy, exposing naked to that enemy some twenty miles of Franco-British flank.

In these direst of circumstances occurred what the free world promptly hailed as "The Miracle of Dunkirk." Hastily plugging the gap opened by Leopold's defection, aided by command errors in the handling of German armor which were inexplicable at the time, the Allies managed successful rear-guard actions against the encircling, more numerous, and better-armed foe; they formed an iron perimeter around the French channel port of Dunkirk and its adjacent wide sandy beaches where myriads of beaten, weary troops were concentrated, their bloodshot eyes turned now toward the sky whence rained the bombs of the Luftwaffe, now toward the sea whence came, in weird armada, their deliverance. By June 4, some 338,000 Allied troops had been removed from Dunkirk to England by a fleet of 861 wildly various vessels in what, if not a miracle, was certainly a masterpiece of improvisation aided by the significant fact

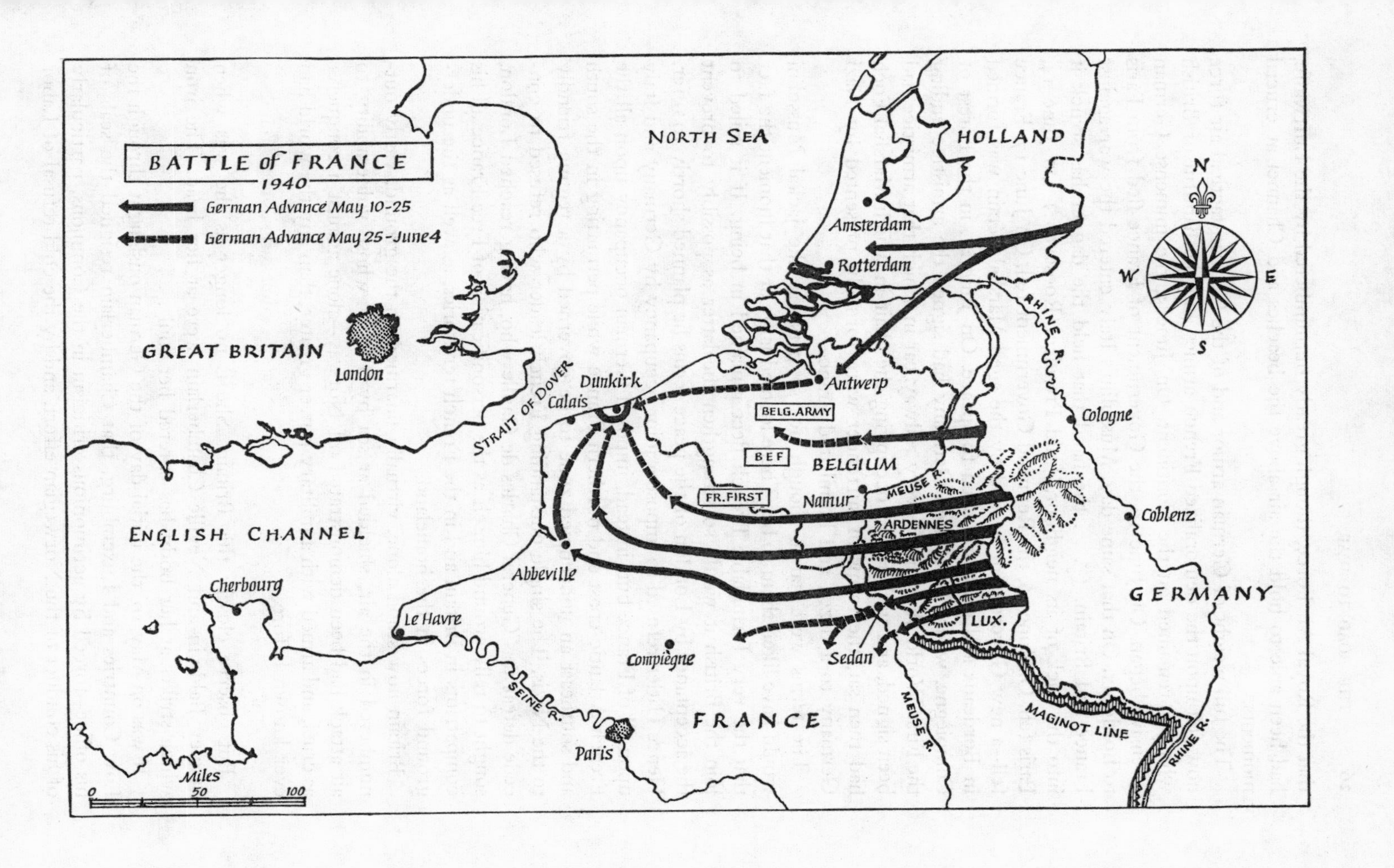
BATTLE of FRANCE
1940
German Advance May 10-25
German Advance May 25-June 4
NORTH SEA
HOLLAND
Amsterdam
Rotterdam
N
W
E
S
GREAT BRITAIN
London
RHINE R.
Antwerp
Dunkirk
Calais
STRAIT OF DOVER
BELG. ARMY
Cologne
BEF
BELGIUM
MEUSE R.
FR. FIRST
Namur
Coblenz
ARDENNES
ENGLISH CHANNEL
Abbeville
GERMANY
Cherbourg
Le Havre
LUX.
Compiègne
Sedan
SEINE R.
MEUSE R.
MAGINOT LINE
RHINE R.
FRANCE
Paris
Miles
0
50
100

that the Royal Air Force, though greatly outnumbered by the Luftwaffe, had been able to hold the air above the beaches and Channel at crucial moments.

The full weight of German armor and of the German tactical air force now fell upon the demoralized French armies and the handful of British who yet remained on the Continent. On June 5, the immense German offensive began. On June 10, the Government of France fled from Paris to Bordeaux. On that same day, Mussolini's Italy entered the war against France and Britain. (". . . the hand that held the dagger has struck it into the back of its neighbor," said President Roosevelt.) On June 14, Paris fell. On June 16, the Reynaud Government fell. On June 17, France fell—a new Government headed by the aged Marshal Pétain was formed in Bordeaux and promptly sued for peace. On June 21, in the Forest of Compiègne, where a defeated Germany had signed the armistice ending the First World War, in the very railway car in which that armistice had been signed, and with Hitler occupying the chair in which Marshal Foch had then sat, the terms of surrender were formally presented by Nazi Germany to a dazed and humiliated France.

The terms were harsh, though not so harsh as the jackal Mussolini would have liked them to be. There loomed large at that moment the fact that the very formidable French fleet remained in being. If it sailed to join the British it would so strengthen the latter as possibly to prevent the acceptance by London of the peace terms he planned shortly to offer. Hence Hitler refused to impose a joint occupancy by Germany and Italy upon all of France but, instead, imposed German occupancy upon all the French Atlantic coast and northern France while permitting in the south and southeast an unoccupied zone to be governed by a regime friendly to the Nazis. The single outstanding French leader who refused to concede defeat was General Charles de Gaulle who, having reached London, sought to rally around himself as the personification of Free France all his compatriots in Britain and in the French territories, as well as the underground forces in the homeland.

Britain now stood alone, virtually unarmed on the ground, vastly outnumbered in the air, shielded at sea by a navy whose vulnerability to air attack had been demonstrated off Norway—alone against a conquerer as cruel, and armed with a military power greater, than any the world had ever known before.

But observe closely this Britain! She is no longer as she was when Stanley Baldwin and Neville Chamberlain were at her head. The iron which strikes at her body has entered her soul . . .

It was on May 10, the initial day of the German onslaught through the Low Countries and Luxemburg, that Chamberlain resigned the seals of his office—forced by acrimonious criticism in the Commons, particularly of his conduct of the Norwegian effort, and by the cold refusal of Labor leaders to join any coalition Government headed by him. In his place now rules a man whose words, whose person, whose every public gesture and almost every act expresses the spirit of a whole people with a perfection seldom seen in history, and never save at those moments of crisis when every possibility can be measured against a single supreme necessity. To Winston Churchill, history is drama, his office a stellar role, himself mystically identified with an author who is also extended vastly beyond him in space and time, embracing the martial ardors and genius of his ancestor Marlborough, the poetry of Shakespeare and Milton, the prose of Gibbon and Macauley, and all the glories of what he so often calls "our ancient island race." Sentimentality on so grand a scale ceases to be sentimental—it becomes an authentic emotion of heroism and, of itself alone, a force that shapes human destiny.

See him, hear him in his first public address as Prime Minister on the day before Holland's surrender, the day prior to Hitler's sword-thrust through the Ardennes into the body of France. Jut-jawed and glowering, he stands in Parliament and declares: "I have nothing to offer but blood, toil, tears and sweat. . . . You ask, What is our policy? I will say: It is to wage war, by sea, land, and air, with all our might and with all the strength that God can give us: to wage war against a monstrous tyranny, never surpassed in the dark, lamentable catalogue of human crime. That is our policy. You ask, What is our aim? I can answer in one word: Victory . . ." See him again three weeks later, on June 4 (the last Englishmen were being taken off the beach at Dunkirk), as again he addresses Parliament and the world, defiance flashing from his eyes like lightning from an ominous cloud and rumbling through his voice like thunder: "[We] shall fight in France, we shall fight in the seas and oceans, we shall fight with growing confidence and growing strength in the air, we shall defend our island, whatever the cost may be, we shall fight on the beaches, we shall fight on the landing-grounds, we shall fight in the fields and on the streets, we shall fight in the hills; we shall never surrender. . . ."

Only once during these initial days of power does Winston Churchill seem to stumble out of step with the march of great events, his mood jarring with that of his time and place—and this may be a false seeming. It is certainly for but an instant. It occurs on June 15. With France now far gone toward total collapse without having managed to deploy effectively one-fourth of her total military strength, with Reynaud struggling desperately to persuade the Council in Bordeaux that the French Government should go to Africa with the Fleet and from there continue the war, a radical proposal is put forward in London, not by notoriously impractical dreamers but by such sober-minded national patriots as Lord Halifax and General de Gaulle, Sir Robert Vansittart and M. René Plevin. It calls for the "indissoluble union" of Britain and France, an actual fusion into one of their separate identities and sovereign powers: "Every citizen of France will enjoy immediately citizenship of Great Britain; every British subject will become a citizen of France."[10]

The instant is one in which a gap opens through the black fury of present time to reveal deep underlying trends, a gap through which those not blinded by ancient tradition may catch a glimpse of the future. Winston Churchill is outraged. He sees, he smells something akin to treason. But he is under the pressure of events, he is presented with choices, for which there are no clear precedents and he soon yields this point to the majority of his Cabinet, chiefly on the ground that "some dramatic statement" is needed "to keep the French going." The hope is overwhelmed by past enmities and present terror, however, in the Council meeting which Reynaud summons in Bordeaux. England within three weeks "will have her neck wrung like a chicken," says Pétain: the proposed Union would be tantamount to "fusion with a corpse." The Council refuses even to vote on the proposal, so that Reynaud, having staked the last coins of his prestige upon it, is forced to resign.

Thereafter, through all the long summer and autumn of Britain's solitary defiance, there is no question but that Churchill's character, in its salient features, is at one with that of the people he leads. Hitler's peace overtures rebuffed (the tyrant is at first incredulous, then furious); the French Fleet forcibly neutralized (there is brisk naval action at Dakar and Oran); the Luftwaffe in full force met and defeated by the R.A.F. between mid-July and late September in the Battle of Britain; the island's home defenses strengthened as the danger of invasion is weakened; the U-boat menace increased as the Battle of the Atlantic begins on terms initially unfavorable to the Royal Navy; these are the major open events of Britain's war as the weeks pass. To each, Churchill makes his contribution. From each his eloquence extracts the last full measure of propaganda power, shrewdly directed toward the west.

But it is to a war effort largely hidden from public view, an effort whose means is a series of cables signed "Former Naval Person," that he makes his unique and greatest contribution. They go, these messages, from the Prime Minister of Great Britain to the President of the United States: they plead, they argue, they flatter, they cajole, they inform, and in several instances, sharpening with their eloquence the logic of events, they persuade. They persuade in the sense that, without them, their recipient might have postponed important action that was immediately needed.

For though Roosevelt is now more than ever convinced that his country's vital interests demand a British victory, though he is determined to do all in his power to insure that victory, he is also in the throes of an election campaign. He is running for an unprecedented third term as President of the United States. It behooves him to avoid so far as possible every appearance of exceeding his Constitutional authority in the conduct of foreign affairs.

iii. *In the Commodore Hotel, November 1940*

"This generation of Americans has a rendezvous with destiny."

FRANKLIN DELANO ROOSEVELT

There were two men in the room, and anyone who saw them for the first time, not knowing who or what they were, would have known at once that they were brothers. Each was a large, heavy man, brawny, broad-shouldered; each had thick, tousled dark hair, clear gray eyes, and an unusually long upper lip; each was in his forties and either might (so far as appearance went) have been the elder, though by no more than a year or two. The chief difference apparent to a casual glance was that the one who knelt before the television set (a new-fangled gadget in that year) was in his shirt-sleeves whereas the other—slumped back in a lounge chair, feet propped upon a straight-back—had on a coat and vest. Indeed, the coat looked as if it had not been off that beefy back in a long week, so rumpled it was, so flaked and streaked with cigarette ash, though in actual fact it had been freshly pressed and newly put on barely twelve hours ago, at the outset of what was for its wearer the most important of all the days of his life.

When the kneeling man stood up, however, and his brother stood up also, heaved himself up out of the chair to prowl restlessly around the room as he had been doing from time to time all evening, the apparent difference between the two increased. The shirt-sleeved one was a veritable giant of a man. He towered several inches over his brother, who himself stood an inch above six feet in his stocking feet. And his physical movements were more relaxed, as his face to a closer look appeared younger (his eyes more clear, his color fresher) than his brother's. Moreover, it became apparent that in the relationship between the two the taller man willingly and even eagerly subordinated himself to the shorter; he was protective, he gave service, he ran interference. He had been especially valuable in the latter role, both figuratively and literally (he had been an All-American tackle on the Navy football team a quarter-century before), for many hectic weeks now—ever since that late June day in Philadelphia when his brother, who had been a registered Democrat in 1938 and who still (in 1940) occasionally addressed supporters as "you Republicans," had become the Republican candidate for President of the United States.

The shirt-sleeved one spoke now with determined cheeriness.

"They generally pile up big majorities early in the evening, don't they, Wen?" he asked.

"Almost always," the other said, hoarsely, pausing in his bearlike prowl. "The Eastern city vote is always the first in, and it's Democratic."

The door opened. A harried-looking young man entered, bearing a sheet of paper which he handed to the shirt-sleeved one who took it, glanced at it, and passed it on to his brother with a wide grin. Through the open door, coming across the suite's living room from the corridor beyond, entered also a murmurous rise and fall of many voices threaded through by a steady pounding of teletypes. Someone ran panting along the hall. Then the harried young man left, closing the door behind him. The candidate, reading the sheet, grinned too.

"Looks good, Ed," he said. "They'd have to carry New York City a lot bigger than it looks like they're going to . . ."

And he flung himself into the lounge chair and ran a hand through his hair, a lock of which nevertheless promptly tumbled down upon his forehead. But his grin became uncertain as (the television sound being turned down) he listened to a radio news analyst's latest interpretation of the voting trend. Soon the grin faded out altogether. Grimness replaced it.[11]

There was a pattern, a distinctive rhythm and sequence, in the events of Wendell Willkie's adult life, determined by a typically American polarity of idealism and pragmatism. The latter was identified with the feminine principle in its influence upon him, for if he did not inherit through his mother's bloodstream an intensely competitive spirit and a veritable passion for success, he certainly had these instilled in him by his mother's conscious teaching and, even more, by her example. The first woman to be admitted to the bar in Indiana, she was also the first woman to smoke cigarettes in Elwood, Indiana, where she practiced law in partnership with her husband, Herman Willkie; and if her nonconformity served freedom, widening the limits of possible action for more timid souls, this was on her part inadvertent. She asserted her egoistic will, she overcame opposing wills, when she flouted conventions: a Germanic lust for power (she was born Henrietta Trisch) ruled her days. She "exercised a dread power at the family hearth," a biographer has written,[12] and also "continuously dinned into [the] . . . young minds" of her children her ambitions for their "success."

It was in the tradition of his mother that Lewis Wendell Willkie, corporation lawyer, played Big Business as a game all through the Roaring Twenties, and played it to win the highest stakes. In the era of Coolidge and Hoover, he climbed from a minor legal post with the Firestone Tire and Rubber Company in Akron to a commanding position on Wall Street—the presidency and board chairmanship of Commonwealth & Southern, a giant utility holding corporation with total assets of well over a billion dollars—and then, as the youngest major corporation executive in America, sprang into national prominence by waging stubborn and skillful war upon the New Deal's electric power policies as manifest in the Tennessee Valley Authority, the holding company "death sentence" clause, and the proposals (which his influence helped to defeat) for other river authorities modeled on TVA. In this character he was an eloquent advocate of individualism and free enterprise at the same time as his talent for large-scale organization and administration served those processes of collectivization, those tendencies toward monopoly, which were inherent in the development of public utilities.

But there was also alive in him the very different tradition of his father, a small-town lawyer who, as Joseph Barnes writes,[13] "had no ambition to be anything more than he was, to get anywhere, to pile up any fortune." Herman Willkie (the family name was originally "Willcke") was of that German stock which rebelled against militarism and despotism in 1848 and then, in search of freedom, emigrated to America. From the Old World, Herman carried to the New a vivid memory of the whipping given him by a Prussian officer who, forcibly quartered upon the civilian household, had stumbled over him as he, who was hardly more than an infant, played upon the floor. This beating represented to him the whole brutal meaning of the Prussian State and of all tyranny. He spoke of it often to his children, who knew him as one passionately devoted to liberty, to justice as liberty's guardian, to education as liberty's handmaiden, and to the unfettered mind as liberty's essence.

It was from his father that Wendell Willkie derived his profound commitment to civil liberties, his political ideals and values, his strongly partisan devotion to the Democratic party. Through his father came persuasive echoes of the Populist Revolt and the struggling rise of labor unions, of William Jennings Bryan and the Cross of Gold, and (directly and strongly) the influence of Woodrow Wilson with his New Freedom and his later martyrdom for the League of Nations. Largely in emulation of his father he decided to become a lawyer, entering the Indiana law school after he had received his A.B. degree. In his father's tradition he delivered a slashing attack upon the political conservatism of the State Supreme Court and the law school faculty when, as the school's Class Day orator in 1916, he spoke on "The New Freedom." (His oration so outraged the school authorities that they refused to award him in public ceremony the LL.B. degree he had earned; they gave it to him privately several days later.) In the same tradition he, while in Akron, challenged and helped to break the political power of the Ku Klux Klan in Ohio, and dared take issue in public speech with the arrogant, seemingly omnipotent Samuel Insull of Chicago after Insull, at a 1929 meeting of utility executives, had bitterly denounced the "radical agitators" who criticized Big Business and had urged upon his hearers the need to find means of silencing them.

When he resigned his Firestone post to enter private law practice in 1921, he was told by Harvey Firestone himself that he would probably never amount to much because he was a Democrat, and no Democrat ever did. The warning, which might also be deemed a bribe, had gone unheeded at the time and for many years thereafter. A delegate to the Democratic National Convention in 1932, he had voted for Roosevelt and the promised New Deal in November, despite the candidate's proposal to regulate utility holding companies and develop public electric power wherever private power was inadequate or overpriced; and his first response to TVA was an attempt to come to such terms with it as would give maximum protection to the stockholders he represented. It was not until well into 1934 that he came to the forefront of Big Business's war upon That Man in the White House, and it was not until almost the end of 1938 that the Man became so closely identified with the party in his mind that he ceased to consider himself a Democrat.

Thus the polarity, the tension, the basic plot of that drama of the self on which millions of eyes suddenly and intently focused in the spring and summer of 1940. The Republicans, faced by their quadrennial problem of finding a Presidential candidate who might win an electoral majority while representing (essentially) a single minority interest, had presented to them this double-character, this charming ambiguity, this intermittent war of self-on-self within a physical presence so ruggedly handsome and a personality so warmly engaging that only a very penetrating psychologist could have sensed its possibly fatal dangers. A powerful, bearlike physique, evidently unaffected by lack of exercise and the chain-smoking of cigarettes; a visible and audible effect of great virility and of seemingly inexhaustible energy (men found him impressive, women sexually attractive); a quick wit sustained by a wide range of information and a notable talent for debate; a sophistication which appealed to Eastern intellectuals joined to an untidy homespun Hoosier quality which promoted easy communication with farmers and workingmen—these formed a compendium of campaign assets which could not be matched by New York's sharp, hard prosecuting attorney, Thomas E. Dewey, nor by Ohio's dry, lean Senator Robert A. Taft, who were the other two leading contenders for the nomination.

What happened in Philadelphia was richly ironic.

The Republicans who first gathered together on a rainy June Sunday did so in the shadow of a political event as gloomy for most of them as the clouds that hung low over the City of Brotherly Love. A Democratic President, responding to the fall of France to Nazi Germany and the threat to lonely Britain, had just appointed two leading Republicans to his Cabinet: Frank Knox, the Republican Vice-Presidential candidate in 1936, was named Secretary of the Navy; Henry L. Stimson, a Cabinet member in former Republican administrations, was named Secretary of War. A Republican convention then proceeded to nominate as its Presidential candidate a lifelong Democrat whose conversion to Republicanism was so recent and limited that many among the party's professional hard core doubted its sincerity.

(Former Senator James E. Watson of Willkie's home state of Indiana was among those who doubted. When Willkie asked him for support, prior to the convention's opening, Watson flatly refused. "If a whore repented and wanted to join the church," he said, "I'd personally welcome her and lead her up the aisle to a pew, but, by the Eternal, I'd not ask her to lead the choir the first night."[14]) Moreover, the nominee won over his rivals more on the grounds he held in common with Roosevelt, in opposition to his party's hard core, than he did on the grounds he shared with his party in opposition to the New Deal. And this irony was extended and enriched by the selection of the candidate for Vice-President. Charles L. McNary of Oregon, the Senate Minority Leader, was an isolationist (if less fervently so than some), a supporter of TVA and every other Federal power project, an opponent of the reciprocal tariff agreements which Willkie strongly favored, and an opponent of Willkie's candidacy when the convention opened.

If the campaign which followed was not uniquely revealing of the American mind and character in confused suspense between different kinds of world, it was certainly an instructive demonstration of the manner in which the American political system operates in an election year to blur real issues, introduce false ones, and thereby frequently prevent the making of clear choices by the electorate.

Having been nominated because he more closely resembled his Democratic opponent in essential respects than did any other available Republican, Wendell Willkie must now convince the millions that the difference between him and Roosevelt—and between his philosophy of government and the New Deal—was as great and crucial as that between life and death. It was difficult to do this in the field of foreign policy. His hatred of Nazi-Fascist tyranny was as deep as his father's blood in him; so was his conviction that the survival of American democracy required the total defeat of the Axis. He was therefore determined at the outset to say and do nothing that would reduce American aid to Britain or give the slightest encouragement to Hitler. And in the lurid light of the flames that consumed western Europe he adhered to this determination through July, August, and most of September. He supported the President's demand for immediate enlargement of the Army, Navy, and their air arms. He approved the first peacetime military conscription in American history (introduced on June 20 and passed in September after the President, fearing the political effects of isolationist attacks, promised that no drafted troops would be "sent to take part in European wars"). He even approved, against the increasingly angry pressures of Republican professionals, the arrangement whereby the United States presented fifty "over-age" destroyers to Great Britain in return for the donation and lease by Britain to the U.S. of naval bases in the Western Hemisphere. Indeed, his earliest campaign charge against the Administration's conduct of foreign affairs was that it had been weak and vacillating in the face of Nazi-Fascist aggressions.

This strategy, however, was quite obviously self-defeating, as Willkie himself soon recognized. It bitterly alienated the isolationists at the core of his own party and it was wholly inconvincing to others who, of course, had pointed out to them the undeniable fact that the chief Republican spokesmen and the overwhelming majority of the Republicans in Congress had opposed every effort to strengthen the national defense and to join in the only kind of concerted international action which might have deterred the aggressors abroad.

Willkie's major stress, therefore, was on domestic affairs—but since such differences as he had in this area with the New Deal were nearly all of detail, degree, and emphasis rather than of substance, his prophesies of doom, should the New Deal be continued, had in general the quality of a *non sequitur*. "He agreed with Mr. Roosevelt's entire program of social reform," said Norman Thomas, commenting on Willkie's acceptance speech, "—and said it was leading to disaster." Interior Secretary Harold L. Ickes focused the Willkie dilemma more picturesquely if no more sharply when he spoke of the Republican candidate as "the rich man's Roosevelt, the simple, barefoot Wall Street lawyer" whose proposal that the President meet him in public debate of the issues before the country would have made more sense had it been made to his own "running-mate, Senator McNary, with whom he is at greater variance . . . than . . . with the President." Abundantly clear was the fact that Willkie had no positive program of his own to offer in contrast to, or in comparison with, the New Deal.

Perhaps it was his inward sense of inadequacy in a false role, his need to submerge in action the doubts which gnawed at him—it may have been this that determined the amount and kind of effort he devoted to his campaign. Certainly the campaign was arduous beyond any waged before by a Presidential candidate. In fifty days he made 560 speeches, all save the first few in a rasping croak over a microphone; for his normal speaking voice was gone by the first day of his official campaign, a fact which may have had (as some said at the time) a psychological significance. It was as if he sought to have the means justify the end, instead of the other way around. Would he be devoting such great and painful effort to the pursuit of a goal not supremely important? Obviously not. *Therefore* the goal he pursued was supremely important, and not just to himself but to all mankind.

The most maddening thing was that Roosevelt refused to answer. The President presented no immediate and specific targets at which a straight-shooter might aim; he raised no personal resistance against which the Republican might define himself in the eyes and ears of the populace. "Events move so fast in other parts of the world," Roosevelt had said in his speech in Chicago accepting nomination for an unprecedented third term, "that it has become my duty to remain either in the White House itself or at some nearby point where I can reach Washington and even Europe and Asia by direct telephone—where, if need be, I can be back at my desk in the space of a very few hours. . . . I shall not have the time or the inclination to engage in a purely political debate." As Commander-in-Chief he made brief inspection tours of defense plants and naval installations; as Executive resident in the White House he was absorbed in the problems incident to a vastly expanding defense production, the reshuffling of his Cabinet following the nomination of Secretary of

Agriculture Henry A. Wallace as his running mate, the destroyer deal, the Selective Service legislation and administration. He ignored Wendell Willkie.

And so, as September waned, Willkie faced once again a choice between pragmatism and idealism, in such circumstances as to make his choice of some world-historical importance. By then he was in the state typical of Presidential candidates in the closing weeks of a campaign, a state aggravated in his case by unprecedented expenditures of personal effort. He was tired, so tired as to be deprived of the use of his higher critical faculties. His compulsive energies were focused upon the single limited goal of election victory; with whatever lay beyond that he was increasingly prone to take gambler's chances; and by then the pressures upon him to take chances with America's stakes in the war were intense. They came not only from the professionals within his own party but also, in the form of provocations, from the professionals of the opposition party. Scarcely had he been nominated before leading Democrats were striving to link his cause with that of Nazi-Fascism in the popular mind. On July 5, Roosevelt used the term "corporate government" in such a way as to imply (or so many believed) that Willkie, a corporation executive, might seek to establish a "corporate state," on the fascist model, in the interests of "efficiency." In late September, Governor Herbert H. Lehman of New York asserted in a public speech that nothing could give greater aid and comfort to Hitler, Mussolini, and the militarists of Japan than Roosevelt's defeat. In early October, Henry Wallace (typically) went to the farthest extreme. "The Nazi support of Wendell Willkie is part of Adolf Hitler's plan to weaken and eventually conquer the United States," the Democratic Vice-Presidential candidate flatly declared. These assertions could not but stimulate Willkie's temptation to charge that Roosevelt, in seeking a third term, evinced an ambition to himself become a dictator, and that he would involve the United States in war in order to achieve this ambition.

Willkie yielded . . .

At first he yielded only a little, possibly as an inadvertence. At least he *may* have been more concerned to impugn Roosevelt's honesty in general and deficit financing in particular than he was to inject the war issue into the campaign when he said in late September: "If his [Roosevelt's] promise to keep our boys out of foreign wars is no better than his promise to balance the budget, they're already almost on the transports." But it was as if he opened a crack in a dam during flood season—soon the dam gave way completely and he was himself swept away by the torrent. By mid-October the war issue was central to his campaign; the man on whom he'd tried to pin an "appeaser" label only a few short weeks before had become a "warmonger," who, he darkly hinted, might already have made "secret agreements" to bring America into the war. And his new campaign oratory, though dismaying to those who judged it by idealistic standards, seemed to pass with flying colors the pragmatic test of "truth."

One reason for this, helping Willkie (no doubt) to rationalize his conduct, was that by October the Battle of Britain had been won by the R.A.F., and everyone knew that the Luftwaffe had failed despite an all-out effort to win, that control of British skies which was necessary for successful invasion. Everyone knew that Britain would not give in but was determined and able, within as yet unmeasured limits, to defend herself. Hence charges of "warmonger," which would have gone unheeded by men who felt immediately threatened by Nazi-Fascist aggression became persuasive to men who felt there remained a chance to survive in freedom without war and that full advantage of that chance might not be taken.

The Gallup Poll, which had showed Roosevelt leading Willkie by a comfortable 10 per cent of the popular vote in late September, showed a sharp reduction of this margin in the third week of October, when Roosevelt at last announced that he would make five addresses in the two weeks preceding Election Day in order to answer "deliberate falsifications of fact" by the Republicans. Professional Democrats hailed the news, but were by no means completely reassured. They felt the tide running strong against them; their chief may have delayed too long . . .

What followed, as regards foreign policy, was a lowering spiral of action-reaction that sucked the campaign, the candidates, and the nation into disgraceful and dangerous depths.

Roosevelt made his first campaign address on October 23 in Philadelphia, laying equal stress upon his love of peace, his devotion to neutrality, and his record on national defense.[15] On October 28, at a huge rally in Madison Square Garden, he assailed Republican leaders for "playing politics with national defense" (a charge whose effective gravity was increased by Mussolini's unprovoked invasion of Greece from Albania just a few hours before), and again stressed his devotion to "neutrality," going so far as to take credit for that Neutrality Act of which he had always disapproved and for whose repeal he had fought so hard and long! It was in this speech that he joined the names of three Republican conservatives and isolationists, "Martin, Barton, and Fish," in a rhythmic refrain whose iteration was chanted with him by a delighted audience. On the following day, despite the attempts of jittery politicians to dissuade him, he personally presided over the drawing of the first draft numbers from a huge goldfish bowl in Washington while cameras clicked and whirred. He then entrained for Boston. Through the daylight hours of October 30, he made rear-platform talks at frequent train stops, worked with his writers on the speech he would deliver that night, and received a steady stream of messages from frightened politicians all over the country warning him that the election was lost unless he flatly guaranteed to "American mothers" that their "boys," though they might be called to the Armed Services, would never be called upon to fight.

For it appeared that Willkie was making startling gains as he continued to hammer away at Roosevelt's record of "broken promises" which, he reiterated, boded ill for the present promise to stay out of "foreign" wars. The latest Gallup Poll showed the two candidates running virtually neck and neck nationally. The Republican candidate was, however, jarred by Roosevelt's Madison Garden effort, and his immediate response was that of a poker player who, having already bet more than he can afford to lose, doubles his opponent's bet. On October 30 he rasped out in a kind of hoarse frenzy the prediction that "on the basis of his [Roosevelt's] past performance with pledges to the people, you may expect war by April, 1941, if he is elected."

That night, in Boston, the President of the United States and Commander-in-Chief of its Armed Forces referred to the Army in terms applicable to a summer camp for boys, assuring fond mama and papa that their sons would be well-fed and -housed, their health well cared for during their year of service. "And while I am talking to you mothers and fathers, I give you one more assurance," he went on. "I have said this before, but I shall say it again and again and again: Your boys are not going to be sent into any foreign wars."

(Always before he had added the phrase "—except in case of attack," but, reminded of this while the speech was being drafted, he responded irritably, "If somebody attacks us, then it isn't a foreign war, is it? Or do they want me to guarantee that our troops will be sent into battle only in the event of another Civil War?") It was a statement that would plague him "again and again and again" during the months ahead, and so would his flat statement in Buffalo, "Your President says this country is not going to war."

Willkie, too, would be plagued in the months ahead by the predictions he had made of war and dictatorship, should the President win his third term. He might at that later date find a certain wry symbolism in the fact that the green-carpeted suite in which he had awaited the election returns on the night of November 5, 1940, was on the fourteenth floor of New York's Commodore Hotel, the fourteenth being actually the thirteenth since the Commodore, like most hotels, skipped the "unlucky" number following twelve. Wendell Willkie, through all his public career, had occupied an anomalous position . . .

At a little after eight o'clock, John B. Hollister entered the room where Wendell and Ed Willkie watched television while listening to the radio returns.

Hollister, Robert Taft's law partner, had just talked to Taft in Ohio by long-distance phone. He said so, and shook his head gloomily in response to Wendell Willkie's questioning gaze. Though it was still early, the Ohio returns were sufficient to show a decisive trend: Taft estimated that Roosevelt would carry the state by a hundred thousand votes. It meant that the election was lost, in Hollister's view.

"I recommend an early concession," Hollister said.[16]

Cigarette smoke writhed around Willkie's drawn gray face as he shook his head.

"I still have a statistical chance," he said. "The rural vote . . ."

That had been discounted, Hollister said; Taft had done so when he made his estimate.

"I can still win," Willkie said, and relapsed into grim silence.

At about the same time, in his home at Hyde Park, Roosevelt sat in the dining room with tally sheets spread out before him, sheets on which he recorded the figures announced by the radio. He, too, was haggard. His coat was off and his tie loosened and he was sweating heavily. He sat alone: he had ordered his bodyguard to permit no one, not even his immediate family, to enter that room. Later the bodyguard, Mike Reilly, would say that this was the first and only time he ever saw the President lose his nerve—for Roosevelt, obviously, at that moment, despaired of victory.[17]

Hours passed. The big city majorities for Roosevelt, unusually slow to accumulate early in the evening, now piled up well beyond the levels predictably necessary for his victory. (The post-election statistics showed that of the nearly fifty million Americans who had voted, a record-breaking total, 27,243,466 had voted for Roosevelt, and 22,304,755 for Willkie. The electoral vote was 449 to 82. Willkie, however, had gained nearly 6,000,000 votes over the Landon total of 1936, had reduced Roosevelt's total below that of 1936, and had whittled down to 224,000 the Roosevelt majority in New York. It was the narrowest margin of victory in New York for Roosevelt since his election as Governor in 1928 and, nationally, the smallest plurality of any victorious candidate since 1916.) The President, with a wide grin, called to Reilly to open the door.

And on the fourteenth floor of the Commodore, Mrs. Willkie and the Willkie son, Philip, a Princeton undergraduate, came into the bedroom for a brief, unhappy visit with the uncommunicative candidate. Others came, from time to time, all prominent people, most in evening dress. Thomas E. Dewey came, and publisher Roy W. Howard, and editor Russell Davenport. Davenport was there at eleven o'clock when Elmer Davis announced over the radio, in his flat, homely, Midwestern voice, that Roosevelt appeared definitely to have been re-elected. Willkie's face sagged, but he said nothing. A few minutes later the radio said that McNary, out in Oregon, had conceded. Willkie blinked as though slapped, but said nothing. He lit another cigarette—the room's air was now blue with his cigarette smoke.

Mrs. Willkie spoke to a woman reporter in the outer room.

"I've no hope now," she said wearily. She looked at the closed door behind which her husband sat. "I wish Wendell would get ready to go home."

But by then people had stopped asking him to concede. He sat in gloomy silence, for the most part; even his brother Ed seemed walled away from him.

At twenty minutes after midnight he went down to the hotel's grand ballroom where fifteen hundred campaign workers, some of them weeping, awaited his appearance. He spoke to them in a hoarse whisper, painful to hear. "Don't be afraid and never quit," he said. "I am not afraid nor disheartened." He congratulated them on being "a part of the greatest crusade in this century." At 1:30 A.M. he went to bed in his suite, still stubbornly refusing to concede defeat.

Not until nearly noon of Wednesday, November 6, would the traditional message of congratulations go from vanquished to victor.

To the Roosevelt mansion at Hyde Park, that night of Election Day, came the traditional torchlight parade from the village center (SAFE ON THIRD, said one of the placards), the flames bright and unwavering in the mild November air as the torches were held high. The President stood upon his porch with his happy family, lifting his arm again and again in response to the cries of photographers. He spoke to his neighbors: "I will still be the same Franklin Roosevelt you have always known . . ."

III

The Undeclared War

1. *Garden Hose and Hydrant*

The weather on that first Tuesday in December was as brightly warm in Miami as Florida travel folders proclaimed Florida weather always to be. And since the event occurred at a time of day convenient for the gathering of crowds, large crowds were on hand both at the railway station and at Pier 3, where the Navy cruiser *Tuscaloosa*, down from Norfolk, had been tied up in still blue water since before dawn. Hundreds also lined the palm-shaded white-walled streets through which the open car would drive. These crowds grew steadily as the noon hour passed, and with them grew a cheerful excitement.[1]

At precisely 1 P.M. the train arrived. Breathing clouds of smoke and hissing jets of steam, with iron shrieking against iron in an anguish of braked power, the locomotive loomed above and past the station, causing those who stood upon the platform's edge to draw back instinctively or, instinctively, to brace themselves. Terrific, the black monster had hell-fire in its belly: a man near it might in empathy feel flame searing flesh, bones breaking on a huge wheel, and, for just a second, a shattering of the very soul. Then the gleaming steel coaches slid by—slowing stopping—and the weather's mood, split asunder by the passage of the engine, flowed softly and sweetly together again. But it was not quite or wholly the same as before. The mild air's contradiction still breathed and hissed down the tracks, its boiler clanking, while on the platform white-gloved Marines came to attention, presenting arms.

Almost at once came a hoarse cry of recognition and welcome from the crowd, applause punctuated by cheers which the President acknowledged with smile and wave before being helped down from the train to an automobile. Additional thousands of people cheered his arrival, a few minutes later, upon the gangplank which leaned into the gray cruiser's side. At 2 P.M. the ropes were cast off and the cruiser moved rapidly away from the pier, drawn by four tugs through narrow waters toward the bay. Roosevelt, on the quarter-deck, in high good humor, lifted his hat at arm's length above his head and waved goodbye to the crowds.

Mystery, seemingly transparent, shrouded both the purpose and the itinerary of this cruise. The White House had announced late Saturday afternoon that the President "expected" to be absent from Washington for "about fifteen days" but left unconfirmed and undenied the rumor that he would "combine rest with a tour of inspection of defense works in the vicinity of Puerto Rico." The reporters aboard his train had been unable to find out more than this. They noted that he was being accompanied only by the most immediate of his "official family"—his personal physician and Navy Surgeon General, Admiral Ross T. McIntire; his crony and confidant, Harry L. Hopkins, who had been living in the White House since the day Hitler invaded the Low Countries; his military aides—and that all the train talk they heard among these intimates had to do with fishing sites and fishing tackle. All of which led them to conclude that no important news was likely to come from the *Tuscaloosa* during the next two weeks.

Indeed, the Chief Executive had made remarkably little news since that early November night at Hyde Park when he had acknowledged his election to an unprecedented third term. His display of a carefree spirit on that occasion had added to the reassurance of a public which daily read and heard of Greek victories over Mussolini's reluctant warriors, of an impending offensive against the Italians in North Africa by Britain's General Wavell, and of England's buildup of home defenses against a Nazi invasion which seemed daily less imminent and, if ultimately attempted, less likely to succeed.

The President's relatively few public words had been reassuring, too. When Lord Lothian, the British Ambassador, returned to Washington from a London on which Nazi bombs rained nightly, he at once conferred with the President. It was presumed he had presented specific requests for additional American aid to Britain. Not so, said the President airily to his press conference on November 26: ". . . [Nothing] was mentioned in that regard at all, not one single thing—ships or sealing wax or anything else."[2]

In the same airy spirit he'd dealt with the long-matured problem of Joseph P. Kennedy's embassy to the Court of St. James. Kennedy had flown back to the United States six weeks before amidst widely publicized rumors that he would not return to London. These had not been allayed by Kennedy's public statement on Roosevelt's behalf in the last days of the election campaign—a statement in which he asserted that the United States had no valid reason for entering the war, and warned that if she did she might be compelled to transform herself into a totalitarian state as Britain, with her Emergency Powers Act (passed May 1940), seemed about to do. If this had helped to blunt Willkie's sharpest campaign weapon, it had also further impaired Kennedy's usefulness as Ambassador, especially when it was related to his espousal of Chamberlain's "appeasement" policies at Munich and after, and to his thinly veiled conviction that Britain must inevitably lose the war. Hence there was no surprise in the announcement *per se*, made on the day before Roosevelt's departure and immediately following a lengthy conference at the White House, that Kennedy had resigned his post. There was surprise, however, in the form this announcement took. Kennedy told newsmen he intended now to devote all his time "to the greatest cause in the world today, to help the President keep the United States out of war"—and Roosevelt gave every appearance of welcoming this "help." The meeting of the two men had been perfectly "amicable," Stephen Early told reporters on the morning of Roosevelt's departure, adding that the President had "no objection whatsoever" to Kennedy's announced plans.[3]

But if all this was reassuring to a superficially informed and war-fearful public, it was profoundly disturbing to those who saw Britain's cause as America's also and who knew that, beneath the surface of events, the tide of war now ran strongly against her. Among these was Winston Churchill. Immediately upon receipt of the news of Roosevelt's re-election, the "Former Naval Person" had dispatched a message to the White House: "I did not think it right for me as a foreigner to express any opinion upon American politics while the election was on, but now I feel you will not mind my saying that I prayed for your success and that I am truly thankful for it. . . . We are entering upon a sombre phase of what must evidently be a protracted and broadening war, and I look forward to being able to interchange my thoughts with you in all that confidence and good will which has grown up between us. . . ." But now, barely a month later, the Prime Minister had cause to wonder if his thankfulness, his "confidence" in Roosevelt's "good will," were actually justified. It puzzled him, hurtfully, that his words had met with no response: the cablegram had not even been acknowledged.[4] It perturbed him to see the President seemingly relaxed into a warm bath of optimism, acting (or failing to act) as if he had any amount of time in which to implement his election-endorsed policy of all aid to Britain short of war. There was, in fact, no time at all. Unless the amount of American aid reaching British shores was promptly and vastly increased, the British cause was doomed.

To this increase of aid there were three major obstacles, none of which could be removed without vigorous and novel action by the American Executive. One was the typically Rooseveltian administrative tangle in which American rearmament was now enmeshed. Having set up a National Defense Advisory Commission, the President had failed to appoint a responsible head for it even after he'd established within it (by Executive Order on October 21) a Priorities Board administered by Donald M. Nelson. No one could define with any certainty the powers and responsibilities of this NDAC, least of all the Commission's members; the President was in effect the Commission's only chairman, though he "has not the time to run it," as Secretary of War Stimson complained;

and the inevitable result was that decisions necessary to speed the sadly lagging defense effort were simply not made.[5]

A second obstacle was Britain's lack of dollars, or of gold and U.S. investments that could be transformed into dollars, with which to pay cash for American aid as she was required to do by the Congressionally enacted "Cash and Carry" policy. The dollar assets amounting to four and a half billions which Britain had had in September 1939 were all paid out by November 1940. Nearly two billion dollars more had been procured with great difficulty during the war's first year, but most of these were frozen in forms not readily liquefiable. It would not be possible, therefore, for Britain to pay cash for half of what she had specifically ordered from America by the autumn of 1940—and it was clear she would need at least ten times as much before the conflict ended.

The third obstacle—and the most serious of all—was the destructive power which the Nazi U-boat, surface raider, and bombing plane now focused upon Britain's lifeline across the Atlantic to America. As Roosevelt departed from Washington, signals being received in New York indicated that eight British merchantmen were under simultaneous U-boat attack about four hundred miles off the northwest coast of Ireland and that two other ships, near the Irish coast, were being attacked by planes. "Our shipping losses . . . have been on a scale almost comparable to that of the worst year of the last war," the "Former Naval Person" was writing at about this time in what he later deemed the most important letter of his life. "In the five weeks ending November 3, losses reached a total of 420,300 tons. Our estimate of the annual tonnage which ought to be imported in order to maintain our effort at full strength is forty-three million tons; the tonnage entering in September was only at the rate of thirty-seven million tons, and in October, of thirty-eight million tons. Were this diminution to continue at this rate, it would be fatal. . . ."

Yet here was the President of the United States, climaxing weeks of post-election doldrums with a blithe vacation cruise into placid tropic seas! Cuban cigars were purchased at Guantánamo Bay for a smoker tendered the Presidential party by the officers of the *Tuscaloosa.* A radio signal was received from Ernest Hemingway (whose *For Whom the Bell Tolls* was the great literary event of that season) advising of "many big fish" in a certain portion of the waters between the Dominican Republic and Puerto Rico; the *Tuscaloosa* sailed there, but though the President trawled with a piece of pork rind on a feathered hook, as Hemingway had recommended, he caught nothing. In the evenings the party played poker, watched boxing matches between crew members, heard ship's band drummers in a "hot swing" contest, listened to hillbilly music, and watched motion pictures.

On Saturday, December 7 (a date not yet "infamous"), correspondents aboard the accompanying destroyer *Mayrant* reported the President "working" for the first time since leaving Washington: he sat in his shirtsleeves in the *Tuscaloosa's* flag quarters reading and answering mail that had been delivered by Navy plane the day before. Next day the *Tuscaloosa* anchored at 9 A.M. off Britain's St. Lucia Island, in the Windward group, where the President inspected one of the naval base sites recently acquired by the U.S. and whence could be seen with the naked eye, to the north, the blue-hazed outline of Martinique, whose possession by Vichy France was a source of anxiety to Washington. Later that same day, Roosevelt conferred aboard ship with naval and diplomatic officials from Fort-de-France, Martinique, while members of his party focused curious binoculars upon the French aircraft carrier *Bearn*, three miles away. They were acutely aware of the damage this ship, armed with U.S.-made warplanes, might do the Allied cause should she become a weapon of the Nazis.

Then the pleasure cruise resumed, its fun only briefly and mildly interrupted, so far as watchful reporters could see, by a second Navy plane mail delivery on December 9. Roosevelt fished some more (and with no more luck), "inspected" in sightseeing fashion another base, gave lunch aboard ship to the Duke and Duchess of Windsor (the Duke, abdicated King of England, was now Governor and Commander-in-Chief of the Bahamas), held a press conference with the three reporters as he sailed for home (he talked of the importance of bases in a general war), and docked in the late afternoon of Saturday, December 14, at Charleston, South Carolina.

The only serious note he publicly struck in all these lazy, sunwashed days was on December 12 . . .

In Baltimore, on the evening of the eleventh, a major address by Lord Lothian was read to a dinner of the American Farm Bureau Federation by Neville Butler, Counselor of the British Embassy, who explained that a "slight illness" prevented the Ambassador's appearing in person. The address predicted that 1941 would be the critical year of the war and that spring would see an all-out attack on British sea communications, an attack whose dangers were grave since the British Navy was already "strung out terribly thin." England alone "cannot be sure of the result," he said, and concluded by putting the question up to America. "It is for you to decide whether it is in your interest to give us whatever assistance may be necessary to make certain that Britain shall not fail . . ." he said bluntly. "The issue now depends largely on what you decide to do."[6] A few hours later, the British Ambassador, aged fifty-eight, died of his "slight" illness, which turned out to be a uremic infection. The news, sent by Secretary of State Hull via radio to the *Tuscaloosa*, genuinely shocked and grieved the President, who said so at once in a message to King George VI. He had been on unusually warm and friendly terms with the Ambassador; he knew he spoke Lord Lothian's "conviction" as he said that British victory must and would come in this war.

When, however, a reporter asked him a specific question concerning further aid to Britain, shortly after he had landed in Charleston, he refused to answer it.

At that moment there was probably but one man in all the world, aside from Roosevelt himself, who knew that this cruise had had any more important effect than the rest and restoration of a tired and spent Chief Executive. That man was Harry Hopkins . . .

He, Hopkins, had sat upon the *Tuscaloosa's* deck on the morning of December 9 when Navy seaplanes came roaring out of the brilliant sky which arched the low, rolling, pale-green hills of Antigua. He had felt a quickening of interest, even a mild tightening of his nerves, as the planes (there were two) glided down to rest upon the waters beside the ship. It seemed to him probable that in one of the mail pouches aboard those planes would be found a long-heralded, long-awaited letter from Churchill, who had cabled Roosevelt that he was writing it as long ago as November 16. A "very long letter on the outlook for 1941," Churchill had described it, adding that Lord Lothian would deliver it in person "in a few days."[7] Lord Lothian had not done so: the letter was still in preparation when the envoy returned to Washington, and it was deemed to be of such importance as to require careful checking by the British Treasury and Chiefs of Staff, and by the War Cabinet, whose formal approval of it was also deemed necessary. Naturally, Roosevelt's anticipatory interest had been heightened—which meant that Hopkins's had been also. For by the late autumn of 1940, Harry Hopkins had become a virtual extension of the President's eyes and ears, and of the President's mind and will also.

Once, Hopkins had been personally ambitious and not overly scrupulous in his pursuit of power—though even when the fever of ambition raged highest in him he had wished for power to serve and uplift his fellow man, not to rule over them, for he was a welfare worker by deep conviction as well as profession and had been one ever since his arrival in New York City from his native Iowa in 1912, when he was twenty-two. Once he had actually aspired to the Presidency, an aspiration which would have seemed absurd to a public fed on the Hopkins-hating propaganda of a business-dominated press. It had not seemed absurd to Franklin Roosevelt. Indeed, the President had personally favored Hopkins as his successor, or had at least indicated to Hopkins that he did, even after cancer had laid the latter under a surgeon's knife in the summer of 1937 (most of the sick man's stomach had been removed) and the chances of a recurrence of the malignancy were placed by the Mayo Clinic at fifty-fifty. Now all such ambition was ended. For a year or so, Hopkins had seemed to be recovering from the effects of his drastic surgery. Then came a series of nutritional maladjustments (this in the crucial summer of 1939) necessitating a second prolonged stay at Mayo's, where his life was despaired of, followed by many Washington months of what he called "heroic treatments" prescribed by Admiral McIntire and a former Navy Surgeon General, Admiral Edward R. Stitt. He emerged as a man from whom all but the vital essence had been burned away, cut away—a skeletal figure on whom clothes hung almost as loosely as a scarecrow's garb, his eyes like glowing coals in a face of pale-yellow parchment and his voice a thin reed that often hardened and broke into quick jagged pieces of impatience. Pills and hypodermics kept him slenderly alive.

He had been miserably sick following dinner at the White House on the evening of May 10, 1940 (he was living then a lonely life, his second wife having died of cancer in the same year as his own malignancy was discovered). Roosevelt had prevailed upon him to spend the night there. Thus had been initiated a "visit" destined to last five years and an American Executive relationship which, though precedented to a small degree in Woodrow Wilson's friendship with Colonel House, was historically unique in its quality and in the importance of its effects. Living every moment at the edge of death, Hopkins was irritable, irascible, profane, often cruelly disregardful of the sensibilities of those with whom he dealt. He was also brave, gallant, self-sacrificial beyond belief in his dedication to his job; a man of great sweetness beneath his often sour surface, able to laugh with a wry contempt at his frailties and sufferings; incurably idealistic, a lover of mankind armored in protective cynicism; utterly devoted to Roosevelt as man and as President—all in all, one without whom Roosevelt could not have functioned as he was now, in the last month of 1940, beginning to do. He could act on some occasions as the President's hatchet man, on others as the President's conscience. He seemed often to know what Roosevelt wanted and needed and thought before Roosevelt did himself, for his empathic understanding of the Chief was implemented by a quick, shrewd, operator's mind. ". . . When a man knows he is going to be hanged in a month, it concentrates his mind wonderfully," Samuel Johnson once said—and the Hopkins mind, always abnormally concentrated upon whatever task was at hand, was now as a rapier that thrust directly into the heart of matters which the diffuse Roosevelt approached circuitously, deviously, with a repetitious calculation of "angles."

The President, who trusted few men and revealed himself wholly to none, could and did trust Hopkins absolutely. He trusted him, as a matter of course, with Churchill's letter, which was indeed in one of the airborne pouches that came aboard the *Tuscaloosa* on the morning of December 9.

It was a letter every bit as long and important as Hopkins, with Roosevelt, had been led to anticipate. "As we approach the end of this year, I feel you will expect me to lay before you the prospects for 1941," Churchill began, as if he wrote on tacit assignment from the President. "I do so with candor and confidence, because it seems to me that the vast majority of American citizens have recorded their conviction that the safety of the United States, as well as the future of our two Democracies and the kind of civilization for which they stand, is bound up with the survival and independence of the British Commonwealth of Nations." He then proceeded to present in some four thousand words a survey of Britain's strategic situation in the Far East, Africa, and Europe; the grim facts of Britain's war economy (her shipping losses, the impossibility of achieving maximum industrial output for at least another year and a half, the utter exhaustion of her dollar supply); and specific suggestions for American action. Two things, obviously, were necessary: the increased production of desperately needed materiel (heavy bombers were stressed since this was "the weapon on which . . . we depend to shatter the foundation of German military power"); and the safe delivery of this production across submarine-infested seas. The latter, Churchill suggested, required the armed American protection of "lawful trading" on the high seas by "escorting battleships, cruisers, destroyers, and air flotillas."[8]

If no single item of information in this message was new to Roosevelt and Hopkins, there was stimulating novelty in the manner of its presentation and in the breadth of its view; it evinced a kind of thinking few Americans seemed able to do, organically linking each specific item to all the others in a single global panorama. Roosevelt admitted to Hopkins that he was immensely impressed. He said little more about it in the days immediately following, but Hopkins noted unwonted silences and a faraway look in Roosevelt's eyes when, to others, the Chief seemed merely to be loafing in the sun.

And Hopkins, too, was impressed—especially by Churchill's unprecedented, all-revealing frankness, and the boldness with which he asserted an identity of interest between Britain and the United States. "If, as I believe, you are convinced, Mr. President, that the defeat of the Nazi and Fascist tyranny is a matter of high consequence to the people of the United States and to the Western Hemisphere, you will regard this letter not as an appeal for aid, but as a statement of the minimum action necessary to achieve our common purpose," Churchill had closed. The message as a whole, writes Robert E. Sherwood, "filled Hopkins with a desire to get to know Churchill and to find out how much of him was mere grandiloquence and how much of him was hard fact."[9]

But if the letter's impact justified the attention Churchill had given its preparation, this was certainly not because it provided solutions to Roosevelt's problems. The essential problem was political. It concerned not *what* should be done but *how* it could be done within the framework of organic law, given the present state of public opinion, given the degree to which isolationism might operate in Congress without regard to majority opinion outside. It was by no means a simple problem.

Roosevelt brooded over it. He reviewed in his mind the "destroyers-for-bases" deal and the more recent proposal to build merchant ships in the United States and then lease them for a stated period to Britain. He recalled an 1892 statute uncovered last summer by a Treasury lawyer, Oscar S. Cox, empowering the Secretary of War to lease Army property "not required for public use" for a period of not more than five years "when in his discretion it will be for the public good." He shaped homely arguments which might persuade a majority of the public (it must be a large majority) to back a proposal which would irrevocably commit his nation to British victory (or Nazi defeat) at whatever cost. "Then, one evening, he suddenly came out with it—the whole program," Hopkins said later.[10]

When Secretary of the Treasury Henry Morgenthau, Jr., first heard about it at a White House luncheon on December 17, it seemed to him one of Roosevelt's "brilliant flashes." Hopkins was equally convinced of its brilliance, but he knew it was not a flash.[11]

Unusually large, unusually impatient was the crowd of reporters who packed the President's Oval Study that afternoon of Tuesday, December 17, just a few hours after the luncheon at which Morgenthau, with British visitors, had been a guest.[12] There had been such a dearth of news from the White House for so long a time that surely the present press conference would produce a flood of it. So the reporters felt. And only the newest and greenest among them lost this feeling when a tanned, jovial President greeted them with the offhand remark, "I don't think there is any particular news." The others braced themselves.

"Of course," the President began, "there is no doubt in the minds of a very overwhelming number of Americans that the best immediate defense of the United States is the success of Great Britain in defending itself; and that, therefore . . . we should do everything to help the British Empire defend itself." He then denigrated as "narrow-minded" the proposal to make outright money loans to Britain in her present circumstances, and as "banal" the proposal of outright money gifts to her. Both proposals implied a banker's faith in the power of money which was, he indicated, unjustified. He reminded the reporters that in 1914, when the First World War broke out, some bankers had said the conflict would probably end in three months and certainly in six because by that time one side, or both, would have run out of money. "Well, you know what happened."

He paused, he leaned forward slightly. There was a notable rise in the room's emotional temperature.

"Now, what I am trying to do," he said, "is eliminate the dollar sign. That is something brand new in the thoughts of everybody in this room, I think—get rid of the silly, foolish, old dollar sign."

He explained. In America, factories turned out munitions, some of which were bought by the British, some by the U. S. Government. He proposed that our Government, from now on, should place *all* the contracts for munitions manufactured by our factories, using some of the products ourselves, but either leasing or selling others of them, "subject to mortgage, to the people on the other side" whenever we decided that these products "would be more useful to the defense of the United States if they were used in Great Britain than if they were kept in storage here."

Puzzlement showed on some of the reporters' faces.

"Well, let me give you an illustration," said the President. "Suppose my neighbor's house catches fire, and I have a length of garden hose four or five hundred feet away. If I can take my garden hose and connect it up with his hydrant, I may help him to put out the fire. Now what do I do? I don't say to him before that operation, 'Neighbor, my garden hose cost me $15; you have to pay me $15 for it.' What is the transaction that goes on? I don't want $15—I want my garden hose back after the fire is over. . . ."

The legal details of all this had not yet been worked out, he told the conference, so there was "no use" asking legal questions about it. In any case he was sure all his listeners would "get" the essential idea, which was simply that of substituting for the dollar sign "a gentleman's obligation to repay in kind."

During the question period that followed, the President dealt adroitly with a number of probing questions. Implementation of his plan would, he admitted, require revisions of the Neutrality Act and also "various types" of new legislation "in addition to appropriations." But there was absolutely "no idea" of sending the "American flag" into war zones in order to deliver the goods. Yes, a great speedup of defense production was needed, as William S. Knudsen of the National Defense Advisory Commission had been publicly saying. The objective, the President said, was "to keep all the machines that will run seven days a week in operation seven days a week." But it was "premature" to generalize about lengthening the work week in defense plants. Moreover, he remained opposed to the appointment of a single "production czar" as head of the now headless seven-man NDAC: such an arrangement might create more problems than it solved, especially in the field of labor relations.

The conference ended. The "post-election doldrums" had certainly ended. The newsmen rushed from the room.

All of them were aware that the occasion they were to report was of immense immediate importance. The more thoughtful among them, possessed of a historical imagination, might see it as of even greater long-term importance. For not only would the proposed "Lend-Lease" (as it was soon called) be a new departure in the external relations between Britain and the United States, initiating a tie of such intimacy and working interdependence as to make the two powers virtually one in the shaping and carrying out of foreign policy; it would also mean a virtual fusion of considerable elements of the two powers' domestic affairs, since obviously the planning and administration of defense production must be done by both nations in the closest concord. Already the two countries had agreed* to standardize their basic designs for planes, tanks, guns, and military vehicles, so that these could be used interchangeably between the two armed forces. Already (though this was a closely guarded secret in the highest circles of government) the American Chief of Naval Operations, Admiral Harold R. Stark, with the President's approval, was inviting the British Chiefs of Staff to send representatives to Washington

* The Stimson-Layton Agreement between the U. S. Secretary of War and Sir Walter Layton, special envoy of the British Ministry of Supply, signed November 29, 1940. It involved an offer of the British to work with the Americans in developing new weapons and redesigning old ones for both nations.

for lengthy formal military staff talks on the premise that the United States might "be compelled to resort to war against Germany" and that, therefore, it behooved the two powers "to reach agreements concerning . . . the major lines of military strategy" and "satisfactory command arrangements."[13]

Nor was the announcement of the "Lend-Lease" proposal the only major news the President made in the historic ten days following his return to Washington.

The "neighborly analogy" of the garden hose may well have "won the fight" for this proposal, as Robert E. Sherwood believed,[14] but it was a far from perfect analogy. What of the hydrant to which the hose must be connected? Roosevelt had indicated that it belonged to the "neighbor" but in actual fact it, too, was on the American side of the Atlantic and unless a sufficient water pressure was built up in it, the hose could be of no help toward putting out the fire. To increase this pressure was the urgent necessity that brought Secretaries Stimson and Knox into the White House's Oval Study on the afternoon of December 18 (Knox accompanied by Navy Under Secretary James V. Forrestal, Stimson by Judge Robert P. Patterson, named Under Secretary of War the next day), armed with a concrete proposal for reconstituting the NDAC as an executive agency with a responsible head and a clear delegation of authority. Stimson, at least, feared the session would be difficult if not fruitless. Not only was Roosevelt acutely sensitive to criticisms of his administrative arrangements (such criticism was unavoidably personal, since the arrangements were obviously designed to keep the reins of power in his own hands); he had also, in Stimson's view, a mind which "does not follow easily a consecutive chain of thought, but . . . hops about from suggestion to suggestion."[15]

What happened that afternoon was therefore a pleasant surprise to the Secretary of War—one suggesting that Roosevelt's "hopping about" may have been an evasive tactic, deliberately employed, rather than a manifestation of mental weakness. For Roosevelt had not only thought his way through the general problem which brought his Secretaries to him that day, he had done so in a wider context than they, and to a greater depth. He, for instance, had taken into account (as they had not) the need to build into the over-all program of industrial expansion devices which would prevent unlimited price rises followed by a deep depression when the war had ended. Moreover, he wanted to go farther and faster than Stimson and Knox suggested in their reorganization plan. The Director of the Budget, Harold D. Smith, had told him of an old statute "which nobody seemed to know about" authorizing the President to set up "a managing bureau for all kinds of emergencies." By its terms he could, he believed, establish a three-man board of Knudsen, Knox, and Stimson to replace the seven-man Commission. He wanted to announce this drastic reorganization as soon as possible, and not later than Sunday, December 22!

As it turned out, the announcement of an Office of Production Management, with full authority to organize and administer defense production, was made on Friday, December 20, with Knudsen of General Motors as Director General and Sidney Hillman of the CIO (he had also been a member of the NDAC) as Associate Director General. The addition of Hillman to the three men originally proposed was made by Roosevelt to insure a maximum cooperation of labor and management in the defense effort and with the assurance, derived from a studious observation of both Knudsen and Hillman, that the two men could and would work together in close harmony.

Thus swiftly did the President now act to remove two of the three great obstacles to effective aid to Britain—namely, Britain's lack of dollars, and the inadequacy of American industrial mobilization. Against the third obstacle—that of the U-boat menace to British shipping—no direct immediate action could be taken by the United States, Roosevelt indicated. He announced that the British Government was being permitted to place orders for sixty cargo vessels to be built in American shipyards; he explored with his associates the possibility of seizing the ships of Axis and Axis-conquered nations which were not immobilized in American ports, then turning these over to the British; but he was unwilling if not unable to assign American warships and warplanes to convoy duty, thus initiating at the very least a limited "shooting war" which would almost inevitably expand, sooner or later, into full-scale conflict.

Indeed, the steps already taken might, in his view, have gone beyond the outermost limit of popular approval had not Adolf Hitler chosen this precise moment to "warn" the United States through a "Wilhelmstrasse spokesman" of dire consequences should she continue her "attitude of . . . friendliness" toward Britain while employing "towards the other [warring nation] . . . a policy of pinpricks, challenges, insults, and moral aggression which has reached a point at which it is insupportable." The seizure of the seventy thousand tons of German shipping now immobilized in U.S. ports in order to turn them over to Britain could only be interpreted as an act of war, the "spokesman" continued. The effect was to increase the American public's support of the President's recent acts, and to swell the size of the radio audience to which he made, on December 29, a historic "fireside chat." "There will be no 'bottlenecks' in our determination to aid Great Britain," he said. "No dictator, no combination of dictators, will weaken that determination by threats of how they will construe that determination. . . . If Britain should go down, all of us in all the Americas would be living at the point of a gun, a gun loaded with explosive bullets, economic as well as military. We must produce arms and ships with every energy and resource we can command. . . . *We must be the great arsenal of Democracy.*"

It was none too soon. Even as the President spoke, the fire his garden hose aimed to put out was raging in literal flames through the ancient and historic heart of the British capital. From Nazi warplanes incendiary bombs rained down that night of December 29 and 30 in the most savage of all air raids thus far in the war, setting more than fifteen hundred fires in the City of London. But already the first task, that of putting into precise legal form the general idea of Lend-Lease, was under way. The bill was introduced in the House and Senate by the respective majority leaders (a deliberately unusual procedure) at noon on January 10, 1941, and was stamped by the Clerk of the House of Representatives, H.R. 1776.

The Committee to Defend America by Aiding the Allies made the most of the bill's number, appealing to every patriotic ardor in an effort to mobilize public opinion behind the proposal. But of course the actual significance of Lend-Lease was exactly opposite that of the historic document dated July 4, 1776—it was in effect a Declaration of Dependence, or Interdependence—and the proposal's opponents, spearheaded by the America First Committee, were not loathe to point this out. The issue, at any rate, was now presented to the people with a clarity rare in American politics, and both sides might agree that the Great Debate which at once began was the most crucial to national survival since that provoked by Senator Stephen A. Douglas's Kansas-Nebraska Bill of 1854. If not as acrimonious on the whole as that earlier debate, it often seemed only slightly less so. Senator Burton K. Wheeler of Montana promptly dubbed the bill a "triple-A foreign policy; it will plough under every fourth American boy." President Roosevelt promptly replied: ". . . the rottenest thing that has been said in public life in my generation!"

ii. *In the Senate Caucus Room, February 11, 1941*

Never in the memory of Capital employees had so large a crowd of spectators assembled for a Congressional hearing. The hallway of the Senate's Office Building was jammed long before the main doors of the Caucus Room were opened; when that happened, something very like a stampede occurred. Many more policemen than usual were on hand, but they were too few to control the throng—and by the time thirty more had been rushed to the scene, some eighteen hundred citizens, good-humored but determined, had shoved their way into a room designed to accommodate no more than five hundred. At least as many more remained outside, disappointed but still hopeful of catching a glimpse of the day's star witness who was, indeed, the star witness of the whole of the formal hearings. It was dramatically fitting that he should appear at the very last session, having flown back for the purpose across the menaced and menacing Atlantic from the ruins, the glories of England . . .

Heretofore much the largest crowd to be attracted by the current hearings had assembled in and immediately outside the Ways and Means Committee Room of the new House Office Building on a Thursday morning in late January when a lean and boyish Colonel Lindbergh, clad all in blue (blue suit, soft blue shirt, a dark-blue knitted tie), sat in the witness chair before the House Foreign Affairs Committee. He appeared (and made a "good appearance") at the request of Representative Fish, Jr., of New York, ranking Republican member of the Committee. With a persuasiveness compounded of present earnestness, past heroism, and the "Lindy" stereotype long impressed on the popular mind, he had said precisely the things Ham Fish most wanted his countrymen to hear. And since by far the greater part of the crowd was made up of his worshipful supporters, he had been repeatedly applauded and cheered despite the stern efforts of Chairman Sol Bloom of New York to maintain order.

Far different would be the testimony of that day's principal witness who, indeed, might not have appeared had not his influence been deemed necessary to overcome that of the great hero of the 1920s and early '30s. For though Lindbergh was unlikely to persuade an American majority to his view, he (or the magic myth of him) might well hold together a minority sufficiently large to delay the bill's passage until, in desperation, its proponents had agreed to crippling amendments. There was so little time!

A door at the rear of the room opened. Policemen pushed in, trying with imperfect success to clear a path for the familiar bearlike figure—broad of shoulder, broad of face, broad of smile, a lock of hair drooping over one eye despite a recent haircut—whose appearance raised a gale of sound in the room: excited whisperings, applause, cries of welcome. Photographers' flashbulbs burst with machine-gun rapidity as, with difficulty, he made his way around the table where the Senators now stood up in his honor. He laughed, he shook hands with Senators, he paused to kiss the cheek of a late Congressman's widow. When at last he reached the witness stand he cheerfully turned this way and that for the benefit of the massed photographers whose bulbs now burst simultaneously and continuously in a kind of sheet lightning. Gradually the tumult died.[16]

But there was still no formal call to order. Wendell Willkie, typically, had left behind his prepared statement; someone had to rush back to his hotel room to get it and bring it to him before he could begin.

Then, into the room's sudden silence, came the familiar voice, almost as hoarse as it had been when most of those in the room had last heard it over their radios in early November. He read his statement quickly, the words coming faster than those of any earlier witness (stenographers noted the fact for the benefit of newsmen)—and he maintained this speed, imparting a sense of extreme urgency to what he said, as he responded to the Senators' questions. He spoke as one who could hardly be deemed a partisan of Franklin Roosevelt but whose visit of several weeks to England had been publicly blessed by the President, whose returning plane had touched down at the Washington airport as recently as twelve-thirty that very afternoon, and who carried in his mind the vivid memories of three long private talks with Churchill and of literally dozens of other conversations with British leaders.

He backed Lend-Lease with a fervor that was predictable; he always went all out for whatever he supported. He did propose certain modifications: a stipulation that aid should go only to Great Britain, the British Empire, Greece, and China, with Congress reserving the right to include other nations; a redrafting of certain phrases and the addition of others to reassure those who feared that too much power was being given to the President. But "if aid to Britain is what is going to get us into war," the United States was already in it; the only real question now was how to make that aid most effective. Hitler was unlikely to make war on this country while Britain yet stood, but should Britain fall "we will be at war in a month" or at most "sixty days." He did not believe that Britain, with our aid, would fall. "The people of Britain are united almost beyond belief. They are a free people.† Millions of them will die before they give up that island. When the going gets tough they'll force that bunch of robbers to give up." He advocated the sending to Britain of *all* our bombers save those needed for training here. He advocated also the sending of five or ten destroyers a month!

There followed a question period during which the justice called "poetic" was administered to him, chiefly by Senators Bennett Champ Clark of Missouri and Nye of North Dakota, for the pragmatic excesses which had marked and marred his recent campaign for the Presidency.

Senator Nye quoted from the Republican candidate's prediction of last October 30 that "on the basis of his [Roosevelt's] past performance with pledges to the people, you may expect war by April, 1941, if he is elected." Well, Roosevelt had been re-elected. Did Willkie still believe his prediction was accurate?

The witness, visibly uncomfortable, lit another cigarette, having just stubbed out his last one.

"You ask if I said that?" he addressed Nye.

"Are those still your views?"

"It might be . . ." he paused, and then a sudden broad grin spread over his face as he shrugged his beefy shoulders. "It was a bit of campaign oratory," he said.

And the laughter which swept the room seemed to clear away the malice, the doubts, the exasperations spread by this line of questioning, a line which it was now obviously useless to continue.

By the time the witness was dismissed it was evident to every astute observer that his testimony had been more effective among the theretofore undecided than any other given in the whole of the hearings, though at an as-yet-unmeasured expense of Willkie's standing in his own adopted

† This was doubtless aimed at Joseph P. Kennedy, who had testified against Lend-Lease and had more than hinted on other occasions that Britain, under pressure of war, was well on the way toward becoming herself a totalitarian State.

party. (On the morrow there would be a notable increase in newspaper support of Lend-Lease, thanks to Willkie's testimony. On the day after that, the bill would be favorably reported out of the Senate Committee by a vote of 15–8. And in the succeeding weeks, every amendment that seriously reduced Executive flexibility in the application of Lend-Lease would be defeated in the House and the Senate. Finally, on March 11, at three-fifty in the afternoon, the President would sign the bill into law, it having passed the Senate by a decisive majority of 60–31 and the House by 317–71.)

iii. *The Fire Spreads Eastward*

It is almost four months later, near midnight of a soft warm Saturday. Harry Hopkins is relaxing in the old frayed dressing gown he habitually wears in his White House room—a room that was once Abraham Lincoln's study. He has treated himself to a rare day off, going that afternoon to the races; he feels better physically than for many weeks past. He is also less concerned with world affairs, though these are certainly not less anxious than usual. Indeed, Britain appears to be in as desperate a plight, almost, as she had been a year ago on this same date, which is June 21, the longest day of the year . . .

True (a happy consequence of Lend-Lease, from Hopkins' point of view), there are signs of a turn for the better in the Battle of the Atlantic. Shipping losses mounted to the appalling total of 1,603,000 tons for the three months ending May 1, reaching a peak of 654,000 tons in April, but from that high point they have gone down to 500,000 tons in May and will apparently be considerably less than that in June. Moreover, there is good reason to anticipate a further decline. For with every week that has passed since the decision on Lend-Lease, the American determination and indeed necessity to sustain Britain, even at the risk of war, has grown stronger. In April the President decreed an extension halfway across the North Atlantic of the so-called security zones and patrol areas wherein American naval vessels shadow Axis raiders and report their positions by radio to the British. (He also, on May 27, declared a state of "Unlimited National Emergency," whatever that may mean.) This naval action increases the effectiveness of British improvements in their sea arm—better methods of submarine detection, the use of catapults on merchant ships to launch fighter planes against the heretofore devastating Focke-Wulf 200 bombers (the Focke-Wulfs, in Churchill's words, have now become "the hunted rather than the hunter"[17]), and the increase may provide in actual fact, as well as in Hopkins' view, the margin of force by which the tide seems now to turn.

But disaster has crowded upon disaster for Britain in the Mediterranean, all through the spring, as Hitler has taken over from a fumbling, faltering Mussolini the management of affairs in that crucial area. Nazi legions have swept down through a rebellious Yugoslavia, then Greece, forcing the evacuation with severe losses of a British Expeditionary Force drawn originally from the Army of the Nile, which could ill afford to spare it. Yugoslavia and Greece are now part of the Nazi empire. So is Crete, into which the Germans poured airborne troops on an unprecedented scale in May and from which yet another British army has has to be evacuated with heavy losses to it, to the Royal Air Force, and to the Royal Navy. As for North Africa, the dominating figure there is no longer the British General Wavell; it is the German Lieutenant General Erwin Rommel, the Desert Fox, whose Afrika Korps has driven the British deep into Egypt and who continues to hold the initiative. Alexandria is threatened. The whole Middle East seems threatened as there appear on strategic battle maps the beginnings of a gigantic Nazi pincers, of which one arm thrusts down through the Balkans toward Turkey and Syria while the other thrusts eastward toward the Suez Canal. If the pincers close, all the oil-rich lands of Mesopotamia and Arabia will lie within the Nazi grasp, and Britain's direct sea communications with the Far East will be severed.

The nightmarish quality of the latter possibility is heightened by evidences of impending Japanese aggression in the Southwest Pacific. Under the premiership of Prince Konoye, and with a Foreign Minister (Yosuke Matsuoka) who is deemed by Secretary Hull to be "as crooked as a basket of fishhooks,"[18] Japan linked herself formally if ambiguously to Germany and Italy as long ago as September 27, 1940, when she signed a Tri-Partite Pact in Berlin. The first three articles of it are impressed on Hopkins' mind as on the minds of all others who operate at the summit in Washington:

1. Japan recognizes and respects the leadership of Germany and Italy in the establishment of a new order in Europe.
2. Germany and Italy recognize and respect the leadership of Japan in establishment of a new order in Greater East Asia.
3. Germany, Italy, and Japan agree . . . to assist one another in all political, economic, and military means when one of the three contracting powers is attacked by a power at present not involved in the European War or in the Chinese-Japanese conflict.

And who is meant by "a power at present not involved"? Russia? No, for the closing article of the Pact, Article 5, says explicitly that the terms of the agreement "do not in any way affect the political status which exists at present between each of the contracting powers and Soviet Russia." Who, then? Obviously the United States. The Pact serves notice upon America that, should she go to war with Nazi Germany, she will find herself also at war with Japan; if with Japan, then also with the European Axis. And all through the early months of 1941 Berlin has been urging Tokyo to launch an immediate attack upon Singapore and the Dutch East Indies, the Nazi argument being that the Tri-Partite Pact will deter from intervention an America physically unprepared to fight, in whom isolationist sentiment is still a potent political force. No one in London or Washington can forget that Japan may obtain for the asking, from an enfeebled and essentially pro-Axis Vichy France, bases in French Indo-China from which the assaults urged by Hitler can be launched.

Into all this darkness and grief has come, during the second week of May, a brief but relieving flash of melodrama: Rudolf Hess, Deputy Fuehrer of the Reich, long the closest intimate of Hitler (though the war has reduced this intimacy), has flown alone in an unarmed plane from Germany to Scotland, bailing out near the estate of the Duke of Hamilton, whom he had met during the 1936 Olympic Games in Berlin. He has come on his own authority (he says) to make peace (on Hitler's terms, of course) between the British and Germans, two Teutonic peoples who should be friends with one another and who have a common enemy in Bolshevik Russia. His act has produced a popular sensation, one salutary in its effects on Allied morale. But it is without real significance; Hopkins has learned this from the cables of the Former Naval Person. Hitler's deputy, like Hitler himself, is addicted to astrology; he feels that he has been told by the stars to make this flight which, as an embarrassed Nazi press announces, "will have no effect on the continuance of the war which has been forced on Germany."[19]

No, the world situation, viewed from the White House this night of June 21, remains chock-full of uncertainties, of ominous threats. If Harry Hopkins is less than normally concerned about them it is only because he chooses to be. Out of the black storm of Time he has snatched this bright and placid moment, knowing it must be brief.

And now it ends . . .

For as he lounges in his dressing gown, as the darkness of approaching midnight presses down upon the lamps of Washington, signals come with the speed of light from far around the eastern curve of Earth where already it is Sunday, June 22. In the office of the Soviet Foreign Minister, German Ambassador Schulenburg begins to read aloud to a grimly silent Molotov a long radio message sent in code from the Wilhelmstrasse. It asserts that "the Soviet Government has broken its treaties with Germany and is about to attack Germany from the rear in its struggle for life," and that "The Fuehrer has therefore ordered the German Armed Forces to oppose this threat with all the means at their disposal." These means, aided by complete tactical surprise, are sufficiently great to seem for the moment invincible. While Schulenburg reads, flame erupts and thunder roars along a thousand-mile front reaching all the way from Finland to the Black Sea under the impact of a striking force of 120 German divisions. The German diplomat's personal embarrassment is very great in that hour. His crowning achievement was the Nazi-Soviet Pact, he has sincerely believed in the Pact's efficacy, and he is now utterly, bitterly disillusioned. He hurries to his message's end. Molotov looks hard at him, saying, "It is war. Your aircraft have just bombarded some ten open villages." Then Stalin's Foreign Minister asks a question which will seem very strange, in its plaintiveness, to those who read it years later: "*Do you believe that we deserved that?*"[20]

And it is perhaps at that very instant that the stupendous news comes to Harry Hopkins via a listening post monitoring short-wave radio signals from Europe. The news is not wholly unexpected. As long ago as early January there had come to the State Department a long and detailed report of the German General Staff's plan for an attack on Russia in the spring, a report which, having been carefully checked against its sources in Berlin and deemed probably reliable, was communicated by Sumner Welles to the Soviet Ambassador in Washington on March 20. And for several weeks past, massive movements of German troops toward the Soviet border have been noted by British Intelligence and duly reported to Washington and Moscow. The event itself nevertheless comes as a shock to all the world; and to Hopkins, initially, it comes as a shock of relief. The doom which has seemed so imminently to threaten the British must be at the very least postponed. Nor is the event, for Hopkins, only a relief; it is also a historical effect that illumines and justifies its historical cause, Lend-Lease being of this causality a major part.

"The President's policy of support for Britain has really paid off!" This is his first thought upon receipt of the news. "Hitler has turned to the left."[21]

We who look back upon the event across more than twenty turbulent years know that it has not occurred so simply. We know of a long message written by Hitler to Mussolini on the afternoon of June 21 and delivered to the Italian dictator a bare half-hour before the first Nazi troops cross the Soviet border. In it, the Fuehrer assumes that "England has lost this war," that the United States already "supports our enemy with all the power she is able to mobilize," and that the "elimination of Russia," which is well within the Nazi power, will mean "a tremendous relief for Japan in East Asia, and thereby the possibility of a much stronger threat to American activities through Japanese intervention." If Roosevelt's policy is among the factors influencing the Fuehrer, it is by no means the most important. Certainly it does not *determine* Hitler's action, which not only might have been very different but would have been had he possessed even a slight measure of that intuitive political genius which is widely ascribed to him. As it is, out of his viciousness, his ignorance, his stupidity, he shapes monumental miscalculations of America's war-making potential, of Russia's present strength, of Britain's will to fight.

Certainly, if Roosevelt *were* historically responsible for the mighty clash of arms whose echo is heard by Hopkins at midnight, then Hopkins himself would be also and almost equally responsible. For he is the actual if untitled administrator of Lend-Lease through the critical spring and summer of 1941. Without him—without his unique character, position, abilities—the program might have gotten off to a disastrously slow start. With him, the start has been fast. Urging, pressing, driving; backed by all the power, the prestige of the White House; conducting most of his vast business by phone because other means of communication take too long; making of himself (or being made) "a catalytic agent between two prima donnas," Churchill and Roosevelt; providing through his person unprecedented means of sympathetic cooperation between two heads of Government, each of whom places implicit trust in him; he has managed to put the initial seven-billion-dollar appropriation to effective work with amazing speed and to insure that speed and a maximum possible efficiency (in the circumstances) will rule over what will ultimately become a sixty billion-dollar effort.

Nor does Hopkins now dwell on the happy relief attending Hitler's "turn to the left." Instead he focuses upon the consequent problems which he himself must handle, and will speak of the Russian war, on the morrow, as only "a temporary breather." Yet he does not wholly accept the estimates of military experts, British and American alike, that Soviet armies cannot stand for more than a few weeks against the Nazi legions (the War Department estimates that "Germany will be thoroughly occupied in beating Russia for a minimum of one month and a possible maximum of three months"). Like Roosevelt, he is more sanguine of Russia's present chances than are most Americans, perhaps because he is more sympathetic to the Russian experiment than most; he may even share the President's belief that, as the years pass, the Soviet and American systems will come to resemble one another more and more closely, to the benefit of both.[22] At any rate, the problems to which he immediately turns are precisely those of providing Lend-Lease aid to Russia.[23] He assumes on the instant and without question that such aid must and will be provided: Hitler, not Stalin, is at the moment the gravest possible threat to the survival of Western democracy; the "breather," if that is all it is to be, should certainly be prolonged as far as possible.

In this, Harry Hopkins the political liberal is at one with Winston Churchill the Tory . . .

On that fateful weekend the Prime Minister is host at Chequers, his country estate, to John G. Winant, who has succeeded Kennedy as U. S. Ambassador to the Court of St. James. Winant finds as fellow guests the British Foreign Secretary, Anthony Eden, and the British Ambassador to the Soviet Union, Sir Stafford Cripps. He also finds a Churchill who is convinced that a German invasion of Russia is not only inevitable but imminent and that all who oppose Hitlerism should not hesitate to give the fullest possible aid to Russia. "I have only one purpose, the destruction of Hitler, and my life is much simplified thereby," says the Prime Minister to the American diplomat. "If Hitler invaded Hell, I would make at least a favorable reference to the Devil in the House of Commons."[24]

And on Sunday afternoon, June 22 (it is nine o'clock in the evening in London), Harry Hopkins listens in the White House to the same sentiments expressed in different words as Churchill broadcasts to all the world through the BBC. "No one has been a more consistent opponent of Communism than I have for the last twenty-five years," rolls the Churchillian thunder into Hopkins' room and ear. "I will unsay no word that I have spoken about it. But all this fades away before the spectacle which is now unfolding. . . . Any man or state who fights on against Nazidom will have our aid. Any man or state who marches with Hitler is our foe. . . . That is our policy and that is our declaration. It follows, therefore, that we shall give whatever help we can to Russia and the Russian people. We shall appeal to all our friends and allies in every part of the world to take the same course and pursue, as we shall faithfully and steadfastly to the end. . . ."[25]

Three weeks pass by.

Smolensk, barely two hundred miles from Moscow, is in Nazi hands while, to the north, a German army group thrusts swiftly through the Baltic States toward Leningrad and, to the south, an army group drives toward Kiev, capital of the Ukraine. The Luftwaffe appears to dominate the Russian skies, much of the Soviet air force having been destroyed on the ground in the first hours of surprise attack. But despite immense initial losses of men and materiel, Russia gives no sign of collapse. On the contrary, her resistance grows daily more stubborn, with new divisions hitherto unknown to German Intelligence appearing in greater numbers than old ones can be maimed or destroyed. And eyes informed by history may see shades of Napoleon's lost legions rising from the Russian earth to haunt Hitler's hordes when Stalin in a radio broadcast on July 3 calls for a "scorched earth" policy—the destruction of everything useful to the enemy "in the event of a retreat." Everyone knows that space and time fight on the Soviet side: the distances are vast, the dread Russian winter is coming.

The President on June 24 has publicly supported the British policy of aid to the Soviets, but this for the time being is a mere declaration of principle. What kind of aid? In what amounts? And how are the goods to be delivered?

Early in the morning of Sunday, July 13, Harry Hopkins boards a plane in Washington. He flies to Montreal, thence to Gander, Newfoundland, where he changes to a Lend-Lease B-24 bomber that takes off at once for Prestwick, Scotland. Hour after weary hour he looks down upon the gray waters of the North Atlantic and ponders the events which now rush as a torrent of problems over his aching mind. American troops are now en route to Iceland. The area which the U. S. Navy will police against Nazi warcraft is about to be extended far to the east of its former Atlantic limit. (In Hopkins' briefcase is a map of the North Atlantic torn by the President's hand from a *National Geographic* Magazine just two days ago.[26] On it the President has penciled a line running north along longitude 26° from the South Atlantic through the Azores to a point two hundred miles south of Iceland, where it turns eastward at right angles to curve around the Icelandic coast two hundred miles out before heading north into the Arctic. This is the proposed new limit of responsibility for the patrolling U. S. Navy.

British naval units will thereby be freed to escort shipping around Norway's North Cape through the Barents Sea to Murmansk, the nearest possible Soviet port and one of the only two ice-free ones in the north. But will this really help? It may mean only greater losses to a British Navy already extended to the utmost, for the Murmansk run is bound to be dreadful to all who attempt it, the ships being under incessant attack for hundreds of miles from land-based Nazi aircraft.

Then there is the problem of the Middle East. American military opinion, from the Chief of Staff (General George C. Marshall) on down, strongly opposes Britain's military commitments in that area and is inclined to insist that no more Lend-Lease materiel be sent there. Especially no more U.S. tanks should be sent there; if the U.S. is drawn soon completely into the war, as Marshall (like Hopkins) is convinced she will be, she will need those tanks for her own armies and they are all too likely to be lost in defeat on the deserts of Syria. The British, however, though admitting the risks, insist that risks must be run in war and that they have in the present instance a good chance to hang on. The issue has become sharp, explosive. When Roosevelt recently sent Churchill a telegram questioning the Middle East strategy, Churchill's reply made Roosevelt "hit the roof," as Hopkins will say to the British Major-General John Kennedy a few days hence. "But I smoothed the President down," Hopkins will go on to say. "I said to him, 'Remember you sent that telegram to a man who is fighting for his life. Think of the blitzes in London and all that and the United States still sitting outside the war.' Roosevelt softened at once, and sent a very friendly telegram back to Winston."[27] The issue, however, remains acute. It will constitute a principal item on the agenda of Hopkins' talks in London.

There are also serious difficulties arising from Lend-Lease operations in the British Isles. Chief of these at the moment is a very delicate, tedious, and worrisome problem of investigating malicious charges, made in the United States, that the British are diverting Lend-Lease materials from their legitimate purpose in order to use them in export trade, especially with South America. To gather detailed factual refutation of this charge must consume many hours of Hopkins' and Winant's limited time, it involves the virtual certainty of giving personal offense to important British officials, yet the refutation must be made in order to protect Lend-Lease appropriations against the attacks of isolationist Congressmen.

The plane descends. When it lands upon the Scottish field, Hopkins is almost too ill to move. Nevertheless he goes at once to Churchill; he plunges at once into his historic tasks.

To a meeting at No. 10 Downing Street with the British Chiefs of Staff—Churchill as chairman—he presents the facts without committing himself as to the merits of America's military opposition to the Middle Eastern operations. He does so in such a way as to elicit from the British a carefully written appreciation of the situation which is not only effective in providing a meeting ground for divergent military views but is also of great value to the future planning of over-all war strategy.

In the Downing Street garden, sitting alone with the Prime Minister one sunny afternoon, he tells Churchill of the President's wish for a meeting with him aboard ship "in some lonely bay or other," in the Atlantic, as soon as it can be arranged—and it *is* almost at once arranged to take place on Saturday, August 9 in Placentia Bay, Newfoundland, with the Prime Minister and his colleagues to come on His Majesty's newest battleship, *Prince of Wales*.[28] (Hopkins subsequently urges Roosevelt to bring with him General Marshall and his deputy, General H. H. [Hap] Arnold, for consultations with their British counterparts.)

In the American Embassy, he goes into the matter of alleged diversions of Lend-Lease supplies, garners facts to answer false charges, and smooths ruffled feathers.

But over all that he does, over all that anyone of high position does and thinks in London and Washington, looms the Russian enigma. It casts thick shadows of doubt and uncertainty. No sound bases exist in either capital for estimating the Russian strength and need; what information is at hand is fragmentary and evidently full of falsehoods. In such circumstances how can valid decisions be achieved at the forthcoming Atlantic Conference? Hopkins comes to a sudden decision. Can Russia be reached from Britain by air? he asks Churchill. It can, the Prime Minister replies: PBY (Catalina) flying boats have made a few flights from Invergordon, Scotland, around the North Cape to Archangel. The route, however, is of great length and danger, subject to violent and unpredictable weather as well as to attacks from Nazi fighter planes. Hopkins brushes this aside. Does Churchill believe it would be valuable for a personal representative of the President to engage in face-to-face talks with Stalin? Yes, replies the Prime Minister, albeit reluctantly; the value might be immense. Very well, says Hopkins, he will go if the President agrees to it, and he at once dispatches a cable "For the President Only."

"I have a feeling that everything possible should be done to make certain the Russians maintain a permanent front even though they be defeated in this immediate battle," he writes. "If Stalin could in any way be influenced at a critical time I think it would be worth doing by a direct communication from you through a personal envoy." He also says: "Air transportation good and can reach there [Moscow] in twenty-four hours." He is at Checquers the following evening (Saturday, July 26) when he receives the President's reply: "Welles and I highly approve Moscow trip. . . . I will send you tonight a message for Stalin."[29]

First the long anguish of the northern flight in the comfortless interior of a PBY stripped for war: Arctic cold penetrates to the very marrow of his thinly fleshed bones, for it has been impossible in the time available to obtain proper clothing for a civilian passenger. Then the ordeal of Russian hospitality aboard an admiral's yacht, anchored off Archangel in the azure Dvina River. A four-hour banquet, with multiple toasts of vodka, torments his remnant of a stomach and denies depth to the brief sleep he snatches, less than two hours of it, before he is awakened for transport to the airfield. Then the flight southward in an American Douglas piloted by Russians through brightening light of morning, over broad rivers and lakes that wink, that glitter among endless forests of pine and birch. Until at last he is over the capital of mystery, the round heart of enigma.[30]

Despite his illness and near-exhaustion he looks eagerly down as his plane begins to land.

Moscow is a giant wheel of concentric circles through which spokelike roads and railroads thrust out in all directions into the surrounding woods. Ancient Moscow glows red-gold in the summer sun—scores of miles of red-brick wall, hundreds of gilt-domed churches—while modern Moscow rises among and above the old in an intermittent drabness of gray concrete: office buildings and apartments rear up in a heavy architectural style long outmoded in the West. The plane lands. There is enormous handshaking at the airport, a drive through nearly treeless streets to Spaso House, a nap, a long private talk with the Ambassador . . .

He, Ambassador Laurence A. Steinhardt, is a harried and frustrated man. Though he disagrees with expert military opinion in London and Washington to the extent that he sees in Russia no swift and easy conquest for Adolf Hitler, if indeed Hitler conquers at all, he has few facts with which to sustain his belief. Facts are hard to come by in the Soviet capital. This Embassy compound, this double-structure in which the diplomatic corps lives and works, is an island-prison within a sullen sea of distrust and suspicion, double-walled against communication with ordinary Russian citizens and against any information save the meager and dubious quota doled out by Kremlin officialdom. Moreover, every native servant that the Americans hire must be regarded as a possible agent of Soviet espionage.

Hopkins nods. At Archangel the British airmen who flew him from Scotland are confined on a houseboat in the Dvina, their requests to go ashore bluntly denied. One must admit, however, that the passion for conspiratorial secrecy which (judging from history) is in the Russian blood, and is evidently raised to highest pitch in the inscrutable Stalin—this passion has been repeatedly encouraged by Western words and deeds since the October Revolution of 1917. Distrust breeds distrust. Hate breeds hate. For instance, the town to which British fliers are denied access in July of 1941 is the same Archangel at which British and French troops were landed in August of 1918 to fight the Bolsheviks (they were not withdrawn until September 1919); and the Roosevelt whom Steinhardt represents to the Soviet Chief of State was a not-unimportant member of the Administration of Woodrow Wilson which, in 1918, sent an American expeditionary force into Siberia to aid the foes of the Bolsheviks. These episodes may be forgotten in London and Washington; they are remembered in Moscow.

All the same, Hopkins is determined to break through the barriers to needful exchanges. Perhaps he has a better chance to do so than anyone else since Stalin came to power, for his credentials are unique. The circumstances are unique. Dire Soviet needs cannot be alleviated unless they are first revealed, and out of such revelations must come unprecedented knowledge of Soviet strengths and weaknesses; nor can they be alleviated without unprecedented Soviet cooperation on the highest levels.

Steinhardt feels inclined to agree, with reservations. At any rate, says he, they will soon find out. The first meeting with the Russian dictator is scheduled to take place at 6:30 the following evening. Hopkins (the Ambassador eyes his guest with concern) should be well rested for it. Hence a light dinner, an early bed for the exhausted traveler. From long before sunset until long after sunrise, the summer dusk and dawn being nearly together in that latitude, Hopkins sleeps deeply . . .

And awakes to strangeness in a harsh, strange land. It is Wednesday, July 30.

He drives sightseeing with the Ambassador through the streets of Moscow, and sees some part of what peacetime visitors were expected to see. Everywhere there are weird juxtapositions and interminglings. Bleak austerity is interspersed with Oriental opulence; barbaric splendors, vestiges of savage superstitions, evidences of a Slavic lust for punishment (both the giving and receiving of it)—all these exist side by side with the most enlightened institutions of Western science and culture. A moody violence, a latent cruelty seem to flow off the ancient cobbles of Chinatown, through the narrow, twisting lanes of the Old City, onto the broad asphalt of Gorky Street where (one senses) it may burst at any moment through some gap in the prevailing discipline. It is as if a high wind swept off the barren steppes of Central Asia to snarl and howl through isolated patches of European forest, bending great boughs and, now and then, breaking one off or even uprooting a whole tree in sudden insensate fury.

Everywhere, too, the signs and agents of war. Tanks rumble through the streets. Soldiers march westward. Planes roar overhead. Anti-aircraft batteries bristle in the parks. In the suburbs are gangs of heavy muscular women who dig ditches, who throw up barricades.

And to the very center of all this—to the symbol of all, the focus of all—comes the American Embassy car as the appointed hour draws near. The nineteen dark towers of the Kremlin wall, the cathedrals, the palaces, the belfry, are silhouetted against a slowly declining sun.

Hardly noticeable beneath the tall wall of a palace is a plain yellow house of three storys, its every window white-bordered and its upper ones hung inside with white linen curtains. Hopkins looks closely at it as the car comes to a stop before it. No doubt his nerves grow tighter; no doubt his breath comes shorter. He leaves the car. He accompanies Steinhardt into the house . . .

And into Stalin's office.

It is a room of no great size, plainly furnished. There is a bookcase containing, apparently, statistical reference works; a death mask of Lenin under glass against one wall; an unadorned writing desk with a phone upon it; some homely but comfortable-looking armchairs.

If any of this meager detail impresses itself upon Hopkins in that moment, however, it does so at the margins of his consciousness. His attention is focused upon Lenin's successor.

He is surprised by what he sees.

He had expected the Soviet dictator to be more impressive physically; he had expected him to be, if not actually tall, at least well above medium height. As it is, Hopkins looks *down* on Stalin. And quite far down. Though the dictator stands erect beside his desk, his head is an inch below his visitor's eyes. Nor is there anything impressive in the dress of the Man of Steel, unless it be the high gloss of polish upon his knee-high boots. Above his boots, his trousers of stout plain cloth are baggy; above his waist, his plain blouse fits snugly; and nowhere upon him is an ornament, a decoration.

Stalin's handclasp, however, is sufficiently impressive; his hand is large, hard, strong. There is authority, too, in his harsh voice, greeting his visitors with brief words (swiftly translated by the interpreter) through lips that widen in what Hopkins will later term a "managed smile"—a rather sardonic smile that narrows the eyelids without moderating the steely cold directness of the gaze. And when all are seated, whatever psychological advantage Hopkins may derive from his physically "looking down" upon his host (Stalin insists upon the relationship of host and guest, saying, "You are our guest; you have but to command.")—this advantage, if any, is lost. Stalin is short-legged but long-waisted; when seated, with Hopkins and Steinhardt before him, his eyes look level into theirs and it becomes evident that he is, physically, a powerful man. He is thick of chest, broad of shoulder. He must weigh close to one hundred and ninety pounds, no pound of it flabby fat, and this weight is evenly distributed over a frame standing no higher than five feet six inches when upright. "He is built," thinks Hopkins, "like a football coach's dream of a tackle. . . ."[31]

The dictator offers Hopkins a Russian cigarette and accepts in return an American. He thereafter smokes one cigarette after another, his consumption of them more than matching Hopkins' and accounting, perhaps, for the hoarseness of his voice, since he deeply inhales every puff. He wastes no words. He answers questions shortly, makes statements flatly. Now and then he laughs, a sardonic bark of a laugh. He sticks to the point as closely as ever Hopkins inclines to do, so that the latter has a rare and delicious feeling of much business of immense importance being dispatched in the shortest possible order.

Stalin needs 20- to 37-mm. anti-aircraft guns in great quantity, with ammunition for them. If he had twenty thousand such mobile, rapid-firing pieces right now he could shift some two thousand pursuit planes from defensive to offensive duties. He understands that the United States has available large stocks of rifles of the caliber used by Soviet troops; he could use a million or more of them. He already has enough ammunition for these. He needs high octane aviation gasoline. He needs aluminum—especially aluminum. For the construction of airplanes, he says.

"Give us anti-aircraft guns and the aluminum . . ." He looks hard at Hopkins. "Give us these, and we can fight for two or three years."

He welcomes the two hundred Curtiss P-40s which are now in process of delivery to him, sixty of them directly from America and the remainder by way of England, but he is evidently far better off in terms of aviation than Hopkins has been led to believe. Admittedly, the initial loss of Soviet planes was great, caught as they were on the ground, but they were for the most part old, relatively slow fighters. (The Germans, too, in ignorant contempt of Soviet air power, used outmoded plane types at first; they now send in their best types.) Soviet air reserves and construction capabilities are large—much larger than Washington or London has suspected—and the new Soviet bombers and fighters now flying into battle prove themselves equal in quality to the best of the Germans. Soviet pilots prove equal also. The greatest aviation need at the moment is for short-range bombers which can be used tactically, in support of ground troops.

As for routes and ports of delivery, Vladivostok is unsuitable for several reasons. It is too far from the scene of battle, says Stalin. It is too near a possibly hostile Japan, says Hopkins. The route up the Persian Gulf and through Iran is also unsuitable. Iranian highways and railroads are inadequate, the attitude of the Iranian Government uncertain. This leaves Murmansk and Kaldalaksha as the only permanently ice-free ports, with Archangel a port that can be kept open with ice-breakers. The route to these is so hazardous that a large proportion of the material shipped along it is bound to be lost at sea. They represent, nevertheless, the best available possibilities . . .

Thus the specific items of their first talk. More important, in historic effect, are the general impressions each makes upon the other, or derives from the other.

"I expressed to him the President's belief that the most important thing to be done in the world today was to defeat Hitler and Hitlerism," Hopkins will write in his report. "I impressed upon him the determination of the President and our Government to extend all possible aid to the Soviet Union at the earliest possible time. . . . I reiterated to Mr. Stalin the appreciation of the people of the United States of the splendid resistance of the Soviet Army. . . ."

As for Stalin, he gives Hopkins the impression, the conviction even, that he contemplates a long, costly war. Why, otherwise, would he lay such stress on aluminum? There is, in other words, no possibility of his negotiating a peace with the "Hitlerites" (as his interpreter calls them) on any basis save that of their abjectly profitless withdrawal from Soviet soil—and of course there is no possibility of such a withdrawal.

That Stalin is eager for the closest cooperation with the United States—of this, too, Hopkins is convinced. Or *almost* convinced. There remain doubts as to Stalin's willingness to disclose, frankly and fully, needed information about the situation at the front. Steinhardt (Hopkins is reminded) has been denied access to such information; no Ambassador, no military attaché, not even a war correspondent has been permitted to go to the front; and it is increasingly evident that the pessimistic estimates by foreign military observers in Moscow are tissues of guesswork so darkly tinted with anti-Communist prejudice as to hide rather than reveal truths.

To the removal of these doubts, to the alleviation of this need, Hopkins directs his attention next day. In the afternoon he has, with Steinhardt, an important conversation with Vyacheslav Molotov, Stalin's Commissar for Foreign Affairs. They discuss the situation in the Far East, and Hopkins seeks in terms of it to discover more facts about Soviet war strengths and prospects. He seeks in vain. The doubts and need remain when Hopkins comes at six-thirty that evening to his second meeting with the Communist dictator.

This time Steinhardt does not accompany him. Only an interpreter is with Stalin in the office as Hopkins enters—an interpreter who turns out to be none other than smiling, moon-faced Maxim Litvinov! The gesture is, of course, deliberately significant; but it does not produce upon the American the precise effect at which the Russian aims. It produces unease, a vague sense of shame. The sometime Soviet Commissar for Foreign Affairs, prophet of collective security against Nazi-Fascism, of friendship with Western democracy, long cast down into hazardous and silent nether darkness, seems to Hopkins "like a morning coat which has been laid away in mothballs . . . but which had now been brought out, dusted off, and aired as a symbol of completely changed conditions." A man, thought Hopkins, ought not to be used in this way. Implicit in the operation is a certain contempt, not only for Litvinov but also (more faintly) for Hopkins and, indeed, for all humanity. Implied by it is a government of coercion, a policy rooted in violence, implemented by terror. Later Hopkins will remember the impression this gesture makes upon him as being of a piece with that made the night before when, having left Stalin, he entered into technical discussions (at ten o'clock) with one General Yakolev concerning the specific amounts and kinds of material aid the Red Army might receive from America. The general was afraid, Hopkins felt—he was literally afraid to go one step beyond the rigid instructions given him, the agenda provided him. And it seemed to Hopkins consistent with this that the blackout into which he stepped at midnight, going back to Spaso House, was the deepest, the blackest he had ever witnessed, far more so than London's. One might expect Stalin's Russia to have a special genius for blackouts.

Yet in the private conference this night, the dictator "comes clean with a vengeance" (as Hopkins might put it), giving as frank and complete an "appreciation and analysis" of the Nazi-Soviet war as anyone had a right to expect.

Item. The Russians had 180 divisions in being when Hitler attacked with approximately 175, but many of these were too far behind the front to go at once into battle. Hence the "inadequate" initial defense. Now, however, there are 240 Soviet divisions at the front, plus twenty more in reserve, and the present front line is much more "propitious" for the defense than the western frontier would have been.

Item. The front is fluid, with "very many Russian and German troops . . . fighting far forward from their respective lines because of the advances made by both sides with their mechanized forces. . . . Merely because German forces pierce the Russian line does not mean the Russians are lost. They fight behind the Germans, are adept at the use of cover, and fight their way out in the night."

Item. The Germans give evidence of war-weariness (captured troops say they are "sick of war") and are certainly, at the moment, involved in grave logistical and communications difficulties. Some of their reserves are as far as 400 kilometers behind the front and communications between these and the front are continuously menaced by what Stalin, or Litvinov, calls "insurgents" (Hopkins would call them "guerrillas"). The pressure on the Russian front has "become considerably less . . . in the last ten days," the reason being, in Stalin's opinion, that the Germans have been unable to supply their mechanized divisions and air forces adequately with fuel.

Item. Russia had 24,000 tanks and 60 tank divisions, with 350 to 400 tanks per division, when the war began, as compared with 30,000 Nazi tanks. Russia can produce about 1000 tanks per month, fewer per month than the Germans can produce. Hence there is urgent need for tanks and steel from the United States during the winter, while the Soviets increase their capacity. As for planes, the Germans produce between 2500 and 3000 fighters and bombers per month, the Russians 1800 per month, but by January 1 this latter rate will increase to 2500 per month, 60 per cent of them fighters, 40 per cent bombers.

Item. Though Stalin does not reply "in detail" to Hopkins' questions as to "the location of his munitions plants," he indicates that "about 75 per cent of the sum total . . . [are] in the general areas of which Leningrad, Moscow, and Kiev . . . [are] the centers." "I gained the impression," Hopkins will report, ". . . that if the German army could move some 150 miles east of each of these centers, they could destroy almost 75 per cent of Russia's industrial capacity."

Item. But the Russians are dismantling and moving eastward, out of bombing range, many of their factories and machine tools—and the Germans (Stalin is convinced) will be stopped before Leningrad, Moscow, and Kiev by the time winter closes in, probably along a line "within 100 kilometers of their present position."

The items add up to an impressive sum, weighty enough to sink through the Hopkins mind into a deep conviction that Russia, far greater in present strength than the West believed, has a gigantic, swiftly realizable potential. He is also convinced that a full working cooperation with Stalin can and must be established, and he will now proceed with unflawed confidence to a discussion of aid details. Before he does so, however, he listens closely to a "personal message" which Stalin asks him to convey to the President, a message of whose report Hopkins makes a single copy, accompanying it with a recommendation that it not be permitted to leave the President's office, though its contents might be given orally to Secretary Hull.

"Stalin said Hitler's greatest weakness was found in the vast numbers of oppressed people who hate Hitler and the immoral ways of his Government," Hopkins will write. "He believed these people and countless other millions in nations still unconquered would receive the kind of encouragement and moral strength they needed to resist Hitler from only one source and that was the United States. He stated that the world influence of the President and the Government of the United States was enormous. . . . Stalin said that he believed it was inevitable that we should finally come to grips with Hitler on some battlefield . . . and he wanted me to tell the President that *he would welcome the American troops on any part of the Russian front under the complete command of the American Army*."‡

The talk lasts for more than three hours, with Litvinov so self-effacing and effaced as to be virtually forgotten by Hopkins. Litvinov is not *personally* (it seems) in the room. Not once is his opinion asked for; not once does he volunteer a remark of his own. He is a machine, utterly ignored by Stalin who does not so much as look at him but instead looks straight into Hopkins' eyes when he speaks—"as though I understood every word that he uttered," Hopkins will say. Similarly with the secretary who, two or three times during the long conversation, when Hopkins asks a question to which Stalin cannot reply precisely, appears in the room in response to pressure from the dictator's finger upon a button on his desk. This secretary appears instantaneously, silently, and stands at attention as Stalin repeats to him the question Hopkins has asked. Then the secretary replies quickly, as if by rote, and leaves as swiftly and silently as he came.

In the months ahead, Hopkins, in company with Churchill and Roosevelt, will habitually refer to Stalin as "Uncle Joe," as if the dictator were essentially a kindly, humorous, salty character whose innate suspiciousness and distrust is but a foible, annoying on some occasions, amusing on others. He will admire Stalin's toughness, his decisiveness, his succinct-

‡ Author's italics.

ness of statement, his refusal to waste precious time in "small talk." But always there will be in the back of his mind this sense he has had of Litvinov-as-machine, of the anonymous secretary-as-machine, of Yakolev-as-machine—a sense too of the brooding atmosphere of terror within which this machinery works—and hence of the price paid in loss of humanity and resiliency for Stalin's seemingly absolute power of decision. "Before my three days in Moscow ended," he will write, "the difference between democracy and dictatorship was clearer to me than any words of a philosopher, historian or journalist could make it."

And even as he flies north from Moscow on August 1, in the Russian-piloted Douglas—and looks down again for the last time upon the fields, the villages, the immense forests and thousand lakes—he may suspect that totalitarian Russia, frozen by fear to the rigid consistency of ice in the Arctic, must soon have shattered under the hammer blows of the Nazis if it were not in a sense *worn* (rendered somewhat flexible despite itself) by a Mother Russia possessed of passionate loves, passionate hates, and all the give and spring of vital tissue. He may suspect, even this early (for the suspicion is consistent with his vague but strong sense of Stalinist terror), that the iron dictator's power of decision is not in fact as absolute as it has seemed in the Kremlin to be. If so, he will not be altogether surprised by the discrepancies which will soon begin to appear between Stalin's clearly expressed will and the events that supposedly follow from it. Hopkins will credit these to the mysterious, incalculable workings of the Politburo and may well wonder if Stalin is not himself a victim—enslaved, driven—by the terror he seems to inspire, the naked power he seems to wield.

The flight from Archangel to Scapa Flow, Scotland in the PBY is a major test of Hopkins' courage and fortitude. By some horrid mischance, the satchel containing his medicines (he cannot live long without them) has been left in Moscow, so that he is desperately ill as well as exhausted by the time the Douglas touches down. Moreover, the weather reports for the route of the homeward flight are incomplete and unfavorable: there will certainly be strong headwinds all the way, and rough waters for the landing. But Hopkins turns down the recommendation by the Catalina's captain that takeoff be delayed until the weather is more favorable; he knows he must board the *Prince of Wales* on August 2 if he is to sail with Churchill to the secret rendezvous off Argentia, knows too that his presence at the Atlantic Conference is important to its success. Churchill and Roosevelt have not yet met one another. He alone is equipped to serve as buffer between their possibly clashing personalities while at the same time focusing their attentions upon crucial tasks at hand—and he alone, among all those on the U.S.S. *Augusta* and H.M.S. *Prince of Wales*, will have talked to Stalin about the war.

For twenty-four hours he is in troubled air, his sick body tossed and buffeted. He has barely strength enough to jump from the plane to the slippery deck of an admiral's launch, at Scapa Flow, when at last the flying boat comes down. A sailor with a boat hook hauls him sprawling across the deck to the safety of the cabin. But he laughs! He laughs at this undignified arrival of the President's personal envoy upon a British boat. He laughs at his sickness, his weakness. He waves a cheery farewell to the crew of the PBY, whose captain will later speak in awestruck tones of his passenger's "unbelievable courage," his "unparalleled devotion to duty."[32]

IV

To the Day of Infamy

i. *A Game of War*

Upon the swamps of Louisiana the September dawn emerged, not as a gradual brightening of the land under an eastern sky, not as light from any source or direction, but as an abrupt precipitation of gray and wavering objects out of a shrieking, streaming, liquid night. No object seemed quite solid, rigid. The trees with their tatters of Spanish moss flung out upon the wind, the tents bulging and flattening beneath them, even the trucks whose stubborn immobility in the deep red mud of the roads provoked the curses of myriad weary men—all these seemed fluid and tentative shapes in the rain. They might redissolve at any moment into the element from which they came.

But the "war" would go on.

There was a colonel who stood under a canvas awning on which the rain fell in sheets, fell with the sound of sheets being torn, and this colonel was especially determined that there be no end today since it was the "enemy" who attacked and must be stopped before (on the morrow, the colonel hoped) a decisive counterattack could be launched. He stood for several minutes under the awning. There was no perceptible increase of the sourceless light. Nevertheless more and more objects emerged to his vision, and the space between him and the farthest of them grew steadily wider. There was a sodden field beyond the sodden wood. Men moved across it bent in the rain under the weight of their weapons, their packs, their tiredness. There was a water-slicked red clay road along which trucks crawled and men marched and beside which was a ditch brimful of swiftly running muddy water.

The colonel turned and entered the caravan, to which the pole-propped awning formed a porch.

Though he would be fifty-one years old three weeks from now, he appeared ten years younger. Though nearly six feet tall, he appeared no more than of middle height. Though bald, with only a few thin strands of blond hair around and across the back of his skull, he somehow did not *seem* so, for the shape of his head was such, and his complexion was such, as to prevent the nakedness of his scalp from becoming a salient feature of his appearance. His step still had the poise and elasticity of youth. He carried his hands as a boxer does, his elbows slightly bent, giving the impression that he could bring them into action fast and that his reaction time in general was very fast. His eyes were a bright blue, his mouth wide and mobile, with a flat, slightly overhanging upper lip, and his skin was unwrinkled and had a healthy glow of suntan. It was an interesting face to watch when he talked because it changed expressions often and the range of its expressiveness was great. His smile was frequent, wide, and disarming, his frown rare, yet one sensed that he might have a fiery temper and that his anger—red-faced, fist-clenched—could be fearsome to see and dangerous to its objects. There was in him the kind of tension produced by an effortful self-control, as in a harp string drawn taut; one felt that this might increase his vibrant responsiveness to physical stimuli—to sights and sounds and tactile perceptions—while inhibiting his as-yet unmeasured capacity to absorb generalized knowledge and intellectual abstractions.

The caravan had been made into a headquarters war room. Upon its walls were large-scale contour maps of western Louisiana and eastern Texas, with pins having different colored heads to mark the various unit positions. The colonel looked at them. Above and to the left were the organizations so far identified of Lieutenant General Ben Lear's attacking Second Army (the "Reds"); below and to the right were the organizations of Lieutenant General Walter Krueger's Third Army (the "Blues"). There were squads and platoons and companies, battalions and regiments and divisions, mostly grouped in blocks of three in accordance with the new triangular setup. On paper each was a disciplined unit of force acting as an integral part of a larger force that defined against opposition the mind and will and skill of a commander. But in reality—in the swamps of Louisiana, swept by the fringes of a hurricane roaring into Texas from the Gulf—they must still be viewed through eyes trained in the military profession as civilians in uniform. No one could say they were as inadequate to the needs of modern war as the four sticks they used in lieu of real anti-aircraft guns, the wooden forms that represented tanks, the white flags they waved to indicate the firing of guns; but neither could anyone say that they were what they must become if they were to win or even survive a battle. They were not yet solid elements of an army.

Indeed, there had been exasperated moments during the last three weeks when the actual troops had appeared to the mind's eye of the colonel to be almost as wavering and tentative as they had appeared that morning to his physical eye, blurred under wind-driven sheets of rain in a gray and streaming dawn. Nor was it unnatural in the circumstances that they seem so, or even be so. They were the arms of a people whose collective mind was still flawed by contradictions, whose will was not yet hard enough for war. The national policy they implemented remained essentially ambiguous, wavering still in the blasts of an outraged, embittered isolationism.

True, there had emerged from the Atlantic Conference a joint declaration, the Atlantic Charter, whose eight points, if as meaningless *per se* as they were high-sounding, added up in effect to an alliance with Britain for "the final destruction of the Nazi tyranny" and the making of a just and lasting peace. True, the U. S. Navy had been ordered to "shoot at sight" any Axis raiders operating in American "defensive waters," an order following hard upon a Nazi U-boat attack on the U.S. destroyer *Greer* on September 4. (Wendell Willkie promptly applauded the order, at further cost to his standing in the Republician party.) True, also, the United States and Britain had joined in freezing all Japanese funds and assets in their countries, in the denunciation of all existing trade treaties with Japan, and in the imposition of other economic sanctions—this in response to Japanese occupation of bases in French Indo-China, recently granted them by Vichy France. But against these evidences of increased commitment must be balanced the fact that the Selective Service Extension Act, without which the half-trained conscripts of the new Army must be literally redissolved into the civilian element from which they came, had barely squeaked through Congress in August. In the House, where only 21 Republicans voted for the Act while 133 voted against, the margin of passage was a single vote! This gave a disturbing plausibility to predictions by some isolationists that next month would see mass desertions by draftees to whom the Government had "broken its promise" of release after a year's service. "OHIO," chalked on walls and sidewalks, was alleged to have a sinister meaning—"Over the Hill In October."

There were other signs that isolationism, though weakened, remained a potent factor in national life. They were particularly ugly signs in that they expressed an anti-Semitism whose effective strength was as yet incalculable but whose aim was certainly subversive of essential American freedoms. While final preparations for the great "Battle of Louisiana" were going forward, a special subcommittee of the Senate Interstate Commerce Committee was launching an investigation of the motion picture industry. It was an investigation whose premise was that Hollywood's Jewish producers (". . . born abroad and animated by the persecutions and hatreds of the old world," to quote Senator Nye) had been injecting "pro-war propaganda" into films. Wendell Willkie had at once sprung to the defense of the film industry, and as special counsel for it at the hearings he managed to transform these into a kind of courtroom trial obviously embarrassing to both Nye and Senator Bennett Champ Clark. Nevertheless, the investigation continued to make newspaper headlines dismaying to all who were committed to religious and racial tolerance in America. These last were even more dismayed by a speech Charles A. Lindbergh made at an America First rally in Des Moines on September 11. The great hero of the twenties declared that "the three most important groups who have been pressing this country toward war are the British, the Jewish, and the Roosevelt administration," and that the warmongering Jews were a "danger to this country" chiefly because of "their large ownership and influence in our motion pictures, our press, our radio, and our government." This had provoked a storm of protest from leading national figures, including several who were not famous as battlers for liberal causes—William Randolph Hearst, for instance, and Thomas E. Dewey—but its possibly great hidden persuasiveness was indicated by the evident reluctance of the America First Committee to disavow any part of it.*

Add these things up, and one achieved a general sense of America's psychological unpreparedness for war.

When the simulated "Battle of Louisiana" began with an attack by Krueger's Third Army in mid-September, the most significant difference between the opposing forces had been in the weight and distribution of their armor. Lear, of the Second Army, was armor-heavy. Assigned to him at the outset of the games—which were by far the greatest in United States history—had been the First Armored Corps, the only complete organization of tanks and armored vehicles in the nation. It consisted of two divisions having three hundred tanks each, plus 2000 other armored vehicles. Krueger's numerical superiority was considerable—near 250,000 troops versus Lear's 150,000—and he was of course not without armor: he had a few hundred tanks. But his armored weight was much less than Lear's, he possessed not a single completely armored division, and to many a trained observer, impressed by examples of Nazi blitzkrieg, it appeared that the real advantage lay with the Second Army. Yet four days later the first phase had ended in decisive victory for Krueger. Lear had seemed not to know what to do with his preponderance of armored strength. It was apparently not used at all on the initial day. On the third day, when his armored units managed to penetrate the Blue line at a couple of points, a skilled use of Blue reserves nullified his gains: the reserves were not committed until the tank strength was spent, whereupon they pinched off the salients and plugged the gaps. By the afternoon of the fourth day, the entire Second Army had its back against the Red River, following a retreat that was nearly a rout: its communications across the river were imperiled by air attacks (Blue planes dominated the skies), its armor was utterly immobilized (a Blue cavalry thrust at midnight had captured the Red gasoline dump). "Had it been real war,"

* The Committee, in fact, never did disavow it but merely deplored "the injection of the race issue into a discussion of war or peace." It was not Lindbergh who had done this, according to them, but "the interventionists" who had criticized Lindbergh's speech.

reported Hanson W. Baldwin in the New York *Times*, "Lear's forces would have been annihilated."

For this event, a considerable portion of the credit had been given by knowledgeable observers to the colonel who now stood before the war room maps, who turned now to receive, by phone and messenger, reports from the developing "front." His name had even figured in the national news (if very obscurely), for the first time in his life. For instance, Drew Pearson and Robert S. Allen had announced in their syndicated column that it was "Colonel [Dwight D.] Eisenhower . . . who conceived and directed the strategy that routed the Second Army," he being Krueger's Chief of Staff, and that Eisenhower "has a steel-trap mind plus unusual physical vigor [and] to him the military profession is a science and he began watching and studying the German Army five years ago."[1] If Third Army strategy proved as effective in the second phase of the games (the phase opening this rain- and wind-swept morning) as it had in the first, the colonel could expect very soon a general's stars upon his shoulders and (probably) a staff job under Marshall, Chief of Staff of the U. S. Army, in Washington. Nor would this sudden emergence from obscurity be especially surprising to him, or to many other Army career men. Ever since the spring of 1926, when he had graduated first of about 275 men from the Army's very tough Command and General Staff School, at Fort Leavenworth, he had known that his name was high on the General Staff Corps Eligible List, kept there by an unbroken succession of "Superiors" upon his annual efficiency ratings. He knew, too, that Marshall and Lieutenant General Lesley J. McNair, Chief of the newly organized General Headquarters, were in search of general officer material, that they hoped to find it in Louisiana, and that their assignment of him to Krueger on the eve of the great maneuvers meant that he was being put to the test.

If the colonel were at all worried as this long day began, he hid the fact well—and as the day wore on and the dispatches poured in from the far-flung lines, it became increasingly clear that he and Krueger had, in fact, nothing to worry about. Lear's strategy contained no surprises; his armor continued ineffective. The Blues yielded here and there under the shock of attack, but with no loss of resilience: whenever and wherever the pressure of the Reds slackened, the Blues again sprang forward, pressing hard against the flanks of salients and forcing, often, a withdrawal from them. By nightfall there had been no significant shifts of position.

Next morning the Blues counterattacked over the whole front, and by the afternoon of September 27 the "battle" had ended in a decisive victory, again, for Krueger's Third Army. Again, the Third Army's staff work was given high praise by professional observers from Washington; again the name of Eisenhower appeared (not at all prominently) in the public prints, along with that of Lieutenant Colonel LeRoy Lutes, Krueger's G-4 (Supply), who had also done an "outstanding job."

McNair's critique of the exercises would stress deficiencies in the command of small units in both armies: generally speaking, company and platoon leadership had been inadequate, as was to be expected in a citizen army hastily assembled; but this had markedly improved between the first preliminaries and the final "battle." Both McNair and Marshall were especially pleased by the degree of ground-air coordination achieved by Third Army; both made a point of meeting and talking with Eisenhower.

There was a single great surprise for Eisenhower himself in the last phase of the maneuvers. This was on the morning following an afternoon in which the Blue's Second Cavalry Division had driven deep scallops into the Red's Second Armored ("Hell on Wheels") Division.

The commander of Second Armored was Major General George S. Patton, Jr., whom Eisenhower had known as a friend ever since the spring of 1919, when both were stationed at Camp Meade, Maryland. Patton, though but five years older than Eisenhower, was a legendary figure among Army professionals even in that early year. Everyone knew he could make deadly use of the pearl-handled .45 revolvers he habitually wore in violation of uniform regulations: he had done so in Mexico one March day in 1916 when, sent by Pershing to capture a principal lieutenant of Pancho Villa, he had killed the man in a gunfight. Everyone knew of heroic deeds he had performed, wounds he had suffered, and medals he had won during the St. Mihiel and Meuse-Argonne offensives in France two years later. Everyone knew of his passionate devotion to tanks, he having been commander of a tank brigade on the Western Front—a devotion which helped cement his friendship with Eisenhower, who had commanded the Tank Corps Training Center at Camp Colt, Gettysburg, Pennsylvania, during the war. They had agreed in 1919 that the "tank is in its infancy," to quote an article Eisenhower was then writing for the *Infantry Journal:* "The clumsy, awkward, snail-like pace of the old tanks must be forgotten, and in their place we must picture a speedy, reliable, and efficient engine of destruction."[2]

But even in that earlier year Eisenhower had *not* wholly agreed with Patton's theory of command (Patton believed that troops fight best out of a combined fear and hero-worship of their commander), nor had he been altogether sympathetic with the brand of personal showmanship, the ostentatious "toughness," the intense and ruthless competitiveness, with which Patton as professional soldier sought to realize his dream of glory. These qualities had caused troops of the Second Armored to nickname their commander the "Green Hornet," not always in admiration. They had also caused Eisenhower to keep an especially wary eye upon the Second Armored from the moment the maneuvers began.

On this particular morning a report came to Third Army headquarters that Patton's division, in desperate straits only last evening, was now on a ridge commanding miles of country behind Third Army lines! Eisenhower stared; Eisenhower swore. It was a logistical impossibility, he said to Krueger. To be where he was, Patton would have had to move his division some 380 miles around the Blue Army in the night, and he could not possibly have had enough gasoline for such a drive. Krueger agreed. But the report checked out: Patton was indeed upon that ridge, claiming he had "won the war" for the Second Army, and "what the hell are you going to do about it?" What Krueger did was to protest vigorously to the umpires who, indeed, needed no persuasion. They ruled out the forced night march: they ordered Patton back to his former position.

Later it was learned that Patton, a wealthy man, had arranged to have his tanks "gassed up" at filling stations along the route of his night march, paying for the gasoline out of his own pocket. It was also learned that several men had been killed and injured in traffic accidents as his division roared at high speeds, without lights, over the dark roads. Patton refused to bow to the blasts of popular criticism which this fact focused upon him, insisting that armored troops must learn to move swiftly at night under combat conditions and could learn only by doing, and his argument had weight with his superiors. From first to last, out of 400,000 men involved, some scores were accidentally killed during the maneuvers, a cost deemed not excessive by the top command.

ii. *A Meeting of Scientists*

At ten o'clock in the morning of the first Saturday in December 1941, four men met together in an office of the Carnegie Institution of Washington, at 1530 P Street, N.W. The room was in no way distinguished from a thousand others: its walls were without pictures, its floor was covered by the plainest of durable carpets, and the table at which the men sat was a severely plain oaken one with a dozen straight-backed chairs drawn up to it. Nor would an observer unaware of its context have found the meeting itself markedly different from a thousand other business sessions he might have witnessed that day in America. One of the four men, chairman of a special committee, had submitted a report with recommendations to the head office; it was to hear the head office's reply that these four were gathered here; and because the meeting was so small, and all the men had known each other long and well, it was completely informal.[3]

This same observer would have soon sensed, however, if he were at all acute, that these men, though they differed widely from one another in appearance and in the mannerisms by which personality is revealed, more closely resembled each other in their professional characters—in their basic attitudes toward their work, in their habits of thought and feeling about it—than is normally the case. He would have sensed, too, that their work was itself partially responsible for this. It was of such a nature as to set them apart, in ways both subtle and profound, from the common bureaucracy of Big Business, Big Labor, and Big Government. They were administrators, but the field in which they performed administrative functions required of them a degree of genuine disinterestedness and also a quantity of knowledge, a quality of intelligence beyond the professional needs and personal capacities of most men. These four were men of transition from one age to another, builders of bridges between heretofore widely separated worlds, and they engaged in shaping a final link between science and government after which, if present anticipations were realized, nothing in the whole social and economic life of mankind could ever be quite the same again.

Though informal, the meeting was not formless. Its loose structure had a head, James B. Conant, a man of narrowly angular body and plain face who looked somehow a little unkempt even when he was at his neatest, his tidiest. He was tall and thin; his clothes hung loosely upon him. His abundance of dark hair grew low upon his forehead and seemed almost never to be neatly combed. He had wide-spaced gray-blue eyes behind steel-rimmed spectacles, and an unusually wide mouth (smile wrinkles curved around it) above a vertically narrow chin. It was easy to picture him in the occupation that had brought him his first recognition, white-smocked in a laboratory of organic chemistry, his fingers on the pet cock of a titration tube or holding a smoking test tube over a Bunsen burner. He fitted the part, in appearance. He did not fit at all the popular conception of how a president of Harvard University should look.

Had popular stereotypes chosen a Harvard president from among those in the room, by appearance alone, the choice might well have fallen upon Lyman J. Briggs, though he was in fact the only one who had made his career wholly outside academic circles. He was also, at sixty-seven, the oldest man present. He had received his Ph.D. from Johns Hopkins in 1901, and had then done valuable research work in the Department of Agriculture. During the First World War he had been detailed to the Bureau of Standards, in the Department of Commerce, and had been, since 1933, the Bureau's Director. A tall, erect, dignified man, his thin hair white with years, he had in general the appearance popularly associated with the Ivy League.

Or the choice might have fallen upon Arthur H. Compton, a strikingly handsome man in the prime of life, with the powerful build and relaxed physical movements of an athlete. Simultaneously chairman of the Department of Physics and dean of the Division of Physical Sciences at the University of Chicago, he had the physical impressiveness, the personality that generally characterizes the successful man of affairs and might easily have been (as indeed he was destined to become) the chancellor of a university. But Compton's greatest distinction had been earned in a physics laboratory. In the early 1920s, experimenting with the scattering of X-rays beamed upon graphite, he had first observed what became known as the *Compton effect*, which became a major verification of Einstein's 1905 theory that light consists of specific quanta, tiny bundles of energy

—that light, paradoxically, has a corpuscular as well as a wave nature. The discovery won for Compton, in 1927, a Nobel Prize for Physics. Since then his most important work had consisted of precise measurements of variations in the intensity of cosmic rays at different latitudes and altitudes.

The fourth man in the room, Ernest O. Lawrence, was, at forty, the youngest. He was also physically the largest. Everything about him was oversize, including the hard-driving energy evident in his movements as he shifted his giant bulk in his chair, and the focused intelligence evident in his eyes as they gazed upon his colleagues through rimless glasses. He had, somehow, in his mind and character, the quality of the landscapes he had known as a boy in South Dakota—the largeness of outline coupled with a rigorous economy of detail which characterizes the open, windswept plains with their far horizons, their enormous skies. He had the single-mindedness, the self-reliance, the truly rugged individualism encouraged by vast solitudes and the frontier psychology in which he had been raised. It was therefore paradoxical, though typical of the times, that the work that was his obsession should make a pioneering individualism virtually obsolete in his field of scientific research. For Lawrence was the creator of the epoch-making cyclotron, a machine for accelerating (that is, imparting increased energy to) subatomic particles, and the cyclotron as it developed was so huge and expensive that the acquisition and operation of it was necessarily a function of organizations rather than of individual men. Lawrence himself, as director of the University of California's Radiation Laboratory at Berkeley, had proved to be a rare combination of creative mind, inspired teacher, and super-salesman.

Thus, as befits bridge men, each of the four in the room had strongly within him elements of the two ages and worlds that were to be joined together. Each had known the sharp pangs and incommunicable joys of solitary, self-disciplined, dedicated effort. But each was also experienced in the biology and behavior of big organizations and, knowing the pangs of frustration that these inevitably impose on creative men, knew also that they are not unbalanced by certain deep joys of belonging, of being a member of enterprises large beyond any individual's attainment and of having (as a concomitant of such membership) a clearly defined place in the total scheme of things. If each knew through experience that some types of neuroses are encouraged by the organization's thwarting of individualism, he also knew that other types, bred by a solitary freedom, are reduced. A sharing of responsibility, for instance, may lessen the anxieties of moral choice as well as the burden of individual guilt for decisions that prove to be wholly evil when judged by the individual's private moral code . . .

Not that such thoughts were actively present in the minds of the four men that morning. They had long ago accepted the fact that the whole tendency of science and technology was toward larger and larger organizations, they had adjusted to it more easily than many if not most of their scientific colleagues, and they were that morning wholly concerned with an immediate specific challenge.

This last was the outcome of an interaction between two lines of development in American science through the last two years, under the impact of world crisis. One line had to do with governmental administrative organization and may be said to have begun with Dr. Sachs' visit at the White House in October 1939, immediately following which the President authorized and nominally appointed an Advisory Committee on Uranium, with Briggs as chairman. The Committee had accomplished little and was almost moribund when the President ordered it reconstituted as a subcommittee of a National Defense Research Committee (NDRC), whose establishment he announced in June 1940.

The chief inspiration of NDRC was the man who became its chairman, Vannevar Bush, a former dean of Engineering at the Massachusetts Institute of Technology who was now president of the Carnegie Institution of Washington. Bush had heard Lindbergh at private meetings in 1939 and 1940 present terrifying "inside facts" about the organization of German science and technology for war by the Nazis, indicating that the Allies should come to terms with them to avoid destruction.[4] Bush reacted in an opposite sense: he proposed that the Nazi threat be faced by a mobilization of America's scientific resources for national defense. He discussed this with, among others, Conant at Harvard; Karl T. Compton, president of the Massachusetts Institute of Technology (he was a brother of Arthur); and Frank B. Jewett, board chairman of the Bell Telephone Laboratories, who was president of the National Academy of Sciences. The group worked out a plan. Bush outlined it clearly and briefly in a memorandum. He then sought and obtained audience with Harry Hopkins.

As Robert Sherwood points out,[4] Bush was a man not unlike Hopkins in several ways that made for a rapport between them. Both were thin of body and sharp of mind, with fast reaction times and an equivalent impatience with the slow and ponderous. They liked and understood one another at once. The fact was of some (if incalculable) importance to history since Hopkins, in the absence of it, might not have arranged at once for Bush to see the President and then have so prepared the President's mind that it was made up in favor of the Bush proposal before Bush himself had so much as crossed the threshold of the Oval Study. Within minutes after Bush and Roosevelt first met their meeting amicably ended, Roosevelt having scrawled "O.K.–F.D.R." across the memorandum Bush had given to Hopkins.

A few days later (it was June 15, 1940, the day after Paris fell to the Nazis), the President signed a letter authorizing establishment of the NDRC with Bush as its head, a letter addressed to Bush and largely written by him in collaboration with Hopkins. "Recently I appointed a special committee, with Dr. Briggs . . . as Chairman, to study into the possible relationship to national defense of recent discoveries in the field of atomistics, notably the fission of uranium," the letter said in part. "I will now request that this committee report directly to you, as the function of your Committee includes this special matter, and your Committee may consider it advisable to support special studies on this subject. . . ."

Thus, at last, a truly effective working alliance between science and government in America was begun. The initiative had come from science, and initially the working scientists—those actually engaged in developing the new knowledge that was to be applied to war—were the ones who exercised control over the allocation of Government funds. They made the decisions as to what research projects were to be pushed, to what extent, and by what universities or industrial laboratories. For instance, the uranium subcommittee, as reconstituted, no longer included Army Ordnance and Navy Bureau of Ordnance representatives but was made up wholly of active and very distinguished scientists, Lyman Briggs continuing as chairman. Later it was enlarged and became known as the Uranium Section (S-1) of the NDRC.

The scale of its expenditures, however, remained extremely modest compared to those of other projects under the Research Committee. By the time Conant met with his three colleagues on that first Saturday of December 1941, total expenditures of some $300,000 for sixteen S-1 projects had been approved. This compared with millions of dollars approved for research on other problems in a single laboratory, the Radiation Laboratory, at the Massachusetts Institute of Technology.

Even so, there were key figures in NDRC who felt that too much emphasis was being given nuclear research as a government-sponsored wartime enterprise. Conant himself, in the summer of '41, was urging Bush to drop this line of research altogether on the grounds that it was keeping many top scientists from work far more likely to contribute importantly to the national defense. He continued to hold this view, according to Arthur Compton, when he came to the University of Chicago in September of that year to receive an honorary degree during the University's fiftieth anniversary celebration, and it was in the living room of the Compton home, on a crisp, cool night, that his mind was changed.[5]

Ernest Lawrence was largely responsible for this conversion. Like Conant, Lawrence was in Chicago to receive an honorary degree from the University. He, too, was a guest in the Compton home. And as the three men sat before a wood fire in the fireplace, Lawrence (with Compton's strong support) discussed the lighting of atomic fires in terms of the latest experimental results in his Radiation Laboratory, and of the latest intelligence from England, whose physicists were at this time farther advanced toward a solution of the problem than the Americans were.

Actually, the problem was twofold. First was the problem of achieving a self-sustaining and controllable chain reaction within natural uranium.

Second was the problem of separating the rare isotope U-235, which is fissionable by slow neutrons, from the much more abundant U-238, which is not. The first problem was difficult enough, but by the time Conant, Lawrence, and Compton sat together before the wood fire in Compton's Chicago home, Fermi and his associates at Columbia had initiated experiments with a lattice structure or "pile" of pure graphite bars into which lumps of pure natural uranium were inserted at regular intervals; the results of these had convinced Fermi that the chances of achieving the chain reaction were now considerably better than fifty-fifty.

Less certain of solution at that moment seemed the problem of separating U-235 from U-238. It presented enormous technological difficulties. The overcoming of them had been retarded (paradoxically) by the fact that those initially concerned with the project were nuclear physicists working in the United States, a nation whose genius for large-scale technology, conditioned by a peculiarly American type of private-profit economy, has evolved an abnormally intense specialization of function, an abnormally rigid compartmentalization of knowledge. It was "the compartmentalization of information, which was practiced in the atomic-energy project from November 1940 on, that was the cause of our failure to recognize that light uranium [U-235] might be produced in quantities sufficient to make atomic bombs," Leo Szilard would testify before a Senate Committee in a later year.[6] "We should have known that in the fall of 1940. We might have failed to realize this altogether, just as the Germans failed to realize it,† if we had not had the good fortune that the British scientists were not compartmentalized. They were able to put two and two together and communicated their conclusions to the United States Government in the middle of 1941."

Szilard here referred primarily to the method of separating U-235 from U-238 by gaseous diffusion through a porous barrier. It is a method that depends upon the operation of a principle known as Graham's Law, which says that under identical conditions, different gases will diffuse through a porous medium at rates inversely proportional to the square roots of their molecular weights. Applied to uranium it presented complicated problems of chemical engineering, "a subject wholly alien to nuclear physicists," to quote William L. Laurence of the New York *Times*. In America, physicists and engineers were not normally on speaking terms in their professional capacities. Laurence finds it significant that the only leading physicist in America who actively recognized in 1939 the "great potentiality" of the gaseous diffusion process was John R. Dunning of Columbia; Dunning was not only a physicist but also a trained engineer.[7] In consequence, research toward development of the process was under way at Columbia

† Responding to questions from Senator Millard E. Tydings of Maryland, Szilard said it was merely "luck" that the German scientists also failed to "put two and two together." Their failure to do so was inexplicable, in Szilard's view. "It is true that they were split up in small groups," he said, "but they were not compartmentalized."

by 1940, directed by Harold Urey, the world-famous discoverer of heavy water.

But this work might never have become influential of high governmental policy had there not been a crucially important exchange of information between British and American scientists in the summer of 1941. At that time, physicist M. L. E. Oliphant of England, who had played an important role in the development of radar, came to America. He brought with him British research data indicating that a chain reaction could be achieved in a much smaller amount of U-235 than had been deemed minimum, until then, by the Americans. He also brought information on the gaseous diffusion method developed in the Clarendon Laboratory, Oxford, where physicists, chemists, and chemical engineers had been working intensively on the problem, as a team, for many months. The British—and particularly James Chadwick, the discoverer of the neutron—were now convinced that a nuclear bomb could be made, and soon enough to be used with a possibly decisive effect in the present war. They were acutely worried by intelligence that the Germans were striving to increase the production of heavy water in Norway and had ordered the making of considerable quantities of heavy hydrogen paraffin. Obviously, these were intended for use as "moderators" of neutron speed. Thus the British scientists imparted not only their research information but also a sense of extreme urgency to the American scientists, two of whom were soon to be sent to England by NDRC on a fact-finding mission.

Another important development discussed by Lawrence, Conant, and Compton before the Compton fireplace this chilly September night had been summarized in a memorandum from Lawrence dated July 11, 1941, addressed to a special review committee of the National Academy of Sciences, a committee of which Arthur Compton was chairman and Lawrence himself a member.[8] Experiments in the Berkeley Radiation Laboratory had apparently confirmed the theory that a new "trans-uranic" element (plutonium), which "presumably behaves like U-235" and could therefore be used as the explosive material in a nuclear bomb, would be produced in a chain-reactive pile, or "nuclear reactor," as this was beginning to be called. It would be imbedded in the uranium; its extraction would not be easy. But Glenn Seaborg and his colleagues in nuclear chemistry at Berkeley were already addressing themselves to the problem and were confident of its solution . . .

All this was presented so forcefully, so convincingly, to Conant, that before the fireplace conversation had ended he had completely reversed his policy views. The line of development having to do with governmental administrative organization thus met and interacted with the line of development whose substance was the actual progress of nuclear research—and the interaction became definitely effective for government policy through that special review committee of the National Academy of Sciences already mentioned. Having made a review of existing knowledge, this committee strongly recommended an all-out effort to make nuclear bombs and presented rough cost estimates which, though huge by any standard and especially so for what the scientists admitted was an "untried prediction," seemed by the scientists not incommensurate with other current military expenditures.

Compton presented his committee report personally to Bush on November 6, 1941. Bush now headed an Office of Scientific Research and Development (OSRD) which had been established by Executive Order (June 28, 1941) in response to the expansion of scientific war effort. His place as Chairman of NDRC, now a part of OSRD, had been taken by James Conant, and both men became members of a so-called Top Policy Group to which general policy discussions regarding the scientific effort were confined. Its other members included the President, Vice-President Wallace, Secretary of War Stimson, and Army Chief of Staff Marshall. It was to this Group that the review committee report was assigned for discussion, after Bush had presented it to the White House. It was of course the President himself who must make the final decision. And it was to learn what the President had decided that three of the four men whom we have met were gathered together on the morning of the first Saturday in December.

The fourth man, James Conant, already knew . . .

Years later, when the four men strove to recall in detail what they had said and done that morning, it might seem to them that they had all been in the center of a vast echo chamber which was also a hall of mirrors, for by then every word and gesture would be blurred (to memory) in endless reiteration and reverberation—endless ramification, extension, reflection in magnified form—down lengthening corridors of time. One might easily believe that the terror and wonder and dismay that would later invest the event, in the light of its consequences, invested it at the instant of its emergence. They did not, however. Upon the ordinary oaken table fell an ordinary wintry morning light, split by venetian blinds. Everything was as it had often been before, accustomed and homely—save that at the outset the suspense of three of the men, their anxiety to learn what the fourth had to tell them, was perhaps somewhat greater than they ordinarily felt at such meetings. They did feel, all of them, a sense of great and threatful challenge, and they braced themselves as Conant opened the proceedings by explaining that he spoke on behalf of Bush, who had intended to be present but, at the last moment, had been required elsewhere.

The President of the United States, Conant went on matter-of-factly, had accepted the review committee's recommendation: the Government proposed to make an "all-out" effort toward the atomic bomb.

And the men shifted in their chairs, looked at one another. Their suspense, however strong or mild, was ended.

The effort, said Conant, would be financed to begin with from a special fund assigned to the White House for use at the President's personal discretion. It was on the *bomb*, Conant emphasized, that all attention must now be concentrated. Only a bomb as potent militarily as had been predicted could justify an enterprise so immense and costly at such a time, an enterprise which must inevitably absorb materials, energies, skills, and minds that were badly needed elsewhere in the defense effort.

There followed a discussion of the first things to be done, and an assignment of responsibilities for these.

Nothing had been said about plutonium in the review committee's final report. Little was said about it this Saturday morning, though Lawrence (it was agreed) should press certain studies of the properties of the plutonium nucleus. But after the meeting had ended, Compton and Conant met Vannevar Bush and walked with him to the Cosmos Club, then housed in a century-old red brick building on Eighth Street—and there, over lunch, Compton brought up the subject of Lawrence's memorandum of the previous July 11.[9] Further thought should be given, said he, to the possibility of producing plutonium as Lawrence had suggested. The fact that plutonium could be extracted by chemical means, that no isotopic separation of it would be required, might well give it a great advantage over U-235 as the material of the bomb. Bush and Conant raised reasonable doubts, and Compton acknowledged the difficulties.

"Nevertheless," he said, "Glenn Seaborg claims he can have the plutonium available for use in the bomb within six months of the time it is first produced."

Conant shook his head.

"Seaborg," said he, "is a very competent young chemist—but he isn't *that* good . . ."

Before the three had finished their lunch, however, Bush and Conant had given Compton full authority to pursue the problem of plutonium production. The final decision was to pursue simultaneously four distinct ways of obtaining the explosive stuff of the bomb. Three of them—the centrifuge, the electromagnetic, the gaseous diffusion—aimed to produce pure U-235. The fourth aimed to produce plutonium. Later, as a result of the intensified research now about to begin, a decision would be made as to which of these four should be used in the actual manufacture.

It was to the plutonium problem—an afterthought of the morning's discussion—that Compton devoted his first attention that afternoon. He drew up an initial budget of some $300,000 for the first half of 1942, and had it approved by Briggs and Conant. He talked by telephone with physicist George Braxton Pegram at Columbia and arranged to confer with him, Fermi, and others of the Columbia group on the following afternoon. That would be a Sunday afternoon, but Pegram and his colleagues were agreed that there was no time to be lost.

Meanwhile, Lawrence was proceeding with similar speed . . .

They were men of ideas who had been given a unique opportunity to translate their ideas into acts, and on a huge scale. There had as yet been raised across their special field none of the barriers which normally (and especially in America) separate creative ideation from practical administration. Ideas, for the time being, were identical with acts; from them would spring, ultimately, three immense plants, three secret cities. And their anticipatory sense of this could hardly fail to give to these particular men an exhilarating sense of power. Godlike power. Would it also give them, in the lonely reaches of the night, an equivalent sense of terrifying moral responsibility?

By the time the possibility of making atomic bombs was first presented to Arthur Compton, his duty seemed perfectly clear: as Christian and patriot he could not do other than serve his country to the utmost of his ability in a war of civilization against barbarism. "If bombs can be made, we must make them first." The alternative—Adolf Hitler in unique possession of atomic warheads—was pure evil. . . . But Compton knew that others found the problem not only real but so difficult they could shape no clear answer to it.

In his own physics department at the University of Chicago was a young and valued assistant professor named Volney C. Wilson, to whom Compton turned in the early summer of 1940 when, following a stimulating conversation with Lawrence at Berkeley, he (Compton) wanted a precisely calculated opinion as to the feasibility of a chain reaction in ordinary uranium. Volney Wilson made the calculation—it was of necessity a rough one, since certain properties of the uranium nucleus that must be precisely known were then imprecisely measured—and concluded that the reaction could probably be made to work. He asked, however, that he be taken "off this job" because "it is going to be too terribly destructive."

"I don't want to have anything to do with it," he said.[10]

Late in the Sunday morning following the meeting we've witnessed, Compton took a taxi to Washington's Union Station, where he entrained for New York. At Wilmington, Delaware, a passenger who had just boarded the train told him of a report on the radio that the Japanese were attacking Pearl Harbor, Hawaii.

iii. *War!*

At a little after nine o'clock that Sunday morning, December 7, 1941, a gray, sad-faced Cordell Hull, his manner no more weary nor less resigned than usual, left his apartment at the Wardman Park Hotel in Washington. He breathed a frosty air. He looked into a cloudless sky. He saw bright sunlight upon green lawns and bare trees in the park, and upon quiet streets beyond the park. Few people were as yet abroad; those few betrayed no special excitement. He entered his chauffered limousine. By nine-thirty he was deep in conference in his office, with the Department's three top Far Eastern experts . . .

Over the country as a whole that morning, there was a slight relaxation of the extreme tensions of the last several days. A week before, on November 29, the public had been mildly soothed to learn that the President had arrived in Warm Springs, Georgia for a brief rest, after weeks of mounting crisis in the Far East and increased American naval involvement in the Battle of the Atlantic. He told reporters as he left the capital that the Japanese situation might call him back at any moment, but the fact that he left at all seemed to indicate that no immediate outbreak of hostilities was expected. But on November 30, following a long telephone conversation with Hull, he had abruptly ordered his special train readied. Grim-faced and silent, he had boarded this train at three-twenty that afternoon—and by the time he arrived in Washington's Union Station next morning, December 1, the impression was general that Japan might at any moment launch attacks upon Southeast Asia, based on Indo-China. War warnings were said to have been dispatched from Washington to all Army and Navy commanders in the Pacific (such warnings had indeed been sent on November 27), and every American military outpost in the far-flung area—in Hawaii, Wake Island, Guam, Midway, the Philippines—was reported to be on the alert against possible surprise attack. Not that a direct attack upon United States possessions was deemed likely. What *was* likely, and what the public was led to fear, was an assault upon Siam, the strategic gateway to British Malaya and the Burma Road over which American supplies moved into beleaguered China; and an invasion of the Dutch East Indies. Such events, in the Administration view (there were isolationists who vehemently disagreed), would force the United States to fight. Nor had anything happened to relieve this hypertension in the days immediately following the President's return.

On Saturday, December 6, however, newsmen reported "some slight hope" the crisis would "subside" enough to permit a renewal of the negotiations that, a few days earlier had seemed hopelessly deadlocked. On December 2, the two greatest British battleships, *Prince of Wales* and *Repulse*, had arrived at Singapore. This, it was believed, coupled with American firmness, might have given the Japanese pause. The belief or hope was reinforced Saturday night when radio broadcasts told an anxious public that Roosevelt had just sent a personal message to Hirohito, the Emperor of Japan. Perhaps new channels of communication between the two governments were about to be opened. Perhaps a new basis for an understanding would now be established.

But if the public still grasped at such straws of hope, Cordell Hull did not. He knew there was no longer any hope at all. He had tried for peace in the Pacific; as God was his witness, no one could have tried harder for a peace that was not tantamount to abject surrender. When he thought of the fifty-odd lengthy conversations he'd had with the Japanese Ambassador and associates since early last March, most of them in his hotel apartment (first in the Carlton, then in the Wardman Park) at night, after hard days in the office—when he thought of these, his very bones ached with weariness. Perhaps he had purchased valuable time—he believed that he had—but that was all.

And now the time had run out.

In backward look it seemed that there had never been a real chance for peaceful agreement—certainly not since Matsuoka led the Japanese into the Tri-Partite Pact in September 1940; probably not since he had led them out of the League of Nations in February 1933, when the League censured Japan's brutal seizure of Manchuria. A path had been entered from which there was no turning back, though Hull had worked to open up possible byways and provide possible halting places whence, gradually and with no loss of face, Imperial Japan might reverse her direction. Without prejudicing the future, he had repeatedly opposed any American action in the present that might drive Japan, or make her feel driven, into those armed adventures advocated by her militarist clique.

He had done so, often enough, against the vehemently expressed wishes of his own colleagues in the Cabinet. Secretary of the Treasury Morgenthau, Secretary of War Stimson, Secretary of the Navy Knox, and Secretary of the Interior Ickes—all these had pressed at various times, and to varying degrees, arguments for a stronger line against Japan than Hull deemed wise.

For the most part, these arguments had had to do with economic sanctions. Japan was peculiarly vulnerable to these—and Morgenthau especially had been embittered by the State Department's reluctance to employ them with full rigor. Logic and morality were alike outraged, in his view, by the continued shipment to a Hitler-allied Japan of well over half her needed strategic war materiel, including items the United States herself needed now, or would shortly need, for her defense buildup against Hitler and this same Japan. Take steel and scrap iron, for example. By July 1940—when Britain stood alone against the Nazi fury, a dismembered France was sunk helpless into the disgrace of Vichy, and Japan was issuing ultimatums to the French in Indo-China—by then it was perfectly clear that the United States should be saving every ton of her iron and steel for her own defense industry. Yet we continued to provide Japan with about 90 per cent of her scrap, and Hull continued to oppose an embargo on it! Equally if not more outrageous, in Morgenthau's opinion, was the oil situation. By practicing the most rigorous economies, Japan had managed to accumulate by 1939 a strategic oil reserve of some fifty-five million barrels; this would have lasted perhaps a year and a half if she had been forced to rely exclusively upon it. Her natural and synthetic oil production totaled some three million barrels annually, or only 10 per cent of her estimated minimum needs. The remaining 90 per cent she imported from the Caribbean, the Dutch East Indies, and the United States. Most of all, the United States! In mid-1940 we were shipping oil to Japan at the rate of twenty-three million barrels annually, about 60 per cent of her total oil imports—and Hull continued to oppose an oil embargo! It was late September 1940—after Japan had bullied Vichy (with Hitler's help) into an acceptance of her demand for bases in northern Indo-China, had actually sent troops into Indo-China, and then had signed the Tri-Partite Pact—before Hull agreed that an embargo on scrap and on aviation gasoline should be announced. The great bulk of the oil exports from this country to Japan were permitted to continue.

Morgenthau's diary recorded the angry disgust he felt at that time. "My own opinion is that the time to put pressure on Japan was before she went into Indo-China and not after," said his entry for September 23, "and I think it's too late and I think the Japanese and the rest of the dictators are just going to laugh at us. The time to have done it was months ago and then maybe Japan would have stopped, looked and listened."

Would she have?

Much more likely—indeed, almost certain in Hull's well-informed opinion—would have been a swift and massive drive by Japan to the south at a time when Britain teetered on the brink of extinction and the United States had barely begun to arm herself. If the risk run by imposing a scrap embargo was less in late September than it had been before, it remained great enough to breed anxieties in Cordell Hull. Both Presidential candidates were at that time proclaiming their determination to keep America out of "foreign wars." Candidate Roosevelt, who was also President and Commander-in-Chief, was saying in public speech that he stood by every word of the Democratic platform plank which flatly promised: ". . . we will not send our Army, naval or air forces to fight in foreign lands outside the Americas, except in case of attack." What, then, could we have done in response to a Japanese invasion of Malaya and the Dutch East Indies? Could this have been construed as an "attack" upon the United States? Hull doubted it—doubted that the country would have awakened to its peril before the Japanese Empire had been established on an economically self-sufficient basis and we faced across the Pacific a power as strong and hostile as the Nazi Europe whose glare across the Atlantic was so frightening.

No, a successful power politics required a much more realistic appraisal of the enemy's psychology and power political resources *vis-à-vis* our own than Morgenthau admitted to his (in Hull's acid view) self-indulgent emotionalism. The Secretary of State had relied heavily these last eight years upon the judgment of the American Ambassador in Tokyo, Joseph C. Grew, surely one of the ablest career diplomats ever to serve United States interests. Grew knew the Japanese people well, and liked them; he knew the Japanese political system well, and feared it. He had stressed over and over again that the lawful Japanese Cabinet was far from being in full control of Japanese foreign policy, that extremists in the armed forces were fully capable of independent action (they had taken it repeatedly), and that death by assassination was the all-too-frequent fate of political leaders who stood out against the designs of the militarists. "Unless the United States is willing to back economic sanctions with armed force, she should impose no such sanctions on Japan." This (in paraphrase) had been the burden of Grew's message during the years immediately preceding the crisis summer of 1940. "They [the Japanese] are a hardy race, accustomed throughout their history to catastrophe and disaster," he had said in a telegram dated December 5, 1938; "theirs is the 'do or die' spirit, more deeply ingrained than in any other people." And even in what was now famous in American diplomatic circles as his "Green Light" telegram, dated September 12, 1940—a telegram wherein he announced his reluctant conclusion that "a show of force, together with a determination to employ it if need be" could "alone contribute effectively" to a maintenance of "the status quo in the Pacific"—even in this Grew had counseled caution.[11]

The halting of sales of iron and steel would register our disapproval of Japanese policy in a way disturbing to some key makers of that policy, Grew believed—but since it was obviously justified by "our own newly instituted program of national preparedness," it need not be construed in Tokyo as an "outright" sanction. "On the other hand," Grew had gone on, "we must envisage the possibility that drastic embargoes on the export of such important products as petroleum, of which the United States is known to possess a superabundance, would be interpreted by the Japanese Government and people as actually sanctions which might and probably would lead to some form of retaliation. The risks . . . will depend less upon the careful calculations of the Japanese Government than upon the uncalculated 'do or die' temper of the Army and Navy. . . ."

Such considerations indicated the policy that Hull in fact pursued—a policy firm in general structure but not unyielding in detail; patient, balanced as precisely as possible upon the point of diminishing returns so far as deterrent effects were concerned; a policy that aimed to raise doubts and give pause, avoiding the one-step-further that would inflame the passions and inhibit the intellect of Japan; a policy based on the premise that, if war must come, the longer it was postponed the better for us, since time was on our side.

Thus Hull had been cautiously but definitely open to a suggestion which came to him, in early 1941, through Postmaster General Frank C. Walker. At that time, Matsuoka and other Japanese officials were making extremely bellicose statements, reaffirming their ties with Hitler. Ambassador Grew had just cabled (January 27) a warning rumor he had received from the Peruvian envoy in Tokyo to the effect that "a surprise attack on Pearl Harbor was planned by the Japanese military forces in case of 'trouble' between Japan and the United States," a plan that seemed "fantastic" to the Peruvian but which had been rumored to him from many sources.[12] (Hull had promptly passed the cable's contents on to the War and Navy Departments.) The surface scene in the Far East had seemed cold and dark indeed. To two Catholic priests then in Japan, however, certain highly placed Japanese had revealed secret fires or at least sparks of hope for peace. Upon their return to this country, the two priests hastened to communicate to Postmaster General Walker, a leading Catholic in the Administration, their belief in the possible existence of a firm basis for negotiating the issues between the United States and Japan. Walker, in turn, arranged an interview between the priests and the President. Hull and Walker were both present, Hull concurring in the President's decision that the priests should maintain their contacts with the Japanese Embassy, though solely and strictly as private citizens, providing thereby an unofficial channel of communication between the American Executive and Japanese diplomats. The upshot of this had been the opening of the wearisome talks between Hull and the new Japanese Ambassador, Admiral Kichisaburo Nomura, shortly after the latter arrived in Washington in mid-February. Hull was from the first pessimistic concerning them. "I estimated right at the outset that there was not one chance of success . . . in a hundred," he later recorded. ". . . but . . . we believed we should not throw the chance away, however microscopic it was."[13]

He might well have been encouraged in this attitude by a major victory in that secret war of espionage and counterespionage which is waged inevitably and incessantly among all sovereign powers in the absence of world law, and which was especially intense at that time between Japan and the United States. Manifesting phenomenal ingenuity, Army and Navy cipher experts had managed to break the most secret of the Japanese communications codes. Decoding machines in Washington were thus enabled to operate with remarkable swiftness upon intercepts of communications between Tokyo and her various embassies, often delivering these to responsible American officials under the code name of "Magic" before they were seen by the Japanese to whom they were addressed. Of course Japanese cipher experts were simultaneously at work upon the five American codes then being used; it was believed possible that they had broken four of them. The fifth, however, remained intact. Convincing evidence of this—and of the sharp divisions in the Japanese Government at the highest levels—was the fact that Prince Konoye had actually warned Grew on one occasion *not* to entrust certain types of information to any but the "one code" we possessed which, he had been told, was unbreakable! Obviously Prince Konoye had been told this by the Japanese military police, and he issued his friendly warning to the American Embassy "in view of certain types of intelligence which it was not in his interest to have known to the police."[14]

"Magic" had of course given Hull a distinct tactical advantage over his conversational opponents, especially during the last ten weeks or so. He knew what they were going to say before they said it; the possibility of surprise or deception was denied them. But it had had no effect upon over-all strategy nor final outcome since no real strategic choices had been open to either side. Hull had begun by stating "four basic principles" on which any agreement must rest: "(1) Respect for the territoral integrity and sovereignty of all nations; (2) support of the principle of non-interference in the internal affairs of other countries; (3) support of the principle of equality, including equality of commercial opportunity; (4) nondisturbance of the status quo in the Pacific except as the status quo may be altered by peaceful means."[15] On these principles we could not yield: they were of the essence of our commitment to China, to the Philippines, and Britain in her extremity. But they were not acceptable by Japan: their application would have required her to renounce the Tri-Partite Pact, withdraw her forces from China and Indo-China, and wholly abandon, in an abject confession of defeat, the dream of empire to which she had already sacrificed much blood and treasure and whose swift realization seemed more likely at that moment than at any other since the dream began. The negotiations, though serious to those engaged in them, were but a mask. Behind it was the reality of bitter stalemate and approaching war.

The mask had wholly slipped in July, or been jerked off by the Nazi invasion of Russia—an event that occurred despite urgent pleas from Tokyo to Berlin that it be prevented. (Matsuoka lost his office in consequence.) It was promptly followed (July 2) by an Imperial Japanese Conference from which issued a policy statement whose essence was duly communicated to Berlin and promptly intercepted and decoded by "Magic." It contained an "Outline of . . . Policy . . . in View of Present Developments" that, to Washington's eyes, was ominous in the extreme:

1. The Imperial Government is determined to follow a policy which will result in the establishment of the Greater East Asia Co-Prosperity Sphere and world peace, no matter what international developments take place.
2. The Imperial Government will continue its effort to effect a settlement of the China Incident and seek to establish a solid basis for the security and preservation of the nation. This will involve an advance into the Southern Regions and, depending on future developments, a settlement of the Soviet Question as well.
3. The Imperial Government will carry out the above program no matter what obstacles may be encountered.[16]

A summary of the program to be based on this policy included the flat statement: "First of all, the plans which have been laid with reference to French Indo-China and Thai [Siam] will be prosecuted, with a view to consolidating our position in the southern territories."

Thus the powder train had been finally laid to the fatal magazine, and the match applied—for the Japanese Government's "first of all" was immediately "prosecuted." On July 21, Japanese troops were sent into southern Indo-China, giving them possession (in Hull's later words) "of the whole of France's strategic province, pointing like a pudgy thumb toward the Philippines, Malaya, and the Dutch East Indies."[17] On July 23, Hull, recuperating at White Sulphur Springs, West Virginia from an illness, asked Sumner Welles to break off the conversations with Nomura which Welles had continued in Hull's enforced absence from Washington. On July 24, the President proposed to Japan that Indo-China be designated a "neutralized" country, Japan withdrawing her troops from it and joining with the United States, Britain, China, and the Netherlands in a guarantee of this "neutrality." On July 26, the President issued an Executive Order, to which Hull agreed (though only because he could see no alternative), freezing all Japanese funds and assets in the United States, thus in effect‡ initiating the total embargo which Morgenthau and most political liberals in this country had long favored. On that same day the British renounced their trade treaties with Japan and imposed financial restrictions on Japanese trade, as did the Dutch Government in exile, in London, two days later.

The latter act, the imposition of economic sanctions, appeared in retrospect as decisive as Hull had thought it would be—and in just the ways he had feared. While much of the American press was cheering the end of "appeasement" in the Far East and assuring the public that this meant the end of the Japanese threat ("[Japan] in the end . . . can only whimper and capitulate," wrote Kenneth G. Crawford in *PM* on July 27[18]), Hull contemplated with foreboding alternative possibilities well expressed by Wilfred Fleischer in the New York *Herald Tribune:* "Japan must move quickly to consummate her conquests in Asia or face economic ruin and defeat. . . . The Japanese are now with their backs to the wall and they must carry on with the struggle they have so rashly embarked upon or renounce their dreams of empire in Asia. The die has bent cast."[19] Ambassador Grew also contemplated grim alternatives and deemed it likely Japan would feel forced to choose that one which was most grim for her, and for us, but which alone was consistent with her policy of the last dozen years. Indeed, the power to alter the course of events no longer existed in either Tokyo or Washington, he feared. "The vicious circle of reprisals and counter-reprisals is on," he confided to his diary. "Unless radical surprises occur in the world, it is difficult to see how the momentum of this downgrade movement in our relations can be arrested, nor how far it will go. The obvious conclusion is eventual war."[20] And "Magic" provided confirmation of this dark view. On August 4, a telegram from Tokyo to the Japanese Ambassador in Berlin was intercepted and decoded in Washington. It said: "Commercial and economic relations between Japan and other countries, led by England and the United States, are gradually becoming so horribly strained that we cannot endure it much longer. Consequently, the Japanese Empire, to save its very life, must take measures to secure the raw materials of the South Seas. It must take immediate steps to break asunder this ever-strengthening chain of encirclement, which is being woven under the guidance of and with the participation of England and the United States, acting like a cunning dragon seemingly asleep."[21]

Two days later, on August 6, Nomura delivered to Hull Japan's reply

‡ For it was followed very soon by orders prohibiting the shipment to Japan of any of the materials, including petroleum, she most critically needed.

to the President's Indo-China "Neutralization" proposal (it had by then been extended to include Siam)—a reply whose terms were wholly unacceptable by Washington but which the Japanese Government could only (or did only) reiterate in one form or another during the four months of growing tension that followed. Japan would not evacuate her troops from Indo-China until a settlement had been reached between China and Japan; even then, she must be recognized as having a special position in Indo-China. She made two major requests: *First*, that the restrictions on trade with her be removed (this was crucial); *Second*, that the United States employ her "good offices" to bring about direct negotiations between Japan and Chiang's China. The implication was that we would threaten Chiang with a withdrawal of our aid to him if he did not agree to negotiate.[22]

There matters stood—or there the powder train flared—at the time of the Atlantic Conference where, unknown to the public, the Japanese problem was a major item of discussion between Roosevelt and Churchill.

As he sat with the American President upon a British warship's deck—as his gaze wandered over the chill blue waters of Placentia Bay, aglitter in August sunlight—the Prime Minister's concern over the Pacific situation was little short of desperate. If Japan moved south, war between her and Great Britain was unavoidable—and unless the United States at once entered that war, Japan "immediately would be in a position through the use of her large number of cruisers to seize or destroy all the British merchant shipping in the Indian Ocean and in the Pacific, and to cut the lifelines between the British Dominions and the British Isles."[23] Only a prompt and emphatic warning that the United States *would* fight beside Britain in the Pacific if the impending southward drive were made—only this, Churchill vehemently argued—could have a deterrent effect upon Japan. Accordingly he had brought with him a draft Declaration which he proposed should be issued simultaneously from London and Washington to Tokyo. Its key sentence said: "Any further encroachment by Japan in the Southwestern Pacific would produce a situation in which the United States Government [His Majesty's Government, in the London version] would be compelled to take counter measures even though these might lead to war between the United States [Great Britain] and Japan."[24]

Roosevelt had agreed that a warning should conclude the statement he proposed to hand personally to the Japanese Ambassador immediately after his return to Washington. He may even have agreed, while aboard H.M.S. *Prince of Wales*, to Churchill's blunt wording; certainly Churchill believed that he had.[25] But if so, his mind was quickly changed by Cordell Hull upon his return to the White House. The Secretary of State, continuing his strategy of carefully balanced risks, aiming to buy the maximum possible amount of time, argued that so sharp a warning as Churchill proposed might easily be interpreted in Tokyo as a hostile challenge immediately provocative of a war we were far from prepared to fight. (It was on August 12, be it remembered, that the House of Representatives almost rejected the extension of Selective Service, finally passing the bill by a majority of one.) Accordingly, the note actually handed Nomura by Roosevelt on August 17 made no direct mention of the possibility of conflict, closing instead with a murky ninety-one-word sentence saying that if Japan persisted in her present course the United States would be "compelled to take immediately any and all steps which it might deem necessary toward safeguarding the legitimate rights and interests of the United States and American nationals and insuring the safety and security of the United States." Even this had seemed "too provocative" to Hull unless "balanced by a more friendly gesture,"[26] namely a second note, also handed Nomura by Roosevelt that August 17, offering to resume what Hull, with a wary eye upon Congress, called "the informal exploratory conversations" with Japan.

So the wearing round of talks had begun again.

For Hull, the experience was rather like watching a dreary play in which one also participated as an actor and which repeated itself over and over again as the stage beneath it was undermined. "Magic" not only provided him with the script from which Nomura spoke and with the cues for his own major lines, all of which (because of "Magic") could be devised well in advance of each nightly conversation; it also revealed to him the accelerating progress of the undermining, the inexorable approach of a collapse that would throw all the players into the abyss. He was given a unique opportunity to measure the skill with which the Japanese admiral played his diplomat's role. The admiral, he concluded, played most ineptly.

Nomura was physically of a type uncommon in his country, a tall man with thick chest and shoulders, and he seemed to Hull different in other ways (admirable ways, in Hull's view) from many Japanese Hull had met. Solemn of face and disposition, but "much given to mirthless chuckling"[27]; concerned to be personally honorable, hence burdened and stricken with conscience; slow in his mental processes, but firm and tenacious in his grasp of the ideas he held; doubting his own capacities even more than he did the wisdom of the policies he served, though his doubts of the latter were profound; he was a figure often personally pitiful in Hull's eyes and, in the eyes of history, perhaps tragic in the Greek sense of tragedy since he appeared a good man driven into evil ways by a malignant Fate. He was transparently honest in his personal relations, he was incapable of convincing dissimulation in his official capacity—and this diplomatic disability was augmented by the fact that he knew just enough English to make him trust overmuch his ability to understand and communicate in that language. His reports to Tokyo, intercepted by "Magic," showed often his failure to understand precisely what had been said. He had entered upon his present role with reluctance; he disliked and distrusted Matsuoka. He had felt some relief when Matsuoka was dropped. But by late August he certainly would have agreed with Hull that their talks together—no matter what innovation was introduced, what fresh approach attempted—seemed always "to come to a certain point and then start going around and around in the same circle."[28]

For instance, there had been introduced to the talks by then the new idea of a personal meeting between Konoye and Roosevelt. Prince Konoye made the initial proposal through Nomura, and Washington promptly agreed to it "in principle." But what, precisely, were the two heads of state to talk about?

That Konoye sincerely and even desperately wanted the meeting, there could be no doubt; his political life was at stake§ as the economic squeeze on Japan grew daily tighter. On August 23, the Dutch cut off not only all oil exports from the Indies to Japan but also all bauxite, from which aluminum is derived and of which Japanese reserves were meager—barely enough to last seven months at the rate of use required by an expanded program of airplane production. On August 26, "Magic" intercepted a cable from the Japanese Foreign Minister, Soemu Toyoda, to Nomura, saying in part: "Now the international situation as well as our internal situation is strained in the extreme and we have reached the point where we will pin our last hopes on an interview between the Premier and the President. . . ."[29] But from an Imperial Conference called in September at Konoye's instigation there could only issue, as suggested bases for negotiation at the proposed Konoye-Roosevelt meeting, substantially the same terms of "settlement" previously rejected by the United States. It became clear that Konoye—bound by the conclusions of the conferences over which he had presided, driven by the momentum of events he had helped to launch, unable to achieve a balance of power between the Navy (which did not actively want war) and the Army (which did)—could not provide the required assurances. On October 2, Hull informed Nomura that the Japanese proposals were still too vague and ambiguous, where not too definitely antagonistic to our interests; hence the proposed meeting should be "postponed."

For Konoye this was the end. Two weeks later he was out of office.

He was replaced as Premier by General Hideki Tojo, the former Minister of War, who was a chief architect and had long been the principal spokesman of the Japanese Army's expansionist policy. Toyoda was replaced as Foreign Minister by Shigenori Togo. And Nomura, in utter despair, sought to resign his post on the grounds that he had failed in his mission, was now out of touch with his Government, and could have no influence upon Hull and Roosevelt because they believed him to be without influence in Tokyo. "I cannot tell you how much in the dark I am," he said in one of the "Magic" intercepts of cables from him to Togo.

§ His actual life also. On September 18 an attempt was made to assassinate him. Though easily frustrated, and kept very secret, the attempt pointed up once again the fact that passionate Japanese imperialists set a severe limit upon the area of possible genuine negotiation with the United States and were fully capable of killing a head of Government who, they felt, was going beyond these limits.

"Now that I am a dead horse," he also said, "I do not want to continue this hypocritical existence, deceiving myself and other people."[30] But the Tojo Cabinet, seeking no doubt to make use of his deserved reputation as an honest man (the Americans would be loathe to doubt the personal sincerity of his struggle for peace), begged him to stay on, and out of patriotism he did so.

For though both sides now believed that war was inevitable, both wished to continue the talks—Japan in order to mask her war moves, insuring a perhaps decisive initial surprise; the United States in the hope of gaining more time in which to prepare. "Magic" now began to intercept messages which, for the first time, set a deadline. "Both in name and in spirit this offer of ours is indeed our last,"[31] telegraphed Togo to Nomura in the first week of November as he sent forward a "new" proposal. If it provided a basis for agreement, well and good—but all arrangements for signing that agreement *must* be completed by November 25. Nomura was also informed that a request he had repeatedly made for the assistance in Washington of a top-flight professional diplomat was now being granted. His personal friend, Ambassador Saburo Kurusu, was being sent by Trans-Pacific Clipper.

During this same week (on November 5, within hours of the Japanese Government's final decision to resort to war if the offer which was "our last" was rejected), General Marshall and Admiral Harold R. Stark, Chief of Naval Operations, presented to the President a memorandum reaffirming the "basic military policies and strategy agreed to in the United States-British Staff conversations" of early 1941. "The primary objective of the two nations is the defeat of Germany," the memorandum said. "If Japan be defeated and Germany remain undefeated, decision will still not have been reached. In any case, an unlimited offensive war should not be undertaken against Japan, since such a war would greatly weaken the combined effort in the Atlantic against Germany, the most dangerous enemy." Stark and Marshall urged that no military action be taken against Japan unless the latter committed a "direct act of war . . . against the territory or mandated territory of the United States, the British Commonwealth, or the Netherlands East Indies," or unless Japanese armed forces moved into Siam "to the west of 100° East or South of 10° North; or into Portuguese Timor, New Caledonia, or the Loyalty Islands." They specifically recommended "that no ultimatum be delivered to Japan."[32] Since Hull had shaped his diplomatic strategy from the first in the light of the realities of the military situation, as represented to the Executive by Stark and Marshall, there was no contradiction between it and these latest opinions.

Thus the stage, now thoroughly undermined, was set for the last act.

Kurusu, who arrived in Washington in mid-November, was disliked and distrusted by Hull and Roosevelt even before they met him personally. A former Japanese Ambassador to Nazi Germany, he had been one of the signers of the Tri-Partite Pact. The "Magic" intercepts more than suggested that his present mission was a cover operation, designed to deceive—else why would he be sent "with no additional instructions" (as Nomura had been informed) to land in Washington barely a week before the November 25 deadline? And this prejudice against him was reinforced by the sight and sound of the man. He struck Hull as in every way the antithesis of Nomura—a small man physically, his gaze shifty behind horn-rimmed spectacles, his grin toothy, his manner sly and deceitful. "His only recommendation, in my eyes," Hull later said, "was that he spoke excellent English, having married his American secretary."[33]

Nor was the "final" Japanese offer any more satisfactory. As Hull and Roosevelt knew (via "Magic") before Nomura presented it, the offer comprised two sets of proposals. Proposal "A" was to be presented first; its rejection was obviously anticipated. Then the other, labeled "B," was to be presented as a *modus vivendi* or temporary arrangement, whereby war would be avoided while the quest for a permanent solution continued. But it, too, was wholly unacceptable to Washington. Japan promised that she would make no further southward move and would even withdraw her troops from southern Indo-China *provided* that the United States removed the recently imposed trade restrictions, undertook to supply Japan with "a required quantity of oil," halted her buildup of defensive forces in the Philippines and elsewhere in the Pacific, and (most unacceptable of all) promised "to refrain from such measures and actions as will be prejudicial to the endeavors for a restoration of general peace between Japan and China"[34]—this at a time when frantic messages from Chiang Kai-shek warned of an impending attack from Indo-China upon Yunnan Province whose success would close the Burma Road, utterly isolate China from the outside world, and probably encircle and destroy the Chinese armies. Such terms could only be regarded in Washington as terms of surrender. The United States was required to do a number of definite things at grave risk to her national interests and in violation of her moral feelings and commitments. Japan in return promised *not* to do something: she would not, she said, move south. As an earnest of this she would at once withdraw her troops from southern Indo-China. The earnest required her to sacrifice no real strategic power, however: from northern Indo-China troops could be returned to their southern posts in full force within a day or so. And no limit whatever was placed upon the troop buildup which threatened Yunnan, nor upon Japan's action to the north. She would be free to butcher a Nationalist China from which the United States had withdrawn all material and moral support, free also to launch an attack at any time upon an already desperately struggling Soviet Union.

Hull could only play for time. "We groped for anything that might offer any possibility for keeping serious conversations going," he would later say.[35] The "final" Japanese offer was formally presented on November 20. During the days immediately following, Hull and his associates struggled to prepare counter-proposals with which to offset the rejection of Japan's *modus vivendi.* The first effort was to shape an American *modus vivendi,* in which Britain, China, and the Netherlands concurred, whereby the peace between Japan and the West would be guaranteed for three months. This effort was abandoned after Chinese Ambassador Hu Shih, on instructions from an angry and suspicious Chiang Kai-shek, objected strongly to the fact that twenty-five thousand Japanese troops would be permitted to remain in northern Indo-China by the terms proposed, and that no pledge was required of Japan that she refrain from launching any further invasion of China during the next three months. Hull had no real hope that Japan would have accepted the offer anyway. He had even less hope that she would accept the ten-point general peace settlement which, after consultation with the other governments concerned, he handed to Nomura and Kurusu on November 26. One of its points pledged the governments of the United States and Japan to support no other "Government or regime in China . . . than the National Government of the Republic of China, with capital temporarily at Chungking." Another pledged Japan to a withdrawal of "all military, naval, air and police forces from China and Indo-China."[36] Both Japanese envoys read these proposals with evident dismay, and Kurusu vigorously protested them, saying that his Government would "throw up its hands" when it learned of them.

Meanwhile, the "Magic" intercepts revealed clearly that Japan was preparing to attack, had set in motion the forces for attack, and that the blow would fall very soon. When Hull informed the Japanese envoys that he could not possibly present the American reply by November 25, as they begged him to do, they telegraphed Tokyo pleading for an extension of the deadline. Tokyo replied: "There are reasons beyond your ability to guess why we wanted to settle Japanese-American relations by the 25th; but if within the next three or four days you can finish your conversations with the Americans, if the signing can be completed by the 29th . . . , if the pertinent notes can be exchanged, if we can get an understanding with Great Britain and The Netherlands, and in short if everything can be finished, we have decided to wait until that date. This time . . . the deadline absolutely cannot be changed. After that things are automatically going to happen."[37]

It was at this juncture that Secretary of War Stimson proposed the sending of a "final alert" to General Douglas MacArthur, commandant of the Philippine Department of the Army, and to the other Pacific commanders. With President Roosevelt's approval, the messages went out on November 27. The one to Lieutenant General Walter C. Short, commandant of the Hawaiian Department, said in part: "Japanese future action unpredictable but hostile action possible at any moment. If hostilities cannot, repeat, cannot be avoided, the United States desires that Japan commit the first overt act. This policy should not, repeat, not, be construed as restricting you to a course of action that might jeopardize your defense. Prior to hostile action you are directed to undertake such reconnaissance and other measures as you deem necessary but these measures should be carried out so as not, repeat, not, to alarm civil population or disclose intent."[38] The message to Admiral Husband E. Kimmel, Commander-in-Chief of the Pacific Fleet, based at Pearl Harbor, said in part: "This dispatch is to be considered a war warning. Negotiations with Japan looking toward stabilization of conditions in the Pacific have ceased and an aggressive move by Japan is expected within the next few days. The number and equipment of Japanese troops and the organization of naval task forces indicates an amphibious expedition against either the Philippines, Thai [Siam] or Kra Peninsula or possibly Borneo. Execute an appropriate defensive deployment. . . ."[39]

On November 28, Nomura and Kurusu (and the Washington readers of "Magic") were informed: "With the report of the Imperial Government that will be sent to you in two or three days, talks will be de facto ruptured. This is inevitable. However, I do not wish you to give the impression that the negotiations are broken off. . . . From now on do the best you can."[40] On November 29, the day Roosevelt arrived in Warm Springs for his brief vacation, Hull read extracts from speeches to be given by Tojo and Togo in Tokyo on November 30. Tojo's speech asserted that Chiang Kai-shek was "dancing to the tune of Britain, America, and Communism" and that "the honor and pride of mankind" required Japan to "purge this sort of practice from East Asia with a vengeance."[41] (It was upon reading and pondering this that Hull decided to phone the President, suggesting he return as soon as possible to Washington.) To all this was added a note, dated November 30, from Tokyo to the Japanese Ambassador in Berlin: "Say very secretly to them [i.e., to Hitler and Foreign Minister Joachim von Ribbentrop] that there is extreme danger that war may suddenly break out between the Anglo-Saxon nations and Japan through some clash of arms, and add that the time of the breaking-out of this war may come quicker than anyone dreams."[42]

Meanwhile, too, had come reports of the sighting of Japanese troop convoys and warships heading south along the coast of China, and of large troop movements in Indo-China. They became more and more numerous during the days of ominous pause that succeeded Roosevelt's return to the capital, adding to the extreme tension which gripped official Washington—the sense of being caught helpless between implacable enmity abroad and disunity at home.

Of the latter—of the extreme lengths to which a Roosevelt-hating isolationism could go—dismaying evidence was presented on Thursday, December 4, when Colonel Robert R. McCormick's Chicago *Tribune*, endeavoring to "prove" that Roosevelt plotted to involve us in war, published to all the world the top-secret war plans of the Army and Navy calling for raising an armed force of ten million, five million to be used for the invasion of Germany in July 1943. The *Tribune* also published the estimated production requirements of a so-called Victory Program, information of vital military importance to potential enemies. The making of such plans was the clear Constitutional duty of the Executive in the circumstances then prevailing, and the publishing of them was as clearly an act of treason, in the opinion of the Cabinet, most of whom strongly believed that those responsible should be prosecuted under the Espionage Act. The President, however, declined to press such action. He may even have felt helpless to do so at that moment, being convinced that a head-on clash between the leading spokesman of Midwest isolationism and the Government could only increase national disunity.

In any case, the mounting Pacific crisis required all Roosevelt's attention. On December 6 Admiral T. C. Hart, Commander-in-Chief of the Asiatic Fleet, reported the sighting of large Japanese forces apparently sailing toward Kohtron. One twenty-five-ship convoy had an escort of six cruisers and ten destroyers; another ten-ship convoy was escorted by two cruisers and ten destroyers. The Asiatic Fleet's scouting force also reported thirty ships and one large cruiser anchored in Cam Ranh Bay, Indo-China.

Hull summoned three State Department experts on Far Eastern affairs to confer with him Sunday morning, December 7. He laid before them the draft of an address the President planned to make to Congress, and the country, either the next day (December 8) or on the day following. It was deemed a crucially important speech, being designed not only to emphasize the warning to Japan, contained in the just-dispatched personal message from Roosevelt to Hirohito, but also to prepare Congress and the American public for the declaration of war which, it had been decided, in agreement with the Marshall-Stark memorandum of November 5, must follow a Japanese attack on Siam. That the Japanese *would* move first upon Siam was the almost universal belief in official Washington that morning, if only because this move would be the one most difficult for the United States to counter in the present seemingly unchangeable state (a divided state) of American public opinion. In the face of intransigent isolationism, how convince the needed majority of Americans (it must be an overwhelming majority) that an attack on Siam was in effect an attack upon the United States?

While this question was under discussion there arrived in Hull's office, via Army courier, the "Magic" intercept of Japan's anxiously awaited reply to America's ten-point peace proposal. It was a lengthy document transmitted in fourteen parts from Tokyo to Nomura with instructions to the Ambassador to keep it secret until further notice. Hull skimmed through it, noting the increasing truculence of tone as arguments long worn threadbare were again gone over.

The first thirteen parts of this message had been received and decoded by early the previous evening and had been delivered by Navy courier to Roosevelt in the Oval Study of the White House at nine-thirty that night.

Hopkins had been present, had paced slowly up and down, up and down the room as Roosevelt read, and then had read the message himself very swiftly, grimly. When he handed it back to the President, the latter said, "This means war." Hopkins had agreed, adding that it was too bad, in the circumstances, that we could not strike the first blow and so avoid being surprised. Roosevelt had nodded; it was impossible, however. "We are a democracy and a peaceful people," the President had said and then, lifting his head and his voice, "But we have a good record."[43]

The fourteenth part of the message had been sent only this morning, after an ominously deliberate delay of some twelve hours, and it removed whatever lingering doubt the first thirteen parts may have left as to the imminence of war. Hull read it with the closest attention: "Obviously it is the intention of the American Government to conspire with Great Britain and other countries to obstruct Japan's efforts toward the establishment of peace through the creation of a New Order in East Asia. . . . Thus the earnest hope of the Japanese Government to adjust Japanese-American relations and to preserve and promote the peace of the Pacific through cooperation with the American Government has been lost. The Japanese Government . . . cannot but consider that it is impossible to reach an agreement through further negotiations."[44]

Hull's mind was sharply stimulated by this when, at ten-thirty, Secretaries Knox and Stimson arrived for a conference which had been arranged the night before, after Knox had read (as Hull had not yet then done) the first thirteen parts of the Tokyo message. For many months these three had met weekly in a so-called "War Council" to review current developments and shape diplomatic moves that were consistent with Army and Navy capabilities. Now they devoted themselves to the same effort as had occupied Hull and his Far Eastern experts: they strove to develop the argument of the President's proposed speech. At Stimson's suggestion, both Hull and Knox dictated statements which might be used in preparing the speech's final draft, Hull's saying in part: "At this moment of serious, threatened, and imminent danger, it is manifest that control of the South Sea area by Japan is the key to the control of the entire Pacific area, and therefore defense of life and commerce and other invaluable rights and interests in the Pacific area must be commenced within the South Sea area at such times and places as in the judgment of naval and military experts would be within sufficient time and at such strategic points as would make it most effective." Knox's draft was more succinct: "(1) We are tied up inextricably with the British. . . . (2) The fall of Singapore and . . . Malaya will . . . not only wreck [Britain's] . . . Far Eastern position but jeopardize her entire effort. (3) If the British lose their position, the Dutch are almost certain to lose theirs. (4) If both the British and the Dutch lose their positions, we are almost certain to be next. . . . (5) [Hence] . . . any serious threat to the British or the Dutch in a serious threat to the United States. . . ."[45]

While these earnest deliberations proceeded, another "Magic" intercept was delivered to Hull. It instructed Nomura to "submit to the United States Government (if possible to the Secretary of State) our reply to the United States at 1:00 P.M. on the 7th, your time."[46]

The officer in charge of the Navy section which translated and distributed "Magic" to the small number of high officials authorized to receive it (there were seven, including the President, on the Navy Department's distribution list; six, including Hull, on the War Department's list) was one Alwyn D. Kramer, a lieutenant commander and a very alert, industrious young man. He was at once struck by the fact that a specific time was mentioned in this latest intercept. One P.M. in Washington, he noted, coincided with 1:00 A.M., December 8, on the Malay Peninsula and with 7:30 A.M., December 7, or shortly after dawn on Sunday ("the quietest time in the week," he said aloud) in Hawaii. He strove to impress the significance of this on those to whom he delivered the intercepts, his attention being chiefly focused, as he would later testify, upon Kota Bharu, Malaya, on the east coast of the peninsula. His success was imperfect. Admiral Stark, asked if a further warning should not be sent the Philippines, made no response. Meanwhile, on the Army side, a combination of luck and lower-echelon sluggishness kept the crucial intercept from General Marshall's eyes until after eleven that morning—and he did not see the instruction as to time until eleven-thirty, just an hour and a half before (as was at once clear to him) war would almost certainly begin somewhere in the Pacific. His immediate impulse was to send another warning to MacArthur in the Philippines and to Short in Hawaii. He phoned Stark, who at first thought no further warning to Hart or Kimmel was needed but who called back a few minutes later to ask Marshall to tell MacArthur and Short to pass on the new information to the appropriate Navy commanders. Marshall then wrote out in longhand a message saying in part: "Just what significance the hour set may have we do not know but be on the alert accordingly. Inform naval authorities of this communication." This was filed with the Army Message Center at precisely twelve o'clock noon.¶[47]

To Hull, Knox, and Stimson, Tokyo's specification of time was but further confirmation of what they already believed, that war might come at any moment—though it also prevented Hull's being surprised when Nomura phoned, at noon, to ask if he and Kurusu might see the Secretary at one o'clock. Hull said yes. Shortly afterward, Stimson and Knox departed, the former returning to his home for lunch, the latter going to his office in the Navy Department. Hull waited. The Japanese envoys did not appear at the appointed time, however. Instead came another call from Nomura, at a few minutes past one, asking if the appointment might not be postponed until one forty-five. Hull again said yes. Again he waited.

¶ When static prevented Army radio communication with Pearl Harbor, the message was sent commercially via Western Union which (a boy on a bicycle was sent to deliver it in Hawaii) managed to get it into Short's headquarters eight and one-half hours later.

Meanwhile, across the street, Roosevelt and Hopkins were lunching together in the White House's Oval Study when, at a few minutes before two, a call came from Secretary Knox. The Navy radio station in Washington had just received an astounding signal from Admiral Kimmel's headquarters. Knox read it over the phone: "AIR RAID ON PEARL HARBOR. THIS IS NOT DRILL."

"I thought it must be a mistake," Knox said, "that they must mean the Philippines. But Stark says no, it's Pearl."[48]

Hopkins, too, thought there must be some mistake. Surely the Japanese could not be attacking at Honolulu! Roosevelt, however, thought the report probably true. It was just what the Japanese *would* do, he believed—strike at the most unexpected place, without warning, while negotiations yet continued. He also said that the Japanese had taken matters out of his hands, if the report were true: they had made for him the decision he had long been reluctant, and helpless, to make. And if he felt relief as he said this, who can blame him? Now, at long last, the United States would be truly united, with all her energies focused upon the utter defeat and destruction of the Axis governments, an object crucial to her survival as a free society.

Then he phoned Hull. It was five after two. Nomura and Kurusu, twenty minutes late for their postponed appointment, were just arriving at the State Department and being shown into the diplomatic waiting room.

"Has the report been confirmed?" Hull asked.

"No," said Roosevelt. "But I think it's probably true."

Hull thought so, too. The Japanese envoys were waiting at that very instant to see him, he said. Should he receive them? The President thought he should, but that he should not mention the news he'd just received.

"Just accept their reply formally and coolly," Roosevelt advised. "Then bow them out."

At precisely two twenty, Nomura and Kurusu entered Hull's office, Nomura explaining at once, apologetically, that they had been delayed by decoding and transcription difficulties. Hull nodded coldly. Coldly he accepted the document they handed him. He asked them curtly if they presented it under instructions from their Government. Nomura said yes. The two envoys remained standing (for Hull pointedly did not ask them to sit down) through the several minutes required for the Secretary's perusal of the document. When he had finished reading, he looked hard at Nomura, and spoke to him in a voice quivering with cold rage.

"In all my fifty years of public service," he said, "I have never seen a document that was more crowded with infamous falsehoods and distortions—infamous falsehoods and distortions on a scale so huge that I never imagined until today that any government on this planet was capable of uttering them."

Nomura's face was a frozen mask. He started to speak. Hull stopped him with lifted hand and nodded toward the door. The two went out, their heads bowed.

On Massachusetts Avenue, later that afternoon, more than a thousand grimly silent Americans gathered beside the iron fence enclosing a side-yard of the Japanese Embassy to watch Embassy employees burn great stacks of official papers and secret documents. On Pennsylvania Avenue that evening the highest officers of Government pondered in dismay the mounting reports of disaster at Pearl Harbor where, it was now clear, the Army and Navy had been taken completely by surprise. In Pittsburgh, Pennsylvania, that night, Senator Nye, following an America First rally, said that the Japanese attack was "just what Britain had planned for us . . . since 1938" and accused his own government of "doing its utmost to provoke a quarrel with Japan."

And in the House Chamber of the Capitol next morning, before microphones which broadcast his words to the world, the President of the United States said to Congress: "Yesterday, December 7, 1941—a date which will live in infamy—the United States of America was suddenly and deliberately attacked by naval and air forces of the Empire of Japan. . . . With confidence in our armed forces—with the unbounded determination of our people—we will gain the inevitable triumph—so help us God. I ask that the Congress declare that since the unprovoked and dastardly attack by Japan on Sunday, December 7, a state of war has existed between the United States and the Japanese Empire."

There followed three days of anxious waiting in Washington. On November 29, "Magic" had intercepted a message from Berlin to Tokyo assuring Japan that, should she "become engaged in a war against the United States, Germany would of course join in the war immediately." Aware of this, Roosevelt had declined to mention Germany and Italy in his War Message to Congress, though he was urged to do so; he could not but feel jittery thereafter over the possibility that Hitler would violate the Tri-Partite Pact as he had violated so many others. What, in that case, could America do? Victory over Japan would mean nothing, would mean less than nothing, if gained at the price of a Hitler-dominated Europe. . . . These jitters were at last ended when, on December 11, Germany and Italy declared war upon the United States.[49]

Book Two

THE TURNING TIDE

V

Pacific Defeat and Global Strategy

i. *Pearl of the Pacific*

Sweet somnolence of a Sunday morning, pleasantly warm as always, perfumed as always by banks of flowers. Quiet the city streets, almost empty the country roads through the long green washes of cane, the brown-and-green mulched fields of pineapple. A few scattered fleecy clouds over the valley where Honolulu lies, with lake-like Pearl Harbor to the west of it, but for the most part a clear and brightening sky. Cumuli massed as usual, however, over the peaks of the Koolau Range at the eastern edge of Oahu. Resting upon dark heaves of volcanic rock, these banked clouds may appear to valley dwellers (the few who are up and about) as stupendous billowing pillows of white upon which rests in its turn a sky that abruptly shifts from dark velvet to vivid blue when, with the suddenness characteristic of tropic dawns, the sun comes up.

Surely there are few scenes in all the troubled world more pacific than this one as long shadows are shortened by the rising sun. A languid peace broods even over the warships at anchor in Pearl Harbor. Three task forces have put to sea. One, under Vice Admiral William F. Halsey, Jr., consists of the aircraft carrier *Enterprise*, three heavy cruisers, and nine destroyers. Its mission is the reinforcement of Wake Island with Marine fighter planes—a response, in part, to the "War Warning" message sent from Washington on November 27, though it is probable that Halsey has knowledge of this message only because he had been with Admiral Husband E. Kimmel when the latter received it. Certainly the commander of a second task force, Rear Admiral John Henry Newton, has no knowledge of it as, with the carrier *Lexington*, three cruisers, and five destroyers, he is on his way to Midway Island to reinforce the patrol plane strength there. Yet Newton, now moving hourly nearer Japan, had not sailed until two days ago, or six days after the "War Warning" was received. (Halsey keeps his planes bombed up; Newton does not.) The third task force is under the command of Newton's immediate superior, Vice Admiral Wilson Brown, who will later recall that he had "learned" of the "War Warning" before Newton sailed but failed to mention it to his subordinate. This third force contains no carriers (the *Lexington* has been temporarily detached from it) as it heads for Johnston Island to conduct landing exercises. The remaining carrier assigned to the Pacific, the *Saratoga*, is undergoing repairs in San Diego. Otherwise the whole of the U. S. Pacific Fleet, some eighty-six combat and service vessels, is now in Pearl Harbor. The eight battleships are there for the first time since last July 4. One of them, the *Pennsylvania*, is drydocked in the Navy Yard on Oahu's mainland, while the others—*California*, *Maryland*, *Oklahoma*, *Tennessee*, *West Virginia*, *Arizona*, *Nevada*—are anchored off Ford Island, lined up mostly two-by-two along Battleship Row. They are in "Condition 3," which means that about one-fourth of the anti-aircraft batteries are manned and all watertight doors are closed—all save those in the *California*, opened for maintenance purposes. Nine cruisers, twenty destroyers, and five submarines are also moored in the still, blue-green water, none of them alerted for immediate action, few of them fully manned. Approximately one-third of the captains of this vast array of fighting ships, and one-third to one-half of all other officer personnel, are ashore for the weekend.[1]

A similarly lazy peace broods over the military airfields of the island. At Wheeler, most of the Army's fighter planes are neatly ranked on concrete aprons for the easiest possible protection against sabotage by Japanese Hawaiians. This is the only anticipated danger to them. At Bellows, across Oahu to the east, a fighter squadron that has been engaged in target practice has parked its planes in rows, emptied their gasoline tanks, and dismounted their guns for cleaning. The pilots, most of them, are off on weekend leave. At Hickam, the Army's bomber base adjacent the Navy's installations at Pearl Harbor, a considerable number of B-18s (deemed obsolescent) stand in rows along with twelve of the valuable new B-17s (Flying Fortresses), only six of which are operable; in addition there are a dozen A-20s, with but six operable. Here the only excitement is the imminent arrival of a flight of twelve unarmed B-17s from California, an excitement too mild to disturb at all deeply the prevailing languor. The same languor prevails over Haleiwa, on the northwest shore of the island some eight miles from Schofield Barracks, where a fighter squadron, its planes as neatly ranked as those on other fields, takes its ease. As for the Army's chief anti-aircraft weapons (three-inch guns), most of them are so far unready that from one to four hours would be required to get them into action.

Nor is the Navy's air arm more strongly flexed. At Kaneohe, the Navy patrol plane base eastward across Oahu from Pearl, most of the thirty-three PBYs are moored in the bay. At the Naval Air Station on Ford Island twenty-nine PBYs are parked in a row. Similarly on Ewa, the

Marine airfield to the west of Pearl, where forty-nine planes, mostly fighters and scout bombers, are lined up.

Everywhere, within each of the two services almost as much as between them, is a failure to make connections, a failure of communication, so that what should be (and what the world has been told is) a taut-nerved organism ready for instantaneous coordinated action is actually a loose collection of organisms, almost none of which is fully awake.[2] Command arrangements both reflect and determine a vast confusion. Nominally there are two top commanders: Lieutenant General Walter C. Short commanding the Hawaiian Department of the Army; Admiral Husband E. Kimmel commanding the Pacific Fleet. As the latter will later point out,[3] however, these two are not in any real sense "opposite numbers" having equivalent duties and responsibilities. The Fleet's assignment is "farflung and offensive," the Army's is "local and defensive"; and there is no machinery for meshing the two commands into anything approaching a single directing unit. The coordination of Army and Navy activities, to the extent that it exists, largely depends upon, and derives from, the voluntary cooperation of the two nominally supreme commanders. Something of its essential nature will be inadvertently revealed in a later year by Kimmel: "Mindful of the necessity of mutual understanding and cooperation between the two services in a situation where their interests were so intertwined as they were in Hawaii, I called upon General Short in civilian clothes at the quarters in Honolulu he was temporarily occupying before he took over the duties of commanding general. I found him then and later to be a man of sound judgment and a competent soldier. . . . Our official and social relations were friendly, . . . [and] we frequently conferred on official matters of common interest and invariably did so when either of us received messages which had any bearing on the development of the United States-Japanese situation. . . ."[4] No doubt each believes he is cooperating with the other in the most admirable fashion and that his doing so indicates a tolerance of attitude and a breadth of mind which many colleagues, beset by interservice jealousies, do not possess.

But these two nominally supreme commanders of the Hawaiian area are not wholly, in actual fact, supreme. They share the over-all command with a third man who operates on virtually an equal basis with them. He is Rear Admiral Claude C. Bloch, commandant of the 14th Naval District, which includes the physical facilities of Pearl Harbor. On paper he is in part responsible to Kimmel and in part directly to the Navy Department in Washington. But neither he nor Kimmel feels that he is in reality a subordinate of the Fleet commander since he has more seniority than Kimmel and has himself been a commander of this Fleet. If he is outranked at the moment it is, they both feel, quite possibly *only* for the moment. Bloch's assigned duties clearly include the administration of the Naval base (which exists "solely for the support of the Fleet"), but if they also include the *defense* of the base the fact is far less clear. According to an agreement drawn up between the services in 1935, headed "Joint Action Army and Navy," the Army is responsible for the security of Pearl Harbor.

Nevertheless, the only air elements available for distant sea searches, crucially important to Pearl Harbor's defense against external attack, are assigned not to the Army but the Navy. These are the PBY long-range seaplanes, organized into two Patrol Wings as elements of the over-all air command of Rear Admiral P. N. L. Bellinger. Bellinger's place in the chain of command is impossible to determine with any precision. He is the Fleet Air Wing Commander and, as such, responsible to Kimmel. But as commander of the PBYs and of the Naval Base Defense Air Force he is also responsible to Bloch and to the base command in San Diego. Altogether, he has five different superiors to whom he is in some part responsible—but neither Short nor any other Army officer is among them. He is supposed to "cooperate" with Major General Frederick L. Martin, commander of the Army's Hawaiian Air Force (Short's air arm), but here again the cooperation must be informal and largely voluntary since no specific objective means have been devised for achieving it.

Finally, within each command, there is the problem of balancing the incalculable need for an alert total defense against the obvious, calculable need for training personnel. Green pilots and reserve officers, green troops and sailors have been poured into the islands in unprecedented numbers, and every time there is a full alert the carefully planned training schedules for these is disrupted. Short has therefore divided the alert into three phases: Number 1, against sabotage and subversive activity; Number 2, against sabotage, subversion, and air attack; Number 3, against sabotage and subversion, air attack, and invasion from the sea. It is only alert Number 1 that is now in force. He has so informed Washington in reply to the November 27 "War Warning" and Washington has given no indication that this is deemed inadequate. Nor has Kimmel received an indication that the arrangements he has made are unsatisfactory to his Washington superiors.

In sum, the Army and Navy with their respective air forces continue to operate in Hawaii as sovereign powers, on this lazy Sunday morning, their working relations determined by treaty and characterized by the polite, formal, and practically inefficient usages of diplomacy. It is virtually as a head of state about to consort with another head of state, his every gesture *vis-à-vis* the other being heightened in significance by his (and the other's) sovereign power, that Admiral Kimmel prepares now for an early round of golf with General Short.

The Admiral has risen with the sun, having been in bed shortly after 9:30 the night before, following a quiet dinner party in a Honolulu hotel given by one of his immediate subordinates. He is a handsome man; few would call him a warmly friendly one. Most deem him rather coldly proud and rank-conscious, self-contained within an almost impervious shell—a man who finds it hard to relax at any time into a casual give-and-take with other men, and impossible to do so here and now. His eyes are a steely gray, his hair iron-gray, his jaw firmly set below full-fleshed cheeks, his posture erect. His smile is seldom and rather bleak: though his lips are full, they are normally pressed together in a hard double-line that turns down a little at each end. He is notable for bureaucratic efficiency, for attention to detail and channel and correct procedure, but he is not without creative ingenuity: he is justly proud of the role he played years ago in the development of a photographic system for the analysis of gunnery scores. He has been long in the service of his country—ever since he left his native Kentucky to enter Annapolis in 1900—but though his climb through the Navy hierarchy was at a satisfactory pace, it was not spectacular until January of this year, eleven months ago, when suddenly, unexpectedly, he was jumped over thirty-two of his seniors to his present post. He is acutely if not anxiously aware of the challenge and opportunity now presented to him. His devotion to duty (and ambition) is austere and single-minded. Most senior officers bring their wives with them on Hawaiian tours of duty; he has left his on the mainland because her presence, or the social engagements her presence would entail, might too much distract him. He lives alone, save for the servants attendant upon his rank, in a bare new house on a slope of Makalapa overlooking Battleship Row, just a few minutes' drive from his headquarters at the submarine base.[5]

A gentle wind (ten knots) now caresses the valley from the north. The sun stands now well above sea and mountain, and its light is brooding down in peace through the eastern windows of the Admiral's house when, shortly after 7:30, he is called to the phone. What he hears through the receiver causes him to stiffen. The duty officer at Fleet headquarters relays a report that the destroyer U.S.S. *Ward* has attacked a strange submarine operating in the defensive area, and there is also a report that a PBY has attacked an unidentified submarine. The Admiral asks, crisply, if the reports are fully confirmed. They are not. *Ward* has been asked to amplify but the amplifying report has not yet been received. The Admiral decides to wait for it before proceeding to headquarters. There have been so many false reports of submarine contacts in recent weeks . . .

And the golden sunlight continues to pour through the open windows. The gentle wind stirs the young palms in the lawn. The air which the Admiral breathes beside the phone is perfumed by flowers.

Yet the shooting war has already begun in the Pacific. It is now almost an hour old.[6]

It was at precisely two minutes before four o'clock that morning that the *Ward*, on patrol just outside Pearl Harbor, received a blinker signal from the nearby minesweeper *Condor*, informing her of the sighting of a suspicious object believed to be a submerged submarine (it was the white wake of the periscope that was seen) proceeding "on westerly course, speed nine knots." At once the *Ward's* commander, Lieutenant William Woodward Outerbridge, sounded general quarters. Three minutes later every man on the ship was at his battle station and remained so for a tense three-quarters of an hour while the indicated area was searched in vain. The search was continued by the regular watch after the rest of the crew was released (at 4:43), but nothing was seen until 6:37. At that instant Outerbridge (the *Ward* was his first command; he was on his first patrol with her) was again called to the bridge to view what he at once recognized as the conning tower of a submarine which was following the target ship *Antares* as the latter sailed toward the entrance to Pearl Harbor. Almost simultaneously the *Antares* signaled her suspicion that she was being followed. Again Outerbridge sounded general quarters. By his orders the *Ward* was headed toward the submarine at maximum possible speed (she was a four-stacker relic of 1918, operating now on only two of her four boilers), on a course designed barely to avoid a collision, while the guns were loaded and aimed. At 6:45, when the destroyer was within one hundred yards of the submarine, the first shot of the Pacific war was fired by the *Ward's* number 1 gun, a 4-inch rifle in the destroyer's bow. The shell missed by inches. Thirty seconds later the second shot was fired, from the number 3 gun mounted on the galley roof. It scored a direct hit into the base of the conning tower. Then, as the *Ward's* stern passed over the bow of the now-diving submarine, four depth-charges were dropped. The submarine appeared to run directly into the first of them as the charge exploded.

At 6:51, Outerbridge signaled Pearl Harbor in code: "Depth-bombed sub operating in defensive sea area." Two minutes later, mindful of the number of false alarms there had been in the past and of the skepticism with which reported submarine sightings were consequently received ashore, he sent a second message, designed to impress upon Pearl Harbor's command the fact that a real submarine had been really engaged and really destroyed. Signaled Outerbridge: "Attacked, fired upon, depth-bombed, and sunk, submarine operating in defensive sea area." A minute later he added: "Stand by for further messages."

Alas, the communications system at Pearl Harbor was far too sluggish and inadequate, the personnel of the base were far too sunk in Sunday lethargy and too conditioned to slackly routine procedures, to respond with swift action to any message, however urgent. The *Ward's* report was received at 7:12 (twenty-one minutes after its dispatch) by the duty officer of Bloch's 14th Naval District. He attempted to reach Bloch's aide but couldn't. He then called the duty officer at Fleet headquarters, read him the message, and spent approximately ten minutes trying to reach Bloch's chief of staff. When at last he did, the staff chief refused to believe the report and demanded further confirmation from *Ward*. Bloch's chief of staff then called Bloch and spent several minutes in talk with him, trying to decide (in his own later words) "what other action should be taken." Bloch, like his chief of staff, doubted the authenticity of the

Ward message; he took no action, pending receipt of further information. It was at about this time that Kimmel was called. Nobody bothered to inform the Army.

Nevertheless, the Army also received a warning, and through its own warning system. The warning went unheeded.[7]

Admittedly the system was in an embryonic state and was being operated at this time solely as a training facility. It was designed to rely primarily upon radar. This device for using radio waves instead of light waves to "illuminate" distant objects and plot their precise positions in relation to an observer owed much of its initial development to research scientists in the U. S. Naval Laboratory in Washington. (Its name was coined by two U.S. naval officers, F. R. Furth and S. M. Tucker, from the words *R*adio *D*etection *A*nd *R*anging.) The British had developed it much further for air defense purposes, and by early 1939 had established a chain of twenty radar stations along England's eastern coast, linked to a central interception center whence a swiftly and fully coordinated defense, making a maximum possible use of available planes, could be directed. This had played a major, perhaps a decisive, role during the air battle for Britain. The fact had not impressed itself, however, on the professional military minds in charge of the Hawaiian defense. To the top commanders on Oahu, radar remained an esoteric new-fangled gadget whose capabilities were unproved: they gave to its installation a relatively low priority (the Air Corps major to whom this duty was assigned later testified to a lack of cooperation from his superiors),[8] and did not attempt to use it to make up for their lack of reconnaissance planes—a lack they repeatedly complained of to Washington.

Five mobile radar units were set up at strategic points above Oahu's shoreline, whence they could "spot" planes as far as 150 miles away. They were connected by direct telephone wire to an information center at Fort Shafter, at the edge of Honolulu, where, on a large plotting table, the information received could be spread out in immediately visible form before a "control" officer. The plan was for this officer to become (as in Britain's air battles) the vital center of air defense operations, transmitting orders to the various commands and keeping them informed of each other's activities and whereabouts. Obviously the system could work in a combat situation only if the control officer knew which of the planes he "saw" on his plotting table were friendly and which hostile—but no arrangements for making this crucial distinction were yet in force. The Army officer in charge might be kept informed of where Army planes were operating, but he had assigned to him no liaison officers who could tell him where the Navy and Marine planes were.

And on this Sunday morning, the information center was not fully operational even as a training facility. Only one officer was on duty, First Lieutenant Kermit A. Tyler. He was there solely as a trainee, assigned the hours from 4:00 to 8:00 A.M., and his opportunities to learn during the first two hours of his duty were meager indeed. Not until 6:10 was any radar contact reported at all. There was another at 6:45—some planes (necessarily unidentified) about 130 miles north of Oahu. At seven all the enlisted men went off to breakfast, the direct lines to the field stations were closed down, and the lieutenant was left alone in the center save for the switchboard operator who remained to handle calls coming through on the regular phone network. Six or seven minutes later this operator, a private named Joseph McDonald, came to the lieutenant in some excitement with a report from the radar installation at Opana, a remote spot on the northwestern shoulder of the Koolau Mountains, a few miles southwest of the most northerly point (Kahuku Point) of the island.

The Opana radar was being manned by a couple of privates, Joseph Lockard and George Elliott, whose assigned Sunday morning duty ran from four to seven but who had kept the set operating beyond the latter time because one of them, Elliott, wanted to practice with it until the breakfast truck arrived. Lockard, who had had experience in set operation, was explaining the procedure to Elliott, who had been operating as a plotter, when abruptly, at 7:02, there appeared on the radar screen by far the largest "blip" (radio-wave echo) that either of them had ever seen. A huge flight of planes (at least fifty) was approaching Oahu from a point 137 miles to the north, three degrees to the east, at a speed of 180 miles an hour. This was the information which McDonald at the Shafter Information Center relayed to Lieutenant Tyler; McDonald thought it important enough to justify calling the enlisted men back from breakfast.

But Tyler didn't think so. He knew that the carriers *Enterprise* and *Lexington* were at sea; the planes might well be theirs. Or they might be Flying Fortresses coming in from California. In either case there was no need to get excited, and this was the response which McDonald reported back to Opana. Lockard protested. He and Elliott had been plotting the incoming flight, which now seemed bigger than ever and was only ninety-two miles away. He asked to speak directly to the lieutenant and tried hard to impart to the officer the sense of urgency he felt. He had never seen anything like this before; surely it required attention. Tyler remained unmoved.

"Don't worry about it," he said.

So Lockard, feeling a little crushed, turned back to the screen and, with Elliott, plotted the incoming flight until, at 7:39 A.M., its "blips" disappeared from the screen. The approaching planes were then just twenty-two miles away, and radar's vision of them was cut off by intervening hills.

Meanwhile, the *Ward* continued her war. At sunrise she sighted a motor-driven sampan, ostensibly a fishing boat, operating in an area where none save U. S. Navy craft could rightfully be; she bore down upon it as it attempted to flee. The sampan, from Honolulu, with three Japanese aboard, then surrendered under a white flag and was turned over to a

Coast Guard cutter while the *Ward*, listening intently through her sonic equipment as she continued to search the defensive area, depth-bombed every suspicious echo.

7:55 A.M.

Through the windows of Admiral Kimmel's house comes a faint sound like rolling thunder far away, as if a violent electrical storm raged on the other side of the Koolau Range. Then the phone rings and the Admiral, receiver to ear, listens to his duty officer's report of the *Ward's* capture of the sampan. The report is interrupted. There's a message from the signal tower, says the duty officer! Pearl Harbor is under attack "and this is no drill!" Simultaneously, Makalapa's Sunday peace is shattered by a roar of planes, followed within seconds by the house-shaking *crump-crump-crump* of explosions not a mile away—explosions whose concussions may well strike the admiral as so many sickening blows to his solar plexus even before he runs out onto his lawn, clad in the white uniform traditionally worn on Sundays, knotting his tie as he goes, to see planes with red circles on their wings and torpedoes slung to their bellies flying low over his house, slanting down toward Battleship Row. He sees the splash the torpedoes make as they hit water and begin their brief streaking runs into the steel sides of the ships for whose security and fighting efficiency he is directly responsible. Dive bombers are roaring down, too. Night burst out of flame into the morning air, rising in tall black columns over the planes and hangars, the docks and ships of Ford Island. Similar columns rise over Hickam, farther away, at the admiral's left.

He stands for a long minute, watching the death of his men and ships, the ruin of his career, the destruction of the whole meaning of his life up until now, then climbs into his car and is driven to the headquarters of the Commander-in-Chief of the Pacific Fleet.

And it is almost precisely at that instant that Lieutenant General Walter C. Short, in his quarters at Fort Shafter a few miles from Makalapa, first learns of the attack.

The general, a man of sixty-one with an honest homely face and a reputation for high efficiency as a staff and training officer, has climbed to his present post without the benefit of an initial push from a Service school. He is no West Point man but a Phi Beta Kappa graduate of the University of Illinois (class of '01) who began his Army career as a second lieutenant in 1902. During the First World War he served as a staff officer with the First Division and as assistant chief of staff of the Third Army; he was decorated with the U. S. Distinguished Service Medal and, by France, with the ribbon of an Officer of the Legion of Honor. Thereafter, through the starved and stunted peacetime Army of the twenties and early thirties, he advanced to the rank (in 1936) of major general. His promotion to lieutenant general came with his appointment to the command of the Hawaiian Department last February.

If he is a warmer personality than Kimmel—less proud, more approachable—his dedication to his job is as great as the admiral's. He, too, sought an early bed after a far from gay Saturday evening, having been worried by the transcript of a suspicious-sounding transpacific telephone conversation between a Tokyo newspaper and a Japanese dentist in Honolulu, reported to him by his counterintelligence officer. (Was the dentist a secret agent of Japan? Did his strange talk of the flowers now blooming on Oahu presage a planned uprising by the nearly 160,000 Japanese-Hawaiians? Such an uprising, timed to coincide with a Japanese attack in the Far East, is the general's greatest dread. Against it he has taken all possible defensive measures.) And like the Admiral, he has arisen early, in anticipation of his golf date.

The first sounds of the Japanese attack surprise him, though he quickly interprets them as emanations from an unusually large and realistic Navy battle practice. When he goes outside, he is puzzled by the amount of smoke that rises and spreads over the western sky. But it is not until several minutes after eight o'clock that his chief of staff comes to him in great excitement with the news that both Wheeler and Hickam fields are under attack and that "it's the real thing."

Thus begins for him, as for Kimmel, the worst day of his life. By 8:30 the initial intense attack by torpedo planes and dive bombers is ended, though sporadic attacks by individual planes continue. Ten minutes later comes a large-scale high-level bombing attack on Pearl Harbor's ships, an attack that continues for thirty-five minutes. Before it ends, dive bombers again appear in great numbers. By 9:45 it is all over; the last Japanese planes disappear into the northwest. But of course the Americans on Oahu do not know that it is over. All through that sickening day they prepare feverishly for an expected renewal of the air attack and of landings by Japanese troops. General Short establishes a command post in an ordnance storage tunnel sometime before noon and there, as he tries to draw the scattered defense forces into coherent and focused fighting units, he receives the reports of damage done, casualties inflicted, and Japanese carriers sighted (though in actual fact none were) at sea.

In the light of the setting sun, that awful day, the smoking ruins of Pearl Harbor and of the airfields of Oahu—all of them with the exception of small Haleiwa—appear to be a graveyard for hope of victory in the Pacific war. The Fleet, it appears, is destroyed as an effective force in opposition to Japan's designs. The balance of naval power, it appears, is decisively tipped toward the Rising Sun. And even when, days later, the damage done is more accurately assessed, and realized to be less than at first appears, it is bad enough. Of the eight great battleships, the very heart of the Pacific Fleet, not one is now capable of sea duty. The *Arizona* (blown up when a bomb went down one of her stacks) and *Oklahoma* are totally destroyed. The *West Virginia*, *California*, and *Nevada* are beached or sunk: perhaps they can ultimately be salvaged, but they are certainly out of action for many months. The *Maryland* is not so severely damaged that it cannot be restored to service within (perhaps) a few weeks, but the *Tennessee*, though not much more seriously damaged, is jammed against massive blocks of concrete by the sunken *West Virginia* and must take much longer to repair since the work cannot begin until the concrete blocks are blasted away. A direct bomb hit has damaged the dry-docked *Pennsylvania*, flagship of the Fleet, but less seriously than any of the other battleships: its repair, since it is already in drydock, should be relatively swift. Two destroyers and a target ship have been totally destroyed; three cruisers, a destroyer, and three auxiliary vessels have been seriously damaged. The Americans may thank God, or happy circumstance, that none of the carriers is in the harbor, else they too would be out of action and nothing would be left with which to strike back at sea for a long time to come.

There is now, for the moment, no effective air force in Hawaii. A total of 188 planes (96 Army, 92 Navy) have been destroyed; 159 planes (128 Army, 31 Navy) have been damaged.

Some 2008 Navy officers and men have been killed, 1102 of them on the *Arizona*. Seven hundred Navy men have been wounded. The Marines count 109 dead, 69 wounded. Of the Army, 218 have been killed and 364 wounded. There have been civilian casualties, too—68 killed and 35 wounded. Altogether, 2403 American lives have been lost.

And all this has been achieved by the Japanese at what, in terms of war, is a trifling cost. Years later it will be learned that the Japanese striking force consisted of 31 ships: 6 carriers, 2 battleships, 2 heavy cruisers, a light cruiser, 9 destroyers, 3 submarines, and 8 tankers. These ships, under the over-all command of Vice Admiral Chuichi Nagumo, rendezvoused with extreme secrecy in remote Tankan Bay of the Kurile Islands and sailed from there on the morning of November 26. Early in the morning of December 7 (December 8, Tokyo time) the carriers were at their fly-off point two hundred miles north of Oahu, and from there the first flight of attackers took off at 6:00 A.M. When the mission was completed (the last plane to return, at 1:00 P.M., was piloted by the leader of the attack, Commander Mitsuo Fuchida), it was found that twenty-nine Japanese planes with fifty-five men had been lost, out of a total striking force of 343 planes. Also lost were a large submarine and five midget submarines, each of the latter having a crew of two.

It was at one of the midgets that the U.S.S. *Ward* had fired the first American shot of World War II.

ii. *Mr. Churchill Comes to Washington*

The transport plane from Hampton Roads, Virginia, an unscheduled and highly secret flight, turned into the wind and slanted down out of the last light of day into the darkness that covered the earth, down into a pale lane defined by parallel straight necklaces of lights. Its tires shrieked on the runway of the Washington airport as it braked to a stop.

The time was precisely two minutes before seven o'clock in the evening of Monday, December 22, 1941.

Secret Service men moved as the wheeled stairway moved up to the plane's door, then stood at the foot of the stairs looking to the right and left as, behind them, the plane's door opened. Seconds later there came through that door a short, stocky man with a huge cigar clamped between his teeth. He trudged rather heavily down the stairs and across the concrete to the waiting car of the President of the United States. The President, sitting in the car, smiled broadly as he extended his hand to the Prime Minister of Great Britain.

"I clasped his strong hand with comfort and pleasure," Winston Churchill later recorded.

By a quarter past seven, the President's car had turned in through the gates on the south grounds of the White House and rolled to a stop at the porticoed entrance looking out, across lawn and Mall, toward the Washington Monument. Reporters and photographers, alerted by the White House press secretary, were gathered there. In silence and without photography they watched the brief awkwardness that always accompanied the President's emergence from an automobile, his slow progress on the arm of a naval aide, Captain John R. Beardall, to the mansion's doorway. There he turned, right hand resting on ivory-handled cane, the Prime Minister beside him, and smiled his famous smile through the few minutes that both posed for pictures. Now and then, looking down (for Churchill was almost a full head shorter than he), he addressed a laughing word to his distinguished guest.

One reporter, curious about the nautical garb which Churchill wore now as he had generally done in his outdoor photographs these last eighteen months, took pains to discover that the knee-length double-breasted coat, "buttoned high in seaman fashion," and the flat cape with a circled insignia in front, was the uniform of a semi-governmental British organization known as the Elder Brothers of Trinity House, whose concern was with life-saving and the operation of lighthouses. All the reporters noted that the Prime Minister was much more subdued, much less buoyant in his apparent attitudes than was his host. He did not smile into the camera eyes as the flashbulbs exploded. He looked, indeed, rather grim and tired as, evidently impatient, he waited for the picture-taking to end. Then he thrust his cigar again between his teeth and, preceding his host, stalked into the White House—a building "painted white," as the Associated Press dispatch would say, "to cover up fire marks made when another British mission arrived for a different purpose in the War of 1812."

There were good reasons why the Prime Minister might appear grim and tired. His eight-day voyage across the storm-tossed, submarine-infested Atlantic had not been without acute anxieties, and it had been a period of heavy and incessant labor.[9]

On the day following the Pearl Harbor attack, whose sad consequences were more than offset in his mind by the happy fact of America's entrance at last into the war as a full belligerent, the King's first minister had written to his King: "I have formed the conviction that it is my duty to visit Washington without delay, provided such a course is agreeable to President Roosevelt, as I have little doubt it will be. The whole plan of the Anglo-American defense and attack has to be concerted in the light of reality. We have also to be careful that our share of munitions and other aid which we are receiving from the United States does not suffer more than is, I fear, inevitable. . . . These reasons were accepted by my colleagues in the Cabinet unanimously today, and I therefore ask Your Majesty's permission to leave the country."[10] The King, having no real power to say "no," of course said "yes." The President, however, had raised the question of personal danger to the Prime Minister, especially on the return journey when the Germans would be alerted to intercept him. "We do not think there is any serious danger about the return journey," Churchill had replied. "There is however great danger in our not having a full discussion on the highest level about the extreme gravity of the naval position, as well as upon the production and allocation issues involved."[11] Roosevelt had then expressed his "delight" that the Prime Minister would be his guest in the White House, though he reiterated his sense of the personal risk involved.

And so, on December 12, the Prime Minister had left London in a blacked-out train, accompanied by Lord Beaverbrook, the Minister of Supply; Admiral Sir Dudley Pound, First Sea Lord; Air Chief Marshal Sir Charles Portal, Chief of the Air Staff; and Field Marshal Sir John Dill, who had just been replaced as Chief of the Imperial General Staff by Sir Alan Brooke. Two days later they had sailed from the mouth of the Clyde, in Scotland, on the battleship H.M.S. *Duke of York,* heading down through the Irish Sea into the Bay of Biscay, accompanied by a flotilla of destroyers. They were forced to cross routes which U-boats followed going out from and returning to bases on the French Atlantic coast. This meant that the great battleship could not leave its escorting protective vessels behind, though these in heavy seas slowed its pace to a petty six knots. The most anxious moment of the voyage, so far as immediate danger was concerned, seemed to Churchill to be when the flotilla passed under clearing skies within four hundred miles of Brest. ". . . I could not help remembering how the *Prince of Wales* [on which the Atlantic Charter had been signed] and the *Repulse* had been destroyed by shore-based torpedo-aircraft attack the week before."[12]

The loss of these mightiest of British warships off Malaya on December 10 had been a grievous blow to both Britain and the United States. The two battleships had sailed from Singapore on December 8, hoping to attack massive Japanese landings then taking place on the peninsula; had turned homeward after nightfall on the ninth, when theretofore overcast skies cleared and there was reason to believe that Japanese search planes had seen them; and had been sunk shortly after noon the next day when attacked by more than four-score bombers and torpedo bombers. The event, coming hard upon the Pearl Harbor disaster, seemed in that dark hour to mean that the Japanese would have full command of the sea approaches to the Far East for a long time to come, a period during which she could expand and consolidate her gains almost without opposition. "In all the war I never received a more direct shock," said Churchill years later, of the telephone call that informed him of the disaster. ". . . As I turned over and twisted in bed the full horror of the news sank in upon me. There were no British or American capital ships in the Indian Ocean or the Pacific except the American survivors of Pearl Harbor, who were hastening back to California. Over all this expanse of waters Japan was supreme, and we everywhere weak and naked."[13] There loomed, now, as the *Duke of York* sailed westward, the possibility that all Malaya might soon be in Japanese hands. Already the Japanese were one hundred and fifty miles south of the positions they had first held on the peninsula; they fought their way southward, with increasing strength and incredible speed, toward Singapore, the key British bastion in the Far East. As for Hong Kong, its garrison fought with great valor but with no hope of relief or reinforcement; its doom was obviously imminent by the time Churchill had reached the mid-Atlantic.*

All this, however, did nothing to change Churchill's conviction of what the basic Anglo-American global strategy ought to be, and indeed *must* be if the war were to be won. His greatest dread was that the successive Pacific tragedies, and those which now clearly impended in the Philippines and Southeast Asia, would cause the Americans to revise *their* basic strategic conceptions, so arduously worked out and concerted, through joint staff talks, with the British. The dread had been fed by official reports and the summaries of American press opinion which had come from America during the last two weeks. These "gave the impression that the whole fury of the nation would be turned upon Japan. We feared lest the true proportion of the war as a whole might not be understood. We were conscious of a serious danger that the United States might pursue the war against Japan in the Pacific and leave us to fight Germany and Italy in Europe, Africa and the Middle East."[14]

Spurred by this felt danger, the Prime Minister had consumed most of his working hours (which were many) aboard the battleship in the composition of three papers outlining his view of the present status and future course of the war. These were to serve as the prepared bases for his conferences with Roosevelt.

The first of them had North Africa as its principal focus.[15] Here the situation had markedly improved, from Britain's point of view, since last summer, when Harry Hopkins had come to London with strong American arguments against British military commitments in the Middle East. Then, under the gallant Wavell, British forces in North Africa had stood

* Hong Kong fell on Christmas Day, 1941.

on the defensive at the gateway to the Nile Valley. Now it was the British under General Sir Claude Auchinleck who took the offensive against Rommel's badly overextended Afrika Korps, and with such success the Prime Minister anticipated an early advance by the British Eighth Army all the way across the desert to the borders of French Tunisia. If that happened, it seemed distinctly possible that the French in North Africa might be persuaded to invite, or at least connive in, the Allied occupation of all northwest Africa, an operation (it had been given the code name GYMNAST) which Churchill had first proposed to the British military chiefs last summer. Full preparations, he now argued, should be made to seize this opportunity should it present itself. The United States and Britain should promise "to re-establish France as a Great Power with her territories undiminished" and "offer active aid by British and United States expeditionary forces, both from the Atlantic seaboard of Morocco and at convenient landing-points in Algeria and Tunis, as well as from General Auchinleck's forces advancing from the east." The French should also be promised "ample supplies" for themselves and "the loyal Moors" in North Africa, and Vichy "should be asked to send their fleet from Toulon to Oran and Bizerta and to bring France into the war again as a principal." This would of course mean the prompt occupation of all France by the Nazis, an event which would not, Churchill said (and perhaps believed) worsen greatly if at all the daily lives of the French people "since it does not seem that the conditions in the occupied and hitherto unoccupied zones are widely different."

Otherwise in this paper, Churchill stressed as "the prime fact of the war at this time" the "failure and losses" of Hitler in Russia. The failure was great, the losses (though impossible to estimate with accuracy) obviously enormous. For the first time, a Nazi blitzkrieg had been frustrated: Moscow and Leningrad remained firmly in Russian hands. The Nazis had actually been forced to retreat from their farthest advanced positions before the Soviet capital where their troops, inadequately equipped for the extreme rigors of a Russian winter, were suffering now some of the torments that Napoleon's Grand Army had suffered in 1812. Even in the south, where the climate did not fight on the Russians' side, the German hordes had received checks. After taking Rostov they had been forced to abandon it and retreat forty miles to the west. Churchill, with all this in mind, gratefully anticipated for Hitler "a winter of slaughter and expenditure of fuel and equipment on the largest scale." But ". . . neither Great Britain nor the United States have any part to play in this event, except to make sure that we send, without fail and punctually, the supplies we have promised. In this way alone shall we hold our influence over Stalin and be able to weave the mighty Russian effort into the general texture of the war."

(As Churchill composed this brief résumé and conclusion, Anthony Eden, the British Foreign Secretary, was in Moscow attempting to shape closer and firmer ties with the Russians for the conduct of the war. He was having his difficulties with Stalin, who insisted upon agreements *now* regarding postwar political settlements. Stalin wanted Britain to agree [1] that the Polish-Soviet frontier existing when Germany attacked Russia would be re-established—which is to say all eastern Poland, as constituted before World War II, would become Soviet territory; [2] that the Finnish-Soviet frontier would also be as it had been when Germany attacked Russia—which is to say the line would be the one established at the close of the Russo-Finnish War in 1940; [3] that the position of the Baltic States would be as it had been at the time of Hitler's attack on Russia—which is to say these States would no longer exist, being incorporated in the Soviet Union; and [4] that the same would be true of Bessarabia—which is to say this portion of Rumania would become part of Russia, as it had been in 1914. To this, Churchill, in his own words, "reacted violently." Two days before the *Duke of York* docked at Hampton Roads he sent a message to the British Cabinet which he "hoped" would be transmitted to Eden. He said: "Stalin's demand about Finland, Baltic States, and Rumania are directly contrary to the first, second, and third articles of the Atlantic Charter, to which Stalin has subscribed. . . . The time has not yet come to settle frontier questions, which can only be resolved at the Peace Conference when we have won the war. The mere desire to have an agreement which can be published should never lead us into making wrongful promises. . . . The Russians have got to go on fighting for their lives anyway, and are dependent upon us for very large supplies, which we have most painfully gathered, and which we shall faithfully deliver.")

The second of the three papers was headed "The Pacific Front" and faced unflinchingly the prospect that the Allies would be "deprived one by one of our possessions and strong-points in the Pacific, and that the enemy will establish himself fairly easily in one after the other, mopping up the local garrisons." This seemed the inevitable consequence of Pearl Harbor and of the loss of *Prince of Wales* and *Repulse*. It must, however, be regarded as an "interim period" during which "our duty is one of stubborn resistance at each point attacked, and to slip supplies and reinforcements through as opportunity offers," since this would force Japan "to make ever-larger overseas commitments far from home," exposing to Allied attack lines of communication far too long to be everywhere adequately protected. The root of Pacific strategy was a recognition of the fact that Japan's resources "are a wasting factor," that the country had "long been overstrained by its wasteful war with China," and that the Japanese were "at their maximum strength [i.e., in terms of the possibility of immediate deployment] on the day of the Pearl Harbor attack." The "interim period," in any case, must be brief. It should end with "the forming of a definitely superior battle fleet in the Pacific" in May 1942, when "two new American battleships" were supposed to "be fit for action." This event, Churchill continued, in tangential reference to his greatest fear at that moment, "would reassure the whole western seaboard of the American continent, and thus prevent a needless dissipation on a gigantic defensive effort of forces which have offensive parts to play."

The third paper was headed "The Campaign of 1943" and was based on the assumption that the military operations forecast in papers I and II would be successfully completed in 1942. Thus, by 1943, the Allies would again have naval superiority in the Pacific and the Japanese would be paying the bitter price of overextension; the British Isles "would remain intact and more strongly prepared against invasion than ever before"; and the "whole West and North African shores from Dakar to the Suez Canal and the Levant to the Turkish frontier would be in Anglo-American hands." The Allies would be in a position to liberate "the captive countries of Western and Southern Europe" by landing "during the summer of 1943 of United States and British armies on their shores." Churchill did not, however, propose a single massive assault upon some one segment of what Hitler boastfully called "Fortress Europa." All too vivid in his mind was the memory of the stalemate and wholesale butchery on the Western Front during the First World War. It had bred in him a profound aversion for massive confrontations. He sought instead the indirect approach wherever possible and would hazard the final event not on one huge battle, but on a sequence of engagements that had definable limits in terms of space, time, and manpower commitments—engagements that might be broken off whenever they threatened to become (as the Western Front of 1915–18 had become) all-consuming furies beyond the control of any of their alleged commanders. In the present instance he sought to use Anglo-American sea superiority to release for Allied use the revolutionary energies of peoples now held captive by the Nazis. "By themselves they will never be able to revolt, owing to the ruthless countermeasures that will be employed," he wrote, "but if adequate and suitably equipped forces were landed in several of the following countries, namely, Norway, Denmark, Holland, Belgium, the French Channel coasts and the French Atlantic coasts, as well as in Italy and possibly the Balkans, the German garrisons would prove insufficient to cope both with the strength of the liberating forces and the fury of the revolting peoples. It is impossible for the Germans, while we retain the sea power necessary to choose the place or places of attack, to have sufficient troops in each of these countries for effective resistance." He proposed these landings for the summer of 1943. "In principle . . . [they] should be made by armoured and mechanised forces capable of disembarking not at ports but on beaches, either by landing-craft or from ocean-going ships specially adapted. . . . The vanguards of the various British and American expeditions should be marshalled by the spring of 1943 in Iceland, the British Isles, and, if possible, in French Morocco and Egypt. The main body would come direct across the ocean." Churchill then revealed to all who had eyes to see the deep motive of his strategy. "It need not be assumed," he wrote, "that great numbers of men are required. If the incursion of the armoured formations is successful, the uprising of the local populations, for whom weapons must be brought, will supply the corpus of the liberating offensive."

Thus the Prime Minister's preparations for ARCADIA, which was the code name given this conference—and though none of these papers could be given to the President on the evening of Churchill's arrival at the White House (Roosevelt would not then have had time to read them in any case), the British leader was relieved of his greatest anxiety concerning strategy before that first evening ended.

He was installed in a large bedroom across the hall from Harry Hopkins' room. He partook of the nightly cocktail ritual (Roosevelt always made a great deal of this, engaging in lighthearted banter while personally mixing the drinks). He ate with his usual hearty appetite his first White House meal (though the "White House cuisine did not enjoy a very high reputation," according to Robert Sherwood, the food "was always better when Churchill was there"). And then he was taken to the Oval Study for what amounted to the opening session of ARCADIA.

Present, in addition to Roosevelt and Churchill, were Cordell Hull, Sumner Welles, Harry Hopkins, Lord Beaverbrook, and Lord Halifax, the British Ambassador who had succeeded Lord Lothian. The principal subject was the situation in North Africa, and upon it all the conferees, Churchill was delighted to discover, were in substantial agreement. It was agreed that Hitler, frustrated in Russia, being the kind of man he was, would be likely to attempt a move through Spain and Portugal into Northwest Africa, especially since he might obtain among the prizes there the great French battleships *Jean Bart* and *Richelieu* moored in Casablanca's harbor. It was agreed that to "forestall the Germans" in this attempt was "vital" to Allied interests. "Accordingly," says Churchill's report home,[16] "the discussion was not "*whether*, but *how*." And even as regards this there was basic agreement. Vichy France's enmity toward Britain precluded from success any British effort to persuade her to cooperate or connive in an Allied occupation of North Africa, but an American effort in this direction might succeed. If the United States approached Pétain or General Weygand† in Vichy with a pledge to restore France to her Great Power status, should she now cast her lot boldly with the Allies, the pledge might be accepted. On the other hand this approach might lead to "smooth promises from Pétain and Weygand" who, meanwhile, covertly informed the Nazis of Allied intentions. Hence preparations should be made for entering North Africa forcibly, in case peaceable entry was denied, and these should be completed before any approach to the Vichyites was made. On this, Churchill and Roosevelt found themselves in full agreement. "The President said he was anxious that American land forces should give their support as quickly as possible

† Weygand had just been recalled to Vichy and dismissed from his North African command, an event disturbing to the Allies since it indicated the growing power in Vichy of fascist-minded Admiral Jean-François Darlan.

wherever they could be most helpful," Churchill reported, "and favoured the idea of a plan to move into North Africa being prepared for either event, i.e., with or without invitation."

Clearly, the Americans continued to regard Hitler's Germany as their chief enemy: the Pacific remained in their conception a secondary theater wherein an active strategic defense was, for some time to come, all that could be supplied or hoped for. They had no intention to revise the agreed-upon basis of global strategy, so that on this score the Prime Minister might go to his bed that night with an easy mind.

iii. *Global Strategy: The Process of Decision*

And indeed he himself had long recognized a difference between the American and English mentalities, or temperaments, which should have kept this particular anxiety from preying seriously upon him. It was much more likely, much more in keeping with national character, for the British to shift ground strategically than for the Americans to do so.

When dealing wih matters of business or commerce, Churchill had noted,[17] the Americans were inclined toward large-scale and fundamental conclusions, logically derived from a detailed survey of existent and clearly defined factors. These last, however fluid they might be in objective reality, were solidified in the American mind through the very process of precisely defining them; they were then dealt with as static entities when the "broad, sweeping, logical conclusions on the largest possible scale" were bodied forth as plans for action. Moreover, the Americans demonstrated great faith—an excessive faith, by Churchill's view—in the practical efficacy of any such plan; they seemed convinced that it in itself had the power to anticipate if not actually to determine the course of future events. (As Churchill put it, "They [the Americans] feel that once the foundation has been planned on true and comprehensive lines all other stages will follow naturally and almost inevitably.")

Different in this respect—and by the same token more sophisticated, in Churchill's view—was the British mind. Englishmen had relatively little faith in a rigorous logical consistency as a guide to practical action or as a key to practical success. At the base of their outlook upon the world was an acute sense of the "swiftly changing and indefinable." Hence they seldom aspired to "dominate the event" through "fundamental decisions," preferring instead to take their cues from the "unfolding event" and then to rely upon "opportunism and improvisation" to see them through. They of course shaped plans for action, but (unlike the Americans') these were for the most deliberately loose and vague and subject to change; they left plenty of room for swift responses "in accordance," not with a detailed and prior "fundamental decision," but with the unforeseen external occurrence. (No doubt the notorious "perfidy" of Perfidious Albion was rooted in this English mental trait, of which the instinct for privacy and a tolerance of eccentricities were part and parcel.)

This difference between the British and the Americans, manifest in their differing approaches to commerce and industry, was expressed in intensified form in their attitudes toward and practical dealings with the problems of war. As the ARCADIA conference opened, the British had no real strategy of their own for winning the war.‡ Their nearest approach to what might be called an "end-game" plan was a proposal coded ROUNDUP which no one took very seriously in its early form. It called for an invasion of the Continent by ground forces, but only after (or *if*, an unlikely "if" as things looked in 1940–41) Germany's position in Europe had so far deteriorated that she no longer hoped for victory and sought to withdraw her forces from conquered territory in order to concentrate on defense of the Fatherland. ROUNDUP was designed, not to force this retreat, but to frustrate its orderly performance and exploit the opportunities it opened for inflicting mortal wounds. The scale of the operation would appear absurdly small to later planners, the total forces consisting of six armored divisions, six and one-third infantry divisions, and six tank brigades, plus supporting troops.[18] Aside from this, as the war spread to the Pacific, the British had in the realm of grand strategy only the basic conception of Germany as the prime enemy, Japan the secondary one upon whom overwhelming force might be turned once Germany's fighting power was destroyed—and this was a conception forced upon them by geography and the timing of events.

The Americans, on the other hand, had worked out on paper by December of 1941 a fairly definite grand strategical plan, with (in rudimentary form) implementing operational plans, and they had done so, not in forced response to immediate hostile pressures, but in a calculated anticipation of these.[19]

The strategy had evolved out of a succession of so-called "Color Plans" devised in the 1920s and early thirties by a Joint Planning Committee of Army and Navy officers who reported to the Joint Board, which was the agency of "cooperation" at the highest level between the Army and Navy. (The Board was to be superseded by the Joint Chiefs of Staff in early 1942 when the hazards of mere "cooperation" between the two services were recognized in the lurid light of Pearl Harbor.) Of the Color Plans, the one receiving the greatest attention was ORANGE, based on the assumption that Japan would be the enemy and that each nation would fight without allies and without attacking the territory of any third power. Such a war would be primarily a naval war, fought out in the Pacific. Far less likely, but nevertheless considered and planned for as a possibility, was a war with Britain, brought on by commercial

‡ "Until the end of 1941 Britain can scarcely be said to have had a strategy for winning the war except to fight back with all she had and hold her European foes in a ring of salt water and desert. Beyond that she could only, as Churchill had taught her, hope for some change in the tide of world affairs that might weaken her enemies. She lived by the faith he gave her, and from hand to mouth, for she had no other choice." Arthur Bryant, *The Turn of the Tide* (New York: Doubleday, 1957), p. 15.

rivalries. For this, RED was prepared—a naval war in the Atlantic but (unlike ORANGE) involving also large-scale ground operations to deprive the enemy of bases in the Western Hemisphere. The least likely contingency of all, in the international situation that prevailed in the twenties and early thirties, was a war in which Britain and Japan were allied against the United States. Yet it was the plan§ for this contingency (RED-ORANGE) which, of all those made during this period, was most useful as a strategical preparation for the situation that actually developed as the 1930s drew to a close. It called for a two-front naval war, involved the use of large ground forces to repel invasion, and made the pregnant decision "to concentrate on obtaining a favorable decision in the Atlantic" while standing on the defensive, with minimum forces, in the Pacific. The reason for this was that Britain was considered the stronger of the two hypothetical enemies, and the vital northeastern section of the United States was most vulnerable to an attack from the Atlantic. "It is not unreasonable to hope that the situation at the end of the struggle with RED may be such as to induce ORANGE to yield rather than face a war carried to the Western Pacific," the planners said.

Thus the American planners had already wrestled with the complexities of a two-front offensive-defensive war when, in November of 1938, they were directed by the Joint Board to consider what the United States should do militarily in case she faced simultaneously a threat in the Pacific, stemming from Japanese aggressions in Southeast Asia, and a threat in the Atlantic, stemming from German-Italian aggression in Europe. They began by defining five different possibilities presented by the existing international situation and ended, nearly six months later, by proposing a specific plan to deal with each of them. These were called the RAINBOW plans, numbered 1 to 5 inclusive, and of them RAINBOW 5 came the closest to anticipating the conditions of World War II from September 1939 to June 1940. RAINBOW 5 assumed that the United States, Britain, and France would act together against the Axis Powers. It proposed that a strategic defensive be maintained in the Pacific while American forces were sent across the Atlantic to Africa or Europe "in order to effect the decisive defeat of Germany, Italy, or both"—an event which would be followed (if Japan then refused to yield) by a transfer of major force to the Pacific for an offensive against Japan.

The fall of France and, as it then seemed, the imminent defeat of Britain caused a shift of American planning emphasis from RAINBOW 5 to RAINBOW 4, which assumed that the United States would stand alone against the Axis Powers and must therefore confine her initial effort to an active defense of the whole of the Western Hemisphere. (This plan called for U. S. Army forces to be sent to the southern part of South America and other Army forces to be used in joint operations with the Navy in eastern Atlantic areas, while a strategic defensive was main-

§ Actually it was only a "recommended" plan, since it was never formally adopted as a war plan.

tained against Japan behind the line Alaska-Hawaii-Panama. The Philippines were written off as indefensible.) Not until it became evident that Britain might continue to stand for a long time to come, with American aid, was the emphasis shifted back to RAINBOW 5—but when this happened the circumstances were such as to make the planners' work more important than ever before.

For by that time the process of final basic strategic decision was approaching its conclusion. Such decisiveness was, of course, beyond the purview of the Joint Planning Committee, whose work was influential of concrete acts only to the extent that it was persuasive of those in executive authority. In the present case the authority was chiefly exercised by three men: General Marshall, Army Chief of Staff; Admiral Stark, Chief of Naval Operations; and (ultimately) President Roosevelt in his Constitutional capacity as Commander-in-Chief of the nation's Armed Forces. Hence the shaping of RAINBOW 5 was of far less importance, so far as actual decision-making was concerned, than the conclusions which General Marshall was reaching as he watched the darkly "unfolding event" in Western Europe through early June of 1940. On the morning of June 17, the day France fell, he called a meeting of his top assistants in his office and addressed to them the following words: "Are we not forced into a question of reframing our naval policy, that is, purely defensive action in the Pacific, with the main effort on the Atlantic side? We have to be prepared for the worst situation that may develop, that is, if we do not have the Allied fleet in the Atlantic." Nor was Marshall's essential opinion changed on this point by subsequent events whereby the British continued to wield their fleet in the Atlantic and the French Fleet was neutralized, at least for the time being.

Meanwhile, Admiral Stark was approaching the same basic conclusion. In the autumn of 1940, after the Battle of Britain had ended in R.A.F. victory, the Chief of Naval Operations presented to his colleagues a written analysis of the war situation as it affected American security, stressing at the outset his view that "if Britain wins decisively against Germany we could win everywhere; but . . . if she loses the problem confronting us would be very great; and while we might not *lose everywhere*, we might, possibly, not *win* anywhere." He then stated in the form of questions the four alternative courses of action which in his view were open to the United States, listing them alphabetically, A to D. He phrased the last of them (paragraph "Dog" in naval parlance) as follows: "Shall we direct our efforts toward an eventual strong offensive in the Atlantic as an ally of the British, and a defensive in the Pacific?" His own answer was an emphatic "yes," in case the United States became actively involved in war with the Axis, as he had little doubt she soon would be. He further urged that Plan Dog, as this proposal came to be called, be worked out jointly by the Army and Navy on the basis of a "clear understanding between the nations involved as to the strength and extent of the participation which may be expected in any particular theater." To this end he recommended secret staff talks with the British "to reach agreements and lay down plans for promoting unity of Allied effort should the United States find it necessary to enter the war."

It could be expected that Stark's recommendation, and Plan Dog itself, would find hearty acceptance by General Marshall. Similarly with Churchill and the British Chiefs of Staff, who presumably heard of it through Rear Admiral Robert L. Ghormley. (Ghormley had been stationed in London during the summer as an observer and as a liaison officer with the British.) Less heartily affirmative, however, and indeed decidedly ambiguous as regards Plan Dog, was the response of Roosevelt. In the aftermath of his election victory of 1940, he approved Stark's proposal for secret staff talks.¶ These were accordingly set up to open in Washington on January 29, 1941. But he declined to approve or disapprove a statement of national defense policy which had been prepared by the Joint Planning Committee and accepted by the Joint Board as the basic "position paper" of the American delegation to the forthcoming conference. It called for an immediate entrance by the United States into war with the European Axis in case she was forced into war with Japan, this in order "to permit prompt movement to . . . [the Atlantic] of forces adequate to conduct a major offensive in that ocean." Meeting to discuss this paper with the Secretaries of War, Navy, and State, and with the Service Chiefs, less than two weeks before the international staff talks began, Roosevelt was evasive of the crucial strategic question. He thought there was no more than "one chance in five" that the United States would be forced to act simultaneously against Japan and the European Axis; he refused to commit himself as to what the basic strategy should be (i.e., whether the major initial effort should be in the Pacific or Atlantic) if this unlikely event should occur. On the other hand, he did insist that aid to Britain must not be curtailed even if the U.S. became involved in a two-ocean war. Thus he tacitly or by implication concurred in the major premise of Plan Dog, which was of course the *raison d'être* of the upcoming talks.

On this basis a conference agenda, and instructions for the American delegation, were prepared. The talks were to be rigorously "non-political." No specific commitments could be made, even in the exclusively military sphere, save as regards "methods of cooperation." The agreements reached and plans made must be confirmed by the British Staff Chiefs and the American opposite numbers; they could become operative only on the basis of political agreements between the two governments.

The talks opened on schedule and continued through fourteen formal sessions until March 29, 1941, when the agreements and conclusions reached were embodied in a final report, soon known as ABC-1. Essentially the Allied strategic plan under ABC-1 was identical with the American RAINBOW 5, on which work went forward rapidly after the staff

¶ See page 50.

talks ended. Both were formally approved on May 14, 1941, by the Joint Board, and by the Secretaries of War and of the Navy on May 28 and June 2 respectively. But when they were presented to the President for final approval they became entangled in what Robert Sherwood has called Roosevelt's "densely forested interior," and could be disentangled at last only through bold action, taken on their own responsibility and in the absence of a commensurate authority, by the very men who had presented them in the first place.

It was characteristic of the later Roosevelt that, entering a new room of policy, he should seek to keep doors open behind him through which he might beat a hasty retreat if the room proved too full of hazard. It was also characteristic of Roosevelt, early and late, that he almost always, as if by deliberate intent, presented his subordinates with terms of reference for specific jobs, and with delegations of authority, so blurred that they necessitated executive creativity at the risk (often excessive) of bitterly personal power struggles within the areas of overlap. In the present instance he studied with care the documents presented to him and indicated his awareness of their great importance. He then declined to approve them. He had an excuse: the British Government had not yet approved ABC-1, and RAINBOW 5 was based on ABC-1. But the excuse seemed lame to the American military chiefs, who were left in a quandary. The plans demanded that arrangements be made and actions taken *at once* by both the Army and Navy, in cooperation with the British or on the assumption that such cooperation (definitely promised by ABC-1) would be forthcoming if the U.S. entered the war. Dire events would not be deterred by quibbles, nor wait upon any administrator's convenience.

Well, then, said the Army Chief of Staff, we must act.

It was at such moments that George Catlett Marshall demonstrated those qualities which made him so immensely valuable to his country and to the free world. He was in that year sixty-one years old but he appeared and acted much younger. His sandy hair was but slightly streaked with gray; his trim body, just under six feet tall, was youthfully vigorous and erect; and there was nothing of an old man's weariness in the direct gaze of his clear gray eyes. None would have called him handsome of face: his nose was too blunt, his upper lip too long, his mouth too wide: but his features were cast in a mold of rugged honesty and courage and they were lighted by an intelligence that, if far from brilliant, was soundly logical and respectful of objective fact. In his total character he bore a striking resemblance to Robert E. Lee, who was one (if not the chief) of his heroes. Like Lee he was grave of mien and aloof of manner, pleasant but holding himself so much in reserve that few could claim to know him, personally, with any real intimacy. Like Lee he adhered with stern self-discipline to a very high and difficult code of honor: when as a freshman at the Virginia Military Institute in 1897 he was run through with a bayonet wielded by a sophomore during a particularly vicious hazing, he refused to report the man who had injured him. Like

Lee, he was utterly selfless in his devotion to duty, his high example inspiring the best in those who worked with him.

There had been high officers in the skimped Army of the 1920s, General Fox Conner among them, who regarded Marshall as "close to being a genius" and, even thus early, predicted for him the supreme command of Allied armies when, as Conner believed inevitable, a Second World War engulfed the United States. Conner said as much repeatedly to his Executive Officer in the Panama Canal Zone in the early 1920s, his "exec" being then Major Dwight D. Eisenhower. Conner was convinced that, in the next world war, the principle of "coordination" or "cooperation" between the commanders of the armies of allied nations would not work. "Systems of single command will have to be worked out," Eisenhower would later quote Conner as saying.[20] ". . . We must insist on individual and single responsibility—leaders will have to learn how to overcome nationalistic considerations in the conduct of campaigns. One man who can do it is Marshall. . . ." And as Chief of Staff, Marshall had done nothing to dim the luster with which he had shone before Conner's eyes. He had displayed a talent for large-scale administration along with a profound understanding of, and commitment to, the Constitutionally defined role of the professional soldier in the American democracy. He was at the present moment contemplating without dismay the difficult task of completely reorganizing the War Department, streamlining procedures and reshuffling personnel, to make it an effective agency for waging war. He had learned his way through the intricacies of proliferating New Deal bureaucracy, neatly balancing or fusing military and political considerations as he did so. And, above all, he had learned how to work with Roosevelt, whose full confidence and affectionate respect he had earned.

He was thus prepared to answer, at a meeting in Secretary of War Stimson's office on June 10, 1941, the question raised by the President's ambiguous response to ABC-1 and RAINBOW 5. Were the Army and Navy authorized to proceed with their own planning under RAINBOW 5? They were, said Marshall—or at least (he would not presume to speak for the Navy) the Army was. He pointed out that the President had not *dis*approved of the two plans. As a matter of fact, had Roosevelt not specifically requested that both be brought to him *for* approval "in case of war"? Surely this was in effect a final decision and a sufficient authorization for doing what now so obviously needed to be done.

So it was that Admiral Stark and General Marshall, at the first ARCADIA session of the Chiefs of Staff, were enabled to submit as the basis for all future plans two brief paragraphs reaffirming the conclusions reached at the "A-B Staff Conversations in February, 1941," this despite the fact that the decision implied a willingness to accept the loss to Japan of the Philippines, Guam, and Wake Island in the opening months of the struggle.

And on this basis, the Americans and British were able to achieve quick and firm agreement regarding the largest outlines of grand strategy. It was agreed that, in the Pacific, the main objectives in 1942 would be to keep sea and air lanes open in order to supply the strategic defense—a defense requiring tactical offensives by Allied warships and -planes whenever and wherever possible in order to keep the Japanese off balance, delaying if not preventing the consolidation of their initial gains. But the greatest Allied emphasis would be placed during the coming year on closing a ring around Germany with a view to crushing her in (hopefully) 1943. Three paragraphs drafted during ARCADIA provided the over-all framework within which all planning in detail was to be done:[21]

15. In 1942 the main methods of wearing down Germany's resistance will be:
    a. Ever-increasing air bombardment by British and American Forces.
    b. Assistance to Russia's offensive by all available means.
    c. The blockade.
    d. The maintenance of the spirit of revolt in the occupied countries, and the organization of subversive movements.
16. It does not seem likely that in 1942 any large scale land offensive against Germany except on the Russian front will be possible. We must, however, be ready to take advantage of any opening that may result from the wearing down process referred to in paragraph 15 to conduct limited land offensives.
17. In 1943 the way may be clear for a return to the Continent, across the Mediterranean, from Turkey into the Balkans, or by landings in Western Europe. Such operations will be the prelude to the final assault on Germany itself, and the scope of the victory program should be such as to provide means by which they can be carried out.

Within this very general framework, however, and especially as regards paragraph 17, there were many openings for disagreements—many wide spaces within which differences in national temper, mind, and experience could be expressed—and disagreements there were even in this first and, on the whole, most harmonious of top-level strategy conferences. The British were psychologically prepared to wage a very long war, having repeatedly done so in the past, and victoriously, against nations which upset or threatened to upset that balance of power on the Continent required by England for her own security, her own effectiveness as a world power. They were prepared to postpone (indefinitely, as it would often seem to her ally) the hour of final decision, Micawberlike in their hope that meanwhile "something" would "turn up" to make the final decision more surely favorable to them, and less costly. Behind this attitude was their awareness that, after nearly two and a half years of war, they were fully extended. Having achieved virtually the maximum of their manpower and industrial mobilization, they had perforce so distributed their strength in response to the enemy's initiative that any increase of their effort at one point must mean a decrease at others.

Not so the Americans. They placed far less faith in chance or circumstance, far more in their own decisive strength and will, than the British in their present historic position (just one generation following the massacre of the First World War) could afford to do. As always, the Americans were in a hurry to get the job done. They demanded to get at once to the root of the matter: in this respect Harry Hopkins, whom Churchill once dubbed "Lord Root of the Matter," was the personification of his countrymen. Pressing for the earliest possible victory, they were willing to risk a high rate per unit-time of casualties and materiel losses in order to gain it, being convinced that the total losses would then be less than in a long war and knowing that, in any case, initial losses could be made up out of the nation's vast manpower and industrial reserves.

Americans, military and naval professionals shied away from the blurred loose command arrangements which their ally was often willing to accept: they wanted equal portions of responsibility and authority to be bound together in each command assignment, and the chain of command to be unmistakably defined from the highest to the lowest level. An instance of this difference occurred on the day after Christmas, 1941, when the chief subject of discussion at a major meeting in the White House was a proposal by General Marshall that a single supreme commander be appointed over what was then known as the ABDA Area. (The initials derived from American, British, Dutch, Australian, and the Area was a geographically vast theater of war extending from the Bay of Bengal to Australasia, including Burma, Singapore, and the Dutch East Indies.) The proposal was a response to the unexpectedly swift Japanese drive to the south and west whereby it appeared that the immense natural resources of the Dutch East Indies might soon fall into Japanese hands; Australia might be invaded, and the Allies presented with the appalling threat of a Japanese drive through India into the Middle East. Said Marshall: ". . . I feel very strongly that the most important consideration is the question of unity of command. The matters being settled here [at ARCADIA thus far] are mere details which will continuously recur unless settled in a broader way. . . . I am convinced that there must be one man in command of the entire theater—air, ground and ships. We can not manage by cooperation. . . . If we make a plan for unified command now, it will solve nine-tenths of our troubles." He pointed to the Allied experience of the Western Front in World War I, where a supreme commander was at last appointed, though not until "much valuable time, blood, and treasure had been needlessly sacrificed."[22]

Churchill disagreed. The analogy between the Western Front in 1918 and ABDA in 1942 was wholly false, he said. In France there had been a single continuous line of battle; in ABDA the Allied forces were widely scattered, with a thousand miles between the farthest separated of them. "The situation out there is that certain particular strategic points have to be held," he said, "and the commander in each locality is quite clear as to what he should do. The difficult question is the application of resources arriving in the area. This is a matter which can only be settled by the Governments concerned."[23] Nor was he more inclined to accept the arrangement when it was made known to him that the man whom the Americans wished for the supreme command was the British General Wavell. The "honor" seemed to him an empty one since it required Wavell to preside over a theater of certain defeats and possible disaster.** But Roosevelt backed Marshall and so, if covertly, did Beaverbrook. Robert Sherwood records how Beaverbrook at the climactic moment of disagreement passed a note to Harry Hopkins saying: "You should work on Churchill. He is being advised. He is open-minded and needs discussion." Whereupon Hopkins arranged a private meeting between Churchill and Marshall, who convinced the Prime Minister of the merits of his proposal not only as regards the conduct of affairs in ABDA but also (and more importantly) as establishing a precedent for future Allied operations. Wavell was then appointed, the announcement being made simultaneously with that of the appointment of Generalissimo Chiang Kai-shek to Supreme Command of Allied Forces in the Chinese Theater.

The Americans shied away, too, from all proposed offensive operations which seemed to them "peripheral" or overly diffuse. If a proposed action could not be clearly perceived by them as an organic element or indispensable preliminary of the finally decisive one, they opposed it. They gave short shrift, for example, to Churchill's proposal for scattered landings of British and American forces "in several" European countries in the hope (overly slender, in American opinion) that the conquered peoples would then rise up in effective revolt against their oppressors. Nor were they much more favorably inclined at the outset toward GYMNAST or, as it was soon renamed, SUPER-GYMNAST—the occupation of North Africa proposed for the early spring of 1942. Roosevelt was intrigued by this, largely on political and psychological grounds: GYMNAST, providing early employment to American troops, would boost American morale, give needed battle experience to the armed forces, and encourage the suspicious Russians (already beginning to press for a "second front") to believe their Western allies intended to do everything possible at the earliest hour to relieve the intense Nazi pressure on the eastern front. American military professionals, however, emphasized the "difficulties of troop movements and logistical support by sea" of the operation (the quotation is from a memorandum to Marshall by Colonel Matthew B. Ridgway of the Army's War Plans Division, dated December 23, 1941) and doubted the strategic value of North Africa to the Allies. How or to what extent would its occupation con-

** The British Chiefs of Staff deemed the "honor" worse than empty—they suspected it was filled up with malice, being inspired by Roosevelt's desire to shift to British shoulders the responsibility for the tragedies which almost certainly impended. They unanimously favored an American for the ABDA supreme command, if supreme command there must be in that tormented area—an attitude which angered Churchill since it insulted the President and threatened Allied unity.

tribute to the final decision against Germany? Would it be worth its probable cost? Such doubts were reinforced a few days after Churchill's arrival in Washington by the fact that Auchinleck's offensive, for which the Prime Minister had had such high hopes, failed to produce the expected victories in the Libyan desert. Far from driving the Desert Fox westward in headlong retreat, after capturing large numbers of his troops, the British Eighth Army was forced by the end of December to stand against an astonishingly strong Rommel counterattack. Thus it became increasingly unlikely that Weygand or any other high French official under Vichy would welcome the Allies into North Africa.

Less controversial than GYMNAST was Churchill's request for American troops to be stationed in Northern Ireland. MAGNET, as this operation was coded, received final approval by Roosevelt and the Prime Minister on New Year's Day, 1942, and so did the movement of American Army units to Iceland (INDIGO) to release for duty elsewhere the British troops and U. S. Marines formerly stationed there. But even these relatively minor operations were viewed askance, in the light of events in the Far East, by key members of the American military. The Assistant Chief of the War Plans Division spoke irritably of the MAGNET decision on the very day it was made. Newly appointed Brigadier General Dwight D. Eisenhower wrote on his desk memorandum pad for January 1, 1942: "I've been insisting that the Far East is critical—and no sideshows should be undertaken until air and ground there are in satisfactory shape. Instead we are taking on Magnet, Gymnast, etc." Three days later he wrote on his memo pad: ". . . we've got to have ships—and we need them now! Tempers are short, there are a lot of amateur strategists on the job. I'd give anything to be back in the field."[24]

Certainly Eisenhower had good and sufficient reasons for his concern. They were urgent enough to force, very soon, an indefinite postponement of GYMNAST and a drastic downward revision in the initial scale of both INDIGO and MAGNET.

He had been summoned to Washington in the week following Pearl Harbor from Fort Sam Houston in San Antonio, Texas, where he had continued as Chief of Staff of the Third Army following the 1941 Louisiana Maneuvers. His specific assignment under his old friend Brigadier General Leonard T. Gerow, Chief of WPD, was the improvisation of a maximum possible support of the Philippines defense effort. It was a task for which he was fitted by the fact that for more than four years ending in mid-December 1939, he had been General Douglas MacArthur's chief assistant on detached service to the Philippine Commonwealth in Manila. There he had helped to plan defenses and train troops under the Philippine National Defense Act of 1935. The aim had been to make Philippine defenses so strong by 1946 that the cost of reducing them (an estimated half-million casualties and five billion dollars) would be prohibitive for Japan. Alas, this date of "full fruition" of the defense buildup was still a half-decade away. In the present circumstances the most that could be hoped for was a holding action that would upset the Japanese timetable and permit the organizing of effective defenses for the East Indies, Singapore, and Australasia.

Eisenhower's train had arrived at Washington's Union Station at seven o'clock Sunday morning, December 14, 1941. He was met there by his younger brother Milton, who for sixteen years had been a top administrator in the U. S. Department of Agriculture (he was the Department's Land-Use Coordinator in 1941) and in whose Falls Church, Virginia, home Dwight Eisenhower was to stay during his Washington assignment. Milton drove him at once to the old War Department building on Constitution Avenue (the Pentagon in that year was still abuilding) where he was succinctly but fully briefed on the Far Eastern situation, and on his own assignment, by Marshall himself.[25]

The Pacific Fleet had been so badly mauled at Pearl Harbor, said Marshall, that months must pass before it could engage in offensive operations. The carriers were still unharmed but they lacked the supporting vessels necessary for their full employment. Nor was Hawaii itself considered free from the danger of invasion: against this imminent possibility the battered Army garrison and the air forces there must be reinforced.

As for the Philippines, the situation there was every bit as desperate as Eisenhower had anticipated it would be. A bombing attack by the Japanese had severely damaged the Cavite Navy Yard, adjacent to Manila, on December 10. The U. S. Navy's Asiatic Fleet was no more than a task force whose strength was much too slight to interfere seriously with the buildup of Japanese invasion forces; its surface vessels were being withdrawn to prevent their destruction, leaving only submarines to harass (with probably negligible effect) Japanese shipping and naval units. Altogether General MacArthur, the Philippines commander, had in his entire theater a mere sixty thousand inadequately trained native troops, some eleven thousand first-rate Philippine Scouts, and approximately nineteen thousand U. S. Army troops with whose formations the Scouts were integrated. Outnumbered and unsupplied, these forces could not long deny to the Japanese, continuously reinforced and fully supplied, the conquest of the Philippines.

"Well, that's it," Marshall had concluded abruptly, looking hard at his subordinate. "What should be our general line of action?"

Eisenhower asked for a "few hours" in which to think about it.

When he returned to Marshall's office, according to his own account, he lay stress on "the psychological effects of the Philippine battle upon the people of the United States" and upon those of China, the Dutch East Indies, and the Philippines itself. "They may excuse failure but they will not excuse abandonment," he said to the Chief of Staff. "Their trust and friendship are important to us." He therefore proposed the establishment of an Allied base on Australia and the security of a line of communications to it at whatever cost might be required of money and risk. "In this . . . we dare not fail."[26] Marshall said merely that he agreed and told Eisenhower to go ahead with the proposal; but it was evident that he was pleased by this first effort of his new staff adviser on Far Eastern affairs. Eisenhower had thus far justified the high estimate of his abilities made by Pershing, Conner, and others under whom he had served in the past. He did the kind of thinking necessary at the very top of the chain of command, where psychological, political, and military considerations were necessarily fused, one with the others.

Three days later, on December 17, Marshall formally approved the "Plan for Australian Base" presented to him by Eisenhower in memorandum form.

Thereafter, the Assistant War Plans Chief was absorbed from early morning until late each night in the problems of establishing the Australian base and getting supplies from it to the beleaguered Philippine forces. A convoy of seven ships carrying troops, aircraft in crates, ammunition and other materiel, escorted by the cruiser U.S.S. *Pensacola*, was at sea Manila-bound on Pearl Harbor Day. It had then been redirected to Brisbane, Australia, where its arrival on December 22 marked the beginning of what was ultimately to become an enormous Allied base, the springboard for attacks to the north, though these seemed incredibly remote in the closing hours of 1941. On the following day, MacArthur made the hard decision to declare Manila an open city, withdraw all his forces on Luzon into the Bataan Peninsula, and establish his headquarters on the tiny fortified island of Corregidor—all this according to what had been designated long ago as War Plan Orange 3 (WPO-3). In the face of strong enemy pressures, the maneuver was exceedingly difficult. It required miracles of timing and coordinated movement on the part of initially scattered units, many of them untrained and operating under fire. Its swift accomplishment might be deemed a tactical victory to the extent that it denied to the enemy for months to come the use of Manila Bay, which was a principal fruit of a victory he believed he had won in the third week of December. But there was no hiding the fact that it was a last-ditch desperation move and it gave persuasive power to what MacArthur in a cable to the War Department, on December 28, called a "crescendo of enemy propaganda" used with "deadly effectiveness" on the Filipinos. "I am not in a position here to combat it," he said, in one of the great understatements of that year. Roosevelt responded with a proclamation to the people of the Philippines, renewing his "solemn pledge . . . that your freedom will be redeemed and your independence established and protected." Two days after, he sent a memorandum to Secretary of War Stimson saying: "I wish that War Plans would explore every possible means of relieving the Philippines. I realize great risks are involved but the objective is important."

No amount of "exploration" could discover "possible means" which did not exist, however, and Eisenhower, by the time he learned of Roosevelt's memo, was face to face with this bitter truth. He turned, perforce, to "impossible" means. A special fund of ten million in cash was provided for the purpose of hiring, at whatever fantastic fee, men with ships who were willing to attempt a running of the Japanese blockade, delivering desperately needed supplies to Bataan and Corregidor. A former Secretary of War, Brigadier General Patrick J. Hurley, was flown to Australia to supervise this bizarre enterprise. It failed. Only three of seven ships sailing from Australia reached Cebu, in the southern Philippines, whence all efforts to transship to the north were frustrated by Japanese control of the seas. Of the hired blockade runners, at least fifteen ships totaling forty thousand tons were either sunk or captured. Nor did the overage destroyers which were then assigned to blockade-running duty have more success. None of them reached Bataan. A few submarines managed to get through—and that was all. Bataan's defenders were on half rations (Filipino rations, at that) by mid-January, and Eisenhower was condemned to watch helplessly, sick at heart, the approaching doom of men who were his friends and with many of whom he had worked hopefully and hard across the very terrain of their present hopeless struggle.

Obviously the Allies had drastically underrated Japan's initial war making power. The Far Eastern situation as a whole had been sufficiently disturbing to them when Marshall first proposed a single supreme command for ABDA. By the second week of January it was actually terrifying to Allied students of global strategy, coupled as it must be with Rommel's imminent renewal of the attack toward Alexandria, Cairo, Suez, and (ultimately) the Middle East with all its riches of oil and strategic advantage. If Japanese and Nazi forces should meet on the plateau of Iran, what human power could deny them the conquest of all the Earth?

Wavell, it appeared, might soon become a supreme commander without a theater of command, for ABDA was being shattered into fragments by the incredibly swift hammerblows of Japan's army, navy, and air force working closely together as America's armed services had yet to learn to do. Singapore, that prime agent and symbol of European White Supremacy in the Orient, that "impregnable" bastion of Empire in the Far East—Singapore, it now appeared to astonished eyes, could not long be held. Sloth and smug complacency, born of a conviction of the essential inferiority of colored peoples, had prepared the ruin of this key citadel—if, indeed, it could properly be called a "citadel." The British had assumed that the Malayan jungle was impenetrable by troops armed with modern weapons, and had failed to consider the possibility of leapfrog amphibian attacks by an enemy who could dominate the air above small craft working close inshore. The same neglect of hostile possibilities had kept them from training troops for jungle fighting. Hence they were unable seriously to delay, much less to halt, the drive of some two hundred thousand highly trained Japanese jungle fighters down the Malay Peninsula toward Singapore's back door.

And the door itself stood wide open! There were no adequate defenses on the northern side of Singapore island. The reservoirs upon which the island's millions depended for their water supply lay naked to an attack from Johore, soon to be overrun by the Japanese, and so did the northern limits of Singapore town. All the heavy fortifications—the mighty guns, the formidable barricades—faced toward the sea!

This defensive lack was not yet known to Churchill on January 12, when the next-to-last major session of ARCADIA was convened in the White House. He has recorded the profound shock, the utter dismay with which he first learned of it upon his return to London early in January's third week. ". . . the possibility of Singapore having no landward defenses no more entered my mind than that of a battleship being launched without a bottom," he has written.[27] But he was of course acutely aware of the general deterioration of the Allied position in the Far East and he concurred in the decision, reached January 12, to divert most of the MAGNET-INDIGO convoy to ABDA, though this meant a postponement of SUPER-GYMNAST until the last of May at the earliest since the shipping needed for the North African operation could not be returned from the far Pacific before that time. Such a postponement was in any case indicated by the difficulties Auchinleck was now encountering with Rommel at the Egyptian border.

There was, however, no expressed wish at this meeting to shift the major strategic emphasis from the Atlantic to the Pacific. On the contrary, there was complete agreement among Roosevelt, Churchill, and the British and American Staffs that "only a minimum of forces necessary for safeguarding vital interests in other theaters should be diverted from operations against Germany." Thus the secret music of ARCADIA ended as it had begun, on a note of harmony.

iv. *In Mountainous ARCADIA the United Nations Is Born*

That it should so end would have come as no surprise to the general public, from whose eyes and ears every discussion of strategy was necessarily walled away. The public indeed would have been surprised to learn that seeds of discord were buried in the common ground, where some of them were already beginning to sprout—for in those aspects visible, those sounds audible to the great masses of Britain and the United States the conference demonstrated an Allied solidarity that was absolute and sacred.

Witness on 1941's Christmas Eve, as the public did, the ceremonial lighting of the national Christmas tree in the White House garden. Churchill joined Roosevelt in the ceremony, the two appearing side by side on the White House balcony whence they addressed a great throng assembled in the darkness below them while millions listened beside radio sets throughout the land. Introduced by the President as "my associate, my old and good friend," the Prime Minister addressed his listeners as "fellow workers in the cause of freedom," saying that though he was far from country and family on "this anniversary and festival" he did not feel far from home. "Whether it be the ties of blood on my mother's side," he said, referring to the fact that his mother was born a Langhorne of Virginia, "or the friendships I have developed here over many years of active life, or the commanding sentiments of comradeship in a common cause of great peoples who speak the same language, who kneel at the same altars, and, to a large extent, pursue the same ideals, I cannot feel myself a stranger here in the center and at the summit of the United States." Instead he felt that he had "a right to sit at your fireside and share your Christmas joys."

Next day, Christmas Day, he and the President went to church together, an interdenominational service, and sang together there a hymn the Prime Minister had never heard before, "O Little Town of Bethlehem," whose words, he confessed, stirred him deeply:

> Yet in thy dark streets shineth
> The everlasting light;
> The hopes and fears of all the years
> Are met in thee tonight.

Together they listened with bowed heads to a prayer in which the Prime Minister was spoken of as one who "continues to lead his valiant people even through blood and sweat and tears to a new world where men of good will may dwell together, none daring to molest or make afraid."[28]

Witness, too, as the public most emphatically did, the appearance of the Prime Minister before a joint session of the Congress of the United States on the day after Christmas. Republicans and Democrats alike laughed and cheered his opening words: "I cannot help reflecting that if my father had been American and my mother British, instead of the other way around, I might have got here on my own." Grave were his listener's faces as he said: "Twice in a single generation the catastrophe of world war has fallen upon us; twice in our lifetime has the long arm of Fate reached across the ocean to bring the United States into the forefront of battle. If we had kept together after the last war, if we had taken common measures for our safety, this renewal of the curse need never have fallen upon us. . . . Still, I avow my hope and faith, sure and inviolate, that in the days to come the British and American peoples will for their own safety and for the good of all walk together side by side in majesty, in justice, and in peace." Afterward, Congressional leaders of both Houses and parties crowded up to shake his hand, to praise him and his words, until the Secret Service men, whose zeal sometimes seemed to him excessive, closed around to conduct him in safety back to the White House.

And though the success of his Congressional address was immense, it was no greater than that of his speech four days later to the Canadian Parliament in Ottawa.

To the Parliament he spoke of Vichy and North Africa (the Canadian Government had galled Whitehall by continuing diplomatic relations with

Vichy); he raked over the yet-glowing embers of his resentment at the French Government's refusal to go to North Africa in 1940. "It was their duty and it was also their interest to go. . . . In Africa, with our aid, they would have had overwhelming sea power. . . . If they had done this, Italy might have been driven out of the war before the end of 1940, and France would have held her place as a nation in the councils of the Allies and at the conference tables of the victors. But their generals misled them. When I warned them that Britain would fight on alone whatever they did, their generals told their Prime Minister and his divided Cabinet, 'In three weeks England will have her neck wrung like a chicken.' " Churchill looked up across the lectern and the years, his jaw thrust out, his voice deepening. "Some chicken!" he growled. "Some neck!"

And was wildly cheered.

Thus, even before the old year had died, the public was encouraged by the two great leaders of the English-speaking world to view what was happening in Washington as the emergence of something more, a great deal more, than another international military alliance. An alliance, after all, implies discrete national entities with a space between them across which it operates. But in the present instance this space appeared to the public (was made to appear to the public) to be virtually annihilated. It was as if essential elements of nation-states that were formerly definite of outline, rock-hard of core, had been melted down in the fires of war and now flowed together in new and unprecedented forms. What obtained was no mere linkage of temporary convenience between the states but a union of them, a perpetual if partial union in which relations formerly external were internalized. ARCADIA might be likened to an iceberg floating in a sea of secrecy, with much of its bulk submerged and hidden from the public gaze, but it nevertheless thrust into the sun of publicity two high peaks of achievement. One—and it received far more publicity than the other at its inception—was the signing at the White House of a "Joint Declaration" by twenty-six nations on (aptly) New Year's Day 1942, an event which may be deemed the conception if not the beginning of the actual birth of the United Nations. The other was the creation of the "Combined Chiefs of Staff Committee," an unprecedented fusion of national command authorities into a single supreme authority through which the whole of the Allied military effort was thereafter directed.

The language of the "Joint Declaration" was a blending of two separate drafts, one prepared by Roosevelt, the other by Churchill. It was Roosevelt who substituted "United Nations" for the term "Associated Powers," theretofore used to designate the nations at war with the Axis. (Churchill then called to the President's attention a line from *Childe Harold's Pilgrimage* wherein Byron speaks of "the sword United Nations drew."[29] It was Roosevelt, too, at Harry Hopkins' insistence, who in a long, private session with Maxim Litvinov tried to persuade this newly appointed Soviet

Ambassador to the U.S. that the phrase "religious freedom" must appear in the Declaration as one of the goals for which the United Nations fought. (He succeeded to the extent that Litvinov finally asked Moscow for instructions on the point and was told by Stalin—"as a matter of course," in Churchill's words—that the phrase was acceptable.)

It was Churchill who, at the insistence of Labor members of the coalition Government he headed, inserted in the semi-final draft "social security" as one of the objectives for which the struggle against the Axis was being waged. He also tried to insert the word "authorities" in the sentence referring to the "Governments signatory hereto," his purpose being to open a way whereby De Gaulle's Free French could sign the document. Neither insertion remained, however, in the final draft. Apparently no great issue was made over "social security" which, as an "ideal," was clearly of a different order than the others listed, but the word "authorities" was much argued about when it met opposition from both Secretary of State Hull and Litvinov.

Hull had developed a personal antipathy to De Gaulle, whose concomitant was an insistence, against overwhelming evidence to the contrary, that the U.S. could influence Vichy against the Nazis. He felt personally insulted by the recent action of the Free French in seizing from Vichy, through bloodless naval action, the Western Hemispheric islands of St. Pierre and Miquelon, after De Gaulle under State Department pressure had promised not to do so. The Free French had been enthusiastically welcomed by the islanders, of whom 90 per cent voted against Vichy in a plebiscite, and the action was hardly less enthusiastically applauded by the American public. Hull, however, had issued a statement on Christmas Day in which he branded "arbitrary" the "action taken by the so-called Free French," said it was "contrary to the agreement of all parties concerned," and added that the Canadian Government was being queried by "this Government . . . as to the steps that government is prepared to take to restore the status quo of these islands."†† This provoked such a storm of popular anger against Hull and his "so-called State Department" as he had never faced before, and Hull, smarting under it, was in no mood to permit the entrance of Free France into the United Nations in any guise whatever. The President, however, shrugged this off: the incident seemed to him relatively trivial, and Hull's attitude petulant to the point of absurdity. He overruled the Secretary's opposition to Churchill's desire for the insertion in the United Nations Declaration of the term "authorities."[30]

Litvinov's opposition, however, was decisive. He had no grounds for it save that Moscow had by then approved the document, and he as Ambassador had no authority to agree to further textual changes in it. After a somewhat heated argument with Churchill, he is said to have asked for, and received, approval of the insertion from his Government, but if so

†† This incident gave special significance to Churchill's Ottawa speech of December 30, in which he excoriated Vichy and praised the Free French.

the approval arrived too late. The document had by then been signed, and Churchill had sent an explanatory message to the War Cabinet in which he said that "Litvinov is a mere automaton, evidently frightened out of his wits by what he had gone through."

The full text of the final draft was as follows:

A Joint Declaration by the United States of America, the United Kingdom of Great Britain and Northern Ireland, the Union of Soviet Socialist Republics, China, Australia, Belgium, Canada, Costa Rica, Cuba, Czechoslovakia, the Dominican Republic, El Salvador, Greece, Guatemala, Haiti, Honduras, India, Luxembourg, the Netherlands, New Zealand, Nicaragua, Norway, Panama, Poland, South Africa, and Yugoslavia. The Governments signatory hereto,

Having subscribed to a common program of purposes and principles embodied in the Joint Declaration of the President of the United States of America and the Prime Minister of the United Kingdom of Great Britain and Northern Ireland, dated August 14, 1941, known as the Atlantic Charter,

Being convinced that complete victory over their enemies is essential to defend life, liberty, independence, and religious freedom, and to preserve human rights and justice in their own lands as well as in other lands, and that they are now engaged in a common struggle against savage and brutal forces seeking to subjugate the world, DECLARE:

(1) Each Government pledges itself to employ its full resources, military or economic, against those members of the Tri-Partite Pact and its adherents with which such Government is at war.

(2) Each Government pledges itself to cooperate with the Governments signatory hereto, and not to make a separate armistice or peace with the enemies.

The foregoing declaration may be adhered to by other Nations which are, or may be, rendering material assistance and contributions to the struggle for victory over Hitlerism.‡‡

As for the second of the great public achievements of ARCADIA, namely the creation of the Combined Chiefs of Staff, it would seem in retrospect a natural and hence inevitable evolution out of the Anglo-American staff talks of the year before; since it was an obvious historical necessity, dictated by circumstance, the arrangement was bound to be made—

But was it?

One has only to compare what happened in Washington in early 1942, as regards provisions for the supreme direction of a coalition war, with what happened in France in the spring of 1918 to see how false is this ascription to circumstance of a causal efficacy which, in actual fact, in-

‡‡ The closing sentence incorporated a change made in the original text by Moscow. As first drafted, the sentence had referred to "contributions toward the defeat of members or adherents of the Tri-Partite Pact," and the Russians had feared their signing it might commit them to war against Japan at a time when they were fighting for their lives against Germany. In any case, said Litvinov, "Hitlerism" in his country meant Italian Fascism and Japanese militarism as well as German Naziism.

volved a character-testing, intelligence-testing decisiveness on the part of individual men. The situation on the First World War's Western Front "demanded" a unified Allied command from the moment Germany invaded Belgium in August 1914. Yet no serious effort toward such unification was made through three and a half years of bloody stalemate. And even when the attempt was at last made, its achievement—that is, the degree and efficiency of the unification achieved—fell considerably short of the need which had "dictated" it. The Beauvais Agreement under which Foch operated as supreme commander through the closing months of World War I made a distinction, difficult to define in words and almost impossible to define in action, between the "strategic direction" of military operations and the "tactical employment" of military forces. Foch was "entrusted" with the former while "full control" of the latter was retained by British, French, and American commanders-in-chief. Each national commander, moreover, had the right of appeal to his Government if, in his opinion, the safety of his army or the over-all interests of his country was compromised by any order of Foch's. The whole arrangement reflected the human natures and free choices of Clemenceau and Foch, of Lloyd George and Haig, no less than it did the general situation inciting it—and it was flawed with ambiguity. If 1942's Combined Chiefs of Staff was not similarly flawed the credit is due, not to blind-and-deaf circumstance, but to a small handful of men who in mountainous ARCADIA displayed acute intelligence and high moral courage at the ultimate peak of decision.

For it was by no means a foregone conclusion that a truly unified supreme command, rigorously guarded against a dispersal of its powers through the competing channels of economics and politics, would be set up in the Washington of January 1942. On the contrary, the force of circumstance operating through Churchill *vis-à-vis* Roosevelt would seem to have dictated a much looser and less authoritative arrangement. There was, for instance, the ticklish question of where the headquarters of the supreme command, if established, should be located. Should it be in London? Or in Washington? The latter place was indicated by the fact that it was geographically placed between the Pacific and Atlantic war zones, was safe from enemy air attacks, and was the capital of the ally who must furnish the bulk of the manpower and industrial production with which the decisive blows would be struck. But a frank and open recognition of this last point was difficult for the British, who had stood for a long year alone against the European Axis, who were still bearing the brunt of the battle in the West, and who were accustomed by history to regarding themselves as a world power second to none. Small wonder, therefore, that two such canny international politicians as Churchill and Rooosevelt should wish to avoid meeting the question head-on, if such avoidance were at all possible. Small wonder that the general belief in high circles, when ARCADIA opened, was that what would emerge as the top international military organization would be (in Robert Sherwood's words) "a sort of joint secretariat to pool records and intelligence and serve as liaison between the British Chiefs in London and their American opposite numbers."[31]

Marshall, more than any other single man, seems to have been responsible for the very different organization that actually emerged. The American Staff Chief made it essentially the same argument he had made for the establishment of a single supreme command over ABDA. Liaison was not enough, he said. Cooperation was not enough. Look, for horrid example, at what happened to Pearl Harbor! The Japanese had hit and run, leaving ruin in their wake, before the arrangements for "cooperation" between Army and Navy had begun to work—and this despite the close physical proximity of Kimmel and Short! There was simply no margin of time or resources, for the Western Allies of 1942, within which disagreements between linked staffs could be settled. Ergo, the staffs must be welded into one. . . . Once made, the argument encountered no effective resistance. The "logic of the situation" was all on its side. But a historian of process must insist that the argument might *not* have been made with sufficient persuasiveness by an officer of sufficient stature at that moment of "necessity." If the force of circumstance prevailed, it was in large part because it was joined by the force of Marshall's mind and character.

Even greater was his decisive importance in the days immediately following the formal establishment of the Combined Chiefs organization. The American members at the outset were Marshall in his capacity as Army Chief of Staff; Lieutenant General Henry H. (Hap) Arnold, Commanding General of the Army Air Forces and Deputy Chief of Staff for Air; Admiral Stark in his capacity as Chief of Naval Operations; and Admiral Ernest J. King, Commander in Chief of the U. S. Fleet.§§ The British members were General Sir Alan Brooke, Chief of the Imperial General Staff; Admiral Sir Dudley Pound, First Sea Lord; and Air Chief Marshal Sir Charles Portal, Chief of the Air Staff. Since the British Chiefs necessarily maintained their headquarters in London, close to their own Government, they were represented by officers of high rank stationed permanently in Washington but maintaining "daily, and indeed hourly, touch with London," as Churchill said.[32] Also a member of the Combined Chiefs, stationed in Washington, was Field Marshal Sir John Dill, former Chief of the Imperial General Staff, who was designated the personal representative of the Prime Minister.

Marshall, and indeed all others in key positions both in Washington and London, would come to regard the Dill appointment as a most fortunate one. The field marshal was a man of high abilities and warm

§§ There was at this time no American organization equivalent to the British Chiefs of Staff Committee, but when one was established as the Joint Chiefs of Staff (March 1942) the two offices formerly held by Stark and King were combined under King while Stark went to London to take command of U. S. Naval Forces in Europe.

personality—tactful, discreet, selfless—who soon commanded Roosevelt's confidence no less than Churchill's and was perfectly equipped in the military sphere to interpret the British to the Americans and the Americans to the British in ways that reduced, when it did not eliminate, friction between them. The feeling that the Americans developed toward him would be indicated by the fact that when he died in 1944, following a long illness, he was buried among American heroes in Arlington National Cemetery. But when the appointment was first made, Marshall was highly critical of it, not out of any dislike for Dill as a man (he liked him from the first) but as a matter of policy. As active agent of Britain's political head, Dill must operate on a level different from that of the British and American Service Chiefs, Marshall thought, and the distinction between political and military authority, which he was concerned to make as definite as possible, would be blurred. The objection was effective. After returning to London, Churchill was required to set forth by cable clear terms of reference for Dill in Washington, excluding from the latter's field of authority all matters save those which were the common responsibility of the Staff Chiefs.[33]

At the same time as he insisted upon a rigorous exclusion of all nonmilitary concerns from the Combined Chiefs' sphere of responsible action, Marshall insisted upon the *inclusion* of all that was necessary to secure its full authority over the military conduct of the war. This involved him in a historically significant controversy over the setting up of what became known as the Munitions Assignment Board, whose function was to allocate materiel among armies and theaters of war.

Let us look in upon a scene in the White House's Oval Study late in the Wednesday afternoon of January 14, just before the opening of the last formal session of ARCADIA[34]:

The President, lounging back in his chair, his cigarette tipped upward jauntily in it long holder, lifts a paper from the cluttered desk before him. He looks at Harry Hopkins, who sits like a collapsed scarecrow, cloth-draped sticks below thin, pale face with burning eyes, in a chair drawn up on the other side of the desk. He looks at blunt-faced General Marshall, militarily erect in another chair before him. It is to Marshall that he directs his words as, having crushed out his cigarette, he reads slowly, distinctly, from the paper in his hands.

The document, as Marshall knows, is the result of an effort by Roosevelt and Churchill to resolve the sharp issue that has arisen between the British and American Chiefs of Staff regarding the designated authority of the proposed Munitions Board. Such a unified international board—and others dealing with shipping, food, production and resources, raw materials—is clearly indicated by the establishment of the Combined Chiefs. The British Chiefs have proposed, for munitions, an allocation system whereby Britain and the United States would each have certain "protegé" countries "for which it has accepted responsibility." Protegés of the United States would be the Latin American countries and China. Protegés of Britain would be the countries of Continental Europe including France (Free France), the countries of the Middle East including Turkey, and of course the British Dominions and colonies.

To Marshall, this British proposal seems an obvious attempt to deny real substance to the accepted concept of the Combined Chiefs organization. It means that the allocation of American-produced materiel throughout the admittedly crucial theater of global war would be directed from London; its net effect would be the retention in British hands of supreme command over the Allied war. He therefore listens intently, outwardly impassive, to the words Roosevelt reads. He assumes as he listens that these words have been concurred in by both Beaverbrook and Hopkins, and this does nothing to soothe the feelings of anxiety, and even of outrage, which rise in him as the reading proceeds. What Roosevelt and Churchill now propose is that Munitions Assignment be divided between two equal agencies, one to be headquartered in London and directed by Beaverbrook, the other in Washington and directed by Hopkins. Beaverbrook would report directly to the Prime Minister, Hopkins to the President.

The reading finished, Roosevelt places the paper on his desk and looks at his Army Chief of Staff. He invites comment. And Marshall, looking hard at his Commander-in-Chief, minces no words. His opposition to this proposed arrangement is absolute and unalterable; so great is it, in fact, that he will feel compelled to tender his resignation as Chief of Staff if the proposal is finally accepted. The allocation of munitions, involving the assignment of priorities among war theaters, is obviously an intrinsic element of grand strategy. How can any commander direct any campaign unless he has full control of the materiel needed to fight it? To place munitions assignment in independent agencies operating on the same level as the Combined Chiefs is to prevent a proper functioning of the latter.

Well, then, asks Roosevelt, what does Marshall propose?

And Marshall, replying, does more than propose; he *insists* that the Munitions Assignment Board be clearly and completely subordinate to the Combined Chiefs of Staff. His resignation is the alternative.

Then Roosevelt turns to Hopkins who, much to the general's surprise, reveals that he has not, after all, had a hand in the preparation of this Roosevelt-Churchill proposal. Beaverbrook may have been consulted, probably has been, but Hopkins evidently has not. For Hopkins' scarecrow body is now pulled upright in his chair, as if by the force of mind-and-feeling that blazes in his dark eyes, as he vehemently supports Marshall's position, saying that if things are not arranged as Marshall says they should be, he himself cannot accept any responsibility in the matter; he'll refuse to serve as head of the proposed Washington office.

If Roosevelt does not squirm visibly in his chair as he faces the hours immediately ahead of him, he must squirm inwardly. What Marshall and

Hopkins insist upon is nothing less than a public recognition and acceptance by the British of the fact that London is no longer the capital, the power center of the English-speaking world. Washington is. And however great the emphasis upon the Combined Chiefs and subordinated Combined Boards of various kinds as a pooling of national sovereignties to form a federal "union," a kind of two-in-one "third power" superior to each of its members, the fact remains clear that the greater part of this pooled sovereignty is, in origin and in terms of actual power, American. The preponderance of administrative force is American. The upcoming session, in which this fact is to be underscored, cannot fail to be painfully embarrassing to Churchill, Beaverbrook, and the British Chiefs; and it can be but slightly less so to Roosevelt personally since, if he backs Marshall and Hopkins (and he can hardly do otherwise in the circumstances), he will be placed in the position of demanding for himself the top direction of the joint war effort. No doubt he is casting around in his mind for some device to save face for the British when the door opens to admit the Prime Minister, the British Minister of Supply, the staffs, the U. S. Secretaries of War and Navy, and the others who participate in ARCADIA's plenary sessions.

But no face-saving device presents itself. The meeting, opening at 5:30 in the afternoon (darkness falls outside the windows), becomes quickly as embarrassing as Roosevelt has feared it would be. Marshall reiterates his insistence that the Munitions Assignment Board function as a subcommittee of the Combined Chiefs. Hopkins reiterates his uncompromising support of Marshall. And Roosevelt is forced to indicate, if diffidently, that he sides with his Army Staff Chief and his principal personal assistant. Churchill and Beaverbrook argue vehemently, but the most they can gain is a seeming postponement of the final decision. They finally suggest that the American-proposed "system be set up and tried for one month," the Board to be a single agency headquartered in Washington with Hopkins as its chairman, its acts to be (as Hopkins again insists) simply "recommendations" to the Combined Chiefs who, if they do not like them, "can alter them or throw them out." Roosevelt, perhaps with an inward sigh of relief, is quick to accept this suggestion. "We shall call it a preliminary agreement," says he, "and try it out that way." For there is small doubt in his mind, and none at all in Marshall's, that the "preliminary agreement" is in actuality the final one. And so it will prove to be. Established on a one-month trial basis, the "system" is destined to persist to the end of the war.

Thus was substantial directing power firmly invested in what might otherwise have been a mere form. And the power and effectiveness of the Combined Chiefs would grow with exercise as the war continued. Before the war ended the Combined Chiefs would hold some two hundred formal meetings, eighty-nine of them face-to-face meetings of British and American principals at conferences where Roosevelt and Churchill were also present at least part of the time—conferences in such far places as Casablanca, Teheran, Cairo, the Crimea. Nor was the historical significance of this development unperceived by those who were most intimately involved in it.

"I had little faith in this organization at the time [it was set up]," Sir Alan Brooke, Chief of the Imperial General Staff, would later write,[35] "I think mainly due to the fact that it had been set up in Washington with the U.S.A. as the predominant partner whilst they had . . . not much knowledge in the running of a war and certainly little experience. My views altered completely as time went on and I grew to have the greatest faith in the Combined Chiefs of Staff organization as the most efficient that had ever been evolved for coordinating and correlating the war strategy and effort of two allies."

Speaking at Harvard, where he was awarded an honorary degree in early September 1943, Winston Churchill stressed the historic significance of the Combined Chiefs even more strongly. He said: "This Committee, with its elaborate organization of Staff officers of every grade, disposes of all our resources, and in practice uses British and American troops, ships, aircraft and munitions just as if they were the resources of a single state or nation. . . . This is a wonderful system. There was nothing like it in the last war. There never has been anything like it between two allies. . . . Now in my opinion it would be a most foolish and improvident act on the part of our two Governments, or either of them, to break up this smooth-running and immensely powerful machinery the moment the war is over. For our own safety, as well as for the security of the rest of the world, we are bound to keep it working and in running order after the war—probably for a good many years, not only until we have set up some world arrangement to keep the peace, but until we know that it is an arrangement which will really give us that protection we must have from danger and aggression, a protection we have already had to seek across two vast world wars."[36]

VI

The Heroism and Economics of War

i. *Agony on the Rock: Corregidor, May 5–6, 1942*

He had always been thin. His nickname had been "Skinny" since long before he entered West Point as a youth of eighteen, forty years ago. But never since he reached his full growth had there been less flesh on his bones than there now was. Nearly four months of meager rations, of far less sleep than usual, of such strains upon every fiber of his being as few men are required to bear, these had refined him to his essence. His essence was military. It was as *soldier*, professional soldier—just that, virtually nothing else—that he limped now along the dank stone corridor of Malinta Tunnel, leaning a little on the cane General MacArthur had given him when MacArthur departed this Rock of torment.

He walked amidst pain and death: passing the entrance to the hospital quarters, he could hear the faint moans of wounded men, some of whom must soon die. He walked toward pain and death: his destination was an observation post near the east entrance to the tunnel whence he must soon watch shells bursting along the island's only shore, killing and maiming his troops and shattering what was left of defenses never adequate against a Japanese attack across the narrow waters that separated Corregidor from the foot of Bataan. He walked beyond the bounds of hope: there was no glimmer of light at the end of this gloomy tunnel, only terror-filled darkness from which any man might by instinct shrink away. There were almost no outer props at all to sustain a flagging spirit. He was thrown upon inner resources, and even these, he might feel, were near to being used up as harsh experience clawed away one layer after another of his inwardness.

The military tradition and the West Point code, for instance, had been for him a major resource. It was his by heritage. Two former Jonathan M. Wainwrights had died in battle against enemies of the Republic—his paternal grandfather, a member of the first class ever to graduate from

Annapolis, had been killed in Galveston Harbor on New Year's Day 1863 while commanding the U.S.S. *Harriet Lane;* his Uncle Jonathan, ensign on the U.S.S. *Mohican,* had been killed in action against a pirate vessel off the coast of Mexico in 1871. His father, Robert Wainwright, had been a West Point cadet at the time Uncle Jonathan died. A certain inevitability therefore characterized his own entrance into the Military Academy as Cadet Jonathan M. Wainwright IV. Since boyhood he had been dedicated to the code of Duty, Honor, Country, knowing it as not only the code of West Point but also of the Spartans at Thermopylae ("O passer-by, tell the Lacedmonians that we lie here in obedience to their laws") and of the Texans in the Alamo ("Thermopylae had its messenger of defeat, the Alamo had none"); of the knights of medieval chivalry, and of Saladin at Jerusalem in 1187. It required of a man that he stand and fight to the death whenever his commander ordered him to do so or whenever he himself knew that, in terms of the over-all battle, his life was more expendable than the position he held and the time he gained for his comrades-in-arms by holding it. It also required him to deal humanely, magnanimously with wounded or vanquished foes. These were the rules of war.

But General Wainwright, commander of American forces on Bataan, driven back step by bloody step to a final defense line barely ten miles from the peninsula's southern tip, must confess that in early February of '42 the "old rules of war began to undergo a swift change in me."[1]

In late January, some fifteen hundred Japanese troops had been landed at Quianuan Point on the west coast of Bataan, far behind the American line. They had been landed against an alert defense that covered them with heavy fire; hundreds of them had been killed during the landing operations, and those who remained were quickly pocketed. Their position was hopeless since no arrangements had been made for their evacuation by sea. Nevertheless they fought on, inflicting hideous casualties upon the Americans in the process of being killed themselves (some companies of Philippine Scouts lost 50 per cent of their men in a few days of this action) before the last remnants of them were driven to the edge of the South China Sea where they took refuge in a cave washed out by water erosion into the base of a sheer cliff. There they could no longer offer effective resistance. They had no alternative to surrender save death, and their deaths could serve no useful purpose.

Yet they refused to surrender!

Wainwright had found this impossible to believe when it was first reported to him. ". . . You must remember that these were the early days of our war with Japan," he later explained, "and the men in that cave were some of the first Japs—if not *the* first—thus pocketed." At his orders, another opportunity for honorable surrender was given the trapped soldiers; they fired upon the troops who brought the offer. It was then necessary to have a gunboat shell the cave from the sea while engineers ashore lowered electrically fused mines from the top of the cliff, blasting the trapped men into bloody bits. A single dazed prisoner was taken. "It had at last dawned on me, as it was to dawn on so many commanders who followed me in the Pacific war, that a Jap usually prefers death to surrender."[2]

Usually!

To this discovery a Western soldier, however brave, might respond with some dismay. Certainly no fighting man's morale could be raised by his contemplation of an enemy of disciplined millions, armed with every weapon of Western science, to whom Thermopylaes and Alamos were nothing extraordinary—commonplace, in fact—and who was prepared to duplicate them at any time as a matter of course. Such toughness in an enemy lessened one's own chances of survival.

The dismay, however, had a deeper root than this. Involved in it was a strong if undefined feeling that the cave of Quianuan somehow degraded and befouled the meaning of Thermopylae and Alamo, calling into question the code by which Spartans and Texans had fought and died. For if the act of ferocious self-sacrifice was glorious in the cavern-like rooms of a Franciscan Texas mission in 1836, how could it be (as it seemed) a kind of obscenity in the cave by the South China Sea in 1942? If it was the highest heroism in the former place, arousing profound admiration, how could it be (as it seemed) an inhuman fanaticism in the latter, arousing only disgust? Faced by such questions, one either doubted the validity of the value-scale by which human glory and heroism are measured, or he doubted that the Japanese soldier was a creature who could be judged in human terms. In either case, important portions of the ancient code did not apply in the present conflict.

And of the above alternatives, it was the last which most of the Americans on Bataan and Corregidor were inclined to accept. To them the Japanese soldier was a beast who ran with the pack, as wolves do, and who was actually fused or identified with his social function, as ants are. He had no respect for individual life, his own or anyone else's. He existed and acted almost wholly en masse—as a creature of instinct rather than intelligence. He was capable of a solitary viciousness, like a mad dog's, but even when physically detached from the man-swarm, the teeming yet single organism which was his militaristic state, he remained an integral part of it. His appetite for death was insatiable. If you paused to help him as he lay wounded on the battlefield, like as not one of his fellows feigning death nearby would spring up to shoot or bayonet you, knowing and not caring that this would mean not only the loss of his own life but also of the lives of future wounded Japanese who might otherwise have been saved. If you surrendered to him, if he had you wholly within his power, he would starve you, beat you, torture you, like as not kill you, for no reason save his delight in the infliction of pain and death.

For this view of the enemy, for these conclusions as to his nature, an abundance of bitter tangible evidence had accumulated since the noon hour of last December 8 (December 7, Pearl Harbor time) when General Wainwright had seen his first action of this war. He had that day watched some eighty Japanese bombers unload on Clark Field where—despite hours of warning from Pearl Harbor, despite the example provided by Hickam Field—virtually every American plane was caught and destroyed on the ground. A sense of helplessness had gripped him then—and this, with a growing hopelessness joined to it, had become a prevailing part of his mood during the days and weeks and months which, since then, had flowed together in his remembering mind to freeze as an almost solid mass of pain and weariness, horror and despair. No small part of the horror was the impression made upon him by enemy actions.

Take, for instance, the action of the enemy against Philippine Scout positions on the Abucay Line, on the moon-drenched night of January 11–12. Japanese troops shouting "*Banzai*" had rushed forward from a cane field into murderous American fire and had flung themselves upon barbed wire before the Scout positions, deliberately offering their dead bodies as stepladders over the wire for the Japanese who followed them. Was this "courage" by the Western definition of the term? No American was likely to think so. It seemed an action contemptuous not of death but of life, since (as the enemy must have known) the Abucay Line was by then indefensible and would soon be abandoned. It was doubtful that so much as an hour's time was gained by the wanton self-immolation of those *Banzai* attackers. Next morning, when the full light of day had come to that sector, a Philippine Scout was fatally shot by a Japanese who, playing dead, had watched the Americans bandage a badly wounded fellow Japanese.

Far more horrible than these incidents, however—and more convincing evidence of the enemy's bestiality—was the treatment meted out to the seventy-six thousand Filipino and American troops in Bataan (twelve thousand of them from the United States) who—starved, sick, exhausted, driven into a position where further fighting would have meant useless loss of life—at last surrendered to the Japanese on April 9. The full story was of course not known to the general as he limped this May night along Malinta Tunnel, but enough was known to provide a clue to the rest. Some who had escaped their captors had managed to reach Corregidor; the story they had to tell of enemy savagery was almost incredible, yet undeniably true.

On April 15, six days after the surrender, there had begun what would become known to the world as the Death March of Bataan. Despite their terrible physical condition, the prisoners were driven on forced march under a tropic sun from Mariveles at the southern tip of Bataan to the railroad line at San Fernando—some sixty miles—and were then jammed into inadequately ventilated freight cars for transport to a point seven miles from Camp O'Donnell, which had been transformed into a prison stockade. They staggered into the camp, utterly exhausted. The whole of the journey was a nightmare. Men who fell exhausted on the road were beaten, prodded with bayonets—often clubbed or stabbed or shot to death. At the slightest provocation, or with none at all, they were beaten. Many who, thirst-crazed (for the Japanese had confiscated their aluminum canteens), broke line in order to drink foul water from roadside ditches had their brains beaten out with rifle butts. At one stage, those far down the line of march saw scores of headless corpses scattered along miles of road, victims of Japanese swords. There were men, not a few men, who halted by the roadside to relieve themselves (about half the troops suffered from dysentery) and were ordered by their guards to eat their excrement. They were killed if they refused to do so. Of the seventy thousand who began the march, only fifty-four thousand reached the Camp O'Donnell; some had escaped along the way, but around ten thousand had died. Nor was a happier fate in store for those who made it to the camp. It was unprepared for the numbers crammed into it. The water supplies and facilities for sanitation were inadequate, the prisoners were fed a starvation diet, and the guards were brutal beyond belief. In the three months following their arrival there, more than 40 per cent of the Death March survivors were doomed to die of disease, starvation, torture, and wanton murder.[3]

Yes, from all this it was easy to conclude that the Japanese were not human creatures, hence not to be judged in human terms: the code did not apply to them and could not be called into question by their conduct.

But this was not the whole of the evidence, even as regards the prisoners of Bataan, some few of whom (it appeared) had been treated with little more harshness than harsh circumstance imposed, had been fed enough to prevent actual starvation, had been given enough safe water to prevent maddening thirst, and had personally witnessed few acts of barbarism throughout the whole of their long march to San Fernando. Moreover, even those escapees who had suffered the worst cruelties could report valid if rare instances of kind acts, merciful acts, perpetrated by men as incontestably Japanese as the most sadistic of the guards. There were officers who, passing by, ordered a halt to the cruelties and apologized to the prisoners for the treatment given them. Kindness, indeed, was the rule among the guards who shepherded the sick, exhausted men from the freight cars along the last few miles of hot dusty road that separated the railroad from the camp.

The Japanese, then, as type, must be judged to be at least intermittently human, even humane—which is to say he was not, after all, wholly a type whose existence derived from and depended upon the organized State. He was instead a composite of individuals who might in some respects vary more widely among themselves than Americans did—might, in these respects, have more "individuality"—since the extremes of possible action and hence of self-definition were for them, it seemed, so much wider than for us. (Consider the moral and aesthetic distance separating the Japanese tea ceremony—so exquisitely beautiful, so sensitively polite—from the actions of those soldiers of the Rising Sun who killed helpless captives for refusing to eat feces! Yet both operations were permitted, even encouraged within the Japanese culture.) And once this admission of the enemy's human quality was made, a door was opened to all those doubts which one had sought to exclude, unconsciously perhaps, because they ate at the very roots of the Western soldier's code and tradition. For if the Jap was human—as human as the American, though different in ways and outlook—then his flinging of himself upon the barbed wire of the Abucay Line, his insistence upon being killed in the Quianuan cave, these *did* cheapen the values and challenge the universal validity of Thermopylae and Alamo. They did so to the degree that they seemed to the Western man a travesty of "glory," an ugly fanaticism, an obscene expression of a love for death. To this precise degree the ancient code and tradition were shown to be, not the absolutes they had theretofore appeared to be, but (instead) relativities whose validity derived, ultimately, from something outside themselves.

And so another and very deep layer of inwardness, another seemingly basic psychic resource, was clawed away . . .

The doomed Americans on this Rock were now stripped almost naked of belief in anything outside themselves. Outside their *essential* selves. General Wainwright himself might hesitate to ask why he and they now did as they did since the "why," insofar as it called for a statement of external purpose, had no clear answer. One behaved now as a brave soldier in extremity because this was the way a brave soldier in extremity behaved. There was no other reason: the "why" was identical with the act; nor was there any choice save, perhaps, in the vital attitude one took toward his inevitable fate—though even this seemed to be determined by what one *was*, as if it were part and parcel of one's essential nature.

And for most of those who had suffered Bataan and now suffered Corregidor, the attitude was one of defiance, grim and rock-hard but not without a certain peculiar gaiety, a certain wild wry humor. At its core was a kind of fierce pride in being able to "take it." Frank Hewlett, war correspondent, had caught some of this in a piece of rude doggerel he had composed in late January when the Americans were executing their dangerous withdrawal from Abucay to a final Bataan defense line some eight or ten miles to the south:

> We're the battling bastards of Bataan
> No momma, no poppa, no Uncle Sam
> No aunts, no uncles, no nephews, no nieces,
> No rifles, no guns or artillery pieces,
> And nobody gives a damn.[4]

The lines had been often quoted by General Wainwright, aloud and to himself. Others quoted the far more felicitous verse of a junior officer in the Headquarters Company of the Philippine Division, composed at the same time as Hewlett's doggerel. Bataan, wrote Lieutenant Henry G.

Lee,[5] had been saved by the successful retreat and reformation in a more defensible line—

> . . . saved for another day
> Saved for hunger and wounds and heat
> For slow exhaustion and grim retreat
> For a wasted hope and sure defeat. . .

But though they felt themselves forsaken, ignored, and abandoned by those for whom they suffered and died—though they were indeed convinced that "nobody gives a damn"—they continued to perform to the best of their ability under extreme pressures. They would maintain their stubborn integrity to the end, knowing how very bitter the end might be, despite the lack of "a reason why." And this, too, Lieutenant Lee had put into words:

> I see no gleam of victory alluring
> No chance of splendid booty or gain.
> If I endure—I must go on enduring.
> And my reward for bearing pain—is pain.
> Yet, though the thrill, the zest, the hope are gone
> Something within me keeps me fighting on.

All this, or much of it, might have been seen in the general's face and figure by a sensitive and knowledgeable observer from the world beyond this beleaguered island, had such an observer witnessed the general's limping progress down the stone corridor. In his precarious narrow verticality was a grim refusal of the horizontal, a stubborn refusal to be flattened. His trousers flapped around knifelike shanks. His shirt hung loosely down from narrow bony shoulders on each of which were three stars (he had been a Lieutenant General since March 19, when he was designated Commander-in-Chief of United States Forces in the Philippines) over a chest in which every rib was visible when his shirt was off. Above his opened collar, his neck with its stringy muscles and relatively huge Adam's apple seemed too scrawny to hold up, as it did, his long, thin, acid-looking face with its tight little chin and thin mouth and sharp, thin nose; with its pouched eyes from the corners of which deep squint lines radiated; with its puckered forehead and oversized ears, one of which was deaf now, the eardrum having been burst a few days before by the explosion of a shell at the Tunnel entrance; and with its thin, hollowed cheeks down each of which curved from eye to jaw a seam so deep it looked as if a knife might have cut it in flesh too rough, too leathery to bleed.

He went out the Tunnel entrance, out into the hot, dark night; clouds hid the almost full moon. He climbed effortfully into his observation post and looked away to the north, waiting. He knew he would not have to wait long.

All through these last hellish days evidence had mounted that the long-feared invasion from the mainland was imminent. In Manila a Philippine

Army officer operating a clandestine radio broadcasting unit—risking torture and death—had reported the completion by the Japanese Fourth Division of landing maneuvers near what had been the U. S. Naval Base at Cavite, across Manila Bay from Bataan, and had also reported the construction by the Japanese of many thousands of bamboo ladders, obviously designed for use upon the cliffs of Corregidor. Even without such direct secret intelligence, the imminence of invasion would have been clearly indicated by the increased tempo of the air bombardment and artillery shelling of the fortress island. Six days ago, on April 29, the birthday of Japanese Emperor Hirohito, a theretofore unprecedented concentration of artillery fire had blown up two artillery dumps—and though it had seemed impossible that the intensity of fire could be increased from this high pitch, it actually had been during the days since then. There were two key batteries on the island whose silencing was essential to the success of a Japanese invasion attempt; all but a couple of the ten-ton mortars in one of them had been destroyed by May 2, and on that day seven of the eight mortars in the other were blown to pieces (one huge mortar barrel landed on a golf course a full hundred yards away) when a high-angled howitzer shell exploded the battery's powder room.

Two days, later, May 4, the shelling had reached an almost incredible intensity. In five hours no less than thirty-six hundred shells, each weighing five hundred pounds, had fallen on Corregidor at a steady drum-fire rate of one every five seconds, twelve every minute—enough shells to fill six hundred trucks with a weight of 1,800,000 pounds, according to calculations made (to "amuse" themselves) by Wainwright and his principal subordinate, Major General George F. Moore. In twenty-four hours some sixteen thousand enemy shells had exploded on the island. Long before this ordeal ended every one of the thousand beds in the Malinta Tunnel hospital was filled; hundreds of shell-wounded were laid out in makeshift beds in the aisles. Obviously all this was the climactic "softening up" of island troops preparatory to the inevitable landings. Equally obvious was the fact that the beach defenders (there had been four thousand of them three weeks ago; now shell-fire had reduced them to three thousand) were no longer strong enough to repel invasion. They lacked both light and heavy guns, they were very tired, and their morale was lowered by the incessant punishment they had taken and continued to take. The bitter end must come very soon.

Suddenly, as the general watched, there fell upon the island's northern shore an artillery barrage so heavy that the flashes and sounds of the explosion ran together in a continuous sheet-lightning, a continuous roll of thunder. The fire was most intensely concentrated, he noted, a mile and a half to the east of him, near North Point. The time, he noted, was 8 A.M. He watched for several minutes, then turned away and left the post and went back into the Tunnel, back to the two little cells with whitewashed walls (each measured seven feet by nine) which had been his living quarters for the last several weeks. There, again, he waited . . .

Perhaps as he did so his weary mind ran back to that noon hour almost two months ago (it was on March 10) when, on orders from his immediate superior, he had boarded a motor launch at Mariveles and crossed over to this island, here to be informed, first by MacArthur's chief of staff (Major General Richard K. Sutherland), then by MacArthur himself, that he, MacArthur, was about to depart for Australia. Sutherland had called him "Skinny," MacArthur had called him "Jonathan" (no one else ever did), and both of them had been concerned—a bit excessively in the circumstances, Wainwright thought—with the public relations aspects of MacArthur's impending move. Again and again it had been impressed upon the battle-weary and hungry Wainwright that his superior officer was leaving against his will, "pursuant to repeated orders of the President." Sutherland said the President had been "trying to get" MacArthur to leave for several days but that "until yesterday the general kept refusing." MacArthur said that matters had "gotten to such a point that I must comply with these orders or get out of the Army." He also said that his plan was to divide the total Philippine command into four parts, with Wainwright in command on Bataan and he himself exercising overall command from Australia—an arrangement that had been countermanded by Marshall's order on March 20 despite (as Wainwright suspected) protests from MacArthur's headquarters.

Almost the last thing MacArthur had said that day to the man he left behind as the doomed commander of a lost cause was: "I want you to make it known throughout all the elements of your command that I'm leaving over my repeated protests." Wainwright had of course promised to do so—and had kept his promise.[6]

But this had not done much if anything to make MacArthur's action more palatable to the men of Bataan and Corregidor when they heard of it. MacArthur had never been popular with the rank and file Americans of his command, or indeed with any considerable group of Americans save the members of the extreme political Right. Almost everything about him grated on those who were committed to the practice as well as the theory of the American democracy. They resented his haughty demeanor; his insistence upon wearing a distinctive uniform; his addiction to calculated dramatic gestures, including the "purple prose" of his public utterances; his evident lust for a personal power and glory; his more than willingness to claim all manner of special privilege for himself, including a safe and comfortable home life with wife and son in a house on Corregidor, amidst such luxuries as good liquor and expensive cigars, while the hungry men of Bataan fought and died in misery. This feeling against him was especially strong among junior officers and enlisted men, but it was by no means limited to them. Wainwright himself was not wholly free of it, as he would reveal—perhaps unwittingly, perhaps with a slyly deliberate irony—in a book he would later write about his war experiences;*

* *General Wainwright's Story* (New York: 1946).

a book in which every MacArthur incident and conversation reported would seem to have been selected with a view to revealing the arrogance and egotism of the man.

Especially irritating to many of the troops was MacArthur's statement to reporters who greeted him at Alice Springs, Australia, after he'd been taken with his party in PT boats to the southern Philippine island of Mindanao and flown from there to his destination. "The President of the United States," he then said, "ordered me to break through the Japanese lines. . . . I came through and I shall return." It became standard practice in one Bataan regiment to say: "I am going to the latrine, but I shall return." Others sang with enthusiasm the sarcastic lines composed by some anonymous cynic (versifying seems to have been a favorite pastime on Bataan) and set to the tune of "The Battle Hymn of the Republic":

> Dugout Doug's not timid, he's just cautious, not afraid
> He's protecting carefully the stars that Franklin made.
> Four-star generals are rare as good food on Bataan
> And his troops go starving on.
>
> Dugout Doug is ready in his Chris-Craft for the flee
> Over bounding billows and the wildly raging sea.
> For the Japs are pounding on the gates of old Bataan.
> And his troops go starving on.[7]

But if such matters as these entered Wainwright's weary mind as he waited in his whitewashed cell they must have done so only fleetingly, tangentially. More relevant to this dominant thought was his memory of the orders from MacArthur, even from Roosevelt, which had determined the broad outlines of his action through these last weeks. The earliest of these required "no surrender" on Bataan, no matter what the circumstances. In early April this had been supplemented, reinforced by a message from MacArthur in Australia: "When the supply situation becomes impossible there must be no thought of surrender. You must attack."[8] And when Wainwright on Corregidor was informed on the evening of April 9 that Major General Edward P. King, Jr., on Bataan had sent a surrender offer to the Japanese he reacted promptly, as his orders required him to do. He specifically ordered King *not* to surrender; he ordered him instead to attack. King, of course, had deliberately disobeyed—and even at the time Wainwright had not blamed him for it. He had even been grateful to him for it, since King's action not only saved the lives of hundreds, perhaps thousands of Americans whose death would have served no purpose, but also absolved Wainwright personally of any possible blame for the capitulation. "It [King's] was a decision which required great courage and mental fortitude," Wainwright would write in a later year, adding, "I was soon to find out that it is not easy for an American to surrender."[9]

He was finding it out this bitter night as he waited for the inevitable news that the Japanese had landed on Corregidor. But at least he would not have to surrender, now, in defiance of specific orders from his superiors. As Bataan fell, Roosevelt had messaged MacArthur and, through MacArthur, the Philippines commander, saying: "Am keenly aware of the tremendous difficulties under which you are waging your great battle. The physical exhaustion of your troops obviously precludes the possibility of a major counterstroke unless our efforts to rush food to you should quickly prove successful. . . . I am still hopeful that the efforts of the Navy to supply you by submarine will be effective and in time and that at least one or more of the surface vessels attempting to run the blockade will reach you shortly. Nevertheless I feel it proper and necessary that you should be assured complete freedom of action and of my full confidence in the wisdom of whatever decision you may be forced to make."[10]

At 11:15 (he made a precise note of the time), his phone rang. The Japanese were landing near North Point, he was told. He went at once to his Tunnel command post, and from there to the command post of the Marine Corps units, located just inside the east entrance to Malinta. He shifted from one to the other all through the dark early morning hours, wherein the single bright spot for him was a message to him personally from the President. "During recent weeks," said Franklin Roosevelt, "we have been following with growing admiration the day-by-day accounts of your heroic stand against the mounting intensity of bombardment by enemy planes and heavy siege guns. . . . The American people ask no finer example of tenacity, resourcefulness, and steadfast courage. The calm determination of your personal leadership in a desperate situation sets a standard of duty for our soldiers throughout the world. . . . You and your devoted followers have become the living symbols of our war aims and the guarantee of victory." By daylight, advance units of the Japanese were within five hundred yards of the Tunnel's eastern entrance. By ten o'clock word came that the Japanese were landing more tanks and that the tanks were moving toward the line. The American troops were pinned down by the intense shelling, virtually all American artillery was knocked out, communications were knocked out, and the Japanese could now make whatever landings they chose, unopposed. The situation, Wainwright knew, was now utterly hopeless; he had a nightmare vision of tanks nosing into the Tunnel to massacre the wounded in the hospital and the nurses who remained. Nevertheless he paced up and down, up and down the Tunnel corridor for several minutes before he turned back to his headquarters.

He ordered the broadcast of the surrender message prepared, against the inevitable, some time before. He ordered white flags run up two hours later, when Japanese fire showed no sign of slackening despite the broadcast. And at about the same time he prepared and sent a message to the President:

"With broken heart and head bowed in sadness but not in shame I report to Your Excellency that today I must arrange terms for the surrender of the fortified islands of Manila Bay. . . . There is a limit to human endurance and that limit has long since been past. Without prospect of relief I feel it is my duty to my country and to my gallant troops to end this useless effusion of blood and human sacrifice.

"If you agree, Mr. President, please say to the nation that my troops and I have accomplished all that is humanly possible and that we have unheld the best traditions of the United States and its Army.

"May God bless and preserve you and guide you and the nation in the effort to ultimate victory.

"With profound regret and with continued pride in my gallant troops I go to meet the Japanese commander. Goodby, Mr. President."[11]

ii. "*We Must Be the Great Arsenal of Democracy*"

Tuesday, January 13, 1942 dawned cheerlessly upon Washington, D.C. The rising sun was hidden behind a dull gray mantle of cloud; the air had that peculiarly penetrating chill characteristic of the Capital's humid clime in winter; and the weather's gloomy mood was all too perfectly in accord with that likely to rise in any American patriot who listened, as everyone in Government did, to the morning radio news reports. Especially disturbing to those concerned with the production and delivery of Allied war materiel was the news of ship sinkings off the Atlantic coast of North America, where the U. S. Navy was obviously unprepared to deal with a sudden onslaught of U-boats.

One such patriot, having switched off his radio, stands shaving before a bathroom mirror in a suite of the Broadmoor Hotel, on upper Connecticut Avenue, when we first see him.[12] He presents to our gaze, and to his own, no romantic figure. Though not fat, he would be better looking if he carried less flesh on his large frame; though not bald, his brown hair is very thin and its forehead line recedes up his oval skull at a rate alarming to vanity. His mild eyes, beneath eyebrows arched rather more than normally high, are made to seem milder still by the round rimless glasses he wears. The cheeks from which he scrapes lather are pink and so plump that his mouth, though full-lipped, seems a trifle small in relation to them; and the appearance of forceful character which his well-shaped jaw might otherwise make is reduced by a deep dimple at the center of his chin and by the visible possibility that this chin may soon be joined by another, a flabbly one directly below it. All in all, so far as appearance goes, he might have been the model for Sinclair Lewis's George F. Babbitt.

Nor are the broad outlines of this man's career, up until recently, such as would have distorted seriously the conception of Babbitt's character. Like Babbitt, Donald M. Nelson is a product of the American Middle West—that vast region of in-between whose generally flat, featureless landscape seems to many observers to stamp itself indelibly upon the characters of the human beings raised in it, flattening them, too, into a standardized monotony. Like Babbitt, Nelson is an alumnus of his State university, where he concentrated on "practical" courses to the exclusion of all save a smattering of the humanities. And of him as of Babbitt it might be said that he has "made nothing in particular, neither butter nor shoes nor poetry," in the pursuit of his main line of work. Merchandizing—the buying and selling of goods made by others—has been his business. He has been engaged in it since 1921, when he became manager of the men's and boys' clothing department of the great mail order house of Sears, Roebuck & Company in Chicago. He has prospered at it. A dozen years ago he became a Sears vice president in charge of merchandising, and a director of the firm. Just three years ago he was named Executive Vice-President and chairman of the company's executive committee.

But appearances may deceive. The impression made by broad outlines, by the exclusively salient features that present themselves to a casual glance or distant view, is often contradicted by a closer look. And when such a look is focused on this man and his career (the whole country will be looking at him through press and radio before another twenty-four hours have passed; he now begins what he will always remember as "the most eventful day of my life"), it will be seen that his resemblances to Babbitt are superficial whereas his differences from him are profound.

For instance, though he is of the Middle West, the landscape of his boyhood was no featureless prairie; its central theme was the mighty Mississippi—the islands dotting its bosom, the wooded bluffs towering above its flanks. He was born and raised in Mark Twain's home town of Hannibal, Missouri, where he took piano lessons (reluctantly, at his mother's insistence) in the very house Sam Clemens had lived in as a boy—the "Tom Sawyer house"—and where, one day, his lesson was happily interrupted by a visit from Tom's creator in person.[13] Moreover, though his salesman's talents are considerable, he has never been (as Babbitt was) exclusively or chiefly a salesman "nimble at the calling" of selling things "for more than people can afford to pay."

At the University of Missouri he majored in chemical engineering; he developed there an interest in physical chemistry which has enabled him to follow more closely than most "laymen" the progress of nuclear physics; and his first employment at Sears, in 1912, was as a scientific technician engaged in testing, and devising ways of testing, the quality of textiles and other products sold by his company. A little later he was assigned the job of persuading Sears' merchandise supervisors that they should use the company's laboratory findings as checks upon the accuracy of their catalogue descriptions of the items they handled. It was a job that tested his own quality. He was then a young man who looked young and had no authority whereby the hard-boiled supervisors, naturally resentful of his implied doubt of their truthfulness, might be compelled to do his bidding. The arts of diplomacy and the force of logic were his only weapons, and these often failed him. "I was undoubtedly kicked out of more offices than anyone else in the history of Sears," he later wryly recalled.[14] But in the end he won his point: the laboratory findings were ultimately accepted by the supervisors as sacrosanct and binding.

Thus Nelson functioned through his first working years, not as a specialist whose work area has long been clearly defined, but as a coordinator, a synthesizer, an innovator in areas *between* specialties, shaping there new definitions whereby heretofore separate functions were organically linked one with another. And he did not cease to function in this way when he entered the merchandising field. Having been recommended for advancement to his new post by his success in relating the objective accuracy of physical science to the pricing and advertising of goods, he was forced quickly to realize that his success as merchandise executive required him to know almost as much about the production as about the distribution (the buying and selling) of the stuff he handled. Sears was a mass merchandising firm operating upon a very narrow margin of profit per unit-item sold. Hence its merchandising executives had to know precisely, not only which of thousands of manufacturers were most efficient, but also what it was in the way of production and management techniques that made them so. Often the letting of a big Sears contract required the conversion of a manufacturing concern's production from many lines to a single one, or from one to another; and often Sears' merchandising executive must preside over this conversion. Often, too, he must act as purchasing agent for the manufacturers of the goods he sold, going into the commodities market to buy such raw materials as steel, lumber, aluminum, wool, in greater quantity and hence at higher discounts than any one of his suppliers could obtain. Altogether, Sears' top merchandise executive had dealings with more than five thousand manufacturing concerns, including twenty-five owned outright or in large part by Sears itself.

Few men in America, therefore, could have had a wider or more precise knowledge of the actual workings of the American economy—of its ways and means of producing and marketing and transporting goods—than Donald Nelson when, in May of 1940, he was called to Washington by Secretary of the Treasury Morgenthau to serve as Treasury's Director of Procurement. His specific task at that time was to facilitate British and French purchases of desperately needed American war materiel—especially airplanes. A month later, after the fall of France, the President himself had asked him to serve as Coordinator of National Defense Purchases for the newly organized National Defense Advisory Commission—and ever since, Nelson has been in the thick of the battle (often a bitter battle) to convert a reluctant American economy from peace to war. When NDAC was superseded by the Office of Production Management (OPM) in January of 1941, Nelson, at Roosevelt's request, was asked by its Director General, William S. Knudsen, to head up OPM's Division of Purchases and to serve *ex officio* as a member of OPM's Priorities Board. When a Supply, Priorities, and Allocation Board (SPAB) was superimposed upon a faltering OPM in typical Rooseveltian fashion, late in August of 1941,

Nelson became its Executive Director. At the same time, relieved of his duties as OPM's purchasing director, he was appointed Director of Priorities of that agency. He continues in this dual capacity—giving orders to the heads of OPM in his capacity as Executive Director of SPAB; taking orders from the heads of OPM in his capacity as Priorities Director—on this gray January morning.

His experience at Sears has stood him in good stead through these long months of hectic activity and harassment. An instance of its practical value occurred in his first days as priorities boss. He found his new offices literally flooded with mail from businessmen seeking the materials they needed for industrial production. Some one hundred thousand letters were piled up in stacks so high and wide that the physical movements of office workers were interfered with. His staff was dismayed. He was not. While the truckfuls of correspondence were being moved at his orders to a nearby police court, he put through a long-distance call to Sears in Chicago, asking that company experts in the handling of correspondence (Sears had long ago learned how to manage expeditiously sudden deluges of mail) be sent posthaste to Washington to help him with his immediate "crisis" and establish a system whereby future crises of this sort would not occur. A day or so later, three Sears "correspondence experts" were greeted by Nelson in his office; within a week thereafter, the backlog of mail was reduced to manageable proportions and all incoming priorities mail was being handled swiftly and efficiently through means Sears had perfected.

He has had, alas, other problems more fundamental and serious which were not so easily solved. So far, indeed, they have proved to be insoluble, and they must evidently remain unsolved so long as present administrative arrangements for economic mobilization remain in force. Or, to be more precise, remain *without* force. For it is the absence of centralized direction toward clearly defined goals—it is the failure to plan the national economy in terms of accurately conceived needs, then implement the plans with effective governmental controls—it is this that has caused the whole defense effort to lag so terribly far behind what it ought by now to be and must quickly become if the war is to be won.

The lag, realized as extremely dangerous in the late fall of '41, has become recognized as very nearly catastrophic during the five weeks that have passed since Pearl Harbor Day. Even if production had reached the goals set for it in the preceding year—and it has fallen short of these—the situation would be perilous in the extreme, for it is now realized that the goals themselves have been set far too low. Nelson is not likely to forget the shock he and his colleagues felt when in the first days of the ARCADIA conference Britain's Minister of Supply, the dynamic and driving Lord Beaverbrook, told them what, in his informed opinion, would be needed in the way of American production to insure the final victory. The Beaverbrook figures for planes and tanks, for ships and guns and ammunition, had seemed so fantastically large that the Americans had stared in disbelief when they first heard them, had protested vehemently that the volume demanded was impossible to achieve—and many American production men continue to doubt that it is possible.

Nevertheless these Beaverbrook figures, in some cases actually and arbitrarily increased by Roosevelt, are now the official goals of American production for '42 and '43, having been announced by the President in his State of the Union Message to the Congress on January 6 and incorporated on that same day in a White House directive. Prior to Pearl Harbor the goal had been 28,600 operational aircraft and 20,400 tanks in 1942; now it is 45,000 aircraft in '42, to be upped to 100,000 in '43, and 45,000 tanks, to be increased by 75,000 in '43. The earlier goal for anti-aircraft guns had been 6300 in 1942; now it is 20,000, with 35,000 more in '43. Instead of 6,000,000 deadweight tons of new merchant ships, the goal for '42 is now 8,000,000 tons, to which 10,000,000 are to be added in '43. The originally scheduled production of anti-tank guns for '42 is now to be doubled (from 7000 to 14,000), the number of machine guns is nearly tripled (from 168,000 to 500,000), and the number of long tons of airplane bombs (originally 84,000) is now nearly nine times as great (720,000).[15]

And each of these specific increases implies increases in the production of relevant items. For instance, an increase in rubber production far beyond anything heretofore contemplated is implied by the new schedules for plane, tank, and ship production. The existing stockpiles of natural rubber are much smaller than they should be. Jesse H. Jones' Reconstruction Finance Corporation (RFC) has been provided with ample funds for the needed rubber purchases, but the bankers of that agency have evidently been more concerned with saving money than saving time—and time has now run out: the sources of natural rubber in the Far East are either lost or soon will be to the Japanese. The deficiency must be made up with synthetic rubber, and Nelson is by no means certain that this can be done in time since the synthetic rubber program is just beginning to get under way. Somewhat less serious, but surely serious enough, is the gasoline situation. If the 100,000 planes produced in '43 are to take to the air they must be fueled with quantities of 100-octane gasoline many times greater than have been produced before within a single year. New gasoline plants must be built, and these, like the synthetic rubber plants, must use up other materials that are in critically short supply: steel, aluminum, copper, and so on.

For the accomplishment of this immense task, the prevailing administrative arrangements are wholly inadequate. The double-headed OPM has little more real authority than the no-headed NDAC had had; its terms of reference are essentially those of a planning and advisory body; while SPAB is, in essence, but an expansion of OPM's board of directors. Ever since Pearl Harbor, OPM and SPAB have been improvising, going beyond their assigned authority, struggling desperately to give substance to what, legally, are the merest shadows of power. The same is true of the

Office of Price Administration and Civilian Supply (OPA), under the colorful, dedicated, immensely capable Leon Henderson.

OPA's designated function is to prevent inflation and in general protect the civilian economy against war pressures that threaten to crush it utterly. Henderson and the brilliant young men he has gathered around him in key OPA positions have been convinced from the first, as Nelson himself has been, that rationing to civilian consumers is an indispensable tool of price control and that rationing authority over the civilian economy, now apparently vested in OPM as an aspect of its far from clearly defined powers to establish and enforce priorities, should be transferred to OPA. Lacking such authority, OPA's top people—notably Henderson and J. Kenneth Galbraith, who is among the brightest of Henderson's bright young men—feel themselves compelled to act as if they had it. Just a few days ago, Galbraith learned from someone in OPM that OPM's Rubber Division was about to issue an order limiting the sale of tires to four per customer. He was aghast. Obviously, such an order would have an effect opposite to its intention; virtually every car owner, regardless of his immediate needs, would rush to the nearest tire dealer to purchase his four permitted tires. So Galbraith had persuaded OPA's attorney to visit the OPM offices and come back with a copy of this disastrous order which, when he had it in hand, became the subject of earnest consultation between him and Henderson. The upshot was that OPA issued the Rubber Division's order as its own, but only after having struck out the provision permitting four tires per customer. *All* tire sales to civilians are now, for the time being, suspended . . .[16]

Obviously this chaotic operation, this enforced resort to extralegal procedures in order to get essential jobs done, cannot be permitted to continue. Obviously the days of OPM-SPAB are numbered.

For the time being, however, SPAB remains alive and active. It is to meet this very afternoon in a session over which Donald Nelson is to preside at Vice-President Henry A. Wallace's request (Wallace is chairman of SPAB as he is also of the Economic Defense Board). And it is of the agenda for this meeting that Nelson's mind is full as he completes his shaving, breakfasts hurriedly on scrambled eggs, and then drives through the morning mists of Rock Creek Park toward his office in the Social Security Building. He ticks off the items: "Stockpile Program," "Synthetic Rubber," "Douglas Dam," "Aluminum Requirements of the U.S.S.R.," "Copper," and, finally, "Increased Copper, Lead and Zinc Production through Price Incentives." He concentrates on the first of these, since he is to open the meeting with his own report on stockpiling . . .

When all are settled into their places in the SPAB board room, immediately after lunch that day, he notes with satisfaction but no surprise that few who might be there are absent and all who should be are present.[17] His glancing gaze takes in bluff, hearty Secretary of the Navy Knox; astringent-looking Secretary of War Stimson; good, gray, kindly

Director General Knudsen of OPM; dreamy-eyed, tousle-haired Vice-President Wallace, looking (as always) as if he had just come in from an Iowa cornfield; huge, white-haired, tight-lipped Jesse Jones, looking (as always) like a banker about to refuse a loan; OPA's Leon Henderson, a dark-visaged yet jolly-looking man whose great paunch presses the table's edge even when he sits far back in his chair—all these are at hand along with the chiefs of all the divisions and branches of OPM.

They listen intently to the report with which Nelson opens the meeting. What he has to say can do nothing to heighten the optimism of his hearers and may be personally offensive to Jesse Jones. Jones has had more responsibility than any other in the room for building up stockpiles of strategic materials, and Nelson must stress the fact that these stockpiles, particularly as regards quinine and rubber, are dangerously low. But if Jones is offended he gives no outward sign of it; he votes with the others for a motion embodying Nelson's recommendation "that our whole list of stockpile objectives be reviewed and revised and that ways and means be found to attain the new objectives at a greatly accelerated pace."

And, indeed, the discussion of the next item on the agenda, "Synthetic Rubber," indicates that RFC no longer "drags its feet." The RFC has promised financial backing of an expansion of synthetic rubber production to 400,000 tons annually, whereas SPAB has thus far formally approved a plan to increase production to only 120,000 tons annually. Here, as the discussion continues, scientific technology has direct impact on Government policy. The proposed expansion is of the production of the synthetic known as Buna S., which is much better suited to use in tire casings than other synthetics are—and recent laboratory discoveries, developing new formulas, have made it unnecessary to use chlorine in Buna S. production. Chlorine is scarce and much needed, hence expensive. The new discoveries, applied through mass production, should reduce the per-unit cost of synthetic rubber to a point not much higher than the current fixed price of crude (natural) rubber. Wallace at this point urgently recommends that the new rubber-making plants financed by the Government be owned by the Government. Only thus can "unfair and uneconomic competition with the crude-rubber industry be avoided" after the war's end. Moreover, the pooling of patents in ways fair to all competitors, and to the immense benefit of the national war effort, is easier to achieve if the Government owns the plants than if private corporations do.

The meeting proceeds. Leon Henderson is speaking of acute and even desperate shortages of copper (severe rationing of this commodity is clearly implied; soon the Government will cease making pennies out of copper) when Nelson's secretary enters the room. She hands her boss a note from the White House: the President wants to see him and Vice-President Wallace as soon as this meeting adjourns . . .

It was 5:30 and the shadows of evening had fallen upon the White House lawns and gardens when the limousine bearing Wallace and Nelson passed through the iron gates into the curved drive of 1600 Pennsylvania Avenue. A few minutes later, genial and flawlessly courteous Major General Edwin M. (Pa) Watson, the President's appointments secretary, showed the two visitors into the Oval Study.

To Nelson, the President seemed unwontedly worn and weary that evening, though his handclasp was firm as usual and his smile as warm. Nor did the President begin the talk, as was usual, with a wisecrack or a funny story or a comment (often hilarious, sometimes acid) on the doings of the Congress and the press. Instead he spoke of the general war situation, which was serious enough for the Allies, in all conscience; and —very solemnly, almost religiously—of his personal faith in democracy, his own profound belief in the resilience and flexibility and survival capacities of a free society. He spoke of the effort which must now be made to transform America truly into the "Arsenal of Democracy" he had proclaimed a year ago. "I wasn't just making a phrase," he said.

Then, abruptly, the subject of his monologue (for that is what it was; neither Wallace nor Nelson was able to say a word for almost an hour after shaking hands with Roosevelt) became the administrative organization of the economic war effort. He reviewed the history of the agencies he'd set up for industrial mobilization, pointing out with precision their structural deficiencies—deficiencies of which his critics generally had deemed him unaware. He discussed, too, and surprised Nelson by discussing, the merits and deficiencies of the man who had been in charge of these agencies. He praised Hillman, he praised Knudsen—but it became evident that he did not consider Knudsen the right man for supreme direction of the industrial effort.

Of Knudsen's abilities as a production man there could be no doubt. He had proved them abundantly and repeatedly as president of General Motors. Nor could there be any doubt that the prestige he had earned in the industry, joined to the warm personal affection he inspired in men who had worked with him in Detroit, had become a great asset to the country when he was NDAC's Director of Production and throughout the early days of OPM. Probably no other man, in October of 1940, could have called an impromptu meeting of the major automobile executives in Detroit at which all of them, save the executives of Ford, were persuaded that they could and should engage in the manufacture of airplane parts. At that same meeting, Ford's tough production genius, Charles E. Sorensen, was stimulated to consider and later lay definite plans for the mass production of four-engined Consolidated (B-24) bombers at Willow Run. (The giant Willow Run plant, built in just eleven months, was a mile long and a quarter-mile wide—larger than the combined plants of all three major airplane manufacturers before the war.) Last April, Knudsen had persuaded auto manufacturers to voluntarily cut their production of passenger cars to 80 per cent of that at the beginning of the

1940–41 model year. His persuasive powers had operated as one of the major causes of such conversion of basic industries to war production as had been achieved. Nevertheless, only a fraction of the needed conversion *had* been achieved, and for this fact many (not including Nelson) were inclined to blame Knudsen.

Nelson himself was more acutely aware than the President was likely to be of the difficulties and risks of converting a mass production industry from one line of production to another. Among the prices paid for the great economic advantages of mass production was a loss of flexibility in production techniques. Craftsmen, and industries dominated by craftsmanship, might quite easily turn their skills and relatively simple tools to new uses. But a mass-production line, with its huge jigs and conveyor systems and complicated machine tools, was geared to the making of certain items to the exclusion of all others and could not be converted piecemeal to new uses; it had to be converted wholly and all at once or not at all. The reluctance of carmakers to do this in 1940 and early '41 was certainly understandable—especially since neither the Army nor the various defense agencies could tell them definitely and authoritatively what kind of war goods they should make nor in what amounts.

Now, however, the goals had been set and announced to the world by the very man who leaned forward in his chair at this moment to look closely into Nelson's face, and Wallace's. He spoke earnestly. Our lives as a free people, and the lives of our Allies, depended upon our reaching these goals, he said—and to insure that industry met the challenge he, the President, had decided to create a new Government board, wider in scope and greater in authority than any he had ever set up before. To head that board (Nelson's heart was now beating fast) he wanted a man who could bring naturally discordant and even conflicting interests together in a single harmonious effort, using persuasion whenever possible but coercive authority when this was necessary.

Roosevelt spoke of an occasion when Abraham Lincoln as President called for a vote of his Cabinet on a measure he had proposed and found, as expected, that every single Cabinet member opposed it. "All in favor vote 'Aye,'" Lincoln then said. "*I* vote aye.'" He looked around with a wry smile. "The 'ayes' have it," he concluded. . . . The board Roosevelt now wanted would be made up of strong-minded, strong-willed men, as was Lincoln's Cabinet, and the man who ran it should be able to operate as Lincoln had done on the occasion just referred to.

There followed some talk of the name to be given the new super-agency. Nelson suggested calling it the "War Production Administration." The President considered this for a moment, then shook his head emphatically. The agency's initials would then be WPA, he pointed out. "That wouldn't do at all!" he said with a loud laugh. He proposed instead the name "War Production Board." He asked if this met with Nelson's approval, and Nelson said that it did. Whereupon the President gave Nelson what the latter called, afterward, "the shock of my life"—though by that point in the interview he must have at least halfway expected it.

"I'm glad you approve the name," said Roosevelt, "because *you* are the chairman of the War Production Board."

Nelson stared. The job was too big for him, he averred; it was "too big for any man I ever heard of," but in the circumstances he could only say he would do his best. The President then asked him to draft the Executive Order setting up the agency and defining its authority, an Order that would become legally effective upon the President's signature. He also asked Wallace to resign the chairmanship of SPAB, since SPAB was now being absorbed into WPB. Wallace of course agreed to do so. He, Wallace, was to retain his chairmanship of the Economic Defense Board, whose scope was widened and authority increased as its name was changed to the Board of Economic Warfare.

When he arrived back at the Social Security Building, Nelson had another shock. He found that the news of his new appointment had already gone out over the wires, and was already being broadcast as a "Flash Bulletin" by radio announcers. And such elation as he felt upon receiving the congratulations of colleagues was tinctured with a dismayed concern for his erstwhile superior in OPM, Bill Knudsen, whom he greatly liked and admired. Surely Knudsen, who had done his best—and on the whole, not done badly—had earned the right to be at least informed of the new arrangement before it was proclaimed to the world! He hadn't been. Nelson, going at once to Knudsen's office, found the old man sitting alone at his desk, his face and voice revealing the deep hurt which had been given him. Nelson revealed his own dismay, begging Knudsen not to leave the Government. The old man expressed his appreciation of Nelson's concern but made no promises. Nelson then went to his own office where, before he left for his Broadmoor apartment, he phoned Jesse Jones, who was as close a friend of Knudsen as anyone in Washington, urging Jones to call on Knudsen and persuade the latter not to "quit and go home."

Nor was Nelson the only one who, in his concern for Knudsen, phoned Jesse Jones that evening. Harry Hopkins did also, with a definite proposal he hoped Jones would present to Knudsen in a way that would encourage Knudsen to accept. The proposal, already cleared with Under Secretary of War Robert P. Patterson, was that Knudsen be commissioned a Lieutenant General in the Army and assigned the task of helping Patterson with Army procurement problems. Jones promised to do what he could —and in the end, Knudsen did accept the proposed commission.[18]

iii. *Freedom and Organization*

Next morning, listening to the radio as he shaves, Nelson finds himself and his appointment to be the top news of the day. He hears himself described as "the man who has to tackle the biggest job in all history," and it gives him a sinking feeling. (". . . I had a deeper feeling of humility than I had ever experienced," he will later say.) He also hears himself described as "arms czar" and "dictator of the economy," and this stimulates thought about the general strategy as well as the immediate tactics of the economic war he must command.

It is clear that the economy must be socialized to a degree never before contemplated seriously by responsible Government officials. The distinctions between private and public enterprise must be, for the time being, much reduced, virtually all economic enterprise becoming public to the extent that its energies can be harnessed to the single overriding national purpose of victory in war. The year 1941 has seen the gathering together in usable form of most of the hard data, the accurate and vastly detailed economic information, on which realistic plans can be based. Now the plans must be boldly and firmly shaped. The year has also witnessed the devising and initial testing of most of the Government controls needed for the achievement of planned goals: priority ratings, materials allocations, consumer rationing, price and rent controls, confiscatory taxation of "excess profits." Now these controls must be extended and rigorously applied in every segment of the economy. Full rein must be given the American genius for large-scale organization and administration, for mass production and mass distribution—a genius whose expression in practice has long ago rendered obsolete much of the "rugged individualism" in which most Americans *believe* they believe—but the guiding rein and driving whip must now be firmly in Government hands.

All this may seem to constitute, of itself alone, a radical departure from what most American businessmen are fond of calling "The American Way." Donald Nelson does not see it so. It may *become* a radical departure. Of this he is well aware. And if it is permitted to do so—if it changes the very roots of the American society—then of course the character of that society as a whole will be greatly and permanently altered. The event, however, is by no means inevitable. Everything depends on *how* the vast, intricate job is done, and Nelson's conviction is that it can and must be accomplished "within the framework of the American tradition." The war challenges us, says he, "to prove, once and for all, that our system of political and economic freedom is in fact more efficient, more productive, more able to respond to the demands of a great emergency than the dictatorial system of our enemies."[19]

In this connection he has been often reminded, and will be often reminded in the future, of a conversation he had with Roosevelt in the late autumn of 1940. To be strictly accurate, it wasn't a conversation but an hour-long Rooseveltian monologue—a barrier of talk put up by the President against the resignation from NDAC (and the arguments for resigning) which Nelson had come to the Oval Study prepared to present. The most memorable part of this monologue had to do with Soviet-American relations. Roosevelt told of talking with a Soviet official who came to him in 1933 with a plea for diplomatic recognition of the U.S.S.R. by the United States.† The President had pointed out half-jokingly that, since

† Recognition was formally announced on November 17, 1933, after much haggling over terms.

Russia was a Socialist State and the U.S. a capitalistic democracy, there seemed to be no harmony of interests between them. The Russian had countered by saying that, as time went on, the actual difference between the systems of the two countries was steadily reduced. "A few years ago we were 100 per cent communistic and your country was 100 per cent capitalistic," said the Russian. "Now we are 80 per cent communistic and you are only 80 per cent capitalistic. A few years hence we shall be 60 per cent communistic; you will be 60 per cent capitalistic, and when that time comes we won't be so far apart!"[20]

But for Roosevelt as for Nelson, the 40 per cent difference that will yet remain, should the Russian's prediction come true, will continue to be crucial if there lies within it the issue of human rights and freedoms vs. totalitarian dictatorship. And this, of course, as Nelson sees it, is the essential issue of the present war. Hence the test now is not only of courage and energy, on the economic front as on the battlefield; it is also and even more a test of basic commitments, of sound value judgments implemented by swift, acute, logical intelligence.

Excessive impatience is a weakness, a danger . . .

There have been moments of exasperation since the summer of 1940 when Nelson himself has felt that the President ought to yield to the demand that he appoint an economic boss whose orders to industry would have the full force of law—someone whose coercive powers would be virtually equivalent to those of the head of state and Commander-in-Chief in this emergency. But this feeling with him was transitory. Unlike many Big Businessmen brought into Government since the fall of France, he has come to understand and sympathize with the President's reluctance to permit any such concentration of authority in a single agency, a single administrator, as his critics often demand. The cause of this reluctance, he has become convinced, is not so much Roosevelt's appetite for personal power, great though this undoubtedly is, as it is his concern to preserve in practical operation the basic tenets of a free society.

This conclusion of Nelson's has derived in large part from his experience and observation of some key figures in the War Department and in the Army's Services of Supply. These men, in his view, display a ruthlessness of will and a narrow singleness of purpose which, were they invested with the coercive authority they obviously lust for, would irrevocably sacrifice the ends for which the war is being fought to the means of winning it on the battlefield. And the means they advocate are themselves of dubious efficacy, even in the military sense. It is far from certain that they would increase America's fighting efficiency: their net effect might be precisely the opposite—a lowering of national morale, a dissipation of economic energies. What *is* certain (so Nelson thinks) is that the country "saved" in this way would be fundamentally transformed; it would have become a kind of mirror-image, in essential respects, of the totalitarianism we loathe in our enemies.

Oversimplification—this is the great error of these men, Nelson thinks.

They ask of every proposal a single simple question: Does it contribute *directly* to an increase of America's armed strength, serving the Army's bureaucratic interests by giving it a wider margin for error and hence a greater freedom of choice? If it does, they favor the proposal; if it does not, they oppose it; and in either case their view has been decisive since, by the administrative arrangements prevailing until last evening, no civilian defense agency (certainly not Nelson's Priorities Board) has had the power to stand against them.

Nelson vividly remembers, he always will remember, a "lively little fracas" with the Army and Under Secretary of War Patterson over their insistence that two big aircraft manufacturing concerns, Lockheed and Douglas, be forced to cancel their contracts to provide between thirty and forty new commercial transports to major airlines.[21] The Army's argument was that this civilian "business as usual" interfered with the fulfillment of Army contracts for war planes. Douglas and Lockheed vehemently denied that this was so, and were sustained by reports from production men sent out by the Priorities Board. The airlines placing the orders argued that the new planes were urgently needed to handle the increased traffic bound to result from the war emergency; they (the planes) should therefore be deemed an integral part of America's war strength, especially since they might be transferred to the Army for troop transport if this should prove necessary. But Patterson and the Army remained adamant. It was more *convenient* for the Army to have the plane factories wholly at its disposal—and the convenience of the Army took precedence in these men's minds over any civilian agency's wish or (even) necessity. So it appears to Nelson. It also appears to him that the arbitrary cancellation is motivated in part by a simple egoistic powerlust; the top echelon of Army and War Department gains satisfaction from demonstrating to mere civilians in other agencies, and outside of Government, the fact that they have inferior status, they play subordinate roles, in the great drama of war.

Or consider the case of the first big contract-award for the manufacture of the sturdy, powerful, all-purpose, four-wheel-drive vehicle which has become known to the world as the "jeep." This was back in the days of NDAC, when all Army and Navy contracts had to clear through Knudsen's office (in his capacity as NDAC's Director of Production) before the final award could be made. Knudsen found that, of the three firms which had submitted bids for jeep-making, namely, Ford, Bantam, and Willys, the latter's bid was lowest by some $560,000. Nevertheless, the Army proposed to award the contract to Ford. Knudsen refused to clear it. He insisted that the contract go to Willys, and stood firm in this decision against a delegation of high War Department officials who called upon him the next day. (He used his industry-gained prestige to overcome the delegation's vehement protests, saying: "If I know anything about production at all I know about producing motor cars. . . . This jeep is a motor car—and, gentlemen, I say Willys can make it."[22]) The episode, in Nelson's view, is a case in point. It was more *convenient* for the Army to deal with the giant Ford Motor Company than with relatively tiny Willys; the Army had often worked before with Ford personnel, and there could be no doubt of Ford's ability to meet specifications. Of course this kind of operation throughout the war emergency would mean the use of taxpayers' money to extinguish small industry and promote monopoly. It might well lead toward a political economy closely similar to that envisaged in Mussolini's Fascism. But such considerations seemed not to enter into the decision-making of the Army's top echelon.

Both episodes, Nelson thinks, are examples of oversimplification. They point up the dangerous error of selecting any single factor out of the enormous complex of variable factors in the present situation, assigning to it the status of an absolute, and then determining the value of every other factor altogether in terms of it. The only valid absolute is the *whole* of which the factors are integral parts and from which, as separate and distinct items, they are artificial abstractions. One must learn, therefore, to think "wholistically," determining the priorities of particular interests and acts by measuring them, ultimately, against the total need, the total action of the Republic as it fights for its survival as a democracy. One must learn to think in terms of balance and proportion within the whole, making often (necessarily) very close decisions as to which particular factor has or should have the greater weight when compared to another but doing it always in terms of the whole, the total process. If, for example, one is faced with the question of whether or not an aluminum-making plant should be expanded, he must answer it not only in terms of the need for more aluminum but also in terms of competing demands for structural steel, of which the supply is limited. The question becomes: Is the additional aluminum which the expanded plant will produce needed more than the steel that must be used in the plant's expansion? The answer can be arrived at only by considering both steel and aluminum as factors in the total Allied war effort.

Similar to such questions are *where* a defense plant should be located. Some months ago Nelson, as chairman of OPM's Plant Site Committee, reviewed an Army proposal to purchase a twenty-thousand-acre block of the richest farmland in America in order to build upon it a big ordnance works. Judged solely in Army Engineering terms the selected site was ideal—but Nelson questioned whether its superiority in this respect over other possible sites on marginal or submarginal land was great enough to justify the removal from agricultural production of so much fertile soil. He raised the question with Ordnance, pointing out that a maximum production of food might well become of major importance to the total war effort. He indicated specifically other possible sites, only slightly less ideal than this one for Ordnance's special purpose, which had little or no value as farmland. Ordnance soon agreed with him; the plant site was shifted.

Labor vs. management, Big vs. Little Business, craft vs. mass production—under these general headings rise innumerable specific issues, and each must be resolved, not as a simple halfway compromise between two opposing interests but, rather, in terms of the national purpose which both serve.

As regards labor vs. management, Nelson will attempt to achieve solutions through the establishment of "labor-management" committees in war plants. These are not to be grievance committees, or collective bargaining committees; they are to be wholly devoted to ways and means of achieving a maximum efficiency of production. It must be noted in passing that labor, thus far, has been pressing harder than management for a full conversion of basic industries to war production. Everyone knows of the "Reuther Plan" for converting the auto industry (this industry is ultimately to account for some 20 per cent of the total war production)—a "plan" put forth by Walter P. Reuther, Director of General Motors' United Auto Workers of the C.I.O.

As regards Big vs. Little Business, Nelson is forced to admit that Little Business has been getting and will continue to get "the dirty end of the stick." It suffers from the need to achieve speed and more speed in production. This need dictates the granting of giant contracts to industrial giants and the allocation to them of the materials needed to do the job, materials thereby denied the smaller firms having no war work to do. The latter, if they live at all, must generally live on subcontracts from the giants. On the other hand, insofar as the preservation of "The American Way" is the general objective of our war, Little Business must be granted the maximum possible protection—and Nelson with his colleagues must devote much attention to the problem of doing so through the granting of prime contracts to smaller firms whenever possible, through a proper distribution of subcontracts, and by stimulating small businessmen to "get in and fight" boldly and creatively for a share of the great work to be done. To this end, small businesses will increasingly pool their resources and augment their persuasive powers by working through local community "defense committees," designed to facilitate the obtaining of war contracts.

As regards craft vs. mass production, the most precise calculations of relative benefits must be made in terms of the total effort, the ultimate objective. In general the decision will be in favor of mass production. When Packard, for instance, puts into mass production the Rolls-Royce motor used in British Spitfires—a motor built in England by highly expert hands—there may be some loss of perfection in individual motors, but this will be more than offset by having at hand unprecedented numbers of approximately perfect Rolls-Royce engines. The same kind of reasoning will lead Ford's Sorensen to do all he can to freeze airplane designs once the Willow Run plant begins to turn out Consolidated bombers in huge numbers at great speed. He argues that the overwhelming numerical superiority we thus achieve in the shortest possible time more than offsets the advantages we might gain if we ripped production lines apart, interrupting output, every time a real or fancied design improvement appears on drafting boards.[23] But of course this statistical approach to the matter does not appeal to individual combat pilots who may lose their lives because they encounter in battle enemy planes whose performance is superior to theirs. Nor is it possible wholly to ignore the improvements urged by battlefield experience, or by the design engineering of our enemies. At a certain point, quantitative superiority *is* offset by qualitative superiority, and the location of that precise point at which craftsmanship should prevail for the moment over mass production requires a very careful measurement of relative factors (the particular) against and within the whole (the general) of which they are elements.

Indeed, of all the questions Nelson will have now to deal with on the top policy level, only one, though of an importance overriding all the rest, seems to him answerable as a flat choice between opposing alternatives. This is the question of which is to have supreme control over the national economy as the war proceeds, the military or the civilian branches. The American democratic system, as established by the Constitution, requires all ultimate warmaking powers to be vested firmly, unambiguously in civilian hands—and Nelson has found this principle, as applied to economics, to be accepted in practice as in theory by the officers of the chief Army procurement agencies: the Quartermaster Corps, the Ordnance Department, the Corps of Engineers, the Signal Corps, the Medical Department. But on the top policy-making level of Army and War Departments, superior to these "working branches" of the Army (he so designates them in invidious comparison with their superiors)—on this level he has encountered powerful men whom he suspects of a willingness if not a determination to break with American tradition and Constitution on this matter. His suspicion is destined to grow during the next two years into a conviction that these men (though they vehemently deny it) aim to impose military control upon the economy. Moreover they seem to him perfectly willing to use whatever means are at hand, fair or foul, to crush anyone who opposes them. Their manipulation of public opinion in order to further their aims or interests seems to him especially reprehensible; they have no compunction whatever about spreading through the channels of mass communication stories that are half-true, or distorted in emphasis, or even (on crucial occasions) largely false. Already he is preparing to do battle against them, a battle whose tactics will be at first sub rosa and indirect but which (as we who look back may see) must lead ultimately into a head-on collision.

Part and parcel of Nelson's opposition to military control of the economy is his insistence that the widest possible latitude be maintained within which free choices and creative initiative can operate. The Army, as a necessarily authoritarian organization, gives orders: its tendency is to tell a given industry not only *what* it is to make but also *how* the thing is to be made. Nelson is determined to avoid this. He is convinced that no man or group of men can possibly keep track of all the details, or distribute accurate emphases among all the interests, of the vast American economy. He therefore favors a kind of economic planning whereby definite goals are set and broad patterns of activity are applied but within which details and interests are left free, so far as may be, to call attention to themselves and even to take care of themselves.

And, indeed, as he breakfasts and then rides again through Rock Creek Park toward the Social Security Building, as he plunges into the details of his new assignment and is immersed in these through a long workday, a practical justification of his point of view is beginning to work itself out among airplane manufacturers on the West Coast. Last May the Congress had established a committee, headed by Senator Harry S. Truman of Missouri, "to make a full and complete study and investigation of the operation of the program for the procurement and construction of supplies, materials, vehicles, aircraft, vessels, plants, camps and other articles and facilities in connection with the national defense." In the immediate aftermath of Pearl Harbor, when a deluge of orders poured in upon eight planemakers of Southern California, the Truman Committee recommended that the President appoint a "czar" of the airplane industry. To prevent this, the heads of the companies "decided to offer the President an eight-president soviet to regiment our part of the industry," an organization that became known as the Aircraft War Production Council.[24] Now cooperation has replaced competition among Lockheed, Douglas, Vultee, North American, Ryan, Consolidated, Vega, and Northrup. They have pooled their resources of material and talent and "know-how," so that none of them has its production limited for lack of something another may have in good supply.

An important instance of this cooperation is about to be provided by Douglas and North American. The Douglas plant in El Segundo is manufacturing dive bombers for the Navy, a rush order—and on a day that is in the near future as Nelson begins his work as WPB chairman, Douglas finds its tight production schedule threatened by a shortage of some two thousand feet of binding braid wire without which the planes cannot be bound into solid metallic units, thereby preventing dangerous buildups of static electricity during power dives. The crisis is acute, but the schedule is saved when the needed wire is found in a stockroom of North American. The dive bombers are then delivered in time for use in the mid- and far Pacific, where great and decisive naval actions impend.

iv. *A Test of Nerve for Allied Strategists*

Japanese war lords, poring over maps of the Pacific and East Asia on May 1, 1942, could not but be highly pleased by what they saw. Through an uninterrupted series of victories, the empire of the Rising Sun had been extended over some twelve and a half million square miles. The richest, best-developed portions of China; Burma and Siam; the Malay Peninsula tipped by "impregnable" Singapore; the Philippines, save for the tiny and doomed speck of resistance on Corregidor; the Dutch East Indies, including Java and Sumatra, with their fabulous wealth of natural resources; the Gilberts, the Marshalls, the Carolines, the Marianas, with Guam; Wake Island; the Admiralties; and, far to the west, the strategic Andamans in the Bay of Bengal; all these were now within the empire's perimeter.

A slower rate of advance at a higher cost in blood and treasure had been envisaged in the initial war plans. It had been then assumed that, following Pearl Harbor, six months would be required for conquests actually achieved in five. It had also been assumed that, following the occupation of the Dutch East Indies, six more months would be required to restore their oil fields to production, since a "scorched earth" policy would undoubtedly be applied; but in fact no such policy had been effectively implemented, and oil from these fields already flowed into the Japanese war machine. As for the costs, they had been but a fraction of that which war plans had anticipated. Instead of the pre-estimated 20 to 30 per cent of the engaged naval strength, the actual price to Japan had been a mere twenty-three naval vessels totaling 26,441 tons, of which no vessel was larger than a destroyer. Other losses had been proportionately light: some 315,000 tons of transport and merchant shipping, some thousands of soldiers and sailors, some hundreds of airplanes. The enemy's losses of ships and planes and men had been immensely greater.

There had been only two disturbing episodes in all these months of glory.

On the morning of March 10, American planes had swooped suddenly through a narrow pass in New Guinea's Owen Stanley Range to bomb Lae and Salamaua on that island's outer coast, achieving complete surprise. One large convoy was unloading, and another coming into port, when the attack began. When it ended, five transports and cargo ships had been sunk, a destroyer had blown up when a bomb exploded among its depth charges, a minelayer had been set afire, and two heavy cruisers, two destroyers, two gunboats, and a seaplane tender had been more or less seriously damaged. The airfield had been left pockmarked by bombs, its buildings a shambles—and most of the shore anti-aircraft batteries had been knocked out. All this had been accomplished by the Americans at the cost of a single plane in which two men died. This success had undoubtedly emboldened the Americans to hold onto Port Moresby, some 170 miles to the south, earlier regarded by many of them as indefensible. Certainly it had strengthened the determination of the war lords to take Moresby, from whose airfield the bombers had been launched. (Or so they believed. They would have been astonished to learn that the bombers had in fact flown off two U.S. carriers, *Lexington* and *Yorktown*, in the Gulf of Papua—an unprecedented operation in which one naval force attacked another across a fifteen thousand-foot mountain range!) The episode had had another effect: it frustrated the Japanese attempt to take Moresby from the landward side. With the loss of the cargo ships it became impossible to supply the troops which had been scheduled to press through narrow mountain passes to the side of New Guinea facing Australia.

The second disturbing episode had occurred just thirteen days ago, on April 18. Sixteen U. S. Army B-25 (two-motored) bombers had raided Tokyo, inflicting considerable damage and causing something very like panic among the capital's populace! What most disquieted the war lords, initially, was the apparent impossibility of this feat. Where could the bombers have come from? Surely not from a carrier: none had been sighted in the closely patrolled Japanese waters and, besides, two-motored planes had never been flown off a carrier. (Actually these B-25s, specially altered for the purpose, and led by the famous Lieutenant Colonel Jimmy Doolittle, had flown off the carrier U.S.S. *Hornet* which was accompanied, for scouting and protection, by the carrier U.S.S. *Enterprise,* flagship of Vice Admiral William F. (Bull) Halsey. All but one of them had been wrecked when they ran out of gasoline, or developed motor trouble, before reaching the Chinese airfields at which they aimed. This was because they had been forced to fly off hours before the appointed time; the carriers were sighted by a Japanese vessel which, though promptly sunk, could easily have signaled its sighting to Japanese naval units before it went down. Immediately after the fly-off the two carriers, whose loss would have been a final blow to the possibility of major American fleet action in the Pacific for months to come, had turned and headed for Pearl Harbor at top speed.)

But these raids, after all, had no decisive importance. They were as nothing, compared with the offensive achievements of the Japanese arms.

Nor was there apparent reason to assume that the limit of expansion by these arms had been reached for the time being, that a pause must now ensue during which the fruits of conquest were digested and a strength depleted by mighty exertions was restored. On the contrary, feeding on what she conquered as she thrust outward from her home islands across vast reaches of sea and jungle, transporting the released energies of her rich spoils along interior lines of communication, establishing herself in new strong bases at dozens of far-flung strategic points, Japan maintained a superiority of force over her enemies which, at every point of contact with them, seemed at least as great now as it had been on the first day of war. Not yet, then, had she reached even a temporarily "natural" frontier, since the boundary of an empire (by the "natural law" describing the essential lawlessness of unmitigated State sovereignty) is always *ultimately* a line of equilibrium between opposing forces and must become so *immediately* in time of war.

The apparent fact seemed decisively demonstrated by the fate of Port Darwin on Australia's north-central coast. As the nearest of all Australian ports to the southern fringe of Japanese conquests, Darwin might be deemed the best suited for buildup into a base for Allied counteroffensives. But when a fast convoy of four troop transports escorted by a U.S. light cruiser and a U.S. destroyer left this port in mid-February, bound for Kupang, Timor, to reinforce the Allied garrison there and establish a base, it was forced to turn back, severely damaged, by Japanese air attacks. And four days later Darwin itself was eliminated as a possible Allied base for several months by a massive air strike during which the airfield, the port facilities, the warehouses, and virtually every ship in the harbor (including the destroyer U.S.S. *Peary*) were destroyed. While she thus eliminated a potential strong point against her, Japan established a strong point of her own at Rabaul on New Britain, off the eastern coast of New Guinea. Rabaul, easily captured in January, was now a base for further offensive action to the south, action that was prepared by May 1 and about to be launched with every confidence in its success.

The fair prospect presented to the eyes of the war lords was not dimmed when they turned their gaze from maps of their own theater of war to those of the theaters of their Axis partners. In the Atlantic, Britain's lifeline to America was increasingly damaged and threatened with utter disruption by Nazi submarines. By Pearl Harbor Day, Admiral Karl Doenitz had had a fleet of nearly 250 U-boats, nearly one hundred of them operational, and he had since been adding to it at a rate of fifteen new submarines per month minus the few (much fewer than fifteen) which the Allies were able to destroy in the same period. With a handful of these he had been able to make the United States pay a bitter price for her failure to develop adequate defenses of her freighters and tankers against underwater attack. A mere half-dozen of the largest U-boats had sunk, virtually at will and without hazard, some thirty-one ships totaling nearly 200,000 deadweight tons in January, most of them tankers moving vital oil from the oil ports of Latin America to the United States. In February, no fewer than seventy-one Allied ships had been lost to U-boats in the Atlantic—a total of 384,000 tons—and of these, thirty-four of the largest (again mostly tankers), totaling 365,000 tons, had been sunk in the Caribbean and in the American naval patrol area west of the 40th meridian. The slaughter had been even greater in March and it yet continued, though less concentratedly in American coastal waters since early April when, at last, the U. S. Navy had been able to establish a partial convoy system.[25] Japanese war lords could smilingly imagine the desperate messages flashing between Washington and London as the Battle of the Atlantic went more and more in the U-boats' favor. What benefit could come to the Allied cause from America's vaunted industrial might if the goods could not be delivered to the fighting fronts?

And upon these fronts, in the European and African theaters, the situation of the Allies appeared little short of desperate. All continental Europe, from the Atlantic to a line deep in Russia, was in Nazi-Fascist hands, with the exception of neutral Sweden, Switzerland, Turkey, and Portugal, and of a Franco Spain whose "neutrality" was heavily weighted on Hitler's side. On the crucial Russian front, the line established by the German attack of the autumn of '41 had been here and there pushed back by a Soviet winter offensive, but it was certain that a renewed German offensive would score great gains during the coming summer and might well drive all the way to the Caucasus, capturing the rich oil fields of Baku and perhaps knocking Russia completely out of the war by year's end. In North Africa, too, the Germans (Rommel's Afrika Korps) were preparing to renew the offensive; they aimed to do more than gain back the Libyan ground lost to the British offensive of last January: they aimed to bring Egypt and the Suez Canal into the Nazi empire by autumn. Thus Nazi forces driving south through Iran into Iraq might connect, somewhere along the Euphrates, with Nazi forces that had driven north through Palestine and Syria, sweeping then over the whole of the Middle East to assure the European Axis of inexhaustible supplies of Arabian oil. A Nazi thrust eastward across the Persian plateau toward India would thereafter be feasible.

By then, Japan herself might be firmly established in India, whose disaffection from the British Empire, and lack of internal political stability, was again being demonstrated by Congress Party agitation for immediate and unqualified Indian independence.‡ The conquest of Burma had of course meant the closing of the Burma Road to the Allies, the single land communication between the Western Allies and Chiang Kai-shek's China. The latter's already precarious situation was thus rendered even more precarious, and the possibility of a total collapse of Chinese resistance within a few months seemed very real. If that happened, some twenty Japanese divisions would be freed for further conquest—and certainly the island of Ceylon, and the Indian coastal regions of Madras, Andhra, and Orissa were vulnerable to attacks mounted in Burma, Sumatra, or the Andamans.

As a matter of fact, for almost the whole of April, or up until just a few days ago, the Japanese Navy had been master of the Bay of Bengal and of whatever other portions of the Indian Ocean it cared to enter. Five aircraft carriers, four fast battleships, a number of cruisers and destroyers, accompanied by tankers for refueling—all under the command of Vice Admiral Chuichi Nagumo of Pearl Harbor fame—had conducted a raid and demonstration frightening to the British, who could

‡ Somewhat over three months later, in August of '42, this agitation would become violent, involving large-scale riots all over the subcontinent and repeated acts of sabotage against railroads. Gandhi, Nehru, and other leaders of the Congress Party would then be arrested and imprisoned by the British, as they had often been before.

of course not be sure that it was not the prelude to an actual invasion of Ceylon. An air raid upon Colombo, capital of that big, rich, and strategic island, had seriously damaged port installations and cost the British nineteen fighter planes shot down, plus six Swordfish planes of the Fleet Air Arm—twenty-five planes in all—at a cost of twenty-five Japanese aircraft. British ship losses included two destroyers, two cruisers, a small aircraft carrier and an armed merchant cruiser sunk, plus a merchantman seriously damaged. Simultaneously, upwards of ninety-three thousand tons of merchant shipping, bound outward from Calcutta, had been sunk. And all this had been accomplished without damage to a single Japanese vessel. Alas (from the war lord's point of view), that portion of the British Fleet assigned to the Indian Ocean§ had shied away from full-scale naval combat, else it would certainly have been annihilated by the vastly superior Japanese.

But, after all, this whole Indian Ocean operation *had* been but a demonstration, a probing operation, profitably filling the interim between the conquest of the Dutch East Indies and the next moves definitely indicated by that Japanese Basic Plan which had been completed well over three years before the Pearl Harbor attack. Had the air resistance at Colombo been negligible (it had in fact been surprisingly strong), a radical revision of the Basic Plan might have been indicated. As it was, no such grandiose conception as the conquest of India could be deemed operationally feasible until further Japanese victories were gained in the Pacific—and those war lords trained to think in naval terms might now regret that (largely due to the action at Colombo) three of the five carriers Nagumo had used in the Indian Ocean operation had had to be sent to Japan for refitting and re-equipment. Their availability for the immediately pending operation, south of Rabaul, would have been a virtually final assurance of success. Their absence, on the other hand, caused few serious qualms, since they seemed by no means *necessary* to success.

Indeed, on this May 1, there appeared no convincing reason to believe that all three of the next objectives in the Basic Plan would not be achieved in swift, relatively easy succession. The *first* of these, now prepared in the command headquarters at Rabaul for launching from that point and from Truk some 750 miles north, was the conquest of Tulagi near Guadalcanal in the Solomons, well suited to the establishment of a strong seaplane base, and Port Moresby on the Papuan peninsula of New Guinea, directly opposite and but a few hundred miles from the Cape York Peninsula of Australia's state of Queensland. At Port Moresby, a sizable number of Army troops were to join with a naval landing force to make this point not only a base for ships and planes but also a port of embarkation for establishing control over the Great Barrier Reef and,

§ It consisted of four old and slow battleships, three aircraft carriers (including the light carrier *Hermes*, which was the one sunk at Colombo), seven cruisers (one of them Dutch), and sixteen destroyers.

soon thereafter, for the invasion of key points on the Australian mainland. The *second* of the three objectives was divided geographically between two widely separated land areas but was single in conception and ultimate purpose. Midway Atoll in the central Pacific was to be conquered and occupied. So were the western Aleutians (the island chain extending toward Japan from Alaska). And it was expected that a concomitant of this would be a decisive encounter with the U. S. Fleet before its severe losses at Pearl Harbor and in subsequent actions in the East Indies had been made good by American shipyard production. Such an encounter would (hopefully) result in the Fleet's destruction by greatly superior Japanese naval forces. The *third* and final objective of this phase of operations was the conquest of New Caledonia, Fiji, and Samoa, which would effectively cut the vital lines of communication between Australia and the United States across the Pacific, destroying the possibility of a counteroffensive from Australia northward (since the necessary buildup of troops and materiel could not be achieved) and probably forcing Australia out of the war.

Thus the bright view—past, present, future—seen through war lords' eyes . . .

The same facts and prospects, seen through Allied eyes, took on, of course, a very different hue: they were enshrouded in gloom, they provoked the liveliest anxieties. The threat to Australia was acutely felt and loudly proclaimed by the Government of that island continent, whose fears were echoed and in some cases amplified by nervous residents of the U. S.'s West Coast. Especially had this been so since the fall of Java on March 8. "The Pacific situation is now very grave," the normally sanguine Roosevelt had cabled Churchill on the day after Java's surrender,[26] indicating that he, like the Prime Minister and the Combined Chiefs of Staff, was undergoing during these anxious weeks an increasingly severe test of nerve. Great was the temptation to modify drastically, if not to shift wholly away from, the fundamental strategy of "beat Hitler first." But the temptation was resisted; the strategists at the Allied summit remained unwavering in their basic commitment.

At the height of the crisis in the Indian Ocean, Churchill pointed out to Roosevelt that nearly a third of the Japanese battle fleet and half their total number of carriers had been diverted from the Pacific to the Bay of Bengal and that, therefore, the U. S. Pacific Fleet must have in its assigned area a preponderance of strength over its enemy. The "situation would seem to offer [to the U. S. Fleet] an immediate opportunity," the Prime Minister cabled on April 7.[27] A week later his plea for diversionary action by the U. S. Fleet was more explicit and urgent. The British, he insisted, supporting his insistence with convincing data, were "unable to fight a fleet action" with any chance of success against Nagumo's powerful force. There was therefore "no reason" in the absence of an American diversion "why the Japanese should not become the dominating factor in the Western Indian Ocean. This would result in the collapse of our whole position in the Middle East, not only because of the interruption to our convoys to the Middle East and India [such convoys were forced to sail around Africa's Cape of Good Hope, since the Mediterranean was controlled by the enemy], but also because of the interruptions to the oil supplied from Abadan, without which we cannot maintain our position either on sea or on land in the Indian Ocean area. Supplies to Russia via the Persian Gulf would also be cut." Roosevelt could only reply with the definite promise of some land-based bombing planes and a hint of important "measures now in hand by the Pacific Fleet" which could not as yet be communicated in detail "because of secrecy requirements" but which "we hope . . . you will find . . . effective.[28]

Yet on the very day that the Prime Minister cabled the President his blackest forebodings, he resisted heavy pressures from his own countrymen who wished to divert bombers from the attack on Germany to defenses of the Middle East and India. On April 12, three days before the Churchill cable last quoted above, General Wavell in India had sent a bitter message to the Chiefs of Staff in which he said: "It certainly gives us [in India] furiously to think when, after trying with less than twenty light-bombers to meet attack which cost us three important warships and several others and nearly 100,000 tons of merchant shipping, we see that over two hundred heavy bombers attacked one town in Germany." Churchill had admitted that such views "are certainly fashionable at the moment," but had dismissed them. The Prime Minister's faith in the efficacy of strategic bombing was not shared by every close student of war (though the preponderance of "expert" opinion was with him), but in terms of it he remained unshaken in his adherence to the strategy that gave Hitler's Germany the status of Enemy Number One. He refused to do anything that would weaken the "great plant" which "we have built up . . . here for the bombing of Germany, which is the only way in our power of helping Russia."[29]

Roosevelt, too, had resisted strong pressures from his countrymen for a major shift of emphasis from hostilities with Germany toward hostilities with Japan. It was a general though by no means universal characteristic of prewar isolationists that their aversion to Hitler was less strong than their aversion to the "Yellow Peril." Many of them were racists at heart. Lindbergh, for instance, had reportedly felt few "misgivings" about an all-out war of the United States upon Japan, provided Germany were not too closely allied with her, since Japan was an aggressive "spearhead" of those "Asiatic hordes" threatening "Western civilization." People holding such views found it easy to conclude, in their public expressions, that Roosevelt supported the strategy of "Hitler first" only because Churchill had "sold" him a "bill of goods." He was, they allegedly believed and certainly loudly said, a puppet of Perfidious Albion—a conclusion sympathetically received if not actually encouraged by MacArthur's headquarters. Such charges the President could easily ignore, knowing that they would be proved wholly false by the historical record when this was ultimately spread before the public gaze.

Harder for him to resist was the pressure from Admiral Ernest J. King. When the U. S. Joint Chiefs of Staff was set up to parallel the British arrangement, in March, King had assumed the supreme naval post that combined the formerly separate offices of Chief of Naval Operations and Fleet Commander-in-Chief. He was vigorously opposed to the global strategy of which Admiral Stark, now in London, had been a principal architect—the strategy which made the Pacific a theater secondary in importance to the Atlantic—and he capitalized on the undeniable emergency in the Pacific to obtain a considerably greater diversion of men and supplies to that ocean than would (probably) have otherwise obtained. He did not, however, force any fundamental strategical change. On this the President stood firm, sustained by General Marshall who in turn was sustained by the newly appointed Assistant Chief of Staff in charge of War Plans, Brigadier General Eisenhower.¶ When King formally proposed to General Marshall in mid-February that the Army garrison many more Pacific islands than had previously been planned for, Marshall made formal reply (initially drafted in War Plans) indicating that "a change in basic strategy, as already approved by the Combined Chiefs of Staff," seemed to be implied and that therefore "the entire situation must be reconsidered before we become involved more seriously" in the kind of Army deployment wanted by the Admiral.[30] Eisenhower's personal, private response to the proposal was confided to his diary on February 17: "The Navy wants to take all the islands in the Pacific—have them held by Army troops, to become bases for Army pursuit and bombers. Then! the Navy will have a safe place to sail its vessels. But they will not go farther forward than our air [Army] can assure superiority. . . . The amount of air required for this slow, laborious and indecisive type of warfare is going to be something that will keep us from going to Russia's aid in time!!"[31]

Eisenhower had been, as we have seen, the chief War Department operations officer for the Pacific when he first came to Washington immediately after Pearl Harbor. In this capacity he had insisted in January that reinforcement of ABDA must take precedence over all else for the time being. But *only* for the time being. Never absent from his mind, even during the period of his most intense preoccupation with the Pacific war, was his sense of the crucial importance to the Allied cause of keeping Russia in the war and his conviction that every element of grand strategy must either contribute directly to this end or be consistent with it. "We've got to go to Europe and fight—and we've got to quit wasting resources all over the world—and still worse—wasting time," he wrote in his diary on January 22. "If we're to keep Russia in, save the

¶ Leonard T. Gerow, promoted to major general, was assigned to command the 29th Division on February 16. On that date his place as head of War Plans was taken by Eisenhower.

Middle East, India and Burma; we've got to begin slugging with air at West Europe; to be followed by a land attack as soon as possible."[32] A little over a month later he prepared a memorandum for Marshall in which, accepting the conclusions arrived at during the ABC-1 conversations and confirmed at ARCADIA, he made cogent logical arguments for them. The decision to concentrate on Hitler, said he, was an application of the "strategic axiom" that a commander facing a divided enemy should first attack and defeat the weaker force.** Though Germany with her satellites was certainly "stronger in total combat power" than Japan, she was "relatively" weaker than Japan since she was heavily engaged with Russia whereas Japan was still at peace with the Soviets. Moreover, it was much harder to attack Japan in force than to attack Germany: three or four times as much shipping was needed to transport and maintain a given American unit in the Pacific as was required in the Atlantic area. Hence "logistic reasons" concurred with the "strategic axiom" in the present situation.

In pursuit of the over-all strategy "we must," Eisenhower went on to say, "differentiate sharply and definitely between those things whose accomplishment in the several theaters over the world is *necessary* to the ultimate defeat of the Axis Powers, as opposed to those which are merely *desirable* because of their effect in facilitating such defeat." Necessary, in his view, were "(a) Maintenance of the United Kingdom. . . . ; (b) Retention of Russia in the war. . . . ; (c) Maintenance of a position in the India-Middle East Area which will prevent physical junction of the two principal enemies. . . ." Desirable, but not essential to winning the war, were the maintenance of "a reasonably safe line of communications to Australia" and of "the most advanced bases possible for eventual offensives against the Japanese Empire," as well as the denial to Japan of "free access to the Southeastern Pacific and its natural resources." It was his conception of the "necessary" which led him to urge "immediate and definite action" to aid Russia through increased lend-lease and "through the early initiation of operations that will draw off from the Russian front sizable portions of the German Army, both air and ground." On the latter point, he was both emphatic and specific, saying: "We should at once develop, in conjunction with the British, a definite plan of operations against Northwest Europe. It should be drawn up at once, in detail, and it should be sufficiently extensive in scale as to engage from the middle of May onward, an increasing portion of the German Air Force, and by late summer an increasing amount of his ground forces."[33]

From the Eisenhower memorandum of February 28 evolved what became known as the Marshall Memorandum, which was presented to Roosevelt by the Chief of Staff and Secretary Stimson on April 1, 1942. Its conclusion was that all plans and preparations should be directed to the "single end" of "an attack, by combined forces of approximately 5800

** This in fact is the "opposite" of that "strategem axiom" on which the RAINBOW 5 and ABC-1 were actually based. See page 133.

combat airplanes and 48 divisions against western Europe as soon as the necessary means can be accumulated in England"—estimated at April 1, 1943. Eisenhower's stated belief that a major cross-channel attack could and should be launched in 1942 had had to be modified in the harsh light of realities. There would not be enough ships and landing craft,†† there would be too many urgent competing demands for almost every resource, to permit serious consideration of a European invasion target-date earlier than the spring of 1943. The Marshall Memorandum *was*, nevertheless, a definite proposal for decisive action. Roosevelt approved it on the day it was presented to him, and promptly arranged for Hopkins and Marshall to go to London with it to secure the concurrence of the Prime Minister and British Chiefs. When they returned in mid-April it was with the belief that a firm operational agreement had indeed been reached. Eisenhower was jubilant, noting that ". . . at long last, and after months of struggle, . . . we are all definitely committed to one concept of fighting!"

Thus, at a time when victory-flushed Japan was at the very height of her power, being now assured of an abundance of oil, rubber, and other sinews of war—and at the very moment when she prepared new and decisive actions against forces much weaker than her own—the supreme command of the Western Allies maintained and even increased its over-all emphasis upon the war in Europe. But in so doing it was aware that it took in the Pacific calculated risks of the utmost gravity. The statistical assessment of probabilities that characterizes a large and distant view of current events—the kind of view that men at the summit of directive authority must necessarily take—led to the conclusion that Japan, despite obvious appearances, lacked sufficient strength at the outer margin of her conquests to prevail over the defenses that could be mobilized against her. Every one of her earlier objectives had been achieved; the next would be denied her. No person, however, was absolutely sure of this, since such certainties are always after the fact. They could derive now only from the battles that impended, battles wherein the fighting skills and self-sacrificial courage of thousands of individual sailors and airmen would be tested to the utmost.

†† Eisenhower had been pressing for a speed-up of landing craft production since January. His diary records that on January 24 he "went to Bill Somervell [Lieutenant General Brehon B. Somervell, commandant of Army Service Forces] this a.m. to find out what he knows about this landing craft business. He has known nothing to date—but is having the matter looked up."

VII

Crisis and Turning Point in the Pacific

i. *South From Rabaul*[1]

Though no remarkable prescience was required of the top strategic command in Washington and London to surmise in a general way the Japanese intentions, it was impossible to determine by logic alone the precise forms of action these intentions would assume. Plenty of room remained for tactical surprise—and if the enemy were able to add surprise to his formidable superiority of weapons the outcome could be another and perhaps final Allied disaster in that theater. Indeed, the Americans must themselves make a maximum possible use of surprise—the tactic of the surprise carrier raid—if they were to stop the enemy. It was therefore fortunate for the American Pacific command that the Japanese—perhaps as a result of overconfidence and contempt for their enemies—were now careless of security and that the United States had managed since Pearl Harbor Day to break the Japanese naval code.*

Early in the third week of April 1942, Admiral Chester W. Nimitz, headquartered at Pearl Harbor, where he had replaced Admiral Kimmel as CINCPAC (Commander-in-Chief of the Pacific Fleet), was informed by his Naval Intelligence that several Japanese troop transports accompanied by the light carrier *Shoho* and a striking force that included two large carriers, were being gathered together for (apparently) a move into the Coral Sea. A few days later he had in hand enough hard intelligence to determine that the Japanese force would enter the Coral Sea on or about May 3. By that time it seemed obvious to him, as it did to MacArthur, that Port Moresby was the major Japanese objective. Equally obvious (to MacArthur even more than to Nimitz) was the necessity, the imperative necessity, of retaining Moresby in Allied hands, not only as a key element of Australia's outer defenses but also as a base

* The code broken by "Magic" was the diplomatic code.

essential to that "return" to the Philippines which MacArthur had so flamboyantly promised. Nimitz felt therefore compelled to respond to the challenge as strongly as he possibly could.

He was a handsome, white-haired, scholarly-looking man, quiet of manner. His nerves were steady, his will strong, his mind clear and incisive. And he had need of such inner resources at the present juncture, since his outer resources, when measured against the enemy's, were so severely limited. Moreover, he was hampered to a degree by the command setup made by the U. S. Joint Chiefs when MacArthur arrived in Australia. As we have seen, MacArthur was assigned direction of all Allied forces in the Southwest Pacific Area, which included virtually the whole of the Coral Sea. Nimitz was assigned direction of all American forces in the Pacific, military as well as naval, outside MacArthur's designated command area. Within the latter, the arrangement was somewhat ambiguous. CINCPAC, by order of the Joint Chiefs, had strategic control of all naval operations anywhere in the Pacific, which of course included the waters in MacArthur's area; but MacArthur retained absolute strategic control of all ground forces and land-based airplanes in his area. Hence Nimitz, when operating in Southeast Asian waters, could not order searching flights by land-based planes but must depend upon the cooperation of MacArthur to obtain these, insofar as he obtained them at all. The enemy, on the other hand, for operations in the Coral Sea, had under a single tactical command all land-based planes as well as seaplanes and (of course) carrier-based planes.

By noon of April 29, Nimitz had gathered together all the forces available to him for Coral Sea operations and had ordered them to proceed to that battle zone at their best speed. Based at Nouméa, New Caledonia, was Task Force 17 commanded by Rear Admiral Frank Jack Fletcher. It consisted of the carrier *Yorktown*, three heavy cruisers (*Astoria*, *Chester*, and *Portland*), six destroyers, and a tanker (*Neosho*). It was physically ready for combat, after a week of repair and replenishment at Tongatapu. Nimitz ordered it to rendezvous on May 1 at a designated point west of the New Hebrides with a task force which, when the emergency arose, was westward bound from Pearl Harbor. This latter was Task Force 11, under the command of Rear Admiral Aubrey W. Fitch. It was built around the carrier *Lexington* and included the heavy cruisers *Minneapolis* and *New Orleans*, plus five destroyers.

Also ordered to join Fletcher was Task Force 44, which was a part of what had become known as "MacArthur's Navy," based at Sydney, Australia. It was unique in that it was an amalgam of Australian and American naval vessels under the command of the British Rear Admiral J. G. Crace of the Royal Navy. Two of its vessels, the heavy cruiser U.S.S. *Chicago* and the destroyer U.S.S. *Perkins*, were in port at Nouméa as Nimitz was collecting his tactical forces; they were sent to join Fletcher at the rendezvous point on May 1. At Sydney were the three Australian cruisers of this task force, one of which, H.M.A.S. *Canberra*, was being refitted and hence was unavailable for action. Crace was ordered to come up from Sydney with the other two, H.M.A.S. *Australia* and H.M.A.S. *Hobart*, escorted by the destroyer U.S.S. *Whipple;* he was to join Fletcher and Fitch on May 4.

Nimitz also dispatched from Pearl Harbor to the Coral Sea, on April 30, Admiral Halsey's Task Force 16. It consisted of *Hornet* and *Enterprise*, which on April 25 had arrived back at the Hawaiian base from the Doolittle Tokyo strike. The two carriers were accompanied by four cruisers. There was only a slim chance that this force would arrive in the Coral Sea (some forty-three hundred miles from Honolulu) in time to take part in the battle. Certainly it could do so only if the Japanese delayed, for some reason, the move south of Rabaul. If Halsey did arrive before or during the battle he, as senior officer present, would take over tactical command of the operation.

Otherwise, the over-all tactical command would remain vested in Admiral Fletcher, a sandy-haired man possessing many of the qualities traditionally associated with redheads: great fighting courage, quick temper, and a sharp, fast mind whose judgments were occasionally erratic. His April 29 orders from Nimitz were broad and simple. He was to "operate in the Coral Sea commencing 1 May"; there he was to "destroy enemy ships, shipping and aircraft at favorable opportunities in order to assist in checking further advance by the enemy in the New Guinea-Solomons Area." How he did it was up to him and must be in response (a surprising response, to succeed) to what the Japanese did.

Very different was the Japanese plan, for whose execution Vice Admiral Shigeyoshi Inouye, remaining at Rabaul, had over-all command responsibility. The strategic objectives of Operation "MO," as it was called, were simply stated: "With the cooperation of the South Seas Army Detachment and the Navy, we will occupy Port Moresby and important positions on Tulagi and in southeastern New Guinea. We will establish air bases and strengthen our air operations in the Australian area. Successively, an element will carry out a sudden attack against Nauru and Ocean Islands and secure the phosphorus resources [for phosphate fertilizers] located there." But the tactical plan for the achievement of these objectives was complex in the extreme, requiring for its success not only a close coordination of movements by widely divided forces but also a refusal by the American forces of any response not called for by the Japanese script.

Assigned to the Tulagi invasion was a Navy transport, escorted by two destroyers, three converted minesweepers, two minelayers, two converted subchasers, and two special minesweepers. This group was to initiate the action by sailing directly from Rabaul to Tulagi, covered by the light carrier *Shoho*, a destroyer, and four heavy cruisers, one of which, *Aoba*, was the flagship of Rear Admiral Aritomo Goto, who was in command of this covering group. The actual occupation of Tulagi on May 3, and the establishment of a seaplane base there, would do much to blind

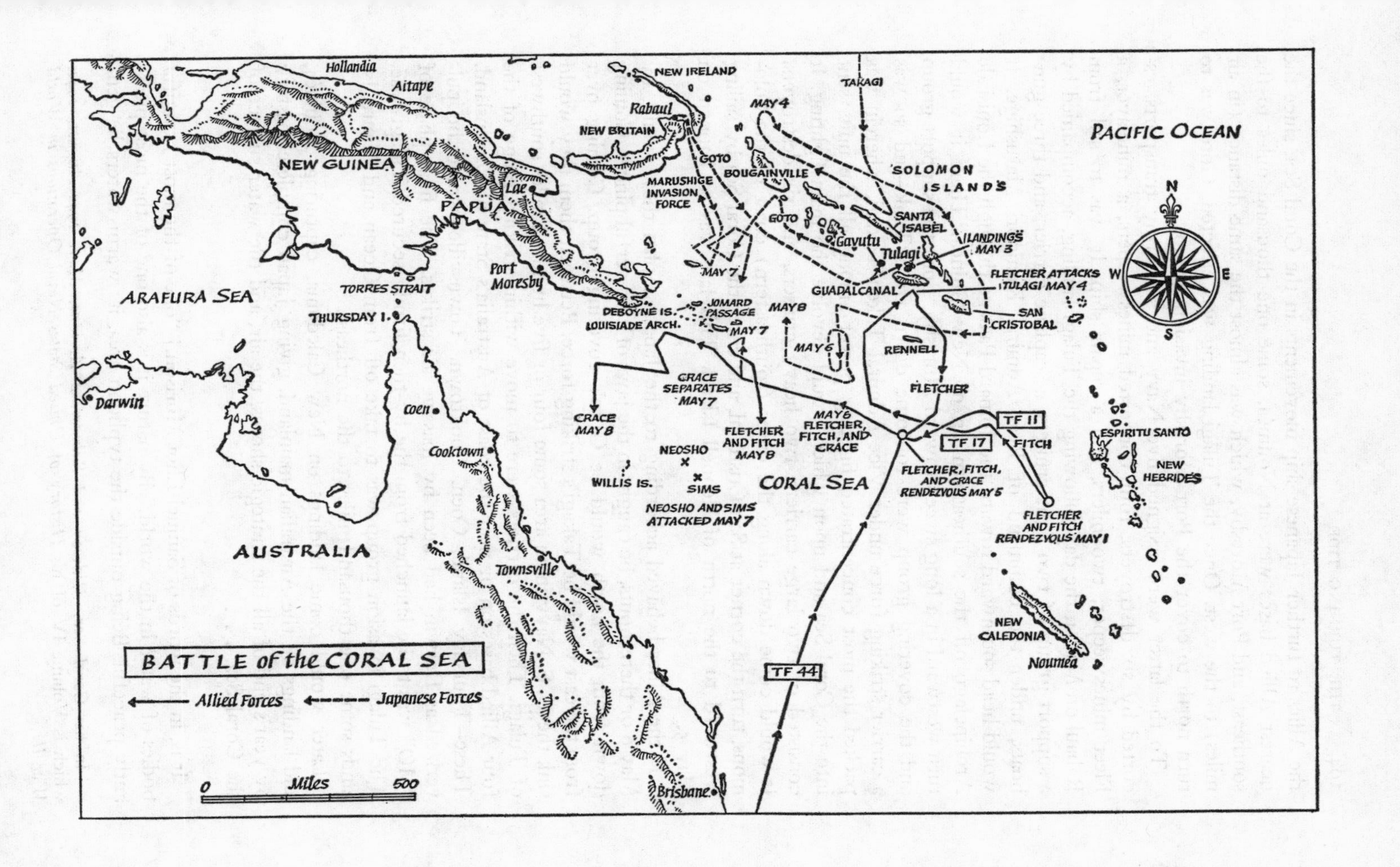
BATTLE of the CORAL SEA
Allied Forces
Japanese Forces
0
Miles
500
PACIFIC OCEAN
N
E
S
W
Hollandia
Aitape
NEW GUINEA
PAPUA
Lae
Port Moresby
TORRES STRAIT
THURSDAY I.
ARAFURA SEA
Darwin
Coen
Cooktown
Townsville
Brisbane
AUSTRALIA
NEW IRELAND
Rabaul
NEW BRITAIN
GOTO
MARUSHIGE INVASION FORCE
BOUGAINVILLE
GOTO
SOLOMON ISLANDS
SANTA ISABEL
Gavutu
Tulagi
LANDINGS MAY 3
FLETCHER ATTACKS TULAGI MAY 4
GUADALCANAL
SAN CRISTOBAL
RENNELL
TAKAGI
MAY 4
MAY 7
DEBOYNE IS.
JOMARD PASSAGE
LOUISIADE ARCH.
MAY 7
MAY 8
MAY 6
FLETCHER
GRACE SEPARATES MAY 7
GRACE MAY 8
FLETCHER AND FITCH MAY 8
MAY 6 FLETCHER, FITCH, AND GRACE
NEOSHO
WILLIS IS.
SIMS
NEOSHO AND SIMS ATTACKED MAY 7
CORAL SEA
TF 11
TF 17
FITCH
FLETCHER, FITCH, AND GRACE RENDEZVOUS MAY 5
FLETCHER AND FITCH RENDEZVOUS MAY 1
ESPIRITU SANTO
NEW HEBRIDES
NEW CALEDONIA
Nouméa
TF 44

the Allies to further Japanese ship movements in the Coral Sea, since the nearest Allied bases were at Nouméa, some one thousand miles to the southeast, and Port Moresby, which was almost the same distance (in air miles) to the west. Once the Tulagi landing was effected, Goto was to turn north to cover the Port Moresby invasion group.

To the latter were assigned five Navy and six Army transports, escorted by six destroyers, four converted minesweepers, a minelayer, a Fleet minesweeper, two oilers, and a repair ship. It was to sail from Rabaul on May 4, the day following the Tulagi landing, accompanied by a support group of two light cruisers, a seaplane carrier, and three gunboats, under the command of Rear Admiral Kuninori Marushige. It would head southward toward the Jomard Passage through the Louisiade Archipelago off the southeastern tip of New Guinea. There it would turn westward in a long sweep toward Moresby. Both the support group and the covering group were to come down from Truk—and so was a carrier striking force under Vice Admiral Takeo Takagi, wherein was packed the most concentrated fighting power among all the units sent into the Coral Sea and upon which would devolve the main fighting. It consisted of two large carriers, two heavy cruisers, and six destroyers. It would come down along the outer (southeastern) coast of the Solomons, turn the corner at San Cristóbal, and enter the Coral Sea by sailing westward to the north of Rennell Island. This last was to happen on May 5.

If the Allies behaved according to the Japanese plan they would, by May 6 or thereabouts, be caught in the jaws of a powerful pincer. Coming down from the north would be Goto's covering group. Coming over from the east would be Takagi's striking force. Between them they would sink the U. S. Navy in an area some four or five hundred miles southwest of Tulagi. Then the carriers were to move within striking range of the four Allied bases on or near the coast of Australia's State of Queensland. These—Thursday Island, Coen, Cooktown, Townsville—would be pulverized as Darwin had been by massive air strikes. The final phase of "MO" was to be launched from the by-then firmly secured Tulagi base. The Tulagi invasion group was to take off from Ocean and Nauru Islands some one thousand miles to the northeast.

Later would come landings on New Caledonia, capturing Nouméa, and landings on the Australian mainland, giving Japan complete mastery by year's end of all the strategic shores, the air, and the water surface of the Coral Sea. . . .

It is, in the words of Samuel Eliot Morison,† "one of the most beautiful bodies of water in the world." By nature it is also one of the most pleasantly peaceful. Being outside the typhoon area, its warm waters lie gen-

† In his *Coral Sea, Midway and Submarine Actions, May, 1942–August, 1942,* which is Volume IV of his *History of United States Naval Operations in World War II.*

erally calm, mildly swept by the southeast trade winds, under bright blue skies—and they wash the shores of some of the loveliest of South Sea Isles. "Almost all the islands on its eastern and northern edges," writes Morison, ". . . are lofty, jungle-clad, and ringed with bright coral beaches and reefs. Here the interplay of sunlight, pure air and transparent water may be seen at its loveliest; peacock-hued shoals over the coral gardens break off abruptly from an emerald fringe into deeps of brilliant amethyst. Even under the rare overcasts that veil the tropical sun, the Coral Sea becomes a warm dove-gray in color instead of assuming the bleak foul-weather dress of the ocean in high latitudes." And what nature here blessed had been heretofore undisturbed, in any serious way, by man; happy is the sea that has no history, and before this spring of 1942, world history had paid small heed to the Coral Sea.

On May 1, at 6:15 in the morning, at a point some 250 miles southwest of Espíritu Santo, Fletcher's *Yorktown* force rendezvoused with Fitch's *Lexington* force, and with the two vessels of Crace's force that had come up from Nouméa. Fletcher's first order to his newly joined forces was that all ships fuel—Task Force 17 from the tanker *Neosho*, Task Force 11 from the oiler *Tippecanoe*. It was a time-consuming operation, especially for the *Lexington* group which was very thirsty for fuel after the long, fast run from Pearl Harbor—and Fletcher decided in the afternoon of May 2 that he could not wait for its completion.

All that day, from MacArthur's headquarters, he had been receiving intelligence of Japanese movements southward. They confirmed earlier estimates of enemy intentions—something big indeed was shaping up—but they gave no clear information as to the enemy's present whereabouts. Fletcher had reason to believe that his own whereabouts, on the other hand, were well known to the enemy, one of whose submarines, surfaced, had been sighted by a *Yorktown* scouting plane at 3:30 that afternoon and probably sunk by three other *Yorktown* planes a short while later. (Actually, Admiral Inouye at Rabaul received no report from this submarine; he remained unaware that an Allied carrier force had entered these waters.) Meanwhile, Fletcher had been informed by Fitch that fueling of the *Lexington* group could not be completed until noon of May 4. He therefore ordered Fitch to rejoin him on May 4 at the point previously designated for rendezvous with Crace's force coming up from Sydney (it was some five hundred and eighty miles off the Queensland coast, near the Willis Isles). He then, at six o'clock, set his course westward toward the middle of the Coral Sea, his aim being to find the enemy by plane search and, if the "opportunity" were "favorable," engage him.

At eight o'clock on the morning of May 3, while Fletcher was a half-thousand miles away, the Tulagi invasion group of the Japanese began to land at its objective. The landing was unopposed; the Australians had had a very small garrison there until May 1 when, told that a Japanese attack was probably imminent, they had begun to evacuate it, an operation that was completed before the Japanese force appeared. Fletcher knew nothing of this until seven o'clock that evening. He was fueling his destroyers from *Neosho*, as he had been doing since dawn, when he received from MacArthur's headquarters a report that planes based in Australia had sighted troop transports debarking soldiers at Tulagi. They had also sighted a half-dozen or so Japanese warships in the waters between Tulagi and Santa Isabel twenty or thirty miles to the north. Within a few minutes thereafter, Fletcher decided to launch an air strike against Tulagi.

Abruptly he terminated the fueling. He ordered *Neosho*, accompanied by the destroyer *Russell*, to meet Fitch and Crace at the rendezvous point near the Willis Isles where, informed of his change of plans, they were to be directed to meet him at a point three hundred miles south of Guadalcanal at dawn on May 5. He did not know that Fitch had completed fueling from *Tippecanoe* by shortly after noon that day, nearly twenty-four hours ahead of the previously estimated time. The necessity to maintain radio silence denied Fitch this means of communication, and he evidently saw no need to send a plane up to *Yorktown* with a drop-message. Had he done so he would undoubtedly have been directed to come north at once to support the strike Fletcher was about to make.

At 8:30, Fletcher turned to the north and moved at top speed (twenty-six to twenty-seven knots) toward a point at which he could launch planes against Tulagi. Well before he reached that point at seven o'clock next morning (May 4)—a point about one hundred miles southwest of Guadalcanal—he ran into weather uncommon in the Coral Sea. A cold front one hundred miles wide had been moving up from Australia and had now reached the northern coast of Guadalcanal. Fortunately for the Allies, it had not extended to Tulagi a few miles to the north. This meant that Tulagi enjoyed its usual beautiful day—brilliant sunlight, calm and sparkling seas—while *Yorktown* and her accompanying ships wallowed in rough seas under cloudy skies which, at frequent intervals, emitted heavy rain. The weather increased the difficulty of launching planes but, on the whole, prospered Fletcher's plan; it screened his approach and militated against retaliatory attacks by the enemy.

He began to launch *Yorktown's* planes just before sunrise on May 4—an attack group consisting of a dozen torpedo planes and twenty-eight dive bombers divided among squadrons which flew independently to the target and operated independently over it.‡ He accepted grave risks as he did so, in *Lexington's* absence. He could not provide fighter escorts for his bombers. He had a mere eighteen Wildcats aboard in operating condition; these must provide protection, a dangerously slim protection, for the carrier itself by flying combat air patrols in three shifts of six planes each. The bombers must defend themselves against whatever fighters rose against them, and they had only .30-caliber machine guns with

‡ This lack of tactical coordination, whereby the defensive and offensive values of mutual reinforcement were lost, soon gave way to more sophisticated and effective naval air tactics—in part as a result of lessons learned over Tulagi.

which to do so. It was therefore fortunate for them that the Japanese strength, like Fletcher's, was now widely dispersed.

In the overconfidence born of easy conquests in Java, the Japanese command had assumed that the Allies would not dare attack a secured base and, on this assumption, in accordance with MO's complex plan, had sent northward before noon of May 3, to cover the Port Moresby invasion group, both Admiral Goto's group and Admiral Marushige's. They were now too far away to respond to the base's frantic cry for help. So was Admiral Takagi with his carrier striking force. Takagi was north of Bougainville, fueling, at noon on May 4, when he first learned of Tulagi's ordeal—and though he at once headed southwest at full speed, he was yet far north of the outer coasts of the Solomons when the last plane to return from the last Tulagi assault had been recovered by *Yorktown*.

Hence no fighters came up to challenge the American bombers as they roared out of foul weather into bright, clear skies and soon saw below them, in early morning light, Tulagi Harbor and adjacent Gavutu Harbor crowded with enemy shipping. Nor were they challenged in their two later assaults, of which the last began its fly-off at two in the afternoon. At a cost of just three planes,§ the Americans inflicted upon the Japanese painful losses: a destroyer, a cargo ship, five anchored seaplanes, three minesweepers (two of them small), and four landing barges, plus another destroyer and a patrol craft damaged. These were meager compared to the losses the jubilant returning fliers *believed* they had inflicted: two destroyers, a freighter, and four gunboats totally destroyed; a light cruiser, a destroyer, a freighter, and a seaplane tender severely damaged. They seemed meager, too, when considered in terms of the weight of metal and explosives that had been discharged at the enemy. Altogether, the Americans that day launched twenty-two torpedoes, dropped seventy-six half-ton bombs, and fired some eighty-three thousand machine-gun bullets at an enemy whose only defense was heavy though (in the event) ineffective anti-aircraft fire. (When Admiral Nimitz endorsed the action report six weeks later, he would comment on the disappointing disproportion between "ammunition expended" and "results obtained," saying it indicated "the necessity for target practice at every opportunity.") Obviously the Tulagi strike was not the Allied success it might have been and would have been had the same pilots made it under the same circumstances a few months later.

Nevertheless it *was* a success, undeniably, in a season that had seen few of them, and it heartened Task Force 17 as Fletcher turned it to the south. He ran fast through the evening and night of May 4, and into the morning of May 5 when, at 8:16, be rendezvoused at the appointed place with the *Lexington* group and Crace's. On that morning, one of *Yorktown's* patrol planes shot down a four-engined Japanese seaplane—but this was the last action for Fletcher's force for two days.

§ One, lost at sea, was never seen again. The other two crash-landed on Guadalcanal; their pilots were rescued that night by the destroyer *Hammann*.

They were now well south of the weather that had protected their approach to Tulagi. They sailed again upon bright blue water under a bright blue sky, caressed by a wind that was soft and warm. Into this southeast wind they steamed at a leisurely pace, both the speed and direction of their movement being dictated by the fact that Fletcher was again refueling from *Neosho*. At nightfall he changed course to the northwest and ran in that direction through the darkness in order to close the distance he had opened during daylight hours between himself and the enemy, assuming, as he did, that the latter was coming out of Rabaul. At dawn next day he turned again into the southeast wind and resumed fueling.

This next day was May 6, the black Wednesday of Corregidor's fall.

At seven in the morning Fletcher put into effect the operation order he had drawn up on May 1, integrating Fitch's and Crace's groups with his own to form a single enlarged Task Force 17. Thereafter he could use his cruisers and destroyers as a unified circular screen for his two carriers, and was as well organized for battle in the Coral Sea as he would ever be. Nearly five hours later, or shortly before noon, the code room of his flagship, *Yorktown,* intercepted a radio signal beamed "in the clear" (that is, in plain English) from Corregidor to Honolulu, saying, GOING OFF THE AIR NOW. GOODBYE AND GOOD LUCK. CALLAHAN AND MC COY. Thus flatly, in words without eloquence or grace, was announced the end of Wainwright's command on The Rock, indicating that the fortunes of U.S. arms in international war had reached their lowest ebb since the burning of Washington by the British in 1814.

Such bitter news, coming to an American Navy professional, could not but harden his determination to do all in his power to reverse the tide.

But where was the enemy? Alas, as it had the day before, Fletcher's search group sought and did not find. For one thing, its eyes were too few; the group consisted of the seaplane tender *Tangier*, operating out of Nouméa, and a mere dozen Catalina patrol planes. For another, its range of vision was triply limited: first, by the cruising range of these seaplanes, which could not fly far enough to search the Solomons; second, by the division of the Coral Sea between the South Pacific and MacArthur's Southwest Pacific Area (the western three-fourths of the sea was supposed to be searched by Australian-based Army planes, though these were too few and too far away to do the job adequately); and third, by the stationary cold front whose stormy mists were as a curtain, one hundred miles in width, dropped down upon the sea between Fletcher's present position and the area where the Japanese were making their next major move. Who could tell what forces were hidden within this curtain's folds? Certainly his carrier-based reconnaissance planes could not; the results of their search that morning and again that afternoon were negative.

All that day, however, from Brisbane and from Pearl Harbor, Fletcher received bits of intelligence out of which, by midafternoon, a consistent pattern of enemy activity had begun to emerge. At 10:30 that morning, four U. S. Army Flying Fortresses (B-17s), staged at Moresby, sighted the light aircraft carrier *Shoho* some sixty miles south of Bougainville. They attempted to sink her with bombs, but no one of the twelve they dropped before being driven off by fighters came near enough to do her the slightest harm. At noon, another flight of Allied planes sighted *Shoho* and other vessels of Admiral Goto's covering group heading to the south. Then, at two that afternoon, these planes sighted the Port Moresby invasion group which had come out of its base only a little while before and was not yet far south of Rabaul. This item of information completed the picture for him. His staff Intelligence said definitely that the Moresby group was to establish an advance seaplane base in the Louisiades, off the tip of New Guinea, and then proceed through the Jomard Passage west and north toward their invasion objective.

So by 6:30 that evening Fletcher had cut short his fueling and dispatched *Neosho* (with her destroyer escort *Sims*) to the point where she was normally scheduled to be on odd-numbered days, shortly after sunrise, to serve as "gas station" for whatever Navy craft needed her. He himself headed north in order to be within plane-strike distance of the Moresby invasion group by dawn on May 7.

What he did *not* know was that a third enemy force, and by far the most potent of the three, was indeed hidden from his searching eyes by the weather to his north. Admiral Takagi's powerful striking force, centered on the big carriers *Shokaku* and *Zuikaku*, had made the turn around San Cristóbal at seven o'clock the preceding evening and, heading west to the north of Rennell Island, had penetrated far into the Coral Sea by the dawn of the present day. Takagi was then slanting to the northwest, a course he held until 7:30 when he turned to his left and headed due south under the cold front's clouds.

Only by chances that were lucky for Fletcher and unlucky for Takagi had an encounter between the two been missed that day. Chance one occurred an hour or so before noon when a Rabaul-based search plane sighted Fletcher and reported the Allied position precisely. This information reached Admiral Inouye—it satisfied him that the Allies thus far were responding as the Japanese plan of envelopment required them to do, and encouraged him to adhere rigidly to this plan—but for some unknown reason it failed to reach Takagi. Chance two was Takagi's evident dependence on seaplanes, carried by his escorting cruisers, for such searches as he made that day. Had he launched long-range searches from his carriers that afternoon he probably would have found Fletcher refueling in sunlight, hence in no position to make the most effective defense against attack, while he himself remained hidden beneath clouds.

As it was, Takagi had reached a point only seventy miles from Fletcher by six o'clock that evening when, having to refuel, he turned away and headed into a light evening breeze from the north. He continued northward until two o'clock the following morning, turning then, again, to the south. Four hours later, or at six o'clock in the morning of May 7, he launched a plane search southward: he wanted to make sure that no Allied carrier force would be operating behind him after he had turned back to cover the Moresby invasion group.

With the launching of this search the maneuvers preliminary to the Battle of the Coral Sea may be said to have ended. Now the actual man-killing conflict begins.

ii. *The Battle of the Coral Sea*

There exists in certain streams of the Amazon Basin an incredibly voracious carnivorous little fish called piranha which, drawn by the taste or smell of fresh blood, will attack a wounded animal in vast numbers and devour it alive. A slight cut, even a scratch emitting a drop of blood, dooms to frightful death any solitary warm-blooded animal entering waters that contain these thronging and insatiable creatures; every vestige of flesh is stripped from its bones with amazing swiftness amidst a horrible stuttering turbulence of bloody water. Nevertheless a single large animal will occupy all the piranhas in the vicinity for a good many minutes, and this fact is made use of by cattle drovers who must cross a piranha-infested stream. They deliberately wound one of their animals, drive it bleeding into the water, and while the piranhas are occupied with it make their crossing a safe distance away.

For us there is analogy here: what the wounded animal does for the remainder of its herd poor *Neosho* and *Sims* are now about to do for the remainder of Task Force 17, not because anyone has planned it that way but because of a Japanese pilot's mistake in recognition and a Japanese admiral's gullible overeagerness.

The pilot is of the search sent out at dawn this May 7. At 7:36 he reports the sighting of an Allied carrier accompanied by a cruiser near the eastern edge of the assigned search area—a point some eight hundred miles east and a little south of Townsville on the Queensland coast. We who see it all from afar know that no cruiser is there, and no carrier. What the pilot sees so inaccurately is, of course, the tanker *Neosho* and the destroyer *Sims* as they arrive at their fueling rendezvous. But Takagi's chief air officer, Rear Admiral Tadaichi Hara, in direct command of the two Japanese carriers and their destroyer escorts, has suspected the presence of a hostile carrier or carriers in this area, which prejudices him in favor of the searcher's report. He therefore accepts it at face value and orders at once an all-out attack.

Thus is sealed the doom of *Sims*, and of *Neosho* a mile or so behind her. Neither nor both together are worth, in the circumstances, the effort now spent on their destruction; neither can survive it.

General quarters is sounded on both vessels at a little after nine when a single plane aims a single bomb at *Sims*, and misses. She manages to dodge or be missed by all the bombs aimed at her in two succeeding attacks—by fifteen high-flying planes at 9:30, by ten low-flying ones a little over an hour later—but at noon no fewer than three dozen dive bombers appear and soon thereafter, for all her swift maneuvering, she is struck simultaneously by three half-ton bombs. Her wounds are immediately fatal. Within a few minutes she sinks and, just as the water is about to close over her, explodes in a terrific tower of flame and smoke and debris that kills nearly all her crew (there are only fourteen survivors) and shatters the nerves of many a witness on nearby *Neosho*. For they, too, are under vicious attack. Twenty dive bombers concentrate on the tanker with deadly accuracy—far more deadly than American pilots have yet been able to achieve. In a few minutes she takes seven direct hits and eight damaging near-misses and is left a staggering wreck, her decks swept by flaming gasoline from a Japanese plane that has struck and exploded against one of her gun stations. Her captain at once orders preparations to abandon ship, whereupon many of his men, panicking in anticipation of *Sims'* dreadful fate, jump overboard and are drowned.¶ But *Neosho* doesn't sink. Not now. For four days she will drift with the wind, burying her dead, caring for her wounded as best she can—until, on May 11, a searching Catalina finds her and tells destroyer *Henley* where to go to take off her 123 survivors (including the fourteen from *Sims*). *Henley* will do so in the afternoon, then sink her.

This extinction of two American ships and some scores of American lives is purchased at the price of a half-dozen Japanese planes. Do the Japanese make a net gain by this bloody transaction? They do not. Takagi will need every plane he can lay hands on tomorrow; he will sorely miss the six lost today. Far more important than this, however, is the loss of opportunity. *Neosho* and *Sims* in their agony have indeed served the function of a sacrificial animal in a piranha-infested stream; they have diverted forces which, if employed elsewhere, might well have won for Japan the Battle of the Coral Sea.

For witness what is happening to the north and west . . .

Let us go back to the dawn of this day. As the sun rises above the ocean's rim at 6:45, Fletcher's Task Force 17 has reached a point some hundred-odd miles south of the outermost island of the Louisiades—a good position from which to attack the Moresby invasion group as it attempts to slip through the Jomard Passage. Fletcher makes at this point a curious decision, one which will in the future subject him to severe criticism from naval strategists. He divides his forces. He detaches Crace's support group (three cruisers, three destroyers) and sends it straight on to the northwest. Why? Out of prudence, he will later explain. He is practically certain to be soon engaged in a deadly duel with enemy carriers and wishes to make sure that the Moresby invasion is thwarted no matter what happens to him. But does his decision serve this pur-

¶ Others managed to clamber aboard life rafts thrown out to them. A week later, out of sixty-eight men on four rafts that had managed to stay together, four men (on one raft) were picked up alive by a U.S. destroyer. One of them later died.

pose? Most naval strategists will insist it does not. Crace is deprived of carrier-based air cover as he moves into a zone where he is vulnerable to massive attacks by land-based planes, and Fletcher's main force is deprived of elements badly needed in his carrier anti-aircraft screen. If, as Fletcher's prudence deems possible, he is destroyed by the main carrier action, what is to prevent Crace's from being subsequently destroyed also? Nothing, obviously. On the other hand, if Fletcher wins his carrier battle, an outcome more likely if his anti-aircraft screen (weak at best) is kept at its strongest, he will have destroyed the most effective protection of the Moresby-bound transport with their auxiliaries. These he might then overtake and destroy, for his speed is greater than theirs and his destructive power much greater.

The criticism seems just: there are evident contradictions in the reasoning on which Fletcher says he based his decision. But there is another line of reasoning, taking account of factors he seems in fact to have ignored, that would have issued in the same decision and perhaps justified it as a logically calculated risk.

One factor is the need to surprise and confuse the enemy. Certainly Inouye at Rabaul *is* surprised, *is* confused. He is essentially a timid man who leans excessively, as timidity is wont to do, upon the crutch of a preconceived and rigid plan. What Fletcher now does has not been anticipated in this plan and Inouye can perceive no reason for it; there is induced in him the wary hesitation of a chess player whose opponent, logically coherent in his game up to this moment, suddenly offers to exchange a rook for a pawn without gaining any apparent advantage in position. By 8:30 the Japanese admiral knows precisely where Fletcher's main force is, and precisely where Crace is, the former having been sighted a little after eight by a carrier-based plane, and the latter at about the same time by a twin-float monoplane. By nine he had ordered the invasion group, now approaching the Jomard Passage, to turn aside. It is an order whose execution enables us to mark in space and time, within a few minutes and feet of absolute accuracy, the point at which Japan's conquest reached its limit to the south.

A second factor Fletcher might have considered in his decision to detach Crace is the need to prevent, so far as possible, attacks on his carriers by land-based planes. Certainly Crace's movement tends toward this effect. His cruisers and destroyers draw off attacks that might otherwise have been directed upon *Yorktown* and *Lexington*—the tactic, again, of the sacrificial animal in a piranha-infested stream—and if luck must be added to Crace's superb tactical skill in order to save him from the fate of *Neosho* and *Sims*, this too is a factor Fletcher might have considered, carefully weighed, and then counted upon. Anyway, the actual importance of historical acts derives not from their intentions but from their consequences, which often enough have little relation to their intentions—and the consequences of Crace's detachment are, on the whole, good for the Allies.

At shortly before two, when the Crace support group is south and a little west of the Jomard Passage, it is attacked by eleven single-engined land-based planes, all of which are driven off by the ship's anti-aircraft fire. At two, twelve land-based two-engined bombers are seen on Crace's radar screens while they are yet seventy-five miles away. The British commander orders radical maneuvers, to dodge bombs and torpedoes, and he does dodge eight torpedoes dropped by these planes when they come in low. Five of the bombers are shot down. Within minutes afterward comes a bombing attack by nineteen high-flying planes; all these bombs, too, are dodged. This ends the enemy's action. Crace continues on his westerly course and will do so until the early hours of tomorrow when, learning that the Moresby invasion has been turned aside, he himself will turn and head south for Australia.

As he does so he will carry with him the vivid memory of an ironical and dangerous closing episode that is not without significance, viewed in terms of world-historical developments. The last high-flying plane of the last Japanese attack of the preceding afternoon had just retired when, suddenly, one of Crace's destroyers, U.S.S. *Farragut*, was attacked by three planes whose bombs narrowly missed her. The dodging destroyer watched these planes with astonishment, with outrage. They were not of the enemy! They were B-26s of the U. S. Army Air Force! The evident fact was confirmed by the planes themselves when, back at their base in Townsville, the photographs they had taken of their target were developed. But will MacArthur's headquarters admit the fact? It will not, nor will it accept the plans subsequently drawn up by the American commander of "MacArthur's Navy" (Vice Admiral Herbert F. Leary) to improve Army pilots' recognition of naval vessels. Instead, all further discussion of the matter will be prohibited! What does this indicate? That sovereignty of the kind making for violent conflict is not necessarily national. That it may be easier for those engaged in a common profession in two different nations to cooperate closely with one another, even to unite with one another in pursuit of a common end, than it is for two services, two rival bureaucracies within the same nation to do so. Crace's force, after all, is a combination of ships from two nations which nevertheless operates as a beautifully coordinated tactical unit.** Between MacArthur's and Nimitz's commands in the Coral Sea, however, are gaps wherein grow misunderstandings, coordination failures, even actual enmities. . . .

But we must now return to Fletcher and his main force on the morning of May 7. Fortunate it is for him that Crace's force is already claiming the attention of Japanese land-based planes and that Hara, with the two

** Morison, in op. cit. p. 39, points out that the Japanese attack upon Crace's group "was of the same type and strength as the one that sank H.M.S. *Prince of Wales* and *Repulse*, on 8 December 1941," indicating that Crace's escape "without a single hit is a tribute to the Support Group's training, and to the high tactical competence of its commander."

large carriers of Takagi's striking force, is launching an all-out attack against a mere destroyer and tanker when, at 8:15, Fletcher himself launches an all-out against what he believes to be, on the basis of scout plane reports, "two carriers and two heavy crusiers." Not long after, when his scout planes return to *Yorktown,* he discovers that a coding error has garbled the sight-report: the scouts actually claim to have seen only a couple of cruisers and a couple of destroyers.†† Should he call back the attack, or let it proceed? The question is difficult, dangerous, possibly even fatal, but he quickly answers it with a bold intelligence that does much to wipe out the error critics will find in his detachment of Crace. He permits the attack to proceed. He bets that it will find profitable targets before it reaches the nominal one, a bet encouraged by the fact that he has now again entered the cold front and so is again somewhat protected against enemy attack by the stormy skies under which he sails. On the other hand he knows from decoded intercepts of enemy radio communications that his position is well known to the Japanese. His time of waiting for the event, after having made his decision, is an anxious one. It is, luckily, also brief. His gambler's courage is rewarded when, at 10:32, he receives from a *Lexington* scout a report that an enemy carrier accompanied by heavy cruisers is only thirty-five miles southeast of the feeble ships at which the massive strike was originally, mistakenly aimed.

The carrier is the 12,000-ton *Shoho* and the cruisers are the four heavy ones that, with a destroyer, complete Admiral Goto's covering group. They are out of the weather; they cruise under clear skies. At once the Allied attack is diverted to the new target—the first enemy carrier ever to be engaged by American carrier-based planes. The initial assault is by three of these, one of whose bombs scores a miss so near it blows five planes off *Shoho's* flight deck. Other attacks quickly follow until, very soon, no fewer than ninety-three planes have dropped bombs, launched torpedoes, and fired guns at this single hapless vessel, many of whose planes (few at best) are off on reconnaissance or on coverage of the Moresby-bound transports. Direct hits by two half-ton bombs disable her and set her aflame. Other hits soon complete her doom. At about 11:36 her fate is announced to tense listeners in *Yorktown's* and *Lexington's* radio rooms by a jubilant lieutenant commander whose words, shot with the speed of light from his swooping plane at the scene of action, are soon to be invested (if only temporarily) with the legendary quality of John Paul Jones' or Oliver Hazard Perry's most famous remarks.

"Scratch one flattop!" cries he. "Dixon to carrier: Scratch one flattop!"

By a little after 1:30, *Yorktown* and *Lexington* have recovered all their planes save the three lost in the action. By a little before five these planes

†† What they really saw were two old-aged cruisers and two, possibly three, converted gunboats of Marushige's relatively weak support group.

are ready for a second strike against what remains of Goto's covering group—four heavy cruisers and a destroyer, now retreating to the northeast—but Fletcher takes account of the bad flying conditions, the lateness of the hour (some of his planes might have to attempt landing after dark on a heaving carrier deck), the relative unimportance of the target, and his ignorance of Takagi's whereabouts compared with Takagi's knowledge (as Fletcher believes) of the Allied position. He cancels the strike.

This, however, does not mean the end of the day's action. While the American admiral is making his decision, the Japanese admiral, Takagi, is looking for him with a flight of twelve bombers and fifteen torpedo planes that have flown off the two big Japanese carriers, *Shokaku* and *Zuikaku*, at 4:30. These planes, if they find him, are to attack him at sundown. But they do not find him. They fly into the bad weather which has discouraged the Allied strike, and while they see nothing of Task Force 17 while passing very near it they are themselves seen on Force 17's radar screens as they head for home. Vectored out by radar, a device with which Japanese ships are not yet equipped, fighters off *Yorktown* and *Lexington* intercept the homing Japanese and, in a series of furious dogfights, shoot down nine of them at a cost of but two of their own number.

And this is but the beginning of an evening of disaster for Takagi's aviation. By happy accident—happy, that is, for the Allies—the frequency employed by American radio telephones jams that used by the Japanese pilots, who must in consequence attempt to find their carriers by sight alone amidst the swiftly deepening gloom. Six of them actually attempt in their confusion to land on *Yorktown*, one of them being shot down by *Yorktown* fire. Eleven others, trying to land after dark, miss their carriers and splash into the sea, so that in the end Takagi recovers just six planes out of the twenty-seven sent out.

There follows a night of hard decision and tense waiting for both the Japanese and American commands. Each knows that the other's main force is within striking distance in the darkness. Each considers seriously the possibility of initiating a night surface action with his destroyers and cruisers. Each decides instead to keep his forces concentrated. Fletcher's decision is in part a consequence of his earlier decision to detach Crace. It is certain that the decisive carrier action toward which all the actions in the Coral Sea have been tending will be fought on the morrow, and the American is justly worried about the weakness of his anti-aircraft screen. This screen would not now be so weak if Crace's three cruisers and three destroyers remained a part of it.

All now depends upon finding the enemy at the earliest possible moment on Friday, May 8, and each commander is acutely aware of this. He who first locates the other will have a possibly decisive advantage since, in other respects, the two forces are of remarkably even strength. Each has two big carriers. Each has a little more than ten dozen planes to fight with: Fitch, who is to have tactical command of the American air battle, has 121; Hara, Takagi's air admiral, has 122; and the American superiority in bomber numbers is offset by the Japanese superiority in fighters and torpedo planes. The Americans have radar and homing devices which the Japanese lack, but the latter have better torpedoes—faster, with fewer duds—and their pilots have, also, more combat experience. The Japanese seem to have only one distinct over-all advantage as the shades of night begin to melt into dawn, but one which adds to the possibility that they can find the enemy before the enemy finds them: they are out of the frontal area where yesterday Fletcher had been, whereas Fletcher, having pursued a southeasterly course through most of the night, is now again out in the clear.

This last fact is to have its effect on the action that begins at six o'clock, an hour before sunrise, when Hara launches a search mission that is followed, an hour later, by an attack group of ninety planes. His purpose in sending the attackers out before the searchers return is to gain time, and in this he succeeds when the attack group, following the median line of the designated search arc, has the great good fortune to encounter the search planes as these head for home, having found Fletcher. The search planes then guide the attackers to *Lexington* and *Yorktown.* Meanwhile, at 6:25, search planes have flown off *Lexington* and, at 8:15, one of them (despite the overcast) has managed to find the Japanese striking force. By 8:38 he has reported its composition, its speed, and its direction. Fletcher doesn't hesitate. Within a minute he has ordered both his carriers to launch strikes and, minutes after that, he turns over to Fitch tactical command of the air battle.

What follows may be likened to a boxing match between two evenly matched opponents in which each rushes at the other pell-mell at the sound of the bell and each swings with all his might a right-hand punch whose effectiveness is somewhat broken by the other's parrying left but, nevertheless, lands on the other's jaw with a force sufficient to paralyze him for the time being. The two then withdraw to opposite sides of the arena. Neither feels strong enough to renew the combat before both, if for different reasons, climb through the ropes. And so the battle ends.

First, let us follow the American strike. The fly-off from *Yorktown* begins at around nine, and by 9:15 thirty-nine of her planes are winging their way toward the Japanese carriers. The dive bombers, having more speed than the torpedo planes, are the first to arrive. By 10:30 they have sighted through a wide gap in the clouds both *Shokaku* and *Zuikaku* heading toward the southwest some nine miles apart, each of them screened by two heavy cruisers and at least two destroyers. But they do not at once attack. Instead they climb three and a half miles into the air, above cloud cover, and fly there in orbit until their torpedo-bearing companions arrive. It is shortly before eleven when all the *Yorktown* flight is assembled, and by that time *Zuikaku* with her screening vessels has disappeared into a rain squall. Only *Shokaku* remains as a visible target, and it is toward her that the torpedo planes, protected against Japanese fighters (Zeros) by Wildcats, swoop down low over the water to launch their explosive fish. They launch, however, from too far away; the torpedoes are too slow; and if *Shokaku* does not dodge all of them, the ones which strike her fail to explode. (The torpedoing pilots, through that process of wishful thinking characteristic of such men in such circumstances, convince themselves they have scored three hits.) The dive bombers do better, though not as well as they should have done, in the opinion of their critics, nor as well as they themselves believe they have done. They score two direct hits (they'll report having scored six). One of these sets gasoline stores afire and so damages the flight deck that planes can no longer be launched, though they can still be recovered. The other destroys the repair compartment for airplane motors.

Lexington's group, flying off ten minutes after *Yorktown's*, has trouble finding the target: most of the dive bombers, flying into thick clouds, are forced by fuel shortage to turn back without ever seeing the enemy. The planes also have trouble keeping together: three fighters escorting the torpedo bombers lose them in the clouds and are eventually forced to turn back without taking part in the attack. Thus the attacking force from *Lexington* is reduced to eleven torpedo planes, four dive bombers, and six Wildcat fighters, of which three are shot down by Japanese fighters who greatly outnumber them. Not a single torpedo hit is scored, and only one bomb hit. But the attackers are well pleased. As they turn back, heading for their own carriers, they see *Zuikaku* burning furiously and (they believe) sinking. As regards this last, they are mistaken. The Japanese carrier is badly damaged—she comes near to capsizing as she makes her painful way back to her base—but she doesn't sink, her fires are soon brought under control, and she can be repaired. She will see action again.

Now let us turn to the Japanese strike.

It is at about the time when the *Yorktown* group begins its attack on *Shokaku* (or shortly before eleven) that *Lexington's* radar screen shows an enemy attack headed toward her out of the northeast, some seventy miles away. The event is, of course, expected. Fitch, nevertheless, is not well prepared for it. How can he be? He has far too few fighters, and the twenty-three dive bombers he now presses into service for defense of the carriers against low-flying torpedo planes are not fast enough, nor sufficiently well armed, to do the job. At eleven a combat patrol has just landed. A mere eight fighters remain in the air as cover for the carriers, and they are so low in gasoline that they cannot be sent out to intercept the incoming attack of (as we know, who watch from afar) seventy torpedo and other bombers guarded by twenty "Zero" fighters. Nine Wildcats are at once ordered up as a relief combat patrol, and they head in the direction of the enemy, but only three of them manage to make themselves felt at all as interceptors. Nor do these three do any damage to the Japanese who, twenty miles from their target, divide into three groups: two of torpedo planes, one of bombers.

They roar in at 11:18. Four of their torpedo planes are shot down by Fitch's dive bombers doubling as fighters (four of these are shot down, too, in the process), after which the fight becomes one of anti-aircraft fire and carrier maneuverability against aerial torpedoes and bombs. And as the two carriers engage in radical evasive maneuvers they draw farther apart, each necessarily accompanied by the destroyers and cruisers assigned to her protection, so that the circular screen which originally surrounded the carriers is torn apart. The break in the circle, preventing mutually reinforcing anti-aircraft fire in every direction, aids the attackers. *Yorktown* is, by a few minutes, the first vessel attacked. She manages by a maximum use of her speed and tight turning radius to dodge eight torpedoes. She manages also to dodge all save one of the bombs aimed at her. This one is an eight hundred-pounder that goes through her flight deck and on down into the fourth deck, killing or seriously injuring sixty-six men and starting fires which, however, are quickly brought under control. Two near misses do additional damage.

Meanwhile, *Lexington* has come under attack. She is far less maneuverable than *Yorktown* and this relative cumbersomeness makes her an easier target. Moreover, the torpedo attackers use on her the "anvil" technique—that is, they attack her simultaneously on both bows—so that as she dodges torpedoes coming in from one side she swings into the path of those coming from the other. The wakes of no fewer than eleven fast torpedoes are counted streaking toward her as, desperately, she maneuvers. Two of them hit her, the first at 11:20, the other seconds later, and both on the port side. Nor is this the limit of the concentrated fury poured on the big ship during these few minutes. There is also the dive bombing attack, undisturbed by American fighters and only slightly so by anti-aircraft fire. From well over three miles in the air the Japanese planes dive down, down, down, to less than a half-mile over the *Lexington* where they release their bombs and level off. Fountains of water rise all around the ship while two direct hits are scored—one on the smokestack structure, one on the port side of the main deck forward—and two near misses that buckle plates.

By 11:47, or just nineteen minutes after it began, the Japanese attack has ended.

Who won the battle? It is impossible to say with any assurance, even tactically, in the noon hour of May 8; this is an interim period during which the effects of the collision are working themselves out. The Japanese *believe* they have won as they begin to recover their planes out of the clouds above their ships. True, one of their two carriers has been put out of action: soon (at 1:00 P.M.) *Shokaku* will be ordered on her way out of the Coral Sea. True, their plane losses have been heavy: *Zuikaku* cannot take aboard all the planes that should have homed on *Shokaku*, and those she cannot take must be jettisoned. Hara will soon discover that he has, for the moment, only nine aircraft operational!

These losses appear minor, however, compared to those inflicted upon the enemy, if the returning pilots' report be accepted as true—for the pilots claim that both American carriers rest by now upon the bottom of the Coral Sea. And this report *is* accepted as true. It is accepted by Hara, by Takagi, and (most important of all) by Inouye at Rabaul.

But what effect does it produce in Inouye's deciding mind? One would normally expect him to order at once a continuation of the Moresby invasion. Instead he orders its indefinite postponement! Why? Because he is, as we have said, a timid man—much too timid to operate (as he is now required to do) at the outermost margins of power, opportunity, and responsibility. He continues to lean upon the preconceived plan. This requires Takagi, as the next step, to launch "Darwin-type" bombing raids upon the Allies' four Queensland bases, and Takagi no longer has the air strength to do it. Hence the Moresby landing troops will continue nakedly vulnerable to attacks by land-based planes; hence (so Inouye's mind works) the whole operation must be put off until a new plan can be made and new forces gathered for its implementation. In the late afternoon he orders Takagi with his entire striking force to retire from the Coral Sea. (The order is one with which Inouye's superior, Admiral Isoroku Yamamoto, Commander-in-Chief Combined Fleet, flatly disagrees when he hears of it and which, this coming midnight, he will countermand. He will order Takagi, then heading north, to turn again south, find what is left of Fletcher's force, and annihilate it. But by then Fletcher, too, will have retired. And during the next two days, May 9–10, the U. S. Army Air Force will provide some justification of Inouye's fears by destroying the advance seaplane base established by the Japanese on Deboyne Island off the tip of Papua.)

The Allied estimate of the battle event, in its immediate aftermath, is precisely the opposite that of the Japanese. As the American carriers begin the recovery of their planes at one o'clock, Fletcher sees reason to believe *he* has won the fight, definitely, even if it be considered solely as a tactical operation. He is informed that one of the two Japanese carriers has been left in a sinking condition—a permanent loss to be added to that of *Shoho* yesterday. Neither of his own carriers, on the other hand, appears damaged to the extent that it is no longer operational. Certainly *Yorktown* is not. Her speed, her steering, her flight deck, her elevators are unimpaired. *Lexington* is in a sadder way. As the last attacker departs she is listing seven degrees to port, three of her boiler rooms are partially flooded, she is afire in three places, and her elevators are out of commission. Her wounds, however, receive a swiftly effective first aid. In a little over an hour her damage control officer is able to report to her captain that the holes in her side have been temporarily stopped, her list is rapidly being corrected by the shifting of oil, her fires have been extinguished, and her flight deck is in shape to recover and launch planes. He does wryly suggest to the bridge that "if you have to take any more torpedoes, you take them on the starboard side."

But scarcely has damage control made this optimistic report than there occurs, deep inside *Lexington*, a terrific explosion quickly followed by others even more terrific, causing many casualties and much damage. An electric motor has been left running in an area that, as a result of torpedo damage, is gradually filled with gasoline fumes; a spark from this motor has ignited these fumes. For a brief time thereafter it appears that even this deep injury will not be fatal, for the ship continues to make twenty-five knots and to recover her planes from the *Shokaku* strike; but at 2:45 a new series of internal explosions begins, starting uncontrollable fires and forcing soon a suspension of all flight operations. This is the end for "Lady Lex," as her men have long called her. At a little after five the order is given to abandon a ship which, by now, wallows dead in the water. The abandonment is carried out in a manner that contrasts strikingly with *Neosho's*. It is perfectly disciplined (yeomen are said to have tidied up and dusted their filing cabinets, sailors and Marines are said to have placed their shoes in a precise line on the deck before going over the side), and not a single life is lost in the process. When it is completed, a destroyer, on Fletcher's orders, sinks the burning and exploding ship with torpedoes.

So ended one of the decisive naval battles of the world—the first sea fight in all history in which the ships of the opponents were never within sight of one another. It must be recorded as a tactical defeat for the Allies. The Japanese lost more planes; they also lost a twelve thousand-ton carrier, a destroyer, and several minesweepers and landing barges, and had suffered severe damage to one of their large carriers. But they had destroyed the thirty thousand-ton *Lexington*, which more than offset all their own losses, and to this must be added their destruction of *Neosho* and *Sims*.

A tactical defeat, however, may be a strategic victory, and this the Coral Sea definitely was for the Allies. It could be deemed so as early as the dawn of May 9, for by then its obvious result was the thwarting (at least temporarily) of the conquest of Moresby, and of the destruction by air of the Queensland bases—events which might well have constituted a breakthrough to final Japanese victory in the Southwest Pacific. But the full measure of this American victory could not be taken—its final confirmation and ultimate scope could not be realized—until it had had its effect upon that action in the mid-Pacific to which it was organically linked in Yamamoto's grand strategic design. This effect was to weaken the carrier strength of the forces Yamamoto now gathered together for his thrust toward Midway and into the western Aleutians. Because of the Coral Sea, Nimitz had one less carrier with which to defend the mid-Pacific than he would otherwise have had—but Yamamoto had *two* less with which to attack. *Shokaku's* grievous wounds could not be healed, nor could *Zuikaku's* mauled air groups be reformed in the few brief and crowded weeks that separated the important decision of May 8 from the even more important decision—indeed, as historical perspective reveals, the crucial decision—of June 4, 1942.

iii. *Midway: Preparations and Approach*

They were, for Admiral Nimitz at Pearl Harbor, the most tense and anxious weeks of the entire war. His logic, which assumed that his opponent was (in the face of obvious facts) equally logical, told him that the Japanese would seek to force at the earliest possible moment a general fleet engagement. This same logic told him what move the enemy would almost certainly make in order to gain this end.

We have seen that the global strategy devised by British-American staff talks before Pearl Harbor, and confirmed at ARCADIA, had assumed that Wake, Guam, and the Philippines could probably not be held against the initial Japanese attacks. Their loss, though painful in the extreme, had therefore been discounted in advance. But Midway was in an entirely different category. As a piece of natural real estate it was worthless—an atoll just six miles across with but a few score acres of dry land divided between two islets inside the encircling reef. Its location, however, some 1135 miles to the northwest of Honolulu, gave it a strategic value that had been recognized as early as the 1860s and had begun actively to be realized soon after the turn of the century. In 1903, by order of President Theodore Roosevelt, it had been placed "under the jurisdiction and control of the Navy Department," and in that same year it had become a station on a commercial cable line running from Honolulu to Guam to Manila. The cable, of course, increased Midway's strategic value. The possibility of exercising effective command is almost directly proportionate to the speed and accuracy of communications, and, through the cable, communication from Honolulu to this central point in the Pacific became virtually instantaneous and as faithful to a commander's intention as his clarity of thought and expression (the two are practically the same) would permit. But it was not until the airplane had been developed into a potent instrument of war—a means of extending the maximum range of fire from a score or so miles to many hundreds of them—that Midway came wholly into its own as a strategic key to the whole mid-Pacific. Commerce heralded the event, in 1935, by establishing on one of the atoll's two islets an airport used by Pan American's "China Clippers." Since then the United States had spent some hundreds of millions to develop a big airfield, a seaplane base, an artificial harbor, a ship channel between the two islets and into the central lagoon, and the shore defenses needed for the protection of these.

Thus Midway had become unexpendable. Not only was it the "sentry for Hawaii," as Japanese Admiral Nagumo would describe it; it was also, as the most westernmost of U.S. mid-Pacific bases, important for offensive action toward Japan. For Midway, therefore, Nimitz was bound to fight with every resource at his command, which is to say that nothing could more certainly force the all-out battle desired by Yamamoto than a serious attack upon this far outpost of the Hawaiian island chain.

And what logic concluded seemed factually confirmed, almost without contradiction, by the swelling stream of Intelligence reports that began to flow into Nimitz's headquarters within two days after the end of the Coral Sea action. Allied aviators operating in the South Pacific suddenly found the skies over New Guinea and the Solomons strangely empty of enemy planes. Virtually all enemy naval activity in that area ceased. This must mean a gathering of forces for a major assault elsewhere very soon—and message intercepts by Allied Naval Intelligence not only supported this but also pointed definitely toward Midway as the main objective: a massive air strike was to be followed by the conquest and occupation of the atoll. There might also be a feint toward Alaska—a raid on Dutch Harbor in the eastern Aleutians, perhaps, or even the occupation of a western island or two of that bleak, chill, mist-shrouded archipelago —and this possibility grew into a very high probability as more and more Intelligence reports came in. The Aleutian move was to be launched a few days before the main assault in the mid-Pacific, in order to confuse the American commander and tempt him to divert to the north some of his relatively meager forces. This, at least, was the appearance, which Nimitz accepted as reality, not because it seemed to him strategically or tactically sound but because it accorded so well with his growing knowledge of the Japanese naval mind. The enemy's was a tricky mind, enamored of the devious, distrusting (or bored by) the obvious, and hence (luckily for Nimitz) loathe to use with simple concentrated directness the massive superiority of force it now controlled. It had a penchant (witness the Coral Sea) for pincer movements and envelopments requiring for their success more tactical competence in every subordinate unit, and more over-all good luck, than a wise prudence at the summit should count upon, in Nimitz's opinion. It had also an inordinate faith in the possibility of achieving complete surprise and of predicting with precision what the enemy would do in response to it.

But if logic, knowledge, and Naval Intelligence concurred in this assessment of the immediate future, there were high offices in Washington and on CINCPAC's own staff who did not. These men were as suspicious of obvious indications as ever a devious Japanese could be. They were vehement in their conviction that the enemy—more subtle in his deceptions, more stupid in his grand strategy, than Nimitz believed him to be —designed in reality an assault upon Pearl Harbor or even, perhaps, upon the West Coast of the United States. It was for this that the huge Japanese preparations were being made, these officers asserted; the signs so clearly read by Naval Intelligence were deliberately put up to mislead. In the face of such strong assertions, some hardihood of spirit and steadiness of mind were required of Nimitz in order to prepare unequivocally, as he did, to meet the challenge he and his Intelligence officers believed imminent. And having thus made what the leading American naval historian of World War II calls "the first vital decision of the campaign,"‡‡ he dismissed from his mind all doubts as to its validity.

Other doubts, however, remained. They added up to a general doubt (or their counterparts added up to considerably less than a comfortable certainty) that Cervantes' adage of "fore-warned fore-armed" held true in his present circumstances. He was warned, all right—and accurately, he was convinced. But to what extent did this "forearm" him? He could be glad his enemy chose to send a carrier, maybe two carriers, into the northern mists and storms where plane launching and recovery were too hazardous and target visibility was too uncertain to make carrier operations predictably profitable. The presence of that additional carrier strength in the mid-Pacific must have assured Midway's conquest and his own fleet's disaster. But the fact remained that the enemy could and would still assign four or five carriers to the Midway campaign whereas all the "fore-warning" in the world would not enable him to muster more than three. None of these could be spared for the defense of Alaska; he could only (as he did) dispatch to the north, to parry the Japanese thrust there, five cruisers, fourteen destroyers, and a half-dozen submarines under the command of Rear Admiral R. A. Theobald, who perforce must limit his operations to the area that could be covered by American land-based planes.

Indeed, on May 27, when he issued his operation order to his tactical commanders, Nimitz feared he might have just two carriers to fight with, *Enterprise* and *Hornet*, the latter with an air group that had had no combat experience whatever. The carrier *Saratoga*, badly damaged by a torpedo in January, was now repaired; she was training off the West Coast; but the escort she required for sailing into dangerous waters could not be formed in time to permit her to arrive at Pearl before the predicted date of the Japanese attack upon a point well over a thousand miles *beyond* Pearl. As for *Yorktown*, Admiral Fitch's estimate (made by his damage control officers) was that a minimum of ninety days would be required to repair the damage she had suffered in the Coral Sea—an estimate that seemed not all excessive to those who watched the battered ship's slow and painful entry into the Pearl Harbor Navy Yard in the afternoon of this same May 27. But a miracle had been prepared at Nimitz's orders, and this miracle was now performed. *Yorktown* went at once into drydock where more than fourteen hundred highly skilled workmen labored on her night and day, supported by hundreds of other skilled workmen in the Yard shops. Within less than forty-eight hours the dock was flooded, *Yorktown* moved out into the narrow waters between Ford Island and the mainland, and on the afternoon of May 29 she fueled while hundreds of repairmen continued to work on her. By the morning of May 30 she was ready to sail, and did sail, from Pearl

‡‡ Morison, op. cit., p. 80.

Harbor, bound with her escorting vessels (Task Force 17) for the zone of battle. She carried an air group hastily assembled from three carriers, men who had never before operated together as a unit.

She carried, too, the tactical commander of American operations. Ordinarily, Vice Admiral Halsey of Task Force 16, as the senior officer present, would have commanded from his flagship *Enterprise*, but a skin disease evidently caused by months of unremitting nervous strain had put him in the hospital. Fletcher, as the next senior, was therefore to command from *Yorktown* as soon as Task Force 17 had rendezvoused with Task Force 16 (*Enterprise-Hornet*) on June 2 at a point some 325 miles northeast of Midway—a point carefully selected as being the best suited to a surprise interception of the Japanese carrier force. In this position, American forces would remain beyond the range of enemy carrier-based searches until some time after the enemy, slanting down toward Midway from the northwest, was within the seven hundred-mile range of search planes based on Midway.

Three carriers, then, with their screening vessels (seven heavy cruisers, one light cruiser, fourteen destroyers), fueled by two tankers that were protected by two destroyers, and supported by nineteen submarines, were all that Nimitz could oppose at sea to what he knew by the end of May to be a truly massive enemy force. In a major surface engagement he would, he knew, stand no chance. In every category of ship that he possessed he was greatly outnumbered and in one category, the big, fast battleship, of which the Japanese had several, he had not a single vessel.

To offset this great disadvantage, however, he had certain assets. For one thing, he had Midway itself—an unsinkable aircraft carrier whose defenses had been so greatly strengthened since early May that a Japanese landing attempt there might very well be repulsed; in any case it would now be, for the Japanese, a very costly operation. For another, he had much less distance between his forces and their base than his enemy had. For a third, he had direct cable communication with the prime objective of the battle—he need not burden the airwaves with that great increase in radio traffic which would otherwise have been necessary to deploy and control and support his forces and which would have indicated to the enemy that the "surprise" assault was anticipated. Finally, he had over-all, and most important of all (protected in part by the cable) a distinct intelligence superiority over his enemy: he knew fairly precisely what the enemy was doing and planned to do whereas the enemy neither knew that he knew nor had means of finding out what his own movements were. Surprise! This factor, so heavily counted upon by the Japanese, might yet tip the scales toward the Americans—for there is none more dismayed and powerless to act (for the moment) than the trickster tricked, the thief robbed, the adulterer cuckolded, the liar deceived.

Whether such tipping of the scales occurred or not, however, depended very largely on the relative capacities of the opposing tactical commanders to keep their heads in crises and employ, in panic-inducing situations, a calmly calculating logic. In this context it was perhaps fortunate for the Allies that Halsey's illness, coupled with the peculiar circumstances of the battle, would make of Rear Admiral Raymond A. Spruance virtually a free agent as commander of Task Force 16. He was a man of no very impressive appearance; no one meeting him on a crowded street would be likely to remember him. But an acute, humorously self-deprecating intelligence looked out through his far-spaced blue eyes, and men who had seen and heard him operate under pressure trusted him implicitly. Few men could have differed more from Halsey, in temperament and character, than he did. He was unassuming where Halsey was self-assertive; quiet where Halsey was vocal; coolly colorless where Halsey was flamboyant; cautious where Halsey was impetuous. Yet he was a man whose personal courage and capacity for decision were as great as Halsey's. He differed from Fletcher, too, in that he was steady, patient, and consistent of judgment at times when Fletcher, out of impatience or overeagerness, was inclined toward rashness. Spruance would seize chances, but never without first measuring them logically against whatever hard information might be at hand. A lack of such information did not paralyze him, however. He knew that there are times, and quite frequently in war, when a man (particularly a commander) must make decisions that might be called "pure" in that they are naked assertions of will—decisions that are in the nature of "first causes." They determine a chain of events without being themselves perceptibly an "effect" of, or determined by, anything outside themselves.

A sense of the quality of the man is conveyed by the visual signal he made from *Enterprise* to his other ships on June 1, the day before his scheduled rendezvous with Fletcher. In it he succinctly stated the enemy's object, the enemy's probable strength, and the hopeful possibility, if secrecy could be maintained, of making "surprise flank attacks on enemy carriers from positions northeast of Midway." He frankly admitted, in effect, that the American command had and could make no definite plan of operations but must take its cue from immediate events. After the initial surprise attacks, said he, "operations will be based on the result of these attacks, damage inflicted by Midway forces, and the information of enemy movements." His next sentence was the most character-revealing of all in that it was his nearest approach to the "inspirational." Many a commander deems "inspiration" the main function of such messages as this, and labors to achieve it through a moving eloquence of statement. Spruance said: "The successful conclusion of the operation now commencing will be of great value to our country." If carriers became "separated during attacks by enemy aircraft," he concluded, "they will endeavor to remain within visual touch."[2]

In substance, the June 1 signal of Spruance to the men under his command was, as it should have been, an expression of Nimitz's operation order of May 27 and of the special Letter of Instruction which Nimitz had appended thereto. Fletcher and Spruance were ordered by Nimitz to "inflict maximum damage on the enemy by employing strong attrition tactics" but, in carrying out their assignment, they were to "be governed by the principle of calculated risk, which you shall interpret to mean the avoidance of exposure of your force to attack by superior enemy forces without good prospect of inflicting, as a result of such exposure, greater damage on the enemy." Few orders could be more difficult to execute successfully; none could be better designed to measure the inner resources—the judgment, the nerve, the self-control—of a commander.

Having refueled at sea (Spruance on May 31, Fletcher on June 1), and having rendezvoused at the designated point by four o'clock in the afternoon of June 2, Task Forces 16 and 17 could only search through their plane-and-radar eyes, and listen through their radio ears, for the first sight or the first news of the enemy's approach. And at Pearl Harbor, a tense CINCPAC could only watch, and listen, and wait.

The ships and planes that Japan had gathered together for the triple purpose of occupying the western Aleutians, taking Midway, and destroying the U. S. Fleet comprised nothing less than the whole of her Combined Fleet. Four large fast carriers, five light ones, five seaplane carriers; 131 fighter planes, 107 bombers, 124 torpedo planes, three dozen seaplanes (some 400 altogether); eleven fast battleships, eighteen cruisers, twenty-two submarines, fifty-six destroyers; four converted minesweepers, several small minesweepers, six subchasers; numerous transports and cargo vessels, fourteen oilers, a repair ship—all this was committed to the execution of Admiral Yamamoto's grand design. And of it all, over-all, he exercised command—a directly personal command over what was designated on his operational organization chart as the Main Body. His flagship was *Yamato*, by far the largest battleship ever built (64,000 tons).§§ Its main batteries had nine 18.1-inch guns firing a 3200-pound shell that was 50 per cent heavier than the 16-inch shells of the biggest American naval guns; its side armor was more than sixteen inches thick. No doubt the admiral—immediately environed by such awesome power, watching from his bridge the six other battleships which, with a light carrier, two seaplane carriers, and two light cruisers, made up his Main Body—was encouraged to believe that his Combined Fleet was invincible.

And so it might have been.

Had Yamamoto been content to wait until the carriers *Shokaku* and *Zuikaku* were again ready for combat, and had he then concentrated wholly on Midway, it is as certain as anything can be in war that Midway would have been his and the U. S. Fleet, forced into a general engagement with him, would have suffered disaster. Even without *Shokaku* and *Zuikaku* he could have achieved this, if only he had concentrated! Instead, he scattered his force piecemeal all over the central and northern Pacific in accordance with a plan even more complex, and even more

§§ *Yamato's* sister ship *Mushashi*, also of 64,000 tons, was then still under construction and would not be completed until sometime in July.

dependent for its success upon accurate prediction of enemy response, than that which had so dangerously weakened Inouye south of Rabaul.

As Nimitz's Intelligence officers had deemed probable, Yamamoto's plan called for the initial action in the Aleutians. On June 3 there was to be a carrier strike on Dutch Harbor, followed (in following days) by landings on Adak, Attu, and Kiska in the western Aleutians. Ships assigned to this were designated the Northern Area Force and included three heavy cruisers, four light cruisers, two light carriers, six submarines, and eleven destroyers. This operation, which could not be technically termed diversionary since it was to be so closely succeeded by imperative action in the mid-Pacific, was nevertheless designed to render the American command confused and hesitant.

On the next day, June 4, the main carrier striking force (four big carriers, two battleships, two cruisers, fourteen destroyers, under the command of the Vice Admiral Nagumo, who had struck Pearl Harbor last December 7), approaching from the northwest, was to launch at dawn a major air strike upon Midway—one which would destroy the planes there and serve in general as an "artillery preparation" (*à la* World War I) for the landing of some five thousand troops on the night of June 5. This Midway Occupation Force comprised twelve transports and freighters, covered and supported by two battleships, eight cruisers, and nine destroyers, under the command of Vice Admiral Nobutake Kondo.

And where was the so-called Main Body of heavy surface vessels to be during these actions? It (under Yamamoto's immediate tactical command) was to stand off to the northwest of Midway, well behind Nagumo, until Midway and the Aleutian objectives were secured. It would not, however, stand intact during this crucial period but instead would be divided into two widely separated parts. Only three of its original seven battleships would remain with Yamamoto. The other four—together with both of the cruisers, the light carrier and the two seaplane carriers originally included in this Main Body—would be detached and sent north under Vice Admiral Shiro Takasu, there to occupy a position about halfway between the Midway and Aleutian forces. This detachment was designated an Aleutian Screening (Support) Force, but its planned placement was such as to enable it to turn either south or north, depending upon which combat area (if either) needed it.

No phase of the entire plan was more revealing of Japanese command psychology than this handling by the Supreme Commander of his Main Force. Witness his mingling of excessive caution with excessive rashness! He attempted to anticipate in detail every possible contingency. If a major American force were sucked north by the Aleutian action, the preponderance of Yamamoto's surface power would shift northward. But the more likely contingency, hence the one on which the plan most counted for success, was that Nimitz would react to the conquest of Midway, on which landings were to be made during the night of June

5, by concentrating his forces for an attempt to retake that atoll. This movement could not lead the Americans into the vicinity of Midway until June 7 or 8, Yamamoto calculated, and ample warning of it would be given him by one or the other of two lines of submarines patrolling to the north and to the west of the Oahu base. Upon receipt of this warning, Nagumo's carrier striking force was not only to engage the Americans but also to maneuver in such a way as to get between them and their base. By that time the Main Body would be again all together and would come in to annihilate with its terrific firepower whatever was left of the enemy. No allowance whatever was made for the possibility that the Americans would not be surprised—this despite the recent events in the Coral Sea, which might well have made Yamamoto suspect the adequacy of Japanese security arrangements.

In fact, however, Fletcher and Spruance had both crossed the lines to be patrolled by Japanese submarines a full two days before these submarines arrived (June 1) at their stations, and when the two American commanders rendezvoused they had fairly accurate knowledge of the strength and approach movements of the enemy. The latter knowledge, however, was of a general nature only. It was rendered imprecise by a stationary weak front which spread thick clouds across some thousands of square miles of ocean, beginning three hundred miles northwest of Midway. Under these clouds, through heavy curtains of mist dropped down to the very surface of the sea, Nagumo's carrier striking force steamed southeastward on June 2 toward its objectives. Search planes had not found it as night fell. Nevertheless, it was Nagumo who was about to be surprised.

iv. *Midway: The Battle*

At a little before nine o'clock in the morning of Wednesday, June 3, the first American air contact with the approaching enemy was made by an ensign flying a Catalina from Midway. Seven hundred miles southwest of the atoll, or well south of the weak front, he sighted, then tracked for several hours, "six large ships in column" (as he first reported; he later counted five more) sailing eastward at nineteen knots. He believed them to be the "main enemy force" and said so at eleven o'clock. Actually he had sighted Admiral Kondo's Midway Occupation Force, whose transports and cruisers were attacked by nine B-17s (Flying Fortresses), based on Midway, at a little before 4:30 that afternoon. The attackers scored neither hits nor near misses, though they claimed to have hit two heavy cruisers (or battleships) and two transports. Only slightly greater success was achieved by four Catalinas from Midway which found the formation sailing in bright moonlight at 1:15 the next morning, June 4, and attacked with torpedoes. An oiler was struck and appeared to blow up in a terrific explosion, though in reality she was only temporarily slowed. Before the four Catalinas had arrived back at Midway, the atoll was under heavy air attack.

And thus the great battle began.

Admiral Nagumo had initiated his operations according to plan at 4:30 that morning, when he with his carrier striking force was approximately 240 miles northwest of Midway. From the flight decks of his four carriers—*Akagi, Kaga, Hiryu, Soryu*—he launched toward Midway thirty-six dive bombers, thirty-six torpedo planes armed with heavy bombs, and thirty-six fighters, or 108 planes in all. By a little before six o'clock this force had been seen by a PBY pilot and had made its appearance on Midway search radar screens. It was then ninety-three miles from its target. At once air raid warning sirens shrieked on Midway, every anti-aircraft gunner was drawn tensely alert at his post, and every plane that was in shape to fly was ordered into the air. The Catalinas and bombers, sent up to prevent their destruction on the ground, were ordered out of the way of the attack, which they could do nothing to frustrate, though the bombers were armed for a strike against enemy carriers as soon as these (from which the Midway strike was being made) could be located. Midway's Marine Corps Fighter Squadron, twenty-six planes in all, were sent out to intercept.

They did intercept. When they were thirty miles from their base they saw the attacking bombers flying in V-formations, with Zero Mark-1 fighters (later called "Zekes") above; they climbed, then dove down from seventeen thousand feet. This initial dive, however, was the sum total of the attention they were able to give the bombers. The improved fighter types that were beginning to come off U.S. production lines had not yet reached Midway; the Marines perforce flew outmoded Buffaloes and Wildcats that had less flat speed, a slower climb, and a wider turning radius than the planes which at once fastened on their tails and greatly outnumbered them. Most of the Marine fliers died during the next few minutes. When the Midway strike had ended and the fighters were ordered to land for refueling, only nine of the twenty-six were able to do so—and of these survivors, seven were severely damaged.

Midway, too, was severely damaged by that time. At 6:30 the first bombs from high-flying Japanese began to explode on island installations, swiftly followed by dive-bombing attacks. Twenty minutes later, when the last attacker headed back to his carrier, huge columns of smoke towered over his target. Midway's oil tanks were afire. So were the hospital and storehouses. The Marine command post and mess hall were smoking ruins, the seaplane hangar was destroyed, and the power station was damaged. The defenders believed they had inflicted a high percentage of casualties on their attackers while suffering remarkably few of their own (actually all but six of the attacking planes returned to their carriers); they could draw some comfort from the fact that the airfield runways, a prime target, remained virtually undamaged; but none could deny that the raid had weakened Midway's defenses against the expected invasion attempt.

And these defenses were being further weakened, far out at sea, while the men on Midway were making their first assessments of the damage they had suffered. At 5:52—just a couple of minutes after the attacking planes that had flown off them made their first appearance on Midway's radar screens—two of Nagumo's carriers had been sighted. Their location was erroneously reported: the PBY pilot who saw them had placed them forty miles southeast of their true position; but since they moved toward Midway in order to shorten the distance that must be flown by their returning planes, they were easily found by the four Army Marauders (B-26s) and the six Marine Avengers (TBF-1s), all armed with torpedoes, sent out from Midway to attack them. At 7:10, having been themselves already seen by patrolling Japanese fighters, the Americans sighted their intended prey. Bravely they bore down upon the carriers through curtains of anti-aircraft fire, low over the water with Zeros upon their tails; and thus bravely, in a minute or so, most of them joined their Marine fighter comrades in death. Five of the six Avengers and two of the four Marauders were shot down, many if not most of them before they had a chance to launch their torpedoes. The three surviving planes were so badly shot up that, arrived back in Midway, they were no longer usable. And not a single hit had been scored (though the survivors reported four).

Nor was this the full extent of the weakening of Midway's air defenses. Some fifteen minutes before the Midway torpedo planes reached their carrier targets, sixteen Marine dive bombers took off from Midway toward the same objective. The men who flew them had never flown dive bombers before. Their commander therefore decided they should make, not a dive-bombing, but a glide-bombing attack upon the carrier *Hiryu*. By this maneuver their vulnerability to both fighter and anti-aircraft fire was greatly increased, and half of them were abruptly shot down in an attempt that did no damage whatever to the enemy. Of the eight dive bombers that managed to return to Midway, six were so badly damaged they would never fly again. More fortunate were the Flying Fortresses which, fifteen minutes after the dive bombers had departed, began to aim their bombs at Nagumo's carriers from a safe height of twenty thousand feet. They suffered no losses whatever, but they did no damage to the enemy either. In this, as in their report of having made no fewer than four hits on two carriers (from nearly four miles up, it was utterly impossible to distinguish a hit from a quite distant miss), the Fortresses repeated their futile past and anticipated their futile future as attackers of ships. By 8:30, therefore, as Nimitz would later observe, ". . . most of Midway's fighters, torpedo planes, and dive bombers—the only types capable of making a high percentage of hits on ships—were gone,"[3] and without having inflicted the slightest material hurt upon the Japanese.

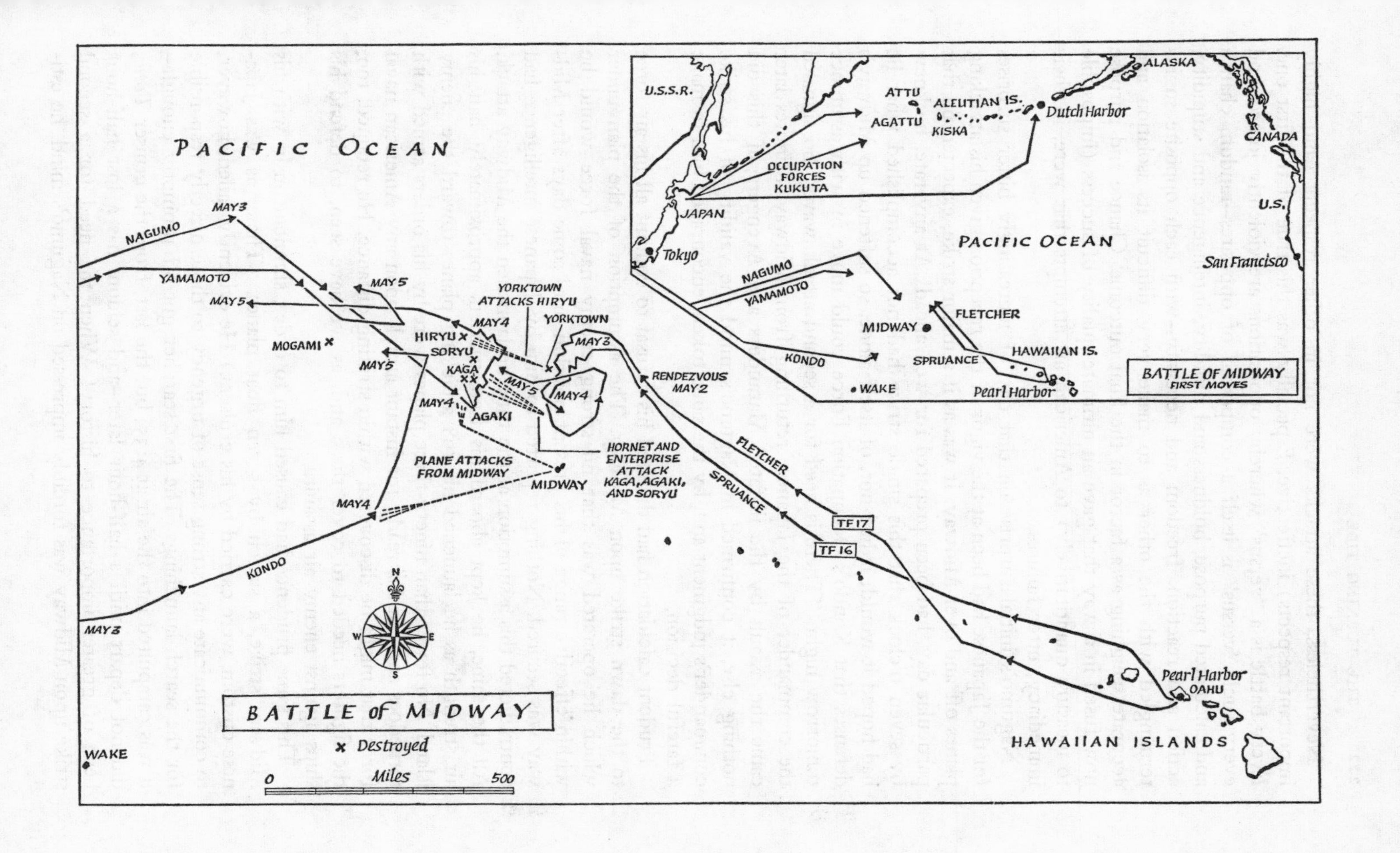
BATTLE of MIDWAY
× Destroyed
Miles
0
500
PACIFIC OCEAN
NAGUMO
MAY 3
YAMAMOTO
MAY 5
MAY 5
MOGAMI ×
MAY 5
YORKTOWN ATTACKS HIRYU
MAY 4
HIRYU ×
SORYU
KAGA
MAY 5
MAY 4
AGAKI
YORKTOWN
MAY 3
MAY 4
PLANE ATTACKS FROM MIDWAY
HORNET AND ENTERPRISE ATTACK KAGA, AGAKI, AND SORYU
MIDWAY
MAY 4
RENDEZVOUS MAY 2
FLETCHER
SPRUANCE
TF 17
TF 16
KONDO
MAY 3
WAKE
N
W
E
S
Pearl Harbor
OAHU
HAWAIIAN ISLANDS
BATTLE OF MIDWAY
FIRST MOVES
U.S.S.R.
JAPAN
Tokyo
OCCUPATION FORCES
KUKUTA
ATTU
AGATTU
ALEUTIAN IS.
KISKA
Dutch Harbor
ALASKA
CANADA
U.S.
San Francisco
PACIFIC OCEAN
NAGUMO
YAMAMOTO
KONDO
MIDWAY
WAKE
FLETCHER
SPRUANCE
HAWAIIAN IS.
Pearl Harbor

Nevertheless, these attacks were not in other respects (and highly important respects) ineffective. Especially was this true of the first one. Every battle is a "versus" whereby oppositions are violently joined, and every such "versus" is itself a compound of opposites—random chance and calculated purpose, boldness and timidity, intelligence and stupidity, action and reaction, freedom and necessity—with each opposite so intermingled with the other as to make very difficult its isolation and accurate weighing as a factor in the final outcome. Chance and purpose now fused in a way that gave an ultimate quality of success (impossible to measure quantitatively) to American air attempts that were, in their immediacy, utter failures.

Nagumo's initial surprise on that day of increasingly bitter surprises for the Japanese had been at the vigor of the reception given his attacking planes off and over Midway. It was as if a major strike, expected on that particular day, had been prepared for well ahead! At any rate, he knew by seven o'clock that this single strike had not accomplished what he had hoped it would; it had not, of itself alone, so softened up Midway's defenses that Kondo's Occupation Force could move in with assurance tomorrow night. "There is need for a second attack wave." So signaled the commander of the Japanese returning from Midway. Minutes later came the assault by the ill-fated Marauders and Avengers; if this did nothing else, it confirmed in Nagumo's mind the validity of his strike commander's judgment and, by the same token, encouraged him to make a fateful decision.

Prudent calculation had dictated his refusal to commit all his air force to the dawn strike upon Midway. The assumption of the plan under which he operated was that no strong enemy naval force would be within effective range of his present position until some days after Midway was secured. Nothing reported to him by Japanese intelligence had contradicted this assumption at the time he launched the Midway attack. All the same, he kept aboard his four carriers approximately half his air strength as he launched his 108 attacking planes toward the enemy island. No fewer than ninety-three planes were by his orders armed with torpedoes and bombs, ready for instant attack upon any American naval force that might be discovered within striking distance. He retained, too, the fighters needed to cover these and, as we have seen, to defend his ships against enemy air assault.

This same prudence had caused him to order, simultaneously with his Midway strike, a search by seven float planes. (These, as was Japanese custom, were carried by his cruisers.) He evidently failed, however, to communicate any strong sense of urgency to those directly responsible for the search launchings. The first searcher got off promptly enough—it was catapulted into the air at 4:35; but the last, from the cruiser *Tone*, did not depart until a half-hour later—and seldom has a lost half-hour been of greater importance to history! When the need for a second strike upon Midway was forcibly impressed on Nagumo's mind, he estimated that his searchers, having been out for two and a half hours (whereas the *Tone* plane had been out for only two), must have covered an area with a radius of at least two hundred miles. They had found nothing. He waited another quarter-hour. They had still found nothing. So at 7:15, several minutes after the three surviving planes of the assault from Midway had disappeared into the northeast, he took what seemed on the evidence a reasonably safe chance. He ordered the ninety-three planes heretofore kept ready for instant launching be taken below, and that those armed with torpedoes for attacks on ships be relieved of these and rearmed with bombs for attacks on the atoll. After all, he argued with himself, the planes returning from Midway would begin to arrive around 8:30, at which point necessity would take over from choice his handling of his flight decks: these *must* then be cleared for plane recovery. He gambled, therefore, with a mere hour or so of time (an hour of hard labor was required for the rearmament he had ordered), and at the moment the probability of his winning the gamble seemed overwhelming.

Then, at a little before 7:30, when his carriers and their planes were in a state of nearly maximum confusion between two kinds of readiness, his estimation of odds was abruptly changed. The belated *Tone* search plane had found what it would have found thirty minutes sooner had it been promptly launched, namely "what appears to be ten enemy surface ships" some two hundred miles to the northeast. Nagumo was startled. He was also apprehensive. But since the *Tone* plane's pilot had made no mention of a carrier or carriers among the enemy ships, he concluded that none was present and that, therefore, no immediate air strike upon the enemy ships was necessary. He could deal with them later, being meanwhile in no danger of air attack from them. He permitted the rearming of his planes to continue. But as the minutes passed his apprehensions grew until, at 7:45, he felt compelled to amend his earlier order. "Prepare to carry out attacks on enemy fleet units," he signaled. "Leave torpedoes on those attack planes which have not as yet been changed to bombs." Two minutes later he ordered the *Tone* search planes to "ascertain ship types and maintain contact."

The timing of these two acts would seem to indicate the beginning of that loss of nerve and capacity for decision which, later in the battle, would become patent in Nagumo. As his orders now stood, he could be for some time only partially prepared for a strike on Midway and partially for one on hostile ships. He would be fully prepared for neither. And it would seem to hindsight that he should definitely have ascertained the composition of the hostile fleet—measuring thus the threat to himself and the extent of the hurt he might give the enemy—before he risked adding (as in fact he did add) to the confusion of his air arm. Was the enemy fleet sufficiently powerful to justify a major strike? Above all, were carriers present? The search plane's pilot did not respond to the admiral's request until more than twenty minutes had passed, and even then he failed to report the one fact Nagumo needed most to know. The enemy force, said the pilot at 8:09, consisted of "five cruisers and five destroyers." Not until 8:20 did he report that the "enemy is *accompanied* by what *appears to be* a carrier"!¶¶

This was disturbing. Highly disturbing. But normally, assuming the pilot reported the whole truth, it would have been no valid cause for Japanese dismay. The odds of one carrier against four would normally spell disaster for the former and no great danger to the latter. The great trouble was that Nagumo at that moment was about as far from being ready either to deliver or repel a major carrier attack as he possibly could be. He had few anti-ship attack planes available for immediate launching—and he could not have launched immediately in any case, since at the time he first learned that an enemy carrier was within striking distance of him, he was himself under attack by Midway-based planes. Scarcely had the Marine dive bombers departed when the Flying Fortresses appeared, forcing a continuation of evasive action. And in the brief interval between the two assaults, if not simultaneously with the latter of them, an American submarine (*Nautilus*) increased the noisy confusion by thrusting her periscope above the waves, attracting intense if inaccurate fire from the carrier screen, and firing two torpedoes at a battleship. Neither torpedo hit and the submarine at once submerged, but the turmoil she had initiated continued for several minutes as destroyers circled over her presumed location dropping depth charges. (*Nautilus* survived unscathed.) By the time all this had subsided it was 8:30 and the carriers had begun their recovery of planes from the Midway strike, a task which kept them occupied until 9:18. When the last returned plane had been struck below, Nagumo prepared at last his attack against the American ships—he began to bring up from the hangar deck those planes that had been armed with torpedoes all along; those that had been disarmed of torpedoes and then rearmed with them again; and dive bombers. During the latter part of this period of recovery he changed course, withdrawing to the north.

These circumstances, so frustrating to Nagumo, vastly augmented the importance of decisions taken many hours earlier by Admirals Fletcher and Spruance. Indeed, the first of them had been made as long ago as the day before, when Fletcher decided to give no credence to the Midway PBY report that the "main enemy force" had been sighted at 11:00 A.M. approaching Midway from the southwest. Fletcher chose instead to believe that American Naval Intelligence had been correct in its prediction that the main fighting force would come in from the northwest under cover of the bad weather which normally prevailed there, in a wide belt, at this time of year. He therefore maintained the highly fortunate position that had been originally chosen, well beyond the range of Nagumo's search planes, and was rewarded some nineteen hours later

¶¶ Italics the present author's.

by a seemingly clear-cut opportunity for surprise. At a little before six o'clock on this morning of June 4, his flagship's code room had begun to intercept those PBY reports of "enemy carriers" which incited the Midway plane action just described. The final report underrated the enemy carrier force: only two of Nagumo's four carriers were seen. It also misstated the enemy position, as has been said: Nagumo was actually forty miles or so northwest of where the PBY said he was. But this incompletion and inaccuracy but slightly reduced the immense advantage which Fletcher and Spruance now had, namely the possession of approximate knowledge of the enemy's strength and location at a time when the enemy had no inkling that they were anywhere in the vicinity.

Fletcher, moving at once to seize this advantage, then made a second major decision—one whose importance, like that of his first, had been increased by Nagumo's search incompleteness and (consequently) ill-informed command activity. Fletcher decided to divide Task Force 16 from Task Force 17, temporarily. At 6:07 he ordered Spruance to "proceed southwesterly" with *Hornet*, *Enterprise*, and screening vessels, in order to "attack enemy carriers when definitely located." He would follow in *Yorktown*, he promised, "as soon as planes recovered." This last referred to the fact that *Yorktown*, whose turn it was to conduct that day's dawn search, had sent out ten Dauntless dive bombers at 4:30 and could not recover all of them until 6:30 or thereabouts. The need to recover planes, however, was by no means the sole reason for Fletcher's decision. According to Naval Intelligence, four or five enemy carriers were operating in the mid-Pacific. Only two had been sighted. Where were the other two, or three? Until he knew, or had a sound basis for guessing, Fletcher very properly refused to make a full commitment of his forces. As a matter of fact he declined even a partial commitment of *Yorktown's* planes for a full two hours after he had turned to follow Spruance. All this was in accordance with that "principle of calculated risk" which Nimitz's order of May 27 had defined, and its fortunate concomitant was that Spruance exercised a virtually independent command throughout the carrier battle that now ensued.

It was Spruance, therefore, who made the next major decision, whereby the possibilities opened by the *Tone* searcher's delayed and overly conservative report, and by Nagumo's confusion of his attack forces, were promptly and fully exploited. This decision was far from easy. His original plan had been the prudent one of launching his strike only after he knew he was close enough to the enemy to insure recovery of his surviving torpedo planes. These had a combat radius of only 175 miles. But when radio reports of the Japanese attack on Midway came in, it appeared that he might catch enemy carriers in the act of refueling and rearming their planes for a second assault upon the atoll, hence in their most vulnerable state, provided he launched two hours sooner than he had planned. He would thus increase the chance of inflicting major damage on the enemy.*** Alas, he would also increase the hazard to his own planes. He would be operating at the outside limit of his torpedo plane range: many planes which might safely return from the strike if he adhered to his original plan would, if he launched now, splash into the sea for want of gas. Swiftly, with an enforced icy coldness and calm, he weighed the chances, including that of achieving complete surprise—for he believed (it seemed very probable) that he had not as yet been sighted by the enemy. The risk, he decided, was well worth taking.

So, at seven o'clock, he ordered the strike to be launched. Moreover he ordered it to be launched in full force, leaving with the carriers only enough fighter planes (thirty-six of them) to maintain combat air patrols above his ships. This further increased the probable loss of pilots and planes from fuel shortage, for it required the planes first in the air to orbit above the carriers for nearly an hour awaiting planes that must be (as nearly half the total force must be) brought up to the flight deck from the hangars below: but it also increased the probability of inflicting fatal wounds on Japanese carriers.

The die was now cast. That phase of battle had been reached in which decisive power over the event is shifted from the commander to his men. Outwardly impassive, Spruance watched these men take off, knowing well that, by his orders, many would soon die in flaming agony. He continued outwardly impassive when, at 7:30 or so (not more than half his strike was yet in the air), his attention was called to a float plane distantly circling. He put binoculars on it. It was of the enemy, beyond doubt (we know it to have been *Tone's* laggard searcher); it meant that surprise was now lost, almost beyond doubt. Nevertheless, his strike must proceed as ordered. . . .

Meanwhile, Fletcher on *Yorktown* had recovered his morning search and turned to follow Spruance. He remained justifiably worried over the possibility that two or three unreported enemy carriers were lurking within striking distance of his two task forces, and it was not until sometime after 8:30 that, having received no further enemy contact reports, he decided that the chance of gain outweighed the chance of loss if he launched at least a portion of his air force in support of the *Hornet-Enterprise* strike. He issued the necessary order. By 9:06, all *Yorktown's* torpedo bombers, half her dive bombers, and a half-dozen fighters were on their way toward Nagumo. On *Yorktown's* flight deck, ready for

*** In his Introduction to *Midway, The Battle that Doomed Japan*, by Mitsuo Fuchida and Masatake Okumiya (U. S. Naval Institute: 1955), Spruance says (p. iv) that he does not deserve credit "for being able to choose the exact time for our attack on the Japanese carriers when they were at their greatest disadvantage. . . . All I can claim credit for, myself, is a very keen sense of the urgent need for surprise and a strong desire to hit the enemy carriers with our full strength as soon as we could reach them." This "strong desire," however, certainly contained a sense of the possibility of catching the Japanese in the state in which they were in fact caught.

instant launching against any other Japanese carriers that might be found, were the rest of Fletcher's bombers and the fighters needed to protect them.

Thus it happened that at a little after 9:00 in the morning, this Thursday, June 4, 1942, 152 American planes were winging their way toward the Japanese carrier striking force.

A total of 118 planes had been committed by Spruance. Off *Enterprise* had come thirty-three dive bombers, fifteen torpedo planes, and ten fighters. Off *Hornet* had come thirty-five dive bombers, fifteen torpedo planes, and ten fighters. But these added up to no single attack by well-coordinated, mutually reinforcing units. Instead, by accident rather than design, they were divided into four distinct and independently operating groups as they proceeded toward their target. Spruance, to gain a little time as a hedge against his apparently lost surprise, had ordered *Enterprise's* bombers to start out before all her torpedo planes were launched. That made two groups. Then *Hornet's* torpedo and dive bombing squadrons, flying at different altitudes, became separated. That made two more. Widely separate, of course, was the attack group off *Yorktown*, though this was so aided by clearing weather that it had almost caught up with its predecessors when these were at last on target.

The target was not promptly found. The forty-mile error originally made in the first PBY sight reports—an error compounded by Nagumo's withdrawal to the north—now became a major hazard to American carrier success. Not only were the Japanese out of sight of the spot at which they were supposed to be, they were also moving in a direction different from that the Americans presumed for them. One very serious result was that the high-flying *Hornet* dive bombers—all thirty-five of them, with fighter cover—missed the fight completely. The attack group commander, seeing nothing below him as he reached the designated location, turned toward the southeast and flew toward Midway until his planes' fuel ran low. Twenty-one of the bombers then returned (barely) to the carrier, the other fourteen going on to Midway where three crash-landed. Every one of the accompanying fighters, having less range than the bombers, was forced to come down at sea.

Hornet's torpedo squadron had far more luck in one sense, far less in another. Lieutenant Commander John C. Waldron was its leader, and when he failed to find the enemy where the enemy was supposed to be, he turned to the north instead of southeast. Soon (at 9:20) he sighted Nagumo's ships. Just as soon, the enemy's combat air patrol found him —and so did Japanese anti-aircraft gunners, whose shells began to burst on every side. At that instant he with his fifteen-plane squadron was yet a full eight miles from the nearest Japanese carrier and was wholly without fighter protection. But he did not hesitate. Instead he initiated an epic of raw courage unsurpassed in American war history as, wiggling his wings in signal to his comrades, he dove straight down full throttle, leveled out low over the water, and then bore in through clouds of bursting shells and streams of machine-gun bullets toward the point at which he might successfully launch his torpedo against the nearest carrier. Whether he was able to launch or not, no one knows. All that is certain is that he and his rear gunner soon died, his plane shot down. And all fourteen of the planes that followed his were also shot down, each with a two-man crew, most of them before they had had a chance to launch. Of the thirty men there was a single survivor, Ensign George H. Gay, who was only slightly wounded and managed to fight his way to the surface as his shattered plane sank into the sea. (All the rest of that day he remained in the water, hiding from Japanese eyes under a rubber seat cushion, and was rescued the following day by a Catalina.) Not a single torpedo hit was scored.

The same raw courage was displayed with almost the same fatal consequences by *Enterprise's* torpedo squadron, which arrived less than a quarter-hour later. Its leader, Lieutenant Commander Eugene F. Lindsey, aware that he now operated very near if not beyond the limit of his planes' combat radius, bore straight down upon carrier *Kaga* without waiting for the dive bombers that were supposed to attack simultaneously. He, too, with his squadron, was wholly without fighter protection, for the Wildcats assigned to cover him had, on the way, attached themselves by mistake to Waldron's *Hornet* torpedo squadron.††† Fire-spitting Zeros flocked around him. A polka-dot pattern of bursting anti-aircraft shells spread around him. Still he with his squadron bore in. Soon ten of the fourteen planes in the squadron had been shot down. Again very few torpedoes were launched—and none hit.

It was then *Yorktown's* turn. Her twelve torpedo planes, led by Lieutenant Commander Lance E. Massey, arrived at eleven o'clock and at once made a level attack on carrier *Soryu*, as courageously as the *Enterprise* squadron had done and even more disastrously. This time there was some fighter protection, but very little and very briefly. A mere half-dozen Wildcats accompanied the *Yorktown* group and these were soon overpowered by Zeros. Hence Massey, like Waldron and Lindsey, flew into murderous Zero and anti-aircraft fire and, like them, died in flames. Six others of his planes were shot down, too, before they could launch torpedoes. And of the five that did manage to launch, three were immediately afterward shot down. Two planes out of twelve survived and, again, no hits were scored.

Thus, when the attack by Massey's squadron had ended, six torpedo planes survived of the forty-one that had attacked three carriers—*Akagi*, *Kaga*, *Soryu*—and not one torpedo had reached its target. Nevertheless,

††† All the time that Waldron with his squadron was being slaughtered, this fighter group orbited futilely high above the battle, where no Zeros were, awaiting the signal to come down which had been prearranged with Lindsey and which, of course, never came. It was by radio message from the leader of this fighter group that Spruance and Fletcher learned at eleven o'clock, for the first time, that the Japanese force had been found and attacked.

in terms of their purpose, these brave young men had not sacrificed themselves in vain. They had sucked out of the sky, down to within a few score feet of the sea, the Zeros which otherwise would have been circling high to intercept the American dive bombers that attacked a few minutes later. These attackers, writes the Japanese historian of Midway, "got in unimpeded because our fighters, which had engaged the preceding wave of torpedo planes . . . , had not yet had time to regain altitude. Consequently it may be said that the American dive-bombers' success was made possible by the earlier martyrdom of their torpedo planes."[4]

This "success" was very great—great enough to reverse the whole trend of the naval war in the Pacific. It was at a little after ten that Lieutenant Commander Clarence McClusky, commanding the thirty-eight bombers of the two *Enterprise* squadrons, saw from a height of nineteen thousand feet all four of the Japanese carriers. *Akagi*, *Kaga*, and *Soryu* were fairly close together, whereas *Hiryu* was some miles ahead—and he selected the first two as his targets, dividing his forces fairly evenly between them and encountering, as they circled and then made their shrieking dives, no fighter opposition and relatively little anti-aircraft fire. Almost simultaneously the *Yorktown* dive bombers, under Lieutenant Commander Maxwell F. Leslie, arrived and, by accident lucky for the Americans, happened to select *Soryu* as his target. The decks of all three carriers were in precisely the condition Spruance had hoped they would be in —crowded with planes being fueled and serviced—and very soon all three were flaming wrecks, having suffered repeated direct hits and near misses. "Looking about," writes one of the officers of *Akagi* (Nagumo's flagship), "I was horrified at the destruction that had been wrought in a matter of seconds. There was a huge hole in the flight deck just behind the amidship elevator. The elevator itself, twisted like molten glass, was dropping into the hangar. Deck plates reeled upwards in grotesque configurations. Planes stood tail up, belching living flame and jet-black smoke. . . . Climbing back to the bridge, I could see that *Kaga* and *Soryu* had also been hit and were giving off heavy columns of black smoke. The scene was horrible to behold." Soon there were repeated induced explosions of gasoline and ammunition on *Akagi*. "As fire spread among the planes lined up wing to wing on the after flight deck, their torpedoes began to explode, making it impossible to bring the fires under control. The entire hangar area was a blazing inferno, and the flames moved swiftly toward the bridge."[5] Admiral Nagumo—near despair, his nerves jangling and his judgment flawed—was forced to transfer his flag to the light cruiser *Nagara* and his tactical command to the admiral who had been and remained in charge of the striking force's battleship and cruiser screen.

This was Rear Admiral Hiroaki Abe. He promptly ordered an air strike from the one Japanese carrier that remained operational, *Hiryu*, upon what he believed to be the single carrier the Americans had (only one had been reported) in the mid-Pacific. (The Japanese believed that the planes off this carrier had been reinforced by land-based planes.) While her three sister carriers were still reeling under dive-bombing attacks, *Hiryu* began to send aloft eighteen dive bombers and six fighters; and at eleven o'clock she launched ten torpedo planes with an additional six fighters.

This force made its appearance on *Yorktown* radar screens when it was just fifty miles from Fletcher's flagship, where fighters of her combat patrol were being fueled and preparations made for recovering the planes that had struck Nagumo. Abruptly, refueling was halted, planes on the flight deck scrambled into the air, and the returning dive bombers were waved away. Since combat air patrols from *Enterprise* and *Hornet* had joined *Yorktown's*, no fewer than twenty-eight fighters went out to intercept, and they did so with such deadly effectiveness that the Japanese were split into small groups of which only eight bombers managed to reach the carrier screen. There two of them were shot down by anti-aircraft fire. Of the six that reached their target, one was shot down by *Yorktown's* guns, but as it shattered into pieces a few feet above the carrier's flight deck its bomb exploded on the deck. This was one of three direct hits made by the attackers on *Yorktown*. A second, exploding in the smokestack, ruptured boiler uptakes and extinguished fires in five out of six boilers, reducing the carrier's speed to zero within twenty minutes. The third and final hit exploded on the fourth deck, forcing an immediate flooding of magazines in the vicinity to prevent their blowing up. Many men were killed or maimed by these hits and raging fires were started, one of which demolished the carrier's radar equipment and so disabled communications facilities that Fletcher was forced to transfer his flag to the cruiser *Astoria*. But soon thereafter damage control had worked to such good effect that the fires were limited or put out and four boilers had been restored to operation, enabling the carrier to make from eighteen to twenty knots.

Then, at around 2:30, one of the screening vessel's radar saw *Hiryu's* torpedo planes with fighter escort coming in. They were forty miles away. *Yorktown* was again refueling fighters and again abruptly terminated this operation, but she was still launching these fighters when the attack came in. Five out of ten torpedo planes, three out of six fighters, were lost by the Japanese as they bore in, but two out of four torpedoes (despite the carrier's maneuvering) hit *Yorktown* amidships on the port side. Again the carrier's speed was slowed to zero and, this time, there developed a heavy list to port (twenty-six degrees) with no possibility of correcting it by shifting fuel or counter-flooding, since the power required for these actions was not available. It appeared that *Yorktown* must soon capsize. Her captain therefore ordered abandon ship, destroyers took off her crew, and by evening the derelict was escorted by a single destroyer, *Hughes*, which was to sink her if her capture by the Japanese became imminent. Not *Hughes* but a Japanese submarine caused the carrier's end, however: torpedoes from the submarine sank not only *Yorktown* but the destroyer *Hammann,* which had by then come to her aid—this in the early afternoon of June 6.

But by the time *Yorktown* at last went down, *Hiryu* (whose planes had sunk her) had been for nearly thirty-six hours a sunken vessel. She had drowned at Spruance's orders. Simultaneously with the close of the attack on *Yorktown* came a report from a *Yorktown* scout plane that *Hiryu* with accompanying ships was now about one hundred miles to the northwest of the doomed American carrier. Spruance immediately ordered an attack on this sole unhurt Japanese carrier, and *Enterprise* began in the late afternoon of June 4 to launch a strike by twenty-four dive bombers, ten of them planes that belonged normally to *Yorktown. Hornet* launched sixteen. No fighters accompanied them: all the fighters (thought Spruance) were required to protect the American carriers; but only three of *Enterprise's* dive bombers were shot down by Zeros before the bombing dives on carrier *Hiryu* began. At a little after five o'clock, four hits were made on the Japanese carrier. When the *Hornet* group arrived a little later, *Hiryu,* aflame from stem to stern, was so obviously done for that no further attack on her was needed. They shifted their bombing attention to an escorting battleship on which they inflicted minor damage.

The destruction of *Hiryu* brought to an end the decisive action of June 4, 1942—again, for the second time in history, a naval battle in which surface vessels of hostile fleets never came within sight of one another, though submarines played some part.

As night fell, there seemed to remain to the Japanese a slight chance that victory might yet be snatched from the jaws of crushing defeat. Admiral Yamamoto's main body of heavy surface vessels had not been engaged: if somehow he could obtain a surface action with the Americans in the night, when the latter's plane superiority was neutralized by darkness, he might annihilate them with his big guns. Or the Americans might be destroyed if they could somehow be enticed within plane range of Wake Island, where Japanese air forces had been concentrated for transference to Midway once the latter had been conquered. Yamamoto moved in the early darkness to seize this apparent chance. He ordered his scattered forces to converge upon an area north of Midway.

This last chance existed, however, only to the extent that the American tactical command made mistakes, and Spruance, to whom tactical command of the entire American force had now been transferred,‡‡‡ made none. "I wished to have a position from which either to follow up retreating enemy forces or to break up a landing attack on Midway," said he in his battle report. "At this time the possibility of the enemy having a

‡‡‡ Fletcher made this transfer after he'd been forced to move his flag from *Yorktown* to *Astoria.* He did so because command of a carrier task force could be effectively exercised in battle only from a carrier and because Spruance had by then abundantly demonstrated his command abilities.

fifth CV [big aircraft carrier] in the area, possibly with his Occupation Force or else to the northwestward, still existed." So instead of pursuing the shattered Japanese striking force at the risk of encountering battleships in the dark, he slanted down toward Midway for several hours, then turned back to the west in order to achieve the offensive-defensive position he desired. By dawn he was within air strike distance of the area in which Japanese forces would have been concentrated had Yamamoto held to orders issued the evening before.

But the Japanese admiral had not so held. He had grown increasingly aware of the risks he ran as the first hours of June 5 passed without enemy contact. The possibility of his finding the Americans in the dark was very small. The probability that they would find him in daylight was very great if he continued in his present direction. Lacking air cover, his mighty battleships and cruisers might then go the way of Nagumo's carriers. "Enough is enough," he muttered to his staff officers as, a little before 3:00 A.M., he definitely canceled the Midway occupation and ordered a general retirement, thus conceding the first major Japanese defeat in battle in three and a half centuries. An eyewitness has described his "ashen face" and "strangely glittering eyes" at this time. He had suffered from stomach trouble and nervous depression as his ships sailed from Japan, and this sickness now returned to him, worse than before. Soon he was forced to take to his bed, where he would remain for a week, subsisting exclusively on rice gruel.

Meanwhile his forces suffered another grievous loss. The heavy cruisers *Mikuma* and *Mogami*, two of the fastest and most powerful ships in the Japanese Navy, each armed with ten 8-inch guns, collided in early morning darkness as they maneuvered to avoid attack by an American submarine, the *Tambor*. Both were damaged, *Mogami* losing a large section of her bow. The retiring Japanese were forced to leave them behind, cripples limping over dangerous waters escorted by two destroyers. American planes soon found them. *Mikuma* was then sunk by bombs and *Mogami*, after six direct hits, was kept afloat only by superhuman efforts on the part of her damage control crew. She barely managed to make her way back to port, so severely damaged that a year would pass before she was again ready for action.

Spruance continued his pursuit of the retreating Japanese through June 5 and the daylight hours of June 6. It was a cautious pursuit. He was well aware that disaster could yet overtake him. If he ran into a concentration of enemy submarines, if he ran out of fuel as a result of battle-imposed maneuvers, if he pushed his aviators beyond the limits of their endurance, if he encountered planes from an unsuspected carrier (Yamamoto, as a matter of fact, had two light carriers with him), the tide of battle which now ran so strongly in his favor could be abruptly reversed. By the evening of June 6 he was convinced that these risks outweighed the possibility that he might catch up with the retreating Japanese and inflict further major damage on them. Accordingly, on the evening of

June 6, he broke off his pursuit and turned back toward Pearl Harbor. The Battle of Midway was ended.

And it ended in a Japanese defeat whose dimensions were realized far more accurately by Yamamoto, tossing and turning on his sickbed, than they were by his victorious opponent. The Aleutian operation achieved some success. There were damaging air strikes on Dutch Harbor, June 3 and 4, followed by the occupation of the islands of Kiska and Attu a few days later. But these island bases depended for their strategic importance upon the conquest of Midway, and Midway remained now more firmly in American hands than it had ever been before. Yamamoto knew well that the margin of Japanese superiority over the Americans in the Pacific was now dissipated. The limits of Japanese expansion had been reached, and passed. From now on she was condemned to fight a defensive war.

VIII

A Dangerous Quarrel among Friends

i. *On a Hot Afternoon at Hyde Park, June 20, 1942*

To Winston Churchill, fresh from the green coolness of an English June, the summer heat of the Hudson River Valley, trapped in this dark and tiny room, was almost unendurable. He soaked a handkerchief with the sweat of his brow, he stained a cigar with the sweat of his fingers, he longed for the air-conditioned bedroom that would be his on the morrow when he came down with the President from Hyde Park to the White House—and he found it irritatingly difficult to bring his mind to a sharp focus on the subject at hand. Though he was well prepared for this afternoon's conversation, he was grateful for the fact that there was to be, apparently, no sharp encounter of opposing views. In any such encounter he would have been, he felt, at a distinct disadvantage amidst this stifling gloom.

For his two American friends seemed marvelously unaffected by the temperature.[1] Franklin Roosevelt, seated behind a desk so large it occupied most of the room's meager floor-space, was as full of buoyant energy as ever. Harry Hopkins, prowling the narrow background or sitting in a chair a little behind his chief, appeared not even to perspire. And both moved with their customary zest upon a problem he faced, for the moment, rather wearily . . .

It was Harry Hopkins who had first indicated to him that the Americans wished him to make the trip (his second to the United States since Pearl Harbor)—a trip he himself had already decided was necessary. Hopkins had written to him on June 6, soon after the first definitive reports of the Battle of Midway had been received from Nimitz.[2] "Whether the beating they [the Japanese] have taken is going to force them to withdraw [from the Central Pacific] we do not know," Hopkins had said in his letter, "but it rather appears so. When you add this to the Coral Sea business, it will change the relative value of our naval forces in our favor very substantially. The Japs simply cannot stand the attrition. . . ." But this lessening of a tension that had heretofore been increasing in the Pacific—increasing to a point where it threatened to force a fundamental shift in global strategy—did nothing to reduce the need for another face-to-face meeting between President and Prime Minister. On the contrary, to the extent that it permitted more attention to European needs and possibilities, it made such a meeting even more imperative. "I am sure there are certain matters of high policy which you must come to grips with the President on," Hopkins had gone on to say, "and he is hopeful that you can make a quick trip and I fancy he will be cabling you about it at once."

Chief among these "certain matters" was a growing disagreement between the British and Americans over the strategy of the European war. Hopkins had made only oblique reference to it, saying that Washington's "anxiety" about the Russian front "is heightened by what appears to be a lack of clear understanding between us as to the precise military move that shall be made in the event the Russians get pushed around badly. . . ." and that he himself was "somewhat discouraged about our getting into the war in a manner that I think our military strength deserves. . . ." But, to take any possible sting out of his words, he had quickly added that he had "always been an impatient person" and had "no doubt that our time will come." He had also spoken of the "thrill and encouragement which the Royal Air Force bombing has given all of us here"—a reference to the first one thousand-plane bombing attack on a German city (Cologne), made by the British on the night of May 30.

At the time of Hopkins' letter, Soviet Foreign Minister Vyacheslav Molotov had just concluded a visit to Washington. ("I liked him better than I did in Moscow," said Hopkins. "Perhaps it was because he wasn't under the influence of Uncle Joe!") He came at the President's request to confer on Lend-Lease delivery problems, and he did so, but he also seized the opportunity to impress upon the American Government the desperate need for a "second front" operation that would force the Germans to withdraw forty divisions from the Russian front in 1942. Roosevelt had responded by telling Stalin, through Molotov, to expect a second front in 1942, though he had not specified when or where. A few days later, Admiral Lord Louis Mountbatten, British Chief of Combined Operations (the Commandos) was in Washington, primarily to deal with landing craft problems. He had conversations with Roosevelt in which the President (almost casually, it seemed) mentioned the possibility that a "sacrifice" cross-Channel attack might have to be made by the Western Allies in the autumn in order to relieve pressure on the Russians. These words had aroused great alarm in Churchill; they were a major incentive for his present visit.[3]

Both he and the British Chiefs of Staff had had from the first many reservations concerning the agreement on strategy reached in April on the basis of the Marshall Memorandum (see p. 189). This agreement, which the British had regarded as provisional but which the Americans insisted upon regarding as ironclad, called for concentration upon a huge buildup of troops and materiel in the British Isles (BOLERO) in preparation for a massive cross-Channel assault upon the Continent (ROUNDUP) to be launched in the early spring of 1943. In the meantime there was to be a limited cross-Channel assault (SLEDGEHAMMER), in September of 1942, if this was deemed necessary to save the Russians.

It was on SLEDGEHAMMER that disagreement had thus far focused, and with such intensity as to generate a good deal of heat. A June renewal of the German offensive on the Russian front, though expected, was depressing in fact. Particularly so was the all-out attack upon closely invested Sevastopol in the Crimea. This key port city was obviously doomed, its fall would obviously be but a prelude to a powerful Nazi thrust toward the Volga River and the Caucasus Mountains, and all this further confirmed the opinion of most British and American military professionals that the Allies would be lucky if the Soviets were still in the war by the end of 1942. Paradoxically, it was this mutually agreed estimate of the situation which was the basis for the Anglo-American disagreement. By the American view, the threat to Russia was a conclusive argument for SLEDGEHAMMER. By the British view, it was a conclusive argument against it. On April 16, the very day on which Marshall believed he had achieved a firm agreement on strategy, Field Marshal Sir Alan Brooke, Chief of the Imperial General Staff, had noted in his diary: "Should Germany be getting the best of an attack on Russia, the pressure for invasion of France will be at its strongest, and yet this is just the most dangerous set of circumstances for us."[4] For what would happen if Russia collapsed? Obviously the Germans would at once concentrate the bulk of their forces in France. To attempt a landing against such an overwhelming superiority of force would be suicidal folly. Or if the landing had already been made, the invaders would face annihilation unless —against immense hazards, with inevitably immense losses—they could be withdrawn by sea.

Marshall, thought Brooke (who impressed his view upon a sympathetic Prime Minister), had "not studied any of the strategic implications of a cross-Channel operation." For instance, he had argued "that the main difficulty would be to achieve a landing."[5] Brooke had agreed that "this would certainly present grave difficulties." The "real troubles," however, "would start after the landing," the British Staff Chief had gone on to say. "We should be operating with forces initially weaker than the enemy and, in addition, his rate of reinforcement would be at least twice as fast as ours. . . . His formations were fully trained and inured to war whilst ours were raw and inexperienced. I asked him [Marshall] to imagine that his landing had been safely carried out, and asked him what his plans would then be. . . . I found that he had not begun to consider any form of plan of action or . . . to visualize the problems that would face any army after landing. . . . Nor could he understand that until the Mediterranean was opened again we should always suffer from the crippling shortage of sea-transport."* None of these objections had been removed from Brooke's mind when the conversations with Marshall ended on April 16. "The plans are fraught with the gravest dangers," he confided to his diary that evening. ". . . The prospects of success are small and dependent on a mass of unknowns, whilst the chances of disaster are great and dependent on a mass of well-established facts."

Nothing had happened since to change Brooke's mind. Much had happened, or been learned, which should (he felt) have changed Marshall's mind. Perhaps he had counted on such a change when he agreed "in principle" with the American proposals and gave his relucant assent to the preparations they implied. (He had *not*, he insisted, committed himself to a cross-Channel attack in 1942 or even 1943: he had simply agreed that such an attack should be made as soon as there was good chance for its success.) Certainly it had then seemed to him that the Americans must of their own accord give up SLEDGEHAMMER once they had begun realistically to plan for it, facing up to its abundance of dangers and difficulties amidst an acute proverty of resources. Instead, the Americans not only continued to adhere to every term of the April agreement but also denied that this agreement had been made with any reservations. Indeed, they invested in it a moral fervor that distorted perspective and logic—as if the agreement were a kind of sacred vow, binding on all future action, from which every departure (no matter how clearly indicated by fresh estimates of conditions) was cowardly, dishonest, even wicked.

These, then, were the circumstances in which the President's promise to Molotov and Stalin of a second front in 1942, followed by his remark about a possible "sacrifice" operation in September, disturbed Churchill so profoundly.

The Prime Minister understood and even shared the motives impelling Roosevelt. The need to help Russia, the need to provide actual battle experience for the new armies, the need to maintain at a high level the morale which would certainly be lowered through a long period of inaction, the need to prevent the fundamental revision of global strategy which might result from the pressure of American public opinion in the long-continued absence of important action against the Nazis—all these argued strongly for Roosevelt's contention that operations in the European Theater were "essential . . . in 1942."[6] But they argued only for a

* This because of the necessity to send around Africa into the Indian Ocean the shipping which would otherwise have passed through the Mediterranean and the Suez Canal. A shortening of turn-around time was equivalent to an increase in the number of ships.

successful operation. By the very terms that impelled it, a failed effort would be worse than none at all. It would "not help the Russians whatever in their plight, would compromise and expose to Nazi vengeance the French population involved, and would gravely delay the main operation in 1943," as Churchill had written in a note he planned to give the President before their conversation had ended on this fervid afternoon of June 20.[7]

He had said, he would often say again, that an Allied disaster on the shores of France provided almost "the only way in which we could possibly lose this war"[8]—and it was chiefly to prevent what seemed to him (and the British Staff Chiefs) a foolish courting of this disaster that he had come again to America. His opposition to SLEDGEHAMMER was now adamant and unalterable. If he must nakedly exercise the full force of his office against it, he would do so. But he hoped he could achieve his object through persuasion, and to this end he was prepared initially to cushion his hard purpose with relatively soft words wherein he pretended an openness of mind that did not exist.† Said he, in the note he would soon place in the President's hand: "We hold strongly to the view that there should be no substantial landing in France this year unless we are going to stay. . . . No responsible British military authority has so far been able to make a plan for September, 1942, which has any chance of success unless the Germans become utterly demoralized, of which there is no likelihood. Have the American Staffs a plan? At what points would they strike? What landing-craft and shipping are available? Who is the officer prepared to command the enterprise? What British forces and assistance are required? If a plan can be found which offers a reasonable prospect of success, His Majesty's Government will cordially welcome it, and will share to the full with their American comrades the risks and sacrifices. This remains our settled and agreed policy."

But he knew that no very acute perception would be required to see that, in his "settled" opinion, no such plan would or could be "found." What, then, should be done? "Can we afford to stand idle in the Atlantic theater during the whole of 1942? Ought we not to be preparing within the general structure of BOLERO some other operation by which we might gain positions of advantage, and also directly or indirectly take some of the weight off Russia?" He then made his opening move toward a revival of that project which had never died from his mind, and which Brooke was inclined to favor, namely, the invasion of North Africa (GYMNAST). "It is in this setting and on this background," he wrote, "that the French Northwest Africa operation should be studied."

† In his *The Hinge of Fate*, p. 346, Churchill says that he "did not have to argue against SLEDGEHAMMER myself," that it "fell of its own weakness," but this is contradicted by his note of June 20, quoted above. At that time he evidently did not know that active opposition to the September operation was no longer necessary; at any rate he *did* "argue against" it.

Certainly there were good reasons for Allied concern over the situation in North Africa at that moment. Near the end of May, Rommel had launched his Afrika Korps in all-out attack upon the British Eighth Army and, after an initial setback, had won a decisive tank-battle victory on June 13. The main British strength had been forced to withdraw from Libya across the Egyptian border a few days later, leaving behind in the coast town of Tobruk some thirty-three thousand troops with supplies sufficient to maintain them for three months. So long as Tobruk was held, the Allies need not despair. Until this strength-draining thorn in his flank had been transformed into a strength-giving means of blood transfusion, the enemy could not move successfully against Alexandria—and last year, with a British garrison of about the same strength as now remained, Tobruk had withstood a siege of thirty-three weeks. All the same, Churchill could not but wonder if the arguments being made for an invasion of Western Europe to aid the hard-pressed Russians might not be made with far more cogency for an invasion of western North Africa to aid the hard-pressed Eighth Army. He was in fact sure they could be. The African invasion was clearly a feasible operation of war, whereas the French invasion as clearly was not, and if it did not fulfill Stalin's major requirement for a second front—namely, that it compel the withdrawal of forty German divisions from Russia—it would definitely aid the Russians in other important ways.

But he well knew that his view could not easily prevail. Marshall and Secretary Stimson would never accept his bland assertion that GYMNAST preparations could be made "within the general structure of BOLERO." They were bound to insist that BOLERO was explicitly and exclusively tied to the cross-Channel assault. They would have to be overruled; to this end he would have to exploit to the full that predilection for North Africa manifest by the President ever since the opening days of the ARCADIA conference.

Yet at the same time he must take care, he must exercise every art of diplomacy and committee politics to insure that his opposition to SLEDGEHAMMER did not place weapons of conclusive argument in the hands of that tough, uncompromising old sea-salt, Admiral King, who would certainly use them against the whole basic concept of "Germany First." Such weapons could not be shaped by logic out of a realistic appraisal of the Allied situation. Churchill was sure of this. But they might be shaped by pride, impatience, and anger out of the mutual distrust and distorted views engendered by a violent quarrel. Quarrel must therefore be avoided, or at least confined within literally reasonable limits. Marshall and Stimson must not become so antagonized that they listened sympathetically to King's conceptions of global strategy or (more dangerously) to those put forth from Melbourne by the glamorous General Douglas MacArthur, Supreme Commander of Allied Forces in the Southwest Pacific.

He had had recent opportunity to measure the lengths to which the imperious MacArthur might go to have his own way. There were lengths that reached if they did not surpass the outermost limits of a prescribed subordination. In late April, when the threat of Australian invasion was greatest (though Churchill himself had never believed it imminent), he had received from Australia's Prime Minister John Curtin a proposal to divert to Australian defense two British divisions (one of them armored) that were scheduled for India, to add a British aircraft carrier to "MacArthur's Navy," and to assign more shipping to the supply lanes running to Australia from the United States. That Australia's anxious political leader should present such a proposal was natural enough, though Churchill regarded it as unsound (India was in more danger than Australia, he was convinced). What was unnatural, and dangerously so, was that Curtin made his proposal, so he said, at the *request* of MacArthur! Churchill, whose relations with Curtin were difficult at best, had found it necessary to query Roosevelt on the matter. Had MacArthur "any authority from the United States for taking such a line?" No, he had not, the President had replied in effect; the Prime Minister could rest assured that "any request reaching you from Mr. Curtin is made upon his own responsibility." Simultaneously, MacArthur had been advised by the War Department to transmit all future requests of this nature to the Joint Chiefs of Staff in Washington, under whose direction he operated.‡

Nor had the Coral Sea and Midway actions reduced perceptibly the pressures exerted through King and MacArthur for a shift of strategic emphasis by the United States from the Atlantic to the Pacific. The argument was now made that these victories indicated the certainty of Japan's defeat in a relatively near future, if only the major effort were made against her, whereas no such certainty attached to a major effort against Hitler's Germany. Churchill might suspect that MacArthur bolstered his strategic conclusions with frequent references to a "public opinion" that would be satisfied by "an adequate effort in the only theater which is charged exclusively to the United States"[9]—though this stratagem, to the extent of its effectiveness, weakened the foundations of coalition warfare.

It was all very ticklish. The impending debate would be long, complicated, wearisome—and (mopping his brow) Churchill was very glad he would not have to engage in it today. The heat of it, added to that already enclosed in this dark little room, would have been more than he could bear. Sufficiently hard was it to follow with his two American

‡ MacArthur "took very ill the War Department's statement of policy concerning his relations with Curtin" since ". . . as he observed, it seemed 'to imply some breach of frankness' on his part." He said he had merely answered specific questions put to him by Curtin, "in the belief that it was his duty to do so and 'for [no] other purpose.'" The quotations are from pp. 213–14 of *Strategic Planning for Coalition Warfare*, by Maurice Matloff and Edwin M. Snell (Washington: 1953).

friends a conversational path laid out quite smoothly toward an end already substantially agreed upon. . . .

Admittedly this path ran through strange country. Weird mysteries were at either hand, and ahead of them—beyond the point they would reach this afternoon—lay a darkness unalleviated by the slightest glimmer of precedent. What hazards lurked there, none could know.

For Roosevelt, the path had begun with the Einstein letter delivered to the White House by Dr. Sachs in October 1939. For Churchill, it had begun at about the same time with certain undated and unrecorded conversations between himself and F. A. Lindemann (The Prof) who, since the 1920s, had been his intimate friend and principal adviser on all scientific matters. It was by Lindemann that he had been first apprised of the possibility (it had then seemed remote) that an unprecedentedly powerful "atomic" weapon was presaged by the Hahn-Meitner-Strassmann experiments, published in January 1939, and that the Germans would doubtless do their utmost to realize this possibility. It was with Lindemann's advice that, upon becoming Prime Minister, he had committed His Majesty's Government to a major effort of scientific research coordinated through the Ministry of Aircraft Production and guided by a committee of leading scientists whose chairman was Sir George Thomson. It was Lindemann—now become Lord Cherwell (though still The Prof)—who had kept him informed of the progress of this research and, in August of 1941, had recommended definite action toward the production of an "atomic" bomb. By that time the chances of making such a weapon before the war's end were "reasonably good," Churchill was told.

Accordingly, on August 30, 1941, he had sent a minute to the Chiefs of Staff Committee expressing his opinion that "action should be taken in the sense proposed by Lord Cherwell," this despite the fact that he "personally" was "quite content with existing explosives."[10] ("I feel we must not stand in the path of improvement," he said.) He recommended that Sir John Anderson, Lord President of the Council, be appointed "the Cabinet Minister responsible." The Chiefs of Staff Committee had promptly agreed, whereupon there had been set up what was designated (for security purposes) the "Directorate of Tube Alloys" whose operations were given a "maximum priority." Since October 1941 these operations had been loosely concerted with those of American scientists working toward the same end under the auspices of their Government—this in accordance with a suggestion made by the President in a letter to the Prime Minister.

And now the time had come when a decision must be made whether or not to go forward with the construction of plants for the production of fissionable materials and of the bombs that might employ them. It was a decision hard to make in one sense, easy to make in another. No scientist was absolutely certain that a controlled self-sustaining chain reaction could be induced in a mass of ordinary uranium. None as yet had been. No one could know with absolute certainty that an explosive effect would be achieved if enough of the rare isotope, uranium-235, or of the plutonium derived from the much more abundant U-238§ were brought together. There were myriads of difficult technological problems to be solved before the great plants required to produce the needed amounts of pure U-235 or of plutonium were operational; no one could be absolutely sure that all these problems were soluble. Amidst this forest of uncertainties, the one absolute certainty was that the necessary effort would be hugely expensive. It would cost hundreds of millions of pounds sterling. It would divert from other war uses vast quantities of materials and energy. It would commit to this single purpose a large proportion of the best available scientific and engineering talent. Considered exclusively in these terms, the decision was very hard.

Nevertheless there was no real doubt in Churchill's mind—and he knew there was none in Roosevelt's mind—that the production effort would have to be made. The risk of not doing so was too great. If Nazi Germany obtained the atomic bomb while the Allies were without it, and the bomb was as destructive as scientists predicted, she would win the war. All that had gone before would not count. The issue was as starkly simple and conclusive as that. And Nazi Germany, with a head start, had presumably been working hard toward such a bomb ever since the war began.

Evidence of it was the emphasis placed by the Germans on the production of heavy water (the very term seemed to Churchill "sinister . . . , eerie, unnatural") immediately after the Nazi conquest of Norway. Pure heavy water could be obtained through an exceedingly prolonged electrolytic process that required prodigious amounts of electricity, and since hydroelectric power was abundant in Norway it was there that most of the heavy water in the world (almost all of it, in fact) had been accumulated by the late spring of 1940. It totaled perhaps one hundred gallons by that time. The Germans had at once ordered a great increase in heavy water production by the Norsk Hydro plant at Vemork, according to British Intelligence. A production of three thousand pounds a year had been ordered in May 1940 and, just a few months ago, this had been upped to ten thousand pounds a year. It was doubtful that these quotas had been or could be met, but there was no doubt about why the heavy water was wanted: it was wanted for use as a moderator of neutron speed in a uranium pile, wherein the Germans sought to induce a self-sustaining atom-splitting chain reaction. Very special attention was therefore being given this Vemork plant by British secret agents and, in response to their reports, by scientists who advised the War Cabinet. Under consideration by the Cabinet at this very moment was the advisability of

§ See pages 85 and 86.

ordering an attack upon the plant by Combined Operations, despite the extreme dangers and difficulties of this.¶

But of course the only real defense was to get the bomb first, assuming one could be made. On this, Churchill and Roosevelt could not but agree. They might have disagreed, however, about the degree of Anglo-American cooperation through which the effort was to be made. Obviously the huge installations required could not be built in England, where they would be seen by the enemy's air reconnaissance and be subject to enemy air attack. If the British and Americans were at this point to divide their effort, each attempting to make its own bombs, the necessary plants might be secretly built in Canada or perhaps in Australia, now that the Japanese threat to that island-continent appeared to be removed, but the strain thus imposed on British resources would be very great and must limit the scope of the enterprise. By far the best arrangement, in Churchill's view—and certainly the one implied by developments thus far in this field—was a joint effort in which all the information obtained by British and American scientists was pooled, the great plants were built in remote areas of the United States, and "the results, if any [were shared] equally between us." He "strongly urged" this view upon the President.

He had told Hopkins the day before that he wanted to bring up the subject of "Tube Alloys." Hopkins had so informed Roosevelt. The President had then postponed the present discussion until he could receive from Washington the special information he needed. This was now at hand and, having digested it, the President promptly accepted the Prime Minister's conclusion. "We therefore took this decision jointly, and settled a basis of agreement," Churchill would later say.** ". . . I have no doubt that it was the progress that we had made in Britain, and the confidence of our scientists in ultimate success, imparted to the President, that led him to his grave and fateful decision."[11]

But we who look upon the scene from afar can see that Churchill was in error if he believed that the President's decision rested upon facts and opinions and judgments "imparted" that afternoon. The essential decision had already been taken by then.

¶ The attack was actually made in late February 1943, in one of the heroic exploits of the war. Some three thousand pounds of heavy water were destroyed and the plant severely damaged. In November 1943, planes of the Eighth U. S. Bomber Command, based in England, made a major attack on the plant and power station, inflicting much damage and destroying some 120 pounds of heavy water. The Germans then sought to dismantle the heavy-water installations and take them to Germany, but a ferry steamer on which the equipment was loaded was sunk by a Special Forces party in February 1944. William L. Laurence tells the story in considerable detail on pp. 94–115 of his *Dawn Over Zero, The Story of the Atomic Bomb* (New York: 1946).

** Later it would appear that the agreement was not as complete or wholehearted as Churchill initially believed—either that, or Roosevelt retreated from it under pressure from the U. S. Army and War Department.

During the last year, aided by earlier information provided by scientists in England, great progress had been made in various laboratories in the United States, under Government auspices. A relatively cheap method of producing uranium of the needed purity had been developed. Methods of separating U-235 out of natural (though purified) uranium, and of producing plutonium, had been much advanced. Continuing experiments by Fermi's group had confirmed his earlier view that graphite, though not as good a moderator as heavy water, was good enough to enable the construction with its use of so-called "nuclear reactor" or chain-reactive pile. (At the same time, as Churchill knew, the Canadian Government was cooperating in the building of a heavy water plant in British Columbia; it could not be in production for some time to come but might then supply the deficiency in case, for some reason, graphite proved unsuitable.) Responding to all this, the Top Policy Group (see p. 85) had recommended just a few days ago that the whole effort be now greatly expanded and accelerated. Accordingly, plans for the production plants were already going forward, several possible sites for them having been selected during the spring, and to the Army Corps of Engineers had been assigned the task of constructing them. As a matter of fact, Colonel J. C. Marshall of the Corps had only yesterday been ordered to establish a new Engineer District esoterically designated as the DSM Project (the initials stood for "Development of Substitute Materials"), which ultimately was to take charge of the entire atomic bomb program.

Small wonder, therefore, that Roosevelt found no difficulty in reaching a general policy agreement on this matter with his distinguished visitor who, grateful for it, sighed his relief into the hot dark still air.

ii. ". . . *A Very Black Hour*"

Late that night the President's special train bore Churchill, Roosevelt, and Hopkins from Hyde Park southward toward the Capital. At eight o'clock next morning—Sunday, June 21, the longest day of the year and the first anniversary of Hitler's attack on Russia—they arrived in Washington's Union Station and were taken in heavily guarded automobiles to the White House. The Prime Minister moved at once into the huge bedroom which had been his last December and early January and for whose air-conditioning he was now profoundly grateful. "I dwelt in comfort," he would later record, "at about thirty degrees below the temperature of most of the rest of the building."

He had a briefly peaceful and restful time, breakfasting, reading newspapers, perusing telegrams of no particularly memorable import, crossing the hallway to chat with Harry Hopkins. Then he went with Brooke and Major General Sir Hastings (Pug) Ismay, the Minister of Defense's Chief of Staff,†† to the Oval Study where the President awaited him and where, inevitably, his restful interlude ended.

He had been only a little while in the room when a telegram was given to the President who, having read it, handed it to the Prime Minister without a word.[12] Churchill read through shocked eyes: "Tobruk has fallen, with twenty-five thousand men taken prisoners."‡‡ He couldn't believe it; he asked Ismay to phone London for confirmation. Ismay departed, but returned almost at once with a message from Admiral Sir Henry Harwood commanding the British Fleet at Alexandria in which the admiral said that, because of Tobruk's fall and the general deterioration of "the situation," he was withdrawing "all Eastern Fleet units south of the Suez Canal" to protect them from the "heavy air attack on Alexandria" that seemed possible "in the near future, . . . in view of approaching full moon." It was true, then. The British were back where they had been two years ago in Africa. All their conquests in Cyrenaica and Libya were lost; they stood on the defensive, almost naked of armor, against an enemy whose tanks could now run on captured British oil and petrol, whose guns could fire captured British ammunition, whose infantry could be carried forward in captured British lorries. "This was one of the heaviest blows I can recall during the war."

Brooke, too, was staggered—especially so because it seemed a black reflection upon the fighting qualities of British armies. How could it have happened that, within a day after the attack began, Tobruk's garrison had surrendered to a force of perhaps half its size? "Defeat is one thing," said Churchill; "disgrace is another." And Brooke could not but agree as he contemplated the terrible global implications of this disaster. Another major battle might destroy the British forces in Egypt and give to the enemy the Valley of the Nile, Suez, the whole of the Middle East. How, then, could the British be maintained in India? How could Chiang Kai-shek be sustained in China? How could sufficient material aid be gotten to Russia?

Neither man tried to hide his dismay—and both were intensely grateful for the reaction of Roosevelt and Marshall to their distress. "Nothing could exceed the sympathy and chivalry of my two friends," writes Churchill. "There were no reproaches; not an unkind word was spoken." Brooke could not later recall "what the actual words were that the President used to convey his sympathy" but vividly remembered "being impressed by the tact and real heartfelt sympathy which lay behind these words. There was not one word too much nor one word too little." Nor was sympathy all that was offered.

"What can we do to help?" asked Roosevelt.

†† Which is to say he was Churchill's Chief of Staff, since Churchill held the combined posts of Prime Minister and Minister of Defense.

‡‡ Actually the number of prisoners taken was thirty-three thousand.

"Give us tanks," was Churchill's prompt reply. "All the tanks you can spare. And ship them to the Middle East as quickly as you can."

Roosevelt turned to Marshall.

Marshall first proposed sending the American Second Armored Division at once to the Middle East, under the command of General Patton; but in view of the fact that this division was only partly trained, he soon decided instead—a very hard decision—to deny to this and other U.S. armored divisions, many of the few hundred Sherman tanks that were then available. (The Shermans were then just coming into assembly line production.) Three hundred of these, plus a hundred 105-mm. self-propelled guns, were ordered dispatched at once to the Middle East. Later, when one of the six ships bearing this materiel was sunk by submarine action off Bermuda, Marshall and Roosevelt, "without a single word" from London, put another seventy Shermans aboard another fast cargo vessel, which got through safely.

"I always feel," wrote Brooke many years later, "that the Tobruk episode in the President's office did a great deal toward laying the foundations of friendship and understanding built up during the war between the President and Marshall on the one hand and Churchill and myself on the other."[13]

But the episode did nothing to reduce the strategic disagreement between Britain and the United States. Nor did the kindly feeling generated by it prevent the military discussions which followed from becoming often as heated amidst the humid Washington heat as Churchill had feared they would be . . .

He was initially annoyed to find that, while he was with Roosevelt at Hyde Park, Brooke at a meeting of the Combined Chiefs of Staff had reportedly agreed with Marshall and the other Americans that the North African proposal was a "diversion" from BOLERO which should not be countenanced. (Brooke recorded in his diary entry for the day that Churchill had been "a bit peevish, but not too bad and, after an hour's talk with him, had him quiet again.") This made more difficult the advancement of his position against the formidable opposition of Marshall and Stimson.

Stimson was not present at the first meetings, but his argument certainly was—in a letter to the President, dated June 19, which the President permitted Churchill to read.[14] "Geographically and historically," argued Stimson, BOLERO provided "the easiest road to the center of our chief enemy's heart." The "greatest danger" to the plan had lain "in the Pacific" but this had now been "greatly alleviated" by the victory at Midway. BOLERO preparations were already exerting strong "psychological pressure" on the enemy; there were "unmistakable signs of uneasiness in Germany as well as increasing unrest in the subject populations" of France and other conquered countries. "Under these circumstances an immense burden of proof rests upon any proposition which may impose the slightest risk of weakening BOLERO. . . . When one is engaged in a tug of war, it is highly risky to spit on one's hands even for the purpose of getting a better grip. No new plan should even be whispered to friend or enemy unless it . . . is so sure of immediate success and so manifestly helpful to BOLERO that it could not possibly be taken as evidence of doubt or vacillation in the prosecution of BOLERO." His concluding words were not calculated to endear him nor recommend his argument to His Majesty's First Minister; he no doubt would have used different words had he known that Churchill would read them. "To my mind," said he, "BOLERO in inception and in its present development is an essentially American project, brought into the war as the vitalizing contribution of our fresh and unwearied leaders and forces. My own view is that it would be a mistake to hazard it by any additional expeditionary proposal as yet brought to my attention."

Churchill was unswayed. He made that day what Marshall later reported to Stimson to have been "a terrific attack on BOLERO"[15]—a characterization of his argument which the Prime Minister would never have accepted. He did argue strongly against a "premature" attempt to land in France, stressing the fact that the shortage of landing craft would make impossible the landing of more than four thousand troops in the first wave of an assault upon the strongly fortified coast of France, should such an assault be made in September. But SLEDGEHAMMER, he was agreeably surprised to learn, was no longer ardently pressed: evidently (from his point of view) the Americans were at last beginning to recognize the reckless folly of this proposal. What, however, was proposed in its place? Apparently nothing. The evident intention of the Combined Chiefs was to take no offensive action whatever in the Atlantic Theater in 1942, concentrating everything instead on ROUNDUP in 1943. This disturbed him. He put forth his arguments for GYMNAST, which he persisted in regarding as no "diversion" from the preparations for a cross-Channel assault but, rather, as a logical part of them. He pointed to the benefits which would accrue to the Russians if the Mediterranean were opened to Allied shipping, as it would be if North Africa were conquered and Italy fell in likely consequence. The shipping lanes over which supplies flowed from America to the Soviets would in that case be shortened by thousands of miles, would be open the year around, and would be far less hazardous than any now available: the event would be equivalent to the capture by the Soviets of millions of tons of desperately needed materiel. He emphasized, too, as he knew Roosevelt did, the values of a North African operation as a dress rehearsal for the cross-Channel assault. Raw green troops would go into North Africa; battle-hardened veterans in efficient tactical formations would come out, ready for the supreme test in France. Moveover, a sound basis would be provided for determining who among the available general officers should command the forces invading France. Finally, he pointed to the immediate situation in North Africa. Did it not argue persuasively, even imperatively for GYMNAST?

All this was presented by the Prime Minister with his customary eloquence. His eloquence, however, did not help his cause against opponents who had an almost instinctive distrust of rhetorical brilliance and who suspected that it now served to hide rather than reveal basic motives and purposes.

What Marshall suspected and feared was that the British were opposed not just to a cross-Channel assault in 1942 but also (secretly) to one in 1943—that, indeed, they would (through Churchill) continue to postpone this one great decisive operation in favor of peripheral nibbling indecisive actions whereby the war would be indefinitely prolonged. It might even, in that case, be lost. For though the Allies now possessed potential advantages over the enemy—more industrial power, more men, greater natural resources—these might count for naught in an end determined by devices of war which no man had yet seen. Given enough time, who could be sure that those terrible "secret weapons" that were Hitler's constant boast and threat, and toward which we ourselves were working, might not actually be placed in his hands while we, lacking them, continued to rely on conventional arms?

Surely (thought Marshall) the Prime Minister was being less than candid, he was being considerably less than wholly honest, when he indicated that GYMNAST could be fitted into the general plan agreed upon in April. That plan did not apply to an undefined future. A definite time schedule was of its essence. The BOLERO buildup was to be at a rate sufficient through the summer and autumn of 1942, and through the following winter, to launch the major assault in the spring of 1943. And how could any man honestly believe that the GYMNAST proposal was not a contradiciton of this? If the North African operation were undertaken it would obviously divert from the United Kingdom to the Mediterranean area an immense amount of shipping, in addition to troops and air forces and naval units, that would otherwise be devoted to the cross-Channel buildup. The diversion might well continue beyond the fall of the present year into the winter of 1942–43; even if it did not, it would prevent enough buildup in Britain to make a cross-Channel attack possible in the spring of 1943. What Churchill proposed was, therefore, not a matter of "both/and," as he tried to make it seem. It was a question of "either/or"—a sharply pointed question that probed to the very heart of Allied strategic conceptions.

Marshall's own answer to this question had of course already been given. Everyone in the room knew what it was. Nevertheless he reiterated it with conviction and force, making "a very powerful argument for BOLERO, disposing of all the clouds that had been woven about it by the Mountbatten incident"—as Stimson was told immediately after the session and wrote into his diary that night. The Secretary of War also noted that "towards the end [of the meeting] it was agreed that we should go ahead full blast on BOLERO until the first of September. At that time the Prime Minister wanted to have a resume of the situation to see whether a real attack could be made (in 1942) without the danger of disaster. If not, why then we should reconsider the rest of the field." But just how firm was the agreement for a "full-blast" pursuit of BOLERO through August? Stimson evidently had doubts about it—and doubts, too, about the precise accuracy of his diary statement concerning it—for he added, rather lamely: "At any rate that seems to have been the substance so far."[16]

Somewhat different from this was the British estimate of the military conclusions reached that day, summarized in a note evidently dictated by Churchill that evening.[17] There had been general agreement that preparations for a major cross-Channel operation in 1943 were "to be pushed forward with all speed and energy," this note said. At the same time, it had been recognized as "essential" that Great Britain and the United States be prepared also "to act offensively in 1942." There had been general agreement that operations "in France or the Low Countries in 1942 would, if successful, yield greater political and strategic gains than operations in any other theater"; planning and preparation of such operations were "to be pressed forward with all possible speed, energy, and ingenuity." At the same time, it had been recognized that "we must be ready with an alternative" in case no "sound and sensible plan" for 1942 cross-Channel operations could be "contrived." Hence plans and preparations for GYMNAST were *also* to go forward, it being agreed that whatever forces were employed in North Africa would "in the main be found from BOLERO units which have not yet left the United States." Also to be "carefully considered" by the Combined Chiefs was the possibility of operations in Norway and on the Iberian peninsula. (Churchill had made the Norwegian proposal, coded JUPITER, the first of May, to the considerable dismay of Brooke, who thought it had no merit at all.)

Thus there was, from the American point of view, a continuing ambiguity in Churchill's position, expressive of the wiliness and subtlety in the man himself which often struck simpler natures and narrower minds as deliberately, maddeningly deceitful and dishonest.[18] And of this ambiguity, this wile, this subtlety, an apparent instance was provided immediately following the meeting that afternoon of June 21.

At five o'clock, two American major generals whom Churchill had not met before were brought to his air-conditioned room. One of the two was Dwight Eisenhower, the other Mark Clark. Harry Hopkins had told Churchill immediately after lunch that the President wanted particularly for him to meet these two men. This obviously meant that they were intended to play a major role in future European operations; it may also have meant that they were regarded by Marshall as remarkably articulate exponents of American strategic views who might exert a persuasive influence upon the Prime Minister. At any rate they talked to him almost exclusively about ROUNDUP, and with a missionary zeal, as if they sought to convert him. They encountered no opposition: he was already among the converted, his zeal as great as theirs, and he expressed no reservations concerning the timing of the operation. The assault should be made, he agreed, in the spring or summer of 1943. As evidence of his zeal he gave them a copy of a paper he had prepared for consideration by the British Chiefs of Staff on June 15, just two days before his departure for the United States—a paper in which he stressed "the qualities of magnitude, simultaneity, and violence" that were "required" for ROUNDUP's success. He contemplated "at least six heavy disembarkations . . . in the first wave" and "at least half a dozen feints" in order to take advantage of the enemy's inability to be strong everywhere at once. There should be "not less than 400,000 men ashore and busy" within a week after "zero," and within a week after that there should be 700,000. ". . . if [by then] air supremacy has been gained, if the enemy is in considerable confusion, and if we hold at least four workable ports, we shall have got our claws well into the job."[19]

This *seemed* straightforward enough. But was it (the Americans asked themselves) truly an expression of personal commitment to ROUNDUP? Was it not, instead, a subtle argument *against* ROUNDUP insofar as this operation bore a target date in 1943? "The object of the above notes," concluded Churchill's paper, "is to give an idea of the scale and spirit in which alone they [the cross-Channel operations] can be undertaken with good prospects of success." It was a scale vastly greater than that envisaged by American and British planners who had been at work on this project in London's Grosvenor Square, since early April, and to whose first outline plan Churchill's paper was a response. The planners, indeed, who must fit ends to means in terms realistic for 1943, found it impossible to take Churchill's conception seriously.

And there the strategic issue remained—somewhat clarified, perhaps, but certainly unreduced—when the Washington talks ended two days later.

On June 24, as Marshall's personal guest, the Prime Minister went with Ismay, Brooke, and Dill to Fort Jackson, South Carolina, to inspect American troops being trained there. Both he and Ismay were favorably impressed by a battalion parachute drop in the morning, but neither was by a field exercise with live ammunition in the afternoon. Ismay, in fact, was discouraged by it. Asked for his opinion, the general told Churchill that "it would be murder to pit . . . [these troops] against continental soldiery." Churchill nodded: the troops were certainly "immature": but they were "wonderful material" and would "learn very quickly."[20] Not quickly enough, though, in his opinion, to make SLEDGEHAMMER possible or ROUNDUP an acceptable risk. To Marshall and the other Americans he spoke in praise of the "miracle" whereby divisions were being "mass-produced" by a country which, only a few years back, had possessed an Army of less than two thousand. But he kept insisting that at least two years were required to train a competent soldier.

On the evening of the following day, in Baltimore, he boarded his flying boat and took off on his flight home, having cut short his visit by several days.

He was forced to do so by the political repercussions of Tobruk's fall. He faced a Vote of Censure in the House of Commons. And though he won this test of confidence very decisively on July 2 (the vote was 457–25), he had to hear and answer some harsh criticisms of his conduct of the war in the debate that preceded the division of the House. The whole experience could not but add to his reluctance to take major incalculable risks in the near future. More than ever was his heart hardened and his mind set against any cross-Channel effort whatever in 1942. More than ever was he doubtful of the feasibility of such an effort in 1943. More than ever was he convinced, on the other hand, that the risks of a long period of inaction were also too great to be accepted. There must be important offensive action in the fall of 1942, or else the alliance with Stalin's Russia would be subjected to intolerable strains, and circumstances seemed to him to point more imperatively than ever toward North Africa as the proper theater for this action.

As July 1942 opened and advanced, the Allies remained in the shadows of what Marshall later called "a very black hour."

In the south of Russia, Sevastapol fell on July 2, and the Germans then drove powerfully toward the Caucasus, capturing one key point after another. In North Africa the British Eighth Army retreated all the way to El Alamein, just forty miles west of Alexandria, where it was spread dangerously thin along a thirty-five-mile front between the sea to the north and the impassable salt flat known as the Qattara Depression to the south. The specter of a linkage of Nazi forces coming down from the Caucasus with forces coming up from Egypt continued to haunt London and Washington. In the Atlantic, Allied merchant shipping losses to U-boat attacks mounted toward unprecedented rates. During May, 120 ships with a gross tonnage of nearly 602,000 had been sunk, and this rate had been surpassed in June, when more than 627,000 tons went down. The sinkage rate continued into July, reaching a peak in the second week of this month when 400,000 tons were sunk—"a rate unexampled in this war or the last," as Churchill cabled Roosevelt grimly on July 14. This was 2.5 times the rate at which new shipping would be built if Roosevelt's production quotas (then deemed absurdly optimistic) were met (they were ultimately surpassed).

Only in the Pacific was the prevailing gloom penetrated by a few faint rays of light. Here the Japanese continued to hold the strategic initiative. They still possessed a sufficient numerical superiority over the Americans to permit their concentrating in one area without exposing themselves to an overwhelming American concentration in another; they still operated along interior lines of communication. And it was to be expected that they would exercise this initiative at the earliest possible moment by resuming the movement south from Rabaul which had been, from their point of view, only temporarily frustrated by the Battle of the Coral Sea—a movement whose strategic objective was the severing of

American lines of communication with Australia. But the Midway action, besides denying the Central Pacific to Japan, had reduced Japanese superiority in aircraft carriers while demonstrating that these were the decisive weapons in present-day naval warfare. It had disorganized and scattered forces which otherwise could and would have been concentrated for the southward drive. It had undoubtedly damaged the morale of the Japanese high command, introducing to its councils debilitating doubts and hesitations that had been absent from them. And all this meant that the Americans were now presented with an opportunity to seize the tactical initiative whereby they might further disarray Japanese plans while strengthening their own defensive positions against the expected next enemy move. They must, however, act quickly. They must also accept grave risks, since they could not effectively strike in the Southwest Pacific (the area of maximum strategic importance) without weakening their forces in the Central and North Pacific or else reducing their commitments to BOLERO and the emergency in the Middle East.

As July opened they decided to grasp the opportunity, with all its risks, being strongly urged to this course by both King and MacArthur. On the second day of the month the Joint Chiefs of Staff issued a directive prescribing offensive operations in the area of New Ireland, New Britain, and New Guinea, to be conducted in three successive phases or "tasks." Task One was to take the Santa Cruz Islands, Tulagi, and adjacent positions in the lower Solomons, one of which was Guadalcanal. Task Two was to take Lae, Salamua, and the northeast coast of New Guinea. Task Three was to take Rabaul and adjacent positions in the area of New Ireland-New Britain. August 1 was set as the target date for Task One.

Much of the intensive discussion preceding this directive had been concerned with the question of whether the Army or the Navy should command the operations. As we have seen, the command arrangements that had been made to accommodate Australian politics in terms of the talents, temperament, and prestige of MacArthur had badly blurred the line separating the Army's authority and responsibility from the Navy's in the Southwest Pacific. Abundant opportunities for inter-Service disagreement were to be found there, and neither King nor MacArthur was the kind of man likely to overlook them, each being intensely jealous of his own and his Service's prerogatives. Inevitably the question had at last been settled, by Marshall for the most part, in a compromise wholly pleasing to neither Service. Nimitz was assigned command of the first phase (Task One) and MacArthur of the last two. MacArthur of course complained of the difficulty of assuming a command transferred between phases, but a harassed and weary Marshall, intensely preoccupied with other and larger problems, was in no mood to listen. In a message characterized by official Army historians as both "hopeful" and "anxious," the Chief of Staff told MacArthur that in his opinion a "workable plan" had been made and "a unity of command established without . . . precedent for an offensive operation." He went on: "I wish you to make every conceivable effort to promote a complete accord throughout this affair. There will be difficulties and irritations inevitably but the end in view demands a determination to suppress these manifestations."[21]

He himself was forced to live on an almost exclusive diet of "difficulties" and "irritations" through these hot, humid summer days. On the very day of the Southwest Pacific directive, he was in communication with Hopkins, then at Hyde Park with the President, concerning the need to brace the public against the dire consequences of a German conquest of the Upper Nile Valley, believed to be imminent by nearly all American military men. (G-2, Army Intelligence, predicted that Rommel would be in Cairo within a week.) The United Nations must "present to the world a solid front," said Marshall, suggesting that "the President guide public comment so as to indicate that the United Nations stand together in adversity as they ultimately will in victory."[22] He was also involved in the difficult decisions which the President then had to make concerning the diversion to the British, in their desperate need, of war materiel that happened at that moment to be passing through the Middle East en route to Russia and China.

The question of diverting heavy bombers originally consigned to China was particularly hard. And dangerous . . .

When Wavell's ABDA Theater was shattered by the Japanese advance, there had been set up an Allied China-Burma-India Theater. To it had been assigned one of the most remarkable soldiers in the American Army, Lieutenant General Joseph W. Stilwell, nicknamed "Vinegar Joe" in recognition of his tart temper, acid intelligence, and hard-bitten countenance. He was a brave and honest man, a sound strategist and tactician, though unfortunately not the kind of personality congenial to Roosevelt, on whose nerves he seemed occasionally to act as an abrasive. Indeed, he was temperamentally a "loner" who found it difficult to work with others, and the difficulties he faced in Chungking, where he served *ex officio* as Chiang Kai-shek's Chief of Staff, were immense. Inadequately supported and supplied, he must build armies out of widely diversified units of Chinese, Indian, British, and American troops; direct their operations over mountains and through jungles in unhealthy climates; and (perhaps worst of all) deal continuously with the authoritarian temperament and autocratic power of the Chinese dictator and with the graft and corruption that were rife in Chinese Government. It was Stilwell who must bear the brunt of the dictator's displeasure (and Madame's also) whenever the Generalissimo felt slighted by Washington and London, which was often; and Stilwell's recent messages to the War Department clearly indicated that any such delay in the Chinese air buildup as was now contemplated would risk the threat if not the actuality of a separate peace between China and Japan.[23]

The bombers were nevertheless diverted, the risk accepted.§§ And on the next day—and the next, and the next—Marshall perforce dealt with other questions no less hard, no less risky. There was no end to them.

But there was an end to his patience—or, rather, to that iron control he imposed on his impatience. This end was reached during the second week of July. The event was like the one drop too many in a chemical solution: it precipitated a sudden salt of decision out of which came the next great event in the Allied war against Nazi-Fascism.

iii. *TORCH Is Lighted Amidst Darkness*

George Catlett Marshall's was not a naturally passive disposition, easily yielding to outer influences and devoid of personal ambition. His natural self-will, on the contrary, was probably greater than most and so were his natural energies and passions. The selflessness, the calm purposefulness which impressed all who came in contact with him were the products of a self-mastery achieved in terms of his very high code of honor—and self-mastery had been for him (and remained) difficult. It was this which gave to him his rare distinction, causing associates to trust him as they did few men. They sensed the remarkable degree to which he ruled himself according to the generally recognized, but too seldom observed, laws of honor; they felt that whatever had been sly or slippery in his character had been crushed under the heel of his honorable self; they knew, therefore, that he would not lie nor cheat nor accept credit due others.[24]

He was not endowed to any unusual degree with the instincts, intuitions and manipulatory skills of a politician. He was not gregarious. Popular acclaim meant relatively little to him. He would not zestfully or even willingly stake his life on the chances of public opinion, as an elected official must constantly do. Nor was he especially blessed or cursed with creative imagination: he was no dreamer of mighty dreams. He was a practical man, a solid man, a logical man, a clear and definite man, and he wanted everything in his environment—all that pertained to him, at least—to be as clear and as definite as possible.

He had had, however, a long and arduous experience of "fluid situations" and of the discrepancies that are often so wide between the ap-

§§ The effect in Chungking was as Stilwell had predicted: a storm was raised. If there was "crisis" in Libya and Egypt, there was also "crisis" in China, said Chiang to Stilwell in bitter anger. The Tenth Air Force, from which the heavy bombers were diverted, had been promised to China and Chiang had a right to expect to be notified *before* any part of it was taken away from him. "Do the Allies want the China Theater maintained?" he asked—and Madame added significantly that there was a great deal of pro-Japanese sentiment and activity in Chungking. All this was communicated through Stilwell to the President, who promptly sent a message to the Generalissimo stressing the urgency of the crisis in the Middle East, the importance of this area to the lines of communication with China, and the importance attached to the United States and the other Allies to China as "a vital part of our common war effort."

pearances and realities of power. He had learned in a hard school, through the twenties and thirties, what MacArthur as Chief of Staff had so signally failed to learn, namely, that the principal officer of the U. S. Army must accept in his heart and brain, and not merely with his lips, the fact of his subordination to civilian political control. He had learned that War Department organization charts—their neat compartments, linked by horizontal and vertical lines—were far from literal representations of the channels through which power actually flows or of the offices in which decisions are actually made. (He had seen the President himself put down in a head-on collision with the Army Engineers, whose lobby of hungry contractors and localized "interests" was more persuasive of the Congress than the White House could be regarding many a hugely expensive public work.) He had doubtless been disillusioned; he could hardly have expected the world to be as in fact he found it—but he had not been embittered. Indeed, it is unlikely that the nation ever had an Army Chief of Staff who assessed more sympathetically or (on the whole) more accurately the motives which impelled, and the pressures which played upon, the men outside his Service with whom he must work: the President, the Presidential assistants, the Cabinet members, the members of Congress, the admirals, the bureaucrats, the Big Businessmen, the journalists. He had studied: he had learned. And of the essence of what he had learned was the fact that few of the realities with which his high office must deal, and those few not the most important, could be precisely defined or clearly perceived as solid entities; they existed instead as shifting intangible relations between personalities that continually changed, among centers of force that continuously fluctuated.

He must therefore *feel* his way, and with a severely limited control over the general direction and speed of his official labors. It was as if he rode a raft down a river in a fog. He had a rudder and he had a pole. He might use these to steer wide of jagged rocks that loomed up now and again through the mist, or to turn toward or veer away from the river bank. And on this bank, through occasional rents in the curtain of fog, he could glimpse landmarks that were noted on his chart, calculating from them how far he had come and how far he had yet to go to reach a prescribed destination. Such landmarks, glimpsed by him, were bound to be few. They must, however, be solid and permanent; his need required that they not dissolve in the mists, or constantly change their shapes and positions, as Englishmen accustomed to fogs and raised in a magic forest of ambiguities seemed quite willing for them to do.

The principal landmark for him in this early July of 1942 was the agreement with the British on strategy, arrived at last April and reaffirmed with some modification during Churchill's visit in late June. His inward need (an almost desperate need) endowed this agreement with a sharper definition and a greater solidity than it would ever have appeared to have to less interested eyes. He was even inclined to regard the outcome of the late June conversations as a kind of *quid pro quo* whereby the extraordinary aid given the British in the Middle East paid for their continued adherence to the basic April agreement. "The Prime Minister favored an attack on Africa to ease the pressure on the British in this theater," he had said to a War Council meeting on June 29. "The result of the conferences, however, was that we managed to preserve the basic plan for BOLERO."[25] Not only was BOLERO to be pressed with all vigor; SLEDGEHAMMER was also to be mounted during the summer on a "contingency" basis (that is, its actual launching would depend upon developing circumstance) until September, when it would be reviewed and a final judgment made concerning it. This was the agreement: it was his only guide and only basis for purposeful activity in the eastern Atlantic.

Then, abruptly, it ceased to exist.

On July 8, the British Joint Staff Mission in Washington was notified that the War Cabinet in London had decided *not* to mount SLEDGEHAMMER. The Cabinet hoped that the United States would agree to the invasion of North Africa! Reasons were given. The mounting of SLEDGEHAMMER would tie up a quarter of a million tons of shipping and all the landing craft in the British Isles, preventing any large-scale raids by Mountbatten's forces and suspending the amphibious training of any forces not committed to SLEDGEHAMMER. It would delay preparations for the major cross-Channel assault in 1943. It could be justified, therefore, only if its actual launching were assured—and the launching could be justified only in circumstances so unlikely as to verge on the impossible. The Germans would have to be utterly demoralized as a result of reverses in Russia (where, in point of fact, they had just broken through the Kharkov front and forced the Soviet armies into a general withdrawal in the Don Basin).

All this was initially communicated to Marshall by Field Marshal Dill, who found the experience memorable.[26] Marshall's reaction was explosive—and Marshall in eruption was an event as awesome as it was rare. He was sick and tired of arrangements that were made, then unmade, then made again and unmade again. He was sick and tired of meaningless words and empty gestures. He was sick and tired of proposed operations that, though costly and risky, could have no important effect on the outcome of the war. He regarded the situation on the Russian front as an argument *for* rather than *against* SLEDGEHAMMER. Had not this been deemed from the first an "emergency" operation? Did not the evident inability of the Russians to halt the German offensive constitute an "emergency"? Surely the need for an assault that would force a diversion of German strength from the Russian front grew swiftly toward that point at which it would become precisely the "contingency" upon which SLEDGEHAMMER was designed to be launched. For if the German advance through the Don Basin continued at its present rate it would soon render "negligible in magnitude" Russia's "participation in the war," enabling a German concentration in the West that would destroy the meaning of ROUNDUP plans and BOLERO movements. Thank God, GYMNAST was not the only alternative to SLEDGEHAMMER. There was also the offensive now being mounted in the Southwest Pacific—an offensive severely limited by available resources but capable of expansion if future American commitments to the United Kingdom were reduced.

This last disturbed Dill profoundly.

Admiral King, who of course would welcome Marshall's change of mind and heart, happened to be out of town that day and the next; the Joint Chiefs of Staff did not again meet until the afternoon of July 10. Marshall then read to his colleagues the British War Cabinet dispatch but (it is a measure of the anger which still gripped him) ignored the reasons given for the proposal. Instead he presented for discussion two questions, one of which was clearly raised by the dispatch while the other as clearly implied a breach of faith and a continuing perfidy. The first question: Should the United States agree to the North African invasion? The second: Did the British really want to invade the Continent in 1943? His own answer to both questions was, "No." GYMNAST would be an "expensive and ineffectual operation," as he had often said before; and the very fact that it was now again proposed meant, obviously, that the British had never really intended BOLERO-SLEDGEHAMMER and did not now intend BOLERO-ROUNDUP. What, then, should be done? The United States, he believed, should make one more effort to secure from the British the "full and wholehearted . . . support" without which BOLERO and the operations linked to it could not possibly succeed. The effort should be forceful; the British should be presented with what amounted to an ultimatum. They should be bluntly told that if they refused to adhere to an agreement they had now twice made, the United States would shift her major emphasis from the Atlantic to the Pacific "and strike decisively against Japan; in other words, assume a defensive attitude against Germany, except for air operations; and use all available means in the Pacific."[27] This from the soldier who, more steadfastly and effectively than any other high officer on either side of the Atlantic, had been the prophet and architect of Anglo-American unity in the war effort!

And what he proposed, the others at the meeting quickly accepted. He had already prepared a memorandum intended for submittal to the President, in which he stated his case and made his recommendations. Its substance had been "cordially endorsed" by Secretary Stimson that morning. (The peppery Stimson had welcomed what he called a "showdown" in which the Americans threatened "to turn . . . [their] backs on" their Ally.[28]) This paper was now signed by all three of the Joint Chiefs and dispatched to the President, who was then at Hyde Park.

Its effect upon Roosevelt was electric. He at once phoned Washington with a request designed to put Marshall and King on the defensive concerning what he called "your Pacific Ocean alternative." He wanted "a detailed comprehensive outline of the plans"—and of course there were none. He wanted to know what effect the proposed shift would have on the disposition of forces and shipping—and one effect, as the Joint Chiefs had to reply, was greatly to reduce the rate of Army deployment; even if all the ships now assigned to BOLERO were transferred to the Pacific (and half this shipping was British), the number of troops that could be transported from the United States to a theater of war would be cut from one hundred thousand to forty thousand per month. He wanted to know what effect the change would have on the defense of the Soviet Union—and the Joint Chiefs had to reply that this effect would be unfavorable in present circumstances, though establishment of a strong Far Eastern front would of course aid Russia in case of war between her and Japan.

On the day after he had received the memorandum containing this information, Roosevelt telegraphed Marshall: "I have definitely decided to send you, King and Harry to London immediately. . . . I want you to know that I do not approve the Pacific proposal."[29]

The President gave his reasons the next morning when, returned to Washington, he met with Marshall and Stimson in the White House. He held to the logic that had led to the "Germany First" decision months ago, adding that decisive action against Japan could not be taken in any case until the Navy was greatly strengthened and that American concentration in the Pacific this year or next must inevitably increase "the chance of complete German domination of Europe and Africa." It continued to be true that Japan's defeat did not mean the defeat of Germany, whereas Germany's defeat meant the defeat of Japan very soon thereafter, perhaps "without firing a shot." As for the use of the Pacific alternative as a threat "to force the British into accepting a concentrated effort against Germany" (so Marshall had put it in an informal message accompanying the Joint Chiefs memorandum), Roosevelt was dead set against it. It was "something of a red herring." It was like "taking up your dishes and going away"—by which he meant that there was a childish petulance in it.[30]

Not that he was unsympathetic with Marshall's exasperation. His talk clearly revealed that he was. He himself was "absolutely sound on BOLERO" and wished it to be pressed unremittingly. He insisted on this in response to Stimson's half-accusing questions. But his talk also revealed his human sympathy with the principal cause and target of Marshall's exasperation. Winston Churchill was at that time being subjected to severe domestic political pressures, and the President of the United States would not sanction any effort which, whether or not it achieved its stated aim, must personally humiliate and weaken the domestic position of the Prime Minister of Great Britain. Indeed, he was opposed to one ally's presenting ultimatums to the other on any question. Each should of course have definite views and press them strongly, but neither should refuse to negotiate on the basis of them in order to arrive at workable compromises. Neither could afford to forget for a moment that the one absolutely indispensable condition of victory was Allied unity.

Hence his decision to send Marshall and King to London, along with Harry Hopkins as his personal representative. The mission was to meet with Churchill and the British Chiefs of Staff and shape with them a truly definite decision regarding Allied operations in the eastern Atlantic—one that, this time, would stay made. The three would have plenary powers within broad limits, but they must not stake everything on their initial effort (which he favored) to persuade the British to reinstate SLEDGEHAMMER. "It is of the highest importance that U.S. ground troops be brought into action against the enemy in 1942."[31] The Americans therefore must be prepared to consider and agree with the British upon a less satisfactory alternative if, as seemed highly probable, Churchill and Brooke proved adamant in their opposition to any cross-Channel movement in 1942.

In private conversation with Hopkins after dinner that evening, the President was more specific. If SLEDGEHAMMER could not be launched, consideration must be given North Africa and the Middle East as theaters "where our ground and sea forces can operate against German ground forces in 1942." GYMNAST had many things in its favor, one of them the fact that it would be "a purely American enterprise." In the Middle East "we would possibly have no resistance" and could use "our forces either in Egypt or from the head of the Persian Gulf" where both "Russia and England" were "sorely pressed." Of course operations in either theater would "require a substantial reduction in BOLERO for the next three months." He was "prepared to accept this."[32]

On the following day, July 16, Marshall, King, and Hopkins boarded a TWA Stratoliner at Washington's National Airport and took off for the British Isles. They landed at Prestwick, Scotland, late in the afternoon of Friday, July 17, and boarded a train for London since the weather over England was too bad for flying. With them went a memorandum of instructions from Roosevelt as Commander-in-Chief. Its closing words were: "Please remember three cardinal principles—speed of decision on plans, unity of plans, attack combined with defense but not defense alone. This affects the immediate objective of U.S. ground forces fighting against Germans in 1942. I hope for total agreement within one week of your arrival."

The "hope" was in large part realized.

Precisely one week later, on Friday, July 24—after incessant and sometimes bitter argument in Claridge's Hotel, where sixteen rooms on the fourth floor had been converted into a temporary United States military headquarters; at 20 Grosvenor Square, the apartment building that had been converted into the headquarters of United States forces in the European Theater (ETOUSA); in the British War Office in Whitehall;

at No. 10 Downing Street, where Churchill opened the first formal meeting on the Monday after the Americans arrived—the British and Americans, meeting as the Combined Chiefs of Staff, projected a combined operation against the north and northwest coast of Africa, to be launched not later than December 1, 1942. Moreoever, the memorandum which became the instrument of this agreement was submitted, not by the British who had always favored GYMNAST, but by Marshall (with King) who had always opposed it!

The manner of this happening is instructive in the tactics of committee politics. All week long, Marshall had been dealing with questions to which his own emphatic answers were overruled—questions that were in effect the objects of a battle wherein his own unhappy lot had been that of a soldier forced to retreat. At no point had he easily yielded; stubbornly he had fought to hold as much ground as he could and, for every step of his withdrawal, make his opponents pay a price in concessions. Nor was his July 24 memorandum a departure from these tactics.[33] It was designed, not as an act of surrender, but as a bold tactical maneuver whereby the whole tide of battle might be reversed and every position that he had given up might, in one sweep, be regained.

The crucial memorandum divided naturally into three parts. Part One proposed that the planning of ROUNDUP proceed on the assumption that the operation would be launched by July 1, 1943. It further proposed that preparations for SLEDGEHAMMER also be continued but (this in answer to the major British objection) only to the extent that they did not "seriously interfere with training for ROUNDUP." Part Two proposed the African operation, but with the understanding "that a commitment to this operation renders ROUNDUP, in all probability, impracticable in 1943 and therefore that we have definitely accepted a defensive, encircling line for the Continental European Theater, except as to air operation." This was designed to force an overt acceptance by the British of Marshall's basic contention that ROUNDUP and GYMNAST were contradictory and that a choice must therefore be made between them. If this were accepted, the choice might very well go against North Africa and for the Continental invasion, especially if the making of the choice could be postponed. Part Three proposed this postponement: the choice to abandon ROUNDUP and accept the strategic defensive was not to be made until September 15, and would then be guided by an assessment of the "probable course" of the war in Russia and of the effects this would have upon the prospects for a successful invasion of the Continent in the first half of 1943. This meant, of course, on the premise stated in Part Two of the memorandum, that September 15 would be the earliest date on which a final decision could be taken on whether or not to go ahead with the African operation; in Marshall's view, it reaffirmed the agreement of April as modified in late June.

The British, however, chose to regard the memorandum as (in Brooke's words) "a paper containing almost everything we had asked them [the Americans] to agree to at the start." They interpreted it as a flat proposal to substitute GYMNAST for SLEDGEHAMMER, and they were willing at least tacitly to accept the conclusion that going into North Africa this fall would preclude going into Continental Europe during the first half of '43. Indeed, Admiral of the Fleet Sir Dudley Pound indicated openly that, in his opinion, GYMNAST and ROUNDUP were as contradictory of one another as the Americans claimed. Neither Brooke nor Air Chief Marshal Sir Charles Portal would go this far, but Brooke (as his official historian says) had always "doubted whether" the cross-Channel assault "would be possible in 1943" and therefore "made no attempt to challenge . . . [the American] view."[34] He did press with his British colleagues for a modification of the language of the memorandum to indicate that the decision for North Africa constituted no break in the continuity of Allied strategy. The modification was accepted—another tactical defeat for Marshall, whose basic contention was that North Africa *did* constitute precisely such a break. The defeat was confirmed by the approved addition to the memorandum (at British insistence) of a clause saying "that the organization, planning, and training, for eventual entry in the Continent should continue so that this operation can be staged *should a marked deterioration in German military strength become apparent, and the resources of the United Nations, available after meeting other commitments, so permit.*"¶¶

Thus all that remained to serve Marshall's tactical purpose in the memorandum formally adopted by the Combined Chiefs was the provision that a final decision on ROUNDUP be put off until September 15. On the basis of this, Marshall, King, and Stimson could later insist that the June 24 decision was not final: the final decision would not be taken until mid-September.

But this last-ditch delaying tactic, whereby it was hoped that BOLERO-SLEDGEHAMMER and BOLERO-ROUNDUP might yet be saved, was doomed to failure from the start. It foundered on Roosevelt's insistence and Churchill's agreement that major offensive action *must* take place in '42—a necessity which Harry Hopkins, as the President's personal representative, had emphasized and re-emphasized all week long.

On Saturday, July 25, Hopkins dispatched a personal message to the President in which he observed and deplored the tendency in the London discussions to regard the preceding day's decision on North Africa as merely tentative. He urged that the President set a target date of "not later than 30 October" for the invasion. "What I fear most is that if we do not make a firm decision on GYMNAST and fix a reasonably early date there may be procrastinations and delay," he said. "Although I

¶¶ Italics the present author's.

believe the intention here is to mount the operation aggressively, unless the written language of the orders is precise there may be difficulties when it comes to carrying out the orders by the secondary personnel."[35] The President thoroughly and promptly agreed. He sent word that the landings should be no later than October 30 and asked Hopkins to tell the Prime Minister that he was "delighted" with this final decision and that the orders now were "full speed ahead."

Meanwhile, that Saturday morning, the Combined Chiefs had reconvened for the last formal meeting of the conference. They discussed command arrangements for the North African venture. It was no longer true that the operation would be "purely American," if indeed it had ever been. The amphibious assault troops were to be exclusively American, this in order to reduce if not avoid forcible opposition by the African French. (If the assault forces were British, the French would be bound to resist to the utmost—or so the Combined Chiefs believed.) But British naval units and British aircraft would be involved even in the initial assault phase, while later operations inside the Mediterranean would be primarily British. This, in other words, was to be the first active instance, a testing instance, of Anglo-American coalition warfare—and because the American commitment to it would be much larger than the British, the Combined Chiefs had agreed that its Supreme Commander should be an American. Under him were to be two task force commanders, one from the United States to command proposed landings at Casablanca, one from the British to command landings at Oran and possibly Algiers. The Deputy Supreme Commander was also to be British.

At this same meeting a new code name was given the operation—in part for security reasons and in part, one suspects, because memories of acrimonious discussion clustered too thickly around GYMNAST. The new name was TORCH.

Even then, Marshall would not give up.

The American mission arrived back in Washington on Monday, July 27. Three days later was held in Washington a meeting of the Combined Chiefs—the first such meeting to be presided over by blunt, honest, elderly Admiral William D. Leahy, who had been Ambassador to (Vichy) France until a few weeks ago and was now installed in the unique post of Chief of Staff to the Commander-in-Chief of the U. S. Army and Navy. The position, wherein Leahy's relationship to the President became roughly parallel to Dill's relationship to the Prime Minister, had been originally suggested by Marshall and opposed by King. The Army Chief of Staff had been concerned to establish a clearly defined liaison between the White House and the Joint Chiefs; the Chief of Naval Operations had been concerned to defeat another effort by the Army (as he saw it) to gain ascendancy over the Navy;—and the admiral's objections had quite miraculously melted away when the general, with that adroit large-mindedness characteristic of his operation, proposed a former Naval Operations Chief as the man to fill the post.

The post's value, if not Leahy's adequacy for it, was demonstrated at this first of the many Combined Chiefs sessions over which the Admiral, as the senior American officer, was destined to preside. He opened the meeting by stating his "impression" that both the President and the Prime Minister regarded the decision to invade North Africa as now finally and firmly taken; both believed that "all preliminary arrangements are proceeding as rapidly as possible in order that the operation may be undertaken at the earliest possible date." Dill said that he, too, understood that the final decision had been taken. Marshall doggedly disagreed. With weary patience he tried to force his way through the one loophole that remained open to him in the July 24 memorandum, now officially designated as document CCS 94. The decision to mount the North African invasion would be a decision to abandon ROUNDUP, and the decision to abandon ROUNDUP was not to be taken until mid-September. So said CCS 94. Marshall now agreed (for it was obvious) that the definite choice between ROUNDUP and North Africa could not be so long delayed. It must, in fact, be made almost immediately. Logistical considerations demanded this—the fact, for instance, that an estimated ninety-six days would be required to convert ships for combat loading. But he insisted that the final decision had not yet been made, and was supported in this contention by King. Both King and Marshall proposed that this final decision be postponed for a week, in order to permit more staff study of the problems involved.

The President, however, would have none of this.

When Leahy returned to his office in the White House he at once reported the inconclusive results of the meeting to his chief, and Roosevelt at once called for a meeting in the Oval Study that evening, to be attended by Leahy, by the President's Naval Aide, by General "Hap" Arnold of the Air Force, and by Brigadier General Walter Bedell Smith, who then served as Secretary of the U. S. Joint Chiefs and, in this capacity, as the American Secretary of the Combined Chiefs. Smith had been one of the Americans journeying to London with Hopkins the week before; and it was he who reported Roosevelt's words in a memorandum to the Joint Chiefs.[36] "The President stated very definitely that he, as Commander-in-Chief, had made the decision that TORCH should be undertaken at the earliest possible date," Smith wrote. "He considered that this operation was now our principal objective and the assembling of means to carry it out should take precedence over other operations as, for instance, BOLERO." The implication in CCS 94 that September 15 would be a date of final decision was false. If the record was confused, the President as Commander-in-Chief proposed to clear it by sending immediately a message to the Prime Minister in which he stated his decision and asked for the Prime Minister's specific concurrence.

iv. *What Might Have Been*

Thus ended a three-week period during which basic Anglo-American unity was more seriously threatened than at any other time in the war. Had a different decision been taken, had the Americans actually made the shift in global strategy which the Joint Chiefs proposed, the main course of world history would probably have been changed.

Consider what might have been. The narrow margin by which the Russians managed to maintain themselves against the German onslaught as summer waned and autumn began might have been reduced to nothing, in consequence of the diversion of shipping from Russian to vastly extended Pacific lines of communication. The collapse of Russian resistance might have been followed by a successful German invasion of Britain while the United States was still so heavily engaged against Japan that she could not come effectively to her Ally's aid. If that had happened, and while it was happening, reactionary politics in America, rendered impotent in the actual event by Allied victories, might well have grown so strong—feeding on the fears and hates and selfishness on which reaction always feeds—as to force a negotiated peace with the Axis. This would have meant the death of democratic society and the establishment of totalitarian government in the United States. The spirit of scientific humanism which had animated Western civilization would have been greatly enfeebled if not wholly destroyed and the death of the body of that civilization would probably soon have followed.

Or assume that these dire consequences had been somehow avoided. Suppose that the Russians had, after all, remained effectively in the war. Suppose that the defensive strategy in the West, in North Africa, in the Middle East had successfully contained Nazi-Fascist power. Suppose that Japan had been crushed by 1944 and that the United States had then concentrated her power upon the European enemy. What, then, would have happened? The enemy would have been much stronger in relation to the Allies than in fact he was when at last the decisive actions occurred; Italy, for one thing, would have remained Germany's active partner. Hitler would have had more time with less harassment in which to consolidate his earlier gains and create in concrete fact that Fortress Europa of which he continually boasted. The ultimate decision would then truly have depended upon that dread secret weapon to whose development the Allies had, as we have seen, firmly committed themselves by July of 1942—and the targets for this weapon would have been key cities of Germany and, possibly, Italy. What effect would this have had upon the postwar relations between the Western Allies and Soviet Russia?

The shadow of these "might-have-beens" lay heavy upon the memories of this three-week crisis that remained to Marshall and Stimson after the war had ended. Stimson's published words show him to have become uneasy if not a little ashamed as he later contemplated the role he had played in the drama. He then insisted that he had always regarded the Marshall proposal, which he so "cordially endorsed," as a "bluff" whose sole purpose was to force British agreement with BOLERO-ROUNDUP. This does not jibe with entries made at the time in Stimson's diary—and even as a "bluff" the proposal, in Stimson's later view, was "hasty." (Robert Sherwood's impression, published after the war, was that "the plan was far more than a bluff in General Marshall's mind and certainly in Admiral King's"[37]; and the validity of this impression is attested to by the immensely detailed and documented histories of the strategic controversy later issued through the Office of the Chief of Military History of the U. S. Department of the Army.) Marshall, characteristically, when the war ended, published neither vindication of judgment nor confession of error. His code of personal honor would not permit it. He let the record speak for itself. But the record, closely read in the light of a knowledge of Marshall's character, plainly reveals this three-week period to have been, for him personally, among the unhappiest of the war.

Almost the only bright memories he retained from this unhappy time were centered on the man he had chosen to command American forces in the European Theater.

IX

The Emergence of Eisenhower

i. *Marshall Finds a Commanding General*

During the first visit to London with Hopkins the previous April, Marshall had had little opportunity to observe the work and abilities of the American officers then stationed in the British capital. He had come away with the distinct feeling, however, that they had little understanding of what BOLERO required of them in terms of global strategy. This was not their fault. They had been isolated from that process of argument and decision in which the top echelon of the War Department had been engaged since Pearl Harbor. Nevertheless it *was* a fault, a serious one, and as a first step toward correcting it he had sent Eisenhower to London in late May, accompanied (at Eisenhower's request) by Major General Mark W. Clark, with instructions to study the situation and make recommendations.

Behind this openly avowed purpose had been another, secret one. The trip was in the nature of a final test of the man who was then his War Plans Chief and to whom he had just about decided to assign a much larger and more difficult responsibility.

When summoned to Washington a week after Pearl Harbor, Dwight D. Eisenhower came highly recommended by every officer under whom he had served. One of these had been Pershing for whom, when Pershing was Chairman of the American Battle Monuments Commission, thirty-six-year-old Major Eisenhower had written on special assignment an excellent guidebook to the battlefields where Americans had fought in France during the First World War. ("In the discharge of his duties, which were most difficult . . . , [Major Eisenhower] has shown superior ability not only in visualizing his work as a whole but in executing its many details in an efficient and timely manner," Pershing had written the Chief of Infantry in August 1927. "What he has done was accomplished only by exercise of unusual intelligence and constant devotion to duty."[1]) His concrete achievements, so far as Marshall could assess them, had fully justified the high praise bestowed upon him. The Chief of Staff himself, as we have seen, had taken note of Colonel Eisenhower's work during the Louisiana Maneuvers of the preceding summer, and been impressed by it.

In the six months of his 1942 assignment, during which he had worked under the personal eye and (to a degree) the personal tutelage of the Chief of Staff, Eisenhower had fitted well into the routine and risen nobly to the crises of the War Department. He had learned through actual experience as well as intimate observation how the Chief of Staff worked with the Joint Chiefs, the Combined Chiefs, the Secretary of War, the White House, and the complex of civilian war agencies. He had demonstrated his firm grasp of the basic principles of global strategy, as Marshall conceived them, along with an ability to apply them realistically to specific situations in terms of actual and potential resources. He seemed to be able to balance military against political considerations in pursuit of an assigned goal far more accurately than most professional soldiers—or most politicians—were able to do. He had executive ability. He had shown, within the limits of his administrative assignment, an ability to organize and direct efficiently the work of other people. He had shown, too, in Marshall's opinion, an ability to pick the best available man for a specific job; when asked for personnel recommendations, his answers generally coincided with Marshall's judgments.

Over-all, he seemed to understand far better than most soldiers the essential nature of high command, and what was required of the man who would fill high command posts with success, in an age when mechanized combat forces, though vast in numbers, were but a fractional component of the organization required for "total war." Necessarily the top command function in such circumstances must be exercised not by single individuals, but through large groups of men working together so closely as to constitute an integral as well as an integrating force. Here as elsewhere, individualism yielded ground to the collectivizing forces inherent in an advancing technology. Eisenhower himself, in a later year, would specifically deny "that the influence of the individual in war has become submerged, that the mistakes of one responsible officer are corrected or concealed in the mass action of a great number of associates."[2] He would insist that "personal characteristics are more important than ever before in warfare." But he would then immediately go on to indicate that many of the "characteristics" most important to successful modern command are the opposite of individualistic. ". . . the teams and staffs through which the modern commander absorbs information and exercises his authority must be a beautifully interlocked, smooth-working mechanism," he would say. "Ideally, the whole should be practically a single mind; consequently misfits defeat the purpose of the command organization essential to the supply and control of vast land, air, sea, and logistical forces that must be brought to bear as a unit against the enemy." Such a "misfit" in a modern command organization, he indicated, would be Wellington, "a crusty, unapproachable individual who found one of his chief delights in penning sarcastic quips to the War Office." Since the direction of modern armies had become a function practically equivalent to the direction of large-scale industrial enterprises or a huge Government bureau, the supreme commander must have the basic attitudes, the mental processes of an organization man. He must operate in many respects as a "chairman of the board."

Not only did Eisenhower seem to understand this far better than most, he seemed also unusually well equipped to act effectively upon his understanding. Marshall was practically convinced of it by the time he ordered his War Plans Chief to London, with Clark, the last week of May.

The two men flew the Atlantic, landing in Scotland on May 25, and spent ten crowded days in the British Isles where both of them, and Eisenhower especially, made very favorable impressions upon the British. (Eisenhower shared a railway compartment from Glasgow to London with Lieutenant General Sir Humphrey Gale of the British General Staff, and Gale later reported that never had he met a man he liked better on first acquaintance. He spoke of the American's sense of humor, simplicity of manner, candor, and soundness of judgment.) Immediately upon his return to Washington, Eisenhower made an oral report to the Chief of Staff on what he had observed. A European Theater should be at once formally established, said he. Its top commander should be someone who not only knew thoroughly the plans and purposes of the American Government but also had "a working knowledge of our capabilities in the production of land, air, and naval units and materials to support them in offensive fighting." When asked for a name, he specifically recommended Major General Joseph T. McNarney of the Army Air Force for the assignment, though McNarney had been recently appointed Deputy Chief of Staff and was badly needed by Marshall in that post.

A few days later, Eisenhower came into Marshall's office with a paper he had prepared, one important enough, he said, to require Marshall's close personal study. It was a proposed "Directive for the Commanding General, European Theater of Operations." Marshall glanced at it, agreed as to its importance, and asked Eisenhower if *he* were satisfied with it. Eisenhower was.

"That's good," Marshall said, "because you're the man who is going to execute it. Whom would you like to take with you? When can you leave?"[3]

ii. *A Portrait of Eisenhower*

The War Department communiqué announcing the establishment of the European Theater of Operations, with Major General Eisenhower commanding, was issued on June 25, 1942—the day Rommel drove across the Egyptian border. On that same day, in London, where he had arrived with Major General Clark a few days before, the new commanding general held his first press conference during which, as the New York *Times* observed, he gave "an excellent demonstration of the art of being jovially outspoken without saying much of anything."

At once the name and image of Dwight D. Eisenhower, hitherto virtually unknown outside his profession, became among the most famous in the world. Journalists avid for "background information" descended upon his family, his friends, his associates past and present; and a deluge of printed and spoken words impressed the main outlines of his life upon the public mind.

It became common knowledge that he was born in Texas in 1890, the third eldest of seven brothers (one of whom died in infancy) and was taken as a baby to Abilene, Kansas, famous in Wild West folklore as the scene of Wild Bill Hickok's greatest gunfights; that his parents were of German Mennonite stock, pious and pacifistic, imposing much Bible-reading and prayer upon their children; that he had grown up in humble circumstances, his father's income being limited to a meager wage earned as a "stationary engineer" (mechanic) in a local creamery, and had therefore been required to work hard at home chores and odd jobs all through his boyhood and 'teens; that he had nevertheless been active in sports, playing (though not starring) on the high school football and baseball teams, and had made a better-than-average grade record in his classes; that by the time he had decided to try for a Service academy appointment he was too old to be accepted at Annapolis, his first choice, and so had gone to West Point where his record was good but not outstanding; that his wife Mamie (née Doud) came of a prosperous family formerly of Boone, Iowa, now of Denver; that of the two sons born to them the elder had died of scarlet fever at the age of three and the younger, John, was now a cadet at West Point; that he had commanded America's only tank training school, at Camp Colt near Gettysburg, during World War I (he had just received his orders for overseas duty when the war ended), and had immediately thereafter seriously considered asking for a transfer to the Air Corps; that he was deemed an "expert" in mechanized warfare; that he was also considered to be one of the Army's "best brains," having made top grades in the Service schools he had attended since West Point (the fact that he had graduated number one from the Command and General Staff School was stressed) and having proved his mental abilities in a succession of increasingly responsible and difficult staff assignments.

In all this, the public could see nothing glamorous or heroic. Apparently, out of a standard American background, he had emerged as the All-American boy who grows up to become the standard American man, an exponent of all the standard virtues, "making good" by performing assigned duties in a manner pleasing to those in a position to advance him.

He was a warrior who had never seen a battle, a commander who had scarcely ever exercised a field command, and from all accounts he made an immediate personal impression that was not particularly dashing or brilliant or awe-inspiring. Yet perceptive observers might see this very lack of obvious distinctions as advantageous to the process by which he could become, in his present assignment, a great hero of democracy. After all, it is a major premise of democratic theory that the governor and the governed—he who makes and he who submits to just law—are the self-same person, so that there can be no question of total inferiority or superiority but only a difference of function between the man who commands and the man who obeys. Of this premise, Eisenhower appeared to be an incarnation. He was "American as pumpkin pie." He was "comfortable as an old shoe." He associated easily with G.I. Joe and equally so with the King and Prime Minister of England. His nickname, by the happiest possible accident, was "Ike"—a sobriquet perfectly suited not only to his surname but also to the wide, boyish, infectious grin which showed so often in photographs of him. Hence, if his sudden fame were confirmed by future triumphs, his public self might "satisfy the paradoxical demands which a democracy makes of its heroes" (to quote one of his biographers): he might become the ordinary man who is exceptional, his exalted image a mirror in which the average man saw himself reflected in the shapes and colors of greatness.

A perceptive observer, becoming personally acquainted with him in the summer of 1942, might also have noted how environmental influences upon his early life, as journalism described them, seemed designed to mold him for the kind of job he had now to do.

He had grown up within a few miles of the exact geographic center of the United States; and the Kansas of his formative years was a curious balance of opposing regional traditions, as befitted a State poised halfway between every pair of national geographic extremes. A crusading Puritanism had been introduced to the eastern portion of the State by immigrant New Englanders in the days of "Bleeding Kansas": it had been sustained by such religious colonies as the Mennonite River Brethren, whose immigration from Pennsylvania had brought the Eisenhowers to Dickinson County in the 1870s; and it continued to manifest itself in a disposition to legislate the private morality of citizens. But western Kansas, a high, flat tableland of little rain, accepted to a degree the cavalier traditions of the Old South—a combative "code of honor," an emphasis on the skillful handling of horses and weapons, an insistence upon untrammeled personal liberty—as it developed the gambling "rugged individualism" of cattlemen, wheat farmers, and oilmen.

In Abilene, during the years of Eisenhower's growing up, the opposing traditions were mingled in approximately equal proportions. The town still retained some of the flavor and, among its boys especially, many of the vital attitudes of its wild cowtown past. The boys played "cowboys-and-Indians" as a favorite game while in grade school (the man Eisenhower's favorite recreational reading continued to be Western pulp magazines) and their fistfights, in several of which the boy Eisenhower was a principal, were of a ferocity almost incredible to later generations. But Abilene was also a town of churches, and in the Eisenhower family home—a white, two-story frame house at the southeastern edge of town, where the eighty-year-old Mother Eisenhower still lived in the summer of 1942 (the father had died in March)—all pride of combat, bred by lawless violence, was opposed by a deeply religious pacifism. The Eisenhower parents insisted that each of their sons be self-sufficient, self-reliant; they made no effort to dictate careers to them; but they could not hide their disappointment and hurt when young Dwight Eisenhower announced his decision to try for a Service academy appointment. When he won his appointment, his mother reportedly went upstairs to her room and wept. . . .

It might be expected that the professional soldier who came out of such an environment would retain a "civilian mind," that there would be in him a balanced tension of frontier pragmatism and religious idealism, and that he would have (so to speak) a psychology of "middleness" and "togetherness." There would have been encouraged in him a tendency to seek always for common denominators among diverse people and things and forces, then to employ these for the achievement of coalitions, amalgamations, homogenizations. And this, of course, was required for success in his great new assignment. Of the very essence of his task was the discovery and cultivation of "middle grounds" where forms of active creative compromise might grow out of initial oppositions.

In terms of what was now demanded of him, four of his personal qualities were outstanding. One was an amazingly quick and accurate sensitivity to the personalities and current moods of those with whom he dealt in face-to-face situations, whether as individuals or in groups. He could, so to speak, "tune in" a wider range of frequencies in the sphere of empathic communication than most men could. His War Department colleagues, for instance, were generally agreed that he could think "like" Marshall. What they referred to was an apparent ability to do more than this. On some occasions and in some respects he seemed actually to feel himself to *be* Marshall—so much so that, in terms of what Marshall wanted said and done, he could not make mistakes. In this sense he could also "be," it seemed, people very different from Marshall. And yet he remained always himself, a distinct individual, in the eyes of others; while receiving impressions, he himself made a "good" one. This, combined with his other qualities, made him a practically perfect chairman of group enterprises. In the conference room, he could measure and respond to very slight changes in the emotional temperature and pressure. He could take his cue from a sign too slight for most men to notice. He could sum up a discussion, he could define a consensus, with clarity and force, bringing order out of chaos: conclusive action emerged out of what would otherwise have been separate, inconclusive expressions of opinion. He therefore often served the chairman's function, guiding and focusing discussion, even in meetings where the chairmanship was nominally assigned to another.

Closely joined to this quality of sensitivity was that of flexibility. He could not have received and retained impressions as he did had he opposed to them no inner resistance at all; a stone dropped into a river disappears without a trace. But neither could he have done so had he opposed them with an absolute inner rigidity. Not rigidity nor fluidity, then, but a rarely achieved state somewhere between the two was what gave him his peculiar brand of sensitivity. He possessed psychic viscosity of a degree (not too much, not too little) that seldom occurs—and though this *need* not have been linked to an over-all flexibility of character, a viscosity of total self (the "power [in a solid] of yielding continuously under stress," as Webster's defines it), it *was* so linked in his case. He differed in this respect from Marshall: he yielded to pressures or, to change metaphors, bent with winds that had no effect on Marshall's posture.

Whether this flexibility, considered in the abstract, was admirable or contemptible must largely depend on point of view. Those friendly to Eisenhower and critical of Marshall might say that Eisenhower remained tolerant and cooperative (large-minded) in circumstances where Marshall showed as stubbornly intolerant (small-minded). Those friendly to Marshall and critical of Eisenhower might say that the latter was weak and timid and self-contradictory where the former was brave, strong, and perfectly self-consistent. But honest and disinterested observers, looking at Eisenhower in the context of 1942, considering him in terms of his historic assignment at that time, are likely to conclude that his rare kind of flexibility was, on the whole, very fortunate for the Allies. What Eisenhower was now about to do, Marshall in all probability could not have done as well—and we shall encounter later indications that Marshall himself realized that this was so.

A third quality that had recommended Eisenhower to Marshall was articulateness. The War Plans Chief never mumbled nor hesitated in a search for words when presenting information or proposals orally to the Chief of Staff. Men who did were not likely to last long around Marshall, no matter what other qualities they might possess; under the burdens he must bear, he had neither the time nor the energy to search for definite meanings amidst jumbles of words nor the patience to wait through long gaps between words.[4] Eisenhower spoke always rapidly and forcefully, employing a wide range of facial expressions (he had an unusually mobile countenance) and bodily movements (shrugs and hand gestures and pacings of the floor) to give his words greater meaning and importance than they sometimes seemed to have when his physical presence had been withdrawn. His written communications on concrete matters (and he then dealt with no others) were lucid and succinct. He was somewhat addicted to the exclamatory, both in speech and writing, and had a way of stressing as his own most profound convictions those views he knew to be most strongly held by the man with whom he communicated. (For instance, he wrote Marshall on March 27, at a time when he knew Marshall to be exasperated by the failure to reach agreement on cross-Channel operations, that unless the plan to concentrate American forces in Britain were adopted "as the ultimate aim of all our efforts, we must turn our *backs* upon the Eastern Atlantic and go, full out, as quickly as possible against Japan!"[5]) But this was no conscious ingratiation. It was sincerely expressive of himself at that moment. And it was therefore genuinely flattering to those whose opinions he stated so emphatically; it increased the general happiness of his human relations.

These relations were very happy, very fortunate, in part because of the three qualities already described, but mostly in consequence of a fourth, which enhanced the value of all the rest. This was a quality of personal charm through which was projected, as its very heart, a sense of moral goodness. He made men *want* to please him, not only because his pleasure was extremely pleasant to perceive, not only because he could and did convey an unusually heartwarming personal gratitude, but also because he made men feel that he was good and right in the moral sense, so that in pleasing him they served a moral idea. Better, perhaps, than any man Marshall had known before, Eisenhower was able to use his warmly human personality, his really remarkable likeableness, as a medium for friendly communication and cooperation among men of widely various backgrounds and strongly individual characters. The personal affection and confidence he was capable of inspiring might well become a cement of Allied unity and, by that token, a factor of importance to victory in coalition warfare.

He must first of all, and most important of all, develop a command organization without precedent in history. He must join together armies of different sovereign nations in such a way as to make them parts of a single supranational army; he must weld together air, ground, and sea forces, with their respective specialized services of supply, so that they operated as mutually reinforcing functions of a single body. Inevitably there would be frictions as these disparate parts were brought into close contact; he must insure that the heat energy they produced became a vitalizing rather than inhibiting force.

He had made a good beginning even before his new post had been announced. While yet in Washington he had met and favorably impressed the President and the Prime Minister, as we have seen. He had met and equally impressed Secretary Stimson, whose impatience for a "second front" he had sought to restrain. Perhaps most important of all was the meeting he had had with Admiral King who, willing to pay with Navy concessions in the Atlantic for Army concessions in the Pacific, and obviously pleased by what he saw in Eisenhower, assured the new commanding general that European naval forces should and would be under the single responsibility and authority of the Theater Commander.

King, in his abrupt and crusty way, was emphatic about it: he wanted to hear no "foolish" talk about the commanding general's authority depending upon "cooperation and paramount authority," as set forth in the Joint Regulations for control of Army-Navy forces in the field.[6] In London, Eisenhower immediately established intimately friendly relations with King's predecessor as Chief of Naval Operations, Admiral Stark, now commander of American naval forces in the European area. "Call me 'Betty,'" said Stark, "a nickname I've always had"—having asserted that his office existed solely for the purpose of assisting U.S. fighting forces in Europe. Eisenhower himself publicly signalized and symbolized an unprecedented Army-Navy command arrangement when he had a naval lieutenant commander assigned to him as a personal aide, though he had another, personal reason for doing so. The naval aide he asked for, and got, was a longtime friend of his, Harry C. Butcher, now on leave from his duties as vice president of the Columbia Broadcasting System in Washington. Butcher, whom everyone called "Butch," was a handsome man of great personal charm, an expert and indefatigable storyteller, who had a trained talent for public relations and with whom the commanding general could be completely himself, relaxed and at ease, in such private life as he could rescue from the consuming demands of his job.

By the time Marshall arrived in London for the late July strategy conference, it was evident to him that Eisenhower ran an efficient headquarters, that he had obtained the confidence and respect of the ranking British and Americans with whom he must work, and that, as proof of his ability to be as "tough" as circumstances required, he was winning his way on the only important matter within his sphere of responsibility on which the Americans and British had disagreed thus far, namely the use of Flying Fortresses for daylight precision bombing of the Continent. (The British opposed this as unfeasible. General Carl [Tooey] Spaatz, Eisenhower's top air commander, strongly favored it. And Eisenhower firmly supported Spaatz, stressing it as a necessary preparation for a successful invasion of the Continent.) Best of all, he had made remarkable headway toward the Anglo-American solidarity which he and Marshall deemed prerequisite to victory.

In his first conference with Ismay,[7] after assuming his command, he had asked whom he should talk to about ways and means of establishing good relations between his troops and British civilians. That this should be his initial question was "a revelation," an admiring Ismay told Marshall; it expressed a sense of relative values not commonly met with in professional soldiers. And of course Eisenhower was right to give a very high priority to the solution of this problem. The incoming thousands of American troops had better pay and snappier uniforms than British soldiers; they had, at first, the glamor of visitors from a distant land, giving them advantages over their British rivals for the favors of English girls; and in their ignorance of what the war had meant to the British they would be inclined to swagger and condescend in the manner of "privileged crusaders" come to "help Britain out of a hole." The British, on the other hand, were convinced they had saved Western Civilization by standing courageously alone against the Nazi-Fascist tyranny at a time when the United States had hesitated to do her part; they were in no mood to be patronized by arrogant young provincials whose myriad presence on their already overcrowded islands required of them further sacrifices of comfort and convenience. The opportunities for serious trouble were manifold.

The man to see, Ismay had said, was Brendan Bracken, head of the Ministry of Information (its American counterpart was the Office of War Information [OWI] headed by Elmer Davis). And Eisenhower had promptly seen him. The upshot was a developing intensive program for the information and education of incoming young Americans, employing printed materials, films, lectures, tours of bombed areas, and "home entertainment" of G.I.s by English families. To prevent these families from using up a week's supply of severely limited food ration coupons in order "properly" to entertain American soldiers on weekends, the latter were encouraged to bring their own rations while the former were told why this was done. To reduce the difference between the amount of ready money in G.I. and Tommy pockets, at the same time fostering international good will, the U. S. Army newspaper *Stars and Stripes* was encouraged to sponsor a fund-raising drive among U.S. troops for the benefit of war orphans in the British Isles; and an intense, continuous program to sell U. S. Government bonds to the troops was conducted. The British, too, through Bracken's organization, which worked closely with the London office of OWI and with the Public Relations Section established by Eisenhower at ETOUSA headquarters, were informed of the attitudes and behavior patterns of their allies.

Meanwhile, among his own staff, and everywhere within the radius of his direct personal influence, Eisenhower sought to elevate Anglo-American friendship above the level of mere practicality into that of a religious patriotism, himself its major prophet—and woe be it to heretics! There was at that time in London a senior American officer who, in his cups, boasted that his troops would show the British how to fight. He did so on several occasions and, though he was popular among his British colleagues, the resentment his alcoholic talk aroused in them was at last great enough to be brought to Ismay's attention. Ismay, in turn, and "in strictest privacy," brought it to Eisenhower's attention, shortly after the new commanding general had arrived. Eisenhower, Ismay later recounted, "went white with rage," told one of his aides to have the "officer in question" in his office at seven the next morning, and "hissed" as the aide left the room that he would "make the son of a bitch swim back to America." Ismay protested. He hoped that a warning and rebuke would be the limit of Eisenhower's discipline; he would not have brought the matter up at all if he'd thought such extreme measures would be taken. Eisenhower then relented, but "turned his wrath" on Ismay for having threatened by implication to remain silent regarding such matters in the future.

"If we are not going to be frank with each other, however delicate the subject," he said, "we will never win this war!"[8]

James Warburg of OWI told of an incident witnessed by one of his men at breakfast in London's Mt. Royal Hotel. An American officer entered the breakfast room ostentatiously juggling two grapefruit, an item of food rarely seen by the British in wartime. He had the grapefruit cut for him by a waiter, took a sack of sugar from his pocket, and poured it lavishly upon the fruit halves, even spilling some upon the tablecloth, though sugar was also scarce in wartime England. The story aroused anger in Eisenhower. He repeated it to a meeting of his personal staff.

"If I had been present," he said, "I would immediately have ordered that officer home. By slow boat. Preferably unescorted."[9]

In the strategy meetings during the last week of July, Eisenhower had played his part as a firm adherent of the cross-Channel strategy he had helped design; but he was more flexible than Marshall concerning the precise timing of the operation, and somewhat less inclined than Marshall to impugn the motives of the British who set their faces as flint against SLEDGEHAMMER. He shared Marshall's suspicion that the British were considerably less than wholehearted in their support of BOLERO-ROUNDUP. He was well aware that Churchill's determination not to risk "another Passchendaele," his predilection for "eccentric" and "back-door" operations, coupled with Brooke's estimate of the extreme hazards of a frontal assault, might result in commitments to indecisive operations in the Mediterranean which would postpone the decisive operation indefinitely. He quoted Napoleon on the importance and difficulty of adhering steadfastly and exclusively to a big plan which takes time to develop, avoiding temptations in the interim to engage in "inconsequential side shows." But he also shared to a degree the British view that SLEDGEHAMMER had a less than fifty-fifty chance to succeed. He told Marshall that his only reason for favoring it (as he did when the meetings opened) was that it *might* divert German troops from the Russian front and *would*, if a tenable bridgehead were established on the Cherbourg Peninsula, commit the British absolutely to a major cross-Channel effort in '43.[10] When SLEDGEHAMMER was finally rejected, he was able to see more merit in the North African alternative than Marshall could, and to adjust more easily than Marshall to the increasingly evident fact (in view of British attitudes, and the indispensability of a wholehearted British commitment to the operation) that no major cross-Channel attack could be made before 1944. When the TORCH memorandum was adopted by the Combined Chiefs on July 24, and approved by President and Prime Minister the following day, he at once accepted it as a final operating decision whereas Marshall, as we have seen, did not do so until Roosevelt acted as Commander-in-Chief.

His differences from Marshall during this crucial week were never substantial. They had to do with emphasis, timing, degrees of willingness to accept the words of others at face value—or at least to act as if one did so. And he clearly understood (Marshall could see he understood) that these subtle differences derived for the most part from differences between his and Marshall's proper functions in the total Allied command. It was Marshall's function at the very pinnacle of command to press strongly for his and his Government's strategic views, within the framework of the Combined Chiefs organization. He must do so at the risk of personally antagonizing, now and then, the British who held with equal strength to contrary views. But it was Eisenhower's function to forge the instrument of the Combined Chiefs' will in his theater, and he must therefore never permit differences between him and his British colleagues to prevent the close working cooperation which the service of this function required. More than this, when the will of the Combined Chiefs was so flawed by disagreements that it could not decisively operate, and the effect of this was a frustration of needed action on his own level of command, he must attempt to compose the differences. Here as elsewhere he was the intermediary: he must use his office, he must make his very person, a bridge that joined together what would otherwise remain dangerously separate.

At the end of that week Marshall had had no hesitancy in appointing Eisenhower as Allied Supreme Commander of the TORCH expedition, a decision that was his to make since TORCH was to be primarily an American operation. He told Eisenhower of this decision on the afternoon of Sunday, July 26, in his headquarters at Claridge's, just a few hours before taking off with Hopkins and King on his return flight to Washington. (At the Combined Chiefs meeting the day before, when the question of who should command was up for discussion, Admiral King had said with typical emphasis: "The best man you can possibly get is right here and available—General Eisenhower!"[11]) The decision was final, Marshall had said; from that moment forward, Eisenhower was to regard TORCH as his primary immediate command responsibility, though several days must necessarily elapse before a formal directive on it could reach him through the official machinery of the Combined Chiefs. He also continued for the time being in command of the plans and preparations aimed toward an eventual return to the Continent.[11]

In the crowded weeks that followed, Marshall was given no reason to regret this decision. Eisenhower's flexibility, self-control, and genius for cooperation were tested to the utmost as serious disagreements arose between British and Americans concerning the time, place, and scope of the North African invasion.

iii. *What Shape Should TORCH Have?*

SLEDGEHAMMER would have been primarily a British "show." TORCH was to be primarily an American "show." And it may be evidence of the sobering effect of responsibility that Americans who had boldly pressed SLEDGEHAMMER in the face of its certain and immense hazards turned cautious as they faced the considerably smaller, less certain hazards of TORCH.

The British were willing to assume major initial risks in order to achieve surprise and a quick conquest of the key strategic area, Tunisia. They wanted the whole of the expeditionary force to be landed inside the Mediterranean, at Oran, Algiers, and Bône—the latter only a few miles to the west of the Tunisian border. "We must have occupied the key points of Tunisia within twenty-six days of passing Gibraltar," they insisted, "and preferably within fourteen days."[12] Moreover they wanted these landings to be made in early October despite the fact that this gave barely enough time for the combat loading of ten transports and no time at all for amphibious rehearsals as a climax to the training of assault troops. They argued that tactical efficiency was far less important in the circumstances than swift early action: Tunisia must be taken before the Germans could build up forces there—and the advent of winter on the Russian front might permit such a buildup to become massive through the diversion of troops from that theater. They acknowledged the danger that Franco Spain might yield to Nazi pressure and enter the war as an Axis partner, rendering Gibraltar untenable and so sealing off the western gateway to the Mediterranean after the expeditionary force has passed through it. But they argued that the danger would become relatively negligible if a swift conquest of the strategic area presented the Spanish dictator with the accomplished fact of a North Africa substantially in the hands of the Allies. Only if the landings, despite their American complexion, were strongly and effectively opposed by the North African French, who might then in their folly go so far as to bomb Gibraltar from the air (they had done so in 1940 when the British attacked Dakar)—only then would Franco be likely to cast his lot irrevocably with those of Hitler and Mussolini. This, however, constituted a further argument for Allied concentration at key points inside the Mediterranean: such resistance as the French made must be swiftly overcome.

At the heart of the British conception of the operation was the necessity to hold Malta, some fifty miles south of Sicily, as a base essential to the defense of Egypt and the reopening of the Mediterranean.[13] The British hold on this island was rendered increasingly precarious by the enemy's dominance of the air over the Malta Channel, through which supply convoys from Gibraltar must pass, and by the incessant air attacks to which Malta itself was subjected. (Of seventeen merchant ships sailing in two convoys with large naval escort in mid-June, only two had managed to get through the curtain of fire dropped down upon Malta's approaches by enemy air and sea power.)

The American view of all these matters was very different. The U. S. Joint Chiefs wanted to keep the initial risks to a minimum in this first important venture of American arms against Nazi-Fascism. Their minds dwelled upon the worldwide consequences of an American disaster at this juncture (Stimson all through this period was gloomily certain that disaster was far more likely than success)—consequences so horrible that they must *at all costs* be avoided, including (if necessary) a sacrifice of the possibility of swift and easy Tunisian conquest. They insisted, therefore, upon a hedging of their bets. They flatly refused to attempt possibly opposed amphibious operations without at least one set of master exercises for the troops who must engage in them; this meant that the earliest date for the landings must be in the first week of November. They also flatly refused to commit all their forces inside the Mediterranean; this meant a major landing at Casablanca, on the Atlantic coast of French Morocco, despite the heavy surf which could normally be expected there in the autumn and which, in the British view, would make an opposed landing there extremely hazardous if not actually impossible.

Gnawing at the heart of the American conception of the operation was a continuing doubt (not to be openly confessed after the Commander-in-Chief had made his decision) that it was worth doing at all. Eisenhower, as he wrestled with problems that must be solved, yet seemed insoluble, might remember the emphatic and by no means unique professional opinion of an American lieutenant general that the Mediterranean could not be opened to Allied shipping in any case so long as the Axis held air bases in the south of Europe; the attempted conquest of North Africa would therefore be a piece of "idiocy" that could contribute absolutely nothing to the winning of the war. Eisenhower had disagreed with this opinion when he first heard it, before he departed for London. It was not shared by either the American or British Navy, whose officers (especially the British officers) were certain they could put convoys through the Mediterranean with little loss if they were assured of land-based air cover off North Africa.[14] But the opinion nevertheless remained as a disguised element in the over-all American attitude.

Conditioning this general disagreement between Washington and London was the former's commitment to offensive action in the Southwest Pacific, where U. S. Marines invaded Florida Island (which included Tulagi) and Guadalcanal in the Solomons on August 7, just a week after the target date set for Task One in the U. S. Joint Chiefs' directive of July 2. Complete tactical surprise was achieved by the Americans. They quickly captured their prime objective on Guadalcanal—an airstrip constructed by the Japanese at great expense—but their situation was promptly rendered dangerous in the extreme by a naval action off the tiny island of Savo, just north of Guadalcanal, on the night of August 9, in which the U. S. Navy suffered one of the worst defeats in its history. Japanese warships on that black night managed to slip between the Allied fleet and the island shore, their presence rendered invisible on radar screens by the mountains before which they moved. Suddenly, star shells arched over the Allied vessels and exploded behind them, silhouetting them as perfect targets. Within a few minutes the Japanese had sunk three U.S. cruisers and an Australian cruiser with torpedoes and gunfire, and with virtually no damage to themselves. Thereafter the gap between the initial occupation and the final securing of Marine positions on Guadalcanal seemed actually to widen with the blood and fury poured into it because, in the race of island buildup and supply which now ensued, the Japanese held great initial advantages. The effect of this on North African operations was to limit their scope. The British assigned every warship they could spare from other duties to the escort of North African convoys and the protection of their landings; they went so far as to weaken India's naval shield in order to strengthen the spear being launched toward Tunis. But there remained a shortage of escort vessels which the U. S. Navy was unable to make up, despite the new vessels which now came down the ways of American shipyards in increasing numbers. Especially serious was the shortage of aircraft carriers. Until airfields in North Africa were obtained, the only land-based air cover for the Allies must fly off the single small field at Gibraltar.

There began between London and Washington what Butcher dubbed a "trans-Atlantic essay contest."[15] Eisenhower, whose task it was to reconcile British and American views, saw as their common denominator the agreed necessity for landings at Oran and Algiers as two of the initial three objectives. The question at issue was one of ". . . fixing the flanks."[16] Should the third landing be at Casablanca, some 450 miles west of Oran, or should it be at Bône, some 220 miles east of Algiers? Washington favored the former, London the latter. Eisenhower's first effort toward a working compromise was an outline plan for TORCH, completed August 9, which went much farther toward satisfying Washington's demands than it did toward satisfying London's, but to which, typically, he attached a message indicating his own inclination to agree with British criticisms of it. The plan called for a Casablanca landing to be made simultaneously with landings at Oran and Algiers in early November, as favored by the Americans, rather than early October, as favored by the British. There would be no landings east of Algiers save for a regimental combat team which would be put ashore at Bône. This choice of time and place reduced the initial risks to limits acceptable to the Americans. The landings could be made on a larger scale with better-trained troops in November than in October; and if the Strait of Gibraltar were closed by Franco's collaboration with Hitler, Allied forces inside the Mediterranean would still have a port at their back (though admittedly very far back) and a single rail line from there over which supplies and reinforcements might come into northern Algeria (though admittedly a rickety line capable of bearing but a fraction of the traffic which would then be required). The British, criticizing this, reasserted the position they had taken from the first: Tunisia was the prime objective, it must be quickly seized, and a major landing must therefore be made at Bône as well as at Algiers and Oran, and at the earliest possible moment, preferably by October 7, even though the force available for the initial assault would then be but a third of that which would become available a month later. The Casablanca landing, which was "unfeasible and irrelevant," should be canceled or, at the very least, postponed.

An immediate effect of these criticisms, and of Eisenhower's agreeable attitude toward them, was a directive from Roosevelt to Marshall and King for a restudy of the operation with a view to launching it October 7. This was issued August 12. On the following day, Eisenhower messaged the War Department that he and his staff were now convinced of the soundness of the British view; he was drawing up a new plan whereby the Casablanca landing was canceled, the landing at Bône was added, and the target date was advanced into October. But he was by no means adamant in this new conviction. When Marshall gave it as Washington's opinion that an operation planned as Eisenhower now proposed to plan it had a less than fifty-fifty chance for success, Eisenhower promptly (August 15) concurred in the estimate. So did Clark and Patton, he said. (Clark was now his deputy as commander of TORCH; Patton, who was to command TORCH forces sailing directly from the United States, had come to London to confer with Eisenhower.) Nevertheless, he and his staff continued to plan along the lines favored by the British, completing the outline on August 21.

The new version called for landings on October 15 at Oran, Algiers, and Bône. The troops to be landed at Oran were designated as the Western Force; they were to be brought across the Atlantic in a convoy sailing from the United States. The troops landing at Algiers and Bône were designated the Eastern Force; they were to sail from the United Kingdom in a single convoy which divided after it was inside the Mediterranean. And since this new version reversed the emphasis of the earlier one, going much farther toward satisfying London's demands than it did toward satisfying Washington's, Eisenhower accompanied it (again typically) with personal comments in which he anticipated and largely agreed with Washington's criticisms of it. The October 15 date was probably too early, he said. The size of the assault force at this early date would be too small to discourage or to cope with a determined French resistance. The expedition's right flank and rear would be dangerously exposed as it drove toward Tunis. "It was, he declared, his personal opinion that simultaneous landings inside the Mediterranean and at Casablanca would make a great difference, supposing the two governments could find any way to cut their commitments elsewhere so as to provide the additional naval cover to make the landings possible."*

* Maurice Matloff and Edwin M. Snell, *Strategic Planning for Coalition Warfare* (Washington: 1953), p. 289.

The British Chiefs of Staff responded to this in a spirit of compromise: they indicated their willingness to postpone the operation until November; but the Joint Chiefs in Washington reacted so violently against it that the possibility of reaching any working agreement seemed more remote than ever. The Joint Chiefs now proposed (August 25) to eliminate not only the landing at Bône but also the one at Algiers! The objective was to be limited to "the early and complete military domination of Northwest Africa from Rio de Oro [Spanish Sahara], exclusive, to Oran, inclusive." This fell upon the British Chiefs as (in Churchill's words) a "bombshell." Wearily, hopelessly, they pointed out that its risks, if initially less than those of the August 21 outline plan (and this was far from certain in view of the surf conditions on the Atlantic Coast in November), were at least as great as these ultimately, and would be run for nothing worth having.

It became necessary for Roosevelt and Churchill to settle the matter between them.

In all probability, the wrangle would not have been permitted to sink to the level of impasse and near-despair it had now reached if Churchill and General Brooke had remained in London while it was going on. Instead the Chief of the Imperial General Staff had departed on July 31, and the Prime Minister had departed on August 2, on what Brooke justly described as a "momentous journey," first to Cairo, then to Moscow.

At Cairo they made decisions directly affecting Eisenhower's command arrangements for TORCH. They removed a weary and disheartened Auchinleck from the Middle Eastern Command and replaced him with General Sir Harold Alexander, whom the British Chiefs had designated only a few days before as commander of the ground troops which were to drive for Tunis according to their conception of TORCH. Alexander's place in TORCH was assigned to General Sir Bernard Montgomery. But scarcely had Eisenhower been informed of this when Lieutenant General W. H. E. Gott, who had been assigned command of the British Eighth Army under Alexander, was killed in a plane shot down by the Germans, whereupon it was decided that Montgomery should be the Eighth Army's commander and that Lieutenant General Kenneth A. N. Anderson, who had made a name for himself during the retreat to Dunkirk, should be the TORCH ground force commander. (It was Ismay who had to inform Eisenhower of these swiftly successive changes. He has recorded that the American commanding general, having listened to glowing accounts of Alexander's, then Montgomery's, and finally Anderson's qualities, remarked "rather sadly" that the British seemed to have "a lot of Wellingtons" in their Army. But he had a question. "Tell me, frankly, are the British serious about TORCH?"[17])

In Moscow, Churchill had participated in, and Brooke among others had witnessed, an unforgettable scene. The Prime Minister came to the Soviet capital as a bearer of bad news, and at a time when the Soviet dictator, surfeited with bad news, was a prey to the most acute anxiety about the immediate future. Hundreds of thousands of the best German troops, armed with superior numbers of tanks and guns and planes, were massing on the steppe west of Stalingrad, toward which city they would launch very soon an all-out attack. Stalin himself doubted that the city could be held against it. Never had he felt more desperately the need for the "second front" which, he insisted, had been promised for the autumn of 1942. Never, he insisted, would there be a more favorable opportunity for the success of a "second front" than existed at this moment, when nearly the full strength of the German Army was concentrated against Russia: there remained in France not a single first-class German division. (Actually, according to British intelligence, there were twenty-five German divisions in France, of which nine were of the best quality.) Yet Churchill had now to tell him that there was to be no real "second front" in 1942 but only a relatively minor operation in North Africa from which the hard-pressed Russians could derive no immediate benefit whatever.

The Prime Minister performed this unhappy task on August 12, just a few hours after his plane landed in Moscow. But it was not until more than twenty-four hours later that he was compelled to bear the full brunt of the dictator's wrath. At midnight, in a large bare echoing room in the Kremlin (it reminded Brooke of a railway station waiting room), with language blunt and rough and abusive, Stalin accused the Western Allies of a breach of faith. He went farther: he accused the British of cowardice. "Why," he wanted to know, "are you so afraid of the Germans?" Wars could not be won by men who were unwilling to accept risks and losses, he said in harshly insulting tones. Churchill's jaw jutted out, his lower lip curling over the upper, as these words were translated. He brought his fist down hard upon the table "and poured forth one of his wonderful spontaneous orations," as Brooke wrote later.[18] "It began with: 'If it were not for the fighting qualities of the Red Army . . .' And then went on to tell Stalin precisely what his feelings were about fighting and a lot more. . . ." At one point, the British interpreter was so carried away by Churchillian eloquence that he forgot to take down notes for translation, an omission which Churchill promptly noticed and for which he "dressed down" the interpreter very smartly. He then repeated what he had said. He wanted Stalin to hear every word. The Soviet dictator suddenly got to his feet, grinning broadly around the large bent pipe he was sucking. He interrupted the Prime Minister with a gesture in order to say through his own interpreter: "I do not understand what you are saying, but by God I like your sentiment!"

Brooke was convinced that "Stalin insulted Winston with the purpose of finding out what his reactions would be. . . . He very soon discovered what Winston was made of, and I am certain that this outburst of Winston's . . . impressed Stalin and started feelings of admiration for what he discovered was a true fighting man. At any rate, from that moment onwards the relations between the two improved. . . ." Cordiality prevailed at a great banquet, replete with the usual multiple toasts in vodka, given the visitors the following night. And on the night after that, the eve of the British departure from Moscow, Stalin invited Churchill to his private house in the Kremlin for a talk- and drinkfest that lasted six hours and was conducted in an atmosphere of friendship. Very pointed questions were asked and frankly answered by the two before, in the wee hours of the morning, they said goodbye to one another.

From Moscow, Churchill and Brooke flew back to Cairo, where they were occupied for several days with Middle Eastern problems. They did not arrive back in London until August 24, landing then in the midst of the TORCH plan imbroglio.

The Prime Minister, sensing the danger that the operation might be abandoned altogether, and that there were those in Washington who would shed no tears if it were, took immediate steps to save it. He had Eisenhower and Clark to dine with him at No. 10 Downing Street the following evening, and thoroughly canvassed with them the confused state of TORCH affairs. It was his impression that Eisenhower "fully shared the British view that powerful action inside the Mediterranean, above all including Algiers, was vital to success" but that the American commanding general's views, "so far as he may have pressed them, did not seem to influence his military superiors."[19] There was dispatched to the White House the next day the first of a series of "Former Naval Person" messages which, with the President's replies, had by September 5 definitely and finally fixed the places and relative strengths of the TORCH landings. It was mutually agreed by the two political heads of government that there would be simultaneous landings at Casablanca, Oran, and Algiers, and that the initial landing forces would be wholly American. Some thirty thousand assault troops, sailing directly from the United States, were to land at Casablanca, with an immediate follow-up of twenty-four thousand more. ("Bad surf conditions on the Atlantic beaches is a calculated risk," said Roosevelt to Churchill. "The use of numerous small lightly defended ports may be necessary.") Twenty-five thousand assault troops, immediately followed by twenty thousand more, all from U.S. forces stationed in the United Kingdom, were to land in Oran. Ten thousand U.S. troops from the United Kingdom were to land at Algiers, to be quickly followed by British troops.

Eisenhower, "cheerfully" accepting the decision, nevertheless took care to point out that the weakness of the Algiers landing and the elimination of the Bône one meant that "early capture of Tunis was . . . removed from the realm of the probable to the remotely possible."[20]

It was now at last possible for him, Clark, and the planning staff that had been established at Norfolk House in St. James's Square, a mile or so from Grosvenor Square, to make firm plans for the operation; with sighs of relief they plunged into their complex and anxious task, their target date for the assault landings being November 4. But the commanding general was already convinced that the actual date—at once as early as could be, and as late—would be November 8. He told Churchill so when he and Clark again dined at No. 10 Downing Street on September 8, their regular Tuesday meeting with the Prime Minister. Two weeks later, at a meeting of the British Chiefs of Staff over which Churchill presided and at which Eisenhower was present, the November 8 date was set as official and final.

He had by then gone far toward developing an instrument and process of command that was historically unique and, in the spirit which imbued it, uniquely his own. "There may have been other American or British generals who could have wrought this miracle of cooperation," writes Ismay, "but I cannot name them."[21] Indeed, it was more than "cooperation" that he achieved. "Americans and Britons in alternating layers" were "fused together like a plywood board," says Major H. A. DeWeerd[22]—and both the force which pressed the layers together and the glue which thereafter bound them were, for the most part, products of Eisenhower's mind and will and, above all, his moral character as refracted through a personality so appealing that it was virtually impossible to dislike him. He was by no means incapable of stern action. He relied whenever possible, as wisdom must, upon voluntary persuasions: these were the positive stuff of the supranational patriotism he sought to create. Over and over again he stressed that "this is an Allied battle" which must be fought "shoulder to shoulder" and that, therefore, no praise or blame would be given to the "British as British or the Americans as Americans." But he could and did on occasion use force and the threat of force, ruthlessly, to protect his conception against outward threats and inward flaws. As a result, to act or think on purely nationalistic grounds became reprehensible, while to permit a quarrel to express itself in nationalistic terms became a crime punishable by instant dismissal and disgrace.

In the first serious dispute between an American and a British officer on his staff, the former in a flash of temper called the latter a "British son of a bitch." Eisenhower, reviewing the evidence, decided that neither man was wholly right or wholly wrong about the matter on which they quarreled. Nevertheless, he relieved the American of his duty and ordered him home. The British officer, his anger cooled, protested what seemed to him excessive harshness, saying: "We've all learned, sir, that the phrase he used is an American colloquialism which should not be taken too seriously." Eisenhower agreed that this was so. "But he called you a *British* son of a bitch!" he explained. "For that, he goes home."

Other quarrels he handled in such ways as to make their energies serve the common cause. He did nothing to discourage the frank, open expression of differences, so long as the terms of the expression were not such as to prevent or seriously inhibit the shaping of final (generally compromising) decisions. Quite the contrary. He knew well that minor irritations, if too rigorously repressed for too long, add up to major emotions of explosive power; they may then be released with disastrous effects at critical times by trivial causes. Better by far to vent irritations at the time of their occurrence, and in the situation which provoked them; their flares of temper might then light the way to immediate understandings and solutions. He had a device for encouraging this happy outcome. When staff sections failed to agree, he had them virtually locked in an office together until they arrived at satisfactory solutions or proved up to the hilt the impossibility of their doing so. In the latter case, which was rare, and if the matter were sufficiently important, he himself made the decision, and in any case the men thus forced to work closely with and against one another came to know one another well, to understand the other's idiosyncracies and tastes and reaction patterns, and to develop tolerances for those irreducible differences which might otherwise have harshly grated.

The ultimate effect of this process, if it were long continued, could hardly fail to be a loss of individual personality on the part of those engaged in it: so much forcible insistence upon "getting along" with one another, upon "selflessness" and "cooperative attitudes," must have as its counterpart, in the long run, a certain blandness of essential character, a loss of all that varied widely from the norms—all, in other words, that made for truly unique selves and self-expression. But its immediate effect involved no such loss: it was a command mechanism in which individual men used themselves, consciously, deliberately, as forces acting and reacting on one another along prescribed lines toward an agreed-upon goal—a mechanism geared, not to the "lowest common denominator," but to the capabilities of the highest and best as measured by the scale of values that coalition warfare imposed. Strong characters remained strong, weak ones were strengthened, and all were animated by the ideal of international solidarity which Eisenhower personified while remaining (and, paradoxically, in part *because* he remained) as "American as pumpkin pie."

Certainly, from among the men with whom he had been personally acquainted for some time, none whom he chose as a principal subordinate was especially notable for "smoothness" of manner or easiness of disposition. Each was a sharply defined personality requiring special handling by the commanding general, on occasion, to insure a continued valuable service.

Consider, for major instance, his Chief of Staff, Brigadier General Walter Bedell (Beetle) Smith, whom he had come to know well in Washington during the early months of 1942, when Smith served as U. S. Secretary of the Combined Chiefs of Staff. Stern of countenance, aloof of manner, abrupt of speech, Smith seemed about as different from Eisenhower as one man may be from another. He described himself in what he obviously deemed unflattering terms as "the Prussian type of officer," having a quick temper which, to quote Ismay, "he was wont to vent on friend and foe alike" though, as Ismay quickly adds, "the storm generally blew over quickly and left not a vestige of ill-feeling."[23] At work he drove himself and others mercilessly, despite a physique that was none too robust, paying for it with a recurrently active stomach ulcer. Shy by nature, indifferent to "mere" appearances, he had, as he himself said, no talent whatever for "public relations" (one suspects that the Army had attracted him in part because it provided him with a clearly defined pattern of human relationships), and he was generally as inclined toward pessimistic views as Eisenhower was toward optimistic ones. On purely military matters, however, he and Eisenhower thought "exactly alike," as Eisenhower often remarked, so that the natural tendency of his intellect toward probing analyses—a tendency much stronger in him than in Eisenhower—could make his mind a valuable extension of the commanding general's. He expressed himself easily and well, both in speech and in writing. He was naturally self-effacing in public—an asset in a staff officer. And when one knew him well, he revealed himself as a sensitive man, thoughtful of others, shrewdly humorous, with wide intellectual interests, capable of complete dedication and absolute personal loyalty. Eisenhower saw in all this his own perfect complement—a man whose personal characteristics would serve to check and balance those of his own which, unchecked, unbalanced, might lead him into error. Smith was destined to become, in Eisenhower's own words, "one of the great Staff Chiefs of history, worthy of rank with Gneisenau."[24]

Consider, for a second major instance, Eisenhower's deputy commander of TORCH. Churchill, who called Smith "the American bulldog" (Eisenhower's Staff Chief, thought Ismay, had "a face like a bulldog and many of the characteristics of that attractive breed"), dubbed Clark "the American eagle." And indeed the very tall, lanky Clark was in appearance a hawklike man. His eyes had a piercing, hawklike gaze above a beaklike nose that cleaved the air a soaring six feet above the ground, and his long-fingered hands, swooping in great arcs at the ends of very long arms, were as talons that might rend as well as grasp his prey. Nor did his general character belie his appearance. He was a fighting man of immense physical courage and energy—a man of the open air, a man of action, fierce as an eagle—who chafed at desk work and grew irritably impatient with whatever or whomever prevented direct and immediate action against the enemy. Impatience was his besetting sin, he realized; it would probably have incapacitated him for his London assignment if Eisenhower, an old and close friend, had not been there to restrain him ("Now just keep your shirt on, Wayne," Eisenhower was constantly saying) and to smooth his ruffled temper. For, to quote his own words, he found the "situation" in London "almost intolerable" during the weeks of TORCH planning and preparation, no small part of his troubles stemming from his enforced close working relationship with British General Anderson, whose nature and manner grated upon him. (Anderson's personality grated on others, too, the British finding him even more "difficult" than the Americans did, according to Eisenhower, who had often to smooth Anderson's ruffled feelings as well as the feelings that Anderson had ruffled. But Eisenhower and Clark agreed that Anderson was professionally competent and both realized—Eisenhower especially—that he must be worked with in any case. A senior American officer might be removed by an American commanding general at this early testing juncture of Allied unity, but a senior British officer could not be.[25])

For a third major instance, consider Eisenhower's choice as commander of the American troops which were to land on the African Atlantic coast. George S. Patton, Jr., whom we met during the Louisiana Maneuvers of 1941, was a tall man of splendid physique whose favorite facial expression, when he faced a camera in battle dress, was the slit-eyed, tight-lipped grimness of a professional killer about to gun down an adversary with the pearl-handled revolvers he habitually wore on his hips. It pleased him to outrage Christian moralists and liberal humanitarians by extolling the glories of war, proclaiming his own lust for battle, and boasting of the joy to be derived from the slaughter of enemies. He flavored his speech with profanity, and even obscenity. He was notorious for lectures to his troops delivered in language so foul it could not be repeated by many among his hearers, much less published to the world at large. But Eisenhower understood (or believed) all this to be a pose. Patton didn't "really mean" half the shocking things he said and did; he indulged his belief in shock tactics. It was as if Georgie, when a long-legged boy, a son of wealth and privilege, an inheritor of the honor code of Virginia's aristocracy, had been called a sissy, had feared that he actually was a sissy, and had ever since been trying to prove to himself and others that he was not but, on the contrary, was the toughest fighting man in the toughest army in the world. He was playing a role in a heroic drama he had written for himself. He lived his part, however. He was obviously willing to die for the warrior values he so loudly proclaimed (he had been wounded and decorated for valor in World War I). And his trained intelligence had enabled him to become a truly brilliant "blitzkrieg" tactician, capable of exploiting to the full the possibilities of mechanized armor. He had, in short, the virtues of his defects, and Eisenhower counted upon himself to prevent or moderate the ill effects of the latter.

The only principal American subordinate whom Eisenhower chose from outside his personal acquaintance was the commander of the Central Task Force, which was to land at Oran. For this post, from a list submitted by Marshall, Eisenhower chose Major General Lloyd R. Fredendall.

iv. *Firelight on Their Faces: An Evening at Telegraph Cottage, October 17, 1942*

Butcher had found this place in the last week of August—a small, unpretentious house on a ten-acre tract completely covered with woods, save for a lawn and rose garden at the house's back, and a small vegetable garden. Intensely English, intensely private, its quiet solitude protected by a golf course that reached out beyond the woods on either side, it seemed as remote from London's traffic and modern war as if it lay in a northern province and an earlier century. In point of fact, it was only forty minutes or so by car from 20 Grosvenor Square. It was also only a half mile—as Butcher later discovered, to his great chagrin—from a decoy designed to flame automatically whenever radar reported night bombers near, tempting them to unload in this unpopulated area. Five small bedrooms it had, but only one bath. Fireplaces provided its only source of heat.[26]

It had seemed perfectly to fit Ike's requirements for a retreat. When he first came to London as commanding general he was assigned a plush suite in Claridge's; its gilded walls made him feel, he complained to Butcher, as though he were "living in sin." Butcher had then arranged their moving in early July into a much less ostentatious three-room suite in the Dorchester, across Park Lane from Hyde Park and only three short blocks from Grosvenor Square, but though this was an improvement it was no place for easy, inconspicuous relaxation. No hotel in the West End could be for a man in Eisenhower's position. So Butcher had hired Telegraph Cottage, as it was called, for thirty-two dollars a week, and been much relieved when Ike declared it to be what he wanted and needed. They continued to live in the Dorchester but came here whenever they could get away, often bringing with them as guests men with whom the commanding general wanted to have long, uninterrupted talks.

On this Saturday night the guests were two who had been often here before—Wayne Clark and Beetle Smith—and they sat now after dinner before an open fire whose radiant warmth pushed back into the corners of the room the chill shadows of October and whose red, smoky light made even Beetle's pale face take on a rosy glow. It had been a near thing with Beetle. On a night nearly three weeks ago now, Eisenhower, with Smith, had dined (Smith on milk only) at No. 10 Downing Street. After dinner the commanding general had been engaged by his host in an animated discussion of JUPITER, which Churchill continued to urge as necessary for the protection of Murmansk convoys, when, abruptly, the Prime Minister got to his feet and broke off the talk, ending the visit at a little after 1:00 A.M.—early for a "PM session." He took Eisenhower alone into the Cabinet Room and there advised him that Smith appeared to be really "frightfully ill." "You should order him into a hospital at once, or you will lose him altogether."[27] So into the American General Hospital in Oxford Beetle had gone the next day—and not a moment too soon: two blood transfusions within forty-eight hours had been required to restore the loss he'd sustained from his bleeding stomach ulcer.

But now Beetle was saying to them all, in the firelight, that he felt fine. He boasted with a laugh about his "new blood" which, said he, had so "recharged" his "batteries" that he was ready to "electrify the world."[28] Eisenhower, looking at him, hoped so; of Smith's value to him and the whole command he was now absolutely convinced.

And certainly Smith seemed less tense, less fine-drawn than he had been when first he sat before this fireplace, last September 7, only a few hours after he'd arrived from Washington to assume his new duties. He had been so keyed up that night that he couldn't sleep despite a virtually sleepless night before on the plane that had brought him across the Atlantic. Butcher had been in the kitchen at seven the next morning, fixing coffee, when Beetle came in from hours of wandering through the pines and rhododendrons, and over the golfing meadow, having heard (he said) a pheasant cock crowing at four o'clock and, his huntsman's blood thus stirred, been able no longer to lie abed. . . . And Eisenhower, if his mind cast back to that earlier firelit night, might remember how Smith had already begun to prove his value as he sat for the first time where now he sat, in that selfsame lounging chair, talking then with shrewd judgment and a wealth of factual information about the "global picture" as seen from Washington and about domestic politics as they impinged upon the war effort in this midterm election year.

They had talked, too, that night, about the man Marshall, laughing a little—with affection, with admiration—at his idiosyncracies. One of them was an inability to recall the names of people. "Get me what's-his-name," he'd say to Beetle. "You know who I mean. Red eyes." Whereupon Beetle would have to decide, and quickly, which among the men Marshall might conceivably want to see could best he described as red-eyed. Marshall's confidential assistant was a man named McCartney whom, after years, he persisted in calling "McCarthy," and his secretary, a woman named Nason, was always addressed by him as "Mason." He never used nicknames at all. It was as if doing so would imply or invite a degree of personal intimacy he could not permit between himself and men whom he must regard, always, as expendable. Smith had said that night that the pressures on Marshall hadn't let up for an instant since the London meetings; if anything they had increased; and Eisenhower had said flatly that Marshall was a great man who had never been greater than during these recent weeks of divergence over TORCH. And then and there he, Eisenhower, had taken a solemn vow, swearing that "come hell or high water," once TORCH was firmly set, he would carry it through within the limits of shipping and air cover and materiel and men assigned to it, without "whining to the War Department" because there wasn't enough of whatever it was he needed or because there were crucial factors outside his control which could affect the operation disastrously.

He had kept that vow, too, thus far. It had not been easy.

For God knew there had not been enough of anything, least of all time, with which to mount TORCH properly. Of anxieties or reasons for anxiety, on the other hand, there had been and remained a superabundance. One might feel them as almost physical presences thronging in the dark outside the windows, lurking in the shadowed corners of the room, kept only narrowly at bay by the light and warmth of the open fire. The operation's success seemed to depend so completely upon uncertainties: that Spain would remain neutral, that French troops in North Africa (there were some four hundred thousand of them) would put up no determined resistance, that the Germans would not capture with airborne troops the vital Algerian airstrips before the Allies could do so—above all, conditioning all, that surprise would be achieved. The worries about security were, at this stage of the dangerous game, the most acute of all. So many golden opportunities to discover the vital secret had been given the enemy!

The first of them had occurred only a few days after the final shape of TORCH had been decided upon. A Top Secret letter from Smith to the Governor of Gibraltar, giving the date and places and strength of the landings, was carried by a British naval officer courier in a plane that was shot down by the Germans off the coast of Spain. The courier's body was washed ashore, found by Spaniards, and turned over to the British by Spanish authorities. Inside the officer's buttoned tunic was found the letter, still sealed. Had it been opened, its contents transmitted to the Germans, and then sealed up again? British security experts didn't think so: the presence of sand in the tunic's buttonholes seemed to them fairly conclusive evidence that the body had not been examined; but no one could be absolutely sure.

Then there was the case of the Top Secret minute from the Prime Minister to the Chiefs of Staff urging that Bône be added to the list of TORCH landings. In an almost incredible breach of regulations and common sense, a confidential secretary had carried this out of his office and lost it from his pocket as he boarded a bus. It lay on the street for anyone to pick up, and it *was* picked up by a charwoman who took it to an airman lodging in her house. This airman, evincing an intelligent security-sense almost as remarkable as the secretary's lack of it, had taken it at once to the Air Ministry where he stubbornly refused to give it to anyone but the Chief of the Air Staff personally. Who else had seen it by then? Security experts were almost sure that no one had, for though rain had begun to fall as the secretary mounted his bus, the paper he had lost was dry. It must have been picked up within seconds after it hit the pavement. All the same . . .

There was also the incident of the maps of North Africa that had been printed in a country town and were being trucked to military headquarters when a package of them was accidentally broken open, scattering a great number of them upon the road. Had an enemy agent witnessed this, or been informed of it, and correctly assessed its significance? Highly unlikely, thought security experts, but barely possible, of course. A greater security risk, of a wholly different kind, was involved in the action taken by local police after the lost maps had been gathered up and before the proper military authorities were aware of the accident. The police, seeing that the maps were of French North Africa, had phoned De Gaulle's headquarters in London to find out if the Free French had lost them. Luckily the Frenchman who answered the phone was not suspicious, or possessed of a lively curiosity; he merely replied that the Free French had lost no maps. For just suppose he had asked to see one of them before he answered! He must then at once have recognized it for what it was, a military operational map, and could hardly have failed to deduce that a North African operation impended.[29]

What would have made this so dangerous as well as acutely embarrassing was the fact that General de Gaulle with his Free French had been and continued to be rigorously excluded from all knowledge of TORCH. The decision to do so was a political one of whose wisdom Eisenhower had formed no very firm opinion. There was seemingly no need for him to; he must accept it in any case as ironclad, it having been taken at the highest level of the governments he served. But it was certainly very near the forefront of all their minds this evening since it was part of the reason why one of the four men before the fire was about to depart on a highly secret mission of great importance and grave danger. The dinner had been in the nature of a farewell to Mark Wayne Clark who on the morrow, weather permitting, would take off in a B-17 on a journey that might well cost him his life.

The argument for excluding De Gaulle from any major overt role in TORCH seemed to all these men a strong one. He was hated by the officers of the French troops in North Africa with that special hatred men feel toward anyone who makes them feel a guilt they refuse to acknowledge to themselves. They had sworn a solemn oath of personal loyalty to Marshal Pétain as French Chief of State; through him and the Vichy Government they had made their peace with the Axis; and if De Gaulle were right, if he really did symbolize and act on behalf of a truly sovereign France, what they had done was contemptible and they themselves were cowardly traitors. Rather than admit this they would destroy their accuser if they could; and if they saw De Gaulle's Free French among the Allied forces upon their shore they, who might otherwise welcome (at least tacitly) their "liberators," would almost certainly be moved to resist them.

Less strong was the argument for denying to De Gaulle a covert role in the operation, or even any knowledge of what was afoot. Churchill himself regarded it as in large part an expression of "President Roosevelt's prejudices against General de Gaulle"[30]—prejudices encouraged by Admiral Leahy and, even more, by Secretary of State Hull, whose personal hostility toward the leader of the Free French had become almost pathological since the St. Pierre-Miquelon episode of last December. Roosevelt, at any rate, was adamant on the subject: De Gaulle must be permitted no slightest shred of information about TORCH, no matter how "irritable and irritating" he became as (inevitably) he began to suspect that something "big" was being prepared behind his iron-stiff back.[31]

There were two ostensible reasons for this. One was that De Gaulle and his associates could not be trusted with a secret, that the Free French were (as Churchill said, laughing at the indelicacy) "leaky."[32] And certainly this was a reason that had weight in the minds of the British, who remembered only too vividly that, back in the dark days of September 1940, their attempt to take Dakar from the Vichy French was frustrated in part because De Gaulle's Free French, who joined in the ill-fated expedition, were careless of security. But the *second* ostensible reason contradicted the first, as even the four remarkably "unpolitical" men now gathered in Telegraph Cottage might have suspected. It was that De Gaulle, if he knew of the enterprise, would make it impossible for Allied agents to deal with Vichy French officials who were in a position to facilitate the bloodless entry of the Allies into Algeria and French Morocco. But surely these same Vichyites were also in a position to facilitate *resistance* to the landings and to betray the whole operation to the Germans! Surely they were far poorer security risks than the Free French! And surely it was naïve to suppose that they could be of much aid to the Allies unless they were given information which, however vague in detail, would destroy the possibility of strategic surprise if it were conveyed to the enemy.

Nevertheless, these were the lines along which a fantastic conspiratorial politics had proceeded toward the present flamelit moment. A month ago, on the Wednesday afternoon of September 16, a Ferry Command plane from America had landed at Hendon Airport bearing a tall, slightly stoop-shouldered man, invincibly civilian within the Army uniform he wore, whom Beetle Smith greeted as "Colonel McGowan." Actually he was forty-seven-year-old Robert D. Murphy, a veteran of some twenty-five years in the American diplomatic corps, who had been counselor of the American Embassy in Paris when France fell, had later served in the same capacity in Vichy, and in recent months had been American consul general in Algiers. Beetle had at once taken him to Telegraph Cottage where that night, in this very room, a highly secret meeting had been held. All four of the men now present here had been present then ("I served in my usual role of kibitzer, water boy, cigarette girl, and flunky," wrote Butcher in the diary he was keeping for Eisenhower). So had been Ambassador Winant, Averell Harriman, and representatives of the British Foreign Office and British Military Intelligence—some ten in all.[33]

By the time that meeting ended, near midnight, Murphy had been quite thoroughly briefed concerning the impending operation and repeatedly warned by Eisenhower against disclosing any more of this information to the Frenchmen with whom he would deal than was absolutely necessary for their effective cooperation. (Later, through official channels, Murphy would be specifically ordered not to disclose the time and places of attack until four days before the landings.) In return, Murphy had presented his view of the facts, possibilities, and probabilities of French politics as these could affect and might be used to aid Allied military operations.

Of central importance was the finding of a French leader who would work with the Allies and whose orders French forces in North Africa would obey; and, though the fact went unmentioned that evening, and would always be vehemently denied by the State Department, Murphy had been severely limited in his search for such a man by the anti-Gaullist policy he himself had helped to shape.[34] There was a growing army of underground resistance fighters in both Occupied and Vichy France, but its members and activities were inevitably linked to De Gaulle; nearly all Frenchmen who believed in democracy and loathed fascism were either actively or passively Gaullist, despite the general's personally authoritarian tendencies; and since these men were ruled out of account by the policy directive under which Murphy worked, he perforce dealt with Frenchmen whose commitment to democracy was either highly questionable or obviously nonexistent and whose hostility to the Nazis began to manifest itself only when, with the entry of the United States into the war and the refusal of Russia to collapse on schedule, they began to doubt that Nazism, after all, would win the final victory. To the extent that they had actively collaborated with the Nazis, they were now moved toward secret activities that would place them on the possibly winning side, but in such a way as to save their lives and property from the vengeance which must certainly overtake them if De Gaulle and his followers became the rulers of postwar France. They embarked upon a game of double-cross and double-deal, an intriguing game for which most of them were well equipped by natural talent and past experience. Chief among them—the center of a group of them—was one Jacques Lemaigre-Dubreuil.

Before the war, Lemaigre-Dubreuil had been head of the Taxpayers' League, one of the most powerful of those reactionary pressure groups that contributed so much to the impotence of the French Republic. He was widely believed to have been secretly involved in the fascist march on the French Chamber of Deputies in 1934 and to have helped finance from his ample resources the Cougoulard attempt to overthrow the Republic in 1937. This belief may or may not have accorded with the facts, but it was certainly not inconsistent with his known views and political actions. He was now, according to the Free French, among the most viciously effective of all the French collaborationists—and indeed there could be no doubt that he did in fact collaborate. He continued as top executive of Huiles Lesieur, the largest vegetable oil company in France (he had been permitted to open his company's Dunkirk plant soon after the French surrender), selling his company's products profitably to the Germans. He continued as regent of the Bank of France and became a partner of the Banque Worms, through which the French economy was enslaved by the Third Reich. He was on friendly, actively cooperative terms with the hated traitor Pierre Laval. And though he lived in the occupied zone he was permitted to travel with complete freedom through Vichy France and French North Africa, where were raised the peanuts from which most of his company's oil was produced. But *why* did he collaborate? Was it because he was himself a Nazi at heart, or an opportunist perfectly willing to sacrifice his fellow countrymen in order to maintain his own accustomed privileges, powers, and profits? Of course not, said he to Murphy, who was convinced that Lemaigre-Dubreuil had been "cooperating" with him since the autumn of 1940 and that the wily, wealthy Frenchman's sole purpose in all these activities was to maintain a front (it just *happened* to be highly profitable for him) behind which he could work for the liberation of his country.[35]

As a matter of fact, Murphy was soon to say† that Lemaigre-Dubreuil had deliberately "established, with my knowledge and approval, a deceptive police record" showing him to be "a collaborationist" while obtaining from Laval, Otto Abetz (Nazi Ambassador to France), and others whom he "cultivated . . . , useful information . . . which I included in my State Department reports." He also "functioned as a liaison between myself and General Giraud."

For it was upon General Henri Honoré Giraud that the choice had at last fallen as the French leader who might open North Africa's doors to the Allies. It was of him that "Colonel McGowan" had spoken at greatest length, here in this room, on the night of September 16. A tall, mustached, ramrod-stiff, sixty-three-year-old hero of World War I (he still limped from a wound suffered in that war), Giraud had served honorably if very briefly in World War II, having been captured almost at the outset by the Germans. He had been imprisoned in the fortress at Königstein from which, recently and dramatically, he had escaped, his feat being engineered in part by the Lemaigre-Dubreuil group, according to some accounts, and by the Deuxième Bureau (the French intelligence service), according to all accounts. Associated with the latter had been General Charles Emmanuel Mast, who was now Chief of Staff to the commanding general of French forces near Algiers. Mast, with a profound personal loyalty to Giraud, was in constant touch with his hero, now ensconced in the house of a sister near Lyons; he was also in constant touch with Murphy in Algiers, having convinced the latter of his devotion to the Allied cause; and it was through Mast as well as through Lemaigre-

† In a letter written to Colonel (later General) William J. Donovan, Jan. 11, 1943. Quoted by William L. Langer, *Our Vichy Gamble* (New York: 1947), p. 230.

Dubreuil that Murphy had been informed of Giraud's possible willingness, under certain conditions, to join in Allied operations.

One of these conditions appeared to be that Giraud be assigned supreme command of any North African venture. At least, Giraud's friends (said Murphy) "had always made the point that the command in North Africa must be French," according to Butcher's notes of the September 16 conversations. Over this, Eisenhower of course had shaken his head. The contemplated buildup of TORCH would put a half-million American and British troops into North Africa within a short time after the landing day. It was wholly unrealistic to expect that the command of this massive enterprise would be given a French general who had had no part in planning or mounting it and of whose professional competency Allied authorities had only the sketchiest information. On the other hand, if Giraud could (as Murphy seemed sure he could) actually prevent French resistance, if his prestige and authority were such that French troops would rally to his standard, then surely his services were worth a price, a high price if necessary, though at that moment indeterminate. Eisenhower had therefore suggested that the question of command be held for the time being in abeyance, so far as Murphy's dealings in Algiers were concerned. The diplomat might say that it was "too early" for final detailed decisions on this matter; his one definite promise should be that any French troops who joined in the battle would serve under the command of a French general.

It was on this note that the night conference had ended.

Next morning, having spent the night in Telegraph Cottage, "Colonel McGowan" had been returned to Hendon where a plane awaited him. He had flown back to Washington for a few more days of consultation there before again crossing the Atlantic, this time flying to Lisbon and thence to his post in Algiers. Ever since, he had been engaged with his colleagues in intense, covert negotiations, their results reported to Washington and then to London in a series of rather breathless messages transmitted in the most unbreakable of secret codes. The culminating three messages had arrived only today, just a few hours before Eisenhower greeted Smith and Clark at the Cottage, and while these messages were, on the whole, heartening, they were also disturbing; they would have been even more so to men better backgrounded in French politics and personalities, and more aware of ideological issues and significances, than was any of those upon whom the firelight now played.

Giraud had agreed to join in the forthcoming operation. He was to be spirited away from his sister's house to a specified spot on the southern shore of France. There a submarine (he stipulated that it be an American, not a British submarine) was to pick him up and take him to Gibraltar, where the supreme headquarters of the expedition was to be maintained until the landings had been secured. What was disturbing about this was Giraud's continued evident expectation that he would be in command of the whole operation. The proposal made through Mast was that a unified command be set up, with Giraud at its top, Eisenhower retaining "complete command" of the American forces. Had Murphy, violating instructions, promised this in order to obtain Giraud's cooperation? The Americans gathered before the fire could only hope not.

Equally disturbing, while also opening up the most exciting of hopeful possibilities, was the introduction into "Colonel McGowan" messages, just today, of a name hitherto absent from them—that of Admiral Jean François Darlan. It was the most hated name in France, with the exception of Laval's, among common folk. Darlan had been among the very first of the 100 per cent collaborationists, was generally believed to have betrayed Republican France into the bloody hands of her enemies, and had certainly been directly or indirectly responsible, since then, for the imprisonment and torture and death of a large number of brave Frenchmen (Gaullist, most of them) who had dared actively to resist the peace that Vichy had accepted. His hatred for the British was notorious. He was, however, commander-in-chief of the Vichy French armed forces, and especially of the French Fleet, the fourth most powerful in the world, which yet remained in Toulon as a great unredeemed prize of war. He was also the most powerful figure in the Vichy Government, under the aged figurehead, Marshal Pétain, his only serious competitor for this dubious distinction being, again, Laval, who had been named Premier several weeks back (the event had caused the President to call home Ambassador Leahy) but whose office and influence depended wholly upon the Nazis. Hence the excitement over the news that a representative of Darlan had been in touch with Murphy in Algiers to advise him that the admiral *might* have a message for him.

"Darlan apparently wants to play ball," was the interpretation put on this by the Americans—and by the most fervent of the French supporters of Giraud also. The latter had obviously reacted with some alarm to the appearance of so formidable a rival of their hero. Mast had sought at once to impress upon Murphy the alleged fact that the French Army "preferred" Giraud to Darlan (who was, he indicated, a cheap opportunist, thoroughly untrustworthy) and that the Americans could "gain entry practically without firing a shot through Giraud's command."[36] He went further. He asserted that the French Navy, despite having been long under Darlan's command, would go where the Army went.

Nevertheless, Murphy recommended that Darlan's overtures be "encouraged" while a formula was worked out for the admiral's cooperation with Giraud—and to the development of a possible formula, Eisenhower promptly devoted a concentrated hour or two, submitting it then simultaneously to Marshall, the British Chiefs of Staff, and the Prime Minister. The latter had congratulated him upon his "sagacity," he said now, in flickering firelight, with a wide grin and a touch of pride.[37]

His scheme was for Giraud to be named governor of French North Africa, responsible for all civil and military affairs under the protection of Allied forces and, so far as military matters were concerned, under the guidance of the supreme Allied command. Darlan was to be accepted by Giraud as commander of the French military and naval forces in North Africa, serving in this capacity as a principal subordinate of the Allied supreme commander. Once North Africa had been firmly secured as a base for further Allied operations, Darlan was to be named Deputy Allied Commander-in-Chief, replacing Clark who, in satisfaction of his continuing urgent request for a transfer from staff work to battle command, was to become commanding general of a newly organized Fifth Army.

The formula was perfectly satisfactory to Clark, at any rate. He had latterly referred to his "pants" (he had "ants" in them) as often as Ike had to the "shirt" he was supposed to "keep on," for he was now weary indeed of the paper work and the talk, talk, talk in which, it seemed to him, the British way of doing things—always in conference, in committee—wasted valuable time. He craved action of the kind a Fifth Army command would give him . . .

But at the moment he was not thinking that far ahead. He was thinking—they all were thinking as they sat in the Cottage living room—of the morrow and the days immediately after that, during which he would be having all the action he could possibly crave, if of a kind he had never anticipated, and beyond which there was a distinct possibility (none of them spoke of it) that he would no longer be around to engage in any kind of activity whatever.

The journey on which he was about to embark would take him with four other officers, one a U. S. Navy captain, in two Flying Fortresses to Gibraltar. This in itself would be hazardous enough: the bombers would be flying airlanes continuously threatened by Nazi aircraft and, at the end of their flight, must land on an airfield where no B-17 had ever landed before. No one knew for sure that it could be done. At Gibraltar, the travelers were to board a British submarine which would take them to a point off the Algerian coast some fifteen miles west of a tiny port named Cherchell where, on the night of October 20, precisely three days from now, the submarine was to surface and watch for a signal from the shore. If and when a "single steady white light" showed in the "seaward dormer window" of an isolated house upon the shore, Clark and his party were to go ashore and there, in the lonely farmhouse, they were to meet with Murphy, General Mast, and members of Mast's staff.

The purpose of this secret meeting, called for in one of the three "Colonel McGowan" messages received that day, was an exchange of necessary information between those who were to land and those who were to aid (ashore) the landings in North Africa. And while the meeting was being held, or at the instant of approach to it, the danger would be at the maximum. After all, there could be no certainty that the whole arrangement was not a trap whereby the enemy might have delivered into his hands a "senior general officer" of the American Army who was thoroughly familiar with the details of the upcoming operation (these were among Murphy's stipulations) and from whom, by means too unpleasant to contemplate, information might be extracted which would destroy absolutely the possibility of either tactical or strategic surprise.

Not that the latter order of surprise appeared now likely. The man who had represented Darlan to Murphy had also reported that both German and Japanese Intelligence were telling their Governments that an Allied military operation would be launched soon against Casablanca or Dakar, or both. The Germans were urging Vichy to take necessary precautions. "The Germans appear determined to settle the western Mediterranean issue during the coming weeks and will have the use of the Spanish mainland and of Spanish Morocco for this purpose," said this particular "McGowan" cable. "Gibraltar is under constant surveillance. In French opinion, definite action is not a question of weeks, but days. The French political situation is extremely delicate and collapse may be expected in as little as ten days. There is no question that the situation in North Africa is moving fast. Information indicates the Axis has raised about 100,000 troops along the Tunisian frontier."

Only tactical surprise–surprise as to time and place–remained a possibility. Was it a strong possibility still? The four men talked of this, staring into the bed of glowing coals as if upon the bright red face of danger, its hot breath upon their faces. . . .

Bad flying weather prevented the takeoff of Clark and his companions at the scheduled time the next morning.[38] Not until the following morning, October 19, did the two B-17s get away for Gibraltar, where they landed after an uneventful flight, and not until near dawn of October 21 did they arrive off the shore where the signal light burned. It was by then too near daylight to risk a landing; a new rendezvous time had to be arranged, for the night of October 21–22, at further hazard to security.

Hence it was near dawn of October 22 before, at last, Clark and Mast were face to face. Detailed discussions were at once begun and continued until midafternoon, when a telephone call informed the owner of the house where they met that French police, evidently told of mysterious activity in this normally quiet spot, were on their way to investigate. The French officers fled abruptly while Clark and his companions hid in a dark wine cellar empty of wine (Clark in his report stressed the word "empty") until the police, successfully misled by Murphy and the house owner, departed after a cursory search of the upstairs.

That night a heavy surf was breaking over the beach from which they must depart; it was by the narrowest of chances, in pitch darkness and an angry sea, that they made their way back to the submarine, Clark leaving on the beach his trousers (whatever "ants" remained in them were certainly drowned by then) and a money belt containing some hundreds of dollars in gold.

But the mission was a success. Clark and his associates arrived back in London on October 25 with a mass of written information, prepared by Mast and his staff, about the location and strengths of North African troop units, and about the storage places and quantities of supplies, ammunition, gasoline. The Americans had been told, too, where resistance was likely to be heaviest and where Allied airborne troops might safely land.

X

The End of the Beginning

i. *On a South Sea Isle*

Let George do it, the saying goes. So call him George.[1]

He is listed on muster rolls and incorporated in organization charts as (let us say) Smith, George A., serial number such-and-such, private first class in a certain squad of a certain platoon of a certain company of a certain battalion of a certain regiment (the Fifth, let us say) of the United States Marines. He is a tiny interchangeable part of the war machine, a unit of physical force expendable to the degree that he is replaceable or, by being used up, helps to achieve certain stated objectives. What George is now doing, with others like him, is described as securing or attempting to secure an island in the Southwest Pacific, of which neither he nor the others had ever heard until six weeks ago—though God knows that now seems to him an eternity.

He is also trying, with difficulty, to stay alive.

For if George as we first glimpse him is a type, a composite, a statistic, he becomes to us on closer look—he remains always in his own eyes, his feeling and thought—a unique person, himself and none other, possessing and possessed by his own memories, fears, hates, loves, desires, attitudes, tendencies, and (less strongly, less tenaciously) ideas. Call him, then, not a type but a representative man: if he stands for a million who are "like" him it is because he remains himself, and it is of the essence of his sense of his own uniqueness, his sense of being himself alone, no other, that he longs to live and fears to die.

After all he is yet very young, barely twenty, and all his young life until two years ago was lived (let us say) in a middle-sized town of the Middle West where as a boy during long summer evenings he used to lie upon his back on the front porch rail of his middle-class home watching shadows darken across the lawn toward a quiet street and then the wink and dart of fireflies across the night while his father's voice, and his mother's, talking in random murmur above the porch swing's rhythmic creak, came into his hearing not as words but as a slow, sweet music of time—summer time, peaceful, lazy time—interweaving with a private dream he had. Night wind caressed his cheek, softly, and he dreamed of a slender brown-eyed black-haired girl on the next street over, whom he had loved ever since the eighth grade and never dared ask for a date. An easygoing even-tempered dreamy boy he was, who made average grades in school, and was satisfied with that, and played in their successive seasons football-basketball-baseball-tennis without starring in any of them, but was *not* satisfied with this, if only because he wanted so terribly to impress that girl on the next street over—a boy of medium height, rather stockily built, with a mop of brown hair so coarse it was difficult to comb neatly, far-spaced gray eyes, a snub nose, and a wide, gentle mouth that smiled oftener than his eyes did, though his were often-smiling eyes—a boy who took things and people pretty much as they came and went pretty much in the same direction they did, and at the same speed.

How, then, had it happened that on a hot afternoon in late June 1940, when he was just out of high school and working in a filling station to earn money for college next fall (though he wasn't at all sure he would actually enroll), he suddenly asked leave of his boss to go across the street to the post office and into the room where a traveling Marine recruiter had set up shop and where he, George, enlisted in the Corps, signing the papers without hesitation, with a flourish, even, as if he had thought about it a long time before reaching his firm conclusion? He hadn't really thought about it at all. He was hard put that evening to persuade his parents they should confirm with their signatures an act for which their only son, just turned eighteen, could give no clear reasons. Of course, there was a war on, and his father grumbled that we'd probably get in it because we'd never learned to mind our own business and had always been suckers for British propaganda, but that was no good reason for doing what he had done, and he never said so. He could only say he wanted to do it; if he had acted on impulse, the impulse ran deep: and it was not until later, in boot camp, that he connected up his act with an episode that had occurred on the day before his enlistment. At noon that day a flashy red Buick convertible with its top down had been driven into the filling station by a self-assured, smooth-looking young man whom George had never seen before but who had beside him in his sporty car the raven-haired girl of the next street over. Her face was glowing with sun and wind and happiness. Her dark gaze, turning from right to left as it lifted to her companion's downward look, swung a lash of unrecognition across George's face as, servile, he scraped a butterfly off the windshield . . .

He made the connection in a state of shock as he stood at rigid attention in September sunlight on a Parris Island drill field, his cheek burning from a slap given him by his outfit's D.I. There had been two slaps, in fact—hard ones—because in response to the D.I.'s barked question as to *why* he had volunteered for the Marines he had replied that he didn't know, he could think of no good reason. He had never been struck before without striking back, not since he was a small child, and to stand there and take it from that ugly-faced Leatherneck sergeant ("Don't you crack wise to me, mister!" the sergeant snarled) was about the hardest thing he had ever had to do until then. There had been harder things afterward, before he left training camp. Once when they were on forced march under full pack on an unseasonably hot day, his particular buddy, nauseated by exhaustion, had puked in the road during a brief rest stop and then been forced by that same goddamned D.I. to kneel down and lick up his vomit![2] George had been nauseated himself at the sight of it and had barely kept himself from vomiting, being helped to do so by a once-furious hatred of the D.I. that had now become a cold-steel constant of his life—but neither he nor anyone else had dared say a word or lift a finger to help his buddy.

He hated the D.I., no doubt of that, but by the time of the forced march his resentment of insults and injuries had begun to be tempered by a realization that they were not truly *personal.* They were part of a design, crude but effective, to overlay the unique George A. Smith and his comrades in arms with the kind of "likeness" to each other necessary to their function, and then to drive this "likeness" deeply enough into them to make it actually *of* them and not just a uniform to be put on and taken off. By that time, too, he had begun to realize that, though there was certainly a connection between the filling station episode and his sudden decision to join the Marines on a hot June afternoon, this episode—whatever it was that the girl's dark-eyed look had meant to him—was by no means the sole cause of his act. Maybe it wasn't even the principal cause. Maybe there had been, all the time, a deep desire or need to prove himself to himself, prove that he was tough enough to make the grade in what everyone said was an elite corps. At any rate he looked back now with a certain contempt upon the civilian he had been only a few short months ago—soft, dreamy, lazy, undisciplined—and was deeply proud of his now-proved ability to take it and dish it out, of the unprecedented hardness and endurance of his body, and of the skills he had so perfectly acquired by endless repetition that they virtually performed themselves through his body while his mind, undistracted, dealt in split-second reaction time with the unforeseen, the unexpected, in combat situations.

He was a Marine. And it was as a member of a regiment whose name had become legendary during World War I that he first saw the island which he and his comrades are now (he hopes) in process of securing from the Japs. A sergeant of the Fifth Marines it had been who, rising from a ravine in Belleau Wood on a June day in 1918, shouted to his squad, "Come on, ya bastards! D'ya wanta live forever?"—and Pfc. George Smith of the Fifth it was whose belly knotted with fear (though he said quietly, "Well, cheers!") when he saw a black shadow looming out of the curiously pale darkness of a tropic night, shortly before dawn of this Friday, August 7, 1942, and heard the fellow jammed next to him at the transport's rail explain that what they saw must be the cape.[3] Cape Esperance. This, he knew, was the northernmost point of ninety-mile-long, twenty-five-mile-wide Guadalcanal; the transports and warships would now, he knew, slant down for some twenty-odd miles along the island's northeastward shore; and perhaps in broad daylight he would have seen Guadalcanal as beautiful, viewed for the first time across a blue sea from the coasting transport. Certainly beauty was there for the seeing —in the jagged, lofty, blue-green mountains of the interior; in the dark-green jungles opened here and there by wide, pale sweeps of grassland, shoulder-high grasses flowing there in the wind like sea waves; in the tall, swaying cocoanut palms spread in mile after mile of groves along the northern shore; in the dazzlingly white beaches or coral sand with surf breaking gently upon them, rhythmic as a porch swing's stroke across summer night in a now lost and ancient past. But probably George would have been blinded to all this, however bright the day, by his fear-breeding knowledge that the spot toward which his transport now aimed was designated on operation maps of Guadalcanal as Beach Red, a strip of shoreland lying near the mouth of the Tenaru River, just a few miles east of the airstrip the Japs had almost completed and would presumably defend to the death; yes, and that the 1st Battalion, Fifth Marines, Reinforced, his own particular outfit, was to be the very first to hit Beach Red . . .

As things turned out, the landing was unopposed. Shortly after sunrise, George in full battle dress heard the shriek of shells arching from Navy cruisers onto Japanese positions around the airfield, saw the lightning flashes and heard the thunder-roar of their explosions, then watched the shelling, and the bomb-bursts and flame-red lines of tracers when Navy dive bombers and fighters came in, watched it in much the same way and mood as a country child, scared but fascinated, might watch the ominous growl and flicker of a thunderstorm approaching across a Mid-western prairie. Only he was the one (of many) who did the approaching, after a tense hour or two. He piled with others of his platoon into a Higgins boat which became one of dozens of landing craft of various types and sizes circling in a rendezvous area until, abruptly, the signal was given and they all headed in a line of boats straight for a shore on which, abruptly, the sand began to be churned and the cocoanut palms shredded by a concentrated barrage laid down from a couple of destroyers, the barrage not lifting until a bare minute before George's boat came to a grinding, bottom-scraping halt and he jumped out into the warm shallow water and waded ashore.

It was as simple as that, and as safe. The only thing that slowed down George's outfit afterward was the jungle undergrowth and the fear of ambush there, under the palms. An unjustified fear. Because in a couple of hours of cautious advance enough of the beachhead had been secured to permit a speedup in the landing of supplies and equipment and, a little later, to permit the First Marines to land and come on through the Fifth's position in an advance toward the presumed defense perimeter of the airfield—and still not a shot had been fired by the enemy. Some Jap planes came over in the afternoon, but they didn't attack the beachhead; they focused instead on the shipping offshore but didn't seem to hit anything there. Somebody said a destroyer had been damaged. "I'm beginning to doubt whether there's a Jap on the whole damned island," the First Marine Division commander, Major General Alexander A. Vandegrift, was quoted as saying when he came ashore at four o'clock.[4]

Not until well into the following afternoon, after George's outfit had crossed the Tenaru and moved on west along the shore past the airfield and through the main Japanese encampment at Kukum (it was empty, its installations intact save for the damage done by our own shellfire and bombs)—not until then did they run into any fighting at all, and then it was very light. There were some snipers among the trees and some machine guns in dugouts, quickly silenced. By nightfall the airstrip, Henderson Field,* was ours along with large gasoline and ammunition dumps, radio and refrigeration equipment, an electric power plant, artillery pieces, tinned food, tents—masses of valuable materiel which the Japs had made not the slightest effort to destroy before they, who were supposed never to yield ground or surrender, had apparently fled in panic into the hills. It was all very strange, eerie. And ominous, too. For George just didn't believe it could be that easy. His theory was that the Japs had been caught by surprise, all right, and so were greatly outnumbered for the moment, but they hadn't panicked; they had simply withdrawn to await reinforcements, confident that they would be back here in a few days. They hadn't destroyed anything—and had declined to make a fight here in which things would be destroyed—because they expected to use them themselves . . .

Well, he'd been right about that, God knows. At nightfall came rain, sloshing bucketfuls of rain through the clashing fronds and down the tall trunks of the cocoanut palms into a puddle where he lay (wherever he moved was a puddle; they had no tents that night) and couldn't sleep at all, rifles cracking here and there in the dark as scared soldiers fired at their fears and then at two o'clock a sudden blaze of flat white light from flares floating down from a Jap plane circling straight above them while, out at sea, all hell broke loose.[5] At first he thought it was an air raid on shore—the flashes were so brilliant, the noise of the explosions so loud—but it wasn't. It was a naval battle out toward Savo Island, and we sure as hell hadn't won it! He began to find that out next day when the Navy up and retired. Damned if it didn't! In the morning and then again in the afternoon the transports and cargo ships un-

* Named after Major Lofton R. Henderson, commander of the Marine Aviation Squadron based on Midway on June 4, 1942, when he was killed as he dove his plane into the stack of a Japanese warship.

loading offshore interrupted these proceedings in order to disperse as protection against threatened Jap air attacks, and in the late afternoon they simply hoisted anchor once and for all and sailed away, accompanied by such warships as yet remained afloat (George heard later that the tremendous explosions of red flame he'd seen across the watery dark the night before had been American and Australian cruisers blowing up), disappearing below the southeastern horizon an hour or more before the sun went down on August 9 and taking with them supplies and equipment desperately needed on Guadalcanal. George and his fellow Marines were left with half the ammunition they needed, with barely enough food to last a month if they went on short rations (which they promptly did), with no radar equipment or coastal defense guns, and without the heavy machinery required to expand Henderson Field as planned.

(The Navy did that day what had to be done in the wake of the Savo Island disaster—certainly neither cowardice nor irresponsibility characterized the forced retirement—but the Marines left on the island, unable to retire and denied for a long time the strength and means of victory, remained understandably bitter. Months later some of George's surviving comrades would have made for them in Melbourne a medal one of them had designed. Its "heads" face showed a rear admiral's hand dropping a hot potato into the outstretched hands of a Marine who knelt on an island of palms. Below was printed the motto, *Faciat Georgius*, which is to say, "Let George do it."[6])

Thus it began, days adding up to weeks of hunger and fever and dysentery and bone-deep weariness interspersed with hours of stark terror and the ugliest kind of butchery as the Japs tried desperately to retake Henderson Field from Marines who fought desperately to hold it and (with small success at first) enlarge its defense perimeter. Things had gone terribly wrong, that's for sure. Marines are supposed to be assault troops: they take a place and then the Army comes in to hold it while the Marines are withdrawn to mount a new assault elsewhere. This obviously wasn't going to happen here. At first there wasn't enough aviation stuff at Henderson to operate it as a combat air base, there was no coast artillery, and no PT-boats were around for anti-submarine patrol, so Jap submarines kept popping up offshore, shelling Marine positions with impunity, while Jap planes flew over unopposed by Allied fighters, though AA guns did keep them flying high. There was no barbed wire to string before the line of foxholes, and precious few Marines, as a matter of fact, for the extent of line that must be held. Two weeks passed before the first Marine fighter squadron landed at Henderson. Since then, George has felt a little less nakedly exposed. The fly-boys have done a terrific job, no doubt of that, fighting day after day against superior numbers and shooting down four or five Jap planes for every one lost of their own. But on the ground George and the others have continued to live in hell, with no promise and diminishing hope of relief, amidst torrential rain and knee-deep mud and steaming jungle and tall, tough, sawtoothed kunai grass and swarms of biting, stinging insects.

The things he has seen, these last weeks! On the Ridge on a sunny morning, during the three-day battle there, one of the fellows he knew had his jaw shot off and stumbled forward sprouting a brilliant fountain of blood, and then died in a pool of it in the coral dust. In that same fight—maybe that same morning, maybe later, he can't remember now—he saw a man sitting in a slit trench where a mortar shell had landed whimpering at the sight of his own guts spilling out of his ripped belly into his cupped hands. Once he saw a teen-aged boy staggering into a tree beside a jungle trail, screaming as blood oozed through the fingers he'd clamped over his blinded eyes. Then there were those hundreds and hundreds of torn crushed burned chopped Jap bodies piled up in heeps in the sand of the seashore beside the mouth of the Tenaru, stinking in the hot sun, black with the blow-flies that fed upon them.

And the things he has done, these last few weeks! Long ago he read somewhere that you practically never see the man you kill in modern war, not the specific individual man, the killing being done at such a distance by long-range weapons. It's all abstract, this guy had said—killing has become a mathematical problem—so that modern war is less brutalizing as well as (paradoxically) more inhuman than wars of earlier ages when men killed with ax and sword and spear, hacking and thrusting into living flesh. Well, then, what that tough brute of a D.I. had trained him for, and what he is now fighting on Guadalcanal, is no modern war. He has shot two men at close enough range to see the look of shocked surprise on their open-mouthed faces as they toppled backward, and one of them writhed screaming on the ground for maybe a minute before George finished him off, pumping bullets into the screaming head until it looked like a bloody sponge. He has felt a skull crack and cave in under the stock of his clubbed rifle, and the sickening crunch and slither of his bayonet thrust with all his might through muscle and rib and lung into a red-clay bank, pinning there, as if it were a giant insect in his entomology specimen box back home, what looked like every caricature he'd ever seen of the Jap—a buck-toothed four-eyed bandy-legged creature that twisted and jerked and waved thin crooked little arms before it died with its eyes wide open, glaring at him.

These things he has seen, these done, a boy who not so long ago went to considerable lengths to avoid having to kill a chicken for his grandmother's farm table because doing so always made him a little ill—he, George A. Smith, who crouches now still as a rock behind a flowering shrub on the east bank of the Matanikau River and looks across the water toward a setting late September sun, searching the jungle on the other side for the Japs he knows are there. And not only there. They are on this side, too; they are all around him. His mouth, once wide and gentle and often-smiling, is now drawn into a hard grim line. His far-spaced gray eyes, once full of dreams as they gazed gently upon a world of love, are now narrow slits. He knows he is alone, more terribly fatally alone than he has ever been before. . . .

It has all happened so fast, without warning! But then it always does in the jungle—the stinking jungle. God, how he hates this closed-in, stealthy, dirty kind of fighting in a terrain where there is no freedom of movement and practically zero visibility! It's Jap kind of fighting in Jap kind of country—gloomy, tricky, full of sickness and a sudden stab-in-the-dark kind of death.[7] George is one of those who has always liked open country and the long view; he wants enough empty space around him to give him a distinct definition and the possibility of expansion, space enough for the big thought and the big act and the recognition from afar of friend and foe and the opportunities as well as the hazards of his world. Here all is cramped, narrow, turned in upon itself; an inward-spiraling darkness. Here a man hasn't a chance to brace himself against shock, no time to choose between different possible responses to fatal challenges, and the decision goes not to the fairest and bravest and strongest but to the liar, the sneak, the cheat. The fact that the Jap prefers this terrain to any other, choosing always to occupy it rather than ridge or valley grassland when a choice between the two must be made, is one of the elements of George's belief that the enemy, after all, isn't truly human but a furtive jungle animal. A reptile, say. A poisonous reptile.

What has happened is that George as one of maybe twenty men leading the way for a patrol consisting of two companies has gotten cut off from the patrol's main body. They were working their way cautiously up the east bank of the river, everything quiet and peaceful as could be, when all at once a half-dozen machine guns opened up on them and, within seconds, knocked down a half-dozen Marines dead or wounded in the thick undergrowth.[8] George felt a bullet within an inch of his ear (no more than an inch away, he'd swear it), as he dove into a bramble bush, tearing hands and cheek on thorns, and since the shriek was past his left ear and had prolonged itself at his back he knew it came from this side of the river and from behind him. They had walked into a trap, with no more than an hour left before the main body turned back as per orders requiring a return within the defense perimeter by nightfall. Three times during that hour they tried to break out, but the only result was a lot more Marines dead or wounded—and now they are on their own, those who are left alive.

Maybe they are all dead now, thinks George, except me . . .

Huge white and yellow flowers flare odorless at either hand. He smells the fishy river smell, the stink of vegetable decay. He listens intently with every outer ear for the swish and rustle of leaves, the sound of voices, the click of a rifle bolt. In the deepest part of himself he hears the silent wailing of the blues—so lost, so lonely, so far away—as across the river, behind the trees, he sees the evening sun go down. Then, in the momentary twilight of the tropics, he finds himself again able to act, forces his numbed legs to lift him from his prolonged crouch and carry him scrambling down the river trail, provoking a sudden lethal stuttering of machine guns, until he falls into an abandoned Jap foxhole he happened to notice just before the trap was sprung, and night falls down upon him. A long night. A sleepless night, heavy with danger—Japs all around him in the dark, mopping up. Twice he has to drive them off with rifle fire.

But at break of day he is still alive and the Japs seem to have gone elsewhere. At least he hasn't heard anything of them for a long time. So, very cautiously, he climbs out of his hole—there are no shots this time; they've truly gone—and has just begun to work his way along the trail toward his own lines when he hears a groan from almost at his feet and, looking down, rifle at the ready, sees lying just off the trail a Marine with blood-soaked shirt, a stranger to him, unconscious, evidently badly wounded. He tries to pass on. Common sense tells him he'll be damned lucky to make it back alone and unencumbered through the Jap-infested land; he'll have virtually no chance at all with this burden of sorrow upon his back. But he can't pass on. He just can't. Bonds invisible, but strong beyond his strength to break, tie him to this helpless stranger. George does, then, what George must do (*Faciat Georgius*), dressing the bleeding wound as best he can, taking up his burden, staggering under it down the river trail through hours and miles of a terror blurred at last into numbness by his exhaustion, hiding through one long hour in a thicket while a Jap patrol passes by so near he could have touched the ill-wrapped puttees with an outstretched hand—and he almost makes it! Almost . . .

He is within a half-mile of the nearest Marine outpost when he sees at his left, through the haze of exhaustion and across a narrow swamp, three brown figures moving through green foliage, and is stabbed with pain before he can see (he never does see) a blue flame stammering out of a gun barrel at his right. He is knocked sideways across a fallen log into muck. His blood splashes briefly across slime. He sinks face down into fetid liquid mud, his burden yet heavy on his back, and so disappears forever from the sight and knowledge of the world.

ii. *Mr. Willkie's Vision*

Some two weeks after the representative man we've called George Smith would have been first listed on Guadalcanal casualty lists in the column headed MIAPD (Missing in Action, Presumed Dead), a war correspondent named John Hersey accompanied Company H of the Fifth Marines as it went down from Bloody Ridge through the jungle to the bank of the Matanikau and there tried unsuccessfully to force a river crossing. In his written account of the experience, printed first in *Life* magazine, later expanded into a little book called *Into the Valley*, he told how he asked some of the men he was with what it was they believed they were fighting for "today, here in this valley," and how all of them sat silent for a long time, evidently pondering the question until finally one of them said to the others: "Jesus, what I'd give for a piece of blueberry pie." Another then spoke up in favor of mince pie, and yet another in favor of apple, and all of them, Hersey insisted, were thus answering his question "very specifically" though of course not literally. Pie, he carefully explained, was a symbol, a badge of home. What these men were fighting for was "to get the goddamned thing over with and go home."[9] George Smith, as we have described him, would no doubt have answered in much the same way had Hersey asked him the same question.

The "blueberry pie" phrase was destined to become famous—and not a few of the serious-minded would be disturbed by it. Surely Americans fighting in distant lands, caught up in world history and hurt by it, should see a larger purpose and object for what they did than a "home" defined by them (according to Hersey) as "where the good things are—the generosity, the good pay, the comforts, the democracy [sic], the pie"!

Among those who thought so was Wendell Willkie.

On the very day when Hersey on Guadalcanal heard his companions speak of pie as a war aim, Willkie took off from the airfield at Chengtu, China on the next to the last long leg of a flight around a world at war. The plane in which he flew was a four-engined Consolidated bomber (C-87) converted for transport use, christened the *Gulliver*, operated by a U. S. Army crew, and it had begun its long flight from Mitchel Field, New York, on August 26. When it landed in Minneapolis five days from now, Willkie would have flown some thirty-one thousand miles in forty-nine days, thirty of these days having been spent upon the ground of thirteen different countries in activity so continuously exciting and so little relieved by sleep as to melt a full fifteen pounds of flesh off his great frame and leave him soaked through and through with tiredness. His campaign for the Presidency had been hardly more arduous.

The seminal idea for the journey had been planted in his mind by a cablegram he had received less than three months before from three American newspaper correspondents stationed in Kuibeshev, the wartime capital of the Soviet Union. The three—Eddy Gilmore of the Associated Press, Maurice Hindus representing the New York *Herald Tribune*, and Ben Robertson representing *PM*—urged him to make a good-will visit to Russia. A few weeks later, on August 7, the day the Marines landed on Guadalcanal, he attended a luncheon at the White House honoring visiting Queen Wilhelmina of The Netherlands and there (immediately after the luncheon had ended) he discussed the proposed trip with the President, who promptly gave it his blessing. Thereafter the idea had quickly grown into a plan for a 'round-the-world flight to be made by Mr. Willkie as private citizen paying all his personal expenses but performing a mission for the President of sufficient importance to justify his transportation by the Army. He asked two personal friends to accompany him. One was Joseph Barnes, former Foreign Editor of the New

York *Herald Tribune*, who knew the Russian language well and could serve as both interpreter and secretary; the other was Gardner (Mike) Cowles, Jr., of the family which published newspapers in Des Moines and the Twin Cities, and *Look* magazine in New York. Both were upper-echelon officials of the Office of War Information who were given leave of absence to make the trip but who could legitimately regard it as a continuation of their official duties.[10]

For as conceived by the President, by high officers of the Army and Navy, by the OWI, and by Wendell Willkie himself, three important purposes of "psychological" or "political" warfare were to be served by the journey—and as the journey approached its end, none could doubt that these purposes had indeed been served, and well.

First, the flight had demonstrated in dramatic fashion the fact that the Allies were in control of the strategic air routes of the globe, while also calling attention to the number of peoples now committed to defeat of the Axis through the United Nations. From New York, the *Gulliver* had flown to Puerto Rico; from Puerto Rico to Belém and Natal in Brazil; from Natal across the South Atlantic to the British Gold Coast port of Accra, then to what Joe Barnes called a "fantastic walled city in the middle of Nigeria" named Kano; from Kano to Khartoum in the Anglo-Egyptian Sudan, at the junction of the White Nile and the Blue; from Khartoum to Cairo, and then to the British air base at Lydda; thence to Baghdad and Teheran; from Iran, then, into Russia, landing at Kuibishev and Moscow; from Kuibishev to Tashkent and thence through the back door of China at Tihwa (the Russians called it Urumchi) in the far-western Chinese province of Sinkiang; from Tihwa to Lanchow and on down to Chengtu and Chungking; and now north again to Siberia, to Chita and then the next (also the last) major stop on the journey, in the capital of the Siberian Republic of Yakutsk. From Yakutsk the *Gulliver* would fly to Fairbanks, Alaska, and then back to the United States via Edmonton, Canada. Everyone, friend and foe alike, must realize that no Axis plane could have come anywhere near matching this wide-ranging freedom of movement.

Second, the journey had enabled a recognized leader of American business and industry to impress upon key men all over the world the facts of America's industrial mobilization and to hearten them with statistics on the unprecedentedly vast quantities of war materiel that would soon flow out of American factories and war plants and shipyards into the hands of Allied fighting men. As a salesman of America's industrial power to people who might otherwise have been skeptical of it, Willkie had been, and knew he had been, superb. He was chockful of big statistics and poured them into every ear that would listen. Moreover, as Joe Barnes remarked, when he stepped out of the huge C-87 (a huge man exuding a huge, restless vitality), he appeared the living personification of the big production he preached.[11]

Third, the journey had been a striking demonstration of the unity with which Americans, regardless of their political party allegiance, were supporting the war effort. Willkie had missed no opportunity to point up the fact that he was performing a personal mission for the man who, having defeated him in the election of two years past, remained President and Commander-in-Chief, but that he himself nonetheless remained titular head of the opposition party, determined to do all within his power to defeat Roosevelt at the polls in 1944. . . .

But it was probably not of these three accomplished purposes that Willkie was now thinking. A fourth purpose, overshadowing all the rest, had grown in his mind since he left New York, and it was doubtless this which directed his thoughts as he looked down upon the mountains and wild gorges north of Chengtu, upon the irrigated valley of the upper reaches of the Yellow River near Lanchow, and then upon the Great Wall of China snaking its lonely way across northern China's barren hills. Perhaps he thought of walls in general as he looked down upon this most famous of them, and of the "something" Robert Frost had remarked "that doesn't love a wall." Certainly his mind was full that day as it had been for many days of the problems of walls between peoples and nations, walls of mind as well as of concrete and barbed wire, walls dividing what should be, what must be, and what therefore inevitably would be joined together somehow. It was the dangling "somehow" that most disturbed him. His spirit moved to the "ground-swell" Frost had spoken of that "makes gaps even two can pass abreast," though the groundswell he felt was worldwide and myriad millions would press their way through the gaps it opened.

All over the world the walls were tumbling down as a new kind of organization of human life on earth struggled to be born.[12] Wendell Willkie was both exhilarated by the spectacle and dismayed by the failure of Allied leaders to see it or, at any rate, to comprehend its meaning. British and Americans alike talked and acted as if the world after the war would be much the same as it had been before Hitler, Mussolini, and the Japanese war lords upset the balance of power, with Washington and London exercising much the same kind and degree of world decisiveness as they had before. They seemed not to realize that what was now happening was but one stage in a world revolution that had begun before the first gun of this war was fired and would certainly continue, and at an accelerated pace, after the Axis was defeated. It might continue violently or peaceably, hopefully or catastrophically, but inevitably it *would* continue. And if Britain and the United States failed to recognize it, or tried to prevent its happening instead of helping to guide it toward humane ends, why, Britain and the United States and possibly the whole humane tradition of Western culture would be overwhelmed by it.

He recalled a dinner in the home of British Admiral Sir Henry Harwood in Alexandria, Egypt, a day or so after he had visited the front at El Alamein and been told by General Sir Bernard Montgomery that a defensive battle then still in progress, though in its final phase, was a decisive Allied victory. (This was the Battle of Alam Halfa, in which Rommel's attack toward Alexandria was repulsed and the Afrika Korps left in a weakened condition to cope with the offensive Montgomery planned to launch as soon as all factors appeared to be in his favor. "Egypt has been saved," he kept telling Willkie. He also asserted that "it is now mathematically certain that I will eventually destroy Rommel.") Around the dining table, in addition to the host and Willkie's party, had sat ten men from the British Navy, diplomatic corps, and consular service stationed in Alexandria. In the fashion typical of him, Willkie sought to "draw out these men" on the subject of colonialism and its postwar demise. He had hoped for an enlightened and enlightening discussion of the way in which colonial governments could be transformed gradually but with necessary swiftness into self-government by the now-colonial peoples. "What I got," he would later record,[13] "was Rudyard Kipling, untainted even with the liberalism of Cecil Rhodes. . . . That evening started in my mind a conviction which was to grow strong in the days that followed it in the Middle East: that brilliant victories in the field will not win for us this war now going on in the far reaches of the world, that only new men and new ideas in the machinery of our relations with the peoples of the East can win the victory without which any peace will be only another armistice."

In Beirut he encountered no such "new men" nor "new ideas" among those who governed Syria and the Lebanon under old League of Nations mandates. Instead he encountered the rigidly nationalistic French General Georges Catroux, military ruler of these ancient lands, the still more rigidly nationalistic General de Gaulle, then a house guest at Catroux's official Residence des Pins, and the British Major General Sir Edward L. Spears, head of his country's military mission there—men who sought to embroil him in the quarrel then raging between the Free French and the British over which should govern peoples who clearly intended to govern themselves as soon as the war was over, if not before. Similarly in Jerusalem, where he was the house guest of Sir Harold MacMichael, the British Resident High Commissioner for Palestine and Trans-jordan—a man who was the very type of athletic pipe-smoking English colonialist, beautifully mannered, rather amusedly contemptuous of those over whom he ruled, and indifferent to if not ignorant of the dangerous ferment all around him. The manifold problems of Jew and Arab, filtered through MacMichael's complacently urbane mind, were made to seem (in Joe Barnes' words) "simple and old and eternal, and not much worth bothering about."[14] Far different was the impression gained in the single day during which Lowell C. Pinkerton, the U. S. Consul General at Jerusalem, loaned Willkie his house. It had, this house, a double staircase so arranged that Arabs and Jews could come in alternation, each giving to Willkie in the most violent language his concept of the wrongs suffered by his people and the extreme measures which must be taken to right them.

Willkie's over-all conclusion was that, in the Middle East as a whole, the lives of common folk were bound to "change more in the next ten years than they have in the last ten centuries." The long cultural and political stagnation of ancient lands where Eden was supposedly located, where civilization certainly began, was coming to an end. Evidences of swift transition from old to new were at every hand in Egypt, Palestine, Syria, Turkey, Iraq, Iran. Here working examples of the most advanced technology were set down amidst a primitive economy that was much the same as it had been in Biblical times; here men and women of the highest culture, fastidious and sensitive and aware, mingled in public places with peasants and unskilled laborers who were illiterate, filthy, and diseased, their stunted minds glinting dully through eyes as lusterless as the muddy water they drank and sometimes bathed in. Here he first sensed the "vast leaven" which was, he now knew, "working deep in the lives of something more than half the human race," but neither here nor in the Russia and China he had since visited had he found any "automatic guarantee" that the great world-changes would work in favor of the West.[15] If the political values and ideas which animated Western democracy were to be accepted in the Middle and Far East they must be more consistently practiced, abrogating exploitive economics and all notions of White Supremacy, than they had ever been before within the democracies themselves and within the lands they had held as colonies.

He had no doubt of the moral and practical superiority of democratic institutions and what he called a "free economy" over social and economic institutions founded on Marxist doctrine. He had asserted as much over and over again in arguments with individual Russians as he moved about their country visiting factories, schools, libraries, collective farms, hydroelectric power developments, and, on one memorable occasion, the battlefront near Rzhev. His central argument had been unpersuasive to his hosts, whose rigorously conditioned minds were obviously impervious to all ideas inconsistent with socialist theory. It had made less impression upon them, perhaps, than they had made upon him when they stressed the selfishness, callousness, sensuality, and childish triviality which were the moral consequences, in their view, of capitalism as expressed through the marketplace. (On one occasion, arguing with a young Soviet factory superintendent, his deliberately provocative insistence upon individual monetary profit as the prime motive for all human endeavor embarrassed the listening pilot of the *Gulliver*, who felt it to be unworthy of Willkie and likely to lead the Russian toward wrong conclusions about American values. The pilot had pointed out that, while he had been pleased by the pay raise he received with his promotion from captain to major, the raise meant nothing to him compared to the Distinguished Flying Cross he had received at the same time.[16]) But whenever the argument focused on human rights and human freedoms—what these meant and whether or not, or to what extent, they actually existed in Russia—his faith in democratic principles, in their unanswerable *rightness*, was reinforced. All the Russians he argued with were thoroughly equipped with Marxist answers, and not one was able to define a proper political freedom as being anything more or other than a willingness to accept State-imposed necessities. Most of them, indeed, seemed willing to regard as peripheral and expendable the freedoms of inquiry and conscience and speech which Willkie regarded as central and absolutely essential.

Yet he had been impressed by the practical warmaking efficacy of the Soviet system. "Russia," he would soon write, echoing the Lincoln Steffens of 1919,[17] "is an effective society. It works. It has survival value." He genuinely liked and admired the Russian people—their energy, their courage, their endurance, their seriousness of purpose, their ability to dream mighty dreams and then work creatively to realize them. As someone had said, they were a continental people with a continental outlook, similar to Americans in many ways of temperament. He believed therefore that it would be possible for the two countries to "work together for the economic welfare and peace of the world" after the war had ended. "At least, knowing that there can be no enduring peace, no economic stability, unless the two work together, there is nothing I ever wanted more to believe." He saw no danger to American ideals and institutions in such collaboration. "So deep is my faith in the fundamental rightness of our free economic and political institutions that I am convinced they will survive any such working together."[18] They would be less likely, he might have added, to survive the stresses and strains of an all-out arms race and power competition.

But the needed collaboration could not operate after the war unless it was begun, and well begun on a basis of mutual respect and understanding, *while* the war raged. Now was the time to do it—now while the unifying influence of a common enemy and a common danger was in effect. Willkie's conviction of this had combined with his awareness of Russia's war needs (they were at that moment more desperate than anyone publicly admitted) to dictate a statement he issued in Moscow on September 26 calling for a "second front" in Europe "at the earliest possible moment our military men will approve." Some of these military men, he provocatively added, might "need some public prodding." Next summer, he ominously added, might be "too late."

This demonstration of free speech called down upon his touseled head sufficient wrath from official quarters in London and Washington to indicate the personal responsibility which is—which must be—the core of personal freedom in a world of close interdependencies. Roosevelt told a press conference in Washington on October 6 that dispatches quoting Willkie on matters of strategy were not worth reading, since they were purely speculative. Churchill told the House of Commons that such public speculation "as to the time and places of future Allied offensive operations" was undesirable.† Willkie in his turn had been angered by this reaction, especially by Roosevelt's remark, which he took as a personal insult, but he was neither dismayed nor deterred. He let reporters know exactly how he felt about it when he met with them in Chungking. He had been commissioned by the President to do certain things of a very general nature, he indicated, and he had done them to the best of his ability. "But when I speak for myself I am Wendell Willkie, and I say what I damned please!"[19] Whereupon he proceeded to do just that, issuing to reporters on October 7 in Chungking a prophetic statement whose frankness and sincerity were wholly untempered by discretion and which was destined, he hoped, to have historic effects.

During his journey, his statement said, he had been subjected to a bewildering variety of peoples and ways of life and government, but all "ordinary people" in the thirteen countries he had visited had in common a desire that the United Nations win the war and that they themselves live after the war "in liberty and independence." They also had in common a doubt "in varying degrees" of the readiness of the leading democracies of the world "to stand up and be counted for freedom for others after the war is over." The doubt was vitiating "their enthusiastic participation on our side." What was urgently needed from the Western democracies was a "clear and simple statement of where we stand." The Atlantic Charter was obviously not enough, especially since there was grave doubt that it was intended to apply anywhere outside western Europe.‡ "Some of the plans to which such a statement would lead are already clear, I deeply believe, to most Americans," Willkie then boldly declared: "We believe that this war must mean an end to the empire of nations over other nations. No foot of Chinese soil, for example, should be or can be ruled from now on except by the people who live on it. And we must say so *now*, not after the war. . . . We believe it is the world's job to find some system for helping colonial peoples who join the United Nations' cause to become free and independent nations. We must set up

† Willkie's statement revealed to the British the astounding fact—they found it almost incredible—that he, one of the most influential of Americans, sent abroad on what everyone knew to be a quasi-official mission, since he was transported by Army plane and accompanied by two officials of his Government's information service, had not been briefed by Roosevelt concerning impending operations before he left Washington. Willkie knew nothing of TORCH when he talked to Stalin and Stalin, who (as we have seen) had been told of it by Churchill, said nothing about it to his visitor.

‡ Before Willkie began his journey, Churchill had issued two statements about the Atlantic Charter. The authors of it, according to one of these statements, "had in mind primarily the restoration of the sovereignty, self-government, and national life of the states and nations of Europe now under the Nazi yoke." The Charter's provisions, said the other statement, must not be construed to "qualify in any way the various statements of policy which have been made from time to time about the development of constitutional government in India, Burma, or other parts of the British Empire." Churchill had also told the Commons (September 9, 1941) that he was opposed to the formulation of peace aims or war aims "at this time, when the end of the war is not in sight, when conflict sways to and fro with alternating fortunes and when conditions and associations at the end of the war are unforseeable."

firm timetables under which they can work out and train governments of their own choosing, and we must establish ironclad guarantees, administered by all the United Nations jointly, that they shall not slip back into colonial status."[20]

The wrath brought down upon his head by his Moscow statement was as nothing compared to that he had aroused by this latest one—in London, among the native ruling cliques of the colonial peoples he proposed to liberate (they feared as poison the ideas of personal freedom which Willkie's views might inject into the minds of men whom they proposed to rule and exploit), and in Washington where a prevailing official view was that Willkie was endangering the Anglo-American alliance. He had anticipated this. No special prescience was required to measure the outrage which his remark about "no foot of Chinese soil" would engender in those who had a vested interest in Hong Kong. Easy to anticipate was some such response as Winston Churchill was in fact to make a few weeks hence when (November 10) he growled that "we [the British] intend to hold what we have" and that he had "not become the King's First Minister to preside at the liquidation of the British Empire."[21] Inevitable and, in Willkie's view, contemptible was the charge that he, by boldly speaking his mind, and the interest of oppressed millions, was skirting if not crossing the boundary of treason, "rocking the boat" so greatly as to threaten its capsize. Always those who sought to maintain a status quo of wrong, of injustice, made this assault upon anyone who proposed change: they dared not openly declare their interest in the perpetuation of evil, but they could and always did charge that any proposal for removing the evil was premature—that it was, for one reason or another, inexpedient at the present time.

At the present time . . .

Beyond the Great Wall lay the vast pebbled wasteland of the Gobi, an enormous flat emptiness of brown and gray under an enormous cloudless pale-blue sky, where every mile was so like every other that nothing appeared to move, to slip by or past the wing. The distance was perfectly pure, perfectly open, so that everywhere was here and here was everywhere, and Time ceased. The throbbing plane seemed to hang motionless, suspended on a point of stillness. And as he looked down upon the abstract plain from his plane of abstraction, the world traveler might see all past and all future spread below him in an infinite objectless eternal Now, with nothing to distract him from the inward illumination, the inward vision, and might feel himself opening out to receive it as a religious mystic does who goes into the desert wilderness in search of the experience of God—a felt union with the eternal, all-embracing One.

Perhaps it was here, then, in this long moment of suspension, that Wendell Willkie had most intensely his vision of One World, later to be embodied in a book with that title. Perhaps it was here that he first shaped some of the phrases which, when his book was published in April of 1943, would strike deep into the minds and hearts of millions of men of good will all over the world:

"Freedom is . . . indivisible. . . . If we want to enjoy it, and fight for it, we must be prepared to extend it to everyone, whether they are rich or poor, whether they agree with us or not, no matter what their race or the color of their skin. . . . When I say that peace must be planned on a world basis, I mean quite literally that it must embrace the earth. Continents and oceans are plainly only parts of a whole, seen, as I have seen them, from the air. . . . And it is inescapable that there can be no peace for any part of the world unless the foundations of peace are made secure throughout all parts of the world. . . . When I say that in order to have peace this world must be free, I am only reporting that a great process has started which no man—certainly not Hitler—can stop. Men and women all over the world are on the march, physically, intellectually, and spiritually. After centuries of ignorant and dull compliance, hundreds of millions of people in eastern Europe and Asia have opened the books. . . . They are no longer willing to be Eastern slaves for Western profits. They are beginning to know that men's welfare throughout the world is interdependent. They are resolved, as we must be, that there is no more place for imperialism within their own society than in the society of nations. The big house on the hill surrounded by mud huts has lost its awesome charm."[22]

What he dimly envisioned was a worldwide organization of freedom, a global United Nations within which all elements of national sovereignty inimical to peace and freedom were pooled and through which all men could be assured equality of opportunity and a share of the material benefits that flowed so abundantly from the scientific technology. It would be a unity of rich diversity, a community of mankind wherein creative differences between individuals and groups (he stressed these when he spoke of the role of minorities in a democracy) were encouraged. Moreover he was convinced that the country best equipped to lead mankind toward the new One World was his own, for he came home "certain of one clear and significant fact: that there exists in the world today a gigantic reservoir of good will toward us, the American people."[23] Here, then, was a cement—an inwardly persuasive power, a kind of "fifth column" of democracy—which might be used to bind peoples together in a community of good will. No other country possessed anything like it in quality or extent.

But would the reservoir be used for this purpose? There was a danger, a very great danger, that it would be used up, drained, to no good purpose at all. And perhaps, during this same eternal moment—future and past alike present in the endless monotone below—Wendell Willkie saw or sensed that by the time his book was out the world would have been presented by the Western democracies, and especially by his own country, with glaring and repeated instances of the cynical expediency he personally loathed and knew would be fatal to his One World vision if it set a pattern, established a precedent. They were being prepared, these instances, while he journeyed homeward—and he was being spiritually prepared to fight against them with every resource at his command in a battle for public opinion.

For this was to be his role from now on, the role of prophet and idealist who spoke the conscience and the hope of mankind—he who, at earlier crucial moments of his life, had been himself a battleground between pragmatism and idealism ("sweetheart" vs. "soul") where victory went to the former. He was now to be the stanchest foe of expediency—"military, political, temporary or otherwise"—for he was sure that "the moral losses of expediency always far outweigh the temporary gains" and that "every drop of blood saved through expediency will be paid for by twenty drawn by the sword."[24] In this role he would often disturb Franklin Roosevelt, who could not resist poking fun at him now and then —imitating at a press conference his pronunciation of "reservoir," for instance—ostensibly because he dealt so simply and clearly and directly with matters Roosevelt felt to be immensely complicated and difficult. Actually Roosevelt's motive would seem to have been self-defense: Willkie seemed to spark, deep within the President's complex character, occasional shudders of self-shame. (Robert Sherwood has recorded his conviction that the President was always ashamed of himself for "having yielded to the temptation . . . to indulge in unworthy wisecracks at Willkie's expense."[25])

Significant in this connection is a story told in a later year by Secretary of Labor Frances Perkins of a conversation she overheard between Roosevelt and Madame Chiang Kai-shek when the latter came to Washington in 1943—largely as a response to Willkie's urging. Roosevelt kept pressing his charming guest for her frank opinion of Willkie and she, who had no special penchant for candor, kept putting him off with noncommittal courtesies until finally, driven into a conversational corner, she said: "Well, Mr. President, he is an adolescent, after all." Roosevelt then pressed her for a candid opinion of himself. "Ah, Mr. President," she promptly replied, "*You* are sophisticated." But to the watching, listening, amused Mrs. Perkins it seemed that Roosevelt would have been less obviously pleased and flattered by this remark ("there was a gleam of pleasure, shall I say, and simple human vanity in his eyes") if the remark had been strictly true.[26]

iii. *In a Dank and Gloomy Cave*

Night fell early on Gibraltar this Friday the thirteenth of November, 1942. Rain fell with it, and curtains of mist so low over the airfield that occasional ghostly wisps drifted among the wings and propellers of the planes parked there—too many planes for so small a field—and against the faces of Army Air Force personnel who, huddled in their waterproofs, waited beside the runway.

When the sound of motors came out of those lowering skies, sudden and loud through the wet dark, the waiting men tensed; they prayed that Lady Luck, in defiance of the forces supposed to rule this date, would be riding in the cockpit with the young Air Force lieutenant who would try to bring the bomber down, safely down with her top-brass payload. And evidently she was! For the pilot did what, for all his skill, he could not have done by skill alone, bursting the place through the near-zero ceiling just seconds before its tires screeched and smoked upon the pavement exactly where they would have touched down had he landed in bright sunlight, so that General Eisenhower with British Admiral Sir Andrew Cunningham (naval commander of the North African expedition) and the inevitable Butcher emerged smiling from the plane and, standing again on solid earth, smiled yet more broadly as he was told how very lucky his landing had been.[27] He might later regard it—others certainly would—as almost his only stroke of personal good luck in an otherwise evil day. . . .

He had had almost precisely similar luck a week ago, on November 5, when he came down from England to establish here the supreme headquarters for the impending North African invasion. The plane he rode that day had been the one which took Wayne Clark south on his secret mission in October, a fully armed Fortress dubbed the *Red Gremlin*, and its pilot had been the same as Clark had had on that earlier occasion, Major Paul W. Tibbets, Jr. So foul was the weather in England and all the way down to Gibraltar that Tibbets had advised strongly against a takeoff that had already been twice postponed, asking Eisenhower to make a decision at the English airfield which in ordinary circumstances, when technical considerations were the sole factors, was the pilot's alone to make. They had flown then at an average height of one hundred feet all the way down; Tibbets had had actually to climb to get into the landing traffic when, at last, the mighty Rock loomed through mists wherein, according to report, an enemy plane had been and probably still was lurking.[28] Eisenhower confessed he had never felt greater relief from personal hazard than he did when, near 4:30 that afternoon, he stepped from the plane to shake hands with Lieutenant General Sir F. N. Mason-MacFarlane, Gibraltar's Governor, and to be whisked in the governor's car to Government House where, ever since, he had had his private quarters. (Technically—the thought of it tickled him—he, Texas-born and Kansas-bred, was now the commander of Britain's mightiest bastion, and would be until he moved to Algiers, though the actual functions of command continued, of course, to be exercised by MacFarlane.)

So it was to Government House, to an early bed in their rooms on the top floor of what had once been a convent, that he and Butcher were driven immediately after their dangerous landing on this black Friday the thirteenth. And next morning he came early from that house to the damp and dismal little room that had been his office, the supreme command post of TORCH for a week now. It was deep in the bowels of the mighty Rock—one of a series of chambers carved out under fourteen hundred feet of limestone (the largest one, a full thirty feet tall, used as a war room, had now a huge operations map of North Africa on one wall)—and to reach it he had to pass through a half-mile or more of perpetually chilly, dripping, ill-lit tunnel. He had walked sedately enough through that tunnel on his first day here, but this morning, as he had on every other since the first, he trotted the whole distance to arrive, not breathless, but breathing deeply and gratefully warm, at the dreary spot where were focused these days a seemingly irreducible cluster of anxieties. No sooner had one anxiety-breeding difficulty been removed than another, or more than one, emerged out of North Africa, France, England, or the United States to take its place.

But at least the anxieties were less acute, less crucial now than they had been at first. He was sure that nothing could exceed in number and crushing weight the psychological burdens he had had to bear during his first two days here, and especially during the long, long hours intervening between the absolutely final commitment of forces to the North African operation and his first definitive news of how the operation was going. Measured solely in terms of the number of ships and men, of planes and tons of materiel, this commitment would no doubt seem small at a later date: much larger ones would have to be made in future operations before the enemy's great strength was at last overcome. But measured in terms of percentages of available resources, and in terms of imponderables, no later operation would be likely to exceed this one, and the nervous strains it imposed on the commander were not relieved, as later ones inevitably would be, by established precedent. Never before in modern times had so large a force attempted a landing on hostile shores, and never in all history had so much shipping, a million tons of it, been committed to a single operation of war.

Especially thick had been the cluster of anxieties around the Western Task Force, General Patton commanding. It had begun to embark from various American Atlantic ports on October 20 and by October 28 had become the main body of a convoy designated by the U. S. Navy as Task Force 34, Rear Admiral H. Kent Hewitt commanding. This main body, consisting of some twenty-five large transports, accompanied by tankers and cargo vessels, bore 35,000 troops and 250 tanks. Bringing it safely across the U-boat-infested Atlantic, dividing it into the three separate landing groups called for by the finally revised operation plan, and then landing the three simultaneously on November 7 at three designated spots on the French Moroccan coast (near Port Lyautey, some seventy-five miles northwest of Casablanca; at Fedala, about twelve miles northwest of Casablanca; and at Safi, some 150 miles southwest of Casablanca) was the Navy's job. To it had been assigned three great battleships, five aircraft carriers (the *Ranger* and four smaller ones), five heavy cruisers and four light ones, three submarines, and more than forty destroyers—an armada that dotted with ships some six hundred square miles of ocean after the final rendezvous had been effected 450 miles southeast of Cape Race, Newfoundland. Nevertheless, the opportunities for disaster were many and great all the way across the Atlantic, and they rose to a terrifying peak of danger at the voyage's end. If the main landing at Fedala had been anticipated by French forces determined to resist it, and if the shore there was pounded by the huge surf normally to be expected in November, the Casablanca operation would certainly be costly and might actually fail.

No such worry about weather had accompanied the huge convoys that passed through the Strait of Gibraltar under cover of night, November 5–6, having sailed from England several days before, but of other worries concerning these there had been an abundance. By then the Germans and Vichy French could not have failed to know that a large-scale operation was being launched by the Allies inside the Mediterranean. Perched on rooftops in Algeciras and La Linea on "neutral" Spanish soil, German observers with powerful binoculars could and did keep Gibraltar's bay and narrow strait under continuous surveillance; and since a wire-net fence was all that separated Gibraltar's airfield from Spain, enemy observers had certainly noted that planes were massed there wingtip to wingtip beside the runway. Eisenhower could only hope that neither the Germans nor the Vichyites knew or guessed the objectives of this so-obviously launched operation—and for this hope, British Naval Intelligence, given him by Admiral Cunningham, provided some basis. According to the blunt, hearty, aggressive-minded admiral, whom Eisenhower now regarded as a close personal friend, the Germans believed that the convoys with their air cover were aimed at reinforcing Malta and/or striking against Sicily, where preparations were being made to repulse the expected landing attempts.[29] This was precisely what the Allies had wanted the enemy to believe: the operation plan called for the Center and Eastern Task Forces to sail on past Oran and Algiers in broad daylight, on toward Malta, and then circle back during the night of November 7–8 to head straight for their designated objectives.

Of course, the over-all African situation had been much improved, the general outlook much brightened by the great victory that General Montgomery had won with his British Eighth Army over Rommel with his Afrika Korps at El Alamein. Here, on the night of October 23, some 882 field and medium guns had opened fire "like one battery," as Montgomery put it, initiating a beautifully conceived and executed "set-piece" battle in which the "Desert Fox," Rommel, was outwitted and forced into repeated, costly tactical errors. Before Eisenhower left London, Rommel was in headlong flight to the west, badly disorganized and pursued by Montgomery, having lost sixty thousand men, one thousand guns, and five hundred tanks. This was more than a good omen for the invasion Eisenhower was launching. It meant that the European Axis, for the first time, was now definitely on the defensive in a major theater of war. It increased the likelihood that Vichy France would not stubbornly resist the Allied landings and that Spain would not actively aid the Germans against Gibraltar.

All the same, things could yet have gone very wrong. What if the French Fleet had come out of Toulon to join the Italian? What if the Germans had concentrated U-boat "wolf packs" in the Mediterranean? (There had been a flurry of dismay when word came of the torpedoing of the combat-loaded U.S.S. *Thomas Stone* inside the Mediterranean, just 150 miles from its destination, on the morning of November 1.) What if the Luftwaffe had concentrated where they could cover our landing points? What if the Algerian French had, after all, put up a truly determined resistance and Spain, after all, had opened her border to the Germans? Any one of these possibilities would, if realized, have greatly added to the losses and hazards of the expedition; a combination of them could have meant the annihilation of the two task forces. The Allied troops, alas, had not been adequately trained for strongly opposed large-scale amphibious operations. A British commando-led raid on Dieppe, on the Channel coast of France on August 19 had suffered a bloody repulse, with some two thousand of the six thousand troops involved (most of them Canadian) being killed, wounded, or captured—and in the light of this demonstration of the hazards of seaborne attacks upon coastal defenses, Eisenhower might actually have shuddered away from his remembrance of the single set of master exercises for TORCH it had been possible to hold, on the shores of Scotland, before the expedition set sail. So many glaring errors had been made! ("But then you never learn anything from a perfect exercise," he had tried to console himself at the time. "You only learn from the bad ones—and this one was surely bad enough to scare the boys into trying harder."[30])

At the very center of these clustered anxieties, for Eisenhower on November 7, had been the worry about Giraud. At first the worry had been that he would not come at all. Eisenhower's political advisers in Gibraltar—H. Freeman Matthews of the State Department and William H. B. Mack of the British Foreign Office—had been as convinced of the French general's importance to the Allied cause as Murphy was; they went so far as to suggest at one point "that the difference between public association and non-association of the Giraud name with the operation might mean the difference between success and disaster."[31] It had been expected by them that a broadcast message from Giraud in Gibraltar to the French in North Africa would be sufficient to reduce the latter's resistance to merely token dimensions if, indeed, it did not cause the French to welcome the Allied troops as "liberators." Naturally, the greatness of the hopes contingent upon Giraud's arrival became the measure of the worry over the possibility of his non-arrival. Hours after he was supposed to have boarded the submarine sent to fetch him off the coast of France there was no solid assurance that he had done so. (The submarine was the British boat *Seraph*, but in deference to Giraud's insistence that he ride only American craft it had been placed for this single dangerous voyage under the command of American Navy Captain Jerauld Wright.) At last had come word that he was indeed on this submarine as it approached the point of rendezvous with the seaplane which would take him to Gibraltar. Finally, a little after four o'clock in the afternoon, this seaplane had landed in the Bay of Gibraltar; and a few minutes later the six-foot-tall, ramrod-stiff French general, clad in a stained and rumpled civilian suit (he had fallen into the sea while transferring from rowboat to submarine a thousand yards off the French coast), made his appearance in Eisenhower's subterranean office.

But such relief as the American had then felt was short-lived. It had ended, in fact, in a matter of seconds, destroyed by the Frenchman's first words.

"General Giraud has arrived," said General Giraud. "General Giraud is ready to assume command of the operation."

He had meant it, too! There followed what must surely have been one of the strangest of all historic conferences. "Deep in the limestone cave—barely twenty-five miles from Cape Trafalgar, whose . . . memory still lived to deny us the French Fleet—two traditions came face to face," one of Eisenhower's biographers would later write; "two vital traditions proceeded to define themselves through opposition. It was one of those moments in which the deepest inner qualities of men are revealed, a moment profoundly symbolic insofar as those inner qualities represent national ideals. On one side of the desk sat the Frenchman, bred in the tradition of Napoleon, his will as sharp and hard and inflexible as a knife, his mind narrowly legalistic in its formulations but soaked through and through with the mysticism of 'la Gloire.' On the other side sat the American from Kansas, bred in the tradition of the Western frontier, his will subordinate to objective needs and flexible in its response to them, his mental energy focused always on the job to be done 'out there.' Giraud was inclined to confuse personal egotism and national patriotism, believing that to gain power and glory for himself was to gain power and glory for France. Eisenhower never employed 'power' and 'glory' as concepts at all. Gazing across at Giraud, trying to 'size up' a creature strange to him, he was thinking only of how this man might be used, how he might be persuaded to help us or at least prevented from hurting us. If he felt a stir of anger at having been put in so compromised a position, he quickly fought it down."[32]

In actual fact, such anger as he felt had not been directed at those (Murphy, and Murphy's colleagues) who had presented him with this weird creature as "problem." Even when Giraud produced a letter signed by Murphy which, he claimed, promised him the command, Eisenhower had not blamed the American diplomat. He had, however, mingled a large measure of pity for Giraud with the intense irritation that the Frenchman's general attitude and exorbitant demands aroused in him. Obviously Giraud was a brave man who loved France and hated Germany. He had risked his life to come here. His family remained in France where they might be seized by the Nazis as hostages if, as expected, the Germans responded to the North African operation with an occupation of all France. And he had been obviously if not deliberately (by Murphy) misinformed as to the role he was scheduled to play in forthcoming events.[33] Placed in a ridiculous, personally humiliating position, he managed to preserve more personal dignity than many could have done, though he did so by sticking adamantly to his original position through hours of reiterative argument, making things hard indeed for Eisenhower.

Patiently, the Allied commander had explained why no French general could possibly be entrusted with the office Giraud demanded. Not a single Frenchman was among the troops which at that very moment approached the landing beaches. On the contrary, if there were fighting in the initial stages of this operation, it would be because French forces chose to be our enemies. To prevent their making this choice was the great function Eisenhower hoped Giraud would perform for the Allies, for his country, and for his place in history—and indeed it was the only function he could attempt to perform at this juncture. From Gibraltar, as soon as the initial landings were under way, Giraud could announce to the world his personal and professional commitment to the enterprise; he could plead with his fellow countrymen in North Africa to rally to him, turning their arms, not against American friends, but against German enemies. Then he would be flown to North Africa to take command of the French troops who heeded his plea. The Frenchman shook his head.

"General Giraud must be given command of this operation," said General Giraud. "General Giraud cannot accept less. His countrymen would not understand his doing so and his soldier's honor would be tarnished."

And so the stubborn argument had continued, prolonged and complicated and exasperated by the fact that Giraud could speak no English and Eisenhower no French, so that every word said by each had to be translated for the other through an interpreter. There had been an interruption when Giraud was taken to dine at Government House while Eisenhower, with Clark, was a guest of the Royal Navy at the Admiralty mess. But then at 10:30 the argument had been resumed, with the Frenchman still as adamant as the solid stone which enclosed them, as stuffily chilly as the air they breathed, as ceaselessly reiterative as the water which dripped, dripped, dripped from the arched ceilings of the passageway outside the office door.

Midnight had come: off Oran and Algiers, young Allied soldiers were climbing into the boats which were to take them ashore; and still the argument continued, with Giraud still refusing to act as he was supposed to do in order to prevent needless bloodshed. Eisenhower's patience—eroded by the dripping seconds, the trickling minutes of wasted and wasting time—had worn thin, and Clark's (he as Eisenhower's deputy had alternated with his chief in the conduct of futile argument) had given way altogether. Finally, convinced that the French general was now playing an opportunistic "waiting game," a thoroughly exasperated Clark had told the interpreter (Colonel Julius C. Holmes acted in this role) to tell Giraud that "from now on your ass is out in the snow," and had stomped angrily from the room.[34]

Shortly afterward, when H-Hour for the Algerian landings (1:00 A.M Gibraltar time, Sunday, November 8) was but three-quarters of an hour away, the session at last ended on precisely the same note as it had begun. Giraud insisted that he be designated commander-in-chief, else he would be "a spectator in this affair." Eisenhower said flatly that Giraud's demand was impossible, and if the Frenchman persisted in it the campaign must proceed "exactly as if we had never met or conferred with you."[35] Whereupon the elderly Frenchman, bone-weary no doubt with the physical and psychological strains of his day, had stood up, bowed stiffly, and limped off to his bed.

Evidently he had slept well, too—much better than Eisenhower had been able to do through the dark hours of the early morning of the most important day of his life until then, for the Allied commander had had to spend the first few of those hours drafting a lengthy report to Marshall of his conversations with the difficult Frenchman, tacitly requesting from Washingon the official support of his stand which, to his relief, had been promptly received. At any rate, when Eisenhower saw Giraud again the Frenchman's disposition had been as much improved over that manifested the night before as the environment in which they now met, a warm, sunlit room of Government House, was improved over the gloomy cavern of their first encounter. Giraud in morning light, refreshed and restored, no longer demanded the supreme position: he announced himself prepared to do what Eisenhower had asked him to do—he would fly to Algiers with General Clark as soon as Algiers was secured—provided he were recognized immediately upon his arrival there as chief of both the military and civil affairs of the French in North Africa. To this a weary Eisenhower had readily agreed. Later, Eisenhower would remember that he had made this agreement contingent upon Giraud's being able to win French support, but a historian may deem it unlikely that he actually overtly did so. Why would he, with his admittedly meager knowledge of French politics, have doubted Giraud's political potency at this early stage of the game when State Department "experts" who advised him were unanimous and emphatic in their conviction that the North African French would rally to the Giraud banner from the moment it was first raised in Algiers?[36]

By that time, numerous reports—maddeningly fragmentary but generally encouraging—had come in from the Algerian landing beaches. By late afternoon a fairly complete picture of military operations there could be put together—a picture with gaps in it, and several black spots, but of an over-all hue sufficiently bright to encourage, among Allied commanders, huge sighs of relief.

At Algiers, the Eastern Task Force, covered (as was the Center Task

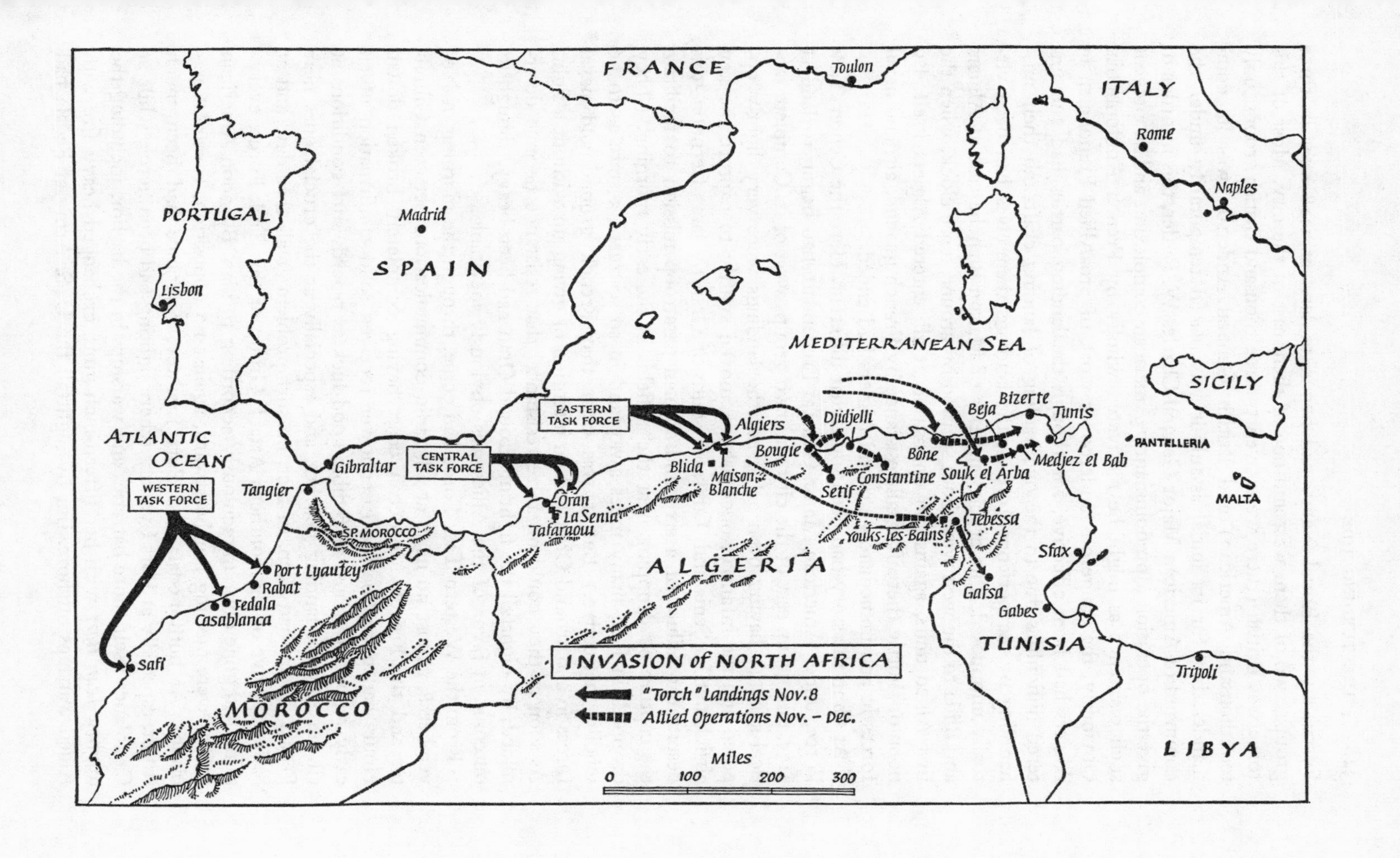
INVASION of NORTH AFRICA
"Torch" Landings Nov. 8
Allied Operations Nov. – Dec.
Miles
0
100
200
300
FRANCE
Toulon
ITALY
Rome
Naples
PORTUGAL
Lisbon
Madrid
SPAIN
MEDITERRANEAN SEA
SICILY
PANTELLERIA
MALTA
ATLANTIC
OCEAN
WESTERN
TASK FORCE
CENTRAL
TASK FORCE
EASTERN
TASK FORCE
Gibraltar
Tangier
SP. MOROCCO
Port Lyautey
Rabat
Fedala
Casablanca
Safi
MOROCCO
Oran
La Senia
Tafaraoui
Algiers
Blida
Maison Blanche
Bougie
Djidjelli
Setif
Constantine
Bône
Youks-les-Bains
Tebessa
Souk el Arba
Beja
Bizerte
Tunis
Medjez el Bab
ALGERIA
Sfax
Gafsa
Gabes
TUNISIA
Tripoli
LIBYA

Force) by the Royal Navy, had begun to land at 1:18 A.M. in three groups, two of them west and one of them east of the city. Most of this force was British (there were twenty-three thousand British troops, only ten thousand American) and British General Anderson was its commander, but for its initial assault it was placed temporarily under the command of American Major General Charles W. Ryder, this in order to give the operation a predominantly American complexion and so prevent such resistance as might be motivated wholly by French Anglophobia. Obviously, the dangerous undercover work of pro-Allied Frenchmen in Algiers had been effective, for though the landing parties had encountered difficulties due to the overloading of landing craft and their mishandling by inexperienced crews, the landings themselves had been virtually unopposed. The crucial airfields of Maison Blanche east of Algiers and Blida to the west were both secured by around ten o'clock, when the first Allied units, against no opposition at all, entered Algiers itself. By noon or shortly thereafter, all resistance by French ground, air, and naval forces in and immediately around Algiers had ended.

At Oran the story had been somewhat different. Here the Center Task Force, under American Major General Fredendall, had begun to land at 1:35, one group east of the city and two groups west of it. Complete tactical surprise having been achieved, the landings were very lightly opposed and the infantry, once ashore, moved swiftly to capture the key airfields at La Senia and Tafaraoui south of Oran by late afternoon—this despite the failure of a six hundred-man paratroop mission to facilitate the capture by dropping near the airfields in the early morning. (They dropped, in fact, many miles away and in so scattered a state as to be wholly ineffective.) But it was clear that French ground and naval forces in and around Oran had no intention of giving up without a fight. As soon as they could organize resistance, that resistance became determined; by nightfall the fighting around Oran had been heavy, though its outcome in favor of the Allies was obviously inevitable.

From the Western Task Force had come, through the morning of November 8, almost no news at all, radio communications between Gibraltar and the French Moroccan coast having completely broken down. Hours had passed before Eisenhower received solid confirmation of an early report of almost incredible good luck as regards surf conditions at all the Atlantic landing beaches, and especially at the crucial ones near Fedala. There had been, in fact, no surf problem at all that day, and at Safi, objective of the Southern Attack Group of this Task Force, everything had gone quite miraculously according to plan. By noon American troops were pushing northeastward, against no opposition, toward Casablanca. At both Fedala and Port Lyautey, resistance had been much stiffer, especially at Port Lyautey where fighting had been fierce, while at Casablanca itself shore batteries and warships in the harbor, including the mighty *Jean Bart* with her fifteen-inch guns, exchanged heavy fire with Allied warships offshore. But by nightfall the U. S. Army at Fedala had secured all the objectives of the attack plan, being in control of the town and its approaches, while at Casablanca the main battery of the *Jean Bart* had been put out of commission, shore defenses had been knocked out or severely damaged, and French air power had been reduced to ineffectuality. There could and apparently would be heavy fighting before the city was secured, but there was no doubt that it *would* be secured.

Thus, by the morning of November 10, there had emerged on the huge map of Gibraltar's war room the outline of Allied victory. To Patton at Casablanca, that morning, went a message from Eisenhower: "Algiers has been ours for two days. Oran defenses are crumbling rapidly. Only tough nut is in your hands. Crack it open quickly." Patton had replied confidently that he was doing so. To Fredendall at Oran went an urgent order, "Clean it up today," and Fredendall replied at 1:00 P.M. with the report that Oran had surrendered.[37] This meant that, by the afternoon of that day, achievement of the invasion's minimum objectives —namely, the capture of the principal ports from Casablanca to Algiers inclusive, and the initiation of action eastward toward Montgomery's westward-driving Eighth Army—had been nearly completed and wholly assured. The anxiety over the possibly total failure of the operation, with its incalculably evil effects on world affairs and its only too calculable effect upon his own career—this anxiety was removed from Eisenhower's mind.

But into its place had sprung another, an anxiety that concerned, not the failure of the operation but, rather, the proportions of its possible success. At its core was the torment of Tantalus. Before Eisenhower's eyes, dangling just beyond his reach, were the fruits of an enormous triumph. It began to appear that, if French civil and military authorities would support or at least not obstruct the operation, its maximum objectives might after all be achieved. He might then extend his reach eastward rapidly enough and strongly enough to grasp Bizerte, Tunis, Sousse, Sfax—all of Tunisia, and all for virtually nothing. Rommel, denied his only dependable ports of supply, would be hopelessly trapped with his Afrika Korps between converging Allied forces. The way would be open for immediate attack on Sicily, employing troops that would otherwise have to be used for North African reinforcement; there was even a remote possibility that Italy would be knocked out of the war. Time, however, was of the essence of this possible victory. In the afternoon of November 9 the Germans began to bring troops into Tunisia by air, and they were building up there as rapidly as possible. Days, hours, even minutes counted heavily against the Allies—and in Algiers they were being used up, wasted in a continuing, complicated, exasperating political wrangle. . . .

Let us review it, not from the viewpoint of Eisenhower in Gibraltar, but from our own of a later time.

Shortly after Eisenhower reached his agreement with Giraud on the morning of November 8, a surprising message came from Algiers. Admiral Darlan was there! He had come, it was said, to visit his son, who lay desperately ill with infantile paralysis in an Algiers villa. Was this a piece of great good fortune for the Allies? Or did it merely complicate the political situation by initiating a competition for power between Darlan and Giraud? Such questions were sharpened in Gibraltar when, later that day, the armistice terms for Algiers came through: Eisenhower noticed they were "approved" by Darlan. Nevertheless he continued to regard Giraud as the man most likely to rally the French to the Allied cause; he did so even after it was clear that Giraud's radio broadcast appeal for a cease-fire had been without effect.

His disillusionment was swift, his disappointment bitter.

For within an hour after Giraud, flown from Gibraltar, landed in Algiers on the morning of November 9, he went into hiding to avoid arrest as a traitor! Marshal Pétain's reply to Roosevelt's personal plea for cooperation with the Allies had been: "France and her honor are at stake. We are attacked; we shall defend ourselves; this is the order I am giving." And it was Pétain who was being obeyed. Soldiers, sailors, and officeholders would take their orders, initially, only from the marshal or one of the marshal's designated representatives; they were bound to regard all who aided the Allied landings as enemies of the State.

The key figure in French North Africa, it now appeared, was Admiral Darlan. With him, on November 8, Murphy had conducted negotiations leading to a cease-fire order; when that order was signed by Darlan and issued, fighting in Algiers ceased; and Murphy seems to have had no slightest doubt that the former event caused the latter.§ Others (not Clark, not Eisenhower) were less certain of the admiral's efficacy in this matter. They saw significance in the fact that (a) Darlan did not sign until late in the morning, when Allied troops were in the streets and the city was obviously already in Allied hands, and (b) the order had no effect on any other battleground in Algeria or Morocco. It seemed to them that the admiral, who had long lived by wits uninhibited by principle, merely demonstrated here his remarkable talent for accommodating himself to a *fait accompli* in such a way and at such a time as would give him credit for determining the event.

Clark, delayed in Gibraltar by bad flying weather for some hours after Giraud's departure, landed in Algiers at five o'clock in the afternoon of November 9, just as the port was undergoing its first German air raid—and he missed death by an uncomfortably narrow margin when one of the Junkers 88's, struck by anti-aircraft fire, plummeted directly toward the Bren-gun carrier in which he was riding from the airfield. Exploding when it was within a thousand feet of the ground, it rained a lethal debris all around him.[38] The experience added urgency to Clark's sense of the importance of a quick dash in maximum possible strength toward

§ He certainly remembered no such doubt when he wrote his *Diplomat Among Warriors* (New York: 1964), pp. 138–39.

the Tunisian air base from which these bombers had come; it proportionately reduced his slender patience with the political quarrels and finagling in which he found himself at once involved. We had bet on the wrong horse, he was quickly convinced: Giraud at this juncture was worth nothing to us. Accordingly he called for a meeting with Darlan, General Alphonse Juin, who commanded French ground forces, Admiral Raymond Fenard, who was top commander of French naval units, and other ranking French officers on the morning of November 10.

With Murphy at his right hand and Darlan at his left, Clark opened this meeting at ten o'clock with a demand for an armistice covering all French North Africa. He fixed his fierce eagle-gaze on Darlan as he did so. He saw a plump, bald, pale-eyed little man who "seemed to cower even when things were peaceful" and whose first words insured that things at this meeting, given Clark's notoriously short temper, would be far from peaceful.[39] Replying to Clark's demand, Darlan said with an oily, apologetic smile that he had sent a message to Pétain in Vichy asking for instructions but so far had received none; therefore he was powerless to do as Clark asked. Pointedly, heatedly, the American reminded the Frenchman that diplomatic relations between Washington and Vichy had been broken off following Pétain's order to resist and that the present negotiations were being conducted, not with Vichy, but with the North African French. Darlan shook his head: he was sorry, he wanted hostilities to cease, but he could not order them to do so on his own authority; he must be authorized by Pétain and such authorization could not come until that afternoon when the Council of Ministers met in Vichy. Clark brought his fist down upon the table. If Darlan would not issue the order he, Clark, would "end this conference in thirty minutes," place the admiral in "protective custody," and "go to General Giraud" who would "sign the terms and issue the necessary" order. Darlan smiled his suave, apologetic smile. Giraud might do so, said he, but Giraud would not be obeyed. "This will only mean the loss of more time and there will be more fighting," said the admiral, regretfully. Whereupon Clark pounded the table again. Finally, when the hands of the clock on the conference room wall were coming together at high noon, Darlan asked for "five minutes with my staff for discussion." Clark granted the request with the understanding "that no one is to leave here or to communicate with anyone outside."

Consider the actual battle situation at this time.

Algiers had been in Allied hands for more than forty-eight hours. At Oran, General Boisson and Admiral Rioult, respectively commanding French Army and Navy forces, had accepted the terms of a provisional armistice, were issuing a cease-fire order, and would within fifteen minutes meet with Fredendall to negotiate the formal terms of surrender. At Port Lyautey all major resistance had been overcome, though sporadic fighting (sniping) continued. At Casablanca, Patton's forces drove toward the southeastern edge of the city while an all-out offensive, its success as certain as the sunrise, was being prepared for dawn tomorrow, November 11.

And what of French Tunisia, the decisive strategic ground?

Here military and civilian authorities continued to vacillate, playing both ends against the middle in ways far more helpful to the Axis than to the Allies. For example, full use of the ports of Tunis and Bizerte had been denied the Axis by sinking vessels in the harbor approaches, but the measures were not of such a nature as to make a full opening of these ports either difficult or time-consuming; Italian engineers were already at work on the clearance job and Italian troop transports would, in a day or so, sail unhindered into the ports. General Barre with his French Tunisian Division could easily have overwhelmed the German contingents being flown into the area he "defended." Instead he remained passive, doing nothing effectively to obstruct the German troop buildup, and this despite the fact that he personally was pro-Ally in sentiment. Admiral Jean Esteva, Resident Governor General of Tunisia, pro-Nazi in sentiment, was so confusedly indecisive that he spread a vast confusion through the area of his administration; he appeared unable to handle the simplest details of matters requiring his attention.

One may be sure that Darlan was sufficiently well informed concerning this general situation to weigh its main factors in his scheming brain as he retired for private talk with his staff. It was certainly clear to him—though not to Clark nor, evidently, Murphy—that no order issued by him from Algiers would be likely to have the slightest effect in Tunisia. This left Casablanca as the only spot in North Africa where his order might appear to decide events, *provided* he could manage to issue that order not a moment too soon nor too late.

And in his calculation of the precise right moment he was aided by his personal knowledge of Auguste Noguès, the French Resident General of Morocco, who had been charged by Darlan himself, late in the afternoon of November 8, with control of French operations in western Algeria as well as Morocco. (The order had been confirmed by Vichy next day.) Noguès was a man whose value-system and reaction-pattern were not unlike Darlan's own. He had no aversion toward buying what he called "honor" (meaning his own advantage) with the blood and agony of men under his command, or of civilians under his "protection." He would resist long enough to be able to say to Vichy and Berlin, should the Axis win the war, that he had capitulated only when further resistance was obviously futile; he would *not* resist so long as to incur perpetual enmity from Allied commanders whose troops were sacrificed to his personal interest and who could, if they chose, treat him as a prisoner of war. In other words, Noguès would wait until the very last moment before the final crushing attack was launched and would then make such terms with the inevitable as would be most advantageous to himself.

When Darlan returned to the conference table he placed before Clark an "order" which said merely that further battle was futile and that he (Darlan) wished to inform Marshal Pétain that, because of the fighting, France would probably lose North Africa. Would this do? the admiral asked, all innocence. Clark exploded. Of course it wouldn't do, he said angrily, using his fist again upon the table. The paper was meaningless. Whereupon Darlan, obviously convinced that his tactics of total evasiveness had reached the point of diminishing returns, drew a sheet of paper toward him and began to write, asking questions as he did so. At last he placed in Clark's hand the specific order the latter had been demanding and now, with slight changes, accepted, subject to Eisenhower's review and possible revision.

Thus was initiated what the world soon knew as the "Darlan deal." Its organic document, this order Darlan had written out in his own hand, contained four main provisions: (1) "Engagements having been fulfilled and bloody battle becoming useless, the order is given to all the land, sea, and air forces in North Africa to cease the fight against the forces of America and her allies (the last three words were inserted at Clark's insistence) as upon the receipt of this order and to return to their barracks and observe strictest neutrality"; (2) the French commanders were ordered to "put themselves in liaison with local American commanders on the subject of terms for the suspension of hostilities"; (3) it was announced that Darlan had assumed authority over French North Africa "in the name of the marshal" and that "the present senior officers retain their commands, and the political and administrative organizations remain in force" unless or until (this reservation was at Clark's insistence) a "fresh order" on the matter came from Algiers; (4) all prisoners were to be exchanged.[40]

Point 3 of this order was of course the crux of the "deal." A storm of protest and bitter controversy was bound to center upon it—a storm whose proportions would be far beyond any Clark anticipated that day and whose essential nature (its moral and ideological base) he would perhaps never fully understand.[41] Point 3 meant that the Frenchmen who had actively aided the Allies must remain in disgrace and actual danger of their lives *because* they had aided us. No sooner had Clark accepted Darlan's order than the admiral insisted that Mast and the others who had facilitated the Algiers landings must be deprived of French command. "It is to your interest to agree that I can't tolerate these men not obeying my orders," said he threatfully. And one of his colleagues promptly added, "You had better put them in a safe place. They are bitterly resented." In Morocco, General Emile-Marie Bethouart, who had been of immense aid to the American landings, had been imprisoned by Noguès and faced a court-martial which would sentence him to death if the Americans did not (as in fact they did, belatedly) intervene. Point 3 also meant the perpetuation in North Africa for an indefinite time of Vichy laws, Vichy officialdom, and Vichy institutions. Among the laws were those denying human rights to Jews, suppressing freedom of speech and the press, and denying freedom of assembly and movement. Among the officials were the brutal police required to implement such inequities. Among the institutions were concentration camps on the Nazi model where brave and honorable men were continuously humiliated, often tortured, and sometimes killed.

Moreover, Clark's acceptance of these terms failed to buy him even a temporary relief from political troubles. After the cease-fire order had gone out but before there was any evidence it would be obeyed in Morocco, Pétain in Vichy announced by radio that Darlan had been removed as head of the French armed forces and replaced by General Noguès. "In view of this I shall have to revoke my order," said Darlan to Clark. Instead Clark placed Darlan under house arrest, ordering a platoon of Americans to surround Admiral Fenard's villa where Darlan was staying and to prevent any communication between him and the outside. Giraud now came forward with a demand that Eisenhower's promises to him in Gibraltar be fulfilled: he wanted to be named "Commander-in-Chief of all French Forces in North Africa or any place in the French Empire." Instead Clark attempted to bring about a working agreement between Darlan and Giraud, but with no notable success.

"I now have two Kingpins," he cabled Eisenhower rather plaintively early that afternoon, "but hope to wiggle out of it somehow. I deemed it of the utmost importance to do anything to secure an order that would be obeyed to cease hostilities."[42]

But was it being obeyed? There was no sign that it was or would be at Casablanca, when Clark went to bed that night. Patton was completing preparations to attack the city at 7:30 next morning with naval fire, air bombardment, and infantry assault. On the other hand, applicable portions of it were evidently being obeyed in areas where the fighting had already ceased, and this despite messages addressed to individual commanders by Pétain specifically contradicting Darlan's order. Clark interpreted this to mean that "in an out-and-out trial of strength with Pétain, Darlan had prevailed." This "convinced [him] . . . all the more that Darlan would have to be our man for the present."[43] And the conviction would be sustained when he learned that Casablanca had indeed surrendered, a cease-fire agreement having been reached just before Patton's all-out attack was about to be launched. (It was a near thing there. American battleships were positioned for firing, American planes were actually over their targets, when Patton received the French commander's request for an armistice.)

This event was not yet known to Clark, however, when he breakfasted on the morning of November 11. Communications between Algiers and Morocco were very bad and, according to his own later account, he believed "some fighting" yet continued in Casablanca as late as the evening of the following day. What he did know at breakfast time was that the expected move of the Nazis into southern France had begun. German troops had begun to march into hitherto unoccupied France the night before and this movement continued apace, unresisted by Vichyites whose concern for national "honor" had required them to order battle against the Americans. Great possibilities for good or evil to the Allied cause were thus opened up, and Clark's concern over them caused him to hasten at once to Fenard's villa. There, pointing to the fact that Vichy France was rapidly ceasing to exist, he presented Darlan with two demands: first, that the admiral order the French Fleet at Toulon to sail for North Africa; second, that he order Esteva in Tunisia to resist the German buildup in his province. When Darlan refused to issue either order, Clark stormed from the house in such fury that the admiral, who well knew how completely he was in the American's power, soon had second thoughts. After lunch he asked to see Clark again and, this time, agreed to do as Clark wished. Even then, however, he did not issue an order to the Toulon fleet commander but merely an "invitation." He *did* by telephone, under direct pressure from Clark, order Esteva to resist the Germans in Tunisia.

A few hours later, though neither the invitation nor the order had produced the slightest perceptible effect, Clark decided to remove the guard from around Fenard's residence, restoring freedom of movement and communication to Darlan. The admiral and Juin employed this freedom to revoke the order to Esteva while Clark slept (literally and figuratively) through the night of November 11–12. Whereupon Clark, roused from his bed at five o'clock in the morning to learn of the revocation, summoned the French admiral and general to his presence and threatened them with a firing squad for treachery if they did not at once reinstate the order of the day before.[44] Of course the order was reinstated, and equally of course it had no effect in Tunisia.

Obvious to hindsight—and, indeed, equally obvious to honest and knowledgeable observers at the time—was an absurd discrepancy between the facts of North African politics and the fictions by which Clark continued to guide his acts and policies. Darlan was in fact his captive. At any point he could have put his captive under lock and key, held him incommunicado, and issued whatever orders he pleased in his captive's name to Tunis, Oran, Port Lyautey, Rabat, Casablanca. Only when he threatened to use force did he obtain any "cooperation" at all from the oily admiral. Yet even when he caught Juin and Darlan in an outright piece of treachery which might (and did, to the extent of its effectiveness) cost the lives of Allied soldiers moving that day toward Tunisia, he persisted in treating with them as if their political effectiveness were a match for his own military might, as if they meant what they said when they proclaimed their eagerness to fight the Germans, and as if he had no alternative choice.

And where was Robert Murphy, the State Department's local political "expert," while all this was going on? He was, as people say, "around." He remained, however, curiously passive, as if he were either stunned by the failure of events to move in the direction he had planned or (on the whole) were content to have them move as they did in the direction of the political Right. He now asserted that the "problem" was no longer "political" but "military" and must therefore be solved by the Allied commanders on the basis of military "necessity"—in other words, in local and immediate terms without regard to worldwide or long-range effects. He was present at every decisive meeting in Algiers, but if he gave advice to Clark which would enable the American general to anticipate Darlan's words and acts—or Juin's, or Noguès'—and to handle these men in ways beneficial to Allied long-term interests there is no clear record of it and neither Clark nor Eisenhower, in the memoirs they were later to publish, would recall it. (They *would* recall that, in Eisenhower's words, "we had our written orders from our governments to cooperate with any French government we should find existing at the moment of our entry into Africa."[45] These, however, were not truly "orders" in the strict military sense. They were instead elements of a State Department paper issued as a guide to policy at a time when it was hoped the North African French would welcome the Allies or at least not resist them; they did not deny Eisenhower the freedom to make such political arrangements as seemed to him necessary in whatever circumstances he encountered.)

The meeting in which the ultimate terms of the "Darlan deal" were tentatively decided upon was held in the afternoon of November 12 immediately following the arrival in Algiers of Noguès. The general from Morocco came with the evident intention of assuming the top spot in North African affairs by virtue of Pétain's vesting in him the power and office formerly vested in Darlan. Clark would have none of this. He refused to "recognize" the authority of either Pétain or Noguès and, in consequence, would not deal with Noguès privately, as Noguès demanded, prior to the general meeting. At the same time Darlan, Noguès, and their colleagues would have no truck with Giraud who, to begin with, was excluded from the meeting. The stormy session which followed was opened by Clark with the bleak announcement that if those assembled did not arrive at a working agreement acceptable to him by the time the meeting ended, they would all be locked up in a warship in the harbor. He then suggested that Darlan assume the top political office for the time being; that the present governors general of Morocco (Noguès), Algeria (Yves Chatel), and Tunisia (Esteva) be retained in office; and that Giraud be appointed to raise a volunteer army to fight against the Axis—an army that would be armed and otherwise equipped by the United States. There followed an hour's fruitless wrangling. Then Clark insisted that Giraud be called in and that Noguès and Darlan shake hands with Giraud. (The American placed, in the circumstances, a quite remarkable faith in the practical efficacy of "shaking hands.") Shortly afterward Clark left them "to battle it out with themselves." When he returned he found that they were inclined—as well they might be!—to accept his suggestion; they asked only that a final decision be postponed until tomorrow.[46]

Meanwhile Eisenhower in Gibraltar had taken bold decisions. On November 11 he had ordered General Anderson and his British First Army to drive eastward at maximum speed by land and sea, supported in the Mediterranean by Cunningham's naval forces, despite uncertainty concerning the attitudes of French soldiers and civilians in the areas through which Anderson must move. He had also ordered American troops eastward from Oran, despite uncertainty concerning the attitude of Franco, who might yet (conceivably) open Spain and Spanish Morocco to German air and land forces, and despite the fact that the military situation in French Morocco remained obscure to him. (He counted on Patton, who was too far away to participate in the drive toward Tunis, to guard Spanish Morocco.) By the night of November 12 the main ports of eastern Algeria, including Bône, had been or were being occupied, as were the inland towns of Sétif and Constantine. The forces which had accomplished this were vulnerable to flanking attacks from their right and to a severance of the long communications at their rear should the French troops in the area become actively hostile. Naturally the possibility was acutely worrisome to Eisenhower; he was prone to do whatever was necessary, politically, to prevent it.

It was on the following morning, Friday the thirteenth, that he came with Admiral Cunningham to Algiers. He was met at the Maison Blanche Airport by Clark, who told him that the final decision-making conference had been in session for some time and who, with Murphy, brought him up to date on developments. Murphy repeated once again what he had repeatedly said to Clark: "The whole matter has now become a military one. You will have to give the answer."

Of course Eisenhower's answer was by then already prepared, already virtually given, and largely by forces outside his control. Roosevelt had insisted that De Gaulle and the Free French be excluded from the operation. The State Department had advised the military to cooperate with "existing" governments in North Africa. Murphy in an October "Colonel McGowan" message had suggested that Darlan might "play ball." Everyone said that French Army and Navy professionals demanded a "legitimate succession of authority" which could be achieved only by a top official who might plausibly claim to derive his power from Pétain. Noguès was now willing publicly to transfer back to Darlan the power Pétain had "temporarily" transferred to him during the period of Darlan's "confinement." And by all these things it was determined that Eisenhower's answer must be to endorse without modification the agreement finally reached by the French shortly after the lunch hour this day.

He took no part in the discussions that led to this agreement. He remained deliberately aloof; Clark called him into the conference room only after all was settled. He shook hands with everyone, permitted photographs to be taken of him with Darlan and the others, and approved the proclamation Darlan was to make later that day of his resumed "responsibility for French interests in North Africa." ("I have the approval of the American authorities, with whom I intend to guarantee the defense of North Africa," said Darlan's proclamation, in part. "Every governor or resident has to remain in his place, and is to take care of the administration of his territory according to the laws in force, as in the past. Frenchmen and Moslems, I rely on your complete discipline. . . . Long live the marshal! Long live France!") He, Eisenhower, then flew back from the warm sunlight of Africa into the wet, chilly gloom of Gibraltar.[47]

iv. *The Waters of Time*

So again we see him on the morning of November 14, a Saturday, as he comes at a trot to the door of his dungeon cell of an office and, entering, finds piled upon his narrow desk messages from Washington, from London, whose tone and urgency surprise him. Nothing in the response made by Churchill or by his own staff advisers to the plan he prepared in October for making use of Darlan, should Darlan become usable, has prepared him for the storm of opposition to the admiral which (judging from the tone of the messages) is rising in the British and American capitals.

To answer these messages becomes his first order of business and he senses that the future of his authority, the whole of his career, may turn upon the quality of his answer. He must persuade. He must convince. And though he has an immense and justified confidence in his abilities to do this in any situation he is given pause by the novelty of the present circumstances and the size of the stakes for which he plays. He sits pen in hand, poised over blank paper, while water drips ceaselessly upon the passage floor outside and (the sound of it) upon his taut nerves.[48] He suffers a Chinese water torture in the chill depths of the Rock, his thoughts all scattered for the moment by unexpected anxieties, until with an effort he brings his mind to a focus and begins to write out in his tight, small script the main points of the argument he will soon develop into a long radio message to Marshall.

Let us look at them in their rough form:

"Completely understand bewilderment in London, Washington over turn negotiations have taken. Existing French sentiment does not remotely agree with prior calculations. . . . Pétain's name something to conjure with here and all French agree Darlan only man with obvious right to Marshal's mantle in North Africa. Noguès stopped Morocco fighting by Darlan's order. Cannot escape recognition of this. . . . Without strong French government, Patton says would take 60,000 Allied troops just to keep Moroccan tribes pacified. Think of how tribal disturbances might affect Spain! . . . Gist of agreement: French will do what they can to help us take Tunisia; selected forces will be organized for war under Giraud; every effort will be made to get Toulon fleet; we will support Darlan in controlling, pacifying country. . . ."[49]

Note how this argument, grounded altogether in military expediency, rests upon four main points of which three seem obviously invalid and the fourth, to say the least, highly questionable.

Noguès stopped fighting because Darlan ordered him to? He will never say so: on the contrary he will tell a reporter weeks later—a very astute reporter, who knows how to ask the right questions—that the decision to surrender Casablanca was reached long before the Darlan order was received. "On Monday [November 9] I called Wuledth, the German representative, and asked him whether in his opinion we had any possibility of resisting," Noguès will say to William Stoneman of the Chicago *Daily News* in early February. "He replied that we had fought well but that our position was hopeless. 'Now you see,' I told him, 'what you have done by taking our weapons away. It is entirely your fault.'"[50] It appears from this that the military situation and a Nazi official's opinion were what determined the surrender, which was decided upon some thirty-six hours before the Darlan order was received, and that the wily, ruthless French general continued the hopeless fight until just before seven Wednesday morning, as Darlan would have done, in order to maintain himself in a "safe" position if the Germans at last won the war. And indeed by the time the Moroccan general had received the admiral's "order," Darlan had no authority that Noguès could recognize. By then the general had been notified of Pétain's repudiation of Darlan and the appointment of Noguès himself in Darlan's place as French North Africa's supreme authority. That he accepted this, the Vichy order repudiating Darlan, is evidenced by the fact that he showed up in Algiers on November 12 determined to exercise his Pétain-bestowed office and was deterred only by Clark's refusal to recognize him.

Esteva will obey Darlan's order to resist the Germans and aid the Allies in Tunisia? There is no sign of it as Eisenhower writes his message to Marshall, nor even any evidence that Esteva has made such promise as Eisenhower mentions. Whence did the Americans derive such dubious information? No doubt from Darlan himself, directly or indirectly. At any rate, while Eisenhower writes and the British First Army pushes across the Tunisian border, the governor in Tunis is doing the precise opposite of what Eisenhower says he will do: he assists the Germans and prepares resistance to the Allies, and will continue along these lines, frustrating so far as he can Barre's belated battle against Nazi invaders, in obedience to what is at first a Vichy order and later (all camouflage stripped away) a naked command from Der Fuehrer. He is committed to a path which will lead him ultimately into a court of law where he will be convicted of treason to France.[51]

The deal with Darlan will help the Allies to obtain the Toulon Fleet? Eisenhower's belief that it may is as futile and almost as ludicrous as the fervent prayer Clark will make tomorrow, Sunday, in Algiers' Holy

Trinity Church. "Oh, God, let me get the fleet from Darlan," Clark will pray; "let me get the fleet from Darlan; oh, God—!"[52] The Fleet remains in Toulon. It will remain there, making no slightest effort to get away, until the morning of November 27 when the Germans move in to occupy the port. Then this powerful force, so badly needed by the Allies, will commit what De Gaulle calls "the most pitiful and sterile suicide imaginable,"[53] blowing up under stupendous clouds of flame-shot smoke no fewer than three battleships, eight cruisers, seventeen destroyers, sixteen torpedo boats, sixteen submarines, seven dispatch vessels, three patrol boats, sixty-odd transport vessels, tankers, minesweepers, and tugs.

Darlan's political authority is indispensable to the maintenance of law and order in North Africa? Let us admit that this "law and order" depends to a large degree upon the attitude of the French Army in North Africa. Let us admit also that these professional soldiers are greatly if not primarily concerned at this point with their pay and pension rights and are therefore anxious to maintain a "legitimate" continuity of authority across the gap which now opens between Vichy France and whatever French state may succeed it. Surely these admissions do not argue the necessity for a deal with Darlan! What "legitimacy" does he retain from the past, after all, who has been explicitly repudiated by Pétain? And how can he of himself alone guarantee any kind of future? Consider the alternative choices, the only choices, which are now open to French soldiers. They may join the Allies, whereupon their pay will continue and they will remain free men; *or* they may refuse to join, whereupon their pay will stop and they may be locked up in war-prisoner stockades. Darlan, regarded from this point of view, has precisely as much political power as the Allied command chooses to bestow upon him—no more, no less.

And what of those over whom "law and order" is to be maintained? Many if not most of the press correspondents in Algiers agree with John MacVane, one of the most knowledgeable of them, when he says that "whomever the Americans and British want to name as boss of North Africa will have the support of the majority of North Africans—whether he be De Gaulle or an insignificant member of the Blida town council."[54] It is obviously De Gaulle, however, who is favored by the great majority of those whom the Allies now "liberate" into Darlan's hands. Eisenhower himself will soon be forced to recognize that, though "local antagonism in the French Army and in all echelons of government against De Gaulle" is intense, De Gaulle enjoys "a distinct popularity with the civilians."[55] A *distinct* popularity? It is in fact overwhelming, not only with civilians but also among enlisted men and lower officers of the Army, and it will, as a growing political force, overwhelm every governmental arrangement that does not take account of it. . . .

Charles de Gaulle! Here truly is a name "to conjure with" in North Africa—and not only there—for what is here named is a rare combine of living man and increasingly potent symbol. Tall, austere, arrogant, aloof, unsmiling, though not without a certain wry deep humor—likening himself in history to Joan of Arc (his Cross of Lorraine is among "the heaviest" Churchill has had to bear, says a Churchillian whisper heard around the world), likened by others in appearance to a collie dog (his face seems absurdly small and narrow in relation to his body)—he is a creature so different from Eisenhower in every essential respect that the ceremonial handshake of the two at Bastille Day exercises in London last July 14 came very near being laughable, insofar as the essence of humor is a juxtaposition of incongruities. By then it had been already established by State Department policy that these two would be estranged from one another in their public lives, but De Gaulle would have been and must forever remain strange to Eisenhower in any case. What moves the one is without meaning to the other. They might have come from different planets.

Americans and British, though more Americans than British, find it easy to laugh at him, at this Charles de Gaulle who is so touchy, so massively egotistical, so monumentally self-righteous, so utterly incapable (it seems) of laughing at himself. Do his bowels move as another man's do? Do his armpits stink as any man's might after physical exertion? Is it conceivable that he might be led by unleashed lust into the wrong bed? His attitude seems to answer such questions in a flat negative, and is thereby annoying, irritating to ordinary fallible mortals. His insistence upon being "above and beyond," his person the very Spirit of France, is to many eyes ridiculous. But it is to be noted that the initially easy laughter at him tends to become after awhile *un*easy, becomes a trifle shamefaced, as if it felt itself to be a betrayal, at least of a certain triviality of soul, on the part of him who laughs. It is as if the laughing one suddenly recognized in his laughter a lamentable rejection of greatness. And at the point where laughter ends, hatred often begins. Many there are who find this man to be literally bristling with accusing fingers thrust toward the sorest spots of their egoes, and they flinch away from him even as they long to cut him down to size, to lay him low and trample him into the mire of contempt. This is the way Pétain feels about him, yes, and Laval, Darlan, Noguès, Yves Chatel, Lemaigre-Dubreuil, and every other Frenchman who has made personal profit of one kind or another out of accommodating himself to Nazi-Fascism. Alas, this is the way Cordell Hull feels about him too (why? one wonders; why, at any rate, so vehemently?), along with every aristocratic-minded career diplomat in the State Department who has actively favored—sometimes unwittingly, always covertly—the kind of Catholic-flavored fascism that Franco and, to some extent, Mussolini have espoused. Is Robert D. Murphy to be numbered among these?

But others there are, millions of others, who come near to taking De Gaulle at his own apparent self-valuation, believing he has come close to earning this with deeds. Or, to be more specific, by example—for surely there have been in all history few greater demonstrations of the *force* of example. He came "naked and alone" into exile,[56] possessing nothing in 1940 save himself, his own ideal commitments, his own uncompromising will, his own profound if narrowly focused intelligence, yet has become the center and leader of a great historic movement. How did it happen? In somewhat the same way as particles of dust, according to scientists, become nuclei of water-molecule clusters in the atmosphere, ultimately precipitating rain out of humid skies. He is, so to speak, a burst of silver iodide particles into a gathered cloud, triggering a downpour. "We are the core of national unity," he has said (and just three days ago, on November 11, in London's Albert Hall), "we are the France that fights." The "cement" of this "unity," he has also said, "is the blood of Frenchmen who have never recognized the armistice. . . ."[57]

Thus the millions who follow him see him as not only the personification of "the France that fights" but also as the possessor of a quality lacking in most of the political leaders of his time, the quality of moral grandeur. There is nothing cheap about him. With the latter-day Wendell Willkie, lonely among the major figures of the West, he shares an unyielding conviction that the politics of true realism must be a politics of morality. Churchill said to De Gaulle not so long ago (at a luncheon in Cairo it was, last August 7), "My conscience is a good girl, I can always come to terms with her"—a remark sufficiently shocking to the Frenchman, and regarded by him as despicable, being so utterly at variance with his own vital attitudes.[58] He, as the Joan of Arc of the 1940s, is ruled by conscience. He has a clear conception of moral ideas as major determinants of history. And if this conception is from Willkie's point of view sadly limited—De Gaulle's central commitment is not to mankind, not to One World, but to a mystically conceived French national sovereignty—it is perfectly sound as far as it goes and, thus far, strong as steel. It is in fact bringing him and Willkie into a communion of adamant hostility to the "Darlan deal" at this very moment when Eisenhower, in his dank cavern, dictates from notes his explanatory apology to Washington.

Vain has been the effort of Churchill and Anthony Eden to arrange an agreement between De Gaulle and the new "high commissioner" of French Africa. On TORCH's D-Day—despite snubs from the American Government, despite circumstances deliberately designed to humiliate him personally and emasculate him politically—the Free French leader agreed to accept Giraud's command and broadcast an eloquent appeal "to the leaders, soldiers, sailors, airmen, officials and French *colons* of North Africa" to "rise up and help our allies, join them without reservations" and without worry "about names or formulas." But he refuses to regard Darlan as a mere "name" (else Goering or Goebbels or Himmler be also so regarded) or the arrangement with Darlan as a mere "formula" (else negotiations whereby Nazis are maintained in power by Allied arms may [later] be also so regarded). Two days past, which was the day before Eisenhower's flying trip to Algiers, he made his refusal formally and flatly to both the British and American Governments, and two days from now, on Monday, November 16, he will refuse again in a memorable conference with Churchill and Eden who then reveal to him, if only tacitly, the personal embarrassment they feel over their enforced acceptance of American policy. His words on this occasion will be well worth our heeding. "You invoke strategic reasons [for the arrangement with Darlan], but it is a strategic error to place oneself in a situation contradictory to the moral character of this war," he will declaim. "We are no longer in . . . the Italian Renaissance when one hired the myrmidons of Milan or the mercenaries of Florence. In any case we do not put them at the head of a liberated people afterwards. Today we make war with our own blood and souls and the suffering of nations." He will then show the Prime Minister and Foreign Secretary a sheaf of messages from France, accumulated over the bitter weekend, revealing the stupefaction and outrage of French popular opinion. "Think of the risks you may be running!" he will cry. "If France one day discovers that because of the British and Americans her liberation consists of Darlan, you can perhaps win the war from a military point of view but you will lose it morally, and ultimately there will be only one victor: Stalin."[59]

Which, save for the recognition of Stalin as a threat, is precisely the view of Wendell Willkie also. In New York that same Monday, Willkie —having put the finishing touches on the manuscript of an address he is to give at a *Herald Tribune* current affairs forum, his climax a ringing denunciation of the Darlan agreement couched in the same moral terms as De Gaulle employs—will receive from Washington an urgent phone call just forty-five minutes before his speech is to begin. The Secretary of War, concerned to protect the Army against politicians who (as Eisenhower puts it) "do not understand the harsh realities of war," has assembled at that moment in the Stimson home several important members of the Administration who "do not understand" and must therefore learn from Stimson to regard what has happened as no betrayal of fundamental principle but, instead, a wholly military expedient, justified on the ground that it saves time and lives. Perhaps it is from one of those assembled that he, Stimson, gets wind of what Willkie proposes to say. At any rate, it is Stimson who phones to urge Willkie as a patriot to delete from his speech all criticism of the Darlan arrangement. "I told him flatly," Stimson will later recall, "that, if he criticized . . . at this juncture, he would run the risk of jeopardizing the success of the United States Army in North Africa."[60] The speech, if not changed, declares Stimson, might cost sixty thousand American lives! Where, one wonders, did Stimson derive this figure? Was it from the Eisenhower message of November 14 wherein Patton is quoted as saying that sixty thousand Allied troops might be required to maintain peace among the Moroccan tribes unless Darlan-Noguès retained power there?

"I can't believe that," Willkie will reply, "but I guess I can't risk it either."[61]

And makes the deletion Stimson calls for.

Nevertheless transmission of this speech abroad is held up by official censorship for twelve hours. Is this censorship military, or political? A fuming Willkie will have cause to wonder when, before those twelve hours are up, the President of the United States releases his own explanation of the Darlan deal, pulling the fangs of Willkie's criticism by saying, "I thoroughly understand and approve the feeling in the United States and Great Britain and among all the other United Nations that in view of the history of the past two years no permanent agreement should be made with Admiral Darlan." Roosevelt will stress again and again that he has "accepted General Eisenhower's political arrangements" only "for the time being" as a temporary expedient, "justified solely by the stress of battle," applying "without exception, to the current situation only."[62] It is an explanation which will cause Darlan to complain that he is "only a lemon which the Americans will drop after they have squeezed it dry"[63] and cause others to wonder how the American Government dare issue it if Darlan indeed possesses the power to frustrate and delay the operation, or to encourage and advance it, which he is alleged to possess and in the absence of which there is no reason whatever for dealing with him. (One is reminded of the statement of the Cretan who said, "No Cretan ever speaks the truth"—a statement which, if true, must for that very reason, in the circumstances, be false.)

At any rate, the oil thus poured on troubled waters will not quiet them, nor Willkie's voice again be muffled by pillows of "patriotism." The storm-lashed waters will wash higher and higher against the dam which would keep them from their natural course, and Willkie's voice (others joining, a veritable chorus of protest) will boom as thunder across them . . .

Until the dam breaks.

This—or at any rate the first wide fissure of it—will occur on Christmas Eve, some six weeks ahead of the morning when Eisenhower dictates, from longhand notes, to a round-faced warrant officer. What the commanding officer feels and hears in the Gibraltar cave is clock time measured out as drops of water that fall (one drop, one second) in steady ceaseless beat upon the outer passageway—the kind of time that can be traded for space and counted upon to lie still as desert space while it is used up at a perfectly predictable rate—the kind some call money because it must be gained or lost, bought or sold—the kind that Roosevelt, influenced by the Eisenhower message, will describe in his forthcoming statement as a "military objective." Far different will be the Time that Eisenhower feels and hears this coming Christmas Eve! It will then be the liquid flowing Time of current history, that a man must swim or drown in—no ticking, dripping abstraction but a substantial flood—variously thick with things-changing, variously heavy with consequence and responsibility, variously erosive in its action upon all that is—pouring out of a night sky upon the roof and against the windows of a farmhouse at Souk el Khemis, yes, and through his very soul. All day long he will have journeyed at petty pace across the Tunisian countryside, seeing his hopes mired with the vehicles that can no longer move along drowned roads, until night comes as it did during a similar downpour in Louisiana back in 1941, not as a gradual fading out of day but as an abrupt blotting out of the visual world. A tenebrous night, then, full of wind and rain, and death.

By then he will have for a full month been established in headquarters in Algiers, and more than a month will have passed since the so-called Clark-Darlan Agreement, with Darlan legally dubbed High Commissioner of North Africa, was "formalized" in a document having the effect of a protocol, though Roosevelt objects to calling it by that name because "it is not desired to recognize Darlan, either expressly or by implication, as a national plenipotentiary."[64] More than a month will have passed since Pierre Boisson, in command at Dakar in French West Africa, decided—though reluctantly, with important reservations which only the force of circumstance overcomes—to cast his lot with the Allies, a decision for which Darlan, who has pleaded for or requested or maybe even "ordered" it, receives much credit from the American commanding general. (But what other choice does Boisson have, in reality, with Free French forces in control of French Equatorial Africa to the south and east of him and the Allies in Morocco and Algiers to the north?) Eisenhower, assured of firm backing from the Washington which made his Darlan policy inevitable (he being the kind of man he is), will by then be more than ever convinced that he has determined events in the political sphere with courage and sagacity. He reiterates to Churchill, who must defend his arrangements against hostile criticism in a secret session of the Commons on December 10, that "we are not entering a cabal designed to place Darlan at the head of anything except the local organization" where "he is entirely necessary, for he and he alone is the source of every bit of practical help we have received." He will then go on to say: "If you . . . contemplate the situation existing along our lines of communication, which extend five hundred miles from here [Algiers] through mountainous country to Tunisia, you will understand that the local French could, without fear of detection, so damage us that we would have to retreat hurriedly back to the ports from which we could supply ourselves by sea. . . . It was only through Darlan's help that we are fighting the Boche in Tunisia instead of somewhere in the vicinity of Bône or even west of that."[65]

Never will Eisenhower as commander display greater offensive boldness than during this nerve-wracking period. The spearhead of the British First Army consists of little more than three brigades of infantry and a brigade of obsolescent tanks as it thrusts through Souk el Khemis and Béja to the very outskirts of Tunis—and there stops. Is forced to stop, by logistics as much as by the growing strength of German resistance. Is then driven back some miles by local counterattacks as American forces are committed to battle in driblets (there is neither time nor transport for assembling large units in advance) at the price of a dangerous exposure of the rear and a possibly disastrous disorganization of the front if this drive for Tunis fails. His troops fight, he well knows, under great handicaps. The Germans operate from permanent bases in Sicily, some 150 miles from Tunis; the Allies are inadequately based on Algiers, four hundred miles away. The Germans possess a network of railways over which to supply the front, with an abundance of first-class rolling stock; the Allies have a single railway from Algiers to the front, with rolling stock that is both overage and limited in quantity. The Germans have also a network of wide paved highways for supply and reinforcement; the Allies must depend upon roads that are often little more than mountain trails. The Germans possess several all-weather airfields in close support of the front; the Allies have a single good all-weather airfield near the front, at Souk el Arba. Moreover, several unhappy incidents—costly failures, for instance, of ground-air coordination—demonstrate that the Americans are as yet far from ready to engage first-class German troops on even terms. Yet when Anderson indicates it may be necessary to draw back from Medjez el Bab, a key road center the Allies must retain if they are to resume the offensive before winter rains set in in full force, Eisenhower refuses to countenance it. Instead, acutely aware that General Mud fights with increasing effectiveness on the German side, he prepares a final all-out drive for Tunis to be launched on December 24.

Small wonder that he will continue impatient of "political distractions," and by "ill-informed criticisms" be increasingly exasperated, who measures everything now by a single simple yardstick: does it help or hurt the achievement *right now* of this glittering prize? He concentrates all he can of strength and attention upon the desperate race, comforting himself with the belief that victory—Tunis secured without a difficult winter campaign—will justify everything, silence all criticism. "My children, it is permitted you in time of grave danger to walk with the devil until you have crossed the bridge." Thus an old Balkan proverb, quoted by Roosevelt to Churchill apropos Darlan on November 20—and Eisenhower, though he does not see Darlan as devil, agrees with the sentiment. "I must say I think he is a poor creature with a jaundiced outlook and disorganized loyalties who in all this tremendous African episode, West and East alike [Montgomery's Eighth Army now prepares battle against Rommel on the frontiers of Cyrenaica], can find no point to excite his interest except the arrangements made between General Eisenhower and Admiral Darlan." Thus Churchill to the Commons on December 10—and again Eisenhower cannot but agree, most fervently.[66]

Yet the opposition opinion persists—and who can say that even Tunis in hand will (or would) reduce its persuasive power for long, or prove it wrong in terms of history? Those who hold it insist upon a wider perspective in space, a longer view in time, and a greater consistency of argument than (as they believe) is employed by proponents and defenders of Darlan. They insist that North Africa be viewed, not in that isolation where expediency (the shallow self, the short view) may prosper, but in the context of global war and the peace to follow. Consider it, for instance, in organismic connection with the far Pacific where, on Guadalcanal, the first Allied offensive against Japan is now assured of victory, following the decisive defensive naval victories of the Coral Sea and Midway. Consider it in connection with China where Stilwell in the presence of Chinese General Ho, who did not contradict him, said a few weeks back to Willkie that the latter, scheduled to visit the war front near Sian in the great bend of the Yellow River, "would see there one of the great trading operations of modern China, with Chinese Nationalist troops engaged in heavy commerce with the Japanese."[67] Consider it in connection with Russia, where Stalingrad, which seemed to many three months ago an inevitable disaster for Soviet arms, has become a stupendous and increasing triumph over the Nazis, with some three hundred thousand Germans encircled and butchered as they are compressed into a smaller and smaller area. Consider it in connection with the factories and fields and shipyards of America, where war production goals that seemed fantastic a few months ago are now being met, will soon (obviously, on many items) be surpassed, and must give into Allied hands within a year or so an immense superiority in all the *things* with which wars are fought. The war tide seems everywhere to have turned against the Axis; there has been reached what Churchill is soon to call "the end of the beginning." But what is it that begins? Is North Africa the image of that future the Western Allies seek to shape for all the world? Is it then to be in North Africa that these Allies on (let us say) Friday the thirteenth of November, 1942, begin definitely to win the war and lose the peace?

For surely one may justifiably question (so say the critics) whether "time and lives" may properly be "saved" in one theater of war at the expense of principles for which the Allies claim to be fighting in all theaters. The motion which is to be introduced in the House of Commons on November 26, forcing Churchill to "seek refuge" in secret session, expresses this view succinctly. The motion says "that our relations with Admiral Darlan and his kind are inconsistent with the ideals for which we have entered and are fighting this war; furthermore, that these relations, if persisted in, will undermine the faith in us among our friends in the oppressed and invaded nations and impair the military, social and political prospects of the final and complete triumph of the cause of the United Nations."[68] It is an opinion which will be strengthened by events that follow the signing of the protocol (which Roosevelt denies is one) whereby Darlan is in effect recognized as Chief of State "in the name of the Marshal." What the Allies support with their arms in French North Africa is a totalitarian government on the Berlin-Rome-Vichy model—a State wherein fascist organizations, as Churchill complains to Roosevelt on December 9, "continue their activities and victimize our former French sympathizers, many of whom have not yet been released from prison." And the Prime Minister will continue: "The first reaction of these organizations to the Allied landing was, rightly, one of fear, but it seems that they have now taken courage to regroup themselves and continue their activities. Well-known German sympathizers who had been ousted have been reinstated. Not only have our enemies been thus encouraged, but our friends have been correspondingly confused and cast down."[69]

The situation, in short, is intolerable. By violence—violence to the conscience of the West, hence to the logic of history—events have been wrenched from their natural course in Algeria and Morocco, have been dammed up behind a flimsy wall of "expediency," and by violence they will release themselves to seek (with what success none can say) their "proper" channel.

Behold, then, the instrument of collective conscience, who is to perform what blunt Wayne Clark will call "an act of providence" and the "lancing of a troublesome boil."[70] He is an intense, pale, slender youth with burning eyes, Fernand Bonnier de la Chapelle by name, barely out of his 'teens—in occupation a student at the University of Lyons, in political sentiment (by the strange linkages war produces) a Gaullist-Royalist—who enters the Summer Palace in Algiers, where Darlan's office is, in the late afternoon of the day before Christmas, 1942. He seeks audience with the High Commissioner, is told that the admiral has not yet returned from a late and abnormally prolonged luncheon, waits then in the anteroom—thinking what thoughts? a prey to what fears?—until the hated admiral enters, whereupon he rises and takes from his pocket a .22 revolver (a strangely feeble weapon for an assassin) and fires twice point-blank into Darlan's face. Forty-five minutes later, the admiral lies dead on a hospital operating table. He will be not long survived by his assassin. The youth, at once seized and roughly handled, will be tried before a military tribunal on Christmas Day and be executed the following dawn by a firing squad, the whole fatal procedure being conducted with such haste and secrecy (the Allied military imposes at once the most rigid censorship) as to make even the unsuspicious wonder if the executing authorities may not have something to hide which they fear the youth may reveal. (De Gaulle will more than wonder; he will more than halfway believe that Bonnier de la Chapelle, "almost a child," is the dupe and instrument of secret policy on the part of those who, having found Darlan useful as a "temporary expedient," now find the admiral an increasingly dangerous embarrassment.[71])

Some may deem it a piece of the soon-to-be-famous "Eisenhower luck"—whereby he received maximum credit for whatever goes right, is absolved of blame for whatever goes wrong, within the area of his responsibility—that he is not present in Algiers on this Christmas Eve but instead, as we have seen, is four hundred miles away in rainsoaked Tunisia. It is with no sense of good luck, however, that he comes with General Anderson to the cleverly camouflaged farmhouse near Souk el Khemis (hay raked over slit trenches, haystacks tunneled for soldiers' quarters) in pouring rain at just about the time Bonnier de la Chapelle is firing the fatal shots. His spirits droop with disappointment. The attack scheduled to begin that evening has been postponed for at least forty-eight hours and will in all probability have to be called off altogether, because of this rain which beats upon him, as he moves from car to farmhouse door, and drums then, endlessly, upon roof and windows. It is impossible to move even the lightest vehicles through the mud. Eisenhower is sadly convinced of this when, at the Souk el Khemis airfield, he sees four men struggling with all their might to move a mired motorcycle which, for all their efforts, is in the end more deeply mired than before. But what this means is that the race for Tunis is lost! It could even mean disaster for Allied forward forces; these, with units so badly scrambled as seriously to reduce tactical efficiency, must now go on the defensive at the end of overextended communications, their commander not daring (in large part for psychological-political reasons) to order a retreat to positions more easily maintained. It is a black evening for the commanding general, and its anxieties are not relieved by the mysterious phone call from Clark in Algiers, coming just before dinner, saying "all hell has broken loose" and that Eisenhower must return to headquarters at once.

Immediately he suspects and voices to Butcher his suspicion that Darlan is dead, but not until breakfast in Constantine on Christmas morning, after a wild all-night drive over dangerously slippery roads, will he learn for sure that the admiral has been assassinated. Whereupon he will admit to Butcher that the event does "end one problem" though, he gloomily adds, it "no doubt will create many more"[72]—a sentiment correct in that many anxiety-breeding political problems will certainly follow, but wrong (so say political liberals) in that Darlan's death does not in any true sense "create" them. Rather do they flow, these problems, from the same source as Darlan-as-problem came upon him, from that expediency which is "purely military" and "temporary."

To Darlan's place will be appointed, inevitably, Giraud, whose elevation makes at least possible a rapprochement between High Commissioner and De Gaulle, a rapprochement hitherto as impossible as it was (and increasingly is) necessary to the peaceful government of French North Africa. Alas, this first step toward such happy event is a faltering one. Giraud is no believer in the theory or practice of democracy, has indeed never pretended that he was, and has no talent whatever for politics or civil administration. Vichyites will continue to be uplifted, Gaullists continue to be cast down, with the whole of this process being imperfectly hidden from public view by Eisenhower-imposed political censorship—and precisely to the degree that this happens will political troubles continue to come down upon the Allied command, not as the water which drips, drips, drips from the cavern ceiling as Eisenhower dictates his message to Marshall, this morning of Saturday, November 14, but as a flood of Time.

Book Three

FLOOD TIDE OF VICTORY

XI

Atomistic, Organismic

i. *"The Italian Navigator Has Landed . . ."*

Never on a workday morning had Chicago's L trains, buses, and streetcars been more jammed with passengers, not for decades had the city's streets been emptier of private cars, than on this Wednesday, December 2, 1942—the second day of Government-imposed gasoline rationing in the United States. It was a cold day, too. The official temperature reading was 10 degrees, but as usual a raw wind was blowing off the lake to make it seem much colder than that to those who waited on corners for public transportation or who walked—and thousands unaccustomed to walking now thronged the sidewalks—from home to work place. These huddled into their overcoats and rubbed gloved hands every now and then across frost-threatened cheeks and ears.

Especially bitter did Chicago's weather seem to such travelers as had just arrived from warmer, sunnier climes. Four of these were men who came down from a train they had boarded in Berkeley, California, two days before and who, bracing themselves against the icy blasts sweeping around the old Dearborn Street station, managed at last to capture a taxi in which they rode south for miles along windswept Lake Shore Drive and then west a few blocks into the campus of the University of Chicago. There they hurried from cab into a building, Eckhart Hall, that had formerly housed the university's departments of physics and mathematics and now housed a Metallurgical Laboratory engaged (so the University faculty had been told) in a wartime metals research program. The Laboratory (so the University administration had been told) was the central element of a national Metallurgical Project, directed by Arthur H. Compton—and it was to Compton's office that the four travelers now went. There one of them, W. K. Lewis, Professor of Chemical Engineering at the Massachusetts Institute of Technology, produced from his briefcase a several-paged document and placed it in Compton's hand.[1] Compton read it at once, with a close and eager attention . . .

He, Compton, who now began the most memorable day of his life, was ending what had been, all-in-all, by far the most memorable year of his life—one that began with the meeting of four scientists we witnessed in an office of the Carnegie Institution in Washington on the day before Pearl Harbor Sunday.* At that meeting, it may be remembered, the outlines of an all-out Government-sponsored research program aimed at the production of an "atomic" bomb were decided upon and the administrative responsibility for it was divided between Ernest O. Lawrence of the University of California, Harold C. Urey of Columbia, and Compton of the University of Chicago. To Lawrence had been assigned research into the possibility of separating the rare U-235 isotope from the much more abundant U-238 in natural uranium by means of electromagnetism, and of developing (this would be, specifically, a task for Glenn Seaborg) chemical means of separating plutonium from the uranium whose chain reaction (then only theoretically possible) produced it. To Urey had been assigned research into the so-called "centrifuge" and "gaseous diffusion" methods of separating U-235 from U-238. To Compton had been assigned the effort (actually directed by Fermi) to produce a chain reaction in ordinary though very pure uranium, the determination of the "critical size" at which an assembly of pure U-235 or plutonium would explode, and the development of devices by which such an assembly might be instantaneously achieved in an effective weapon.

It was to discharge this responsibility that Compton had established last February the Metallurgical Project and Laboratory, moving from Columbia to Chicago the Enrico Fermi group. Fermi, we may recall, had begun in the summer of 1941 to build experimental piles of uranium and graphite, the latter being used as moderator or "slower-down" of "fast" neutrons to speeds at which they could be easily captured by U-235 nuclei in natural uranium, causing these to split and emit yet more neutrons while a small percentage of their mass was transformed into energy. (Unless the speed was reduced, the neutrons were liable to capture by U-238 nuclei, which, usually, were not split thereby.) When the number of neutrons thus emitted exceeded, at any given instant, the number "lost" through U-238 captures and otherwise—that is, when the multiplication factor *k* became more than 1—a self-sustaining energy-producing chain reaction would occur. Since moving to Chicago, as increasing amounts of unprecedentedly pure uranium and graphite became available, Fermi with his colleagues had come closer and closer to achieving this reaction.

Meanwhile, as we have seen, a decision had been taken at the very highest level of Government to merge the theretofore loosely coordi-

* See page 78 and following.

nated British and American atomic efforts and to build in remote, sparsely populated areas of the United States the huge production plants which would be required.† It had also been decided that construction of these plants should begin at once, which is to say that the engineering phases of the project would be going forward even before the research phases had discovered with absolute certainty that the end aimed for could be achieved. A new District of the Army Corps of Engineers had been established to handle the construction work. This was in June 1942. Three months later, in mid-September, as more became known of the possible if not probable scope and weight of the effort that would have to be made, the Engineer District originally dubbed the DSM Project was expanded into what was called, on organization charts, the Manhattan Engineer District and into which was to be absorbed, gradually but as swiftly as possible, administrative control of all the scientific research and technological development as well as of all the engineering and construction. In other words, this work was being shifted from the Office of Scientific Research and Development to the War Department. Assigned to head (or command, as the Army put it) the whole of this enterprise was an Engineer brigadier general named Leslie R. Groves, who had been in charge of all Army construction in the United States and its offshore bases and who, even after this new assignment, continued in charge of Pentagon building construction until the vast War Department headquarters, nearing completion in the fall of '42, was finished.

Of the process whereby pure science leads into engineering technology and, within the American system, opens gaps between creative intelligence and administrative power, Groves' appointment might be deemed symptomatic. It was protested by Vannevar Bush, Director of the Office of Scientific Research and Development (OSRD), as soon as he heard it was being considered; he "doubted whether . . . [Groves] has sufficient tact for the job." And when the appointment was made anyway by the Secretary of War, and approved by the President, upon the recommendation of the Army Chief of Staff and the Commanding General of the Army Service Forces (Lieutenant General Brehon B. Somervell), Bush's judgment, given flatly, sadly, was that "we are in the soup."[2] He was later to change his mind; like many others who came to know General Groves well, he would ultimately conclude that this appointment was on the whole a fortunate one: but most of the scientists who worked on the atomic bomb project not only concurred in Bush's initial judgment but also maintained it to the end. They might recognize the necessity or at least the inevitability of the organizational arrangements now being made, while disliking these, but they were outraged to find such a man as this in even a nominal control of their work. His very appearance was against him in their eyes. He was said to keep himself

† See page 243.

physically fit by training like an athlete. Nevertheless, in his middle years, he had noticeable jowls and paunch—and there were more than a few of the Project's scientists (nearly all of them young, trim-figured men) who were vocally (and falsely) convinced that the general had as high a percentage of fat above his eyebrows as he had below his chin.

Admittedly he had no competence whatever in atomic physics, nor any awe-filled respect for those who did have. He was convinced that "atomic physics is not an occult science" but one whose "basic laws" the "average layman" could easily grasp. Neither had he any sympathetic understanding of the outlook and general psychology of the fiercely independent intellectuals whose work he was supposed, according to the organization chart, to administer (he was irritated by what he deemed the insolently absurd pretensions of young physicists "that no one who was over forty years old . . . could possibly understand the intricacies of atomic energy"[3]); and his long habit of brusque command and blunt speech seemed perfectly calculated to grate upon them. "You scientists don't have any discipline," he once grumbled to Compton, following a conference with project research leaders upon whom he had failed to impose his will. "You don't know how to take orders and give orders." To which Compton replied—ineffectively, he feared—with an effort to explain the difference between the inwardly imposed discipline of the searcher for truth and the outwardly imposed discipline (obedience) of the subordinate in a tightly knit organization.

"I found myself an intermediary," said Compton later, "between those on the one hand who were schooled in self-reliance and to the questioning of all authority and on the other hand the military and industrial men to whom dependence on orders was second nature."[4]

Thus Compton continued to serve that function of bridge man which we noted when last we saw him at the beginning of this (for him) most memorable of years. Unlike most of the members of his research "team," he recognized qualities in Groves that were as uncommon as they were indispensable to the swift success of the project. The general was in many respects the ideal construction engineer—a hard-driving Big Operator who Got Things Done come hell or high water. His first act of major importance on his new assignment, performed on the first full day of it, aimed at obtaining for his Project 1250 tons of uranium ore from the Belgian Congo, by far the richest such ore in the world (it contained an average of over 65 per cent uranium oxide as compared with an average of two-tenths of 1 per cent in ores mined in Canada and Colorado), which was then stored in some two thousand steel drums in a Staten Island warehouse. It had been mined by the Union Minière du Haut Katanga, whose managing director, M. Edgar Sengier, headquartered in New York since October of 1939, had tried without success on three separate occasions to interest State Department economic officials in the purchase of it. When Engineer Colonel Kenneth D. Nichols appeared in his office on September 18, 1942, Sangier demanded to know if the colonel had come to "talk" or to "do business"—the Belgian had had more than enough of mere "talk"—and was pleased to find Nichols fully authorized by Groves to conclude an agreement whereby Union Minière turned over at once to the United States all the ore stored on Staten Island and shipped to this country "all the richest uranium ore above ground" in the Congo.[5]

Groves' second act of major importance was performed the next day, September 19, when he had a momentous interview with the head of the War Production Board, Donald Nelson. The general was convinced by recent unhappy experience that he "could never get the job done" on his new assignment unless the Project's requests for scarce materials were given top priority, a rating they had not theretofore been granted by WPB. Perhaps put off by the general's peremptory and imperious manner, Nelson at first flatly refused to grant the AAA-rating that Groves demanded, whereupon the general threatened to recommend to the President that the whole project be abandoned "because the War Production Board is unwilling to cooperate with his [the President's] wishes." The threat was effective. The fact that Groves dared make it may have indicated to Nelson, who had an intelligent layman's knowledge of recent developments in nuclear physics, that the Manhattan Engineer District was indeed as important as the general asserted it to be. At any rate, when Groves left Nelson's office he carried in his pocket a letter signed by the WPB chief authorizing him and his principal assistant, the District Engineer (Nichols), "to assign an AAA rating, or whatever lesser rating will be sufficient, to those items the delivery of which . . . cannot otherwise be secured in time for the successful prosecution of the work" for which they were responsible.[6]

Groves dealt thus exclusively in his work with things and people, the latter as adjuncts or functions of the former, eschewing general ideas, for which his orders from his Government were substitute. His commitment to external realities was uninhibited by inner complexities. There were few unsettled and unsettling problems of basic belief in his mind: God, country, and humanity were perfectly fused. Once he was asked by Compton which he would choose if ever he were forced to choose between "the welfare of the United States" and "the welfare of mankind." In his reply he doubted the possibility of such mutual exclusiveness between the two. "Show me if you can an agency through which it is possible to do more for the service of man than can be done through the United States," said he, expressing an opinion not widely at variance with Compton's own, if considerably simpler in texture.[7]

Nor was this the only basis for understanding between these two.

Compton, like Groves, had no such aversion to, nor distrust of, Big Business as was characteristic of most research scientists. He had himself been for years an employee of Big Business. Like Groves, he was convinced that the actual production of U-235 and plutonium must be taken out of the hands of the researchers and placed in those of large-scale industry: he had faced and faced down a near rebellion of members of the Metallurgical Laboratory when, in June of '42, he proposed asking the Army Engineers of the then newly organized DSM Project to choose a suitable industrial engineering company to design and build the production plants. He was therefore prepared to back Groves' prompt decision to assign the engineering, construction, and operation of the plutonium plant—a giant, threefold responsibility—to the giant chemical firm of Du Pont (the separation of plutonium from uranium being a chemical process), though he knew and warned the general that important members of the Metallurgical Laboratory would be vehemently opposed to this move. Not only did the scientists grossly underestimate the magnitude of the engineering effort which must now be made, he said, they also as political liberals loathed Du Pont in particular as a prime symbol and proponent, in Liberty League days, of anti-New Deal political reaction. (Especially would the key foreign-born scientists oppose this move. Their European education had made no such sharp distinction between science and engineering as was made in American education, so that they felt competent to deal with the engineering as well as the research phases of the Project; and it had been their bitter political experience that giant steel and chemical industries were major supporters if not instigators of Nazi-Fascism.[8])

But though he backed Groves against his "team" on this matter, Compton backed the "team"—and to the limit—against those who indicated the slightest doubt of its scientific competency.

Among such doubters (or so it seemed to Compton) was Charles M. A. Stine, Vice-President of Du Pont, who with Crawford H. Greenewalt (destined to become Du Pont's president) met with Groves and Compton in mid-November, after the company's executive committee had voted, despite grave misgivings, to undertake the plutonium project. Stine at this meeting, after eight of Du Pont's key employees had spent several days in the Metallurgical Laboratory reviewing all the work done and information available, reiterated a carefully calculated doubt that the project could succeed. He referred to the many years that had been required by Du Pont to put nylon into mass production after it had been abundantly demonstrated that nylon was a superior product which *could* be mass-produced. He pointed out that a self-sustaining chain reaction had not yet been achieved, that there was no conclusive evidence that such a reaction could be controlled (the reactor *might* blow up in a catastrophe whose limits were immeasurable but certainly immense), that the possibility of separating plutonium from its highly radioactive medium was as yet indeterminate, and that, even if all went as the most optimistic thought it might, "production would be limited to a few grams of plutonium in 1943 and not much more in 1944." Assuming that a workable plant had by then been built, "not until sometime in 1945 could production possibly reach the planned rate"—and of course no determination could be made of the relative practicability of aiming for a plutonium bomb without measuring the Chicago work against the work on U-235 being done by Urey's group at Columbia and Lawrence's at Berkeley. The over-all conclusion reached by Du Pont's experts, said Stine, was that there was no more than one chance in a hundred that the plutonium project would "lead to anything in this war."

Compton was (in his own words) "appalled" by this. One of the alleged reasons for Du Pont's reluctance to undertake the project had been that the company was without experience or expert knowledge of nuclear physics; yet Stine now cavalierly rejected the carefully considered judgment of the most brilliant group of physicists ever assembled in a single laboratory. This group, which included three Nobel Prize winners (Fermi, James Franck, and Compton himself) had found the chances to be "ten to one," as Compton now said emphatically to Stine, "that if we go ahead with full strength we shall have atomic weapons ready before the war can be finished." But how could such "full strength" be achieved if the prime contractor had no faith in the success of the work it undertook? "Immediately my mind turned to means of changing their point of view to one of optimism," Compton would later say. The means arrived at was a five-man reviewing committee appointed by Groves whose majority was composed of Du Pont representatives (T. G. Gary, Roger Williams, and Greenewalt) and whose assignment was to "study the entire program of producing fissionable material and . . . recommend how the project could be best advanced." Its chairman was W. K. Lewis, its fifth member Eger V. Murphree of the Standard Oil Development Company—though as it turned out, Murphree, because of illness, was unable to participate.[9]

Meanwhile, the project as a whole had moved with increasing momentum toward the production phase.

In May of 1942, Compton with others had selected as the potential site for the plutonium production plant an area along the Clinch River in the Great Smoky Mountains of Tennessee where electric power from TVA was available (though far from enough for plant purposes) and where a rugged terrain, sparse population, mild climate permitting winter construction, available rail transportation, and distance from the seacoast combined to fulfill other ideal requirements. The proposed site was personally visited by Groves immediately following his assignment to the Manhattan Project, and arrangements were at once made to take over an area of approximately eighty square miles for what was initially known to the initiate as the Clinton Engineer Works but was destined to become famous as Oak Ridge. Here would be located, not the plutonium works originally planned for, but the vast plants required for the separation of U-235 from U-238 by the gaseous diffusion process. (The site which would be selected for the plutonium plant, early in 1943, was a desert region on the Columbia River in the State of Washington where the Government would take over some seven hundred square miles. Here would be built the enormous Hanford Engineer Works, named after the nearly abandoned railroad town of Hanford which was located near the center of the Government reservation. The site was selected when Du Pont, provided by the Metallurgical Laboratory with statistics on the chances of an accidental nuclear explosion, decided "that even Oak Ridge was in a region of too dense population for the first plutonium plant to be erected with reasonable freedom from fear of a disaster."[10])

In November, Groves, in consultation with J. Robert Oppenheimer, who would be chosen to head the work of designing and producing the bomb itself, had selected for the site of the bomb-making project a remote area in New Mexico whose principal terrain feature was a mesa known as Los Alamos and whose only inhabitants were the proprietors and students of a boys' school which neared bankruptcy. This became known within the Project as "Site Y."[11]

As for the research which was being telescoped in time with production technology, its principal facility was to be a laboratory located in one of Cook County's forest preserves, some fifteen miles outside Chicago, known as the Argonne Forest—a wilderness whose isolation was remarkable considering its proximity to the center of the city. Isolation was deemed advisable for purposes of secrecy, and essential for physical safety, for it was here that Fermi was supposed to build the pile with which the critical experiment, the climax of all the research effort thus far, would be made.

When construction of the facility was begun in the summer of '42, it was with the expectation or hope that the building would be ready for occupancy by October 20. Labor difficulties, however, had delayed what was in the first place an overly optimistic work schedule. The result was that the Argonne Laboratory remained still uncompleted on this December 2, when the reviewing committee, returning from Berkeley to the East, paused between trains in Chicago to visit again the Metallurgical Laboratory and to give into Compton's hand the several-paged document he now eagerly, even anxiously perused . . .

The report was in one respect disappointing to him, as it would be to others in the Laboratory, for it did not recommend the immediate development of production plants for plutonium. The committee had concluded that the best chance for early success lay with U-235, and now recommended that there be built as rapidly as possible a plant for the separation of it from U-238 by gaseous diffusion. The electromagnetic separation process, for which Lawrence had had such high hopes, did not seem to the committee likely to prove useful for large-scale production, though its development should, in the committee's opinion, continue to be pressed. So should developmental tests of plutonium, for which, it was recommended, a pilot plant should be built immediately. Thus the report seemed to Compton somewhat less "optimistic" than the facts justified, but on the other hand it had none of that "pessimism" which Stine (as Compton saw it) had displayed in Wilmington. Its obvious basic assumption was that "the program would go ahead with full vigor," and this was a relief and an encouragement to the director of the Metallurgical Project.

A few minutes after reading the report, Compton with other leaders of the Laboratory met with the reviewing committee in an Eckhart Hall conference room to discuss questions raised by it. They were of course questions in which Compton was intensely interested. Nevertheless, he found it extremely difficult to keep his attention fastened on them that morning. If his colleagues did not notice that he was distracted and unwontedly nervous, it may have been because he hid well the true state of his feelings, or it may have been because they shared those feelings, at least to a degree. Certainly a nervous tension that was not caused by the discussion itself presided over this meeting. It began to do so at the outset, when W. K. Lewis, the committee chairman, looking over those who had assembled, took note of a significant absence.

"Where's Fermi?" he asked. "We'd like to have his opinion on some of these matters."[12]

There was a sudden brief silence. Then Compton said that Fermi had asked to be excused because an "important experiment" required his presence elsewhere—whereupon there was another brief silence during which several of those present glanced at one another, then glanced away. Thereafter the tension mounted.

It was probably more acute in Compton than in any of the others, for he bore at that moment a greater burden of anxious responsibility for what Fermi was now doing—or, rather, for his doing it at this particular time and place—than they did.

Approximately a month before, Fermi had come to Compton's office with a startling suggestion. Obviously, the Argonne Forest building would not be ready for many weeks after enough of the material (the super-pure graphite and uranium) needed to build a reactor was available in Chicago. This meant a several-week delay of the critical experiment, which might prove disastrous to the Allies if German scientists were moving forward as rapidly as they were presumed to be. But was it really necessary for safety reasons that the experiment be performed in the Argonne Laboratory? Fermi didn't think so. Indeed he was convinced "that we can make the chain reaction work safely right here in Chicago."[13]

He then presented to Compton the argument Compton later presented to Stine when the latter, in his "pessimism," spoke of the possibility that a chain reaction, if achieved, could not be controlled. The belief that it *could* be was initially derived from numerous investigations indicating that, when uranium fission occurred, not all the neutrons "boiled off" were immediately emitted. Some of them (approximately 1 per cent) were delayed, being emitted in decreasing quantities over a period of time (approximately one minute). The previous May, this phenomenon had been measured with precision in an experiment conducted by three members of the Metallurgical Laboratory. They found that 1 per cent of the emitted neutrons were delayed by at least 0.01 second and that most of these—approximately 70 per cent of them—were delayed by as much as a minute. In other words, there was "a sort of inertia to the chain reaction," as the official historian of the Project would later put it, and the time required to overcome this "inertia" was sufficient to give controls a chance to operate.[14] The trick was simply to build a pile in which the multiplication factor *k* was only slightly greater than 1, so that the reaction would build up slowly, and to insert in it at calculated intervals rods coated with a substance that would absorb neutrons. In the pile Fermi proposed to build, several minutes would elapse between the instant the reaction started and the instant when its power would be doubled if no controls at all were used. This provided ample time in which to manipulate effectively the single cadmium-coated rod with which the reaction was finally to be managed. The operator would start the reaction by pulling the rod out beyond a certain point, and would regulate its speed or rate of energy production by pulling the rod farther out (increasing the reaction) or pushing it in (decreasing or, beyond the initial point, halting the reaction). There would be, on the basis of all available experimental evidence and theoretical knowledge, no danger whatever of an explosion.

But of course "all available knowledge" did not yet include the actual production and control of a chain reaction. Until it did, there could be no absolute certainty that some as-yet-unknown process would not multiply neutrons more abundantly than was now predicted, once the reaction began. Fermi and Compton agreed that the possibility was exceedingly remote. Even if realized, it could not lead to a true nuclear explosion in a pile of barely critical size whose operation was guarded by every conceivable safety device. The two were convinced of this. There remained, however, the irreducible risk of the unknown, and Compton (since his was the assigned responsibility) must decide whether the running of it in the midst of a great city was justified by the larger risk of weeks of delay.

He had decided that it was . . .

Several years before, President Robert M. Hutchins of the University of Chicago became convinced that American intercollegiate athletics, especially football, having been corrupted into commercialized forms of mass entertainment, were an intolerable contradiction of the proper values, processes, and aims of higher education. Accordingly he had led his institution out of Big Ten intercollegiate sports into an expanded program of intramural sports, a decision fortunate for the Metallurgical Laboratory in that it made the football stadium at Stagg Field available for scientific work on a campus where work space was at a premium. Important research had for many months been conducted in a wooden press box atop the stadium's West Stands.[15] And now Fermi's critical experiment was about to be performed in a slate-walled squash racquets court below these same West Stands. It would be conducted without Hutchins' knowledge. Compton had deliberately refrained from informing him of the matter because he feared that the university's president, if he knew of it, would feel forced to forbid it.

So the top administrative responsibility was now Compton's alone—and he knew, as he sat with the others in the Eckhart Hall conference room, that on the erstwhile squash court the climactic moment approached. It might well be reached that very day. For weeks, Fermi and his group had been engaged in the hard, dirty, careful work of constructing what was originally intended to be a spherical pile of precisely machined blocks of graphite, each of them resembling in shape an overlong loaf of bread, whose alternate layers contained lumps of uranium. As they built, they conducted a continuous series of tests that measured the approach of k to 1; and yesterday they had found to their surprise that—though it was only three-fourths the height that had been deemed necessary, and contained only some twelve thousand of the sixteen thousand pounds of uranium metal that had been thought required—the pile had reached critical size. A single layer had then been added, topping the pile off to shape "an oblate spheroid flattened at the top, i.e., like a door knob."[16] This morning, if all went well, Fermi would order withdrawn from the pile all the cadmium-coated rods save the single one which would be used to control the final experiment, and this final experiment would be begun. Small wonder that Compton awaited anxiously an expected phone call.

It came at midmorning. Volney Wilson called from the West Stands. "I thought you would want to know that Fermi is ready to start," he said, adding that the laboratory was very crowded but that Compton might bring with him a single observer from the reviewing committee if he so desired. Compton did so desire. He chose Crawford Greenewalt to be his companion because, at forty, Greenewalt was the committee's youngest member and should therefore remember longer than any of the others the historic scene which was now about (in all probability) to be enacted.[17]

When the two men arrived at the West Stands they climbed a stairway and passed through a door in a thick concrete wall onto a balcony extending across one end of the squash court. At the other end of the room was the massive graphite-uranium pile. Above one corner of it was a wooden platform on which stood three men and several buckets; if the reaction grew suddenly, unexpectedly violent and the hand- and machine-manipulated control rods failed to halt it, these three men (the "suicide squad," as they were called) would strive to douse atomic fire with their buckets of cadmium solution. The balcony was indeed crowded with men (some twenty of them, in addition to the two new arrivals) and with equipment for the control and measurement of the reaction. But on the floor below, beside the pile, was a single lonely young man,

George Weill by name. In his hand was the end of a 1×3-inch piece of wood, the other end of which was inserted in the pile as the very last of the cadmium-coated rods, all the others having been pulled out.

Compton and Greenewalt took their places beside Fermi, who greeted them with a quick nod and smile before returning his attention to the five-inch slide rule he held in his hands and upon which he now made a swift calculation. He seemed perfectly calm. His voice was matter-of-fact as he called down to the man below.

"All right, George," he said, "pull it to thirteen feet."

The time was 10:37 A.M.

Weill did as he had been told, measuring the distance with a tape measure. Thereafter, as the rod was pulled farther and farther out in carefully measured steps, Compton watched the line traced by a recording meter's stylus climb up a graph, then level off, then climb again as the rod was pulled farther out; watched the light of a galvanometer dance across the scale, then dance back again; heard sudden gusts and dyings-down of the Geiger counters's clatter; and took note of the really amazing precision with which the reactor's performance was coinciding with that which Fermi had predicted for it. There was no sign of any process whereby unexpected neutrons were released. Then, at noon or shortly before, there was a sudden nerve-jarring commotion as the emergency control rod, whose operation was automatic, shot back into its slot with a resounding crash. But it was almost at once realized that this meant nothing save that the safety point had been set too low. As a matter of fact, the imperturbable Fermi seemed to regard the interruption as a welcome one.

"It seems like a good time to eat lunch," said he.

At 2:00 P.M. or thereabouts they were all again assembled in the squash court.

"All right, George," called Fermi from the balcony.

And the experiment was resumed, Weill again pulling the rod out, adding a foot to its exposed length, then six inches, then another six inches, with Fermi making at each step another swift calculation with his slide rule. His lips, Compton noted, grew tighter and tighter, though his manner continued calm, his tone of voice matter-of-fact.

At 3:25, he called: "Pull it another foot, George. This is going to do it."

He turned to Compton.

"Now it will become self-sustaining," he said quietly. He gestured toward the recording meter. "The track will climb," he said, "and continue to climb. It will not level off."

And that is what happened. Compton, fascinated, stared at it, the meter, then glanced at the faces around him. The din of the Geiger counters was almost deafening. Minutes passed. Then the meters showed that a dangerous level of radiation was beginning to be reached on the balcony.

"Throw in the safety rods," Fermi called above the clatter.

And the rods went crashing in. The curve of the recording stylus went down, the light of the galvanometer danced back to zero, the noise of the Geiger counters was reduced to an occasional click—and across this silence came a low-voiced cheer.

Eugene Wigner produced a bottle of Italian wine and, with a little bow, presented it to Fermi.

As Compton walked back to Eckhart Hall with the "dark, tall, slender" Greenewalt, he looked now and again into his companion's glowing eyes while listening to excited and exalted talk of the meaning of the "miracle" they both had witnessed. Greenewalt spoke of atomic energy as an immense boon to mankind, with myriad as yet unimagined uses in industry, medicine, and the everyday lives of all men.

But even as he listened to this outpouring of joyful hope, Compton saw in his mind's eye Volney Wilson's face at the moment when the chain reaction became self-sustaining—saw this, and was disturbed by it. He recalled how Volney Wilson, two and a half years ago, had made at Compton's request calculations indicating that the chain reaction which Fermi had suggested as a possibility could probably be produced, and how Wilson at the instant of submitting these calculations had requested that he himself be removed from all activity which might lead to the release of this awesome power. The request had of course been granted: Wilson had been transferred to the Radiation Laboratory at Cambridge, Massachusetts, where he had done valuable work on the development of radar equipment. Soon after Pearl Harbor, however, he had evidently decided that the times did not permit the kind of private conscience he had formerly acted upon; he had told Compton he was willing to "go where I am most needed," and had at once been transferred back to Chicago where he was put in charge of the instrument section of the Metallurgical Laboratory. He had since worked hard and brilliantly on the project, but always with the secret hope that the Project would fail —that some unsuspected recalcitrance in the atomic nucleus would render a chain reaction impossible. The disappointment of this secret hope had been mirrored in his face, had narrowed his eyes and furrowed his brow as he stared fixedly upon the dials of instruments he had helped to devise.

Where Greenewalt saw bright visions of the future, Volney Wilson saw horror . . .

The early dusk of winter had fallen and the reviewing committee had left Eckhart Hall when Compton put through a long-distance call to James B. Conant, who was working late in the office of the president of Harvard University.

"Jim," he said, when Conant was on the line, "you'll be interested to know that the Italian navigator has just landed in the new world. The Earth was not as large as he had estimated, and he arrived in the new world sooner than he had expected."

"Is that so?" Conant's excitement sounded through his voice. "Were the natives friendly?"

"Everyone landed safe and happy."[18]

But had they, really? Volney Wilson might have said that, from now on, no one was safe—and he, for one, was far from happy.

ii. *Casablanca: The Conduct of War and the Terms of Surrender*

On the day of Fermi's "critical experiment" in Chicago, President Roosevelt in Washington dispatched an urgent message to Marshal Stalin in Moscow, though without much hope it would produce the effect he wanted.

Eleven days before, on November 21, when it appeared that Tunisia might be in Allied hands by Christmas, he had proposed to Stalin that a personal meeting of American President, British Prime Minister, and Soviet Premier, each accompanied by a military staff, be held at the earliest possible date to decide in concert what military actions should follow the conquest of North Africa. Churchill, in a separate message to Moscow, had warmly seconded the President's proposal. At the same time, the Prime Minister had indicated to the President that a meeting of the Big Two prior to a meeting of the Big Three might be advisable, since the Russians would "certainly demand a strong second front in 1943 by the heavy invasion of the Continent either from the west or from the south or from both," a demand which should be met by "a joint and agreed view" on the part of Britain and the United States. From this, Roosevelt had been inclined to demur, ostensibly on the ground that a prior meeting might arouse further suspicions in Stalin's always suspicious mind[19] but also, in all probability, because certain unacknowledged suspicions of British motives had been planted in his own mind by Marshall and Stimson and King.

At any rate, the initial exchange of messages with Stalin had achieved nothing. The Soviet Premier had evinced no eagerness for the proposed meeting. He had suggested instead that the military staffs of the three countries meet together to make joint recommendations which he, the Prime Minister, and the President might deal with through correspondence. But what would be the point of such a meeting? Neither Roosevelt nor Churchill could see any at all. "Certainly if a Russian delegation went to Cairo [a meeting place suggested by Roosevelt] . . . , they would be so tied up that they would have to refer every point of substance back to Stalin in Moscow," said a Former Naval Person message[20] to the President. And if the British and American officers went to Moscow (the other meeting place suggested by Roosevelt) they would be similarly unable to shape a joint recommendation save on terms already agreed upon by their respective Governments.

And so, on Wednesday, December 2, 1942—perhaps at the very moment when the chain reaction became self-sustaining in that crude pile of uranium and graphite on a Chicago squash court—another urgent message flashed from the White House to the Kremlin halfway around the world. "My most compelling reason [for proposing an Anglo-American-Soviet meeting] is that I am anxious to have a talk with you," said Roosevelt to Stalin. "My suggestion would be that we meet secretly in some secure place in Africa that is convenient to all three of us. The time, about January 15 or 20."[21] To which Churchill added his urging the next day. "I earnestly hope you will agree," said he to Stalin. "We must decide at the earliest moment the best way of attacking Germany in Europe with all possible force in 1943. This can only be settled between the heads of Governments and States with their high expert authorities at their side."[22]

Stalin's reply to this second plea from his Western Allies was even more discouraging than his reply to the first had been. Though he claimed to "welcome the idea of a meeting between the heads of the Governments . . . in order to fix a common line of strategy," he himself could not be absent from the Soviet Union "even for a day, as it is just now that important military operations of our winter campaign are developing," operations which "will not be relaxed in January, probably the contrary." He also hinted that, despite his professed welcoming of the "idea" of a meeting, he saw little real reason for it since the future operations of the Western Allies, insofar as they related to Russia, were already determined: the Allies had only to fulfill their "promise" to establish "a second front in Western Europe in the spring of 1943."[23] Roosevelt then proposed a postponement of the meeting until March 1, preceding it with a meeting somewhere in Africa of the military staffs of the three countries, but to this proposal, too, Stalin returned a negative answer. It would be "impossible" for him to leave Russia "even at the beginning of March," he said, and besides he didn't "know what exactly are the problems which you . . . and Mr. Churchill intend to discuss." He also made his suspicions more explicit, saying with a certain irony: "Allow me to express my confidence . . . that the promises about the opening of a second front in Europe given by you . . . and by Mr. Churchill in regard to 1942, and in any case in regard to the spring of 1943, will be fulfilled, and that a second front in Europe will actually be opened by the joint forces of Great Britain and the United States of America in the spring of the next year."[24]

This third Stalin refusal was final, so far as a Big Three meeting was concerned. Even before it was received, however, Roosevelt sent to Churchill by courier a letter in which he assumed that "our Uncle Joe . . . will again decline" and stated his belief that "in spite of it you and I should get together, as there are things which can be definitely determined only by you and me in conference with our Staff people." He was sure, he added, "that both of us want to avoid the delays which attended the determination of TORCH last July." He also thought that, "in view of Stalin's absence," he and Churchill need not have with them any "foreign affairs people . . . , for our work will be essentially military."[25]

As regards the last point, the Prime Minister was not wholly in agreement with the President. He was acutely aware of the political aspect of the military problems, and the military aspect of the political problems, with which the two heads of Government must deal in the months ahead. He would therefore have liked to bring Foreign Secretary Anthony Eden with him. Inextricably involved with several of the "essentially military" matters to be handled at the proposed conference, for instance, was the "essentially political" problem of bringing De Gaulle and Giraud together in some kind of working arrangement. But the Prime Minister could well understand how this very fact might constitute a strong argument in the President's mind against bringing with him Eden's opposite number, Secretary of State Hull, whose personal antipathy toward De Gaulle exceeded Giraud's and whose incapacity or unwillingness to "forgive and forget" was as remarkable as it was regrettable in a high diplomatic officer. Hull would certainly bitterly oppose the personal meeting with De Gaulle that Roosevelt undoubtedly intended and, when his strong views were disregarded, might exude an atmosphere of sulky petulance (he had often done so before) that would hardly be helpful to the general proceedings.[26]

So Churchill, eager for the conference Roosevelt proposed ("the sooner the better," said his reply) made no difficulty about leaving Eden behind, agreed to make all arrangements for it in London "on the basis that it is a staff meeting only," and happily accepted the suggestion that the meeting take place in mid-January in what the President described as "a satisfactory and safe place just north of Casablanca." He further agreed "that some of our military men should precede us by a few days to clear the ground."[27]

Approximately four miles from the harbor of Casablanca and at the western edge of the city, in a suburb named Anfa, stands a knoll. Atop this knoll is a hotel, the Hotel Anfa. Its central structure contains commodious rooms suitable for conferences, its outer wall is flanked by a wide veranda, and around it are dotted spacious villas (they belong to the hotel), each with its own garden and lawn. The hotel commands a magnificent view. From its veranda one may look out across a sea that is of a dazzling blue under the normally bright African sky and, overland, across miles of the gleaming white buildings whence the city derives its name. The dominant notes of the long view are blue and white but there is also a blur of other colors which, near at hand, are separable into the blood-red of exposed soil, the black of great jagged shore rocks over which (on most days) a huge surf breaks, the bright yellow-green of grasses, the dark-green explosion of fronds out of the brown trunks of palm trees, and the various reds and yellows and purples of flowers (begonia, bougainvillea, a dozen others) that bloom here abundantly in mid-January.

When British Major General Sir Ian Jacob saw this place immediately after Christmas, it seemed to him perfect for the conference whose site he had been sent out from Algiers to select.[28] He therefore promptly made the necessary initial arrangements. And though those who participated in SYMBOL (the code name was chosen by Churchill) could unanimously agree on little else when the conference was convened as a session of the Combined Chiefs of Staff on January 13, 1943, all were agreed that the choice of a meeting place had been a most fortunate one. The security officers welcomed a site sufficiently remote from the city to be easily guarded (a high barbed wire fence was quickly erected around the whole area). The principals were glad each to have a comfortable villa assigned to him as private living quarters (there was even a villa reserved for General de Gaulle, though it was far from certain at the outset that he would accept an invitation to attend). And it was generally acknowledged that the visual loveliness spread all around, combined with the mild yet bracing climate of Morocco in January, could not fail to exert a benign influence upon the discussion it environed.

Such influence was needed, for the disagreements between British and Americans as to what military operations should be undertaken following the conquest of Tunisia (an event confidently expected to occur in May) were sharp, if by no means as deep as they appeared at the time to be.

British military leaders, under the chairmanship of the British C.I.G.S., General Sir Alan Brooke, remained convinced that any attempt at a full-scale invasion of the Continent from the west in 1943 would be foolhardy.[29] The Battle of the Atlantic against the U-boat was far from won. As the Casablanca Conference opened, one of German Admiral Doenitz's "wolf packs" had just attacked a slow convoy of nine tankers sailing from Trinidad to Gibraltar with oil for Eisenhower's North African forces, and, despite a protective escort consisting of a destroyer and three corvettes, had sunk all but two. The Allies were losing to German submarines a half-million tons of shipping a month, and though the tonnage of new ships produced in American shipyards during 1943 should exceed the tonnage sunk even if the present rate of loss continued, there would remain through the year a shortage of the shipping, the escort vessels, and (above all) the landing craft which would be necessary for a truly exploitable breach of Hitler's Atlantic Wall.

But if they were thus still adamantly opposed to a "premature" cross-Channel operation, the British were equally convinced that, for obvious if not always openly statable politico-military reasons, there must be no long pause in offensive action by the Western Allies against the European Axis following the final victory in North Africa. The commitment to TORCH last July seemed to them to have logical implications for this coming July. The acceptance of the one meant an acceptance of the other, or else the whole North African enterprise must prove as abortive —as futile and barren—as its American opponents had initially claimed it would be. Nor could the working out of these implications be properly deemed a diversion from or a delay of the supreme and culminating enterprise, the direct massive assault from the west on Hitler's Germany. On the contrary, it was a necessary preparation.

What was implied, said the British, was a prompt and swift exploitation of the advantages which would accrue from the final victory in North Africa. Tunisia must be used at the earliest possible moment as a springboard for a drive northeastward across the Mediterranean through Sicily into Italy—a thrust into what Churchill had dubbed the "soft underbelly" of Hitler's Europe. The virtually inevitable politico-military consequences of such a venture would be worth immensely more to the Allies than the cost of obtaining them could possibly be. Italy would almost certainly be knocked out of the war altogether, and if the Germans then moved major forces down the peninsula in an effort to prevent its occupation by the Allies, Italy might become for Hitler what Spain had been for Napoleon, a "bleeding ulcer" draining away strength which would otherwise be deployed in a truly decisive area.

In any case, the elimination of half the European Axis partnership could not but lower German morale while strengthening in the Balkans an already formidable resistance to Nazi tyranny. Turkey might then be persuaded to enter the war on the Allied side, and this, together with a reorientation toward the West of the Balkan resistance, would reduce what Churchill and his key advisers clearly if only tacitly recognized as a long-term threat but which the Americans seemed not to recognize at all, namely, the postwar power which Stalin's Russia could exert over eastern Europe and the seething, troubled Middle East.

To all this, which the British were prepared to back with cold facts and ruthless logic, the American Joint Chiefs of Staff and their new chairman, Admiral Leahy, could oppose no clear and definite proposal of their own. They were much more loosely organized than their British counterparts. The three Services—Marshall's Army, King's Navy, and Arnold's Air Force—continued to operate, not as three arms of a single central organism, but pretty much as three sovereign powers who had entered into an alliance of convenience, or necessity. They competed with one another (especially the Army and Navy) for available resources; they divided between themselves "spheres of influence," the Pacific being primarily the Navy's war and the Atlantic primarily the Army's; the Navy had control of landing craft, with the result that King's lack of commitment to the basic strategy of "Hitler First" could and did have a hampering, limiting effect upon the Army's European operations; and since every decision of the Joint Chiefs must be unanimous—a minority of one was sufficient to block action—it was likely to be a compromise among differing views rather than the firm expression of a single mind and faith.

The U. S. Chiefs were initially agreed, however, in their opposition to British "Mediterranean strategy"; they refused to regard it either as an inevitable postlude to TORCH or as a logical prelude to ROUNDUP (the code name still applied to the cross-Channel assault) within the

Allied Grand Design. Undiminished was the American suspicion (it could not but have some effect, however unadmitted, on Roosevelt's mind) that the British paid only lip-service to a ROUNDUP which, in their secret hearts, they were determined to prevent through repeated indefinite postponements. And where the British saw Italy as a possible "bleeding ulcer" for Hitler, Marshall saw it as a possible "vacuum into which the resources of the cross-Channel operation would be dissipated." He and his colleagues continued to regard the Mediterranean, with Franco Spain at one end of it, "as a kind of dark hole, into which one entered at one's peril," to quote Sir Ian Jacob. The Americans believed that "if large forces were committed . . . ," Jacob continued, "the door would be suddenly and firmly shut behind" them.[30]

Moreover, the American Chiefs shared with a varying intensity the belief (Admiral King's feeling on this point amounted to a passionate conviction) that the British paid far too little heed to the needs and dangers of the war with Japan. If it was now clear that the limits of Japanese expansion had been overreached, it was by no means clear that her final defeat could be accomplished by the United States, which had assumed the prime and virtually sole responsibility for this task, save at the price of a ruinously long and bloody struggle. The growing superiority of the Americans over the Japanese as regards the materials of war—the tanks, planes, ships, guns, and wheeled transport—counted for relatively little in the mountainous jungles of Southeast Asia and the South Pacific islands. Here terrain favored the defense, climate and disease seemed to exact a smaller toll from the Japanese than from the American, and the troops of the Rising Sun continuously demonstrated their willingness to fight to the death for their divine Emperor even when their position was utterly hopeless. Give them time, relax the pressure upon them for only a few months, and the forces of Japan might so consolidate their gains, might so fully exploit their conquered resources, as to make their defenses almost impregnable.

Hence Marshall and his colleagues were inclined to believe (one can hardly be more specific than that about what was actually a balancing of relative emphases) that, since there was no practical possibility of a cross-Channel attack in 1943 (on this they were forced to agree with the British), the Western Allies should go on the defensive in the European Theater for that year and concentrate upon a major offensive against Japan. The Americans suggested that the British commit themselves to the reconquest of Burma, to insure that Chiang Kai-shek's China remained in the war, while the Americans set for themselves the task of cutting Japanese communications to their outlying conquests in the far-western Pacific. Meanwhile, of course, BOLERO (the buildup of resources in the British Isles for ROUNDUP) would be continued at the maximum possible rate.

Thus the issue between the two Allies.

To aid the presentation of their side of it, the British brought with them what one of their historians has described as "an elaborate staff, cipher and planning organization, with the technical mechanism for presenting every quantitative calculation that might be called for."[31] Several days prior to the conference opening, a six-thousand-ton liner fully equipped to serve as staff headquarters and communications center sailed from an English port; it was safely anchored in Casablanca's harbor on January 13 when the planes bringing Churchill, Brooke, and the other British leaders flew over it at the end of their long flight from England. But no such American ship was anchored in the harbor, nor was any substitute for it present in Casablanca when the U. S. Chiefs arrived, and by the time Roosevelt and Hopkins flew in on January 14, the American military leaders were acutely aware that their mental and physical preparations for this confrontation had been far too meager. Sir Ian Jacob, who served as secretary to the British C.O.S. during the Conference, noted with a kind of shocked surprise that the "American party" had failed to bring with them "any kind of staff who could tackle the problems that were bound to arise in the course of the conversations, and to produce detailed solutions for the Chiefs of Staff." He also noted that "when the U. S. Chiefs saw how the land lay and the size of our party, they suddenly woke up to the fact that they had left most of their clubs behind."[32]

Jacob's choice of metaphor indicates something of the feeling that prevailed over the meeting as it opened. And in these circumstances it was indeed fortunate that there were gardens of flowers in which Marshall could pace back and forth between conference sessions, conversing easily if earnestly with American colleagues or (as often happened) Sir John Dill; that there was a beach along which Brooke and British Major General John N. Kennedy could take bird walks with their field glasses ("Delightful hour and a half," says the entry for January 15 in Brooke's diary,[33] "during which we saw goldfinch, stonechat, warblers of all sorts, white wagtail, and several kinds of waders on the seashore, such as sanderlings, ring plover, grey plover and turnstones."); that there were views wide and narrow of the sort that delighted Churchill's Sunday-painter's eye; that the pleasant surroundings were sufficiently exotic to heighten the sense of adventure in Roosevelt, whose mood so far from Washington was that of a boy let out of school; and that in general the clear, dry air with its salt tang and the brilliant light and warmth of the sun relaxed nervous tensions while stimulating mental processes and sharpening perceptions.

Equally benign and, on balance, probably decisive of the harmony the military talks finally achieved was the influence of Sir John Dill. Dill had by this time gained the absolute trust and warm personal friendship of Marshall and the other U. S. Chiefs. He was equally liked and trusted by his compatriots. And to a meeting of the British Chiefs with the Prime Minister on the evening before the first plenary session of the Combined Chiefs in Casablanca he was able to present fully, exactly, and sympathetically every main point of the American position. He concurred in, if he did not actually originate, the line which Churchill decided should be followed by the British during the discussions. The Conference should open, said Churchill, with a presentation by the Americans of their views, after which the British must restrain their impatience for an agreement, pressing their own views with an even-tempered but relentless reiteration, as in "the dripping of water on a stone."[34] Admiral King should be especially encouraged to report at length on the progress and prospects of the Pacific war. There were, as Jacob noted in his diary, two reasons for this. "Our Chiefs felt that they knew so little of what was really going on in the Pacific, or of what the U. S. Navy planned to do, and of the amount of resources that these plans would absorb, that some enlightenment would be valuable," wrote Jacob. "They also felt that 'Uncle Ernie' would take a less jaundiced view of the rest of the world if he had been able to shoot his line about the Pacific and really get it off his chest."[35]

And Dill's benign influence steadily operated upon the sometimes heated discussion of the next five days. Brooke was a naturally impatient man who had strong opinions, no love for staff work (he had been a brilliant battle commander and longed to return to battle command), and a swift mind whose thoughts came out in a fast, clipped speech that grated often upon men of slower minds and speech. They suspected him of trying "to put something over" on them. Dill was able to interpret him to the Americans in ways that smoothed the feathers he had ruffled. He was also able to interpret the Americans to Brooke in ways that prevented disastrous expressions of the latter's impatience.

On the morning of January 18 there was a particularly heated controversy among the Combined Chiefs over the relative emphases to be placed on the Pacific and European Theaters, during which it seemed to Brooke that no progress whatever had been made toward a valid general agreement and that none could be made against King's stubborn refusal to consider the importance of anything outside the Pacific. ("I am afraid that nothing we ever said had much effect in weaning King away from the Pacific," Brooke later said. "This is where his heart was, and the bulk of his Naval Forces. The European war was just a great nuisance that kept him from waging his Pacific war undisturbed.") By lunchtime Brooke was in despair.

"It is no use, we shall never get agreement with them," he said to Dill as the two walked upstairs together.

Dill took a very different view. "You have already got agreement on most of the points," said he. "It only remains to settle the rest." And he suggested that he come to Brooke's room after lunch to discuss the matter.

So after lunch, sitting on Brooke's bed, Dill reviewed the points already settled and, moving on to those still unsettled, asked Brooke what concessions he was willing to make to the American view on these.

"None," said Brooke. "I won't budge an inch."

Dill smiled. "Of course you will," he said. "You know you have to reach an agreement or else put the whole thing up to the Prime Minister and the President. And you know as well as I do the mess that *they* would make of it." Whereupon Dill outlined the basis on which, it seemed to him, agreement could be obtained and upon which, in fact, it was substantially obtained that very afternoon. Brooke was surprised, relieved, grateful. "I am certain that the final agreement being reached was due more to Dill than anybody else. . . ." he wrote later. "I owe him an unbounded debt of gratitude for his help on that occasion and in many similar ones."[36]

Incorporated in an eleven-page report on "The Conduct of the War in 1943," approved by President and Prime Minister at the last plenary session of the Combined Chiefs at Casablanca (Saturday, January 23), the "final agreement" gave top priority to the security of sea communications across the Atlantic, in recognition of the fact that the shipping shortage constituted, as Brooke had insisted, "a stranglehold on all offensive operations." On this, the British and Americans had agreed at the outset. They had similarly agreed that the North African campaign must be pressed to a complete Allied victory and that the effort to supply Russia must be continued. But as regards the major concrete issue which had separated the Allies when the Conference opened, the agreement represented a triumph of the British over the American Staff view, for it ordered preparations to be begun at once for the conquest of Sicily (code-named HUSKY) at the earliest moment possible following the end of the North African campaign. July of 1943 was the target date. Marshall let it be known at the closing plenary session that he had yielded reluctantly to British pressure on this point; he continued to be "most anxious not to become committed to interminable operations in the Mediterranean" and continued to believe that northern France must "be the scene of the main effort against Germany."[37]

As regards the latter, it was agreed that the buildup of resources in Great Britain for the cross-Channel invasion would be continued through 1943 at the maximum rate permitted by operations elsewhere and that the strategic bombing of Germany would be increased, daylight precision bombing by the American Air Force being added to the night bombing already conducted by the RAF. (This represented a triumph of American over British views, the British continuing to be doubtful about the feasibility of daylight bombing.) More important as an earnest of full Allied commitment to cross-Channel action was the appointment of British General F. E. Morgan as "Chief of Staff to the Supreme Allied Commander (Designate)"—a title promptly shortened to COSSAC—with the assigned task of establishing an Anglo-American headquarters for the future Supreme Commander and preparing an outline-plan for the invasion of northwestern Europe from the United Kingdom. (Morgan's principal colleague, not selected until after the Conference had ended, would be the American Brigadier General Ray W. Barker.)

As regards the war against Japan, the "final agreement" was less final and considerably less specific than it was on European operations, but so far as it went it was representative of American rather than British views. It said that "operations in the Pacific shall continue with the object of maintaining pressure on Japan"[38] throughout the year, though these operations were to be so spaced as to cause no excessive drain on resources that would otherwise go to Europe. Whether or not they constituted such a drain was to be a decision, not of the Combined Chiefs of Staff, but of the U. S. Joint Chiefs—an arrangement far from satisfactory to the British. Nor were the British anxieties much soothed by the rather vague stipulation that the Pacific operations be carried out "with the resources available in the theater." These resources, after all, included the greater part of the U. S. Navy, a very substantial portion of U.S. shipping, and the bulk of the landing craft that would otherwise have been available for operations in Europe.

Provisionally approved, and with extreme reluctance by the British Chiefs, was the U. S. Joint Chiefs' proposal for the reconquest of Burma in order to reopen the Burma Road into China. It was to consist of an amphibious operation to capture Rangoon coupled with a major land offensive in northern Burma. Churchill, whose estimate of the importance of Chiang's China to the Allies was far smaller than Roosevelt's, let it be known at Casablanca that he had no liking for the Burma proposal but he raised no such objection to it as might have prevented the over-all "final agreement." He would prudently wait until after the Conference had ended to express his adamant opposition to the whole Burma conception, an opposition which in the event would prevent its execution and provide further food for the American Staff's belief that the pledged word of Englishmen was not to be trusted.

Thus this "final agreement" on military matters at Casablanca was loose-jointed and, in several respects, ambiguous. Only in the circumstances, only in view of the acrimony which had marked so many of the discussions leading to it, could it be regarded as valid cause for relief and gratitude. Yet it was so regarded by Harry Hopkins no less than by Brooke, and Hopkins no less than Brooke was aware (evidently) of Dill's role in achieving it. At breakfast with Churchill on the morning of January 23, Hopkins gloomily remarked that the whole Conference seemed to him "a pretty feeble effort"—but that afternoon he scribbled a note to "Jack" Dill in which he said the eleven-page report, which he had just perused, was "a *very* good paper and damn good plan."[39]

All the while that the Combined Chiefs were threshing out their differences in the conference rooms of the Hotel Anfa, Churchill and Roosevelt in their villas engaged in discussions of political matters. One of these was the immediately pressing problem of governing French

North Africa; another had to do with the surrender terms to be offered the Axis.

Practically simultaneous with the opening of the Casablanca Conference had been the arrival in Algiers of one Marcel B. Peyrouton, flown in a U.S. plane from South America where he had until recently been Vichy France's Ambassador to Argentina. He was brought on Eisenhower's orders to serve under Giraud as Governor General of Algeria, a post in which he replaced the weakling Yves Chatel and for which he had been strongly recommended by Darlan and Robert Murphy. He became at once the focus of as furious a storm of controversy in Britain and America as had been focused on Darlan. There were reasons. Peyrouton had been a notoriously brutal Minister of the Interior in Vichy France, employing police power to suppress all expressions of democracy and to imprison, torture, and kill Frenchmen who dared oppose totalitarianism. Hundreds of Gaullists had been among his victims. He and Laval were bitter enemies, and this was represented to a remarkably incurious Eisenhower as significant of pro-Allied sympathies on Peyrouton's part, though in fact the enmity was personal and indicated no fundamental difference between the two in political philosophy. Indeed, Peyrouton's activities in Argentina had laid him open to the suspicion that he was, in effect, an agent of Nazi-Fascism. His new appointment, therefore, could not but fill out a pattern first publicly revealed by the "Darlan deal"—and to those who had accepted the Four Freedoms and the Atlantic Charter as sincere expressions of Allied war aims, the pattern was one of betrayal. In their outraged view, the official justification of the original arrangement as a merely "temporary" and "purely military" expedient was now wholly discredited.

The sense of outrage was augmented by the fact that Eisenhower continued to maintain a rigorous censorship of all political news in his theater. "Through every possible outlet open to them the De Gaulle forces in London and central Africa were fiercely attacking every French military and civil official in Africa, and the latter wanted to reply, publicly, in terms no less harsh," the general later explained.[40] "I believed that to permit the growth of such a public name-calling contest would create conditions which would make future reconciliation impossible. By imposing political censorship on all I prevented local French officials from participating in the public quarrel." But of course the censorship applied much more harshly to the critics than to the supporters of the status quo in North Africa and it certainly did nothing toward any "future reconciliation" of Gaullists and Vichyites. On the contrary, by increasing De Gaulle's anger with the Americans, by seeming further to confirm his darkest suspicions, the censorship made more difficult the effort to bring Giraud and De Gaulle together in Casablanca.

This effort succeeded only after Churchill had threatened to force De Gaulle's removal from the "headship" of the French Liberation Committee in London (the Prime Minister would withdrew the support of

His Majesty's Government from any "movement" headed by De Gaulle) unless the haughty Frenchman came to meet Giraud, as both the President and Prime Minister had asked him to do. It is doubtful if this threat, which would have been difficult to implement, had much influence on De Gaulle's decision. His objection to coming to Casablanca was not that he did not wish to meet Giraud: he had on his own initiative been trying for weeks to arrange a private personal meeting with the High Commissioner.[41] What he objected to was the fact that the meeting was being forced upon him in order to gain popular support for political arrangements he abhorred. Nevertheless he did at last (on January 22) arrive in Anfa, where he was installed in a villa next door to Giraud's.

He was in no friendly, pliant mood. He had, on the day of his arrival, a stormy session with Churchill followed by a relatively amicable visit with Giraud, who asserted again and again that he concerned himself exclusively with military matters, never listened to the radio or read a newspaper, and paid no attention to politics—though this did not (of course) prevent his having strong and very reactionary political opinions. Giraud regarded as "reprehensible" the "popular and revolutionary character of the resistance in France."[42] That evening De Gaulle arrived "cold and austere" (Hopkins' words) at Roosevelt's villa for his first meeting with the President, and his disposition was not improved when, as he later recorded, he "noticed shadows in the rear of the balcony and saw curtains moving in the corners" of the large room in which he sat side by side with his host upon a couch. "Because of these shadowy presences, the atmosphere of our first discussion was a strange one." And in point of fact, as Hopkins discovered upon investigation, the French visitor was covered by sub-machine guns in the hands of Secret Service agents during the whole of his supposedly private chat with the President![43]

Not until the last possible moment at Casablanca, at noon on Sunday, January 24—while cameramen and war correspondents flown down from Algiers the day before jammed the little garden of the President's villa—did Churchill (with threats) and Roosevelt (with calculated charm) prevail upon De Gaulle to make a public gesture of reconciliation with Giraud. It was badly needed, by the President especially, at this juncture, for the chorus of angry denunciations of "cynical expediency," led by Wendell Willkie, was being dangerously effective from the Administration's point of view. Stonily ignoring Churchillian thunders, the Free French leader turned at last to a smiling and frankly pleading Roosevelt, in the villa's living room where Hopkins and Giraud also were, saying in English to the President, "I will do it for you."[44]

Then the President in his wheelchair was pushed by two attendants to the top of steps leading down into the garden, where the sight of him with Churchill and De Gaulle and Giraud, all four of them together, brought gasps of astonishment from assembled reporters and photographers. He held up his arms so that the attendants could lift and carry him to one of the four chairs that had been set up in a row facing the correspondents. And when he was seated, with Giraud at his right and De Gaulle at his left, and with Churchill (cigar in hand) at the left of De Gaulle, none of them smiling or wholly at ease, the cameras clicked and whirred. Roosevelt suggested that the two Frenchmen shake hands, and they stood up and did so, rather glumly, repeating the handshake for the photographers who had missed it the first time. And that was that. The two Frenchmen (they were to issue an innocuously worded joint statement later) went away with their staffs, leaving the President and Prime Minister seated now next to each other in the brilliant sunlight, with close-cropped grass beneath their feet and flowers blooming behind them, and with the crowd of correspondents before them, pencils poised over note pads.

Then came words from the President which imparted to this meeting with the press a world-historical importance far beyond that of the temporarily famous handshake of two French generals.

A carefully worded official communiqué had been prepared, approved by all concerned, and, of course, revealing nothing beyond the fact that the conference had been held and military decisions taken. This was given to the press. But Roosevelt, speaking from notes, now added to it some off-the-record background information. He then said, speaking slowly and carefully:

". . . Peace can come to the world only by the total elimination of German and Japanese war power. . . . The elimination of German, Japanese, and Italian war power means the unconditional surrender of Germany, Italy, and Japan. . . . It does not mean the destruction of the population of Germany, Italy, or Japan, but it does mean the destruction of the philosophies in those countries which are based on conquest and the subjugation of other people."[45]

Unconditional surrender!

The phrase, which did not appear in the communiqué and had not been formally agreed upon by the British and American Governments, was destined to ring around the world and echo down corridors of years. It came as a surprise to Winston Churchill. "I would not myself have used these words," he said later.[46] But of course he could not at that moment give the slightest hint of the doubts he felt concerning the wisdom of the remark—and indeed these doubts were not, on balance, very serious—as he made his own statement to the press after Roosevelt had concluded. Instead he perforce presented himself as deeply and fully in accord with all that the President had said, and especially with the demand for unconditional surrender.

Roosevelt later indicated that he himself had been surprised by his words. "We had so much trouble getting these two French generals together that I thought to myself that this was as difficult as arranging the meeting of Grant and Lee—and then suddenly the press conference was on, and Winston and I had had no time to prepare for it, and the thought popped into my mind that they had called Grant 'Old Unconditional Surrender' and the next thing I knew I had said it."[47] Actually the key phrase—which was alleged by critics to have the effect of prolonging the war by strengthening the Axis will to resist—appeared in the notes from which Roosevelt spoke, had been seriously discussed with Churchill (who had queried the War Cabinet for its view of the matter), and as long ago as May 1942 had been recommended by a committee set up by the State Department and chaired by the distinguished diplomat, Norman H. Davis, with high officers of the Army and Navy among its members. "It must be remembered that at that moment no one had the right to proclaim that Victory was assured," Churchill later explained. "Therefore, Defiance was the note."[48]

Moreover, at that moment, there were several sound specific reasons for using the phrase. By so loudly closing the door on the possibility of a negotiated peace ("Negotiation with Hitler was impossible," Churchill later declared. "He was a maniac. . . ."), the "unconditional surrender" formula would allay the worst suspicions aroused, in those committed to democracy, by the "deal" with Darlan and the appointment of Peyrouton; the apparently emergent pattern of "appeasement" was broken. The formula would allay to some extent the suspicions of Stalin, and moderate the anger he was bound to feel and express when he learned (and indeed he had already been informed by the time the press conference began) that the kind of "Second Front" he regarded as "promised" for 1943 was not to be established.

iii. *The Battle of the Bismarck Sea*

A month later, on the other side of the Earth, two U. S. Air Force generals leaned over a large map spread out flat on the table before them.[49] One of the two—the smaller in stature, the greater in rank (he had three stars to the other's one)—tapped with his forefinger, absently, the spot on the map designating their present location: they were in Port Moresby on the southern shore of the Papuan Peninsula of New Guinea or, by that token, at the northern margin of the Coral Sea. His gaze, however, with that of his companion, was focused not on the spot he tapped but on another, much farther up the map. This spot was labeled "Rabaul," at the northernmost tip of New Britain or, by the same token, near the southeastern tip of a sea nameless on that map but soon to be called Bismarck.

Both men (Lieutenant General George C. Kenney, Brigadier General Ennis C. Whitehead) had an acute sense of the two spots as centers of opposing forces—focal points where energies of opposite charge accumulated until they were great enough to spark across the force-field they polarized, each striving to overcome the other and dominate the field unchallenged. Or the map, for them, represented a kind of four-dimensional chessboard, a spatial-and-temporal pattern studded with positions of strength and weakness and with points of equilibrium, between which were lines of fluctuating opposing power. But neither man would have naturally described the map in these terms. For them, force was no such metaphysical abstraction as it had become for the theoretical nuclear physicist. It consisted of tangible things-in-motion—things like planes, tracer bullets, ack-ack shells, falling bombs, sea-plowing ships—with a specific number of skilled brains, skilled hands to operate them. And each of the two was vividly aware through personal experience of the myriad concrete individual realties of which the pattern was but a schematic outline.

Perhaps this was especially true of the shorter of the two, the one with the three stars, General George C. Kenney, Commanding General of Allied Air Forces, Southwest Pacific Area, and Commander, U. S. Fifth Air Force, who had a special distrust of the "merely theoretical," a special loathing for "paper shuffling," a special love for direct physical action, and almost no patience at all with efforts not obviously or immediately related to action. At fifty-three he was an old man by Air Force standards, though his abundant hair was still dark and his step had a youthful spring. He had come late to his vocation. Raised in Brookline, Massachusetts, where he went through high school, he had gone three years to the Massachusetts Institute of Technology, had left without graduating, and had not "found himself" until, in his late twenties, considerably older than most of his buddies, he became a combat pilot in World War I. He flew seventy-five missions in France, shot down two German planes, was shot down himself (his survival was little short of miraculous in those days before parachutes), and emerged from the war a captain with a Distinguished Service Cross, a Silver Star, and a career. Between the wars, while advancing at no spectacular speed to the rank of lieutenant colonel, he had concentrated on the technical phases of war aviation, developing in 1928 a method of fragmentation bombing at low altitudes through the use of parachute bombs having supersensitive fuses; the parachutes delayed the explosive contact until the plane had had a chance to get away.[50]

He was a man much like Mark Wayne Clark in many of his mental and character traits—a truncated Mark Clark, for he stood at least seven inches shorter than Churchill's towering "Eagle," possessing his full share of the truculent cockiness (game cockiness) with which short men often feel compelled to face a world of people they must look up to—and these traits had stood him in good stead during the crowded half-year that he had served as MacArthur's principal air officer. Cockiness joined to an absolute personal loyalty to the Supreme Commander was essential to survival in MacArthur's headquarters. Cockiness joined to real ability had been required to clean up the mess he had found when he first came to his new command. He had not forgotten, he would never forget, his first session with Major General Richard K. Sutherland, MacArthur's Chief of Staff. This had been in Lennon's Hotel on the evening of his arrival in Brisbane. Sutherland had let him know that it was altogether the fault of the Air Commander in the Philippines, Major General Lewis H. Brereton, that nearly all the planes at Clark Field had been wrecked on the ground by the Japanese attack of December 8, 1941, despite hours of warning. After all, Brereton had been "advised" several days before to move his planes to Mindanao and had failed to do so! Sutherland had also let him know that Lieutenant General George H. Brett, whom Kenney was replacing, was absolutely no good and that the men he commanded were no good either, for the most part—at least not those with the rank of colonel and above. All of which "information" Kenney had accepted with a show of polite skepticism: it seemed obvious to him that scapegoats and alibis were being manufactured.[51]

Nor was this opinion changed when, next morning, he had his first meeting with Douglas MacArthur in an office on the eighth floor of what had been before the war the home office of a life insurance company in Brisbane and was now Allied Headquarters for the Southwest Pacific. The office was a large one, luckily, for the tall, handsome supreme commander, his sleek black hair and firm-fleshed aquiline face belying his sixty-three years, had ranged a wide floor space as he expatiated at length and with vehemence on the shortcomings of the Air Force in his theater. Up and down he strode, up and down between his oversized baretopped desk and a portrait of George Washington hanging on the opposite wall, his far-famed corncob pipe unlit in his hand,[52] his voice a kind of hoarse, surging growl which somehow managed at the same time to be incisive, asserting the incompetence not only of Brett but of every ranking officer Brett had promoted during these last months. MacArthur proclaimed, as if it were the Voice of God, to contradict which would be blasphemy, that he with his own staff "could take over and run the Air Force out here better than it has been run so far," and that, to their glaring professional incompetencies, Brett and crew had added the heinous crime of "disloyalty" to the person of the supreme commander.

"I will not tolerate it," said Douglas MacArthur. "I demand loyalty from you, from everyone in the Air Force, and I'll get rid of anyone, you included, who doesn't give it."

Whereupon George C. Kenney had gotten to his feet, raised himself to his full height of five feet six inches, and informed the supreme commander that he "knew how to run an air force as well or better than anyone else"; that he proposed to do so in this theater, correcting whatever he found wrong in his command, from the present moment until he was relieved of his duties; and that he would seek such relief if and when it was no longer possible for him to give the kind of loyalty MacArthur demanded and, in Kenney's belief, had every right to demand. This display of force—or matching of egotisms—had been effective. MacArthur had halted his restless pacing, looked hard at his new Air Force commander, and smiled.

"George," he said, "I think we are going to get along together all right."

And they had, too, ever since. For one thing, Kenney before the end of that first full day had found out for himself that some of the most serious of MacArthur's complaints (and Sutherland's, though Kenney was convinced the Chief of Staff's unfortunate personality was partly responsible for the mess) were justified. The Air Force command organization was hard to comprehend on paper and impossible to manage in action; Kenney promptly streamlined it. There were indeed incompetents in key places—staff officers where operators ought to be, and so on; Kenny promptly had them shipped out. There was far too much emphasis on office procedures—the proper filling out of requisition forms, the proper filing of reports—and far too little on the actual flying of planes in combat; Kenny promptly reversed the emphasis. And as he did these things he had the "enthusiastic approval" and full backing of MacArthur—so much so that he was soon able to match his influence with the supreme commander against that of the arrogant Sutherland, and win.

He had won a showdown encounter with the Chief of Staff at the very outset of his command, as a matter of fact, when Sutherland dared issue to him what amounted to tactical orders for operations over Guadalcanal. Storming into Sutherland's office, he had told the Staff Chief that he, Kenney, was running the air show "because I'm the most competent airman in the Pacific," that the present orders were in effect a personal insult which must be at once withdrawn, and that future orders must be couched in terms of general purposes and objectives, leaving the operating details to him and his own men. Sutherland at first had angrily refused to rescind the orders and issue "proper" ones, but did so after Kenney threatened to take up the matter with MacArthur directly.[53]

But of course Kenney was able to maintain this high line only because his Air Force fighting units, embued with new spirit and supplied with at least a minimum efficiency for the first time (the supply situation steadily improved; Kenney spent a lot of sweat and anger in verbal combat with the Service of Supply) began to win battles—had won many battles since that day seven months before when, not yet formally installed in his new command, Kenney had first seen this place where he and his deputy, Brigadier General Whitehead, now, on the last Friday in February 1943, leaned over a map.

It had been soon after daybreak of the last Thursday in July when in an old beat-up B-17 he flew over Port Moresby for the first time after an overnight hop from Townsville, Australia, the plane going down low over the greenish-blue harbor on one side of which clustered native grass huts on stilts at the water's edge and on the other of which were the wharves and town that white men had built, then lower still over the short hilly streets northward until, not far beyond the outskirts of the town, the wheels bounced and shrieked upon the much-bombed airstrip known as Seven Mile. He would never forget how spectacularly beautiful New

BATTLE of the BISMARCK SEA

PACIFIC OCEAN
Kavieng
NEW IRELAND
BISMARCK SEA
Rabaul
NEW GUINEA
FIRST ATTACK MAR.2
CAPE GLOUCESTER
Madang
VITIAZ STRAIT
NEW BRITAIN
HUON PENINSULA
Lae
Finschhafen
MAIN ENGAGEMENT MAR.3
Salamaua
Wau
SOLOMON SEA
PAPUA
Gona
Buna
Dobodura
KAKODA TRAIL
OWEN STANLEY RANGE
Port Moresby
PAPUAN PENINSULA
MILNE BAY
JOMARD PASSAGE
N
W
E
S
CORAL SEA
Miles
0
200

Guinea had seemed that morning, viewed from the air in slanting early light.[54] Twenty miles inland, but dominating the landscape, were the peaks of the Owen Stanley Range rearing straight up to well over two miles into the sky, their lower slopes covered with the dark green of tropical rain forest that spread unbroken in undulating waves toward the coast. Near at hand, the rugged foothills rimming harbor and town were treeless for the most part, covered with yellowish green grasses that looked short and soft from afar but were actually taller than a man and tough and sharp enough to cut human flesh. The fact was typical, symptomatic. Within five hours after his landing, Kenney had developed an acute sense of the danger, suffering, and death that brooded over this savage wilderness, what with the swarming mosquitoes, the poisonous snakes, the jungle fevers, the humid heat . . .

And the Japs.

There had been a Jap air raid on Seven Mile a little before noon that day, as there was on every clear day at that time. Kenney had watched it as he crouched in a crowded slit trench that was half full of muddy water—a dozen bombers from Lae or Salamaua on the north shore, laying their eggs almost lazily, it seemed, from nearly four miles up, destroying on the ground three dive bombers and a couple of damaged fighters and setting fire to several drums of gasoline before flying away unharmed, with seeming contempt, escorted all the while by fifteen fighters that had come perhaps from the airstrip at Buna, directly across the mountains from Moresby, and had had nothing at all to do above Seven Mile save watch the show. On a bare four minutes' notice, ten American fighters had managed to get into the air by the time the first bombs fell, but there they were unable to climb to anything like twenty thousand feet before the Japs had turned back to their home base. The anti-aircraft fire had been equally ineffective; the shellbursts had looked to be well below the height at which the Japs were flying, and were scattered at seeming random all over the sky.

That's the way things had been, just six months ago. The Japanese air arm punished the Allies with impunity while Japanese ground forces pushed overland across the mountains on the Kakoda Trail from Buna toward Moresby, driving the greatly outnumbered Australians before them. All through August and early September the Japs had moved forward, steadily though ever more slowly, until on September 17 they had reached a point only a little more than thirty miles from Moresby and less than twenty air miles from the nearest of the three airfields Kenney was by then developing in that vicinity. There, at last, the Australians stopped and held them.

But, meanwhile, Kenney had so improved his Air Force that it was able to play a key part in the defeat of an attack the Japs made on Milne Bay at the southeastern tip of New Guinea. The attack was originally designed to form one arm of a pincers, the Kakoda Trail attack being the other, which would close on Moresby and pinch off the whole of Papua.

Instead, Allied planes had forced Japanese troop transports and supply vessels out to sea before they were completely unloaded and, by strafing the troops already ashore and bombing the supply dumps, had enabled Australian infantry to establish a defense line relatively so strong that the Jap assault broke futilely against it, with heavy loss of life. A savagely cruel fight it had been in a savagely cruel rainsoaked jungle. The Australians, driving into areas the Japs had briefly held, found that the enemy, who had been ordered to "kill without remorse," had tied Australian captives to trees and used them for bayonet practice, leaving the butchered bodies sagging in ropes beneath placards crudely lettered in English saying, "It took them a long time to die."[55] The Aussies, after that, were as little inclined to take live prisoners as they were to surrender themselves; they, too, killed and killed "without remorse." By the end of the first week in September, the Japanese survivors (some thirteen hundred were left of the two thousand that landed, but hundreds of these were incapacitated by wounds or disease) had been evacuated at night from Milne Bay.

And that had been the turning point in Papua.

A week later, north of Moresby, the Aussies were strong enough to counterattack and drive the Japanese back over the Kakoda Trail in what, aided by U. S. Army troops, became ultimately a rout during which thousands of the Japanese died of fever, exhaustion, starvation, and during which their commanding general was drowned in a river crossing. Then, in November—aided by primitive but surprisingly educable New Guinea natives who helped to ferry Allied troops in commandeered fishing vessels up the northern coast to a beach twenty-five miles south of Buna—MacArthur had launched a brilliantly conceived, bloodily executed campaign whereby the Japanese were driven from Buna and Gona and the Allies left in possession not only of the small Buna airstrip but also of the strategically important Dobodura plain, a level, grassy stretch just six miles inland where Kenney promptly set about constructing a huge airfield within easy striking distance of Rabaul.

So now, by this last Friday in February, a little over a month after the last organized resistance had ceased in the Buna-Gona area, the enemy had perforce gone over definitely to the strategic defensive in New Guinea. He no longer thought in terms of capturing Moresby but rather in terms of holding Lae and Salamaua and the Huon Peninsula some 150 miles up the northern coast from Buna, positions important if not essential to the defense of Rabaul. And as he thought in these terms he was increasingly disturbed by the fact that the Australians still held an airbase in the former gold-mining boom town of Wau, high up in the mountains just thirty miles southwest of Salamaua. Wau was completely isolated, in the heart of wild headhunter country; its garrison was supplied wholly by air; but all through February it had withstood the strongest attacks the Japs could mount with troops then available in that area. Hence the decision of the Japanese high command to move some seven thousand fresh troops into Lae by sea convoy, tripling the size of the force there—a movement so large that preparations for it in both Lae and Rabaul could not be hidden from Allied Intelligence. Broad hints of it had been conveyed to Kenney in Brisbane only yesterday, February 25, and it was this which had brought him flying up to Moresby today to consult with Whitehead. Already he had ordered the cancellation of a big strike that had been planned for Rabaul and had advised his deputy to move the bulk of his fighters (P-38s) and medium bombers (B-25s) to Dobodura, and to have his reconnaissance planes cover with special alertness the sea approaches to New Guinea from not only Rabaul but also Kavieng, at the northwestern tip of New Ireland, and the Admiralties, on the northwestern edge of the Bismarck Sea.

"The thing we've got to do now, Whitey, is think like Japs," he said as his gaze focused on the map spot labeled "Rabaul." "How would we run this convoy if we were Japs?"

And they decided that, in view of the beating taken from the air by the large convoy sent down to reinforce Guadalcanal last November (this had been practically decisive in the Allied conquest of Guadalcanal), they as Japs would certainly take advantage of a weather front which, according to meteorologists, was due to blanket the northern coast of New Britain with heavy rain and thick mists driven by winds of gale force during the first few days of March. This meant that they'd take the northern route, the one they'd taken so often before that there was a line for it on the map, moving west as though aiming for Madang before cutting sharply down through Vitiaz Strait into Huon Gulf. By then the weather front might well have moved into the Gulf also, and they'd be hidden by it all the way to Lae. In any case, by the time the convoy was within range of Allied fighters and medium bombers (as Japs they'd probably have little fear of high-flying B-17s which, Kenney was forced to admit, had practically never hit a moving ship), they would cover with all the planes (there must be about two hundred) available at bases in Rabaul, Madang, Wewak (some 190 miles up the northern New Guinea coast from Madang), Cape Gloucester (on the western tip of New Britain), and Kavieng. They would figure this was enough to overwhelm any attacking force the Allies could put into the air.

"That's one surprise we have for them," said Whitehead grimly, resuming his identity as an American general.

For in point of fact, before this weekend was over, the U. S. Air Force would have 129 fighters and more than two hundred bombers poised, ready and waiting, on Papuan bases.

But this wasn't the big surprise that had been prepared, the one that made Kenney more eager for the approaching action than he had been for any other since he came out here. The big surprise was a new method of attack, called "skip-bombing," making use of five hundred-pound bombs having five-second delay fuses which, like the parachute fragmentation bombs Kenney had devised, enabled bombers to make low-level "can't miss" approaches and clear away before their bombs went off. The tactic, developed primarily by Major William Benn, called for flat approaches to target ships at masthead heights by B-25s that had been specially modified by a "character" (Kenney's term) named Major Paul I. ("Pappy") Gunn.

Gunn, as Kenney had discovered within forty-eight hours after his arrival in Australia, was a phenomenally skilled "gadgeteer" who had been a civilian flier in the Philippines when war came (he looked well over forty years of age, though he blandly declared his age to be thirty) and whose wife and four children were still in Manila, which gave him a very special grudge against Japs. Before Kenney first met him, he had devised a "package installation" of five .50-caliber machine guns for the noses of A-20 light bombers, multiplying their strafing power. This had suggested to Kenney that a similar installation might be made in the noses of B-25s, replacing the bombardier who normally rode there. He had asked Gunn to work on it, and Gunn had come up with a nose-installation of eight .50-caliber machine guns which could rake the deck of a ship with deadly effect while the bomb run was being made.[56]

As regards this convoy supposedly coming out of Rabaul, then, Kenney's plan was to find it with his reconnaissance just as soon as possible, then to keep hitting it with heavy bombers night and day, weather permitting, until it came within range of the fighters and A-20s and B-25s. Meanwhile, light bombers and other short-ranged aircraft would keep Lae under attack, in order to reduce the number of fighters coming up from there. The climax would be a coordinated attack of maximum force using both the Flying Fortresses and the B-25s, with accompanying fighters, and with everything timed to the split second. The B-17s were to come in much lower than they usually did, bombing from eight or ten thousand feet instead of twenty thousand, followed within seconds by masthead skimming skip bombers, and over all this would be an umbrella of P-38 fighters. The effect, if the timing were right—and there was to be a full-dress rehearsal of the show tomorrow, off Moresby—should be devastating.

Kenney and Whitehead, leaning over their map, receiving a report that seven medium and small Japanese vessels had been sighted at eight o'clock that morning moving at eight knots about a hundred miles southwest of Rabaul (it was miraculous that reconnaissance had found anything at all in the weather up there), decided that the climactic attack would be made at ten o'clock in the morning of some day during the first week of March, when the convoy had passed through Vitiaz Strait and was off Finschhafen on the eastern tip of Huon Peninsula.

They could hardly wait . . .

First the prelude, as eight Japanese transports combat-loaded with seven thousand troops and their materiel, escorted by eight destroyers, sixteen ships in all, plow west and south (more west than south) through heavy seas under clouds so low they merge now and then with flying spray cast up by the slicing bows, every aspect of the convoy's operation planned in the most minute detail and everything going according to plan, the weather included, until at four o'clock in the afternoon of March 1 there is a brief break in the clouds and the convoy's commander, Rear Admiral Masatomi Kimuri, sees (has pointed out to him) an American bomber thrusting in and out of the cloud banks, circling, playing hide-and-seek then among the clouds for hours, until the ceiling drops down again and the plane disappears once and for all.[57] Regrettable! thinks the admiral; but he is only mildly worried as the storm continues to rage. Naturally he had hoped for complete surprise—it would have been wonderful to slip all the way into Lae unseen by enemy eyes—but he hasn't expected this to happen. Nor is the loss of surprise a serious matter if the enemy is unable to attack anyway, as he certainly cannot for as long as the present weather holds. It shouldn't be too serious even if the weather clears, for in that case he will have assigned to his protection (his superior officer at Rabaul, Vice Admiral G. Mikawa, has promised him) enough Imperial Army and Navy planes to cover against Allied planes which, inferior in number to begin with (according to his belief), will by then have been further reduced by bombing and strafing attacks on their bases.

Night falls. It is pitch black on heavy seas for the convoy until, sometime after midnight, the wind dies down and stars begin to peep through breaking clouds. The storm, from Kimuri's point of view, has ceased to cooperate, is instead perversely slanting down across New Britain into the Solomon Sea—and when the sun comes up at dawn, March 2, it is into a sky containing far too few clouds, far too few defending fighters (Zekes) for Kimuri's liking. He is in an unfortunate position so far as air defense is concerned. The Zekes, coming from air bases on New Britain and New Guinea, use up so much gasoline reaching him that they can cover for only a little while before turning back to refuel. Hence the admiral regards it as rather more than regrettable—it is a cause of actual anxiety—when at 8:15 a B-24 is seen circling high above the convoy, which is now thirty miles north of Cape Gloucester, heading westward at nine knots toward almost certain trouble.

And trouble is reached, or comes upon them, two hours later in the form of a dozen B-17s and a dozen and a half other heavy bombers from Allied bases (the convoy is still out of the range of P-38s and B-25s) who make flat bombing runs at the surprisingly low altitude of five thousand feet through thick clouds of flack put up by Kimuri's destroyers, through streaming patterns of tracers fired from thirty circling, stabbing Zekes, up and over the now frantically maneuvering ships. Bombs fall as a huge blasting hail so thick that not all of them can be dodged. Within a half-hour one transport, hit squarely amidships, has broken in two and gone down, casting 950 survivors, many of them badly injured, into the sea (a couple of destroyers are ordered to gather them up and push ahead full speed into Lae, where they will unload under cover of night); two other transports are burning, badly damaged by direct hits; three Zekes have been shot from the sky; and all of the bombers have turned back toward their bases, ten of them damaged but none of them so seriously that it cannot get home.

Should he go on? The admiral might well ask himself that question, having been (his command having been) hit and badly hurt by heavy bombers of a sort whose attacks he had learned through earlier experience to regard as little more than annoyances, then seeing Allied reconnaissance over him all afternoon and knowing that if he makes the planned turn into the Strait he'll bring himself by not long after sunup tomorrow well inside the most effective range of Allied fighters and medium and light bombers from Dobodura and Moresby, in addition to heavy bombers. But he has his orders—and Mikawa at Rabaul, though Mikawa knows what he has suffered, does not change them. So on he goes into the sunset and through a night made anxious, even dangerous by an Australian Catalina that hovers over the main convoy and now and then drops a bomb, as if to make certain that there is little sleep among the ships' responsible officers, until the sky brightens with approaching dawn.

So now on the morning of Wednesday, March 3, 1943, he steams southward through calm waters in brilliant sunshine, his convoy loosely sprawled over miles of sea under far fewer Zekes than he'd like to see up there—of the two hundred assigned to cover him, only forty or so can be over him at any one time; they fly high in anticipation of high- and medium-altitude bombing attacks—as the two destroyers that unloaded the survivors at Lae rejoin him. He is now only a few minutes, only a few thousand yards away from the precise time (ten o'clock) and place (fifty miles southeast of Finschhafen) that were named by Kenney and Whitehead, marked on the map spread before them, at Moresby five days ago—the point (spatial, temporal) of fatal execution. The minutes pass. The distance is closed. And there and then he begins to see his fate written in moving dots above the southern horizon as eighteen heavy bombers and twenty medium bombers come toward him at seven thousand feet, with sixteen P-38s above them. Abruptly the sea is no longer calm: it is churned by exploding bombs. The sky is no longer clear: it is pocked by clouds of exploding shells. The scattered ships are swept by a tempest of flame and fragmented steel, and men begin to die upon them by the dozens, by the score, soon (minutes later) by the hundreds.

Men die in the sky also, for here too is a tempest of fire and steel. P-38s rush upon Zekes, guns stuttering, and patterns of smoke and flame are traced upon the clear air (the lightly armored Zekes fall one after another, fall two at a time, blazing coffins for their pilots) in a roaring melee out of which history will pluck for vivid remembrance a single vivid moment, brutal and heroic. It is while the heavy bombers are making their initial attack and the P-38s strive to keep the Zekes off of them. One of the Flying Fortresses, piloted by a Lieutenant Moore, is hit, its wing enveloped in flame, but is held on course steadily to the bomb-release point, at which point, as the bombs fall out of the bay, the wing breaks off and the B-17 plunges downward. Of its nine-man crew, seven bail out and are hanging helpless in their parachutes when ten Zekes dive toward them from the fighter battle above. They die, then —all seven of them die, their bodies riddled by Zeke machine gun bullets—though the last of them to die sees as his last sight on Earth three P-38s swooping down upon the murderous Zekes, the P-38 machine guns speaking the vengeful fury of their pilots. And these also—a Captain Ferrault with his two wingmen, Lieutenant Easton and Lieutenant Schifflett—soon die. They are shot down by an enemy who at the outset outnumbers them three to one, but take with them in death five of the Zekes.

Meanwhile, at the surface of the sea, hard upon the first bomb explosions, comes a swift low-level pass by thirteen Beaufighters of the Australian Air Force, machine guns spraying crowded decks with deadly effectiveness, and immediately after this come a dozen of the renovated B-25s with their skip bombs, Major Ed Larner leading them, followed by a dozen of the renovated A-20s, also armed with skip bombs, roaring in so low that their propeller blasts leave ruffled trails upon the water not unlike the wakes of torpedoes. And torpedoes are what the Japanese ship commanders fear as they watch the wave-skimming approach. They swing their helms hard over to present only bows or sterns, instead of broadsides, to the explosive "fish" they expect the planes to launch; their troops line up on the decks, rifles in hand, facing planes that are low enough to be hit by them; and Larner with his men exult at the sight. The Japanese do just what they are supposed to do in order to get themselves killed by the eight machine guns now carried in the nose of each B-25 and the five in the nose of each A-20. The machine guns open up. They rake the decks from stem to stern, from stern to stem, before the planes are within the range of rifle fire. The Japanese troops are mowed down in rows like wheat by a scythe; the decks are red and slippery with their blood by the time the five hundred-pounders are released to skip like flat stones across the water, angling then into the ships' sides below the water line and exploding there with the effect of mines, tearing gaping holes. It is less a battle than a slaughter. Not since Pearl Harbor has there been such a killing of ships! Of thirty-seven bombs dropped by the dozen B-25s, seventeen score direct hits; of twenty-nine bombs dropped by the dozen A-20s, eleven score direct hits; so that within half an hour every Japanese transport is hit at least once and is either sunk, sinking, or so badly damaged that it can never make port. Of the eight destroyers, one is sunk and three others are badly damaged. (Meanwhile, thirty-eight P-38s are raiding the airfield at Lae, knocking out a half-dozen Japanese planes while losing none of their own and so delaying the replacement of Kimuri's air cover that he is, for a crucial time, deprived of any; the Zekes remaining aloft above him—

and half their original number are shot down—are forced by fuel short-age to retire.)

The slaughter continues.

There is a second major coordinated attack by Allied planes at 3 P.M. when sixteen heavy bombers, a dozen medium bombers, ten skip-bombing B-25s (Larner again leads them), and five Australian light bombers, all covered by eleven P-38s, roar in to finish off one after another of the crippled ships. And even this is not the end. By the evening of March 3 the sea off Huon Peninsula is strewn with rafts and lifeboats bearing Japanese survivors of the sunken convoy, and when these are spotted by Allied planes or by PT boats that night and all through March 4 and 5, they are raked by machine gun fire, blown up by depth charges, shelled. Of those men cast into the sea within swimming distance of the shore and struggling desperately to get there, scores are shot in the water with deliberate ruthlessness. The massacre of hundreds of defenseless human beings is a "grisly task," the U. S. Navy's principal historian will later admit, but "a military necessity since Japanese troops do not surrender."[58] (This same historian, speaking of the few hundred survivors who manage, after all, to reach shore, will say that "for a month there was open season on Nips in Papua," the natives having "the time of their lives tracking them down as in the old head-hunting days.")

At three o'clock on the morning of Thursday, March 4, 1943, in Brisbane, George C. Kenney knocked at the bedroom door of a sleeping Douglas MacArthur who, thus awakened to receive the "final talley" of the battle as reported by Whitehead in New Guinea, shared at once and fully his airman's jubilation.

This "final talley," as we know, greatly overestimated Japanese losses. According to Kenney there had been at least eleven and maybe fourteen merchant vessels in the convoy, of which every one had been sunk. Another merchant ship had been destroyed in Lae's harbor, and yet another in Wide Bay. Six destroyers, some of which had been inflated to the dimensions of light cruisers in Kenney's belief, had been sunk, two others damaged. Sixty aircraft had been definitely destroyed, twenty-five others probably destroyed, ten damaged. And somewhere between ten and fifteen thousand Japanese had been killed. All this had cost the Allies only thirteen dead and a dozen wounded. Four Allied planes had been shot down—Lieutenant Moore's B-17 and the three P-38s that had come vainly to his rescue; two other planes had made crash landings at their home base. ". . . a magnificent victory . . . has been achieved," said MacArthur in a radio message heard around the world. "It cannot fail to go down in history as one of the most complete and annihilating combats of all time."[59]

Actually the Japanese had lost only twelve ships (the eight transports in the convoy and four of the escorting destroyers); between twenty and thirty aircraft; and something over three thousand men. Even so, the victory was great in itself, and greater still in its effects. Never again would the Japanese enemy dare send a convoy, or any merchantman of any size, into waters covered by American planes. Never again would he seriously contemplate any such offensive in New Guinea as he had planned to launch against Wau. From this time forward all his efforts would be designed to hold what he had or, if lose it he must, to make the Allies pay a maximum price for what they gained. Soon, in the immediate aftermath of this Battle of the Bismarck Sea, the Americans would initiate what had been designated in the U. S. Joint Chiefs' directive of July 2, 1942,‡ as Task Two and Task Three and which had been combined by the planners in MacArthur's headquarters into a plan code-named ELKTON.

Prepared in response to instructions issued MacArthur by the Joint Chiefs shortly before they left Washington for the Casablanca Conference, ELKTON called for the capture of Lae and Salamaua and all the airfields of the Huon Peninsula, of Munda Point and other key airfields on New Georgia, in the Solomons, and of airfields on New Britain and Bougainville to support climactic operations against Kavieng and the key base at Rabaul. Within three hours after Kenney had completed his report of triumph to MacArthur, he with Sutherland and Major General Stephen J. Chamberlin, Sutherland's Operations officer (G-3), was in a plane headed toward Washington where, after some days of heated wrangle, much of it centered on the precise division of authority between Nimitz and MacArthur, approval of a considerably revised (reduced) ELKTON was obtained from the Joint Chiefs, along with the additional planes and other weapons and materiel needed to implement it.

On March 28, the Joint Chiefs issued a directive which—superseding that of July 2, 1942—ordered MacArthur as commander of the Southwest Pacific Area to seize the Lae-Salamaua-Finschhafen-Madang portion of New Guinea and to send occupation forces into western New Britain. It also ordered Admiral W. F. (Bull) Halsey as commander of the U. S. Naval Forces in the South Pacific to occupy the Solomon Islands up to and including southern Bougainville, operating in this campaign under MacArthur's "strategic direction." All forces in the Pacific Ocean not specifically assigned to these operations were to remain under the supreme command of Admiral Nimitz. Thus was established the outline which events would follow in the South and Southwest Pacific through the remainder of 1943.

Out of this directive came a formal "Strategic Plan for the Defeat of Japan" which the Joint Chiefs presented to the Combined Chiefs at a top-level conference in Washington in May—a conference called at Churchill's insistence and upon which he bestowed the code name TRIDENT . . .

‡ See page 252.

iv. *A Luncheon at the British Embassy*

The Prime Minister during this conference, as on his earlier visits to Washington, was a personal guest of the Roosevelts, and was assigned the same room in the White House as before. But on this Saturday, May 22, 1943, he was staying in the British Embassy as guest of the Ambassador, Lord Halifax. He had asked the Ambassador to arrange for him the luncheon to which he now, late in the noon hour, descended—had asked that invitations to it be issued such leading Americans as were most necessary for fruitful discussion of a set topic of which they (the Americans) were to be apprised beforehand—and as he entered the dining room he was gratified but by no means surprised to see that every invitation had been accepted.[60]

He shook hands with tousle-haired, dreamy-eyed Henry Wallace, Vice-President of the United States; with thin-visaged, dispeptic-looking Henry Stimson, Secretary of War; with clamp-jawed and bespectacled Harold L. Ickes, Secretary of the Interior; with the shaggy Texan, Tom Connally, Chairman of the Foreign Relations Committee of the Senate; and with the urbane and coldly handsome Sumner Welles, Under Secretary of State. (Conspicuously absent was Welles' superior, Secretary of State Hull, uninvited in recognition of the continuing and increasingly acrimonious feud between Hull and Welles, and of the fact that Welles was the more highly regarded of the two by the British, both as a mind and as a man. Soon Roosevelt would be forced to request Welles' resignation, however, for the Secretary and Under Secretary could no longer work together at all and the President could not afford the loss of Hull's rare influence over a Senate in which he had served several terms.) A few minutes later all were seated at the long table, conversing over their food while spring breathed softly through opened windows, stirring the long draperies. There spread through the room a sweetly mingled scent of roses and new-mown grass. Then the meal was ended and all the fresh, clean odors from out-of-doors were drowned abruptly in the smoke of Churchill's huge black cigar and of the cigarettes which several of the other men lit.

Discussion of the assigned topic was begun. . . .

It was a topic not indicated on the formal conference agenda but very strongly indicated, its urgency continuously augmented, by the turn and march of world events since the Prime Minister's last visit to the American capital. At the opening session of the Conference, in the President's Oval Study ten days ago, Churchill referred to the "striking change" that had occurred in the general situation since he had last sat where he now did, beside the President's desk, less than a year ago. "It was here that I heard the ominous news of the fall of Tobruk," he recalled, adding that he would "never forget the manner in which the President sustained me at that time."[61] Different indeed was the news coming out of Africa as he spoke on the afternoon of May 12. At that very moment the newspapers and radios of the world were proclaiming the final collapse of Axis resistance in Tunisia where Montgomery's British Eighth Army, having driven all the way from Egypt, had at last formed a juncture with Alexander's British, American, and French forces in the second week of April, coming then under the over-all command of Eisenhower and forming an iron chain around the Italian and German troops (including all that remained of the once invincible Afrika Korps) who stood in Tunisia with their backs to the sea and their sea communications virtually destroyed by Allied naval units and air power. The iron chain had swiftly tightened. On May 7, the Allies had thrust into both Tunis and Bizerte. On the day TRIDENT opened, the Axis forces were squeezed, helpless and hopeless, into the small Cape Bon Peninsula where, on the morrow, their commander, Colonel General Jürgen von Arnim (he replaced Rommel, who had been called to Germany) would surrender them and himself unconditionally.

So TORCH had ended in a final brilliant blaze of triumph. More than 340,000 of the enemy had been killed, wounded, or captured; in the culminating acts of surrender, some 252,000, including fifteen German and seven Italian generals, became prisoners of war. A total of 1969 enemy aircraft had been destroyed while 633 had been captured intact on the ground (the Allied air loss totaled 657 planes), and 184 enemy ships had been sunk—95 by air attack, 47 by submarines, 42 by surface forces. And there was every reason to believe that HUSKY, the upcoming invasion of Sicily, now being mounted with an immensely wider margin of safety than TORCH had had, would also produce triumph.

But what was to follow HUSKY? How was the inevitable and probably swift conquest of Sicily, following hard upon the conquest of North Africa, to be exploited? By the invasion of Italy itself, Churchill was convinced and most forcefully said as TRIDENT opened. The fruit, ripe for the plucking, would include the Italian Fleet, the loss to Germany of the twenty-six divisions with which the Italians now garrisoned the Balkans in aid of their Axis partner, and possibly Turkey's permission of Allied bases on her soil within easy air reach of the great Ploesti oil fields in Rumania. Moreover, as in the case of the defection of Bulgaria at the end of the First World War, "the collapse of Italy would cause a chill of loneliness to pass over the German people, and might be the beginning of their doom."[62] The alternative, in view of the fact (agreed upon by all) that a cross-Channel assault upon France could not be launched with a reasonable chance of success prior to the late spring of 1944, would be a full year's disengagement from the enemy in Europe by British and American forces at a time when they were magnificently equipped, with battle-hardened troops and a growing superiority of air and sea power, to strike telling blows, and at a time when the "prodigious" Russian effort was costing the Russian people "torrents of blood" and placing the Western Allies greatly "in their debt."

As for the Far East, where Britain bore a major share of the responsibility, the Prime Minister (as the Conference opened) had made it abundantly clear that he opposed adamantly any operation that might seriously reduce the force available in Europe for action exploitive of the confidently expected conquest of Sicily. The offensive in Burma, approved at Casablanca and code-named ANAKIM, was a physical impossibility; it must be recognized as such by anyone who realistically balanced Allied capabilities in that portion of the world against those of the Japanese. And it had been ill-conceived in the first place. "Going into the swampy jungles to fight the Japanese is like going into the water to fight a shark," the Prime Minister had written in a paper addressed to the British Chiefs of Staff as he and they were in midpassage of their Atlantic crossing to this meeting, on the *Queen Mary*. "It is better to entice him into a trap or catch him on a hook and then demolish with axes after hauling him out on to dry land."[63]

Though he did not explicitly say so, Churchill was convinced that the estimated costs and dangers of overcoming the Japanese in the Pacific, by forces available to Nimitz and MacArthur, were exaggerated through Admiral King's influence in decisions taken by the U. S. Joint Chiefs. What had happened in Europe might be likened to the blunting and then the cutting off of a pincers movement by Nazi Germany; one arm of the pincers had thrust through North Africa toward the Middle East, the other had thrust down through southern Russia toward the same objective. Both were now definitely defeated—by the magnificent Russian stand and counterattack at Stalingrad, by the annihilating conquest of Axis empire in Africa. And much the same thing had happened in the Pacific. The Japanese had designed a huge pincers movement which would pinch off all the Pacific from the Hawaiian Islands westward while a sword was thrust directly into the Hawaiian Islands. This design had been frustrated by the battles of the Coral Sea and Midway last year and by the conquests of Guadalcanal and Papua this year.

As for the enfeebled northern prong of the pincers in the fogbound Aleutians, which could in any case be little more than a nuisance to the Allies in the absence of a southern prong, it was at that very moment being nipped off by an American attack which bypassed the main Japanese base on Kiska and focused on Attu, the westernmost island. The newspapers were full of it on that day of TRIDENT's opening, for the assault had been launched by two U.S. forces just the day before, May 11. (It was destined to end some three weeks later in a Japanese act which sent a thrill of horror through the Allied world, a thrill of pride through the Japanese homeland, and which defined as sharply as any event of the war the basic differences between Japanese and Western attitudes toward life and death. Trapped on a ridge between Chichagof Harbor and Sarana Bay, a thousand Japanese troops under the command of Colonel Yasuyo Yamasaki made a wild *Banzai* charge, screaming "Japanese drink blood like wine" and forcing the Americans to butcher them like animals in a slaughter pen. The few who managed to penetrate the American lines, and those who lay wounded on the ground, held hand grenades against their bodies and blew their intestines out in a bloody mess. Later were found many of the "final letters" of those who thus destroyed themselves. "Is war such a thing as this?" said one of them. "Soon after firing ceases, birds are singing and flying around above the quiet and frozen ground." Said another: "I will become a deity with a smile in this heavy fog. I am only waiting for the day of death!"[64])

The military staff talks which started the day after the initial session in the President's office resembled those at Casablanca in that they began in harsh discord but now, ten days later, promised to end in (considering the initial divergence of views) a surprising harmony. In part this was because the initial divergence was not wholly along nationalistic lines. Certainly it was not as regards the Far East.

This was the first major strategy conference to be attended by field commanders from the China-Burma-India Theater, and the three principals who came—British Field Marshal Wavell of India and American Generals Stilwell and Claire L. Chennault from China—were at odds with one another in their strategic concepts. Especially was this so of Stilwell and Chennault. The former, driven out of Burma a year ago in a heroic but disastrous retreat ("The Japs ran us out . . ." he said flatly. "We took a hell of a beating!") and struggling now to train and equip a modern Chinese army, was convinced that the recapture of Burma with a consequent reopening of the Burma Road was essential to the success of any large-scale offensive against the Japanese in China. He therefore insisted that the Burma campaign be given top priority, though he differed from his British colleagues as to its nature and timing, and that the bulk of the supplies being flown into China from India over the "Hump" (the Himalayas) should be assigned to his ground-force training center in Yunnan. Chennault, who had gained deserved fame as commander of the American volunteer "Flying Tigers" fighting in China against Japan prior to America's entry into the war, and who had come nominally under Stilwell's orders when this volunteer group was incorporated into the U. S. Fourteenth Air Force of which he (Chennault) was given command, was convinced that top priority should be given his air operations. The Air Force, as he was not loathe to point out, had gained the only Allied victories over the Japanese in China; it would achieve decisive victories, in Chennault's view, if it received the emphasis, the material support, which Stilwell sought to obtain for his ground operations. As for the danger of provoking a Japanese offensive which, in the absence of strong Allied ground forces, could capture the Allied air bases—a danger of which Marshall, who supported Stilwell, was acutely aware—Chennault refused to countenance it. If such an offensive occurred, he indicated, he could defeat it with his Air Force, provided this was strengthened as he asked.

The issue was sharp.[65] Its cutting edge went all the deeper into living flesh because of the personalities who defined it. For Chennault was approximately as acid and irascible as Stilwell, and the quarrel between the two had already produced some legendary shouting matches. ("It's the ground soldier slogging through the mud and fighting in the trenches who will win the war!" shouted Stilwell. And Chennault shouted back: "But God damn it, Stilwell, there *aren't* any men in the trenches!") It was not a quarrel on even terms, however, as TRIDENT opened. To do what Stilwell proposed to do would have required abrupt and drastic reforms in Chiang Kai-shek's government; Stilwell daily encountered as an enemy more frustrating than the Japanese the graft and corruption which permeated Chiang's political party and ruling clique, the Kuomintang. To do what Chennault proposed to do, on the other hand, required no disturbance of the Chinese political and economic status quo; the Generalissimo and his entourage had only to watch, applaud, and enjoy a victory won for them, without effort on their part, by the American Air Force. Hence Chiang was a strong supporter of Chennault's strategic concept and of Chennault personally against Stilwell, whom he had actually come to hate and who in turn had for China's dictator the most profound contempt ("Vinegar Joe" continuously referred to Chiang in private and not-so-private communications as "The Peanut"). Moreover, Chiang's views and prestige were aided at that moment in Washington by the charming presence in America of Madame Chiang.

The upshot was that Chennault prevailed over Stilwell in such harmony as finally emerged from TRIDENT's initial dissonance. "The Conference is not justified in ignoring the possibility of a Chinese collapse," the President had said in his talk following Churchill's on May 12, indicating (if vaguely) his support of the Burmese operation. But the British thought the possibility remote that China would be knocked out of the war, and in any case continued to place no such weight on the value of China's contribution to the total Allied effort as the Americans did. Out of this balancing of opposing views came the decision that there should be "vigorous and aggressive land and air operations at the end of the 1943 monsoon in Burma" but that merely "administrative" preparations were to be made for ANAKIM and that Stilwell could not have the American infantry divisions for which he was begging. Chennault, on the other hand, did receive a large portion of the increased air strength that he asked for.

Insofar as the initial divergence of views was along nationalistic lines (and as has been said, it was not wholly so), the Far Eastern decision might be judged a compromise between the British and American positions. Concerning operations in the Pacific, however—a theater virtually removed by circumstance, and Casablanca agreement, from effective control by the Combined Chiefs—the decision was wholly an expression of American views. The U. S. Joint Chiefs' "Strategic Plan for the Defeat of Japan," including those portions of it which were weakened in the event by the decisions made concerning Burma and China, were approved with some modification; it called for the capture of the Marshall and Caroline Islands as well as of the Japanese positions yet remaining in the Solomons, the Bismarck Archipelago, and New Guinea.

As regards the European Theater, where the initial divergence between British and American views was great, compromise again ruled and issued in decisions that were, in Winston Churchill's opinion, much too precise in their design upon the distant future and much too vague in their design upon the future lying immediately ahead. Despite the triumph in North Africa, the American Joint Chiefs continued to regard Mediterranean operations as "peripheral" and "indecisive," and openly regretted the fact that the British insistence upon TORCH last summer and upon HUSKY at Casablanca had committed them to these enterprises. ("What strategy would you have preferred?" Brooke asked Marshall with some asperity as the two, accompanied by Dill, walked to one of the meetings. "The cross-Channel attack," Marshall promptly and predictably replied. "We should finish the war more quickly." "Probably so," said Brooke, "but not in the way we hope to finish it!"[66]) The Americans were vehemently opposed to any large-scale operations in Italy, flatly refusing (as at Casablanca and before) to regard these as an organic element of the strategy whose climax would be the invasion of France. Upon the latter, now code-named OVERLORD, they wished to concentrate all effort in the European Theater, and they were determined to bind the British into a hard and fast decision as to the date and scale of this culminating operation. From this American pressure came a TRIDENT agreement that D-Day for OVERLORD should be May 1, 1944; that the initial assault should be made by nine divisions, two of them airborne; that these nine, having secured the bridgehead, should be immediately followed by twenty others; and that in preparation for this event, four American and three British divisions would be moved from the Mediterranean to the United Kingdom after November 1. Further preparation for the great invasion would be a vastly increased air offensive against Germany and German-occupied Europe, to proceed in four phases of which the last and greatest would be reached in April 1944. It was intended to destroy Germany's fighter planes and, through massive and incessant bombing, her production and transportation facilities and the morale of her people.

There remained the question Churchill had raised on the conference's opening day. HUSKY would be launched in a few short weeks; what was to follow it in the Mediterranean? On this the Combined Chiefs had not been able to agree, ten days later, as the Prime Minister met with his luncheon guests in the British Embassy. Nor would they reach any precise agreement by the time TRIDENT ended three days later. Their nearest approach was a formal resolution:

"That the Allied Commander-in-Chief North Africa [Eisenhower] will be instructed, as a matter of urgency, to plan such operations in exploitation of HUSKY as are best calculated to eliminate Italy from the war and to contain the maximum number of German forces. Which of the various specific operations should be adopted, and thereafter mounted, is a decision which will be reserved to the Combined Chiefs of Staff."[67]

The Prime Minister would not, could not let the matter rest there. He had already decided to fly from Washington to Algiers as soon as TRIDENT ended, there to consult with Eisenhower on post-HUSKY operations and to throw all his considerable weight on the side of an invasion of Italy and against the invasion of Sardinia which the U. S. Joint Chiefs favored. With the President's permission, Marshall would accompany him on this important journey.

But though Churchill was far from satisfied with many of the details of TRIDENT, he was impressed and gratified by the conference's prevailing mood—a mood of calm and utter confidence. Surely it was justified by events! Six months of disaster had been followed by six months of triumph, and there was every reason to believe that (as he would later write) "this agreeable change" would continue "to the end of the struggle." On the very Saturday of the British Embassy luncheon, morning newspapers reported that General Jimmy Doolittle's Strategic Air Force, operating under Eisenhower's supreme command, had bombed throughout the central Mediterranean the day before, paying special attention to the heavily fortified Italian island of Pantelleria, about forty miles from Tunisia, destroying 113 enemy planes (most of them on the ground) at a cost of a single Allied plane; that Attu was now secured, though "mopping up" continued; and that Tokyo had announced the death of Admiral Isoroku Yamamoto, the greatest of her naval leaders, in airplane "combat with the enemy." (Yamamoto was supposed to have boasted he would dictate peace terms to the United States from the White House. His death was a "planned kill" by U. S. Army Air Force fighters flying off Henderson Field on Guadalcanal. They had been assigned the task by Nimitz upon receipt of remarkably precise intelligence of Yamamoto's decision to fly on an inspection trip to a Japanese base in the northern Solomons. The two bombers carrying him and a half-dozen of his key staff officers were shot down as they came in to land on April 18, 1943.) The Allies had climbed out of the valley of the shadow of death into uplands lighted by the sun of armed victory. For the first time, large operations could be planned in the assurance that there would be a sufficiency of manpower and materiel for their successful execution (there was a troubleseome shortage of steel needed for landing craft, but this was the only serious one). The initiative had passed wholly out of the hands of the Axis, and it seemed no longer possible that the Allies could lose the war.

They might, however, lose the peace. Even this possibility appeared greatly reduced by an announcement from Moscow that morning, a political announcement of such importance that it crowded much battle news off the front pages of newspapers. Since the early 1920s, a principal obstacle to friendly relations between the U.S.S.R. and other nations had been the active existence of an organization known as the Communist International (the Comintern), an agency through which the Communist parties of the various countries were knit together into a single international revolutionary party directed from Moscow and dedicated to the subversion and overthrow of existing governments elsewhere. It was in effect a hostile action and propaganda arm of the Soviet Government. But today it was announced that the Executive Committee of the International, meeting in Moscow, had on May 15 proposed its own dissolution! This was said to mean that the separate Communist parties, freed from their "duties and obligations" to the Third International, would be enabled "to adapt their . . . programs and political activities to the conditions prevailing in the various countries where they exist." Washington and London "hailed" this "step" as a "great gain for the Allies." Earl R. Browder, chief of the U. S. Communist Party, had expressed himself as gratified, stressing at the same time that American Communists had not been members of the Comintern since 1940. Wendell Willkie had also expressed himself as gratified, provided the announcement really meant what it seemed to mean: it made him "hopeful of better Allied relations."

Nevertheless, a real possibility remained that the peace following victory over the Axis Powers would prove as illusory as that which had followed the German defeat of 1918, and it was upon the making and keeping of a genuine world peace that the discussion at this Embassy luncheon was focused. What should be the structure of a postwar settlement? What kind of international organization was required to prevent the ruthlessly aggressive nationalism that had produced World Wars I and II? How was it to be brought into being? This was the "immense theme" that Churchill wished to consider with his American guests, and of it he now made, at the "formally expressed desire" of these guests, a statement of his own views.

The first or at any rate the most immediate consideration must be the prevention of armed aggression by Germany or Japan, said he. Everyone agreed that both nations must not only be disarmed but also kept from rearming. Stripping Japan of her conquests should effectively inhibit her in this respect; she lacked in her home islands the iron with which to build and the oil with which to run a modern war machine. But Germany, having greater natural resources within her prewar boundaries—possessed of an overweening national egotism, a population energetic and capable, an advanced technology, and a General Staff that (behind thick cloaks of secrecy) was a maker as well as an executor of government policy—presented a more menacing problem requiring a more drastic solution. Churchill favored the separation of Prussia from the remainder of a country over which Prussian militarism had exerted so baneful an influence ever since the formerly independent German States had been unified by Bismarck's ruthless genius just seventy-odd years ago. He acknowledged, as an aside, that there were "many people who wish to carry the process of division further, dividing Prussia itself into component parts."[68]

(Did he look at Sumner Welles as he said this? He might well have done so. For Welles had made no secret of his personal conviction that not only should East Prussia be wholly detached from Germany and made an integral part of Poland, but also that the main body of Germany should be broken into three parts whose boundaries would be "determined primarily by cultural, historic, and economic factors."[69] One of these, a State of Southern Germany, of which the largest unit would be Bavaria and comprising the Rhineland and Saar regions, would have a population predominantly Catholic. The other two would be predominantly Protestant. There would be a State of Eastern Germany, of which the largest unit would be Prussia [minus East Prussia], and a State of West Central Germany, comprising Hanover, Oldenburg, Hamburg, and a congeries of small former principalities.)

"But on this," said Churchill, "I reserve judgment."

He hurried on, then, from the negative to the positive aspect of his "immense theme." The heads of the United Nations, and all present in this room, were agreed that a world organization was required to keep the peace, and that this organization must be founded on the principles of justice and freedom and upon a revived prosperity. Only as regards the formal structure of this organization was there disagreement. His own view (he stressed that it was a personal view, not the view of His Majesty's Government) was that the supreme authority should be vested in an association of the United States, Great Britain, and Russia, to which might be added China, if the United States insisted upon it, though China was not a Power comparable to the other three. "On these Powers would rest the real responsibility for peace." They would constitute, with "certain other Powers" whose membership would be a rotating one, a Supreme World Council.

Subordinate to the World Council would be three Regional Councils—one for Europe, one for the Pacific, one for the Western Hemisphere—upon which would devolve the responsibility for the earliest efforts to settle quarrels and prevent hostilities within their respective areas. "It is only the countries whose interests are directly affected by a dispute who can be expected to apply themselves with sufficient vigor to secure a settlement," he said. "If countries remote from the dispute are among those called upon in the first instance to achieve a settlement, the result is likely to be merely vapid and academic discussion." He readily admitted (in response to a question from Wallace) that disputes might arise which could not be settled on a regional basis, these being precisely the disputes most threatful of world conflict. But in such cases the quarrel would inevitably pass swiftly from the purview of the Regional Council to that of the Supreme World Council, whose rotating members were to be elected as representatives of the three regions.

A palpable weakness of the League of Nations—the principal cause, in fact, of its collapse into the abyss of World War II—had been its inability to impose effective sanctions, economic or military. The world organization which Churchill proposed would have sufficient armed force to deter and suppress aggression. He suggested that there be an agreement among the nations concerning the size of the armed forces each would maintain, and that the forces of each country be divided into two contingents, one to constitute the national armed forces, the other to become part of "an international police force at the disposal of the Regional Councils under the direction of the Supreme World Council." Each of the national contingents assigned to the police force would "be bound, if it were so decided by the World Council, to undertake operations against any country other than its own."

When Henry Wallace raised the question of bases for the Regional Council contingents (were there to be internationalized zones and forts occupied by the internationalized forces?), Churchill made vague reply. Within the world security organization he proposed there would be, said he, plenty of room for "special friendships" between nations so long as these were "devoid of sinister purpose against others." Such a "special friendship" should certainly continue between the United States and the British Commonwealth. Indeed, referring to wartime ties so close the two great Powers were virtually bound into one, he ventured to suggest that there be "some common form of citizenship, under which citizens of the United States and of the British Commonwealth might enjoy voting privileges after residential qualification and be eligible for public office in the territories of the other, subject, of course, to the laws and institutions there prevailing." As regards bases, a precedent had been set in the destroyer-bases deal of 1940—a precedent he hoped would be followed in the future. "I look forward to an extension of the common use of bases for the common defense of common interests. In the Pacific are countless islands possessed by enemy Powers. There are also British islands and harbors. If I have anything to do with the direction of public affairs after the war, I shall certainly advocate that the United States have the use of those that they might require for bases."

In the discussion following Churchill's presentation there was no outspoken disagreement with his conception of regional organization. Welles, whose official duties included work with an Advisory Committee on Postwar Foreign Policy established by the Secretary of State in 1942 and who therefore had devoted more time and thought to the problems of organized world security than had any of the other Americans around the table, was already committed to the idea of "building the world organization upon a foundation of regional systems."[70] He knew, for one thing, that this conception was much more likely to find favor with the President than would the conception of a single strong world authority, though even it went a good deal farther toward a pooling of sovereignties in an international peace-keeping agency than Roosevelt was yet prepared to go.§ Lord Halifax wondered if the formation of a European Regional Council would have the effect of "disinteresting" U.S. public opinion in European affairs, especially since the U.S. would be simultaneously involved in the Regional Council for the Western Hemisphere. He asked Welles if this might not be the case. Welles did not think so. After all, each Regional Council would operate under the supreme authority of the World Council, and the United States would be a permanent member of this as well as the leading member of its regional bloc. American public opinion would therefore have to concern itself with world as well as with regional affairs. Stimson interjected at this point his strong conviction that, whatever the form finally decided upon for the world security organization, the decision must be made *before* the war ended. Speaking out of his bitter experience as a Republican supporter, in 1919 and 1920, of American participation in the League of Nations, he gave it as his emphatic opinion that Americans would "relax" as soon as hostilities had ended and would thereafter be "reluctant to embark upon new international experiments"; if an effective world security organization were not actually in being by the time the last shot of this war was fired, it never would be. With this, the other Americans around the table were inclined to agree. They did definitely agree that plans for future cooperation among the United Nations could be most easily and surely laid while the urgent need for it was daily manifest on the battlefields of the world.

But if the Americans at this luncheon were inclined to agree in general with the "regional" approach which Churchill, and Welles, took toward the problem of postwar organization, there were other Americans who most emphatically did not. Among these (as Welles well knew) was Secretary of State Cordell Hull.

The State Department's Advisory Committee had a membership carefully designed by Hull to represent a fair cross-section of American public life. Both Republican and Democratic Senators and Representatives served on it. Personal representatives of the Secretaries of the Treasury, War, and Navy; two members of the President's personal staff (David K. Niles and Lauchlin Currie); and the Librarian of Congress (Archibald MacLeish) served on it. Also serving were such eminent Americans as James T. Shotwell of the Carnegie Endowment for International Peace; Brooks Emeny, director of the Foreign Affairs Council; William Green, President of the American Federation of Labor; Philip Murray, president of the Congress of Industrial Organizations; Walter P. Reuther, director of the General Motors Department of the

§ Roosevelt in the spring of 1943, impressed by the wartime collaboration between the heads of the four Great Powers, wished to perpetuate it in an establishment whereby the United States, Britain, Russia, and China would police the world with their armed forces, all other nations, France included, being disarmed. To deal with special international problems of food, relief, health, economics, and so on, he favored establishing specialized agencies. These would function separately. He saw no need to subordinate them to a single coordinating body.[71]

United Automobile Workers; and Eric A. Johnston, president of the United States Chamber of Commerce. Membership from the State Department was deliberately severely limited, but Sumner Welles was appointed committee chairman.

Early in 1942, this body decided that an interim international political organization, to be known as the United Nations Authority, should be created at the earliest possible moment so that machinery for international collaboration would be in operation when the war ended. It was to consist not only of the four Great Powers (including China) but also of all the other United Nations, though the manner of the latter's participation remained undetermined. The Committee also decided that war relief, though the bulk of it must necessarily be provided by the United States, should be administered through an International Relief Council composed of representatives of the United Nations, headed by an American, and that it should *not* be used for political purposes but should aim solely at feeding, clothing, housing, and curing the ills of war-ravaged peoples. In this way the United Nations would become more than a temporary wartime alliance between sovereign States. It would have actual operating substance of its own.

Having arrived at these conclusions, with all of which Hull thoroughly agreed, the Advisory Committee ceased to meet in plenary sessions. Its various subcommittees continued active, however, their reports and recommendations being reviewed by a Subcommittee on Political Problems. Of this, too, Welles was chairman until late January 1943, when Hull decided that (in his own words) "a stage had been reached when we should begin to arrive at definite decisions, and that I should therefore take charge."[72] He did so, Welles continuing as chairman of a Special Subcommittee on International Organization set up by the Political Subcommittee.

Two months later, the Special Subcommittee submitted to its parent body a draft of a proposed charter for an international organization, and it was then that the issue of "regionalism" became sharp and clear between Hull and Welles. The Executive Council of the proposed organization, according to the charter Welles' group had drafted, would have eleven members, but only four of these would represent individual nations. These four, the Great Powers, were to be permanently represented. The other seven members would represent, not individual nations, but different specified regions of the world. Hull feared that a Council so constituted could not be truly executive. It would function as a coordinating body, the actual key decision being made in the regions. Indeed, Welles described it in terms properly applicable to a committee of executives (rather than an executive committee), each of whom had an organization or constituency of his own to which he gave his first allegiance. Thus no provision was made for a permanent headquarters; though the Council "should remain in permanent session, . . . it might sit at such places as it may consider most expedient"[73]; and nothing was said about a United Nations Authority secretariat. What, then, would happen if a quarrel arose, not between two nations within a region, but between two regional blocs? Surely this was not impossible. The very factors that promoted harmony within a region—the commonality of interest—implied differences between regions, and it was out of differences that disagreements grew into serious disputes. In the face of such disputes, a Council constituted as Welles proposed to constitute it would be helpless. The relative power emphasis was all wrong, Hull believed. Instead of deriving from the "regional systems" such powers as it possessed, the central authority should bestow upon these "systems" such powers as *they* possessed, insofar as they were institutionalized within the world organization—though of course there was always a large measure of reciprocity in arrangements of this sort.

Accordingly, Hull directed the Political Subcommittee, which he now chaired, to set aside the Special Subcommittee's draft for the time being and concentrate instead upon "a detailed consideration of international organization . . . on the basis of fundamental issues." There followed a period of profound study and discussion out of which emerged the conviction, formally expressed by the group, that the basis of international organization should be "universal" rather than "regional." In other words (Hull's own later words), "we should have a strong world organization which would be supreme over any regional associations, and . . . the latter should not be constituted in such a way as to interfere with the authority or work of the general organization."[74]

To this idea, by the time of Churchill's Embassy luncheon, Cordell Hull had committed himself absolutely, his activity in its service being spurred by his fear of the Prime Minister's influence upon the President's thinking. Months before TRIDENT opened he was well informed of the British leader's views on the matter. In early February, Roosevelt had given him a copy of a long message from Churchill entitled "Morning Thoughts: Note on Post-War Security." In late March he had listened to a radio broadcast by Churchill in which regional organizations for Europe and the Far East were proposed while "only a vague and secondary role" was assigned to "an over-all world organization." This luncheon of May 22 to which Welles was so significantly invited while he himself was not, could only intensify his conviction that the "trend toward regionalism" was growing perilously strong and that it must be resisted with the utmost vigor, while the superior claims of the "universal" approach were asserted, if any validly organized peace and security were to emerge from the war. From now on he would devote himself to the task with the same single-minded energy, zeal, and stubborn patience that had enabled him to win Congressional approval of the first Federal income tax law, of which he was the author, in 1913, and of the Trade Agreements Act of 1934, of which he was the principal inspiration and for whose implementation in tariff-reducing reciprocal trade agreements between the United States and a score of other countries he was almost wholly responsible. He had always regarded his struggle toward international free trade as a struggle for world peace: high tariffs were the chief weapon of "economic wars" and these, he had told the Congress as long ago as 1918, were "but the germs of real wars." The crusade on which he embarked in this spring of 1943 might therefore be deemed a logical sequal to his crusade of 1933, and it was destined to be equally effective . . .

In appearance, Cordell Hull had changed imperceptibly since Pearl Harbor Day, when we last focused upon him. He presented himself to the eye and ear in the spring of 1943 as the same tired, gray, sad-eyed man who had conducted those interminable talks with the Japanese envoys in the fall of 1941—a little grayer, perhaps, and tireder and sadder, his frail health somewhat more frail than it was then. There still clung to him the aura of a Southern gentleman of the old school, reminiscent in several respects of Andrew Jackson, a bit quaint as befitted the last major figure in public life to be born in an authentic log cabin, normally soft-voiced (he lisped slightly), courteous, and mild-mannered, but giving frequent hints, and occasional full-scale demonstrations, of an abnormally fiery temper. Nor had he been changed to any perceptible degree in his essential nature, these last two years. He had, however, under the strains of war, revealed more clearly than ever before certain character traits which his critics found less than admirable. High-minded and much given to the enunciation of pious platitudes, he had always been convinced beyond doubt of his own rectitude and inclined to insist with a special vehemence upon the moral rightness of precisely those of his public acts which seemed to others most questionable on moral grounds. He knew that whatever he had done was right; if it had not been, he could not have done it. And as regards De Gaulle, especially, and the morass of French African policy in which so many bright hopes for a free world seemed then to be sinking, his self-righteousness had been joined to a petty vindictiveness, an insistence upon personal vengeance for what he considered to be personal slights, and an eagerness to impugn the motives of anyone who dared criticize his State Department, which even his well-wishers often found seriously alarming.[75]

It was therefore fortunate for his high place in history that he was now turned by the turn of events into an area of activity for which he was best fitted by education and experience and lifelong belief. It would not be his sole area of activity, of course: he would strive to extend his Vichy policy to Italy, repeating errors that had plagued North African operations, and would continue to do all in his power to block that acceptance of De Gaulle as French leader which might have made the general relatively easy to work with and was certainly indispensable to any valid solution of the "French problem." Here the least admirable sides of his character would continue to show in the most unfavorable light. But in his dealings with postwar world organization, even his defects, many of them, would become virtuous in their effect. His self-righteousness would become the core of an uncompromising spirit at a point where compromise would have been disastrous to the haltingly, tentatively emerging world order. His feuding temper would force a removal of Sumner Welles from the corridors of power at a moment when Welles' brilliant presence was becoming a major hazard to the emerging order.

The first task to which he addressed himself, in the weeks following the TRIDENT Conference, would be the difficult one of shifting the current of the President's fluid mind away from "regionalism" and toward a definite and firm resolve for "universality." To this task he would bring the same weary patience that had won victories in his struggle against international trade barriers. He would also often bring, for conferences in the President's Oval Study, his companions in argument for a central world authority, such men as Isaiah Bowman, Leo Pavlovsky, Norman Davis, James C. Dunn, Green H. Hackworth, and Myron C. Taylor. And by the time midsummer had arrived, the President would be nearly convinced. By that time, too, a dozen State Department staff experts would be hard at work on a tentative "Draft Text of the Charter of the United Nations" which would be completed in early August, along with "seven fundamental policy analyses, each dealing with a basic function of an international organization." Two months later, in October, would be held the Moscow Conference, attended by Hull for the United States, Foreign Secretary Eden for Great Britain, and Foreign Minister Molotov for Russia. To it Hull would come armed with the draft of a Four-Nation Declaration, of which he had prior approval from his Government and that of Britain, pledging its signatories to establish at the earliest possible date "a general international organization, based on the principle of the sovereign equality of all peace-loving nations, and open to membership by all such States, large and small, for the maintenance of international peace and security."[76] The signing of this document in the Kremlin on October 30, 1943, by the three foreign ministers and by the Chinese Ambassador to Moscow, would be generally regarded by historians as the actual inception of the United Nations Organization. . . .

But all this lay in the future as, on Saturday afternoon, May 22, the British Embassy luncheon discussion drew toward a close. Winston Churchill made two parting suggestions. "After the war we—you Americans and we British—should continue the practice of Combined Staff conversations," said he. "We should also by constant contact take whatever steps are necessary to ensure that the main lines of our foreign policy run closely together." He looked at one after another of his guests —at Henry Wallace, whose gray eyes had an unwonted sparkle and who seemed less shy, less awkward then usual; at Stimson and Ickes and Welles; at Tom Connally who was destined, in the immediate aftermath of the Moscow Conference, to author a momentous Senate Resolution committing the United States, upon being passed by a vote of 85–5, to collaboration in a world organization. All indicated their warm agreement with what the Prime Minister had just said. They arose, then, to depart—each in a glow of good humor, exhilarated, perhaps even exalted.

Of none was this more true than of Henry Wallace.

The Vice-President of the United States, among all those in the Embassy dining room that day, was the one most susceptible to a sense, a *feeling* of world unity (the One) arising out of, without destroying, diversity (the Many). He was a strange, discordant mixture of scientist and mystic—a geneticist whose work with hybrids was revolutionizing corn production in America; a half-believing dabbler in the religious mysteries of the Orient—expressing thus in his own person the opposition of intellect and emotion, of the methods of reason and the processes of faith, which made the essential difference between the cultures of West and East. He remained a divided self, painfully striving for personal integrity. And it was no doubt because of this that the motto on the Great Seal of the United States, *E Pluribus Unum*, had always had for him a special if inexpressible significance. It was joined in his mind with the vision of the Old Testament prophet Micah who sang of the "last days" when "it shall come to pass" that "the house of the Lord shall be established in the top of the mountains" and the peoples and nations shall go there to be taught the ways of God. "And He shall judge among many people, and rebuke strong nations afar off; and they shall beat their swords into plowshares, and their spears into pruning hooks: nation shall not lift up a sword against nation, neither shall they learn war any more. But they shall sit every man under his vine and under his fig tree; and none shall make them afraid." Had these "last days" now come?[77]

If so, how climb the mountain, and how descend? Where ran the pathway of the Lord? It ran, the same path, up and down, Wallace might have said (he had a taste for mystical language). It ran from the particular to the general, but it also ran from the general to the particular—ascending in the first instance, descending in the last. Today, at this luncheon, the assembled group had concentrated discussion upon the general, tacitly assuming that particular solutions of particular problems of world organization would derive from an over-all general solution, whether or not the latter were "regional" as Churchill wished it to be. But the contrary process was equally valid: the solution of the general problem might equally well derive from particular solutions of particular problems. There was, indeed, a reciprocity.

Consider, for instance, the decision of a few months ago to convene at Hot Springs, Virginia, an international conference on food and agriculture, to which the members of the United Nations would send delegates, and to convene other conferences on other economic problems at later dates. Out of such meetings, limited to the consideration of specific problem areas, would almost certainly develop the technical specialized international agencies which Roosevelt favored, under the aegis of the Great Powers, in lieu of a single over-all international authority. But these could not effectively operate for long as entirely separate entities, Roosevelt to the contrary notwithstanding. The problems they would deal with were interdependent: what an international agency did in the field of food and agriculture was necessarily affected by what other agencies did concerning relief and rehabilitation, health and population, labor, technical education, money and trade barriers. Their work must be coordinated. Hence they (the particular) implied an over-all organization (the general). And Henry Wallace, more than most, was in a position to see certain advantages which might accrue from a start in this way, ascending from particulars to the general. (Different advantages would accrue from a start in the other way, descending; the best approach was a double one, ascent and descent in balance.)

It would be difficult, for instance—it might be impossible—to obtain in the 1940s any agreement between Russian Marxists and Western democrats concerning the precise meaning of such abstract words as "freedom," "justice," "democracy." Insofar as a valid organization depended upon such agreement, therefore, the hope for it was dim. But ideological differences were unlikely to keep Marxist and Jeffersonian democrats from seeing the same thing when they looked at a gully and measured its rate of erosion, or compared the yields of two plots of wheat to which different fertilizers had been applied, or compared the milk production of two similar dairy cows fed on different diets. Nor were ideological differences likely to cause serious disagreement as to the best technical means of reducing soil erosion, improving fertilizers, increasing milk production. Working agreements on such matters would be quite easily achieved, and with them a certain amiability was bound to enter into the human relations of those who worked together. Tensions would be reduced. Mutual respect and trust and understanding would be increased. And the latter would provide fertile ground in which the seeds of a genuine friendship could sprout and grow.

God knew that such friendship between Russia and the West was more than desirable; it was absolutely necessary, and must manifest itself through active collaboration, if civilization were to survive for long beyond the present war. Wallace was even more convinced of this than Wendell Willkie was. His conviction fed on a knowledge denied Willkie and shared by few (Stimson among them) even in the uppermost levels of Government, for he was fully informed concerning the work of the Manhattan Engineer District and, by virtue of his acute scientific intelligence, was able to assess the importance of that "critical experiment" of Fermi's in Chicago last December 2. He knew that one of the matters with which Churchill was dealing during his present visit to Washington was the restoration, or attempted restoration, of that full interchange of research information between Britain and the United States which had prevailed when ORSD had been in charge of American atomic work but which had been disrupted by American security arrangements when the Army took over. (Four days hence, Churchill would cable London, for Lord Cherwell's information, that the President had agreed to a resumption of "the exchange of information on tube alloys" since it now appeared "that this weapon may well be developed in time for the present war and . . . [therefore] falls within the general agreement covering the interchange of research and invention secrets."[78]) Like Volney Wilson, Henry Wallace felt and saw "terrifying potentialities," and knew that only through the building of a friendly, peaceful world order could the realization of these potentialities be avoided.

He made his way to the door. And there, bidding goodbye to Lord Halifax, he shook hands and spoke with rare warmth.

"This has been the most encouraging conversation in which I've taken part during the last two years," he said, and went out into the soft sweet flower-scented brightness of a Washington spring.[79]

XII

Preludes to the Final Assaults

i. *Sicily Farewell*

The mountains of Sicily, brown as the autumn hills of his native Missouri, veiled by the same kind of pale blue haze as had enwrapped those hills of home when he looked at them from afar on golden days of his boyhood, shrank into the distance as Lieutenant General Omar N. Bradley watched from the window of a climbing C-47 in the morning light of Wednesday, September 8, 1943. Soon Sicily was as a drift of smoke from a distant fire, a soft brown blur upon the eastern horizon, and the general peered down from nearly two miles in the air upon a seemingly boundless expanse of seemingly empty sea.

But it wasn't empty.

Twenty minutes out of Trapani, the wings of the C-47 suddenly dipped and rose and dipped again as the pilot made friendly salute to nine LSTs (landing ship tanks) and three escort vessels that were barely visible through the veil of mist. They were seemingly stationary upon the blue stillness of the Mediterranean, but this apparent immobility was also an illusion. Squinting his eyes, the general could discern faint white streaks reaching across the water from the ships southwestward toward Oran, toward Algiers, evincing a forward movement toward the coast of Italy—and of course he knew what these ships were and where they headed. They were the lead units of U. S. Vice Admiral H. Kent Hewitt's fleet of troop transports and fighting ships which, as a part of the naval command of British Admiral of the Fleet Sir Andrew Cunningham, operating under the Supreme Allied Commander in the Mediterranean (Eisenhower), were to carry the VI Corps of General Mark W. Clark's U. S. Fifth Army across the Tyrrhenian Sea through this mellow day and through a bright clear night into the dawn of tomorrow, September 9, when assault troops were to land upon the white sands of a beach that curved, long and wide, around the Gulf of Salerno some thirty miles southeast of Naples. AVALANCHE was the code name of the operation, its aim was the capture of Naples, and its hazards were very great. The general, looking down, reviewed them in his mind, measuring them against those of the great amphibious operation in which he himself had been engaged two months ago. He felt helpless in his present exaltation; he could only hope and pray for the success, the survival of those men far below.[1]

But he did not look down for long upon the invasion fleet. The pilot veered away from the path of "friendly" ships; the general was glad to have him do so. . . .

Less than two months had passed since, on the night of July 11, which was D plus one of HUSKY, the plane in which the general now rode had been among 144 C-47s that had taken off from Tunisian airfields loaded with two thousand paratroopers of Major General Matthew B. Ridgway's 82nd Airborne Division. The pilot now at the controls was the same as had flown it then. To reach the assigned drop zone near Gela, Sicily, where the troops were to provide temporary reinforcement of the 1st Division of General Patton's invading U. S. Seventh Army, these planes must pass over the offshore anchorage area of the Navy. The naval command, informed of the time and path of the flight, had given assurance of safe conduct. Alas, this had not kept trigger-happy AA-gun crews on the ships from opening up with deadly effect on the C-47s when they came in low immediately following a German air attack. Of the 144 troop carriers, twenty-three were shot down; of those who made it back to Tunisia, half were severely damaged; and more than four hundred of the paratroopers were dead or wounded. The pilot was not likely to forget that hellish night.

Nor would the general.

Bradley, then commanding the U. S. II Corps, had watched the tragedy from a temporary command post set up in what, until the day before, had been headquarters of the local *carabinieri* in a tiny fishing village named Scoglitti on the southern coast of Sicily, a place to which he had come by ways that were psychologically as well as physically exhausting. Late in the afternoon of July 5 he had been on the bridge of the same ship from which Admiral Hewitt now commanded the U. S. Naval Task Force headed for Salerno, and on which Mark Clark was now embarked, the *Ancon,* a converted luxury liner of ten thousand tons. Standing beside Rear Admiral Alan G. Kirk, U.S.N., he had watched the sandstone cliffs of Oran sink below the horizon while, over the loudspeaker system, the voice of Lieutenant John Mason Brown, U.S.N., told the ship's company for the first time precisely where the invasion fleet was going and what the assault forces were going to do.[2] (The U. S. Seventh Army was embarked in scores of vessels from Oran, Algiers, Bizerte. Montgomery's Eighth Army sailed in additional scores of vessels from Tripoli, Benghazi, Alexandria, Port Said, Haifa, Beirut. The vast armada converged upon the southeastern tip of Sicily, the Americans on the left and

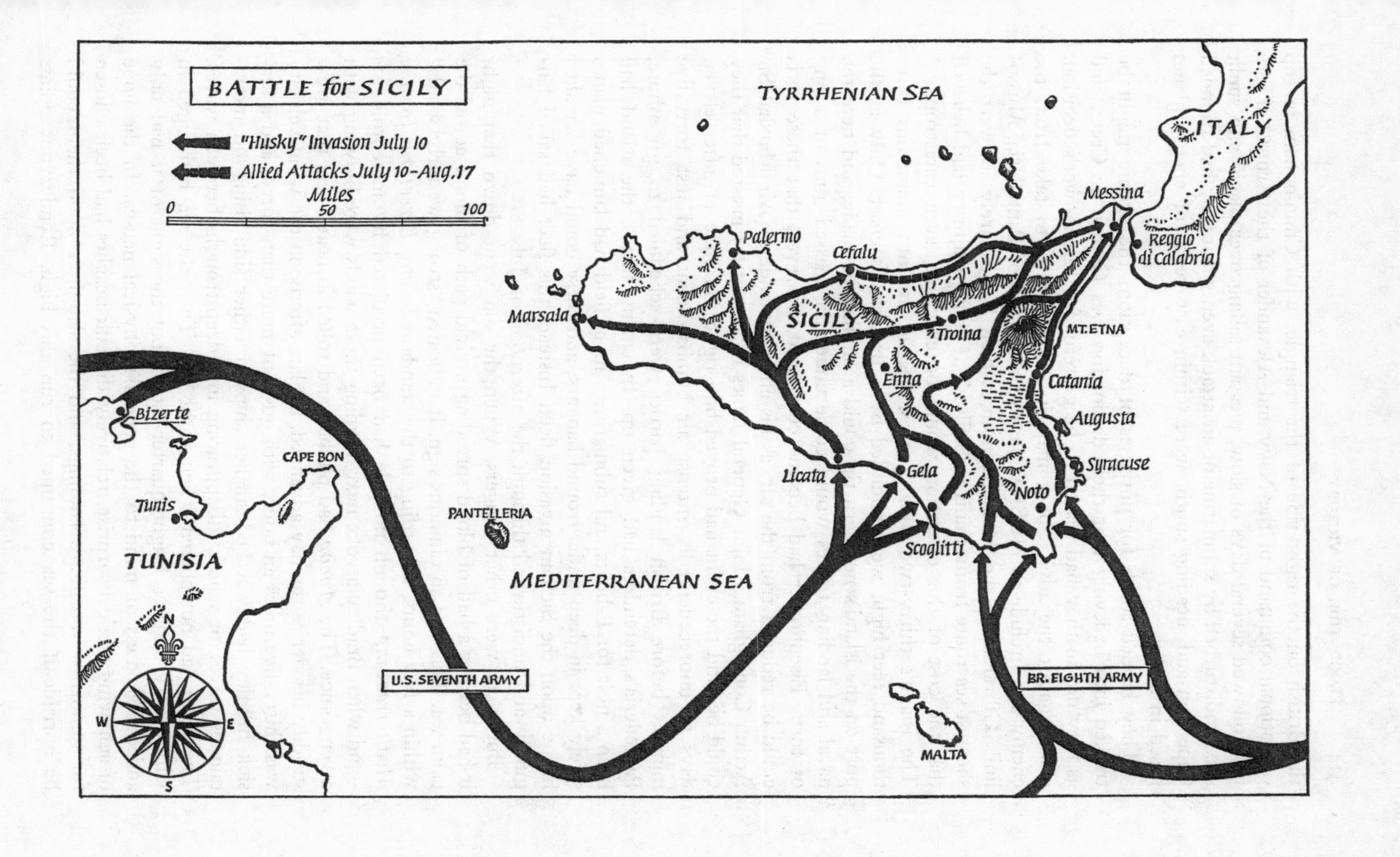
BATTLE for SICILY
"Husky" Invasion July 10
Allied Attacks July 10–Aug.17
Miles
0
50
100
TYRRHENIAN SEA
ITALY
Messina
Reggio di Calabria
Palermo
Cefalu
Marsala
SICILY
Troina
MT. ETNA
Enna
Catania
Augusta
Syracuse
Licata
Gela
Noto
Scoglitti
Bizerte
CAPE BON
Tunis
PANTELLERIA
TUNISIA
MEDITERRANEAN SEA
N
W
E
S
U.S. SEVENTH ARMY
BR. EIGHTH ARMY
MALTA

the British on the right side of the triangle, with Cunningham in top operational command of the Navy and Alexander of the Army.) There had followed several days of slow, pleasant sailing over placid and sunlit seas, undisturbed by submarine or air attack even when they had rounded Cape Bon and, heading south, were within easy reach of enemy planes based in Sicily.

They headed south for purposes of deception: the enemy might be tricked into believing that their destination was Greece or Crete: and as they did so they had reason to be grateful for Eisenhower's decision, made against the advice of a majority of his staff, to take from the enemy as a prelude to HUSKY the fortress island of Pantelleria, Mussolini's Gibraltar of the Mediterranean, which lay squarely athwart the shortest sea route from Tunis to Sicily. The staff's majority had believed that the cost of this operation would be excessive, even catastrophic.[3] The island's thirty-two square miles, heaped up into mountains three thousand feet high, were bounded by a precipitous coast. Only at the port on the island's northern tip could a landing be made, and here the naval and landing forces would come under the massed guns of a ring of forts. Eisenhower had become convinced, however, that these forts could be reduced from the air, as his air commanders (Air Marshal Sir Arthur Coningham, Major General James H. Doolittle) insisted that they could be—and the event had proved him right. On June 11, after eleven days of unprecedentedly intense air bombardment and just forty-five minutes before British landing parties were scheduled to go ashore, Pantelleria's defenders had given up. In enemy hands, the island had been a nest for E-boats and submarines: its airfield had launched planes safely kept in deep underground hangars; and these could have wreaked havoc upon the Sicilian invasion fleet. Instead, this fleet had sailed languidly and undisturbed through the afternoon of July 8.

But there were other dangers. When the sun went down that night it had been as a ball of blood spreading a vivid path of blood across the calm sea. This was an ominous sign. It indicated "strong westerly winds" within a few hours, according to the standard *Sailing Directions for the Mediterranean*,[4] though no gale had been predicted by meteorologists—and when Bradley awoke next morning those winds were blowing with a vengeance. The *Ancon* had pitched and rolled in heavy seas that grew steadily heavier as the day advanced. By late afternoon the wind velocity was thirty-five miles an hour, with gusts of more than forty, and a seasick Bradley had watched smaller ships at either side rising on mountainous waves, or wholly disappearing into deep troughs between waves. The wind had not abated when night fell. Then the sea had raged in wild beauty under a bright quarter-moon, but the sight of it had only added a sickness of mind to the general's physical nausea. In the hope of achieving tactical surprise, relatively difficult beaches had been chosen for tomorrow morning's landings, and the slaughter upon them could be horrible if the sea continued to run this high. Rendezvous points might be missed. Some of the large transports might not even be able to lower landing craft. Certainly the air drop which was to be made in early morning darkness by elements of Ridgway's 82nd Airborne—a drop which was supposed to capture key points, spread dismay and confusion among the enemy, and delay his counterattack—would have to be canceled. The seasick general had been frankly and badly frightened as midnight approached.[5]

Then, abruptly, the wind had dropped. Tossing seas had smoothed out into long rolling swells. And the gale which had threatened disaster was thereby transformed into a piece of great good fortune for the Allies insofar as it convinced the Sicilian coast defenders that, in such weather, no hostile fleet would sail upon them.

Next day, July 10, the landings had been made by both British and American assault troops with unexpectedly light losses. Because the wind continued dangerously high for air operations, the airborne units (the British even more than the Americans) had had a rough time. Few paratroopers or gliders had come down anywhere near their designated objectives; they were scattered all over the landscape. But even this was in some ways a good thing for the invaders since it caused the enemy to vastly overestimate the size of the air drops, adding thus to his fearful surprise. He, the enemy, *was* definitely surprised. He had believed that, if the landings were attempted in Sicily, they would be made on the northwest coast, which was nearest Tunisia, or possibly on the northern coast as close as possible to Messina. Separated by a strait barely two miles wide from Reggio di Calabria on the Italian mainland, Messina was the inevitable ultimate objective of any invading force; its capture could effectively prevent the defenders' escape from the island. Hence the bulk of the best Italian and German troops remained concentrated in the north and west—a fact which had become clear to the Allies by noon of D-Day. By nightfall all the Allied beachheads were wide and secure enough to permit landing of the materiel required for swift exploitation of the initial success.

Less happy was the situation early next morning when, near Gela, the tough, brawling American 1st Division, commanded by the colorful Major General Terry Allen with the no less colorful Brigadier General Theodore Roosevelt, Jr., as second-in-command, was hard hit by German panzers, a hundred of them, including several dozen 26-ton Mark IVs. They broke through the infantry lines and pressed savagely in converging columns toward Gela where, had they met, they would have cut off the division from its sea support and endangered the whole American beachhead. When a weary and anxious Bradley arrived at Terry Allen's makeshift command post near the beach late that morning, some of the Mark IVs had penetrated to within two thousand yards of the sea and the units they attacked stood precariously in last-ditch positions, desperately in need of antitank weapons.[6] But there the Americans had held as the cruisers *Boise* and *Savannah*, with a couple of destroyers, moved close in and, their gun crews directed by fire-control parties ashore, knocked out much of the Axis armor with salvos of amazing accuracy.

Bradley had returned to Scoglitti that afternoon grateful to the Navy for this unprecedented instance of close tactical interservice coordination. Gratitude was replaced by helpless fury a few hours later, however, for it was then, after dark on July 11, that the tragedy of the 82nd Airborne units occurred. The same Navy which had saved Army lives on the ground in daylight destroyed them in the air at night, Bradley watching sick at heart as "the sky exploded in AA fire" and "spent fragments of AA shells clattered on our tiled roof."[7]

Thus, auspiciously on the whole, though not without tragic error, had begun the whirlwind campaign which conquered Sicily in thirty-eight days. It was a campaign during which Bradley had admittedly learned a great deal about battle command, not only from his own personal exercise of it but also from observing and contrasting the command techniques, the tactical concepts of Patton and Montgomery. Georgie and Monty were both showmen: each was an exponent of personalized command, each was the player of a heroic role in a self-composed drama: but there the similarity of the two ended. Where Montgomery was cautious sometimes to the point of timidity, Patton was bold sometimes to the point of rashness. Where Montgomery looked upon a battle as a set piece, a work of art in which the action was dominated by the opposing commanders' preconceived plans and from which victory emerged (other things being equal) as the reward of the superior plan, Patton regarded a battle as a violent encounter in situations fluid beyond the comprehension of any rigid preconception and in which victory went to the side that moved the fastest and hit the hardest. Where Montgomery always laid great stress upon artillery preparation and flank protection as he launched his attacks, Patton often counted upon sheer audacity and speed of movement to obviate the necessity of both. As an appreciative Eisenhower would later say, speaking of Patton in Sicily, ". . . speed makes possible the full exploitation of every favorable opportunity and prevents the enemy from readjusting his forces to meet successive attacks. Thus through speed and determination each successive advantage is more easily and economically gained than the previous one. Continuation of the process results in demoralization of the enemy. Thereupon speed must be redoubled—relentless and speedy pursuit is the most profitable action in war."

This principle Patton "clearly appreciated" and applied in Sicily.[8]

Montgomery, in the original over-all campaign conception, was to drive swiftly up the eastern coast of Sicily through Syracuse, Augusta, and Catania to the key objective of Messina. He was also to swing one arm up through the center of the island to capture there the ancient fortress town of Enna, a communications hub of major importance, and then curve back eastward toward the back door of Messina. His capture of the latter place would crown the campaign with its final victory. It was expected that he would engage the best and most experienced Axis troops; these would inevitably be withdrawn from the strategically barren ground of western Sicily to defend the decisive area. Meanwhile Patton's relatively inglorious assignment was to occupy a great deal of real estate which was defended feebly if at all. He was to take Palermo, the island's capital and a port essential to the logistical support of the American Seventh Army. Otherwise his assigned objectives were of little strategic importance. Insofar as he contributed to the final decisive action it would be by diverting enemy troops from Montgomery's front to his own in the campaign's closing stages.

But within a week after D-Day this campaign conception has been rendered obsolete. Montgomery, having swiftly taken the logistically essential port of Syracuse, was pinned down by some of the toughest units in the Nazi Army at the edge of the malaria-infested plain of Catania and it was obvious that he would not be able, with available forces, to push through Catania and along the single narrow coastal road that ran northward along the precipitous eastern slope of Mount Etna. Accordingly he was shifting strength to his left wing; his main effort would become the swing inland around Etna toward Messina; but there was slight chance that this advance would be rapid, in view of Montgomery's cautious temper, the rugged terrain highly favorable to the defense, and the inevitable response of crack German forces operating along interior lines. The U. S. Seventh Army, on the other hand, was "several days ahead of schedule," as Patton noted in his diary on July 18. "This has been due to the fact that having once got the enemy started, we have not let him stop, but have, so to speak, kept him on his heels." (It was "also due to the fact that the Italians and Germans spent tremendous effort in time, labor, and money, building defensive positions," he added, characteristically. "I am sure that, just as in the case of the Walls of Troy and the Roman walls across Europe, the fact that they trusted to defensive positions reduced their will to fight."[9]) When he wrote this, just twenty-four hours had passed since he and the logic of the situation had persuaded Alexander, with Eisenhower's concurrence, that the battle orders must be drastically revised to permit the U. S. Seventh Army to operate either alone or parallel to the British Eighth Army in the Messina "neck."

Thereafter, Patton's demonstration of the efficacy of his often expressed "theory" of war, which was simply to "go like hell," was increasingly impressive. "Remember that we as attackers have the initiative," he had said in his order of the day for July 10. "We must retain this advantage by always attacking rapidly, ruthlessly, viciously, without rest. However tired and hungry you may be, the enemy will be more tired, more hungry. . . . God is with us. We shall win." And win they had! Within five days, Palermo had been taken, splitting the island in two. Marsala, the westernmost port on the island, fell the next day. Five days after that, Cefalù on the coastal route from Palermo to Messina had been taken. The going had become slower and tougher as July ended and the Axis forces were concentrated in excellent defensive terrain on the northwestern slope of Mount Etna and the mountains north and east of it. The battle for Troina, during which Terry Allen's division fought back no fewer than two dozen vicious German counterattacks in six days, was particularly fierce and bloody. But there was no slightest slackening of the Seventh Army's offensive pressure.

On August 17, with the thrust of the American 3rd Division into Messina, followed by a detachment from the British Eighth Army, the conquest of Sicily was complete. The original hope had been that the British Eighth Army would close so swiftly upon Messina that, in conjunction with naval and air units, it would put a stopper into the Messina bottleneck before Axis forces could make their escape. The revised hope had been that Patton's army would perform this function. Alas, this hope was disappointed. The Germans, using Italians ruthlessly as sacrifice troops to screen their own retreat, managed to conduct an orderly withdrawal to Messina despite Patton's speed and the unprecedented virtuosity with which his flying columns changed their direction in midflight. From Messina, covered by anti-aircraft batteries massed on either side of the scarcely more than river-wide strait, and covered also by the darkness of night, the Germans had been ferried with their armament into the toe of Italy; they would now stand between the Allies and Rome unless events in Rome, presumably under way as Bradley flew toward Tunisia, effected the immediate capture of that focus of ancient history and present power.

But if victory was not as great as Allied planners had initially hoped it would be, it was nonetheless a famous one. Its purely military consequences comprised the capture of some 135,000 Axis troops, most of them Italian; the killing and wounding of 32,000 more of the enemy; the securing of air bases from which to pummel Italy and the Balkans; in general, the possession of a springboard for possible assaults on Sardinia and the Italian mainland. And if the victorious campaign had thus impressed upon Bradley the positive value of Patton's offensive boldness and relentless drive in fluid situations (twice Patton had ordered the II Corps forward when its commander paused to rest and regroup; in both cases the event had justified the action), he had also had impressed upon him certain grave weaknesses—palpable falsehoods and dangers—that were implicit in other elements of Patton's psychology and technique of command.

For one thing, Patton carried much too far into action his belief that sheer momentum, keeping the enemy continually off balance, could substitute for adequate supply support. He was inclined to "brush aside" as "minor details" logistical problems which were actually crucial. It was fortunate for him that his II Corps commander held a contrary view; otherwise the line of supply from Palermo to the front on the road to Messina might have snapped altogether in early August. Even more basic and serious was Patton's egoistic conviction that the average combat soldier identifies himself with the "glory" of his commander—that the soldier's desire to enhance such "glory" combines with his awe and fear of the commander to incite brave, efficient battle action. Bradley knew that this is simply not so. ". . . a man who lives each day with death tagging him at the elbow lives in a world of dread and fear," he would later write. "He becomes reproachful of those who enjoy rear-echelon security and safety." Of those who so enjoy, the army commander is supreme. Hence when Georgie in immaculate uniform flaunted the "pageantry of his command" before battle-weary troops, the emotion he inspired in most of them was not awe but resentment. And when his command car, "gaily decked with oversized stars" and followed by a parade of staff vehicles, roared past soldiers who drearily plodded from one fatal hazard toward another along the Sicilian roads—when they were forced to breathe the clouds of dust he raised in seemingly callous disregard or contempt for them—their resentment was inflated by angry disgust into actual hatred. Between Patton and his men there was, on this score, a total failure of empathy.[10]

Nor was this the limit of empathic failure joined to an erroneous command psychology. Of all the episodes of the Sicilian campaign, none would be more vividly remembered by Bradley—nor by the world at large when knowledge of it was broadcast—than one that occurred on August 10 at a II Corps evacuation hospital, visited by Patton on his way to call upon Bradley at the latter's command post. Bradley first heard of it from Patton himself. Explaining his lateness of arrival, the Seventh Army commander said he had stopped at the hospital and that, while touring wards full of wounded men, he had encountered a "couple of malingerers," one of whom he had "slapped . . . to make him mad and put some fight in him." He spoke casually, with no slightest sign of regret, and Bradley had thought little of it at the time. Not until two days later, when a full eyewitness report of the incident came to corps headquarters through channels (Bradley promptly had it sealed, marked to be opened only by him or his chief of staff, and locked in a safe)—not until then did he learn that the "malingerers" were two men suffering from battle-induced nervous collapse.[11]

Far more afraid of his own fear than most men are, Patton had always insisted that "battle neurosis" was not a euphemism for cowardice and that the only proper treatment for the weakness was a shock so insulting, so painful that it stimulated the "individual's sense of shame." The corps commander had assumed, however, that his superior officer recognized the difference between applying such treatment at the front when the neurosis is just coming on and applying it to a hospitalized casualty. In the former case, the treatment is often curative; in the latter, it is sheer brutality. Yet appallingly brutal Patton had been, according to the unquestionably authentic report. Encountering the first of the two nerve-shattered men, he had flown into a profane rage, calling the patient a "yellow bastard" and "son of a bitch" in a loud voice, evoking shocked protests from doctors and nurses. Encountering the second man, who was running a temperature of 102, he had lost control of himself entirely. Purple with fury, he had struck the sick man twice across the face with the gloves he was carrying before hospital attendants intervened, physically, between him and his helpless, crying victim. By then the hospital was in an uproar, nor was this quieted by Patton's further progress through the wards during which he shouted his admiration for brave wounded men and his contempt for the two "cowards."

Soon, of course, stories of the episode had spread all over Sicily and North Africa. Eisenhower had learned of it in detail from incensed war correspondents, all of whom knew the Seventh Army commander's act had been a general court martial offense, none of whom believed Patton could ever command troops again, and one of whom asserted there were "at least fifty thousand American soldiers who would shoot Patton if they had the slightest chance."[12] Eisenhower had been forced to send a blistering reprimand to his best ground-gaining general in that general's moment of greatest triumph, ordering him to apologize in person to the enlisted man he had struck and to do it in front of as many of the original witnesses as could be gathered together. Patton was further ordered to visit the various staff headquarters under his command, apologize to the assembled officers, and have them convey his apologies to the troops. Eisenhower had then called the correspondents together to tell them what he had done. He would impose no official censorship on the story, he had said, but he hoped the correspondents would impose a voluntary one since he needed Patton to "cover" impending operations. So high was Patton's prestige among the Germans, he said, that they watched his movements closely; hence these might, of themselves alone, be as effectively deceptive as large-scale feints. The correspondents, presented with such a request from the supreme commander, their major news source in a theater of war, had of course done as he wished.*[13]

And there the matter rested as Bradley winged his way through morning light toward the coast of Africa.

The whole sad episode might be deemed by him a further object-lesson in the dangers inherent in any highly personalized command wherein major reliance is placed on showmanship, on histrionic displays. "Colorful" characters were almost always highly egoistic and emotional, inclined to achieve their effects at the expense of self-discipline and of the attitudes of cooperation and willing subordination necessary for teamwork. A case in point, though far different from Patton's, was that of Terry Allen and

* Equally of course, this effort to deny the public information to which it was entitled—and, indeed, required for the proper conduct of public business in a democracy at war—ended in failure. Drew Pearson broadcast the story in full over a national radio hookup in late November, when it caused a greater furor, more damage to Patton's career, and more "trouble" for the Allied high command than would have resulted from an honest handling of the news at the time it occurred.

the 1st Division. Even before the Sicily landing, Bradley had decided to relieve Allen of the division command at campaign's end—and he had done so, separating Ted Roosevelt from the division at the same time and for the same reasons. The task had been one of the most unpleasant he had ever performed but necessary, he was convinced, in order to "save Allen both from himself and from his brilliant record and to save the division from the heady effects of too much success." The division, under Allen, "had become increasingly temperamental, disdainful of both regulations and senior commands." It had become the victim of "too much brilliance, too much success, too much personality." It would simply have to learn to "subordinate itself to the corps mission and participate willingly as part of a combination," for it had already been selected as one of the key American units in the invasion of France next spring. There it would have to fight "at the side of inexperienced divisions and under the command of an inexperienced corps," and if it were to do so well it "desperately needed a change in its perspective." This Bradley proposed to achieve by placing the division under the command of Major General Clarence R. Huebner, who had none of the "color" of Terry Allen or Roosevelt but was known throughout the Army as a particularly "flinty disciplinarian."[14]

He, Bradley, had good personal reasons for concern over the 1st Division's performance during the cross-Channel assault and the subsequent climactic operation of the European war. . . .

On the day of Messina's fall (August 17), President Roosevelt and Harry Hopkins had arrived in Quebec, Canada, to meet with Churchill and the Combined Chiefs of Staff in a conference code-named QUADRANT. Its major purposes and chief accomplishments had been a study and general approval of the outline plan which General Morgan and his COSSAC staff had prepared for OVERLORD (it narrowed down the choice of Channel beaches, emphasizing those of Normandy, and confirmed the target date of May 1, 1944); a review of major technical aspects of this culminating enterprise (these included the swift creation of artificial harbors on the invaded coast through the use of portable breakwaters, code-named "mulberries," which could be towed in sections across the Channel); a confirmation of the earlier decision by Roosevelt and Churchill to concentrate work on the atomic bomb in the United States and reopen channels of communication between British and American scientists on this subject ("We have settled a number of hitherto untractable questions, e.g. . . . 'Tube Alloys,'" cabled Churchill to the British War Cabinet on August 25[15]); and a decision that, in view of the great preponderance of American troops and materiel to be employed in the buildup after the beachheads were secured, the supreme commander of OVERLORD should be an American (Churchill himself had proposed this, though the earlier understanding had been that the commander would be British since the assault must be mounted in Britain and would initially consist of British and American troops in approximately equal numbers, and since the North African and Mediterranean commands had gone to an American). If British, OVERLORD's commander would have been Alan Brooke, the Chief of the Imperial General Staff. It was now assumed, being intended by both Roosevelt and Churchill, that the assignment would go to Marshall.

At the close of this conference, Marshall had radioed Eisenhower that the time was come for choosing the commander who would prepare and lead U.S. troops in Great Britain and across the Channel. He asked for recommendations. Eisenhower had replied without hesitation: "The truth of the matter is that you should take Bradley and moreover I will make him available to you on any date you select."[16]

So it was that Omar Bradley—as he looked down from his lowering C-47 upon the African shore, as he then saw emerge from the light blue haze below him an increasingly detailed landscape of brown hills and green fields and white villages where once were spread the gardens and palaces of luxurious Carthaginian suburbs—was approaching the end of the first leg of a journey to England where he was to form a U. S. Army Group† and, as commander of it, "keep pace with British planning" for OVERLORD. He would remain in command of this Group, of which the 1st Division would be an element, when OVERLORD was executed.

Already his attitude toward the Mediterranean Theater had become that of a spectator who, intensely interested in the players and their actions upon the stage, was nevertheless detached from them. His plane came down in the late morning upon an airfield near the site of Carthage. He drove through those ruins to a cluster of villas atop a high hill overlooking the Gulf of Tunis, where Eisenhower now maintained his Advanced Command Post. He then awaited Eisenhower in the villa assigned the supreme commander, who was detained in his office well beyond the noon hour. And as he did so, basking in warm sunlight upon the terrace, looking far across the sea toward an invisible Italy, it was as if the present scene and even tomorrow's event upon the flaming beaches of Salerno were things remembered out of a receding past. . . .

Far different was Eisenhower's attitude that day. When the supreme commander at last arrived at the villa for his lunch, it was nearly two o'clock and he was wholly absorbed in his theater's immediate concerns. His eyes were wearied, his cheeks lined with worry over them. He greeted his old friend and West Point classmate warmly but abstractedly. He reverted almost at once to his anxieties of the moment. He seemed to need to talk about them.[17]

† At this period of the war, an Army normally consisted of two corps, each with two or more divisions. An Army Group would consist of two or more armies. By the early months of 1945, an Army Group might comprise as many as four armies, including ten corps and forty-three divisions.

ii. *The Axis Is Broken*

They had come flooding in upon him in the immediate aftermath of an event that had begun to occur in Rome late in the afternoon of July 24. This was just two weeks after the initial landing in Sicily and only six days after Allied heavy bombers appeared in great numbers and broad daylight in the skies over Rome, theretofore deemed immune to air attack, and rained destruction upon the Littorio railroad station and airfield, the Ciampino airfield, and other military targets, incidentally killing many hundreds of civilians for whom no air raid shelters had been prepared. These events climaxed an unbroken series of catastrophes for Italian arms. All Italy reeled under their impact that late July afternoon, a Saturday, as a world-historic scene began to unfold at the Palazzo Venezia in Rome.

Let us view the scene contemporaneously . . .

It is shortly before five o'clock when members of the Fascist Grand Council begin to arrive at the palace for the first Council meeting to be held in three and a half years.[18] Creatures of darkness they are, each in pitch-black uniform, and they move as so many strokes of night across the waning but brilliant afternoon. They move furtively. Their cars are driven through a gate into the interior courtyard, are parked there instead of (as formerly) in that great square, the Piazza Venezia, where so often in the past the Roman populace has gathered by the ten thousand to shout *Il Duce! Il Duce! Il Duce!*, faces uplifted to the high balcony where the new Caesar has been wont to stand looking down upon them contemptuously—legs far apart, fists on hips, huge jaw outthrust—accepting adulation as his due. The square is almost empty now. For this the Council members are grateful. Some of them have been to confession, several carry concealed weapons; all are in a state of nerves as they anticipate a violent outcome to this meeting, and all are anxious to avoid popular attention. They have been accustomed to regard the people as a tame beast harnessed to their will. It is all the more fearful, therefore, that this beast has now grown savage.

They go into the council chamber. It is a mighty room with a towering ceiling and tall windows, its marble-pillared walls lined with blue velvet and hung with huge paintings in heavy gilt frames, its floors of ornate mosaic so highly polished that footing upon them is uncertain (everything is now slippery, tricky, uncertain). And there they stand at a U-shaped table below a raised dais covered with red brocade where the Duce will sit upon a thronelike chair that is flanked on either side by chairs of more modest mien—one for each of the surviving members of the *Quadrumviri* of the 1922 March on Rome, one for the President of the Senate, one for the Secretary General of the Fascist Party, Carlo Scorza. It is Scorza who calls them all to attention at precisely five minutes past five. A door has opened. Mussolini is entering. "Salute the Duce!" cries Scorza, and the others chorus, "We salute him!" each raising his right arm stiffly.

He enters, this Benito Mussolini, from the adjoining *Sala del Mappamondo* where since 1929 he has maintained his office. It is an even larger and more imposing room than the council chamber, and the Duce has had his writing table placed in a far corner of it beside a fireplace built for giant logs, under a candle taller than a man in an ornate holder taller than a man—placed in such a way that visitors must advance across a vast empty space to reach it. Many have recorded the feelings that afflicted them as they advanced, have told how their physical stature seemed to diminish while mingled awe and apprehension grew with every step they took until they arrived at last as pygmies—subservient, worshipful, short of breath—at the desk of the Giant of Destiny. Has he watched them come, remarking their faltering steps, their shrinking presence? They do not know. They only know that he is not looking at them as they reach the end of their journey but, instead, is gazing with a frowning concentration upon a document held in his hands or lying on the table top. (Sometimes the table is piled high with papers, to show the vast complexity of rule over the Roman Empire; sometimes it is almost bare, to show the superhuman efficiency of the New Caesar.) They must wait through an intimidating pause before, raising eyes that burn and pierce, he deigns to notice them. Whatever time is lost (lost?) is then abruptly made up, however; for with him, to notice is to order and to order is to dispose. He listens. He considers briefly. He speaks, and his every word is a word of law.

How different is the man who now enters the council chamber from the awesome figure of legend and memory! Where are the firm step, the erect bearing, the absolute self-assurance of the mighty ruler of men? "Sawdust Caesar," a contemptuous journalist[19] once dubbed him, and this same journalist might now have seen sawdust leaking out through holes torn by the slash of events in a fabric not half so tough as it had once seemed to be. There is stuff in him yet, of course: his egotism, his vanity remain an almost undiminished inner resource. Nevertheless he appears shrunken, flabby, a tired old man beginning to cave in upon himself, as he raises his hand in acknowledgment of the ritual salute and takes his place upon the throne.

Nor is this impression contradicted by the speech he begins at once to make. It is, in the circumstances, an incredible speech. This meeting has not been called of his own free will; it has been forced upon him by Council members who are convinced that bloody revolution will engulf them all unless "Mussolini's War" is terminated. Repeatedly he has been warned of a plot against him by some among the twenty-eight who now gaze upon his face, and he knows that Count Dino Grandi is prepared with a resolution which, if adopted by the Grand Council, will request him to resign his power. Yet, in his overweening egotism, he has made not a single note, has not even prepared his mind seriously for an effort that would have had to be persuasive indeed to save him. Instead he gives a rambling two-hour discourse—by turns accusatory, self-justifying, arrogant, petulant—shot through and through with misrepresentation and the most blatant falsehood, delivered in a strangely dead monotone and evidently designed, insofar as it was designed at all, to absolve himself of blame for military disasters ("I did not in the least desire the delegation of the Command of the Forces in the Field given me by the King"), to place that blame on Army chiefs (the "initiative belongs to Marshal Badoglio"), and to convey the impression that no radical decision can now be taken anyway since the only choice is between "unconditional surrender," which is impossible, and "resistance to the end." He seems no longer to care, deep down, whether or not he is believed, or believed in. His voice is the voice of dull despair.

And his listeners—sitting at first in shocked silence, then in a silence restive with angry resentment—cannot but be reminded with increasing vividness of the immense tide of woe that has flowed between this moment and the last meeting of the Grand Council in December of 1939. Albania, Somaliland, Ethiopia, Eritrea, Libya, and Sicily—each has become a scene of bloody loss and humiliation; and soon now, inevitably, the Italian homeland will itself become a battleground. Who is chiefly, personally responsible for this endless and increasing tragedy? Mussolini, surely. For was not he the man who bound Fascist Italy's fortunes to those of Nazi Germany in a Pact of Steel, disregarding the dislike and distrust which hotblooded Latins have always felt toward coldblooded Teutons? Was it not he who dragged an unprepared and reluctant Italy into this tragic adventure on the false assumption that he would thereby pluck without risk the fruits of a victory already won by his ally? And has he not just returned from a meeting at Feltre to which he was abruptly summoned by Hitler and at which he dared not even hint to his master (for Hitler is now clearly his master) that his regime is threatened with collapse unless Italy detaches herself from the Axis and seeks a way out of the war?

At last this gray river of a speech comes to an end. It flows into a sea of discussion which at first is placid enough under a high pressure of embarrassment and unease but which soon becomes agitated, then actually stormy as rising winds of outrage and anger sweep over it.

The storm has grown so violent that many among those assembled are afraid no craft of reason can ride it out when, at last, Count Grandi, "the finest man Fascism produced" as Mussolini himself will later aver (though indeed Grandi was "produced" and molded into his present form of spike-bearded dignity before Fascism existed), stands up to propose his resolution. He speaks in a low tone, solemnly, and immediately commands a respectful and silent attention. His resolution, gravely read, calls upon "the Head of the Government to request His Majesty the King . . . to assume, together with the effective command of the Armed Forces . . . that supreme initiative of decision which our institutions attribute to him and which, in all our national history, has always been the glorious heritage of our august dynasty of Savoy." His speech in support of his resolution, a long hour long, inveighs with embittered eloquence against the "personal rule of one man" whose effect has been "the gradual suppression of personal freedom." Fascism began to crumble, he asserts, from the moment its old motto of "Liberty and Fatherland" was replaced by "Believe, Obey, Fight." He looks directly at Mussolini (the Duce leans forward on his throne, his cheeks pale, his brow dewed with sweat, his hand on his stomach, as if he were cramped by the pain of what some doctors have diagnosed as a duodenal ulcer and others as acute gastritis brought on by prolonged nervous tension), saying: "You have imposed a dictatorship on Italy which is historically immoral. For years you have kept in your own hands the three Service Ministries. And to what effect? The destruction of the spirit of our Armed Forces. For years you have stifled our personalities in these funereal clothes . . ." He gestures with spread fingers toward the uniform he wears. ". . . and for years, among several candidates for any important post, you have invariably selected the worst."

He stops. And Mussolini leans back, fumbling with his collar, his face dead-white and gleaming with sweat under the light of the huge wrought-iron chandelier, shaped like a wheel, that hangs from the ceiling. The Duce raises his hand and nods in recognition of the next speaker.

And the discussion continues. Hour follows hour of mutual recrimination and reproach during which the Duce seems visibly to shrink, his posture shifting wholly from that of lawgiver to that of accused, his tired voice becoming "low, humble, almost pathetic," according to one[20] among those present. Two resolutions in addition to Grandi's are presented—but it is upon Grandi's that the vote at last is taken at half-past two o'clock in the morning of Sunday, July 25, 1943. Its outcome by then is perfectly predictable. Seven vote against the resolution. One abstains. One other virtually abstains since he says he votes for his own resolution, which is not up for vote. Nineteen vote *for* the resolution. Nineteen out of twenty-eight! The defeat, for Mussolini, is overwhelming.

He gathers his papers together and stands up.

"You have brought the Regime into crisis," he says through pale lips, his eyes baleful. "The meeting is adjourned."

"Salute the Duce!" cries Scorza.

But Mussolini makes a gesture of angry protest, saying bitterly, "No! I excuse you from that . . ."

And stalks to a door that, closing behind him, shuts him off forever from the scenes of his glory, the days of his power.

Later that same Sunday, July 25—more than fourteen hours later, or at five o'clock in the afternoon—he goes in civilian clothes for audience with the diminutive King Victor Emmanuel who, clad in the uniform of a marshal, notifies him of his dismissal from office as Head of the

Government and his replacement by Marshal Badoglio. Leaving the palace at 5:20 he is arrested (or abducted) by *carabinieri* who place him in an ambulance and rush him to *carabinieri* barracks, there to begin seven weeks of imprisonment by Badoglio's Government. He is to be held in various secret places. The last will be a hotel at Gran Sasso, high in the Appenines, a former ski resort, whence he will be rescued in a daring operation by German airborne troops on September 12 and flown to Vienna.

Thereafter, for Six Hundred Days considerably less glorious than Napoleon's Hundred (he repeatedly compares himself with Napoleon at this time), he will be Hitler's puppet ruler of that portion of Italy held by German arms.

But it is with Badoglio's accession to the chief governing power of the Italian State that Eisenhower's anxieties began—the ones he discussed with Omar Bradley over a late lunch, high on a Carthaginian hill, on Wednesday afternoon, September 8, while Hewitt's ships carried Clark's army across the Tyrrhenian Sea toward Salerno.

Among his first reactions to the news of Mussolini's fall, received by him just before breakfast on July 26, was to regret the "existence of rapid communications," according to the diary kept for him by Harry Butcher.[21] In the absence of such close ties with Washington and London he would have been able on his own responsibility to offer the Italians "peace with honor, including repatriation of Italian prisoners as rapidly as possible," Butcher went on, "provided, of course, they [the Italians] will complete the overthrow of Fascism and turn and fight the eight or ten German divisions on the Italian mainland." Would or could the "overthrow of Fascism" be completed by a Badoglio whose Government we recognized as an ally in war, whose forces we supplied with arms, and who could protest any fundamental social and political reform on the ground that it would interfere with the war effort? The question, brushed aside as trivial by Butcher's impatient "of course," loomed large and solid in other minds. These other minds would have recognized that rapid communications trammeled Eisenhower's present operation chiefly because his North African political decisions (though he was personally absolved of blame for them) had been so unfortunate. And most of these other minds would have been profoundly grateful for the communications which restrained him had they known that he "hoped," according to Butcher, "to handle the negotiations with Italy as a purely military matter, as he did the Darlan affair. . . ." Apparently he continued to believe that "political" and "military" were separable matters in such situations as now faced him, and that his "deal" with Darlan had been wise.

At any rate he was right insofar as he perceived certain similarities between Marshal Pietro Badoglio and Admiral Darlan. Allied political journalism was quick to do so and to convey these similarities into the public mind.

Like Darlan, Badoglio was no friend of democracy: he had been a member of the Fascist Party since 1936, had led Italian forces against the Ethiopians and Republican Spain, and had protested (privately) Mussolini's 1940 decision to attack France only because Italy was not yet prepared for a major war and could not be before 1942 or 1943 at the earliest. Like Darlan he was, on the record, an intriguer and opportunist who at that very moment was admittedly engaged in trickery and double-dealing. Like Darlan he was supported by politically reactionary elements, the same people who had fervently supported Mussolini in earlier days and would support him now if the war had gone well for Italy. Like Darlan also, he had in fact very little to offer the Allies in terms of military aid and everything to gain from them in terms of personal political power; he had no truly strong support even among the Italian Armed Services‡ and was bound to do whatever the Allies determinedly insisted he do, for he had no alternative. It was inevitable, therefore, that any arrangement with Badoglio whereby he and the morally bankrupt Italian monarchy were kept in power with Allied arms must be compared with the "Darlan deal" and vehemently opposed by the same liberal elements as had hated that "deal." It was incumbent upon the Allied Governments to avoid the appearance of negotiating with Italian Fascism, however disguised it might be by a shift of façade, and to insist in every public pronouncement that the "unconditional surrender" formula announced at Casablanca was being rigidly adhered to.

But what precisely, in the circumstances, did "unconditional" mean? "No surrender was ever made without some conditions," grumbled Butcher in his diary entry for August 12, when he also noted that "what had appeared to be a quick collapse of Italy has disappeared into uncertainty" and that "around headquarters, we are inclined to attribute this to the hard-boiled attitude of the Prime Minister and the President, who publicly insisted upon 'unconditional surrender' as soon as Mussolini was out."[22]

Eisenhower by that time was suffering the same torture of Tantalus as he had suffered at the opening of the North African campaign last year. Before his eyes, just beyond his reach, dangled again immense prizes of war. If only he were free to move, he might at very little cost gain all of Italy, or at least all Italy south of the Po River, along with the formidable Italian Fleet, possibly entrapping at the same time all Nazi troops that continued the battle in Sicily plus all that were now being sent, or about to be sent, south of Rome. Alas, he was not free. Nor were governmental restrictions the only ones imposed upon his movement. On the day he learned of Mussolini's downfall he seriously considered

‡ Rear Admiral Raffaele De Curten, Italian Minister of Marine, looked upon the "new regime" with disgust as "even more Fascist than the old," according to Italian Admiral Franco Maugeri's *From the Ashes of Disgrace* (New York: 1948), p. 165. "Badoglio is running the government just like a field marshal, as if it were the Army," De Curten reportedly told Maugeri in August of 1943. Maugeri's own lack of respect for Badoglio as man and politician is evident in his book.

launching at once a one-division thrust upon Naples, to capture there a large airfield just three miles inland, thus anticipating by several weeks the Salerno operation (AVALANCHE) and the attack across the Strait of Messina into Calabria (BUTTRESS) which were scheduled to follow hard upon Sicily's conquest. There was "so little to be gained by . . . merely getting a toehold on Italy, when a bold kick in the shins might cause Italy to give up the fight," as Butcher noted in his report of Eisenhower's thoughts on July 26. But Beetle Smith, then just returned to Algiers from Sicily, where Montgomery had told him the campaign there must last another month, counseled caution; and British Brigadier Cecil Sugden of his planning staff told him flatly that, due to the shortage of landing craft (so many of these had gone to the Pacific!), "it would be impossible to launch an attack even on the toe of Italy until September 7." In planning conference, later that day, Eisenhower had managed to advance the latter target date to September 3, but no nearer.[23]

So, perforce, Eisenhower waited.

Tentative peace-feelers were put out in early August by Italian emissaries who made contact with British diplomats in Lisbon and Tangier. Then, on August 15, an Italian general, Castellano, arrived in Lisbon and presented the British Ambassador with a letter from Badoglio in which the Italian Head of Government said frankly that his country's situation was desperate, that peace was fervently desired by virtually every Italian, that German troops streamed into Italy through the Brenner Pass and from southern France, that the Italian people hated the Germans intensely, and that he and his Govenment were being closely watched by the Germans. He felt powerless to act as he and his people desired unless he were assured that the Allies would move into Italy in sufficient time and strength to prevent a German takeover. To this, Castellano in Lisbon added: "We are not in a position to make any terms. We will accept unconditional surrender—provided we can join as allies in fighting the Germans." If this proviso were accepted he was authorized at once to give his erstwhile enemies detailed information concerning German and Italian troop dispositions.

But the proviso was *not* acceptable to Beetle Smith and British General Kenneth W. D. Strong, Allied G-2 (Intelligence) in the Mediterranean, who were at once sent from Eisenhower's headquarters to meet with Castellano in Lisbon. Smith and Strong could only present the unconditional surrender terms dictated by Roosevelt and Churchill in a dispatch to Eisenhower on August 18. These, which seemed to Eisenhower "unduly harsh" (he suspected "that our home governments want to make a propaganda Roman holiday"), called for a cessation of hostilities at a date and hour to be determined by Eisenhower and a public proclamation of the armistice by Badoglio *immediately* following its announcement by Eisenhower. Simultaneously with its announcement, the Italian Government must "order their forces and people . . . to collaborate with the Allies and . . . resist the Germans," must immediately release all Allied prisoners "in danger of capture by the Germans," and must "order the Italian Fleet and as much of their merchant shipping as possible to put to sea for Allied ports." Moreover, "as many military aircraft as possible shall fly to Allied bases" and "any ships or aircraft in danger of capture by the Germans must be destroyed."[24] These terms Castellano was required to accept or reject without qualification, though he was helpless, under his instructions, to do either. Moreover, lacking secret radio and code facilities, he had no means of instantaneous communication with Rome. All he could do was adjourn the talks and return to Rome by circuitous route, after having, on his own responsibility, turned over such information as he possessed on German and Italian troop dispositions.

The talks were not resumed until August 31, when Smith and Strong again met with Castellano, this time at Alexander's headquarters in Sicily. The situation on the mainland had rapidly worsened, from the Allied and Italian point of view. German strength had now grown so great that a frightened Badoglio doubted Allied ability to overcome it. He asked, through his emissary, for solid information as to the time, place, and strength of the Allied landings then being mounted. His request was coldly rejected. Smith and Strong could only reiterate the terms they had presented in Lisbon, insisting these were non-negotiable; they refused to trust the Italian with even that minimum of operational information required for a loose coordination of Anglo-American and Italian military movements. Once again Castellano was forced to break off the talks and return to Rome. He came back on September 2, prepared at last to sign the armistice on the following day.

And on that same Thursday, September 2, Eisenhower made two momentous decisions. He decided to permit Montgomery's attack across the Strait of Messina to proceed on the morrow, the British Eighth Army then to move as rapidly as possible northward along the Italian coast toward Salerno; it was an action that made the Salerno landing virtually irrevocable since this was conceived to be strategically of a piece with the Reggio commitment. The second decision was more daring. AVALANCHE's tactical plan called for dropping parachute and glider troops of the U. S. 82nd Airborne Division north of Naples during the night of September 8–9, their mission the blowing up of bridges across the Volturno River. This would prevent Nazi panzer divisions (several were believed to be south of Rome) from rushing down to block mountain passes through which the U. S. Fifth Army must move on its way from Salerno to Naples. Mark Clark counted heavily on this airborne operation as his "left arm."[25] It was therefore not easy for Eisenhower to decide that the 82nd's drop should be shifted from Naples to Rome, where its mission would be to capture airfields and railroad yards and to join with Italian troops in holding the Eternal City against the Germans until Allied reinforcement could be rushed there. The risk was great—but if the operation succeeded it might yet gain the immense prize Eisenhower had envisaged on the day of Mussolini's fall. In Italy, it was still true that all roads led to Rome; the city was a communications center vital to the supply of German forces in the south. Its capture might well force a German withdrawal to the Valley of the Po.

Next day, September 3, Eisenhower was present at the signing of the armistice, though he did not affix his own signature to the document (Smith signed for him, as Castellano did for Badoglio); the Italians were then told that the effective date would probably be sometime between the tenth and fifteenth of September, though in fact Salerno's D-Day had long been set as September 9.

Three days later, September 6, Brigadier General Maxwell D. Taylor, second-in-command of the 82nd Airborne, accompanied by Colonel William T. Gardiner, an American air intelligence officer, departed on a highly secret visit to Rome. They were to obtain precise information concerning the disposition of German troops in the Rome area and the amount of aid the airborne units might expect to receive from Italian forces (had the two been captured by the Germans, they would have been liable to death before a firing squad). What they learned, soon after their arrival at dusk of September 7, was disheartening in the extreme. Italian General Giacomo Carboni, commander of the Rome defenses, was astonished and dismayed to learn that the armistice was to be announced by Eisenhower at 6:30 P.M. of the following day. He told them that German forces immediately around Rome totaled twelve thousand and that no fewer than thirty-six thousand more were within swift striking distance. His own troops were not only outnumbered but also short of gasoline and ammunition—some units had only twenty rounds per gun. He doubted that he could hold off the Germans for as long as twelve hours and, by these circumstances, was most emphatically convinced that both the air drop and the armistice announcement must be postponed.

The Americans then demanded to see Marshal Badoglio himself, and did so at two o'clock in the morning of September 8. The Italian Head of Government was as astonished and dismayed as Carboni by the news that the armistice was to go into effect in just sixteen and a half hours. He begged to know the scale and place of the impending amphibious assault, gratuitously giving his opinion that a landing at Salerno (of which he was supposed to know nothing) would be "too far south" to save Rome. He also begged Taylor to ask Eisenhower to delay the armistice announcement until his Government had had time to make "necessary arrangements." Both pleas were refused. Instead Taylor, after an intense if brief search of his soul in the light of all the information available to him, suggested that Badoglio lay his case directly before the Allied supreme commander in a coded radio message. He himself then dispatched a coded message to headquarters saying, "Situation innocuous"—"innocuous" being the code word chosen, prior to his departure, to indicate that the airborne operation aimed at Rome should in his opinion be canceled. Almost simultaneously, Eisenhower received Badoglio's direct plea for a postponement of the armistice broadcast.[26]

This was the situation, this the cluster of anxieties, which the supreme commander talked over with his guest, Omar Bradley, during a late lunch on September 8.

"Badoglio has gummed up the works," he said glumly, going on to explain that the Rome air drop was being called off so late (some units of the 82nd were about to board the air transports when the stop order was received) that it could not be shifted back to the original objectives north of Naples, and that there was no longer any certainty that the Italian Head of Government would announce the Italian surrender as the armistice terms required him to do. Eisenhower was frankly worried: the already great apparent hazards of the Salerno commitment were now increased incalculably. But as he talked, he became more relaxed. He had no doubt as to his own proper action. He had told Badoglio that he himself would broadcast at 6:30, as previously arranged, and that "if you or any of your armed forces fail to cooperate as previously agreed, I will publish to the world the full record of this affair." What choice did Badoglio have, after all? He would *have* to do as he had promised or be left at the mercy of the Nazis, without a friend in the world. Eisenhower therefore expected to receive at any moment renewed assurance from Badoglio that the armistice terms would be honored.

No such assurance had yet been received, however, when Bradley's plane took off for Algiers from the Carthage airfield in the late afternoon. Nor had it by 6:30 when an outwardly calm and confident supreme commander stepped before a microphone and said to all the world:

> This is General Dwight D. Eisenhower, commander in chief of the Allied forces. The Italian Government has surrendered its armed forces unconditionally. As Allied Commander-in-Chief I have granted a military armistice, the terms of which have been approved by the governments of the United States, Great Britain, and the Union of Soviet Socialist Republics. . . . Hostilities between the armed forces of the United Nations and those of Italy terminate at once. All Italians who now act to help eject the German aggressor from Italian soil will have the assistance and support of the United Nations.

There followed approximately an hour and a half of anxious waiting. Not until eight o'clock did the frightened Badoglio go on the air in Rome, ordering all Italians to cease hostilities against Anglo-American forces and to "oppose attacks from any other quarter." A few hours later he, senior members of his Government, and the Italian Royal Family fled from Rome without having warned their subordinates that they were about to do so and leaving no instructions. They went by automobile to Pescara on the Adriatic coast and there boarded a corvette which took them south to Brindisi—"the first capital of the new Italy," as Badoglio proclaimed. Here the King and Badoglio soon established what Churchill described as "a rump government under the eyes of an Allied Commission and with no effective authority beyond the boundaries of the administration building of the town."[27]

Meanwhile, in obedience to the armistice terms, the Italian Fleet set sail for Malta, the main body coming down from Genoa and Spezia. Off Sardinia it was attacked by German aircraft from southern France, one of whose bombs exploded the magazine of the battleship *Roma*, flagship of the fleet, which sank in twenty minutes. With her went the lives of hundreds of sailors, including the Fleet's Commander-in-Chief, Admiral Carlo Bergamini.

Great but not unalloyed was the rejoicing in the Allied camp. Reflecting upon the Italian surrender a day or so after it had occurred, Harry Hopkins was prey to "grave misgivings about both the King and Badoglio" since, as he recorded, "neither of them, by any stretch of the imagination, can be considered to represent a democratic government." He went on: "It is very easy to recognize these people, but it is awfully hard to throw them overboard later. I surely don't like the idea that these former enemies can change their minds when they know they are going to get licked and come over to our side and get help in maintaining political power."[28]

After the war had ended it would be learned that General Carboni, in his terror of the Germans, had vastly overestimated their strength in the Rome area on September 7–8. Instead of twelve thousand troops with which to wrest control of the Roman airfields from the Italians, German Field Marshal Albert Kesselring had a mere two battalions in position to attack. There were a few anti-aircraft units near the capital, a panzer division was on the shores of Lake Bolsena some sixty-six land miles northwest of Rome, a parachute division was south of the city—and that was all. The one thing Kesselring feared most on September 8–9 was precisely the operation to which the U. S. 82nd Airborne Division had been assigned, the air drop on Rome. Against this, he felt himself to be defenseless. It is recorded that he "kept his binoculars trained on the sky all . . . day [September 9], watching for enemy planes that never came. . . ."[29] Not until he was convinced that the northermost Allied landing was at Salerno did he, with sigh of relief, decide to occupy Rome, and even then he encountered an opposition that was considerably more than token. The Rome garrison, despite abandonment by their King, the Badoglio Government, and many of their own officers, held the Germans back for two days before they were overcome.

From all this it appears that Eisenhower would almost certainly have won the great prize he sought if he had boldly gambled with the 82nd, permitting the Rome drop to be executed despite the forebodings of Carboni and Badoglio and against the advice of Taylor. There are some who claim that the arrival of American paratroopers would have triggered a rising of the Rome civilian population which, of itself alone, could have overwhelmed the relatively few Nazis who then oppressed them. In the event, not only was Rome condemned to eight long months of torture by Hitler's brutes but also the crack 82nd was denied any part in a battle where every available ounce of Allied strength was needed. Clark's loss of the airborne support on which he had heavily counted—the failure, in other words, to block the Volturno crossings over which German reinforcements were poured—brought the Salerno operation very close to disaster.[30]

From the first it had been recognized that the possibility of achieving tactical surprise at Salerno was slight. The Reggio commitment clearly implied an impending amphibious assault somewhere to the north, and Salerno was obviously indicated by the fact that its wide, sloping beaches—eminently suitable to large-scale landings, within easy striking distance of Naples—lay at the farthest range of Spitfire fighter planes based on Sicily. Over Salerno, a Spitfire from the nearest Sicilian field could operate for a maximum of twenty-two minutes! But correct expectation is of no great value to the defender if physical means of defense are lacking. The Germans, even if the inflated estimates of Carboni-Badoglio be accepted, were not yet sufficiently strong in Italy to permit their concentrating on Salerno without dangerously exposing other areas—and they could by no means be certain that Salerno would be the *only* landing place. They must and did, as we have seen, consider the possibility of an airborne assault on Rome. They must and did consider the possibility that the Allies would gamble on initial surprise and swift exploitation to offset a lack of fighter plane cover, in which case an amphibious assault might be made north of Rome, perhaps as far north as Leghorn. (Leghorn had, indeed, much to recommend it as an Allied objective, and some strategists later expressed the opinion that it should have been chosen. Placed at a strategically decisive point, in that a firm Allied lodgment there would force the Germans to pull back from all of Italy that the Allies needed to mount a mighty assault on southern France, Leghorn has at its back a broad, level plain suited to offensive maneuver instead of, as at Salerno, a mountainous terrain easy to defend.)

Hence Allied Intelligence predicted on the eve of the operation that Salerno's landings, which were to be made in four-division strength, half the troops being British, would be sharply resisted by first-class German units known to have replaced the Italian garrison but that dominance of the air over the beaches, close gunfire support by the Navy, and the highly trained skills and courage of the assault troops would enable a beachhead to be established. This beachhead would be far from secure, however, for several days. The greatest danger to it would come on D plus four or on the days immediately following, G-2 went on, for by then the enemy would have concentrated enough strength for a determined effort to drive the invaders into the sea.

These predictions proved accurate.

The enemy was fully alert as British and American troops were loaded in landing craft and headed for the beaches in the early morning darkness of September 9. The British somewhat neutralized this fact in the sectors assigned them by laying down a naval gun barrage upon German posi-

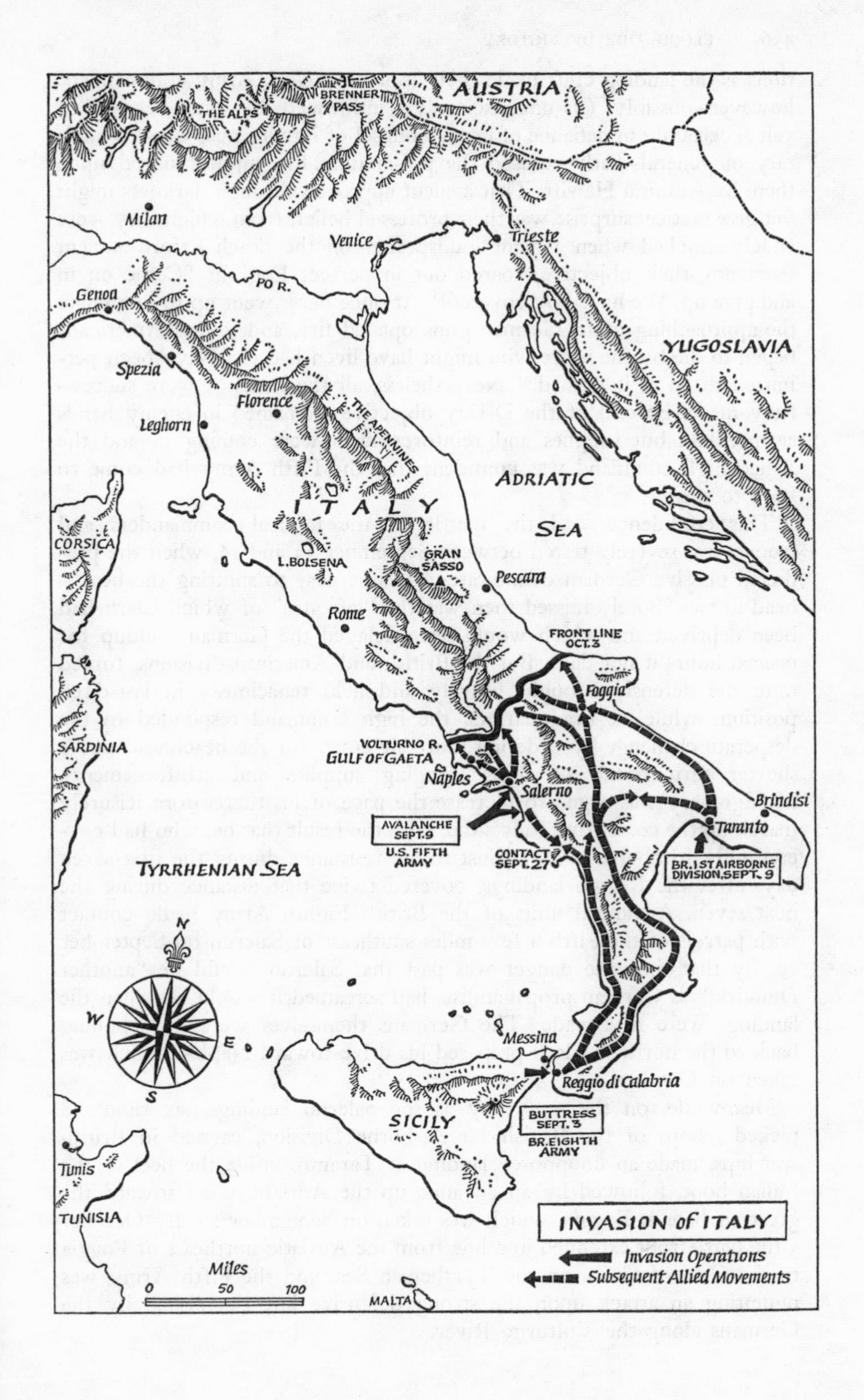
AUSTRIA
BRENNER PASS
THE ALPS
Milan
Venice
Trieste
PO R.
Genoa
YUGOSLAVIA
Spezia
Florence
THE APENNINES
Leghorn
ADRIATIC
SEA
ITALY
CORSICA
L.BOLSENA
GRAN SASSO
Pescara
Rome
FRONT LINE OCT.3
Foggia
SARDINIA
VOLTURNO R.
GULF OF GAETA
Naples
Salerno
Brindisi
Taranto
AVALANCHE SEPT.9
U.S. FIFTH ARMY
CONTACT SEPT.27
BR.1ST AIRBORNE DIVISION,SEPT. 9
TYRRHENIAN SEA
N
W
E
S
Messina
Reggio di Calabria
SICILY
BUTTRESS SEPT. 3
BR. EIGHTH ARMY
Tunis
TUNISIA
INVASION of ITALY
Invasion Operations
Subsequent Allied Movements
Miles
0
50
100
MALTA

tions as the landing craft made their approach. U. S. Army commanders, however—possibly (if unconsciously) influenced by inter-Service rivalry; certainly in defiance of every counsel of intelligence, whether military or general—flatly refused the pre-landing fire support urged upon them by Admiral Hewitt. That a silent approach through darkness might yet give tactical surprise was their professed belief, from which they were rudely shocked when a giant loudspeaker on the beach before ancient Paestrum, their objective, roared out in perfect English: "Come on in and give up. We have you covered!" At once flares went up to illuminate the approaching craft, German guns opened fire, and young Americans began to die by the score who might have lived had the Navy been permitted to do as it wished.[31] Nevertheless, all the landings were successfully made. Several of the D-Day objectives remained in enemy hands at nightfall, but supplies and reinforcements were coming in and the Allied high command was confident that the Fifth Army had come to Italy to stay.

This confidence, and the mettle of the tactical commanders and troops, was severely tested between September 13 and 16, when the predicted massive German counterattacks came near to splitting the beachhead in two. Sorely missed then was the "left arm" of which Clark had been deprived and which would have delayed the German buildup for crucial hours if not days. But the British and American divisions, forced onto the defensive, fought bravely and held tenaciously in last-ditch positions while, at headquarters, the high command responded to the desperate challenge by ordering more air cover for the beachhead and a shorter turn-around of ships bringing supplies and reinforcements. Montgomery was urged to increase the pace of his theretofore leisurely march up the coast from Italy's toe, with the result that he, who had covered only forty-five miles against feeble resistance during the first seven days after the Reggio landings, covered twice that distance during the next seven. Advanced units of the British Eighth Army made contact with patrols of the Fifth a few miles southeast of Salerno on September 17. By that time the danger was past that Salerno would be "another Dunkirk," as German propagandists had screamed it would be when the landings were first made. The Germans themselves were now pulling back to the north as Clark prepared his drive toward Naples, which was taken on October 1.

Meanwhile, on the same day as the Salerno landings, six thousand picked troops of the British 1st Airborne Division, carried in British warships, made an unopposed landing at Taranto, inside the heel of the Italian boot, followed by an advance up the Adriatic coast toward the great air base at Foggia, which was taken on September 27. By October 3 the battlefront extended in a line from the Adriatic northeast of Foggia to the Gulf of Gaeta on the Tyrrhenian Sea, and the Fifth Army was mounting an attack upon the strong defensive line established by the Germans along the Volturno River.

iii. *World Summary and Italian Forecast*

So closed a season of great prosperity for the Allied cause almost everywhere in the world.

In the Pacific, the conquest of the Solomons neared completion, with New Georgia now in American hands (organized resistance on that island ceased August 28), and an attack on Bougainville being prepared with every confidence that it would succeed. Attacks upon Makin and Tarawa in the Central Pacific were also being prepared while, in the far north, amidst the storms and fogs of the Aleutians, what had been a Japanese spear aimed toward Alaska was transformed into an American spear aimed toward the Japanese home islands of Hokkaido and Honshu. Everywhere throughout that enormous theater the Allies were on the offensive, with growing strength, against an enemy who lacked the strength to mount offensives of his own and grew weaker day by day.

In China, Chennault had established forward echelon headquarters for his U. S. Fourteenth Air Force at Kweilin, and from it, with Chiang's blessing, was directing a major air offensive against enemy shipping and port installations. An increasingly frustrated, exasperated Stilwell continued to fear Japanese reactions to this air activity, and continued to struggle vainly to create a Chinese army capable of stopping the ground offensive he knew the Japanese were capable of launching—an offensive that would capture the bases from which Chennault's aviators now operated. In early September, as if deliberately to sharpen the issue between himself and "The Peanut," "Vinegar Joe" had bluntly proposed the use of Chinese Communist as well as Nationalist divisions under Chiang to forestall the expected reaction. It was a proposal in line with the then widespread conviction that Chinese Communism, in addition to producing more effective warriors against the Japanese than did the Nationalist Government, was so far essentially an agrarian cooperative movement, as likely to develop according to Western democratic ideals as it was to become indissolubly attached to Russian totalitarianism. Indeed (so ran the belief) it would be *more* likely to do the former than the latter if it were given even a small part of the friendship and aid which influential Americans sought to lavish on Chiang. Of course, the reaction of Chiang to Stilwell's proposal was one of angry outrage. The Kuomintang had begun a series of determined efforts to force Stilwell's recall, the first of these being a plan for reorganization of the China Theater, presented to Roosevelt by Chinese Ambassador T. V. Soong on September 15, whereby the position occupied by Stilwell would be abolished. In any case, fears for the future must be measured against present realities: no such ground offensive as Stilwell (with Marshall) feared had as yet been launched by the Japanese and, meanwhile, there could be no doubt that the Air Force blows were hurting the enemy.

On balance, the Chinese situation seemed more hopeful to the Allies than it had for a long time past.

In Russia, the year had begun with the annihilation at Stalingrad of Hitler's once-mighty Sixth Army (it had seemed invincible in Belgium and France in 1940)—some three hundred thousand men having been ordered by Der Fuehrer, against all reason and compassion, to hold their ground when only precipitous retreat could have saved them. And Stalingrad had been but the beginning of a series of great Russian triumphs. Since Stalingrad, nearly three hundred thousand square miles of Soviet soil had been retaken from the Germans, including Smolensk, Orel, Kharkov—and the relentless offensive continued toward Kiev and (beyond) the prewar frontier of Poland, toward Nikolayev, Odessa, and (beyond) the prewar frontier of Rumania. An estimated million casualties had been imposed on the Nazi hordes, bringing to near six million the estimated number of Germans killed and wounded on the Russian front. American Lend-Lease—despite the costly hazards of the Murmansk run, despite the meagerness of rail and truck transport through Iran and Siberia, despite the fact that less than three-fourths of the expected shipping had been assigned to Russia's aid—now poured into the U.S.S.R. in ever-increasing volume and was an essential part of that growing strength whereby the Russians could now mount and sustain massive offensives in summer as well as winter. More than four thousand planes, some 138,000 trucks and jeeps, 912,000 tons of steel, and great quantities of other war supplies had gone from America to Russia by July of 1943, in addition to very considerable British shipments of weapons and raw materials.

In the Mediterranean, the Allies now had an unchallenged and unchallengeable supremacy. The seas were dominated by Allied ships, the skies by Allied planes, the land by Allied armies across Africa from Spanish Morocco to the Palestinian border, a fourth of the way up the Italian boot and all the way up the western coast of the Middle East from El 'Arîsh to the Turkish border. Turkey herself wavered in the balance between a dubious neutrality and entry into the war as one of the United Nations—or at least Winston Churchill was convinced that she did and sought, against American opposition, to make the possibility's realization a cardinal aim of Mediterranean policy and strategy. His earlier strategy, he might (but did not) say—a strategy urged upon a reluctant U.S. military—had certainly proved fertile enough. Sicily conquered, Mussolini deposed, Italy invaded and transformed from enemy to de facto co-belligerent—these fruits had been gathered by early September; and to them were now added Sardinia, long favored over Sicily as an invasion objective by the U. S. Joint Chiefs, which had come as a free gift into Allied hands on September 19, and Corsica, which had come almost as free two weeks later, being taken then with no difficulty by the Fighting French.

In the Atlantic, the menace of the Nazi U-boat, which had been so terrifying at the time of the Casablanca Conference and had increased in February and March of '43, when more than one hundred of Doenitz's undersea craft were operating (generally in "wolf packs") every day in the North Atlantic, sinking well over a half-million tons of Allied shipping per month, was now reduced to the over-all status of "nuisance," albeit a fatal one for many touched by it. Radar screens installed in bomber planes, enabling bombardier to "see" surfaced submarines through layers of cloud; the use of rockets by such planes; the transformation of some merchantmen into miniature aircraft carriers; the extension of the convoy system to virtually all shipping—these and other methods had effected a drastic reduction in Atlantic shipping losses in the spring of the year. In March, the losses to U-boats had totaled approximately 515,000 tons; in April they totaled around 242,000 tons; in May they were less than 200,000 tons, and in that month forty U-boats were destroyed. In June, Doenitz was forced to face the bitter fact of defeat: his boats were being destroyed faster than new construction could replace them, and the surviving crews were notably reluctant to press home their attacks. He withdrew his weapons—temporarily, he hoped—from the North Atlantic, and Allied shipping losses for the month fell to less than 22,000 tons. Meanwhile, the curve of production from Allied shipyards had risen steeply; from now on more shipping would be produced than was lost at sea from all causes.

In Germany, night bombing by Britain's Bomber Command had been joined by daylight "precision" bombing by Flying Fortresses of the American Eighth Air Force, forcing a shift of emphasis from bombers to fighters in German aircraft production—the acceptance by the Nazis, in other words, of a defensive posture in the air. Essen and other cities in the Ruhr had been severely damaged by night bombing attacks that began in early March and ended in July, and between July 24 and August 3 the key port and industrial center of Hamburg had suffered the worst injury that, until that time, had ever been done a great city from the air. The second of four raids made on Hamburg during this brief period had produced a new and terrifying phenomenon, a veritable tornado of fire raised by a concentrated mixture of incendiaries and high explosives. It hurled fire miles into the sky, sucked air into itself in a way that created winds of hurricane force through Hamburg's streets, and killed not only with heat (temperatures went as high as 1500° F.) but also with suffocation since it exhausted the oxygen in areas beyond its perimeter as well as those over which it directly passed. Accompanying it had been a sweep fire even more deadly, even more devastating in that it spread on the wind faster than a man could run and struck down those who fled it with a scythe of heat before flame itself had touched them. (Temperatures in the sweep fire mounted to an incredible 1800° F.) Thus twelve square miles of Hamburg had been transformed into utter black ruin over which hung for weeks a nauseating stink of death.[32] Preparations were being made for the massive air attacks on Berlin that were to begin in November. All through the winter and the spring of next year, this bombing of Germany and of the countries she occupied was to continue, and with a rising intensity, as a necessary preparation for OVERLORD. It would be greatly aided by fighter planes—Thunderbolts, Lightnings, Mustangs—coming into major production in America, fighters of sufficiently long range to accompany the Fortresses on daylight raids that, without fighter escort, were proving to be too costly.

In the race for a decisive secret weapon, though Hitler continuously boasted of one, the Allies seemed to be outstripping the Nazis. At least there was no evidence perceptible by air reconnaissance or by secret agent that Germany had embarked on any such massive effort as was now getting under way at Oak Ridge, Tennessee, at Hanford, Washington, and at Los Alamos, New Mexico. There *was* evidence that she progressed in her effort to produce long-range rockets and pilotless aircraft, along with means of aiming and launching them. Intelligence reports supplemented by air reconnaissance had by June indicated that experimental work on these weapons was concentrated at Peenemünde on Germany's Baltic coast, but these same sources also indicated that the development, though possibly far advanced, had not yet reached the production phase when, on the night of August 17, a massive bombing attack was made on the research laboratories and pilot manufacturing plant. Peenemünde was beyond the range of fighter escort. A brightly moonlit night was chosen to assure target visibility. The bomb run was made at the dangerously low height of eight thousand feet to assure accurate aim. And the price of these risks had been the loss of more than two score of the 571 heavy bombers that made the raid, nearly all of them shot down in the light of the moon by German night fighters as the raiders, mission accomplished, headed home. But if the cost had been great, greater still had been the gain. It appeared that effective production of the new weapons had been delayed by several months: the Nazis were now relocating factories as well as experimental works, the former going underground in the Harz Mountains in central Germany, the latter going to Poland where Britain-based bombers could not reach them but where the tough Polish underground, closely linked to British Intelligence, could keep their activities under close surveillance. Nor was the Peenemünde raid the only one discouraging to this Nazi effort: dozens of presumed launching sites for the weapons, in the Low Countries and the Pas de Calais area of France, had also been destroyed from the air. All this had led to a consensus among experts that the blow of these long-range missiles (there was sharp division of opinion between scientists concerning the possible heaviness of the blow) could not fall upon London, the obvious target, until the spring of 1944 at the earliest.[33]

In Italy, however, the season of Allied prosperity, starting late, had lasted just one month, from September 3 until October 3—and this was destined to be the last richly prosperous month on that mountainous peninsula for a long time to come. Any swift, reasonably economical exploitation of the initial success required leap-frogging amphibious assaults up the western shore of Italy, slashing into the enemy flank and threatening his communications, but these in turn required landing craft in the Mediterranean which instead had gone to the Indian Ocean for use in conjunction with the dubiously conceived and ultimately aborted invasion of Burma. Moreover, in accordance with the decision reached at the TRIDENT Conference,§ seven divisions were soon transferred from the Mediterranean Theater to the British Isles, there to become part of the buildup for OVERLORD. Thus the U. S. Fifth and British Eighth Armies were condemned to fight an arduous, bloody offensive campaign in what they knew to be a secondary theater (such knowledge could not fail to lower morale) during which gains, when made at all, must generally be measured in fractions of a mile and in which almost every stony mile was tilted steeply toward or away from bitter winter skies.

In the mountains of Italy, a superiority of armor and mechanized transport often counted for as little as they did in the jungle swamps of Southeast Asia: on narrow and precipitous mountain trails, a mule was more valuable than a tank. Advances must be made by the soldier on foot, climbing step by effortful step against an enemy always above him, always shooting down upon him. One ridge taken, there was always another just beyond. Even complete dominance of the air was of little avail, since thoroughly prepared German defenses on the mountainsides were almost invulnerable to bombing attacks: Clark would later learn that, under one of the most concentrated of all the tactical bombings in Italy, enemy officers played cards calmly and uninterruptedly in an underground bunker.

Indeed, the overwhelming Allied strength in the Italian skies would prove, on at least one occasion, to be the means if not a source of tragic error. . . .

Let us move forward to late January of 1944. Allied troops, having fought their way at the cost of high casualties through the so-called German Winter Line, are discouraged to find themselves up against a much more formidable barrier to their advance on Rome. This obstacle is a line of defenses called the Gustav Line, built by the Germans in such a way as greatly to enhance every natural advantage which steep mountains, high hills, and swift, treacherous rivers offer to the defense. In the face of it—largely upon the urging of Churchill, haunted as always by memories of futile Western Front slaughter in World War I—the decision has been made to attempt a turning of the right flank of the Gustav Line with a "scalloping" amphibious assault, though only two divisions can be initially assigned to it and this, all realize, is not

§ See page 398.

enough for success without amazing luck. There is luck at first. The place chosen for the landing is Anzio, just thirty-seven miles south of Rome; the time, January 22; and on D-Day the assault forces go ashore with light casualties, aided by tactical surprise and by a simultaneous attempt to force a crossing of the Rapido River, which ties up German troops who would otherwise have been available for action against the beachhead. This latter aid, however, is short-lived. Luck runs out. By the evening of Anzio D-Day the Rapido attack is bloodily repulsed and Kesselring is free to shift forces. He does so promptly, establishing his troops in a strong defensive position in the Alban Hills, which dominate the Anzio plain, and then launching counterattacks that very nearly drive the too-few invaders into the sea. Thereafter, far from giving relief, the Anzio beachhead is itself in dire need of it, and British and American armies are condemned to renewed frontal attacks upon the Gustav Line.

It is in these circumstances that an anxious and baleful attention is focused by the Allied tactical command upon one of the most famous buildings in the world, the historic Benedictine Abbey of Monte Cassino. Opened by St. Benedict himself in A.D. 529 upon a hill towering 1715 feet above sea level, just north of ancient Cassino, the Monastery—destroyed by Saracens in 884, rebuilt by the monks and reopened in 914; destroyed again by earthquake in 1349 and again rebuilt—is a huge structure, two hundred yards long, itself a treasure and filled with treasures for the pious Catholic and for lovers of art and history, pious or not. It is an embodiment as well as a symbol of many of the ends—humane, aesthetic, religious—for which the Allies claim to be fighting. Moreover, negotiations conducted by the Vatican Secretariat of State have exacted promises from both Germans and Allies to do all possible to avoid damaging the building, the Germans specifically promising not to make the Abbey a part of their defensive line nor to use it for any military purpose whatever. But who at this late date would trust the word of a Nazi German? Certainly Lieutenant General Sir Bernard C. Freyberg does not. He is commander of the New Zealand Corps which has just been transferred from the British Eighth to the U. S. Fifth Army, his immediate assignment is the breaching of the Gustav Line at Cassino, and he is convinced that the Germans are using the Monastery as an observation and fire-control post. He so informs Clark's headquarters on February 12, insisting that immediate destruction of the building by aerial bombardment and artillery fire is a military necessity.

Clark demurs. He and his staff have no evidence that the building is being used as Freyberg says it is, and they see no military advantage to be gained by its destruction. That the Germans are in the Monastery now is highly doubtful, but "they certainly will be in the rubble after the bombing ends," as Clark says to his superior, Alexander, in a telephone conversation in the late afternoon of February 12.[34] He adds that if Freyberg were an American commander he, Clark, would refuse to authorize the requested bombing: he fears the shock to world opinion that must come out of the deliberate ruin of so sacred a shrine.

But Freyberg is *not* an American. Neither is he an Englishman. And Alexander is perforce as concerned to avoid friction with the New Zealander as Clark is. He also takes note of Freyberg's assertion that "any higher commander who refuses to authorize the bombing will have to be prepared to take the responsibility for the failure of the attack"—a statement so flat, so implicitly threatful that its contradiction must amount to a severe stricture on Freyberg's military competence and the assumption by Alexander of tactical responsibilities not properly his. So, reluctantly, regretfully, the bombing is authorized. Bad weather postpones it for a couple of days. Then, on February 15, 1944, some 255 Allied bombers drop some 576 tons of high explosive on the Abbey, raising enormous solid-looking clouds of smoke and dust above the hill, clouds which continue to hang there after the bombers have left, for then the massed Allied artillery completes the ruin and churns the rubble for hours. Thus a great monument of Western civilization is destroyed in what Clark later calls "a tactical military mistake of the first magnitude" since it "only made our job more difficult, more costly in terms of men, machines and time."[35] The Germans do as Clark has predicted: they, who have not theretofore been in the building, quickly occupy heaps of broken stone more valuable for defensive purposes than the intact Monastery walls would have been, and from the defensive works they fashion there they beat off without serious difficulty every attack that Freyberg launches against them.

The road to Rome remains blocked, and will remain so for months to come.

iv. *In a Villa near the Pyramids*

Cassino's tragedy lay yet two months and more in the future when Franklin Roosevelt went to bed on a Saturday night, far from home. The day he would know as Sunday, December 5, 1943, was rising, not out of eastern Europe as it would have done had he been in the White House, but out of the Valley of the Yangtze to touch with red the mountain peaks of Sikang. He lay for a time sleepless in the strange dark: the problem was yet heavy on his mind (he who had so many had nevertheless come to think of this one as *the* problem): and his tomorrow poured due westward over Minya Konka and the gorges of the upper Salween onto the plateau of Tibet. He slept, and morning rose above the Himalayas, the valley of the Indus, the ruins of ancient Persia. It drove night from the streets of Shiraz, Abadan, Basra. It thrust toward him across a vast wave-heaped sea of sand into Jordan and across Jordan into Sinai, winked its way across the Gulf of Suez onto the domes and minarets of Cairo's mosques, and onto the tips of the Great Pyramids of Giza. Seconds later, it dully glowed upon the silt-laden waters of the

Nile. It was by then sweeping the last shadows of night from the woods west of Cairo, from the garden palaces of corrupt and corrupting Egyptian magnates scattered through these woods, and from the villa of American Ambassador Alexander C. Kirk, where, in a bedroom, its light fell at last upon the eyelids of the President of the United States. He awoke. He gazed out the window into the palm-shaded flower garden. He sighed.

His problem was still with him.

It had seemed so simple, so obvious three months ago—too much so to be accorded, really, the status of "problem." He had anticipated a little personal embarrassment over it in his dealings with the British, had worried a bit about how he should handle it with Churchill, but even this had proved unwarranted when the Prime Minister himself, in Quebec, had volunteered the opinion that supreme command of the cross-Channel invasion should go to an American. This had seemed to solve everything, for there was no question then as to which American would be chosen. He was, in effect, already chosen: he was General George C. Marshall. Even General Brooke, the British C.I.G.S. to whom the assignment had been originally promised and whose view of Marshall's professional capabilities was considerably less exalted than Roosevelt's, and measurably less so than Churchill's, had taken this for granted. Back from Quebec, then, Roosevelt had let those most concerned know that Marshall was definitely selected but would retain his position as U. S. Army Chief of Staff while functioning in Europe as supreme commander. Eisenhower was to be brought back to Washington to serve as Acting Chief.

And so the matter had been settled by the first of September. The British were content; Stimson and Hopkins were elated: the Marshalls began personal preparation for the general's tranfer, secretly removing private property from the Chief of Staff's house at Fort Myer to their family home at Leesburg; and the President's lips daily trembled on the verge of a public announcement of this decision.

Why had he hesitated?

One factor he had had to consider, of course, was the impassioned and highly vocal opposition of Admiral King and General "Hap" Arnold to Marshall's departure from Washington, where he was the unofficial but acknowledged leader of the U. S. Joint Chiefs—an opposition in which Admiral Leahy, the Joint Chiefs Chairman, quietly but firmly concurred. The proposed arrangement (typically Rooseveltian) whereby Marshall would be *both* Chief of Staff and supreme commander was clumsy, they said: it would breed confusion, and out of confusion might come disastrous error: while on the other hand to limit the general to the European Theater would be to deprive the Allies of his counsel on the abundant problems of China-Burma-India and the Pacific. They were convinced that Eisenhower could not possibly function in Washington with anything like Marshall's effectiveness. He was unfamiliar with many crucial matters of global strategy; his relations with the Pacific Theater were bound to be complicated by MacArthur's ill-concealed contempt for him; and he lacked Marshall's prestige with Congressional, governmental, and business leaders.

"We have the winning combination here in Washington," said blunt Admiral King to his Commander-in-Chief. "Why break it up?"[36]

Why? Some there were who believed they knew why, and that the reasons were nefarious—or at least they said they so believed, in radio broadcasts and public prints. For it happened inevitably, in accordance with standard operational procedure of the armed services in such matters, that news of the impending appointment was "leaked" to the press in a way calculated to cause the greatest amount of popular controversy and protest. An editorial appeared in the semi-official *Army and Navy Journal* alleging that "powerful influences would like to eliminate Marshall as Chief of Staff," the clear implication being that the assignment of Marshall to command of the invasion would be a demotion for him since he now had global authority and would then become a "mere" theater commander. Soon thereafter an editorialist for the semi-official *Army and Navy Register* found reason to believe that "Harry Hopkins prefers Lt. Gen. Brehon B. Somervell" as Chief of Staff. The Republican-isolationist press then promptly discerned a "plot" manipulated by the "slimy hand" of the "Rasputin of the White House." Front-page "news" stories and lead editorials told the world that Somervell, then commanding the Army Service Forces, was "preferred" because he as Army Engineer had worked closely with Hopkins on WPA projects and could be counted upon to assign huge war contracts in such a way as to assure Roosevelt's election to a fourth term in 1944.[37]

General John J. Pershing was moved to protest. He wrote Roosevelt that "the suggested transfer of General Marshall would be "a . . . very grave error in our military policy." (Roosevelt replied: ". . . I want George to be the Pershing of the Second World War—and he cannot be if we keep him here.") Even Churchill, in early October, was moved to protest—not against Marshall's transfer, of course, but against "the way in which our great changes in the High Commands are being broken to the public." Fearing a spread of the uproar to the British Isles, he begged his friend, in a Former Naval Person message, to make with him at once a joint announcement of the decisions that had been reached, putting an end thereby to the public's "impression of mystery and of something to be concealed." (Roosevelt replied: "It seems to me that if we are forced into making public statements about our military commands we will find ourselves with the newspapers running the war."[38])

Thus, though Roosevelt continuously reiterated his decision on Marshall to those most intimately concerned with it, he also continued to delay his public announcement of it as September gave way to October. Stimson wrote to him: "I do not think we can safely postpone the date of his [Marshall's] taking command beyond November first. The fatal delays and diversions which may sabotage OVERLORD will begin in the U.K. this autumn and nothing but his direct presence and influence will save us from them."[39] Yet October gave way to November and November advanced, and still the announcement was delayed. What were Roosevelt's reasons for this? Perhaps he himself could not then have given them with any clarity or precision, since they were not arrived at logically. There were multiple factors merging one with the others to form a continuous whole over which his mind played intuitively—and somehow, even in the immediate aftermath of Quebec, the decision he believed he had made hadn't felt right. It had felt less and less so as arrangements were made with great difficulty for his important meetings with Churchill and Chiang Kai-shek in Cairo, and with Churchill and Stalin (at long last) in Teheran—the first to begin on November 22, the second on November 29.

For instance there was this basic argument of Stimson's that only Marshall's commanding presence in London could *force* the British to adhere to their agreement on OVERLORD. The Secretary of War could count upon Marshall to stand firm against the pressures of the British Chiefs and the wiles of the British Prime Minister. But surely this was an argument that cut both ways—and it might well cut deeper as an argument *against* than as an argument *for* the new assignment. The fact that Marshall had learned (rightly or wrongly) to doubt the sincerity of the British commitment to OVERLORD, that he would brook no compromise with them on this matter, that he had the strength of will and force of character to impose rigidity upon a wavering ally—this very fact (if it was one) might indicate that Marshall was not the best man to weld British and Americans into a single Allied Expeditionary Force. In British eyes he might be irrevocably tagged and ticketed as the exponent of an already defined view, one with which they were in strong if only partial disagreement: his opinions would be discounted by a certain crucial percentage before he had so much as formed them. On the other hand, this same fact (if it was one) might well argue that Marshall was absolutely the best available man for the very role he now played as a key member of the Combined Chiefs of Staff. Indeed he might now be, for this role, the indispensable man. To the extent that he held the British steadfast to the purpose and design of OVERLORD he would establish the conditions of success for the supreme commander, whoever he might be, while remaining in a position to guide that commander and to absorb like a blotter the blame which might otherwise divide allies on the fighting front.

Roosevelt may well have arrived at this general sense of realities, may well have felt his way quite far toward this conclusion, by the time he with Harry Hopkins and the U. S. Joint Chiefs set sail from Hampton Roads, Virginia, on the battleship U.S.S. *Iowa*, en route to the Middle Eastern conferences. Certainly by then (November 13), this general sense, this felt conclusion, was encouraged by the interaction of British and American views as to the proper scope and nature of the supreme command.

The understanding reached between Roosevelt and Churchill in Quebec had been that the Mediterranean command was to be kept distinct and separate from the OVERLORD command and was to go to a British general. The Prime Minister had then intended Alexander for this post. Harry Hopkins, however, took a different view. "I feel very strongly that, from the point of view of organization, Marshall should have command of all the Allied forces, other than the Russian, attacking the Fortress of Germany," he wrote in a memorandum to the President on October 4. It was "essential," said he, "that there be one strategic air force and that our bombers not be frozen either in England, Italy or Africa. . . . By the same token, the disposition of ground forces, the use of ships and landing craft should be under a single commander."[40] But the basic intent of this proposal, in which Stimson and the U. S. Joint Chiefs vehemently concurred, was left unstated: it was to prevent Churchill and the British from pursuing at the expense of OVERLORD that "Mediterranean strategy" with its assaults upon the "soft underbelly of Europe" to which they continually recurred. Nor was this intent unperceived by the British when the proposal became fully known to them. It provoked in fact a prompt and strong reaction, albeit a tactically prudent one in that it was effected through the ameliorating influence of Field Marshal Sir John Dill rather than through a direct Former Naval Person message. "You should leave Admiral Leahy in no doubt that we should never be able to agree to the proposal of putting OVERLORD and Mediterranean Commands under an American Commander-in-Chief," cabled Churchill to Dill on November 8. ". . . This would place him above the Combined Chiefs of Staff, and would affect the constitutional control of the movements of forces by the President as United States Commander-in-Chief and by the Prime Minister acting on behalf of the War Cabinet. . . . If I were to attempt to propose anything such as is suggested . . . there would be an explosion. However, this will not occur while I hold my present office. You may at your discretion impart the above to Mr. Hopkins." The U. S. Joint Chiefs—which is to say Leahy, King, and Arnold, since Marshall largely abstained from these discussions—then proposed that the unified European command, which they characterized as "urgent and compelling," might be given a British officer, despite the ultimate preponderance of American forces, "provided the man named is Sir John Dill." A shift of national personalities, however, did not answer the constitutional objections Churchill had raised to the whole arrangement: the new proposal died aborning.[41]

From all this, it had become clear that Marshall, if placed in the supreme command, would be limited in his authority to the western assault upon Germany. In this authority, thus defined, he would be subordinated to the Combined Chiefs of whom, in all probability, he would no longer be one. He would be in no position directly to influence even the Mediterranean Theater, much less those of the Pacific, the Southwest Pacific, the Far East.

These last had been much on the President's mind as the *Iowa* sailed eastward, his sense of their seriousness encouraged by bloody events taking place on South Sea isles far around the world. On the day of his embarkment, heavy bombers of the Seventh Air Force began intensive bombing of the Gilberts and Marshalls in the Central Pacific, in preparation for the scheduled amphibious assaults on Makin and Tarawa. Four days later, when the *Iowa* with destroyer escort was in the mid-Atlantic, preliminary air bombing of the distant islands ceased, some 141 sorties having been flown and some 173 tons of bombs dropped. Three days after that, on November 20, when the *Iowa* arrived at Oran and the President with his party debarked for a flight to Tunis, Makin and Tarawa in the Gilberts were invaded following intense and prolonged naval bombardment. (Next day, a Sunday, while touring Tunisian battlefields with Eisenhower, the President said: "Ike, you and I know who was Chief of Staff during the closing years of the Civil War, but few others do—while everyone knows the names of Grant and Lee. That's one reason why I want George to command the invasion. He's entitled to a place in history as a great general.")[42] On the second day of the Cairo Conference, which opened on November 22, both Makin and Tarawa were secured.

Here in this same villa near the Pyramids where he now was, the President as Commander-in-Chief had heard ten days ago statistical echoes of the thunderous explosions, the roaring motors, the hissing liquid fire sprayed on living flesh, the screaming men who were horribly cut and burned and broken on the other side of the world. And what he heard in numerical figures spoken by Leahy, King, Marshall had had its effect on what he said that day, in a living room of this villa, to Generalissimo Chiang Kai-shek and the oh-so-charming Madame Chiang. It had had its effect, too, upon estimates made by Admiral Lord Louis Mountbatten and his staff, in India, of the force required for an amphibious assault upon the Japanese-held Andaman Islands in the Bay of Bengal—an assault Chiang deemed essential to the success of those proposed Allied operations in Burma which had been a major topic of discussion between himself and the President.

Makin had proved easy enough for the assault troops. A regimental combat team of the 27th U. S. Army Division had climbed from transports into a new kind of landing device called amphtracs (LVTs), never before used in battle—an amphibious tractor which, reaching land, became an armored troop carrier capable of fifteen miles an hour over smooth ground—and had come ashore in perfect order with light casualties. Thereafter their difficulties had been mostly of their own making, derived from excessive slowness of movement and failures of coordination and communications. Expert critics of their performance would later claim, with disgust, that Makin should have been taken by nightfall of D-Day. As it was, the island was wholly occupied by midmorning of November 23, virtually every Japanese defender having by that time been killed, at a cost to the 27th Division of just 64 dead and 150 wounded. Early next morning, however, the carrier U.S.S. *Liscome Bay* operating in Makin waters, was torpedoed by a Japanese submarine, blew up, and sank in twenty-three minutes, taking the lives of 644 men and maiming and burning scores of others.[43]

Tarawa's was a different story. Betio, main island of the twenty-six dotted around the atoll's lagoon, had on it a three-strip airfield whose possession was the key to the Gilberts and which the Japanese were determined to hold. Around it they had built elaborate pillbox defenses having walls of steel-reinforced concrete seven feet thick, further reinforced by cocoanut logs and coral sand. The beaches on the seaward side and the sea approaches were covered by intersecting lines of intense artillery and small-arms fire and by all manner of ugly obstacles; on the lagoon side the fortifications were somewhat weaker but nevertheless very strong. Manning these formidable defenses, which the Japanese considered impregnable, were more than 4500 first-class troops, most of them Imperial Japanese Marines and most of them still very much alive in their bombproofs when the naval gun barrage lifted and troops of the Second U. S. Marine Division, in amphtracs, moved toward beaches on the lagoon side. Americans were killed and wounded by the hundred before the shore was reached and then, pinned down on a narrow strip of coral sand, under broken and shredded palms, were killed and wounded by the hundred more before they could be sufficiently reinforced and supplied to begin the reduction of strong defensive positions that fronted and flanked them. By nightfall of D-Day some 1500 of the 5000 Americans ashore were dead or wounded. Fortunately the enemy was by then too disrupted in his communications (the shelling and bombing had accomplished this) to launch a determined counterattack; had he done so during the night, he would almost certainly have wiped out the precarious beachhead.

Nor was the American position much if any improved when the sun rose on D-plus-one. Reserves headed for Betio's shore that morning, not in amphtracs, many of which had been destroyed, but in landing boats that could not clear the barrier reef (amphtracs could crawl over it); they were condemned to wade ashore through waist-deep water under heavy machine gun fire, with the result that their percentage of casualties was actually higher than that of the first waves to hit the beaches on D-Day. But the beachhead was held. From it the American Marines moved slowly over the island, reducing the defensive positions one by one in the nastiest kind of close-in fighting—roasting Japanese alive with flamethrowers, blasting them into bloody bits with sticks of TNT, and all the while suffering heavy casualties themselves—until, at 1:30 in the afternoon of November 24, Major General Julian C. Smith, the Second Marine

Division's commander, could announce that all organized resistance had ceased on the island. The Japanese defenders had been virtually exterminated: nearly 4700, including some 200 Korean laborers, were killed; a single officer, 16 enlisted men, and 129 Koreans were taken prisoner. On the American side, 980 Marines and 29 sailors had been killed, 2050 Marines and 51 sailors had been wounded—casualty figures that, coupled with sharp criticisms of the operation by eyewitness war correspondents, would provoke cries of protest from the American public when they were released.

Certainly bad mistakes had been made on Tarawa: mistakes were inevitable in an unprecedented and complicated operation. Much was being learned from them. Not enough naval gunfire and air bombing had prepared for the landings. Not enough amphtracs had been available to carry the reserves as well as the initial assault waves (of 125 LVTs used in the landings, 90 were lost). Equipment and supplies had not been moved toward the beaches in the order in which they were required, and this had caused death-breeding congestion, confusion, and delay on the beaches. No amphibious tanks had been available (they would be for future operations), and the need for these had been abundantly demonstrated. Correction of such errors and deficiencies would no doubt reduce the cost of later amphibious assaults.

Even so, the indicated price of future victories might well dismay an Allied global strategist who considered the number of them that must be gained over heavily fortified islands, each fanatically defended, on the way from Pearl Harbor and Australia to the heart of the Japanese Empire, *if* sole reliance were placed on amphibious strength. He must also take account, as Mountbatten certainly did, of the preponderance of Allied force that had been deemed necessary, in the absence of shore-based aircraft, for the conquest of these islands. American troops on Makin had outnumbered the defenders ten to one, on Tarawa approximately four to one, yet victory had barely been accomplished within the four days considered to be the maximum period of continuous effectiveness for carrier-based planes. The President could hardly fail to conclude, though indeed he had by then already concluded, that an "island-hopping" strategy must not be counted upon exclusively to defeat Japan. Any reasonably economical victory—perhaps any final victory at all—seemed to him to require a militarily strong and active China scoring decisive victories over her invaders upon the Chinese mainland, with Anglo-American aid. This in turn required, as Stilwell insisted, a reopening of the Allied supply route through Burma into China and, by that same token, a cutting of Japanese lines of supply and reinforcement from the south.

Hence Roosevelt had greeted with special cordiality the slender, austere-appearing Chinese Generalissimo and the slim, chic Madame Chiang when he met them in Cairo—and he had continued to treat them with deferential courtesy throughout the four-day meeting. He had been determined to make China's ruling couple feel that they were equal partners with himself and Churchill in the war against the Axis. He had held long private conversations with them during which he went so far as to promise flatly a large-scale amphibious operation in the Bay of Bengal within the next few months, as Chiang wished. He had sustained Marshall and the other U. S. Joint Chiefs in their insistence, in sessions of the Combined Chiefs attended by Stilwell and Chiang, that ANAKIM (the Burmese operation) must be carried through in full, as Chiang wished—this despite the disturbing fact that the Generalissimo was notably vague in his answer to questions about the contribution China could or would make to this effort. In short, he with the Joint Chiefs had managed to transform the whole Cairo meeting into primarily a "Chinese Conference."

All this had disgusted Churchill, Brooke, and the British Chiefs of Staff. (The staff talks "were sadly complicated by the Chinese story, which was lengthy, complicated, and minor," Churchill would later recall. "Why the Americans attached such importance to Chiang I have never discovered," Brooke would later write.¶ ". . . He had nothing to contribute towards the defeat of the Germans, and for the matter of that uncommonly little towards the defeat of the Japanese. . . . All he did . . . was to lead them [the Americans] down a garden path to a Communist China."[44] The British had been frustrated in their every effort to obtain Anglo-American agreement upon proposed operations in the Eastern Mediterranean as a necessary prelude, in their view, to the impending meeting with Stalin. In vain, Brooke and Churchill had argued that far more benefit would come to the Allied cause from amphibious action in the Aegean Sea than could possibly come from action in the Bay of Bengal. Indeed, the latter was a fantastic proposal, Brooke bluntly said, which could accomplish nothing of any value whatever. Its sole effect would be to deprive OVERLORD of desperately needed landing craft, or else postpone it for months. Use of these same craft in a properly planned Aegean operation, on the other hand, would force a continued dispersal of German strength which would otherwise be concentrated to resist OVERLORD, fixing hundreds of thousands of troops in areas far from the decisive Russian and Western fronts. Brooke had supported his

¶ "I was very interested in the Chinese pair," wrote Brooke in his diary entry for November 23. "The Generalissimo reminded me of a cross between a pine-marten and a ferret. A shrewd, foxy sort of face. Evidently with no grasp of war in its larger aspects, but determined to get the best of all bargains. Madame was a study in herself; a queer character in which sex and politics seemed to predominate, both being used to achieve her ends." After the war he recalled that Madame Chiang, though "not good-looking . . . certainly has a good figure which she knew how to display at its best. Gifted with great charm and gracefulness, every small movement of hers arrested and pleased the eye. For instance, at one critical moment her closely clinging . . . dress of black satin with gold chrysanthemums displayed a slit which exposed one of the most shapely of legs. This caused a rustle amongst some of those attending the conference, and I even thought I heard a suppressed neigh come from a group of the younger members!" (Quoted on pages 51 and 53 of Arthur Bryant's *Triumph in the West*, based on the war diaries of Brooke.)

contentions with incontrovertible statistics on landing craft, on shipping available for the transfer of divisions, on the number of troops and aircraft now idled in a passive defense of Egypt and the Middle East, and on the capacity of port facilities in the United Kingdom; but he had only succeeded in arousing anger in King and Stilwell, who resented his abrupt "sarcastic" manner, and suspicion in Marshall, Leahy, and Arnold, who remained considerably more than halfway convinced that all Eastern Mediterranean proposals were part of a British "plot" to prevent the timely execution of OVERLORD.

This suspicion had not been at all allayed by Churchill's reiterated emphasis upon the possibility and enormous value of involving Turkey in the war; it was actually increased by the Prime Minister's refusal to regard the May target date for OVERLORD as sacrosanct, and by his insistence that OVERLORD must not be permitted to become a "tyrant" denying all flexibility of weight and timing and objective to Allied operations throughout the spring and winter in the Mediterranean. For instance, what great harm could come to OVERLORD from acceding to Alexander's urgent request, made through Eisenhower, that the transfer of sixty light LSTs from the Mediterranean to the United Kingdom be deferred from mid-December to mid-January? asked Churchill. Alexander desperately needed them for "cat-claw" operations up the Italian boot to Rome. And how could OVERLORD be adversely affected—how, indeed, could it fail to be greatly aided—by the active employment of men and machines now idly defending Egypt (a force which could not be used by OVERLORD in any case) for an assault on Rhodes, whose conquest would mean complete Allied domination of the Aegean and would encourage Turkey to become one of the United Nations? It could be done, Churchill had gone on to say, without modification of the relative proportions of "realizable strength" he had suggested to Eisenhower as a guide to strategy a couple of months ago, namely "six-tenths . . . across the Channel, three-tenths in Italy, and one-tenth in the Eastern Mediterranean." If Turkey then entered the war, immense possibilities would open up: a drive through the Balkans toward Vienna would thrust the horns of dilemma into the very bowels of German strategy, for if the Germans did not resist it their communications with the Russian front would be dangerously threatened and if they did their strength on that front, and in France, would be dangerously sapped. Admittedly, this might mean a postponement of OVERLORD for a couple of months, due to the shortage of landing craft, but look how much easier OVERLORD's task would then be! The road to Berlin would be shortened by a great deal more than two months and the cost of traveling it, in spilled blood and wasted treasure, would be much reduced.

Roosevelt, personally, had been almost persuaded by this. Unlike Churchill, however, he placed no great reliance upon his own competence as a military strategist. He leaned heavily upon his military advisers, especially upon George C. Marshall—and Marshall had been at one with the other U. S. Chiefs in the belief that the Eastern Mediterranean proposals held little merit and much danger. It was the old story: if Churchill were permitted to have his way, the Allies might soon find themselves hopelessly entangled in indecisive operations that weakened and postponed if they did not ultimately prevent OVERLORD. As for the paramount importance of arriving at an agreement with the British before entering into discussions of strategy with Stalin, Marshall had refused to concede it. So had Roosevelt. Marshall had been reasonably sure that Stalin would support the American and oppose the British strategic views during the upcoming discussions in Teheran; and Roosevelt had actually sensed certain advantages to be gained, in terms of political psychology, by confronting the morbidly suspicious Russian dictator in a state of Anglo-American disagreement. The fact would demonstrate to "Uncle Joe" that his two Western Allies dealt with him on the same candid basis as they dealt with each other, and it would enable him (Roosevelt) to become the arbiter of disputes between British and Russians.[45]

Indeed, Roosevelt had long been buoyantly confident that, in a face-to-face meeting, he could "handle Uncle Joe" far better than Tory Churchill could. He was sure he could establish a personal relationship with the dictator, a relationship of mutual trust and confidence, and that many if not most of the difficulties of "working with the Russians" would then fade away. Nor did he now doubt, having returned to Cairo, that what he had anticipated had come to pass. The Teheran meeting had been, from his point of view, an enormous success.

On the day of his arrival in the Iranian capital he had been installed, with Hopkins and Leahy among others, as a guest of the American Minister in the U.S. legation. But the fact that this house was a full half-mile from the British Legation and Soviet Embassy, which adjoined one another and could be easily surrounded and guarded as a unit, caused Stalin (with Churchill's concurrence) to invite the President to come as his guest into the Soviet Embassy, obviating the necessity for a dangerous traversal of narrow streets by one or more of the Conference principals several times a day. Roosevelt had of course accepted, moving into the Embassy on the day after his arrival, and this had facilitated the establishment of those relations with Stalin on which he had so heavily counted. He had judged the Russian dictator to be as Hopkins had described him (Stalin, incidentally, had made a special display of his liking and respect for Hopkins)—a rough, blunt, ruthless man, capable no doubt of great cruelty, but also shrewd, efficient, and inclined to respond in kind to forceful, honest dealings. Stalin shared with Hopkins an impatience with trivia, an insistence upon plunging directly to the "root of the matter," and Roosevelt was convinced that, fairly treated, he could be trusted to keep his promises. Of these, the most important and gratifying at the Conference—so Roosevelt believed—had been contained in an almost casual remark to the effect that, once the final defeat of Germany was accomplished, Soviet troops in sufficient numbers for offensive action could be sent to Eastern Siberia. "We shall be able by our common front to defeat Japan," Stalin had said.[46]

With him, Roosevelt had discussed at length his ideas on postwar organization to keep the peace—ideas now much influenced by Cordell Hull. He had discerned no fundamental disagreement by Stalin with the general concept of a United Nations Organization composed of: (a) an Assembly, of which each nation would be a member and which would discuss world problems and make recommendations concerning them; (b) an Executive Committee of which the "Big Four" (the U.S., Britain, the U.S.S.R., and China)** would be permanent members and of which the rotating members would be two European nations, one British dominion, and one each from the Middle East, the Far East, and South America—the Committee to deal with specific international disputes and with such non-military problems as those of health, economics, food, and so on; and (c) an enforcement body consisting exclusively of the Big Four ("The Four Policemen," Roosevelt called it) which would deal directly, immediately, and forcefully with any overt hostilities. Stalin had raised pertinent questions. Would decisions of the Executive Committee be binding on all member nations? (Roosevelt made vague answer, indicating that he doubted it: the Committee would make "recommendations" in the "hope" that the "nations concerned would be guided thereby.") Did China really qualify as one of the Big Four, capable of performing as a world "Policeman"? (Roosevelt replied that he was thinking of the future: though not yet a power comparable to the other three, China with her four hundred millions of intelligent and energetic people was bound to become a major force in the world as she acquired, inevitably, the tools and skills of Western science and technology.) But since China was not now in fact a great power, and making her one of "The Four Policemen" would increase the hostility which the small nations of Europe were almost certain to feel toward such a body, why not set up instead *two* enforcement bodies, one for Europe and one for the Far East, the former to consist of Britain, Russia, the U.S., and possibly one other European nation? (Roosevelt doubted that Congress would permit American membership in an exclusively European community; he added that Stalin's proposal resembled the "regional" proposals of Churchill—a distortion of Churchill's views which the Prime Minister had later been at some pains to correct in Stalin's mind.[47])

But of course the main business of the Conference had been with military strategy, and in the transaction of it matters had arranged themselves (or been arranged) pretty much as Marshall and the other U. S. Joint Chiefs had hoped they would. Stalin had enlisted himself (or been enlisted) on the American side of discussions of the British Eastern Mediterranean proposals. It had seemed obvious to Roosevelt and the Joint Chiefs soon after the Conference opened that the Soviet dictator and his

** France, at this point, did not qualify in the President's thinking, or in Stalin's, as a Great Power.

military advisers shared to the full the American suspicion of British motives. The Russians had made it clear that, as had been true since 1942, only a full-scale assault upon France would constitute a true "second front" in their view. "I wish to pose a very direct question to the Prime Minister," said Stalin at one of the Teheran banquets. "Do the Prime Minister and the British Staff really believe in OVERLORD or do they only say they do in order to reassure us Russians?" Whereupon Churchill had asserted with a great show of conviction that "when the time comes, we will hurl across the Channel every sinew of our strength." Similarly, Brooke and the other British Chiefs had had repeatedly to insist, in response to Russian questions, that they were indeed committed to this culminating operation and sought only to assure its success through a preponderance of Allied strength over the enemy in France when the invasion was launched.

(Nevertheless, Churchill believed and later wrote that he "could have gained Stalin" in support of his strategy had not the President been "oppressed by the prejudices of his military advisers, and drifted to and fro in the argument." Brooke was not so sure. The C.I.G.S. had become immensely impressed at Teheran with the quality of Stalin's "military brain" and with the dictator's ability to fuse military with political strategy. Stalin, thought Brooke, was now satisfied with his own "defensive position" and was "beginning to feel that the Germans had shot their bolt." Hence there was no longer the urgent necessity, from Stalin's point of view, for a relief by Western action of pressure on his own front. "He no longer had (if he had ever had) any great desire for the opening of the Dardanelles," Brooke would later write. "This would bring in the British and the Americans on his left flank in an advance westward through the Balkans. He had by then pretty definite ideas as to how he wanted the Balkans run after the war; British and American assistance was therefore no longer desirable in the Eastern Mediterranean." At any rate, the Conference ended with no decision regarding Rhodes, Turkey, and the Dardanelles—and indecision at that point was tantamount to killing the proposals. In the event, as Churchill would later write, "the whole of these subsidiary but gleaming opportunities" was destined to be "cast aside unused."[48])

The British *had* gained at Teheran a point as regards the target date of OVERLORD. It had been decided that D-Day for the operation *might* be postponed from May 1 to June 1, to coincide with a Russian offensive promised by Stalin (this would prevent excessive German concentration in France) and enable the assemblage in Britain of much more assault shipping than the early May date would permit. It had also been decided that a supporting operation (code-named ANVIL) would be launched against southern France "on the largest possible scale that is permitted by available landing craft" simultaneously, if possible, with OVERLORD, the two invasions constituting a pincers movement of the kind that had been employed by the Russians so often and so successfully against the

Germans. Further, the British, with facts and logic overwhelmingly on their side, had gained a point as regards the amphibious assault in the Bay of Bengal (code-named BUCCANEER) which Roosevelt had promised Chiang Kai-shek. The matter had been left in abeyance as the Teheran Conference ended—it was to be considered by the Combined Chiefs of Staff upon their return to Cairo—but the inevitable upshot had been that Roosevelt, after lengthy consultation with Marshall, had been forced to conclude that the Andaman Islands invasion could not, after all, be carried out. A deciding factor here had been Mountbatten's estimate, strongly influenced by the American experience of Makin and Tarawa, that fifty thousand British and Imperial troops should be employed in this operation against a mere five thousand Japanese—a demand upon the severely limited supply of landing craft that would have forced a postponement of OVERLORD until well into July at the earliest.

The dispatch of this message to Chungking would be difficult and unpleasant, no doubt of that. But this was weighed in the President's mind, and immensely overbalanced, by the over-all success of Teheran as he saw it.

For as Roosevelt heaved himself into his wheelchair in the master bedroom of Ambassador Kirk's villa on this Sunday morning, December 5, 1943—as he shaved and breakfasted and prepared his mind for the day ahead—it was in the conviction that the foundations of the future peaceful world-order had been firmly laid during his five days in the Persian capital. The needed postwar collaboration of Russia and the West seemed to him assured. Never would he forget the dinner given by Churchill on his (Churchill's) sixty-ninth birthday, in the British Legation, during which Stalin had proposed glowing toasts to Roosevelt and Churchill as his "fighting friends" and to "American production" without which "the United Nations could never have won the war." He was sure that the communiqué issued by the Big Three at the Conference's end expressed the sincere beliefs and wishes of all who signed it. "We shall," it said, "seek the cooperation and active participation of all nations, large and small, whose peoples in heart and mind are dedicated, as are our own peoples, to the elimination of tyranny and slavery, oppression and intolerance. . . . We look with confidence to the day when all peoples of the world may live free lives, untouched by tyranny, and according to their varying desires and their own consciences. . . . We came here with hope and determination. We leave here friends in fact, in spirit, and in purpose."

There remained to oppress him, and to darken an otherwise brilliant day, only that problem which had fetched so deep a sigh from him when his eyes first opened upon this Sunday morning. . . .

Twice in Teheran, Stalin had asked him point-blank, "Who will command OVERLORD?" Twice he had replied that his choice of a commander depended to a large degree upon the outcome of the current

Conference. Twice Stalin had responded that, until the commander was named, he would not be able to believe wholeheartedly in "the reality of the operation." Churchill, too, though refraining from direct questions, had made it clear that he awaited the President's decision with growing impatience. Clearly a final solution of the problem could be no longer delayed—and evidently the solution must be made by himself alone, in utter solitude of spirit, unaided by anything or anyone outside himself.

God knows he had hoped and tried to have the decision made for him by circumstance, by others, by the logic of the situation. Again and again he had made trial balances of the factors for and against Marshall's appointment, praying that the scales would tip definitely one way or the other. But they hadn't, they didn't. On the one hand were the vehemently expressed convictions of Stimson and Hopkins that Marshall must have the assignment; on the other, the equally vehement convictions of three U. S. Chiefs of Staff that Marshall must not have it, certainly not, unless he were given command of the Mediterranean also. On the one hand was Marshall's undeniable right, in simple justice, to the assignment which would give him the greatest personal glory—a right to which was joined the immense personal pleasure Roosevelt would derive from rewarding Marshall as the general deserved. On the other hand was the undeniable need for Marshall's influence upon global war direction at the highest level—a need to which was joined the great personal comfort and convenience which Roosevelt derived from Marshall's continued active presence in Washington. Every factor seemed to be neutralized, canceled out by its opposite.

The problem seemed somewhat more simple, or slightly less insoluble, if couched exclusively in terms of a choice between Marshall and Eisenhower. There was no doubt in Roosevelt's mind of the personal capacity of either man to handle either assignment, that of Chief of Staff or that of supreme commander of OVERLORD—but neither did he doubt that, all things considered, Marshall was measurably the better man for the former post. Eisenhower, entering upon the duties of this post, would have to learn things that Marshall already knew, and in the process of learning would be vulnerable to error; he would have to earn an authority and prestige that Marshall already possessed; he would have to prove what Marshall had already abundantly proved, namely an ability to make hard decisions and then stand by them against extreme pressures, risking the enmity of strong men whose will and ambition he thwarted. All of which meant that Marshall could do more to ease the task of Eisenhower as OVERLORD commander than Eisenhower could do for Marshall if the positions were reversed. Indeed, so long as Marshall remained in his present post, the qualities required for successful OVERLORD command might be to a considerable degree those of a "second" rather than a "first" man. Heightened in value would be precisely those characteristics most distinctive of Eisenhower: flexibility of mind and will, an ability to make himself personally liked by all kinds and degrees of men, a genius for compromise and accommodation, an ability to become the personification (a remarkably attractive personification) of Allied unity, and an ability in moments of crisis to make swift calculations of means toward ends already defined for him by his superiors. Nevertheless, the question remained: Was Marshall's evident superiority over Eisenhower for the position of Chief of Staff sufficiently important at this stage of the war to deny him the glory, the historical fame, of the OVERLORD command?

If only Marshall would express his own thoughts on this matter! If only he would say whether or not he personally desired the OVERLORD assignment! Indeed, he would not have to go that far: he had only to hint or inadvertently reveal through some slip of the tongue that he truly wanted it, and the assignment would be his. He had steadfastly refused to do so. The nearest he had come to it was in Stimson's office one day when the Secretary of War had forced from him the statement —reluctantly made and obviously immediately regretted—that "any soldier would prefer a field command." Just last night, Harry Hopkins as the President's emissary had called upon Marshall for a private visit during which the general had been urged and even begged to express an opinion one way or the other. All Marshall would say was that he would "go along wholeheartedly with whatever decision the President makes" and that the President "need have no fears regarding my personal reaction." He had courteously but firmly refused to express a judgment of his own.[49]

Hence Roosevelt's loneliness of spirit on this bright warm morning.

After breakfast he worked with Hopkins on the message to Chiang Kai-shek. It had to be adroitly worded to give Chiang the impression that he was being consulted and not merely told about the decisions reached concerning Burma and the Andamans; its composition required concentration, its completion was a relief. But even while he worked on it, Roosevelt was adding up again in the back of his mind the various factors involved in the choice of OVERLORD's commander. Again they canceled each other out. Again he sighed. He arranged, then, to have lunch with the general here in the villa, the two alone in complete privacy. He would make one last effort to break down that wall of honorable reticence which Marshall maintained so stubbornly around his personal integrity. Then he would, he must, decide.

Marshall came—grave, dignified, aloof, courteous, reserved, inscrutable. Warmly greeted as "George," he coolly responded. Soon he was sitting across a narrow table from his President and Commander-in-Chief, listening to his host's smiling, pleading blandishments with a respectful attention, his face otherwise devoid of expression. "It will so much help me—you can greatly lighten my heavy burdens of the moment—if you will simply tell me straight out which post you prefer, the one you now have or the OVERLORD command. I promise that your stated preference will be my decision." This was the substance of Roosevelt's plea. And as he made it he strove to penetrate the inner fastnesses of the man opposite him. In vain. Marshall, shaking his head slightly, not smiling but not frowning either, looked out through clear eyes with such forceful (yet mild) directness that Roosevelt could not look deeply into them. He made his reply in a neutral, matter-of-fact tone.

"I will not attempt to estimate my own capabilities," he said, "nor discuss the pros and cons of this matter. Personal feelings might influence my judgment, and the issue is too great for any personal feeling to be considered. It is for you to decide. I can only say that I will cheerfully abide by your decision, whatever it may be."[50]

Such reticence in such circumstances is a form of self-expression. What did it mean in this case?

Roosevelt looked hard at his guest; his smile became a trifle wry as his admiration was touched with exasperation; and perhaps he sensed, after all, what was going on deep within the soldier's breast, and was guided thereby. Marshall's selflessness and code of personal honor required him to keep his personal ambition on a short leash. He would never promote himself out of a purely selfish desire for fame and glory; he would lean over backward to avoid doing so. But this same selflessness and code of honor, joined to his patriotism, also required him to do what he conceived to be his duty even at the expense of that moral taste, that fastidiousness, which goes by the name of "modesty." If he were convinced beyond all doubt that he could serve his country better as supreme commander of OVERLORD than he could as Chief of Staff of the U. S. Army he would be compelled, at that moment, to indicate as much. On the other hand, he *did* want the OVERLORD command, the greatest field command in all history—he wanted it, yearned for it as he had for nothing else in all his military career—and though the leash he kept on his ambition was very short it was perhaps long enough to permit his silence at this moment if he had concluded, objectively, that the best arrangement probably required his continuing as Chief of Staff.

The silence lengthened. Marshall waited through it with no sign of tension, no hint of bated breath. At last Roosevelt spoke.

"Well, then, it will be Eisenhower," he said.

Marshall nodded pleasantly, impersonally. Eisenhower could do the job, he said.

There followed a remarkable psychological event. Roosevelt's reticences were fully as great and impenetrable as Marshall's, if very differently maintained. Only rarely, and then only in brief flashes, did he make the slightest revelation of his deepest self to another man; almost never did he give any hint of the utter loneliness he must often if not always feel in his high office, and of his need for at least *some* external human support. But now he more than hinted of it, he spoke directly out of it in intimate confession.

"I feel I could not sleep at night," he said, "with you out of the country. . . ."

The remark would stick in Marshall's mind, would be treasured by him in his secret heart until he died.

A few minutes later the general rose from the table, shook hands with his host, and walked out of the villa through the brilliant Egyptian sunlight toward his car and the duties that awaited him. He walked erect, briskly—a great soldier, a great man, and never greater than on that day.

XIII

OVERLORD *Triumphant*

i. *Decision at Southwick House*

Six months of world war passed by. They were not uneventful. In the Pacific, victory in the Gilberts was followed by more impressive victories in the Marshalls, where Kwajalein and Eniwetok were taken, and in the Carolines, where the long-famous and -feared Japanese air and naval base of Truk was isolated and, after a severe mauling by a carrier task force, rendered as impotent as Rabaul had become. Saipan and Tinian in the Marianas were being "softened up" by naval and aerial bombardment in the late spring, as prelude to their inevitable conquest. Because lessons taught by Tarawa were well-learned, and the materiel to implement them was at hand (Admiral King saw to that!), "island-hopping" as a form of attrition warfare no longer appeared to be a hopelessly protracted and costly way to final triumph over Japan. In Russia, Red armies on the southern front drove the Nazi invaders from Soviet soil entirely—the front line here now stood across the borders of Poland and Rumania—while in the north only a relatively narrow strip of prewar Soviet territory was yet occupied by the enemy at the beginning of June. In Italy, a winter of bloody stalemate was succeeded by a breakthrough of the Gustav Line (Cassino was at last taken by British and Commonwealth forces on May 18, 1944), and a breakout from the long-confined Anzio beachhead. By the night of June 2 German resistance in the Alban Hills was broken and the road to Rome was open. Two days later, Allied troops were in the Piazza Venezia.

But though these events commanded headlines—though initial anxieties and ultimate joys clustered around them—they were not the major focus of interest for a majority of the American and British people during these six months. The major focus was upon a theater where none save air battles were fought but where impended perhaps the greatest battle, all things considered, in the history of the world. Everyone knew that it impended. Concrete evidence of it weighed so heavily upon the British Isles that they would have been sunk into the sea, according to a wisecrack of the time, if they had not been held up by masses of barrage-balloons. In hundreds of hedge-bordered English fields, by late spring, were parks of camouflaged tanks, trucks, bulldozers, ducks, jeeps, and self-propelled guns. Dozens of airfields were jammed with planes parked wingtip to wingtip beside the runways—nearly ten thousand war planes in all. Dozens of ports large and small were jammed with shipping—well over five thousand ships and landing craft, including seven battleships, twenty-one cruisers, and literally hundreds of destroyers, gunboats, corvettes, and other fire-support craft. Moved or moving into staging areas and embarkation ports were more than a million picked troops especially trained for the forthcoming operation, half of them American and half British and Canadian, organized in thirty-seven divisions.

Awesome indeed was this unprecedented concentration of power, and everyone saw it as the outward manifestation of what must be (and in fact was) by far the most complicated plan ever made for a single operation of war. Eight hundred typewritten pages were required for a terse summary of the overall naval plan alone. A complete set of actual naval orders, with the necessary maps, weighed three hundred pounds. Equally bulky were the plans for ground, air, and (especially) logistical operations. And all these were closely meshed together into a total plan, the so-called "Morgan Plan," for OVERLORD. Originally it had been developed by COSSAC within the severe shipping limitations imposed by Admiral King's demands for the Pacific, by the insistence upon a May D-Day, and by the Cairo-Teheran decision that a simultaneous landing would be made from the Mediterranean upon the south of France (ANVIL). It had projected a three-division landing on a narrow front in Normandy, with only two more divisions afloat at the moment of landing for immediate reinforcement of the beachheads. No provision was then made for the swift capture of Cherbourg. These features, which Morgan himself regarded as risky in the extreme, called forth immediate and strong protests from both Eisenhower as Supreme Commander and Montgomery as operational commander of the Allied Expeditionary Force.[1] As a result, OVERLORD was postponed a month to take advantage of another four weeks of American ship production, ANVIL was postponed until July 15 at the earliest in order that shipping originally allotted to it could be transferred to the United Kingdom, and the D-Day assault force was increased from three divisions to five.

The final plan called for ground-troop landings on five beaches, each three or four miles in length, each consisting of gentle slopes of hard sand or gravel up which wheeled and tracked vehicles could easily move —scattered along some sixty miles of Normandy shore from near the mouth of the Orne River north of Caen to the eastern coast of the Cotentin Peninsula at whose northern tip was Cherbourg, the first major Allied objective. The three eastern landings, on beaches designated

"Sword," "Juno," and "Gold," immediately north of Caen and Bayeux, were to be made by troops of the British Second Army. The two western landings, on beaches designated "Omaha" (north of the village of Trévières) and "Utah" (due east of Ste. Mère Eglise), were to be made by troops of the American First Army. These landings were to be made at dawn. Preceding them by several hours, in the darkness of night (though it was to be a moonlit night), would be landings by airborne troops at either end of the assault front—British glider and parachute forces along the River Dives in tactical support of "Sword" and the general operation against Caen, Americans of the 82nd and 101st Airborne Divisions in the vicinity of Ste. Mère Eglise in tactical support of "Utah" and the general offensive toward Cherbourg.

To decieve the enemy as to the time and place of the main assault, pinning down significant numbers of his troops far from the Normandy battleground, an elaborate cover plan was worked out. It centered on the creation of a fictitious U. S. Army Group (the "First") assembled along the southeastern coast of England for assault across the narrowest part of the Channel, the Pas-de-Calais. False information concerning this Group was fed into German espionage channels through known enemy agents, dummy landing craft appeared in large numbers in the Thames estuary and along the eastern coast, hundreds of dummy tanks were placed where German air reconnaissance could photograph them, huge though actually deserted tent encampments were laid out in East Anglia, a radio network was set up to simulate the traffic of an Army Group preparing to invade, and the pattern of air bombardment of France was carefully arranged to indicate that the Pas-de-Calais area was being "softened up" for the impending assault. Thus the Germans were to be led to believe for weeks after the initial landings that the Normandy operation was in the nature of a large-scale feint and that the main blow was yet to fall in the north. The German Fifteenth Army, nineteen divisions strong, would sit in watchful idleness upon the Calais coast while German forces in Normandy were gradually overwhelmed.[2]

(Incidentally, the first "commander" of this fictive Army Group was Lieutenant General George S. Patton, Jr., whose presence in England was widely publicized and who was in actual fact slated to command an army, heavy with armor, for the swiftest possible exploitation of any major breakthrough of the enemy's containment line in Normandy. Still under a cloud because of the "soldier-slapping" episode in Sicily, Patton in England was specifically instructed by Eisenhower to make no speeches nor statements to the press. He violated this instruction in May by giving an impromptu and supposedly "off-the-record" talk to a small and select group in Bristol during which, with typical flamboyance, he announced that it was the "destiny" of Britain and the United States to "rule the world"—a statement not likely to promote harmony with the Soviet Union or any other of the United Nations. Next day, reports of his remarks appeared under large headlines on the front pages of newspapers in both Britain and the United States, provoking another storm of popular criticism of this "Fascist-minded" general. Nevertheless, Eisenhower, having carefully considered the extenuating circumstances of Patton's remarks, retained him for the army command —though it was decided that "Georgie" should operate "under wraps" [that is, without any publicity at all] until he had gained victories great enough to wipe the stain from his name.)

Once the lodgments were made on the Normandy shore, the Allied troops were to move inland as rapidly as possible, linking up the five landing areas behind a continuous and expanding front. Victory along this front must then depend upon victory in the battle for reinforcement (all thirty-seven of the initial Allied divisions were to be on the Continent within seven weeks after D-Day) and for supply (a single division in battle must be furnished with at least six hundred tons of supplies per day). For this last, elaborate preparations were made, and they included many ingenious devices. "Mulberries" have already been mentioned. These, prefabricated in sections for towing across the Channel, would upon anchorage not only create sheltered water but also serve as large floating docks. They were to be supplemented by blockships—old merchantmen and obsolete warships, designated "gooseberries"—which would proceed to the artificial harbor areas under their own power and be sunk at designated spots. Two large harbors were to be thus created. Another logistical device would supplement the use of tankers to insure the delivery of high-test gasoline to rapidly moving, mechanized Allied forces. There had been manufactured enormous lengths of four-inch pipe so limber it could be coiled and unwound like a rubber hose. This was to be laid across the Channel floor and hooked up to rigid pipe on the shores of the Continent, thereby creating eventually twenty continuous pipelines, most of them hundreds of miles in length, through which gasoline could be pumped from England at the rate of a million gallons a day to Cherbourg, Boulogne, Antwerp, Eindhoven, and Frankfurt. Yet another device, less bizarre but at least as effective, was the manufacture of a complete railway system to be transported across the Channel and set up in a remarkably short time in replacement of air-shattered systems of northern France. There was detailed planning, also, to make the most efficient use of the French road system for the movement of troops and supplies, transforming major highways into one-way traffic arteries of limited access and egress. An outcome of this planning would be the Red Ball Express, soon to be the most famous traffic movement in the world—trucks rolling at high speed from Normandy toward Paris and beyond in all kinds of weather day and night, undeterred, almost unslowed by the blackout.

These devices and others, welded into the over-all plan, would facilitate a buildup huge and rapid beyond the enemy's most extreme calculation of the possible. Despite severe storm damage to the "mulberries" in mid-June, despite the fact that Cherbourg was destined not to be taken until D plus 21, despite the fact that for weeks thereafter Cherbourg (its port facilities initially much damaged) would be the only major usable French port in Allied hands, there would be landed in France during the first 109 days some two million men, a half-million vehicles, and seventeen million ship-tons of supplies, twice the total tonnage supplied Pershing in nineteen months of World War I. Out of logistical surprise would come tactical and even strategic surprise. Because they didn't believe that the Allies could build up so rapidly, German commanders would make last-ditch stands which cost them dearly and accomplished little when an orderly withdrawal from one prepared defensive position to another would have greatly reduced their losses and enabled them to exact a high price in blood for the ground they yielded.

Nor was gigantic buildup the sole source of superior material strength soon to be exerted over the enemy in France. The process of building up within the Allied fighting organism was accompanied by an accelerated process of tearing down within the Nazi—and this, too, was a result of the plan as it began to be applied in early April. For two months thereafter, on every day of permissible weather, Allied air forces conducted sweeping raids upon the French railroad system in the north, with devastating effect. Railroad marshaling yards were ruined. Bridges were destroyed. (Of the two dozen bridges across the Seine between Paris and the sea, eighteen were completely broken and three more damaged.) Some fifteen hundred of two thousand engines in northern France were immobilized. The whole region by the end of May had become a "railway desert." Simultaneously, the coastal radar network designed to give the Nazis warning of an Allied approach to France had been virtually paralyzed, some five-sixths of the installations between the Pas-de-Calais and the Gulf of St. Malo having been destroyed from the air. Moreover, the Luftwaffe, already weakened, forced now again into battle against great odds, had been further reduced in strength—so much so that its operations were no longer a serious hazard to the invasion. Thus as Allied arteries of supply and reinforcement were opened and expanded, those of the Nazis were closed and severed; and as Allied eyes and ears were increased in their range of perception, those of the Nazis were blinded and deafened.

This might have gravely hampered the defensive strategy believed to be favored by German Field Marshal Gerd von Rundstedt, commander of all enemy forces in the West. Rundstedt had no faith in the efficacy of such fixed defenses as the much-touted Atlantic Wall, decreed by Hitler in 1942 for construction from Norway to Spain. Even if it had been completed—and it yet remained in considerable part a propaganda myth, though construction on it had been rushed fanatically and frantically along the French Atlantic coast these last months—it could not defeat a truly determined effort by the Allies to establish a beachhead or beachheads and to expand them inland for several miles. Rundstedt was said to be convinced of this. His strategy was said to concede it. What he would count on, if he had his way, was a large mobile strategic reserve. This, held back in the interior in a position to strike in any of several directions, could be used to fight the decisive battle, not at the time and place of the initial landings (the Anglo-Americans, after all, were at liberty to choose these), but later, when enough troops and materiel were ashore to make their destruction catastrophic.

Rundstedt, however, despite his position at the top of the Western command, was not in actual control of German strategy in this theater. Nominally under him as Commander-in-Chief of German Army Group B was Montgomery's old antagonist of the desert, Field Marshal Erwin Rommel, the most popular and audacious of German generals, who had been sent down to France last November to reorganize the Channel defenses. Rommel not only disagreed completely with Rundstedt's strategic ideas, he had also obtained Hitler's approval of his own: he could and did now ignore such orders from his immediate superior as happened not to jibe with his own conceptions. It was Rommel's conviction that Allied dominance of the air, coupled with the immense weight of naval and artillery bombardment which the Allies could lay down behind the lines, would deny to a strategic reserve the mobility it must have to be effective. Indeed, this reserve might be almost destroyed from the air as it was strung out along roads leading to the front under skies from which the Luftwaffe had been driven. Hence every available ounce of German strength must be massed at or immediately behind the coast, ready to be hurled at the invader while he was yet straddled and vulnerable between the two elements of water and earth. Later would be too late; later the enemy would be invincible. "The war will be won or lost on the beaches," Rommel declared. ". . . the first twenty-four hours of the invasion will be decisive."[3]

Of this view of Rommel's, and of his preparations to implement it, the Allied high command was well informed by British Intelligence. It was known that German troops and conscript workers to the number of half a million had been hard at work on the Atlantic Wall for well over six months, constructing hidden batteries and all manner of fortifications, strewing boat- and man-killing obstacles over tidal stretches, sowing mines by the hundred-thousand before and on and behind the beaches. "Rommel has made a world of difference since he took over . . ." said Montgomery to Brooke in May. "He will do his level best to 'Dunkirk' us."[4] The over-all picture, which showed a wide dispersal of German strength and the complete absence of a central reserve (a mere nine divisions were now in the Fatherland), remained favorable to success of the plan. For this, the "Mediterranean strategy" on which so much controversy had focused, could be given (and was given, by the British) much credit. The enemy has a grand total of some three hundred field divisions. Well over half of these were hard-pressed in Russia. Eighteen were in Scandinavia. Seventy-four were withdrawn from the ultimately decisive areas into southern Europe, eighteen of these being south of the Loire in France. This left forty-one divisions in northern France and the Low Countries, and of these one was withdrawn on June 4 for reinforcement in Italy where, on this day, Clark's Fifth Army entered Rome.

But the fact of this withdrawal, indicating that the Allies would achieve tactical surprise, was of course unknown to the Allies until after OVERLORD was launched. What *was* known had an opposite implication. For in early May, it was discovered that the Germans were reinforcing Normandy. In February, Intelligence had estimated that no more than six German divisions would be in the sector between the Seine and the Loire on D-Day; by mid-May it appeared that at least eight would be there and that four more could be brought against the beachhead within forty-eight hours. Three panzer divisions were within immediate striking distance of the beaches and three more were just south of the Loire or north of the Seine, within a day's travel of the invasion points. Such intelligence, with its implication that the Germans had somehow penetrated the great secret, was disquieting and even alarming to the Allied high command.[5]

This command—directing the final planning, preparation, and execution of by far the greatest amphibious operation in the history of the world—was vested in an organization remarkable in all respects and unique in some, though precedence for most of its features was provided by the Allied Force Headquarters (AFHQ) through which Eisenhower had commanded Mediterranean operations. Eisenhower had been actually functioning as Supreme Commander in England for nearly a month before, on February 12, 1944, he received the directive from the Combined Chiefs of Staff that formally assigned to him this command. "You will enter the continent of Europe," the directive said, "and, in conjunction with the other United Nations, undertake operations aimed at the heart of Germany and the destruction of her armed forces." On the following day, Eisenhower issued his first General Order, establishing the Supreme Headquarters, Allied Expeditionary Force (SHAEF), and on the day after that he publicly announced the names of his principal subordinates. Deputy Supreme Commander was British Air Chief Marshal Sir Arthur Tedder. General Sir Bernard Montgomery, commander of the British Ground Forces, was scheduled, as we know, for top operational command during the opening phase in Normandy; under him would be Lieutenant General Omar Bradley, commander of the American Ground Forces. British Admiral Sir Bertram H. Ramsey was commander of the combined naval forces, with Admiral Harold R. Stark commanding U. S. Navy forces in the theater. (Admiral Sir Andrew Cunningham was now First Sea Lord in the British Admiralty.) The combined air forces were commanded by British Air Chief Marshal Sir Trafford Leigh-Mallory; under him, U. S. Lieutenant General Carl A. Spaatz commanded U. S. Air Forces, with Major General James H. Doolittle commanding the powerful U. S. Eighth Air Force. Eisenhower's Chief of Staff was (as in the Mediterranean) U. S. Lieutenant General Walter B. (Beetle) Smith. There were three Deputy Chiefs of Staff: British Lieutenant General Frederick E. Morgan, who had been COSSAC; British Lieutenant General Sir Humphrey M. Gale, who served as SHAEF's chief administrative officer; and British Air Marshal James M. Robb, who became Chief of the Air Staff. U. S. Major General Ray W. Barker, who had been Morgan's deputy COSSAC, became SHAEF's G-1 (personnel); British Major General Kenneth W. D. Strong became G-2 (intelligence); British Major General J. F. M. Whiteley became G-3 (operations); U. S. Major General Robert W. Crawford was G-4 (supply); and British Lieutenant General A. E. Grasett headed the newly created and highly important G-5 (civil affairs), whose responsibility was the maintenance of economic and political order among civilians behind the battle fronts.

Thus SHAEF, even more than AFHQ, was a self-consistent amalgam of two nationalities—a supranational command organization within which, as Eisenhower insisted in an "off-the-record" press conference on January 17, the "British-vs.-American question . . . does not occur." He had gone on: "I get a directive from the Combined Chiefs of Staff and it is carried out with what I have with a grand team of fighters, both American and British, in the best way we know how, and with the questions solved on a military basis. Nothing else."[6] SHAEF was also a supra-service amalgam within which, to a unique degree, the rivalries of ground, air, and sea fighters were done away with, the three being combined in the headquarters staff with the logistical command to form a truly single, unified, integrated command. Unique, too, and initially vehemently opposed by Churchill and the R.A.F., was the arrangement whereby the Strategic Air Forces (the British Bomber Command under Air Chief Marshal Sir Arthur Harris, the U. S. Eighth Air Force under Doolittle) were placed under SHAEF's Air Commander, Leigh-Mallory—an unprecedented fusion of, or instrument for fusing, strategic and tactical air operations. Eisenhower was influenced in this by what he called the "lesson of Salerno," namely, that "when a battle needs the last ounce of available force, the commander must not be in the position of depending upon request and negotiation to get it."[7]

To facilitate this integration—to insure that SHAEF became truly an organization rather than a collection—Eisenhower insisted that the physical headquarters be set up outside of London, in Bushey Park. Here was established Widewing, a military post of Nissen huts, mess halls, and tents, with in addition two long one-story buildings under mounds of camouflage where the top commanders of SHAEF had their offices. Here was "quickly developed," as Eisenhower would later say, "a family relationship that far more than made up for minor inconveniences due to distance from the seat of Britain's administrative organization."[8] Here the final tactical plans for OVERLORD were confirmed.

Or were they?

In April, an Advanced Command Post of SHAEF was established in a wood near Portsmouth, provided there with a Navy communications system through which the progress of the invasion fleet could be followed in detail. And it was here that the Supreme Commander had to make the truly final decision concerning Utah Beach on the Cotentin Peninsula. That Utah was necessary to the timely capture of Cherbourg, and that Cherbourg's capture was required for the success of the whole operation, had been an early decision of the plan. But Utah Beach could not be attempted unless airborne units landed behind it to capture and hold causeways across a wide lagoon (lowlands flooded by the Germans) which divided the beach from the mainland. If the enemy held these causeways he could pour a murderous fire upon the beach while remaining himself well protected against answering fire. Hence the seriousness of the problem presented to Eisenhower on May 30, at Portsmouth, by his chief airman, Leigh-Mallory, who was convinced that the airborne operation in support of Utah would result in a useless slaughter of the 82nd and 101st. He predicted 80 per cent casualties; he urged that the air landings be called off.

"I went to my tent alone and sat down to think," Eisenhower later recorded.[9]

He added up the factors, weighed them against each other. If he called off the airborne attack he must also, in logic and humanity, call off the Utah landing, thereby increasing the danger to all the other landings and perhaps condemning the entire enterprise to bloody futility. Leigh-Mallory's was of course an expert opinion, but it was *only* an opinion and it was not shared by the perhaps equally expert American airborne commanders. Neither was it supported, in the direness of its predictions, by past experience in Sicily and Italy. The Supreme Commander soon concluded that the airborne operation must "go as planned," and he so informed Leigh-Mallory on the phone and in writing.

By then, every contingency that could be foreseen and controlled by human prescience and ingenuity, and by vast material resources, had been prepared for. Every known risk deemed unavoidable had been carefully calculated and accepted. D-Day was set for Monday, June 5, with the understanding that it might be postponed to the sixth or seventh. An early decision had been that H-Hour should be no *sooner* than thirty minutes after the first daylight and no *later* than an hour and a half afterward; the final decision was that it be at 6:30 A.M. on the western beaches and an hour later on the three eastern ones. The day and hour were determined by a balancing of tidal and moonlight conditions. Moonlight was wanted for the night-drop of airborne units: experience had shown that utter darkness decreased the efficiency and increased the cost of such operations. A relatively low tide was wanted to facilitate the clearance of paths through mines and obstacles that would become too deeply underwater for such work as the tide rose: landing troops must move up over a greater width of beach, under fire, than they would have had to do at higher tide, but this was among the risks accepted.

There yet remained one great factor to condition all the rest in this enterprise—one difficult to predict with accuracy and wholly impossible to control. That factor was the weather.

Six miles from Portsmouth, at the center of a wooded private park, stood Southwick House, a great three-story mansion that had become the Allied Naval Headquarters for the expedition. The former library of this mansion was a large room with nearly empty bookcases lining three of its walls, containing a table covered with green baize, two sofas, and a number of easy chairs. At night, heavy blackout curtains were drawn over its tall windows. Here, beginning on June 1, at 9:30 each evening and four each morning, the Supreme Commander held "weather meetings" with his top commanders and SHAEF's Chief Meteorological Officer, Group Captain J. M. Stagg, whom he described as a "dour but canny Scot." Of course the forecasts they discussed were not made by Stagg alone. They represented a consensus of the SHAEF Meteorological Committee over which Stagg presided and on which sat meteorological officers from the Allied Expeditionary Air Force, the Allied Naval Expeditionary Force, the British Admiralty, the U. S. Army Air Forces in Europe, and the British Air Ministry. But it was primarily from Stagg, all through May, that Eisenhower received the daily forecasts and with whom he discussed them in detail, later measuring them against the event to see what would have happened (as regards weather) had he launched the invasion on the basis of them. By June 1 he had a good idea of how the weatherman's mind worked, of the manner in which he expressed himself, and of the points most to be considered in making meteorological predictions.[10]

As he began to hold the twice-daily conferences with his commanders and Stagg, he hoped that the weather patterns that had generally prevailed throughout May would continue through June. The hope was short-lived. (It would seem to him, looking back, that he always had bad luck with weather. "When I die," he once said to Bradley's aide, "they ought to hold my body for a rainy day and then bury me out in the middle of a storm."[11]) The long-range forecast, generally optimistic on May 29, was pessimistic by Friday, June 2, though the Supreme Commander on that day ordered some invasion units to sail on the following morning from ports on the Irish Sea: they must do so if they were to reach rendezvous points for a June 5 D-Day. On the evening of the following day, Saturday, it appeared almost certain that D-Day must be postponed. There was developing (in early June!) what Stagg described as a "typical December depression"—a series of low-pressure areas marching eastward across the North Atlantic, bringing with them high winds and rough seas and low clouds which would make landings difficult, naval fire support inaccurate, and air support impossible. These conditions would prevail through the next forty-eight hours and there appeared little chance that a "benevolent high" would move in to improve things during the twenty-four hours after that. Nevertheless, it was decided not to make the final decision on postponement until the four o'clock meeting on the morning of June 4.

As that meeting was held, the weather outside Southwick House and the prospects presented by Stagg were as "dirty" as they could be for that time of year. Despite them, Montgomery—fearful of the loss of security, recognizing the extreme difficulty of maintaining morale (the keen fighting edge) of men narrowly cooped up for days in transports and barbed-wire enclosures—favored keeping the June 5 date. No one else did. Tedder and Leigh-Mallory pointed out that air dominance had from the first been deemed essential to success of the plan, and on June 5 there could be no air support at all. The airborne landings would have to be canceled. Admiral Ramsey, though he believed the Navy could probably handle the "mechanics of the landing," stressed the difficulty of handling small craft in the wave-heaped Channel and of adjusting naval gunfire. Eisenhower listened. There was some doubt whether the troop-laden ships already at sea, recalled to port, could be readied for a D-Day twenty-four hours later, but it seemed obvious to him that the postponement must be made. He therefore moved D-Day forward to Tuesday, June 6, and ordered a meeting at 9:30 that evening for review of this decision.

The day thus begun was miserable for the Allied high command. A weeping, wailing gloom settled heavily upon the woods in which the Supreme Commander had his living quarters (a long caravan which he called his "circus wagon") and office tent. Rain fell ceaselessly. Wind sobbed through the trees. Nervous anxiety mounted from hour to hour in Eisenhower's mind. By shortly before 9:30 that evening, when he entered his car to be driven the two miles from his caravan to Southwick House, he was under extreme tension and his face showed it. He could manage only a feeble flicker of a grin as he entered the library where Beetle Smith, Leigh-Mallory, Tedder, Ramsey, and Montgomery were already gathered, with seven other senior officers.

The crucial conference began with a gloomy report on conditions prevailing on the coast of France. There were precisely what the Meteorological Committee had predicted they would be; had the June 5 date been adhered to, despite the forecast, a major disaster would almost certainly have resulted. But then the weatherman made a surprising announcement. There had been "some rapid and unexpected developments in the situation," he said; they permitted a ray of hope to lighten the darkness. A high-pressure area, previously stationary off the coast of Spain, was beginning to push northeastward. It should produce a gradual clearing of the skies and a moderation of the wind over Channel and assault areas throughout the next day and clear or only partly cloudy skies over moderate seas on the morning of June 6. In all probability, this interruption of foul weather would be brief, however. The skies would probably again be cloudy by noon of June 6, presaging a resumption of rain and wind on June 7.

His statement made, Stagg was sharply questioned. What he had given, he replied, was a summary of probabilities, not of certainties. No one could say with absolute certainty what the weather over the Channel would be thirty-odd hours later. No one could have foreseen, twenty-four hours earlier, the break in the weather which his statement that evening described. It was, as he had said, an unexpected development. But his statement had been carefully checked and double-checked, it was one in which all his expert colleagues concurred, and he regarded its probable accuracy as very high.

Quick, nervous discussion followed. If the American Naval Task Force sailing for Omaha and Utah Beaches was to reach its destination by H-Hour of a June 6 D-Day, its commander, Rear Admiral Alan G. Kirk, must receive firm sailing orders within half an hour; moreover, a further postponement must be for a minimum of forty-eight hours, because of the necessity to refuel ships. So said Admiral Ramsey. Eisenhower then asked each of the officers for his opinion. Smith, admitting it was a gamble, favored moving on June 6. So did Montgomery. Tedder and Leigh-Mallory, fearful that the cloud cover predicted for the afternoon of June 6 would prevent necessary air support of the ground forces, were dubious.

The actual decision must be made at once, and Eisenhower alone must make it. He sat in silence for what seemed to the others a long time. When he spoke it was as if he talked, at first, to himself.

"The question is," he said, "how long can you hang this operation on the end of a limb and let it hang there?"

If he postponed again, it would have to be for at least forty-eight hours, and by then, according to present indications, the weather might be just as bad. Nor would conditions of tide and moon be quite "right" on June 8. Tidal conditions would not again be "right," as a matter of fact, until June 19—and then, even if the weather were good, and no one could predict this, the airborne troops would have to drop in darkness instead of in the light of the moon. Nor was it reasonable to conclude that security could be maintained much beyond the present hour, if indeed it were not already lost. (An American major general, over cocktails at Claridge's, had blurted that the invasion would occur before June 15, for which he had been promptly demoted and sent home. A British colonel had told civilians he was training to attack specific targets in, he broadly hinted, Normandy. He too was promptly demoted and disciplined. An envelope of top-secret OVERLORD papers had been mistakenly addressed to a girl in Chicago. Just last night a teletype operator of the Associated Press in London had practice-typed an "urgent flash" on what she thought was a disconnected machine but which instead told New York and, within seconds, the world that "EISEN-

HOWER'S HQ ANNOUNCED ALLIED LANDING IN FRANCE." The slip had of course been promptly corrected, but who could say what German Intelligence had already surmised from it?) If the enemy was not yet aware of the time and place of the landings he would almost certainly be if the invasion were again postponed. After all, hundreds of thousands of Allied troops were now fully briefed on the parts they were to play and it was folly to believe that a "secret" so widely shared could be kept from German Intelligence.

Again Eisenhower spoke, his face drawn.

"I am quite positive we must give the order," he said, speaking slowly. "I don't like it, but there it is." He glanced at the clock on the wall, and at the faces of his commanders. "I don't see how we can do anything else."

And so the orders went out to Kirk and the other naval commanders. The mighty movement toward France began.

But even this was not the absolutely final decision. Another conference, to review weather conditions and confirm or retract the earlier orders, was set for four o'clock next morning, June 5.

The caravan shuddered in gusts of wind, and rain needled into his face as if shot from a gun, when the Supreme Commander came down the aluminum steps and gravel path toward his waiting car. But when he arrived at Southwick House he and the others found that the weather was developing as Stagg had predicted it would six hours before. Even Tedder and Leigh-Mallory at last agreed that the operation should continue.

"O.K.," Eisenhower said. "We'll go. . . ."

ii. *The Great Invasion*

Of all the words in the English language, one of the least widely known in 1944, though destined for a considerable popular currency in 1945, was the word "implosion." The reverse of "explosion" (it is defined as a bursting in rather than a bursting out), it may be used to describe the kind of movement of forces that occurred in the storm-tossed English Channel from early morning until after dark on June 5, 1944. Energies originally scattered over thousands of miles—shaped into active or passive agencies of war in myriads of factories, farms, forests, mines, oilfields, mills, shipyards, and military and naval installations throughout America and Britain—had been brought within the confines of this island, then gathered more closely together in southern England, and at last focused as concentrated units of power in Plymouth, Dartmouth, Torquay, Portland, Southampton, Portsmouth, and some fifteen or twenty other ports on England's southern shore and along the Bristol Channel. From these ports the power units were thrust out upon the sea in more than twenty-seven hundred ships organized into fifty-nine convoys sailing through carefully mineswept lanes into a rendezvous area of five miles radius, nicknamed "Piccadilly Circus," thirteen miles southeast of the Isle of Wight. Thus the implosion.

It was immediately succeeded by an *ex*plosion somewhat analogous to that of a gigantic shotgun shell containing five immense and elongated pellets fired down a five-, then ten-grooved barrel aimed southward. In "Piccadilly Circus," the mighty armada was formed up into five powerful task forces, one for each of the assault beaches and each provided with a buoy-marked mineswept lane that became two lanes halfway across the Channel, one lane for the fast convoys and one for the slow. Down these, in the brief darkness comprising night in that latitude at that season, the ships sailed over rough seas under a wrack of cloud that, flying in the wind, was torn asunder every now and then to permit the moon to show her face. A lucky moon, thought many who saw her in glimpses from the decks of pitching, rolling ships that night. A silver goddess who smiled upon this enterprise, and blessed it. For the whole of this vast and intricate crossing was going almost precisely according to the plan, veritable miracles of seamanship were being accomplished, and no sign appeared that the enemy had any inkling of what was going forward.

At the southern end of the ten-grooved barrel (to complete our metaphor), the immense pellets began to scatter slightly, each seeking its own specific target. With few and minor exceptions, every transport and cargo vessel ticketed for the initial assault—every LST and LCT—was in its assigned place off the coast of Normandy by the assigned hour in the darkness before the dawn of June 6. Landing craft were lowered and net ladders slung over the sides of bucking ships. Down these clambered heavy-laden engineers and signalmen and infantrymen—down into waiting boats which, loaded, began to circle as their crews awaited the signal to head for shore. The preliminary naval bombardment began, German batteries replying tentatively, searchingly at first, then vehemently as definite targets were found. The pre-dawn twilight was full of ominous noise. Dawn came. The signal came. The tempo of naval gunfire increased, shells now bursting so thickly on and immediately behind the beaches as to hide the French coastal landscape behind thick curtains of smoke and dust. The landing craft ceased their circling; they pushed forward in straight lines and at carefully regulated speeds against the vaunted, the long-feared Atlantic Wall. . . .

These first events were essentially the same before every landing area. Thereafter events differed as the landing areas differed in physical feature and in quantity and quality of defense. Let us look briefly at each in turn.[12]

First, the westernmost landing, at Utah Beach, made by the U. S. VII Corps.

As has been indicated, the Utah landing, because the Germans could so easily block the beach exits (nine causeways across a two-mile-wide flooded area), appeared in prospect the most difficult and hazardous of the

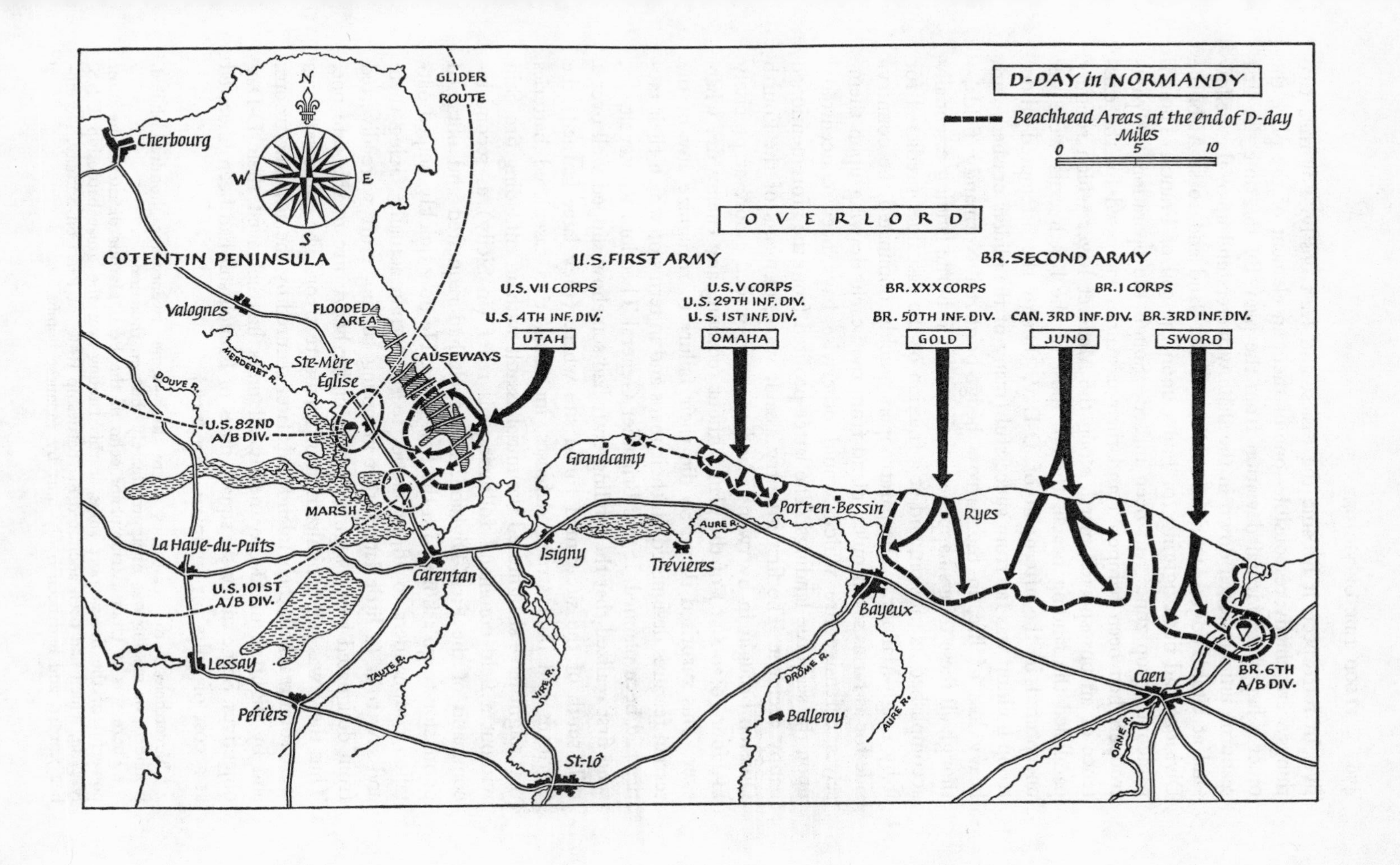
D-DAY in NORMANDY
Beachhead Areas at the end of D-day
Miles
0
5
10
OVERLORD
U.S. FIRST ARMY
BR. SECOND ARMY
U.S. VII CORPS
U.S. 4TH INF. DIV.
UTAH
U.S. V CORPS
U.S. 29TH INF. DIV.
U.S. 1ST INF. DIV.
OMAHA
BR. XXX CORPS
BR. 50TH INF. DIV.
GOLD
BR. I CORPS
CAN. 3RD INF. DIV.
JUNO
BR. 3RD INF. DIV.
SWORD
COTENTIN PENINSULA
Cherbourg
N
W
E
S
GLIDER ROUTE
Valognes
FLOODED AREA
CAUSEWAYS
MERDERET R.
DOUVE R.
Ste-Mère Église
U.S. 82ND A/B DIV.
MARSH
La Haye-du-Puits
U.S. 101ST A/B DIV.
Lessay
Périers
TAUTE R.
Carentan
Grandcamp
Isigny
Trévières
AURE R.
Port-en-Bessin
Ryes
Bayeux
DRÔME R.
Balleroy
AURE R.
VIRE R.
St-Lô
Caen
ORNE R.
BR. 6TH A/B DIV.

five. In retrospect, it became the easiest and least costly. For this, two things were chiefly responsible—one of them an element of the plan, the other a happy accidental deviation from the plan. By the time the first seaborne units touched down in the shallow waters and upon the yellow sand at Utah's edge, American soldiers of the 82nd and 101st Airborne Divisions had been fighting for hours upon the soil of France. Though parachute drop zones had been missed, though the operations of paratroopers had been hampered and their casualties increased by the existence of an unsuspected marsh along the Mederet River which roughly paralleled the landing beach, though most of the beach exits were yet uncaptured in the afternoon of D-Day, though the attempted glider troop buildup was far from successful (many of the gliders crashed, with heavy loss of life, in the narrow hedge-bordered Normandy fields)—though all these things happened, the western airborne landing essentially accomplished its mission, and at a fraction of the casualties predicted for it by Leigh-Mallory.* The paratroopers quickly dominated the countryside for as far as seven miles inland from the beach, drawing upon themselves defensive fire which would otherwise have been concentrated upon the seaborne landings. The latter profited from the aforementioned happy accident. The first infantry assault wave, elements of the Fourth Division brought in by twenty landing craft, waded ashore at precisely H-Hour (6:30 A.M.) of the plan without receiving any enemy fire whatever. This surprised them. So did their failure to recognize any of the terrain features designated on their maps and in terms of which their tactics had been planned. It was Brigadier General Theodore Roosevelt, Jr., who first realized that the landing craft had somehow slipped well over a mile south of the site aimed for—a site where (they later learned) the Germans had built strong defenses, including two casemated batteries that might have slaughtered the initial assault with an enfilading fire. Still without a field command following his relief (in Sicily) as second-in-command of the First Division, Roosevelt had requested and obtained permission to go ashore with the first wave. He now quickly helped battalion commanders to adjust tactics to the terrain actually facing them and saw to it (a little later) that incoming landing craft were diverted from designated beach segments then under heavy fire to this safe one. Thus there was full capitalization of fortunate error. The causeway exits were soon reached, their inland ends later secured by the airborne troops, and by nightfall of D-Day nearly all units had achieved their D-Day objectives. Some thirty-six square miles of French soil had been liberated at a cost of only 197 infantry casualties.†

* Nevertheless, the casualties were high—some twenty-five hundred killed, wounded, or missing out of approximately thirteen thousand.

† There was at Utah a triumphant echo of the Pearl Harbor disaster. The most powerful of the fire-support ships at this landing was the great battleship U.S.S. *Nevada*, which had been anchored in "Battleship Row" at Pearl on Sunday, December 7, 1941, and had been badly hurt by Japanese bombs.

Far different was the story of Omaha.

Unlike Utah, Omaha Beach had been carefully prepared for maximum defense by the Germans; they were aided by a coastal terrain eminently suited to their purpose. A gently sloping strip of sand some three hundred yards in width was bounded landward by a natural shingle sea wall topped, a few yards farther on, by an artificial sea wall, of concrete through half its three-mile length, of piling through the rest, above which was a level, grassy stretch a hundred to three hundred yards wide ending in moderately high bluffs. On the level stretch were two tiny villages whose houses, those the Germans had not demolished, were transformed into defensive strongpoints. The bluffs, edging a plateau extending inland, were much too steep to be climbed by wheeled or tracked vehicles, so that the only exits from the landing area were four ravines up each of which ran an unsurfaced road, or dirt track. The roads had been heavily mined; they were covered by rifle and machine-gun emplacements.

As at Tarawa, though with better reason, since tactical surprise was here essential to the prevention of overwhelming enemy reinforcement, preliminary air and naval bombardment had not been long or intense enough to silence prepared defenses. From them the enemy poured a withering fire upon landing craft as these touched down and upon the troops who floundered out of them into shallow water where many not killed by shot or shell or mine were drowned when they stumbled or were wounded under the heavy burdens they had to bear. All seemed chaos and confusion. Most of the tanks that were supposed to precede the first infantry wave ashore and cover it with their guns never made it: they sank when canvas "bloomers," designed to float them in, collapsed, or they were destroyed by German shells. Wave organization was disrupted; units hit the beach as much as two miles from the segments assigned them. In consequence of these and other misfortunes, nearly all the Americans who survived the bloody approach spent all D-Day morning huddled helplessly, fearfully under the sea wall and behind beach obstacles and stalled vehicles. There was no forward movement at all. For long hours of agony the issue was in doubt. By noon, Bradley, aboard U.S.S. *Augusta*, was seriously considering the possibility that the troops would have to be withdrawn and the Omaha force diverted to Utah.

But even as he considered this dire possibility, the issue was beginning to be decided against it, not by plan or high command, but by the naked courage of a few individual men.‡ A brigadier general strode up and down waving a pistol and shouting, "Now let's get off the beach!" until his bravery was emulated, his words obeyed. A sergeant "got mad" and, rallying his squad, led them pell-mell through a minefield on the bluff's side and, at the top, knocked out a pillbox with his bazooka. Another

‡ The story is superbly told both in Cornelius Ryan's *The Longest Day* (New York: 1959) and David Howarth's *D-Day, The Sixth of June, 1944* (New York: 1959). The specific examples here cited are from pp. 227–28 of the softbound reprint of the former, and from pp. 152–56 of the latter.

sergeant also "got mad" and, cursing furiously, virtually booted men forward. "They're murdering us here!" said a wounded colonel, striding boldly upright among cowering men. "Let's move inland and get murdered!" Another colonel was more vehement. "Two kinds of men are staying on this beach, the dead and those who are going to die," he shouted. "Now let's get the hell out of here!" A lieutenant, angry and disgusted, suddenly climbed atop the sea wall and, looking down at his terror-frozen men, said contemptuously, "Are you going to lie there and get killed or get up and do something about it?"

And so small groups of men began to blast holes in the barbed wire and, often with their own mangled bodies, cleared lanes through the minefields until at last, in the late afternoon, infantrymen managed a general advance up the bluffs and vehicles began to move off the beach up the ravines. Even then a determined German counterattack would have liquidated the beachhead. Instead, by nightfall, the German shore defenses were liquidated, the invasion front had been pushed a mile to a mile and a half inland, and reinforcements and supplies were coming onto Omaha in massive quantities. It became evident that V Corps (the First and Twenty-ninth Infantry Divisions) would stay ashore. The cost had been high, though actually no higher than SHAEF had anticipated for each of the five landings. V Corps lost some three thousand men killed, wounded, and missing.

In the British sector things went better than at Omaha, though considerably less easily than at Utah.

The British 6th Airborne Division—fifty-three hundred paratroopers and airborne infantry—dropped on moonlit fields and woods and marshes northeast of Caen at the same time as the American 82nd and 101st Airborne dropped on the Cotentin Peninsula. Their mission was to seize bridges over the Caen Canal and Orne River and knock out a formidable battery that ranged on Sword Beach. It was only partly accomplished, due to badly missed paratrooper drop zones and the failure of some portions of the glider supply buildup. Nevertheless, at the price of 650 casualties, the division was approximately as successful as its American counterparts in easing the seaborne landings. These last began approximately an hour later than at Omaha and Utah because there were—before Gold in the west, Juno in the center, and Sword in the east—reefs and patches of quicksand that had to be submerged by a higher tide to permit the passage of boats and amphibious vehicles and men afoot (wading the shallows) from sea to shore. The extra time was well employed by the Royal Navy. The British warships had two full daylight hours (instead of half an hour of full daylight, as the American Navy had had) in which to shell shore installations before the first assault wave touched down. The shelling, to which rocket fire was added immediately after the first landing, proved effective—and on the British beaches, in marked contrast to Omaha, a majority of the tanks assigned to support the infantry got ashore with the initial wave and fulfilled their assignment.

This was a three-division infantry assault—the British Fiftieth Infantry, the Canadian Third Infantry, and the British Third—incorporating some Free French units, and it encountered less resistance and suffered fewer casualties than had been feared. Later, resistance stiffened. But the only determined German counterattack of the day failed (it was made by the Twenty-first Panzer Division), and by nightfall the British Fiftieth and Canadian Third were linked up in a continuous front four to six miles inland from Gold and Juno. The British Third had driven inland approximately the same distance from Sword and had made contact with the Sixth Airborne at its left, though it remained separated from the Canadians at its right by a thin wedge (a single German battalion) driven to the sea by the otherwise fruitless counterattack. All this was satisfactory. It was not, however, as deep a penetration as had been hoped for. Bayeux, a D-Day objective, yet remained in German hands (it would be taken the next day, virtually undamaged). So did Caen, which Montgomery had confidently predicted he would take before D-Day's sun went down.

But the over-all picture was bright, from the Allied point of view. SHAEF and the Combined Chiefs of Staff gazed upon it with sighs of relief. The predicted disaster to the two American airborne divisions had not occurred. Complete tactical surprise had, after all, been achieved. (Rommel, the Allies would soon learn, had not even been in France at the beginning of the twenty-four hours he had said would be decisive of the war. On the assumption that the predicted weather would make a major cross-Channel operation impossible, he had gone to Germany on June 4 to celebrate his wife's birthday and confer with Hitler. Receiving word of the invasion by phone in midmorning, he did not arrive back at his headquarters until six o'clock in the evening of D-Day.) Nearly 155,000 Allied fighting men had been established on nearly eighty square miles of Normandy soil at a total casualty cost of from ten thousand to twelve thousand; and Allied dominance of the skies, immediate shipping capacity, and prepared buildup made it unlikely in the extreme that the Germans could push this force back into the sea.

All America breathed sighs of relief that night, and rejoiced.

The first flash report of the invasion had been heard in New York at 3:32 A.M., and on the West Coast (simultaneously) at 12:33 A.M., Tuesday, June 6, 1944. It came by radio from SHAEF's public relations officer: "Under the command of General Eisenhower, Allied naval forces, supported by strong air forces, began landing Allied armies this morning on the coast of France." Immediately thereafter, the Supreme Commander's Order of the Day to the "soldiers, sailors, and airmen of the Allied Expeditionary Force" was broadcast. "You are about to embark on a great crusade. . . . In company with our brave Allies and brothers in arms on other fronts you will bring about the destruction of the German war machine, elimination of Nazi tyranny over the oppressed peoples of Europe, and security for ourselves in a free world. . . . We will accept nothing less than full Victory. Good luck and let us all beseech the blessing of Almighty God upon this great and noble undertaking."

Night shift workers in plants turning out war material, all across the land, paused in their labors: tens of thousands bowed their heads in prayer, hundreds kneeling to chant aloud in unison the Lord's Prayer. Night workers and insomniacs in thousands of towns, hearing the news, called their friends out of bed: streets normally dark and empty at that time of night were suddenly brightened by lighted windows and dotted with people who came together in little clusters, talking in hushed tones. But most Americans did not hear the news until they got out of bed that Tuesday morning and turned on their radios. They heard it thankfully, hopefully, but also anxiously, with a strong mixture of dread. So much had been said about the Atlantic Wall and the huge casualties that must be expected of any effort to pierce it!

The prevailing feeling was religious in tone. At 10:00 A.M., broadcasting from the White House, the President of the United States asked his fellow Americans to join him in a prayer he had composed:

> Almighty God—
>
> Our sons, pride of our Nation, this day have set out upon a mighty endeavor, a struggle to preserve our Republic, our religion, and our civilization and to set free a suffering humanity. Lead them straight and true; give strength to their arms, stoutness to their hearts, steadfastness to their faith.
>
> They will need Thy blessings. Their road will be long and hard. For the enemy is strong. He may hurl back our forces. Success may not come with rushing speed, but we shall return again and again; and we know that by Thy grace and by the righteousness of our cause, our sons will triumph.
>
> And, O Lord. . . . Help us to conquer the apostles of greed and racial arrogancies. Lead us to the saving of our country and with our sister nations into a world unity that will spell a sure peace—a peace invulnerable to the schemings of unworthy men. And a peace that will let all men live in freedom, reaping the just rewards of their honest toil.
>
> Thy will be done, Almighty God. Amen.

All day, wherever and whenever they could do so, Americans stayed within earshot of radio loudspeakers and scanned successive editions of newspapers, eagerly attentive to every snippet of news from France and anxiously awaiting general summaries of the great event. By that evening, the summaries were being made. They spoke of victory; they were full of hope.

For the Allies, the bright face of victory became somewhat tarnished during the days and weeks that followed. Few men feared that the Germans could liquidate the bridgehead, but many feared its containment and, by that token, the nullification of its *raison d'être*. The Germans in fact seemed to be achieving this as the June days passed, then the weeks, finally the month itself. In July developed a veritable chorus of complaint that "command timidity" in Normandy was denying the Allied world the victory that D-Day's boldness had earned.

The plan had contemplated a "swinging door" strategy, with the British forces in the Caen area providing the hinge and the American right wing the door. Caen, a communications hub, lies only 125 miles and slightly northeast of Paris: an Allied thrust through it to the west would drive a wedge between the German Seventh Army fighting in Normandy and the German Fifteenth (the only other major enemy force in northern France) along the Pas-de-Calais. Hence the assumption that the enemy would reinforce promptly and strongly in this area, concentrating there the bulk of his armor. It had been hoped and expected, however, as has been indicated, that Caen itself would be taken in the first rush inland from the sea, opening up to the Allies a terrain well suited to a full exploitation of Allied tanks and combat air power immediately south and southeast of the city. Moreover, many observers and participants in the battle, including the Germans,§ were convinced that Caen *would* have been taken on D-Day evening if a determined effort to do so had been made, for the defenders were then relatively few in number and low in morale. Instead there was a stalemate, a bloody stalemate, for weeks. Caen was not taken until July 9, thirty-three days after the landings, and even then there was no significant forward movement in that area for weeks thereafter. Correspondents began privately to make acid remarks about the "rusty hinge," and SHAEF evinced impatience. (". . . I repeatedly urged Montgomery to speed up and intensify his efforts to the limit," writes Eisenhower. "He threw in attack after attack, gallantly conducted and heavily supported by artillery and air, but German resistance was not crushed."[13])

Nor was dissatisfaction, on the part of knowledgeable Allied observers, wholly focused on the alleged "rustiness" of the "hinge." There was also a quite general feeling that, despite the static situation at Caen, the "door" could swing far more rapidly than it was doing—thus flaking inhibiting rust off the creaking hinge—if it were given the kind of healthy push it ought to have. Bradley, it was felt, should make this push. He of course remained nominally under the command of the cautious Montgomery, but correspondents knew that, from the moment of the landings, he had been operating on virtually the same command level as Montgomery, under Eisenhower. Admittedly he faced grave tactical difficulties. For one thing, the Normandy hedgerow country was wonderfully

§ Among those convinced that the city would be taken that day were the Gestapo guards of Caen's prison. They set up two machine guns in the prison courtyard and, in batches of ten, slaughtered all the male prisoners, ninety-two of them, without making the slightest effort to determine whether or not they had committed the offenses charged to them. Only forty of the ninety-two were in fact members of the French Resistance.

adapted to defensive needs. Some of the hedgerows had been established in Roman times; all were centuries old; and the earthen banks on which the hedges grew (often there was a double bank, a trench between) had hardened to the consistency of reinforced concrete. Each was a wall for the defense: huddled behind it, machine gunners and riflemen could take a heavy toll of troops advancing across the open field before it. Each was a tank trap for the offense: coming against it, a tank was tilted upward, its vulnerable belly exposed, its guns aimed harmlessly at the sky. There were also numerous and extensive bogs. In such country, a superiority of armor, however great, counted for little or nothing.

And this difficulty was compounded by the worst weather to strike Normandy in seventy summers. At midnight of June 18–19, just twenty-four hours after the Americans had reached the west coast of Cotentin, severing the Peninsula, a tremendous and wholly unseasonable storm struck the northern coast of France. It continued with increasing intensity—sheets of rain blown by winds of gale force—all through the nineteenth. The event pointed up, and enhanced, the great good fortune of Eisenhower's decision at Southwick House on June 4–5—for had he then postponed the invasion again, the rescheduled D-Day would have coincided with the breaking of this mighty storm. The operation would have had to be further postponed. Winds averaged thirty-five miles an hour, with gusts of near sixty, all through June 19, and continued to blow with only slight abatement through June 20 and 21. An enormous surf piled up against Omaha Beach; it wrecked the mulberries offshore along with many of the craft anchored within them and caused at once a shortage of supplies for Allied forces, especially a shortage of ammunition. Bradley felt forced to cancel an attack south and southwest along the bogs at Cotentin's neck which had been designed in support of an all-out drive north upon Cherbourg, the latter drive having been launched (perforce without air support, because of the storm) on the morning of June 19. Indeed, all Allied offensive activity on the Peninsula had to be halted (or so Bradley decided) save the Cherbourg drive, whose importance was of course increased by the harbor-wreckage at Omaha. The drive, greatly aided by Navy bombardment of the coastal forts, ended on June 26 with Cherbourg's capture, and the killing or capture of its entire garrison. Within forty-eight hours thereafter, despite German sabotage of the port facilities and the mines and booby-traps they had thickly strewn about, the first Allied cargo ship entered the harbor.¶

But Cherbourg's capture, liberating the entire Peninsula, was not followed by any such rapid advance as must be made if the Americans were to catch up with the phase lines (positions to be occupied on D plus 25, D plus 30, and so on) drawn on SHAEF's maps before the invasion was launched. And informed critics, having admitted the difficulties of terrain and weather, became steadily less inclined to accept the excuses that

¶ The artificial harbor off the British beaches, though severely damaged, survived the storm.

were given by the top field command for the lack of progress. Bradley complained of ammunition shortage, but others pointed to the enormous stockpiles of materiel piled up behind almost all stationary lines, and to the fact that the Americans now outnumbered the enemy on their front by two or three to one and also dominated the air. By July 2, a million Allied soldiers were in Normandy: thirteen American and eleven British divisions, plus one Canadian: and there had been landed some 567,000 tons of supplies and 172,000 vehicles. Surely, with all this strength at their command, the Allied generals should be able to break out of the hedgerows and bogs into country suited to armor and tactical air power! Surely they might then drive east and north through the Pas-de-Calais into Belgium!

Such criticism, and such impatience for a liberation of the whole Channel coast, was given urgency by the effects of a "secret weapon" unveiled by the Germans on June 13. In the early morning darkness that day, a strange sound, rather like a motorcycle "buzzing" at high speed, was heard in the sky over Greater London's Bethnal Green. Looking up, watchers saw above them a swiftly moving yellow-red flame. Suddenly the sound ceased, the flame went out. Some twenty or thirty seconds later there was a terrific explosion in a street, killing six people and injuring nine. Thus began the long-anticipated assault upon London with pilotless aircraft.** It had been repeatedly postponed and was now much reduced in strength by the Allied air raids on Peenemünde, upon German war plants and transportation, and upon the ninety-six known launching sites on the French coast of the Channel. Nevertheless it was a formidable assault by a formidable weapon. The Flying Bomb, jet-engined, with a ton of TNT in its warhead, flew at speeds of up to four hundred miles an hour at heights of around three thousand feet. It was steered by a magnetic compass and had its range determined by a small propeller rotated by the air through which it passed. After the propeller had rotated a certain number of times, measuring the distance from launching site to target, the engine automatically cut off and the bomb tilted down, sometimes diving and sometimes gliding steeply to earth. It exploded on contact with terrific blast effects. Hitler called it the V-1 ("V" for Vergeltungswaffen or "weapons of reprisal") because he hopefully believed it would be but the first of a series of "secret weapons" which, offsetting Allied superiority in numbers and conventional weapons, would enable him to snatch victory from the jaws of defeat.

Nor was this hope as fantastic as it might seem later to be. Eisenhower himself believed that if the V-1 and its successor, the V-2, had been available "six months earlier . . . our invasion . . . would have proved exceedingly difficult, perhaps impossible. I feel sure that if . . . [the enemy] had succeeded in using these weapons over a six-month period, and particularly if he had made the Portsmouth-Southampton area one of his

** See page 440.

principal targets, OVERLORD might have been written off."[14] By the same token, the imminence of the V-1 attack enhanced further the fortunateness of Eisenhower's own D-Day decision. Had the invasion been postponed until July, the launching ports would inevitably have become prime V-1 targets and, in the absence of adequate defense measures, the effect could have been catastrophic for OVERLORD.

As it was, the "buzz bomb" assault, which began in earnest on June 15, killed some sixty-two hundred civilians, injured eighteen thousand, and damaged three-quarters of a million houses (of which twenty-three thousand were wholly destroyed) within the next eleven weeks. Nearly half these casualties and this damage occurred in the first three weeks, before methods of defense by standing fighter plane patrols, radar-directed antiaircraft fire from coastal batteries, and massed barrage balloons began to be worked out. During this period—and, indeed, until the beast was mastered—no small part of the damage done was to the nerves and general morale of the population in the target area. As a terror device, the V-1 was well-nigh perfect. To its very real physical danger was added a chronic dread (the fatal bomb might fall at any hour, day or night, in any weather) which became acute during the brief interval between the engine's cutoff and the explosive impact. Would the bomb glide, or plunge straight down? None could say. But from mid-July onward the defenses against it became increasingly effective. By the last week in August not more than one bomb out of seven launched was getting through to London; on August 28, of ninety-four bombs that approached the English coast, ninety were destroyed; and on September 1, as Allied troops approached the launching sites, the assault in England ended altogether.[15]

This was not the end of London's ordeal, however. Just one week later, at 6:43 in the evening of September 8, unpreceded by a warning sound, two death-dealing explosions occurred miles apart in Greater London. They were the warheads of the first V-2s to come down upon the city, destined to be followed by some five hundred during the next seven months. More deadly than the V-1, though less effective as a terror device, because its approach was unheralded, the V-2 was a thirteen-ton rocket with a ton of TNT in its nose and a range of some two hundred miles, powered by a mixture of alcohol and liquid oxygen.††

†† Ironically, German scientists who developed the V-2 based their work on ideas published and patents obtained, many of them more than a quarter-century before, by Robert H. Goddard of Worcester, Massachusetts. A principal incitement was Goddard's 1919 paper, "A Method of Reaching Extreme Altitudes." He was the first man to develop a rocket engine which (like the V-2s) used liquid propellants (he mixed liquid oxygen with gasoline), and he successfully launched the first liquid-fueled rocket in 1926. He tried repeatedly and unsuccessfully to interest the U. S. Army and Navy in his rocket experiments in the 1920s. During World War II, the Navy used him chiefly in developing "jato" (jet-assisted airplane takeoff), which was somewhat like using the Wright Brothers to develop an improved kite after their Kitty Hawk experiments. In 1960, fifteen years after his death, the U. S. Government paid one million dollars for infringing Goddard patents, specifically acknowledging that the Air Force's Atlas and Thor, the Army's Jupiter and Redstone, and the Navy's Vanguard used what were essentially Goddard rocket engines and Goddard liquid propellants.[16]

Nearly four tons of alcohol and five of liquid oxygen were consumed in the first minute of flight, by which time the rocket had been lifted six miles straight up, then tipped to an angle of forty-five degrees, and boosted to a speed of four thousand miles an hour. It described a gigantic arc as it rose to a maximum height of fifty miles or so and then curved down to strike with terrific force, burying its nose in the earth and forming a crater as its warhead exploded. Its explosive force was thus exerted upward instead of outward, as with the V-1, which meant that it demolished whatever building it happened to strike but did not (as the V-1 did) cause great blast damage beyond a few score yards of its immediate impact. It killed about twice as many people per bomb as the V-1 only because there was no warning of its approach and hence no possibility of taking cover. From first to last, twenty-seven hundred were killed and sixty-five hundred seriously injured in England by the V-2, casualty figures that would have been much higher if the Germans had not been forced to launch from the farthest limit of the rocket's range, with consequent increase in its inaccuracy.

For by September, there had been a dramatic change in the military situation on the Continent. . . .

iii. *Breakout and Pursuit*

As July opened, and as has been indicated, there was a growing fear on the part of some observers that the Germans might after all manage to contain the invasion bridgehead and force upon the Allies the kind of bloody, indecisive trench warfare that had disgraced the military commands and destroyed the manhood of western Europe in 1914–18. The immediate objective of the American First Army at that time was a line along the road which runs sixteen miles southwest from the ancient citadel of St. Lo to Coutances. Once reached, this line was to be the springboard for a major attempt to break out of the Normandy confinement into a war of wide and rapid movement. Alas, the line could not be reached. Early in the morning of July 3, an attack was launched down the west coast from north of La Haye du Puits toward Coutances, some twenty miles to the south. Of these twenty, less than seven had been covered by the attacking force in twelve days, at great cost against heavy resistance, when Bradley ordered the effort discontinued on July 14. Nor had the eastern terminus of the proposed "jump-off" line been reached by then. An offensive launched southward from the Bayeux-Carentan road toward St. Lo had driven across the Vire River on July 18, capturing more than fifty villages, but hampered by weather that seemed to have enlisted permanently on the side of the defense (chill rain fell day after day), it was almost literally bogged down at La Meauffe, five miles north of St. Lo, as the western assault was called off. Not until late on July 18 did the Americans take St. Lo and even then, reduced to rubble, it remained under heavy German artillery and mortar fire.

The American First Army front was thereafter described on operations maps as a generally wavering line that, for five miles or so west of St. Lo, coincided with a road running straight as a ruler across the map from St. Lo to Périers and, beyond Périers, to Lessay, where the western coastal attack toward Coutances had halted. Beyond this initial five miles, the front curved north of the road as it extended westward to the sea. It was a line far less satisfactory for breakout purposes than the line from St. Lo to Coutances—the death-dealing hedgerows continued to bound narrow fields for some score miles south of it—but Bradley decided it would have to do as a springboard. Accordingly a plan code-named COBRA was drawn up by Bradley and his staff, and promptly approved by Montgomery and Eisenhower. It called for one of the most intense tactical air bombardments in history—a carpet of bombs laid by some fifteen hundred heavy bombers and 750 medium and fighter bombers on a rectangle extending for three and a half miles along the road to Périers and a mile and a half south of it. Three shock divisions, a motorized infantry and two armored, supported by more than a thousand guns, were then to plunge through the gap blown in the German defenses and, followed by other divisions, drive as swiftly as possible south and west and east, threatening the enemy rear and forcing his precipitous withdrawal. Weather permitting, the attack was to begin on July 21.

But the weather was not permissive. Low-hanging clouds began to shed heavy rain on July 20, and this miserable weather continued for several days. It was July 25 before, at last, the skies were clear and the ground firm and dry enough for COBRA to be launched.

It did not begin well. There had been no little trepidation on the part of Bradley and his subordinates as they contemplated the unprecedented use of Flying Fortresses and Liberators in such close support of ground troops as the plan required. The heavies, each carrying forty one-hundred-pound fragmentation bombs, were to drop their sticks from eight thousand feet, a vertical distance considerably greater than the horizontal distance separating the forward ground units from the leading edge of the bomb-carpet. There was virtually no margin for error. Bradley later insisted that he approved this portion of COBRA only when he was assured by the air command that the bombers would come in out of the sun—from the east, if the attack were made in the morning; from the west, if in the afternoon—along and parallel to the St. Lo–Périers road, which clearly marked from the air the northern boundary of the carpet.[17] They were not to come in over the American ground troops at all; hence there would be no tragedy if some of the bombs fell short of the target. But if this assurance was given Bradley, there was (as he bluntly charged there was) a breach of faith on the part of the air command, for in the actual event the bombers came in directly from England, directly over the heads of the ground troops. And as the heavy bombers laid down their carpet at the rate of ten bombs per acre,

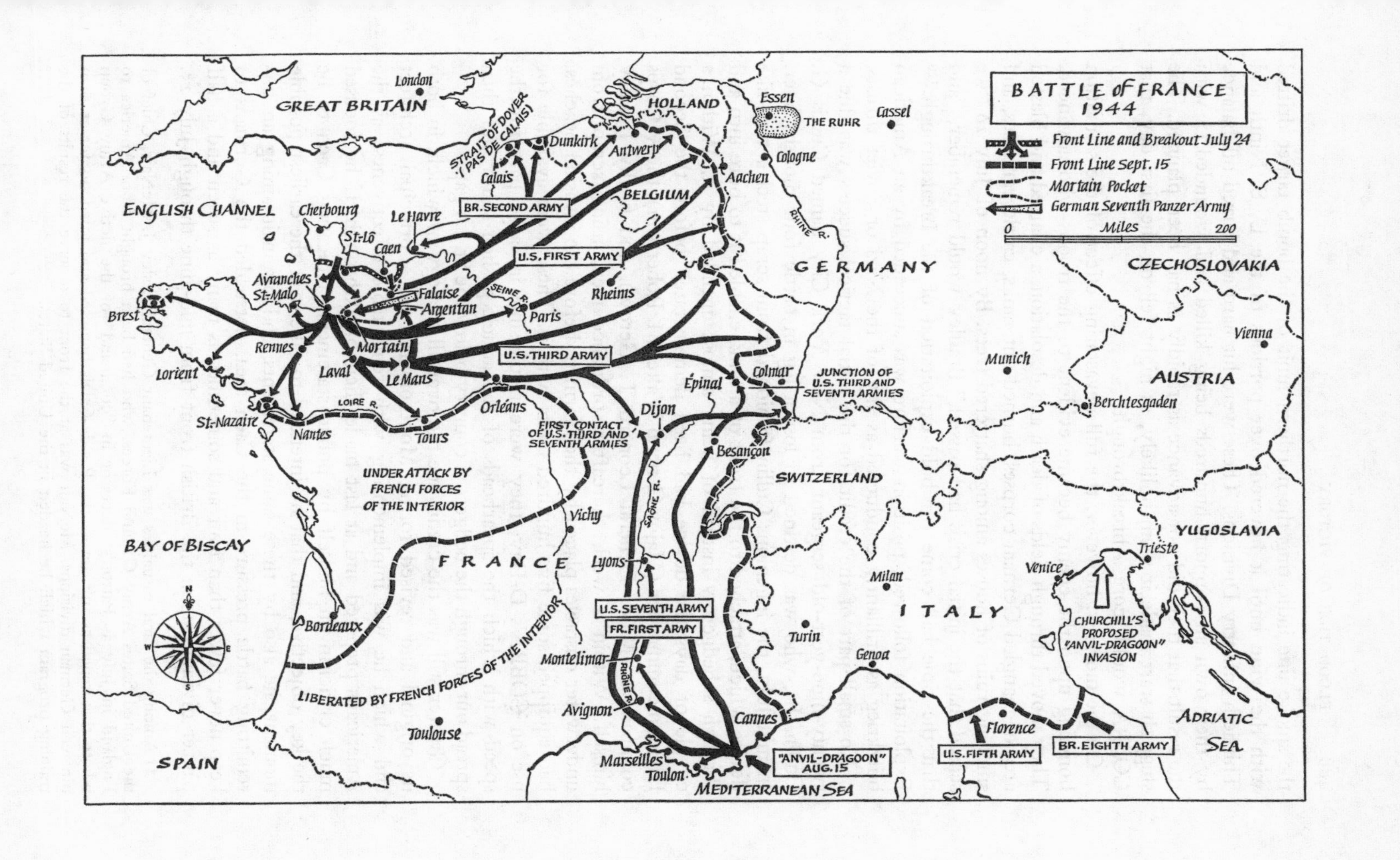
BATTLE of FRANCE 1944
Front Line and Breakout July 24
Front Line Sept. 15
Mortain Pocket
German Seventh Panzer Army
Miles
0
200
London
GREAT BRITAIN
STRAIT OF DOVER (PAS DE CALAIS)
Calais
Dunkirk
Antwerp
HOLLAND
Essen
THE RUHR
Cassel
Cologne
Aachen
BELGIUM
RHINE R.
ENGLISH CHANNEL
Cherbourg
Le Havre
BR. SECOND ARMY
St-Lô
Caen
U.S. FIRST ARMY
GERMANY
CZECHOSLOVAKIA
Avranches
St-Malo
Falaise
Argentan
SEINE R.
Paris
Rheims
Brest
Rennes
Mortain
Laval
Le Mans
U.S. THIRD ARMY
Lorient
LOIRE R.
Orléans
Épinal
Colmar
JUNCTION OF U.S. THIRD AND SEVENTH ARMIES
Munich
Vienna
AUSTRIA
Berchtesgaden
St-Nazaire
Nantes
Tours
FIRST CONTACT OF U.S. THIRD AND SEVENTH ARMIES
Dijon
Besançon
UNDER ATTACK BY FRENCH FORCES OF THE INTERIOR
SWITZERLAND
Vichy
SAÔNE R.
YUGOSLAVIA
BAY OF BISCAY
FRANCE
Lyons
Trieste
Venice
Milan
ITALY
U.S. SEVENTH ARMY
FR. FIRST ARMY
Bordeaux
Turin
CHURCHILL'S PROPOSED "ANVIL-DRAGOON" INVASION
Montelimar
RHÔNE R.
Genoa
LIBERATED BY FRENCH FORCES OF THE INTERIOR
Avignon
Cannes
Florence
ADRIATIC SEA
Toulouse
U.S. FIFTH ARMY
BR. EIGHTH ARMY
SPAIN
Marseilles
Toulon
"ANVIL-DRAGOON" AUG. 15
MEDITERRANEAN SEA

the smoke line indicating the northern limit of the bomb target drifted with the wind until it hovered over portions of the U. S. Ninth and Thirtieth Infantry Divisions. These were hit hard and jarred off-balance by their own air support, hundreds being killed and wounded,‡‡ with the result that they did not advance as rapidly as had been planned. The sluggish start made it seem unlikely, as night fell on the first day, that COBRA would score a breakthrough.

On the morrow, however, the full devastating effect of the saturation bombing upon the enemy became evident to the troops who advanced. They moved through fields of death and desolation, a charred and blasted area of mangled German corpses, burned-out tanks, cattle carcasses, and smoking ruins of houses among shattered trees. By noon of July 26 "we sensed that the initial crisis had passed," Bradley would remember, "and that the time had come for bold exploitation of the breakthrough."[18] Exploitation followed; position warfare was succeeded by an American blitzkrieg as brilliantly conducted as any of the Nazi or Soviet thrusts.

No small part of the credit for the initial tactical success was due a twenty-nine-year-old sergeant from New York City named Curtis G. Cullin, Jr., who was destined to lose a leg in battle four months later. In mid-July, the ingenious Cullin fashioned from scrap steel a tusk-like device which, attached to the front of a tank, enabled it to bore into and through a hedgerow instead of being almost upended by it. Within a couple of days the device had been demonstrated before the Second Division commander (Major General Walter M. Robertson), the V Corps commander (Major General Leonard T. Gerow), and finally Bradley himself. Within a week thereafter, ordnance men, using scrap from underwater obstacles placed by the Germans before the invasion beaches, had equipped some five hundred tanks with it. These were available for use on COBRA's D-Day; they were responsible in large part for the speed with which the spearheads of the attack pushed south and then spread out through the hedgerow country below the St. Lo gap.

Greater still was the credit due the over-all strategy of which, in both its original and revised forms, Montgomery was a principal architect and which he was implementing with remarkable effectiveness as the Americans prepared and at last made their breakthrough. If he focused much criticism on himself by public statements indicating Caen to be the key objective, and that he intended to take it at the earliest possible moment, he also by these same statements, and by maintaining an unremitting battle pressure in the Caen area, persuaded the Germans to keep never fewer than four and sometimes as many as seven and a half panzer divisions upon the British front from mid-June through July 25.

‡‡ Among the fatal casualties was Lieutenant General Lesley J. McNair, Chief of the United States Army Ground Forces, who had been brought from America to England in July as Patton's successor in "command" of the fictive Army Group whose threatened assault across the Pas-de-Calais bemused and idled no fewer than nineteen German divisions. McNair was at the front to observe the results of the training program which he headed in the United States.

During this same period, the number of panzer divisions facing the American First Army on its far longer front varied from none to three, the highest number being reached on July 20. Only two were there when COBRA was launched.

Once the gap had been opened, it was as if the whole vast weight of American war production and manpower were pushing the First Army's spearheads through it with irresistible force. Elements of Major General J. Lawton Collins' VII Corps, which had made the breakthrough, took Coutances, sixteen miles from St. Lo, in a little more than two days. The Germans were forced to pull back south from the areas of Lessay and Périers so rapidly that they had little or no time in which to mine the roads down which Major General Troy H. Middleton's VIII Corps moved. The two Corps met at Coutances, whence armored columns raced to the sea, took Granville, and poured toward Avranches while, to the east, other columns struck down through Percy and Vire. Pockets of stunned Germans were surrounded, captured. And these advances, great and rapid compared to what had gone before, were to seem meager and slow compared to what came after. For at high noon on Tuesday, August 1—as American troops, pouring through Avranches, turned the corner into Brittany; and as the Germans, pulling armor out of the Caen sector, prepared a desperate counterattack toward Avranches from the hills of Mortain—Lieutenant General George S. Patton, Jr. was beckoned forward to play his predestined role.

He had been waiting impatiently for this moment ever since OVERLORD was launched, knowing as he did that the U. S. First Army was to be divided in two when it had been swollen by the buildup to an unwieldy size. There would then be created a U. S. Third Army—armor-heavy, designed for a maximum rapidity of movement—with himself in command. The Third Army would form the outer part, the wide-sweeping right edge, of the swinging door. The First Army, reduced to normal size, was to be commanded by Lieutenant General Courtney H. Hodges, who had been Bradley's principal subordinate since D-Day. A quiet, methodical general, as meticulous in his handling of detail as Patton was careless of it, Hodges was well suited to direct the movement of the inside or narrowly sweeping part of the door, which was joined at its left to the hinge formed by the British, this being a task requiring more of steadiness, relentless perseverance, and dogged adherence to traditional tactics than it did of reckless speed and bold improvisation. The two Armies would constitute Twelfth Army Group, commanded by Bradley, who thereafter would operate officially on the same command level as Montgomery, who commanded the Twenty-first Army Group. When Eisenhower moved SHAEF to France he would assume the over-all operational command theretofore exercised, if only nominally for the most part, by Montgomery.

And Patton's impatience for this event had grown almost frantic since his highly secret arrival in Normandy on July 6. He had watched First

Army grow to twenty-one divisions—a full seven divisions more than a field army ought to have, according to military textbooks—with no clear sign that the predicted division into two armies, of which the breakout would be the incitement, was about to occur. He knew it had been agreed among Bradley, Montgomery, and Eisenhower that the American forces must operate as a single unit until some semblance of order had been shaped out of the disorder that must inevitably characterize the immediate aftermath of the breakthrough, but the cautious postponements of the decisive tactical movement exasperated him. He was convinced that "by pushing harder . . . we could advance faster." As he later wrote: "I stated at the time, and still believe, that two armored divisions, preceded by a heavy artillery concentration using air bursts, and followed by two infantry divisons, could have cut straight down the west coast to Avranches without the necessity of waiting for an air blitz."[19] When COBRA was at last launched, he was ordered by Bradley to follow Middleton's columns, which were to be incorporated in the Third Army, to "aid in unscrambling them should they become entangled"—and on July 28 he was, by oral order, assigned the command which would be officially his at noon on August 1. He was also told how the two corps which would initially comprise his Army, the VIII Corps (Middleton) on the right and the newly created XV (Major General Wade Hampton Haislip) on the left, were to be initially used.

"Georgie, you used to play end on the Army football team," said Bradley in his slow Missouri drawl. "Well, your job is to catch a forward pass and make an end run. You'll be taking over troops which are on the move, and you're to keep them moving. You'll wheel 'em down through Brittany, down to the Loire. . . . It's the kind of war you like. You'll be pretty much on your own. Just so you keep moving in accordance with the general strategical plan."[20]

And Patton did indeed "keep them moving." His flying armored columns took Rennes on August 3 and, in a little more than a week, cleared all Brittany save the four ports of St. Malo, Brest, Lorient, and St. Nazaire, which he was ordered to bypass so that there would be no loss of his forward momentum.§§ Along the Loire, Nantes and Tours became objectives of a Patton column. Other columns thrust south and east from Rennes and Fougères through Laval. In these drives he made much use of fighter bombers of the XIX Tactical Air Command to knock out enemy resistance ahead of his tanks. ("It was love at first sight between the XIX Tactical Air Command and the Third Army," he said.[21] He was also aided by the *maquis* or French Forces of the Interior operating behind enemy lines; these were supplied by night air

§§ The four ports were closely besieged and one of them, St. Malo, the least of the four, soon fell. Brest, whose garrison of fanatic Nazis was dangerously aggressive, was taken after bloody fighting on September 19. The relatively passive German garrisons at Lorient and St. Nazaire, narrowly contained, were permitted to remain in these ports until the war was over.

lifts with guns, ammunition, and even a small column of jeeps, enabling them to deny the use of key roads to the German and so prevent his shifting and concentrating forces. In general, thousands of Allied planes, by maintaining a continuous intense assault on enemy ground forces with rockets and cannon and machine guns, helped create optimum conditions for the attack by both Patton's Third and Hodges' First Army. The latter, during the first week of August, successfully executed an intricate turning movement pointed toward the Seine against far more German strength than Patton faced.

But most important of all to the continuance of Patton's "end run" was a daring decision taken by Bradley as the first week of August ended. At one o'clock in the morning of August 7, with armor withdrawn from the Caen sector and infantry reinforced (at long last) by troops theretofore immobilized along the Pas-de-Calais, the enemy launched his counterattack from the hills at Mortain toward the sea at Avranches. His obvious aim was to split Twelfth Army Group in two: if he reached the sea, he would sever the communications of the twelve U.S. divisions that had by then passed southward through the Avranches corridor—and by noon of August 7 he had made menacing progress into positions held by Major General Leland S. Hobbs' outnumbered Thirtieth Division, the only one between the enemy and Avranches. Bradley's decision had directly to do with four divisions which, having passed through the corridor, were as yet uncommitted to battle on Patton's front. Should they be recalled from Patton to reinforce the First Army at Mortain? Or should he permit them to remain in the Third Army, "beefing up" Patton's drive toward Le Mans? He chose the latter alternative. He gambled heavily on the ability of an initially thin line of battle-weary American troops to contain the German assault, but he gambled for very high stakes—nothing less than the complete encirclement of the German Seventh Army, whose left flank was now temptingly open. He consulted meteorologists. They assured him that several days of fair weather, permitting full exploitation of Allied dominance of the skies, could be expected. He then ordered Patton to move full speed on Le Mans and there turn at right angles to the north toward Argentan where, according to the plan agreed upon with Montgomery, Lieutenant General Miles C. Dempsey of the British First Army, and Lieutenant General Henry D. G. Crerar of the Canadian First Army, a juncture would be formed with British and Canadian forces driving southward from Caen through Falaise. Thus a steel trap would close on all the hundreds of thousands of Germans who fought in the Mortain pocket.

This immense triumph was not wholly achieved. Patton's armor thrust eastward fifty-five miles in thirty-six hours to take Le Mans at little cost. Five days later he stood at his assigned terrain objective near Argentan. But there he was forced by his orders to halt and wait for the British and Canadians to close an eighteen-mile gap which yet separated the two arms of the pincers ("The Germans can't stop me," he once fumed to a correspondent, "only these f-----g phase lines").[22] Montgomery's troops, coming hard against prepared defenses, had covered but half the distance to Falaise; they were stalled there; and panzer units and German infantry were already beginning to stream out of the pocket toward the Seine. Patton begged for permission to proceed northward. He was emphatically refused it. Not only did Bradley fear a tragic head-on collision of the two Allied forces,¶¶ he also doubted Patton's ability to hold a line across the gap, a line necessarily stretched very thin, against the immense tide of Germans that must soon flow against it. "I much preferred a solid shoulder at Argentan to the possibility of a broken neck at Falaise," he later explained.[23] So Patton, nearly maddened by frustration, sat on the "shoulder" and watched helplessly as broken elements of the German Seventh Army fled eastward.

The bag of German prisoners was further reduced, in the immediately following days, by two unfortunate Allied command decisions—one by Montgomery, one by Bradley. Blocked on his first main drive toward Falaise, Montgomery naturally and properly shifted his attack. He did not, however, shift it initially to the east where, at Chambois, against what were then weakly held enemy positions, a junction with the Americans could have been formed to trap Germans who were already strong in the Falaise-Argentan gap. Instead, he shifted to the west where, against this same German strength, he did nothing save (as Bradley bitterly observed) "squeeze the enemy out toward the Seine."[24] A few days later, Montgomery did shift to the east, but by then Bradley, goaded by Patton's angry impatience, and without consulting Montgomery, had ordered the Third Army to drive in three columns toward the Seine. The southern prong of the proposed trap thus failed to come simultaneously against the northern one, and scores of thousands of Germans who might otherwise have been killed or captured managed to escape across the Seine. Especially disappointing to SHAEF was the escape of several panzer divisions, though these lost much of their equipment and many men to incessant air attack. The Allies would meet these units again inside Germany.

Nevertheless the triumph was very great and, in conjunction with the successful launching of the southern invasion on August 15, decisive of the struggle for France. When the trap at last closed, eight German infantry and two panzer divisions were captured virtually intact. Moreover, within the gap as it closed, roads and adjacent fields became what Eisenhower called one of the greatest "killing grounds" for Germans in the entire war. Correspondents who accompanied the Supreme Commander on a walking tour of the Falaise area, a day or so after the battle had moved on, would never forget the indescribably horrible sight and smell of it. Everywhere were clusters and heaps of mangled bodies, dead

¶¶ Patton's phone call to Bradley on the evening of August 12 was not likely to allay this fear. "Let me go to Falaise," he said, "and we'll drive the British back into the sea for another Dunkirk."

men and animals stinking in maggoty corruption amidst the blasted hulks of tanks, trucks, wagons, mobile guns. "It was literally possible to walk for hundreds of yards at a time," as Eisenhower said, "stepping on nothing but dead and decaying flesh."[25]

So ended the Normandy battle. From first to last, between June 6 and August 19, it had cost the Allies 170,000 casualties—68,000 British and Canadian, 102,000 Americans. It had cost the Germans between 250,000 and 300,000 killed or captured, including twenty army, corps, and divisional commanders, along with more than 1000 tanks and 3000 guns. (Rommel himself was critically wounded when a low-flying fighter plane shot up his staff car on July 17.) It had precipitated a headlong retreat of the Germans from northern France—a retreat which did not halt until the front stood beyond Antwerp to the north and on the German border, against the Siegfried Line, to the east. By then the Allied forces that had exploded out of Normandy were joined by Major General Alexander McC. Patch, Jr.'s U. S. Seventh Army and the French First Army which had driven up the Rhone and Saone River Valley to form a juncture with the right wing of the U. S. Third Army and constitute the Sixth Army Group under U. S. Lieutenant General Jacob L. Devers. The Allied line stretched unbroken from Switzerland to the sea—and no reasonable man on either side of it, accurately informed, could any longer doubt that Germany had lost the war. . . .

They were reasonable men, and very brave—though also very belated in their discovery that Nazism was an intolerable evil—who in Germany that summer conspired to eliminate Hitler, seize power from the Nazis, and end the war on whatever terms were procurable from the Allies. They were Army officers, three of them field marshals, several of them generals, and most of them from aristocratic families. Their realization of Nazi evil was, for the most part, a consequence of the turn of the tide of war against Germany in 1943. And after several earlier attempts to assassinate the Fuehrer, all of which miscarried without discovery by the Gestapo, they were galvanized into decisive action by the success of the Western invasion and the even greater successes scored (greater, that is, in terms of territory reconquered and losses inflicted) by the Russian summer offensives.[26]

These last began in early June with a subsidiary but substantial victory in the north. An attack in the Leningrad area, breaching the Mannerheim line and capturing Viborg, was followed by operations that cleared the north shore of Lake Ladoga and soon reopened the railroad from Leningrad to Murmansk. A beaten Finland sued for peace in late August. On June 23, a tremendous offensive opened on the central Russian front between Vitebsk and Gomel, shattering the German defenses and carrying the Russians eighty miles westward within a week. Within five weeks the Russians reached the Nieman River, an advance of 250 miles during which they had destroyed no fewer than twenty-five enemy divisions and cut off as many more. Farther south, a series of Russian attacks begun on July 13 achieved similar triumphs, advancing as much as 120 miles in ten days and thrusting across the Vistula in Poland before the end of July. Here, too, the German losses were enormous, both in men and materiel. Still farther south, the Russians in late August broke through the German line that had theretofore stood between them and Rumania. Soon thereafter, both Rumania and Bulgaria were in their hands, their left flank was on the northern border of Yugoslavia, and Germany was deprived of the Great Ploesti oilfields which she desperately needed.

All these victories were in process of accomplishment, or were unmistakably foreshadowed, as July opened. The German anti-Hitler conspirators were acutely aware that, if they were to save the Fatherland from the full consequences of the Hitlerian madness, they must act at once. They were shaken by the loss of Rommel, who had committed himself to their cause during the preceding winter and upon whom they had heavily counted. Some felt that his wounding left them "deprived of their pillar of strength." But they had a gallant and determined leader in an almost incredibly brave young colonel, Count von Stauffenberg, who was fortified in a moment of doubt by advice he and his colleagues sought from stalwart Major General Henning von Tresckow, Chief of Staff of the German Second Army on the Russian front. "The assassination [of Hitler] must be attempted at any cost," said Tresckow, in a message that shines brightly out of the black evil of Nazi Germany. "Even should it fail, the attempt to seize power in the capital must be taken. We must prove to the world and to future generations that the men of the German Resistance Movement dared to take the decisive step and to hazard their lives upon it."[27]

The attempt was made on Thursday, July 20, 1944.

The day was sunny and hot. Colonel Stauffenberg, recently named Chief of Staff of the German Home Army, had been summoned from Berlin to Hitler's military headquarters at Rastenburg in East Prussia to report on the training of replacements for the shattered German armies in Russia. When he entered the conference room at a little after half-past the noon hour, he carried in his bulging briefcase a time bomb set to go off in six minutes. A long table whose top was covered by a map of the Russian front occupied the center of the room. Hitler was seated near the midpoint of one side of it, and some two dozen others—high-ranking officers, and S.S. security men—were gathered around him. One of these, General Adolf Heusinger, Chief of Operations, was reporting on the situation in Russia, referring constantly to the map, and Stauffenberg, who was to report next, put his briefcase down upon the floor just six feet from Hitler's legs, leaning it against the inside of one of the two solid oaken piers (one at each end) which supported the table top. He then slipped unnoticed out of the room. He was two hundred yards away when the bomb exploded with terrific force, totally wrecking the conference barracks, hurling debris and smoke and dead bodies into the air. Immediately he got into his car, made his escape from the headquarters camp with some difficulty, and flew back to Berlin to superintend the *coup d'état,* for he was convinced that no one could have survived the blast.

He was mistaken.

A colonel, leaning over the table to look more closely at the situation map, had found Stauffenberg's briefcase in his way and moved it to the other side of the oaken pier. This pier was therefore between the bomb and Hitler at the instant of the explosion, a fact which doubtless saved Hitler's life. His eardrums were punctured, his legs superficially burned, his right arm badly bruised and his back lacerated, but he was not seriously injured. He survived to take a terrible vengeance upon the conspirators, their families and friends, and all who dared give them the slightest aid.

Several of the plotters committed suicide as soon as they knew their part had been or would soon be discovered. Eight of the leaders of the conspiracy, after torture by the Gestapo, were summarily "tried" before the Peoples' Court, an instrument of Nazi tyranny that had no concern with principles of justice. Within two hours after their condemnation, they were hanged by the neck in nooses of piano wire suspended from meat hooks until, after five minutes or so of writhing agony, they expired. (Indicative of the inner nature of Nazism—and indeed of all totalitarianism—is the fact that the victims of this barbarity were required to strip to the waist and were deprived of belts or suspenders for their trousers, so that, twisting and turning in their death torment, their trousers fell down. Motion picture films of all this were taken by Hitler's order and viewed by him with evident enjoyment a few hours later.) Rommel, implicated by one of the conspirators who broke under Gestapo torture, was given a choice between suicide and a state funeral, or arrest and trial before the Peoples' Court. The latter would inevitably have resulted in reprisals upon his family, following his meat-hook hanging. He chose the former. It was then announced that he had died of the wounds he had suffered on June 17, and messages of condolence were sent to his widow by Hitler and Goebbels.

For many months, night and day, the screams of tortured men and women, arrested on suspicion of complicity in the plot, echoed through Gestapo dungeons. Seven thousand were arrested in all, according to Gestapo records; some five thousand are believed to have been done to death.

The world learned of the assassination attempt from Hitler's own lips early in the morning of July 21. He broadcast over the radio from his headquarters. Thus the Allied troops who broke out of the Normandy confinement on July 25 did so in the belief that the "Thousand-Year"

Reich, hard-pressed from the outside, was on the verge of internal collapse.

Would this collapse have occurred if the Allied Governments had not committed themselves so adamantly, publicly to "Unconditional Surrender"? Many Americans and Englishmen believed so, then and later. They expressed the conviction that the formula Roosevelt had announced at Casablanca denied to the conspirators the popular support they would otherwise have had in their own country and the aid they might have obtained, as other Resistance movements did, from Allied secret agents. It is perhaps significant, however, that those who expressed this belief most vehemently were, quite often, political reactionaries who in the past had indicated no strong antipathy to Nazism-Fascism.

Political liberals were generally unconvinced that "Unconditional Surrender" had any important effect on popular sentiment inside Germany. Certainly those Germans who became actively anti-Nazi did so in the belief that the war was already lost and that the terms imposed by the victors were likely to become harsher with every week of useless bloodshed that passed. What the Casablanca formula did do was destroy the possibility of a negotiated peace that left the Nazis in power. Such a peace the Allies could certainly have had in that summer of '44. Hitler's last hope was that the British Government, dismayed by the Bolshevik drive from the east while the Anglo-Americans were being held back in the west, would at last return to the policy which, in the days of Baldwin and Chamberlain, had so greatly benefited him.

In any case, it is permitted to doubt that the success of Stauffenberg's brave attempt would have served the stated war aims of the Allied Governments. The Army clique which engaged in the conspiracy was hardly less anti-democratic than it was anti-Nazi. Most of its members had done their bit toward the destruction of the Weimar Republic, and nothing at all to prevent the rise of Hitler; indeed they had aided and abetted him. What kind of government would they have installed in Hitler's place? According to William L. Shirer, ". . . it is indicative of the mentality of the plotters that more than one among them . . . began [in 1943] to see in Himmler a possible replacement for Hitler!"*** Stauffenberg himself, in his moment of doubt following the Normandy invasion (it was during this moment that he sought Tresckow's advice), saw clearly one unhappy consequence of his act, should it succeed: the plotters would be charged by their countrymen with responsibility for Germany's defeat, though this was in fact already substantially accomplished. Hence, had Stauffenberg's bomb destroyed Hitler's person, it might well have restored inviolate for millions of Germans the myth of his heroic genius, have added martyrdom to it, and rendered plausible

*** *The Rise and Fall of the Third Reich* (New York: 1960), p. 1017. Heinrich Himmler, SS Chief, was in this capacity head of the Gestapo and concentration camp system and the active director of programs of mass torture and killing. Millions of helpless men, women, and children died by his orders.

for these millions the lie, a repetition of 1918's, that the German armies had not been decisively beaten on the battlefields but had been betrayed behind the lines.

iv. *The Weighing and Measuring of a Supreme Commander*

It was during this crucial summer and early autumn of 1944 that Dwight David Eisenhower, who had loomed increasingly large in the public consciousness for two years, achieved that immense fame and prestige which, possessing him as much as he possessed it, was destined to become one of the important facts of the postwar world. The fame, the prestige derived from great events in which millions of men played their part. None among the general public at that time could be sure how large or small Eisenhower's own part had been in them. The general public could only be sure that he was the principal architect of SHAEF as an institution, that mighty victories were gained in his name, that he exuded an atmosphere of modesty and sunny good will, that his wide grin was charming, and that strong men of different nationalities and widely differing natures expressed the most fervent admiration and sincere respect for him as a man and as a soldier. A future historian, however, having access to accurate records of events and to memoirs of the leading personalities, might summarize under three heads the tests and revelations of Eisenhower's quality as Supreme Commander during these months. The three: (1) De Gaulle, (2) the invasion of southern France, (3) Allied strategy north of the Seine.

General Charles de Gaulle had developed greatly as a political force since the days when TORCH was being planned and mounted and he was being alternately snubbed and ignored by the Roosevelt Administration and, to a lesser extent, by the Churchill Government. His prestige among his own countrymen had fed on the insults that had been given him, insults earned by the intransigence with which he insisted upon the sovereign rights of France as a Great Power and upon his own prerogatives as the personification of France. Giraud, meanwhile, had faded almost completely out of the picture. Out of the old Free French movement had been developed a Provisional Government of France which had been given a limited recognition (albeit with extreme reluctance, insofar as De Gaulle dominated it) by both London and Washington. Its headquarters was in Algiers. Its ruling body was a Committee of National Liberation, carefully designed by De Gaulle to represent all shades of French political opinion, from Right to Left. Advising this Committee was a Consultative Assembly of one hundred members, most of whom had escaped from occupied France. Though the Assembly had no designated legislative powers, its "advice" in many instances had the force of a legal decree to which De Gaulle bowed against his will.[28]

This was so when, on the eve of the launching of OVERLORD, Churchill invited De Gaulle to come to London, there to cooperate with the

Allied Governments in political phases of the great invasion. De Gaulle was reluctant to accept the invitation, but did so when the Assembly joined with a large majority of the Committee to insist that he accept. He arrived in London on Sunday, June 4, 1944, and thereafter tested severely the patience, self-control, and genius for conciliation of a Supreme Commander whose nerves at that moment were taut with the inevitable anxieties and apprehensions of the impending operation.

De Gaulle, on the eve of his country's liberation, was himself under extreme nervous tension. His feelings were ruffled by the manner in which he had been summoned, which was in accord with the continued refusal by Washington (hence, by London also) to grant full recognition to himself and his Committee as the Government of France. He feared that the slightest weakness on his part, the slightest slackening of his will to power, would result in France's being relegated to the position of a second- or third-class State while he himself was cast aside contemptuously as a tool no longer useful. He was therefore in his most touchy, arrogant, uncompromising mood when his plane landed in London; he was determined to exact a price for every concession he made to the wishes of his Allies; and he was only slightly mollified, accepting it as his proper due, to be met at the airport by a reception committee that included the British Foreign Secretary and SHAEF's Chief of Staff, and to be then taken at once to No. 10 Downing Street for conference with the Prime Minister—a stiff and even "bristling" conference, as Churchill later wrote.[29] Later that day he was taken by train to Eisenhower's headquarters in the woods near Portsmouth where the Supreme Commander received him with ceremonial deference and, exercising all his personal charm, took him to the war room to explain in precise detail the initial phase of OVERLORD. The ice that had bound the French leader's spirit was considerably melted, but not so much so as to prevent his refusal to return to London on Churchill's train. He preferred to motor back, he said, with his own officers.

Next day he added to Eisenhower's anxieties by indicating that he would not issue a proclamation to the people of France, immediately following Eisenhower's, as he had been asked to do and as was necessary if the invaders were to receive the fullest possible cooperation of Frenchmen behind the German lines. He had been given a copy of Eisenhower's D-Day proclamation during his Portsmouth visit and asked to suggest whatever changes in it seemed to him desirable, but this effort at ingratiation backfired when, having made suggestions, he learned that no changes actually could be made since the proclamation was already printed on thousands of leaflets and recorded for radio broadcast. He was humiliated. "I cannot follow Eisenhower," he said, striding from the room and leaving his dismayed listeners in doubt as to his precise meaning.[30] He did broadcast a proclamation of his own, however, a few hours after Eisenhower's, pledging his support to the Allied cause in language that left no doubt that he claimed to be the Government of France. And this was but the beginning of the difficulties he made. On this and following days he objected to the printing of invasion money without consultation with him, claiming it was a clear violation of French national sovereignty. He objected to the Allied plan of having the interim civil government of France administered by the Allied military command. He demanded (and was reportedly refused) permission to visit France to organize the civil administration under his Provisional Government.

All these objections and demands became primarily Eisenhower's to handle (both Churchill and Roosevelt were more than willing to have the burdensome Cross of Lorraine shifted from their shoulders to the Supreme Commander's), and he handled them, and De Gaulle himself, with a seemingly inexhaustible tact and patience. He strove for, and achieved, an agreement with the Frenchman on "military levels." He convinced De Gaulle of his personal frankness, sincerity, and overwhelming concern for Allied unity: the Frenchman later spoke of the "frankness" which was "one of the most appealing qualities" of Eisenhower's "sympathetic character." He told De Gaulle that his G-5 (civil affairs) policy could be summed up in a single phrase, "Let Frenchmen govern Frenchmen," and then accepted gracefully the *fait accompli* with which De Gaulle presented him when, on June 13, the French leader crossed the Channel on a French destroyer and, having been hysterically welcomed by the populace of the Normandy towns through which he drove, left behind him two representatives to secure his authority over the liberated ground. One of the two was to be regional commissioner, the other was to recruit and train a French fighting force in Normandy, and Eisenhower, who might justifiably have regarded all this as a flouting of his own authority, chose instead to thank De Gaulle for "cooperating" with him and ordered General Grasett, SHAEF's G-5, to administer Normandy's civil affairs thereafter through De Gaulle's representatives so far as possible.

Similarly with regard to the liberation of Paris in the last week of August. By that time there could be no question whatever, even among State Department "experts" on French politics, that the French people and especially those of the Resistance were overwhelmingly Gaullist. There *was* question, however, concerning the degree of control that De Gaulle could exert over his demoralized countrymen—especially over loosely organized bodies of armed men who were perforce accustomed to outlawry—during the period of social chaos and confusion that must inevitably follow the release from Nazi tyranny. Nowhere was this question more serious than in Paris. SHAEF would have been glad to defer the capture of the capital until the logistical problems which then plagued the Allies had become less acute. In Allied hands, Paris, a city of four million hungry people, must be fed, and this meant the diversion of transport and gasoline and men desperately needed to maintain the momentum of the drive across the Seine. But SHAEF was given no choice in the matter. There was an uprising of Free French forces within the capital and the high command could not do other than support it by sending in troops.††† The commander of the German garrison in Paris formally surrendered on August 25 and on the following day, though snipers continued their murderous work in some parts of the city, De Gaulle came to the capital. There, amidst ecstatic popular acclaim, he established his headquarters in a government building.

On the day after that, Eisenhower, accompanied by Bradley and the four correspondents assigned to the Supreme Commander's personal camp, entered the city to call upon the French leader, a symbolic gesture of no small importance to France. He was recognized and given a tremendous ovation in the streets. He found De Gaulle troubled, anxious, seemingly unsure of himself. Food and supplies were needed at once, the French leader said, if order were to be restored. Also De Gaulle asked for the "temporary loan" of two American divisions with which to make a show of force that would establish his authority. The Supreme Commander found this ironical. "You fellows raised hell with me when I used existing authority to maintain order in North Africa," he said that evening to the four correspondents. "This time I'm following a hands-off policy. I'm playing along with the people the liberals support—and they now appeal to me to defend them against the excesses of their own group."[31] Nevertheless, he recognized that De Gaulle was "in a tough spot"—and though he could not spare two divisions from the fighting front at that moment he could and did arrange to have two of them, on their way to the front, march in parade through Paris streets past a reviewing stand on which De Gaulle stood, Bradley beside him as symbol of Allied unity.‡‡‡ Paris was fed. De Gaulle's hand was strengthened. The foundations of France's restored greatness were, it seemed, firmly laid. . . .

As regards the invasion of southern France, originally code-named ANVIL and now called DRAGOON, much controversy preceded and was destined to follow it. Churchill and the British Chiefs of Staff held that the operation's value, rendered dubious by the enforced postponement, was destroyed altogether by the Normandy breakthrough. Until the breakthrough there had been obvious need for major ports to supplement overstrained Cherbourg, through which reinforcements and supplies could flow directly from America into France—and Marseilles and Toulon were certainly great ports. They were, however, much farther from the United States than were Brest and the other Brittany ports, soon (said Churchill) to be in Allied hands; they were also much farther

††† Selected for this historic honor was General Jacques Leclerc's famous Second French Division which, nearly three years before, had made an incredible thousand-mile march across the Sahara from Lake Chad to join the British Eighth Army and fight through the closing phases of the North African campaign. This division was destined to take Berchtesgaden, site of Hitler's mountain villa. Since the fall of France in 1940, Leclerc's allegiance had been to De Gaulle and the Fighting French.

‡‡‡ "Because this ceremonial march coincided exactly with the local battle plan," writes Eisenhower in his *Crusade in Europe* (p. 298), "it became possibly the only instance in history of troops marching in parade through the capital of a great country to participate in pitched battle on the same day."

from the zone of decisive battle; the effort to take them might well result in a greater and bloodier "Anzio"; and, even with the best of luck, there could be no true tactical coordination of the two forces for at least ninety days after the southern landings were made. A march of five hundred miles through Lyons and beyond must be completed before Patch could effectively join in the main battle. Hence, argued Churchill with all the eloquence at his command, forces scheduled for ANVIL-DRAGOON could be more profitably used elsewhere, notably at the head of the Adriatic whence—while threatening the German rear in Italy and thus aiding Alexander's advance there—they could strike north through Yugoslavia into Austria. Such a strike would be like that of a match amidst dry tinder: the whole Balkans would "flame into open revolt against Hitler," a revolt the Allies could make effective with supplies of arms and other equipment.

The Prime Minister confined his argument to military grounds. He would not admit that postwar political considerations moved him. And on purely military grounds he and the British Chiefs of Staff lost their case.

Chiefly they lost it to Eisenhower, upon whom (though he expressed Marshall's view and was strongly supported by the U. S. Army Chief of Staff) fell the main burden of answering it and standing firm against the Prime Minister's great and unremitting pressures. The Brittany ports were not yet in Allied hands, the Supreme Commander pointed out, and there was no certainty that they could be immediately taken without paying more for them in casualties than was justified by alternative possibilities. There *was* certainty that, when and if captured, the port facilities would be ruined; they must be rebuilt before they could be fully used.§§§ Marseilles and Toulon were therefore needed, and Eisenhower was convinced that the cost of taking them would be nowhere near as high as Churchill feared. "We know that a large portion of the defending forces have been drawn northward to meet our attacks. Capture [of the ports] should be so swift as to allow little time for demolition."[32] As for the allegation that the southern drive would serve no purpose in the main battle until its forces were physically joined with those in the north, this allegation was simply false. From the moment of its launching, ANVIL-DRAGOON would provide protection and support for the right flank of Eisenhower's forces, protection and support that would increase with every mile of advance. In its absence, many of Eisenhower's divisions would have to be posted along the hugely extended flank in order to protect badly strained communications from enemy raids. Each such division, immobilized, would be lost from the aggressive fighting front. Finally, the United States had armed and equipped a number of French divisions which, stationed in North Africa and Italy, were naturally eager to participate in the liberation of their homeland and could be

§§§ Brest's port was so utterly wrecked by Allied bombers and German demolitions that, upon its capture, no attempt was made to use it.

brought swiftly into the battle for France only through ANVIL-DRAGOON—and it was only in France that these divisions could obtain replacements for their battle losses.

So, on August 15, the landing force went in upon the Riviera between Cannes and Toulon, and the event justified Eisenhower's rather than Churchill's estimate of the tactical difficulties. Resistance was light. Toulon and Marseilles were taken on August 28, by which time one U.S. column was north of Avignon, another was approaching Montelimer, and a third was beyond Grenoble. On September 11, the French First Army was close to Dijon, far up the left bank of the Rhone-Saone Rivers, where it was soon joined by a column of Patton's U. S. Third Army; and the American Seventh Army was north of Besançon. All these swift advances were greatly aided by the French Forces of the Interior. The invaders from the south then wheeled eastward to occupy a front from the northwestern tip of Switzerland to Epinal, where the Sixth Army Group was joined, through Patton's right wing, to the Twelfth Army Group. It came under Eisenhower's command, by direction of the Combined Chiefs, on Friday, September 15. Even Churchill admitted that this "brought important assistance" to Eisenhower. The Prime Minister deplored its "heavy price," however, and stated this price, years later, in terms he had not explicitly used when arguing with Eisenhower. "The army of Italy was deprived of its opportunity to strike a most formidable blow at the Germans," said he, "and very possibly reach Vienna before the Russians, with all that might have followed therefrom."[33]

At this juncture of armies and events, the chief and indeed the only factor preventing a continuation of the Western drive into Germany's heart was logistical. If the Germans had conducted an orderly retreat from Normandy to the Seine and there established a strong defensive line, as had been anticipated in the plan, a proper balance would have been struck between the effective work of the Services of Supply and the operations of the fighting units. In that case the Brittany ports would have been cleared as rapidly as possible and a new port established in Quiberon Bay—planned efforts which Eisenhower boldly canceled in order to maintain the momentum of the pursuit following the breakout. Hence, in September there was an acute famine of supply; every spearhead of attack, having outrun its communications, was forced to slow its speed and lessen its strength. This famine would have been relieved if Allied shipping could have come into Antwerp, which was captured on September 4; but this port could not be used by the Allies until the enemy had been cleared from the Scheldt Estuary, a task destined not to be accomplished (because insufficient forces were assigned to it) until the last week of October.

It was in anticipation of these circumstances and, later, under the actual pressure of them, that Eisenhower made momentous decisions concerning Allied strategy north of the Seine. As early as August 17,

Montgomery began to propose in writing and conference a strategy later described by its author as "the German 'Schlieffen Plan' of 1914 in reverse, except that it would be executed against a shattered and demoralized enemy."[34] It called for "a really powerful full-blooded thrust" of some forty divisions at the northern end of the Allied line to capture the Ruhr, industrial heart of the German war machine, and drive on to Berlin. The drive would of course be made by the Twenty-first Army Group, under Montgomery's command, and his Group's needed strength could be obtained only by attaching to it, as its right wing, an American army of at least twelve divisions. Time was of the essence of success for this operation. The Germans were now off-balance, their forces scattered, demoralized, ill-equipped. They were also very weak numerically: their total force in the West added up to the equivalent of no more than twenty divisions as September opened. Of these, less than three opposed with rearguard actions the drive of the Allied forces up the Rhone-Saone, five stood between Patton and the Saar Basin (which was the second most important industrial center of Germany), and only eleven, a mere two of them panzers, were north of the Ardennes. Some one hundred thousand other troops had been forced to flee from the coast of the Bay of Biscay, but their effective combat strength, by the most generous estimate, added up to no more than a single division's. The enemy, however, had repeatedly demonstrated his ability to make rapid recoveries. He would certainly do so in defense of the Ruhr, which was vital to him. The heavy "left hook," in other words, must be swung with all possible speed and, in view of the supply famine, it "must have all the maintenance resources it needs without any qualification and any other operation must do the best it can with what is left over."[35]

Naturally this proposal was not pleasing to Bradley, whose Twelfth Army Group, reduced to a single army, would be confined by it to an ingloriously passive, secondary role.[36] He had no use whatever for Montgomery, as man or as soldier. And he was now convinced that the British Field Marshal (Montgomery was elevated to that high rank on August 31) was actuated solely by a desire to achieve all possible glory for himself. He was also afraid that Eisenhower might weaken under the weight of Montgomery's massive egotism. "Apprehensive lest Ike give in to Monty's persistent plea for troops," Bradley would later write, "I was adamant that U.S. troops be retained under U.S. command."[37] He went so far as to cite Pershing's flat refusal during World War I to permit U. S. Army units to be distributed piecemeal among British and French commands—though in point of fact this Pershing stand of 1917 provided no true precedent, even in principle, for Bradley's present one. As for Patton, he was predictably infuriated by the notion that the gasoline needed to fuel his swift-driving Third Army should be diverted from him to the cautious, slow-moving Montgomery. Hence the counter proposal by Bradley that the Twelfth Army Group should take the Ruhr by a double-envelopment of it from the south while Twenty-first

Army Group "rimmed" it in the north "across the plains of Westphalia."

He argued that Montgomery's plan for "a single axis of advance" would permit the enemy to concentrate defenses against it whereas, by following Bradley's plan, Eisenhower "could feint and dodge with his double thrust and confuse the enemy on his intentions. . . . As long as we held the initiative on so broad a front, the enemy would find his defenses stretched beyond the breaking point." He also argued that no thrust could be made across the Rhine until the supply problem was solved, and would later remember that he "would have preferred that Monty devote his resources to the Scheldt and the opening of Antwerp."[38] When he learned that SHAEF had approved an operation code-named MARKET GARDEN, designed by Montgomery to implement his strategic conception, Bradley "objected strenuously" to it. MARKET GARDEN, which Bradley admitted was "one of the most imaginative" plans of the war, called for the use of airborne troops to secure crossings of five major water barriers between Antwerp and Arnhem on the Lower Rhine in Holland, the airborne attack being swiftly followed up by an armored drive across the Rhine at Arnhem, outflanking the Siegfried Line and taking the Ruhr. Bradley's objection was that the swerve of British troops from an eastward to a northeastward drive would dangerously expose the left flank of Hodges' U. S. First Army.

Eisenhower's response to these challenging oppositions was reminiscent of the manner in which he had responded to a somewhat similar controversy in the summer of 1942, when TORCH was being prepared.¶¶¶ He at first ordered that priority be given to Montgomery's northern drive. Later, impressed by the ease with which the Twenty-first Army Group moved up the coast to Antwerp, he decided (on September 4) that, though Montgomery's was still to be the main Allied effort, it need not preclude a continuation of Patton's drive toward Metz and the Saar. On that same day, Montgomery messaged him in urgent terms, repeating his argument that "one really powerful and full-blooded thrust towards Berlin is likely to get there and . . . end the German war," that there were "not enough maintenance resources for two full-blooded thrusts," that a choice must therefore be made between a thrust "via the Ruhr and . . . [one] via Metz and the Saar," that the northern thrust was in his opinion the "most likely to give the best and quickest results" and should be given "all the maintenance resources it needs" while any other operation did "the best it can with what is left over," that "time is vital," and that to "attempt a compromise solution and split our maintenance resources so that neither thrust" was "full-blooded" would "prolong the war."[39] Eisenhower replied the next day, though due to communication difficulties (he was at his personal headquarters in Granville on the west coast of the Cotentin Peninsula nursing a sprained knee) his full reply did not reach the British commander in

¶¶¶ See pp. 285–87 and 289–94.

Belgium until September 9. "While agreeing with your conception of a powerful and full-blooded thrust . . . I do not agree that it should be initiated at this moment to the exclusion of all other maneuvers," the Supreme Commander said. He proposed instead to cross the Rhine "on a wide front," seizing both the Saar and the Ruhr, an operation he deemed possible because the "bulk of the German Army that was in the West has now been destroyed." By the time the Saar and Ruhr were achieved, "Havre and Antwerp should be available to maintain one or both of the thrusts you mention."[40] Montgomery, convinced that the Supreme Commander vastly overestimated the possibilities, promptly asked Eisenhower for a personal conference at his (Montgomery's) headquarters in Belgium.

It was significant of the Supreme Commander's lack of "side" that he responded at once to what amounted to a summons from a subordinate. He flew to Brussels on September 10 and there conferred with Montgomery, the meeting taking place in Eisenhower's plane because his wrenched knee made it painful for him to move. He at first insisted that his intention had always been, and still was, to give priority to the Ruhr thrust and the northern route to Berlin. Moreover, said he, this was being done. When the British commander flatly contradicted him ("It is *not* being done," said Montgomery; instead the Saar thrust was being maintained simultaneously with the northern one, the result being that neither could be maintained properly and neither would succeed), he replied that by "priority" he did not mean "absolute priority." To halt absolutely the southern advances in order to give all available supply to the Twenty-first Army Group would be a dangerous absurdity, in his opinion. These forces in the south would then be unable to advance in support of Montgomery's lengthening right flank and would themselves be in a precarious position when he, having outrun the possibility of maintenance, was forced to stop or withdraw. For Eisenhower did not believe—he perhaps did not want to believe—that Montgomery, adequately supported now, could win the war with one sustained drive. On the contrary, since there was a "considerable reserve in the middle of the enemy country," as Eisenhower later wrote, "any pencillike thrust into the heart of Germany" such as Montgomery proposed "would meet nothing but certain destruction." Montgomery heatedly denied that a forty-division thrust could be properly described as "pencillike" or even as a "narrow-front" attack. Rather should it be described as a "major blow" which would knock out the enemy if it were launched while the enemy was still groggy and tottering. It must be launched at once, however; opportunity was reduced with every passing hour.[41]

So the argument raged, with Montgomery insisting on the necessity for an "either/or" decision while Eisenhower clung to "both/and." Upon the latter note the conference ended. The Supreme Commander authorized Montgomery to defer clearance of the Scheldt Estuary in order that MARKET GARDEN could be launched at the earliest possible moment. But he insisted that MARKET GARDEN was to be (in his later words) "merely an incident and extension of our eastward rush to the line we needed for temporary security," a line that, in the north, coincided with the Lower Rhine.[42] He made no promises concerning operations in the south, which presumably were to continue. In other words, as Montgomery saw it, "we parted without any clear decision."[43]

But upon his return to Granville, Eisenhower, as was his frequent wont, "thought aloud" about his problems before the attentive Butcher, who wrote into his diary that day, September 12: "He is thinking in terms of advancing on a wide front to take advantage of all existing lines of communication, . . . Ike has decided that a northern thrust toward the Ruhr under Montgomery is not at the moment to have priority over other operations. Monty is fearful this will give the enemy time to organize better defense and heavier resistance. . . . His prospective attempt to cross the Rhine may have to be postponed until late September, and as winter approaches the weather diminishes the value of our great weight of air power."[44] This was indeed an accurate summary of the message Montgomery had sent the Supreme Commander on September 11, though Eisenhower, because of this very message, was in the process of changing his mind somewhat (not enough, Montgomery would believe) even as he talked with or to his Naval Aide. "I have investigated my maintenance situation very carefully since our meeting yesterday," the British Field Marshal had written. "Your decision that the northern thrust toward the Ruhr is NOT repeat NOT to have priority over other operations will have certain repercussions. . . . The large-scale operations by Second Army and the Airborne Corps northwards towards the Meuse and Rhine cannot now take place before 23 Sep. at the earliest and possibly 26 Sep." He went on to emphasize the sad consequences of this postponement in terms of increasing German strength between his present line and the Rhine.

It seemed to Montgomery that this message "produced results which were almost electric."[45] Next day, Beetle Smith came to Montgomery's headquarters to tell him that Eisenhower had decided to halt the Saar thrust. Patton must stand on the defensive while Hodges' U. S. First Army, on Montgomery's right, was given "the bulk" of the Twelfth Army Group's "logistic support." Moreover, Montgomery was authorized to deal directly with Hodges who thus became, in effect, a part of his command. On the strength of these assurances, the field marshal that day (September 12) ordered the launching of MARKET GARDEN five days thence, weather permitting, and on September 17 his orders were executed. Three airborne divisions—the British First, the American 82nd, and the American 101st—were dropped in column from north (Arnhem) to south, seizing the water-barrier crossings and forming a "carpet" up which the Twenty-first Army Group advanced, at the outset, with swift dispatch.

This event, however, did not end the argument between Montgomery and Eisenhower. Two days before MARKET GARDEN's D-Day, Eisenhower signaled Montgomery concerning "our next move" after the Allies were "in possession of the Ruhr, the Saar and the Frankfurt area," indicating his belief that these objectives would be "soon achieved." Berlin, said he, was "clearly . . . the main prize" and it was his desire to move upon it "by the most direct and expeditious route, with combined U.S.-British forces supported by other available forces moving through key centers and occupying strategic areas on the flanks, all in one coordinate, concerted operation."[46] To which Montgomery replied, on the day following MARKET GARDEN's D-Day, that in his opinion "a concerted operation in which all available armies move forward into Germany is not possible; the maintenance resources, and the general administrative situation, will not allow of this being done QUICKLY." He reiterated his unshaken and unshakable conviction that only one thrust in sufficient strength was possible and that the northern one was best. But "if you consider . . . that the proper axis of advance is by Frankfurt and central Germany, *then I suggest that Twelfth Army Group . . . would be used and would have all the maintenance. Twenty-first Army would do the best it could with what was left over; or possibly the Second British Army would be wanted in a secondary role on the left flank of the movement.*"[47] (Italics are the present author's.) Thus Montgomery continued pressure for a clear-cut "either/or" decision. He didn't get it.

Instead, Eisenhower wrote him on September 20 to say that ". . . generally speaking I find myself so completely in agreement with your letter of 18 September that I cannot believe there is any great difference in our concepts. . . . Never at any time have I implied that I was considering an advance into Germany with all armies moving abreast. . . . I am quite confident that we see this thing almost identically. I merely want to make sure that when you start leading your Army Group in its thrust on to Berlin and Bradley starts driving with his left to support you, our other forces are in a position to support the success of that drive. Otherwise the main thrust itself would have to drop off so much of its strength to protect its rear and its flanks that very soon the drive would peter out."[48] But by the time he read this, Montgomery had learned that what he had taken to be a firm promise that Patton would be halted was not being fulfilled,**** and in any case he could not see in Eisenhower's message any reduction of the issue between them. He said so with typical frankness in a "Dear Ike" signal: "I cannot agree that our concepts

**** According to Patton's *War as I Knew It*, p. 133, "Bradley called [September 17, D-Day of MARKET GARDEN] to say that Monty wanted all American troops to stop so that he, Monty, could make a 'dagger thrust . . . at the heart of Germany.' Bradley said he thought it would be more like a 'butter-knife thrust.' In order to avoid such an eventuality, it was evident that the Third Army should get deeply involved at once, so I asked Bradley not to call me until after dark on the nineteenth." By then Patton was indeed "deeply involved," having launched a major attack toward Metz.

are the same. . . . I have always said stop the right and go on with the left, but the right has been allowed to go on so far that it has outstripped its maintenance and we have lost flexibility. In your letter you still want to go on further with your right [in order to support the northern thrust, etc.]. . . . I would say that the right flank of Twelfth Army Group should be given a very direct order to halt and if this order is not obeyed we shall get into greater difficulties. The net result of the matter in my opinion is that if you want to get the Ruhr you will have to put every single thing into the left hook and stop everything else. It is my opinion that if this is not done you will not get the Ruhr." He signed, "Your very great friend Monty."[49]

Upon receipt of this, Eisenhower summoned a strategy conference to meet on September 22 in his recently established headquarters at Versailles. Montgomery—worried by the Arnhem battle which was going badly that day and aware of his personal unpopularity at SHAEF—did not attend personally (Bradley thought this an "affront to the Allied Chief"[50]) but sent his Chief of Staff fully briefed to represent him. The upshot was that Eisenhower this day at last made the decision for which Montgomery had been pressing him for a month. He rejected Bradley's "double thrust" concept and accepted Montgomery's concept *in toto*. He ordered that Montgomery be given overriding logistical support and that Hodges be given such logistical support as was needed for the task of protecting Montgomery's right flank. Most important of all, he at last specifically directed "the remainder of the Twelfth Army Group to take no more aggressive action than is permitted by the maintenance situation after the full requirements of the *main* effort have been met."[51]

But it was now too late—"exactly one month too late," according to Montgomery. "Nothing could now prevent events taking the course which I had predicted a month before."[52] Even so the margin by which Arnhem became a defeat rather than a victory was slim and would almost certainly have been wiped out if MARKET GARDEN could have gotten under way a few days earlier. Between September 12, when the attack was firmly ordered, and September 17, when it was launched, German strength was doubled between Montgomery's front and Arnhem, and this—joined to bad weather, supply shortage, and tactical mistakes later admitted by Montgomery, was enough to deny the operation its stated objective. A fifty-mile advance was made in the first five days of attack, linking up with the American paratroopers to secure crossings of four of the five water barriers; but British armor was not able to break through to Arnhem where the British First Airborne Division fought desperately against growing odds. On September 24, the survivors of this gallant division were ordered withdrawn across the river. Only twenty-four hundred made it.

Thus was extinguished the hope, which had flamed so brightly, of ending the European war in the autumn of 1944. There had been virtually no defensive forces between Eisenhower's armies and Berlin in the last days of August and the first days of September. Now fourteen German divisions opposed the British Second Army, the Siegfried Line was manned by units reformed and rearmed following their flight from France, and a desperate Hitler—by canceling occupational deferments, calling up sixteen-year-olds, and transferring naval and air personnel to the ground forces—was in the process of creating no fewer than forty new divisions. With these he intended not merely to hold but to strike back decisively against his Western enemies, who were now condemned to weeks and months of bloody frustration and creeping advances until they could again be sufficiently supplied and reinforced to attempt an all-out offensive.††††

It is both interesting and instructive to consider what might have been if Montgomery's strategy had been adopted in August and, as then seemed possible, had been crowned with the final victory by December. The shape of the postwar world would in that case have been very different. Berlin and Vienna would have been taken by the Western Allies rather than by Russia, giving thus to central Europe a Western rather than an Eastern orientation. The stature of Montgomery in contemporary fame and world history would have been vastly increased—he might well have emerged as the greatest single Allied military hero of the European war—and this would have been a symbol and manifestation of a greatly augmented prestige and authority for Britain in the postwar world. For it was not until after September 1 that the overwhelming preponderance of American materiel and manpower over Britain's began to be effective in Europe: had the war ended a few weeks later, the American and British contributions to the final decision would have been approximately equal—and so might have been the persuasive force of the two in postwar councils.

†††† Field Marshal Brooke, the British C.I.G.S., felt himself unhappily confirmed by all this in the judgment he had made of Eisenhower, and written into his diary, on May 15, following the conference that day, attended by King and Prime Minister, at which a final review was made of Normandy invasion plans. ". . . no real director of thought, plans, energy or direction. Just a co-ordinator, a good mixer, a champion of inter-Allied cooperation, and in those respects few can hold a candle to him. But is that enough? Or can we not find all qualities of a commander in one man? May be I am getting too hard to please, but I doubt it." (Arthur Bryant, *Triumph in the West*, p. 139). Ralph Ingersoll, editor of New York's *PM*, who was a lieutenant colonel in the plans section of Bradley's field headquarters in September of '44, records on page 219 of his *Top Secret* the conviction that the Supreme Commander "could have ended the war by Christmas by decisively backing *either* Montgomery or Bradley." But, he goes on, "there was no strong hand at the helm, no man in command. There was only a conference, presided over by a chairman—a shrewd, tactful, careful chairman. . . . The man on whose shoulders the title of Supreme Allied Commander rested had been especially selected for his ability to conciliate, to see both points of view, to be above national interests—and to be neither bold nor decisive, neither a leader nor a general." These were distinctly minority views among those in a position to judge Eisenhower's performance; they gained but slight acceptance among the general public then or later.

As it was, Britain's manpower and economy were extended to the limit and beyond long before victory came, while U.S. strength on the Continent grew to exceed three times Britain's. At war's end, an exhausted Britain was reduced unmistakably to the status of a second-class power, too weak to serve effectively as a "third force" which could mitigate the clash and arbitrate the differences between the Soviet Union and the United States.

Book Four

THE TRAGIC TRIUMPH

XIV

The Edge of Triumph

i. *End of a Long Summer*

All through that long hot summer of 1944, though this was a Presidential election year, politics had run a poor second to the war in a race for popular attention in the United States.

There had been a brief flurry of political excitement in the spring, two months before the launching of OVERLORD, when Wendell Willkie's brave but foredoomed effort to reshape the Republican party in his own internationalist image came to its predestined end in the Wisconsin Presidential primary. Ever since his return from his 'round-the-world flight, Willkie had fought with dogged persistence for his vision of One World and against every word and deed of the Roosevelt Administration or of his own party which seemed to him to work against its realization. He was again a tousle-haired, hoarse-voiced St. George, out to slay the twin dragons of isolationism and "military expediency" at whatever cost to his own political fortunes. When a group of reactionary St. Louis businessmen headed by Edgar M. Queeny of the Monsanto Chemical Company sought at a private luncheon to force his abandonment of vocal internationalism as the price of their support of his candidacy for the '44 Republican Presidential nomination, he replied with blunt anger: "I don't know whether you're going to support me or not, and I don't give a damn. You're a bunch of political liabilities who don't know what's going on anyway."[1] Wisconsin, whose Republicans were destined to choose one Joseph R. McCarthy as their candidate for the U. S. Senate in 1946, was "the worst State for me, except Illinois, in the whole country," Willkie frankly admitted,[2] but circumstances forced him to campaign there. He did so vigorously. He covered the state from end to end and side to side, making fourteen speeches in thirteen days, dividing his verbal fire equally between New Deal domestic policy and Republican Old Guard isolationism, and shaking hands by the thousand. None other named on the Republican primary ballot so much as set foot in Wisconsin during this period, or even admitted that he sought the nomination. All the more devastating to Willkie's aspirations, therefore, were the results of the balloting on April 4—balloting in which seventeen delegates were won by Thomas E. Dewey, four by Harold Stassen, three by Douglas MacArthur, and not a one by Wendell Willkie. Next day, admitting that he could never win the nomination, Willkie had withdrawn from the race, which meant in actual fact that there *was* no longer a race. Obviously the Old Guard, after its discomfiture in Philadelphia in 1940, was again in full control of the party machinery. Hence the nomination of young knife-sharp and -hard Thomas E. Dewey—former "racket-busting" district attorney and, since 1942, Governor of New York—was a foregone conclusion for twelve weeks before it was formally ratified by the Republican convention, in Chicago, on June 28. Nor was there any surprise in the selection of Dewey's running mate, Governor John W. Bricker of Ohio, whom Alice Roosevelt Longworth had once acidly but aptly described as "an honest Harding."

There had been another flurry of political excitement when the Democratic National Convention met, also in Chicago, a few weeks later. Franklin Roosevelt's nomination for a fourth term, in this first Presidential election campaign to be waged in wartime since 1864, was taken for granted by Republicans and Democrats alike, but there had been a considerable question, among the delegates and the public at large, concerning the Vice-Presidential nomination. The incumbent Vice-President, Henry Wallace, whose nomination had been dictated by Roosevelt to a rebellious 1940 Democratic convention, had certainly (from Roosevelt's point of view and by Roosevelt's act) been given great opportunities to "build himself up" as a potent political figure. Perhaps he had done so. But while becoming hero and spokesman of those voters who must support Roosevelt in any case, or not vote at all, for they had nowhere else to go, he had so antagonized the Democratic "regulars" and "professionals" that, according to Robert E. Hannegan, chairman of the Democratic National Committee, he could not be renominated for his present post without a fight at least as bitter as that of 1940 if, indeed, he could be nominated at all. A worn and weary Roosevelt had accepted Hannegan's assessment. "I am just not going to go through a convention like 1940 again," he reportedly said.[3] "It will split the party wide open, and it is already split enough between the North and South; it may kill our chances for election this fall, and if it does, it will prolong the war and knock into a cocked hat all the plans we've been making for the future." A little later he accepted Hannegan's choice for Vice-President. This was Senator Harry S. Truman of Missouri, who had begun his political career as a protégé of Kansas City's notorious Boss Prendergast and was the opposite of impressive in personal appearance and public speech, but who had made a consistently liberal voting record and had gained a national reputation for probity, acuteness, and commitment to the general welfare as chairman of the Congressional Committee Investigating the National Defense Program (the Truman Committee).

But the President had not publicly announced that Truman was his choice. He had not even told Truman so, nor any of the other aspirants for the office, of whom former U. S. Supreme Court Justice James F. Byrnes, director of the Office of War Mobilization, was a principal one. The convention excitement, such as it was, derived from this fact, which in turn derived from one of the most Rooseveltian of Roosevelt's characteristics. His dealings with the world at large, as has been noted before, were not marked to any strong degree by directness, candor, frankness. The straight line from here to there seldom recommended itself to him as a route to be followed through difficult country in the full light of day. In such country, he preferred the circuitous, whereby obstacles were avoided (though left intact) instead of overcome—either that, or the secrecy of night in which to cloak his movements. Joined to this trait was a quite remarkable empathy and capacity for personal affection, and though this was a great asset in personal politics it was also a source of grave weakness in what he himself had called the "politics of principle." When direct, frank dealing in the service of any purpose, however grand, must produce in his presence a direct hurt of any person, however humble (or even mean), he often could not bear to engage in it. He would go to great lengths of subterfuge and deviousness to avoid it. In the present instance, he had much liking for Henry Wallace, a sympathetic appreciation of the humanitarian idealism that was the central theme of Wallace's public life, and an acute awareness that Wallace, a shy and sensitive man who was less at ease in his relations with other people than most men are, was more than normally vulnerable to psychological hurts.

He therefore, typically, asked his personal counsel and principal speechwriter, Samuel I. Rosenman, to meet Wallace upon the latter's return from China, where Wallace had gone on a special mission for the President.[4] Rosenman, as Roosevelt's personal representative, was to tell the returned traveler why it had been decided, with extreme reluctance, that he could not be on the ticket this year. At the same time (Roosevelt's empathy was often thus blunted when he need not feel, with a personal immediacy, another's pain), the President had permitted Ickes, at Ickes' request, to accompany Rosenman in the performance of this unpleasant task, though there had long been an enmity between the Secretary of the Interior and the Vice-President that must now be increased by the former's known "availability" for the latter's post. The negative result of this tactic was predictable, especially since Wallace, before he met with Rosenman and Ickes at breakfast in his Wardman Park Hotel apartment, had already phoned the President, asked for private session with him, and been invited to lunch at the White House on that very same day. "To say that my mission to Wallace was unsuccessful is an understatement," Rosenman later said. Nor was the task accomplished by

Roosevelt, as he and Wallace lunched together. On the contrary, Wallace was led to believe that, though the choice could not be dictated to the convention as it had been four years before, he was Roosevelt's personal choice. Indeed, the event would indicate that the President went so far as to promise a letter to the convention in support of Wallace's candidacy! Certainly a letter *did* go from Hyde Park to the convention's permanent chairman in mid-July, describing Wallace as a "personal friend" for whose "renomination" Roosevelt "personally would vote . . . if I were a delegate. . . ."

Thus fortified, Wallace's candidacy for the nomination became at least as formidable as Byrnes's, especially since his supporters were prepared to pack the galleries and attempt a stampede of the convention. It appeared that the race between the two would be very close if Truman did not enter the lists—and Truman, who was pledged to support Byrnes, for whom he made the nominating speech, flatly refused to enter unless Byrnes first withdrew. On the other hand, if Truman *did* enter while Byrnes remained in the race, he and Byrnes would split the vote of the delegates opposed to Wallace, thereby increasing from possible to probable the latter's ultimate victory with all that this might mean (*would* mean, Hannegan insisted) in terms of party disruption during the campaign and reduced Democratic vote in November. Hence Hannegan's behind-the-scenes labors at the convention had not been easy—but they had been successful. Byrnes was persuaded to withdraw gracefully after labor union leaders flatly refused to support him. Truman was persuaded to become a candidate after Roosevelt told him, through Hannegan, that his refusal to do so would "break up the Democratic party."[5] And the convention nominated Truman for Vice-President after it had been informed of a two-sentence note from Roosevelt to Hannegan saying that he, Roosevelt, would be "very glad to run with either" Harry Truman or Bill Douglas (though U. S. Supreme Court Justice William O. Douglas's candidacy was not being seriously pressed), and that he believed "either one of them would bring real strength to the ticket."

Thereafter, for many weeks, the approaching Presidential election had generated no popular excitement whatever. Dewey began to campaign early, and with a great show of youthful vigor. He of course voiced the standard Republican generalities concerning the sacredness of "free enterprise" and of the "American institutions" which were allegedly being subverted by the "leftists" and corrupt "bosses" who dominated the Democratic party. But he studiously avoided the development of specific issues that might arouse sharp controversy and strong feelings among the populace. The burden of his speeches was that it was "time for a change" from an Administration of old, tired, and quarrelsome men to one composed of fresh minds, youthful hearts, and sound bodies. Meanwhile his supporters, including several of the owners of press and radio, seized every opportunity to foster doubts concerning the President's physical and mental health. A whispering campaign, which Democrats became convinced was carefully planned and highly organized, spoke of Roosevelt's having had a "mental breakdown" in conjunction with (it was more than hinted) an incurable disease that would ultimately, and probably soon, be fatal.

What the Republicans obviously hoped for was an election in which the total vote was relatively small. Their hard-core strength would in any case be augmented by the votes of such "independents" as had formerly supported Roosevelt but were now bored, or frightened, or otherwise alienated by a government that continued to make harsh demands upon them (rationing, price control, the draft, wage limitation) in a war they were increasingly inclined to regard as already virtually won. There was bound to be a considerable protest vote—and if the total vote were small enough, the protest could be decisive of Republican victory.

As for Roosevelt, he had not done anything during these weeks to counteract the opposition strategy, or effectively to answer his opponent's charges. When he made his speech formally accepting the nomination he was on his way to Pearl Harbor, there to adjust differences that had arisen between Admiral Nimitz and General MacArthur concerning the strategy to be followed to the end of the Pacific war. He had broadcast from his special train, secretly parked on a siding in the San Diego naval reservation. "I shall not campaign, in the usual sense, for the office," he said, in words reminiscent of those he had used at the outset of the 1940 campaign.[6] "In these days of tragic sorrow, I do not consider it fitting. And besides, in these days of global warfare, I shall not be able to find the time. I shall, however, feel free to report to the people the facts about matters of concern to them and especially to correct any misrepresentations." It was easy for many among his listeners to wonder if these words were not a confession of weakness on his part—he would not campaign because he lacked the mental and physical strength to do so—and this interpretation was encouraged by an unfortunate photograph taken by one of the cameras focused upon him in the railway car as he spoke. It showed him with his mouth wide open and twisted, his whole face sagging in an appearance of exhausted senility. The opposition press seized upon it with glee.

Shortly thereafter, he and his party boarded a cruiser which took them to Pearl Harbor. There, on July 27 and 28, he sat between Nimitz and MacArthur as the two argued their opposite sides of the issue between them. It was a clear-cut issue. Nimitz and the Navy, committed to a Central Pacific axis of advance upon Japan, wanted to bypass the Philippines and land instead upon Formosa. MacArthur, who had promised the Filipinos that he would "return," wanted to liberate the Philippines and bypass Formosa. MacArthur presented the stronger case, to the President's mind. He argued that possession of the Philippines "would enable us to clamp an air and naval blockade on the flow of all supplies from the south to Japan and thus, by paralyzing her industries, force her to early capitulation." He argued, further, that "it was a moral obligation to release this friendly possession from the enemy now that it had become possible" and that the failure to do so would not only be incomprehensible to "the Oriental mind" but would also "result in death to the thousands of prisoners, including American women, children and men civilians held in Philippine concentration camps." He argued, finally, that to "bypass isolated islands was one thing, but to leave in your rear . . . a large enemy concentration supported by an entire country's resources such as the Philippines involved serious and unnecessary risks."[7] His view prevailed; his plan for a landing on Mindanao, to be followed in succession by landings on Leyte and Luzon, was adopted. A few weeks later it was decided that Mindanao would be bypassed and Leyte invaded on October 20, a decision made possible by the flexibility of MacArthur's planning and the remarkable efficiency of his command.

When news that the President had been in Pearl Harbor was released on August 11, correspondents took occasion to say he had "appeared in excellent health." ("I was shocked at the personal appearance of President Roosevelt," said MacArthur to his staff upon his return to Australia. "I had not seen him for a number of years and he had failed immeasurably. I predict he will be dead within this year."[8]) What the correspondents allegedly saw in Hawaii, however, was in sharp contrast to what a huge crowd actually saw in Bremerton, Washington, upon Roosevelt's return to the United States via Alaska. He had come down the Inside Passage on a destroyer, and from the deck of this destroyer he delivered an address to thousands gathered at the Puget Sound Navy Yard, to millions sitting before their radios. It was, as Rosenman said, a "dismal failure."[9] The President looked tired and ill, partially because he gave the speech standing up in braces he had not worn for a year and which, because of the considerable weight he had lost during that year, fit him poorly. The manuscript from which he spoke had been carelessly dictated by him aboard ship and left virtually unrevised; it was a rambling, superficial discourse on his recent travels, and he delivered it in a "hesitant, halting and indecisive" manner. Taken in conjunction with the San Diego photograph, it dismayed his friends and rejoiced his foes.

Nor was this impression of failing powers contradicted in the public mind, or among Roosevelt's close associates, by his handling of a quarrel within the War Production Board, and between that Board and the Army, which had erupted into big headlines while he was out of Washington. On the contrary, further evidence of indecisiveness, of a halting ineffectiveness, seemed thereby provided.

The quarrel was regarded by Donald Nelson, the WPB chairman, as the culmination of his long struggle to prevent a totalitarian military domination of the civilian economy.* It had to do with the reconversion of American industry from war to peace production, and it began when

* See pp. 181–83, and pp. 173–78.

Nelson on June 18 announced a four-point program: "(1) Revocation of WPB orders limiting the uses of aluminum and magnesium, which had become very plentiful, so that manufacturers would be able to use these metals for the production of essential civilian goods whenever manpower became available. (2) Permission for any manufacturer to make and test a single model of any product planned for postwar production. (3) Provision for advance retooling by manufacturers, through permission for the placing of unrated orders for tools and machinery needed for civilian production. . . . [An unrated order was one that could not be filled until all those with priority ratings had been filled.] (4) A provision whereby a WPB regional director could authorize a small manufacturer to go into production of civilian goods, provided that the materials, the manufacturing capacity, or the manpower involved was not needed for the war effort. ['Spot-authorization,' this was soon called.]"[10] The program obviously meant "that there can be precious little in the way of expanded civilian production in the immediate future," Nelson said. "But in the interest of war production itself, and for the protection of the entire economy, it nevertheless is essential to prepare now for the return to civilian production. Just as industrial preparations for war had to be started long before large-scale fighting began, so also the industrial preparations for peace must be begun in plenty of time before the fighting ends."[11]

The Army and Navy—though chiefly the Army, through Lieutenant General Brehon B. Somervell, Commanding General of the Army Service Forces, and Robert P. Patterson, the Under Secretary of War—reacted violently against this program. It was based on the dangerously dubious assumption that the war was about to end; it would promote an exodus of labor from impermanent war jobs to permanent peacetime civilian jobs, increasing the already excessive labor turnover in war plants; it would divert the attention and energies of management from the present needs of military production to the future possibilities of civilian production; and it would deny to the Army that flexibility as to kind and amount of materiel made necessary by the fluctuating fortunes of war. Its over-all effect could be disastrous on the fighting fronts in the months ahead. So ran the Army argument. Nelson flatly denied every part of it and, indeed, doubted that it frankly expressed the real convictions of those who advanced it. He suspected hidden motives. So did Senator Truman in his capacity as Chairman of the Truman Committee. In a special statement released to the press on July 8, Truman described the announced Nelson program as an effort to bring about "an orderly resumption of civilian production in areas where there is no manpower shortage and with materials that are not required for war production." The program, he went on to say, "has been opposed by some selfish business groups that want to see their competitors kept idle until they finish their war contracts. It has also been opposed by Army and Navy representatives who want to create a surplus of manpower with the hope that the consequent pressure on unemployed workers would result in some of them shifting to occupations or areas in which there is still a manpower shortage."

The latter point was the crux of the openly stated matter, in Nelson's view. There had been increasingly frequent cutbacks in military orders during recent months. These had created localized unemployment, some of it severe. In other areas, and in certain kinds of jobs, there were acute manpower shortages. But to assume as the Army assumed that a deliberate creation of "pools of unemployment" in towns A and B and C would, through forced migration, relieve manpower shortages in towns D and E and F, hundreds of miles away—to assume this was to betray a woeful ignorance of the nature of the labor supply, of American production techniques, and of human psychology in general. "Workers are not all cut to a pattern as were the men of Frederick the Great's Prussian Guards," said Donald Nelson. "They follow many skills and trades, most of which are not learned instantaneously. It does no good at all to cry that you need five hundred workers; the question is, what kinds of workers? If you need welders, the existence of many thousands of unemployed linotype operators will do you no good whatever." The Army argued that there should be no revival of the civilian economy anywhere so long as there was labor shortage in a single war plant, which meant (in Nelson's words) that "you couldn't employ idle die-setters in Cleveland if a factory in Phoenix needed welders."[12]

So obviously fatuous was this openly stated argument that Nelson could not but believe it designed, at least in part, for the achievement of unstated aims. Perhaps its ulterior motive lay among those "selfish business groups" (Big Business) to which Senator Truman had referred and with which officers of the Army Supply Services had close, friendly ties. Certainly there were some in Big Business who argued strongly if privately that the war must not be permitted to "change the pattern" of American industry and that to prevent this the Government should not permit or encourage individual reconversions by relaxing its economic controls but should instead use these controls to insure the restoration, so far as possible, of the *status quo ante bellum.* There should be a precisely defined reconversion period, according to this view. During it each producer would be permitted to manufacture only such kinds of things as he had made before the war, and in numbers that were in direct ratio to his production figures during a stated prewar base period. Thus all manufacturers of a given product would resume its manufacture simultaneously, would not be permitted to shift to new products until the defined reconversion period had ended, and would face no new competition during this period. Small wonder that the proposal was not loudly pressed in public by its most ardent supporters! Its easily discernible effect would be the end of such industrial democracy as yet remained in America. The proposed reconversion period must be, at least at the outset, one of rising unemployment and decreasing supplies of consumer goods—a period of depression during which the incomes of common folk were drastically reduced while the prices of the things they must buy were upheld by Government controls and imposed market scarcities. And at its end there would be few if any small manufacturers left in the country. Monopoly industry would reign supreme over the economy; linked to the Army in a giant industrial-military complex, it might well rule a totalitarian United States.

Indeed, the whole Army approach to manpower and reconversion problems was, in Nelson's view, but another expression of the authoritarian, totalitarian mind against which he had had to struggle for two long years.[13] Such a mind had a penchant for single prescriptions and blanket solutions. It lacked the precision or was too lazy to make the discriminatory judgments upon which the preservation of individual liberty, or of any kind of recognized individualism, depends. And it was driven by a lust for personal power unmitigated by concern for the rights and sufferings of other individual men and women. In actual reality, excessive labor turnover in war plants was a multiple ill for which there could be no single prescription, a multiple problem that could not be adequately covered by any blanket solution. In one plant the problem could be solved simply by lighting a previously unlighted parking area. In another it could be solved by staggering the open hours of grocery stores and other facilities so that night-shift workers could make use of them. In a third, it could be solved by removal of an incompetent or disagreeable plant manager. Each case was different; each required its own unique handling within a general framework of policy. Those who would shape true solutions must apply to each problem, not the romantic's forceful will but the realist's critical intelligence. . . .

When Roosevelt returned from his visit to Pearl Harbor he found that WPB was itself split into warring factions by the quarrel with the Army. Charles E. Wilson,† Nelson's principal subordinate, with the title of Production Vice Chairman of WPB, was inclined to agree with the Army, at least to the extent that he felt the announced reconversion plan might be premature. Other WPB vice chairmen agreed with the Army not only as regards the "when" but also as regards the "how" of reconversion, the Army's "how" being that of a precisely defined and rigorously controlled reconversion period. Wilson and these others soon found themselves attacked in public as enemies of free enterprise and promoters of monopoly who, it was clearly implied, stood to make private profit from the public policy they favored. Moreover, and worse, they believed (were led by the Army to believe) that the attacks upon them had their secret source in Nelson's own office—an allegation Nelson vehemently denied. Meanwhile, Nelson himself was under public attack as the Army released sly stories of an alleged "production crisis" in

† Not to be confused with the Charles E. Wilson who succeeded Knudsen as president of General Motors. The WPB Wilson was former president of General Electric.

contexts indicating that WPB was responsible for it. (In point of fact, according to Nelson, there was no "production crisis," and such materiel shortages as existed were generally due to the Army's own mistakes in making premature cutbacks and then, months later, restoring them.)

Even at this late date, Roosevelt might have restored harmony and avoided further public embarrassment of his Administration in an election year if he had firmly, publicly backed Nelson. For two years he had refused either to do this, as Nelson had repeatedly asked, or to dismiss him, as Stimson and the Army had (on one occasion) virtually demanded. Nor did he do so now. Instead, he called Nelson to the White House and described to him in glowing terms a special mission to China he wished him to undertake with Major General Patrick J. Hurley. Nelson agreed to take it, and agreed also that Wilson should be Acting Chairman of WPB in his absence. But when this was publicly announced, as it promptly was, it had an effect precisely opposite its obvious intention. A flood of telegrams and letters protesting Nelson's departure and Wilson's appointment poured into the White House, leading to press and radio comment that Nelson was being "sent to Siberia" as reward for his defense of the general welfare against predatory interests; and Wilson was convinced that all this was instigated by Nelson, directly or indirectly. He thereupon angrily resigned, held a fuming press conference in which he let the world know what he thought of Donald Nelson, and so produced even bigger headlines than before. The upshot was that Wilson went home, Nelson went to China (he could comfort himself with the fact that he had at least defeated the Army-Big Business reconversion proposals), Julius A. Krug‡ became WPB Chairman, and Dewey was given more live ammunition to use in his attacks upon Roosevelt.[14]

A considerable portion of this ammunition was expended while the President was again away from Washington, attending what became known as the Second Quebec Conference. From September 10 to September 17, in Quebec's Citadel and Château Frontenac, Roosevelt and Churchill met in personal conference and in plenary sessions of the Combined Chiefs of Staff to shape plans for the completion of the European war, the defeat of Japan, and the treatment of Germany after the war. The latter subject produced the most important news to come out of the conference—and again the news was not such as to reassure Roosevelt's well-wishers concerning his mental and physical vigor.

Harry Hopkins was temporarily out of favor with the President—a fact known to very few of the White House inner circle—and he did not accompany his chief to Quebec. Neither did the Secretary of State, though a major item of postwar foreign policy was on the agenda. Instead, on September 12, the President summoned to Quebec his old friend and Hyde Park neighbor, Henry W. Morgenthau, Jr., Secretary of the Treasury, who brought with him a "plan" for treating conquered Ger-

‡ Krug had been WPB Vice Chairman and Director of the Office of War Utilities.

many almost as drastically, as punitively as Rome had treated Carthage at the close of the Punic Wars. It was originally the work of Harry Dexter White, a special assistant to Morgenthau, and its logic was as narrow as it was ruthless; but it had strong emotional appeal for many Allied leaders in that final year of the Hitlerian madness. Had not the German repeatedly proved he could not be trusted with war-making power? Insanely egotistical and (consequently) insensitive to the rights and feelings of other people, save insofar as he derived a dark sexual pleasure from inflicting pain upon them, he had committed in these last years crimes against humanity of such magnitude as to be incomprehensible by civilized minds. Other people produced their fair share of psychopaths capable of the foulest crimes, but among all the heirs of Western culture only the Germans made psychopathic cruelty the central theme of their State, with torture-murder a major and carefully organized activity of government. Possessed of war-making power, therefore, Germany was intolerable in a community of civilized nations. And of what did her war-making power basically consist? Obviously, of her industrial might. Ergo, she must be stripped of her heavy industry and transformed into a primarily agricultural and pastoral country. This was the essence of the soon-notorious "Morgenthau Plan," which was initialed by both Roosevelt and Churchill near the close of the Quebec Conference, though not without prior protest by the Prime Minister. It provided that Russia and other Nazi-devastated countries be authorized "to remove the machinery they require" from Germany, as reparation for their own losses; that the industry of the Ruhr and Saar be "put out of action and closed down"; and that "the two districts . . . be put under some body under the world organization which would supervise the dismantling of these industries and make sure that they were not started up again by some subterfuge."[15]

Weeks before this "plan" became known through a "leak" to the general public, it provoked powerful opposition in Washington among those who realized what its consequences would be, not just for Germany, but for Europe and indeed the world. Henry Stimson voiced this opposition effectively in a memorandum to Hull which Hull passed on to the White House. The Secretary of War found nonsensical the notion that the Saar and Ruhr "with their very important deposits of coal and ore" could be "totally transformed into a nonindustrialized area of agricultural land." The "commerce of Europe" since 1870, he pointed out, had been "very largely predicated" upon the "raw materials" of this region. "I cannot treat as realistic the suggestion that such an area in the present economic condition of the world can be turned into a nonproductive 'ghost territory.' . . . The need for the recuperative benefits of productivity is more evident now than ever before throughout the world. Not to speak of Germany at all or even her satellites, our allies in Europe will feel the need of the benefit of such productivity if it should be destroyed. Moreover, speed of reconstruction is of great importance, if we hope to avoid dangerous convulsions in Europe. . . . Nor can I agree that it should be one of our purposes to hold the German population 'to a subsistence level' if this means the edge of poverty. This would mean condemning the German people to a condition of servitude. . . . Such a program would, I believe, create tension and resentments far outweighing any immediate advantage of security and would tend to obscure the guilt of the Nazis and the viciousness of their doctrines and their acts. By such economic mistakes I cannot but feel that you would also be poisoning the springs out of which we hope that the future peace of the world can be maintained. . . ."[16]

And this view of the matter very soon prevailed. Within a month, Roosevelt was pretending that he knew nothing about the proposal, and on October 20 he sent a memorandum to Hull in which he repudiated the very idea of "making detailed plans for a country we do not yet occupy." The details, he added, were "dependent on what we and the Allies find when we get into Germany."[17] As for Churchill, he apparently initialed the "plan" in the first place only, or chiefly, because he wanted Morgenthau's support of postwar credits for Britain from the United States and felt he could count upon the War Cabinet to prevent the proposal's being carried into effect, if serious efforts to do so were ever made. It was with his "full accord," as he later wrote, that "the idea of 'pastoralizing' Germany did not survive."[18]

All these seeming evidences of Roosevelt's loss of grip (only intermittently did he seem to function with the effectiveness of his former years) were displayed amidst an apathy in the face of young Dewey's challenge which was as puzzling as it was dismaying to the President's supporters. There could be no doubt that the Republican campaign was gaining ground, both on the "high level" where Dewey pitched his verbal shafts (though not without resort to lawyer's tricks of quoting out of context, or making false implications without actually lying) and on the "low level" where malicious rumor was a principal weapon. For instance, there was a story, printed as gospel truth in some Republican papers, that the President's famous Scottie dog Fala had been accidentally left behind when the President embarked from Alaska on his circuitous way back from Hawaii, that this had been discovered when the returning party was far down the Inside Passage, and that a destroyer had then been sent back to pick up Fala at immense cost to the taxpayers. Such stories, unanswered, were effective. Yet Roosevelt did not answer them. He who had formerly gloried in the battle now seemed bored by it, and this attitude was now even more disturbing to Democratic politicians than his somewhat similar one in the early stages of the 1940 campaign had been. In 1940, after all, there had been no question about his ability to campaign effectively, if only he made up his mind to do so, whereas in 1944 this question loomed large indeed. Anxiety had been mingled with relief among his supporters, therefore, when he announced in August that he would make a speech on September 23 that was "political" though "not very," the occasion being a dinner of the International Brotherhood of Teamsters at the Statler Hotel in Washington.[19] A repetition of the Bremerton fiasco, this late in the campaign, would be disastrous. . . .

Instead of disaster was triumph. He made on September 23 what Judge Rosenman forever after regarded as the greatest political speech in his long political career. It began with ridicule of the allegation that he was old and tired to the point of senility. "Well, here we are again—after four years—and what years they have been!" he said, his voice vibrant as of yore with the youthful zest for battle. "You know, I am actually four years older—which is a fact that seems to annoy some people. In fact, there are millions of Americans who are more than eleven years older than when we started in to clear up the mess that was dumped in our laps in 1933." He went on to ridicule the plank in the Republican platform which accepted "the purposes of the National Labor Relations Act, the Wage and Hour Act, the Social Security Act," and all other Federal welfare statutes which, as Roosevelt pointed out, the Republicans had overwhelmingly opposed when they were proposed—a historic fact which rendered dubious the Republican platform "promise" of a "fair and just administration of these laws." "Can the Old Guard pass itself off as the New Deal?" he asked. "I think not. We have all seen many marvelous stunts in the circus but no performing elephant could turn a hand-spring without falling flat on his back." He ridiculed Dewey's charges that the Roosevelt Administration had not adequately prepared for war and was incompetent to make the peace. To do this, he had only to remind his listeners of what the dominant Republican leaders had actually done and said immediately "before and after 1939." And so he came to the climax of his ridicule in a paragraph destined to be remembered in history as the keynote of the campaign:

> These Republican leaders have not been content with attacks on me, or my wife, or my sons. No, not content with that, they now include my little dog, Fala. Well, of course, I don't resent attacks, and my family doesn't resent attacks, but Fala *does* resent them. You know, Fala is Scotch, and being a Scottie, as soon as he learned that the Republican fiction writers in Congress and out had concocted a story that I had left him behind on the Aleutian Islands and had sent a destroyer back to find him—at a cost to the taxpayers of two or three, or eight or twenty million dollars—his Scotch soul was furious. He has not been the same dog since.

And that was the end of Dewey's chance to win.

The campaign became a "race between Roosevelt's dog and Dewey's goat," as the director of publicity of the Democratic National Committee put it[20]—and Dewey's "goat" was obviously "got." The Republican nominee, who had theretofore had everything his own way, was jarred off-balance; he came back swinging wildly. In the end he would do as much to defeat himself as Roosevelt would do to defeat him—though from that moment on Roosevelt would campaign with a vigor that nearly matched his young opponent's. Almost as effective as his "Fala speech" would be his four-hour tour of New York City's streets in heavy rain on Saturday, October 21 ("I felt the crowd," he said that evening to his associates. "It kept me warm. . . . I didn't know I was wet through. . . .")—a display of buoyant, zestful strength that seemed to give the lie to all claims that he lacked the stamina for another four years in the White House. The tour would be followed that evening by an effective speech on foreign policy. And there would be subsequent joyously successful appearances and hard-hitting campaign addresses in Chicago, Philadelphia, Hartford, and Boston, as he made his way to a fourth victorious Presidential election night at Hyde Park (again he would speak to cheering torchlight paraders assembled on his lawn) on November 7. He would carry thirty-six States with an electoral vote of 432 compared to Dewey's twelve States with an electoral vote of 99. Of a popular vote of some 48 million, he would receive 25,600,000 as compared with Dewey's 22,000,000. Dewey, as it turned out, received some 298,000 fewer votes than Willkie had received in 1940.

The latter fact might have given a certain, rather bitter personal satisfaction to Wendell Willkie had he been permitted to know of it. He never knew. When the "Fala speech" was given he was a patient in New York City's Lenox Hill Hospital. When the election was held, he was dead. With him died a great and secret dream which, shared with Roosevelt, might well have given America a new birth of freedom—might well have enabled intelligence to be effective as never before in our modern political life—had it been realized in the months immediately ahead. . . .

Willkie's Wisconsin defeat had put a stop to his personal political ambitions for the time being; it had not put a stop to his newsworthy importance on the national scene. Indeed, public opinion polls indicated that his prestige was actually enhanced among many millions by the gallant effort he had made, the political martyrdom he had endured in the cause of international cooperation. All through that long, hot summer he had tried to use this prestige of his as an instrument of persuasion, or force, upon the Republican party and its Presidential nominee. Prior to the Republican National Convention he wrote a series of seven newspaper articles stating his position on domestic and foreign policy. He called for a wider extension of social security, legislation to protect the civil rights of racial minorities, an "expansionist economic program" to insure full employment after the war, a sharp downward revision of tariffs, and the immediate creation of a Council of the United Nations in which the United States fully participated. This was in intention and effect a platform offered his party on the eve of its convention. It was totally ignored by the Republican platform builders in Chicago.

After that convention he ostentatiously declined to declare his support of Dewey pending Dewey's unequivocal repudiation of isolationism—a repudiation that was never made. Nor did he declare his support of Roosevelt and the Democratic party. In August he wrote two articles, published in *Collier's* magazine early the following month. One of them, entitled "Cowardice in Chicago," attacked both party platforms for dishonesty and evasiveness concerning basic issues of foreign policy, particularly those pertaining to the abolition of colonialism and the creation of a truly effective world organization. The other article focused on the attitude of both parties toward racial minorities in this country, and upon the effect of this upon America's foreign affairs in a world where the white man's exploitive rule over the colored races of Asia and Africa was obviously coming to an end. When these two articles and his seven newspaper pieces were put together as a book, *An American Program*, published in early October, he wrote in a foreword to it that "our attitude on our racial minorities and on our international obligations will constitute a test of our sincerity at home and abroad and of our ability to bring about, with other nations, a world of peace and security."[21]

But though he thus maintained a non-partisan role (he believed this enabled him to exert on both candidates a force counteracting the "growing pressure of nationalism" upon them), there could be no real doubt in his mind that, as between Dewey Republicans and Roosevelt Democrats, the latter were far the closer to his own position on issues he deemed fundamental—and this despite the abhorrent racialism of the Southern wing. After all, the latter could effectively prevent national legislation on Negro rights only because northern Republicans, of the kind who in Wisconsin had so emphatically repudiated his leadership, refused to join with Northern Democrats to overrule it. They *did* join with Southern Democrats, all too often, to prevent enactment of liberal legislation which Willkie strongly favored. As for foreign policy, he had only to look at two crucially important international conferences being held in the United States that summer and fall for evidence of Democratic (or at least Roosevelt Administration) commitment to the kind of internationalism he espoused. One of these was the United Nations Monetary and Financial Conference, meeting at Bretton Woods, New Hampshire. Out of it came proposals for an International Monetary Fund and an International Bank for Reconstruction and Development. The other was a conference of delegates from the United Kingdom, Russia, China, and the United States for the purpose of devising the framework of the proposed United Nations Organization. It met at Dumbarton Oaks, an estate in Georgetown, Washington, D.C., and out of it came the organizational pattern destined to be incorporated virtually intact in the United Nations Charter. Both met with the blessing of the Roosevelt Administration; both carried forward policies and plans developed within or under the aegis of the State Department, though with a careful concern for non-partisanship. They were among the events causing several of

Willkie's closest friends to declare for Roosevelt as soon as it became obvious that Dewey had no intention of risking the support of isolationists, or "nationalists" as they now preferred to call themselves. Why did not Willkie do so after it was clear that his non-partisanship had reached a point of diminishing returns?

One part of the answer was certainly his personal distrust of Roosevelt, whom he regarded, not without justification in terms of personal experience, as a tricky opportunist whose word to him could not be relied upon. In the immediate aftermath of Willkie's Wisconsin defeat there was much press and radio comment to the effect that he might be Roosevelt's choice for the Democratic Vice-Presidential nomination. When Secretary of the Navy Frank Knox died suddenly of a heart attack a few weeks later there were widely publicized rumors that Willkie would be appointed Knox's successor, to make him acceptable as Vice-Presidential nominee by delegates to the convention. Willkie himself refused publicly to confirm or deny that any offer of this kind had been made to him; he told friends that he distrusted Roosevelt too much to accept it. He more than suspected that the White House was attempting to trick him into an announced support, after which it might or might not honor such pledges as had been privately made to him.

The same suspicion colored his reaction to an approach initially made to him, in great secrecy, by Roosevelt himself through the most intimate (save for Hopkins, then out of favor) of the President's associates. In the last week of June he received in his New York apartment a phone call from Judge Rosenman in Washington.[22] The President, said Rosenman, wished him (Rosenman) to come to New York to confer with Willkie on a subject in which Willkie was deeply interested but which had nothing to do with the upcoming election. Willkie agreed to the meeting, with the understanding that all knowledge of it would be withheld from the public. The two had lunch together in a private suite of the St. Regis on July 5 (Willkie took the precaution of absenting himself from the room whenever a waiter appeared); and Willkie then learned that Roosevelt was enthusiastic about an idea Willkie had broached some weeks before to former Governor Gifford Pinchot of Pennsylvania and that Pinchot had passed on to the President. It was an idea for "a new setup in American politics." It coincided perfectly with Roosevelt's own views.

"I think the time has come for the Democratic party to get rid of its reactionary elements in the South, and to attract to it the liberals of the Republican party," Roosevelt had said to Rosenman a few days ago. "Willkie is the leader of those liberals. He talked to Pinchot about a coalition of the liberals of both parties, leaving the conservatives in each part to join together as they see fit. I agree with him 100 per cent and the time is now—right after the election. We ought to have two real parties—one liberal and the other conservative. As it is now, each party is split . . ."

"Both parties are hybrids," said Willkie to Rosenman.

The "idea" had been "growing in the President's mind" ever since the failure of the "purge" attempt in 1938, said Rosenman to Willkie. Roosevelt was convinced "that the real future of progressivism in American politics lies in a realignment of the parties rather than in intraparty conflict. The trouble is that all Democrats get together in a convention hall and the majority adopts a good liberal platform; then, after the election, the Southern conservatives, who do not depend for election on anyone outside their own conservative districts, just run out on the platform. The President learned . . . that he cannot beat them in their own districts. He is now ready to form a new grouping, leaving them out of the new liberal party. . . . He wants to team up with you. . . . If it is impossible for you to start talking with him about it before the election, then you can wait until later; but he wants to do it—whether he wins or loses in November."

Willkie responded warmly. It would indeed be impossible for him to confer directly with the President until the election was over: such a conference could not possibly be kept secret and, publicized, was bound to breed suspicions of a "deal" for immediate campaign gain. But Rosenman was authorized to tell the President that Willkie was "ready to devote almost full time to this. A sound, liberal government in the United States is absolutely essential to continued cooperation with other nations of the world." Rosenman so reported to Roosevelt who, as the judge later wrote, "was pleased and excited at the prospect of this fundamental political fight of nationwide proportions."

The rapport between Roosevelt and Willkie was soon broken, however, by Roosevelt's own action. Yielding to that passion for private personal intrigue which seemed to grow as his grip on public affairs relaxed, Roosevelt dictated a letter to Willkie which was mailed "with great secrecy" as he departed from Washington on his way to Pearl Harbor. He did not tell Rosenman of it, though its function was a repetition of that the judge had already performed. He wanted to talk with Willkie "about the future," he wrote, "even the somewhat distant future," as soon as possible after his return from the trip he was making. The meeting would be "wholly off the record or otherwise, just as you prefer." But the fact that a letter had gone from him to Willkie was promptly "leaked" to the press, and Willkie was convinced that this was done deliberately to mislead the electorate into a belief that he was personally committed to the President's re-election. His suspicion seemed confirmed when the President, returned to Washington, denied in a press conference that he had written the letter, a denial he was forced to retract in another personal note to "Dear Wendell" after Willkie's friends had threatened to publish the controverted document.[23]

Nevertheless, the dream of a party realignment was still very much alive in both Roosevelt's and Willkie's minds when, on September 6, Willkie was taken by ambulance from his New York apartment to the hospital, having suffered a heart attack while on a visit to his old home in Rushville, Indiana. He wanted desperately to live. He was only fifty-two. He knew he was indispensable to the realization of this last great dream. But years of too much tension, too much food, too many cigarettes, too little exercise had taken their toll of his once-strong physique. He remained in the hospital for four weeks and four days, suffering repeated heart attacks and coming down at last with a throat infection and lung congestion that induced high fever. The infection, though it responded to penicillin, used up the last strength of his blood, his heart.

He died of a coronary thrombosis very early in the morning of Sunday, October 8, 1944.

ii. *"I Have Returned!"*

Silently, save for a low, pulsing hum of engines which is as the sound of silence—darkly, under a black sky, upon a black and glass-smooth sea—ships crowd by the hundred past midnight into Friday morning, past small Homonhon Island into Leyte Gulf, feeling their way and each other with invisible radar beams as they slant northeastward until, shortly before dawn, they are in assigned positions off the coastal plain of Leyte.[24] Then the dawn. For the Japanese who watch it from the palm-fringed shore of Leyte Valley, that dawn does indeed come up like thunder across the bay—across San Pedro Bay between Leyte and Samar—to light in flaming fury the day of Friday, October 20, 1944. The sudden sun leaps above clouds like round black hills on the eastern horizon; it burns swiftly through a yellow haze above miles of blue-green water where more than seven hundred ships are lined up in successive rows and columns. And, rising into daylight, the dawn roars with anger. Fire and smoke burst thunderously from scores of rifled cannon on battleships, cruisers, destroyers parked so thickly in three different fire-support areas that they must take turns firing. Smoke and fire erupt from shells bursting on and behind the beach defenses. Whenever the gunfire ceases, at planned intervals, planes roar in from fleet and escort carriers—bombing, strafing. The din is incessant, terrific. Thick curtains of smoke and dust, punctuated with flickering flame at their bases, rise high enough to merge with the broken cloud-cover of natural sky, walling from sight of sea all save the outermost edges of Leyte Valley, as loaded LCIs and LSTs cease their circling two or three miles offshore and form in waves that head straight for the designated landing areas. Their near approach is covered by thick flights of rockets from LCI rocket craft—literally thousands of 4.5-inch rockets launched within a span of two minutes—while, from behind the hills to one side of the sand-strip marked on the maps as Beach Red, Japanese mortar fire comes down. Climactic din! Then the ramps of the landing craft come down; the troops and tanks and motorized artillery plunge ashore.

Yet casualties are few. Save for the mortar fire at Beach Red, the landings are virtually unopposed. The Japanese are not without prepared beachhead defenses: there are well-designed earthworks and concrete pillboxes, many of them damaged slightly or not at all by shells or bombs. They are, however, unmanned. The Japanese have pulled back from them, have retired inland. Why? Have they expected to return when the barrage lifts? (The Chief of Staff of the Japanese Thirty-fifth Army, General Yoshiharu Tomochike, is later to express his amazement at the brevity of the preliminary bombardment.) Have they adopted a new concept of defense in depth in place of the old one of "annihilate the enemy on the beach"? (The latter has never succeeded since the Americans learned the bitter lessons of Tarawa; the former has had some recent partial success.) Are they so greatly outnumbered as to make even the attempt at a defense impracticable until they are reinforced? (It will be later revealed that there are nearly thirty thousand Japanese troops on Leyte that angry morning.) Whatever the reason, the event is lucky for the invaders, else there might have been, as airman George Kenney will write to "Hap" Arnold, "a casualty list that would have rivaled Tarawa."[25] As it is, initial objectives are easily achieved within the allotted time with minimal losses. Before noon, supplies and reinforcements are moving ashore without interference from enemy planes or guns, and there are no signs of impending counterattack.

Offshore, all this is watched all morning as closely as may be from the bridge of the cruiser *Nashville* by one whom the world is about to recognize as the man of the hour ("*Mon Dieu*, what a man!" said an awestruck French soldier of him in 1918) and who himself feels he has reached a climactic moment, perhaps *the* climactic moment thus far, of a career that has not been without glory.

General Douglas MacArthur, clad in freshly laundered, sharply creased suntans, his famed gold be-braided and self-designed cap tilted at rakish angle upon his handsome head, has with punctilio asked permission of the captain (Captain Coney) to stand here.[26] He never fails to ask permission before setting foot on the bridge. It is a gesture that seems to some aboard a strange humility in view of MacArthur's reputation for personal arrogance but, to others, seems not so at all, being only a concern for formal procedures from which he, in his high rank, derives privilege, deference, power. More universally surprising has been his attitude in general during this voyage to battle. He has been almost as a boy engaged in high adventure—eager, happy, affable, and approachable—utterly informal in his relations with sailors and Marines for whom, sitting in his cabin doorway for hours at a time, he has signed his name on such scraps of paper as they hand to him. He smiles, he jokes even, while doing so, this remote and austere dignitary. He is now impatient to go ashore. Through binoculars his gaze sweeps the shoreline, turning often to the northwest where lie the airfield on Cataison Point and, invisible from the ship, the substantial town of Tacloban, Leyte's capital. Today is an anniversary for him, he says to those beside him. By strange coincidence, it was precisely forty-one years ago today that he, a Second

Lieutenant of Engineers, fresh out of West Point, sailed into San Pedro Bay on his first field assignment. As Assistant to Engineer Officer, Department of the Visayas, he began, on that October 20, 1903, a survey of Camp Bumpus, Tacloban.[27]

And perhaps as he speaks of this he has a flashing sense of the career, the Self, developed through the last four decades into the here and now. He cannot truly say that he started "from the bottom" on that far-off October day—nor will he ever say it. His is an aristocratic warrior's pride. He had begun his conscious life as a child of Destiny, a prince of the Kingdom of Glory, being a son of the brilliant and imperious Colonel, later General, Arthur MacArthur who had won fame before he was twenty-one as "Boy Colonel" of the Union Army in the Civil War, had been awarded the Congressional Medal of Honor for valor on Missionary Ridge, had served with well-publicized distinction on the Western frontier, had become a national hero as "pacifier" of the Philippines following the war with Spain, and had been relieved of his Philippines command and returned to the United States in consequence of his reluctance, if not refusal, to yield governing power over the islands to the newly appointed civilian High Commissioner, William Howard Taft. In that quarrel the son had sided, and he still sides, with his father, sharing to the full his father's contempt for civilians in general and politicians in particular, especially those who profess "progressive" or "liberal" sentiments. He is very much his father's son; a colleague of both has testified they were the two "most headstrong men" he ever knew.

But he is equally his mother's son, if not more so. She came of an old and distinguished Virginia family; four of her brothers served with the Confederate armies in the Civil War—and she, who had every typical wile and attitude of the Southern belle, was able and more than willing to exercise her considerable social charms in her son's interests. She doted on him, and he on her—excessively, it seemed to some. When he went to West Point, she did too, taking rooms in the Thayer Hotel just below the reservation and remaining there throughout her son's four years in the Academy: he saw her daily; he was with her every possible moment. When her son was named personal aide to her husband and with him made an inspection tour of the Far East, she went along. After her husband's death in 1912 (he died while addressing a banquet reunion of his old Civil War regiment in Milwaukee), she made her home with her son. Some there are who wonder if this remarkably close relationship, continued long after he became a mature man, had something to do with the fact that Douglas MacArthur did not marry until 1922, when he was forty-two. Certain it is that his mother, a few months after his marriage, fell desperately ill of an ailment the doctors could not diagnose with certainty, though her heart was affected, but recovered with miraculous suddenness after her son had made a ten thousand-mile journey to her bedside (he was on a Philippines assignment at the time). "In less than a week I had her home with me, despite the doctor's dire prophecies," he later said.[28] Certain it is also that his bride of 1922, a very rich society divorcee, divorced him in 1929 after a long separation. (She later married Lionel Atwill, the actor.) Two years after his mother's death, he remarried. According to one account[29] his mother had introduced him to Jean Faircloth of Tennessee aboard the ship carrying them to the Philippines in the fall of 1935; at any rate he met her then, at a time when his eighty-four-year-old mother, failing fast, was within a few weeks of death. The two were married in 1937, when she was thirty-eight and he fifty-seven, and a year later she gave birth to a son, Arthur MacArthur. The marriage was a very happy one.

Yet Douglas MacArthur has never been, nor been regarded as, a sissified "mama's boy." At West Point he had proved his physical toughness and moral courage as well as his mental capacity. He took without whine at summer camp in his plebe year a physical hazing so vicious it would have broken a boy of smaller pride or weaker physique (it caused his tentmate of the time to resign from the Academy in disgust), and later he protected his tormenters from the wrath of both Academy officers and Congressional investigators.[30] He was a natural leader, imbued with that "habit of command" which Southerners, deriving it from their ownership of slaves, long deemed a sure sign of personal and racial superiority. In his First (that is, senior) year he was First Captain of the Corps, the highest possible cadet post, and he graduated number one in the Class of '03, having made the highest scholastic record that had been made at the Point in a quarter-century. In the years since, he has given repeated demonstrations of courage, toughness, brilliance, driving ego, and an insatiable appetite for power and glory.

Especially revealing of his character is an episode in 1914, when the thirty-four-year-old Captain MacArthur was in Vera Cruz as a General Staff officer assigned to obtain information that might be useful to the commander (General Leonard Wood) of an American expeditionary force if one were sent into revolution-torn Mexico. On his own responsibility, without bothering to inform the commander of American-occupied Vera Cruz, General Frederick Funston, who had been specifically ordered to take no action that might provoke the Mexicans into a resumption of hostilities, MacArthur made a daring night reconnaissance through the city's hinterland in search of narrow-gauge railroad engines. He located three. According to his own detailed written account, he fought single-handedly three pitched gun battles during that wild night, engaging fifteen "brigands" in the first of them, five in the second, and three in the third, receiving no fewer than four bullets "through my clothes" while killing or wounding no fewer than eight of his attackers.[31] His report was prepared to support a recommendation that he be awarded the Congressional Medal of Honor, a recommendation made by General Wood who had been told of the exploit in the most glowing terms through a letter from a friend of MacArthur's then stationed in Vera Cruz. The medal was not awarded, however. A three-man review board, after studying the relevant documents, disapproved the recommendation on the ground that MacArthur should not have acted as he did without informing the commanding general at Vera Cruz and also because, in the opinion of one of the three board members, there was "insufficient proof" that the described adventures had actually happened, or, in other words, that MacArthur had truly acted "above and beyond the call of duty."[32] MacArthur, incensed, promptly addressed a memorandum directly to the Chief of Staff protesting the board's findings! The upshot was predictable. The Chief of Staff, General Hugh Scott; the Assistant Chief of Staff, General Tasker H. Bliss; and the Assistant Secretary of War, Henry Breckenridge, reviewed and approved the original board's negative decision—and MacArthur's embarrassment as well as his already considerable reputation for overweening egotism and ambition were further increased.

But glory enough to satisfy most men came to him, well-earned, a few years later, after the United States had entered World War I. An early policy decision in the War Department was that National Guard divisions, set up on a State basis, would join with the small Regular Army to form the nucleus of the AEF. Only two States (New York and Pennsylvania) had complete Guard divisions in the early summer of 1917, however, and Secretary of War Newton D. Baker hesitated, for public relations reasons, to send either of them as the first Guard division to land in France. Major MacArthur, then attached to Baker's office, suggested that a division be formed of "surplus" Guard units from many States—it would "stretch over the whole country like a rainbow," said he—and Baker promptly accepted the suggestion.[33] Thus was born the famed Rainbow (42nd) Division, of which MacArthur was initially Chief of Staff, later (as the youngest general officer in the Army) a brigade commander, and ultimately, after the Armistice, the commanding general. In Secretary Baker's informed opinion he was the finest front line officer in the AEF. War correspondents, delighting in him as a source of colorful copy, called him "the d'Artagnan of the AEF," quoted frequently the lush language he employed in public speech, and told millions how he was constantly at the front under fire, how he was twice gassed but refused even a day's hospitalization, how he disdained to wear a steel helmet (though he ordered his men to do so), how he carried a riding crop under his arm and once captured a German officer by gesturing imperiously with it, and how his men allegedly worshiped him and, under his eyes, performed great deeds. Certainly the Rainbow's combat record was a brilliant one, and he did rather more than his share toward shaping it, winning in the process several decorations for bravery. "On a field where courage was the rule, his courage was the dominant feature," said the citation with which he received the Distinguished Service Cross. The Medal of Honor was again denied him, however. He was strongly recommended for it by a special board in his division, but the recommendation was disapproved at Army

Headquarters because the "acts recited . . . are judged not to meet the standard set for the award. . . ." Typically, the Rainbow's special board members were reported to be "shocked and embittered" by this rebuff of their hero; they were sure it expressed personal "enmity against" him "on the part of certain senior members of Pershing's . . . staff."[34] They protested formally, vehemently, vainly.

When MacArthur returned from France in the early spring of 1919 the outlines of his public self, since filled out in detail, were firmly established, deeply etched into the popular consciousness. His egotism was legendary. He was nothing if not flamboyant. A news photograph taken of him on the deck of a troop transport which landed him in New York showed him facing the camera, a slight smile on his handsome lips, wearing a nearly ankle-length, huge-sleeved, huge-collared raccoon-skin coat with an eight-foot brightly colored wool scarf knotted at his throat, its ends trailing down to his knees.[35] The famed riding crop was in his left hand, and his Army officer's cap had been somehow transformed from its regulation rigidity into a soft-crowned jaunty-looking headgear. Behind his back in the picture sat a row of doughboys, laughing. Did they laugh at him? If so, the picture might be deemed significant of part of the impact he was about to make upon a decidedly non-heroic, pacifistic, pleasure- and profit-bent, postwar America.

For he entered then upon years of frustration. His career continued to be of the maximum brilliance possible a professional soldier in peacetime America. He became the youngest West Point superintendent in history, the third youngest Chief of Staff in history, the first Chief of Staff ever to succeed himself (he served from 1930 through 1935). But professional soldiers were not much honored by leading opinion makers during the Jazz Age—and during the Depression, especially in its opening years, they appeared to many as forceful agents of reaction, potential if not actual threats to civil liberties in a time when Mussolini's Black Shirts and Hitler's Brown Shirts were marching from triumph to triumph. It cannot be said that MacArthur's words or deeds were well calculated to dispel this notion. As Chief of Staff, he was forever discerning "plots" by "subversives" to destroy "the principles hallowed by the blood of our ancestors" and to "set up internationalism in the place of patriotism." In a 1932 commencement address at the University of Pittsburgh, he said: "Pacifism and its bedfellow communism are all about us. In the theater, newspapers and magazines, pulpits and lecture halls, schools and colleges, it hangs like a mist before the face of America, organizing the forces of unrest and undermining the morale of the working man."[36] And when he received from President Hoover via Secretary of War Patrick J. Hurley an order on August 28 of 1932 to "surround . . . and clear . . . without delay" a bedraggled Anacostia Flats camp of so-called Bonus Marchers—several thousand unemployed war veterans who had descended upon Washington in an effort to persuade the

Congress to grant an immediate cash bonus and who had remained there, having (most of them) no better place to go, after the Congress turned down the proposal—he insisted upon carrying out the order personally, though there was no necessity for him to do so and several good reasons why he should not. Certainly his effectiveness as a Chief of Staff who must deal constantly with civilian politicians was reduced by the sight of him in full uniform (Army officers on Washington duty normally wore civilian clothes in those days), leading some hundreds of cavalry and infantry, with a platoon of machine gunners and six tanks, against a disorganized body of unarmed unemployed, driving them from their pitiful shelters, destroying these, and giving every sign of enjoying his absurdly exaggerated show of force. That night he told newspapermen gathered in his office that not "one in ten" of the "insurrectionists" was a bona fide veteran, in his opinion. "Had the President not acted today, had he permitted this thing to go on for twenty-four hours more, he would have faced a grave situation . . ." said MacArthur. "Had he let it go another week, I believe the institutions of our government would have been severely threatened." But there were few who believed that MacArthur in this instance had been instrumental (as he implied) in the saving of his country. There were many who believed that he himself, backed by men of similar mind, was a far graver threat to free institutions in these troubled times than the ragged little "army" on Anacostia Flats had ever been. A veritable storm of popular indignation descended upon him.

Nor was the prevailing view of him as a "fascist-minded militarist" dimmed at all by his proposal to the House Military Affairs Committee in early 1935 that the men in CCC camps be given military training and "used as a nucleus of an Enlisted Reserve." It was pointed out that this imposed military service on precisely that portion of the population which derived the smallest benefits from the American society and economy, namely those who could not find jobs, and was only too closely analogous to the methods by which Hitler and Mussolini "solved" their "unemployment problem."

He himself was of course convinced that he was ringed about by traitorous enemies of "Americanism"—cowardly pacifists, New Deal socialists, Red agents, plus all manner of men who envied him his obvious personal superiority and hated him for it and were utterly incapable of feeling such vibrations of the yearning soul as characterized the address he made to a reunion of the Rainbow Division in Washington in the summer of 1935. "It was seventeen years ago—those days have vanished tone and tint," said he on this occasion, his voice throbbing with emotion. ". . . they have gone glimmering through the dreams of things that were. Their memory is a land where flowers of wonderous beauty and varied colors spring, watered by tears and coaxed and caressed into fuller bloom by the smiles of yesterday. . . . We listen vainly but with thirsty ear for the witching melodies of the days that are gone. . . . Youth . . .

strength . . . aspirations . . . struggles . . . [etc., etc.] far drums beating the long roll . . . the crash of guns . . . the rattle of musketry . . . the still white crosses. . . . And now we are met to remember."[37] He was glad to escape honorably a few weeks later from a decadent America which poked fun at his noble sentiments, was contemptuous of his concepts of Honor and Glory, and found his rhetoric absurd.

The escape was provided by Manuel Quezon, first President of the newly created Philippine Commonwealth. By the terms of the Tydings-McDuffie Act of 1934, the Commonwealth was to become an independent sovereign State in 1946; this raised the vital question of whether the new State would be able to defend herself against a Japan bent on a career of conquest. The prevailing U.S. military opinion was that the islands were indefensible against a truly determined Big Power,§ but with this opinion MacArthur emphatically disagreed. He was convinced a proper effort—the development of a well-trained, well-armed Army and of an intelligent system of defenses—could raise the cost of subduing the islands so high by 1946 that Japan would not be willing to pay it. He told Quezon so when the latter was in Washington in the summer of 1935, whereupon the President-elect asked him to come to Manila to serve as chief Military Adviser during the upcoming six-year Presidential term. He made the offer attractive in terms of money (MacArthur's salary would be higher than Quezon's own) and even more so in terms of Power and Glory. MacArthur, with the approval of Roosevelt and the Secretary of War (Harry H. Woodring), promptly accepted.

He found in Manila a task and an atmosphere far more congenial to his imperious spirit than any America had offered him. "Adviser" was a wholly inadequate and even inaccurate description of the post he occupied. He was head of a mission of officers detached from the U. S. Army for this service, among them Major Dwight D. Eisenhower, who had served on MacArthur's staff in Washington and was now the mission's chief of staff.¶ He was also in effect a combination war minister and commanding general, with the rank of Field Marshal—a higher rank than was possible in the U. S. Army. (He received the commission in a glittering ceremony at Malacanan Palace in August of 1936, Mrs. Quezon handing him a gold baton; he designed a special gold-braided cap and white dress uniform of sharkskin cloth as suitable garb for his exalted station.) He lived in remote grandeur in a penthouse atop the Manila Hotel, rarely appearing at social functions and thus enhancing the effect of such appearances as he did make. He was an arbiter of Destiny, a Giver of Laws to the people, surrounded by such deference

§ See pp. 129–30.

¶ A distinct coldness developed between MacArthur and Eisenhower during the latter's years on the Islands. MacArthur is supposed later to have characterized Eisenhower as "the best clerk I ever had" while Eisenhower is supposed later to have characterized his service under MacArthur as a "four-year study of dramatics."

and adulation as he had never known before and could never know in his native land.

He requested and was granted retirement from the U. S. Army in 1937, after he was confidentially informed by Malin Craig, the Army Chief of Staff, that his authorization to extend his tour of foreign service beyond the normal two years was about to be revoked so that he could be recalled for duty in the States. It suited MacArthur's dramatic temperament to regard this voluntary act on his part as a "virtually forced retirement" imposed by "certain powerful groups" who, for their own nefarious purposes, wished him out of the country.[38] Thus his continued service in Manila became a kind of royal exile. Two years later, when George C. Marshall became Chief of Staff, MacArthur's sense of "personal animosity" toward him in Washington was heightened. Had not Colonel Marshall been denied promotion to brigadier general by MacArthur's special board on promotions when MacArthur was Staff Chief? Had not Colonel Marshall instead been ordered to Illinois as Senior Instructor for the National Guard, an assignment that seemed to end the possibility of the colonel's ever becoming a general officer? Had not MacArthur flatly rejected Marshall's plea (it was the first Marshall ever made for special consideration in the Army) for a change of assignment? And was not Marshall hand-in-glove with New Dealers —Harry Hopkins, for instance—bent on "socializing" America and appeasing Communists?[39] Small wonder, therefore, that MacArthur's efforts to build Philippine defenses with American help were continuously frustrated in Washington! He professed to be sure that the Joint Chiefs' determination to aid Britain and, later, Red Russia against the Nazis at the expense of the Far East had as one of its secret motives a personal enmity toward himself. His histrionic, insatiably ambitious character—his essentially simple if brilliant mind—required this division of mankind into "good guys" (those who admired him uncritically) and "bad guys" (those who did not)—required this dramatic "plot" whereby history became a stage play with himself in the starring role. Heroism of the kind he craved must impose villainy on all who were not his adulators . . .

Not that his life was all play-acting, of course. He worked hard and competently in the real world toward his goal of a Philippine militia of some 400,000 men, organized in forty divisions, strategically placed throughout the Islands for swift mobilization, equipped with modern arms furnished by the United States, covered in the air by 250 planes and, offshore, by a fleet of 50 sixty-five-foot torpedo-launching speed boats —all this by 1946. He continuously exuded an absolute confidence in the efficacy of these arrangements, once they were completed. As late as the fall of 1939, after Hitler's invasion of Poland, he predicted that his plan, fully carried out, would make the cost of a successful invasion "at least a half million men in casualties and upwards of five billions of dollars in money."[40]

Nor did the necessities of dramatic "plot" blind him (he would not permit them to blind him) to the main chance, or prevent his seizing it even when doing so was a tacit admission that the "villains" of his play were fictional. Had he truly believed on the deepest level that Marshall was the kind of man who lets personal feelings dictate official acts he could never have written him as he did in May 1941, asking (with a humility almost unique in the MacArthur career) for a return to active duty in the U. S. Army and also suggesting (this was much more in keeping with MacArthur's standard procedure) that all Army forces in the Far East be consolidated under a single commander, with himself as that commander. Certainly the Marshall of the fictional "plot" would not have replied as the real Marshall did that "your outstanding qualifications and vast experience in the Philippines make you the logical choice for the Army Commander of the Far East" and that Secretary of War Stimson "at the proper moment . . . will recommend to the President that you be so appointed. It is my impression," Marshall added, "that the President will approve . . . [this] recommendation."[41] The President did so a few weeks later.

But of course the event did not prevent MacArthur's immediate relapse into the posture required by his type of heroism. He had by then gathered around him an immediate staff whose common denominator was an unquestioning devotion to him, even a kind of worship of him as a kind of god, and these men accepted and reinforced his professed view that he was being continuously discriminated against, for personal reasons, by men in power in Washington. It became *their* fault that the Japanese had not waited until 1946 to attack him but had struck five years too soon. Had not White House machinations virtually forced Japan to strike before he was ready? It was *their* fault that nearly all his slender air strength was destroyed on the ground at Clark Field on December 8, 1941. Why had they not rushed completion of the airfields needed for a proper dispersal of his planes? It was *their* fault—a betrayal of a sacred obligation to the Filipinos if not treason to the U.S.—that adequate reinforcements and supplies did not pour into Luzon. Were not supplies and shipping that might have made all the difference in the Philippines being employed to aid a Communist Russia whose destruction (devoutly to be wished by all patriotic Americans) might otherwise have been accomplished by Hitler? Oh, the "plot" was nefarious indeed, and it focused on him because the Communists knew him to be, of all Americans, Communism's most implacable and brilliantly effective foe. Even the direct order from Roosevelt as Commander-in-Chief which enabled him honorably to escape the ugly fate of Wainwright and his men on Bataan and Corregidor had, according to the MacArthur canon, the principal purpose of discrediting his personal courage in the eyes of his troops and the American public, and inflicting upon him (further to discredit him) the command in Australia of a cause already virtually lost. That the cause was *not* lost, in actual event, was chiefly due to his lonely, heroic genius. . . .

All this has justified his striking back against his Washington "enemies" while striking against the enemy on his fighting front, with whatever weapons are at hand and suitable. Chief among these is his control of the flow of information out of his theater of command. He has imposed a complete anonymity upon all subordinate American commanders in his theater. Always it is "General MacArthur's Forces" which fight the battles and "General MacArthur's Headquarters" which announces the victories—generally some weeks in advance of their accomplishment and with no accurate indication of their cost. "If you capture Buna," said MacArthur to Lieutenant General Robert L. Eichelberger, later Commander of the U. S. Eighth Army, in late November 1942, "I'll give you a Distinguished Service Cross . . . and [the supreme reward] I'll release your name for newspaper publication." And it is Eichelberger who, though "a great admirer of General MacArthur as a military strategist," will profess years later not to understand the MacArthur "public relations policy," particularly that portion of it which announced a final victory when, in point of fact, only "a first phase . . . [has] been accomplished without too many casualties." ("The phrase 'mopping up' had no particular appeal for a haggard, muddy sergeant of the American Division whose platoon has just been wiped out in western Leyte," Eichelberger will say. ". . . if there is another war, I recommend that the military . . . and everyone else concerned drop the phrase 'mopping up' from their vocabularies. It is not a good enough phrase to die for."[42]) Actually, of course, this public relations policy, implemented through MacArthur's chief PRO—one Colonel (later Brigadier General) LeGrande A. Diller, whom all correspondents concerned with truth in official communiqués have come heartily to despise—has a perfectly simple and obvious intent: it is to portray MacArthur as an omniscient commander whose genius gains enormous victories at almost no cost in casualties: it is to transform the whole Allied struggle in the Far Pacific into "MacArthur's War" . . .

And the purpose has been to a large degree achieved by this flaming morning of October 20, 1944, as he stands on the bridge of the *Nashville* and gazes at the teeming beaches and blasted palm groves of Leyte. It has been achieved at the cost of much hurt, helpless anger on the part of men who earn with their bravery and sacrifice the Glory he wraps around himself. The Marines, for instance, whose role in MacArthur's battles is never mentioned in his communiqués, will soon be chanting a "poem" expressive of their feelings, the last verse being:

> And while possibly a rumor now,
> Some day it will be fact
> That the Lord will hear a deep voice say,
> Move over God, it's Mac.

But such jibes, if known to MacArthur, remain unknown to the general public—and it is the general public whom he is prepared to address as he leaves the bridge and goes to his cabin for an early lunch. "I shall return," he had said some two and a half years ago upon his arrival in Australia (he insisted that precisely these words be published despite objections by the OWI which felt it more appropriate to say, "*We* shall return"), and now the predicted moment, conceived by him to be one of the great dramatic moments of history, is at hand.

Soon he appears again on deck. He wears sunglasses that darken his gaze, that hide his eyes from beholders, that somehow (perhaps for this reason) set him apart in appearance, aloof, from those who accompany him as he descends a ladder to a landing craft and takes his position in the stern "behind and above" the others aboard, as an eyewitness correspondent will report.[43] These others include President Sergio Osmena, who has succeeded Quezon (now dead) as exiled chief executive of the Philippine Commonwealth; Brigadier General Carlos P. Romulo, famous as the "Voice of Freedom" broadcasting from doomed Corregidor in 1942 and now appointed Resident Commissioner of the Philippines; General Sutherland, MacArthur's Chief of Staff; and General Kenney. Photographers are at hand to record the fact that, when the landing craft is grounded and its ramp flops down, MacArthur and his party wade ashore through knee-deep water (some few there are who will profess surprise that the Saviour cannot, after all, walk on water). A portable radio transmitter is set up on the beach to broadcast MacArthur's words.

"I have returned!" says he in deep-voiced chant, addressing millions of Filipinos directly and hundreds of millions of others as eventual listeners-in. ". . . Rally to me. Let the indomitable spirit of Bataan and Corregidor lead on. As the lines of battle roll forward to bring you within the zone of operations, rise and strike! For future generations of your sons and daughters, strike! In the name of your sacred dead, strike! Let no heart be faint. Let every arm be steeled. The guidance of Divine God points the way. Follow in His name the Holy Grail of righteous victory!"

Three days pass by.

Civil government, headed by President Osmena, is declared re-established over that portion of Leyte in Allied hands. The flags of the United States and the Philippine Commonwealth are simultaneously and ceremoniously raised above the now-secured capital of the island, Tacloban. The whole Allied world applauds MacArthur's great victory. (Incidentally, and ironically, the "return" hurts the general's political party in the Presidential campaign at home since it discredits the Republican charge that he is deliberately denied the means of victory by an Administration that hates and fears him.) But aboard the *Nashville* in Leyte Gulf, where MacArthur continues to maintain his headquarters, and on the flagships of the American admirals, the prevailing mood is not one of relief and rejoicing over a triumph achieved; it is instead one of mounting tension in the shadow of approaching events.

For there now impends a series of naval engagements which, considered as elements of a single far-flung action, will constitute what is by far the greatest sea battle of all history, if measured in terms of ship tonnage employed, ammunition expended, and number of men involved. It is also destined to be, in all probability, the last major battle in which surface craft settle accounts with gunfire. . . .

iii. *The Battle for Leyte Gulf*

Preliminary to the invasion of the Philippines—and, indeed, determinative (in its effect) of the decision to land on Leyte in October instead of on Mindanao in November—was a series of great victories gained by American forces in the Marianas, and in the Philippine Sea to the west of them, between mid-June and mid-August of 1944. The Marianas—Saipan, Tinian, Guam—were then conquered, providing bases near enough Japan (1585 miles south of Tokyo) for direct attack by B-29 Superfortresses.**

Particularly bloody, and decisive, was the conquest of Saipan. It meant the cracking of the inner defense perimeter of Japan and was desperately resisted by Imperial troops, who in three bloody weeks were forced back into a small pocket in the north of the island. Here were enacted, on a larger scale than ever before, those gruesome scenes—wholly pointless, nasty, ugly from the Western point of view—that had earlier done so much to convince American fighting men that their enemy was not truly human. The highest Japanese officers present were Lieutenant General Yoshitsugo Saito, military commander, and Vice Admiral Chuichi Nagumo, whose success at Pearl Harbor had been canceled by his failure at Midway and who was now demoted to a relatively small command (the Central Pacific Area, the Fourteenth Japanese Air Force) based on Saipan. These two concurred in ordering the biggest, bloodiest *Banzai* charge of the war when, in early July, death or surrender became immediate alternatives. More than 3000 Japanese troops—some of them wounded, many armed only with bayonets or improvised spears or hand grenades—charged the American positions, overrunning some of them, inflicting heavy casualties in the process of being slaughtered themselves. Saito and Nagumo committed suicide. Nor was this the end, or even the worst, of the horror. Japanese civilians trapped on the northern cliffs refused to surrender. American soldiers were sickened by the sight of fathers and mothers dashing out their small children's brains against rocks before plunging off the cliffs, screaming, to their own deaths. Hundreds of civilians shot one another, plunged knives into one another, drowned themselves, blew themselves up with hand grenades. Some of them,

** These unprecedentedly huge bombers (length, 99 feet; wingspan, over 141 feet), destined for a decisive role in the Pacific war during the months ahead, had a speed of 358 miles per hour, a ceiling of 35,000 feet, and a range of over 4000 miles with a bomb load of 10,000 pounds. The B-29's maximum bomb load was 20,000 pounds and its armament consisted of twelve .50-cal. machine guns, or ten machine guns plus one 20-mm. cannon. They had come into production in July 1943.

armed, holed up in caves and ravines where, at last, they were burned to death by American flame throwers. When it was all over, nearly 24,000 Japanese were dead on Saipan; less than 2000 (though by far the largest number in any battle until then) were taken prisoner. American losses were 3426 killed or missing and 13,099 wounded.

Equally desperate and even more disastrous for Japan was the naval action, the great Battle of the Philippine Sea, which was a corollary of the Marianas invasion. The initial landings on Saipan June 15 caused Japanese Admiral Soemu Toyoda, Commander-in-Chief of the Imperial Combined Fleet, to send north and east into the Philippine Sea a powerful task force under the tactical command of Vice Admiral Jisaburo Ozawa. It included nine carriers, five battleships, eleven heavy cruisers, two light cruisers, seven destroyer divisions, and a dozen supply ships. Awaiting them was an American naval force of fifteen carriers, seven battleships, twenty-one cruisers, and sixty-seven destroyers under the top command of Admiral Raymond A. Spruance, whom we last met directing with calm courage and sagacity the crucial phase of the Midway victory. Spruance's fighting arm in the present operation was powerful Task Force 58 under Rear Admiral Marc A. Mitscher, and Mitscher, informed of Ozawa's approach, wanted to drive west full speed to engage at the earliest possible moment. The prudent, logical Spruance restrained him. "We were sent to take Saipan," he later explained, in calm response to criticism. "Our duty was to protect that amphibious force. If we couldn't do that, then we had no business being there. My feeling was that, if we were doing something so important that we were attracting the enemy to us, we could afford to let him come—and take care of him when he arrived."[44] Certainly they *did* take care of him, if less completely than they might have done if Spruance had been less prudent. As at Midway and the Coral Sea, the opposing surface vessels were never within gunfire range of one another. The battle was fought on June 19–20 entirely with bombers, fighter planes, anti-aircraft guns, submarines—and when it was over the Japanese had suffered a decisive defeat of their surface craft, an annihilating one of their air arm. On June 19 occurred what has become known to the Americans as the "Great Marianas Turkey Shoot." Of the 545 Japanese planes launched that day against Mitscher's task force, 366 were destroyed in the air by American fighter pilots and nineteen were shot down by anti-aircraft fire. Seventeen more were destroyed on Guam landing strips—a total of 402 planes and the lives of hundreds of Japan's best, and irreplaceable, pilots. Japanese naval air power was dealt a mortal wound at the cost of twenty-six American planes, twenty-four American aviators, and thirty men killed on bombed ships. By the end of the battle, the following evening, the Japanese had also lost three carriers and two oilers sunk, plus severe damage to several cruisers and destroyers, whereas the Americans lost no ships sunk and suffered relatively minor damage to only five.

Most of the ships of the Japanese task force escaped destruction, however. Its air groups destroyed, its surface units battered, the force limped away and separated into two parts as it moved into the China Sea. The carriers sailed north to base in Japan's Inland Sea, and they remained there—close to what supply there was (it was meager) of new aircraft and, especially, trained pilots—on the eve of the Philippines "return." The battleships and cruisers turned south toward Lingga Roads off Singapore and Sumatra, where the major portion of the Japanese Fleet, the so-called First Striking Force, including all the heaviest ships, had been based since last February. The ships were transferred there in order to be near the source of fuel oil after U.S. submarines had, through sinkings of tankers and cargo vessels, drastically curtailed the flow of resources from India and Malaya.

One of the major hazards of the Leyte invasion was that MacArthur would be operating well beyond the range of his land-based planes while Japanese airfields would be all around him. To reduce this hazard, Admiral William F. Halsey with the immense and terrific U. S. Third Fleet undertook in early October to sever the "pipeline" through which the Philippines fields could be reinforced from the north. He began with a tremendous strike on Okinawa October 10, eliminating that big island for the time being as a staging base for planes and destroying much shipping. He followed this, on October 12, with an air strike against Formosa which, strongly resisted by Japanese air forces, produced the greatest battle that had yet occurred between carrier- and land-based planes. When it was over, the heavy cruiser *Canberra* and the light cruiser *Houston* were severely damaged and the Third Fleet had lost eighty-nine planes, but the Japanese had lost something over 550 planes and hundreds of pilots while suffering major damage to airstrips and installations.

Thus, as the Americans began their move toward the Philippines, Japanese air capabilities over Leyte were but a fraction of what they would have been a few months before, and the Imperial Navy was divided into two widely separated pieces—the First Striking Force at Lingga under the command of Vice Admiral Tokeo Kurita, with Vice Admiral Shoki Nishimura as his principal subordinate; and the so-called Mobile Force in the Inland Sea, Ozawa's crippled command which included all four of the Japanese carriers still able to operate by October. Though these carriers were truly fine ships, and appeared formidable indeed from the air, they were in effect phantom vessels since they were almost wholly without pilots trained to fly from their decks. . . .

But this impotence of Ozawa's carriers is unknown to the U. S. Navy command involved now in the Leyte operation. What *is* known, what has impressed itself on the mind of every high American naval officer, is the blame that has attached to Spruance for the fact that Ozawa's force continues to exist at all. Ozawa should have been destroyed in the Battle of the Philippine Sea. Spruance, it is charged, was overcautious, first, in not permitting Mitscher to sail farther west to seek battle and, second, in not going all-out in hot pursuit when the Japanese began to retire. Spruance himself bears the sting of criticism with equanimity, without rancor, answering with simple reference to the orders under which he operated. Since they assigned him the overriding responsibility of supporting and covering the amphibious operation against Saipan, and since they said nothing about his seeking out and destroying the enemy fleet, he clearly had no right to attempt the latter at serious risk to the former. And the risk, in the light of information available to him, *would* have been serious. "The Japanese often operated with well separated forces, as at Midway and in the South Pacific previously . . ." he will later point out. He, therefore, could not ignore the possibility that one detachment of the enemy would lure him west "while another made a run around our flank and hit our amphibious shipping at Saipan."

The criticism, however, has been more effective than its answer in shaping plans for the now-impending battle. In consequence of it, an ambiguity, dangerous in the circumstances, has been introduced into the operating orders under which Halsey with his Third Fleet is to "support" and "cover" MacArthur's Southwest Pacific Forces "in order to assist in the seizure and occupation of all objectives in the Central Philippines." His orders from Nimitz, in the preparation of which he has had a part, require him not only to "destroy enemy naval and air forces in or threatening the Philippines Area" but also to accept as his "primary task" the destruction "of major portion of enemy fleet" in case the "opportunity" for it is "offered or can be created."[45] It is left entirely to his judgment to decide when or if this "opportunity" occurs. He alone is to decide which of the two assigned tasks is paramount in case a choice must be made between them. He is not required to seek MacArthur's concurrence in, or even to inform MacArthur of, such changes as he may make in his battle plan. . . .

To understand what is now about to happen it is necessary to know something of the geography of this corner of the world. So far as naval action is concerned, Leyte and Samar constitute a single body of land, being divided from one another only by river-narrow and winding San Juanico Strait, both shores of which were secured by U. S. Army troops on October 21—and since Samar is much the larger portion of this single body, Leyte may be deemed an appendage of it, a southwestern arm whose east coast is the western boundary, as Samar's southwestern coast is the eastern boundary, of Leyte Gulf. Separating Leyte from neighboring Dinagat and Mindanao to the east and south is Surigao Strait, running almost due north and south. Separating Samar from the southeastern tip of Luzon to the northwest is San Bernardino Strait, running from the southwest to the northeast. Hence there are three ways by which the Japanese, from their major base at Lingga Roads and their bases in Japan's Inland Sea, may attempt to attack the amphibious shipping jammed into San Pedro Bay. They may attempt to drive directly into the Gulf by slanting southwesterly down from Japan. They may attempt an entrance with equal directness by coming up northeasterly from Lingga through Surigao Strait. Or they may make an indirect approach by coming up from the south or down from the north through the China Sea, thence across the Sibuyan Sea, to pass through San Bernardino Strait. The latter maneuver requires a curve around the east side of Samar, once San Bernardino is passed, in order to enter the Gulf from the east, but it seems to offer more opportunity for surprise than the other approaches. Both Surigao and San Bernardino must therefore be closely watched and guarded; the outside approach from the northeast must be also. And powerful U.S. naval units are in positions to accomplish this on October 24, 1944.

Inside and at the immediate outside entrance to the Gulf, having accomplished its mission of transporting and landing the invasion troops, is the U. S. Seventh Fleet, commanded by Vice Admiral Thomas C. Kinkaid. By the late afternoon of October 24, Kinkaid, operating under MacArthur's direct command, has his fighting ships disposed to guard both the eastern entrance to the Gulf against such Japanese attack force as may come from that direction and the southern entrance, against such attack as may come up from the southwest through Surigao Strait. The latter task is assigned to Rear Admiral J. B. Oldendorf, who has six battleships, four heavy cruisers (one of them Australian), four light cruisers, and twenty-eight destroyers (one of them Australian). Off the Gulf to the east, in three groups fanned out from north to south, is Rear Admiral Thomas L. Sprague's force of sixteen escort carriers (dubbed "baby flattops" or "jeeps" in invidious comparison with ships of the fast carrier units), nine destroyers, and twelve destroyer escorts. This is a far weaker force than Oldendorf commands, of course—but, then, so is the threat it guards against. There seems no possibility whatever that the full weight of a major enemy force can be brought against it.

Far to the north, guarding both San Bernardino Strait and the direct approaches from Japan, is Halsey with his sixty-five ships, including nine great carriers, four light carriers, a half-dozen battleships, four heavy cruisers, a dozen light cruisers, and scores of escort carriers (with replacement planes), destroyers, destroyer escorts, oilers—Halsey with his hundreds of highly trained and intrepid pilots flying planes at least as good as any in the world. Never before has so much far-ranging fire- and bomb-power been concentrated at sea under a single command. Were the Japanese to challenge it with their entire navy they would risk the navy's destruction; to challenge it with only part of the Imperial Fleet, as they must now do if they challenge it at all, would be suicidal. Sprague, having so bristling a mobile wall between himself and the enemy, has little if anything to fear from that direction as he patrols the waters off the Gulf. Or so it seems.

But it does not always happen in war that victory goes to the numerically or physically stronger, else there would be no need for other than routine administrative talents on the part of generals and admirals. Even a strength that is overwhelming, measured solely in quantitative terms, is on occasion defeated by ruse and stratagem. The Japanese have a plan. It was developed in the aftermath of the Marianas campaign, whose political effect in Tokyo was the fall of the Tojo Cabinet and the succession of a Government primarily concerned to find a way out of the increasingly disastrous war. It was developed simultaneously with the bloody (also, in retrospect, needless) American conquest of the Palaus. It was developed by men having no real belief that their war could still be won, though it bears the brave label of SHO-GO (or SHO-1, in this instance), "sho" meaning "to conquer." The spirit bred by extreme adversity permeates it, its courage being that of despair, its nature that of an all-or-nothing gamble. "If we lose the Philippines, even though our Fleet remains intact, it will be of little use to us," says Admiral Toyoda, stating SHO-1's basic premise. "For with the Philippines in enemy hands, our shipping lane to the south will be completely severed. If we draw the Fleet back into Japanese waters, it will be without fuel. If we leave it in the south, it will be without arms and munitions. There is no sense in saving the Fleet at the expense of the loss of the Philippines."[46]

But if born of desperation, SHO-1 has been shaped by shrewd calculation. From Lingga Roads, the First Striking Force, under Kurita, is to sail northeasterly into Brunei Bay on the northwest coast of Borneo. There it is to be divided into two unequal parts, with Nishimura commanding the weaker part and Kurita the stronger. Nishimura, with two battleships, a heavy cruiser, and four destroyers, is to sail north and east through Surigao Strait into Leyte Gulf. Immediately before or after he penetrates the strait he is to be joined by a force coming down through the China Sea from the north, a so-called Second Striking Force, commanded by Vice Admiral Kiyohide Shima and comprising two heavy cruisers, a light cruiser, and some nine destroyers. Meanwhile, Kurita from Brunei is to move to the north, then curve eastward through the Sibuyan Sea, through San Bernardino Strait, and down along Samar's eastern shore to the mouth of Leyte Gulf. Thus if the plan works, a powerful pincers will close on American shipping in the Gulf, annihilating it. Kurita will command a powerful force indeed. Among his five battleships will be the two largest fighting ships in the world, *Yamato* and *Mushashi*, completed in 1942, each displacing 68,000 tons, each armed with 18.1-inch guns, each capable of 27 knots. He will have also ten heavy cruisers, two light cruisers, and ten destroyers.

Powerful as it is, however, it is (of course) no match for Halsey's Third Fleet. How, then, can it be expected to make its way through the Halsey-guarded San Bernardino Strait? The answer, provided by the most ingenious phase of the SHO-1 Plan, is that Halsey is not to be guarding San Bernardino when Kurita arrives at its western entrance. Instead he is to have been lured northward by some very attractive bait, namely Ozawa's Northern (or Mobile) Force with its four carriers, one heavy, three light. Ozawa's role is sacrificial. He is to drive down deliberately within range of Halsey's air searches, inviting total destruction (he expects total destruction) as the price of Kurita's safe passage through San Bernardino. The price is not great, after all. Of what use are aircraft carriers without aircraft? Of what use are planes without pilots?

A complicated plan, surely, as all Japanese plans are, but sustained by a far more accurate intelligence of American intentions and capabilities than the Americans have of the Japanese, and well designed to take advantage of weakness inherent in the divided American command arrangements. In the original planning, B-29s of the Twentieth Air Force, under Major General Curtis E. LeMay, were to support the invasion, but these are not under the supreme command of either Nimitz or MacArthur (LeMay is directly responsible to "Hap" Arnold in Washington) and so cannot be ordered to bomb Lingga Roads or (at least) to reconnoiter it. MacArthur has strongly urged that this be done, but so far it hasn't been. As for direct aid from B-29s over the Philippines, this is no longer possible; for the China bases from which they were to fly, bases for which inadequate ground troop defense was provided, have now been overrun by the Japanese in an offensive provoked by the aggressiveness of Chennault's Fourteenth Air Force, just as Stilwell had feared they would be.†† Hence, without harassment or observation from the air, Kurita has been enabled to sortie from Lingga Roads on October 18 and to divide his Fleet into the two prescribed forces at Brunei Bay, the two sailing from Brunei on October 22. By that time, Shima with his so-called Second Striking Force is coming down inside Formosa on his assigned mission of "support" and "cooperation" with Nishimura's so-called Force "C," as Nishimura sails toward Surigao Strait and Kurita toward San Bernardino. By that time, too, Ozawa with his decoy ships is well down into the Pacific.

And if well designed to take advantage of the American divided command, SHO-1, now under way, is even better designed to take advantage of that psychological characteristic of the Admiral of the U. S. Third Fleet which has caused him to be dubbed "Bull" Halsey.

Let us focus for a moment on this man; his mind and temperament, and the actions rooted in them, are to determine much of what happens in this mighty Battle for Leyte Gulf.

He is, first and last, a fighting man of the sea, worthy descendant of a long line of "seafarers and adventurers, big, violent men, impatient of the law, and prone to strong drink and strong language." (The description is his own.[47]) Among his forebears is one Captain John Halsey, who received his privateer's commission from the Royal Governor of Massachusetts in 1704, whose voyages and battles were essentially piratical, who once engaged four ships at once with his brigantine and emerged victorious with $250,000 in booty, and with whom (significantly) the Third Fleet's admiral feels a special affinity. His Great-grand-

†† See pp. 396 and 437.

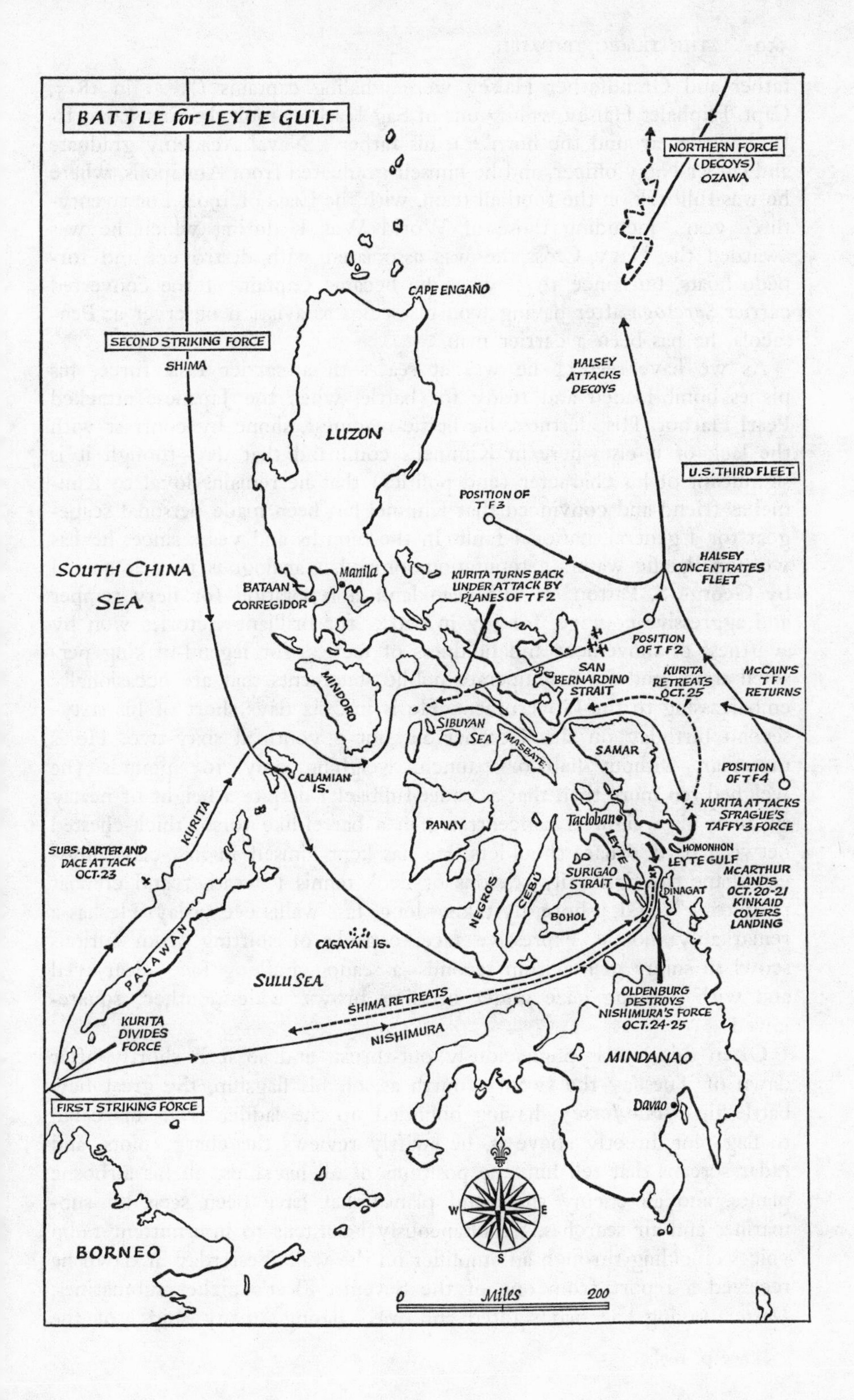

BATTLE for LEYTE GULF
NORTHERN FORCE
(DECOYS)
OZAWA
CAPE ENGAÑO
SECOND STRIKING FORCE
SHIMA
HALSEY
ATTACKS
DECOYS
LUZON
U.S. THIRD FLEET
POSITION OF
T F 3
SOUTH CHINA
SEA
Manila
BATAAN
CORREGIDOR
KURITA TURNS BACK
UNDER ATTACK BY
PLANES OF T F 2
HALSEY
CONCENTRATES
FLEET
POSITION
OF T F 2
SAN
BERNARDINO
STRAIT
KURITA
RETREATS
OCT. 25
McCAIN'S
T F I
RETURNS
MINDORO
SIBUYAN
SEA
MASBATE
SAMAR
POSITION
OF T F 4
CALAMIAN
IS.
KURITA ATTACKS
SPRAGUE'S
TAFFY 3 FORCE
KURITA
PANAY
Tacloban
LEYTE
HOMONHON
LEYTE GULF
SUBS. DARTER AND
DACE ATTACK
OCT. 23
SURIGAO
STRAIT
McARTHUR
LANDS
OCT. 20-21
KINKAID
COVERS
LANDING
NEGROS
CEBU
DINAGAT
BOHOL
CAGAYAN IS.
PALAWAN
SULU SEA
OLDENBURG
DESTROYS
NISHIMURA'S FORCE
OCT. 24-25
SHIMA RETREATS
KURITA
DIVIDES
FORCE
NISHIMURA
MINDANAO
FIRST STRIKING FORCE
Davao
N
W
E
S
BORNEO
0
Miles
200

father and Grandfather Halsey were whaling captains (". . . in 1815, Capt. Eliphalet Halsey, sailing out of Sag Harbor, took the first Long Island whaler around the horn"[48]), his father a Naval Academy graduate and career Navy officer, and he himself graduated from Annapolis, where he was fullback on the football team, with the Class of 1904. For twenty-three years, including those of World War I, during which he was awarded the Navy Cross, he was associated with destroyers and torpedo boats, but since 1935, when he became Captain of the converted carrier *Saratoga* after having won his wings as aviation observer at Pensacola, he has been a carrier man.

As we have seen,‡‡ he was at sea with a carrier task force, his planes bomb-loaded and ready for battle, when the Japanese attacked Pearl Harbor. His alertness, his battle-readiness, shone by contrast with the lack of it elsewhere in Kimmel's command that day—though it is significant of his character (and politics) that he remains loyal to Kimmel as friend and convinced that Kimmel has been made personal scapegoat for a general, national fault. In the months and years since, he has won on Pacific waters a reputation somewhat analogous to that gained by George S. Patton on European land—a reputation for fiery temper and aggressive courage, for joy in battle, for brilliant victories won by swiftness of movement and boldness of tactics, for legend-making personal traits, and for intemperate public statements that are occasionally embarrassing to the Government. He is just six days short of his sixty-second birthday on this October 24, but a youthful sixty-two. He is muscular, without flab or paunch, weighing only 165 pounds (he weighed ten more than that as cadet fullback) despite a height of nearly six feet; his weight is concentrated in a barrel-like torso, thick-chested between hard, square shoulders. He has kept himself in first-class physical shape through daily sessions of deck tennis ("weather and combat permitting") and, ashore, by taking long, fast walks every day. He has a remarkably mobile, expressive face, capable of shifting from furious scowl to sunny grin within seconds—a seadog, bulldog face—clear-eyed and with piercing gaze under beetling brows, wide-mouthed, square-jawed.

Often this jaw is pugnaciously out-thrust, and so it is shortly after dawn of Tuesday the twenty-fourth as, on his flagship, the great new battleship *New Jersey*, having bounded up the ladder from his cabin to flag plot directly above it, he swiftly reviews the charts, plots, and radar screens that tell him the positions of all his ships, all his airborne planes, and all enemy ships and planes that have been seen by submarines and air searches. Simultaneously he listens to intermittent radio voices crackling through an amplifier on the wall. Yesterday at dawn he received a report from one of the Seventh Fleet's picket submarines, *Darter*, saying she had sighted and was chasing "many ships" of the

‡‡ See p. 109.

enemy, including three "probable" battleships down near the southwestern tip of the Philippines. Later, off Palawan, the westernmost of the major Philippine islands, *Darter* and her sister submarine *Dace* attacked what is in fact (as we know) Kurita's Center Force, sinking two heavy cruisers and severely damaging a third. Halsey by then had ordered three of his task groups to close on the eastern shores of the Philippines and from there, at dawn today, send out air searches covering the whole of the western sea approaches to the island chain. So far there are no reports. The admiral descends to his breakfast. He enters the large messroom that adjoins the small office he shares with Rear Admiral R. B. Carney, who is his Chief of Staff, and as he does so all his staff officers, seated at the oblong table, rise to their feet. They always do, and always he says, as now: "Sit down, goddammit! How many times do I have to tell you?"[49] He is again in flag plot when, at 8:20, a thin, sputtering voice comes out of the amplifier, speaking the words he has been waiting to hear: "Four battleships, eight cruisers, thirteen destroyers off southern tip Mindoro Island, course 050, speed 10 to 12 knots . . ." Kurita is sailing eastward between Mindoro and Panay into the Sibuyan Sea! Within minutes Halsey, whose flagship is part of Rear Admiral Gerald F. Bogan's Task Group Two off the eastern entrance to San Bernardino Strait, has ordered Task Group Three (Rear Admiral Frederick C. Sherman), to the north of him off Luzon, and Task Group Four (Rear Admiral Ralph E. Davison), to the south of him off Samar, to move toward him at their best speed, meanwhile launching their planes for strikes upon Kurita's ships. A little later he orders Task Group One (Vice Admiral John S. McCain), heading for replenishment at Ulithi in the Carolines, to reverse course, fuel at sea, and come to him as quickly as possible.

For Halsey is now convinced that the Japanese Navy—which had not been expected to fight hard for Leyte, which had been expected to reserve its "big punch" for the defense of Luzon—is committed to an all-out effort, providing him with that golden "opportunity" which, according to his written orders, makes destruction "of major portion of enemy fleet" his "primary task." He is confirmed in this when he learns, a little after nine o'clock, that two Japanese battleships, a heavy cruiser, and accompanying destroyers have been sighted in the Sulu Sea (this, as we know, is Nishimura's Force C)—and learns also, a little before noon, that another Japanese force of two heavy cruisers, a light cruiser, and four destroyers has been sighted, heading south, near the Cagayan Islands. Now, if he could only find the Japanese carriers! All day long, as he receives one report after another of battle in the Sibuyan Sea—and of battle to the north of him, off Luzon—he wonders and worries about the location of the Jap carriers. Where the carriers are, there will be, in his conviction, the main body of the Japanese Fleet.

Third Fleet planes make five separate strikes that day upon Kurita's ships in the Sibuyan Sea—the first at 10:45 in the morning, the last at around four o'clock in the afternoon—with 259 planes participating in them, circling and diving through intense but inaccurate anti-aircraft fire (Kurita has no air cover) to drop bombs, launch torpedoes, strafe decks with machine gun fire. All save eighteen of them return, bearing glad tidings to Halsey's ears. Mighty *Mushashi*, she of the 18.1-inch guns, world's largest battleship, has been sunk, and so have been three cruisers and a destroyer! Other vessels have been severely damaged. Kurita, after milling around aimlessly for a time, has turned southwest in (it appears) full retreat.

Less cheerful is news from the north, off Luzon, where Japanese land-based planes, fifty or sixty of them, have Sherman's Group Three under attack at almost the very moment when Sherman is receiving Halsey's orders to move south. The light carrier *Princeton*, bombstruck, is set afire, suffers internal explosions, and must at last be abandoned and sunk. But even from the north the news is not all bad—may even be deemed, on the whole, good—since the Japanese pay heavily for their success with *Princeton* and score no others while losing, in their three attacks of four or five dozen planes each, not less than 110 planes they can ill afford to lose, with pilots they can even less afford to lose.

All this has caused Halsey virtually to dismiss from his mind by late afternoon a dispatch issued by him hours earlier—a dispatch he regards, not as an executive order, but as a battle plan to become effective (at his specific direction) in case Kurita, despite the Sibuyan Sea mauling, manages to pass through San Bernardino Strait. The language of the dispatch, however, is misleading. Four fast battleships (including *New Jersey*) are named; so are two heavy cruisers, three light cruisers, fourteen destroyers; and these ships "will be formed" into Task Force 34 under Vice Admiral Willis A. Lee, Jr., and "will engage decisively at long ranges." So says the dispatch.[50] Kinkaid and Sprague of the Seventh Fleet, whose radios intercept the message, interpret it as definite assurance that Lee will be standing guard on the morrow at the eastern opening of San Bernardino. They have need of such assurance. As the afternoon wanes, Kinkaid especially has enough to occupy his mind, surely. A Japanese air raid on Tacloban air strip, uncomfortably near his flagship's anchorage, has set a fuel dump afire. Nishimura, approaching Sarigao Strait, will certainly try to force a passage in the night. Oldendorf, deployed for heavy night action at the eastern entrance of Surigao, is short of ammunition—especially of AP (armor-piercing)—and a night action, in any case, is tricky. Well it is that Kinkaid need not add Kurita to his anxieties, thanks to Halsey.

But Halsey's thoughts have now turned almost wholly from the west to the north. Indeed, a good half of them have been ranging northward throughout the long, action-crowded day. Where, *where* are the Jap carriers? The question, unanswered by the air search that has been proceeding in wide sweeps over the ocean north and east of Luzon, has grown increasingly urgent—has become a source of fuming impatience in Halsey's cramped office—as the sun sinks down the western sky. It is nearly dusk before the answer comes—three enemy carriers, two light crusiers, three destroyers, sighted in a position two hundred miles east of the northeastern tip of Luzon! No doubt there are other vessels, too, in this force, all coming down toward the central Philippines at the leisurely speed of fifteen knots. Halsey has no intention of waiting for them, *à la* Spruance. "Experience had taught us that if we interfered with a Jap plan before it matured, we stood a good chance of disrupting it," he will later explain. "The Jap mind is inelastic; it cannot adapt itself to an altered situation." And he is convinced that he now knows what the Jap plan is—knows the meaning of all those complicated movements by initially widely scattered forces. The slow speed of all of them, never more than fifteen knots, indicates a rigid time schedule. Center Force, Southern Force, Northern Force must plan to rendezvous tomorrow off Samar and then, as a single powerful force, proceed to slaughter the ships in San Pedro Bay, with ultimately disastrous effect on the troops landed on Leyte. Well, Center Force has been so enfeebled by this day's action as to constitute no longer a serious threat. Southern Force is far too weak to get by Oldendorf. It remains for Halsey to take care of Northern Force which is, he is sure, the main body—far stronger than either of the other two—and whose air strength will be supplemented by land-based planes. He may well accomplish the final destruction of Japanese sea power if he strikes with all his force.

He climbs at once the ladder to flag plot.

"Here's where we're going," he says to his Chief of Staff, pointing to Northern Force's charted position. "Mick, start them north."[51]

And Carney begins at once to send out the orders.

There are high officers in Third Fleet who doubt the wisdom of this move, and indicate as much. Some of them remember a Japanese manual on naval tactics, translated and circulated by U. S. Naval Intelligence the previous summer, in which a "gambit strategy" using a decoy fleet built around carriers had been thoroughly discussed. Admiral Lee is convinced that Northern Force is precisely such a decoy and that Center Force's seeming retirement is a temporary maneuver, to be followed by a turnabout toward and through San Bernardino Strait. He sends a visual signal to this effect from his flagship *Washington* to Halsey in *New Jersey* in the last light of day. He receives acknowledgment of its receipt, nothing more. Admiral Bogan, informed by plane reports that Center Force has indeed turned around, that it is now heading east again—informed also that navigation lights in San Bernardino, hitherto blacked out at night, are now lit—believes that Third Fleet should be divided. Only Task Groups Three and Four should go north, in his opinion; they are more than strong enough to overwhelm Ozawa's reported strength. His, Bogan's, own carriers should remain off San Bernardino to cover Lee's Battle Line which, as per Halsey's preparatory dispatch of yesterday, should now be formed. But when Bogan communicates his reconnaissance information to *New Jersey* he is told with brusque impatience that Halsey already has it, whereupon he concludes that Halsey, with all facts in hand, must already have thought through the situation and rejected the proposal he, Bogan, would otherwise make.

But has Halsey truly *thought through?* Would it not be more accurate to say that, as befits his soubriquet, he now *bulls through*—head down, charging—just as he will later bullheadedly insist against all the evidence that he makes no mistake in doing so? Tomorrow night, when the battle is over and he suffers anxieties (though he'll never admit it) over the part he has played, he will say in a dispatch to Nimitz and MacArthur that it seemed to him "childish . . . to guard statically San Bernardino"[52] in view of his pilots' reports of the damage done Center Force. But shouldn't his considerable experience have encouraged in him a healthy skepticism as to the accuracy of pilots' battle reports? Is it not a general rule that aviators overestimate the damage they inflict? Halsey, impatient to seize golden "opportunity," believes what he *wants* to believe. He is like Patton in this—that where other men decide to act, with interval great or small between decision and action, he (like Patton) decides by acting, fusing the two processes into one. And these acts that *are* decisions often produce battle victories that might be lost by more forethoughtful, calculating, prudent men.

But it is the defect of such warrior virtue that is demonstrated this night and next morning. Halsey drives northward at best speed with sixty-four ships against Ozawa's mere seventeen—with nine large carriers and four light ones, their decks loaded with planes, as compared with Ozawa's single large carrier and three light ones, all of whose decks are virtually planeless—leaving behind not so much as a single destroyer to watch the eastern mouth of San Bernardino. And as he does so he uses radar-equipped night-flying planes off carrier *Independence* to find Ozawa for him in the dark. This enables him to launch his first strikes at dawn on October 25. But it also deprives Kinkaid's Seventh Fleet of the means of finding in night's darkness the forces of Nishimura and Shima approaching Surigao Strait, and of keeping track of Kurita as he approaches and passes through San Bernardino.

Not until Nishimura's lead ships run head-on into a darting screen of PT boats, flung out for that purpose at the southern entrance to Surigao, is Oldendorf informed of his enemy's precise whereabouts—this at an hour before midnight. Oldendorf is not surprised, of course. He has had ample warning and is waiting—he has been waiting since before dark—in position to execute the classic naval maneuver known as "crossing the T," probably for the last time in history. Nishimura brushes past the PT boats, unslowed and undamaged, but is then a perfect target for the vastly superior American forces. Destroyers engage him in early morning darkness, when he is well inside the strait, and hurt him badly with torpedoes. Battleship *Fuso* and three destroyers are sunk or left in sinking condition, while battleship *Yamashiro*, Nishimura's flagship, is damaged. But still the Japanese push on in column to form the base of the "T" whose crossbar is formed by Oldendorf's six battleships and eight cruisers (four heavy, four light) steaming back and forth across the northern mouth of the strait. At 3:51 o'clock, the cruisers open a devastating converging fire upon the Japanese ships, followed minutes later by fire from the battleships—a fire to which Nishimura, outgunned and outmaneuvered, can make no effective reply. Within half an hour, *Yamashiro* has capsized and gone down, carrying to their deaths Nishimura and all save a handful of her crew. The heavy cruiser *Mogami*, furiously burning, is fleeing northward, to be finished off in the pursuit phase of the battle—the only phase in which aircraft participate—after daylight has come.

And what of Shima who, with his Second Striking Force, was supposed to join Nishimura in this battle? He arrives in the lower portion of the strait after the slaughter of Nishimura has begun. Seeing the furious lightning of battle on the horizon and hearing its ominous thunder as he passes what he takes to be two burning Japanese ships (actually it is *Fuso*, split in two, both halves burning), he decides abruptly, in most un-Japanese fashion, that discretion is the better part of valor. He retires in haste, his sole contributions to the action being the firing of eight torpedoes at a couple of tiny islands (he sees them on his radar screen as two large ships) and the ramming of damaged *Mogami* with his heavy cruiser *Nachi* as he makes his 180-degree turn from north to south. Next day he loses a light cruiser and two destroyers to air attack but manages to escape with two heavy cruisers and three destroyers.

Of the Japanese Southern Force, then, when the Surigao Strait action has ended, a single destroyer survives; the total Japanese losses include two battleships, a heavy cruiser, a light cruiser, five destroyers, and many thousands of lives. Of Oldendorf's ships, on the other hand, a single destroyer has suffered damage, and that not so serious but what the ship will be ready for further action in the spring. Only thirty-nine Americans have been killed, 114 wounded. . . .

But if Oldendorf is not surprised by the enemy on the night of October 24, T. L. Sprague certainly *is* surprised at dawn on October 25. He is doubly surprised. He has divided his force into three task units, dubbed Taffy 1, Taffy 2, Taffy 3—the first operating in the south off Mindanao, the second in the center off the mouth of Leyte Gulf, the third in the north off Samar—and Kurita is actually within gunfire range of Taffy 3 before the Americans have the slightest inkling that the Japanese have traversed an ungarded strait. That's one surprise. The other is that Kurita's firepower and speed are immensely greater than they should be, on the basis of yesterday's carrier plane reports to Halsey. Actually, as we now know, *Mushashi* has gone down in the Sibuyan Sea, as reported; but it is *not* true that three Japanese cruisers and a destroyer have also been sunk, as reported. Kurita, debouching from San Bernardino, still has four battleships, including *Mushashi's* sister ship *Yamato* with her 18.1-inch guns; he has six heavy cruisers, two light cruisers, some ten destroyers; and his speed, supposed to be drastically reduced by the damage done such of his ships as are left afloat, has evidently been impaired slightly, if at all, else he could hardly have covered (as he has covered) nearly 150 miles through treacherous waters in the last seven hours. The American situation is desperate. Taffy 3, commanded by cool, calm, quiet and iron-nerved Rear Admiral Clifton A. F. Sprague§§ consists of five small escort carriers having a top speed of seventeen knots, each mounting a single 5-inch 38 ("Open fire with the pea-shooters when range is clear," is one of Clifton Sprague's early orders in this battle[53]), screened by three destroyers and four destroyer escorts—a force so meager and slow that Kurita has only to form battle line in order to blast it out of and under the waves with his battleships and cruisers.

But he doesn't do it.

Fortunately for the Americans, Kurita is as surprised by this sudden encounter as they are—though why he should have been in the circumstances is hard to understand—and Clifton Sprague's prompt, superaggressive response to his appearance encourages Kurita's belief that the opposing force is immensely larger than it truly is. He even fears he has run head-on into a major portion of the Third Fleet when Sprague at once turns his carrier escorts into the east wind, launches every available plane for strikes on the enemy, has every ship make smoke, and sends his three destroyers and a destroyer escort forward in a torpedo and gunfire attack that, inflicting grave damage on two heavy cruisers that are also damaged from the air, is as gallant an action as any in American naval annals. It is a good day for smoke screens, the air heavy, humid; and under cover of smoke the Americans, different units of them at different times, run into a rain squall whose curtain of heavy mist, dropped down to the sea, obscures them wholly for from ten to fifteen minutes. This is providential, in the American view. For Kurita, with imperfect radar and no planes, must depend on direct surface sightings for his information as to his opponent's strength and disposition. At moment of first sighting, he begins to suffer a failure of nerve. His ships are in the midst of executing an earlier order to deploy from cruising formation (in column) to anti-aircraft formation (in circle) when, as if frantic, he orders a general attack, throwing everything into confusion. All formation lost, all visibility lost for crucial periods, the Japanese attack is delivered piecemeal, chaotically, dissipating the advantage that Kurita's overwhelmingly superior firepower and speed would have given him had he formed his big ships in line. Moreover, he employs armor-piercing shells designed for use against thick-skinned battleships and cruisers, and these rip through the thin skins of Sprague's ships in many cases without exploding, inflicting only minor damage. This is indeed

§§ No relation to his namesake senior officer, Thomas L. Sprague.

lucky for the Americans. Every one of Taffy 3's ships is repeatedly struck during the wild melee that follows, but only one of the half-dozen escort carriers goes down; two of Sprague's three destroyers and one of his four destroyer escorts are sunk—the price of their highly effective gallantry.

For two and a half hours the confused running fight continues, with Taffy 3 aided by planes launched from Taffy 2 and Taffy 1, the planes often making "dry runs" (that is, without bombs or torpedoes) on enemy ships in order to divert fire from their own. By the end of that time, incredible though it seems, three Japanese heavy cruisers have been so severely damaged they must be abandoned and sunk; another has been so badly hurt she is forced to withdraw from the battle; and most of Sprague's ships are still afloat. Nevertheless, Kurita still has four battleships, two light cruisers, and seven destroyers—more than enough to blast his way through Clifton Sprague and the two "Taffies" behind Sprague, if only he uses them properly. He doesn't. His nerve now fails him utterly. At 9:25, to the Americans' profound astonishment and even more profound relief, he abruptly breaks off the action and retires out of gunfire range. "I could not believe my eyes . . ." Clifton Sprague will later write. ". . . it took a whole series of reports from circling planes to convince me. And still I could not get the fact to soak into my battle-numbed brain. At best, I had expected to be swimming by this time."

Meanwhile, to the south, Japanese land-based planes have unveiled a new and ominous tactic, born of desperation but possessed of a deadly effectiveness. . . .

Japan now lacks means and time to train replacements for the skilled pilots that have been killed by the hundred in battle; there *is* time enough to train men in the relatively simple maneuver of approaching and crash-diving an enemy ship in a bomb-loaded plane, the pilot serving as the living-and-dying instrumentation of a guided missile. As a matter of fact, there are young Japanese airmen already sufficiently trained to do this, and willing to volunteer for such suicidal duty. Accordingly, Vice Admiral Takyjiro Ohnishi, commander of Japan's First Air Fleet, headquartered in Manila, has formed a special suicide attack corps, calling it "kamikaze" after the "heavenly wind" which (according to Japanese account) intervened to swamp a Mongol fleet bent on invading Japan from Korea in 1281—and at 7:40, a half-dozen planes from this corps come in upon Taffy 1 off Mindanao. Four of them manage to go into the planned-for fatal dives and two of them score hits, inflicting serious damage on two escort carriers and causing many casualties. This, the first kamikaze attack of the war is swiftly followed by the second, with battered Taffy 3 as its target. Shortly before 11 A.M., an hour and a half after Kurita has broken off the main action, five kamikaze planes come in upon Clifton Sprague's ships, diving from around five thousand feet to strike four of his remaining five escort carriers, sinking one of them and damaging two others.

Ominous indeed! The new tactic, difficult to guard against, threatens to become the most damaging that Japanese airmen have employed against American ships and sailors since Pearl Harbor.[54]

At 12:36, after circling indecisively for three hours during which he receives false report (believing it true) that an enemy task force is near enough in the northeast to engage him before he reaches San Bernardino, even if he starts north at once, Kurita confesses defeat—confesses it in words sent Admiral Toyoda in Tokyo: "First Striking Force has abandoned penetration of Leyte anchorage. Is proceeding north searching for enemy task force. Will engage decisively, then pass through San Bernardino Strait."[55] He is influenced in this decision by news of Nishimura's disaster in Surigao Strait, by Shima's message (sent at 4:25 in the morning) that he is retiring from Surigao, by the false report already referred to, by his belief that American-held Tacloban airstrip is now operational, and by his continued vast overestimation of the strength of the force that has engaged him. (His staff officers see Sprague's destroyers as heavy cruisers, the slow escort carriers as big carriers with a speed of thirty knots; they even see a Pennsylvania-class battleship among these alleged "fast carriers"!)

But Kurita is also and at least equally influenced by the presumed effect of certain messages relayed to him by the Japanese communications center on Formosa, which has intercepted them. They are Kinkaid's calls for help from Halsey sent out after Kurita's sudden, unexpected appearance before Taffy 3. Some of them have been dispatched "in the clear" (that is, in plain English, uncoded)—a fact evincing urgency, even desperation. Obviously Kinkaid does not know where important elements of the Third Fleet are. Does this mean that the bait offered by Ozawa's carriers in the north has been accepted? Perhaps. On the other hand, if the lure had worked, Ozawa would certainly have come under attack hours ago and would have told Kurita so. No such information has been received. (Later it will be learned that Ozawa sent three important messages to Kurita on Octobor 24 and 25, the last of them telling of an attack upon him by Task Force 38 of the Third Fleet. Due to a faulty radio transmitter, none was received.) Hence, from Kurita's point of view, the only certainty about Kinkaid's cry for help is that it will be answered as promptly, as powerfully as possible—is no doubt in process of being answered at the present moment—which is to say that heavy air blows of the kind that hurt him yesterday in the Sibuyan Sea may soon fall upon him. . . .

As for the commander of the Third Fleet, what effect have Kinkaid's pleas had upon him? What actions do they provoke?

Let us go back in time (to 6:45 this morning) and northward in space (to a point some two hundred miles east of Luzon's Cape Encanto), focusing again on Admiral "Bull" Halsey, aboard the battleship *New Jersey*. He has ordered Task Force 34 to form under Lee and station itself ten miles ahead (or north) of his carriers from which, at 6:30, he has launched his first strike. He has just begun to "sweat it out," impatiently awaiting news he cannot expect to receive for at least an hour and a half from his planes winging their way toward Ozawa's ships, when a dispatch from Kinkaid is handed to him. "Am engaging enemy surface forces Surigao Strait," the dispatch says, then asks a disturbing question: "Is TF 34 guarding San Bernardino Strait?" Halsey at once surmises that Kinkaid has misconstrued the "preparatory dispatch" concerning Battle Line issued by Halsey yesterday, at once tries to soothe the sudden nagging worry about his own responsibility by blaming Kinkaid (yesterday's dispatch "was not addressed to him, which fact alone should have prevented his confusion"), at once replies "negative" to Kinkaid's question ("[TF 34] is with our carriers now engaging enemy carriers"),[56] and then tries to dismiss the matter from his mind as he continues to wait, and wait, and *wait* for the first report from his attacking planes. Before it arrives he has received a second dispatch from Kinkaid telling of enemy retreat from Surigao Strait and then, at 8:22, a third dispatch that is disturbing indeed: "Enemy BBS and cruiser reported firing on TV 22.4.3"—this last being Clifton Sprague's Taffy 3. Center Force, then, has come down undetected out of San Bernardino! Eight minutes later comes Kinkaid's fourth dispatch: "Urgently need fast BBS Leyte Gulf at once." Whereupon Halsey, sensing that he is being bitterly blamed (as indeed he is) for the dangerous situation in the south, unadmittedly aware too that the danger *does* stem from his pell-mell all-out drive to the north, grows angry. He now conceives his assigned mission to have been a wholly offensive one ("It was not my job to protect the Seventh Fleet"), and is convinced that he is now "rushing to intercept a force which gravely threatens not only Kinkaid and myself, but the whole Pacific strategy."[57] He is in any case too far to the north to be of any immediate assistance in the emergency to the south. All he can do, and does do, is order McCain's Task Group One, then fueling to the east of him, to "strike enemy" in the designated location at "best possible speed." He notifies Kinkaid that this has been done. Then he receives from the Seventh Fleet's admiral a fifth dispatch, saying that the attacking force of Samar consists of four battleships and eight cruisers "plus others" and making a double request—that "Lee [Battle Line commander] cover Leyte at top speed" and that "fast carriers make immediate strike." Halsey's anger increases. Where the hell is Oldendorf with his battleships and cruisers? Why aren't they rushing to Sprague's aid? Part of the answer comes to him in a sixth dispatch from Kinkaid, saying that Oldendorf's ships are "low in ammunition." But this does nothing to mollify him.

For now reports have begun to come in of the plane strike on Ozawa, and they indicate to him that he may annihilate the Japanese main body within the next four hours or so if only he is let alone. Already one Japanese carrier is reported sunk and two others badly damaged, along with a light cruiser. Before noon, what is left of the Japanese Fleet will come under the 16-inch guns of Lee's Battle Line, if present course and speed are held, and the Japanese will then be lucky if so much as a single ship survives the slaughter. It is exasperating to a nearly maddening degree to receive at such a moment (at 10 A.M.) a plain-English dispatch from Kinkaid saying: "Where is Lee? Send Lee." And exasperated anger becomes actual madness a few minutes later when Halsey reads a dispatch, not from Kinkaid, but from CINCPAC himself, Admiral Nimitz in Pearl Harbor, saying in words Halsey regards as personally insulting: "The whole world wants to know where is Task Force 34?" Flicked thus with verbal whip on a raw spot of his ego, Third Fleet's admiral snatches his cap from his head, throws it on the deck, and shouts obscenities at the top of his bull-roaring voice until Carney rushes over to him, grasping his arm and crying: "Stop it! What the hell's the matter with you? Pull yourself together!"[58]

Only with great nerve-straining effort can Halsey do so.

Even then he does not at once change course. Lee's advancing Battle Line is permitted to reach a point only forty-two miles from Ozawa, all of whose carriers afloat are now dead in the water, before (at 11:15) he is ordered to reverse course. What is to become known as the "Battle of Bull's Run" then begins. Two of Third Fleet's Task Groups are left in the north to finish off Ozawa (his total losses will be four carriers, a light cruiser, two destroyers sunk; four battleships, two light carriers, four destroyers damaged), while Halsey races southward with Lee's Battle Line and Bogan's carrier group to join forces with McCain, arriving off San Bernardino in the early morning darkness of October 26, several hours too late to block Kurita's retreat. . . .

Next day, planes from Bogan's and McCain's carrier groups repeatedly attack Center Force's retreating ships, sinking a light cruiser and seriously damaging a heavy one, but by nightfall of October 26, when the last action of this great Battle for Leyte Gulf has ended, most of Kurita's ships—including four battleships, a half-dozen crusiers, and ten destroyers—have made their escape. It is for the Japanese a small consolation. They still have a fleet-in-being of sorts—American planners of future battles in the far Pacific will not be able wholly to ignore it—but it is no longer capable of a major fleet action. Japan's days as a major sea power are ended.

Statistics measure the lopsidedness, the crushing nature of her defeat in this single far-flung three-day four-part battle. Of the sixty-four Japanese ships engaged, twenty-eight have been sunk, including three battleships, a large carrier, three light carriers, six heavy cruisers, four light cruisers, and eleven destroyers. Of the 216 American ships engaged, only six have been sunk, all of them small, including a light carrier, two escort carriers, two destroyers, and a destroyer escort.[59]

XV

To the End in Germany

i. *In a Dark Wood . . .*

It is said that a single American soldier in the Ardennes on December 19, 1944, at the deliberate expense of his own life, stopped a panzer thrust which, had it not been stopped at that time and place, might have enabled the Germans to reach if not cross the Meuse.

The story is perhaps apocryphal.

The soldier's name was never learned . . .

So call him Earnest. Call him Sergeant Earnest Morehead of a certain platoon of a certain company of, let us say, a battalion of the 119th Infantry Regiment in the 30th Division.

He is (let us say) a young man very different in almost every trait of character from the George who "did it," and died doing it, on Guadalcanal two years ago.* He is six feet tall, slenderly built, not quite skinny (though "Skinny" was his nickname in junior high), whereas George was of medium height and stocky, inclined toward plumpness. Though only twenty-four, just four years older than George was in 1942, he is worriedly aware that his black hair is already thin and receding, whereas George's was a thick mop of brown. His attitude toward other people tends to be tense and withdrawn, in contrast to George's relaxed gregariousness—and where George naturally inclined to take things easy, Earnest as naturally inclines to take things hard. He is complicatedly self-conscious. He is unable to feel himself very often as a single simple identity in a single simple location, but instead feels himself multiple, as one who operates on several levels that are not parallel but tilt into one another to make jagged slashes, rough discontinuities of being. Often he is literally beside himself, watching himself critically and passing harsh

* See pp. 301–9.

judgments—which is to say his self-consciousness is of a kind that breeds the opposite of self-love, self-pride, even self-respect.

Yet he knows he possesses certain innate faculties of intellect, of imagination that are graded "superior" by the standards of the world he chiefly lived in, from grade school through college, before he entered the Army three years ago. He cannot help knowing it, since the exercise of these faculties in the past has repeatedly won for him prizes, medals, scholarships, and a favorable publicity. But he can and does often wonder if his kind of intellect and imagination are not fatal hazards to "success" in the cruelly real (or is it unreal?) world he now inhabits. They are certainly sources of weakness in this world insofar as they prevent his ready acceptance of martial values and ambitions, inhibit his unquestioning obedience to authority. For instance, he was urged to enter OCS following boot camp. He stubbornly refused, partly because he felt himself unsuited to wielding even a shavetail's authority but mostly because he had conscientious objections to the Army caste system which, in its actual workings, identifies the corrupting pleasures of special privilege with the harsh necessities of command. Or so he believes.

On the other hand, he is aware that, in terms of his present job, not all is weakness that derives from his kind of intellectual imagination. At least two major strengths are developed by it. One is that he knows far more of what this war against Nazi Germany is about, far more of the nature of the enemy, than nine out of ten of his comrades in arms, and his knowledge sustains absolutely his conviction that if ever a war was morally justified and historically necessary, given the conditions that prevailed in 1939–42, this of the Allies is. It is justified, it is necessary in a negative sense: Hitler's Germany must be utterly, ruthlessly crushed in order to maintain the possibility of human decency in the world, and also for the assuagement of outraged natural moral feelings which, unassuaged, might die of their exacerbations. He, Earnest Morehead, who once considered himself a pacifist, equating "evil" with "sickness" (one doesn't hate the sick for their sickness, does one?), has hated Nazis with a deadly hatred, has taken actual pleasure in his imagined self's shooting down the SS guards of concentration camps, long before he donned the uniform he now wears. And this has given him courage in battle. At Mortain, told that the German troops attacking his outnumbered rifle platoon were of an SS regiment, he had felt a cold fury rise in him to counteract the heat, the terror of battle, and had had no wish to run away when his unit was outflanked right and left. He had wanted only to see Germans in his rifle sights as they entered the field before him and had taken a fierce joy in knocking them down with his fire, at least three of them, when they did appear. By his example he had held his squad in place, what remained of it (casualties among the rifle platoons were appalling that day), until the flanks were again secure.

The second major strength relates to the first insofar as his intellectual imagination enables him to be "philosophical"—"philosophical" in the vulgar as in the technical meaning of the term. He has a sense of the mainstream of history as a natural flow-of-world (the Nazis interrupt it; the Nazis must be destroyed) guided by principles of justice that are in natural balance (the Nazis upset it; the Nazis must be destroyed) and from which meaningful patterns emerge for those who can mentally detach themselves from it and view it realistically from a distance. Thus he sees significance in—he even derives a certain excitement from—activities and observations that are wholly meaningless to most of his comrades, and boring to them; and he can maintain a quite high morale during the long morale-erosive periods of "wait" that almost invariably follow the urgent "hurry up!" of the Army.

Latterly, as his outfit rests in the flat, featureless German border countryside not far from Aachen, and as the first snows of December transform the landscape into an abstract pattern of black and white under a gray monotone of sky, he has been idly pondering, in terms of his experience of war, the dichotomies of chaos and order, chance and purpose, freedom and necessity. He has been wondering if the difference between these seeming opposites may not be simply a difference of perspective—the difference, say, between the view of battle taken by a soldier in the front line and that taken by the commanding general far to the rear. At the front, often, all is chaos and confusion, a wild welter of chance occurrences that present to the individual soldier a multitude of free choices. Communications suddenly break down; the soldier does not know where he is in relation to his comrades. An enemy tank suddenly appears where one's own tanks are supposed to be. A flanking fire suddenly pours in from a position held ten minutes before by one's own side. The soldier, feeling himself all alone in the terrible deathly solitude of the battlefield, may do any one (or two, or three) of several different things. He may stay where he is, passively huddled down behind such cover as is available. He may stay where he is while actively exposing himself in order to fire upon those shadowy, menacing figures that flit among the trees over there. He may dodge to the left or right in search of a better position from which to fight. He may beat an orderly retreat; he may panic and run away.

But how differently it all appears—how different it all *is*—to the commanding general! To the extent that accurate information flows swiftly and abundantly into his headquarters, the battle has for the general a clear and definite design. Its movements are an active balancing of discrete, coherent, measurable forces. Turning to the wall map in his war room, with its penciled lines, its flagged pins, he can comprehend it all at a glance. Chaos becomes the substance of order, chance is revealed as the working disguise of purpose, and freedom (an individual quality, wholly unpredictable) is transformed into necessity (a statistical quantity, perfectly predictable within calculable limits)—all this merely by enlarging the perspective, by shifting from the close and narrow view to the view that is distant and wide.

Earnest Morehead had been initially led into this pondering a few weeks ago when he read, in some magazine or other, a retrospective "think-piece" about the action in which the 30th Division, and his particular outfit in that Division, have thus far chiefly distinguished themselves. The article eulogized the "command courage" displayed by Omar Bradley early last August when he decided not to divert strength from Patton's Third Army, then beginning its wide swing from Brittany toward Le Mans, in order to contain the German Seventh Army, then beginning its drive through the hills of Mortain toward the sea. After a swift but careful calculation of relative strengths, Bradley concluded that Major General Leland S. Hobbs' 30th Division, though under great pressure, would be able to "hold the hinge" at Mortain while Patton made his full-force, full-speed flanking drive to the east.[1] But of what did these calculated "relative strengths" consist? It had given Earnest Morehead something of a start to realize that they included not only such countable tangibles as troops, arms, ammunition, planes, tanks, but also such intangibles as his, Earnest Morehead's personal morale—his courage, or that hateful determination to kill SS beasts which amounted to courage. In effect, Bradley had predicted that he, Earnest Morehead, would stand firm and hold his squad in line at the moment of maximum danger—for the issue at Mortain had been very narrowly decided, it was nip and tuck all through that opening day of the battle, and had any one small unit given way the whole line might have been shattered by a panzer-exploited breakthrough. Morehead himself could not have predicted what he would do at the crucial juncture. In precise anticipation of the danger he would be in, he would have placed no heavy bet upon his response to it, one way or the other. . . .

What has chiefly interested and even excited Earnest Morehead about this has been its suggestion that the ancient philosophic question of free will (is it "real" or "illusion"?)—a question at the heart of the *versus* between idealism and materialism, vitalism and mechanism, individualism and collectivism—may be as phoney as the question of whether the library table at home is composed of atoms or of oak. And this suggestion has been strengthened in his mind by a visit made on a two-day pass to nearby Spa, from which he is now returning.

The famous peacetime resort of the wealthy "international set," with its salt baths, its magnificient casino and hotels amidst the low, rolling hills of Aachen, is now headquarters of the U. S. First Army, of which the 30th Division had formerly been a part. (The Division is now a part of the U. S. Ninth Army and is, at the moment, in the Ninth's reserve area.) Sergeant Earnest Morehead went there to visit, in mild violation of regulations against the fraternization of officers and enlisted men, a captain with whom he had roomed while at Amherst and who is now among the few, and by far the closest, of his intimate friends. The captain, now in G-2 of Lieutenant General Courtney H. Hodges' staff, has his full share of the alarmist tendencies, the continuous worries about security, that are characteristic of Intelligence officers. It was therefore significant of the respectful trust as well as affection he has for his college roommate (he has both admired and deplored Morehead's refusal to accept an officer's commission) that on a late afternoon in plush Hotel Britannique where Hodges is headquartered (night fell through chill mist upon the street outside; blackout curtains were drawn then across the windows; great crystal chandeliers glittered in electric light), he pulled out from a table drawer and spread upon a table top a map showing the disposition of Allied troops along the front from the Colmar pocket in the south to the Lower Rhine opposite Arnhem in the north—showing, too, the disposition of German troops facing them insofar as this was known or could be surmised—and explained what these dispositions mean in terms of over-all Allied strategy.

In the south, curving around the troublesome salient of Colmar and running northward for some fifty miles along the west bank of the Rhine, then turning at a sharp angle to run northwestward along the German border for another fifty miles, is the line held by American Lieutenant General Jacob L. Devers' Sixth Army Group, comprising the French First Army (General Jean de Lattre de Tassigny) and the U. S. Seventh Army (Lieutenant General Alexander McC. Patch, Jr.). The left flank of the Seventh Army, on the western slope of the Vosges, adjoins the right flank of Patton's U. S. Third Army whose front extends northwestward to the Luxemburg border. There it adjoins Hodges' U. S. First Army at a sharp angle, First Army's front running generally northward for 115 miles to adjoin the narrow front of the U. S. Ninth Army (Lieutenant General William H. Simpson), squeezed in between First Army and the British Second Army of Field Marshal Montgomery's Twenty-First Army Group. The Ninth Army holds a sector of only eighteen miles.

"The talk around here is that Ninth was put there just to keep Monty from grabbing us," the captain explained, in cheerful revelation of the actual workings of Allied "unity" at the Group level of command. The "us" he referred to was First Army. "It's a cinch that an American Army will soon have to be added to Twenty-First Army Group, to maintain balance, and Brad figured that the Ninth, being the newest and greenest, was the one most easily spared . . ."†

". . . and by that token, of the least help to Monty."

The captain grinned.

As things now stand, the U. S. Third, First, and Ninth Armies constitute Bradley's Twelfth Army Group, comprising altogether thirty-one divisions and holding a front of 230 tortuous miles. But many of these divisions are well below normal strength—are down 25 per cent or more in their front-line rifle strength—due to the excess of casualties over replacements in the rifle platoons.

† Though new as an Army, several of its divisions—the 29th, the 30th, the 2nd Armored, among others—were battle-tested veterans.

"You know about that," the captain said.

"I do," said Earnest Morehead, with feeling.

Bitter experience has taught him that rifle platoons absorb the great bulk of all casualties. In the fifteen days at St. Lo, the eighty-one rifle platoons of the 30th, numbering some 3240 men initially, suffered three of every four of the nearly 4000 casualties inflicted on the whole 14,000-man division—suffered, in other words, over 90 per cent casualties! Morehead properly appreciates the miraculous fact that he himself came through intact save for a shallow flesh wound in his left shoulder.

"And this damned trenchfoot, it hits the riflemen on the line hardest," the captain went on, "and nearly every trenchfoot evacuee is a permanent loss, according to the doctors.[2] Everything's conditioned by the shortage of riflemen, and of ammunition. We sure can't do everything at once, with what we have . . ."

And he mentioned the continuing disagreement ("Hell, call it a quarrel; it's been acrimonious enough, under the politeness . . .") between "Brad" and "Monty" over strategy, the latter still insisting that all possible strength should be concentrated for a single blow, either in the north for a drive through the Ruhr or in the south for a drive through and around the Saar Basin. Bradley's reply remains what it has always been, namely, that concentration for a single thrust would enable the German to concentrate his defense to meet it, whereas a "double thrust," such as the map now described, would "confound the enemy and make better use of the superior mobility of our Armies,"[3] Obviously, Bradley has lately had his way with Eisenhower. For Twelfth Army Group's strength has been concentrated in such a way as to enable the launching of two loosely coordinated offensives during the last six or seven weeks on either side of the Ardennes—that region of steep, wooded hills and narrow, winding valleys, a wild and lonely land, that is geologically an eroded volcanic plateau and has been historically an obstacle, like a boulder in a river, to the flow of commerce and war between Germany and France.

South and west of the Ardennes, Patton has ten divisions on a ninety-odd-mile front, and with this Army, in the second week of November, during a rainstorm that denied him air support (he used massed artillery in lieu of it), he attacked across the flooded Moselle north of Metz and fought his troops through some days of rain, and miles of mud, until they came hard against the Siegfried Line. And there, miles short of the Saar, they were stopped. On a fifty-five-mile front north of the Ardennes, Hodges and Simpson had between them sixteen divisions. According to plan, Hodges was to "ram through to Düren with Simpson on his left flank,"[4] force his way across the Roer River, and push on to Cologne, destroying German forces this side of the Rhine. A necessary prerequisite to a successful crossing of the Roer is the capture or destruction of a network of great earthen dams whose floodgates can be used to control the level of the river downstream (north) of them. It is a prerequisite (the captain indicates) that has been only lately and reluctantly recognized, else there might never have been begun the grim, bloody Battle of the Huertgen Forest that has been raging just south of the Aachen Gap since mid-September; and it is a prerequisite that remains unfulfilled by the attack Hodges launched early in the third week of November, when a break in the foul weather at last permitted intensive air support. In preparation for this attack there was laid a bomb "carpet" reminiscent of that at St. Lo, but with no comparable success. No breakthrough followed. Instead, the attackers advanced less than seven miles in the first two weeks of hard fighting, and they now advanced hardly at all.

Earnest Morehead remarked that the situation seemed to indicate that failure of command intelligence and skill known as "attrition warfare." It seemed also to indicate that Montgomery had been right and Bradley wrong in strategic concept. The captain nodded.

"Of course we can stand the attrition better than the Germans can," he said, "especially since theirs is at a faster rate. We're supposed to be inflicting two casualties for every one of our own."[5]

"Are we actually doing it?"

The captain shrugged. "Our Intelligence reports say so."

Also, he added, one must take account of the fact (certainly Eisenhower must take account of the fact) that Montgomery "is more or less the McClellan type" who doesn't want to move until "he's absolutely certain everything's in his favor"—and absolute certainties are rare in war. Hence the natural reluctance to divert to him who is notoriously slow and cautious, men and materiel that would otherwise go to Patton, who is notoriously swift and bold. To Morehead's question of why, then, Eisenhower did not pursue the Montgomery-suggested alternative, concentrating on Bradley-Patton and a thrust through the Saar, the captain replied with another shrug. It was his guess that this might be "politically impossible," or might seem so to Eisenhower who, as Supreme Commander, had to weigh political as well as purely military factors as he made his decisions.

Then it was that he, the captain, stressed the point that has been of most interest to Earnest Morehead as "philosopher." Tapping with his forefinger the uneven line along the German border across the Ardennes, the captain remarked on the thinness, the "paper-thin" strength, with which this line is held. North of it, First and Ninth Armies dispose a division for every three and four-tenths miles of front. South of it, Third Army disposes a division for every nine miles of front. But across the Ardennes itself, which is well over a third (some eighty miles) of the total front of Twelfth Army Group, there is only a division for every twenty miles of front. Moreover, not one of these four divisions (they comprise Major General Troy H. Middleton's VIII Corps) can be classed at that moment as a first-class fighting outfit. One of them is an absolutely green infantry division: it sailed from the United States just a few weeks ago and has come into the line with no battle experience whatever. Another is an equally green armored division, newly arrived in Europe, held by Middleton in reserve. In this quiet sector, these two outfits are supposed to receive the gentlest possible introduction to combat. The other two divisions are veterans, but have been only recently withdrawn from the bloody, morale-breaking Huertgen Forest fighting in which they were badly mauled; they are battle-weary, their rifle strength seriously depleted.

This over-all disposition, the captain said, represents a calculated risk.[6] The Allied strength might have been distributed in such a way (that is, fairly evenly) over the whole front as to maintain a virtually riskless defensive, but in that case it would have been impossible to maintain offensive pressures as Bradley in fact has done. The recognized risk price of these pressures is the possibility that the enemy, aware of the distribution of Allied strength, will launch a major attack through the Ardennes. No one has forgotten that it was precisely through this difficult region that the Germans exploded their blitzkrieg into Belgium and France in 1940. No one denies that a major attack, if made now, would rupture the thin screen of American troops stretched from northeast of St. Vith to the Moselle in the south. The possibility, the danger has seemed remote to the Allied high command, however, especially since the German commander in the West is wily, prudent Field Marshal Karl Gerd von Rundstedt who is known to have become (wisely, in the circumstances) "defensive-minded."

After all, the Ardennes is itself a profitless ground for the German. Its sole value to him, now as in 1940, is as a door opening out toward the Lowlands and the sea; and the situation and relative strengths of the opposing forces are now far different from what they were in 1940. Then the "door" was an opening framed by static walls, for the French fortress troops of the Maginot Line had no mobility. Now the "door" is an opening between two sliding panels—one to the left, one to the right—which may be slammed hard against the attacker's flanks, for the Allies have a highly mobile strength on either side of the Ardennes. Only if he attacks with such force, such weight and speed, as to burst whole armies into the Allied rear before the mobile strength on the flanks can be brought to bear against him—only then can the German achieve anything decisive through an Ardennes offensive. And to prevent this, in the unlikely event of its being attempted, the Allied high command counts upon the steadfastness, the courageous skill of the Ardennes-screening troops, and upon that of units rushed up from the south or down from the north to plug gaps in the Allied lines. These troops would be greatly outnumbered at the outset, some of them would certainly be overwhelmed, but it is the belief, or bet, of the high command that they would fight effective delaying actions, slowing the monster until a sufficient strength could be deployed to halt him. It would be Mortain all over again. . . .

Quite early next morning, Saturday, December 16, Earnest Morehead hitched a ride in a war correspondent's jeep back to the village where his outfit rested. The Belgian countryside was shrouded in cold mist—a fog so thick, so narrowly confining to the vision, that the jeep seemed almost to be standing still in a white-walled room despite the reckless speed (reckless in terms of the limited visibility) with which it was driven by a dark-visaged sergeant. The sergeant was taciturn by nature, the correspondent was made so by a hangover, the landscape was blotted out by mists, so Morehead was left alone with his thoughts on the hard back seat, undistracted by sight or sound. What he thought of was the "calculated risk" that the captain had described. It strengthened in Earnest Morehead's mind the suggestion that the difference between "freedom" and "necessity"—between an unpredictable "free will" and a predictable causal "determinism"—might be a difference of aspect or perspective rather than a flat opposition.

He was reminded of a chapter on "Uncertainty" in a popular book about modern physics he'd read some months ago, in which the author dealt briefly with the question of whether the universe is ultimately ruled by causality or by pure chance. Radioactivity had been used as illustration. Of a million atoms of radium, the author said, we can predict fairly accurately the proportion that will disintegrate within a given time; but no prediction at all, as to when if ever it will disintegrate, can be made of a single atom. At Spa, at Luxemburg City where Bradley is, at Versailles, where Eisenhower is, the generals think in million-atom terms. To them heroism and cowardice are statistically predictable within fairly narrow limits—they tacitly assume in their strategic plans that a certain proportion of the troops will perform deeds "above and beyond the call of duty," that the great bulk of the troops will perform their assigned tasks adequately, that a few will behave in cowardly fashion. *But I am a single atom,* thought Earnest Morehead, *and there is no way of predicting absolutely what I will do, when the pressure comes. I don't know myself for sure, despite St. Lo and Mortain. For I DO have free will, I have the capacity to choose. I can and will decide, in terms of the actual situation, whether to stand or run away.* And he shivered, for the fog seemed to seep through his flesh to his very bones.

Or is this a shiver of premonition?

Certainly he recalls at that moment (let us say) his friend the captain's expressed fears concerning German intentions, shared by the captain with his superior, Colonel Benjamin Dickson. There have been repeated indications that enemy movements are more massive in the picturesque German Eifel opposite Middleton's front than they have previously been, or would be if this sector were to continue as a rest sector for both sides. There has been heard a roaring of massed motors behind the enemy lines for two nights in a row, and yesterday a woman was sent up to Spa from Middleton's headquarters at Bastogne with the report that she saw the night before a mass of German troops, accompanied by tanks twice as large as any she had seen before, behind the Siegfried Line east of Clervaux, a Luxemburg town some miles south of the center of the Ardennes front. This seemed to the captain particularly ominous because on the very night that the woman saw the things, "Monk" Dickson at an Intelligence briefing had flatly predicted an all-out German offensive through the Ardennes. Of course Dickson had been pooh-poohed by the staff as an alarmist. The prevailing opinion at Twelfth Army Group and First Army continues to be that the Germans might launch a small-scale "spoiling attack" designed to relieve the pressure being exerted by Hodges to the north and Patton to the south, but nothing more than that.[7] They lack the strength . . .

"I'm not so sure," the captain said. "I *am* sure that, if they have the stuff, they could have built up big in the Eifel without our finding out about it—moving at night and hiding in the woods by day. That's damn good country for concealment. Especially with our air socked in day after day by this stinking weather."

And Earnest Morehead, remembering the worried look in his friend's eyes, huddles into his overcoat, shivering again.

Premonition it might be . . .

At that very moment strange and terrible things are happening southeast of him, all along the eighty-odd miles of the Ardennes front.[8] They began to happen at 5:30 that morning when, abruptly, a storm of shell- and rocket-fire burst on and behind Allied lines from hundreds of cannon (including fourteen-inch railroad guns), launching platforms, mortars—a storm that wrecked American telephone communications from one end of the sector to the other and left many a defense installation in smoking ruin. It raged for an hour. Then, as abruptly as it had begun, it ended. Dazed, deafened, the American front-line troops gazed tensely eastward, and their nerves were not steadied when, a minute or so after the barrage had lifted, a ghastly blue-white light from immense searchlights fell upon them. Soon thereafter, the mists before them gave birth to ghostlike figures which, initially fluid and wavering, alternately blending into and emerging from the snow and fog, suddenly congealed into hundreds upon hundreds of white-clad, bucket-helmeted soldiers plodding with ominous steadiness toward them. Tanks roared along the roads, including sixty-ton monsters (Tigers, mounting long-barreled 88s in their turrets), half again as large as the largest American Shermans, while, low in the gray sky above the Losheim Gap, planes that flew faster than any the Americans had seen before streaked by with a weird, shrieking sound.

Well might Earnest Morehead shudder in anticipation of his fate, for it is then being shaped in fire and blood along the eastern edge of the Ardennes. Already, as he rides northward, some American units have been cut off and surrounded. Others are reeling back, fighting desperate rear-guard actions. Still others are in headlong flight, their vehicles bumper to bumper, clogging the narrow, winding roads. All is confusion along and behind a crumbled front.

From a formless welter of violence, fearsome fact and fearful fancy come intermingled in reports to headquarters, making no clear pattern. Days will pass before the battle has on maps a clearly defined outline whence derives its historic name, the Battle of the Bulge. Almost a week will pass before the battle is recognized by the Allied world as an all-or-nothing gamble, analogous to that of the Japanese in the Battle for Leyte Gulf, its aim nothing less than the recapture of Antwerp and the splitting in two of the Allied Expeditionary Force. Months will pass before it is learned that what is initially termed "Rundstedt's Battle" is actually Hitler's, conceived by Der Fuehrer, pressed by him against the reluctance of his top generals (they dare not assert themselves very far amidst the terror yet proceeding from the previous July 20), and, on the grand strategic level, personally directed by him. He intends to reverse the whole tide of war in the West. The Allies are to be put on the defensive with this slashing ground attack and rendered offensively impotent until the skies can be swept clear of Allied bombers by the new jet fighters, now just coming into production in German factories, and new long-range rockets are perfected for use on Allied bases. By then the governments of the West will be more than willing to negotiate a peace which will enable the Germans to turn full-force against the Russians, retrieving everything that now seems lost. Thus the mad dream behind the harsh commanding voice that has spoken through Rundstedt's doubting in this morning's Order of the Day (issued by Rundstedt) to German "Soldiers of the Western Front!" saying: "Your great hour has come. . . . You carry with you the holy obligation to give all to achieve superhuman objectives for our Fatherland and our Fuehrer!"

Fearsome fact indeed, for the Allies, is the initial disparity of opposing forces. Against some fifty thousand American troops in four divisions, two enfeebled by too much recent battle, two by the lack of any battle experience at all, the Germans have launched three Armies comprising twenty divisions totaling a quarter of a million men, with another five divisions soon to be fed into the attack, paced and spearheaded by hundreds of tanks, covered (or to be covered when weather permits) by some 350 planes of which nearly eighty are jet-propelled. In following weeks, the number of planes is to increase to between eight and nine hundred. Gigantic have been the preparations: the operation is amazing in this as in the success with which the whole vast enterprise has been kept from Allied eyes and ears these last several weeks. Despite Allied bombings which are supposed drastically to reduce German production and disrupt her transportation system, nearly six million gallons of fuel and more than 30,000 tons of ammunition have been assembled for the first two weeks or so of this offensive. It is as the Order of the Day has said: "*We gamble everything!*"

As for fearful fancy, it is deliberately encouraged in Allied minds by a so-called Operation GREIF which, violating the accepted rules of war, measures the desperation of this gamble. A special brigade of Germans who can speak English has been formed, headed by the same SS Lieutenant Colonel Otto Skorzeny who, summer before last, rescued Mussolini from his Italian mountain imprisonment. The volunteer members of this brigade have been schooled in current American slang, trained in the use of American weapons, and equipped with American vehicles. Wearing American uniforms they (according to the plan) are to operate behind American lines where they are supposed to seize bridges over the Meuse, cut telephone lines, misdirect traffic, spread panic-inducing rumors, and in general create havoc and confusion.

But in fact, most of this brigade fails to penetrate the American line. Seven jeeploads manage to do so, however, and they operate with an effectiveness vastly disproportionate to their small number before most of them are caught and shot. One group cuts the main telephone cable connecting Twelfth Army Group with First Army headquarters. Another sends a reinforcing American column down the wrong road. Yet another does the most damage of all by confessing its mission under questioning by American Intelligence officers after it has been captured, whereupon the alarm is spread by Allied Intelligence from the Maas to Versailles that *thousands* of Germans in Allied uniforms are roaming the Low Countries and northern France, assigned to all manner of mischief, and that some of them have as missions the assassination of Eisenhower and other top Allied leaders. In consequence, much personnel, much time and energy that would have been better expended on various concrete elements of the enemy attack are now to be expended on shadows. So many men are assigned to protect Eisenhower that he feels himself immobilized, like a prisoner of war, and makes strenuous but futile protest. In the Ardennes, any American soldier riding a jeep or truck or command car not in column is liable to be halted at every crossroads by suspicious G.I. sentries who require answers to questions no German, however well briefed, would be likely to answer correctly. Who won the World Series last year? This year? What position does a football guard play in relation to others in the line? What's the name of Mickey Mouse's girl friend? Bradley himself, having earlier identified Springfield as the capital of Illinois (his interlocutor is initially sure Chicago's the correct answer), is stumped when asked to name movie star Betty Grable's husband. He has been recognized, fortunately: he is waved on with a grin, a salute, and the gratuitous information that blonde Betty's husband is jazz trumpeter Harry James. . . .

Not with such questions, however, nor with those who ask or answer them, is Earnest Morehead's fate directly concerned. He comes at midmorning to his brief journey's end. He reports in to the company CP, and spends the rest of that dull, chill day and all the next in and around the farmhouse where he is billeted. And as he does so, his fate moves circuitously but inexorably toward him in one of the lead tanks (a giant Tiger) of the attack *Kampfgruppe* of the First SS Panzer Division, one of nine divisions of the German Sixth SS Panzer Army.

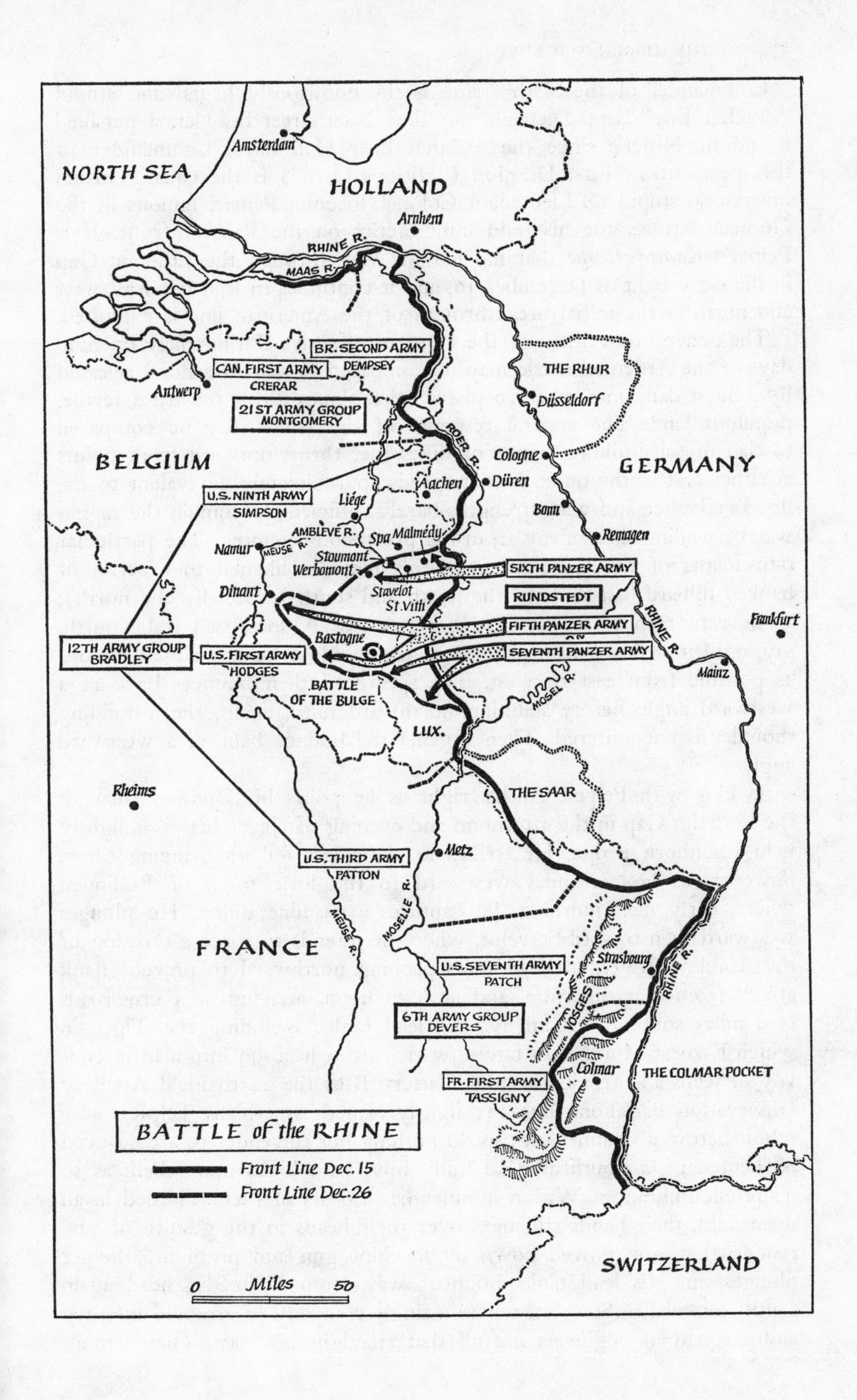

BATTLE of the RHINE
Front Line Dec. 15
Front Line Dec. 26
0 Miles 50
NORTH SEA
Amsterdam
HOLLAND
Arnhem
RHINE R.
MAAS R.
BR. SECOND ARMY
DEMPSEY
CAN. FIRST ARMY
CRERAR
Antwerp
21ST ARMY GROUP
MONTGOMERY
THE RHUR
Düsseldorf
ROER R.
BELGIUM
Cologne
GERMANY
Aachen
Düren
U.S. NINTH ARMY
SIMPSON
Liége
Bonn
Remagen
AMBLEVE R.
Spa
Malmédy
Namur
MEUSE R.
Stoumont
Werbomont
SIXTH PANZER ARMY
RUNDSTEDT
Dinant
Stavelot
St. Vith
FIFTH PANZER ARMY
RHINE R.
Frankfurt
Bastogne
SEVENTH PANZER ARMY
12TH ARMY GROUP
BRADLEY
U.S. FIRST ARMY
HODGES
Mainz
BATTLE
OF THE BULGE
MOSEL R.
LUX.
THE SAAR
Rheims
Metz
U.S. THIRD ARMY
PATTON
MOSELLE R.
MEUSE R.
FRANCE
Strasbourg
U.S. SEVENTH ARMY
PATCH
VOSGES
RHINE R.
6TH ARMY GROUP
DEVERS
FR. FIRST ARMY
TASSIGNY
Colmar
THE COLMAR POCKET
SWITZERLAND

Commander of the Sixth Army is the notoriously brutal and stupid "Butcher Boy" Sepp Dietrich, one-time Nazi street brawler, a personal friend of Hitler's since the Munich Beer Hall days. Commander of the spearhead of First Division ("Hitler's Own") is the equally brutal but not so stupid SS Lieutenant Colonel Joachim Peiper, famous in the German Armies for his bold tank tactics on the Russian front. It is Peiper's *Kampfgruppe* that has led the way through the Losheim Gap in the early light of December 16, and it continues to lead the way west and north as the initial breakthrough of the American line is exploited.

The general movement of the German offensive during these opening days of the Ardennes battle may be compared to that of a flood released by a burst dam onto a barren plateau that slopes down toward a fertile, populous land. The general response of the Allies may be compared to that of self-building levees or dikes that thrust outward from points at either end of the burst dam at speeds approximately equivalent to the flood's advance and with strengths barely sufficient to contain the raging waters, walling them away from the prosperous country. The particular movements of the German spearheads may be likened to a series of banked billiard ball shots to the north and south (especially the north), while center shots are made due westward. A spearhead stabs north, say, until it strikes a firm portion of the shoulder being built as rapidly as possible from east to west. The spearhead then bounces back at a westward angle before stabbing northward until, again, the a-building shoulder is encountered. Then (again) the bounce back at a westward angle.

So it is with Peiper. At his right as he pours his Division through the Losheim Gap in the afternoon and evening of December 16 is lightly held Elsenborn Ridge. He strikes its defenders only a glancing blow, however, as he continues westward to the little town of Bullingen where, early next morning, he captures a gasoline dump. He plunges westward then toward Stavelot, where he intends to force a crossing of the Amblève River, his lead units probing northward to prevent flank attack from that direction—and at high noon, arriving at a crossroads two miles south of Malmédy, the lead tanks, including the Tiger in which Earnest Morehead's fate now rides, run head-on into a little convoy of jeeps and trucks carrying Battery B of the 285th Field Artillery Observation Battalion. The 125 lightly armed Americans, helpless as a rabbit before a steamroller, can do nothing but surrender to a cold-eyed SS lieutenant, a youthful Nazi bully boy, who looks upon them as so many encumbrances. Within minutes he disposes of them. Herded in an open field, their hands still held over their heads in the gesture of surrender, they are mowed down by machine gun and pistol fire. Peiper plunges on. His lead tanks bounce away from Malmédy, head again southwestward to Stavelot, where a single company of armored infantry and a squad of engineers are all that stand in his way. They cannot stop him. Stavelot and the (to him) vital crossing are his early in the morning of December 18.

Thence one arm of his force makes a probing thrust toward Spa, where there is much frantic scurrying as First Army headquarters flees northward. In the dark woods around Spa are the largest gasoline dumps in Europe, some 3,500,000 gallons, whose capture would more than offset the lack of fuel reserves which plagues Rundstedt's Armies. They are not captured. More than a million gallons has been removed before headquarters flees and another 2,225,000 gallons is in process of removal. Some 100,000 gallons is poured into a steep road cut and ignited, a roaring wall of flame leaping skyward just before the panzers reach it, and while tanks from the hastily summoned U. S. Third Armored Division drive through the streets of Spa southward. They turn back, then, the panzers—back to the south and west. It is, for Peiper, no grievous disappointment. Spa was not among his specific objectives anyway. Four miles west of Stavelot is Trois Ponts, where there is confluence of the Amblève and Salm and where highway bridges cross both streams. It is toward these that his main force aims. If he can take these bridges intact he can, he is convinced, drive all the way to the Meuse as fast as his tanks can go, for the Allies now have in all that country westward nothing strong enough to slow him down.

But at Trois Ponts he is given his first serious check since the breakthrough. A single U.S. engineer company—140 men armed with eight bazookas, an anti-tank gun, ten machine guns—manages to halt his lead tanks long enough to prepare the Amblève River bridge for demolition, to retreat across it, and then blow it almost in his face. Furious, he perforce turns northward into the steep and narrow Amblève Valley, seeking another crossing. He finds one four miles south of Werbomont, but this bridge too is blown in his face by a mere handful of engineers, this one only a squad. Again he is forced northward. Meanwhile, some of his men, turning back to Trois Ponts, have perpetrated "frightfulness" in the German tradition that long antedates Hitler whose regime, indeed, it has helped produce. They have dragged twenty-two Trois Ponts civilians from their houses on the riverbank—men, women, even children—and killed them before the horrified eyes of their friends and relatives on the other bank of the river. The atrocity is far from unique: the same sort of thing has happened twice before in this very drive—at Baugnez, at Ligneuville. . . .

And now Peiper may wonder, he has cause to wonder, if his luck is running out.

Heretofore he has been hidden from Allied eyes in the sky by thick, low clouds, but now, on this afternoon of December 18 there is a brief break in the overcast directly above him. Through it a reconnaissance plane sees him—and fighter-bombers of the IX Tactical Air Command are then upon him, diving down below the clouds, bombing, strafing, before he can hide his force in the woods. Within a few minutes he has lost several tanks, several half-tracks, and his location and approximate strength are definitely known for the first time to the Allied command. He bivouacks that night in a dark wood less than a mile from Stoumont, less than twenty-five miles from the fortress city of Liège, and does well to emulate Shakespeare's King Henry on the eve of Agincourt. He passes from one group to another of his men in the darkness, congratulating them, encouraging them, giving them confidence in victory tomorrow.

"Our luck was bad today," says he. "With good luck tomorrow we'll reach the Meuse by nightfall . . ."

And leaves each group boasting exultantly, albeit a bit nervously, of its entrance soon into Antwerp, Paris, even London. . . .

But even as he speaks, his tomorrow's "luck," which is "bad," is encamped in battalion strength on a hill less than a mile away, the hill on which Stoumont stands, having crept stealthily into that village under cover of night; is encamped, too, in battalion strength at Werbomont, having there relieved the valiant bridge-blowing squad of engineers; is encamped finally, also in battalion strength, some miles to the northwest, along the narrow river valley he must fight his way through and out of before he can make swift drive to the Meuse. The three battalions are of the 119th Infantry Regiment of the U. S. 30th Division, alerted in the evening of December 17 for movement into the now a-building Amblève River line.

And a key element of all this "luck" of Joachim Peiper's is centered (according to our apocryphal tale) in Sergeant Earnest Morehead, to whom tomorrow's event presents itself, not as "luck," not as random chance at all, but as iron necessity—a compound of purpose and causality, of Fate and Destiny. Earnest Morehead lies long awake in his sleeping bag that night on Stoumont's hill, under a wind-sighing pine, amidst snow, beside a broken wall, and what yesterday and the day before was "perhaps" a premonition becomes now an absolute one. Ever since he left Spa he has had a fluid sense of impending grave danger; he now has, all at once, a solid conviction of approaching personal doom. *I am going to die tomorrow*, he says to himself,[9] as if repeating dictation from on high, and is both rebellious and afraid in the dark. What is the nature of this fear, this rebellion? Sleepless, his thigh muscles twitching, a knot of dull pain below his ribs, he cannot shut off self-analysis, cannot abstain from the slaughter and dissection of his emotions. He is aware as never before of his doubleness: spirit and body, thought and feeling, actor and acted upon, shaper of the very event which victimizes him: and he finds his fear to be altogether of the physical body, a pure and simple animal terror of pain, of extinction, whereas his rebellion is spiritual, though of spirit flawed by body, and is very far from being either simple or pure. He is complicatedly aware that the death he is fated to die will be of his own choosing, will involve all the anguish of decision when the time comes despite its being *already* decided. And it is against this that he rebels—this bland assumption from on high that he will *choose* to act as fate decrees. *I won't!* he says to the darkness, the silence. He balances all that he might become, he balances the contribution he might make to the on-goingness of the world, for he knows now as never before the creative power that is in him—he balances this against the value of his statistically predictable "heroic self-sacrifice" in battle, and finds the latter immensely outweighed. *I won't!* he says again. *I choose to live, to create* . . .

Yet dies all the same, and of his own free choice, in the afternoon of the following day.

Peiper's main spearhead of more than sixty tanks has no difficulty plunging into and through Stoumont that morning of December 19. The single infantry battalion and ten supporting tanks that stand in his way are quickly overwhelmed, and Morehead flees with the rest of his outfit pell-mell down the hill westward toward the river, into thick fog. But in the afternoon, finding himself alone in a narrow room of mist, for the fog is like miles of distance separating him from his nearest fellow—finding himself alone in a narrow defile of earth and rock where the halting of a single panzer will pile up a whole column—he turns back (all the while standing beside himself, making ironic comment on what he does) to face death looming toward him out of the fog, the lead Tiger, breathing fire and smoke. And he drags death as a string of mines across the road, knowing there is neither space nor time for his own escape, and *laughs* at himself as he does so, laughs defiantly into the very teeth of the Tiger . . .

And dies laughing. Becomes a bloody rag of flesh and shattered bone. Becomes nothing . . .

But stops the lead tank, blasting it into flame, and with it blasting Peiper's last chance for the Meuse. For the blocked panzers can only back up, and they do back up under cover of fog. When they are able they turn around and climb back up the long steep hill toward Stoumont. . . .

Fiction sustained by fact is our story of Earnest Morehead—but it is altogether historical fact that the possibility of Germany's winning the great Ardennes gamble (and it was a distinct possibility on December 16) was destroyed by the courageous tenacity of handfuls of American soldiers, fighting against overwhelming odds, during the first four days of the battle. They slowed the enemy advance, they blocked it at such crucial points as Trois Ponts, Werbomont, Stoumont, until the shoulders north and south of the Ardennes were sufficiently strong to wall in the German tide, channeling it westward, confining it to unprofitable ground. And even this ground was not wholly conquered. At the heart of its road network was Bastogne, where Middleton had maintained his VIII Corps headquarters, and Bastogne was held by the Americans even when completely surrounded by the enemy, short of food, desperately short of ammunition, suppliable only by air drop amidst weather which made air drops impossible for days on end.

The defense of Bastogne has become by historical account the great epic of the Battle of the Bulge. When the full scope of the German attack first began to be realized at First Army headquarters in the morning of December 17, Hodges put through a phone call to Bradley, then visiting Eisenhower in Versailles, asking that the 101st and 82nd Airborne Divisions be assigned to him, both divisions being at that moment resting near Rheims, France. The 82nd was ordered into the Amblève River line at the northern side of the growing salient. The 101st was ordered to Bastogne, where it joined Combat Command B of the 10th Armored Division, sent up from a rest area at Remeling, France, and the 705th Tank Destroyer Battalion, sent down from Kohlscheid, Germany, which was in Ninth Army's sector. The 101st's commander, Major General Maxwell D. Taylor (whose secret mission to Rome will be remembered), was in Washington when this move was made; his second-in-command, Brigadier General Anthony C. McAuliffe, became the senior officer and hence commander of all the beleaguered, outnumbered forces at Bastogne. And it was McAuliffe who, late in the morning of December 22—having been completely encircled the night before—returned to a German offer of surrender terms the single word, "Nuts!" It was a reply at once famous throughout the Allied world.‡ Next day the weather sufficiently cleared to permit air drops, Allied planes were enabled to join the battle, and during the following days the surrounded garrison, employing massed artillery fire with great skill (McAuliffe was his division's chief artillery officer), defeated every German effort to crush it. Then, on the day after Christmas, a slender column of Patton's U. S. Third Army drove into Bastogne from the south, ending the bloody siege.

And on that day, everywhere along the bulged front, the Germans were either stalled or beginning to draw back. The crisis had ended. On January 3, in heavy snow and bitter cold, the Allied counteroffensive was launched; by a little after mid-January the Germans had been driven back to their line of December 15, the Bulge eliminated. What had it accomplished? From first to last, it cost the Americans 76,890 casualties, according to the official figures, of whom 8607 were killed, 47,139 wounded, and 21,144 missing. German casualties totaled 81,834, of whom 12,652 were killed, 38,600 wounded, and 30,582 missing. The Americans lost 733 tanks and tank destroyers as compared to German tank losses of between 350 and 400. The Germans may have gained a little time: the planned major Allied ground offensive was delayed six weeks, ac-

‡ Many were reminded of the single word (considerably more offensive to delicate ears) uttered by one Cambronne near nightfall of June 18, 1815, when he, as commander of the last French square to stand at Waterloo, was called upon by the English to surrender. The square, surrounded, was being slaughtered, its position utterly hopeless, and the call for surrender was made in admiring terms. Cambronne replied, "*Merde!*"

cording to Eisenhower, and the all-out air attack on German industry was delayed four weeks. But even this "gain" is dubious. For one of the effects of the Bulge was to increase the flow of men and supplies to the European Theater beyond what had been theretofore planned (Washington had tended to reduce these in favor of increases of the flow to the Pacific following the reconquest of France), and another effect was to weaken the capacity of the Germans to resist the final offensive when it came. . . .

Perhaps the only true net loss which the Allies suffered from the Bulge was of good will, of wholehearted military cooperation, between the Allies. Certainly Allied unity was severely strained and, on the Army Group level, permanently impaired. But for this the Germans were only indirectly responsible: the prime direct cause of it was the peculiar temperament (with its effect on Bradley's), and the faulty public relations sense, of Field Marshal Bernard Montgomery. On the evening of December 19, when the rapidly increasing depth of the German penetration made it difficult if not impossible for Bradley to maintain close communications with First Army from his headquarters in Luxemburg City, Eisenhower transferred the U. S. Ninth and First Armies to the otherwise exclusively British Twenty-First Army Group. Thereafter the northern portion of the Allied battle was under Montgomery's top command, the southern portion under Bradley's. Inevitably, there was friction between opposing American and British conceptions of how the battle should be run (the Americans opposed making any retreat not directly forced; the British looked upon planned retreats as essential tactical elements of over-all strategy). Inevitably this friction of idea was joined to and augmented by a friction of personality, for Montgomery was a man most Americans found hard to take. He had, indeed, a positive genius for striking attitudes, for making gestures, for saying words that irritated them—and never was this genius more abundantly displayed than in a press conference he held on January 7, 1945, after the tide of battle was turned wholly in the Allies' favor.[10] In his statement to the reporters he made no reference to steps taken by the American command during the first four days of the battle. He indicated that the American situation was desperate when, on the fifth day, he took over and proceeded to "tidy up" the battlefield. "I got reserves into the right place and got balanced—and you know what happened. . . ."[11] He described the battle as "most interesting; I think possibly one of the most interesting and tricky battles I have ever handled, with great issues at stake." His praise of the "good fighting qualities of the American soldier" seemed to many an American, in its context, infuriatingly patronizing.

All this encouraged a clamor in the British press that Montgomery be placed in command of all Allied ground forces, under Eisenhower, as he had been (nominally) in Normandy and had repeatedly asked again to be in recent weeks, in order to mount and launch the "one full-blooded thrust." Bradley feared that Eisenhower might do as the British wished; he said flatly to the Supreme Commander that "after what has happened I cannot serve under Montgomery" (he found it impossible to "forgive Monty for having exploited our distress") and would demand to be sent home if Twelfth Army Group was placed under the Field Marshal's command.[12] As for Montgomery, consistent with the strategic concept he had been pressing since August, he was privately convinced that the American "bloody nose" in the Ardennes "would never have happened if we had fought the campaign properly following the great victory in Normandy, or had even insured tactical balance in the disposition of land forces as the winter campaign developed.[13] Bradley's "calculated risk," in other words, was deficient in logic, excessive in danger, and (Montgomery would later indicate) disastrous in "political consequence" insofar as it prolonged the war in the West until Soviet Russia closed in from the east.

ii. *Yalta*

It was to be the largest, the most important Conference of the war. Dozens of transport planes were required to carry the seven hundred or so persons who comprised the British and American delegations; after an overnight flight from Malta, these planes came down at ten-minute intervals in the morning of February 3, 1945, upon snow-heaped Saki airfield in the Crimea. Churchill's plane arrived before Roosevelt's did. When the latter, *The Sacred Cow*, came to a stop and Roosevelt was carried down from it in the special elevator built for him, he appeared "frail and ill" to Churchill's eyes.[14]

There followed a six-hour automobile drive. Beyond Saki they traversed a wintry, almost treeless plain scarred everywhere by war: they saw blasted tanks beside the road, burned-out freight trains on railway sidings, shattered buildings in every village, on every farm. Then they climbed in bitter cold a mountain range, up into arctic snowfields, before descending with breathtaking swiftness into a different world—a world of bright sunlight, of balmy air, of mountains rising precipitously, in spectacular beauty, from the Black Sea shore, reminding more than one American of the California coast south of Monterey. But the softening of the climate was matched by no softening of the visible effects of war. The only undamaged major buildings in the Yalta vicinity were the three large villas where the three national delegations were headquartered —the Livadia Palace, built for the Czar in 1911 two miles south of Yalta, assigned to Roosevelt and the other American principals (all plenary sessions were to be held there, in deference to the President's difficulty of movement); the Yusupovsky Palace at Koreis, some four miles south of Livadia, an estate once belonging to the Prince Yusupov who was involved in the assassination of Rasputin, assigned to Stalin and his closest associates; and the hundred-year-old Vorontsov Villa at

Alupka, a strange mixture of Gothic and Moorish architecture some eight miles southwest of Livadia, assigned to Churchill and the British. These structures had been left intact, possibly because Nazi generals hoped to return to them, possibly because they were too large and substantially built to be destroyed in the time available. Elsewhere was ruin.[15]

Evidences of wanton destructiveness were not conducive of tender feelings toward the enemy. Roosevelt was outraged by what he saw. In his later report to the Congress he would speak of the "reckless, senseless fury, the terrible destructiveness that comes out of German militarism. Yalta . . . had no military significance of any kind. It had no defenses. . . . Yet when the Red Army forced the Nazis out of the Crimea—almost just a year ago—all these villas were looted by the Nazis and then nearly all of them were destroyed by bombs placed on the inside. And even the humblest of the homes of Yalta were not spared. There was little left of it except blank walls. . . . I had read about Warsaw and Lidice and Rotterdam and Coventry—but I *saw* . . . Yalta! And I know there is not enough room on Earth for both German militarism and Christian decency."[16]

With this sentiment, all the conferees could agree. They would not, however, find it easy to agree what specifically should be done with Germany after the war; and the German problem was but one of many on which Conference agreement would be hard if not impossible to achieve. For not only was this to be the largest and most important of the War Conferences, it was also to deal with the most complex and difficult matters. . . .

The harshest of Roosevelt's critics would soon find it convenient to forget the circumstances in which this Crimean Conference was being held—circumstances that would be left wholly out of account by those in the more distant future who, for their own purposes, would shape a politically potent myth of "treason" and "betrayal" at Yalta by one Alger Hiss and other members of the State Department. Since June of 1944 there had been drastic changes in the balance of power between Russia and the West, and in the degree and nature of their mutual assistance. For three long years before the Normandy invasion, the Russians had borne the brunt of the battle against the Nazis; they had engaged the bulk of Hitler's forces upon their own blood-soaked soil, suffering (and inflicting) immense military casualties while their civilian population in Nazi-occupied territory was victimized by the most hideous large-scale atrocities. They had needed desperately all the Lend-Lease and other material aid they could obtain from the West until the "Second Front" for which they clamored could be established. Simultaneously, the greatest anxiety of Western military leaders had been that the Russians might collapse under the pressure, permitting Hitler to turn full-force against the West. The problems then faced by the East-West alliance—the problems dealt with at Teheran—had been primarily military, answerable in terms of immediate needs and aims that were either complementary or identical among the Big Three.

Far different was the situation in February of 1945. The great Soviet summer offensive, launched in loose coordination with the invasion of Normandy and continued simultaneously with the battle for France and the drive to the German West Wall, had scored sweeping successes, wiping out scores of German divisions; and the forward march since had been interrupted chiefly by the need to regroup and replenish battle-weary troops. By the end of January, the Germans had been driven from Greece and Yugoslavia; the Russians were in military occupation of Bulgaria, Romania, Poland, and East Prussia; and Hungary was a bloody battleground that, despite desperate Nazi resistance, must inevitably be won by the Russians within the next few weeks or months. With the exception of Hungary, then, and northern Italy, where General Alexander's offensive had been stalled for lack of adequate reinforcement and supply, the Germans were driven back within the territory they had occupied in 1939. European victory was in sight. The problems faced by the Big Three at Yalta, therefore, were no longer primarily military; they were political. And they must be dealt with, not in terms of already (and easily) agreed-upon aims and purposes, but in terms that were not yet clearly defined and that must be defined amidst clashes of opposing national interest exacerbated by fundamental differences in cultural outlook and social philosophy. How was Germany to be treated, once the Nazi power was exterminated? How were the postwar governments of Poland and the other nations of east-central Europe to be set up? How were the disagreements that had arisen about the postwar United Nations organization to be removed? To what extent and in what ways would the Big Three work together to keep the peace? What was to be France's status and role in western Europe? These were among the questions handled at Yalta.

Moreover, insofar as purely military needs conditioned the Yalta discussions, they strengthened the Russian position *vis-à-vis* the West. The surprise German attack in the Ardennes had intensified the already serious shortages of riflemen and supplies in Eisenhower's armies and caused the Supreme Commander to make urgent request for information concerning Soviet plans for winter operations. He was disturbed by the shift of German units from the Russian front to his own and had told Marshall on December 21 that if the trend continued it would "affect the decisions which I have to make regarding future strategy. . . . If, for instance, it is the Russian intention to launch a major offensive in the course of this or the next month, knowledge of the fact would be of the utmost importance to me and I would condition my plans accordingly."[17] A SHAEF delegation had then been sent to Moscow, Roosevelt having arranged for its reception by Stalin, and was informed soon after its arrival in mid-January that the major Soviet winter offensive had already been launched. It had been launched three days before—considerably sooner than had been originally planned, Stalin stressed pointedly, because of the need to aid Eisenhower in the Ardennes emergency. By that time, of course, the emergency was over, the Battle of the Bulge was near its end, but it remained true that Eisenhower needed a continued Russian offensive in the east to insure the success of his spring offensive in the west. Otherwise the eighty-five divisions available to him would not, he feared, be enough to defeat Germany. The same note was sounded at the Combined Chiefs of Staff meeting on Malta, immediately prior to the opening at Yalta. "Beetle" Smith had there told the new Secretary of State, Edward R. Stettinius, Jr.,§ that the Russians just *might* have reached the limit of their advance and that, if so, the Germans might retreat into the "redoubt" region of southwest Germany and there, from strongly prepared defenses amidst the mountains, conduct guerrilla warfare for months or even years.[18] Hence Roosevelt and the U.S. civilian delegates arrived in Yalta convinced by the military that, without extensive Russian aid, the European war could not be successfully ended soon.

Even more important, and by far, in the opinion of the U. S. Joint Chiefs of Staff, was the need for Russian military aid in the Far East against Japan at the earliest possible moment after Germany's surrender. Nothing thus far in the bloody Pacific argument had indicated that Japan would crack as the battle approached her home shores. On the contrary, the fanatical resistance on Saipan, the stern fighting that had following the easy initial landings on Leyte, the slowly developed but stubborn resistance to the invasion of Luzon in mid-January, the mounting fury of the battle for Manila that raged while the Yalta Conference was being held,¶ the increasing use of kamikaze tactics whereby forty American lives were lost for every one Japanese and many ships were lost—all these presaged a struggle that would continue until the last possible pocket of Japanese resistance had been overcome. Some high Air Force and Naval officers believed that the Japanese defeat could be accomplished by air bombardment and total sea blockade without invading the home islands, but the prevailing military opinion was that this invasion would be necessary and might cost a million American casualties, especially if Japan managed to return to her shores substantial portions of the two million troops now in China, Manchuria, and Korea, to reinforce the estimated two and a half million under arms at home. Hence the felt need for Russian assistance. General MacArthur shared it. In

§ Stettinius had been appointed Secretary of State when Cordell Hull resigned because of ill-health in October of 1944.

¶ General MacArthur announced on February 6, 1945, that Manila was in American hands, but this was a characteristically premature communiqué. On February 6, U.S. troops had gained only the southern outskirts of the city and all the heaviest fighting lay ahead. Not until March 4, after weeks of the grimmest kind of street battle, was the last Japanese resistance overcome—and what was then in American hands was a tragically devastated Philippine capital.

late February, the Pacific commander would tell official visitors that a bitter struggle was to be expected when the landings were made on Japan and "that as many Japanese divisions as possible should first be pinned down on the mainland, principally by Soviet forces."[19]

All-in-all, then, Stalin at Yalta had as strong a bargaining position as the West, and he of course bargained toughly. He was very far from having all his own way, however, or even from attempting adamantly to do so. Admiral Leahy spoke the general opinion of the American delegation when he later wrote that, though Stalin's "views on the many political questions were usually different from ours, . . . he spoke quite frankly in presenting the Russian attitude. He was friendly, and seemed in many instances willing to compromise in order to reach agreement."[20] There was no factual basis whatever in Leahy's view, or in anyone else's at the time, for the myth to be developed later that the United States "sold out" to the Russians at this Conference or that Roosevelt was mentally incompetent to deal with the stubborn, ruthless Soviet dictator. None there could doubt that the President was indeed "frail and ill." But neither could anyone doubt that he was in full possession of his faculties. Somehow, at whatever expense of inner resources that were no longer renewable, he summoned up a sufficient energy to negotiate diplomatic passages strewn with treacherous shoals, employing as he did so far more patience and understanding than many of his hale and hearty colleagues displayed.

The first question taken up in plenary session by the conferees, this in the late afternoon and early evening of February 5, was that of German policy, and it occupied much time and energy during the following days. Though all were determined to deal severely with Germany, the Russian pressure for severity was met by Western concern to maintain a balance of European power—a concern most acutely felt by Churchill, but concurred in by Roosevelt—with the result that, as regards German policy, Stalin gained not a single one of his initial points. The Russians demanded that Germany be deindustrialized and required to make war damage reparations to the extent of twenty billions of dollars,** the payments to be made not in money but "in kind," half the this amount to go to the Soviet Union. The Western Powers successfully opposed deindustrialization, despite the fact that Roosevelt and Churchill had both initialed the "Morgenthau Plan" at Quebec; and they succeeded in referring the matter of reparations to a Reparations Commission, with no

** Just before the Yalta Conference, at the request of the Department of State, Major General William J. Donovan and his staff in the Office of Strategic Services (OSS) estimated that "Russia had lost approximately sixteen billion dollars of fixed capital in terms of 1937 prices, or twenty-five per cent of the fixed capital in her pre-1939 borders. In addition, Russia had probably lost another four billion dollars' worth of manufacturing inventories and personal property." Edward R. Stettinius, Jr., *Roosevelt and the Russians* (New York: 1949), p. 121.

specific reparations figures mentioned in the Commission's directive. (The Russians were destined to be no more successful in their efforts to obtain a loan from the United States, with which to rebuild their war-ravaged economy.) The Russians pressed for an extension of Poland's frontier westward to include all former German territory east of the line formed by the Oder and Neisse Rivers. The Western Powers agreed that Poland should "receive substantial accessions of territory in the North and West" but successfully insisted that final settlement of the German-Polish frontier should "await the Peace Conference." The Russians pressed for definite decisions regarding the dismemberment of Germany, only to be frustrated by Churchill's insistence (ultimately supported by Roosevelt) that no definite plan for dismemberment could be made until a profound and expert study of the problem had been made, whereupon only the *possibility* of dismemberment was agreed upon "in principle." The single proposal regarding Germany that was adopted substantially as initially proposed had to do with France's role in the postwar occupation of Germany—and this proposal was first made, not by Stalin, but by Churchill. Prior to Yalta it had been agreed that Russia, Britain, and the United States should each be assigned a definite zone of occupation and that over-all control of Germany would be vested in a tri-partite Allied Control Council. The Prime Minister, fearing that the United States would have a very limited "staying power" in Germany once the European fighting had ended, that the whole crushing burden of Western occupation would then fall on Britain, and anxious to have France restored as a balancing Power on the Continent, insisted that France should also have a zone of occupation, to be carved out of the American and British zones. He also insisted that France be made a member of the Allied Control Council, which would thereby be transformed into a four-Power organization. Stalin was strongly opposed to this. France's capitulation in 1940 had "opened the gate to the enemy," he said, and France had "contributed little to this war." She had earned no right, and certainly she lacked the physical strength, to stand as one of the victorious Great Powers. But when Roosevelt, who at first said he would be "just as satisfied if the French are not in on the control machinery," suddenly announced that he had "changed his mind," Stalin just as suddenly gave in.[21] Thus France was to join the Big Three in ruling her ancient enemy—and the prescient, having had experience of De Gaulle, could surmise that the United States might soon have cause to regret it, gratitude being an emotion that (even if it survived a relentless memory of past injuries) was easily stifled by the kind of personal and national pride, the kind of personal and national ambition, that ruled the French leader.

On the day following the opening discussion of the German problem, discussion of the problem of Poland began. Three hard facts conditioned it. One was indicated by Stalin in his opening statement when he said that, for Russia, Poland presented "not only a question of honor†† but also of security." This unhappy land had repeatedly been a "corridor for attack on Russia" in the past, he pointed out; it had been twice used by the Germans in this way within the last thirty years; and this had happened "because Poland was weak." Hence the Soviet Union desired the establishment of a Poland that was "free, independent, and powerful." If the same words had the same meaning for all concerned, therefore, the interests of Russia and the West coincided, for both Roosevelt and Churchill in their opening statements stressed their wish for a "sovereign, free, and independent" Polish State. Moreover, Roosevelt and Churchill both recognized certain realistic limitations on Poland's "freedom" and "independence." Said Roosevelt: ". . . we want a Poland that will be thoroughly friendly to the Soviet for years to come. This is essential." Said Churchill: "I do not think that the freedom of Poland could be made to cover hostile designs by any Polish government, perhaps by intrigues with Germany, against the Soviet."[22]

The *second* hard fact was that the Red Army alone had driven the Nazis from Polish soil and now occupied the country. If Russia chose to dictate the form of Poland's government, if she made herself sole arbiter of the destinies of *all* the eastern European countries from which her troops had driven the Nazi horde, there was little the Western Powers could do to prevent it. That this had indeed been Russia's choice was the conviction (and warning) expressed in two cables from Moscow to Washington by the astute U. S. Ambassador to Russia, W. Averell Harriman, while preparations for the Yalta Conference were being made. On December 28, 1944, Harriman had pointed out that Russia's recent actions proved her to regard as "friendly" and "independent" only those governments on her borders which agreed wholly with her policies; anyone "who disagrees . . . is conveniently branded . . . a 'Fascist.'" On January 10, 1945, Harriman had cabled that the Russians in eastern Europe were employing a "wide variety of means at their disposal—occupation troops, secret police, local Communist parties, labor unions, sympathetic leftist organizations, sponsored cultural societies, and economic pressure—to assure the establishment of regimes which, while maintaining an outward appearance of independence and of broad popular support, actually depend for their existence on groups responsible to all suggestions from the Kremlin. . . ." Harriman had found it "particularly noteworthy that no practical distinction seems to be made . . . between members of the United Nations whose territory is liberated by Soviet troops and ex-enemy countries which have been occupied. The overriding consideration in Soviet foreign policy is the preoccupation with 'security,' as Moscow sees it. . . ." And, added Harriman, the "Soviet conception of 'security' does not appear cognizant of the similar

†† Great Britain had "no material interest in Poland," Churchill had said. "Her interest is only one of honor."

needs or rights of other countries and of Russia's obligation to accept the restraints as well as the benefits of an international security system."[23]

Since the spring of 1942, in communications with Britain and the United States, Stalin had made it clear that Russian "security" in his view required that Poland's eastern boundary be established approximately along the "Curzon Line" (so-called because it was proposed by the British Foreign Secretary, Lord Curzon, at the end of World War I) rather than along the frontier some 150 miles farther east imposed by the Treaty of Riga in 1921. Nor could Stalin's view of the matter be deemed unreasonable *per se*, or historically unjustified. Curzon in Paris in 1919 had been moved to draw his "Line" primarily by ethnic considerations: between the "Line" and the frontier as actually later established, only a little more than a third of the population was Polish. (There were more Ukrainians and Byelorussians in this region than there were Poles.) The dominant treaty-makers in Riga in 1921, on the other hand, had been moved by perfervid nationalist ambitions (few political religions could match Polish patriotism in fanaticism), sustained by a Western desire to make Poland as wide a *cordon sanitaire* against infectious communism as possible: they took this extra slice out of former Russian territory only because a Soviet Union torn by civil strife was too weak to prevent it. Inevitably, the motives that had operated effectively in Riga in 1921 operated in reverse in Moscow in 1945.

But reasonable or no, justified or no, inevitable or no, this Curzon Line proposal ran head-on into the *third* hard fact conditioning Yalta's consideration of the Polish problem. The members of the Polish Government which in 1939 had fled from Warsaw to Romania, thence to France, and finally (in 1940) to London; and which continued to regard itself as the legitimate government of the country it had lost—the members of this Government were intensely nationalistic, often reactionary (even feudalistic) in domestic politics, and predominantly anti-Russian in attitude. They had, certainly, reasons for distrust and fear and hatred of the Soviet Union. To the Russian occupation of western Poland in 1939 had been added the alleged murder in the Katyn Forest a year later of several thousand Polish Army officers who had been interned in camps near Smolensk, and the allegedly deliberate halting of the Russian drive upon Warsaw in the summer of 1944 in order to permit the Nazis to slaughter those (oriented toward the London Government-in-Exile) who had staged an uprising in that city in response to urgings from the Soviet radio.‡‡ It was therefore natural if unfortunate that the London

‡‡ The slaughter of the anti-communist Home Army meant there was no political group in Poland armed to protest the communization of the country when the Nazis were driven from it. On the other hand, it is by no means certain that the Russian halt before the Polish capital was wholly self-imposed. The Russians themselves asserted they were blocked by stiffened German resistance, and support is lent this contention by the fact that they did not actually capture the city until early January 1945—three months after the Home Army surrendered.

Poles should be utterly adamant (most of them) in their refusal to yield territory in the east to the Soviets even if they were compensated with territory taken from prewar Germany in the west. Churchill had pleaded with them to do so during the months preceding Yalta. He felt that the Poles had a claim upon the conscience of Britain because of the valor with which nearly a half-million Polish troops (most of them released from Russian internment after the Nazi invasion of 1941) had fought beside the British in North Africa, Italy, and on the Western Front; yet he was frequently and openly exasperated by the shortsightedness and inflexibility of London Polish politicians and was convinced that only dire consequences, for the Poles and for the West, could flow from an intransigent stand on the Russian border question. When Stanislaw Mikolajczyk, Premier of the Polish Government-in-Exile, tried to persuade his colleagues to agree to the Curzon Line, however, he was forced (in late November 1944) to resign.

Meanwhile, the Kremlin had taken steps to insure that, when Poland was liberated by the Red Army, it would have a pro-Soviet Government. As the Red Army crossed the Vistula and advanced upon Warsaw in July of 1944, it was announced that a Polish Committee of National Liberation, headed by a left-wing Socialist and by a Communist, would administer the reconquered Polish territory from headquarters in Lublin. Thereafter two rival interim governments contended for the ultimate rule of Poland—the London Poles, supported by Britain and (less strongly) the United States, and the Lublin Poles (later headquartered in Warsaw), supported and indeed dominated by the Soviet Union. The Committee of National Liberation was in fact recognized by Moscow as *the* provisional Polish Government only a month before Yalta, a move which seemed designed to remove the question of Polish government from the realm of discussion among the Big Three. Stalin had justified it in terms of military security: he charged that "underground agents" of the London Poles were engaged in "criminal terrorist work against Soviet officers and soldiers" behind the fighting front. Roosevelt had been moved to sharp protest. "I am disturbed and deeply disappointed. . . ." he had said in a message to Stalin on December 30. "I would have thought no serious inconvenience would have been caused your Government or your Armies if you could have delayed the purely juridical act of recognition for the short period of a month remaining before we meet." He further indicated he saw "no prospect" of his country's recognizing "the Lublin Committee in its present form," since it had no established base in Polish popular opinion.[24] As for Churchill, dismayed by an accumulation of unilateral Soviet political decisions in east-central Europe, and especially by Soviet actions in Poland, he had cabled Roosevelt gloomily in January that, in its results, this war "may well prove to be more disappointing than the last."[25]

Thus Britain and the United States approached the Polish question at

Yalta with a special trepidation, even with premonitions of disaster. They were correspondingly relieved and grateful for the agreement which finally emerged from remarkably full and frank discussions. "The Provisional Government which is now functioning in Poland should . . . be reorganized on a broader democratic basis with the inclusion of democratic leaders from Poland itself and from Poles abroad," said the Conference's Declaration on Poland. "This new Government should then be called the Polish Provisional Government of National Unity." A commission composed of Molotov, Harriman, and Sir A. Clark Kerr (the British Ambassador to Russia) was appointed to facilitate this enterprise through consultation with the various Polish leaders. Then the crux of the matter, which might well be deemed an unexpected triumph for Anglo-American views: "This Polish Provisional Government of National Unity shall be pledged to the holding of free and unfettered elections as soon as possible on the basis of universal suffrage and secret ballot. In these elections all democratic and anti-Nazi parties shall have the right to take part and to put forward candidates." As regards boundaries: "The three Heads of Government consider that the eastern frontier of Poland should follow the Curzon Line with digressions from it in some regions of five or six kilometers in favor of Poland. They recognize that Poland must receive substantial accessions of territory in the North and West. They feel that the opinion of the new Polish Provisional Government of National Unity should be sought in due course on the extent of these accessions and that the final delimitation of the Western frontier of Poland should thereafter await the Peace Conference."

Throughout the discussions of Poland, and indeed throughout the Conference as a whole, the main burden of argument from the West was borne by Churchill. Roosevelt, as the only legally designated Head of State among the three principals, was presiding officer at the plenary sessions, a post which facilitated his chosen role as arbiter of the frequent clashes between Stalin and the Prime Minister, though an arbiter whose general weight, at decisive moments, was on Churchill's side. But as regards the Far East, including the terms and timing of Russia's entrance into the war against Japan, the decisions were reached altogether through personal conference between Stalin and Roosevelt. "It was regarded as an American affair and was certainly of prime interest to their military operations," Churchill would later write. "It was not for us to claim to shape it. Anyhow we were not consulted but only asked to approve. This we did."[26] What he approved was a frankly tit-for-tat agreement. Stalin made it clear at the outset that, though there was an obvious identity of interest among the Big Three regarding Nazi Germany, no such identity obtained regarding Japan. Only in terms of definite national gains would he be able to justify to his war-weary people an entrance into Far Eastern conflict. Roosevelt, on the other hand, was concerned not only to gain Russian aid against Japan but also to gain it in such a way and at such a time as to prevent or reduce developments inimical to America's Far Eastern policy. He feared that Russia might enter the Japanese conflict too soon, forcing commitments of American forces to the Asiatic mainland, or (contrariwise) too late, marching in to set up "People's Republics" in Manchuria and Inner Mongolia at no cost to herself after Japan had been overcome at great cost to the United States. He feared also that Stalin might effectively withdraw recognition from Chiang Kai-shek's Nationalist China, throwing all his weight on the side of the Chinese Communists with whom, despite American pressures, Chiang continued to refuse to cooperate in war against the invader. (A considerable number of Chiang's divisions were in fact employed, not against the Japanese, but in a blockade of the Communist-held area of China. At the same time, the Kuomintang, far from making desperately needed domestic reforms, seemed as determined as ever to maintain what Stimson aptly called a "corrupted feudalism.")

The upshot was an agreement, rigorously secret for obvious reasons of military security, that the Soviet Union would enter the war against Japan "in two or three months after Germany has surrendered" on the following conditions: (a) that the status quo in Outer Mongolia (The Mongolian People's Republic) would be preserved§§; (b) that the southern half of the island of Sakhalin, lost to Japan in the 1905 Russo-Japanese War, would be returned to Russia; (c) that the Kurile Islands, extending from the southern tip of Kamchatka to the northern tip of Japan, would also be returned to Russia; (d) that the port of Dairen would be internationalized, "the pre-eminent interests of the Soviet Union in the port being safeguarded"; (e) that the lease of Port Arthur as a naval base to Russia would be restored; and (f) that the Chinese-Eastern Railroad and the South-Manchurian Railroad "which provides an outlet to Dairen shall be jointly operated by the establishment of a joint Soviet-Chinese Company it being understood that the paramount interests of the Soviet Union shall be safeguarded and that China shall retain full sovereignty in Manchuria." As regards Outer Mongolia, the ports, and the railroads, it was "understood, that the agreement . . . will require concurrence of Generalissimo Chiang Kai-shek" and that the President "will take measures in order to obtain this concurrence on advice from Marshal Stalin." In the closing words of the document of agreement, Russia expressed her "readiness to conclude with the Nationalist Government of China a pact of friendship and alliance between the USSR and China in order to render assistance to China with its armed forces for the purpose of liberating China from the Japanese yoke."

The only seriously questionable part of this agreement—questionable on moral grounds and in terms of possible practical effect—had to do

§§ In other words, the twenty-year-old fact of Outer Mongolia's autonomy—its separation from Chinese sovereignty—would be recognized.

with the disposal of Chinese resources at a Conference where no Chinese was present. Certainly China's sovereign power was affected. The Port Arthur and railroad concessions seemed tantamount to giving Russia domination of Manchuria unless (an unlikely event) a strong and united China emerged from the conflict; even a strong China could not really have "full sovereignty" there despite the signed promise that she "shall retain it." Chiang, moreover, was to be given no alternative to "concurrence" in this arrangement, since the President was to "take measures . . . to obtain" it and flatly promised (with Churchill) in the agreement document that the "claims of the Soviet Union shall unquestionably be fulfilled after Japan has been defeated." On the face of it, the United States was buying something she wanted with property that belonged to another.

And yet, if one is to judge this transaction realistically, he must ask to just what extent the "property" in question actually belonged to Chiang's China. Manchuria and the adjoining portion of North China, down to a point well below Shanghai, had been forcibly occupied by the Japanese for years before Pearl Harbor Day, and Chiang, without massive outside aid, would never have been able to repossess them. He might have grown strong enough to do so if "Vinegar Joe" Stilwell's program for building a modern Chinese Army, with all that this implied in the way of social and economic reform, had been carried through. Instead, the program had been continuously frustrated by the corrupt incompetents of Chiang's military entourage and by the well-heeled and none-too-scrupulous "China Lobby" in Washington. Much material support that would have helped Stilwell toward establishment of the ground strength he knew would be needed to halt any major Japanese offensive had gone instead to Chennault, who had pleased the Kuomintang with his assertions that he could drive the Japanese back with air power alone if he were properly equipped. Dire indeed had been the consequences of this mistaken policy in the spring, summer, and fall of 1944. The Japanese, goaded by Chennault's aggressive air strategy, had launched the offensives Stilwell had feared; the inadequately trained and incompetently led Chinese troops had been impotent against them; and within six months nearly half of China, including the forward bases of Chennault's U. S. Fourteenth Air Force, was in Japanese hands.

In the whole dark picture on the Asian mainland during this period, there had been only two bright spots, both the result of Stilwell's initiative and energy. One was his brilliant campaign in northern Burma, where he had used Chinese troops in conjunction with British and American units to defeat the Japanese decisively, capturing Myitkyina in early August 1944.¶¶ Myitkyina was the southern terminus of the incredible 478-mile Ledo Road whose construction Stilwell had insisted upon

¶¶ ". . . this was one of the great and insufficiently noticed military epics of the war," in the opinion of Secretary of War Stimson.[27]

against strong opposition (the project had seemed a fantastic impossibility to most of those who first heard him propose it) and which had been opened to traffic in early January 1945. This last was the other bright spot in the picture. But in Chungking, a proved ability, even a brilliant and possibly China-saving success, weighed little against the threat to personal privilege and profit which Stilwell, just by being what he was where he was, presented to Chiang's superficially charming if far from charmed circle. "Vinegar Joe" had been relieved of his post and recalled to Washington by Roosevelt in October of 1944 after Chiang had indicated readiness to insist upon the recall as a point of personal privilege. Major General Albert C. Wedemeyer had replaced him (Wedemeyer's basic attitudes and political views were much more in line with Chiang's than Stilwell's could ever be), and the weary struggle to achieve a working arrangement between Chinese Communists and Chinese Nationalists had been continued—largely by General Hurley, whose specific assignment was to help China toward political and military unity. The effort, it must be said, had had no truly substantial success.

In view of all this, it could and would be argued that Chiang was lucky to have Roosevelt negotiate for him at Yalta—that the secret accord there gave him a far better deal, on paper at least, than he would have been likely to obtain directly—and Chiang's own later actions would lend credence to this argument. He would not protest the Yalta terms when they were made known to him (the Chinese Communists, who were strong in North China, *did* protest), but would instead enter with alacrity into the Sino-Russian Treaty of August 1945, wherein the China provisions of the Yalta Agreement were embodied. He would be highly pleased to have the Russian agreement facilitate the movement of his forces into the key centers of North China and to have his authority recognized there.

Only later, when it became abundantly clear that the Kuomintang had no real hold upon the people of China and when the U.S.S.R. began systematically to violate every key provision of the Yalta Far Eastern agreement, even to the extent of withdrawing her recognition of the Chinese Nationalists and backing the Chinese Communists (it would be hard to determine to what extent this shift of policy determined, and to what extent it merely reflected, the collapse of Nationalist power) —only then would Chiang and his right-wing American friends discover a "plot" by "subversives" to "betray" him at Yalta. Thereafter the myth of betrayal would grow with what it fed on, which was chiefly irrational fear. When Alger Hiss became the principal in a sensational court trial that resulted in his conviction and imprisonment on a perjury charge, in circumstances such as to make the charge seem identical with a charge of treason, the right-wing myth-makers would discover that the Yalta "plot" had been primarily engineered by Hiss. Actually, though he had gone to Yalta as one of Stettinius's three principal advisers,*** Hiss had had no direct responsibility nor even much active concern for Chinese, Polish, or German policy, nor with any other large immediate problem involving direct power-interest conflicts between Russia and the United States. Instead, he had been absorbed by problems of postwar international organization, the establishment of the United Nations as a permanent world forum and security agency.

And these problems, the intensely felt need for a permanent peacemaking and -keeping organization, had comprised Roosevelt's own overriding concern at Yalta. It was a concern to which urgency was added by the progress he knew was being made by the Manhattan Project. On December 30, 1944, General Groves had given firm assurance that the Project would produce the first atomic bomb for use against an enemy sometime in August, that a second bomb would be available before the end of the year, and that thereafter bombs would be produced at shorter intervals. Project scientists predicted, with an admittedly wide margin for error, that the first bomb would have an explosive force equivalent to five hundred tons of TNT and the second a force of a thousand tons![28]

Should this information have removed Roosevelt's anxiety to insure Russian entry at the proper time into the Far Eastern war? Should it have prevented his making any such deal with Stalin as he had actually made? Later critics would say so: they would not hesitate to condemn him because his foresight failed to discern what to their hindsight seemed obvious. He, however, lived in Time rather than Eternity and had to shape his judgments as to the future in terms of present solid information. And of what did this last consist? He had been informed that Manhattan Project scientists and engineers were convinced that a "practical" bomb would be available that summer—but the facts remained that no such bomb was yet in existence, that there had been no test explosion, and that his closest military advisers were far from unanimous in belief that the bomb would "work." Admiral Leahy, Chairman of the Joint Chiefs of Staff, had no confidence in it whatever.††† Roosevelt had been

*** He was then Deputy Director of the Office of Special Political Affairs in the State Department. Says Stettinius in his *Roosevelt and the Russians* (p. 31): "Shortly after I became Under Secretary of State—October, 1943—with the approval of the President and Mr. Hull I called in the FBI to conduct a security examination of the State Department. . . . I never heard of any questioning of Mr. Hiss' loyalty from anyone inside or outside of the State Department or from the FBI during my time of service in the Department. Hiss performed brilliantly through the Dumbarton Oaks conversations, the Yalta Conference, the San Francisco Conference, and the first meeting of the United Nations Assembly in London. I always had reason to believe that Hiss acted honorably and patriotically in the performance of his duties at these conferences."

††† That summer, just a few days before the first atomic bomb was dropped, Leahy would reportedly say to King George VI of England that he did not think the weapon would be as effective as predicted. Indeed, he would indicate doubt even this late that it was a practicable weapon at all. "It sounds like a professor's dream to me," he would say. (Forrest C. Pogue, "Yalta in Retrospect," in *The Meaning of Yalta*, edited by John L. Snell [Baton Rouge, 1956] p. 199.)

further informed that, by scientific estimate, a single atomic bomb might have an explosive force equivalent to that delivered by a bombing raid of five hundred planes; if so it would be, by Roosevelt's standards, a weapon of fantastic potency. But the fact remained that thousand-plane raids had been numerous over Germany, yet Germany continued to fight fiercely. Indeed, her war production and morale had remained high enough to permit the recent launching of an offensive so massive it had threatened disaster to the Western Allies during its first few days.

No, the information at hand did not justify his counting upon the atomic bomb to bring the war to an abrupt end that summer. What it *did* do was strengthen his commitment to the United Nations concept and his determination to insure full U.S. participation in it, for obviously the weapons available for future wars would be terrible beyond any ever known before. Of every proposal considered at Yalta he asked, in his own mind, the same question: "How will it affect—will it help or hinder—the maintenance of Big Three unity after the unifying effect of a common enemy has been removed?" Upon such unity, all else seemed to him to depend. Without it there could not be achieved that institutionalized balance of force and persuasion which would *be* the United Nations, as envisaged at Dumbarton Oaks.

The general organizational pattern proposed by the conferees at Dumbarton Oaks had as its main elements a General Assembly and a Security Council. The former was to be the UN's organ of persuasion—a deliberative and quasi-legislative body in which every member State, great or small, would be represented by a single voting delegate. The Security Council was to be the UN's organ of force—an executive body to the extent that it could impose sanctions, military and economic, upon peace-breaking nations. Of its eleven members, five (the United States, Great Britain, the U.S.S.R., China, and France, whose seat was being reserved) would be permanent and six would be elected for non-successive two-year terms (three to be elected each year) by the General Assembly. Two large questions had remained unanswered. *One* had to do with Great Power representation in the Assembly. Stalin, believing that Britain with the British dominions and India‡‡‡ would form a solid bloc of six votes and that the United States would control the votes of Latin American countries and the Philippines, had demanded that each of the sixteen Republics comprising the U.S.S.R. be made a voting member—a proposal wholly unacceptable to Britain and the United States. The *second* question had to do with the voting formula for the Security Council. Stalin had insisted that unanimous concurrence of the permanent members be required for deciding *any* matter brought before the Council, thus giving each Great Power an unlimited right of veto while depriving the rotating members of any really decisive power whatever.

These questions were dealt with at Yalta, and if the answer there made

‡‡‡ The proposal that India be given Assembly membership, though it was not a sovereign State, weakened the Western position in opposition to Stalin's demand.

to the first of them was not to Roosevelt's liking, it was better than he had feared it would be. Russia retreated from her demand for sixteen Assembly seats. She settled for only three, one for the U.S.S.R. as a whole, one for the Ukraine, one for Byelorussia—an arrangement Roosevelt felt bound to accept (Churchill, anxious to preserve dominion memberships, had supported it) though it violated logic and was bound to raise political difficulties at home. These last loomed especially formidable in the minds of two of his Yalta advisers, lifelong politicians who prided themselves on "hard-headed realism." One of the two was James F. Byrnes, the former Senator from South Carolina who in the opinion of most New Dealers had, by Roosevelt's need to woo conservative support, been elevated to posts considerably higher than his abilities warranted. (He had resigned as Associate Justice of the U. S. Supreme Court to accept a White House office as Director of Economic Stabilization in 1942 and was later War Mobilization Director.) The other adviser was Edward J. Flynn, Democratic political boss of the Bronx, whose designation as a member of the delegation had seemed inexplicable to most of the other American delegates and would certainly have provoked loud cries of protest had it been known to the general public. These two were convinced that Congressional acceptance of the UN proposals would be imperiled unless Russia's three Assembly votes were matched by three for the United States, and at their urging a tired Roosevelt, at the end of the Conference, had sought and (rather strangely) had obtained without difficulty a promise from Stalin that Russia would support an American request for two more seats if such a request were made at the organizing conference.

Byrnes and Flynn may also have advised Roosevelt to keep the three-vote arrangement secret until he had had time to explain it and the reasons for it to Congressional leaders. At any rate, this is what Roosevelt decided to do. The official communiqué issued to the public at the close of the Conference made no mention of the promise by Britain and the U.S. to support Russia's claim to multiple Assembly seats.[29]

Neither did it mention (no doubt for the same reasons) the agreement reached on the other large question which Dumbarton Oaks had left unanswered—that of votes and vetoes in the Security Council. Months before the Conference opened, Alger Hiss, on behalf of a special State Department committee set up to study the problem, had drafted a recommended voting formula for the Security Council which distinguished between resolutions having to do with "the pacific settlement of disputes between nations" and resolutions calling for "diplomatic, economic or military measures to preserve peace." No State that was a party to a dispute, whether a permanent Council member or not, would be permitted to vote on proposals for that dispute's peaceful settlement. As regards "judicial and quasi-judicial procedures," in other words, there would be no right of veto. But as regards resolutions calling for the application of sanctions, the veto right would be maintained: no such resolution could be adopted without the unanimous consent of the permanent members. This formula, Hiss had written, was based "on the traditional Anglo-American principle that a party to a dispute should not be able to prevent consideration of that dispute" and would at the same time protect the United States against the use of her armed forces "without . . . [her] specific consent." It was substantially this formula that had been agreed upon at Yalta. "Decisions of the Security Council on procedural matters should be made by an affirmative vote of seven members," said the Protocol of the Proceedings of the Crimea Conference. "Decisions of the Security Council on all other matters should be made by an affirmative vote of seven members including the concurring votes of the permanent members. . . ."

This, when it became publicly known, would disappoint those who had hoped the member States would relinquish to the UN such elements of sovereignty as pertained to the use of force in the settlement of international disputes, thus giving to the UN one of the essential elements of a genuine world government. But Roosevelt was convinced that such hopes went far beyond the limit of the possible. Congress, in the first place, would never have permitted such a giving up of sovereignty: if the Russians had not first proposed the Big Power veto, the U.S. or Britain must certainly have done so; and, in any case, the denial of the veto right would probably have greatly increased rather than reduced the chances of world war. Just suppose that a dispute arose between Russia and another State so serious that hostilities were threatened. Suppose that the General Assembly condemned Russia's stand and that the Security Council, by majority vote, recommended a solution which Russia chose to regard as inimical to her vital interests. Suppose, finally, that Russia was then expelled from the UN or withdrew voluntarily (and angrily), or that economic and military sanctions were voted against her by a Council majority? What would be the effect? Either the collapse of the UN into impotence or a world war!

Always in Roosevelt's mind the argument on this matter returned to its starting point. Big Three unity was vital! With it, an enduring peace could be made. Without it, the world faced measureless catastrophe. And he left Yalta exultantly convinced that this unity was now more real than ever before, having survived triumphantly its greatest test thus far. Churchill, at a large dinner given by Stalin on February 8, expressed the feeling that they all stood "on the crest of a hill" with a glorious future stretching before them. Roosevelt felt the same.

There then rang as music in Roosevelt's ears the words of Stalin's toast to the alliance of the three Powers, at this same dinner. "It is good to have an alliance of the principal Powers during a war," Stalin said. "It would not be possible to win the war without the alliance. But an alliance against the common enemy is something clear and understandable. Far more complicated is an alliance after the war for securing lasting peace and the fruits of victory. That we fought together was a good thing, but it was not so difficult; on the other hand, that in these days the work of Dumbarton Oaks has been consummated and the legal foundations laid for organizing security and strengthening peace is a great achievement." Stalin then proposed "a toast for the successful conclusion of Dumbarton Oaks, and that our alliance, born under stress of battle, be made solid and extended after the war, that our countries should . . . defend the cause of unity with as much enthusiasm in peace as during the war."[30]

And so Roosevelt's highest hopes rode out on the words of the "invitation" that formed part of the opening of the final communiqué from Yalta:

"The Government of the United States of America, on behalf of itself and of the Government of the United Kingdom, the Union of Soviet Socialist Republics, and the Republic of China and of the Provisional Government of the French Republic, invite the Government of —— to send representatives to a Conference of the United Nations to be held on 25th April, 1945 . . . at San Francisco . . . to prepare a Charter for a General International Organization for the maintenance of international peace and security."[31]

iii. *The Bright and the Dark*

High hopes. Bright hopes . . .

But then, abruptly, deep disappointments. Dark disappointments, and even despairs . . .

The bright and the dark ran side by side in a rush of contrasting events through the weeks after Yalta; they thrust against one another and tumbled over one another as if struggling for the minds of men . . .

When Roosevelt left Yalta he flew down to Great Bitter Lake, midway along the Suez Canal. Here was anchored the cruiser U.S.S. *Quincy*, which had transported him from America and would return him there. Aboard it were the three wire service newspapermen who normally accompanied him everywhere but who had not been permitted to go from Malta to the Crimea. They all thought he looked dreadfully ill: he seemed (one of them later wrote) to have "aged ten years in ten days." Dark patches were beneath his eyes, his cheeks were hollowed and deeply seamed, loose folds of skin drooped below his chin, and his neck was so shrunken that his shirt collars were now too large. He confessed to Merriman Smith of the United Press that he was very tired and had lost weight "but he refused to take it seriously, said he would gain it back at Warm Springs."[32]

It was easy to believe that he would. Again and again in the past he had demonstrated an astonishing resilience, a wholly amazing recuperative power. He had sustained for weeks on end pressures that would have broken a dozen ordinary men—had sustained them and operated under them until his face was drawn, ashen, and he was obviously on the verge of collapse from nervous exhaustion. Then he'd taken time off—not much time generally, often only a few days. He had gone fishing at sea, had gone up to Hyde Park or down to Warm Springs, or (last year for a whole month) to Bernard Baruch's great estate in South Carolina, and had returned to his crushing job refreshed and restored. It was as if he had within him a reservoir of strength fed by inexhaustible springs; if the well went dry he had only to lean back a little, until it filled up again —and it filled rapidly.

But this time it didn't happen.

Aboard the *Quincy* on Great Bitter Lake he conferred with King Farouk of Egypt, Ibn Saud of Saudi Arabia, and Haile Selassie of Ethiopia on Middle Eastern problems—chiefly on the future of Palestine —and it was noted that his old zest and vital charm lighted these conversations only intermittently. It was also noted by Harry Hopkins, who though desperately ill was present and as acutely perceptive as ever; it was noted by Hopkins that ". . . the President seemed not to fully comprehend what Ibn Saud was saying" in response to his [Roosevelt's] plea that the Arabs "admit some more Jews into Palestine." At any rate Roosevelt repeated his plea two or three times and was each time answered with a flat "no" backed by the clear implication that "the Arabs would take up arms before they would consent" to this. Whereupon Roosevelt became, in Hopkins' view, "overly impressed," going so far as to tell a press conference later on that he had "learned more from Ibn Saud about Palestine in five minutes than he had learned in a lifetime" before. (". . . the only thing he learned," commented Hopkins sourly, ". . . is that the Arabs don't want any more Jews in Palestine.") Hopkins was further displeased by his Chief's response to an irritating incident that occurred while the *Quincy* sailed north out of the lake through the Suez Canal toward Alexandria. The incident centered, as so many irritating incidents did, on De Gaulle. Roosevelt had asked the touchy Frenchman to meet him in Algiers for a friendly visit, but this invitation, conciliatory in intent, was deemed by De Gaulle a summons from superior to inferior which his dignity as leader of a Great Power would not permit him to accept. It rankled the general that he had not been asked to participate in the Crimea Conference; failing that, it seemed to him that the President should call upon him in Paris. Accordingly he curtly declined the invitation. Roosevelt wished to reply through a statement to the press plainly revealing his anger—a show of petulance which Hopkins successfully urged him not to make. Petulance remained the weather of his spirit, however. He displayed it when Hopkins, in dread of adding seasickness to his other miseries, left the ship at Algiers in order to rest a few days at Marrakech and then fly home. Roosevelt, who had counted on Hopkins for help in drafting aboard ship the report he must make on Yalta to the Congress, bade him a cold farewell.§§§[33]

The nine-day voyage home did not perk up Roosevelt as every sea voyage in the past had done. It did not begin well. The irritation with De Gaulle was swiftly followed by the tragedy of "Pa" Watson—Major General Edwin M. Watson—who as military aide had accompanied his Chief to Yalta and who, two days out of Algiers, died of a stroke. The event produced an unprecedented effect on Roosevelt. He who had always maintained a high thick wall of reticence around his private sorrows, and indeed around all his deepest feelings—who had made no open display of emotion when his mother died, nor when such longtime intimates as Louis Howe and Missy LeHand and Marvin McIntyre died—now spoke at length and repeatedly of the sorrow he felt at Watson's passing.[34] He wore his grief as he had his long dark cape at Yalta when official photographs were taken. The cape had given him a funereal appearance, accentuating the ravaged, sunken look of his cheeks and temples, the dark weariness under his eyes; his grief made those who were with him wonder if Watson's death had been for him not only the loss of a beloved friend but also a painful intimation of his own mortality. Certainly it was a bad sign. Another was the swift fading of his shipboard tan after his return to Washington. It was as if days of sitting on deck in the sun spread but a thin powder of color over his face, a powder that dissolved almost at once in the atmosphere of the Oval Study, leaving him again pale and wan.

Nor was his grief over Watson the only unprecedented fissure now opened in the wall of his reticence. When he made his report to the Congress on Yalta, March 1, he spoke sitting down (never again would he have the strength to stand pridefully, defiantly erect in his braces) and began by asking "pardon . . . for this unusual posture." But, he went on, "I know you will realize that it makes it a lot easier for me not to have to carry about ten pounds of steel around on the bottom of my legs; and also because of the fact that I have just completed a fourteen-thousand-mile trip." Never before had he made public reference to his infirmity, much less called attention to it in a way that could be interpreted as a bid for sympathy, even pity. As for the speech itself, it was not up to his usual level either, in the opinion of most of his close associates, despite his realization of its crucial importance to the effectuation of his plans for postwar international cooperation. It was of "prodigious length" for one thing, as was noted in the remarkable diary kept by his confidential secretary, William D. Hassett, "and the President ad-libbed at length—a wretched practice which weakens even a better effort." Robert E. Sherwood found the President's delivery to be "extremely casual." Yet, added Hassett, "to my surprise the reaction of the

§§§ The two were destined not to see one another again. By the time Roosevelt arrived back in Washington Hopkins had flown to Rochester, Minnesota, where he yet remained in the Mayo Clinic as a patient in the second week of April 1945.

senators and representatives—except for the overcautious like Vandenberg and the diehards like Taft—was favorable. . . . I therefore revised my earlier estimate." He might then have wondered, and Sherwood might have wondered, if the "ad-libbed" remarks were really as casual, as unpremeditated as they had at first seemed to those who listened while following the script from which he spoke. Even the opening remark about his legs, which had seemed so impulsively personal, could have been part of a large objective design, for he was appealing for support and was willing to use whatever tools were at hand to obtain it. "It has been a long journey [to Yalta]," he had said. "I hope you will all agree that it was a fruitful one. Speaking in all frankness, the question of whether it is entirely fruitful or not lies to a great extent in your hands. For unless you here in the halls of the American Congress—with the support of the American people—concur in the decisions reached at Yalta, and give them your active support, the meeting will not have produced lasting results."[35]

As he spoke he remained convinced that the Conference had been, on the whole, remarkably successful—that it had resulted in decisions worthy of full American support. It was a conviction shared by nearly all who had been members of the U.S. delegation or who had, otherwise, intimate knowledge of what had actually happened at Yalta. Politically as well as militarily the world picture looked bright to them in the first days of March.

Yet by that time there had already begun for Winston Churchill the strangeness of living in a double world—a public world of rejoicing and triumph, a private world of dark fear and foreboding. "I moved amid cheering crowds, or sat at a table adorned with congratulations and blessings from every part of the Grand Alliance, with an aching heart and a mind oppressed. . . ."[36] And Roosevelt also knew this double world, bright and dark, though with a difference born of a different character, a different outlook. Cheers, congratulations, blessings were everywhere given and received throughout the Allied world because everywhere on Europe's fighting fronts the Allied arms had gained and continued to gain enormous victories. But with military successes came political failures, the latter increasing in nearly direct proportion to the former, shaping a bitter irony. . . .

On the same day as Stalin's large dinner at Yalta, during which he gave his famous toast to Big Three unity, Eisenhower's armies on the Western Front, now comprising eighty-five divisions, had launched the first of a series of coordinated offensives for which the way had been prepared by months of unprecedentedly massive air bombardment.¶¶¶

¶¶¶ Those portions of the air offensive that had concentrated on military objectives had proved highly effective. The attacks on ballbearing plants, plane factories, oil refineries, fuel storage tanks, railway lines and equipment, trucks, etc., had drastically reduced the mobility of the German forces. If all available air power had been

It had been expected that the Germans, under pressure, would fight only delaying actions west of the Rhine—that they would conduct planned withdrawals behind that formidable river barrier and establish there so strong a defensive line that it could not be breached until late April or early May. Instead, Hitler, with the death-loving insanity typical of his "genius," had commanded his armies to stand and fight where they were (to retreat would be "treason"), the inevitable result being that his military strength in the West, already much reduced by his Ardennes gamble, was wholly unable to cope with the Anglo-American forces by the time these had established themselves on the west bank of the Rhine almost continuously from Coblenz northward in early March. Only the steep-walled Rhine, of itself alone equivalent to a powerful defending army, then shielded the heart of Germany.

But not for long. There came to the Allies at that moment one of the great lucky chances—perhaps the greatest—of the fighting war.

In midafternoon of Wednesday, March 7, 1945, a platoon of the U. S. 9th Armored Division reached the crest of a hill above the town of Remagen on the Rhine, midway between Bonn to the north and Coblenz to the south. Theretofore all Allied units to reach the river had found all bridges there destroyed, even when such destruction cut off the only means of retreat for considerable German forces yet west of the Rhine. Hence Sergeant Alexander A. Drabik, commanding this platoon, could hardly believe his eyes when, looking down, he saw that the great Ludendorff Bridge at Remagen was still standing intact. Knowing that explosive charges must have been set upon it and that it could be blown momentarily, he did not hesitate an instant. He led his platoon full speed down the hill, reached the bridge's western end at precisely 3:50 P.M. (a German captain had been ordered to blow it at precisely 4:00 P.M.), and then ran hard down the middle of the bridge under heavy small arms fire, his men following in squad column to the other side. All arrived safely. "We took cover in some bomb craters," Drabik later said. "Then we just sat and waited for the others to come."[37] And the others certainly came! Within ten minutes, a hundred Americans were across. Within twenty-four hours, eight thousand were across. Within five days, several divisions were across. By that time, floating Treadway bridges, which were easily transported in sections and could be laid from bank to bank in a day, had begun to bear the heavy military traffic needed to reinforce and supply the Remagen bridgehead; the Ludendorff, weakened by incessant heavy German air and artillery attack upon it, then ceased to be used. Engineers continued to work on it, however, seeking to repair it, and scores of them were killed or injured when it at last collapsed on March 17.

Meanwhile, to the south of the U. S. First Army sector (the Remagen

---

concentrated on military objectives instead of being dissipated in indiscriminate destruction of cities and civilian lives, Germany might have been rendered militarily impotent before the end of 1944—or so many experts would conclude from the U. S. Strategic Bombing Survey.

bridgehead was in this sector), the U. S. Third and Seventh Armies conquered the Rhineland from Coblenz to Karlsruhe in a continuous series of slashing drives. Patton's Army was especially swift and effective. It reached the Rhine just north of Coblenz only a few hours after the capture of the Remagen bridge, climaxing a march of sixty-five miles in fifty-eight hours. Two days later, First and Third formed a juncture between Remagen and Coblenz (Bonn was captured by the First Army that same day), closing a steel ring around some five German divisions. These successes in the south were aided by Montgomery's operations in the north, where his Twenty-First Army Group played much the same strategic role as it had before Caen in Normandy. Montgomery engaged the Germans on the most vital portion of their front, for the Ruhr lay directly before him; when he applied pressure, therefore, as he did with the Canadian First Army offensive launched February 8, he immediately sucked onto his attack front the available German reserves. The U. S. Ninth Army on the Canadians' right flank was supposed to attack on February 10 but was delayed for two weeks by a Roer River flood produced when the Germans smashed the discharge valves of the only Roer dam that remained uncaptured. The Canadians perforce slogged ahead alone against heavy resistance for seventeen miles in fifteen days before halting to regroup. But when at last the Roer flood receded and the U. S. Ninth attacked, it encountered a weakened, virtually reserveless enemy and, with the aid of complete tactical surprise, scored a great victory at little cost; it broke through the Siegfried Line and had reached the Rhine opposite Düsseldorf by March 2.

There then remained west of the Rhine only narrow and steadily constricting pockets of organized resistance, and within a little more than three weeks the last of these was crushed. The German defeat was overwhelming. Some three hundred thousand troops, the equivalent of twenty divisions, became prisoners of war; at least another hundred thousand were killed or wounded; and vast quantities of tanks, guns, and transports were captured or destroyed. Total German manpower losses between the opening of the Ardennes drive and the reaching and breaching of the Rhine line were upwards of six hundred thousand. There was by then in the Remagen bridgehead a full-strength American Army of three corps, "poised, ready to strike in any direction,"[38] and a second crossing of the Rhine had just been achieved, Patton having sneaked across a division of his Third Army south of Mainz on the night of March 22–23.

On the following night opened the last act of the war on the Western Front. It opened with the thunder and lightning of two thousand guns arching shells across the Rhine in the vicinity of Wesel, north and west of the Ruhr—a canopy of shells under which the assault force of four divisions, two Americans, two British, marched down to the water's edge and there climbed into boats that carried them to the opposite bank. Prolonged, massive, typically meticulous had been Montgomery's prepara-

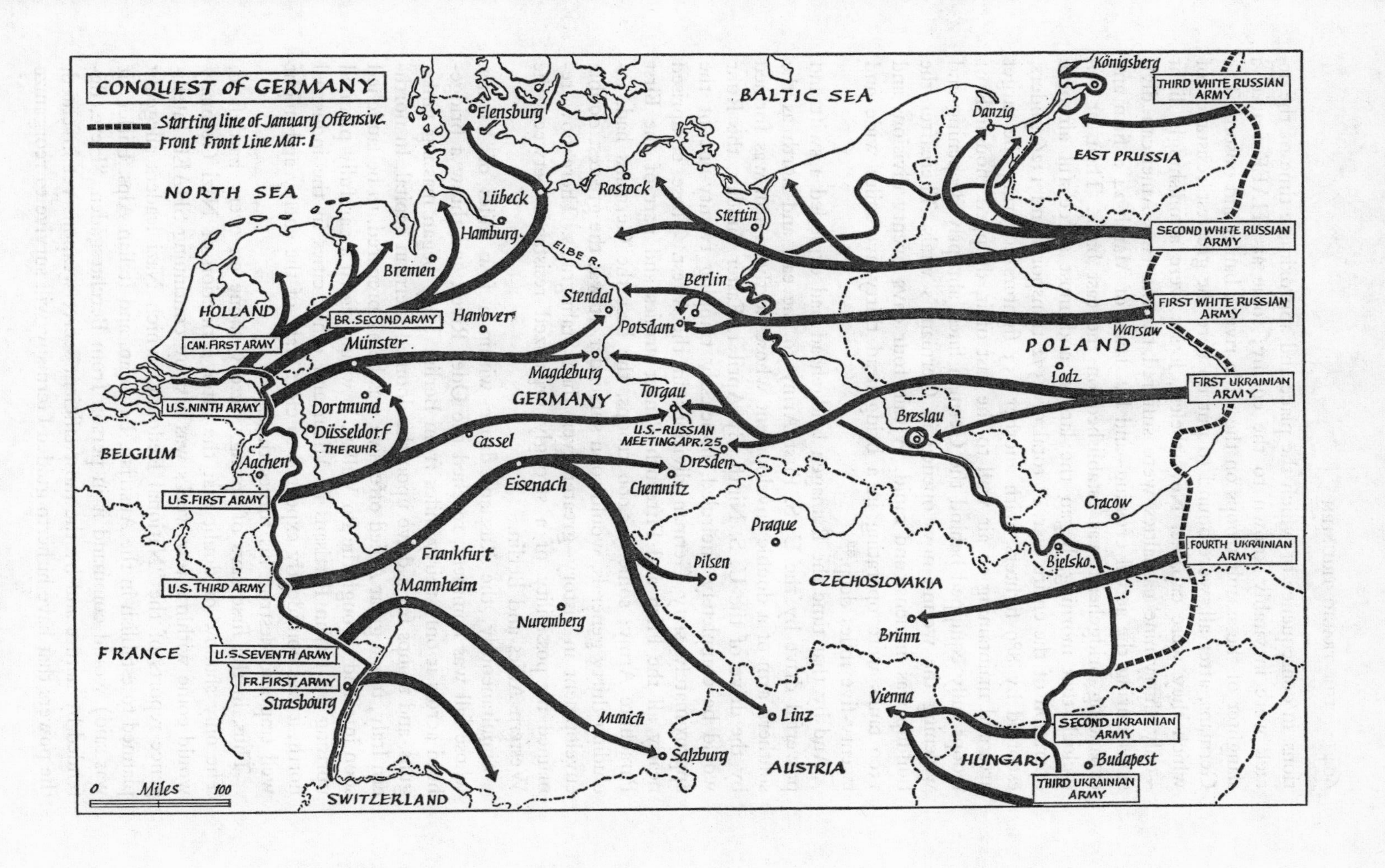

CONQUEST OF GERMANY
Starting line of January Offensive
Front Front Line Mar. 1
NORTH SEA
BALTIC SEA
Flensburg
Lübeck
Hamburg
Bremen
Rostock
Stettin
Danzig
Königsberg
EAST PRUSSIA
THIRD WHITE RUSSIAN ARMY
SECOND WHITE RUSSIAN ARMY
FIRST WHITE RUSSIAN ARMY
Warsaw
POLAND
Lodz
FIRST UKRAINIAN ARMY
Breslau
Cracow
Bielsko
FOURTH UKRAINIAN ARMY
ELBE R.
Berlin
Stendal
Potsdam
Magdeburg
Hanover
HOLLAND
BR. SECOND ARMY
CAN. FIRST ARMY
Münster
U.S. NINTH ARMY
Dortmund
Düsseldorf
THE RUHR
GERMANY
Torgau
U.S.-RUSSIAN MEETING APR. 25
Dresden
Cassel
BELGIUM
Aachen
U.S. FIRST ARMY
Eisenach
Chemnitz
Prague
Frankfurt
Pilsen
CZECHOSLOVAKIA
U.S. THIRD ARMY
Mannheim
Nuremberg
Brünn
FRANCE
U.S. SEVENTH ARMY
FR. FIRST ARMY
Strasbourg
Munich
Linz
Vienna
SECOND UKRAINIAN ARMY
HUNGARY
Budapest
Salzburg
AUSTRIA
THIRD UKRAINIAN ARMY
0 Miles 100
SWITZERLAND

tions, in consequence of which the place and approximate time of the attack were inevitably known to the enemy; some at SHAEF feared a slaughter of the assault troops on the wide river's banks and bosom. The Germans, after all, were bound to put up here the greatest resistance of which they were capable. Nevertheless, losses were astonishingly light —only thirty-nine casualties were suffered by the two American divisions during the actual crossing—and by dawn of March 24 a firm and expanding bridgehead was established on the east bank. Then, at ten o'clock that morning, began the largest and most successful airborne operation of the entire war. A total of 1572 transports and 1326 gliders, escorted by 889 fighters, with another 253 fighters covering the target area and maintaining an air wall to the east of it, dropped thousands of troops fully equipped behind the German lines, abruptly deepening and widening the wound now opened in Germany's vitals. Thereafter the buildup was immense and rapid. Within four days twenty divisions and 1500 tanks were operating in a bridgehead thirty-five miles wide and twenty-five miles deep.[39]

And by that time the Remagen bridgehead had exploded a swift and powerful drive by the U. S. First Army to the east and north as the southern arm of a double envelopment whose northern arm was formed by the drive of the U. S. Ninth. By April 1, Easter Sunday, the Ruhr would be completely encircled, hopelessly trapping twenty-one of the approximately sixty German divisions in the West. These comprised nearly all the Fifth and Fifteenth Panzer armies and part of the First Parachute Army; some 325,000 troops, the best the Germans had, including thirty generals, would soon surrender. It was the greatest double envelopment in history—greater even than Stalingrad's. There now remained no possibility of a strongly organized resistance between the Western Allies and Berlin.

Simultaneously, the Russians drove within a few miles of Vienna, whose fall was imminent, reached the Oder River, and threw a bridgehead across it only thirty miles from Berlin. They began massing tanks, guns, and troops for a drive upon the doomed German capital. In northern Italy, too, a great Allied offensive was being prepared, to be launched soon into and through the Po Valley. It would signal a carefully planned uprising by Italian Partisans in Milan and other cities in the industrial north; it was confidently expected to clear Italy of the enemy and might well trap and destroy his forces there.

Thus, in the first days of spring, victory shone on every battlefield. The only shadow of doubt that the utter extinction of Nazi Germany would come within a few weeks was cast by continuing SHAEF Intelligence reports of the "National Redoubt" which Nazi leaders allegedly planned to establish in the Austrian, Bavarian, and Italian Alps. Hitler (it was said) would command it in person from Berchtesgaden. "Here, defended by nature and by the most efficient secret weapons yet invented, the powers that have hitherto guided Germany will survive to reorganize her resurrection," said a report read by Eisenhower on March 11; "here armaments will be manufactured in bombproof factories, food and equipment will be stored in vast underground caverns and a specially selected corps of young men will be trained in guerrilla warfare, so that a whole underground army can be fitted and directed to liberate Germany from the occupying forces."[40] This was a warning that Churchill, Field Marshal Brooke, and the British Joint Chiefs refused to take very seriously.**** After study, "the general conclusion of our Chiefs of Staff was that a prolonged German campaign, or even guerrilla [operations], in the mountains was unlikely on any serious scale," Churchill would record. "The possibility was therefore relegated by us . . . to the shades."[41] But at SHAEF and in Bradley's headquarters, the possibility was deemed a probability, and it weighed heavily on the dominant minds. ". . . it shaped our tactical thinking during the closing weeks of the war," said Bradley later.[42] Largely in consequence of it, and in ignorance or disregard of political developments that then oppressed Churchill and disturbed Roosevelt,†††† Eisenhower decided that his forces, following the encirclement of the Ruhr, should advance in main strength through the center of Germany on an Erfurt–Leipzig axis to the Elbe River and there halt to await a linkup with the Russians that would split Germany in two. Meanwhile the U. S. Third Army, the U. S. Seventh, and the French First would be driving into the Alpine region to forestall the organization of the National Redoubt. In the north, Montgomery's Twenty-first Army Group, with the U. S. Ninth detached from it and restored to Bradley, would clear Holland and drive east and north through Hamburg and Lübeck to Denmark.

This decision became at once an issue between the British and Americans.[43]

On March 28, in a personal message that had not been cleared through the Combined Chiefs of Staff nor the political heads of the two Governments under which he operated, Eisenhower communicated his intentions to Stalin in order that the Russians might shape their plans accordingly. He felt authorized to do this by an arrangement permitting him to deal directly with Soviet military leaders on exclusively military matters, an arrangement approved by the Combined Chiefs in January. Churchill and Brooke emphatically disagreed. Eisenhower might argue that he addressed himself, not to Premier Stalin as head of the Soviet Govern-

**** It is perhaps not irrelevant to remark that SHAEF's G-2 happened to be British. He was Major General Kenneth W. D. Strong.

†††† Churchill personally informed both Montgomery and Eisenhower of some of the political difficulties then rising between Russia and the West on March 24, when the three were together at Montgomery's headquarters. He showed the two generals an "insulting letter" just received from Molotov concerning alleged negotiations "behind the backs of the Soviet Union" (Molotov's phrase) for the surrender of German forces to the Western Allies. According to Churchill's later account, "General Eisenhower was much upset, and seemed deeply stirred with anger at what he considered most unjust and unfounded charges about our good faith." (Churchill, *Triumph and Tragedy* [Boston: 1953], pp. 442–43.)

ment, but to Generalissimo Stalin as Commander-in-Chief of the Red Army; but such argument—splitting Soviet totalitarian personality, dividing war from politics at this late stage of the struggle—seemed to the British a splitting of hairs, as irritating as it was unrealistic and naïve. After all, Churchill might say in reply, the President of the United States was Commander-in-Chief of his country's armed forces, yet Eisenhower's official communications with Washington were not addressed to Roosevelt but to Marshall. No, the Supreme Commander in this instance had exceeded his authority, in Churchill's view.

And if he objected strongly to the manner of Eisenhower's communication, he objected even more strongly to its substance. The Supreme Commander's strategic decision was by no means exclusively military in its effects; it was also political, and in its political character it was badly mistaken. Such was Churchill's conviction. It meant that the Russians alone would take Berlin—and Berlin was far from having become "nothing but a geographical location," as Eisenhower had said to Montgomery.[44] On the contrary, now more than ever, Berlin was "the prime and true objective of the Anglo-American armies," in Churchill's opinion. Of course Stalin, promptly and cordially approving Eisenhower's plan at a time when cordiality was notably absent from other Moscow messages to the West, expressed agreement with the Supreme Commander's estimate. Berlin, said the Soviet Premier, had "lost its former strategic importance" and the Soviet High Command planned to assign only "secondary forces in the direction" of it. But this did nothing to change Churchill's mind. Stalin's reply, said Prime Minister to Supreme Commander, "should be read in the light of . . . the political aspects. I deem it highly important that we should shake hands with the Russians as far to the east as possible. . . ."[45]

He had his reasons. Good and sufficient reasons they seemed to him to be. They derived from the political events that had begun to form a dark accompaniment to brilliant military victories within two weeks after the close of the Yalta Conference. . . .

Adopted at that Conference, and included in the communiqué issued at its end, was a ringing "Declaration on Liberated Europe" which had been a main bulwark of Western hope, Western optimism as Roosevelt addressed the Congress and Churchill the Commons on Yalta's results. It reaffirmed "a principle of the Atlantic Charter—the right of all peoples to choose the form of government under which they will live—the restoration of sovereign rights and self-government to those peoples who have been forcibly deprived of them by the aggressor nations." It proposed to apply this principle to "the peoples liberated from the domination of Nazi Germany and the peoples of the former Axis satellite states of Europe." Explicit and solemn was the pledge that had been made: "To foster the conditions in which the liberated peoples may exercise these rights, the three Governments will jointly assist the people in any European liberated state or former Axis satellite State in Europe where in their judgment conditions require (a) to establish conditions of internal peace; (b) to carry out emergency measures for the relief of distressed peoples; (c) to form interim governmental authorities broadly representative of all democratic elements in the population and pledged to the earliest possible establishment through free elections of governments responsive to the will of the people; and (d) to facilitate where necessary the holding of such elections."

Thus the words to which Stalin had subscribed. They were promptly and flagrantly contradicted by Soviet deeds.

On February 26, Andrei Vishinsky, Stalin's hatchet man, the notorious prosecutor of the Moscow "purge" trials of the 1930s, arrived in Bucharest, Rumania, on a mission from the Kremlin whose nature was made painfully clear to Rumania's King Michael the next day. Rumania had of course been a Nazi satellite State, and admittedly the Rumanian Government headed by General Radescu was rightist and anti-Soviet in attitude. Admittedly, during its less than three months in power, it had moved slightly and slowly to remove pro-Fascist officers from the Army and to institute land reforms that had been long and desperately needed. Perhaps, as Moscow charged, elements of this Government had sought to provoke extreme actions by the Left which would "justify" a use of the Army to crush the Communists who, through a National Democratic Front organized the previous October, had managed to gain 40 per cent of the Cabinet seats. But though such circumstances might explain they could not obscure the fact that Vishinsky's actions as Kremlin agent on February 27 were in violation of the letter and spirit of the Yalta agreements. He demanded audience with the King. He ordered the King to dismiss *at once* (within two hours) the Radescu Government, from which the Communist ministers had resigned three days before. He pounded the table in threatful anger and, when he left, slammed the office door so hard that plaster was cracked around it. Subsequently (on March 6), after having attempted to appoint a Prince Stirbey in Radescu's place, the King was forced to appoint the Communist Peter Groza as Premier and to accept Groza's list of Cabinet selections. When Ambassador Harriman transmitted to Molotov a Roosevelt request that an Allied Commission be established at Bucharest to insure compliance with the Yalta agreements, the request was brusquely denied.

Churchill saw in this a dark and ugly shape of things to come. They came swiftly. At the very moment that Molotov was rejecting Roosevelt's Rumanian suggestion he was insisting to Harriman and British Ambassador Clark Kerr in Moscow that only Polish leaders acceptable to the Lublin (Communist) Government be invited to consult with the Commission (Molotov, Harriman, Clark Kerr) that had been appointed to facilitate the reorganization of the Polish Provisional Government "on a broader democratic basis with the inclusion of democratic leaders from Poland itself and from Poles abroad," as agreed at Yalta. The only "reorganization" now acceptable to the Kremlin, in other words, was simply an enlargement of the present Lublin Government, and this to Western eyes was as clear a violation of the Yalta agreements as the Rumanian "solution" had been. A Polish Government "reorganized" in this way could hardly be expected to carry out the Yalta pledge to hold "free and unfettered elections as soon as possible on the basis of universal suffrage and secret ballot." Western protests were vain, however. What useful purpose could be served by inviting into the Provisional Government Polish leaders who refused to accept the Curzon Line? Moscow wanted to know. Was not this Line now an established fact, agreed upon at Yalta? And had it not also been agreed at Yalta that Russian security required a friendly Government in Poland? *Ergo*, said Stalin to Roosevelt, only those Poles should be invited who were "really striving to establish friendly relations between Poland and the Soviet Union."[46]

Simultaneously occurred the ominous "Berne Incident."[47] In February, the German SS commander in Italy, General Karl Wolff, had made contact through Italian intermediaries with American OSS personnel, saying that he wished to go to Switzerland to discuss with the Allies the surrender of German forces in Italy. In Zurich, on March 8, he met with Allen W. Dulles, head of the U. S. Intelligence Service in Switzerland, and was bluntly told that the terms remained "unconditional surrender," which is to say that no negotiations, but only arrangements for compliance, were possible. Wolff said he understood. A further "exploratory meeting" designed "to test the credientials and authority" of General Wolff was then arranged, to be held in Berne on March 19. Nothing came of this meeting in the way of troop surrender (Wolff, so far as the Anglo-Americans could discover, was acting altogether on his own limited authority and had not even consulted with anyone else), but much came of it in the way of bad feeling between Russia and the West. Informed of the impending Berne meeting by their Allies, the Russians raised no objection to it but asked that three Soviet officers be permitted to be present. Obviously, they were concerned to have the Italian front surrender arranged in such a way as to prevent any transfer of German troops from Italy to the east. Their request, however, was refused. Harriman advised refusal on the ground that only a military surrender on an exclusively Anglo-American front would be discussed, a matter wholly within the authority of the field command. Major General John R. Deane, chief of the U. S. Military Mission in Moscow, urged refusal on the ground that granting it would be an "act of appeasement" establishing a dangerous precedent. The immediate effect was a dangerous flare-up of Soviet suspicions. The refusal, said Molotov, was "utterly unexpected and incomprehensible from the point of view of Allied relations between our two countries." He demanded an immediate breaking-off of the Berne "negotiations"—a word he persisted in using despite repeated insistence by the Western Allies that only arrangements for a possible unconditional surrender of troops were being discussed.

Clearly, it was now time for the heads of Government to take matters into their own hands, dealing directly with one another on a crucial issue unresolved by their principal subordinates, and this Roosevelt endeavored to do in a cable addressed to Stalin on March 24. "You will, of course, understand that my government must give every assistance to all officers in the field in command of American forces who believe there is a possibility of forcing the surrender of enemy troops . . . ." said he. "It would be completely unreasonable for me to take any other attitude or to permit any delay which might cause additional or avoidable loss of life in the American forces." Such a surrender could have "no political implications whatever" and would constitute "no violation of our agreed principle of unconditional surrender." He therefore could not agree "to suspend investigations" in Berne "because of some objection on the part of Mr. Molotov for some reason that is completely beyond my understanding."

Thus the dark accompaniment of shining victories on the battlefield, and here matters stood on the political front—in the Balkans, in Poland, in London and Washington and Moscow—when Eisenhower made his decisions concerning the military front in the West and messaged Stalin directly concerning it, provoking vehement protests from Churchill.

The protests were ineffective in Washington. For one thing, Eisenhower by his procedure had presented the two Western Governments with a virtual *fait accompli;* nothing, practically, could be done about it. But even if this had not been so, he would not have been overruled by Marshall or the U. S. Joint Chiefs. Certainly he would not have been overruled by Roosevelt. What the general had done—inadvertently so far as politics was concerned, mistakenly so far as military realities were concerned (the "National Redoubt" proved to be the propaganda myth that the British had suspected)—was perfectly in accord with the President's long-considered and deep-seated policy toward the Russians.

For though Roosevelt, like Churchill, came to know in this early spring a double world, dark and bright, and though he raged with his last strength against the dark, he refused to see what was dark as wholly real and what was bright as wholly illusion. Each, he might have said, was real and each illusion—the two intermingled as they always do in anything seen with an earthly vision—but out of both together emerged for him (he might have said) the shape of a future, a *possible* future, that was good beyond all that had been before in the political affairs of the world. To the realization of this future he was dedicated. He was determined to be patient, endlessly patient, when confronted by Soviet mistrust. He was determined to minimize rather than maximize difficulties, making soft reply wherever possible to harsh demands and accusations. He was determined *not* to be trapped in the vicious circle of action-reaction that would, he felt, be the inevitable consequence of the "forceful" policies and tactics being urged upon him by some of his key advisers. In consequence, he spoke and acted as if he had some sympathetic understanding of the dilemma in which the Russians found themselves in the immediate aftermath of Yalta as regards the politics of eastern Europe.

Of what did this dilemma consist? On the one hand was the Yalta promise to hold "free elections" with "secret ballot" and "universal suffrage" among peoples who had not theretofore experienced political democracy nor evinced any strong desire for it. On the other hand was the Yalta pledge that only Governments "friendly to the Soviet Union" would be permitted on Russia's borders. The two promises were not altogether inconsistent when applied to Finland and were in fact fulfilled there,‡‡‡‡ but they were flatly contradictory when applied to Poland and to former Nazi satellites in the Balkans. It was impossible at that time in those places to hold "free elections" (by Western definition) that would issue in Governments "friendly to Russia" (by Politburo definition). Yet it was inevitable, being a felt Soviet necessity, that the latter Governments would be established. Hence the Yalta agreements on this point were, as someone said, futile attempt to compromise between the "impossible" and the "inevitable."[48] If the Governments that inevitably *would* be established were to conform at all to Western conceptions of freedom and democracy they would do so only through a process of evolution, an evolution that had as its prime requisite a reduction of Russian fears and suspicions of the West.

Roosevelt had striven for this reduction from the early days of his Administration. His continuing purpose was "to remove Russia's historic fear of encirclement and exclusion from Europe," as an article in *The Saturday Evening Post* had said more than a year before. He told Edgar Snow in personal interview, shortly after the article appeared, that this statement was accurate. He objected, however, to the article-writer's description of "working with the Russians" as a "Great Gamble." It was instead a Great Necessity. For what was the alternative? he asked. If the two strongest Powers on Earth were not to work together after World War II had ended, preparations should begin at once for World War III! Again, in another interview with Snow on March 3, 1945, a worn and ill President not only reiterated his Russian purpose but also asserted his conviction that it was being achieved. He and Stalin had "got close to speaking the same language at Yalta," he said, adding that many disputes had arisen between Churchill and the Soviet Premier "but Stalin agreed with every single suggestion I made." Hence his absolute confidence that "we are going to get along." Snow found this optimism "so contagious" that "it dispelled most of my fears."[49]

Was it but a manifestation of naïveté, this optimism—rooted in overweening vanity and self-confidence? Or was it kept alive by an act of stubborn faith, by an almost desperate effort of will, as a religious belief born of dread and need? ("I believe! *O Lord, help Thou mine unbelief!*") Or did it actually have a valid life of its own? Did Roosevelt see with

‡‡‡‡ Partly, no doubt, because the Finns had proved to be remarkably tough and stubborn defenders of their own liberty.

prophetic vision that a slender sapling of world organization, now bent and swayed by rising wind, would, if preserved by patience and propped by a steady and strong good will, grow into a great tree of man, deep-rooted in the soil of history as it aspired toward heaven? Such vision he may have had in his mortal sickness. There was a strangeness upon him. Winston Churchill had remarked and was soon to say to the Commons that Roosevelt's face at Yalta "had a transparency, an air of purification, and often there was a far-away look in his eyes."

At any rate, he continued to cling to his determined optimism against strong temptations toward destructive anger and despair as, in late March, he went South to meet the spring. . . .

iv. *When Lilacs in Dooryards Bloom'd*

March 30, 1945. Lilacs breathed a pale fragrance upon warm air, wild flowers bloomed among new leaves of grass, as the special train from Washington ran out of the night over the breast of spring into a Carolina morning. It was Good Friday, and beyond or below the Carolinas the earth of Georgia was a vivid red, the gullies like bloody gashes in living flesh, as the train's whistle cried mournfully across the fields—a long moan, then two aching sighs, again and again. At high noon this cry was heard in Atlanta.[50]

Forty miles south of Atlanta, in west-central Georgia, a crowd of several dozen people was gathered at the railway station of tiny Warm Springs (population 600). It was a curiously mixed crowd. There was in it the country simplicity, the ruddy good health, the sense of permanence, of being deeply rooted in one place, that are deemed characteristic of rural communities. But there was also in it a quality obviously imported, obviously developed in places distant and far different from this—a quality of urbane sophistication, of cosmopolitan sensibility, such as one would find in a pleasure resort, but joined here to pale sickliness, to a refinement of physical suffering. Crippled urbanites mingled with stalwart countrymen; there were men and women on crutches or in wheelchairs, there were children who wore braces on their legs.

Yet the over-all mood, among the crippled as among the sound, was a cheerful one. The sun, leaning westward into early afternoon, shone brightly upon the northwest slope of Pine Mountain, where the village lay. The sky over Bowdell Knob was a deep azure. The soft breeze was sweet-scented by flowers, by new-plowed soil of vegetable gardens ("victory gardens"), by the pine forest on the mountainside. Inevitably it was remarked by many that the day was "perfect" for the event they all awaited.

They awaited it, most of them, with less eager excitement than would have been evoked in any other Georgia town, for the event, which would have been wholly novel to others, was familiar to them. At least twice in almost every one of the last twelve years—in the spring and in the fall—the President of the United States had come in his special train to this station, and many if not most of those who now lounged in the sun, talking and laughing together, had been present on many if not most of those earlier occasions. They remembered how, in the old days, for eight or ten years after he was elected President and for many years before that, when he came here to strengthen his polio-withered legs by swimming in the warm pool of mineral water, he had made each of his arrivals a demonstration of the curative value of Warm Springs. Wearing his steel braces under his trousers, he had come swinging down the ramp from the train, waving, broadly smiling, calling greetings by name to those he recognized, projecting such energetic vitality as dissolved all sense of him as a crippled man. He hadn't done that for a long time now: he had been lowered instead in an elevator built into the rear platform of the train's observation car, then wheeled to the waiting automobile; but the great wonderful smile, the warm life-giving exuberance, had remained the same. It was this that the crowd looked forward to, loving him (most of them) as a personal friend—this and the sense of being again at the vital center of history. For he brought world history with him, did Franklin Roosevelt, wherever he went.

Then the shock . . .

The train came slowly into the station and stopped so that the rear end of the last car rested at the crossing of the track by the highway into town. Secret Service men came down from the cars and, with the expertness of long practice, took covering positions. Their chief, Mike Reilly, moved forward to the observation platform: as usual, Reilly had arrived here several days before in order to arrange personally every detail of the President's protection during the visit. But when, at last, the President himself appeared, it was at once apparent to the crowd that the danger he was in was not of the kind that armed guards, however brave and skillful, can protect against. He was slumped in his wheelchair, inert as a bag of wheat—his huge shoulders drooping, his head down, his hat brim pulled low over his eyes—and for the first time in all the long series of his arrivals here he did not smile and wave. He did not so much as glance at the crowd; he seemed hardly conscious of what was going on. When the chair lurched a little as it was being wheeled from the elevator onto the pavement he swayed weakly, as if he might actually topple over. A hushed murmur ran over the crowd. Then he lifted his hand toward his hat brim, and his hand shook so that he knocked off his pince-nez glasses. A Secret Service man retrieved them for him and irritably, almost angrily, he pinched them back onto his nose. The crowd's low murmur increased. Not until the town's mayor came up to greet him did his head lift, his dull eyes briefly brighten.

"Why, His Honor, the mayor," he said.

And a faint smile touched his lips as he shook hands. It was a limp handshake, the mayor noted worriedly—not at all like the strong grip of earlier years.

For the first time also, here in Warm Springs, Mike Reilly had difficulty getting Roosevelt into the automobile that waited for him. In the past the President's tremendous arms and shoulders had done most of the work, shifting his heavy bulk from chair to car seat easily, swiftly. But this time he didn't help at all. He couldn't. He sagged as a dead weight in Reilly's arms, and there was an awful moment during which it looked as if the Secret Service man might not be able to manage the transfer. He did, though. The car drove off, out of sight of the crowd, toward the six-room clapboard-walled cottage on Bowdell Knob that had become world famous as the Little White House. At the station was left a slowly dispersing crowd whose murmurous anxiety increased with the talk that expressed it.

Tobacco-chewing C. A. Pless, station master, averred that the President "was the worst-looking man I ever saw who was still alive—just like a sitting up dead man."

Ruth Stevens, the thin, angular, burning-eyed manager of the Warm Springs Hotel, grasped in clawlike hand the arm of Merriman Smith who, as always on these trips, was among her paying guests.

"Honey, *is he all right?*" she asked, her intense gaze fastened on the newsman's face.

"Tired to death," Smith replied. He returned her gaze then, and tried to be reassuring. "But he'll pull out of it. He always has . . ."

He did indeed seem to recover some of his departed strength in the country quiet, among the wind-singing pines of the Georgia mountainside, as Easter Sunday came and passed. He loafed in the sun, went for rides through the country, engaged in much light joking conversation with his two maiden-lady cousins, Laura Delano and Margaret Suckley, who were staying with him. His office assistants made the work load upon him as light as they possibly could. But his strength returned very slowly and only slightly compared with former years—and no one could remove from him the crushing weight of his responsibilities or the anxieties that came from them.

A cloud of anxiety as well as a star of hope hovered over San Francisco as final preparations were under way for the United Nations Conference there. He had chosen the American delegation to this Conference with great care, concerned (as he had been from the beginning) to insure bi-partisan support of this venture and so avoid Woodrow Wilson's mistake regarding the League of Nations. From Republican ranks he chose Senator Arthur H. Vandenberg of Michigan, a former isolationist now resoundingly converted to internationalism; Commander Harold E. Stassen of the Navy (he was one of Halsey's staff), former Governor of Minnesota; and Representative Charles A. Eaton of New Jersey. The Democrats named were Secretary of State Stettinius, ex-officio head of this delegation; Cordell Hull, a purely honorary appointment since Hull was much too ill to go to San Francisco; Senator Tom Connally of

Texas; and Representative Sol Bloom of New York. Also named, to insure heterosexual as well as bi-partisan support, had been Dean Virginia Gildersleeve of Barnard College. Immediately after these appointments were made, a program of "popular education" on the need for the UN Organization and on the proposals for it agreed upon at Dumbarton Oaks and Yalta were initiated—a program conducted by Archibald MacLeish and Adlai E. Stevenson as special assistants to the Secretary of State. The choice of delegates was well received by the public, and the "educational" program was producing results. But anxiety sprang through a "leak" to the press on March 29 of the Yalta promise to support Russia's request for three General Assembly votes in return for Russian support of a similar request by the United States if the latter were ever made. Why hadn't the President announced this when he made his report to the Congress? the public wanted to know—and Roosevelt might well ask himself the same question. As it was, the enemies of American participation in international organization were busily sowing dark suspicions of other "secret deals" at Yalta whereby Communism would be helped through the proposed UN toward its goal of world domination.

The cloud was augmented by Moscow's announcement that Molotov would not attend the San Francisco Conference as head of the Soviet delegation. This was a deliberate snub: every other country was sending its principal foreign officer, and Roosevelt was to open the Conference personally with an address. The snub stemmed from the continuing Polish dispute. It was issued in retaliation against a Western refusal to permit Poland to be represented at San Francisco only by the Lublin Government. Personal messages from both Roosevelt and Churchill to Stalin elicited a reply at the end of April's first week that seemed to promise faintly a Polish settlement, ultimately, that was not wholly outrageous of Western principles—but the Soviet Premier had not yet relented to the extent of announcing that Molotov would come to the Conference.

Moreover, by that time Stalin had replied to Roosevelt's message of March 24 concerning the surrender of German troops in Italy. The reply came on April 3; it was personally insulting and wholly alarming. "You insist that there have been no negotiations yet," said Stalin to Roosevelt, in reference to the Berne meetings. "It may be assumed that you have not yet been fully informed. . . . My military colleagues . . . do not have any doubts that the negotiations have taken place, and that they have ended in an agreement with the Germans, on the basis of which the German commander on the Western Front, Marshal Kesselring,§§§§ has agreed to open the front and permit the Anglo-American troops to advance to the east, and the Anglo-Americans have promised in return to ease for the Germans the peace terms. I think that my

§§§§ Rundstedt had been relieved of the Western Front command by Hitler, and replaced by Kesselring, following the Battle of the Bulge.

colleagues are close to the truth. Otherwise one could not have understood the fact that the Anglo-Americans have refused to admit to Berne representatives of the Soviet command for participation in the negotiations with the Germans." Roosevelt made prompt and firm reply, in a message drafted for him by Leahy and Marshall: ". . . I must continue to assume that you have the same high confidence in my truthfulness and reliability that I have always had in yours. . . . I am certain that there were no negotiations in Berne at any time, and I feel that your information to that effect must have come from German sources, which have made persistent efforts to create dissension between us in order to escape . . . responsibility for their war crimes. . . . Frankly, I cannot avoid a feeling of bitter resentment toward your informers, whoever they are, for such vile misrepresentations of my actions or those of my trusted subordinates."[51]

But he was still determined to be patient, to give the Russians the benefit of every doubt. After all, events on the battlefield might well have bred suspicions in the best-intentioned of Russians. As Stalin pointed out in his message of April 7, the Germans had 147 divisions on the Eastern Front and no doubt "could without prejudicing their own position detach fifteen or twenty" of these for reinforcement in the West. Instead they were "continuing to wage a crazy struggle . . . for an insignificant railway station like Zemlyanitsa in Czechoslovakia, which is as much use to them as hot poultices on a corpse, and yet they yield without the slightest resistance such important towns in the center of Germany as Osnabruck, Mannheim, and Kassel." Such behavior was "more than curious and unintelligible." In that same message, Stalin said he had "never doubted your integrity and trustworthiness or Mr. Churchill's either," and he retreated from his earlier charge of bad faith to the extent of saying that the real "point at issue" was a difference of views "as to what is admissible and what is inadmissible as between one ally and another." He asserted that, if a situation similar to the one at Berne had occurred on the Eastern Front, "the Russians would never have denied the Americans and British the right to join in such a meeting."[52]

Roosevelt replied to this on April 11, thanking Stalin for the "frank explanation of the Soviet point of view of the Berne incident, which now appears to have faded into the past. . . ." There must not, he added, "be mutual distrust, and minor misunderstandings of this character should not arise in the future."[53] He sent this message to Harriman in Moscow, through whose office it was to be delivered to the Kremlin—and turned his attention to other matters.

Among these other matters was the latest draft of the address he was to deliver over a national radio hookup on the evening of Jefferson Day, which was April 13. Reference was made in it to Jefferson as a "distinguished scientist" who once spoke of how (and this was a quote from Jefferson) "the brotherly spirit of Science . . . unites into one family all its votaries of whatever grade, and however widely dispersed throughout the different quarters of the globe." Today, the speech draft went on, "science has brought all the different quarters of the globe so closely together that it is impossible to isolate them one from another." But was this "bringing together," this powerful drive toward the integration of peoples into a single world community, actually strong enough to overcome the contrary tendency—that tendency toward a "flying apart," toward disintegration, whose symbol and ultimate expression would be the explosion of the atomic bomb? The question could not fail to rise in Roosevelt's mind as he went on. "Today we are faced with the preeminent fact that, if civilization is to survive, we must cultivate the science of human relationships—the ability of all peoples, of all kinds, to live together and work together, in the same world, at peace. . . . Today, as we move against the terrible scourge of war—as we go forward toward the greatest contribution that any generation of human beings can make in this world—the contribution of lasting peace, I ask you to keep up your faith. . . . The only limit to our realization of tomorrow will be our doubts of today." The draft ended there—on a poor note, it seemed to him. With heavy pencil he crossed out the words "doubts of today." Then, after a pause, he wrote them in again and added a final sentence, the very last he would ever write for intended public speech. "*Let us move forward*," he wrote, "*with strong and active faith*."[54]

He laid the draft aside; he planned to give it a final polishing the next day.

Sometime that afternoon he received from Harriman a message suggesting that the word "minor" be removed as the descriptive of "misunderstandings" in the cable to Stalin closing out the "Berne incident." Next morning, Thursday, April 12, 1945, Roosevelt rejected his Ambassador's suggestion. "It is my desire to consider the Berne misunderstanding a minor matter," he firmly said. And in a cable to Churchill that same morning he said: "I would minimize the general Soviet problem as much as possible because these problems, in one form or another, seem to arise every day and most of them straighten out as in the case of the Berne meeting. We must be firm, however, and our course thus far is correct."[55]

He was in good spirits that bright warm morning in his cottage on Bowdell Knob, though his secretary was shocked by his appearance ("color bad; countenance registering great weariness"). He joked as usual while signing his mail. Of a letter drafted for him in the State Department he remarked that it was a "typical" production of that Department in that it said "nothing at all." At the bottom of the pile of papers was a Senate bill that had just passed both Houses of the Congress, extending the life of the Commodity Credit Corporation and increasing its borrowing power. "Here's where I make a law," he said with a grin (he almost always said this on such occasions) before scrawling "approved" and his signature at the bottom of the page.

At that moment a tall, dark-haired lady of imperious manner entered the cottage carrying an easel. She was an artist, Madame Elizabeth Shoumatoff, come to paint his portrait, as had been previously arranged. He was sitting for her, a blue cape draped over his shoulders, a sheaf of papers in his lap, a freshly lighted cigarette in a long holder in his right hand, when suddenly he made a peculiar gesture. He lifted his left hand to his temple and pressed his temple, then pressed his forehead and rubbed it as if to massage away pain. Then his hand fell loose. His eyes closed. Laura Stuckley was sitting near him in the room, crocheting; she got up and came over to his chair to ask if he had dropped something. She thought he might have dropped his lighted cigarette. His eyes remained closed. "I have a terrible headache," he said very softly—and collapsed unconscious. The time was 1:15 in the afternoon.

He had suffered a massive cerebral hemorrhage. He died two hours and twenty minutes later without having regained consciousness.[56]

Of this death there are many echoes, there is much eventful reverberation around the world. Everywhere among men of good will there is a feeling that the outlook for the future is darkened by it, that hopeful opportunities are diminished by it. . . .

Harry S. Truman first hears of it at 5:30 in the afternoon of this fatal April 12. He enters Mrs. Eleanor Roosevelt's study on the second floor of the White House—a bespectacled, middle-aged, flat-voiced man whose glasses, being thicker than most, provide the only element of his appearance that might distinguish him among a crowd—and finds four people awaiting him. Steve Early, White House press secretary, is there. The Roosevelt daughter Anna is there with her husband, Lieutenant Colonel John Boettiger. Mrs. Roosevelt is there. It is Mrs. Roosevelt who steps forward to say, gently: "Harry, the President is dead." He is stunned. At last he asks Mrs. Roosevelt if there is anything he can do for her. He will never forget her reply as, out of her grief, she looks at him with a sympathy not devoid of pity. "Is there anything *we* can do for *you?*" she asks. "For you are the one in trouble now." And he does indeed feel that the roof of the world has caved in upon him when, less than two hours later, he stands Bible in hand before Chief Justice Harlan F. Stone and solemnly swears that he "will faithfully execute the office of President of the United States" and will to the best of his ability "preserve, protect, and defend the Constitution of the United States, so help me God."

Minutes later, just as a brief Cabinet meeting is about to begin, he makes his first decision as Chief Executive. Early comes in to say the press is clamoring to know if the San Francisco Conference of the United Nations will begin as scheduled on April 25. It will, says the new President without an instant's hesitation. It must. It is "of supreme importance that we build an organization to help keep the future peace of the world." After the Cabinet meeting, during which Truman asks all Department heads to continue to serve, telling them he intends "to continue both the foreign and domestic policies of the Roosevelt Administration," Secretary of War Stimson has private talk with the new President. There is and has long been under way, says Stimson guardedly, a vast secret project for developing a new explosive of fantastic destructive power; this is all he feels free to say at the moment. The President must be fully briefed on this important matter as soon as possible.[57]

In London it is early in the morning of Friday the thirteenth when Winston Churchill is told of Roosevelt's death. His last personal meeting with the President was aboard the *Quincy* in Alexandria harbor on February 13, and he had felt then that a strangely "placid" Roosevelt retained but "a slender contact with life." Nevertheless he is staggered by the news; he feels as if "struck by a physical blow." He at once orders an airplane to be prepared to fly him across the Atlantic to attend the funeral and then confer for two or three days, as Truman wishes, with the new President—but before the day is out he is dissuaded from this by his principal advisers. A crucial debate is about to begin in Parliament: his presence is urgently needed there.

Later he will profoundly regret not having gone anyway, for he is soon to learn, to his utter amazement and dismay, that Roosevelt, even in these last months of mortal illness, had made not the slightest effort to prepare his successor for the burdens that now fall with crushing weight upon him. The Vice-President has not been consulted on any, nor even informed of many, of the major decisions taken since Election Day. As a result, the new President now knows considerably less about the Administration for which he is responsible than do several of his subordinates. Inevitably there must ensue an interregnum fraught with the gravest dangers to the emergence of a peaceful world order. The new man may possess remarkable qualities (Churchill has as yet no way of knowing) but he cannot be expected to make intelligently decisive personal responses to the swiftly changing European situation—to what Churchill regards as a ruthless western thrust of Soviet empire—until he has been for some weeks and maybe months in office.[58]

In Moscow, in the Kremlin, it is later but still very early in the morning of Friday the thirteenth when the fatal news arrives from Warm Springs and Washington. The effect it produces there, both among high officials and upon ordinary citizens, is wholly unprecedented, reports the Moscow correspondent of the New York *Times*. Every morning newspaper appears late upon the streets, its front page made over to feature a black-bordered picture of the late President (neither the Pearl Harbor attack nor the Normandy invasion had been reported on Moscow's front pages which seldom carry pictures of any kind), and when the Supreme Soviet meets that morning it stands in silent tribute to the departed. Over all Government buildings, over many others, is unfurled the black-bordered red flag of national mourning. It flies over Stalin's residence in the Kremlin; and in his office beneath it, the Marshal composes messages of condolence to Mrs. Roosevelt and, through Truman, to the people of the United States. To Mrs. Roosevelt he speaks of her husband as "the leader in the cause of ensuring the security of the whole world." To the new President he speaks of the departed one as "a great politician of world significance and a pioneer in the organization of the peace and security after the war"; he expresses also the "conviction" of the Government of the Soviet Union "that the policy of friendship between the Great Powers who are shouldering the main burden of the war against the common enemy will continue in the future." Later he speaks personally to Harriman, asking if there is anything he can do in that moment of sorrow to promote unity among the Allies. Harriman thinks of many things that might be done but confines himself to one; it would help, he says, if Molotov could come to San Francisco for the Conference. Two days later the suggestion is officially accepted: Molotov is to fly to San Francisco in an American plane, dispatched to Moscow for that sole purpose.[59]

In Third Army Headquarters near Hersfeld, Germany, news of the President's death comes to George S. Patton in his trailer-truck via a midnight BBC broadcast. Eisenhower and Bradley, visiting Patton this day, have gone to bed in a small house nearby. Patton promptly goes to them with the news and the three generals sit together in Eisenhower's bedroom until two o'clock Friday morning trying to comprehend the meaning of this event, trying to determine its probable consequences. For all three of them the news climaxes a most memorable day. They have visited a salt mine at the village of Merkers where troops of the 90th Division, three days ago, discovered a huge cache of Nazi loot—some $250,000,000 in gold (most of it in gold bars) and hundreds upon hundreds of stolen art objects. They have visited, too, the first concentration camp that any of them has ever seen, at Ohrdruf, overrun by the Third Army two days ago.

Ohrdruf is not one of the really big important institutions like Buchenwald, Belsen, Dachau, Erlau, soon to be exposed to the world by the swift advance of Allied arms; it is not a major extermination camp set up for the "final solution" of the "Jewish problem," like Auschwitz with its four huge gas chambers with adjacent crematoriums. Ohrdruf is but a run-of-the-mill example of Nazi German *Kultur*. Nevertheless the sight and the smell of it, and the heard description of its practices, have sufficed to sicken the three generals. (Patton, at one point, stumbled over to a corner and vomited.) The stink of death was thick in their nostrils even before they reached the stockade. It rose from more than three thousand corpses flung into shallow graves and from hundreds of others lying stacked in sheds or scattered along the streets—emaciated, mutilated, putrefying bodies, covered over with maggots and blowflies. A guide shows the visitors a gallows from which prisoners attempting escape were hanged as the German generals who attempted Hitler's assassination were hanged, their necks in a noose of piano wire, their toes just touching the ground. From five to fifteen minutes of delicious spectacle were provided by each hanging for fun-loving Germans. Also seen is the whipping table where a naked man can be made to stand with his feet in stocks while two guards bend him over and a third fun-loving German beats him to a bloody pulp with a thick stick or heavy cowhide whip. It becomes possible to believe what will later be revealed to be true—that the Germans have deliberately, methodically, as a matter of high Government policy, murdered more than six million human beings—men, women, and children—in camps especially constructed for that purpose. Auschwitz in Poland, the largest and most efficient of these camps, killed no fewer than six thousand a day during its period of peak performance.

Eisenhower is determined that what he has seen that day shall be seen, through broadcast and eyewitness report and photographs, by all the world. He is determined to prevent any future dismissal of these horrible realities as "just war propaganda." Accordingly he has sent messages to both London and Washington—he did so as soon as he returned to Patton's headquarters—urging the two Governments "to send instantly to Germany a random group of newspaper editors and representative groups from the national legislatures" to view the obscenity which lies at the heart of Nazi-Fascism and then make uncensored report of it to the public at large.[60]

The ruin at the heart of Berlin that night is compounded by another RAF bombing raid. At midnight, fire rages through the smashed Chancellery while the incredible monster who has loosed upon the world the greatest horrors of all history huddles in his deep bunker beneath the Wilhelmplatz, a rat in a hole. Adolf Hitler, though not yet fifty-six years old (he will be next week, on April 20), has now the appearance and many of the traits of a senile man. His face is gray and slack, his eyes dull, save when insane rage (and insane rage is frequent) distorts his features and transforms his gaze into a baleful glare. Sometimes his head wobbles uncontrollably, often his hands tremble, and his left arm, the one injured by the July bomb, hangs loose and apparently useless. He has lost all contact with reality. He continuously issues orders that cannot possibly be obeyed and raves about "treason" and "betrayal" when they are not obeyed. He turns for slender comfort to astrology, striving desperately to believe that a "miracle" is forecast by the stars to occur in the latter half of April—a supernatural intervention that will save him and his Germany. Meanwhile he does his best to make sure that all Germany will go down with him into the final darkness, for he can no longer really hope. Certainly he can see no basis for hope in the news that has come to him all day from the battlefields. The U. S. First Army has driven into Leipzig. The U. S. Ninth Army has cut north of the Harz Mountains where five German divisions will soon be encircled.

The Americans are on the Elbe, have flung a bridgehead across it to match the bridgehead the Russians have thrown across the Oder in the east. Both to the east and to the west the enemy stands in overwhelming strength just thirty miles or so from Berlin. Soon, inevitably, the capital will be in enemy hands.

And yet, will it?

Sometime after midnight comes a ring on Hitler's private phone and he picks up the receiver to hear Goebbels' excited, exultant voice saying: "My Fuehrer, I congratulate you! Roosevelt is dead! It is written in the stars that the second half of April will be the turning point for us. This is Friday, April the thirteenth. It is the turning point!" Goebbels toasts this death in the best champagne, and others are similarly overjoyed—the Minister of Finance in Berlin, for instance, who feels "wings flutter through the room" when he hears the news, the wings of the "Angel of History" marking the "turn of fortune" for Germany. And Hitler's own crushed spirits are briefly raised.[61]

But only briefly . . .

v. *The End of Nazi Germany*

For there now fell upon the writhing, bleeding body of Nazi Germany the final flesh-shredding lashes of the war. In the north, the British struck through Bremen and on across the Elbe to Hamburg and Lübeck. The Americans, having reached the Elbe, struck southeastward into Czechoslovakia and Austria and to the German border of Switzerland. In Italy, the Anglo-American armies and the Poles struck northward into the Po Valley, Polish troops taking Bologna on April 21 (they there destroyed the famed First German Parachute Division); three days later the Allies were across the Po on a broad front. Simultaneously, the Russians opened their attack across the Oder and drove again westward on a front of more than two hundred miles, scoring great successes everywhere against the hardest resistance the Germans could still make. On April 25, at Torgau on the Elbe, some seventy-five miles south of Berlin, units of the 69th Division of the U. S. V Corps greeted with loud cheers units of the Russian 58th Guards Division, and the slender portion of Germany yet unoccupied was split in two. Next day there was riotous celebration at Torgau, Russians and Americans fraternizing with many spontaneous demonstrations of mutual admiration. Bradley issued a special order of the day in which he praised Marshal Konev's First Ukrainian Army, of which the 58th Guards was an element. "These armies have come down from the ruins of Stalingrad and Sevastopol, across the scorched cities of the Ukraine," Bradley said. "In two years they have smashed fourteen hundred miles through the German Army to drive the enemy from Russia and pursue him to the Elbe. . . ."

On the same day as the meeting on the Elbe came the signal for a general uprising of Italian Partisans in northern Italy. They seized control of Milan, Venice, and many other cities. Mussolini, now a haggard old man, fled northward with a German convoy, accompanied by his young mistress, Clara Petacci. Though he wore a German helmet and greatcoat he was recognized and, on April 28, while ensconced in a farmhouse on Lake Como, was seized by a Partisan band. He and his mistress were stood against a wall and shot. Their bodies were then taken to the Piazza Loretto in Milan and dumped there with the bodies of a dozen other Fascists at or near the spot where fifteen Partisans had been executed by the Nazi-Fascists months before. In the last view the world was to have of him he was hanging by his heels from a meat hook, his mistress beside him, being kicked and stoned and reviled by a huge crowd of the people (very different in temperament and outlook from the Germans) whom he had tricked and cajoled into disaster. Much photographed, thoroughly described in print by eyewitnesses, the scene was gruesome and shocking (Churchill was outraged by it) but perhaps beneficent in its long-term impress upon the popular mind, and upon history. For in the future, whenever power-lustful young egoists animated by childish dreams of "glory" saw pictures of the great Mussolini on his balcony—strutting, arrogant, contemptuously looking down upon a sea of upturned faces—they could not but see also in their mind's eye this final picture of a gaunt old man, his jaw smashed by an angry boot, hung up like butcher's meat before a huge mob that cursed and spat upon him.

Equally sordid—indeed, nastier somehow, and more obscene—was the end of the Nazi Fuehrer.

On April 28, Adolf Hitler learned via a BBC broadcast that Heinrich Himmler, whom he had always deemed the most loyal of his subordinates, had been engaged in secret negotiations with Count Bernadotte, head of the Swedish Red Cross, aimed toward a surrender of all German forces in the West to Eisenhower. (Even in this final hour, Himmler hoped to arrange a peace in the West which would enable German armies to concentrate against the Russians, perhaps with active Anglo-American support.) He raved, frothed at the mouth, turned purple with congested blood, then collapsed into a stupor. After that he was drained, it seemed, of all emotion save a dull, embittered despair. He began to make preparations for suicide and the destruction of his body. Very early in the morning of April 29 he went through the formality of marriage with his mistress of many years, a vapid, bovine young woman named Eva Braun who was determined to die at his side. He then dictated his last will and "Political Testament," repeating in the latter the ugly falsehoods by which he had lived. That afternoon, as the Russians, who had broken into the city on April 23, fought only a block away from the shattered Chancellery, news came to him of Mussolini's death. Everything was finished. . . .

Next day, Monday, April 30, shortly before 3:30 in the afternoon, Adolf Hitler killed himself with a pistol shot through the roof of his mouth, his bride dying beside him of self-administered poison. Their bodies, carried up into the Chancellery garden during a brief lull in the Russian shelling, were soaked with gasoline and burned.

His "Thousand-Year" Reich died with him. All German and Italian Fascist troops in northern Italy and western Austria were surrendered unconditionally to the Allies on May 2, the instrument of surrender being signed in the palace of the Bourbon kings at Caserta, twenty miles from Naples. Next day British forces took Hamburg and on the day after that arrangements between Montgomery and German Admiral Doenitz (whom Hitler had named as his successor) were concluded for the unconditional surrender of all German forces in Holland, northwest Germany, and Denmark. The terms were signed on May 5. On the same morning the First and Nineteenth German armies surrendered to the Allied 6th Army Group in the south. Only shattered remnants of the German Seventh Army now remained in opposition to Eisenhower's forces.

On the afternoon of the following day, a German delegation arrived at Eisenhower's headquarters to arrange the unconditional surrender of *all* German forces, those on the Eastern as well as Western Fronts insofar as the two yet remained separate. The headquarters was in a trade school building in Rheims, France—a dreary, red-brick structure. The delegation was composed of Colonel General Alfred Jodl, recently appointed Chief of Staff of the disintegrating German Army; General Admiral Hans Georg von Friedeburg, commander of the impotent German Navy; and Jodl's aide, Major General Wilhelm Oxenius. Beetle Smith, SHAEF Chief of Staff, acting for Eisenhower, served as chairman of the surrender conference, which was also attended by General François Savez of the French Army and General Ivan Susloparoff of the Red Army. Hours were required to arrange the technical details of surrender but finally, at 2:25 in the morning of May 7, the discussions were completed. Correspondents were assembled in the map-walled war room and here, without ceremony, Jodl, Smith, Savez, and Susloparoff signed the Instrument of Unconditional Surrender. It was 2:41 when the last signature was completed.

Nearly two days later, or at half an hour before midnight of Tuesday, May 8, 1945, this Instrument of Unconditional Surrender was ratified in Berlin in a ceremony designed to express and stress the unity of the Western Allies with the Soviet Union. Here Field Marshal Wilhelm Keitel signed for the German Army, Admiral Georg von Friedeburg for the German Navy, and Colonel General Hans von Stumpf for the German Air Force. Air Chief Marshal Sir Arthur Tedder signed as Eisenhower's deputy, General Carl A. Spaatz of the U. S. Air Force signed for the United States, Lieutenant General Jean de Lattre de Tassigny signed for France, and Marshal Georgi Zhukov signed for the Soviet Union.

After five years, eight months, and seven days of war, a ruined Europe entered upon an uneasy and dubious peace. . . .

XVI

To the End in Japan

i. *Crowded Interlude*

Germany lying prostrate in the dust that summer, naked and bleeding from such a scourging of war as no other major power had received since ancient Carthage, presented a spectacle that appalled mankind. Pity was evoked by it in humane breasts. How could it fail to be by the sight of women and children and old men scrabbling for food in garbage heaps among the ruins of scores of towns, dozens of once-great cities? By the sight of child prostitutes soliciting with words obscene and gestures obscene along rubble-heaped streets of night? By the sight of people without arms, without legs, without eyes, their bodies twisted and their faces scarred by explosive fire and steel? By the evidences everywhere abundant, everywhere reflected in grief-darkened eyes and terror-frozen faces, of what had been suffered by all these people, the physically uninjured along with the wounded, during the long fury that had crushed their nation? Pity was overtly asked for. Jodl had asked for it at the surrender table in Rheims. Granted permission to speak, after having signed the instrument of surrender, he had stood up very stiff and straight and, staring straight ahead, had said in a voice hoarse with emotion: "With this signature the German people and the German forces are, for better or worse, delivered into the victors' hands. In this war, which has lasted more than five years, both have achieved and suffered more than perhaps any other people in the world. I can only express the hope that the victors will treat them with generosity."

But pity was not the only emotion evoked. There was horror and disgust also as, days passing into weeks, more and more was revealed of what these poor suffering Germans had actually "achieved" during the last five and a half years.

Many square miles of countryside had been drenched with the stink of death day after day as crematorium chimneys poured forth white acrid smoke from the burning bodies of human beings killed, not one by one (that might have given their deaths some individual dignity), but in batches of a dozen to two hundred at a time. Doctors of medicine by the score had performed horrible "medical experiments" on living men and women and children and had made reports of them to meetings of medical societies, reports of no scientific value whatever that were nevertheless seriously discussed by the most eminent of the nation's medical practitioners, and with no evidence of personal revulsion. Farmers and industrialists had worked thousands of slave laborers literally to death in mines and fields and factories; bankers had stuffed their vaults with dental gold extracted from the teeth of murdered Jews. Hundreds of bleached human skulls, and of handbags and gloves and lampshades made of the skin of concentration camp victims, were displayed as souvenirs in Nazi German homes. And all these horrors, actively perpetrated by thousands and thousands of these poor suffering Germans, had been passively permitted—without protest, often with approval—by millions upon millions of others.

Such knowledge, falling heavily down upon the Western mind, plunging deep into the individual self, was like a sharp-edged stone dropped into a still pool. Ripples spread out from it in wider and ever-wider circles. "This is what *Nazis* are capable of!" one began by saying, with loathing and with scorn. Later one said, with equal loathing but less certain scorn: "This is what *Germans* are capable of!" One said at last, with loathing still but with a drastic reduction in scorn, since there was now drastically reduced that sense of otherness on which scorn depends: "This is what *men* are capable of!" And as these ripples spread horizontally the stone itself sank down and down until it struck against the very bottom of the soul, its sharp edge cutting deep, and forced upward a cry of anguish that was also a question filled with terror: "This is what *I* am capable of?"

Thus there was an inner as well as an outer necessity, a psychological as well as an objectively historical need, to round up Nazi war criminals following the unconditional surrender of Germany and to arrange for their public trial and stern punishment.

Fat Hermann Goering, long the Number Two Nazi, originator of the concentration camp and commander of the Luftwaffe, surrendered to American troops in Austria a few hours after the Berlin ratification of the instrument of Germany's surrender. By then or shortly thereafter the Allies held captive, among others, Rudolf Hess, the Number Three Nazi, long Hitler's deputy; Alfred Rosenberg, the "philosopher" of the Nazi Party; Joachim von Ribbentrop, the ruthless, overbearing Nazi Foreign Minister; Julius Streicher, notorious sadist and pornographer, editor of *Der Sturmer;* Ernst Kaltenbrunner, one of those with the highest responsibility for the mass extermination of Jews; and Robert Ley, leader of the German Labor Front, under whose administration slave laborers had suffered and died by the thousand. Heinrich Himmler, chief of the Gestapo, the greatest (under Hitler) mass murderer of all time, was captured by British troops near Hamburg on May 20 but promptly committed suicide by biting into a vial of poison concealed in his mouth. Goebbels, having murdered his six children with injections of poison, had had himself and his wife shot to death by an SS orderly on the day following Hitler's suicide. Ley was soon a suicide in his cell.

The others would be among those who sat in the prisoners' dock at Nuremberg with the camera eyes of the world focused on them while their enormous crimes were spread upon the public record in frequently nauseating detail. Sitting there day after day, week after week, month after month (the trial would run from November 20, 1945, to October 1, 1946), they would be denied the possibility of future investment with such glamor of wickedness as invests, say, the mythical Mephistopheles or the historic Borgias. They would become, after a while, boring in a peculiarly horrible way, being so monotonously vicious, so gross and repetitious and unimaginative in their murderous cruelties. They would shrink then in the eyes of the world to their true dimensions as banal, shabby, nasty, craven creatures whose proper fate was to be hustled out of life as quickly as possible and shoveled into holes, like so much stinking garbage.

Nor was all this mere vengefulness: it was also exorcism. There was in it, certainly, the spirit of the Old Testament, a sense of justice as punishment and retribution, but at the same time there was not wholly absent from it the spirit of the New. For in a deep psychological sense, and in a way that might be deemed a bridge between Old and New, the Golden Rule applied insofar as those who sat in judgment did indeed do unto others as they would have others do unto them should they ever be guilty of the least of such crimes as these. The judgment at Nuremberg, in other words—the condemnation of these sordid creatures of hate—was in part a protection of self from self on the part of those who judged. It raised another wall against the possibility that a similar evil might break out of the inner recesses of their own beings into the light and air of the actual world. . . .

The same motive was operative at the San Francisco Conference of the United Nations between April 25 and June 25, 1945. But it operated in a different way. Here too was a clear realization of the dangers of depending too exclusively upon pure self-restraint for the prevention of evil in the world, whether that restraint be exercised by individuals or by sovereign States, but here the emphasis was not upon punitive sanctions but upon the institutionalized implementation of good will, the organized reduction of the incentives and opportunities for national aggression and war. It was an emphasis sadly flawed by continuing and even growing dissension between Russia and the West.

More evident every day of that spring and early summer was the probability that Roosevelt had been correct in his assessment of his personal standing with Stalin, and of his consequent ability to exert an ameliorative influence upon the relations between Stalin and Churchill, and between Molotov and the foreign offices of London and Washington. With his death was lost a medium of fair exchange between East and West. Lost also was a perspective whereby differences that flatly contradicted one another when viewed close up were revealed to be complementary aspects of a larger whole—a perspective that suggested and even imposed a synthesis, a fusion into coherent organism, of what were initially warring oppositions. His successor was determined to follow his policies; no one could have sought with greater humility or sincerity to do so at the outset. But in the face of novelty (and there was certainly for him an abundance of novelty in those days of swift transition), Harry Truman was hard put to find what these policies were. Did they or had they ever in fact existed as clear and definite designs? Roosevelt, it would appear, had approached the problems of war and peace as he had formerly approached the problems of economic depression, not with a set of consistent ideas (an ideology) but with a set of attitudes, of ways of feeling and responding to stimuli. And these, being rooted in the complexities of his character and shaped through his many-leveled ambiguities, could not be transmitted to another. Nor precisely imitated. Gone, then—and mourned by none more than the Russians—was that unique and highly flexible compound of patience and firmness, that "ear" (he had "played it by ear") so sensitively attuned to slight variations of tone and rhythm, that steadily glowing good will, which had done so much to facilitate the work of Yalta and had promised so much for San Francisco.

Truman was a very different kind of man. His was a simpler intelligence, his a much more combative disposition, even game-cocky beneath the temporary humility. He saw the world in primary colors; his spectrum contained few of the subtler shadings. Impulsive and emphatic, he envisaged himself as a man of quick decision, a man who "got things done" with a minimum of palaver and waste motion. Hence his inability, despite his striving, to continue the mixture as before of patience and firmness in his dealings with Soviet fears and suspicions and with the acts rooted in these. Inevitably the proportions were altered. There was less of patience, more of firmness, the latter hardening as the former waned—and of course such personal rapport as there had been between the White House and Stalin was now wholly lost.[1]

Expressive of a part of Truman's character was an episode of his fourth week in office. On the day Germany's surrender was announced, Leo T. Crowley, the Foreign Economic Administrator, and Joseph C. Grew, Acting Secretary of State (Stettinius was then in San Francisco), came to the Oval Study, bringing with them an order drastically and abruptly reducing the flow of Lend-Lease aid to our European allies. They gave reasons. A compelling one for Truman at that time was conveyed through their statement that Roosevelt had "approved" the order but not signed it, the implication being that he certainly *would* have signed it had he continued to occupy the chair in which Truman now sat. It was necessary to do so in order to keep faith with the Congress, whose original intention had been to extend Lend-Lease only to those nations at war with Nazi-Fascism; the European war having ended, European Lend-Lease must be at once curtailed and soon terminated. Perhaps unstated that day but certainly in the minds of Grew and Crowley (it later rankled Truman that these two had arrogated to themselves a policy-making function properly belonging to him) was a conviction that the United States would be foolish to continue aiding a Soviet Union bent on pursuing her own aims in Europe regardless of the wishes and interests of others. To do so, they might have indicated, would be to implement with our resources a policy inimical to ours. At any rate, the reasons actually given "made good sense" to Harry Truman. "I reached for my pen," he later said, "and, without reading the document, I signed it."[2] He promptly regretted having done so. The abrupt slash was palpably unfair to Allies who, after all, had spent a larger proportion of their available blood and treasure in the common cause than the United States had done. It certainly militated against that early entry of Russia into the war against Japan which the Joint Chiefs of Staff continued to deem imperative. And three days after it was issued, while Moscow's prompt and peeved protest to Washington reverberated harshly in San Francisco, threatening to abort the United Nations organization, the order was rescinded. But by then grave damage had been done. Stalin, despite or because of his own penchant for coercive tactics, resented what seemed to him an effort to force Soviet compliance with American wishes regarding the Government of Poland, and regarding the voting procedure in the Security Council of the United Nations—the latter an issue soon to deadlock the San Francisco Conference.[3]

It was in part to undo the harm done by the Lend-Lease order that, two weeks later, Harry Hopkins went to Moscow to confer with Stalin as the President's personal emissary. This was to be the last mission of his life. He had come out of the hospital in Rochester against the strong advice of his doctors in order to attend Roosevelt's funeral. He had remained in Washington in order to give Truman the benefit of his uniquely intimate knowledge of what Roosevelt had felt, had hoped and feared and intended, for the future. He was obviously terribly ill. To Robert Sherwood he "looked like death, the skin of his face a dreadful cold white with apparently no flesh left under it." But his spirit, Sherwood also noted, flamed bright as ever through his frail, emaciated body, and when he talked of the necessity to finish the great unfinished work on which Roosevelt had been engaged, ". . . fire was shooting out of his sharp eyes in their sunken sockets."[4] Truman also took note of the physical illness, the spiritual fire. Was the former too great to permit the latter to be used to thaw the ice forming around Soviet attitudes toward the West? Truman wanted to know. Hopkins was at first dubious; he would have to consult his doctors, he said. But he knew (as others did) that there was no one else in the world who could undertake such a mission to Moscow with equal prospect of success, knew too that the situation was urgent to the point of desperation (the San Francisco Conference was in serious trouble by the third week of May). Accordingly he flew from Washington on May 23, was joined by Ambassador Harriman in Paris, and landed in Moscow on the evening of May 25.[5]

He was Truman's personal emissary—but he was also in a real sense Roosevelt's. He came as a yet-glowing vital element of the dead President; he could speak with Roosevelt's voice as well as his own, his own being that of a man who had proved under great pressure his personal courage, frankness, trustworthiness, and commitment to Soviet-American friendship. This, joined to the authority Truman gave him, constituted his unique qualification for face-to-face negotiations with Stalin. They were fruitful negotiations. A frank and full discussion of the differences between the two Great Powers laid a foundation for limited but substantial agreements. Stalin set the date of August 8 for the Russian invasion of Manchuria, provided the Chinese Government agreed to the proposals made at Yalta. (The Chinese, as has been said, did promptly agree.) He agreed to meet with the President and Churchill in the Berlin area in mid-July. He reaffirmed the Yalta agreement to join Britain and the United States in insuring that the reconstituted Polish Government held free elections and protected individual rights and liberty, though as regards this last there were qualifications whose practical application would soon be regarded by the West as violations of the agreement. There was no clear understanding between Hopkins and Stalin as to the extent to which the "principles of democracy" (which Stalin said were "well known and would find no objection on the part of the Soviet Government") could or would be actually operative in Poland. "He said . . . that in regard to the specific freedoms mentioned by Mr. Hopkins [freedom of speech, assembly, press, and religious worship], they could only be applied in full in peacetime, and even then with certain limitations," says the official record of Stalin's remarks on this point. "He said for example the fascist party, whose intention it was to overthrow the democratic governments, could not be permitted to enjoy to the full extent these freedoms. He said also there were limitations imposed by war. All States when they were threatened by war on their frontiers were not secure and had found it necessary to introduce certain restrictions."[6] More definite, though far from meeting the wishes of Britain and the United States, was Stalin's agreement to honor his Yalta pledge to the extent of including in the reorganized Polish Government certain Polish leaders not of the Lublin-Warsaw group; a list of the names of those to be invited in was made up and approved.

The most resounding immediate success of Hopkins' six long conversations with Stalin was the settlement of the issue of voting procedure in the United Nations Security Council. At Yalta, it will be remembered, the Russians had agreed to a U.S. voting formula whereby a distinction was made between (a) decisions to consider and discuss a dispute between nations (this was deemed a "procedural" matter in that it consisted of deciding upon an agenda) and (b) decisions to investigate and make recommendations for the pacific settlement of disputes or, this failing, to impose sanctions. The former were to require seven affirmative votes (in a Council of eleven) for adoption, not necessarily including all five votes of the permanent Council members, whereas the latter were to require seven votes *including* all permanent members. In other words, the Big Power veto would not apply to "procedural matters" but *would* apply to "all other matters." At San Francisco, however, the Russians retreated from this position. The chief Soviet delegate, Andrei Gromyko (Molotov had by then returned to Moscow and was taking part in the talks with Hopkins) announced that before he could approve the statement incorporating this arrangement in the UN Charter he would have to consult Moscow, and the whole Conference waited on tenterhooks while he did so. If Russia remained adamant, the Conference would surely fail. No Charter could be adopted. There would be no United Nations organization, no machinery whatever for effectively ameliorating the Punic War situation which already seemed in danger of developing between Russia and the United States.[7]

Hence the joy in Washington and San Francisco when, following a conversation in Moscow on June 6, during which it appeared that the opposition to the American position was primarily Molotov's and that Stalin had concurred in it only because he hadn't grasped the question, Hopkins cabled the President that "Marshal Stalin agrees to accept the United States position regarding voting procedure in the Council." According to Robert Sherwood's account, "This was the real news that the San Francisco Conference had been saved."[8]

By June 25 the work was done: on that day, the Charter was unanimously adopted. President Truman addressed the Conference's closing session. "The Charter of the United Nations which you have just signed is a solid structure upon which we can build a better world . . ." he said. "Between the victory in Europe and the final victory in Japan, in this most destructive of all wars, you have won a victory against war itself."

As for Harry Hopkins, having returned from his long journey seemingly none the worse for it physically, he breakfasted with the President in the White House on June 13. Truman was fulsome in his expression of personal gratitude. He urged Hopkins to accompany him to Potsdam where (it had been decided) the Big Three were to meet in mid-July, but Hopkins wisely pointed out that his presence at that meeting would be unfair to James F. Byrnes, whom Truman had chosen to replace Stettinius as Secretary of State as soon as decently possible after the San Francisco sessions ended. If Hopkins were at Potsdam, Churchill and Stalin out of habit and long familiarity would inevitably address to him questions properly addressed to Byrnes, undercutting the new Secretary's prestige and authority. It was a point whose validity Truman could not deny.[9]

So when Hopkins left the White House that morning it was in the knowledge that he was leaving public life, probably forever—and he could congratulate himself on leaving it at a moment of popular triumph such as he, in all his years of dedicated Government service, had never known before. In early July he formally resigned his numerous Government posts. He had by then only a little more than six months of fretful and pain-ridden life remaining to him. He died on January 29, 1946.

ii. *Atomic Decision*

Among those who watched the San Francisco Conference with the greatest anxiety—an anxiety attended by an acute sense of frustration—were key scientists of the Manhattan Project. And of these none was more anxious, none more determined to do something that would relieve anxiety and overcome frustration, than Leo Szilard and James Franck. To them the spectacle of politicians solemnly debating issues of war and peace in utter ignorance* of a force which was about to alter drastically the meaning of the words they used, the scale of the events with which they presumed to deal, had a nightmarish unreality.

Szilard, whose conscience was as sensitive as his intellect was acute, might well feel (as he certainly *did* feel) a special weight of responsibility at that moment. He, it will be recalled, had pecked out on his typewriter in July 1939 the letter to Roosevelt which he had persuaded Einstein to sign on August 2 and which Alexander Sachs had delivered in person to the President, in the Oval Study, on October 11 of that same year. Awesome in both height and reach was the oak which might be said to have sprung, with a rapidity of growth quite unoaklike, from this tiny acorn. Three secret cities had been raised in remote and widely separated sections of the United States since the success of Fermi's "critical experiment" in Chicago on December 2, 1942.† At Oak Ridge in the mountains of Tennessee was a city centered on the vast plants needed for the separation of chain-reactive U-235 from non-chain-reactive U-238 by the gaseous diffusion process. At Hanford in the desert of eastern Washington was a city centered on the vast plants (widely spaced for reasons of safety) required for the production of plutonium by chemical separation from the U-238 in which it was imbedded.‡ At Los Alamos in the deserts of New Mexico was a city centered on the laboratory and plant in which the atomic bomb itself was designed and fabricated.

* Actually the British delegation to San Francisco had been briefed concerning the project coded by their Government as "Tube Alloys," and it would later seem likely that the Soviet delegation, thanks to the activity of Soviet spies, knew a good deal about atomic bomb progress. The U.S. delegation, however, was wholly uninformed.

† See pp. 362–65.

‡ See p. 86.

It was upon the latter, and upon the man in charge of the work there, that Manhattan Project attention had been increasingly focused as the myriad scientific and engineering problems of producing pure U-235 and plutonium were solved. The man, J. Robert Oppenheimer, was in all respects remarkable.[10] Born in 1904 of a prosperous and highly cultured Jewish family in New York (his mother was a talented painter, his father and mother shared a deep love of music and a wide range of intellectual interests), he early manifested genius of the highest order, and every encouragement was given its development. He was fortunate in the high quality of his formal schooling, having been enrolled in the Ethical Culture School founded by Dr. Felix Adler, a school devoted to helping exceptionally brilliant students to realize their potentials. His natural curiosity was insatiable and unspecialized. As a small child he became intensely interested in architecture, then decided that he would be a poet (he wrote much poetry), and simultaneously displayed the kind of mind required by science. He collected stamps, and learned in the process a good deal about geography. He collected butterflies, and learned in the process a good deal about entomology. He collected rocks, and learned in the process a good deal about geology. When he was ten or so, having taught himself to use the typewriter, he entered into correspondence with professors of geology in various institutions who, judging from the form and content of his letters, believed themselves to be dealing with a mature man. One of these professors proposed his name (having never met him personally) for membership in the New York Mineralogical Society; he was elected and, when he was twelve, was asked to deliver a lecture before a Society meeting. He did so, astonishing an audience who had come expecting to hear a man; his paper, printed in the Society's proceedings, became his first publication. Shortly thereafter he developed intense interest in chemistry, his father then providing him with a fully equipped chemical laboratory and hiring the science teacher of the Ethical Culture School as his private tutor for a summer. And simultaneous with his pursuit of these various interests was his gaining of a perfect command of several languages. He learned these as he did all else with amazing swiftness and ease; he intended at one point in his youth to make a career out of studying and teaching languages and their history.

It was at Harvard (he completed the normal four-year course in three; he graduated with, reportedly, the highest grades ever made there) that he decided to become a physicist. During his chemical experiments he had proved to be clumsy with his hands, the opposite of skillful in his use of tools, and this fact about himself was re-emphasized in Harvard's physics laboratory. He was unlikely to succeed greatly as a research experimenter. But for theoretical physics his mental equipment was awesome, and this was promptly recognized by Harvard's leading physics professor, Percy W. Bridgman, who encouraged him to make his career in the science. The encouragement was soon justified. Upon his graduation from Harvard he was given a large sum of money by his father to use as he pleased. It pleased him to go to Cambridge where, in the Cavendish Laboratories, he was in close working contact with Rutherford, Niels Bohr, P. A. M. Dirac, and Max Born. The latter persuaded him to come from Cambridge to Germany's University of Göttingen which was then, in the mid-1920s, a world center of physics, thanks chiefly to the creative presence there of James Franck. Here Oppenheimer collaborated with Born on a paper which contributed substantially to quantum mechanics and earned for him a Göttingen degree of Doctor of Philosophy. Here he made the acquaintance of Arthur Compton, who visited the University. From Göttingen he went for a summer to the University of Zurich, then to Holland's University of Leiden, returning to the United States in August of 1927.

A year later he accepted teaching posts at the University of California and the California Institute of Technology, dividing his time between the two. Soon he was married to a vivid dark-haired girl named Katherine Puening Harrison whom he met at one of the Thursday evening readings of the great Hindu poets conducted by Arthur Ryder (Oppenheimer learned Sanskrit; he, the most intellectual of Western intellectuals when in his laboratory and study, was profoundly attracted by Eastern mysticism). Katherine Harrison opened up to him for the first time the world of politics, the world of "causes" and "movements" between Left and Right, she being wholly of the political Left. He joined many an organization later branded by the Department of Justice as "Communist-front" because he was committed to their openly stated purposes. He was never a Communist, however. His far-ranging intelligence, in which Eastern insight mingled on equal terms with Western outlook, could not be imprisoned within the rigid walls of Marxism, and the attempt of doctrinaire Marxists to force all science to conform to the tenets of Dialectical Materialism could not but seem to him absurd. (He severed his left-wing connections when war came because "I don't want anything to interfere with my usefulness to the nation," he told Arthur Compton—and Compton, an accommodating, conservative, conventional man if ever there was one, was sure that "Oppie," with his background, "would not be naïve with regard to Communism.[11])

During the next decade or so he established himself in the opinion of many knowledgeable people as one of the ten greatest theoretical physicists in the world though, strangely, and unlike any other man on such a list, his name was attached to no single great theory or experiment. He functioned as catalyst, stimulator, creative critic, and left to others the working out of his most fruitful ideas. (Oppenheimer exhaustively criticized Dirac's theoretical work on the positron; Dirac revised his work in the light of this criticism and won with it a Nobel Prize. Oppenheimer exhaustively criticized Carl D. Anderson's theoretical work on the meson; Anderson revised his work in the light of this criticism and won with it a Nobel Prize.) He was a great teacher. His brilliant lectures brought to bear on specific problems a vast erudition gained in a dozen specialized fields. He made connections few others in the world could make. But he had more than brilliance, more than knowledge; he had also living wisdom, a rare, sympathetic understanding of people, a rare sweetness of character. Upon his tall, thin figure, his sensitive, ascetic-appearing face topped by a crew haircut, his students focused a worshipful attention; he moved in an aura of moral goodness, seeming to bear his genius not as a tool or weapon of self-aggrandizement but as a burden of responsibility.

It was this quality of his character quite as much as his brilliance which caused him to be chosen by Arthur Compton and approved by General Groves as head of the work at Los Alamos.[12] And that the choice of Oppenheimer had been fortunate, all were now agreed. "More than any other one man, Oppenheimer is to be credited with the achievement of the completed bomb."§

Remote Los Alamos, though cut off from the outside world as completely as if it were a prison camp, though lacking many of the conveniences of modern life, became a remarkably happy town where difficult work was advanced with remarkable expedition. The "critical size" at which an assembly of pure U-235 or plutonium would become explosive was here precisely determined. By early 1944 the basic bomb designs had been developed. Regarding this, the problem had been to devise a method by which the critical assemblage could be achieved swiftly enough (that is, instantaneously) to insure a reaction that was indeed explosive instead of being so extended in time as to become relatively ineffective. In the event, two methods were devised. One consisted of placing at opposite ends of a gun barrel two masses of fissionable material, each smaller than critical size but both together well above it, and then shooting them together, using one mass as projectile and the other as target. The bomb using U-235 produced at Oak Ridge (it was nicknamed "Lean Boy") was of this type. The second method was one of implosion; it was used in the bomb (nicknamed "Fat Boy"), whose fissionable material was plutonium produced at Hanford. The plutonium was placed in loose pieces, each of sub-critical size, at the core of a large sphere of conventional explosive material over the surface of which were placed many detonators electrically connected in such a way as to be fired simultaneously. The result of such firing from all sides was an implosion—a spherical bursting inward which instantaneously and powerfully compressed into a ball of far more than critical size the theretofore separate pieces of plutonium.[13] The bomb's terrific explosion then occurred.

Long before the actual fabrication of atomic bombs, however—and even before all the problems of pure U-235 and plutonium production were completely solved—Franck and Szilard and most of the most

§ Harry S. Truman, *Year of Decisions* (New York: 1955), p. 418.

eminent of their scientific colleagues took it for granted that the problems *would* be solved, the bombs *would* be built, and they *would* "work." What increasingly concerned them was the question of whether the bomb should be *allowed* to "work" as a weapon of war. Was there no alternative to the actual military employment of so dread a weapon? they asked themselves. What would be the long-term political, historical consequences of its employment if it were employed? In the winter of 1944–45, a group of Manhattan District scientists began to meet together, for the most part in Chicago, to discuss such questions as these, and out of this discussion group emerged a semi-official committee, dubbed a Committee on Social and Political Implications, of which Franck became chairman. They reached conclusions and labored to put them into a concise, persuasive memorandum (Szilard did much of the actual writing of it) addressed to Secretary of War Stimson. It became known, finally, as the Franck Report.[14]

"All of us, familiar with the present state of nucleonics, live with the vision before our eyes of sudden destruction visited on our own country, of a Pearl Harbor disaster repeated in thousand-fold magnification in every one of our major cities," said the preamble to this Report. In the past, the preamble continued, science had been able to develop defensive answers to every aggressive weapon it had previously developed, but this could not be expected to occur in the case of nuclear bombs. The only protection for the human race must come "from the political organization of the world." Certainly, the Report went on, no reliance could be placed on secrecy as a defense against the development of nuclear weapons by other nations. "The experience of Russian scientists in nuclear research is entirely sufficient to enable them to retrace our steps within a few years, even if we should make every effort to conceal them." Inevitably, then, "the race for nuclear armaments will be on in earnest not later than the morning after our first demonstration of the existence of nuclear weapons," after which "it might take other nations three or four years to overcome our head start, and eight or ten years to draw even with us if we continue to do intensive work in this field," unless "efficient international agreement is achieved." Moreover, the United States, whose heavy industry and population were concentrated in a few great cities, would be more vulnerable to nuclear destruction than a country (Russia seemed clearly indicated) "whose industry and population are dispersed over a large territory."

The Report then argued strongly against use of the bomb against Japan without a clear and definite prior warning, for the "military advantages and saving of American lives achieved" by such action "may be outweighed by a wave of horror and revulsion sweeping over the rest of the world." The authors suggested "a demonstration of the new weapon . . . before the eyes of representatives of all the United Nations, on a desert or barren island" after which, "with the sanction of the United Nations and public opinion at home," and having first given Japan an ultimatum to surrender and an opportunity to evacuate certain areas, "the weapon might be used."

Meanwhile, Leo Szilard was making efforts of his own to influence atomic bomb policy. In March of 1945 he prepared a lengthy memorandum urging international control of atomic energy, stressing what he deemed to be America's special vulnerability to atomic bomb attack because of her urban-industrial concentrations, and clearly implying (though he did not specifically say) that actual use of the bomb in the present war would be most unwise. "The strong position of the United States in the world in the past thirty years has been due to the fact that the United States could out-produce every other country in heavy armaments," wrote Szilard. "The existence of the atomic bomb means the end of the strong position of the United States in this respect."[15] He hoped to be able to present this memorandum to Roosevelt personally and persuaded Einstein to write Roosevelt suggesting that the President receive him (Szilard). The Einstein letter went in April to Warm Springs; it was in the Little White House there, presumably unread and certainly unanswered by the President, on the fatal afternoon of April 12. From Warm Springs the letter was returned to the White House, where Truman read it one late April day in the Oval Study.

By that time, or immediately thereafter, there was established by Secretary Stimson, with the approval of Truman, a committee "charged with the function of advising the President on the various questions raised by our apparently imminent success in developing an atomic weapon." It became known as the Interim Committee. James F. Byrnes, who was at that time without Government office, was asked by Truman to serve on it as the President's personal representative—and it was to Byrnes that Truman turned over the Einstein letter. At the same time, the President asked Byrnes if he would arrange to meet with Szilard to discuss the "lack of adequate contact" between atomic scientists and Cabinet policy makers which, according to the Einstein letter, was disturbing Szilard. In due course, the meeting was arranged. On May 28, Szilard came to Byrnes' home in Spartanburg, South Carolina, bringing with him H. C. Urey and, in Byrnes' words, "another scientist."[16] The meeting was, from the scientists' point of view, wholly unfortunate, accomplishing the opposite of its intention insofar as it had any effect at all on policy. There was no basis for real understanding on such a question as this between the politically liberal Hungarian-born physicist and the politically conservative South Carolina politician.

Nor did James Franck fare better in his effort to influence policy. Early in June he came to Washington with the Report of his committee, hoping to present it personally to the Secretary of War. Arthur Compton met him in the capital, reviewed (and disagreed with) the document Franck carried, and tried to arrange the meeting Franck desired. Stimson, however, was out of the city. The Report was then left with Compton for transmittal to the Secretary. Compton, however, was not content to let the Report argue its own case. He attached to it a "covering note" in which, to quote his own words, it was "necessary¶ for me to point out" that the Report made no mention of "the probable net saving of many lives" if the bomb were used "nor that if the bomb were not used . . . the world would have no adequate warning as to what was to be expected if war should break out again."[17] Later, many members of the Franck Committee doubted that the Report was ever delivered to the Secretary of War. There was no evidence at the time, certainly, that it was being seriously considered by official policy makers; and it was unmentioned by Stimson when he wrote out his personal recollections of the atomic bomb decision—recollections published in *Harper's* magazine and his memoirs.

Meanwhile the official machinery of decision-making ground its way inexorably toward a conclusion. The crucial meeting of the Interim Committee in the office of the Secretary of War on May 31, 1945, was attended not only by the official Committee members but also by Generals Marshall and Groves as military advisers and by an advisory Scientific Panel consisting of Oppenheimer, Fermi, Compton, and E. O. Lawrence. It was presided over by Stimson and opened by him with a portentous statement: "Gentlemen, it is our responsibility to recommend action that may turn the course of civilization," he began, according to the vivid memory of Arthur Compton. "In our hands we expect soon to have a weapon of wholly unprecedented destructive power. . . . It is our obligation to use this power with the best wisdom we can command. To us now the matter of first importance is how our use of this new weapon will appear in the long view of history."[18] Three questions dominated the discussions which followed: *First*, was use of the bomb necessary to force Japan's early surrender? *Second*, could arrangements be made to demonstrate the weapon's awful destructiveness without or at least before using it on a "live" target? *Third* (and this was a question more pervasive than specific throughout the meeting), was use of the bomb against a Japanese city actually more reprehensible morally than the use then being made of "conventional" bombs, especially of incendiary bombs of a new design?

As regards the *first* question, there was some difference of opinion among the conferees. On the one hand, there was no sign that Japan's military fanatics who had instigated its aggressions were any less fanatical than before in their determination to fight to the death. Neither was there any sign of a weakening of the will to fight on the part of Japanese troops, sailors, and airmen. Instead, the bloodiest battles of the Pacific war had been fought *since* the cracking of Japan's defense perimeter—on Leyte, on Luzon, on Iwo Jima (invaded February 19), on Okinawa (invaded April 1 at a cost of 35 per cent casualties among the striking force)—and there was no lack of volunteers for the kamikaze planes. These last had exacted a heavy toll of American ships and lives and

¶ Why? his scientific colleagues later asked.

might well have proved disastrous to the U. S. Navy as it approached Japan's home islands had not the newly developed proximity fuse** enabled the shooting down of most of the suicide planes before they could crash into their targets.

On the other hand, there *were* signs that Japan's military fanatics no longer had an iron grip on Governmental policy-making and that high Japanese officials, even the Emperor himself, were seeking for a way out of a war they knew to be lost. A will to fight, however strong, could not be effective if the means of war were lacking, and Japan's physical capacity to wage war was being steadily, swiftly reduced. Her Navy and merchant fleet were virtually destroyed, the latter reduced by submarine and air attack from ten million to one million tons. Her air force lacked trained pilots; it was far too weak to defend the skies over the home islands. Her cities, naval installations, industries, and transportation system were being devastated by increasingly heavy air bombardment as giant air bases went into operation on Tinian, Okinawa, and other islands within easy flying distance of Tokyo; General George Kenney threatened daily air strikes on the home islands with five thousand planes—the surviving populace would become nomads—if Japan did not surrender. And there were American Naval and Air Force officers of high rank who, though utterly ignorant of the atomic bomb, were convinced that Japan *would* surrender before the summer ended. It was a judgment in which Joseph C. Grew, out of his long experience in Tokyo, was inclined to concur, if only the United States modified her "unconditional surrender" formula to the extent of promising the Japanese that they could keep their Emperor. For the Emperor was divine to the Japanese, Grew repeatedly stressed, and so could not by them be dispensed with. Alas, a massive and long-continued war propaganda militated against the acceptance of this recommendation: myriads of posters, billboard signs, slogans, cartoons, and emotion-packed speeches had joined Hitler, Mussolini, and Hirohito together in the popular mind as three of a kind and Grew was attacked as an "appeaser."[19]

All these factors were weighed by the Interim Committee and the Scientific Panel. The balance struck was strongly influenced by Generals Marshall and Groves; neither general had any belief that Japan would surrender unless she were convinced that the only alternative was immediate total destruction. The U. S. Joint Chiefs, said Marshall, were going forward with their plans for an intensification of the air war against

** The proximity fuse was a top-secret development which gave great tactical advantage to the Allies in the last months of the war. An outgrowth of radar, it sent a signal to a target and caught the "echo" of it through a radar receiver, the time interval between initial signal and "echo" being the measure of distance separating fuse from target. Thus a bomb or shell could be set to explode at a specified distance from the object it was aimed to destroy; a "near miss" of a flying object became as effective as a direct hit. The proximity fuse was used to trigger the atomic bombs; the first such bomb to be dropped was set to explode at two thousand feet above the ground.

Japan and an invasion of the home island of Kyushu on November 1 with a force of three-quarters of a million men, to be followed in the spring of 1946 by a landing on Honshu. They continued to expect heavy casualties and were no less convinced than they had been at the time of Yalta that Russia's early entrance into the Japanese war was urgently needed. (Later, several writers†† would insist that the decision to use the bomb had as prime but necessarily secret motive the desire to forestall Russia's entry into Manchuria and strengthen the American position with relation to her in the postwar world. There is no evidence in contemporary records of the decisive discussions nor in the published memoirs of the most responsible participants in them that this motive operated at all.) The Committee's consensus was that the bomb must be used at the earliest possible moment.

As regards the *second* question—that of demonstrating to the Japanese the destructiveness of the bomb before actually dropping it on a live target—the consensus was that such a demonstration was impracticable. If the Japanese were told that a new super-bomb would fall at a specific place at a specific time, they might mass fighter planes over that place at that time. Or they might attack the bomb-bearing plane on its way to the target at a time when delicate adjustments of the firing mechanism were being made, causing a malfunction of the bomb. Or they might move American prisoners of war into the target area. The four scientists of the Panel were asked to meet separately to explore the possibility of devising an effective non-military demonstration, and they did meet at Los Alamos in the second week of June. ". . . we can propose no technical demonstration likely to bring an end to the war," they concluded; "we see no acceptable alternative to direct military use."[20]

As regards the *third* question—the question of whether the use of an atomic bomb was any "worse" morally than the use then being made of "conventional" weapons—it was background to the other two and no specific answer was required to be made to it. But the tendency to answer it negatively was certainly encouraged by a candid look at the air war then being waged against defenseless Japanese civilians. Consider, as outstanding instance, the all-out massive attack with incendiary bombs made on Tokyo by General Curtis LeMay's B-29s on the night of March 9–10, 1945. A total of 334 giant B-29s, sweeping in at six or seven thousand feet, dropped well over two thousand tons of incendiaries on the heart of the highly flammable Japanese capital, raising a fire storm and a "sweep conflagration" more terrible than Hamburg's.[21] B-29 crews, looking down on a tossing sea of flame, found the unpressurized cabins of their planes filling up with a strange red mist permeated by a stink of burning flesh so strong that it caused many a man to vomit before he could thrust over his face the oxygen mask he'd

†† Notably P. M. S. Blackett in his *Fear, War and the Bomb* (New York: 1948), pp. 127–43.

not been wearing because the bomb run was made at so low an altitude. Approximately one hundred thousand men, women, and children were killed, some of them dying in open fields far from burning buildings as oxygen was sucked from the air around them by huge updrafts. Seventeen square miles of the most densely built-up city in the world were utterly devastated, leaving a million and a half people homeless. The charred bodies of children alone, heaped in a single pile, would have formed a broad-based hill a hundred feet high. Nor had the indescribable horror of this holocaust deterred later massive incendiary attacks. On the contrary, LeMay had congratulated himself and been warmly congratulated by others on the great "success" of his initially "daring experiment"; he was now in the process of gutting Japanese cities, two to four at a time, in B-29 raids spaced two or three days apart. (Before the war ended, his B-29s would destroy 178 square miles of sixty-nine Japanese cities and, in six months, cause civilian casualties twice the total of those suffered by Japan's armed forces in forty-five months of war.) If the dropping of an atomic bomb could put a stop to this continuing horror it might even be deemed, relatively, a "good" thing!

And so it was that—despite Stimson's voiced concern over "how our use of this new weapon will appear in the long view of history," despite the agitation of worried scientists of the Franck group, despite the immensely informed and sensitive intelligence of Oppenheimer and the self-avowed Christian piety of Arthur Compton—the conclusion unanimously reached by the Interim Committee and Scientific Panel was precisely that which would have been reached by simple-minded and ignorant men who had no concern whatever with moral issues. To Stimson it was recommended "that the bomb should be used against Japan, without specific warning, as soon as possible, and against such a target as to make clear its devastating strength"—a conclusion "similar to my own," said Stimson, "although I reached mine independently."[22] Far different was the conclusion promptly reached by blunt Admiral Leahy when he was at last forced to accept the fact that the bomb was considerably more than a "professor's dream." Many political liberals had deemed the admiral morally insensitive as Ambassador to Vichy France. His reaction was therefore surprising to them when they learned of it. "My own feeling was that in being the first to use . . . [the bomb] we . . . adopted the ethical standard common to the barbarians of the Dark Ages," he said. "I was not taught to make war in that fashion, and wars cannot be won by destroying women and children. . . . These new and terrible instruments of uncivilized warfare represent a modern type of barbarism not worthy of Christian man."[23]

As for the atomic scientists of the "rank and file"—those who held no high administrative positions and so were not called into high decision-making councils—they continued, even intensified their various agitation. There were polls, there were petitions and counter-petitions, on the question of whether or not the bomb should be actually used in the war. At last General Groves, though he himself had no doubts on the question (*of course* the bomb must be dropped), felt compelled to ascertain in some formal way the predominant opinion of the scientists of the Project, since his superiors wanted to know what it was. Accordingly he asked Arthur Compton to supervise an opinion poll "among those who knew what was going on," and Compton in turn asked Farrington Daniels, director at that time of the Metallurgical Laboratory, to conduct it among the Chicago group. Daniels did so sometime before, though very near the day of the test-bomb explosion.

"At 0530, 16 July 1945, in a remote section of the Alamogordo Air Base, New Mexico, the first full-scale test was made of the implosion type atomic fission bomb. For the first time in history there was a nuclear explosion. And what an explosion!"

So began the memorandum to the Secretary of War signed by General Groves, dated July 18, 1945, reporting the birth of the Atomic Age.[24] The test bomb was a plutonium "Fat Boy" mounted at the top of a structural steel tower one hundred feet high—a tower which was vaporized by the heat of the explosion. What seems most to have impressed every eyewitness was the intensity of the light given out by a vast ball of fire a mile or so in diameter shooting upward, mushrooming, attaining a height of nearly two miles before it began to fade. "For a brief period there was a lighting effect within a radius of twenty miles equal to several suns at midday," said Groves in his report to Stimson, adding that the light "was seen clearly at Albuquerque, Santa Fe, Silver City, El Paso and other points generally about 180 miles away." The thunderous sound "was heard to the same distance in a few instances but generally to about 100 miles. Only a few windows were broken although one was some 125 miles away. A massive cloud was formed which surged and billowed upward with tremendous power, reaching the substratosphere at an elevation of 41,000 feet above the ground, in about five minutes, breaking without interruption through a temperature inversion at 17,000 feet which most of the scientists thought would stop it. Two supplementary explosions occurred in the cloud shortly after the main explosion. The cloud contained several thousand tons of dust picked up from the ground and a considerable amount of iron in gaseous form. Our present thought is that this iron ignited when it mixed with the oxygen in the air to cause these supplementary explosions. . . . A crater from which all vegetation had vanished, with a diameter of 1200 feet and a slight slope toward the center was formed. In the center was a shallow bowl 130 feet in diameter and six feet in depth. The material within the crater was deeply pulverized earth. The material within the outer circle is greenish and can be distinctly seen from as much as five miles away."

Groves also spoke of Oppenheimer's personal reactions as they all awaited the terrific culmination of their terrific two-billion-dollar project. ". . . I got up at 0100 and from that time on until about five I was with Dr. Oppenheimer constantly. Naturally he was very nervous, although his mind was working at its usual extraordinary efficiency. I devoted my entire attention to shielding him from the excited and generally faulty advice of his assistants who were more than disturbed by their excitement and the uncertain weather conditions." (Rain was falling on the desert that early morning; the test, originally scheduled for four o'clock, had to be postponed.) And Brigadier General Thomas F. Farrell, Groves' second-in-command, whose impressions Groves enclosed, spoke of his superior officer's "walking with . . . [Oppenheimer] and steadying his tense excitement. Every time the Director would be about to explode because of some untoward happening, General Groves would take him off and walk with him in the rain, counselling with him and reassuring him that everything would be all right." Thus a picture of the generals as mature men—calm, fatherly, protective—and of the scientists as excitable children at this dawn of the Atomic Age. Groves was not with Oppenheimer at the climactic moment, however. He had by then gone to the Base Camp ten miles away. It was Farrell who, in the control shelter ten thousand yards south of the bomb tower, watched the Director during the last minutes of the first half of the fifth hour. "Dr. Oppenheimer . . . grew tenser as the last seconds ticked off. He scarcely breathed. He held onto a post to steady himself. For the last few seconds, he stared directly ahead and then when the announcer shouted 'Now!' and there came the tremendous burst of light followed shortly thereafter by the deep growling roar of the explosion, his face relaxed into an expression of tremendous relief."

But was relief all that Oppenheimer felt? Was it even his dominant emotion as he saw the giant fireball shooting up into the sky?

By his own testimony (he gave it in answer to a question from William L. Laurence later that day) it would appear that, facing this ultimate expression of Western intellectualism, he recoiled into Eastern mysticism; two passages from the Hindu sacred epic, the Bhagavad-Gita, flashed into his mind. Said one: "If the radiance of a thousand suns were to burst into the sky, that would be the splendor of the Mighty One . . ." Said the other, obverse of the former: "I am become Death, the shatterer of worlds."[25]

While this stupendous event was occurring in the Southwestern desert, hidden from the eyes and ears of the world, much of the world's attention was focused on Potsdam. Here, in the palace and garden city of the Hohenzollerns, here where Einstein had happily worked and lived before Hitler forced him to flee, the Big Three meeting (aptly code-named TERMINAL) was scheduled to begin on this same July 16. The opening was delayed twenty-four hours, however, by Stalin's illness, the marshal having suffered (as would be later learned) a slight heart attack.

In the eyes of the world at that time the Conference loomed large, and certainly questions of utmost importance were indicated by its agenda —Poland's frontier and government, the political reconstruction of Europe along the lines of the Yalta Declaration on Liberated Countries, the political aspect of Germany's military occupation, war reparations, what to do about Franco Spain, Europe's economic rehabilitation. But as it turned out, the Conference was literally inconsequential. So far as major effects were concerned, it might as well not have been held. The nations, East dividing from West, continued along the divergent paths upon which they had already entered, at the same pace as they would otherwise have done.

In some small part this may have been because of the change made in the British Government at this time. Several weeks before, Britain had held a General Election of which the results were unknown at the time the Potsdam meeting opened because the ballot boxes had been sealed until the votes of armed forces personnel overseas could be received and tabulated. When announced, the results astonished the world, the election victors no less than the defeated. Winston Churchill and the Conservative Party, who had confidently expected the election to assure and even reinforce their authority abroad, were emphatically repudiated as Britain's guides into the postwar world. The defeat was overwhelming. Accordingly Churchill and Anthony Eden, having left Potsdam for England on July 25 to await the verdict at home, did not return to the Conference. Their places were taken by Clement Attlee, new Laborite Prime Minister, and Ernest Bevin, new Laborite Foreign Secretary. None of the principals facing Stalin and Molotov at the Conference table as Potsdam drew to a close, therefore—neither Truman nor Byrnes, neither Attlee nor Bevin—was a man experienced in dealing with the Russians nor with the issues that were generating what would later become known (being named by Churchill) as the Cold War.

At any rate, whether or not the British election prevented Big Three settlements at Potsdam, the one Conference action that would appear in retrospect to have some historic significance was taken before Churchill's departure. Its incitement was the giant explosion in New Mexico of which the first news was flashed to Stimson (he had accompanied Truman to Potsdam) in a coded message on July 16: BABIES SATISFACTORILY BORN. The later full report from Groves, which arrived in Potsdam by courier on July 21—a report in which the "conservative" estimate was made that the bomb's explosive energy had been "in excess of 15,000 to 20,000 tons of TNT"—had a tremendous impact upon all who read it. There was considerable discussion among the Western allies as to how much Stalin should be told of the new weapon, the decision being that he should only be told—as he was told by Truman on July 24, in a studiedly casual way—that a weapon of unprecedented destructiveness had been developed. (Stalin evinced pleasure at the news but a surprising lack of surprise, saying merely, in effect: "Fine. I hope you make good use of it against the Japanese."[26] It later seemed probable that the Soviet Premier, through Soviet spy activities, already was informed of the bomb's development; only the report of a successful test was news to him.) There was also further discussion of whether or not, and in what form, the Japanese should be warned of the new weapon's existence and given a chance to surrender before it was used against them. The upshot of this was the one act for which the Conference might remain memorable in history, namely the issuance of the Potsdam Declaration, decided upon before Churchill left for England and published on July 26.

On July 2, anticipating the success of the bomb-test in New Mexico, Stimson had sent an important memorandum to Truman suggesting an ultimatum to Japan which definitely threatened "destruction" if she continued to resist while promising "hope . . . if she surrendered." He had said in this memorandum that the "success" of such an ultimatum would "of course . . . depend on the potency of the warning" and that "personally" he thought the "chances of acceptance" of the opportunity to surrender would be "substantially" increased "if . . . we should add that we do not exclude a constitutional monarchy under her present dynasty."[27] This was a line of thought which Churchill had been simultaneously pursuing and which he was further encouraged to pursue by a private conversation he had with Stalin soon after the Potsdam meeting opened. Stalin told him of an "unaddressed message" from the Japanese Emperor, delivered to the Kremlin through the Japanese Ambassador just as the Russians were about to leave for the Conference, saying that Japan could not accept "unconditional surrender" but that compromise on other terms might be possible. Stalin's reply had been that, since the message made no specific proposals, the Soviet Government could take no action concerning it. In subsequent lengthy conversations with Truman at Potsdam, the British leader emphasized that in his opinion there should be "no rigid insistence upon 'unconditional surrender,' apart from what was necessary for world peace and future security and for the punishment of a guilty and treacherous deed." In the Potsdam Declaration as issued, however, this Stimson-Churchill line was considerably blurred, the "potency" of the threat and the clarity of the promise being much reduced (in the light of the now-certain atomic fires) from what Stimson's memorandum had suggested. "We call upon the Government of Japan to proclaim now the unconditional surrender of all the Japanese armed forces, and to provide proper and adequate assurances of good faith in such action," said the Declaration's closing paragraph. "The alternative for Japan is complete and utter destruction."[28]

That the atomic bomb would be used against Japan if she did not at once surrender was taken for granted at Potsdam. "There was unanimous, automatic, unquestioned agreement [on this] around our table; nor did I ever hear the slightest suggestion that we should do otherwise," Churchill later testified. And Truman has said: "I regarded the bomb as a military weapon and never had any doubts that it should be used."[29] He and Stimson had already agreed on a list of cities—Hiroshima, Kokura, Niigata, and Nagasaki—from which would be selected the first atomic bomb target. On July 24, the same day on which he told Stalin of the "new weapon" and two days before the ultimatum to Japan was published in the Potsdam Declaration, he approved issuance of the formal order to General Carl Spaatz, Commanding General of the U. S. Army Strategic Air Forces, for the dropping of the bomb. (He later insisted that this was designed only "to set the military wheels in motion." The "final decision" was still in his hands and "was not made until . . . we were in the middle of the Atlantic Ocean" on his way back from Potsdam to the United States.) But as late as July 23 there was evidently some question on this matter among high Washington officials—and perhaps even (unexpressed) in Stimson's mind—for on this day an urgent message went from Washington to Arthur Compton at Oak Ridge asking for the results of the opinion poll Daniels had taken of the Metallurgical Laboratory scientists. These results had just been received by Compton.

There then occurred an episode which may or may not have had actual historical effect but which certainly has some historical significance. Of all the principal scientists of the Manhattan Project, Arthur Holly Compton probably came closest to being a "standard American" type. He had been raised in a highly and even professionally religious family (his father was an ordained Presbyterian minister; his mother, of German Mennonite stock, was corresponding secretary of the foreign missionary society in her Middle Western community) and was a serious man, much concerned to be and do good in the world. He had accepted without resistance (for they suited him) the dominant social attitudes, moral values, and general mental characteristics of the American Middle Western middle class. Hence the response he now made to the test he faced may be deemed expressive of a national as well as an individual character.

The poll whose results were now in his hands had not been designed as a professional poll-taker would have designed it.[30] Farrington Daniels had submitted to each of 150 scientists in the Chicago laboratory a single question, *Which of the following procedures comes closest to your choice as to the way in which any new weapons we may develop should be used in the Japanese war?*, and had provided five possible answers. These last, with the distribution of opinion among them, were as follows:

1. *Use them in the manner that is from the military point of view most effective in bringing about prompt Japanese surrender at minimum cost to our armed forces.* (23 votes or 15 per cent of sample)
2. *Give a military demonstration in Japan to be followed by renewed opportunity for surrender before full use of the weapon is employed.* (69 votes or 46 per cent of sample)

3. *Give an experimental demonstration in this country with representatives of Japan present; followed by a new opportunity for surrender before full use of the weapon is employed.* (39 votes or 26 per cent of sample)
4. *Withhold military use of the weapons, but make public experimental demonstration of their effectiveness.* (16 votes or 11 per cent of sample)
5. *Maintain as secret as possible all developments of our new weapons and refrain from using them in this war.* (3 votes or 2 per cent of sample)

The wording of answer number two, which received the most votes, was unfortunate. What was meant by "military demonstration"? But certainly and perfectly obvious was the fact that the scientists who voted for this answer were *not* voting in favor of dropping the bomb without warning upon a Japanese city. Otherwise what was meant by that "full use" which was not to be "employed" until after the "demonstration" had been made and followed by a "renewed opportunity for surrender"? There would seem to be but one possible honest interpretation of the poll results: 15 per cent of the scientists were in favor of using the bomb at once in whatever way was militarily "most effective" whereas 85 per cent, if not flatly opposed to this, at least favored other courses of action. According to the interpretation Arthur Compton chose to make, however, in a message which he intended to be influential of policy, "87 per cent [of the polled scientists] voted for . . . [the bomb's] military use"! (In his memoirs he added a qualification, "at least if after other means were tried this was found necessary to bring surrender.")‡‡[31]

An hour later Colonel Nichols came to him with a second question: "Washington wants to know what *you* think." It seemed to Compton, as he later said, "that a firm negative stand on my part might still prevent an atomic attack on Japan" since he had "been in the very midst of these discussions." But he did not hesitate for long, if at all. (". . . I wanted the war to end . . . I saw a chance of an enduring peace that would be demanded by the very destructiveness of these weapons. I hoped that by the use of the bombs many fine young men I knew might . . . be given a chance to live and not to die.") He replied: "My vote is with the majority [sic]. It seems to me that as the war stands the bomb should be used, but no more drastically than needed to bring surrender."[32]

And so the final decision was taken.

In the immediately following days, no formal reply was made by Japan to the Potsdam ultimatum, which was so phrased as to make its acceptance difficult, but on July 28 the Japanese Premier issued a statement through the Japanese press saying the Declaration was unworthy

‡‡ The poll results and Compton's interpretation of them were top secret at the time, of course. Their release after the war provoked bitter criticism of him by scientists who felt he had deliberately misrepresented their opinions.

of notice. On August 2 the Potsdam Conference ended. "There was no alternative now," says Truman in his memoirs. "The bomb was scheduled to be dropped after August 3 unless Japan surrendered before that day."

Was there operative, throughout this drama of decision, a secret wish on the part of key policy-makers to drop the bomb?

One is reminded that science began to prosper when men like Galileo ceased asking *why* things happen as they do in the natural world and began to concentrate exclusively on *what* happens and *how* it happens. This has not prevented individual scientists from being themselves whole men, of course: the response of *most* Manhattan Project scientists (the overwhelming majority of those not in administrative positions) to the challenge of the bomb in the spring and summer of 1945 shows them to have been highly sensitive and profoundly committed to humane values. But one wonders if, in our society as a whole, a now habitual separation of *how* from *why* and a concentration upon *how* to the exclusion of *why*, extending from scientific research into other fields of human activity, may not be partially responsible for the greatest of our present terrors, those that were born in the summer of 1945. By concentrating on the *what* and *how*, men launched that tide of scientific technological power which has flowed with constant augmentation and continuous acceleration into the twentieth century. By increasingly neglecting questions of *why* that require answers in terms of human or Divine purpose, men also initiated a process whereby this physical power born of science would become increasingly divorced from vital (that is, emotionally informed) intelligence. And to the extent of this divorcement scientific power is a force as independent of individual desire and as indifferent to human values as the tides of the sea or the tremors of the Earth or the storms of the atmosphere.

"The leaders of the modern world are drunk with power," wrote Bertrand Russell in his *The Scientific Outlook* fifteen years before the atomic bomb became a reality; "the fact that they can do something no one else thought it possible to do is to them a sufficient reason for doing it." If a thing can be done, it will be. Progress is inevitable.

iii. *The End in Japan*

As all the world knows, and can never forget, the first nuclear bomb to be dropped on a living city exploded two thousand feet above the Japanese city of Hiroshima at 9:15 in the morning of August 6, 1945. It was a U-235 bomb ("Lean Boy"), carried to the target in a B-29 named *Enola Gay* piloted by Colonel Paul W. Tibbetts, Jr.—the same Tibbetts who flew Mark Clark from England to Gibraltar and, a little later, flew Eisenhower to Gibraltar in the fall of 1942, when TORCH was being mounted.§§ Tibbetts had been carefully selected as Command-

§§ See p. 320.

ing Officer of a special Air Force unit, the 509th Composite Group, established in April of 1945 and arduously trained ever since for the express purpose of dropping atomic bombs. The Group had been shipped to Tinian in May and it was from a Tinian runway that the *Enola Gay* took off at 2:45 that fatal morning.[33]

On the instant the bomb was released, Tibbetts turned the plane as sharply as possible and let it nose down from its bombing height of 31,600 feet in order to gain speed. The importance of getting as far away from the target as possible before the bomb went off had been impressed upon him, and he and his crew saw why when a blinding light filled the plane and, a little later, the plane was jarred as violently as if flak had burst beside it though it was then a full fifteen miles from the explosion point. The crew was astounded, awestruck. "My God!" said one of them. "What have we done?"

What they had done was to destroy instantaneously more than four square miles at the heart of a city of three hundred thousand whose total area had been a little less than seven square miles. Nearly eighty thousand people were killed outright, ten thousand more were missing and destined never to be found, thirty-seven thousand were seriously injured not counting thousands of others doomed to lingering, agonized illness by their exposure to deadly gamma rays; and no one could tell what monstrous mutations might appear in later generations as a result of these same rays. Scenes of indescribable horror were enacted, the dusky air rang with screams of agony along Hiroshima's ruined streets, as the *Enola Gay* flew back to its base. Aboard the U.S.S. *Augusta* in the mid-Atlantic, President Truman spoke excitedly, exultantly to the ship's crew. "This is the greatest thing in history!" he said.[34]

Two days later the Soviet Union invaded Manchuria, and on the day after that, August 9, Truman having again called upon Japan to surrender or suffer a "rain of ruin" from the air, a B-29 of the 509th Composite Group delivered the second atomic bomb upon a living city. This bomb was a plutonium "Fat Boy." The city was Nagasaki, population 250,-000. "Fat Boy" was a much more powerful bomb than the one dropped on Hiroshima but, due to the terrain of its target, it caused less damage and killed fewer people. Still, it was effective enough. In a single flashing instant, the heart of the city was wiped out, thirty-five thousand were killed, five thousand were missing and presumed dead, sixty thousand were injured.

With the dropping of this bomb, the United States exhausted her stock of atomic weapons (though of course Japan did not know this), for Hanford and Oak Ridge had been able by that time to produce only enough fissionable material to make three bombs. But no more were "needed." On August 9, immediately after news of the Nagasaki bomb had reached Tokyo, Japan's Supreme War Council opened a previously scheduled meeting with the Emperor. Admiral Baron Kantaro Suzuki, the Premier, presided and refused to vote to break the deadlock which immediately developed, three votes against three, on the question of whether or not unconditional surrender should be accepted. The great stumbling block was the profoundly felt need of the Japanese for assurance that the Emperor's authority as head of the Government would not be destroyed. At last, at two o'clock in the morning of August 10, Premier Suzuki proposed that, since the Council members could not reach agreement, and since "we cannot afford to waste even a minute at this juncture," they "seek the imperial guidance and substitute it for the decision of this conference." The Emperor, whose station, though exalted above all others, had not previously permitted him to be decisive of Government policy, was now promptly decisive. They had no choice, said he; they must accept the Allied terms, "bearing what is indeed very hard to bear."[35]

There then went to Washington from Tokyo via the Japanese representative in Switzerland a note accepting the Potsdam Declaration with the single proviso that no demand be made in the surrender treaty "which prejudices the prerogatives of His Majesty as sovereign ruler." It was a proviso which Stimson and Leahy, among the President's principal advisers, wished promptly to accept but which Byrnes opposed. "He argued," Truman wrote later, "that in the present situation it should be the United States and not Japan that should state conditions."[36] James V. Forrestal, who had succeeded Knox as Secretary of the Navy when Knox died in the spring of 1944, suggested a compromise in which, while accepting the surrender offer, the United States reiterated that the purposes of the Potsdam Declaration must be accomplished. Truman then asked Byrnes to draft a note to Japan in the light of Forrestal's suggestion. "From the moment of surrender the authority of the Emperor and the Japanese Government to rule the State shall be subject to the Supreme Commander of the Allied Powers who will take such steps as he deems proper to effectuate the surrender terms," said the Byrnes note, which provoked new and intense debate among the Japanese Government, some of whose members were convinced that its acceptance would mean the end of the Imperial system.

Meanwhile, U.S. officials, taking cognizance of officialdom's attempt to keep the negotiations rigorously secret, decided to make a direct appeal to Japanese public opinion. Hundreds of thousands of leaflets containing the Japanese capitulation offer and the American reply to it were prepared, and when these were dropped on Japan from Air Force planes early on August 14 they forced the calling of another Imperial conference. This time the conference was brief. The Emperor listened to statements from both sides of the issue, then said it was his wish that his ministers accept the Allied terms.

The war was over.

The last scene was aboard the forty-five thousand-ton U.S.S. *Missouri*, flagship of the U. S. Pacific Fleet, anchored in Tokyo Bay, on

Sunday, September 2, 1945. General Douglas MacArthur was the dominant figure. When the nine-man Japanese surrender delegation had been piped aboard and stood before him at a table on the galley deck, he addressed to them a speech which, unlike many earlier MacArthur pronouncements, struck what most of the world felt to be the right note and caught what most of those present felt to be the true spirit of the occasion. It was a speech Lincolnian in style and feeling:

"We are gathered here, representatives of the major warring powers, to conclude a solemn agreement whereby peace may be restored. The issues, involving divergent ideals and ideologies, have been determined on the battlefields of the world and hence are not for our discussion or debate. Nor is it for us here to meet, representing as we do a majority of the peoples of the Earth, in a spirit of distrust, malice or hatred. But rather it is for us, both victors and vanquished, to rise to that higher dignity which alone benefits the sacred purposes we are about to serve, committing all of our peoples unreservedly to faithful compliance with the undertakings they are here formally to assume.

"It is my earnest hope and indeed the hope of all mankind that from this solemn occasion a better world shall emerge out of the blood and carnage of the past—a world dedicated to the dignity of man and the fulfillment of his most cherished wish—for freedom, tolerance, and justice."

The instrument of surrender was then signed.

iv. Envoi

And so our long story ends.

One could wish to say that it was brought on that warm Sunday to such a conclusion as was suggested by MacArthur's eloquence. But in our age of anxiety there are, it would seem, no firm conclusions. All is flux and ferment. Out of these has yet to emerge a clear pattern for the future. We have no firm assurance that World War II was other than the next to the last act of a world tragedy whose end will be the death of all. But neither can it be said that all valid reason for hope is gone, that the last act is inevitable.

The question remains, and the quest continues. We are as a man who clings precariously to the side of a sheer cliff, shuddering in terror when he looks down upon black jagged rocks far below, but still climbs, seeing above him hand- and footholds which, though slippery, lead at last to an upland plateau where (he knows) the land is fair and green and bright in the sunlight.

General Sources and Bibliography

In the individual sets of chapter notes, following this general bibliographical note, I have endeavored to give sources for specific items of information and to indicate bases for interpretations made of events and personalities. Here I will list only such books as were found to be, for one reason or another, of definite value to me and might therefore be to other students of the war. I make no effort to list the contemporary news accounts and interpretations in periodicals which were used for scenic and narrative detail, but it will be obvious to the reader that the New York *Times* was much used, as it must always be by anyone writing twentieth-century history. In addition, considerable material was derived from *Time*, *Newsweek*, *The New Yorker*, *Collier's*, *The Saturday Evening Post*, *The Nation*, *The New Republic*, and *Partisan Review*.

I was also greatly aided by an earlier work of mine which took me to warring Europe as a correspondent in the summer and early autumn of 1944 and enabled me to have private interviews at considerable length with (to give their rank as it then was) General of the Army Dwight D. Eisenhower; Lieutenant General Omar N. Bradley; Lieutenant General George S. Patton, Jr.; Lieutenant General Walter B. (Beetle) Smith; Air Marshal Sir Arthur Tedder; Lieutenant General Sir Humfrey Gale; Major General K. F. M. (Jock) Whiteley; Major General Kenneth W. D. Strong; Lieutenant General A. E. Grasett; Lieutenant General Frederick E. Morgan, and all the members of General Eisenhower's "official family" at his personal headquarters, first at Wide Wing and in London, then in Normandy. These last included Eisenhower's two American aides, Captain Harry C. Butcher, U.S.N.R., and Colonel Ernest R. (Tex) Lee, and his British military assistant, Colonel James Frederic Gault. The notes I took of these interviews not only supplied factual information I might not otherwise have had but also aided my recapture, for myself at least, of some of the mood and flavor of those days and events.

Background and Onset of the War

Indispensable, of course, to an understanding of the war in general are the six volumes of Winston Churchill's *The Second World War*, of which the first three volumes—*The Gathering Storm, Their Finest Hour*, and *The Grand Alliance*—tell of how war came to Europe, of America's increasing involvement, and of events leading up to and including Pearl Harbor. Particularly valuable are C. Groves Haines and Ross J. S. Hoffman, *The Origins and Background of the Second World War;* James W. Gantenbein's compilation, *Documentary Background of World War II, 1931–1941;* W. L. Langer and S. Everett Gleason, *The Challenge of Isolation, 1927–1940*, and *The Undeclared War, 1940–1941;* Forrest Davis and Ernest K. Lindley, *How War Came, An American White Paper;* William L. Shirer, *Berlin Diary*, and the same author's *The Rise and Fall of the Third Reich;* A. J. P. Taylor, *The Origins of the Second World War* (though terribly wrongheaded, in my opinion); Herbert Feis, *The Road to Pearl Harbor;* Joseph C. Grew, *Ten Years in Japan*, and also (more importantly) his two-volume *Turbulent Era;* Cordell Hull's two-volume *Memoirs of Cordell Hull;* Francis Biddle, *In Brief Authority;* Robert E. Sherwood, *Roosevelt and Hopkins;* and Robert J. C. Butow, *Tojo and the Coming of the War.*

Focusing specifically on the Pearl Harbor attack are Walter Lord, *Day of Infamy;* Walter Millis, *This Is Pearl!;* Barbara Wohlstetter, *Pearl Harbor, Warning and Decision;* and Adolph A. Hoehling, *The Week before Pearl Harbor.* Highly critical of Roosevelt and in general inclined toward that "plot" or "conspiracy" concept of history typical of the radical Right are George E. Morgenstern's *Pearl Harbor: The Story of the Secret War;* George M. Waller, *Pearl Harbor: Roosevelt and the Coming of the War;* Robert A. Theobald, *The Final Secret of Pearl Harbor;* and Husband E. Kimmel, *Admiral Kimmel's Story.* Reference was also made to Charles A. Beard, *President Roosevelt and the Coming of the War, A Study in Appearances and Realities*, and Charles C. Tansil, *Backdoor to War: The Roosevelt Foreign Policy, 1933–1941.*

Of special value to my effort to recapture the intellectual mood of the time were references to such works as William Henry Chamberlain, *The World's Iron Age;* H. R. Knickerbocker, *Is Tomorrow Hitler's?;* Harold Laski, *Reflections on the Revolution in Our Time;* Anne Morrow Lindbergh, *The Wave of the Future;* Frederick L. Schuman, *Design for Power, The Struggle for the World;* Raymond Gram Swing, *How War Came* and his *Preview of History;* Edmund Taylor, *The Strategy of Terror;* Frederick Lewis Allen, *Since Yesterday;* Isabel Leighton, editor, *The Aspirin Age;* Dorothy Thompson, *Listen, Hans!;* Raoul de Roussy de Sales, *The Making of Tomorrow.*

Much use was also made of Arthur Schlesinger, Jr., *The Crisis of the Old Order, The Coming of the New Deal*, and *The Politics of Upheaval*, the first three volumes of his *The Age of Roosevelt;* James MacGregor Burns, *Roosevelt: The Lion and the Fox;* Alfred B. Rollins, Jr., editor, *Franklin D. Roosevelt and the Age of Action.* Less used but useful were William E. Leuchtenburg, *Franklin D. Roosevelt and the New Deal, 1932–1940*, and Foster Rhea Dulles, *America's Rise to World Power, 1898–1954.*

I should perhaps add that two earlier works of mine, *A Prophet in His*

Own Country: The Triumphs and Defeats of Adlai E. Stevenson, and *The Hero: Charles A. Lindbergh and the American Dream*, contain studies in considerable depth of the battle over isolationism and were therefore helpful in the preparation of the opening book of the present work.

General History of the War

The first and (at this writing) only comprehensive, scholarly account of America in the war, written in the tradition of academic history, is A. Russell Buchanan, *The United States and World War II*, in two volumes. It was published early in the last year of my labor on this work and was most useful. Also used were Walter Phelps Hall, *Iron out of Calvary;* Chester Wilmot, *The Struggle for Europe* (written from the British point of view, this is perhaps the best single book yet written on its subject); Louis J. Snyder, *The War;* Edgar McInnis's running contemporary account, *The War*, in six volumes; and, particularly for certain diplomatic and political developments, Waverley Root's controversial and opinionated but factually accurate and unfailingly interesting *The Secret History of the War*, in three fat volumes. For war diplomacy and grand strategy, Herbert Feis's authoritative *Churchill, Roosevelt, Stalin, The War They Waged and the Peace They Sought*, was constantly used.

To these, add of course Churchill's six-volume op. cit., the several volumes of his war messages and speeches, Sherwood's op. cit., and Samuel Rosenman, editor, *The Public Papers and Addresses of Franklin D. Roosevelt* for the war years.

Political and Economic Aspects

More heavily used in writing about the home front than in writing about any other aspect of our war experience were contemporary newspaper and news magazine accounts. Books found useful in my dealing with political and economic events were the aforementioned works by Biddle, Sherwood, Hull, Rollins, Jr., Schlesinger, Jr., Rosenman as editor of the public papers and as author of *Working with Roosevelt;* James F. Byrnes, *Speaking Frankly;* Harry S. Truman, *The Year of Decision* (Volume One of his *Memoirs*); William D. Leahy, *I Was There;* Frances Perkins, *The Roosevelt I Knew;* William D. Hassett, *Off the Record with F.D.R.;* Rexford G. Tugwell, *The Democratic Roosevelt* and *The Art of Politics;* Joseph Barnes, *Willkie;* Russell Lord, *The Wallaces of Iowa;* Edward R. Stettinius, Jr., *Lend-Lease* and *Roosevelt and the Russians;* Elliott Roosevelt, editor, *F.D.R., His Personal Letters;* Donald Nelson, *Arsenal of Democracy;* Richard E. Courant, *Secretary Stimson, A Study in Statecraft;* Elting E. Morison, *Turmoil and Tradition;* Henry L. Stimson and McGeorge Bundy, *On Active Service in Peace and War;* Eliot Janeway, *The Struggle for Survival, A Chronicle of Economic Mobilization in World War II;* David Novik, Melvin Anshen, W. C. Truppner, *Wartime Production Controls.*

Naval and Military Operations

Much referred to were the War Reports of General of the Army George C. Marshall, Chief of Staff; General of the Army H. H. Arnold, Commanding General, Army Air Forces; and Fleet Admiral Ernest J. King, Commander-in-Chief, U. S. Fleet, and Chief of Naval Operations. These were issued in a single volume in 1947.

The standard reference work for naval operations is Samuel Eliot Morison, *History of United States Naval Operations in World War II*, in fifteen volumes. This is virtually an official history, but Morison was free to make his own judgments and interpretations of men and events and he exercised this freedom in his work. A useful supplement to it is the five-volume *Battle Report*, of which Walter Karig is principal author. The individual volumes are *Pearl Harbor to Coral Sea*, Karig and Welbourne Kelley; *The Atlantic War*, Karig, Earl Burton, S. L. Freeland; *Pacific War: Middle Phase*, Karig, Eric Purdon; *The End of an Empire*, Karig, R. L. Harris, F. A. Manson; *Victory in the Pacific*, Karig, Harris, Manson.

Also extensively used were Ernest J. King and Walter Muir Whitehill, *Fleet Admiral King;* Elmer B. Potter and Chester W. Nimitz, editors, *The Great Sea War, The Story of Naval Action in World War II;* Frederick C. Sherman, *Combat Command, The American Aircraft Carriers in the Pacific War;* Fletcher Pratt, *The Fleet against Japan;* Edward P. Stafford, *The Big E, The Story of the U.S.S.* Enterprise; Mitsuo Fuchida and Masataka Okumiya, *Midway, The Battle that Doomed Japan;* Irving Werstein, *The Battle of Midway;* Thaddeus V. Tuleja, *Climax at Midway;* Robert D. Heinl, Jr., *Marines at Midway;* Robert J. Casey, *Torpedo Junction* and his *Battle Below, The War of the Submarines.*

There appear to be remarkably few American combat units, actively engaged in the war, which have not as yet produced their own particular histories, often in voluminous detail. To read all of these would be a lifetime project. But every historian of the war must make extensive use of the multiple volumes already issued, and continuing (at this writing) to be issued by the Office of the Chief of Military History, Department of the Army.

Most used by me among this series have been Kent R. Greenfield, editor, *Command Decisions;* George F. Howe, *Northwest Africa: Seizing the Initiative in the West;* Charles F. Romanus and Riley Sutherland, *Stilwell's Command Problems*, the same authors' *Stilwell's Mission to China*, and their *Time Runs out in CBI;* Martin Blumeson, *Breakout and Pursuit;* Charles B. MacDonald, *The Siegfried Line Campaign;* Philip A. Crowl and Edmund G. Love, *Seizing the Gilberts and Marshalls;* Philip A. Crowl, *Campaign in the Marianas;* Robert D. Heinl, Jr., and John A. Crown, *The Marshalls: Increasing the Tempo;* Robert Ross Smith, *The Approach to the Philippines;* Louis Morton, *The Fall of the Philippines;* Robert Ross Smith, *Triumph in the Philippines;* Forrest C. Pogue, *The Supreme Command;* Louis Morton, *Strategy and Command;* John A. Miller, Jr., *Guadalcanal: The First Offensive* and his *Cartwheel: The Reduction of Rabaul;* Gordon A. Harrison, *Cross-Channel Attack.*

Nor can the war historian fail to use heavily the six-volume *The Army Air Forces in World War II*, by Wesley Frank Craven and James Lea Cate, with assistants; and the two-volume *History of U. S. Marine Corps Operations in World War II*, issued by the Historical Branch, G-3 Division, U. S. Marine Corps Headquarters. The Marine Corps has issued and continues to issue monographs on specific Marine battles or campaigns, of which several were used in the present work, notably those dealing with Guadalcanal and the central Solomons. Also used was Frank O. Hough, *The Island War, The United States Marine Corps in the Pacific.*

Referred to at various points as I wrote about the Pacific-Asiatic war were Walter D. Edmonds, *They Fought with What They Had;* William L. White, *They Were Expendable,* and his *Queens Die Proudly;* Rekihei Inoguchi, *The Divine Wind, Japan's Kamikaze Force in World War II;* Saluro Sakai, with Martin Caiden and Fred Saito, *Samurai!;* Samuel B. Griffith, *The Battle for Guadalcanal;* Stanley L. Falk, *Bataan, The March of Death;* Richard Tregaskis, *Guadalcanal Diary;* John Hersey, *Into the Valley;* U. S. Strategic Bombing Survey, *The Effects of Strategic Bombing on Japan's War Economy;* Ted W. Lawson, *Thirty Seconds Over Tokyo;* Jack Belden, *Retreat With Stilwell;* Carlos P. Romulo, *I Saw the Fall of the Philippines* and *I See the Philippines Rise;* and Martin Caiden, *A Torch to the Enemy.*

Supplementing official histories of the Atlantic-European war were numerous eyewitness accounts, of which the single most useful compilation, covering all theaters of the war (the war against Japan as well as the war against Nazi-Fascism), was Desmond Flower and James Reeves, editors, *The Taste of Courage.* Individual accounts referred to by me include Frank Gervasi, *War Has Seven Faces;* Curt Riess, *They Were There;* John Gunther, *D-Day* (Sicily); John MacVane, *Journey into War;* Ernie Pyle, *Here Is Your War,* and *Brave Men; The New Yorker* magazine, *The New Yorker Book of War Pieces;* Ralph Ingersoll, *The Battle Is the Pay-off,* and *Top Secret;* and Eric Sevareid, *Not So Wild a Dream.* Use was also made of Martin Caiden, *The Night Hamburg Died;* Cornelius Ryan, *The Longest Day;* David Amrine Howarth, *D-Day, The Sixth of June, 1944;* John Toland, *Battle, The Story of the Bulge;* David E. Merriam, *Dark December;* Robert S. Allen, *Lucky Forward, History of Patton's Third Army;* Walter B. Smith, *Eisenhower's Six Great Decisions;* and U. S. Strategic Bombing Survey, *The Effects of Strategic Bombing on the German War Economy.*

Among the scores of biographies and memoirs consulted, the following were most used: H. H. Arnold, *Global Mission;* Lewis Hyde Brereton, *The Brereton Papers;* Churchill, op. cit.; King, op. cit.; Nimitz, op. cit.; Sir Arthur Bryant, *The Turn of the Tide* and *Triumph in the West;* Claire Lee Chennault, *Way of a Fighter;* Robert Lee Scott, *Flying Tiger: Chennault of China;* Mark Wayne Clark, *Calculated Risk;* Harry C. Butcher, *My Three Years with Eisenhower;* Dwight D. Eisenhower, *Crusade in Europe;* George C. Kenney, *General Kenney Reports;* G. Ward Price, *Giraud and the African Scene;* Harold R. L. G. Alexander, *The Alexander Memoirs;* Bernard L. Montgomery, *The Memoirs of Field Marshal Montgomery;* Correlli Barnett, *The Desert Generals;* George S. Patton, *War as I Knew It;* Omar N. Bradley, *A Soldier's Story;* Sir Frederick E. Morgan, *Overture to Overlord;* Husband E. Kimmel, op. cit.; Elliott Roosevelt, *As He Saw It;* Samuel I. Rosenman, *Working with Roosevelt;* Sherwood, op. cit.; Byrnes, op. cit.; Hull, op. cit.; Elting E. Morison, op. cit.; Stimson and Bundy, op. cit.; Robert Murphy, *Diplomat Among Warriors;* James W. Stilwell, *The Stilwell Papers;* Charles de

Gaulle, *The Complete War Memoirs of Charles de Gaulle;* Galeazzo Ciano, *The Ciano Diaries;* Joesph Goebbels, *The Goebbels Diaries;* Frederick W. Deakin, *The Brutal Friendship, Mussolini, Hitler, and the Fall of Italian Fascism.*

Also, Franco Maugeri, *From the Ashes of Disgrace;* Benito Mussolini, *The Fall of Mussolini;* Pietro Badoglio, *Italy in the Second World War;* Laura Fermi, *Mussolini;* William F. Halsey and J. Bryan III, *Admiral Halsey's Story;* Robert L. Eichelberger, *Our Jungle Road to Tokyo;* Frazier Hunt, *MacArthur and the War against Japan;* Holland M. Smith and Percy Finch, *Coral and Brass;* Courtney Whitney, *MacArthur, His Rendezvous with History;* Joseph E. Davies, *Mission to Moscow;* John R. Deane, *The Strange Alliance;* Ellis M. Zacharias, *Secret Missions;* Charles R. Codman, *Drive;* Leslie R. Groves, *Now It Can Be Told;* Arthur Compton, *Atomic Quest;* Biddle, op. cit.; Lewis L. Strauss, *Men and Decisions;* Leahy, op. cit.; Romulo, op. cit.; Truman, op. cit.

The Atomic Bomb and End of the War

Much used in writing the story of the atomic bomb were the aforementioned memoirs of Arthur Compton, General Groves, and Admiral Strauss, plus Michael Amrine, *The Great Decision;* Robert C. Batchelder, *The Irreversible Decision;* P. M. S. Blackett, *Fear, War, and the Bomb;* Ronald W. Clark, *The Birth of the Bomb;* Robert Jungk, *Brighter than a Thousand Suns;* Fletcher Knebel and Charles W. Bailey II, *No High Ground;* Daniel Lang, *Early Tales of the Atomic Age;* Ralph E. Lapp, *Atoms and People;* William L. Laurence, *Dawn over Zero* and *Men and Atoms;* John F. Purcell, *The Best-Kept Secret;* Henry de Wolf Smyth, *Atomic Energy for Military Purposes;* and Merle Miller and Abe Spitzer, *We Dropped the A-Bomb.*

In planning and writing the story of the end of the war and the making of peace the following were useful: Robert J. C. Butow, *Japan's Decision to Surrender;* Herbert Feis, *Japan Subdued, The Atomic Bomb and the End of the War in the Pacific,* and *Between War and Peace, The Potsdam Conference;* William B. Ziff, *The Gentlemen Talk of Peace;* Emery Reeves, *The Anatomy of Peace;* Wendell Willkie, *One World,* and *An American Program;* Lionel M. Gelber, *Peace by Power, The Plain Man's Guide to the Key Issues of War and of the Post-war World;* Henry A. Wallace, *The Century of the Common Man;* Sir Bernard Pares, *Russia and the Peace;* Sumner Welles, *The Time for Decision;* Michael Straight, *Make This the Last War;* as well as the aforementioned memoirs of Byrnes, Hull, and Truman.

Notes

I. *To the Edge of the Abyss*

1. William L. Laurence, *Men and Atoms* (New York: 1959), pp. xi–xiii, which is a prologue by Laurence's wife, Florence, entitled "The Night the Atom Came to Live With Us." It gives a circumstantial account of this walk. The quotations later made of Laurence are from her account.

2. U. S. State Department, *Peace and War: United States Foreign Policy, 1931–41* (U. S. Government Printing Office: 1943), pp. 364–87, presents full text.

3. C. Groves Haines and Rose J. S. Hoffman, *The Origins and Background of the Second World War* (New York: 1943), pp. 489–90, gives American Institute of Public Opinion poll results on attitudes toward Japan-China at this time.

4. Joseph Alsop and Robert Kintner, *American White Paper: The Story of American Diplomacy and the Second World War* (New York: 1940), pp. 24–25.

5. William L. Shirer, *The Rise and Fall of the Third Reich* (New York: 1960), pp. 470–75, gives a detailed report of Hitler's reply to Roosevelt and of the manner in which the Nazis obtained their assurances from the thirty-one nations that these did not fear an attack from Germany. Rumania and Latvia declined to answer as the Nazis wished, Latvia giving the right answer only after threatful pressure had been applied.

6. Quoted by James MacGregor Burns, *Roosevelt: The Lion and the Fox* (New York: 1956), pp. 391–92.

7. Alsop and Kintner, op. cit., which derived from the long interviews with Administration leaders and was checked in the White House, give on pp. 44–46 a circumstantial account of this meeting. Cordell Hull, *The Memoirs of Cordell Hull* (New York: 1948), pp. 649–53, also describes it, as does Alben W. Barkley, *That Reminds Me*—(New York: 1954), pp. 260–61. Barkley says House as well as Senate leaders were present, but all other accounts, including the New York *Times* report, has only Senators there.

8. Quoted by Gerald W. Johnson, *The New Republic*, June 12, 1961, p. 19, in review of Marian C. McKenna, *Borah* (Ann Arbor: 1961).

9. This direct quote of Roosevelt, and the preceding one (about opening "with prayer"), are from Alsop and Kintner, op. cit., pp. 44–45.

10. This bit of dialogue is from Cordell Hull, op. cit., pp. 649–53. All accounts agree that Hull was close to tears as a result of Borah's comments. Hull says on p. 656, op. cit., that Borah's source of information, which he regarded as more reliable than State Department channels, was an obscure press service in London that was pro-Axis.

11. Quoted by Alsop and Kintner, op. cit., p. 46.

12. Quoted by Hull, op. cit., pp. 640–53. The correctness of the Hull-Roosevelt argument is attested to by Hitler's statement to a secret conference of his generals and General Staff on November 23, 1939, that "because of her neutrality laws" the United States was not as yet dangerous to the Reich and need not be considered as a factor influencing decisions for an attack in the West through Holland and Belgium "at the most favorable and earliest moment." The statement is quoted by Shirer, op. cit., p. 658, from conference notes of an "unidentified participant." It seems evident a repeal of neutrality laws in the summer of 1939, coupled with Mussolini's opposition to the attack on Poland (an opposition which the neutrality repeal would certainly have strengthened), might have given Hitler pause.

13. Quoted by Shirer, op. cit., p. 496.

14. Joseph E. Davies, *Mission to Moscow* (New York: 1941), p. 450.

15. Quoted by Alsop and Kintner, op. cit., p. 1.

II. *In the Valley of Indecision*

1. Geoffrey T. Hellman, "The Contemporaneous Memoranda of Dr. Sachs," *The New Yorker*, December 1, 1945, pp. 73–80.

2. Asked by William L. Laurence, in 1938, whether men would ever be able to harness the power of the atom, Einstein replied: "No. We are poor marksmen, shooting at birds in the dark in a country where there are very few birds!"

3. Samuel Rosenman, ed., *The Public Papers and Addresses of Franklin D. Roosevelt*, 1939, pp. 461–64, 515–16, 518.

4. Charles A. Lindbergh, "Appeal for Isolation." *Vital Speeches*, Vol. 5, pp. 751–52.

5. Lindbergh, "What Our Decision Should Be." *Vital Speeches*, Vol. 6, pp. 484–85.

6. Direct quotes of Sachs and Roosevelt are in Hellman, op. cit. The final exchange between the two is also quoted by Laurence, op. cit., p. 59. The text of the Einstein letter is printed in full in Laurence, op. cit., pp. 57–58.

7. Arthur Holly Compton, *Atomic Quest* (New York: 1956), p. 30. Compton says flatly (pp. 29–30) that the effect "was to retard rather than advance the development of American uranium research."

8. Winston S. Churchill, *The Gathering Storm* (Boston: 1948), pp. 482–83, tells of the French "Plan D" in which this assumption was made, as does William L. Shirer, *The Rise and Fall of the Third Reich* (New York: 1960), pp. 717–18.

9. According to Shirer, op. cit., p. 734, there were thirty-six Allied divisions in the line from Namur to Antwerp against twenty German divisions on May 12.

10. The full text of the Declaration of Union is printed on pp. 208–9 of

Winston Churchill's *Their Finest Hour* (Boston: 1949). Ibid. on pp. 212–14 tells of the Council meeting in Bordeaux, whence derives the direct quotations from Pétain.

11. A highly circumstantial account of election night in the Commodore was carried by the New York *Times* for Wednesday, November 6, and in *Time* magazine for that week, and these were used in the writing of this scene.

12. Mary Farhart Dillon, *Wendell Willkie, 1892–1944* (New York: 1952), p. 17. Joseph Barnes writes in his excellent *Willkie* (New York: 1952), p. 21, that Henrietta Trisch Willkie was still wearing high French heels in the year of her death and that she was "remembered by those who knew her as a driving, restless, not very happy woman, of great ability and almost legendary strength, energy, and ambition."

13. Barnes, op. cit., p. 26. The Barnes biography was heavily leaned upon for the facts of Willkie's career and attitudes. The Dillon biography is in many respects a tract *against* Willkie, composed in flat journalese, full of malicious prejudice against all that has given honor to Willkie's name since his death, but useful (in part for this very reason) to any student of Willkie's career.

14. Quoted by Dillon, op. cit., p. 143 and, in somewhat different form, by Barnes, op. cit., p. 183.

15. Robert E. Sherwood's invaluable "inside" account of the Roosevelt 1940 campaign comprises Chapter VIII of his *Roosevelt and Hopkins* (New York: 1948, 1950). The direct quote is from p. 190. See also James MacGregor Burns, *The Lion and the Fox* (New York: 1956), pp. 422–51.

16. According to Dillon, op. cit., p. 225.

17. Michael F. Reilly (as told to William J. Slocum), *Reilly of the White House* (New York: 1947), p. 66.

III. *The Undeclared War*

1. The New York *Times*, December 3 and 4, 1940, gives a long and circumstantial account of the President's train trip to Miami and his sailing from there.

2. Quoted by Robert E. Sherwood, *Roosevelt and Hopkins* (New York: 1948), pp. 221–22.

3. The New York *Times* report interpreted this as emphasizing "again" the President's "determination to keep this country out of the war."

4. Winston Churchill's *Their Finest Hour* (Boston: 1949), pp. 553–54, presents his congratulatory message in full and adds: "Curiously enough, I never received any answer to this telegram. It may well have been engulfed in the vast mass of congratulatory messages which were swept aside by urgent work."

5. Henry L. Stimson and McGeorge Bundy, *On Active Service in Peace and War* (New York: 1947) pp. 354–55. Stimson's Diary is quoted by William L. Langer and S. Everett Gleason, *The Undeclared War, 1940–1941* (New York: 1953), p. 181.

6. Langer and Gleason, op. cit., p. 213.

7. Churchill, op. cit., p. 559.

8. The letter is printed in full in Churchill, op. cit., pp. 558–67.

9. Sherwood, op. cit., p. 224.

10. Sherwood, op. cit., p. 224.

11. Langer and Gleason, op. cit., p. 238, tell of the White House luncheon

and quotes the *Morgenthau Diaries* (ms.). Roosevelt told Morgenthau and the British guests that it seemed to him "the thing to do is get away from a dollar sign," and then came out with the "essence" of Lend-Lease.

12. Sherwood, op. cit., p. 225; Langer and Gleason, op. cit., pp. 239–40; and Edward R. Stettinius, Jr., *Lend-Lease, Weapon for Victory* (New York: 1944) p. 17 and p. 68, tell of this press conference.

13. "Report of the United States-British Staff Conversations," March 27, 1941 ("Pearl Harbor Attack," XV, pp. 1485–1550), quoted by Langer and Gleason, op. cit., p. 285.

14. "I believe it may accurately be said that with that neighborly analogy, Roosevelt won the fight for Lend-Lease." Sherwood, op. cit., p. 225.

15. Quoted by Langer and Gleason, op. cit., p. 242.

16. The New York *Times* for February 12, 1941, gives long, circumstantial account of the Willkie testimony.

17. Winston Churchill, *The Grand Alliance* (Boston: 1950), p. 148.

18. Walter Millis, *This Is Pearl!* (New York: 1947), p. 16. Millis gives the terms of the Tri-Partite Pact on p. 18, and discusses their significance on that and following pages. Herbert Feis, *The Road to Pearl Harbor* (Princeton: 1950) discusses the making of the Japanese alliance with the Axis on pp. 110–21. Langer and Gleason, op. cit., pp. 30–31, print the third part of the Pact in full.

19. William L. Shirer, *The Rise and Fall of the Third Reich* (New York: 1960), p. 838. Shirer deals with the flight of Hess in some detail on pp. 834–38. Churchill in *The Grand Alliance* covers the episode on pp. 48–55.

20. Shirer, op. cit., p. 848.

21. Sherwood, op. cit., p. 303.

22. Sumner Welles, *Where Are We Heading?* (New York: 1946), p. 38. Langer and Gleason say in op. cit., p. 531, that Roosevelt "had more sympathy than most Americans for the Bolshevik experiment, that he regarded the Communist threat as less grave and certainly less immediate than the Nazi menace, and that he fancied that over the years the Soviet and American systems would approximate each other."

23. Sherwood, op. cit., p. 303: "But if Hopkins had a moment of relief it was no more than a moment; for he was compelled instantly to face the new and gigantic problems of aid for Russia."

24. Churchill, *The Grand Alliance*, p. 370.

25. Ibid., 371–73, presents most of the broadcast.

26. Sherwood, op. cit., p. 308.

27. Sir John Kennedy, *The Business of War* (New York: 1958), p. 155. Kennedy tells of the disagreement over the Middle East on pp. 155–57; Sherwood, op. cit., on pp. 314–16; Churchill, *The Grand Alliance*, pp. 424–25.

28. Churchill, *The Grand Alliance*, p. 427.

29. Sherwood, op. cit., p. 318.

30. The chief source of detailed information on Hopkins' Moscow mission is of course Sherwood, who devotes a chapter to it on pp. 323–48 of op. cit., quoting in full Hopkins' reports of his two meetings with Stalin. *American* magazine for December 1941 featured an article by Hopkins giving the "Inside Story" of his meetings with the dictator. Langer and Gleason cover the mission on pp. 563–67. Reference was made to Nicholas Mikhailov's propagandistic *Soviet Russia: The Land and Its People* (New York: 1948) and to

John Gunther's *Inside Russia Today* (New York: 1958) for physical descriptions of Moscow.

31. Hopkins article in *American* magazine, December 1941. Quoted by Sherwood, op. cit., p. 344.

32. Ibid., p. 348, quoting the report of Flight Lieutenant D. C. McKinley, D.F.C., who piloted the plane which flew Hopkins to Moscow and back.

IV. *To the Day of Infamy*

1. Quoted by Kenneth S. Davis, *Soldier of Democracy* (New York: 1945, 1952), pp. 271–72.

2. Quoted in ibid., pp. 187–88.

3. The meeting is described by Arthur Holly Compton, *Atomic Quest* (New York: 1956), pp. 62–64. Supplementary information, giving circumstantial detail for use in the scene, was provided in a letter to the author from Mr. Compton dated October 10, 1961.

4. Robert E. Sherwood, *Roosevelt and Hopkins* (New York: 1948, 1950), pp. 153–54.

5. Compton, op. cit., pp. 7–9, describes the fireplace conversation.

6. Quoted by William L. Laurence, *Men and Atoms* (New York: 1959), p. 52. Laurence gives verbatim the crucial portions of Szilard's Senate Committee testimony on pp. 52–54.

7. Ibid., p. 40.

8. The Lawrence memorandum is quoted by Compton, op. cit., pp. 49–50.

9. Compton tells of the Cosmos Club luncheon on p. 701 of op. cit. Additional information concerning it was derived from the previously cited letter from Compton to the author.

10. Compton, op. cit., pp. 41–42.

11. The "Green Light" message is presented in full in Joseph C. Grew, *Turbulent Era, A Diplomatic Record of Forty Years*, Edited by Walter Johnson (Boston: 1952), pp. 1224–29.

12. Ibid., p. 1233. Cordell Hull, *The Memoirs of Cordell Hull* (New York: 1948), p. 984.

13. Ibid., p. 986.

14. Grew, op. cit., p. 1275.

15. Quoted by Herbert Feis, *The Road to Pearl Harbor* (Princeton: 1950), p. 178.

16. Quoted in ibid., pp. 215–16.

17. Hull, op. cit., p. 1016.

18. Quoted by William L. Langer and S. Everett Gleason, *The Undeclared War* (New York: 1953), p. 654.

19. Quoted in ibid., p. 654.

20. Ibid., p. 654.

21. Ibid., p. 654.

22. Hull, op. cit., p. 1016.

23. Robert E. Sherwood, *Roosevelt and Hopkins* (New York: 1948, 1950), p. 430.

24. Ibid., pp. 429–30.

25. Winston Churchill, *The Grand Alliance* (Boston: 1950), p. 440.

26. Hull, op. cit., pp. 1018–19.

27. Ibid., p. 987.

28. Langer and Gleason, p. 836.

29. Feis, op. cit., p. 271.

30. Ibid., p. 291.

31. Ibid., p. 296.

32. Quoted by ibid., p. 302. The memorandum is printed in full in the U. S. Government Document, *Pearl Harbor Attack*, Part XIV, pp. 1061–62.

33. Hull, op. cit., p. 1063.

34. Quoted by Langer and Gleason, op. cit., p. 878.

35. Hull, op. cit., p. 1073.

36. Quoted by Churchill, op. cit., p. 589. Summarized by Feis, p. 321.

37. Quoted by Feis, op. cit., p. 313.

38. Quoted by Husband E. Kimmel, *Admiral Kimmel's Story* (Chicago: 1955), pp. 48–49.

39. Quoted in ibid., pp. 43–44.

40. Quoted by Hull, op. cit., p. 1074.

41. Quoted in ibid., p. 1089.

42. Churchill, op. cit., p. 600.

43. Testimony of Commander I. R. Schulz, the Navy courier who delivered the message to the White House, before investigating committee. Printed in *Pearl Harbor Attack,* Part XII, pp. 238–39.

44. Quoted, among many other places, in Walter Millis, *This Is Pearl!* (New York: 1947), p. 336. The Millis work remains, in the present author's opinion, the best written succinct account of the Pearl Harbor attack and the events leading up to it. See also Langer and Gleason, op. cit., pp. 933–34.

45. Both the Hull and Knox drafts are quoted by Langer and Gleason, op. cit.

46. Millis, op. cit., p. 337.

47. Ibid., pp. 340–41.

48. Forrest Davis and Ernest K. Lindley, *How War Came* (New York: 1942). Millis, op. cit., pp. 343–44. Much of the circumstantial detail that follows comes from Davis and Lindley.

49. Sherwood, op. cit., p. 441. Also, Langer and Gleason, op. cit., p. 940. The latter quote the war declaration note handed to the American Chargé d'Affaires in Berlin on December 11, 1941, and point out that no mention was made in it of Japan but that instead it put the war declaration "solely on the basis of German-American relations." They write: "It seems that Hitler's immediate objective, as a matter of prestige, was to declare war before it could be declared upon him." But why, if so, did he wait so long?

V. *Pacific Defeat and Global Strategy*

1. For details of ship anchorage, movement, etc., at Pearl Harbor, Walter Millis' *This Is Pearl!* (New York: 1947), pp. 313–16; Commander Walter Karig, U.S.N.R. and Lieutenant Wolbourn Kelley, U.S.N.R., *Battle Report: Pearl Harbor to Coral Sea* (New York: 1944), pp. 5–21; Husband E. Kimmel, *Admiral Kimmel's Story* (Chicago: 1955). For detailed exposition of how and why the Japanese achieved complete tactical surprise, see Roberta Wohlstetter, *Pearl Harbor, Warning and Decision* (Stanford: 1962).

2. For analysis of command arrangements and confusions, Millis, op. cit., pp. 61–64, 211–13. Kimmel, op. cit., pp. 13–15.

3. Kimmel, op. cit., p. 8.

4. Ibid., pp. 9–10.

5. For details of Kimmel's Saturday night and early Sunday morning, Walter Lord's *Day of Infamy* (New York: 1957), pp. 7–8.

6. For story of Ward's action, Lord, op. cit., pp. 30–39, 38–42; Karig and Kelley, op. cit., pp. 6–8, 12–18; Millis, op. cit., pp. 345–46, 348–49.

7. For story of radar on Oahu, Millis, op. cit., pp. 37, 59–60, 209–11, 352–54; Lord, op. cit., pp. 44–49.

8. Testifying at the Congressional inquiry into the Pearl Harbor disaster, Major Kenneth P. Berquist of the Air Corps (quoted by Millis, op. cit., p. 210), said the lack of cooperation was perhaps due to "a lack of education as to what air defense was and what it could do."

9. Winston Churchill, *The Grand Alliance* (Boston: 1950), p. 662.

10. Ibid., p. 608.

11. Ibid., p. 609.

12. Ibid., p. 626.

13. Ibid., p. 620.

14. Ibid., p. 641.

15. The three papers are presented in full on pp. 646–58 of ibid. The parenthetical description of Eden's difficulties with Stalin in Moscow, and of Churchill's reaction to Stalin's demands is from ibid., pp. 628–31.

16. Report given in full in ibid., p. 664.

17. See ibid., p. 673.

18. Gordon A. Harrison, *Cross-Channel Attack*, a volume of the series on *United States Army in World War II, The European Theater of Operations* (Washington: 1951), pp. 6–8.

19. The evolution of strategy is presented in considerable detail in "Germany First: The Basic Concept of Allied Strategy in World War II," by Louis Morton, which is Chapter I of *Command Decisions* (Washington: 1959). All direct quotes are from it.

20. Dwight D. Eisenhower, *Crusade in Europe* (New York: 1948), p. 18.

21. Quoted by Robert E. Sherwood, *Roosevelt and Hopkins* (New York: 1948, 1950), p. 459.

22. Quoted in ibid., p. 455–56.

23. Churchill, op. cit., quotes from report of meeting, p. 674. The author has changed past to present tense for scenic purposes.

24. Eisenhower, op. cit., p. 22.

25. Kenneth S. Davis, *Soldier of Democracy* (New York: 1945, 1952), p. 281. Derived from personal interviews with Milton S. Eisenhower.

26. Eisenhower, op. cit., p. 22.

27. Winston Churchill, *The Hinge of Fate* (Boston: 1951), p. 49.

28. Churchill, *The Grand Alliance*, p. 669–70. Sherwood, op. cit., p. 443.

29. Ibid., p. 683. On the same page, Churchill speaks of the evident "fear and trembling" with which Litvinov approached Stalin on the matter of "religious freedom" and of how Stalin accepted the phrase "as a matter of course."

30. Sherwood, op. cit., pp. 447–53.

31. Ibid., p. 469.

32. Churchill, *The Grand Alliance*, p. 686.

33. Sherwood, op. cit., pp. 469–70.

34. Scene imagined on basis of ibid., pp. 470–72.

35. Arthur Bryant, *The Turn of the Tide* (based on the Diaries of Field Marshal Lord Alanbrooke) (New York: 1957), p. 254.

36. Winston Churchill, *Closing the Ring* (Boston: 1952), pp. 123–24.

VI. *The Heroism and Economics of War*

1. Jonathan M. Wainwright, *General Wainwright's Story* (ed. by Robert Considine) (New York: 1945), p. 57.
2. Ibid., p. 57.
3. Ibid., pp. 93–94. John Toland, *But Not in Shame, The Six Months After Pearl Harbor* (New York: 1961), covers in detailed vivid narrative the whole action of Bataan and Corregidor, with a chapter on the Death March. This was used as reference by the present author.
4. Wainwright, op. cit., p. 54.
5. Quoted by Toland, op. cit., pp. 171 and 281.
6. Wainwright, op. cit., pp. 3–4.
7. Quoted by Toland, op. cit., p. 280.
8. Wainwright, op. cit., p. 79.
9. Ibid., pp. 82–83.
10. Ibid., p. 118.
11. Ibid., pp. 122–23. The Roosevelt message to Wainwright is quoted on p. 118.
12. Donald Nelson covers in detail his thoughts and movement, the weather, etc., on January 13, 1942, in his *Arsenal of Democracy* (New York: 1946), Chapter 1.
13. Ibid., pp. 58–59.
14. Ibid., p. 62.
15. Robert E. Sherwood, *Roosevelt and Hopkins* (New York: 1948, 1950), p. 474. Winston Churchill, *The Grand Alliance* (Boston: 1951), pp. 688–89; Nelson, op. cit., pp. 186–87.
16. Nelson, op. cit., pp. 191–92.
17. Jesse Jones, *Fifty Billion Dollars* (Houston: 1951), and Hanscom N. Timmons, *Jesse H. Jones* (New York: 1956) were used in the writing of the relations of Jones, Wallace, Nelson, et al. This specific scene (meeting) is covered by Nelson, op. cit., pp. 8–13.
18. Nelson, op. cit., pp. 22–23. Sherwood, op. cit., pp. 475–77. Jones, op. cit., pp. 272–73.
19. Nelson, op. cit., p. 208.
20. Ibid., pp. 114–15.
21. Ibid., pp. 111–12.
22. Ibid., pp. 177–78.
23. Ibid., pp. 226–27.
24. Ibid., pp. 232–33, quoting Henry J. Taylor, *The Saturday Evening Post*, November 22, 1942.

In writing of economic mobilization, the author also used and is indebted to Robert H. Conner, *The Navy and Industrial Mobilization in World War II* (Princeton: 1951); R. Elberton Smith, *The Army and Economic Mobilization*, a volume of *United States Army in World War II* (Washington: 1959); Erna Risch and Chester L. Kiefer, *The Quartermaster Corps: Organization, Supply, and Services*, Vols. I and II (part of same series as above) (Washington: 1962); Richard N. Currant, *Secretary Stimson, A Study in Statecraft*

(Rutgers: 1954); and Elting E. Morison, *Turmoil and Tradition, A Study of the Life and Times of Henry L. Stimson* (Boston: 1960), especially pp. 552–53.

25. Winston Churchill, *The Hinge of Fate* (Boston: 1951), pp. 108–11.

26. Quoted by Samuel Eliot Morison, *Coral Sea, Midway, and Submarine Action*, Vol. IV of *History of United States Naval Operations in World War II* (Boston: 1949), p. 3.

27. Churchill, op. cit., p. 181.

28. Ibid., pp. 183–85.

29. Ibid., pp. 187–88.

30. Maurice Matloff and Edwin M. Snell, *Strategic Planning for Coalition Warfare, 1941–42*, a volume of *United States Army in World War II* (Washington: 1953), p. 155.

31. Ibid., p. 154.

32. Ibid., p. 156.

33. Ibid., pp. 157–59.

VII. *Crisis and Turning Point in the Pacific*

1. Samuel Eliot Morison, *Coral Sea, Midway, and Submarine Action*, Vol. IV of *History of United States Naval Operations in World War II* (Boston: 1949); *The Great Sea War*, edited by E. B. Potter and Chester W. Nimitz (New York: 1960); Walter Karig and Eric Purdon, *Battle Report: Pacific War, Middle Phase* (New York: 1947); Edward P. Stafford, *The Big E, The Story of U.S.S.* Enterprise (New York: 1962); Thaddeus V. Tuleja, *Climax at Midway* (New York: 1960); and Mitsuo Fuchida and Masatake Okumiya, *Midway, The Battle that Doomed Japan* (U. S. Naval Institute: 1955), were the books chiefly used in writing this story of the Coral Sea and Midway battles. There are several discrepancies, minor in nature, between Morison and the Potter-Nimitz-edited book, and the author has preferred the latter (as being more recently published, for one thing) in such cases.

2. Morison, op. cit., p. 98, quotes Spruance's signal.

3. Potter and Nimitz, eds., op. cit., p. 300.

4. Fuchida and Okumiya, op. cit., quoted by Desmond Flower and James Reeves, ed., *The Taste of Courage, The War, 1939–45* (New York: 1960), pp. 503–4.

5. Ibid., p. 504.

VIII. *A Dangerous Quarrel among Friends*

1. Winston Churchill, *The Hinge of Fate* (Boston: 1950), p. 379.

2. Robert Sherwood, *Roosevelt and Hopkins* (New York: 1941, 1950), pp. 580–81.

3. Henry L. Stimson and McGeorge Bundy, *On Active Service* (New York: 1948), p. 423; Gordon A. Harrison, *Cross-Channel Attack* (Washington: 1951), p. 25; Ernest J. King and Walter Muir Whitehill, *Fleet Admiral King* (New York: 1952), p. 394.

4. Arthur Bryant, *The Turn of the Tide*, based on diary of Field Marshal Lord Alanbrooke (New York: 1957), p. 290.

5. Ibid., pp. 289–90, as are quotes that follow.

6. Harrison, op. cit., p. 24.

7. Churchill, op. cit., p. 381. His note is printed in full, pp. 381–82.

8. Sherwood, op. cit., p. 591.

9. Message from MacArthur to Marshall, quoted on p. 215 of Maurice Matloff and Edwin M. Snell, *Strategic Planning for Coalition Warfare* (Washington: 1953).

10. Churchill, op. cit., pp. 378–79.

11. Ibid., pp. 380–81.

12. Churchill tells the story of how he received the news of Tobruk's fall in op. cit., pp. 382–83. Brooke tells it in p. 329 of Bryant, op. cit., and Sherwood in op. cit., p. 591. Brooke's diary seems to indicate the telegram was given Churchill in the afternoon, but this doesn't jibe with timing of the event in Africa, with Churchill's account both on pages cited and in his address to the Commons on July 2, 1942, with Sherwood's reference, nor with the account in *The Memoirs of General Lord Ismay* (New York: 1960), pp. 954–55.

13. Bryant, op. cit., p. 329.

14. Stimson and Bundy, op. cit., pp. 420–23, presents letter in full, saying it was presented with unanimous endorsement of Marshall and Marshall's staff. Elting E. Morison, *Turmoil and Tradition, A Study of the Life and Times of Henry L. Stimson* (Boston: 1960), pp. 484–85, tells of letter.

15. Stimson and Bundy, op. cit., p. 423.

16. Ibid., p. 424.

17. Churchill, op. cit., pp. 383–84. Churchill says that General Ismay "has preserved" the note quoted, but the language of it seems clearly to indicate Churchill's authorship.

18. Cf. Morison, op. cit., pp. 385–86, where he quotes Stimson as saying Roosevelt and Churchill were "too much alike. Both are brilliant. They are both penetrating in their thoughts but they lack the steadiness and balance that has got to go along with warfare." It is interesting to note how much steadier in actual fact Roosevelt was than Stimson (and even Marshall) in the crisis on strategy then developing.

19. Churchill, op. cit., pp. 384–85, tells of meeting with Eisenhower and Clark. The June 15, 1942 paper is presented in full in his op. cit., pp. 353–55. Churchill's memory of the nature of the meeting differs from Eisenhower's. The latter, on p. 51 of his *Crusade in Europe* (New York: 1948), says his call upon Roosevelt and Churchill (as if the two were together at the time) "was no more than an informal chat" and "had no military significance." He adds, however, that it was "gratifying to note" that Churchill like Roosevelt was "thinking of attack and victory, not of defense and defeat," thus indicating that the quality of the visit was probably as Churchill indicates.

20. Churchill, op. cit., pp. 386–87. Ismay, op. cit., pp. 256–57.

21. Matloff and Snell, op. cit., p. 263. The story of the decision is told in detail in ibid., pp. 258–65. See also King and Whitehill, op. cit., pp. 386–89.

22. Sherwood, op. cit., p. 598.

23. Ismay, op. cit., p. 299, characterizes Stilwell, stressing his "individualism" which made it impossible (so says Ismay) for "Vinegar Joe" to cooperate "with anybody." Stimson, who chose Stilwell for the CBI command, characterizes the general in admiring terms on pp. 528–41 of Stimson and Bundy, op. cit., while telling of the difficulties of the China assignment.

24. For assessments of Marshall's character, see Ismay, op. cit., pp. 251–52; Stimson and Bundy, op. cit., pp. 437–38; Elting Morison, op. cit., pp. 497–

99; Robert Payne, *The Marshall Story* (New York: 1951); Forrest C. Pogue, *George C. Marshall, Education of a General* (New York: 1963).

25. Matloff and Snell, op. cit., p. 256, quotes Marshall.

26. Harrison, op. cit., p. 27.

27. Matloff and Snell, op. cit., p. 260. King and Whitehill cover the story of this whole controversy in op. cit., pp. 390–408.

28. Stimson and Bundy, op. cit., p. 424.

29. Harrison, op. cit., pp. 27–28; Matloff and Snell, op. cit., p. 272; King and Whitehill, op. cit., p. 399.

30. Stimson and Bundy, op. cit., p. 425; Sherwood, op. cit., p. 595 and pp. 600–1.

31. From the memorandum of instructions for Hopkins, Marshall, and King, July 16, 1942, reprinted in Sherwood, op. cit., pp. 603–5. The later quote of the memorandum derives from the same source. See also King and Whitehill, op. cit., p. 400.

32. Sherwood, op. cit., pp. 602–3, being quote of Hopkins' notes on the after-dinner conversation with Roosevelt.

33. Memo is summarized along with discussion of it in CCS meeting on pp. 280–81 of Matloff and Snell, op. cit.

34. Bryant, op. cit., p. 347.

35. Sherwood, op. cit., p. 611. Matloff and Snell, op. cit., p. 282.

36. Matloff and Snell, op. cit., pp. 283–84, quotes Smith memorandum.

37. Sherwood, op. cit., p. 594. Stimson and Bundy, op. cit., p. 425. Sherwood also says: "One may indulge in some pretty wild speculation as to the consequences had the plan been followed through–including the thought that the first atomic bomb might have fallen on Berlin instead of Hiroshima."

IX. *The Emergence of Eisenhower*

1. The full letter is quoted by Kenneth S. Davis, *Soldier of Democracy* (New York: 1945, 1952), pp. 220–21.

2. Dwight D. Eisenhower, *Crusade in Europe* (New York: 1948), p. 74. The quotes which follow in this paragraph are from ibid., p. 75.

3. Davis, op. cit., p. 300. Eisenhower, op. cit., p. 50.

4. Harry C. Butcher, *My Three Years with Eisenhower* (New York: 1946), says, p. 92: "The importance of the ability to express oneself lucidly and succinctly . . . was cited as the reason for the failure of some high officers to make good with him [Marshall]. Those who speak slowly and haltingly . . . are soon passed by in the rush to get things done."

5. Maurice Matloff and Edwin M. Snell, *Strategic Planning for Coalition Warfare* (Washington: 1953), pp. 267–68.

6. Eisenhower, op. cit., p. 51. The quote from Admiral Stark which follows is from ibid., p. 54.

7. General Lord Ismay, *Memoirs of General Lord Ismay* (New York: 1960), p. 258.

8. Ibid., p. 259.

9. Butcher, op. cit., p. 65. In the following paragraph, the Eisenhower reference to Napoleon and "inconsequential side shows" is from ibid., p. 30.

10. Eisenhower, op. cit., p. 70. King and Whitehill, *Fleet Admiral King* (New York: 1952), p. 401, say that Eisenhower and the other U.S. officers "were convinced that SLEDGEHAMMER should be undertaken as soon as

possible" but were "equally convinced that the British, from the Prime Minister on down, were unalterably opposed. . . ."

11. Ibid., p. 71. Matloff and Snell, op. cit., p. 286.

12. Matloff and Snell, op. cit., p. 287.

13. Arthur Bryant, *The Turn of the Tide* (based on diaries of Field Marshal Lord Alanbrooke) (New York: 1957), stresses the cardinal importance of Malta in British thinking about TORCH.

14. Eisenhower, op. cit., pp. 72–73.

15. Butcher, op. cit., p. 85.

16. Eisenhower, op. cit., 79. Matloff and Snell, op. cit., pp. 284–93, give a detailed review of the controversy, quoting the original documents extensively. The same ground is covered by Ismay, op. cit., and Bryant, op. cit., from different directions, of course.

17. Ismay, op. cit., pp. 263–64.

18. Bryant, op. cit., pp. 373–74. Winston Churchill, *The Hinge of Fate* (Boston: 1950), tells of this meeting on pp. 486–87.

19. Churchill, op. cit., p. 529.

20. Eisenhower, op. cit., p. 80.

21. Ismay, op. cit., p. 263.

22. H. A. DeWeerd, *Great Soldiers of World War II* (New York: 1944), p. 270.

23. Ismay, op. cit., p. 262.

24. Davis, op. cit., p. 336. The descriptions, not only of Smith but also of Clark and Patton, derive from notes taken by the author in 1944 (Smith and Patton were personally interviewed then) as well as from *Soldier of Democracy*.

25. Mark W. Clark, *Calculated Risk* (New York: 1950), p. 58 and following tells of his impatience and Eisenhower's soothing him. On p. 41 he gives his opinion of Anderson. Eisenhower, op. cit., p. 83, describes Anderson as "honest and straightforward" but "blunt at times to the point of rudeness, and this trait, curiously enough, seemed to bring him into conflict with the British confreres more than it did the Americans." Eisenhower expresses "real respect for his fighting heart."

26. Butcher, op. cit., p. 76. Davis, op. cit., p. 315. The author spent a night or so at Telegraph Cottage in the summer of 1944.

27. Churchill, op. cit., p. 527.

28. Butcher, op. cit., p. 134. The remark was originally made at a dinner on Smith's birthday, October 5. The material about the night of September 7 is also from Butcher's op. cit., pp. 92–93.

29. Ismay, op. cit., pp. 265–66, tells the story of these three security-threatening episodes, which are also recounted in several other books. Ismay's versions are certainly authentic; some of the others are not.

30. Churchill, op. cit., p. 604.

31. Robert E. Sherwood, *Roosevelt and Hopkins* (New York: 1943, 1950), p. 629.

32. Clark, op. cit., p. 54, writes that Churchill, reading aloud a Former Naval Person message he was about to send, chuckled "heartily" as he came to the phrase: "The Free French . . . are leaky. . . ."

33. Butcher, op. cit., pp. 105–11, tells of "Colonel McGowan's" visit to London in detail.

34. In the review of French politics as they affected TORCH the author has leaned heavily upon the cited works of Churchill, Butcher, Eisenhower, Davis (who obtained some of the material from personal interviews on this matter with Eisenhower and his staff), Clark, and Sherwood; Robert Murphy, *Diplomat Among Warriors* (his memoirs) (New York: 1964); William L. Langer, *Our Vichy Gamble* (New York: 1947); Waverly Root, *The Secret History of the War* (New York: 1945, 2 volumes); John MacVane, *Journey into War* (New York: 1944); G. Ward Price, *Giraud and the African Scene* (New York: 1944); and the voluminous contemporary accounts in the New York *Times* after the "Darlan Deal" was made.

35. Robert Murphy, op. cit., says, pp. 116–17, that when he first met Lemaigre-Dubreuil in Algiers in 1940 he found the latter's "melodramatic tale . . . pretty hard to believe" but "passed it on to Washington, sprinkling my report liberally with salt." As time passed, however, and ". . . we tested him out in various ways" (what ways? one wonders), Murphy became thoroughly convinced of the Frenchman's "trustworthiness." In general, Murphy's own account in the cited book supports the view that he was almost incredibly naïve, not only about French politics but also (as he frankly admits) about military matters.

36. Clark, op. cit., p. 71.

37. Butcher, op. cit., p. 146.

38. The best source of information on Clark's mission is of course his own op. cit.

X. *The End of the Beginning*

1. It often happens, when one is writing such a book as this, that one *anticipates* his sources—sometimes in quite startling ways. Having decided to exploit the "Let George do it" phrase, the author read Herbert L. Merrillat's *The Island, A History of the First Marine Division on Guadalcanal* (Boston: 1944) and found that he told part of his story through a hypothetical "George." Merrillat was a captain in the Marine Corps on Guadalcanal, and his is in large part an eyewitness account. Of course the background given "George" is, though "representative," entirely fictional.

2. At the time this section was being written, Los Angeles papers (the author was then in the Los Angeles area) were carrying lengthy accounts of the court-martial of a D.I. on charges of "brutality," revealing that the kind of thing here described, if somewhat extreme, is by no means so much so as to be beyond the bounds of the "representative." Adlai E. Stevenson III, who served a hitch in the Marines, told the author in conversation of seeing men on forced march being made to lick their own vomit. He, however, and typically, felt that the Marine training was highly affective, producing much-needed toughness and a high *esprit de corps.* He was very proud to be a Marine.

3. In describing the Guadalcanal action, reference was made to Merrillat's op. cit.; Samuel Eliot Morison, *The Struggle for Guadalcanal* (Vol. V of his *History of United States Naval Operations in World War II*) (Boston: 1951); Walter Karig and Eric Purdon, *Battle Report: Pacific War, Middle Phase* (New York: 1947); Frank O. Hough, Verle E. Ludwig, Henry L. Shaw, Jr., *Pearl Harbor to Guadalcanal*, Vol. I of *History of U. S. Marine Corps in World War II*); Richard Tregaskis, *Guadalcanal Diary* (New York:

1943); Ira Wolfert, *The Battle of Two Solomons* (New York: 1943); and John Hersey, *Into the Valley* (New York: 1943).

4. Merrillat, op. cit., p. 33.
5. Ibid., p. 37.
6. Morison, op. cit., footnote on page 66.
7. Hersey, op. cit., p. 49.
8. Merrillat, op. cit., pp. 116–18, gives an account of the heroic exploit of Private Harry Dunn, Jr., of the light machine gun section of Company B of the First Marines, September 17–19, 1942. The author used this in part as a pattern for George's experience here. Dunn rescued wounded Private Jack Morrison of his outfit, both of them surviving the battle.
9. Hersey, op. cit., pp. 73–75.
10. Joseph Barnes, *Willkie* (New York: 1952), pp. 289 and 293.
11. Ibid., p. 294.
12. Wendell L. Willkie, *One World* (New York: 1943), softbound edition, pp. 68–74. On p. 78 he writes: "Even Hitler's high racial wall has been breached by the recognition of a common purpose with those 'honorary aryans,' the Japanese."
13. Ibid., p. 8.
14. Barnes, op. cit., p. 298.
15. Willkie, op. cit., pp. 9, 21.
16. Ibid., p. 29.
17. Ibid., p. 23.
18. Ibid., p. 42.
19. Barnes, op. cit., p. 319. Robert E. Sherwood, *Roosevelt and Hopkins* (New York: 1948, 1950), p. 635.
20. Willkie prints verbatim most of his press conference statement in op. cit., pp. 75–76.
21. Quoted by Barnes, op. cit., p. 308.
22. Willkie, op. cit., pp. 78, 84–85.
23. Ibid., p. 65.
24. Ibid., p. 35.
25. Sherwood, op. cit., p. 635.
26. Frances Perkins, *The Roosevelt I Knew* (New York: 1946), as quoted by Barnes in op. cit., p. 353.
27. Harry C. Butcher, *My Three Years with Eisenhower* (New York: 1946), p. 190, says the Fortress "landed at 7 and we had air and other officers nuts because visibility practically nil for landing. Rain, low-hanging mist. Didn't get scared, Ike said, until about 10 that night, so we took a toast to our safe landing." Dwight D. Eisenhower, *Crusade in Europe* (New York: 1948), p. 109, says of landing, "We flew around the Rock in complete blackness, making futile passes at the field. I saw no way out of a bad predicament and still think the young lieutenant pilot must have depended more upon a rabbit's foot than upon his controls to accomplish the skillful landing that finally brought us down."
28. Butcher, op. cit., p. 262. Eisenhower, op. cit., p. 97.
29. Butcher, op. cit., p. 167.
30. Kenneth S. Davis, *Soldier of Democracy* (New York: 1945, 1952), p. 848. Information from personal interview with Harry C. Butcher.

31. Eisenhower, op. cit., p. 100.
32. Davis, op. cit., pp. 357–58.
33. Eisenhower, op. cit., pp. 99–100.
34. Mark W. Clark, *Calculated Risk* (New York: 1950), says, p. 98, that he told Holmes to tell Giraud, ". . . if you don't go along, general, you're going to be out in the snow on the seat of your pants." Butcher, op. cit., p. 171, has a virtually direct quote from Clark on this, and it is, "Old gentleman, I hope you know that from now on your ass is out in the snow."
35. Eisenhower, op. cit., pp. 100–1.
36. Ibid., p. 101.
37. George F. Howe, *Northwest Africa: Seizing the Initiative in the West*, a volume of the series on the *United States Army in World War II* (Washington: 1957), has been deemed authoritative as regards the details of this operation. The messages from Eisenhower to Fredendall and Patton, for example, are given in this volume. Use was also made of Samuel Eliot Morison, *Operations in North American Waters*, Vol. II of his *History of United States Naval Operations in World War II* (Boston: 1947).
38. Clark, op. cit., pp. 103–4.
39. Ibid., pp. 106–12. The quote on Darlan's "cowering" is from p. 115.
40. Clark, op. cit., p. 111. The terms are quoted by Waverly Root, *The Secret History of the War*, Vol. II (New York: 1945), p. 474, and summarized in numerous books, including Davis, op. cit., pp. 371–72.
41. Judgment based on careful reading of Clark's *Calculated Risk*. See, for example, p. 125.
42. Clark, op. cit., p. 113.
43. Ibid., p. 113.
44. Ibid., pp. 117–18.
45. Eisenhower, op. cit., p. 106. It's interesting to note that Eisenhower gives a *source* for this statement (!), as if it came not from his own remembrance, or as if his book were written by someone else who had to look up the details of his life. The source here is William L. Langer's *Our Vichy Gamble* (New York: 1947), which is an apology for the State Department's policy toward Vichy France written at Secretary Hull's request and with the State Department's full cooperation. Moreover, the "order" Eisenhower refers to came not to him but to Robert D. Murphy, as a directive for his activities in preparation for the landings, and it did *not* specifically say that the Allied military must "cooperate with any French government" existing at the time of landing but only that ". . . no change in the existing French Civil Administration is contemplated by the United States" and that salaries, death allowances, and pensions would be guaranteed those French officials "who join with the American expeditionary forces."
46. Clark, op. cit., pp. 119–20.
47. Eisenhower, op. cit., pp. 107–9; Clark, op. cit., pp. 121–22; Butcher, op. cit., pp. 190–93; Howe, op. cit., pp. 256–66. The latter has photographs of Eisenhower and the other principals in Algiers on November 13, 1942.
48. Eisenhower, op. cit., p. 95, describes the Gibraltar cave-office as the "most dismal setting" his headquarters had during the war. He stresses the steady drip "of surface water that faithfully but drearily ticked off the seconds."

49. Sherwood, op. cit., pp. 651–52; Eisenhower, op. cit., pp. 109–10; Langer, op. cit., pp. 357–60.

50. Story in Chicago *Daily News,* February 9, 1943, quoted by Root in op. cit., pp. 464–65.

51. Howe, op. cit., pp. 259–60; Root, op. cit., p. 503. Eisenhower, op. cit., p. 111, obviously concerned to strengthen his case as regards dealing with Darlan, gives Esteva the benefit of every doubt. He indicates that Esteva *would* have obeyed Darlan if the tentative agreement with the admiral in Algiers had been reached hours earlier, but makes no mention of the fact that Esteva did nothing to resist Axis occupation of Tunisia at a time when the Vichy French were fighting the Western Allies.

52. Clark, op. cit., p. 123.

53. General de Gaulle, *War Memoirs: Unity, 1942–44* (London: 1956), p. 54.

54. John MacVane, *Journey into War* (New York: 1943), p. 78. The tense has been changed from past to present, in this quote, for purposes of narrative.

55. Eisenhower, op. cit., p. 131.

56. Refrain used by Thomas Wolfe in *Look Homeward, Angel* (New York: 1930), a novel at the high tide of its reputation in the 1940s.

57. De Gaulle, op. cit., p. 51. What he actually said, in the English translation, was, "We are the core of our unity." I've replaced "our" with "national."

58. De Gaulle, op. cit., p. 21.

59. Ibid., pp. 56–57.

60. Henry L. Stimson and McGeorge Bundy, *On Active Service* (New York: 1948), p. 543.

61. Barnes, op. cit., p. 312.

62. Winston Churchill, *The Hinge of Fate* (Boston: 1950), presents message to Roosevelt of November 17, 1942, wherein he says, "The more I reflect upon it the more convinced I become that it [the arrangement with Darlan] can only be a temporary expedient, justified solely by the stress of battle."

63. The whole of the letter from which this quote is taken is printed in Clark, op. cit., pp. 126–27; also by Butcher, op. cit., pp. 206–7, and Langer, op. cit., pp. 373–74.

64. Langer, op. cit., p. 372.

65. Quoted by Churchill, op. cit., p. 636.

66. The Roosevelt quotation of the Balkan proverb is from Churchill, op. cit., p. 635. The quotation from Churchill's speech to the Commons is from ibid., p. 641.

67. Barnes, op. cit., p. 306.

68. Quoted by Langer, op. cit., p. 372.

69. Churchill, op. cit., p. 638.

70. Clark, op. cit., p. 130.

71. De Gaulle, op. cit., pp. 71–72. Clark says in op. cit., p. 130, that Darlan "had served his purpose, and his death solved the very difficult problem of what to do with him in the future."

72. Butcher, op. cit., p. 229. The circumstantial account of the farmhouse headquarters and of Eisenhower's Christmas Eve is based on Butcher, op. cit., pp. 227–29 and Eisenhower, op. cit., pp. 123–24.

XI. *Atomistic, Organismic*

1. Arthur Compton, *Atomic Quest* (New York: 1956), pp. 139–40.
2. Leslie R. Groves, *Now It Can Be Told, The Story of the Manhattan Project* (New York: 1962), p. 20. Both quotes are from a letter from Bush to Harvey Bundy, a principal assistant of Stimson's.
3. Groves, op. cit., pp. ix and 45.
4. Compton, op. cit., pp. 113–14.
5. Groves, op. cit., pp. 36–37.
6. Ibid., pp. 22–23.
7. Compton, op. cit., p. 113.
8. Groves says in op. cit., p. 45, ". . . there was a small group of scientists, mostly, though not entirely, European born, who felt that they should be given control of the entire project." Compton says, op. cit., p. 160: "[Eugene] Wigner had seen firsthand the action of the Nazis. . . . His concern for the safety of the free world was real indeed. It was very difficult at first, however, for Wigner to believe that anything good could come from cooperation with a giant industrial organization such as Du Pont. Such companies, he had been taught in Europe, were the tyrants of the American democracy."
9. Both Compton and Groves present accounts of this meeting, the former in his op. cit., pp. 133–34, the latter in his op. cit., pp. 52–53. The latter says "Conant" was present, but this is evidently a misprint for "Compton." Groves does not recall the "sharp exchange" between Stine and Compton, and does not believe Du Pont was as "pessimistic" as Compton assumed.
10. Compton, op. cit., p. 166.
11. Groves, op. cit., pp. 66–67. Compton, op. cit., pp. 129–31.
12. Compton, op. cit., p. 140.
13. Ibid., p. 136.
14. Ibid., p. 137. Henry DeWolf Smyth, *Atomic Energy for Military Purposes* (the official report) (Princeton: 1945), pp. 97–98, summarizes the "delayed neutron" experiment, of which the original report, or a substantial portion of it, is printed on pp. 236–38 as Appendix 3 of the book.
15. Ralph Lapp, *Atoms and People* (New York: 1956), p. 36, reports that he was doing his research in the old press box.
16. Smyth, op. cit., p. 98.
17. Compton, op. cit., pp. 141–44, gives a circumstantial account of the first chain-reaction experiment, and there have, of course, been dozens of newspaper and magazine features on this. One of the best, used here, is an Associated Press feature by Sid Moody, printed in numerous papers on the twentieth anniversary of the critical experiment, December 2, 1962. Moody interviewed several of those who had been present as he gathered the material for his story.
18. Compton, op. cit., p. 144.
19. Herbert Feis, *Churchill, Roosevelt, Stalin* (Princeton: 1957), p. 100.
20. Winston Churchill, *The Hinge of Fate* (Boston: 1950), p. 663.
21. Feis, op. cit., p. 100.
22. Churchill, op. cit., p. 665.
23. Feis, op. cit., p. 100. Churchill, op. cit., p. 666.
24. Churchill, op. cit., p. 667.
25. Ibid., pp. 667–68.

26. Feis, op. cit., pp. 101–2.

27. Churchill, op. cit., p. 669.

28. Sir Ian Jacob's *Ms. Diary*, December 28, 1942, quoted in footnote by Arthur Bryant, *The Turn of the Tide* (New York: 1957), p. 444.

29. Bryant, op. cit., based upon and largely consisting of entries in diary of Brooke, presents a résumé of the British position on pp. 439–41.

30. Quoted in Bryant, op. cit., p. 442.

31. Ibid., p. 443.

32. Ibid., footnote, p. 443.

33. Ibid., pp. 446–47. Major General Sir John Kennedy, *The Business of War* (New York: 1948), p. 281, tells of the bird walks. Writes Kennedy: "Harold Macmillan, who was attending the conference as Minister Resident of North Africa, chaffed us one day as we came back with our glasses around our necks: '*Now* I understand why we are taking so long to get any plans made; the birds leave no time for them.'"

34. Bryant, op. cit., p. 445.

35. Ibid., p. 445.

36. Ibid., pp. 449–50.

37. Feis, op. cit., p. 106.

38. Churchill, op. cit., p. 692.

39. Robert E. Sherwood, *Roosevelt and Hopkins* (New York: 1948, 1950), pp. 668 and 691.

40. Dwight D. Eisenhower, *Crusade in Europe* (New York: 1948), p. 131.

41. General de Gaulle, *Unity, 1942–1944*, a volume of his *War Memoirs* (London: 1956), pp. 75–80, tells of De Gaulle's efforts to arrange a meeting with Giraud.

42. Ibid., p. 81. De Gaulle tells of the session with Churchill on p. 82. Churchill tells of it, from his point of view, on pp. 681–82 of op. cit.

43. De Gaulle, op. cit., p. 83. Sherwood, op. cit., p. 685.

44. De Gaulle, op. cit., p. 89. Actually the English sentence was in answer to Roosevelt's request that De Gaulle agree to shake hands with Giraud before the cameras. De Gaulle said: "I shall do that for you." Sherwood tells of the meeting in detail, quoting a long memorandum by Hopkins, in op. cit., pp. 691–93.

45. Samuel I. Rosenman, ed., *The Public Papers and Addresses of Franklin D. Roosevelt*, Volume for 1943. Also quoted by Rosenman, *Working with Roosevelt* (New York: 1952), p. 370.

46. The quote is from a letter by Churchill to Robert Sherwood, printed by the latter in his op. cit., p. 696.

47. Sherwood, op. cit., p. 696.

48. Ibid., p. 697. The parenthetical quote in the following paragraph is also from ibid., p. 697. Feis, op. cit., and Rosenman's *Working with Roosevelt*, stress that "unconditional surrender" phrase was by no means the frivolous remark which Roosevelt later indicated it was, but had instead been carefully considered.

49. George C. Kenney, *General Kenney Reports* (New York: 1949), pp. 199–200, tells of his meeting with Whitehead on February 26, 1943.

50. Ibid., pp. vii–xiii, gives biographical data. Quoted on pp. ix–x is a "cover" story on Kenney in *Time* magazine for January 18, 1943.

51. Ibid., pp. 27–30, tells of meeting with Sutherland and MacArthur.

52. John Miller, Jr., *Cartwheel: The Reduction of Rabaul*, a volume in the official series, *United States Army in World War II* (Washington: 1954), p. 25, quotes Admiral Halsey's impression of MacArthur wherein is mentioned the general's "large bare desk," the "portrait of George Washington that faced it," and the corncob pipe he carried in his hand but "rarely smoked."

53. Kenney, op. cit., pp. 52–53.

54. Ibid., pp. 34–39, tells of Kenney's first impressions of New Guinea and of the Japanese air raid he experienced that first morning.

55. Samuel Eliot Morison, *Breaking the Bismarck Barrier*, Vol. VI of *History of United States Naval Operations in World War II* (Boston: 1950), p. 38.

56. Kenney, op. cit., pp. 76–77 and 155. Morison, op. cit., pp. 57–58.

57. Description of battle based on Kenney, op. cit., pp. 197–206; Morison, op. cit., pp. 54–65; and Miller, op. cit., pp. 39–41.

58. Morison, op. cit., p. 62.

59. Quoted by Kenney, op. cit., p. 206.

60. Churchill, op. cit., p. 802.

61. Ibid., p. 790.

62. Ibid., p. 791.

63. Ibid., p. 786.

64. Louis L. Snyder, *The War, A Concise History 1939–45* (New York: 1960), p. 335.

65. For story of Chennault-Stilwell feud, see Claire Chennault, *Way of a Fighter* (New York: 1949); Joseph Stilwell, *The Stilwell Papers* (New York: 1948); Charles F. Romanus and Riley Sunderland, *Stilwell's Mission to China*, a volume in the official series, *United States Army in World War II* (Washington: 1963), especially pp. 189–90; 251–52; 253–61; Henry L. Stimson and McGeorge Bundy, *On Active Service* (New York: 1948), pp. 528–41; Sherwood, op. cit., pp. 730–31 and 732.

66. Bryant, op. cit., p. 508.

67. Quoted by Churchill, op. cit., p. 810.

68. All direct quotes from Churchill and summary of his presentation to the luncheon are from op. cit., pp. 802–7. The tense is changed from past to present.

69. Sumner Welles, *The Time for Decision* (Cleveland and New York: 1944), p. 352.

70. Ibid., p. 378.

71. Cordell Hull, *The Memoirs of Cordell Hull* (New York: 1948), Vol. II, pp. 642–43.

72. Ibid., p. 1638.

73. Sumner Welles, op. cit., p. 377.

74. Hull, op. cit., p. 1640.

75. Arthur M. Schlesinger, Jr., *The Coming of the New Deal*, Vol. II of *The Age of Roosevelt* (Boston: 1959), pp. 190–91, presents a succinct portrait of Hull's personality and character. Sherwood, op. cit., repeatedly refers to one or another of Hull's character traits, summarizing the quarrel with Sumner Welles on pp. 756–57 and saying that Hopkins "would rather deal with Welles than anyone else in the State Department." Hull tells of his quarrel with Welles in op. cit., pp. 1227–31.

76. Hull, op. cit., p. 1646. Amry Vandenborsch and Willard N. Hagan, *The United Nations* (New York: 1953), p. 78.

77. Russell Lord, *The Wallaces of Iowa* (Boston: 1947), pp. 167, 589. Dwight MacDonald, *Henry Wallace: The Man and the Myth* (New York: 1948), Chapter VII. Arthur Schlesinger, Jr., op. cit., pp. 29–35.

78. Churchill, op. cit., p. 809.

79. Ibid., p. 807.

XII. *Preludes to the Final Assaults*

1. Omar Bradley, *A Soldier's Story* (New York: 1951), p. 165.

2. Ibid., p. 122.

3. Harry C. Butcher, *My Three Years with Eisenhower* (New York: 1946), pp. 311, 319–30; Dwight D. Eisenhower, *Crusade in Europe* (New York: 1948), p. 165; Kenneth S. Davis, *Soldier of Democracy* (New York: 1945), pp. 425–26—the latter based on personal interviews with British Major General Kenneth Strong, Harry Butcher, and General Eisenhower.

4. According to Samuel Eliot Morison, *Sicily-Salerno-Anzio*, which is Vol. IX of his *History of United States Naval Operations in World War II* (Boston: 1954), pp. 66–67.

5. Bradley, op. cit., p. 126. Morison, op. cit., p. 67. Ernie Pyle, *Brave Men* (New York: 1944), p. 14.

6. Bradley, op. cit., pp. 129–31.

7. Ibid., pp. 133–34.

8. Eisenhower, op. cit., p. 176.

9. George S. Patton, Jr., *War as I Knew It* (Boston: 1947), pp. 57–58.

10. Bradley, op. cit., pp. 159–60.

11. Ibid., p. 160.

12. Butcher, op. cit., p. 393. The correspondent was Quentin Reynolds.

13. Davis, op. cit., p. 438. Based on 1944 interviews with Patton, Butcher, and Merrill Mueller of NBC.

14. Bradley, op. cit., pp. 154–57.

15. Winston Churchill, *Closing the Ring* (Boston: 1951), p. 93.

16. Eisenhower, op. cit., p. 179.

17. Bradley, op. cit., p. 166.

18. Though no formal minutes were kept of the Fascist Grand Council meeting described in the following pages, several accounts of what was said, in fairly close agreement with one another, have been published, along with detailed descriptions of the event and its setting. The author has used Christopher Hibbert, *Il Duce, The Life of Benito Mussolini* (Boston: 1962), pp. 173–91; F. M. Deakin, *The Brutal Friendship, Mussolini, Hitler, and the Fall of Italian Fascism* (New York: 1962), pp. 439–56; Laura Fermi, *Mussolini* (Chicago: 1961), pp. 422–27; Benito Mussolini, *The Fall of Mussolini* (New York: 1948), being the American translation of a work called by Mussolini *History of a Year*, edited with an introduction by Max Ascoli, pp. 55–64.

19. George Seldes, *Sawdust Caesar* (New York: 1941).

20. Guiseppe Rottai, as recorded in his *Vent'enni e un giorno* (1949), quoted by Hibbert, op. cit., p. 183.

21. Butcher, op. cit., p. 372. The later quote in the paragraph, referring to the "Darlan affair," is from ibid., p. 406.

22. Ibid., p. 386.

23. Ibid., pp. 372–73. Eisenhower, op. cit., p. 184.

24. Churchill, op. cit., p. 103, gives the direct quote from Castellano in his August 16, 1943 message to Roosevelt. The armistice terms as quoted are from op. cit., pp. 105–6, where the Roosevelt-Churchill message to Eisenhower is printed. The quotations giving Eisenhower's opinion is from Butcher, op. cit., p. 405.

25. Mark W. Clark, *Calculated Risk* (New York: 1950), p. 181.

26. The story of the Taylor-Gardiner mission is told in detail by Franco Maugeri, *From the Ashes of Disgrace* (New York: 1948), pp. 170–81, Admiral Maugeri being the man who brought the two to Italy in a corvette. See also Pietro Badoglio, *Italy in the Second World War* (London: 1948), pp. 71–72.

27. Bradley, op. cit., pp. 166–68; Eisenhower, op. cit., p. 186; Davis, op. cit., pp. 446–47 (based on personal interview with Eisenhower). The quote of Churchill is from his op. cit., pp. 116–17.

28. Robert E. Sherwood, *Roosevelt and Hopkins* (New York: 1948, 1950), p. 744.

29. Morison, op. cit., p. 241.

30. Maugeri, op. cit., pp. 182–92, sharply criticizes Allied strategy in Italy, placing the blame for it, however, on London and Washington rather than on Eisenhower in Algiers. Morison, op. cit., pp. 241–42, critical of the cancellation of the air drop on Rome, does *not* criticize Eisenhower for it but blames Taylor, who "had neither the wit nor the information to call Carboni's bluff."

31. Clark, op. cit., p. 188; Morison, op. cit., pp. 249–50, 259–60, and 265.

32. Martin Caiden's *The Night Hamburg Died* (New York: 1960), gives a vivid, detailed description of the incendiary attacks on Hamburg.

33. Churchill, op. cit., pp. 226–40.

34. Clark, op. cit., p. 318.

35. Clark, op. cit., p. 312.

36. Sherwood, op. cit., p. 759.

37. Ibid., pp. 759–65, tells the story of the controversy over Marshall's reassignment in detail. The quotation from Pershing and Roosevelt's reply are on p. 760. See also Forrest C. Pogue, *The Supreme Command*, a volume in the series *United States Army in World War II* (Washington: 1954), p. 25.

38. Churchill, op. cit., pp. 302–4, gives in full the interchange of messages between Prime Minister and President from which direct quotes are made.

39. Sherwood, op. cit., p. 762.

40. Ibid., p. 764.

41. The Churchill quote is from Churchill, op. cit., p. 305. The quotes from U. S. Joint Chiefs are from Sherwood, op. cit., p. 767.

42. Sherwood, op. cit., p. 770. Eisenhower, op. cit., p. 197.

43. For descriptions of Makin and Tarawa operations, Samuel Eliot Morison, *Aleutians, Gilberts and Marshalls*, Vol. VII of *History of United States Naval Operations in World War II* (Boston: 1951), pp. 121–86. Captain James R. Stockman, U.S.M.C., *The Battle for Tarawa* (Washington: U. S. Marine Corps).

44. Churchill, op. cit., p. 328. Arthur Bryant, *Triumph in the West* (New York: 1959), p. 50.

45. Sherwood, op. cit., pp. 798–99; Bryant, op. cit., p. 59; Stimson, op. cit., pp. 439–40.

46. Sherwood, op. cit., p. 779.
47. Ibid., pp. 785–87.
48. Bryant, op. cit., p. 52. Churchill, op. cit., p. 346.
49. Sherwood, op. cit., p. 803. Stimson, op. cit, pp. 440–41.
50. Sherwood, op. cit., p. 803. The other direct quotes are verbatim from or obviously implied by the Sherwood account and by Stimson, op. cit., on pp. 441–43.

XIII. *OVERLORD Triumphant*

1. Frederick E. Morgan, *Overture to Overlord* (New York: 1950); Bernard L. Montgomery, *The Memoirs of Field Marshal Montgomery*, softbound edition (Signet, New York, 1959, by arrangement with World Publishing Co.), pp. 192 and 199; Dwight D. Eisenhower, *Crusade in Europe* (New York: 1948), p. 217; Winston Churchill, *Closing the Ring* (Boston: 1951), p. 585.
2. Omar Bradley, *A Soldier's Story* (New York: 1951), pp. 344–45; Samuel Eliot Morison, *The Invasion of France and Germany*, Vol. XI of *History of United States Naval Operations in World War II* (Boston: 1957), pp. 74–75; Walter Bedell Smith, *Eisenhower's Six Great Decisions* (New York: 1956), pp. 25–26 and 48.
3. Cornelius Ryan, *The Longest Day* (softbound edition reprinted 1960 from edition of New York: 1959), pp. 27–28.
4. Arthur Bryant, *Triumph in the West* (New York: 1959), p. 148.
5. Ibid., p. 148.
6. Kenneth S. Davis, *Soldier of Democracy* (New York: 1945), p. 465. The author was furnished a transcript of Eisenhower's remarks when gathering his material.
7. Eisenhower, op. cit., p. 222.
8. Ibid., p. 220.
9. Ibid., p. 246.
10. The D-Day decision has been most authoritatively described by Harry C. Butcher, *My Three Years with Eisenhower* (New York: 1946), pp. 561–62; Alan A. Michie, "The Great Decision," *Reader's Digest*, August 1944; Kenneth S. Davis, op. cit., pp. 477–79 (this account derived from Michie and from personal interviews with Eisenhower, Butcher, and Lieutenant Colonel James F. Gault, who was Eisenhower's British Military Aide); Eisenhower, op. cit., pp. 248–50; Cornelius Ryan, op. cit., pp. 48–58; Walter Bedell Smith, op. cit., pp. 51–55; Morison, op. cit., pp. 79–83; Montgomery, op. cit., p. 226; and Chester Wilmot's excellent *The Struggle for Europe* (New York: 1952), pp. 220–26.
11. Bradley, op. cit., p. 343.
12. In writing these brief accounts of D-Day action, use was made of Morison, op. cit.; Ryan, op. cit.; Bradley, op. cit.; David Howarth, *D-Day, The Sixth of June, 1944* (New York: 1959); Eisenhower, op. cit.; Butcher, op. cit.; Gordon A. Harrison, *Cross-Channel Attack*, a volume of the official *U. S. Army in World War II* (Washington: 1951); Charles H. Taylor, *Omaha Beachhead*, a volume in the series, *American Forces in Action* (Washington: 1946); Roland G. Ruppenthal, *Utah Beach to Cherbourg*, a volume of the last-named series (Washington: 1947); S. L. A. Marshall's *Night Drop* (Boston: 1962).
13. Eisenhower, op. cit., p. 267. It should perhaps be added that the author

was in England and Normandy during most of this period, as a correspondent assigned to Eisenhower's personal headquarters, and writes of the period in part from memory and notes taken at the time.

14. Eisenhower, op. cit., p. 260.

15. Winston Churchill, *Triumph and Tragedy* (Boston: 1953), describes "The Pilotless Bombardment" on pp. 38–56. The statistics are from him.

16. *The New York Times Magazine,* Oct. 23, 1960.

17. Bradley, op. cit., pp. 330, 338–41, and 346–49. Lieutenant General Lewis H. Brereton, commander of the U. S. Ninth Tactical Air Force, insisted that Bradley had been told of the plan to come in *over* the troops.

18. Ibid., p. 358.

19. George S. Patton, *War as I Knew It* (New York: 1947), p. 95.

20. Davis, op. cit., p. 503, derived from interview with Bradley in August 1944.

21. Patton, op. cit., p. 99.

22. Patton said this to the author, as he must have to many other correspondents. In August 1944 a strict censorship was made of *all* direct quotes from Patton, on orders from Eisenhower; Patton was "under wraps."

23. Ibid., p. 377. The footnote quote of Patton is from ibid., p. 376.

24. Bradley, op. cit., p. 377.

25. Eisenhower, op. cit., p. 279.

26. Story of assassination attempt and its aftermath is told in detail by William L. Shirer, *The Rise and Fall of the Third Reich* (New York: 1960), pp. 1042–82.

27. Quoted by Shirer, op. cit., p. 1043.

28. Charles de Gaulle, *Unity,* second volume of *The War Memoirs of Charles de Gaulle* (New York: 1955), pp. 170–79.

29. Churchill, *Closing the Ring* (Boston: 1951), p. 628.

30. Davis, op. cit., p. 494.

31. Ibid., p. 512. The author was present at this conference and the quote is verbatim.

32. Eisenhower, op. cit., p. 282. Tense changed from past to present.

33. Churchill, *Triumph and Tragedy,* p. 100.

34. Montgomery, op. cit., p. 243.

35. Ibid., p. 249.

36. Bradley struck most observers, including the author in 1944, as an unusually modest, unassuming, and common-sensical man, but a perusal of his book leads to the unavoidable conclusion (at least by the author) that there was in him a hard core of self-interest and self-righteousness which effectively prevented his seeing merit in any proposal that might, if adopted, detract from his own importance in history. Smug self-satisfaction permeates his book. He did, when the author talked with him in 1944, express harsh criticism of Montgomery—exceedingly harsh—but so many at SHAEF were of the same opinion that the author accepted the judgment more fully than he now does and deemed it no evidence of malice on Bradley's part.

37. Bradley, op. cit., p. 418.

38. Ibid., p. 418.

39. Montgomery quotes this signal in full on p. 249.

40. Ibid., pp. 250–51.

41. Eisenhower, op. cit., p. 306. Montgomery, op. cit., p. 262.

42. Eisenhower, op. cit., p. 307.
43. Montgomery, op. cit., pp. 252–53.
44. Butcher, op. cit., pp. 661–62.
45. Montgomery, op. cit., pp. 253–54.
46. Ibid., pp. 254–55.
47. Ibid., p. 256.
48. Ibid., p. 257.
49. Ibid., p. 258.
50. Bradley, op. cit., p. 422.
51. Ibid., p. 423.
52. Montgomery, op. cit., p. 259.

XIV. *The Edge of Triumph*

1. Joseph Barnes, *Willkie* (New York: 1952), p. 342.
2. Ibid., p. 359.
3. Samuel I. Rosenman, *Working with Roosevelt* (New York: 1952), p. 439.
4. Rosenman, in ibid., tells the story in detail, pp. 438–43.
5. Ibid., p. 451.
6. Samuel I. Rosenman, ed., *The Public Papers and Addresses of Franklin D. Roosevelt, 1944–45* (New York: 1950), address accepting the nomination, July 20, 1944, p. 202.
7. Charles A. Willoughby and John Chamberlain, *MacArthur, 1941–1951* (New York: 1954), pp. 233–34, wherein is a supposedly verbatim transcript of MacArthur's report to his staff upon his return from the Pearl Harbor meeting.
8. Ibid., p. 235.
9. Rosenman, op. cit., p. 462.
10. Donald M. Nelson, *Arsenal of Democracy* (New York: 1946), pp. 401–2.
11. Ibid., pp. 409–10.
12. Ibid., pp. 403–5.
13. Ibid., p. 405, describes the Army's way as the use of "a blunderbuss" when a "rifle-shot approach" was necessary.
14. For a radically different view of Nelson than Nelson took of himself, or than the author takes of him, see Henry L. Stimson and McGeorge Bundy, *On Active Service* (New York: 1948), pp. 494–95.
15. The memorandum of agreement ("Morgenthau Plan") is given verbatim in Stimson and Bundy, op. cit., pp. 576–77.
16. Ibid., pp. 572–73.
17. Robert E. Sherwood, *Roosevelt and Hopkins* (New York: 1948, 1950), pp. 818–19.
18. Winston S. Churchill, *Triumph and Tragedy* (Boston: 1953), p. 157.
19. Excerpts from transcript of Nine Hundred and Sixty-sixth Press Conference of President Roosevelt, August 29, 1944, in *Public Papers and Addresses*, pp. 247–48.
20. Rosenman, *Working with Roosevelt*, p. 479.
21. Wendell Willkie, *An American Program* (New York: 1944), closing sentence of Foreword, on unnumbered page.
22. The story is told in detail by Rosenman's *Working with Roosevelt*, pp. 463–70. The direct quote of Roosevelt in following paragraph is from ibid.,

p. 463. The direct quote of Rosenman is from ibid., pp. 465, 467—and quote of Willkie is from ibid., p. 466.

23. Roosevelt's letters are printed on pp. 467–68 of ibid., and on pp. 372–73 and 377 of Barnes, op. cit.

24. M. Hamlin Cannon, *Leyte: The Return to the Philippines*, a volume of the official series *U. S. Army in World War II* (Washington: 1954), pp. 60 ff.; Walter Karig, Russell L. Harris, Frank A. Monson, *Battle Report: The End of an Empire* (New York: 1948), pp. 309–21; Samuel Eliot Morison, *Leyte*, being Vol. XII of the *History of United States Naval Operations in World War II* (Boston: 1958), pp. 127–48; *The Army Air Forces in World War II*, Vol. V, entitled *The Pacific: Matterhorn to Nagasaki*, W. F. Craven and J. L. Cate, eds. (Chicago: 1953), pp. 355–57.

25. Craven and Cate, op. cit., p. 356.

26. Karig et al., op. cit., pp. 314–15.

27. George C. Kenney, *The MacArthur I Know* (New York: 1951), p. 164. Francis Trevelyan Miller, *General Douglas MacArthur* (Philadelphia: 1942), p. 58.

28. Frazier Hunt, *The Untold Story of Douglas MacArthur* (New York: 1954), p. 115. In April of 1964, after MacArthur's death, his first wife, Louise Cromwell Heiberg, told a Washington columnist that "it was an interfering mother-in-law who eventually succeeded in disrupting our married life." The columnist, Betty Beale of the Washington *Star*, said in an AP story published April 21 that "Mrs. Heiberg is trying to write her memoirs while confined to her Georgetown house by illness." She (Mrs. Heiberg) was married four times, three of the marriages ended by divorce and one, to Lionel Atwill, by her husband's death.

29. Miller, op. cit., pp. 19–26. Hunt, however, in op. cit., says (p. 180) that the two did *not* meet.

30. Hunt, op. cit., pp. 19–26, gives a detailed account of the hazing and verbatim quotes from the transcript of the Congressional Committee hearing on West Point hazing at which MacArthur testified.

31. The report to Major General Leonard Wood, dated September 30, 1914, detailing the events of May 6, 1914, is reported in full by Hunt, op. cit., pp. 52–56.

32. Ibid., p. 59.

33. Direct quote of letter from Newton D. Baker to Henry J. Reilly, official historian of the 42nd Division, reprinted by Hunt, op. cit., p. 66. Also Miller, op. cit., p. 96.

34. Hunt, op. cit., pp. 97–98.

35. The photograph is reproduced in Miller, op. cit., facing p. 104.

36. Hunt, op. cit., p. 136.

37. Quoted by Richard H. Rovere and Arthur Schlesinger, Jr., *The General and the President* (New York: 1951), p. 37. Also Kenneth S. Davis, *Soldier of Democracy* (New York: 1945), p. 231.

38. Hunt, op. cit., pp. 187–89, in a chapter entitled by this MacArthur eulogist, "The Long Years of Exile." Also pp. 174–75.

39. Rovere and Schlesinger, Jr., op. cit., pp. 36–37. Hunt, op. cit., pp. 160–63.

40. Rovere and Schlesinger, Jr., op. cit., pp. 43–44.

41. Quoted by Hunt, p. 205.

42. Robert L. Eichelberger, *Our Jungle Road to Tokyo* (New York: 1950), pp. 181–82.

43. Morison, op. cit., pp. 136–37. The correspondent's article appeared in *Fortune*, XXXI, No. 6, June 1945, pp. 157–58.

44. Karig, et al., op. cit., p. 236.

45. Morison, op. cit., p. 58. He quotes Commander Third Fleet Operation Order 21-44 of October 3, 1944.

46. Quoted by Karig, et al., op. cit., p. 335.

47. William F. Halsey and Julian Bryan III, *Admiral Halsey's Story* (New York: 1947), p. 2.

48. Ibid., p. 2.

49. Ibid., pp. xii and xiii of Introduction by J. Bryan III.

50. Ibid., p. 214. Morison, op. cit., pp. 290–91.

51. Halsey, op. cit., p. 217.

52. Morison, op. cit., p. 193.

53. Ibid., p. 276.

54. Rikihei Onoguchi, Tadashi Makajime, Roger Pineau, *The Divine Wind: Japan's Kamikaze Force in World War II* (Annapolis: 1958), gives most complete history in English of kamikazes.

55. Quoted, Morison, op. cit., p. 300.

56. Both parenthetical quotes are from Halsey, op. cit., p. 218.

57. Ibid., p. 219.

58. Ibid., pp. 220–21.

59. Reference was also made, in writing of the Battle for Leyte Gulf, to E. B. Potter and Chester W. Nimitz, eds., *The Great Sea War: The Story of Naval Action in World War II* (Englewood Cliffs, N.J.: 1960), pp. 371–400.

XV. *To the End in Germany*

1. Omar N. Bradley, *A Soldier's Story* (New York: 1951), pp. 371–72.

2. Ibid., pp. 444–45. Charles B. MacDonald, *The Battle of the Huertgen Forest* (Philadelphia: 1963), p. 139. Trenchfoot is caused by prolonged, unalleviated dampness or soaking of the feet and produces symptoms similar to frostbite. Circulation of blood through the peripheral vessels is inhibited, swelling occurs, toes become purple; amputation is sometimes necessary—and many a G.I. lost his toes, even his feet to this malady.

3. Bradley, op. cit., p. 435.

4. Ibid., p. 439.

5. Ibid., p. 441.

6. Ibid., pp. 454–55.

7. John Toland, *Battle, The Story of the Bulge* (New York: 1959), softbound edition by New American Library, 1960, pp. 20–21. Bradley, op. cit., pp. 463–64, denies that Dickson predicted the Bulge, but immediately goes on to say that First Army G-2 "observations could have been read so as to suggest the *possibility* of attack in the Ardennes" and that Dickson "like most G-2s . . . was often a pessimist and an alarmist. Had I gone on guard every time Dickson . . . called wolf, we would never have taken many of the riskier moves that hastened the end of the war."

8. In writing this account of the Battle of the Bulge, the author referred chiefly to Toland, op. cit.; Bradley, op. cit.; Robert E. Merriam, *Dark Decem-*

ber (Chicago: 1947); *The Memoirs of Field Marshal Montgomery* (New York: 1958); Laurence Critchell, *Four Stars of Hell* (New York: 1947); Dwight D. Eisenhower, *Crusade in Europe* (New York: 1948); Forrest C. Pogue, *The Supreme Command*, a volume of the official *U. S. Army in World War II* (Washington: 1954).

9. Toland, op. cit., p. 17, tells of Captain Fred Aringdale of the U. S. 2nd Division who told a friend suddenly, on the night of December 15, that he was "going to be killed tomorrow." Aringdale was killed on the northern shoulder of the Bulge on the afternoon of December 17.

10. Montgomery in his *Memoirs* gives in full the notes from which he addressed the press conference, on pp. 285–88 of the softbound edition, published by New American Library in 1959. He says, p. 288: ". . . I should never have held that press conference. So great was the feeling against me on the part of the American generals, that whatever I said was bound to be wrong. . . . Secondly, . . . the general impression I gave was one of tremendous confidence. In contradistinction to the rather crestfallen American command, I appeared, to the sensitive, to be triumphant—not over the Germans but over the Americans."

11. These words, which do not appear in Montgomery's *Memoirs* account, are from the account printed in the American press at the time, quoted by Kenneth S. Davis, *Soldier of Democracy* (New York: 1945), p. 530.

12. Bradley, op. cit., p. 487.

13. Montgomery, op. cit., p. 289.

14. Winston S. Churchill, *Triumph and Tragedy* (Boston: 1953), p. 344.

15. Ibid., p. 345. Edward R. Stettinius, Jr., *Roosevelt and the Russians* (New York: 1949), pp. 81–82.

16. Samuel I. Rosenman, ed., *The Public Papers and Addresses of Franklin D. Roosevelt, 1944–45* (New York: 1950), pp. 576–77.

17. Quoted by Forrest C. Pogue in *The Meaning of Yalta*, John L. Snell, ed. (Baton Rouge: 1956), p. 27. See also Forrest C. Pogue, *The Supreme Command* (Washington: 1954), pp. 391–93.

18. Stettinius, op. cit., p. 74.

19. United States Department of Defense, "The Entry of the Soviet Union into the War Against Japan: Military Plans, 1941–45" (mimeographed report issued October 19, 1955), quoted by Pogue in op. cit., pp. 32–33. See also D. F. Fleming, *The Cold War and Its Origins, 1917–50*, Vol. I (New York: 1961), pp. 197–98.

20. Fleet Admiral William D. Leahy, *I Was There* (New York: 1950), p. 322. See also James F. Byrnes, *Speaking Frankly* (New York: 1941), pp. 44–45.

21. Stettinius, op. cit., pp. 127–28, John L. Snell in *The Meaning of Yalta*, p. 69. *Yalta Papers*, pp. 899–900; Byrnes, op. cit., p. 28.

22. Churchill, op. cit., pp. 367–69; Charles F. Delzell in *The Meaning of Yalta*, pp. 103–6. *Yalta Papers*, 678–79.

23. Delzell in op. cit., p. 94, quoting *Yalta Papers*, pp. 64–66.

24. Churchill, op. cit., p. 334.

25. Delzell in *The Meaning of Yalta*, p. 97.

26. Churchill, op. cit., p. 390.

27. Henry L. Stimson and McGeorge Bundy, *On Active Service* (New York: 1948), p. 536.

28. Herbert Feis, *Churchill, Roosevelt, Stalin* (Princeton: 1957), pp. 501–2.

29. Stettinius, op. cit., p. 281, says the reason for not announcing this was that "the President wished to have the opportunity of explaining his agreement personally to the Congressional leaders, and he also wanted to give the Prime Minister similar opportunity to decide how to deal with it in the House of Commons. The matter was also kept secret because . . . some members of the delegation had hoped that the Soviet Union might be persuaded to withdraw its request."

30. Quoted by Churchill, op. cit., p. 363.

31. Protocol of the Proceedings of the Crimea Conference, reprinted from *Yalta Papers* in *The Meaning of Yalta*, pp. 209–10.

32. A. Merriman Smith, *Thank You, Mr. President* (New York: 1946). Quoted by Bernard Asbell, *When FDR Died* (New York: 1961), p. 26 of softbound edition published by New American Library, 1962.

33. Robert E. Sherwood, *Roosevelt and Hopkins* (New York: 1950), pp. 871–74. Sherwood reprints here a memorandum on the Great Bitter Lake meeting written by Hopkins and says that when Roosevelt said "goodbye" to Hopkins at Algiers it was "not a very amiable one."

34. Ibid., p. 874.

35. Ibid., pp. 874–75. William D. Hassett, *Off the Record with FDR, 1942–1945* (New Brunswick, N.J.: 1958), pp. 318–19; Rosenman, op. cit., p. 570.

36. Churchill, op. cit., p. 456.

37. Quoted by Louis L. Snyder, *The War* (New York: 1960), p. 412.

38. Eisenhower, op. cit., p. 386.

39. Ibid., pp. 387–90; Churchill, op. cit., pp. 412–17; Arthur Bryant, *Triumph in the West* (New York: 1959), pp. 327–34.

40. William L. Shirer, *The Rise and Fall of the Third Reich* (New York: 1960), pp. 1105–6.

41. Churchill, op. cit., p. 457.

42. Bradley, op. cit., p. 536.

43. The story of this dispute is based on Churchill, op. cit., pp. 458–68; Eisenhower, op. cit., pp. 399–403; Bryant, op. cit., pp. 337–38; and Feis, op. cit., pp. 603–7.

44. Message from Eisenhower to Montgomery, March 31, 1945, quoted by Montgomery, op. cit., p. 503.

45. Churchill, op. cit., p. 467.

46. Ibid., p. 437.

47. The "Berne Incident" account is based on ibid., pp. 440–54; Feis, op. cit., pp. 583–96; Fleming, op. cit., pp. 212–14. Quotations from message are from Churchill.

48. Samuel L. Sharp in an article in *The Nation*, February 12, 1949, quoted by Fleming, op. cit., p. 238.

49. Fleming, op. cit., pp. 214–15.

50. The account of Roosevelt's Warm Springs homecoming is based on Turnley Walker, *Roosevelt and the Warm Springs Story* (New York: 1953), pp. 286–87; and Asbell, op. cit., pp. 22–23. The quote from Roosevelt to the mayor and the quote of Pless are from Asbell; the quote from Ruth Stevens is from Walker. Michael R. Reilly (as told to William J. Slocum), *Reilly of the White House* (New York: 1947) tells, pp. 226–27, of his difficulty in moving the President's inert weight from wheelchair to car.

51. Churchill, op. cit., quotes Stalin's message of April 3, 1945, in full on pp. 446–47, and Roosevelt's reply of April 5, 1945, in full on p. 447.

52. Ibid., pp. 451–52, reprinting Stalin's message of April 7, 1945, to Roosevelt.

53. Ibid., pp. 453–54.

54. Sherwood, op. cit., pp. 879–80, tells of looking up the Jefferson quotation for this speech and says that though "I did not know it at the time" he "realized later that . . . Roosevelt . . . was undoubtedly thinking of the imminence of the atomic age." Samuel I. Rosenman in *Working with Roosevelt* (New York: 1952) tells of this last speech on p. 551. The draft of the undelivered address is reprinted on pp. 613–16 of *The Public Papers and Addresses of Franklin D. Roosevelt,* which has also, facing p. 616, a facsimile of the last page of the draft on which Roosevelt worked on April 12, 1945, with his penciled strikeouts and additions.

55. Feis, op. cit., pp. 495–96; Fleming, op. cit., p. 213; Churchill, op. cit., p. 454.

56. Account of Roosevelt's death based on Hassett, op. cit., pp. 333–37; Walker, op. cit., pp. 289–92; and Asbell, op. cit., pp. 36–43.

57. Harry S. Truman, *Year of Decisions,* Vol. I of his *Memoirs* (New York: 1955), pp. 5–11.

58. Churchill, op. cit., p. 471 and pp. 478–80.

59. Message from Eden to Churchill, April 15, 1945, reprinted in Churchill, op. cit., p. 483.

60. George S. Patton, *War as I Knew It* (Boston: 1947), pp. 292–95; Bradley, op. cit., pp. 539–41; Eisenhower, op. cit., pp. 407–10.

61. Shirer, op. cit., p. 1110. Also H. R. Trevor-Roper, *The Last Days of Hitler* (New York: 1947).

XVI. *To the End in Japan*

1. Harry S. Truman, *Year of Decisions* (New York: 1955), pp. 70–82, dealing with the Molotov visit to Washington in late April 1945, shows an attitude and manner in dealing with the Russians that is in marked contrast to that Roosevelt pursued in the last weeks of his life.

2. Ibid., p. 228.

3. Herbert Feis, *Between War and Peace, The Potsdam Conference* (Princeton: 1960), emphasizes the unfortunate effect of the Lend-Lease slash on American-Soviet relations, pp. 26–30.

4. Robert E. Sherwood, *Roosevelt and Hopkins* (New York: 1948, 1950), p. 881.

5. Truman, in op. cit., tells of his decision to send Hopkins to Moscow on pp. 557–58. Feis, op. cit., pp. 83–85. The letter covers the Hopkins-Stalin talks in detail on pp. 97–118, citing among sources not seen by the present writer Document 26 of the Potsdam Papers and Charles E. Bohlen Memorandum of Stalin-Hopkins talk, May 28, 1945. Sherwood, op. cit., covers the Hopkins' mission in even greater detail, quoting extensively from the transcripts of the conversations, in op. cit., pp. 883–916.

6. Sherwood, op. cit., p. 906.

7. Feis, op. cit., pp. 94–96.

8. Sherwood, op. cit., p. 912. Truman, op. cit., p. 287, quotes Hopkins message.

9. Sherwood, op. cit., pp. 915–16.

10. For biographical detail on Oppenheimer the author is indebted to J. Alvin Kugelmass, *J. Robert Oppenheimer and the Atomic Story* (New York: 1953).

11. Arthur Holly Compton, *Atomic Quest* (New York: 1956), p. 126.

12. Ibid., p. 125. Compton explained that a top-flight theoretical physicist was required for the post; a theory of fission explosion must be worked out. "But experiments also would have to be done, and some of these would be extraordinarily difficult." Compton said, "What is more, this work would necessarily be carried out under conditions of almost unprecedented seclusion. The leader of this enterprise must be a person of such human understanding that he could keep a group of high-strung specialists working monthly together while largely separated from outside contacts."

13. Henry DeWolf Smyth, *Atomic Energy for Military Purposes*, The Official Report of the Development of the Atomic Bomb (Princeton: 1945), p. 212. William L. Laurence, New York *Times* for Sunday, August 7, 1960, p. 32 of news section.

14. The story of the Franck Report, and extended quotations from it, are in Michael Amrine, *The Great Decision* (New York: 1959), pp. 102–7; Fletcher Knebel and Charles W. Bailey II, *No High Ground* (New York: 1960), pp. 106–8; Medgord Evans, *The Secret War for the A-Bomb* (Chicago: 1953), pp. 119–23 (Evans quotes extensively an article by Robert M. Hutchins, "The Bomb Secret is Out!", *American* magazine, December 1947); P. M. S. Blackett, *Fear, War, and the Bomb* (New York: 1949); Robert Jungk, *Brighter than a Thousand Suns* (New York: 1956), pp. 183–85; and Eugene Rabinowitch, *Minutes to Midnight* (New York: 1950). The Franck Report was printed in the *Bulletin of the Atomic Scientists*, May 1946.

15. Quoted by Evans, op. cit., p. 119.

16. The story of this visit is in Amrine, op. cit., pp. 97–98; Knebel and Bailey, op. cit., p. 102; and James F. Byrnes, *All in One Lifetime* (New York: 1958), pp. 283–85.

17. Compton, op. cit., p. 236.

18. Ibid., p. 219.

19. Henry L. Stimson and McGeorge Bundy, *On Active Service* (New York: 1948), p. 626.

20. Quoted in ibid., p. 617. Also in Stimson's article, "The Decision to Use the Atomic Bomb," *Harper's* magazine, February 1947, p. 10; which is quoted by Compton, op. cit., p. 240; Truman, op. cit., p. 419.

21. A graphic and detailed account of this most devastating air raid in history is Martin Caiden's *A Torch to the Enemy* (New York: 1960).

22. Stimson and Bundy op. cit., p. 617.

23. William D. Leahy, *I Was There* (New York: 1950), pp. 441–42. The closing note in my paragraph is from ibid., p. 442.

24. Feis, in op. cit., prints in full General Groves' report on pp. 165–71, including General Farrell's account. Appendix 6 of the Smyth op. cit., pp. 247–54, is the War Department news release on the test explosion, written by William L. Laurence, Science editor of the New York *Times*. William L. Laurence, *Men and Atoms* (New York: 1959) tells of the test on pp. 115–17.

25. Laurence, op. cit., p. 118. Jungk, op. cit., p. 201.

26. James F. Byrnes, *Speaking Frankly* (New York: 1947), p. 263; Truman, op. cit., p. 416; Feis, op. cit., p. 117.

27. The Stimson memo is printed in full on pp. 62–64 of his op. cit.

28. The Potsdam Declaration or ultimatum to Japan is printed in full in Winston Churchill, *Triumph and Tragedy* (Boston: 1953), pp. 642–44.

29. Ibid., p. 639. Truman, op. cit., p. 419.

30. The story of the poll is told by Amrine, op. cit., pp. 146–49; by Knebel and Bailey, with a notable reticence concerning Compton's handling of it, in op. cit., pp. 112–13; and by Compton, op. cit., pp. 243–44.

31. Compton, op. cit., p. 244. Compton does *not* in his book, report verbatim Daniels' question and five possible answers, with the distribution of votes among them. He says merely that the "questionnaire had five procedures, graded from no use of the bomb in this war to its military use in the manner most effective in bringing prompt Japanese surrender."

32. Ibid., p. 247.

33. Accounts of the Hiroshima and Nagasaki bomb-droppings are too numerous to mention here.The author consulted, in addition to the works by Amrine, Knebel and Bailey, and Jungk, Merle Miller and Abe Spitzer, *We Dropped The A-Bomb* (New York: 1946); the United States Strategic Bombing Survey, Physical Damage Division, *The Effects of the Atomic Bomb on Hiroshima, Japan*, issued in Washington, May 1947; and from the same source, *The Effects of the Atomic Bomb on Nagasaki, Japan*, issued in June 1947; and *The Effect of the Atomic Bombs on Hiroshima and Nagasaki*, a report of the British Mission to Japan, published by His Majesty's Stationery Office, London 1946.

34. Truman, op. cit., p. 421.

35. Toshikazu Kase, *Journey to the Missouri* (New Haven: 1950), quoted by Amrine, op. cit., p. 216.

36. Truman, op. cit., p. 428.

Index

U.S.S.R.
The WAR in the PACIFIC
Japan and conquered territory
Allied Attacks
SEA OF OKHOTSK
MONGOLIA
MANCHURIA
KURILES
Peiping
CHINA
JAPAN
Hiroshima
Tokyo
Nagasaki
Shanghai
EAST CHINA SEA
Chungking
PACIFIC
RYUKYUS
Changsha
Kunming
OKINAWA
APR.'45
Hong Kong
IWO JIMA FEB.'45
MARCUS
BURMA JUNE '45
TAIWAN
INDOCHINA
HAINAN
LUZON JAN.'45
WAKE
MARIANAS
THAILAND
SOUTH CHINA SEA
Manila
PHILIPPINES
PHILIPPINE SEA
SAIPAN JUNE-JULY '44
ENIWETOK FEB.'44
MINDORO DEC.'44
GUAM JULY '44
BIKINI
PALAWAN FEB.'45
LEYTE OCT.'44
YAP
ULITHI SEPT.'44
CAROLINES
JUNE '45
PONAPE
TRUK
Brunei
MINDANAO APR.'45
NGULU OCT.'44
PALAU SEPT.'44
Singapore
MOROTAI
NEW GUINEA MAY-SEPT.'44
BORNEO
ADMIRALTY FEB.-MAR.'44
NAURU
Rabaul
SUMATRA
CELEBES
Hollandia
NEW BRITAIN DEC.'43
Wewak
SOLOMONS JUNE-NOV.'43
Batavia
JAVA SEA
Lae
TULAGI
JAVA
SEPT.'43
GUADALCANAL
DUTCH EAST INDIES
Port Moresby
SANTA CRUZ
Buna NOV.'43
TROBRIAND JUNE '43
AUG.'42
Darwin
Coen
Cooktown
ESPIRITU SANTO
INDIAN OCEAN
NEW HEBRIDES
CORAL SEA
Townsville
NEW CALEDONIA
Nouméa
AUSTRALIA
Brisbane